539.33-8338 IRENNE ROBINSON

W9-BBZ-889

USED BOOK

REVIEWERS

C. ALLEN BARRETT
California State University, Los Angeles

DEBORAH BASKIN
John Jay College

STEVEN G. BRANDL
Georgia State University

W. GARRETT CAPUNE
California State University, Fullerton

JANET DE LAY
Southwestern College

DAVID DUFFEE
State University of New York at Albany

LORIE FRIDELL
Florida State University

LOIS A. GUYON
Illinois State University

DENNIS JAY KENNEY
University of Nebraska at Omaha

JOHN M. KLOFAS
Rochester Institute of Technology

PETER B. KRASKA
Kent State University

ELLEN MCKINNON
Loyola University
Delgado Community College

STEPHEN D. MASTROFSKI
Visiting Fellow
National Institute of Justice

FRANK MORN
Illinois State University

M. G. NEITHERCUTT
California State University, Hayward

EDWARD SELBY
Southwestern College

CATHY STREIFEL
Purdue University

DONALD WALKER
Kent State University

MEL WALLACE
McHenry County College

RICHARD J. WAUGH
Georgia Southern University

ALISSA POLITZ WORDEN
State University of New York at Albany

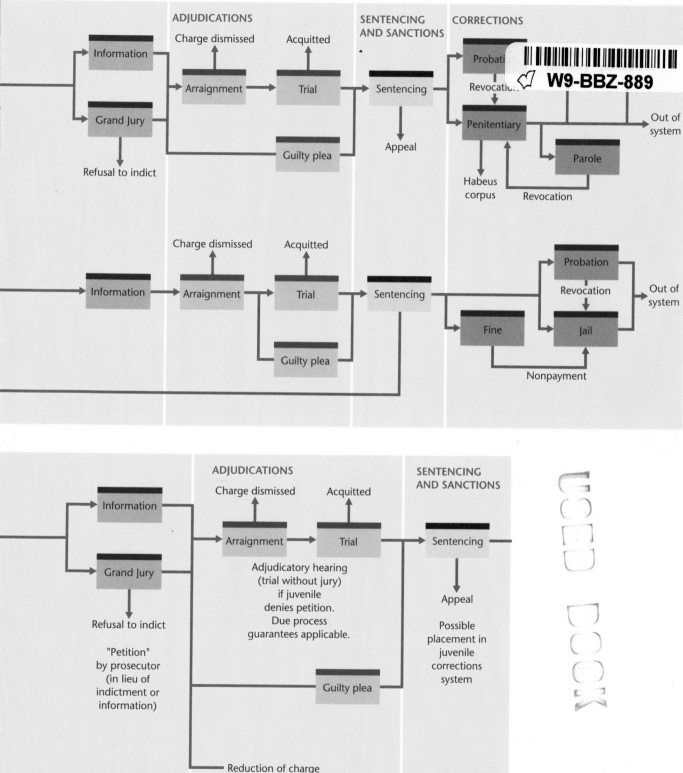

CRIMINAL JUSTICE

Freda Adler
Rutgers University

Gerhard O. W. Mueller
Rutgers University

William S. Laufer
University of Pennsylvania

McGRAW-HILL, INC.

New York   St. Louis   San Francisco   Auckland   Bogotá   Caracas   Lisbon
London   Madrid   Mexico City   Milan   Montreal   New Delhi   San Juan   Singapore
Sydney   Tokyo   Toronto

This book was set in New Aster by York Graphic Services, Inc.
The editors were Phillip A. Butcher, Jeannine Ciliotta, and Bob Greiner;
the designer was Joan Greenfield;
the production supervisor was Annette Mayeski.
The photo editor was Barbara Salz.
Von Hoffmann Press, Inc., was printer and binder.

Cover photo: P. Chauvel-Sygma

Criminal Justice

Copyright © 1994 by McGraw-Hill, Inc. All rights reserved. Printed in the United States of America. Except as permitted under the United States Copyright Act of 1976, no part of this publication may be reproduced or distributed in any form or by any means, or stored in a data base or retrieval system, without the prior written permission of the publisher.

Acknowledgments appear on pages 569–571, and on this page by reference.

This book is printed on acid-free paper.

1 2 3 4 5 6 7 8 9 0   VNH VNH   9 0 9 8 7 6 5 4 3

ISBN 0-07-000457-9

Library of Congress Cataloging-in-Publication Data

Adler, Freda.
    Criminal justice / Freda Adler, Gerhard O. W. Mueller, William S. Laufer.
        p.   cm.
    Includes bibliographical references and index.
    ISBN 0-07-000457-9
    1. Criminal justice, Administration of—United States.
I. Mueller, Gerhard O. W.   II. Laufer, William S.   III. Title.
HV9950.A35   1994
364.973—dc20   93-28243

ABOUT THE AUTHORS

FREDA ADLER is Distinguished Professor of Criminal Justice at Rutgers University, School of Criminal Justice. She received her B.A. in sociology, her M.A. in criminology, and her Ph.D. in sociology—all from the University of Pennsylvania. Dr. Adler began her career in criminal justice as an evaluator of drug and alcohol treatment programs for federal and state governments. Teaching since 1968, her subjects include criminal justice, criminology, comparative criminal justice systems, statistics and research methods. She has served as criminal justice advisor to the United Nations, as well as to federal, state and foreign governments. Dr. Adler's published works include seven books as author or co-author, eight books as editor or co-editor, and over sixty journal articles. She has served on the editorial boards of the *Journal of Criminal Justice, Criminology,* and the *Journal of Research on Crime and Delinquency.* Dr. Adler serves as editorial consultant to the *Journal of Criminal Law and Criminology,* and is co-editor of *Advances in Criminological Theory.* She has recently been elected President of the American Society of Criminology (November 1994–95).

GERHARD O. W. MUELLER is Distinguished Professor of Criminal Justice at Rutgers University, School of Criminal Justice. After earning his J.D. degree from the University of Chicago, he went on to receive the L.L.M. degree from Columbia University. He was awarded the degree of Dr.Jur.(h.c.) by the University of Uppsala, Sweden. His career in criminal justice began in 1945, when he served as a C.P.O. in the British Military Government Water Police, where he commanded a Coast Guard Cutter. His teaching in criminal justice, begun in 1953, was partially interrupted between 1974 and 1982, when, as Chief of the United Nations Crime Prevention and Criminal Justice Branch, he was responsible for all of the United Nations' programs dealing with problems of crime and justice worldwide. Professor Mueller has been a member of the faculties of law of the University of Washington, West Virginia University, New York University, and of the National Judicial College, with visiting appointments and lectureships at universities and institutes in the Americas, Western and Eastern Europe, Africa, Asia and Australia. He is the author of some 50 authored or edited books and 250 scholarly articles.

WILLIAM S. LAUFER is Anheuser-Busch Term Assistant Professor of Legal Studies at the Wharton School of the University of Pennsylvania. Dr. Laufer received the B.A. in social and behavioral sciences at the Johns Hopkins University, the J.D. at Northeastern University School of Law, and the Ph.D. at Rutgers University School of Criminal Justice. Teaching since 1987, his subjects include corporate crime and business ethics, criminal law and criminal procedure, criminology, and correctional law. Dr. Laufer's research has appeared in law reviews and a wide range of criminal justice, legal and psychology journals, such as the *Journal of Research in Crime and Delinquency, Law and Human Behavior,* and the *Journal of Personality and Social Psychology.* He is co-editor of the *Handbook of Psychology and Law, Personality, Moral Development and Criminal Behavior,* and *Crime, Values and Religion.* Dr. Laufer is co-editor of *Advances in Criminological Theory,* with Freda Adler.

CONTENTS IN BRIEF

CONTENTS

LIST OF BOXES

PREFACE

Fifty years ago, there were no college courses on criminal justice. Of course there were police officers, and there were judges, prison administrators, and guards. But none of these officials had any formal education in "criminal justice," nor did they think of themselves as working within something called "the criminal justice system." Unlike medicine or law, which evolved as disciplines and subjects of higher education over a period of thousands of years, the notion of criminal justice as a field of study or as a government system appeared on the scene a mere half century ago.

Since that time, there has been literally an explosion of knowledge of the structure, functions, and power of the institutions that comprise criminal justice in the United States. No longer is the response of criminal justice institutions viewed as arbitrary, driven by untested ideas of what society should do about crime and punishment; it is now seen as a complex and rational response, based on knowledge and data gleaned from countless studies by criminal justice researchers.

It would be a mistake to think of criminal justice as a static system or as a U.S. invention. The criminal justice "explosion" coincided with the globalization of the world: advances in communications and commerce, transportation, and industrial technology have turned separate nations and regions into a global village in which every society is affected by every other society. Independence has been replaced by interdependence, and that has had an enormous impact on crime and criminal justice.

AUDIENCE AND APPROACH

This book is intended for a wide audience: college students who strive for participatory citizenship and need an understanding of criminal justice; students who have chosen criminal justice as their profession and need basic tools; professionals who want to sharpen their skills and need a broad overview of the entire field.

To reach such an audience, and to present the field of criminal justice within a framework that will help students learn and study, we have chosen to focus on three facets of criminal justice today:

Criminal Justice in Action: The field of criminal justice is constantly in motion: new developments, new techniques, new perspectives, new programs, and new ideas fuel an ever-changing, living system.

Criminal Justice on Trial: At the same time, this evolving system faces challenges that far exceed its human and capital resources. Events such as excessive use of force by police, disparity in judicial sentencing, and overcrowded jails and prisons make all of us question how a social institution, its processes and professionals, could have strayed so far from minimal standards or acceptable custom.

Criminal Justice Abroad: And as criminal justice in the United States evolves and is called into question, we must consider all successes and failures, all problems and solutions, in global terms. For what happens in Havana or Bogotá or Naples has an effect on what happens in Miami or Los Angeles or New York, and vice versa. Today, every professional—and every ordinary citizen—needs to understand crime and justice as international and comparative problems as well as national, regional, or local ones.

Criminal justice now takes place within an evolving human system that faces intractable challenges in a borderless world.

FEATURES

The approach we have chosen, the focus on three themes, is designed as a learning experience:

Organization: Basic Structures and Complementary Systems

The text contains nineteen chapters arranged within five parts. Following the first part (Chapters 1 through 5), which is intended to acquaint the student with crime as a social problem, its measurement, and its conceptualization under law, we present Parts 2 through 4, which are devoted to law enforcement (Chapters 6 through 9), courts, (Chapters 10 through 13), and corrections (Chapters 14 through 16), respectively. These are the basic structures of the criminal justice system. To these we have added a fifth part on the criminal justice processes for juveniles, victims, and international and transnational offenders (Chapter 17 through 19), processes that parallel the path of adult offenders through the system.

Multiple Paths: Criminal Justice Systems

For the normal path of defendants through the criminal justice process, we have used as a basis the flowchart of the President's Commission on Law Enforcement and the Administration of Justice (1967). We have also made our own adaptations for the processes for juveniles, victims, and international/transnational offenders. For easy reference, the flowcharts illustrating the four paths appear on the endpapers of the book, as well as within the appropriate chapters.

Focus: Past and Present

Each chapter begins with recent criminal justice events that have captured the imagination of the nation or the world, or that present unique challenges to contemporary criminal justice. Within each chapter, we have also endeavored to present the most up-to-date statistics and studies, as well as the most recent real-life examples. So that students can easily perceive criminal justice in the 1990s as a continuation of historical processes, we have included coverage of the past in both text and box material. Each of the opening chapters for the three central players in the system—law enforcement (Chapter 6), courts (Chapter 10), and corrections (Chapter 14)—contains a historical background. This background is summarized in the Milestones boxes, which contain an illustrated chronology of significant events from ancient times to the present day.

Box Learning Modules: In Action, on Trial, Abroad

Each chapter contains a two-page box on each of the three themes. These boxes develop current thinking or controversy on events and problems in detail. Text, tabular material, line art, and photographs, along with questions for discussion and source listings, are designed to create a "teaching module" that can be used for class discussion, for group projects or papers, or as springboards for further study.

A Double Glossary

Important terms defined in the text are highlighted with boldface; definitions appear in the margin at the point of introduction. An end-of-book Glossary lists all these terms and definitions in alphabet order for ease in reviewing material.

More Features and Scholarly Support: References, Statistics, Tables, Illustrations

Extensive notes for each chapter contain references to the entire literature of criminal justice, both classic studies and current cutting-edge work. The latest available statistics are used in the text and as a basis for numerous graphs and charts. Photographs have been carefully chosen to amplify the text.

SUPPLEMENTS

The supplements package includes an *Instructor's Manual, Test File,* and *Study Guide,* all prepared by Marie Henry of Sullivan County Community College. The *Instructor's Manual* offers both summary and practical material. It includes a list of chapter objectives, a chapter outline, classroom activities, five student projects, two of which are geared to the critical thinking and writing assignments in the companion *Study Guide,* audiovisual resources, and activities tearout sheets that can be reproduced as handouts for students. The *Test File,* which offers 55 test items for each chapter, will also be available on disk in IBM compatible and Macintosh formats. The *Study Guide* is designed to reinforce comprehension of chapter material and, by means of practical exercises, to encourage students to analyze the information and communicate what they have learned.

Finally, to find out about McGraw-Hill's policy regarding the overhead transparencies that have been produced for use with *Criminal Justice,* as well as our policy regarding videos, contact your local McGraw-Hill representative.

IN APPRECIATION

We gratefully acknowledge the assistance and support of a number of dedicated professionals. At Rutgers University, the librarian of the NCCD/Criminal Justice Collection, Phyllis Schultze, has been most helpful in patiently tracking and tracing sources. We thank Lorraine Green (Northeastern University), Carolyn Cass (Rutgers University), and Jane Siegel (University of Pennsylvania) for their contributions to the development of various chapters, and Joan Schroeder for her superb word processing work on the manuscript. Our reviewers, who provided us with so many helpful comments and insights, are listed opposite the title page. We thank them here as well.

We owe a special debt to the team at McGraw-Hill. Executive editor Phil Butcher saw *Criminal Justice* through from conception to completion with extraordinary skill and devotion. Development editor Jeannine Ciliotta's expertise assured its smooth transformation from ideas and first drafts to final manuscript. Carolyn Kroehler helped shape and polish the box material. Editing supervisor Bob Greiner's attention to context and detail deserve very special appreciation. The photo program owes its success to manager Safra Nimrod and researcher Barbara Salz. And production supervisor Annette Mayeski oversaw the production of this text as an attractive four-color book.

We cannot think of a more important and exciting profession than that devoted to the creation, management, and constant improvement of a criminal justice system, and to crime control and the administration of criminal justice in a humane, effective, and efficient manner, and we can only hope that many students using this book as their first experience will choose criminal justice as their career.

Freda Adler
Gerhard O. W. Mueller
William S. Laufer

PART 1

THE UNIVERSE OF CRIME AND JUSTICE

P*art 1 of this book is the gateway to the universe of criminal justice, a universe that is vast, frightening, and exciting. This part also provides a map to help readers explore and understand this universe. Chapter 1 previews the book as a whole and also describes the origin and evolution of the field and profession of criminal justice. Chapter 2 explains how crime is defined and how and by whom it is measured. Chapter 3 focuses on the causes of crime; the classical and positivist schools; and the biological, psychological, social, and economic factors that explain who commits crime and why.*

The law that underlies our criminal justice system is the focus of Chapter 4. When a crime appears to have been committed and authorities such as police or prosecutors have been notified, a legal apparatus is set in motion. This apparatus is the criminal justice system, and it is the subject of Chapter 5. This final chapter in Part 1 describes the system as a whole, with all of its component parts, paths, processes, and outcomes. ■

CRIMINAL JUSTICE: AN OVERVIEW

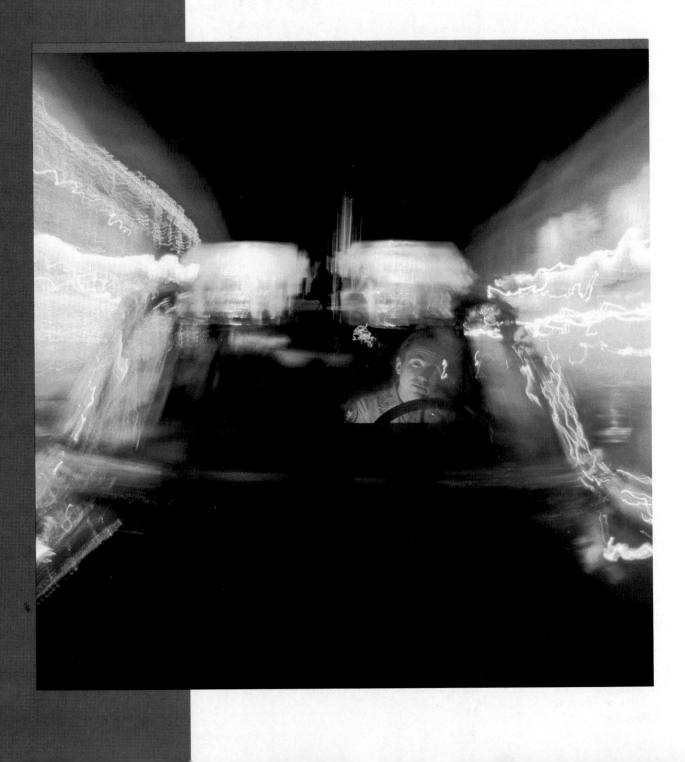

"**I**f New York police Sgt. Andrew McGoey were conducting business as usual, it would probably mean cruising Brooklyn's Sunset Park neighborhood in his patrol car, listening for calls on the radio and waiting for trouble in an area plagued by drug dealing and prostitution.

"But instead of muggers and drug dealers, . . . [E]ach week McGoey and his officers take three dozen elderly women from nursing homes on shopping expeditions. . . . McGoey's men also provided nighttime lighting for a schoolyard, the better to drive away heroin addicts who left their needles and feces for children to discover in the morning. . . .

"Across the country, police officers like McGoey are drawing a new blue line in the war against crime. It's called community policing. . . ." (Newsweek, *August 27, 1990.*) ∎

"Heroin distribution earned Rosalind Coleman seven to 24 years in D.C.'s prison system, but it's pretty clear she's not going to serve her term. No, she won't be released early. She's not planning a breakout. She'll be dead.

"Coleman, convicted in 1988, has AIDS. Today she's serving a good portion of her sentence shuttling back and forth between her cell at D.C.'s Correctional Treatment Facility and D.C. General Hospital. Because of a severe reaction to AZT, Coleman can't take the drug to slow down the disease; because she's an inmate she can't take any of the other experimental AIDS drugs either. As a result, her condition is quickly deteriorating; now she's wheelchair-bound for months at a time. Still, the D.C. Department of Corrections will not let Coleman—or any other prisoner with AIDS—go home to be with family and die in peace.

"One can quibble, of course, over the moral imperatives of the Rosalind Coleman case. . . . The fiscal implications, on the other hand, are crystal clear. Thanks to what appears to be stunning indifference to the prison epidemic by city corrections officials, Coleman and fellow prisoners with AIDS may be on the verge of busting the District's bank." (The Washington Post, *January 31, 1993.*) ∎

"At 11:13 a.m. on Wednesday, July 29, 1992, Manhattan District Attorney Robert M. Morgenthau walked through the back door of his office, followed by several staff members and representatives of the U.S. Justice Department and the Federal Reserve, to face a waiting crowd.

"The slim, white-haired D.A. read in a quiet, halting voice from his prepared text: 'A New York County grand jury has returned two indictments, charging six individuals, including Clark M. Clifford and Robert A. Altman, for criminal conduct arising out of the operation of the Bank of Credit and Commercial [sic, Commerce] International—BCCI.' This bank, Morgenthau said, was 'a criminal enterprise' that had 'bribed central bankers, government officials, and others worldwide to gain power and money.' . . .

"BCCI had outwardly seemed like a normal financial institution, with attractively designed branch offices, its own traveler's check business, and a reputation for financing international trade. But behind this convincing facade, BCCI was a criminal enterprise that catered to some of the most notorious villains of the late twentieth century, including Saddam Hussein, the bloodthirsty ruler of Iraq; leaders of the Medellín drug cartel, which controls the bulk of the world's cocaine trade; Khun Sa, the warlord who dominates heroin trafficking in Asia's Golden Triangle; Abu Nidal, the head of one of the world's leading terrorist organizations; and Manuel Antonio Noriega, the drugdealing former dictator of Panama. . . ." (Newsweek, *December 7, 1992.*) ∎

*"A sea of change is sweeping U.S.
law enforcement. It's called community-oriented policing—the
new-old idea that cops should
work closely with citizens to stop
crime before it happens. . . ."*
Conrad deFiebre, *Star Tribune,*
October 11, 1992.

*"Instead of simply processing
more cases through an already
overworked criminal justice system, some district attorneys are
now asserting themselves in a
new role—that of 'justice minister.'"*
Sean P. Murphy, *The Boston
Globe,* March 16, 1992.

*"While many United States pris-
ons are mired in crisis, here at
McKean, Luther and his staff
have created a culture that management expert Tom Peters calls a
'remarkable experiment.'. . .
After three years of operation . . .
there have been no escapes, no
murders, no serious assaults
on inmates or staff, . . . no suicides. . . ."*
David Holmstrom, *The Christian
Science Monitor,* July 21, 1992.

Criminal justice is the sum total of society's activities to defend itself against the actions it defines as criminal. Today in the United States, criminal justice functions as a system, run by professionals and constantly assessed, evaluated, and advanced by social scientists.

As a science, criminal justice is concerned with achieving the goals of criminal justice systems in a humane, effective, and cost-beneficial manner.[1] It includes scientific studies of decision-making processes, operations, and such justice-related concerns as the efficiency of the police, courts, and corrections; the fair treatment of offenders; and the needs of victims. The system has come under close scrutiny not only by specialists in the field, but also by the media and the general public.[2] There is a growing awareness of its successes and failures, and of the efforts and frustrations of dealing with a global crime problem using methods designed for the local level.

We began this chapter with three examples—community policing, the AIDS prison/inmate crisis, and the BCCI scandal. They reflect three themes that practitioners and academicians constantly encounter in their work: the advances and innovations in the system; the challenges to the system; and the issues arising from globalization. We call these three themes criminal justice *in action,* criminal justice *on trial,* and criminal justice *abroad,* and they are the guidelines we have used in examining and presenting issues throughout the book.

The first example focuses on criminal justice in action. Community policing is a strategy designed to bring about a closer relationship between the police and the community they serve. Police departments across the country are using this technique to prevent crime by building public confidence and citizen cooperation. Law enforcement is changing, moving forward—and so, too, are courts and corrections—with new policies and programs, innovative practices, and systematic evaluations of these programs and practices. Criminal justice is constantly evolving as public opinion, philosophies, laws, and research make an impact on our institutions and practices.

Criminal justice scholars, however, admit that while there have been significant advances, there are just as many limitations, questionable practices, and failures in the system. Our second example illustrates how criminal justice remains on trial for its inadequacies, and for its inability to find better ways of accomplishing its goals. Through the decade of the 1980s and into the 1990s administrators have been confronted with the enormous financial burden AIDS imposes on correctional budgets. Management of dying prisoners, poorly equipped prison hospitals, and avoidance of patient inmates by staff and other inmates are growing concerns. As of now, the system offers few solutions.

And there are a host of other unmet challenges and failures resulting from inequalities, unjust laws, poorly conceived programs, and financial or bureaucratic constraints. It is clear that we have much to do and a long way to go.

The successes and failures of the American criminal justice system are closely linked to events in the rest of the world. The BCCI scandal, the third example with which this chapter opened, targets the range of problems when a bank with offices in seventy-three countries comes under investigation for crimes that include fraud, theft, and money laundering. Clearly our criminal justice system, designed to function at the county and state (and sometimes national) level, is incapable of dealing with a criminal scheme covering half the world. Neither our laws, nor our law enforcers, nor our courts have the power, capacity, and resources to achieve anything in the nature of crime control beyond county lines and national borders. The effects of the globalization of society have made criminal justice abroad a major focus for criminal justice researchers and practitioners.

CRIMINAL JUSTICE IN ACTION

Developments in the criminal justice system, shifting emphases, and the replacement of one strategy with another often are the result of debates between politicians and policymakers, scholars, and opinion makers. Fundamental to these debates has always been a clash between liberal and conservative philosophies. This clash is perhaps best illustrated by comparing the liberal approach to crime control advocated by the Johnson administration in the 1960s, with its emphasis on attacking poverty as the root of crime, with the Reagan administration's rejection of "social engineering" in the 1980s, and emphasis instead on the stepped-up prosecution and imprisonment of criminals. At any one moment in history the clashes between liberal and conservative criminal justice philosophies may be quite pronounced, the battle lines clearly drawn, and the accompanying rhetoric often hostile.[3]

Yet what is liberal in criminal justice today may be viewed as conservative tomorrow. For example, the policy of indeterminate sentencing was hailed as liberal in its time. Today this policy is seen as conservative and is rejected by liberal thinkers favoring predictable and due-process-oriented standards. Such philosophical questions, though old and often rephrased, are of considerable practical significance to criminal justice policy. They have produced major changes in legislation and practice and will continue to do so.[4]

In recent decades there has been a lively political debate about the justice of the criminal justice system. If the system is based on the consensus of all citizens, it can hardly be argued that it is unjust (the consensus model). But critics, often using Marxist principles, argue that in fact there is no consensus on what behavior is to be punishable, who is to be prosecuted, and who is to be punished. They argue that the making of laws, and their enforcement, has been the privilege of upper classes who abuse their power to keep lower classes in their place, using the agents of criminal justice as tools.[5] This argument cannot be dismissed lightly, even at the time when statues and statutes of Marx and Lenin have been toppled in the Eastern and Central European countries. In every country, laws are often the result of pressure from powerful interest groups, from lobbies, and from party and partisan elites.

In the United States, politicians and academic critics have brought about reform on such issues as police abuse of power, discriminatory treatment of minority group offenders, and inhumane prison conditions. Over the years, the scholarly community of criminal justice specialists has been involved in improving or altering the criminal justice system. To do this, they rely on a body of accumulated knowledge from many disciplines—law, criminology, sociology, political science, economics, public administration, management, computer science, information sciences, police science, penology, and criminal justice as a science in its own right. As we demonstrate in this book, criminal justice scholars have devised research-based solutions to troublesome problems ranging from police minority recruitment at one end of the system to sentencing guidelines and parole prediction schemes at the other. Yet vast areas of criminal justice remain unexplored, and other areas stand in need of drastic change.

CRIMINAL JUSTICE ON TRIAL

It is almost impossible to find a period in history in which crime was not popularly thought to be a problem of crisis dimensions, calling for instant and drastic solutions. Crime has been a problem since humans built the first cities. Through

Bank robbery wanted posters. Bank robberies and bank robbers use the energies and resources of all criminal justice agencies—police, courts, and corrections.

PAY ATTENTION TO

"Much of what explains the plight of criminal justice today lies beyond the police and courts. . . . The growing number of single-parent households, violence on television, reduced funding for social and recreational programs in the inner city—all . . . contribute in varying degrees to the problem."
David Freed, Los Angeles Times, December 11, 1990.

"Increasingly, the criminal justice system must question many of its traditional ways of addressing the problems which we are facing . . . Currently, however, there is no forum for determining, on an ongoing basis, the philosophy, mission, goals, objectives, and policy directions of the criminal justice system as a whole."
"Chief Fulwood Takes a Look at the Courts," Legal Times, June 24, 1991.

Heath Wilkins, wearing shackles, at the Clay County Detention Center in Liberty, Missouri, in 1989. Wilkins was sentenced to death for a murder committed in 1985, when he was 16.

the centuries, political solutions have been proposed and implemented, in alternating cycles of harsh and more humane policies, but usually without any positive impact or lasting change.

Consider the following facts about our current criminal justice crisis: In 1960 the American crime rate, as measured by the FBI's Uniform Crime Reports, was 1,887 per 100,000 of the population. In 1991 it was 5,897.8—a little more than a threefold increase. (And the increase may be much greater, according to the National Crime Survey; see Chapter 2.) White-collar and organized criminals are stealing so much of our property that, for the 1980s Savings and Loan frauds alone, American taxpayers will have underwritten an estimated $500 billion by the year 2021. That crime bill amounts to a debt of $1,000 for each American citizen, from the newborn infant to the last survivor of the Spanish-American War. More likely it translates to $10,000 for each American wage earner. Add to the crime bill the cost of cocaine bought by the estimated 4 million citizens who regularly use this drug, and the 22 million who have tried it, the cost of our "drug wars," the families ruined, lives lost, and earning power wasted. The impact on the national economy is devastating. Consider also that twenty times more people are killed criminally (per 100,000 of the population) in the United States than in Denmark, Germany, England, or France.

Because of the high crime rate in the United States, the intake into our criminal justice system is so bloated and clogged that only a third of all reported crimes lead to imprisonment, after nine out of ten cases have been diverted out of the system. Yet the prison population has increased more than threefold between 1960 and 1990, so that the United States now has the highest rate of imprisonment in the world (see Chapter 14). And while great strides have been made in introducing due process into the American criminal justice system, we are the last remaining Western country to use capital punishment (see Chapter 13). Legislatures have created many more crimes and increased the punishment for old crimes, yet law enforcement, despite massive personnel increases, must limit its focus almost exclusively to the most serious crimes.

Finally, crime was once a matter of purely local concern. Now it has become so globalized that any one nation's criminal justice agencies are no longer able to control it effectively.

CRIMINAL JUSTICE ABROAD

"The Maastricht treaty . . . declaration on police cooperation . . . will give governments a powerful set of tools to deal with sophisticated multinational crime."
Barry James, *International Herald Tribune*, October 5, 1992.

A few construction engineers building a nuclear power plant in Chernobyl, Ukraine, embezzled contract money and substituted inferior materials in construction. It was a local crime. But then a meltdown of the reactor occurred, with a huge nuclear explosion. The result: death, destruction, nuclear contamination of food, and health hazards for millions of people all over Europe and Alaska.

Groups of peasants in Bolivia decided to switch their major crop from alfalfa to coca leaves. That was not even a local crime. But the decision has affected crime rates all over the world, with North America and Europe hit the hardest, through the illegal importation, distribution, and consumption of cocaine. The drug money, "laundered" through secret numbered bank accounts in a dozen or more countries around the world, flows back into the United States, where it permits members of organized crime groups to buy legitimate businesses.

Just as commerce and communications, trade and transport, have become totally globalized during the last three decades, so has crime. An increasing number of "local" crimes actually have an international connection. For example, many thefts, robberies, and burglaries are committed because of the need to buy drugs, which are smuggled into the country from abroad. What often appears as local crime is just the visible tip of an immense iceberg—worldwide crime. To

A drug bonfire in Colombia: Getting rid of drugs at the source is part of the world-wide "war on drugs" that crosses so many borders and affects so many lives.

some extent technology or its abuse can be blamed for the globalization of crime. It takes little time and effort to exchange information by computer, or to transfer vast amounts of money. International computer transactions have become as much a tool for criminals as guns and ski masks. Computer criminals can access legitimate systems, enrich themselves through fraudulent transactions, or destroy legitimate data bases. Perpetrators may sit thousands of miles away from the scene of the crime. The impact of such crimes may be felt anywhere in the world, including in your home town. But this is hardly the kind of crime for which you can dial the operator or 911 for immediate help from local law enforcement.

We are all too keenly aware of the complete globalization of life on earth, and with it of crime on earth. In this book, we describe the emerging international criminal justice system through which nations—and their criminal justice agencies—cooperate to deal with international and transnational crime.

Before beginning our exploration of these aspects of criminal justice, it is worth noting how the field of criminal justice was created, and how the professions that serve the criminal justice system emerged.

"BCCI crimes were on a grand scale, and included . . . 'support of terrorism, arms trafficking and the sale of nuclear technologies, management of prostitution, the commission and facilitation of income tax evasion, smuggling and illegal immigration and the illicit purchases of banks and real estate.'"
Rupert Cornwell, *The Independent*, October 2, 1992.

THE ORIGIN OF CRIMINAL JUSTICE

Creating a System

For centuries, everywhere in the world, criminal justice was a fragmented, chaotic process or event. Law enforcers would round up suspects for offenses, real or imagined, in violation of laws enacted for the supposed good of all the people but without any basis in the real needs of the society. Judges would adjudicate as many or as few defendants as their time, or the capacity of their courtrooms, would permit. Those convicted would then be turned over to administrators of the penal system. Sometimes these administrators had little to do; at other times they would be swamped with convicts and literally have to farm them out (to prison farms) or sell them as slaves on prison galleys.

By the twentieth century the system had not improved much. In the United States the chaos was exposed by a series of crime commission studies in the

"The findings, known as the Wickersham Report, were devastating: There was little justice in the criminal justice system."

1920s and 1930s, carried out by some of the best legal minds of that era. Following city and statewide studies in Baltimore, Chicago, Cleveland, Memphis, and Philadelphia; and in California, Georgia, Illinois, Michigan, Minnesota, Missouri, New York, Oregon, Pennsylvania, Rhode Island, and Virginia, former Attorney General George W. Wickersham was instructed to conduct a nationwide study of prevailing conditions in the administration of justice (1929–1931). The findings, known as the Wickersham Report, were devastating: There was little justice in the criminal justice system. There was no agreement on principles or objectives. There was no coordination among the different agencies and departments. Most officials were untrained and haphazardly selected, and many were corrupt and brutal. Scholarship was practically nonexistent. In his message to Congress submitting the report, President Herbert Hoover expressed the hope that its revelations would help to cure many abuses.[6]

But the Great Depression of the 1930s and World War II intervened. Only in the 1960s, a decade of civil disturbances on a wide spectrum of social issues, did the movement for reform again gain momentum. Another presidential commission was appointed, the President's Commission on Law Enforcement and Criminal Justice (1967). Under the chairmanship of Nicholas de Belleville Katzenbach, a former attorney general, the commission's staff included some of the most renowned scholars in criminal justice and criminology. Nine task forces reported on specific issues or areas, such as police, courts, corrections, and juvenile delinquency and youth crime. The general report was called *The Challenge of Crime in a Free Society*.[7] It was the first public document to view criminal justice as a system—one that needed development, but still definitely a system. This system was depicted in a now-famous flowchart reproduced in this and many other criminal justice texts since (see Chapter 5 and inside front and back covers), and widely used in the profession. It demonstrates the variety of entrances and exits in the criminal justice process.[8]

Systematic thinking had entered criminal justice. Law enforcement officers, lawyers, judges, corrections officers, and administrative staff could now perceive themselves as playing a role in a defined process. But it is a long way from the recognition that criminal justice might be or should be a system to the perfection of such a system. The National Advisory Commission on Criminal Justice Standards and Goals (1977) moved in that direction with its emphasis on planning and evaluation as a means of creating a system.[9]

The President's Commission report led to the passage of the federal Omnibus Crime Control and Safe Streets Act of 1968, which, among others, created the Law Enforcement Assistance Administration (LEAA) in 1969. During its brief existence (seven years) this federal agency spent nearly $7 billion on a wide variety of national and statewide projects that examined the functioning of criminal justice, investigated solutions to intractable problems, and assisted in training officials. The work of LEAA has been widely criticized, yet even the harshest critics acknowledge that, without the LEAA, there probably would be little criminal justice education in America. Perhaps there would not even be a recognized criminal justice profession.

"Without the LEAA, there probably would be little criminal justice education in America."

Creating a Profession

During the 1950s and 1960s Americans began to realize that many of the rights, and access to opportunities, that the Constitution provided on paper were in fact not granted equally to all citizens. It was clear, for example, that blacks continued to live as second-class citizens, and that women were not afforded the same rights and privileges as men. Citizens charged with crime were denied the due process guarantees the Constitution provided. The U.S. Supreme Court, under the leadership of Earl Warren, chief justice of the United States, squarely addressed these problems, and in case after case ruled that constitutional guarantees must be honored.[10]

In *Gideon v. Wainwright* (1963), for example, the Supreme Court mandated that every criminal defendant—in whatever court—is entitled to the assistance of counsel.[11] In a series of related decisions, culminating in *Miranda v. Arizona* (1966),[12] the Court placed the burden on the police to warn arrestees of their Fifth Amendment right to remain silent and their Sixth Amendment right to have counsel appointed. The cost of not advising arrestees of their rights includes having the defendant's statements excluded from evidence at trial—not to mention any and all evidence obtained as a result of those statements. *Miranda* was a rude awakening for law enforcement agencies all across the country. Poorly selected and inadequately trained officers could not cope with the demands the Supreme Court imposed. Improved recruitment procedures and training were needed. The Supreme Court also invaded the field of corrections by granting prisoners rights they had not had before and placing new managerial burdens on correctional administrators and staff. This created the need for intensive training of corrections officers.

"Poorly selected and inadequately trained officers could not cope with the demands the Supreme Court imposed."

At this point the LEAA stepped in. With grants under the Law Enforcement Education Program (LEEP), postsecondary school training became available for criminal justice personnel, and hundreds of thousands benefited. Moreover, the LEAA grant program encouraged the establishment of schools, colleges, and departments of criminal justice throughout the country. The chances are that you are students in such an educational program and therefore direct beneficiaries of the LEAA and the LEEP program. By now the United States can boast of 18 doctoral academic programs,[13] as many as 157 master's degree programs, and somewhere between 600 and 1,000 college-level educational programs in criminal justice, criminology, and related fields.[14]

"The chances are that you are a student in an educational program begun under the LEAA and thus a direct beneficiary of the LEAA and the LEEP program."

A profession has hallmarks in addition to educational attainment. Professional organizations like the American Medical Association, or the American Bar Association, set standards, encourage compliance with them,[15] and provide a forum for members to meet and to exchange ideas and information. It is true that the component segments of criminal justice have had such professional organizations for a long time. There are the International Association of Chiefs of Police and many other professional police associations. There are the Criminal Law Section of the American Bar Association, the Criminal Trial Lawyers Association, and the International Association of Penal Law. In corrections, the first professional organization was the American Prison Association (founded 1870), now called the American Correctional Association. Many other specialist associations have also been formed. What had been lacking was a general association of specialists in criminal justice. In 1970, the Academy of Criminal Justice Sciences was established. Its title emphasizes that it is concerned with all the professionals working in what is a very practical profession, and that it is indeed a profession, an academy, concerned with scientific inquiry.

Like all professions, criminal justice has its forum, its annual congresses; and it has its journals, including the *Journal of Criminal Justice, Justice Quarterly*, and the *Journal of Criminal Justice Education*.[16] Over the years an impressive body of scientific information has been created by criminal justice researchers, and the field has its acknowledged core of classic works.[17]

"Over the years an impressive body of scientific information has been created by criminal justice researchers."

Careers in Criminal Justice

Criminal justice now has its own distinct career paths. Many criminal justice agencies require a diploma (a two-year college associate degree) or a bachelor's degree in criminal justice for entrance-level appointments. Many others, while not requiring such academic preparation, nevertheless give preference to candidates with an associate or bachelor's degree for appointment to line or operational levels. In 1960, law enforcement agencies (the largest employers in the criminal justice system) required no college education and, in fact, 80 percent of law enforcement officers had no college education. By 1988, two-thirds of all law

· · · · · · · · · · · · · · · · · ·

"By 1988, two-thirds of all law enforcement officers had some college education, in contrast to 20 percent in 1960."

"Understanding criminal justice and the criminal justice system is an important part of responsible citizenship."

"We are all fortunate to be part of the action, at the historical moment when criminal justice emerges as a profession."

The American romance with vigilantism: Actor Steven Segal in a typical scene from one of his many films. Segal portrays Americans as obsessed with the idea that the only way to deal with violent crime is with an even more violent response.

enforcement officers had some college education, a quarter had diploma-level education, and another quarter had bachelor's degrees, mostly from criminal justice-related programs.[18] Many criminal justice agencies, especially police departments, recruit only from among candidates with some college education, whether required by law or not. Graduate degree holders aspire to teaching and research positions. Many also become managers of criminal justice agencies or direct research organizations.

Career opportunities are associated with the quality of the academic program from which aspirants graduate, as well as the quality of the applicant's own background and work. In the past, these career opportunities in criminal justice were exclusively in government service (police, courts, corrections) or at the "criminal justice level" (agencies at every level of government created during the past twenty-five years). The latter are charged with coordinating tasks for the criminal justice system; research into the functioning of agencies within the system; budget and program planning and evaluation; assistance to agencies within their jurisdiction; and policy formulation. More recently, the private sector has absorbed increasing numbers of criminal justice specialists. Private organizations work with agencies of the criminal justice system to provide research and consulting assistance. Private industry now requires an increasing number of criminal justice specialists for protection systems and services, the planning and direction of security systems, the protection of electronic communications, ensuring the inviolability of banking facilities, and a host of other functions.

But while emphasizing the professional and career aspects of criminal justice education, we do not wish to neglect the significance of an understanding of criminal justice as a part of responsible citizenship, and therefore as a part of a liberal arts education.[19]

Accreditation for Criminal Justice Programs

One hotly debated question is whether, to gain professional status, the educational programs in criminal justice that produce practitioners should be subjected to an accreditation system.[20] Other professions have taken this route— medicine, law, nursing, dentistry, engineering, optometry, forestry, social work. Some scholars want accreditation so that those in the criminal justice field can police themselves rather than being policed by those outside the profession.[21] Others argue that criminal justice should be considered a liberal art or a social science like sociology, psychology, political science, or criminology—fields that are not governed by accreditation standards.[22]

But no matter which side of the argument you agree with, we are all fortunate to be part of the action, at the historical moment when criminal justice emerges as a profession.

LOOKING AHEAD

This chapter has previewed the book that will be your guide and companion for a semester. It has acquainted you with the emergence of criminal justice as a strategy, as a system, as a science, and as a profession. It has also described the perspective we use in the book. We focus on three recurring themes: *criminal justice in action,* society's often exciting efforts to deal with the crime problem by proven or innovative means; *criminal justice on trial,* the problems, shortcomings and failures—but also hopes for the future—of contemporary criminal justice; and *criminal justice abroad,* the fact that our crime problems no longer exist in isolation, but rather are shared worldwide.

In the chapters of this first part of the book you will find basic information necessary for a more detailed study of the criminal justice system. Chapter 2 looks at who commits crime and what crimes they commit, Chapter 3 presents sociological and psychological explanations for crime, and Chapter 4 discusses the basic requirements of criminal law. We introduce the system as a whole in Chapter 5.

In Parts 2, 3, and 4 (Chapters 6–16), we examine the component parts of the criminal justice system—the police, the courts, corrections—to see how these have evolved and how they function today. Part 5 (Chapters 17–19) focuses on three complementary criminal justice systems: for juvenile offenders, for victims, and for international and transnational criminals.

Within the last three decades, criminal justice has become an elaborate machine, a system, a science, and a profession. Yet criminal justice is still a process in formation. With all the advances of recent decades, we nevertheless find ourselves in a crisis perhaps without precedent. And the fact that the crisis is global, with rising national as well as international crime rates, only reinforces the sense of urgency to find ways to relieve society of this growing burden.

NOTES

1. Marvin Zalman, *A Heuristic Model of Criminology and Criminal Justice* (Chicago: Joint Commission on Criminology and Criminal Justice Education and Standards, 1981).

2. Harry Marsh, "A Comparative Analysis of Crime Coverage in Newspapers in the United States and Other Countries from 1960–1989: A Review of the Literature," *Journal of Criminal Justice* 19 (1991):67–79.

3. See Otwin Narenin, "Making a Tough Job Tougher: The Legacy of Conservatism," *ACJS Today* 10(1) (1991):1,17–19.

4. See James F. Gilsinan, "Public Policy and Criminology: An Historical and Philosophical Reassessment," *Justice Quarterly* 8 (1991):201–216.

5. Richard Quinney, *Class, State and Crime: On the Theory and Practice of Criminal Justice* (New York: David McKay, 1977).

6. Gerhard O. W. Mueller, *Crime, Law and the Scholars* (London: Heinemann; Seattle: University of Washington Press, 1969), pp. 95–104.

7. The President's Commission on Law Enforcement and Administration of Justice, *The Challenge of Crime in a Free Society* (Washington, D.C.: U.S. Government Printing Office, 1967).

8. Ibid., pp. 8–9.

9. National Advisory Commission on Criminal Justice Standards and Goals, *A National Strategy to Reduce Crime* (Washington, D.C.: U.S. Government Printing Office, 1973).

10. Aptly described in Charles H. Whitebread and Christopher Slobogin, *Criminal Procedure*, 2d ed. (Mineola, N.Y.: The Foundation Press, 1986), pp. 1–14.

11. *Gideon v. Wainwright*, 372 U.S. 335 (1963).

12. *Miranda v. Arizona*, 384 U.S. 436 (1966).

13. Timothy J. Flanagan, "Criminal Justice Doctoral Programs in the United States and Canada: Findings from a National Survey," *Journal of Criminal Justice Education* 1 (1990):195–213.

14. "Criminal Justice Major Programs of Study in American Colleges and Universities, by Type of Program, Level of Degree, and State, 1988–89," *Journal of Criminal Justice Education* 1 (1990):261–262. See also Mittie D. Southerland, "Criminal Justice Curricula in the United States: An Examination of Baccalaureate Programs, 1988–1989," *Journal of Criminal Justice Education* 2 (1991):45–68.

15. See Joint Commission on Criminology and Criminal Justice Standards, *Report of the Joint Commission on Criminology and Criminal Justice Standards* (Chicago: University of Illinois Press, 1980). There is by no means agreement on the need for, or type of, accreditation for criminal justice education. Contrast Stan Shernock, "Social Control and Criminal Justice Education," *ACJS Today* 10 (1991):2, 24–26, with Arnold Binder, "Comments," *ACJS Today* 10 (1991):2, 18.

16. For the focus of criminal justice journals, as distinguished from criminology journals, see Malcolm D. Holmes and William A. Taggart, "A Comparative Analysis of Research Methods in Criminology and Criminal Justice Journals," *Justice Quarterly* 7 (1990):421–437.

17. Larry J. Siegel and Marvin Zalman, "'Cultural Literacy' in Criminal Justice: A Preliminary Assessment," *Journal of Criminal Justice Education* 2 (1991):15–44.

18. David L. Carter and Allen D. Supp, "The Evolution of Higher Education in Law Enforcement: Preliminary Findings from a National Study," *Journal of Criminal Justice Education* 1 (1970):59, 66.

19. Alexis M. Durham III, "Observations on the Future of Criminal Justice Education: Legitimating the Discipline and Serving the General University Population," *Journal of Criminal Justice Education* 3 (1992):35–52.

20. Binder, "Comments."

21. Shernock, "Social Control and Criminal Justice Education." For accreditation of the graduate level, see Leslie T. Wilkins, "The Future of Graduate Education in Criminal Justice: Keeping Curriculum Fashionable? A Personal View," *Journal of Criminal Justice Education* 1 (1990):21–31.

22. Binder, "Comments," and see John B. Bennett and J. W. Peltason, *Contemporary Issues in Higher Education* (New York: Macmillan, 1985); Frederick S. Weaver, *Liberal Education: Critical Essays on Professions, Pedagogy, and Structure* (New York: Teachers College Press, Columbia University, 1991).

CHAPTER 2

EXTENT AND TYPES OF CRIME

"*P*olice lore is rich with examples of officers fighting crime by changing the numbers. In New York City in the 1940's, the joke was that unloved and unwanted cases were assigned to Detective McCann—that is chucked in the garbage can and never reported, said Thomas A. Reppetto, president of the Citizens Crime Commission, a watchdog group.

"After the Federal Bureau of Investigation criticized the department's statistics in 1950, police headquarters began checking all precinct crime reports. That year, robbery reports jumped 400 percent.

"But the fictitious Detective McCann returned to duty in the early 1960s, Mr. Reppetto said. After a new police chief cracked down in 1966, reported robbery figures climbed again.

"As recently as 1983, an audit of reports by the Chicago police revealed widespread underreporting. 'We were cheating and lying,' said Dennis Nowicki, who, as Chicago's Deputy Superintendent for the Bureau of Investigative Services, conducted the audit. 'It just became an institutionalized practice.'

"According to police officials and outside experts, computers and careful checking have made New York City's crime reports as reliable as possible.

"Patrol officers file the initial reports. After going to the scene of a robbery, say, they fill out a police complaint form with such details as whether the victim was shot or stabbed and the value of the stolen property.

"The officers' supervisor then checks the form, signs it and sends it to headquarters in lower Manhattan, where it is checked again for missing information or inconsistencies. Clerks feed the information into the department's computers, and then microfilm the original report."[1] ∎

Detective McCann has long retired from the police department, but the problems have not disappeared with his retirement. How accurate is the assessment by the officers at the crime scene as to what crime—if any—has occurred? Are three stab wounds suffered by one victim three felonious assaults? Who changes the report when the victim dies? How good is the supervisor in following up on complaint reports, reassessing them, correcting them? How skilled is the computer operator? Are today's figures comparable to those compiled by last year's officers? Have any political, budgetary, or election concerns affected the counting of crimes (for example, the need for more police)?

Getting accurate measurements of the number of crimes and criminals is extremely difficult. In fact, questions about how to measure crime and what those measurements tell us about the types and amount of crime and the people who commit them are among the most important issues in contemporary criminal justice. This chapter begins with a look at the objectives and methods of collecting information. We then consider the limitations of the three sources of information that are used most frequently to estimate the nature and extent of crime in the United States: police statistics, victimization surveys, and self-report information. We next explore the measurement of the characteristics of criminals: gender, age, social class, and race. Last, we discuss specific types of crimes: violent crime; a range of crimes against property; white-collar crime; crimes committed by corporations; organized crime; and a variety of drug-, alcohol-, and sex-related crimes.

MEASUREMENT METHODS

On September 28, 1991, eight persons died in separate shooting incidents in Manhattan. An item in the local press reported on that fact and the public took note of this record high number of homicides in their city in a single night.[2] But criminal justice specialists see much more in the events of that evening. They note that all eight homicides occurred in impoverished areas of the inner city; all occurred between 10 P.M. and 1 A.M.; all victims were in their twenties and thirties; seven were men. All but one of the deaths appear to have occurred in the course of a robbery; all were caused by a handgun. To the criminal justice specialist, these details have considerable operational and policy significance.

Measurement Objectives

There are two important reasons for gathering information about crimes and criminals: to help in policy and planning decisions, and to learn more about how and why crimes are committed. Criminal justice agencies need this information for daily operations and for planning and evaluation of various legislative and policy decisions. Their questions include: How many police officers are needed in given areas? How long does it take between arrest and trial? How many people will be incarcerated? For how long? Other questions pertain to policy and legislative decisions. If, for instance, a law changes in a given jurisdiction, what effect does the change have on the amount of victimization? Consider rape laws. Some legislatures have broadened the scope of these laws to include persons not previously covered, such as spouses and persons of the same gender. Obviously, with the widened net the number of reported rapes will increase.[3] In another area, policymakers may need estimates of the changing rates of HIV infection among sexually active inner-city youths and those using intravenous drugs in order to make decisions about targeting these groups for education/prevention/intervention programs.[4] All these changes need to be evaluated—and evaluation requires measurement.

The second objective of measurement is to enhance our knowledge of why people commit crimes and why some offenses are more likely to be committed than others. For instance, researchers may want to study whether people become criminals by learning the criminal values of the groups to which they belong. Or researchers may investigate whether situational factors, such as time of day or type of place, influence the commission of specific offenses. The kinds of information collected and the way they are collected are crucial for daily operation and planning in the criminal justice system; for evaluation of legislative and policy decisions, including verification and updating of such information; and for research on crime causation.

Crime Trends

Experts frequently present crime data in terms of crime rates. These rates are computed with the following formula:

$$\text{Crime rate} = \frac{\text{Number of reported crimes}}{\text{Total population}} \times 100{,}000$$

If we say, for example, that the robbery rate is 257.0, we mean that there were 257.0 robberies for every 100,000 persons in the population under consideration (e.g., all persons over 18 years of age; the total U.S. population). Calculating crime in terms of rates enables us to show whether changes in the population have changed the amount of crime or whether the actual prevalence of crime has changed.

To be prepared for changing demands on the various sectors of the criminal justice system, administrators and policymakers need information about trends. Will there be greater demands on the police force in the years to come? If so, which units of the police will have to work harder? The homicide squad? The juvenile unit? Will more judges and courtrooms be needed? And what of detention facilities and prison space?

Data show that the U.S. crime rate increased slowly between 1930 and 1960 and then began to rise much more quickly. This trend continued until 1980, when the rate was 5,950 per 100,000 (Figure 2.1). From that peak the rate steadily dropped until 1984, when there were 5,031.3 crimes per 100,000. Since then, however, the crime rate has steadily increased.

Several reasons have been presented for the changes in the crime rate over

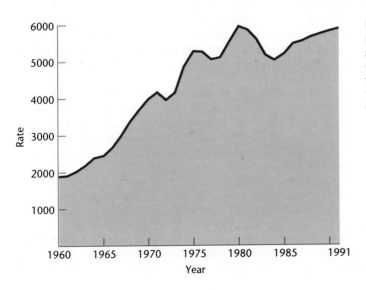

FIGURE 2.1 *Uniform Crime Reports: Rate of all index crimes per 100,000 population, 1960–1991* (*Source:* U.S. Department of Justice, Federal Bureau of Investigation, *Crime in the United States, 1975; 1991* [Washington D.C.: U.S. Government Printing Office, 1976, 1992], pp. 49, 58.)

time. One important factor in the decline from 1980 to 1984 was the age distribution of the population. Given the fact that young people tend to have the highest crime rate, age distribution of the population has a major effect on the number of crimes committed. After World War II, the birth rate increased sharply (in what is known as the "baby boom"). As the baby-boom generation reached its crime-prone years in the 1960s, the crime rate rose; as the baby-boom generation grew older, the crime rate became more stable and in the early 1980s began to decline.

However, the crime rate may have gone down in the early 1980s because of other changes in society. For one, a tougher crime-control policy included mandatory minimum prison sentences for some offenses and less frequent use of parole. In addition, crime prevention programs began to make citizens more aware of what they could do to protect themselves and their neighborhoods.

While these and other reasons (like reporting practices) have been put forth to explain changes in the crime rate, we have no definitive answers. We are not able to explain with any certainty why the rate falls and rises. The rise since 1984 has been linked to drug-related crime against persons and property; an increasing number of the children of baby-boomers reaching their crime-prone years; and the economic recession.

"We are not able to explain with any certainty why the crime rate falls and rises."

Collecting Information

Depending on the questions asked, administrators and researchers collect facts, observations, and other pertinent information—called **data**—on the criminal justice system, criminals, victims, and types of crimes. Given the importance of these data, researchers work constantly on ways to improve the means and methods of collection. Criminal justice data are collected using the normal social science research techniques: survey, experiment, observation, case study. Familiarity with the types of data that are collected and the way in which they are collected will help you understand many of the topics discussed in this book. For much in the field of criminal justice—theories, analyses, predictions—is based on these collected data.

data
Collected facts, observations, and other pertinent information from which conclusions can be drawn.

Surveys. Most of us are familiar with survey research through public opinion polls, marketing research, and election predictions. A **survey** is the systematic collection of answers to questions asked of respondents in questionnaires or interviews; interviews may be conducted face-to-face or by telephone. Typical surveys measure the amount of crime, attitudes toward police, fear of crime, changes in abuse of drugs, and so forth.

survey
The systematic collection of information by asking questions in questionnaires or interviews.

Experiments. **Experiments** demonstrate how two or more variables (factors that may change) are related. If you change one variable while keeping all others the same and then find that another variable also changes, you can assess the extent to which the change in the second variable was caused by the change in the first. New Jersey's Scared Straight! project is an excellent demonstration of the technique.

In the late 1970s, a field experiment (an experiment done in the real world rather than a laboratory) was done at East Jersey State Prison to study whether young boys would avoid committing crimes if they were familiar with the frightening reality of prison life. (The project became known as Scared Straight! because the goal was to scare young people out of crime.) First, several agencies were asked to suggest male youths for the experiment. These boys were then tested to ascertain their attitudes toward punishment, the police, prison, and so forth. Afterward some of the boys were placed in an experimental group that would actually go into the prison. The rest went to a control group, which would not go.

After the experimental group had learned about the horrors of prison life (including rape and other brutalities) from inmates serving life sentences, both groups were again given the attitude tests to find out if the prison experience had

experiment
Research technique in which an investigator introduces a change into a process in order to measure or observe the effects of the change.

FBI employees at work in the fingerprint division. Criminal justice specialists collect many kinds of data, from fingerprints to survey information.

changed the attitudes of the experimental group. It had not. Six months later the juvenile records of both groups were checked to determine how many boys in both the experimental and control groups had committed offenses during the six-month period. Had the youngsters who supposedly were "scared straight" in prison been arrested fewer times than those who had not made the visit? No, according to criminologist James Finckenauer's analysis. In fact, they had been arrested more often than the control group boys.[5] Experiments like this help scientists to determine cause and effect, and educators and corrections personnel to make policy decisions.

Observation. When investigators engage in **observation** they record the activities of the groups they are studying in the groups' natural settings. Since the 1960s this technique has been used to provide information on police behavior, particularly behavior on patrol.[6] Trained observers accompany officers on duty, make observations, and record these observations. These studies have become increasingly sophisticated. A recent one, for instance, has added a debriefing at the conclusion of the encounter. In addition to making observations, investigators record what the officers report they perceive, think, and feel during the incidents that occur.[7]

observation
Recording the activities of groups being studied in their natural settings.

Case Study. A **case study** is an analysis of all pertinent aspects of one unit of study, such as an individual, an institution, a group, or a community. Sources of information are biographies, letters, and diaries. Darrell Steffensmeier's *The Fence: In the Shadow of Two Worlds* and Carl Klockars' *The Professional Fence*, each based on the life of a particular fence (a person who buys stolen goods on a regular basis), demonstrate the kind of detailed information that a researcher can get using this technique. Vincent Swazzi (Klockars' fence) is quite proud of his status in the community: "The way I look at it, this is actually my street. I mean I am the mayor. I walk down the street an' people come out the doors to say, 'hello.' "[8]

case study
Analysis of all pertinent aspects of one unit of study.

"The way I look at it, this is actually my street. I mean I am the mayor."
Vincent Swazzi, in *The Professional Fence.*

Available Data. It is not always feasible, or necessary, to collect new information by use of surveys, experiments, observation, or case study. Vast amounts of data, gathered by individual researchers and private and public organizations for their own purposes, are already available.[9] The police, the courts, and corrections officials, for example, publish reports on the number and characteristics of

NEW CONCERNS—NEW CRIMES

On New Year's Eve, 1991, you had no trouble getting an order of eggs sunnyside-up at any New Jersey restaurant.

On New Year's Day, 1992, you had to go to Pennsylvania or New York for your favorite breakfast treat. Overnight, serving raw or runny eggs had become a crime in New Jersey. The new law, meant to protect people from eggs contaminated with salmonella bacteria, imposed a fine from $25 to $100 on restaurants for serving any dish containing raw eggs, including Eggs Benedict, Steak Tartar, or Caesar Salad (1).

The recognition of certain acts as crimes typically evolves over a period of time, although the enactment of laws may catch some people unaware. Which acts will be made crimes is established through social and political processes. Currently we are witnessing the emergence of two new types of crime: stalking and hate crimes. Neither has been considered a crime in the past. So how does an act come to be defined as a crime by society?

Stalking

Stalking, which Webster's defines as following or pursuing another in a stealthy, furtive, or persistent manner, was not a crime at common law. The harm in stalking would have been rejected as too slight to warrant its prohibition under threat of punishment. Indeed, the common law of crimes punished nothing as an offense against a person that was not at least "an attempt or offer with force and violence to do a corporal hurt to another" (2). But recent and highly publicized cases have alerted the public and the legislatures to the potential danger in stalking. Women have been pursued persistently by jilted partners or by men who simply fancied an actual or potential relationship with them. Some stalkers have maimed and killed their targets. But even people merely harassed by stalkers have suffered anguish and distress (3).

Society's response has been to define stalking as a crime. According to the National Conference of State Legislatures, twenty states have created the crime of stalking and at least a dozen others have similar legislation pending. It has not been easy to delimit the new crime. Newspaper reporters, private detectives, the police, supervisors, and examination monitors do "stalking" for a living. Most laws require that there be a "credible threat of violence" against the victim and that the victim actually suffers anguish. There has been no agreement on penalties, either: The California law provides for a possible one-year jail term and a $1,000 fine (4); in some other states stalking has become a felony, subject to imprisonment in the state penitentiary. As yet no one knows the effect these new laws will have on would-be stalkers: Some are undoubtedly emotionally disturbed and therefore less likely to be deterred by provisions of the criminal law.

Hate crimes

Hate crimes also did not exist under common law, which assumed that civilized society would resolve its problems of prejudice by civil rather than criminal means. But crimes against ethnic groups and against groups defined by sexual preferences other than those of the majority have recently become the focus of public concern—acts such as chasing down and beating up a man simply because he is gay, for example, or spray-painting "Nigger Go Home" on a family's garage door. Whether these acts actually have increased in number is a more difficult question (see Figure 1); in any case, concern about them has increased.

This concern has generated three types of responses: first, law enforcement agencies have categorized these acts as hate crimes to permit assessment and the planning of community or educational responses; there is now a National Hate Crime Statistics Act. Second, some states have created a new "hate crime," a misdemeanor, for which an offender could be convicted in addition to whatever other crime he or she may have committed (for example, an assault). An Illinois statute falls into this category (5). Third, specific laws may penalize particular acts deemed inherently hate crimes. One such law, a municipal ordinance in St. Paul, Minnesota, banning cross burnings, was held unconstitutional by the Supreme Court as violating the First Amendment (right to free speech) (6).

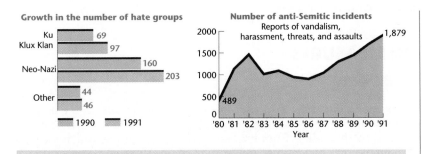

Growth in the number of hate groups

Group	1990	1991
Ku Klux Klan	69	97
Neo-Nazi	160	203
Other	44	46

Number of anti-Semitic incidents
Reports of vandalism, harassment, threats, and assaults

489 ... 1,879

'80 '81 '82 '83 '84 '85 '86 '87 '88 '89 '90 '91
Year

FIGURE 1. Hate Groups, Crimes Increase
(*Source:* Figures from Southern Poverty Law Center; Anti-Defamation League, B'nai B'rith; in *U.S.A. Today,* March 13, 1992, p. 3.)

Do numbers and types of crimes ever decrease?

Are such new laws likely to change the national crime statistics? Probably not. None of them falls within the eight categories of the Part I offenses of the Uniform Crime Reports (UCR). Few of the new crimes can find a place among the twenty-one Part II offense types of the UCR, except the category "all other offenses." But even if they did fit the UCR categories, the new crimes are not likely to change the statistics by much. Most hate crimes will probably be reported within the categories of the principal offense committed—for example, homicide or arson.

Is an old crime ever taken off the statute books? It happens rarely, but it did happen with the end of Prohibition. No crime problem had vexed Americans as much as the illegal manufacture and sale of alcoholic beverages. This crime nightmare ended on December 5, 1933, with repeal of the Eighteenth Amendment. A similarly drastic demise of criminal laws occurred in the wake of the collapse of the Soviet Union in 1991, when market economy criminality became legitimate business. But short of a constitutional decision by a supreme court, a constitutional amendment, or a revolution, the number of crime types will continue to increase as new problems arise in society and as old problems are redefined.

SOURCES

1. Reuters news release, January 13, 1992.
2. Hawkins, *Pleas of the Crown,* 6th ed., Vol. I (London, 1787), p. 263.
3. Elizabeth Ross, "The Problem of Men Stalking Women Spurs New Laws," *The Christian Science Monitor,* June 11, 1992, p. 6.
4. California Penal Code S 646.9 (1992).
5. Illinois Rev. Stat. Ch. 38, 12-7.8 (1991).
6. *R.A.V. v. City of St. Paul, Minnesota,* No. 90-7675, 1992.

QUESTIONS FOR DISCUSSION

1. Criminal laws may be enacted by legislatures under public pressure or at the initiative of powerful lobbies. What should legislatures do before enacting a law to ensure that it is reasonably calculated to prevent a significant harm?
2. Present an example of something not currently considered a crime that you think should be one. Why would you propose it as a new crime?
3. Salmonella bacteria may cause gastrointestinal illness, and since 1985 46 eggs among the trillions sold in America have caused salmonella deaths. Cigarette smoking is linked to death from lung cancer. Do you think selling cigarettes should be a crime? Defend your position.

persons passing through the criminal justice system at various points. But while it may be cost effective to use these kinds of data, it is risky. Many official records are incomplete or have been collected in such a manner as to make them inadequate for comparative purposes.

MAJOR MEASURES

Estimates of the extent and nature of crime in the United States come primarily from the Federal Bureau of Investigation's Uniform Crime Reports, based on data compiled by the police; from the National Crime Survey, which measures crime through reports by victims; and from various self-report surveys that ask individuals about criminal acts they have committed, whether or not these acts have come to the attention of the police. After we look at the police statistics and their limitations, we will explore the usefulness of victimization and self-report studies.

Uniform Crime Reports

The FBI collects data on crimes known to the police, which it then compiles into the Uniform Crime Reports (UCR), published annually. Each month approximately 16,000 city, county, and state law enforcement agencies, covering 97 percent of the total population, voluntarily send information on twenty-nine types of offenses brought to their attention, whether or not an arrest has been made.

Part I and Part II Offenses.   The UCR separate offenses into two major groups: Part I and Part II. Part I offenses include eight crimes divided into crimes against the person (criminal homicide, forcible rape, robbery, aggravated assault) and crimes against property (burglary, larceny-theft, motor vehicle theft, and arson). Because these **index crimes** are serious, they tend to be reported to the police more reliably than others, and they are used collectively as a *crime index*, or indicator, of changes in crime rates over time. Except for traffic violations, all twenty-one other offenses are Part II crimes. They include fraud, embezzlement, weapons offenses, vandalism, and simple assaults. Since crime definitions differ from state to state, the UCR uses a rather broad set of descriptions that may not be legally correct in any one state, but that encompass most criminal events in each category. Moreover, there are some crimes that are not included in any of the UCR categories (see the Criminal Justice in Action box).

In addition to the number and rates of reported crimes, the UCR include the number of crimes "cleared by arrest," information about the circumstances of crimes (such as time, place, and geographic region), descriptions of offenders (age, sex, and race), and the distribution of law enforcement personnel.

index crimes
The eight major crimes included in Part I of the UCR: criminal homicide, forcible rape, robbery, aggravated assault, burglary, larceny-theft, motor vehicle theft, and arson.

Limitations.   The UCR cannot, however, be relied on unquestioningly. They have limited usefulness in categories where the majority of crimes go unreported; they do not differentiate between completed and attempted acts; and where two or more offenses occur in a single event (e.g., robbery and homicide), only the most serious is included. In addition, the UCR do not include federal crimes or most white-collar offenses. Apparent fluctuations in crime rates may also be due to a politically motivated desire on the part of a particular police department to show that its crime rate went down (effective policing) or went up (to justify need for more officers).[10]

"Fluctuations in crime rates may also be due to the desire of a particular police department to show that rates went down."

Improving the Uniform Crime Reports.   In 1986 the International Association of Chiefs of Police, the National Sheriffs' Association, and the state-level UCR programs joined forces with the FBI to deal with the limitations of the UCR. A new reporting system was developed, called the <u>National Incident-Based Reporting</u> <u>System (NIBRS)</u>. Reporting to the NIBRS is voluntary and will coexist with the <u>UCR.</u> Each offense is considered an "incident" and information is recorded about the offender, victim, property, and so forth. There are fifty-two items of information about twenty-two types of crimes.[11] The implementation of NIBRS depends on the resources and abilities of law enforcement agencies. Thus far four states contribute data in the NIBRS format, thirteen states are testing the system, and twenty-seven states are in various planning stages.

The NIBRS is a major attempt to improve the collection of crime data. But it deals only with crimes that come to the attention of the police. What about those crimes that remain unreported? For this "dark figure of crime" we have to rely on victimization data and self-report studies (see the Criminal Justice Abroad box).

Victimization Surveys

<u>Victimization surveys measure crime by interviewing individuals about their</u> <u>experiences</u>. The best-known national study, compiled annually by the Bureau of the Census in cooperation with the Bureau of Justice Statistics, is called the National Crime Survey (NCS). The NCS estimates the total number of offenses committed by asking individuals from a national sample of about 47,000 households about their experiences as victims during a given time period.

NCS Information. The NCS includes victimization by rape, robbery, assault, larceny, burglary, and motor vehicle theft. Nationwide, NCS data give us variations of crime rates by region, season, time of day, and specific places, among others.[12] The survey gathers information about crimes (where and when they occur, use of weapons, number of offenders), about offenders (perceived age, gender and race), and about the victims themselves. Interviewers also try to identify the reasons why people do not report crimes to the police. The reasons victims give include, among others: believing the offense too minor, judgment that the police will do nothing about it, red tape surrounding the reporting process, and fear of reprisal.[13] (We will return to a detailed discussion of victims in Chapter 18.)

Data from the NCS (Figure 2.2) show that the number of crimes reported to the police and the number reported in the victimization survey are far apart. According to the NCS data for 1991, there were 34.7 million victimizations. But the UCR show that only 14.8 million index crimes (excluding arson) were reported to the police.

Limitations. While victimization surveys give us information about offenses that individuals do not report to the police, these data have major limitations. The NCS includes only six offenses, whereas there are eight offenses in Part I of the UCR and twenty-one more in Part II. Since the NCS is based on personal reporting, it suffers from the fact that memories may fade, interviewees may try to please interviewers by fabricating crimes, or respondents may move crimes that happened at an earlier time into the time period under study. Further, the NCS is conducted by interview, and there is the possibility that recording styles may differ, resulting in the recording of the same information in different ways.

Self-Report Studies

A third method of determining the extent and types of crime committed is to ask people to report their own delinquent and criminal acts in an anonymous questionnaire or, occasionally, in a confidential interview. This method of collecting data is called the **self-report survey.**

self-report survey
Survey that respondents answer by confidential interview or anonymous questionnaire.

Self-Report Information. In one of the earliest self-report studies (1947), close to 1,700 seemingly law-abiding people were questioned on whether they had

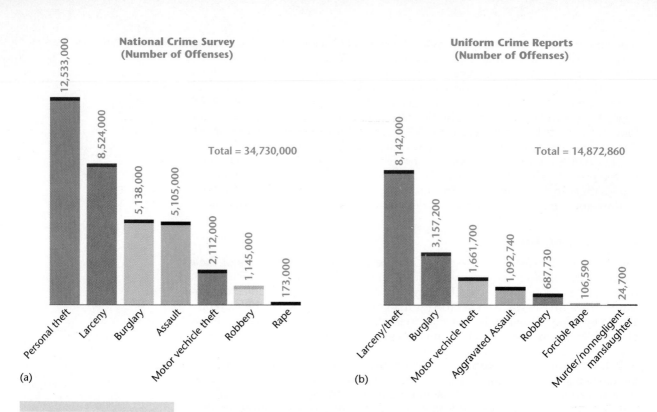

National Crime Survey
(Number of Offenses)

Uniform Crime Reports
(Number of Offenses)

Total = 34,730,000

12,533,000 — Personal theft
8,524,000 — Larceny
5,138,000 — Burglary
5,105,000 — Assault
2,112,000 — Motor vechicle theft
1,145,000 — Robbery
173,000 — Rape

(a)

Total = 14,872,860

8,142,000 — Larceny/theft
3,157,200 — Burglary
1,661,700 — Motor vechicle theft
1,092,740 — Aggravated Assault
687,730 — Robbery
106,590 — Forcible Rape
24,700 — Murder/nonnegligent manslaughter

(b)

FIGURE 2.2 *National Crime Survey and Uniform Crime Reports: A comparison of number of crimes reported [a] National Crime Survey: Total number of victimizations, 1991** (*Source:* Adapted from U.S. Department of Justice, Bureau of Justice Statistics, *National Update* [Washington D.C.: U.S. Government Printing Office], 1993, p. 8.)
[b] Uniform Crime Reports: Total number of index offenses, 1991 (*Source:* Adapted from U.S. Department of Justice, Federal Bureau of Investigation, *Crime in the United States, 1991* [Washington D.C.: U.S. Government Printing Office, 1992], p. 58.)

*Victimization rates are calculated on the basis of the number of victimizations per 100,000 persons aged 12 or older or per 100,000 households.

committed any of forty-nine crimes that were serious enough to require a maximum sentence of not less than one year.[14] Eighty percent of the men reported committing such offenses. This study provided one of the earliest challenges to the conventional wisdom that only a small proportion of the general population commits crime. Since the 1940s, self-report studies have continued to provide information on "hidden delinquency." It appears, for example, that an estimated 90 percent of all youngsters commit delinquent or criminal acts, and that there is a wide disparity between official and self-report data as regards age, race, and gender of offenders.[15]

Limitations. One of the major drawbacks to self-report surveys is that the questionnaires are often limited to petty acts, such as truancy, and therefore are not representative of the range of criminal acts people may commit. Criminologists have argued that discrepancies with respect to gender, race, and class between official statistics and self-report data are due to the fact that different *kinds* of behavior rather than different *amounts* of the same behavior are being measured.[16] Other criticisms relate to the fact that most of the studies involve high school or college students; moreover, those who choose not to participate may have good reason not to discuss their activities.

Police reports, victimization surveys, and self-report studies provide different dimensions to our measurement of crime. They also allow us to examine issues relating to who commits crime. Are crime rates related to gender, race, and socio-economic status? We now turn to this question.

WHO COMMITS CRIME?

Behind each crime is a criminal, or several criminals. These criminals can be differentiated by gender, age, social class, race, and other criteria. These charac-

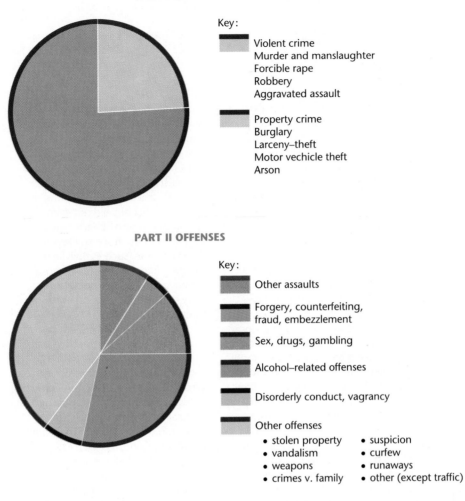

PART I OFFENSES

Key:

▬ Violent crime
Murder and manslaughter
Forcible rape
Robbery
Aggravated assault

▬ Property crime
Burglary
Larceny–theft
Motor vechicle theft
Arson

PART II OFFENSES

Key:

▬ Other assaults

▬ Forgery, counterfeiting, fraud, embezzlement

▬ Sex, drugs, gambling

▬ Alcohol–related offenses

▬ Disorderly conduct, vagrancy

▬ Other offenses
  • stolen property   • suspicion
  • vandalism   • curfew
  • weapons   • runaways
  • crimes v. family   • other (except traffic)

FIGURE 2.3 *Distribution of total number of arrests, 1991 (estimated)* (*Source:* U.S. Department of Justice, Federal Bureau of Investigation, *Crime in the United States, 1991* [Washington D.C.: U.S. Government Printing Office, 1992], p. 223.)

teristics enable us to group criminals into categories, and it is these categories that criminal justice agencies and researchers find useful. In 1991 there were 10,743,755 arrests for all crimes except traffic violations. Figure 2.3 shows how these arrests were distributed by offense. Now let us take a closer look at the individuals behind the statistics.

Gender and Crime

Until the 1970s the subject of women and crime had received little attention from criminal justice administrators, the research community, and the mass media. All tended to perceive female offenders as misguided children who had deviated, primarily for psychological reasons, from the roles assigned to them by society. This perception has been considerably transformed. The criminality of women has become a recognized area of concern in an increasing body of knowledge dealing with contemporary problems. Administrators and researchers are analyzing current female criminality in relation to the criminal justice system, to historical stereotypes, and to women's particular socioeconomic problems in contemporary society.

Except for such crimes as prostitution, shoplifting, and welfare fraud, males traditionally appear to have committed more crimes than females at all ages, although the proportions have changed in recent decades: Women have gone

"The criminality of women has become a recognized area of concern in an increasing body of knowledge dealing with contemporary problems."

23

COLLECTING WORLD CRIMINAL JUSTICE DATA

Crime problems do not stop at national borders. The production and sale of illegal drugs is a transnational operation, and terrorist and organized crime groups often work across national borders. These and other global crime problems, affecting the quality of life worldwide, cannot be resolved without international cooperation. But such cooperation is difficult when the dimensions of the problem are unknown. Just as a government cannot plan for the development of the country—and that includes crime control—without all the facts before it, neither can the United Nations come up with a plan to deal with the world crime problem without a solid core of basic information.

The U.N. surveys

The idea that effective international cooperation is necessary to solve crime problems was behind the first effort to collect data worldwide. In the mid-1970s, United Nations officials in the Crime Prevention and Criminal Justice Branch of the Secretariat were told by the General Assembly to prepare a worldwide statistical report on crime. Some 150 countries were to be surveyed. They had widely divergent legal systems, were at the extreme ends of the socioeconomic development scale, and had widely differing views on the extent to which the incidence of crime should be publicly known.

Questionnaires about the extent of crime, grouped in a few very broad categories, were prepared by the U.N.'s Crime Prevention and Criminal Justice Branch. They were reviewed and amended by its Committee on Crime Prevention and Control, a body of twenty-seven crime experts representing all regions of the world. The questionnaires, in Arabic, Chinese, English, French, Russian, and Spanish, were sent to the ambassadors of all countries at U.N. headquarters in New York City and from there to Foreign Ministries (State Departments) in individual countries. The questionnaires then went to the Ministries of Justice or Interior (responsible for police), the correctional institutions, and the statistical offices in each country. The first crime survey, covering the years 1970–1975, appeared in 1977. Just under a third of the world's countries—forty seven—provided responses that could be analyzed.

Responses were better for the second survey, covering the years 1975–1980. Seventy countries replied, and sixty-five responses were analyzable (see Figure 1). One important change had occurred: While some countries had insisted on anonymity at first, this demand was no longer made. The third survey was even more successful: ninety-five governments responded, and seventy-eight replies, representing half of the world's countries, were analyzable (1).

Analyzing levels of participation

A researcher at Rutgers University has tried to ascertain why some countries did not participate in the first three world crime surveys (2). He discovered that crime statistics are being kept by countries ac-

counting for almost all of the world's population. Sixteen of these countries did not participate in any of the world crime surveys, including China, which alone accounts for one-fifth of the world's population. But sixty-six countries and autonomous jurisdictions did not even respond to this researcher's request for information. It seems likely that some of these, such as Bolivia, the Peoples' Republic of Korea, and Monaco, do keep crime statistics. Why do they not respond to requests for information?

Some of the countries are so small that their administrative staffs may not be able to cope with the requests—perhaps Andorra, Liechtenstein, and Sikkim. Others, such as Afghanistan and Cambodia, are embroiled in wars and civil strife and cannot keep track of their crime problems. Countries such as Angola, Gambia, Guinea, Mali, and Niger have emerged from colonial rule so recently that they have not been able to collect statistics on their crime problems. Some countries simply will not participate, perhaps because of the notion that the incidence of crime reflects negatively on a nation's standing, or because it may affect the tourist trade, or because crime rates contradict a philosophy that crime disappears with the achievement of national goals. Others cannot participate because there are no criminal justice statisticians to count crimes. These countries can be helped through training courses, manuals and guides for collecting crime statistics, and technical assistance, and the United Nations has been supporting such efforts.

Interpreting results

The increase in participation with

each survey is a positive sign, but researchers also face problems in interpreting world crime statistics. Reported crime rates may reflect "real" rates of crime, or they may reflect the efficiency and veracity with which crimes are detected, reported, and recorded in a particular country. Some offenses go unreported in most countries (corruption, white-collar crime, and use of illegal drugs, for example) and therefore do not appear in the world crime surveys. Countries differ in the way they categorize crime, and that affects the ability of researchers to make comparisons among countries.

But these problems are almost trivial in comparison with the very real cultural and political differences among countries. Differences in culture include differences in norms and values, and that leads to different laws. The difference in laws causes a profound difference in what is seen as crime—and what would be reported on a question-naire as crime. In most countries, alcohol consumption is a perfectly legitimate leisure activity. Yet in some countries it is a crime. In most countries, the crime of rape does not exist between spouses. In the United States, by contrast, recent laws have extended the definition of rape (often called sexual assault) to include forced sexual relations between spouses and even persons of the same gender.

Political differences among societies also complicate the task of compiling useful statistics on global crime. What one society defines as an act of terrorism—and hence a crime—another society may call an act of liberation. A civil or human rights violation in one country—for example, the imprisonment of suspects—may be defined as "crime control" by another.

Predicting the future

Despite all the caveats, researchers have been able to determine some very general trends in broad cate-gories of crimes—thefts, homicides, assaults, and drug-related crimes, for example. The third U.N. world crime survey (3), released in 1990, has been used to project a doubling of the overall world crime rate from 1985 to the year 2000 (4,000 per 100,000 population to 8,000 per 100,000). Of course, international efforts to curb crime may be able to prove that prediction incorrect.

SOURCES

1. U.N. Committee on Crime Prevention and Control, *The United Nations and Crime Prevention* (New York: United Nations, 1991).
2. G.O.W. Mueller, World survey on the availability of criminal justice statistics (Newark, N.J.: Rutgers University, 1992).
3. *Third United Nations Survey of Crime Trends, Operations of Criminal Justice Systems and Crime Prevention Strategies* (New York: United Nations, 1990).

QUESTIONS FOR DISCUSSION

1. Give an example (from a newspaper, magazine, or history book) of an act that is seen as a crime in one society and not in another. Is the disparity caused by political or normative differences? Explain.
2. The Rutgers researcher found that countries may base their published crime rates on a variety of information sources: national victimization surveys, sentenced offenders, arrest rates, conviction rates, crimes reported to the police, and imprisonment figures. How would these sources of information affect the estimate of crime rates for each country? Explain.
3. If you were in charge of the next United Nations world crime survey, what would you do to try to get more countries to respond to the questionnaire? Give three suggestions.

FIGURE 1. Replies to Three U.N. Surveys of Crime Trends

Note: For the First Survey: 64 replies received, 47 analyzed.
For the Second Survey: 70 replies received, 65 analyzed.
For the Third Survey: 95 replies received, 78 analyzed.

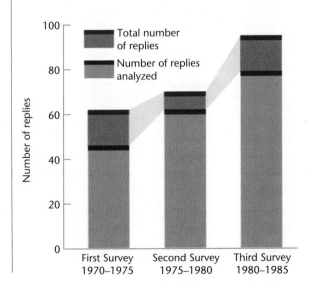

from 11 percent of the total number of arrests in 1960 to 19 percent in 1991. According to the UCR for 1991, for example, female arrestees accounted for 22 percent of the index crime arrests, 12 percent of violent crime arrests, and 25 percent of property crime arrests.[17]

A quarter of a century after the last of a small number of books on female crime appeared, authored by Otto Pollack in 1952, two researchers, working independently, decided to take a fresh look at female crime in light of social changes for women in contemporary society. In 1975 Freda Adler argued that the stresses, challenges, strains, and temptations to which women have been increasingly subjected would be reflected in their crime rates, especially in the area of property offenses.[18] In other words, as the social and economic roles of women changed in the legitimate world, women's participation in crime would also change. Rita Simon took a similar position. She hypothesized that since the propensity of men and women to commit crime is not basically different, as more women enter the labor force and work in a broader range of jobs, their property crime rate will go up.[19]

Since then there has been scholarly debate on the role of women in crime. Some contend that the extent of female criminality has not changed, but that crimes committed by women are more often making their way into official statistics simply because they are reported and prosecuted more often than previously.[20] Others argue that the rate of female criminality has indeed increased, but they attribute the increase to petty property offenses.[21] Moreover, some claim that the increase in these petty property offenses suggests that women are still economically disadvantaged.[22]

The questions currently being raised are not just theoretical; empirical answers are of considerable practical significance for the criminal justice system. If there is an increase in the number of female offenders, what adjustments will have to be made in correctional institutions? If young mothers are incarcerated, what will happen to their children? Thus far there are many questions, and very few answers.

Age and Crime

Though persons under 18 years of age comprise about 8 percent of the population, they account for almost one-third of the arrests for index crimes. Arrest rates decline after age 30 and taper off to about 2 percent or less from age 50 on.[23] This decline in criminal activities with increasing age is known as the **aging-out phenomenon.** A lively scientific debate currently centers on whether crime decreases with age for *all* offenders, even for those who commit frequent offenses. Michael Gottfredson and Travis Hirschi contend that people have a certain inclination to commit crimes, which inclination peaks in the middle or late teens and then declines through life "regardless of sex, race, country, time, or offense."[24]

The opposing side of the argument is that the decline in crime rates after adolescence does not mean that the number of crimes committed by *all* individual offenders declines. In other words, the frequency of offending may go down for most offenders, but some chronic offenders may continue to commit the same amount of crime—or an increased amount—over time. Factors that influence each individual to give up criminal activity vary. Therefore, the relationship between age and crime is not the same for all offenders and offenses. To learn more about how the causes of crime vary at different ages, Alfred Blumstein and his colleagues suggest that we study criminal careers, a concept that encompasses the onset of criminal activity, types and amount of crime committed, and the termination of such activity.[25] Starting in the 1960s, researchers at the Sellin Center at the University of Pennsylvania began studies in this area. Marvin Wolfgang, Robert Figlio, and Thorsten Sellin described the criminal careers of 9,945 boys born in Philadelphia in 1945. Their major finding is that 6 percent of the total number were chronic repeaters who had committed five or more offenses,

aging-out phenomenon
The concept that offenders commit less crime as they get older.

and this group was responsible for over half of all the offenses known committed.[26] Presently, the National Institute of Justice, along with private foundations, is funding another major longitudinal study.

The policy implications of the research on criminal careers is quite clear. If a small number of offenders commit a large percentage of all crime, the crime rate should decrease if we incarcerate those chronic offenders for long periods of time. A number of jurisdictions across the country are changing their sentencing policies to do just that, but this is a highly controversial policy (see Chapter 13).

Social Class and Crime

Relating social class to crime is more difficult than relating gender or age to crime. First, the term "class" is hard to define. If "lower class" is determined by income, then unemployed bank presidents, students on small allowances, and welfare mothers might be in the same category. Second, some researchers claim, any association found between class and crime could be related to bias on the part of the police, who may be more likely to arrest a lower-class suspect than a middle-class suspect.[27] While there are debates on the social class of persons who commit crime, there is no debate about the social class of prisoners. The average male inmate is unskilled, unemployed, and undereducated (has not completed high school). If he has been working, his average annual income is about $5,600.[28]

Race and Criminality

Data on race and crime show that while blacks make up approximately 12 percent of the population, they account for 29 percent of all arrests for index crimes.[29] Blacks account for 45 percent of all arrests for violent crime. Fifty percent of black urban males are arrested for an index crime at least once during their lives, compared with 14 percent of white males. Moreover, the leading cause of death among young black men is murder.[30]

Criminal justice specialists need to look carefully at these statistics because they raise a number of important questions about how the criminal justice system operates. Are blacks picked up as suspects more often than whites? Is there more police surveillance in black neighborhoods? Do blacks receive different treatment in the courts? In prisons? And last, if blacks commit a disproportionately higher number of offenses than whites, what are the reasons?[31] (In subsequent chapters we shall return to these issues.)

Thus far, we have demonstrated the importance of collecting data on crime and criminals. In the next part of the chapter we take a closer look at specific types of crimes and the people who commit them: we look at violent crimes, property and economic crimes, organized crime, and crimes against public morality.

Increasing attention is being paid to the effects of social class on the response of the criminal justice system.
Source: *The New Yorker*, October 8, 1990, p. 44.

VIOLENT CRIMES

The taking of life is the most serious harm one human being can inflict on another. Consequently, we begin this section on violent crime with criminal homicide. Serious attacks that do not result in death are assaults of various types, including sexual assault (rape) and the forceful taking of property from another person (robbery). The penal codes do not define as crimes some other patterns of violent behavior, but these are important enough in practice to warrant separate explanation. One such pattern is terrorism, which encompasses a variety of crimes.

"It was a command and I followed it. Sam told me what to do and I did it."
Serial murderer David Berkowitz, "Son of Sam," *Time*, August 22, 1977.

HANDGUN VIOLENCE AND HANDGUN CONTROL

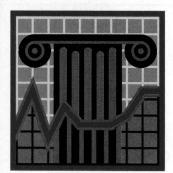

By any standard, the United States leads developed countries when it comes to homicides, and by far the largest number of homicides are committed with handguns. Americans kill twenty-two fellow citizens for each 100,000 of the population, compared with 1.4 citizens in Switzerland and 0.33 in Austria (see Figure 1). The statistics are just as disturbing if we make a city-by-city comparison among cities of equal size in developed countries. For example, Atlanta, Georgia, has ten times as many murders as Copenhagen, Denmark, and New York has more than twenty times the murder rate of London, England.

The United States had nearly 9,000 handgun murders in 1991, and a hotly debated question is whether tighter controls on the availability of handguns would reduce the rate of violent crime. The debate escalated after the 1981 attempted assassination of President Ronald Reagan that permanently disabled his press secretary, James Brady.

Many of those who oppose regulation, including the 3 million members of the National Rifle Association (NRA), argue that it is people who kill, not guns. Gun control opponents claim it is their constitutional right to own firearms. Many display their convictions on bumper stickers that read, "When guns are outlawed, only outlaws will have guns." And many contend that gun ownership helps deter crimes, an argument that has found support in the sociological literature.

Gun control advocates include the twelve major law enforcement groups in the United States, the private organization Handgun Control, and an estimated three-quarters of the American public. They say that regulation or even prohibition of gun ownership is a much quicker way to reduce gun-related criminality than such long-term attempts as changing the causes of social problems.

Does handgun control reduce handgun-related crime? A variety of methods of controlling handgun use have been tried; some 20,000 laws that regulate firearms already exist in the United States. Three methods have been studied in detail.

- A prohibition against carrying guns in public seemed to be related to a drop in gun crimes in Boston (1) and a leveling off of handgun violence in Detroit (2).
- Sentence enhancement, a gun control method that provides additional sentences for crimes committed with a gun, has been studied in six U.S. cities. Homicides committed with firearms decreased in all six cities after sentence enhancement laws took effect, although the decline in homicides was large in some cities and small in others. The researchers studying sentence enhancement point out that its effectiveness is related to how closely judges follow the law. An additional three years in prison may deter criminals from using guns, while an additional month may not (3).
- A third method of gun control, a total ban on handguns, was tried in Washington, D.C., beginning in 1976. Both gun homicides and gun suicides dropped visibly after the ban took effect, while no change occurred in homicides and suicides not committed with guns (4).

All three of these methods did result in some decrease in handgun-related deaths, but none caused drastic reductions. As two gun control researchers point out, the important question to be answered with regard to gun control is this: How many deaths must be prevented by a gun control method to justify its use? Very few of the millions of people who own guns commit crimes with them, and control policies will affect legitimate owners as well as criminals. David McDowall and Alan Lizotte ask:

Is the legitimate happiness of 10 million gun owners worth the lives of 10,000 murder victims? One hundred murder victims? One murder victim? In another context, Is a highly restrictive measure that would save 200 lives better than a less restrictive measure that would save 100? There is no obvious answer to these questions, and different people will draw the line in different places (5).

One technique for controlling handguns that some communities have tried is a buy-back program. St. Louis, San Francisco, Philadelphia, New York, and several other cities have embarked on such programs to reduce the number of handguns in circulation in the community. Police departments buy guns, no questions asked, for $50. In October of 1991, the St. Louis Police Department bought 5,371 guns from citizens in ten days. The Philadelphia police received 1,044 guns within a two-week period. Whether the programs have reduced gun-related crime has not been studied, and McDowall and Lizotte point out a general lack of careful gun control research.

Perhaps we can learn from the countries with low gun-related homicide rates. Many citizens of Switzerland and Israel, for example, have army-issue firearms at their constant disposal by virtue of citizen-army requirements, yet these weapons are not being used for homicides. What factors control the use of handguns in these countries? Even if comparative studies come up with useful findings, the political problems surrounding gun control in the United States will probably continue to hinder the development of nationwide, or even statewide, gun control policies for some time to come (6).

SOURCES

1. Glenn L. Pierce and William J. Bowers, "The Bartley-Fox Gun Law's Short-Term Impact on Crime in Boston," *Annals of the American Academy of Political and Social Science* 455 (1981):120–137.
2. Patrick W. O'Carroll, Colin Loftin, John B. Waller, Jr., David McDowall, Allen Bukoff, Richard O. Scott, James A. Mercy, and Brian Wiersema, "Preventing Homicide: An Evaluation of the Efficacy of a Detroit Gun Ordinance," *American Journal of Public Health* 81 (1991):576–581.
3. David McDowall, Colin Loftin, and Brian Wiersema, "A Comparative Study of the Preventive Effects of Mandatory Sentencing Laws for Gun Crimes," Discussion Paper 6 (College Park, Md.: Violence Research Group, Institute of Criminal Justice and Criminology, University of Maryland, 1991).
4. Colin Loftin, David McDowall, Brian Wiersema, and Talbert J. Cottey, "Effects of Restrictive Licensing of Handguns on Homicide and Suicide in the District of Columbia," *New England Journal of Medicine* 325 (1991):1615–1620.
5. David McDowall and Alan Lizotte, "Gun Control," in Calhoun and Ritzer, *Introduction to Social Problems* (New York: Primis Database, McGraw-Hill, 1993).
6. James D. Wright, Peter H. Rossi, and Kathleen Daly, with the assistance of Eleanor Weber-Burdin, *Under the Gun: Weapons, Crime and Violence in America* (New York: Aldine, 1983), p. 244.

QUESTIONS FOR DISCUSSION

1. One problem with prohibiting carrying arms in public is the difficulty of enforcing such a law; most handguns can be concealed easily. What measures could be taken to enforce such a law? Would such measures be justified by a slight decrease in gun-related homicides? Defend your position.
2. Another handgun control strategy is to prohibit ownership only for people who might use them to commit crimes. How would you determine who should not be allowed to own guns?
3. Do you or someone you know own a gun? Would you or your friend accept restrictions on its use if you thought such restriction would reduce the homicide rate? Would you give up ownership entirely if you thought that would help? What do you think makes some people reluctant to do so?

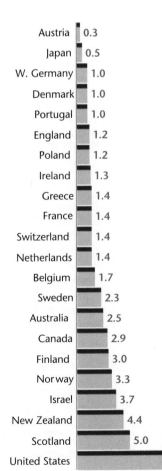

FIGURE 1. Homicide and Young Males
Homicides per 100,000 population for males 15–24 years of age, 1986 or 1987
(*Source:* National Center for Health Statistics, World Health Organization, and country reports.)

Austria	0.3
Japan	0.5
W. Germany	1.0
Denmark	1.0
Portugal	1.0
England	1.2
Poland	1.2
Ireland	1.3
Greece	1.4
France	1.4
Switzerland	1.4
Netherlands	1.4
Belgium	1.7
Sweden	2.3
Australia	2.5
Canada	2.9
Finland	3.0
Norway	3.3
Israel	3.7
New Zealand	4.4
Scotland	5.0
United States	21.9

Homicide

Homicide is the killing of one human being by another. Unjustified, unexcused killings are **criminal homicides.** They are subdivided into three categories: murder, manslaughter, and negligent homicide (a lesser form of involuntary manslaughter). A premeditated and deliberate, intentional and malicious (with malice aforethought—meaning that the perpetrator knew of no justification or excuse for the killing) killing is **murder in the first degree.** Absent premeditation and deliberation, it is **murder in the second degree.**[32] In some states recently, the charge of murder in the first degree has been reserved for the killing of a law enforcement officer or a corrections officer, and for the killing of any person by a prisoner serving a life sentence. Additionally, when death is caused during the commission of a felony, the law considers it murder on the part of all participants. This is called **felony murder,** and most statutes rank it as a murder in the first degree. Most states require that the felony in question be dangerous to life, for example robbery or sexual assault.

Voluntary manslaughter is a killing committed intentionally but without malice, as in the heat of passion or in response to strong provocation without an opportunity to cool off. The rationale is that in such situations a defendant's awareness of the unlawfulness of the act is grossly reduced by passion, fear, or, in some states, gross intoxication. A crime is called an **involuntary manslaughter** when a person has caused the death of another unintentionally but recklessly by consciously disregarding a substantial and unjustifiable risk that endangered the other person's life.

Extent of Homicide. The American murder rate has always been high. In the 1930s, in the midst of the Great Depression, there were 9.8 homicides per 100,000 of the population. Nearly sixty years later, the rate was still 9.8 per 100,000 (see the Criminal Justice on Trial box). The total number of arrests for these crimes in 1991 was 18,654, with a total of 2,626 perpetrators under the age of 18. Of those arrested, 55 percent were black and 44 percent were white.[33]

Victim–Offender Relationship. In the 1950s Marvin Wolfgang investigated homicide situations, offenders, and victims in the Philadelphia area.[34] He found that many of the victims had actually triggered the incident that led to the homicide, by bodily movement, use of force, or verbal abuse. Wolfgang coined the term **victim precipitation** for such instances, which may account for a quarter to a half of all intentional homicides.

Most homicides (61%) occur between relatives and friends.[35] Of intrafamily homicides, killings by women of their mates have received particular attention. Some recent findings in this area are noteworthy: The incidence of long-term abuse suffered by women who subsequently kill their mates is high, and the number of women who kill in domestic encounters is increasing.[36] While **stranger homicide**—a killing in which killer and victim have had no known previous contact—remains significantly less frequent than intrafamily and friend homicide, the impact this crime has on the fear of crime in urban areas is far greater than the small numbers suggest.[37] This increased fear has been attributed to the randomness of the attack, which surprises the victim and renders him or her helpless.

Mass and Serial Murder. In Killeen, Texas, on October 16, 1991, George Jo Hennard smashed his Ford Ranger pickup truck into a cafeteria, got out of the cab, and killed twenty-two people with a semiautomatic pistol. This **mass murder,** the killing of multiple victims in one event or in rapid succession, became the worst mass murder in U.S. history (Table 2.1). Jeffrey Dahmer, a 31-year-old laborer in a chocolate factory, committed another type of murder that is particularly unnerving to the community: **serial murder,** the killing of several victims over time.[38] Dahmer, sentenced to a minimum of 936 years in prison for the 1991

---

homicide
The killing of one person by another.

criminal homicide
Unjustified, unexcused killing of another human being.

murder in the first degree
Killing done with premeditation and deliberation or, by statute, in the presence of other aggravating circumstances.

murder in the second degree
Killing done with intent to cause death but without premeditation and deliberation.

felony murder
Criminal liability for murder for one who participates in a felony that is dangerous to life and causes the death of another.

voluntary manslaughter
Intentionally but without malice causing the death of another person, as in the heat of passion.

involuntary manslaughter
Unintentionally but recklessly causing the death of another by consciously taking a grave risk.

victim precipitation
Opening oneself up, by direct or subliminal means, to a criminal response.

stranger homicide
Murder and nonnegligent manslaughter committed by a person unknown and unrelated to the victim.

mass murder
The murder of several persons, in one act or transaction, by one perpetrator or a group of perpetrators.

serial murder
Killing of several victims over a period of time.

TABLE 2.1 Worst Mass Shootings in U.S. History

October 16, 1991 Twenty-two people are killed in a Killeen, Texas, cafeteria with a semiautomatic pistol by George Jo Hennard, who then killed himself.

July 18, 1984 Twenty-one people are fatally shot in a McDonald's in San Ysidro, Calif., by James Oliver Huberty, an out-of-work security guard, who is killed by a police sharpshooter.

December 1987 Sixteen people are killed. The slayings are discovered after R. Gene Simmons Sr. is arrested Dec. 28 in the killings of two people in Russellville, Ark. A search of his home uncovers the remains of 14 relatives, who authorities say were killed by Mr. Simmons before Christmas. Mr. Simmons is convicted of murder on two charges May 12, 1988, and executed June 25, 1990.

August 1, 1966 Sixteen people are killed in Austin, Tex., by Charles Whitman. Most are hit after he climbs to the top of a tower at the University of Texas. He is killed by police.

August 20, 1986 Fourteen people are shot to death at a post office in Edmond, Okla., by Pat Sherrill, 44, a postal worker who authorities say was about to be dismissed. After police sharpshooters arrive, Mr. Sherrill kills himself.

February 19, 1983 Thirteen people are fatally shot in the head in a robbery at a gambling club in Seattle's Chinatown section. Willie Mak and Benjamin Ng are later convicted of murder.

September 5, 1949 Thirteen people are fatally shot in 12 minutes in Camden, N.J. Howard Unruh, who told police, "I'd have killed a thousand if I'd had enough bullets," was found insane and committed to a mental institution.

September 25, 1982 Twelve people, including five children, are killed in Wilkes-Barre and Jenkins Township, Pa. George Banks, 43, is convicted on 12 counts of murder and sentenced to death.

March 30, 1975 Eleven people are killed at a family gathering in Hamilton, Ohio, on Easter Sunday. A relative, James Ruppert, is convicted of two killings and found not guilty by reason of insanity in nine others.

April 15, 1984 Ten people, including eight children, are killed in a Brooklyn apartment on Palm Sunday. Christopher Thomas is convicted of first-degree manslaughter, with the judge citing "extreme emotional disturbance."

SOURCE: *The New York Times,* October 17, 1991, B10.

murders of fifteen men, had dismembered the bodies of his victims and kept the dismembered parts in his home.

Mass and serial murderers pose a particularly difficult problem for the criminal justice system. They may have no apparent motive. Law enforcement officials thus have few leads to their identity, and yet pressure from community and press to solve the case may be intense. Moreover, while mass and serial murderers commit bizarre acts, juries are reluctant to find these offenders not guilty by reason of insanity, and they then become a problem for prison officials and corrections officers.

Gang Murder. Just after sundown on a warm California evening in 1988, shots were fired from an automatic rifle that rested on the window of a car cruising in South Central Los Angeles. A young woman was killed instantly; eleven others, including a 4-year-old, were wounded.

This comes as no surprise to the police of Los Angeles, where in a single year, 1991, 771 murders were committed by members of the 1,000 gangs that fight to protect their turf.[39] Homicides by gangs of offenders differ from homicides by single offenders with respect to age of the offenders (gang killers are five years younger), ethnicity (more likely to be intraethnic), and victim–offender relationships (gang killers are twice as likely not to know their victims).[40]

These cards look like the traditional baseball (or football or basketball) trading cards—but they show mass and serial murderers, and the backs of the cards contain descriptions of their killings in graphic and gruesome detail.

Armed gang members cruising in Los Angeles. The score: 771 gang murders in one year.

Gangs are so numerous in Los Angeles that the Lakewood county sheriff station has bulletin boards covered with homemade IDs showing gang members and their affiliations.

Assault

assault
Unlawful offer or attempt with force or violence to hurt another.

simple assault
Attack that inflicts little or no physical harm on the victim.

aggravated assault
Attack on a person in which the assailant inflicts serious harm or uses a deadly weapon.

An **assault** is an attack on another person with apparent ability to inflict injury and at least the intent to frighten. Modern statutes usually recognize two types of assault: a **simple assault** is one that inflicts little or no physical harm; a felonious or **aggravated assault** is one in which the perpetrator inflicts serious harm on the victim or uses a deadly weapon. The crimes of homicide and assault share many characteristics. Both are typically committed by young males (disproportionately from minority groups), in urban areas, during the summer months, in the evening, and in the South. Assault victims, too, often know their attackers.

The National Crime Survey estimates that 5,105,000 assaults were committed in 1991.[41] These figures, however, grossly underestimate the real number of assaults because many persons prefer to keep such incidents private—especially if the assault occurred within the household or family. But attitudes about reporting assaults began to change in 1962 when five physicians examined x-ray photographs of young patients in the emergency rooms of seventy-one hospitals across the country. They found three-hundred cases of child abuse (11% resulted in death). This study awakened the public to the gravity of the "battered child syndrome."[42] Child abuse usually occurs in the home, and the children rarely report their victimization to the police.[43] Therefore, it is difficult to measure its extent accurately. The American Humane Association's 1984 national study of child abuse and neglect reported that 30.6 children per 1,000 are maltreated (physically abused, emotionally abused, sexually abused, or neglected) annually.[44]

"The American Medical Association last week declared that domestic violence against women is a true epidemic."
Time, July 29, 1992, p. 57.

During the 1960s the battering of wives also changed from a private matter to a criminal justice problem.[45] According to a national survey of 6,002 households, one member of every six couples experiences a spousal physical assault.[46] But until recently spousal abuse was perceived as a problem more of social service than of criminal justice. As the criminal justice system pays increasing attention to family-related violence, more persons are reporting such violence to the police.

Police officers work to defuse a domestic dispute. Family violence, once thought to be a social rather than a criminal justice problem, is now recognized as a significant law enforcement concern.

Rape and Sexual Assault

According to the Uniform Crime Reports, 106,590 (42.3 per 100,000 population) forcible rapes were reported in 1991. The number had risen 35 percent between 1982 and 1991. Of those arrested for this crime, 16 percent were under age 18; 55 percent were white, 43 percent were black, and 2 percent were of other racial groups.[47] The extent of the problem is largely unknown. The UCR do not include most rapes of wives by husbands or rapes among acquaintances. Consider, for example, the difficulty of estimating the amount of date rape. Estimates indicate that from 25 to 40 percent of all female students have experienced rape, yet only one-tenth of these rapes are reported to the police.[48]

The common law defined rape as an act of forced intercourse by a man of a woman, not his wife. While most laws in our penal codes have retained their original form, the law on forcible rape has changed drastically in many states. This change includes the name of the crime, its definition, the rules of evidence and procedure, and society's reaction to it.

In the past, victims of rape were often treated as the accused by the criminal justice system. Defendants routinely claimed that the victim precipitated the event in some way. Nor did the victim's testimony suffice to convict the defendant, no matter how unimpeachable that testimony may have been. There had to be "corroborating evidence" such as semen, bruises, or eyewitness testimony. No wonder, then, that few victims filed charges or testified, and that few rapists were actually convicted.

The feminist movement has had a major effect on changing laws and attitudes concerning rape.[49] The first state to respond to pressure for reform was Michigan. In 1975, Michigan created the new crime of "criminal sexual conduct" to replace the traditional rape laws. The new law recognizes four degrees of assaultive sexual acts, differentiated by the infliction of injury, the amount of force used, and the age and mental condition of the victim. Recent legislation in several states has also removed some of the difficulties women encountered in rape prosecutions. In some states they are no longer required to reveal prior sexual activity; the requirement of corroborative evidence has been reduced or eliminated; and a wife may now charge her husband with rape.[50]

robbery
The taking of the property of another, or out of his or her presence, by means of force and violence or the threat thereof.

THE FAR SIDE By GARY LARSON

Most robbers victimize people who seem to be in no position to resist.
Source: Gary Larson, *The Far Side, Gallery 2* (Kansas City: Andrews and McMeel, 1988), p. 29.

terrorism
Use of violence against a target to create fear, alarm, dread, or coercion for the purpose of obtaining concessions or rewards.

The aftermath of the terrorist bombing at the La Belle disco in Berlin, April 1986, which killed 2 and injured 200.

Robbery

Robbery is the taking of property from a victim by force and violence or by the threat of violence. In essence, it is the crime of larceny committed by means of a violent assault. Over time, armed robbery has taken many forms. In transportation we have witnessed the passage from stagecoach holdups, to train robberies, to armed carjackings, which in some U.S. cities have reached epidemic proportions. For example, Dallas experienced 687 cases over a six-month period in 1992, and in Los Angeles carjackings accounted for about 7 percent of all robberies. In the District of Columbia area, over an eight-month period in 1992, carjackings were accompanied by four fatal shootings. In addition, in a particularly notorious case, Pamela Basu was dragged to her death. The carjackers threw her infant daughter out of the car into the roadway.[51]

Close to 688,000 robberies were reported to the police in 1991.[52] The average prison sentence on conviction for one charge of robbery is 6.4 years. It increases to 17.6 years if the charges number four or more.[53] Offenders show weapons, primarily guns and knives, in almost half of all robberies.[54]

Research demonstrates that potential victims and establishments can do quite a bit to decrease their likelihood of being robbed. Following a series of convenience store robberies in Gainesville, Florida, a city ordinance required store owners to clear their windows of any objects that obstructed the view of the interior, to place cash registers where they could be seen from the street, and to install electronic cameras. Convenience store robberies decreased 64 percent within a little over a year.[55] Individuals can also reduce the risk of being victimized by adopting behavior patterns that lessen a would-be robber's opportunity to commit the crime. Research is ongoing in this area.

Terrorism

Terrorism is a resort to violence or a threat of violence on the part of a group seeking to accomplish a purpose against the opposition of constituted authority. Neither the individual penal codes nor international law recognizes terrorism as a crime by itself. But the various forms terrorism may take, ranging from murder to assault, arson, and hostage-taking, are crimes. The last is an international

crime that has now been incorporated into American federal law. Like the traditional crime of **kidnapping,** it is the seizing and holding of a person for ransom or reward, by violence or threat of force.

The main objective of terrorists generally is to generate publicity for their cause. They may also aim at mass destruction to demonstrate their power. Consider the following acts of terrorism that have taken place within the last decade:

- On October 23, 1983, a suicide terrorist in a TNT-laden truck blew up U.S. Marine Corps headquarters in Beirut, Lebanon, killing 241 marines and sailors. A second truck blew up French paratrooper barracks two miles away, killing 58.

- October 7, 1985, five hijackers seized the Italian cruiseliner *Achille Lauro*. They held some 400 persons for ransom and killed a wheelchair-bound American passenger.

- On April 5, 1986, terrorists blew up a bomb in a West Berlin disco frequented by American service personnel, killing 2 and injuring 200. The incident prompted an American air strike against Libya in retaliation.

- On December 21, 1988, terrorists exploded Pan Am flight 103, en route from Frankfurt, Germany, to New York. Two-hundred-seventy passengers, crew, and people on the ground at Lockerby, Scotland, died.

- On February 26, 1993, a terrorist bomb in the basement garage of the World Trade Center in New York City killed 6 people, injured over 1,000 people, and caused extensive damage to the building.

In the last few years, the number of spectacular terrorist acts has declined, due perhaps to declining support for terrorist groups in Eastern Europe, where they had earlier found help and sanctuary.

Murder, assault, rape, robbery, kidnapping, and many terrorist activities all have a common component: violence against the person. The victim of violent crime experiences the act immediately, personally, and directly. But the victim of property crime also may feel an immense sense of violation, as victims of burglaries know when they walk into their homes to find them ransacked and looted. The law, however, recognizes a difference in harm between crimes against the person and crimes against property.

PROPERTY AND ECONOMIC CRIMES

Traditional property crimes include larceny (theft, stealing); obtaining property by fraud; burglary; and arson, which not only deprives the owner of property but also can endanger lives. Larceny is the property crime committed most frequently.

Larceny

The crime of **larceny** has several elements. It is

- a "trespassory"
- taking and
- carrying away of
- personal property
- belonging to another
- with the intent to deprive the owner of the property
- permanently.

In the law of larceny, trespass means any absence of permission or authority for the taking. Second, the property must be taken, as by placing a hand on mer-

kidnapping
The seizure and abduction of a person by force or threat of force and against the victim's will; under federal law, the taking of a person across state lines and holding of that person for ransom.

"The law recognizes a difference in harm between crimes against the person and crimes against property."

larceny
Trespassory taking and carrying away of personal property belonging to another with the intent to deprive the owner of the property permanently.

35

shoplifting
Stealing of goods from stores or markets.

chandise, and (third) must be carried away—even if only an inch. Fourth, the property, at common law, has to be personal property, not real estate. Fifth, the property has to belong to another, and (sixth) the taker must intend to deprive that person of rightful ownership permanently. (In many states, however, the law no longer requires proof of this intention.)

The UCR reported 8.1 million thefts in 1991, or a rate of 3,228.8 for each 100,000 of the population.[56] Most thefts do not include personal contact (e.g., pocket-picking and purse-snatching). **Shoplifting,** the stealing of goods from retail merchants, makes up about 15 percent of all larcenies (Figure 2.4). While shoplifting may appear to be a rather insignificant crime, the cost to the public is high. Consider theft from grocery stores and supermarkets. Each thief may steal goods with average value of only $11.19, but all thefts together add up to over $2.2 billion a year.[57] As shoplifters decrease store profits, the price of merchandise goes up in order to pay for more security personnel and electronic monitoring devices.[58]

Fraud

fraud
Acquisition of the property of another through deception.

Fraud is the acquisition of the property of another person through deception. Deception includes false pretenses, confidence games, check forgery, and illegal credit and cash transactions. The amount and types of fraud have changed through the years with technological developments. For example, automated bank teller machines have become common throughout the developed world. As the legal use of such machines increases, so does their illegal use, including the accessing of funds by counterfeit cards and making of false deposits to accounts.[59]

Burglary

burglary
At common law, the nighttime breaking and entering of the dwelling house of another, with the intention to commit a crime or larceny therein; a felony.

The common-law definition of **burglary** is

- the breaking
- and entering
- of the dwelling house
- of another person
- at night
- with the intention to commit a felony or larceny inside.

Statutes have added buildings other than dwellings to the definition, and no longer limit the offense to night attacks. There were over 3 million burglaries reported to the police in 1991. Although these crimes still account for over 20 percent of all index offenses, the number of burglaries committed has declined substantially since 1980.[60]

Criminal justice experts believe that the decline may be due to greater awareness on the part of homeowners about the risks of leaving doors and windows open or newspapers on a doorstep. Or it may be because of greater use of burglar alarms, street lights, and other devices that limit opportunities for burglars to commit crimes.[61] Lawrence Sherman, Patrick Garten, and Michael Buerger, for example, found that burglaries tend to be concentrated in certain "hot spot" areas.[62] Their study of 323,979 calls to the Minneapolis police over a one-year period showed that whereas all calls came from 155,000 addresses and intersections, the 15,901 burglary calls among them came from only 11 percent of the addresses and intersections.

arson
The malicious burning of the dwelling house of another, or the burning of other structures or even personal property.

Arson

The common law defines **arson** as the malicious burning of or setting fire to the dwelling of another person. Modern statutes have increased its scope to include

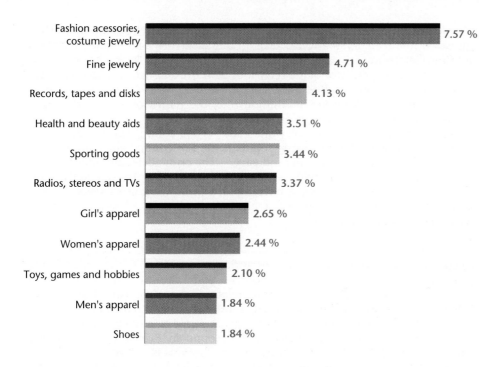

FIGURE 2.4 *Shrinkage: Unexplained losses as a percentage of retail sales in each category** (*Source: The New York Times*, September 19, 1991.)

*Shrinkage or unexplained losses from shoplifting, paperwork errors, or theft by employees. Based on responses of 180 retailing companies to a survey published in *Chain Store Age Executive*.

Chart data:

Category	Percentage
Fashion acessories, costume jewelry	7.57 %
Fine jewelry	4.71 %
Records, tapes and disks	4.13 %
Health and beauty aids	3.51 %
Sporting goods	3.44 %
Radios, stereos and TVs	3.37 %
Girl's apparel	2.65 %
Women's apparel	2.44 %
Toys, games and hobbies	2.10 %
Men's apparel	1.84 %
Shoes	1.84 %

other structures, insurance fraud, and even personal property, such as automobiles. Arson is a fairly infrequent offense. Nevertheless, the amount of damage is great. The National Fire Protection Association estimates annual property loss at close to $6 billion, and adds 4,985 civilian lives lost.[63] The latest approach to the problem of arson is similar to the one used in the research on burglary: It seeks to identify high-risk areas.

The traditional property crimes just discussed are typically committed by a lone perpetrator with a single target—house, automobile, merchandise. In the next section we deal with offenses that present an even greater challenge to criminal justice experts: crimes committed by a person or group of persons in the course of an otherwise legitimate occupation or business enterprise.

White-Collar and Corporate Crime

Initial reports of a crisis in the U.S. savings and loan industry appeared on front pages of newspapers across the country in 1989. They alleged that some savings and loan officers had ruined their institutions financially for personal profit, thereby causing the greatest amount of **white-collar crime** ever uncovered. To bail out insolvent banks may cost an estimated $300 to $500 billion by the year 2021.[64]

Unlike violent crimes and property offenses, which penal codes classify quite neatly, white-collar and corporate offenses include a heterogeneous mix of corporate and individual crimes, from fraud, deception, and corruption (as in the S & L case) to pollution of the environment. They are committed by individuals or by organizations operating locally, nationally, and internationally.

White-Collar Crime. As society becomes more complex, the relation of buyer to seller (or of service provider to client) has become less personal. The anonymity of such relations creates a basis for potential abuse.[65] For example, employees of large entities may use their authority illegally for private gain, by making their services to the public contingent on bribes, kickbacks, or other favors. Consider the insurance adjuster who doubles the estimate of damage in exchange for half the insurance payment. Commercial transactions too are hidden in a maze of

white-collar crime
A sociological concept, encompassing any corporate or individual criminal activity marked by fraud and deception.

"These guys commit their crimes with a pencil instead of a gun."
Mario Merola, district attorney, Bronx, New York, *The New York Times*, June 9, 1985.

"Crime is a logical extension of the sort of behavior that is often considered perfectly respectable in legitimate business."
Robert Rice, *The Business of Crime* (Farrar, Straus, 1956).

insider trading
Use of material, nonpublic financial information about securities to obtain unfair advantage.

complexity. One of them, **insider trading**—the use of material, nonpublic information to obtain an unfair advantage in trading securities—has made front-page headlines in recent years after the arrest and conviction of Dennis Levine, a 34-year-old managing director of the securities firm Drexel Burnham Lambert, and of Wall Street tycoon Ivan Boesky, who on November 14, 1986, pleaded guilty to fraud charges, accepting a $100-million fine, the return of all profits, and a prison sentence. (He has since been released from prison.)

The forms and dimensions of white-collar crime committed by individuals have increased with the increasing sophistication of commercial transactions, technology (computer fraud), and industry.[66] The crime-detection mechanisms on which the police traditionally rely seem inadequate for this vast body of offenses. Moreover, though people have learned to be wary of strangers on the street, they are often unaware that white-collar crimes are being committed, even when they are the victims.[67]

corporate crime
Criminal act committed by one or more employees of a corporation that is subsequently attributed to the organization itself.

Corporate Crime. **Corporate crime** is defined as a criminal act committed by one or more employees of a corporation that is attributed to the organization itself. Between 1984 and 1990, 2,000 corporations were convicted in federal courts for offenses ranging from tax law violations to environmental crimes (see Table 2.2). A vast majority of these companies were small- to medium-sized privately held corporations. One problem with corporate crime is definitional.[68] In 1989 the supertanker *Exxon Valdez* ran aground in Prince William Sound, Alaska, spilling 250,000 barrels of oil. The spill became North America's largest ecological disaster. Prosecutors were interested in determining the guilt or innocence of the captain, his officers, and his crew. But there were additional and

TABLE 2.2 Number of Corporations Sentenced between 1984 and 1990 in Federal Courts

Type of Offense	Year of Sentencing (Number of Offenses)							
	1984	1985	1986	1987	1988	1989	1990	Total
Against persons	1	0	0	0	0	0	0	1
Property	5	8	15	9	12	12	11	72
Public officials	5	4	6	4		6	4	29
Drugs	1	4	2	2		3	0	12
Racketeering	12	4	5	2	10	4	3	40
Fraud & deceit	116	94	128	105	109	82	55	689
Obscenity	0	4	1	1		15	8	29
Civil rights	2	1	3	2		0	0	8
Administration of justice	7	0	2	2		2	0	13
Public safety	5	3	1	0		2	2	13
Immigration	0	1	1	0		4	0	6
National defense	11	6	4	4	18	6	4	53
Food & drug laws	38	37	32	23	9	14	14	167
Environmental	10	24	17	8	28	28	21	136
Antitrust	93	70	47	68	98	58	23	457
Monetary transactions	0	0	0	0	8	5	3	16
Taxation	21	35	16	26	14	26	16	154
Other offenses	17	16	22	13	21	6	2	97
Total	344	311	302	269	328	273	173	2,000

SOURCE: United States Sentencing Committee Guidelines for Organizations, Supplementary Report, 1991, D-10.

far-reaching questions. Did the Exxon Corporation sacrifice the environment by putting profit above safety? If so, was this a corporate crime? The marketing of an unsafe medicine can cause crippling deformities in thousands of persons.[69] Violation of environmental standards can cause suffering to generations of people who will be exposed to polluted water, toxic air, or the consequences of land exploitation.[70] Catastrophic releases of radioactive substances can cause grave hazards to entire countries, as the Chernobyl disaster in the Ukraine demonstrated.[71] Are these corporate crimes?

Detecting corporate criminality is a formidable task.[72] Day-to-day corporate activities have a low level of visibility. Industries are reluctant to volunteer information, especially about their own illegal acts. Offending corporations may operate in many different jurisdictions, some of which regard a given activity as illegal and others do not. Multinational corporations may prefer to move into countries where jobs and development take precedence over protecting the environment or the worker.[73]

"Detecting corporate criminality is a formidable task."

ORGANIZED CRIME

Organized crime got its start in the United States when Sicilian immigrants replicated their traditional family structure in organizing criminal activity.[74] During the early years of Prohibition, Al Capone, Lucky Luciano, Frank Costello, and many other Sicilians became well-known mobsters. Sicilian families (frequently referred to as Mafia) were so successful in controlling bootlegging, gambling, loansharking, prostitution, labor racketeering, drug trafficking, and other illegal enterprises that they were able to take over many legitimate businesses.[75] In recent years other organized crime groups—Latin Americans, Jamaicans, Israelis, Japanese, Russians, Chinese—have gained major influence.[76]

Starting in the 1930s and continuing to the present, major investigations have established the magnitude of organized crime in the United States.[77] Specific legislation has been designed to control it. Many cases have been successfully prosecuted under the Racketeer Influence and Corrupt Organizations Act (RICO). This statute attacks racketeering activities by prohibiting the investment of any funds derived from racketeering in any business that is engaged in interstate commerce. In addition, witnesses from within organized crime have been more willing to testify since, under the **Federal Witness Protection Program** enacted as part of the Organized Crime Control Act of 1970, they are assured of a new identity. Currently over 14,000 persons are in this program.[78] By 1992 organized crime had become globalized. The shadow economies of the formerly socialist countries, particularly Russia, are dominated by organized crime. In Western countries the traffic in drugs is largely responsible for the growth of organized crime networks.[79]

"Out in the ocean, a rope is put around a man's neck. The other end of the rope is attached to an old jukebox and it is thrown overboard. The man invariably follows."
Jimmy Breslin, *The Gang Who Couldn't Shoot Straight* (Viking, 1969).

Federal Witness Protection Program
Program under the Organized Crime Control Act of 1970 to protect witnesses who testify in court by relocating them and assigning them new identities.

CRIMES AGAINST PUBLIC MORALITY: DRUGS, ALCOHOL, AND VICE

The category of "crimes against public morality," as it is called by contemporary criminal-law textbook writers,[80] includes a variety of criminal activities that were once known as "victimless" crimes. Perhaps that is because it was assumed that people who engage in them choose to do so: they include drug use, alcohol abuse, and prostitution and other sex acts between consenting adults. Often no one complains to the police about being victimized by such consensual activities.

But contemporary forms of these activities may entail massive victimizations. And that is especially true of a broad range of drug-related crimes.

Drug-Related Crime

Our "drug problem" is not a single problem but a broad range of problems that involve all social classes and in one way or another touch most people's lives. Moreover, it is a global problem involving vast international networks. There are growers, smugglers (who import drugs from foreign countries), wholesalers and dealers (who sell drugs on the streets); there are corrupt criminal justice officials, abusers who endanger people's lives through negligence (pilots, bus drivers), addict mothers, and even addict unborn babies. Many of the crimes discussed in this chapter are often drug-related.[81]

Extent of Drug Abuse. A wide variety of drugs have been abused in the United States. Historically, the illegal substance most frequently abused has been marijuana. It remains the most frequently abused substance even though annual surveys of high-school students show that the percentage of abusers has gone from 46 percent in 1981 to 17 percent in 1990.[82] A national household survey that measured drug use among the American population aged 12 and older in 1991 found that over 75 million (37% of the population) had used illicit drugs at least once in their lifetime and 13 percent had used drugs within one year of the survey.[83] Today cocaine has become the major drug problem in the United States: an estimated 22 million persons have tried it, and another 4 million are thought to be using it regularly.[84] It is difficult to even estimate how many people are abusing newer drugs such as crack cocaine and the so-called designer drugs.[85]

A crack house in the South Bronx. The widespread use of newer and more powerful drugs like crack cocaine has simply multiplied the problems associated with drug abuse.

Drug Crime-Related Activities. There is no official category of crimes called "drug-related offenses," yet several investigations give us some idea of their extent. The National Institute of Justice's Drug Use Forecasting (DUF) Program issued statistics in 1990 on the percentage of arrestees who tested positive for drugs in twenty-three cities (Figure 2.5). In another study, 35 percent of state prison inmates reported that they had been under the influence of drugs when they committed the crimes for which they were incarcerated.[86]

Before the 1980s drug abusers were arrested primarily for property offenses. Since that time there has been an increasing amount of violent crime related to the use of drugs, especially crack, and to competing drug dealers settling territorial disputes.

Drug Control. Drug control efforts take place on both the international and the national levels. But there is little evidence that any strategy has been successful.

To combat international drug trafficking, the U.S. government has provided funds for bilateral cooperation. Colombia, Bolivia, and Peru have received assistance from the U.S. Army to help curb the activities of the Medellin cartel. These efforts extend to crop eradication programs.[87] The U.S. Coast Guard also has a program of interdiction that seeks to stop drugs from coming into the country by sea and air. A major United Nations program to deal with the international narcotics problem has had only limited success, largely due to lack of financial support.

On the national level, the so-called federal war on drugs provides funds pri-

FIGURE 2.5 *Drug use by male and female booked arrestees** (*Source:* Figures from National Institute of Justice/Drug Use Forecasting Program, *Drug Use Forecasting, Drugs and Crime,* National Institute of Justice, 1990 Annual Report [August 1991], p. 5.)

*January through December 1990.

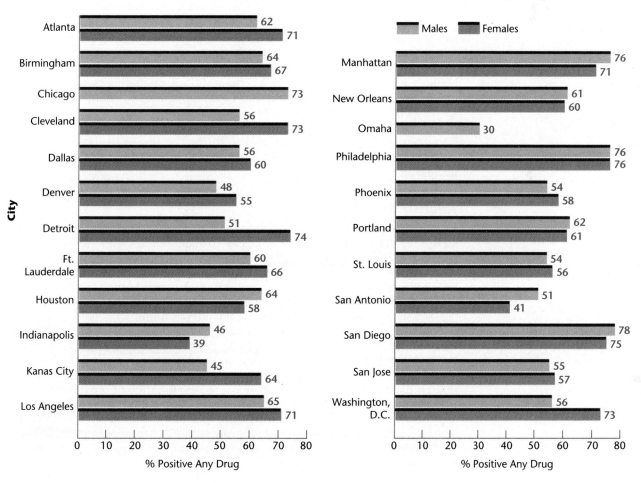

marily to state and local police for street-level attacks on drug users and dealers. The program also involves expansion of prison capacity, the use of alternative punishments such as boot camps (short but harsh military-style discipline programs), and increased enforcement of forfeiture laws, under which property (including real estate, boats, planes, cars, and bank accounts) is confiscated from offenders if it is derived from the drug trade. Drug treatment programs for addicts, and educational programs to prevent the use of drugs to begin with, have received only a fraction of the funds allocated to the overall efforts to combat drugs.[88]

Alcohol and Crime

Alcohol abuse is another major social problem. In the United States, the average annual consumption of alcoholic beverages by each person 14 years of age and over is equivalent to 591 cans of beer, 115 bottles of wine, and 35 fifths of liquor; this is more than the average individual consumption of milk and coffee.[89] Some of the alcohol-related problems that affect the criminal justice system are violent crime, drunken driving, negligence at the work place, and public intoxication.

National surveys of inmates in prisons and jails show that over half of the offenders incarcerated for violent crimes (particularly assaults) used alcohol and/or drugs immediately before the crimes (Figure 2.5).[90] Thirty-four to forty-five percent of inmates convicted of homicide, assault, rape, and robbery described themselves as heavy drinkers.[91] Criminologists have studied various aspects of the association between alcohol and violence. Marvin Wolfgang, for example, in a study of 558 homicides in Philadelphia, found alcohol present in two-thirds of all homicide cases.[92]

Each year there are over a million arrests for driving under the influence of alcohol and over 650,000 persons are injured in alcohol-related crashes.[93] Various citizen groups (for example, MADD [Mothers Against Drunk Driving]) have pressured the federal government into conditioning the distribution of state highway funds on compliance with various anti-drunk-driving measures. States have raised the minimum drinking age to 21, limited "happy hours" (when bars serve drinks at reduced prices), increased penalties for drunk driving, made hosts and bartenders liable for damages if their intoxicated guests or customers become involved in an accident, and so forth. The results of these efforts are mixed,[94] but traffic deaths, especially those that are alcohol-related, have been decreasing.

Sex-Related Offenses

The last group of offenses to be mentioned are those existing under statutes that seek to regulate sexual morality, or at least to document society's views on sexual morality.[95] These range from the prohibition of sexual activity other than consensual spousal intercourse (thus covering "adultery," "fornication" or "lewd cohabitation," and "sodomy"; "prostitution" offenses; and others) to the sale and distribution of obscene or indecent material.

Such legislation has had no discernible effect on human behavior, and law enforcement agencies have always dreaded the task of enforcing it. Officers often find such enforcement efforts to be futile, demeaning, and corrupting. Legislative statements of morality often lack popular support and consensus. However, in recent years the feminist movement has tried to shape public attitudes on such matters as prostitution (more particularly the exploitation of prostitution), sexual harassment, and pornography. Thus, feminists, along with others, have supported—or even worked to strengthen—the moral standards implicit in old legislation on sexual morality, with the overall objective of discouraging male-female exploitation. In this respect they have had an impact on the possible emergence of a popular consensus.[96]

REVIEW

There are two main objectives for collecting data about criminals and crime: to run the criminal justice system on a daily basis and to make policy for its long-term operation. Researchers also need data to test their theories about why people commit crimes.

Data are collected by surveys, experiments, observation, and case studies. It is often cost-effective to use repositories of information gathered by public and private organizations for their own purposes. The three main sources of data are the Uniform Crime Reports, victimization surveys, and self-report questionnaires. Though each source is useful for some purposes, all three have limitations.

Data on criminals show that there is a disproportionate number of young black males in the criminal justice system. Data on crime show that, of the total number of index crimes, violent crimes make up only about 12 percent. Murder, assaults of various kinds, rape, robbery (as well as kidnapping and the other nonindex crimes)—all share the common characteristic of violence, though they differ in the harm they cause, the intention of the offender, the punishment they warrant, and other legal criteria.

The traditional property crimes are larceny, obtaining property by frauds of various sorts, burglary, and arson. Some property-oriented crimes deprive people of their property through business operations of legitimate enterprises. Individual or corporate white-collar offenses include securities-related crime, consumer fraud, computer fraud, and tax fraud, among others. In the twentieth century, corporations have been subject to criminal liability for an increasing number of offenses, including environmental offenses.

There are also property-oriented crimes that deprive people of their property through use of illegitimate business practices. Organized crime groups were so successful in controlling bootlegging, gambling, prostitution, drug trafficking, and other illegal businesses that they were eventually able to control many legitimate businesses.

Some illegal activities—drug-, alcohol-, and sex-related—once were commonly called victimless crimes. But contemporary forms of such activities entail massive victimization. Heroin and cocaine are associated with a variety of crimes including smuggling, property offenses, and violent offenses connected with drug gangs. Alcohol is linked to violence and the harm done by drunk driving. Sex-related offenses such as prostitution and pornography remain hotly debated issues.

Notes

1. James Bennett, "New York Crime Statistics vs. Reality," *The New York Times*, August 16, 1992, p. L39.

2. Kieran Crowley and John Harney, "Death Stalks the Apple as Eight Are Slain in Night of Violence," *New York Post*, September 28, 1991, p. 8.

3. Martin D. Schwartz and Todd R. Clear, "Toward a New Law on Rape," *Crime and Delinquency* 26 (1980):129–151; Andrew Z. Soshnick, "The Rape Shield Paradox: Complainant Protection Amidst Oscillating Trends of State Judicial Interpretation," Comment, *Journal of Criminal Law and Criminology* 78 (1987):644–698;

Ken Polk, "Rape Reform and Criminal Justice Processing," *Crime and Delinquency* 31 (1985):191–205; Gilbert Geis, "Rape-in-Marriage: Law and Law Reform in England, the United States, and Sweden," *Adelaide Law Review* 6 (1978):284–303.

4. James A. Inciardi, Anne E. Pottieger, Mary Ann Forney, Dale D. Chitwood, and Duane C. McBride, "Prostitution, IV Drug Use, and Sex-for-Crack Exchanges among Serious Delinquents: Risks for HIV Infection," *Criminology* 29 (1991):221–235.

5. James O. Finckenauer, *Scared Straight and the Panacea Phenomenon* (Englewood Cliffs, N.J.: Prentice-Hall, 1982).

6. Albert J. Reiss, Jr., "Stuff and Nonsense about Social Surveys and Observation," in *Institutions and the Person*, eds. Howard S. Becker, Blanche Geer, David Riesman, and Robert S. Weiss (Chicago: Aldine, 1968); David H. Bayley and James Garofalo, "The Management of Violence by Police Patrol Officers," *Criminology* 27 (1989):1–25.

7. Stephen Mastrofski and Roger B. Parks, "Improving Observational Studies of Police," *Criminology* 28 (1990):475–496.

8. Carl Klockars, *The Professional Fence* (New York: Free Press, 1974), pp. 110, 113; Darrell Steffensmeier, *The Fence: In the Shadow of Two Worlds* (Totowa, N.J.: Roman & Littlefield, 1986).

9. See, for example at the international level, Richard R. Bennett and James P. Lynch, "Does a Difference Make a Difference? Comparing Cross-National Crime Indicators," *Criminology* 28 (1990):153–181.

10. Michael Couzens, "Getting the Crime Rate Down: Political Pressure and Crime Reporting," *Law and Society Review* 8 (1974):457–493. For a comprehensive discussion of automated crime information systems, see J. Van Duyn, *Automated Crime Information Systems* (Blue Ridge Summit, Pa.: TAB Books, 1991).

11. Patrick G. Jackson, "Sources of Data," in *Measurement Issues in Criminology*, ed. Kimberly L. Kempf (New York: Springer-Verlag, 1990).

12. Steven P. Lab and J. David Hirschel, "Climatological Conditions and Crime: The Forecast Is . . . ?," *Justice Quarterly* 5 (1988):281–299. The article resulted in an interesting scientific exchange. See James L. Le-Beau, Comment, "Weather and Crime: Trying to Make Social Sense of a Physical Process," ibid., pp. 301–309; Steven P. Lab and J. David Hirschel, " 'Clouding' the Issues: The Failure to Recognize Methodological Problems," ibid., pp. 312–317.

13. For a discussion of the consistency between UCR rates and NCS rates over time, see Alfred Blumstein, Jacqueline Cohen, and Richard Rosenfeld, "Trend and Deviation in Crime Rates: A Comparison of UCR and NCS Data for Burglary and Robbery," *Criminology* 29 (1991):237–263; A. D. Biderman and J. P. Lynch, *Understanding Crime Incidence Statistics* (New York: Springer-Verlag, 1991).

For a comparison of victimization data with official police data, see Scott Menard and Herbert C. Covey, "UCR and NCS: Comparisons over Space and Time," *Journal of Criminal Justice* 16 (1988):371–384; Robert M. O'Brien, "Comparing Detrended UCR and NCS Crime Rates over Time: 1973–1986," *Journal of Criminal Justice* 18 (1990):229–238. For the deterrent effect of clearance rates, see Mitchell B. Chamlin, "A Longitudinal Analysis of the Arrest-Crime Relationship: A Further Examination of the Tipping Effect," *Justice Quarterly* 8 (1991):187–199.

14. James S. Wallerstein and Clement J. Wyle, "Our Law-Abiding Law-Breakers," *Probation* 25 (March–April 1947):107–112.

15. Franklin Dunford and Delbert Elliott, "Identifying Career Offenders Using Self-reported Data," *Journal of Research in Crime and Delinquency* 21 (1984):57–86; D. Wayne Osgood, Lloyd D. Johnston, Patrick O'Malley, and Jerald Bachman, "The Generality of Deviance in Late Adolescence and Early Adulthood," *American Sociological Review* 53 (1988):81–93.

16. Michael Hindelang, Travis Hirschi, and Joseph Weis, *Measuring Delinquency* (Beverly Hills, Calif.: Sage, 1981).

17. U.S. Department of Justice, Federal Bureau of Investigation, *Crime in the United States*, 1991 (Washington, D.C.: U.S. Government Printing Office, 1992), p. 230, hereafter cited as *Uniform Crime Reports*. For a scholarly analysis of the theoretical issues, the

most recent research findings, and their implications for practice, see Meda Chesney-Lind and Randall G. Shelden, *Girls, Delinquency, and Juvenile Justice* (Pacific Grove, Calif.: Brooks/Cole Publishing, 1992).

18. Freda Adler, *Sisters in Crime* (New York: McGraw-Hill, 1975), pp. 6–7.

19. Rita Simon, *The Contemporary Woman and Crime* (Rockville, Md.: National Institute of Mental Health, 1975).

20. Meda Chesney-Lind, "Female Offenders: Paternalism Reexamined," in *Women, the Courts, and Equality*, eds. Laura Crites and Winifred Hepperle (Newbury Park, Calif.: Sage, 1987).

21. Darrell J. Steffensmeier, "Crime and the Contemporary Woman: An Analysis of Changing Levels of Female Property Crimes, 1960–1975," *Social Forces* 57 (1978):566–584.

22. For a discussion of female crime in countries around the world, see Freda Adler, ed., *The Incidence of Female Criminality in the Contemporary World* (New York: New York University Press, 1981). For an historical view of female arrest rates, see Helen Boritch and John Hagan, "A Century of Crime in Toronto: Gender, Class, and Patterns of Social Control, 1859 to 1955," *Criminology* 28 (1990):567–599. For an explanation of self-reported criminality of black and white young females, see Gary D. Hill and Elizabeth M. Crawford, "Women, Race, and Crime," *Criminology* 28 (1990):601–623. See also Steven Box and Chris Hale, "Liberation/Emancipation, Economic Marginalization, or Less Chivalry," *Criminology* 22 (1984):473–497. For a discussion of the internalization of gender roles by female prisoners, see Edna Erez, "The Myth of the New Female Offender: Some Evidence from Attitudes toward Law and Justice," *Journal of Criminal Justice* 16 (1988):499–509; Meda Chesney-Lind, "Girls' Crime and Woman's Place: Toward a Feminist Model of Female Delinquency," *Crime and Delinquency* 35 (1989):5–29; see also Nanci Koser Wilson, "The Masculinity of Violent Crime—Some Second Thoughts," *Journal of Criminal Justice* 9 (1981):111–123; Josefina Figueira-McDonough, "A Reformulation of the 'Equal Opportunity' Explanation of Female Delinquency," *Crime and Delinquency* 26 (1980):333–343. On the topic of women and criminal justice education, see Lynn Goodstein, "Feminist Perspectives and the Criminal Justice Curriculum"; Michael J. Lynch, Jackie Huey, J. Santiago Nuñez, Billy R. Close, and Carolyn Johnston, "Cultural Literacy, Criminology and Female-Gender Issues: The Power to Exclude"; Carole Gozansky Garrison, Averil McClelland, Faye Dambrot, and Karen A. Casey, "Gender Balancing the Criminal Justice Curriculum and Classroom"; Richard A. Wright, "From Vamps and Tramps to Teases and Flirts: Stereotypes of Women in Criminology Textbooks, 1956 to 1965 and 1981 to 1990"; M. Joan McDermott, "The Personal is Empirical: Feminism, Research Methods, and Criminal Justice Education"; Vicky E. Dorworth and Marie Henry, "Optical Illusions: The Visual Representation of Blacks and Women in Introductory Criminal Justice Textbooks"; Sue Mahan and Aimee Michelle Anthony, "Including Women in Corrections Texts"; Nanci Koser Wilson and Imogene Moyer, "Affirmative Action, Multiculturalism, and Politically Correct Criminology"; Helen Eigenberg and Agnes Baro, "Women and the Publication Process: A Content Analysis of Criminal Justice Journals"; Susan K. Hippensteele, Alison K. Adams, and Meda Chesney-Lind, "Sexual Harassment in Academia: Student Reactions to Unprofessional Behavior"; Elizabeth A. Stanko, "Intimidating Education: Sexual Harassment in Criminology"; Elizabeth M. Jenkins, "Documentary Film as a Resource in Teaching Criminal Justice: The Case of Women Terrorists." These articles are in a special issue entitled "Women and Criminal Justice Education," *Journal of Criminal Justice Education*, Vol. 3 (1992).

23. See Kyle Kercher, "Causes and Correlates of Crime Committed by the Elderly," in *Critical Issues in Aging Policy*, eds. Edgar F. Borgatta and R. J. W. Montgomery (Beverly Hills, Calif.: Sage, 1987).

24. Michael Gottfredson and Travis Hirschi, "The True Value of Lambda Would Appear to Be Zero: An Essay on Career Criminals, Criminal Careers, Selective Incapacitation, Cohort Studies, and Related Topics," *Criminology* 24 (1986):213–234; Lawrence Cohen and Kenneth Land, "Age Structure and Crime: Symmetry versus Asymmetry and the Projection of Crime Rates through the 1990s," *American Sociological Review* 52 (1987):170–183. For a critique of Hirschi and Gottfredson's contentions, see Darrell J. Steffensmeier, Emilie Anderson Allan, Miles D. Harer, and Cathy Streifel, "Age and the Distribution of Crime," *American Journal of Sociology* 94 (1989):803–831. For a test of those contentions, see Yossi Shavit and Arye Rattner, "Age, Crime, and the Early Life Course," *American Journal of Sociology* 93 (1988):1457–1470; see also James Q. Wilson and Richard Herrnstein, *Crime and Human Nature* (New York: Simon & Schuster, 1985), pp. 126–147.

25. Alfred Blumstein, Jacqueline Cohen, and David Farrington, "Criminal Career Research: Its Value for Criminology," *Criminology* 26 (1988):1–35. See also Julie Horney and Ineke Haen Marshall, "Measuring Lambda through Self-Reports," *Criminology* 29 (1991):471–495; Rolf Loeber and Howard N. Snyder, "Rate of Offending in Juvenile Careers: Findings of Constancy and Change in Lambda," *Criminology* 28 (1990):97–109; David Greenberg, "Modeling Criminal Careers," *Criminology* 29 (1991):17–46; Daniel S. Nagin and Raymond Paternoster, "On the Relationship of Past to Future Participation in Delinquency," *Criminology* 29 (1991):163–189.

26. Marvin Wolfgang, Robert Figlio, and Thorsten Sellin, *Delinquency in a Birth Cohort* (Chicago: University of Chicago Press, 1972). For a discussion of how each delinquent act was weighted for seriousness, see Thorsten Sellin and Marvin Wolfgang, *The Measurement of Delinquency* (New York: Wiley, 1964); see also Marvin Wolfgang, Terrence Thornberry, and Robert Figlio, *From Boy to Man, from Delinquency to Crime* (Chicago: University of Chicago Press, 1987); Paul Tracy, Marvin Wolfgang, and Robert Figlio, *Delinquency Careers in Two Birth Cohorts* (New York: Plenum, 1990); Kimberly L. Kempf, "Career Criminals in the 1958 Philadelphia Birth Cohort: A Follow-up of the Early Adult Years," *Criminal Justice Review* 15 (1990):151–172.

27. Charles R. Tittle and Robert F. Meier, "Specifying the SES/Delinquency Relationship," *Criminology* 28 (1990):271–299; see also David Weisburd, Stanton Wheeler, Elin Waring, and Nancy Bode, *Crimes of the Middle Classes* (New Haven, Conn.: Yale University Press, 1991), for sentencing of white-collar offenders. For neglect of white-collar crime in criminal justice curricula, see Richard A. Wright and David O. Friedrichs, "White-Collar Crime in the Criminal Justice Curriculum," *Journal of Criminal Justice Education* 2 (1991):95–115.

28. U.S. Department of Justice, *Report to the Nation on Crime and Justice*, 2d ed. (Washington, D.C.: U.S. Government Printing Office, 1988), pp. 48–49.

29. *Uniform Crime Reports, 1991*, p. 231.

30. Joan Petersilia, "Racial Disparities in the Criminal Justice System: A Summary," *Crime and Delinquency* 31 (1985):15–34; James W. Balkwell, "Ethnic Inequality and the Rate of Homicide," *Social Forces* 69 (1990):53–70.

31. Robert J. Sampson, "Urban Black Violence: The Effect of Male Joblessness and Family Disruption," *American Journal of Sociology* 93 (1987):348–382. For an historical look at racial disparities in incarceration, see Martha A. Myers, "Economic Threat and Racial Disparities in Incarceration: The Case of Postbellum Georgia," *Criminology* 28 (1990):627–656.

32. G. O. W. Mueller, "Where Murder Begins," *New Hampshire Bar Journal* 2 (1960):214–224, and "On Common Law Mens Rea," *Minnesota Law Review* 42 (1958):1043–1104.

33. *Uniform Crime Reports, 1991*, pp. 58, 217, 223, 231; Kathleen J. Block, "Age-Related Correlates of Criminal Homicides Committed by Women: A Study of Baltimore," *Journal of Crime and Justice* 13 (1990):42–65. See also Peter C. Kratcoski, "Circumstances Surrounding Homicides by Older Offenders," *Criminal Justice and Behavior* 17 (1990):420–430; Derral Cheatwood, "Black Homicides in Baltimore 1974–1986: Age, Gender, and Weapon Use Changes," *Criminal Justice Review* 15 (1990):192–207; M. G. Neithercutt, "The

Death Penalty: Its Relation to Murder and Suicide," *Journal of Contemporary Criminal Justice* 5 (1989):199–219, at pp. 206–207.

34. Marvin E. Wolfgang, *Patterns in Criminal Homicide* (Philadelphia: University of Pennsylvania Press, 1958).

35. *Uniform Crime Reports, 1990*, p. 13. See also Colin Loftin, Karen Kindley, Sandra L. Norris, and Brian Wiersema, "An Attribute Approach to Relationships between Offenders and Victims in Homicide," *Journal of Criminal Law and Criminology* 78 (1987):259–271.

36. Angela Browne, "Assault and Homicide at Home: When Battered Women Kill," *Advances in Applied Social Psychology* 3 (1986):57–79; Coramae Richey Mann, "Getting Even? Women Who Kill in Domestic Encounters," *Justice Quarterly* 5 (1988):33–51.

37. Marc Riedel, "Stranger Violence: Perspectives, Issues, and Problems," *Journal of Criminal Law and Criminology* 78 (1987):223–258. For a discussion of the *Supplementary Homicide Report* (SHR), see Colin Loftin, "The Validity of Robbery-Murder Classifications in Baltimore," *Violence and Victims* 1 (1986):191–204; see also Robert A. Silverman and Leslie W. Kennedy, "Relational Distance and Homicide: The Role of the Stranger," *Journal of Criminal Law and Criminology* 78 (1987):272–308; Margaret A. Zahn and Philip C. Sagi, "Stranger Homicides in Nine American Cities," *Journal of Criminal Law and Criminology* 78 (1987):377–397.

38. Jack Levin and James Alan Fox, *Mass Murder: America's Growing Menace* (New York: Plenum, 1985); Eric W. Hickey, *Serial Murderers and Their Victims* (Pacific Grove, Calif.: Brooks/Cole, 1991); Ronald M. Holmes and James de Burger, *Serial Murder* (Newbury Park, Calif.: Sage, 1988). For a criminal justice response to serial murder, see Pierce R. Brooks, Michael J. Devine, Terence J. Green, Barbara L. Hart, and Merlyn D. Moore, "Serial Murder: A Criminal Justice Response," *Police Chief* 54 (1987):37–43.

39. Sylvester Monroe, "Life in the 'Hood,'" *Time*, June 15, 1992, pp. 37, 38.

40. Cheryl L. Maxson, Margaret A. Gordon, and Malcolm W. Klein, "Differences between Gang and Nongang Homicides," *Criminology* 23 (1985):209–222; see also G. David Curry and Irving A. Spergel, "Gang Homicide, Delinquency, and Community," *Criminology* 26 (1988):381–405. See also Craig H. Collins, "Youth Gangs in the 70's . . . An Urban Plague," *Police Chief* 42 (1975):50–54.

41. U.S. Department of Justice, Bureau of Justice Statistics Bulletin, *Crime and the Nation's Households, 1991* (Washington, D.C.: U.S. Government Printing Office, 1992), p. 2.

42. C. H. Kempe, F. N. Silverman, B. F. Steele, W. Droegemueller, and H. K. Silver, "The Battered-Child Syndrome," *Journal of the American Medical Association* 181 (1962):17–24.

43. Edna Erez, "Intimacy, Violence, and the Police," *Human Relations* 39 (1986):265–281.

44. American Association for Protecting Children, *Highlights of Official Child Neglect and Abuse Reporting, 1984* (Denver: American Humane Association, 1986). See also James Garbarino, "The Incidence and Prevalence of Child Maltreatment," in *Family Violence*, eds. Lloyd Ohlin and Michael Tonry (Chicago: University of Chicago Press, 1989), vol. 2, pp. 219–261; Mildred Daley Pagelow, "The Incidence and Prevalence of Criminal Abuse of Other Family Members," in ibid., pp. 263–311; Robert A. Silverman, Marc Riedel, and Leslie W. Kennedy, "Murdered Children: A Comparison of Racial Differences across Two Jurisdictions," *Journal of Criminal Justice* 18 (1990):401–416. For an encompassing coverage of issues related to child abuse see Charles Patrick Ewing (ed.), "Child Abuse," *Behavioral Sciences and the Law* (Symposium issue) 9 (1993)(1):1–83, with contributions by Murray Levine and Lori Battiotoni, Catherine Brooks and Madelyn Simring Milohmen, Margaret-Ellen Pipe and Gail S. Goodman, Cathy Meen, Nathan Pollock and Judith Hashmall, R. A. Lang and R. Langevin, and Bernard Kahan and Beatrice Crofts Yorker. America's high rate of child homicides is analyzed by Katherine K. Christoffel and Kiang Liuv, "Homicide Death Rates in Childhood in 23 Developed Countries: U.S. Rates Atypically High," *Child Abuse and Neglect* 7 (1993):339–345. See also Beverly Rivera

and Cathy Spatz Widom, "Childhood Victimization and Violent Offending," *Violence and Victims* 5 (1990):19–35.

45. Elizabeth Pleck, "Criminal Approaches to Family Violence, 1640–1980," in *Family Violence*, eds. Ohlin and Tonry, pp. 19–57. Richard M. Tolman and Larry W. Bennett, "A Review of Quantitative Research on Men Who Batter," *Journal of Interpersonal Violence* 5 (1993):87–118.

46. Murray A. Straus and Richard J. Gelles, "How Violent Are American Families? Estimates from the National Family Violence Resurvey and Other Studies," in *Family Abuse and Its Consequences*, eds. Gerald T. Hotaling, David Finkelhor, John T. Kirkpatrick, and Murray A. Straus (Newbury Park, Calif.: Sage, 1988). See also Scott L. Feld and Murray A. Straus, "Escalation and Desistance of Wife Assault in Marriage," *Criminology* 27 (1989):141–161; David Levinson, *Family Violence in Cross-Cultural Perspective* (Newbury Park, Calif.: Sage, 1989). On underestimation of rape rates, see Helen M. Eigenberg, "The National Crime Survey and Rape: The Case of the Missing Question," *Justice Quarterly* 7 (1990):655–671. See also Ida M. Johnson, "A Loglinear Analysis of Abused Wives' Decisions to Call the Police in Domestic-Violence Disputes," *Journal of Criminal Justice* 18 (1990):147–159.

47. *Uniform Crime Reports, 1991*, pp. 58, 229, 232. For a discussion of clearance rates, see James L. LeBeau, "Patterns of Stranger and Serial Rape Offending: Factors Distinguishing Apprehended and At Large Offenders," *Journal of Criminal Law and Criminology* 78 (1987):309–326.

48. Andrea Parrot, *Coping with Date Rape and Acquaintance Rape* (New York: Rosen, 1988). See also John E. Murphy, "Date Abuse and Forced Intercourse among College Students," in *Family Abuse*, eds. Hotaling et al., pp. 285–296; M. P. Koss, C. A. Gidycz, and N. Wisniewski, "The Scope of Rape: Incidence and Prevalence of Sexual Aggression and Victimization in a National Sample of Higher Education Students," *Journal of Consulting and Clinical Psychology* 55 (1987):162–170; R. Thomas Dull and David J. Giacopassi, "Demographic Correlates of Sexual and Dating Attitudes: A Study of Date Rape, *Criminal Justice and Behavior* 14 (1987):175–193; Joanne Belknap and Sandra Evans Skovron, "Public Perceptions of Date Rape" (1988), report on file with National Council on Crime and Delinquency–School of Criminal Justice Library, Rutgers University, Newark, N.J.

49. For a discussion of rape and inequality, see Julia R. Schwendinger and Herman Schwendinger, *Rape and Inequality* (Beverly Hills, Calif.: Sage, 1983); M. Dwayne Smith and Nathan Bennett, "Poverty, Inequality, and Theories of Forcible Rape," *Crime and Delinquency* 31 (1985):295–305; Ruth D. Peterson and William C. Bailey, "Forcible Rape, Poverty, and Economic Inequality in U.S. Metropolitan Communities," *Journal of Quantitative Criminology* 4 (1988):99–119; Robert M. O'Brien, "Sex Ratios and Rape Rates: A Power-Control Theory," *Criminology* 29 (1991):99–114.

50. Andrew Z. Soshnick, "The Rape Shield Paradox: Complainant Protection amidst Oscillating Trends of State Judicial Interpretation," Comment, *Journal of Criminal Law and Criminology* 78 (1987):644–698; Cassia Spohn and Julie Horney, "The Law's the Law but Fair Is Fair: Rape Shield Laws and Officials' Assessments of Sexual History," *Criminology* 29 (1991):137–161. In some African societies the crime of rape is unknown. Its closest approximation might be a trespass for violating a woman who is the property of another. See Edna Erez and Bankole Thompson, "Rape in Sierra Leone: Conflict between the Sexes and Conflict of Laws," *International Journal of Comparative and Applied Criminal Justice* 14 (1990):201–210.

51. Tod W. Burke and Charles E. O'Rear, "Armed Carjackings: A Violent Problem in Need of a Solution," *Police Chief* 60 (1993):18–24. On robbery-violence, in general, see Philip J. Cook, "Robbery Violence," *Journal of Criminal Law and Criminology* 78 (1987):357–376; Colin Loftin, "The Validity of Robber-Murder Classifications in Baltimore," *Violence and Victims* 1 (1986):191–204.

52. *Uniform Crime Reports, 1991*, p. 58.

53. U.S. Department of Justice, *Report to the Nation on Crime*

and Justice, 2d ed. (Washington, D.C.: U.S. Government Printing Office, 1988), p. 97.

54. Terry L. Baumer and Michael D. Carrington, *The Robbery of Financial Institutions*, for U.S. Department of Justice (Washington, D.C.: U.S. Government Printing Office, 1986); Philip J. Cook, "Is Robbery Becoming More Violent? An Analysis of Robbery Murder Trends since 1968," *Journal of Criminal Law and Criminology* 76 (1985):480–489; Frederick H. McClintock and Evelyn Gibson, *Robbery in London* (London: Macmillan, 1961).

55. Wayland Clifton, Jr., *Convenience Store Robberies in Gainesville, Florida* (Gainesville, Fla.: Gainesville Police Department, 1987), p. 15.

56. *Uniform Crime Reports, 1991*, p. 58.

57. Roger Griffin, *Shoplifting in Supermarkets* (San Diego: Commercial Service Systems, 1988); see also Richard Moore, "Shoplifting in Middle America: Patterns and Motivational Correlates," *International Journal of Offender Therapy and Comparative Criminology* 28 (1984):53–64.

58. For the deterrent effect of such techniques, see John Carroll and Frances Weaver, "Shoplifters' Perceptions of Crime Opportunities: A Process-Tracing Study," in *The Reasoning Criminal*, eds. Derek Cornish and Ronald V. Clarke (New York: Springer-Verlag, 1986), pp. 19–38.

59. James M. Tien, Thomas F. Rich, and Michael F. Cahn, *Electronic Fund Transfer Systems Fraud*, for U.S. Department of Justice, Bureau of Justice Statistics (Washington, D.C.: U.S. Government Printing Office, 1986).

60. *Uniform Crime Reports, 1991*, p. 58.

61. George Rengert and John Wasilchick, *Suburban Burglary: A Time and a Place for Everything* (Springfield: Ill.: Charles C. Thomas, 1985).

62. Lawrence W. Sherman, Patrick R. Gartin, and Michael E. Buerger, "Hot Spots of Predatory Crime: Routine Activities and the Criminology of Place," *Criminology* 27 (1989):27–55; see also Ronald Clarke and Tim Hope, eds., *Coping with Burglary* (Boston: Kluwer-Nijhoff, 1984); Paul F. Cromwell, James N. Olson, and D'Aunn Wester Avary, *Breaking and Entering: An Ethnographic Analysis of Burglary* (Newbury Park, Calif.: Sage, 1991); and Garland F. White, "Neighborhood Permeability and Burglary Rates," *Justice Quarterly* 7 (1990):58–67.

63. Michael J. Kartes, Jr., "A Look at Fire Loss during 1986," *Fire Journal* (September-October 1987), p. 40; Patrick G. Jackson, "Assessing the Validity of Official Data on Arson," *Criminology* 26 (1988):181–195. See also Frederick Mercilliott, "The Effectiveness of Alternative Approaches to Investigating Arson: A Study of 155 Cities" (Ph.D. dissertation, City University of New York, 1988); Howard F. Jackson, Susan Hope, and Clive Glass, "Why Are Arsonists Not Violent Offenders?," *International Journal of Offender Therapy and Comparative Criminology* 31 (1987):143–151; Wayne W. Bennett and Karen Matison Hess, *Investigating Arson* (Springfield, Ill.: Charles C. Thomas, 1984), pp. 34–38.

64. Kitty Calavita and Henry N. Pontell, " 'Heads I Win, Tails You Lose': Deregulation, Crime, Crisis in the Savings and Loan Industry," *Crime and Delinquency* 36 (1990):309–341; Gilbert Geis, *On White Collar Crime* (Lexington, Mass.: Lexington Books, 1982); Marshall B. Clinard and Richard Quinney, *Criminal Behavior Systems*, 2d ed. (New York: Holt, Rinehart & Winston, 1973); August Bequai, *White Collar Crime: A 20th Century Crisis* (Lexington, Mass.: Lexington Books, 1978), p. 3. See also James W. Coleman, *The Criminal Elite: The Sociological White-Collar Crime*, 2d ed. (New York: St. Martin's Press, 1989).

65. See, for example, Gilbert Geis, Henry N. Pontell, and Paul Jesilow, "Medicaid Fraud," in *Controversial Issues in Crime and Justice*, eds. Joseph E. Scott and Travis Hirschi (Newbury Park, Calif.: Sage, 1988).

66. See Richard C. Hollinger and Lonn Lanza Kaduce, "The Process of Criminalization: The Case of Computer Crime Laws," *Criminology* 26 (1988):101–126. For an empirical test of insurance fraud, see Paul E. Tracy and James A. Fox, "A Field Experiment on Insurance Fraud in Auto Body Repair," *Criminology* 27 (1989):589–603.

67. For an outline of a general theory of crime causation applicable to both street crime and white-collar crime, see Travis Hirschi and Michael Gottfredson, "Causes of White-Collar Crime," *Criminology* 25 (1987):949–974. See also James W. Coleman, "Toward an Integrated Theory of White Collar Crime," *American Journal of Sociology* 93 (1987):406–439; James R. Lasley, "Toward a Control Theory of White Collar Offending," *Journal of Quantitative Criminology* 4 (1988):347–362; Donald R. Cressey, "The Poverty of Theory in Corporate Crime Research," in *Advances in Criminological Theory*, eds. William Laufer and Freda Adler (New Brunswick, N.J.: Transaction, 1988), vol. 1. For a response to Cressey, see John Braithwaite and Brent Fisse, "On the Plausibility of Corporate Crime Theory," in *Advances in Criminological Theory*, eds. William Laufer and Freda Adler (New Brunswick, N.J.: Transaction, 1990), vol. 2. See also Travis Hirschi and Michael Gottfredson, "The Significance of White-Collar Crime for a General Theory of Crime," *Criminology* 27 (1989):359–371; Darrell Steffensmeier, "On the Causes of 'White Collar' Crime: An Assessment of Hirschi and Gottfredson's Claims," *Criminology* 27 (1989):345–358.

68. Gerhard O. W. Mueller, "Mens Rea and the Corporation: A Study of the Model Penal Code Position on Corporate Criminal Liability," *University of Pittsburgh Law Review* 19 (1957):21–50. William S. Laufer, "Culpability and the Sentencing of Corporations," *Nebraska Law Review* 72 (1992):1049–1094; William S. Laufer and Allison Cohen, "Corporate Crime and Corporate Sanctions in Japan," *Business in a Contemporary World* 4 (1992):106–125. For a general overview of the corporate crime problem, see Francis T. Cullen, William J. Maakestad, and Gray Cavender, *Corporate Crime under Attack: The Ford Pinto Case and Beyond* (Cincinnati: Anderson, 1987), pp. 37–99.

69. Phillip Knightly, Harold Evans, Elaine Potter, and Marjorie Wallace, *Suffer the Children: The Story of Thalidomide* (New York: Viking Press, 1979). For more information on crimes against consumer safety, see Raymond J. Michalowski, *Order, Law, and Crime* (New York: Random House, 1985), pp. 334–340.

70. Donald J. Rebovich, *Dangerous Ground* (New Brunswick, N.J.: Transaction, 1992).

71. James E. Oberg, *Uncovering Soviet Disasters* (New York: Random House, 1988), p. 254.

72. See Russell Mokhiber, *Corporate Crime and Violence: Big Business Power and the Abuse of the Public Trust* (San Francisco: Sierra Club, 1988); Susan P. Shapiro, *Wayward Capitalists: Target of the Securities and Exchange Commission* (New Haven, Conn.: Yale University Press, 1984); M. David Ermann and Richard J. Lundman, *Corporate and Governmental Deviance: Problems of Organizational Behavior in Contemporary Society*, 2d ed. (New York: Oxford University Press, 1982); W. Byron Groves and Graeme Newman, *Punishment and Privilege* (Albany, N.Y.: Harrow & Heston, 1986).

73. Gerhard O. W. Mueller, "Offenses against the Environment and Their Prevention: An International Appraisal," *Annals of the American Academy of Political and Social Science* 444 (1979):56–66. For a discussion of the problems of multinational corporations operating in developing countries, see Richard Schaffer, Beverly Earle, and Filberto Aguste, *International Business Law and Its Environment*, 2d ed. (St. Paul, Minn.: West, 1993). John Braithwaite, "Challenging Just Desserts: Punishing White-Collar Criminals," *Journal of Criminal Law and Criminology* 73 (1982):723–763; Stanton Wheeler, David Weisburd, and Nancy Bode, "Sentencing the White-Collar Offender," *American Sociological Review* 47 (1982): 641–659. For an analysis of corporate illegality, see Nancy Frank and Michael Lombness, *Corporate Illegality and Regulatory Justice* (Cincinnati: Anderson, 1988). Mark H. Haller, " 'Illegal Enterprise': A Theoretical and Historical Interpretation," *Criminology* 28 (1990):207–235.

74. See Howard Abadinsky, *Organized Crime*, 2d ed. (Chicago: Nelson Hall, 1985). For a debate on the existence of a Sicilian-based

American crime syndicate, see Jay Albanese, *Organized Crime in America* (Cincinnati: Anderson, 1985), p. 25. See also Francis A. J. Ianni, *A Family Business: Kinship and Social Control in Organized Crime* (New York: Russel Sage Foundation, 1972); Joseph Albini, *The American Mafia: Genesis of a Legend* (New York: Appleton-Century-Crofts, 1971); Merry Morash, "Organized Crime," in *Major Forms of Crime*, ed. Robert F. Meier, (Beverly Hills, Calif.: Sage, 1984), pp. 191–220.

75. For a discussion of predicting which legitimate businesses will be infiltrated by organized crime, see Jay S. Albanese, "Predicting the Incidence of Organized Crime: A Preliminary Model," in *Organized Crime in America: Concepts and Controversies*, ed. Timothy S. Bynum, (Monsey, N.Y.: Willow Tree Press, 1987), pp. 103–114. See especially President's Commission on Law Enforcement and Administration of Justice, *Task Force Report: Organized Crime* (Washington, D.C.: U.S. Government Printing Office, 1967), p. 9. For a discussion of violence in organized crime, see Kip Schlegel, "Violence in Organized Crime: A Content Analysis of the DeCavalcante and DeCarlo Transcripts," in Bynum, *Organized Crime in America*, pp. 55–70.

76. Jeffrey Fagan, Ko-lin Chin, and Robert Kelly, "Lucky Money for Little Brother: The Prevalence and Seriousness of Chinese Gang Extortion," paper presented at the Annual Meeting of the American Society of Criminology, San Francisco, November 1991; "New Dimensions of Criminality and Crime Prevention in the Context of Development," working paper prepared by the United Nations Secretariat, A/CONF. 121 (1985), p. 20. For a global perspective, see Robert J. Kelley, ed., *Organized Crime: A Global Perspective* (Totowa, N.J.: Rowman & Littlefield, 1986); Gerald L. Posner, *Warlords of Crime: Chinese Secret Societies: The New Mafia* (New York: McGraw-Hill, 1988); Richard W. Slatta, *Bandidos: The Varieties of Latin American Banditry* (New York: Greenwood, 1987); Francis A. J. Ianni, "New Mafia: Black, Hispanic, and Italian Styles," *Society* 11 (1974):26–39, and *Black Mafia: Ethnic Succession in Organized Crime* (New York: Simon & Schuster, 1974).

77. For a perceptive analysis of the changing focus of national commission reports, see Jay S. Albanese, "Government Perceptions of Organized Crime: The Presidential Commissions, 1967 and 1987," *Federal Probation* 52 (1988):58–63; James M. Buchanan, "A Defense of Organized Crime," in *The Economies of Crime and Punishment*, ed. Simon Rottenberg (Washington, D.C.: The American Enterprise Institute, 1973), pp. 119–132.

78. Fred Montanano, "Protecting the Federal Witness," *American Behavioral Scientist* 27 (1984):501–529.

79. James Walston, "Mafia in the Eighties," *Violence, Aggression, and Terrorism* 1 (1987):13–39. For a critical analysis see Tom Mieczkowski, "Drugs, Crime and the Failure of American Organized Crime Models," *International Journal of Comparative and Applied Criminal Justice*, 14 (1993):97–106. See also Richard F. Sullivan, "The Economic Organization of the Nicotine, Heroin and Other Drug Industries," *Journal of Drug Issues*, 3 (1993)(3):231–239.

80. For example, M. Cherif Bassiouni, *Substantive Criminal Law* (Springfield, Ill.: Charles C. Thomas, 1978), pp. 355–397.

81. Howard Abadinsky, *Drug Abuse: An Introduction* (Chicago: Nelson Hall, 1989), pp. 30–31, 54.

82. Lloyd D. Johnston, Patrick M. O'Malley, and Jerald G. Bachman, *Drug Use among American High School Seniors, College Students and Young Adults, 1975–1990*, National Institute of Drug Abuse, table reprinted in *Bureau of Justice Statistics National Update* (October 1991), vol. 1, no. 2, NCJ 131778, p. 9.

83. U.S. Department of Health and Human Services, National Institute on Drug Abuse, *National Household Survey on Drug Abuse: Population Estimates, 1991* (Washington, D.C.: U.S. Government Printing Office, 1992).

84. Michael D. Lyman, *Narcotics and Crime Control* (Springfield, Ill.: Charles C. Thomas, 1987), p. 21.

85. Robert J. Michaels, "The Market for Heroin before and after Legalization," in *Dealing with Drugs*, ed. Ronald Hamowy (Lexington, Mass.: Lexington Books, 1987), pp. 311–318.

86. Christopher Innes, *Drug Use and Crime*, for Bureau of Justice Statistics (Washington, D.C.: U.S. Government Printing Office, 1988). See also Stephanie Greenberg and Freda Adler, "Crime and Addiction: An Empirical Analysis of the Literature, 1920–1973," *Contemporary Drug Problems* 3 (1974):221–270; Cheryl Carpenter, Barry Glassner, Bruce D. Johnson, and Julia Loughlin, *Kids, Drugs, and Crime* (Lexington, Mass.: Lexington Books, 1988); David N. Nurco, Thomas E. Hanlon, Timothy W. Kinlock, and Karen R. Duszynski, "Differential Criminal Patterns of Narcotics Addicts over an Addiction Career," *Criminology* 26 (1988):407–423; M. Douglas Anglin and George Speckart, "Narcotics Use and Crime: A Multisample, Multimethod Analysis," *Criminology* 26 (1988):197–233; M. Douglas Anglin and Yin-ing Hser, "Addicted Women and Crime," *Criminology* 25 (1987):359–397; Douglas A. Smith and Christina Polsenberg, "Specifying the Relationship between Arrestee Drug Test Results and Recidivism," *The Journal of Criminal Law & Criminology* 89 (1992):364–377.

87. See Mark Moore, *Drug Trafficking* (Washington, D.C.: National Institute of Justice, 1989); James Inciardi, *The War on Drugs: Heroin, Cocaine, Crime, and Public Policy* (Palo Alto, Calif.: Mayfield, 1986).

88. Freda Adler, Arthur D. Moffett, Frederick B. Glaser, John C. Ball, and Diana Horwitz, *A Systems Approach to Drug Treatment* (Philadelphia: Dorrance, 1974).

89. James B. Jacobs, *Drunk Driving: An American Dilemma* (Chicago: University of Chicago Press, 1989), p. xiii.

90. *Profile of State Prison Inmates* (Washington, D.C.: U.S. Government Printing Office, 1989).

91. U.S. Dept. of Justice, *Report to the Nation*, 2d ed., p. 50.

92. Marvin E. Wolfgang, *Patterns in Criminal Homicide* (Philadelphia: Univ. of Penn., 1958). See also R. A. Goodman, J. A. Mercy, R. Lova, M. L. Rosenberg, J. C. Smith, M. H. Allen, L. Vargas, and R. Kotts, "Alcohol Use and Interpersonal Violence—Alcohol Detected in Homicide Victims," *American Journal of Public Health* 76 (1986):144–149; James J. Collins, "Alcohol and Interpersonal Violence," in *Pathways to Criminal Violence*, eds. Neil Weiner and Marvin Wolfgang (Newbury Park, Calif.: Sage, 1989). For a comprehensive review of aggression and drug abuse, see Jeffrey A. Fagan, "Intoxication and Aggression," in *Crime and Justice: An Annual Review of Research*, vol. 13, *Drugs and Crime*, eds. James Q. Wilson and Michael Tonry (Chicago: University of Chicago Press, 1990).

93. Lawrence A. Greenfeld, *Drunk Driving*, for Bureau of Justice Statistics (Washington, D.C.: U.S. Government Printing Office, February 1988), p. 1.

94. Joseph R. Gusfield, "The Control of Drinking-Driving in the United States: A Period of Transition," in *Social Control of the Drinking Driver*, eds. Michael D. Laurence, John R. Snortum, and Franklin E. Zimring (Chicago: University of Chicago Press, 1988); Gerald Wheeler and Rodney Hissong, "Effects of Criminal Sanctions on Drunk Drivers: Beyond Incarceration," *Crime and Delinquency* 34 (1988):29–42; Dale E. Berger and John R. Snortum, "A Structural Model of Drinking and Driving: Alcohol Consumption, Social Norms, and Moral Commitments," *Criminology* 24 (1986):139–153.

95. U.S. Department of Justice, Attorney General's Commission on Pornography, *Final Report* (Washington, D.C.: U.S. Government Printing Office, 1986), vols. 1 and 2. For the current state of the law on pornography see William Eich, "From Ulysses to Portnoy: A Pornography Primer," *Marquette Law Review* 53 (1993):156–171.

96. *Regulating Morality? An Inquiry into Prostitution in Queensland* (Queensland, Australia: Criminal Justice Commission, 1991). See Joan Hoff, "Why Is There No History of Pornography?," in *For Adult Users Only: The Dilemma of Violent Pornography*, eds. Susan Gubar and Joan Hoff (Bloomington: Indiana University Press, 1989), p. 18.

CHAPTER 3

UNDERSTANDING CRIMINAL BEHAVIOR

Richard Franklin Speck, 49, died of a heart attack on December 5, 1991, at Silver Cross Hospital in Illinois, near the prison that held him for a quarter century. In the summer of 1966, Speck had broken into a Chicago town house, where he gathered eight student nurses in one room and bound them with bed sheets. One by one he took them to another room. There he spent at least a half-hour alone with each victim, brutally stabbed or strangled her, ritualistically washed his hands, and then went back for the next one. Speck was sentenced to death—a sentence that was eventually (by a Supreme Court ruling) changed to 400 to 1,200 years in the maximum-security Stateville Correctional Center in Joliet.

No one knows why Richard Speck committed these brutal murders. We know that this crime was not his first. Born in Kirkwood, Illinois, in 1941, he was one of the eight children of Margaret and Benjamin Speck. Richard, who never went to high school, spent much of his time drinking excessively and reading comic books.[1] By the spring of 1966 he had been arrested thirty-seven times, on charges ranging from trespassing to burglary.

The murders prompted a massive hunt for the killer. Speck was arrested a few days later at the Cook County Hospital, where he went for treatment of a self-inflicted knife wound. Oddly enough, it was a tattoo on his left forearm (described to police by a sole survivor who had hidden under a bed) that led to his arrest. It read: "Born to Raise Hell."[2]

Was Richard Speck "born to raise hell"? In other words, was he predestined from birth to commit violent crimes? Or can Speck's behavior be traced to the conditions in which he lived, his poor family life, poverty, lack of education, and other environmental factors? ■

Since ancient times scholars have speculated about the causes of crime and the possible remedies. Our current theories are based on an accumulation of knowledge. These theories have a significant impact on how the criminal justice system operates and how it treats individual offenders once they enter the system. They also underlie our efforts at crime prevention and control.

In this chapter we will discuss explanations of criminal behavior that focus on biological, psychological, and social factors. Biological and psychological theories assume that criminal behavior results from physical or mental conditions that distinguish criminals from noncriminals. These theories yield insight into individual cases, but they do not explain why crime rates vary from place to place and from one situation to another. Sociological theories differ from biological and psychological theories in that they look for causes of criminal behavior in the environment in which a person grows up.

The chapter also presents three alternative sociological explanations of criminal behavior: labeling theory, conflict theory, and radical theory. These theories do not focus on individual criminal characteristics or on the social environment; they explain how people become criminals because of what others with power, especially those in criminal justice, do. Labeling, conflict, and radical theories focus on the impact of lawmaking and law enforcement on the creation of criminals.

criminology
Study of the causes, detection, correction, and prevention of criminal behavior.

Criminology is the study of criminal behavior and its causes, detection, correction, and prevention. In this chapter we concentrate on the causes. Understanding the foundations of modern criminology's search for the causes of crime can help us understand contemporary developments in the field. So we begin with a discussion of the two leading schools of criminological thought, the classical and the positivist, both products of the intellectual and scientific thinking of the eighteenth and nineteenth centuries.

CLASSICAL CRIMINOLOGY

Classical criminology grew out of a reaction against the barbaric system of justice that existed in Europe before the French Revolution of 1789. Due process (a fundamental mandate that a person should not be deprived of life, liberty, or property without reasonable and lawful procedures) in the modern sense did not exist; brutal punishments included branding, burning, drowning, and beheading.[3] The death penalty was frequently used for what today we call petty theft. Public punishments such as hangings were popular events for which one might even purchase seats. While Europe grew increasingly modern, industrial, and urban in the eighteenth century, it still clung to these medieval practices.

Principles of the Classical School

By the mid-eighteenth century, social reformers were beginning to suggest a more rational approach to crime and punishment. One of them, Cesare Beccaria (1738–1794), a young radical intellectual, introduced a coherent, comprehensive design for an enlightened criminal justice system. According to Beccaria, the crime problem could be traced not to bad people but to bad laws. The arbitrary system that had been in place for centuries needed to be replaced by a system that would guarantee all people equal treatment before the law. In his famous treatise, *On Crimes and Punishment* (1764), Beccaria proposed among others the following principles:

- All people should be treated equally.
- Judges should impose punishment only in accordance with the law.
- Punishment should be prompt and effective.

"Make the pain of punishment greater than the pleasure of the criminal gains."
Cesare Beccaria, *On Crime and Punishment* (1764).

The execution of Marie Antoinette, queen of France, in October 1793. Cesare Beccaria and other Enlightenment reformers campaigned against the use of brutal punishments and public executions as popular entertainment.

• The type of punishment should be based on the act (the injury done to society), not on the person who committed it.

• Punishment should be based on the pleasure/pain principle—the pain of punishment should be greater than the pleasure of the criminal gains.

The **classical school of criminology,** based on the principles set forth by Beccaria, focused mainly on reform of criminal law, criminal procedures, and penalties. It was built on the assumption that criminals choose to commit crimes after weighing the consequences of their actions. According to classical criminologists, individuals had free will. They could choose legal or illegal means to get what they wanted. Fear of punishment could deter people from committing crime. Moreover, since human beings had the capacity to choose between good and evil, there was no need to ask *why* people behave as they do. Questions about motive or about the specific circumstances surrounding criminal acts were therefore pointless.

classical school of criminology *Criminological perspective suggesting that criminals choose to commit crimes after weighing the consequences of their actions, and that crime can be controlled by criminal sanctions.*

Impact of the Classical School

Toward the end of the eighteenth century, classical principles served as a guide for the drafting of the French penal code, the Russian and Prussian codes, and the code of the Austrian empire; they also influenced the first ten amendments to the U.S. Constitution. Substitution of the rule of law for human whims spread rapidly in Europe and in the United States. Of no less significance was the influence of the classical school on penal and correctional policy. The classical principle that the punishment must be appropriate to the crime was universally accepted during the nineteenth and early twentieth centuries.

POSITIVIST CRIMINOLOGY

During the century that followed the introduction of the classical approach, science underwent rapid development. Significant advances in knowledge of both

· · · · · · · · · · · · · · · · · · ·

positivist school of criminology
Perspective that uses the scientific methods of the natural sciences and suggests that human behavior is a product of social, biological, psychological, or economic forces.

"If only there were evil people somewhere insidiously committing evil deeds,... [B]ut the line dividing good and evil cuts through the heart of every human being."
Aleksander Solzhenitsyn, *The Gulag Archipelago.*

"Heredity is nothing but stored environment."
Luther Burbank, p. 209.

the physical and the social world also influenced the study of crime. Criminology was permanently transformed from an abstract philosophy of crime control through legislation (the classical approach) to a modern science of investigation into causes. The **positivist school of criminology** assumed that human behavior is determined not by free will but by forces beyond the control of individuals, and that it is possible to measure those forces scientifically. Unlike classical criminologists, who claim that people rationally choose to commit crime, positivist criminologists viewed criminal behavior as stemming from biological, psychological, and social factors.

Biology and Crime

The pioneers of the positivist school of criminology were three Italians: Cesare Lombroso (1835–1909), Enrico Ferri (1856–1929), and Raffaele Garofalo (1852–1934).[4] Lombroso measured the physical features of thousands of prisoners and argued that it was possible to identify "born criminals" from a variety of these features, such as huge jaws and strong canine teeth, (characteristic of creatures at an earlier stage of development, before they became fully human). Though his theory did not stand up to subsequent scientific scrutiny, Lombroso replaced the concept of free will as the principle that explained criminal behavior with that of determinism. The fact that he turned to empirical research in his search for the causes of crime changed the nature of the questions asked by generations of scholars who came after him.

There were a number of other pioneers in the positivist school of criminology. In 1939 Ernest Hooten (1887–1954), a physical anthropologist, published a massive study comparing American prisoners with a noncriminal control group. He concluded that "in every population there are hereditary inferiors in mind and in body as well as physical and mental deficients . . . ."[5] He argued that from these inferiors, "criminal stock" is derived. For such individuals, he recommended segregation and sterilization. Other scientists, the physician William Sheldon among them, related body build to illegal behavior. Sheldon's father was a dog breeder who judged animals in competition, and Sheldon worked out a point system of his own for judging humans.[6] One could actually measure on a scale from 1 to 7 the relative dominance of each body type in any given individual. People with predominantly mesomorph traits (physically powerful, aggressive, athletic physiques), he suggested, tend more than others to be involved in illegal behavior.

But while some investigators were measuring skulls and bodies of criminals to find a link to crime, others were arguing that criminality was an inherited trait. To support the theory, they traced family histories through several generations. Richard Dugdale (1841–1883), for example, studied the lives of more than a thousand members of the family he called Jukes. The extremely high number of criminals among the descendants of Ada Jukes led him to refer to her as "the mother of criminals," and to argue that she had passed down a degenerate trait.[7]

These early studies of the physical and mental determinants of crime have been discredited on the grounds that the work was not scientifically sound and that genetic and environmental influences could not be separated. But in the early twentieth century, they were taken very seriously and were the basis for sterilization laws passed by some states and upheld by the Supreme Court in 1927.

Biologically based explanations of criminality were popular in the late nineteenth century, fell out of favor in the early part of the twentieth century when sociologists began to study urban-related crime problems, and emerged again in the 1970s at a time of major advances in biochemistry and neurophysiology. Modern research focuses on genetic predispositions to act with violence or aggression, the intelligence and crime debate, the relationship between biochemical factors (for example, diet) and criminality, and neurophysiological factors that result in criminal behavior.

Genetics and Criminality. To discover whether certain people are genetically predisposed to engage in criminal or violent behavior, researchers have compared identical and fraternal twins. Identical twins develop from a single fertilized egg that divides into two embryos. These twins share all genes. Fraternal twins develop from two separate eggs, both fertilized at the same time; they share about half of their genes. Since the prenatal and postnatal family environments are, by and large, the same, greater behavioral similarity between identical twins than between fraternal twins would support an argument for genetic predisposition. In the 1970s, Karl O. Christiansen and Sarnoff A. Mednick studied 3,586 pairs of twins in Denmark. Reviewing serious offenses only, Christiansen and Mednick found that the chance of finding a criminal twin when the other twin was a criminal was 50 percent for identical twins and 20 percent for same-sex fraternal twins.[8] These findings lend support to the hypothesis that some genetic influences increase the risk of criminality. But while the evidence from these and other twin studies appears persuasive, such research has weaknesses. Might it not be that identical twins are treated more alike than fraternal twins? If this is true, environment, not just genetic influence, becomes an important factor.

Among other studies of genetically predisposed violence are those related to the chromosomes that determine gender. Sometimes a defect in the production of sperm or egg results in a genetic abnormality like the xyy syndrome, which is found in males born with an extra male chromosome. Initial studies done in the 1960s found the frequency of xyy chromosomes to be about twenty times greater than that of normal xy chromosomes among inmates in maximum-security state hospitals.[9] Supporters of these data claimed to have discovered the mystery of violent criminal behavior. The xyy syndrome received much public attention and concern because of the case of Richard Speck, who was originally diagnosed as xyy. (The diagnosis later turned out to be wrong.)

Although convincing evidence appears to be slight, it is nevertheless possible that aggressive and violent behavior is at least partly determined by genetic factors. The problem is how to investigate this possibility. To do so, one would have to separate environmental factors from genetic ones, a task scientists have so far been unable to accomplish.

The IQ Debate. The relationship between IQ and criminal behavior is the subject of an ongoing debate. Some researchers conclude that IQ is an even more important predictor of criminality than is either race or social class.[10] According to this argument, low IQ ultimately results in association with similar nonperformers, dropping out of school, and delinquency. Not all researchers agree: The debate over the relationship between IQ and crime has its roots in the controversy over whether intelligence is genetically or environmentally determined. Many people believe IQ tests measure cultural factors that are learned rather than the innate biological makeup of an individual.

"The debate over the relationship between IQ and criminal behavior has its roots in the controversy over whether intelligence is inherited or learned."

Biochemical Factors. In a highly publicized case involving the 1979 murder of San Francisco mayor George Moscone, the impact of the amount of sugar in the blood was used as a defense in the trial. The testimony showed that when Dan White, the defendant, was depressed, he departed from his normal healthy diet and indulged himself with high-sugar "junk" food, including Twinkies, Coca-Cola, and chocolate candy. Afterward his behavior became less and less controllable. The jury found White guilty of manslaughter, rather than murder, due to diminished capacity. His defense was promptly dubbed the "junk food defense," "Dan White's defense," or "Twinkie defense." (White served five years in prison and committed suicide after his release.)

To study the relationship between behavior and diets high in sugar, in the 1980s a series of studies was conducted on institutionalized offenders in the United States. Inmates were placed on a modified diet that included very little sugar. They received fruit juice in place of soda and vegetables instead of candy.

The results showed a decline in disciplinary actions and a significant drop in aggressive behavior in the experimental group.[11] Other research on biochemical factors has investigated vitamin deficiencies, food allergies, and hormonal problems.[12]

Neurophysiological Factors. Investigations into the relationship of neurophysiology to crime include studies of brain waves, minimal brain dysfunctions, brain lesions, and brain tumors. An English case serves as an example of the problem.[13] In the mid-1950s, a father beat his son and then tossed him out of a window, which resulted in his death. Instead of pleading insanity, as many people expected the father to do, he presented evidence of a brain tumor which, he argued, resulted in uncontrollable rage. A jury acquitted him on the grounds that the brain tumor had deprived him of control over or knowledge of the act he was committing.[14]

Psychology and Criminality

"Guns are neat little things, aren't they? They can kill extraordinary people with very little effort."
John W. Hinckley, Jr., *Time*, May 17, 1982.

The psychological approach to understanding crime, like the biological, focuses on the differences between criminals and noncriminals. Psychological theories all assume that criminal behavior results from underlying psychological problems. The case of John Hinckley, Jr., is a good example.

On March 30, 1981, a young man stood in front of the Hilton Hotel in Washington, D.C., and mixed with the crowd that had gathered to see President Reagan. As the nation watched television coverage of the president leaving the hotel, the young man drew a gun and fired several shots, wounding the president and several members of his entourage. The assassination attempt was related to the fact that Hinckley had developed an obsession with one of the characters, played by Jodie Foster, in the movie *Taxi Driver*. The plot involves a lonely taxi driver who plans to kill a presidential candidate over a failed relationship with one of the candidate's workers. Hinckley believed his only hope of winning Foster's admiration lay in killing the president. After the assassination attempt, Hinckley was acquitted by reason of insanity and was committed to a mental hospital.

Source: *The New Yorker*, Dec. 9, 1991, p. 43.

"So, while extortion, racketeering, and murder may be bad acts, they don't make you a bad person."

Developmental Issues. **Psychoanalytic theory,** founded by the famous Viennese psychiatrist Sigmund Freud (1856–1939), suggests that criminality may result from an overactive conscience that produces excessive guilt feelings. In treating patients, Freud noticed that those who were suffering from unbearable unconscious guilt committed crimes in order to be caught and punished.[15] Once they had been punished, their guilt feelings were relieved. Psychoanalysts today offer two additional explanations for persistent criminal activities: One is a conscience that is not too strong, but too weak. Because conscience is an internalized parental image, it follows that the absence of such an image may lead to delinquency. The other explanation deals with the need for immediate reward and gratification. A defect in the character formation of delinquents may drive them to satisfy their desires at once, regardless of the consequences.

The psychoanalytic approach is still a prominent explanation for both normal and asocial behavior. Psychoanalytic treatment techniques—unraveling the interaction between behavior and unconscious motives—have been used with success since their introduction by Freud. Since analysis involves a one-to-one relationship, therapist with patient, for an extended period, it holds little promise for clients of the criminal justice system. But short-term psychotherapy and group therapy are well suited for use in the criminal justice system—and have been used successfully.

Another psychological approach to criminal behavior focuses on moral reasoning. You may know that it is wrong to steal, but you may believe there are times when the law should be circumvented (e.g., it is OK to steal bread for a starving child). Or is it always wrong to steal, no matter what the circumstances? Regardless of what you decide, the way you reach the decision reveals much about your moral development. The psychologist Lawrence Kohlberg, who pioneered **moral developmental theory,** has found that moral reasoning develops in stages from childhood to the adult years.[16] Children's moral rules, for example, consist of the dos and don'ts that avoid punishment. Adolescent moral reasoning involves a belief in society's rules. Adults critically examine social rules according to their own moral principles. According to Kohlberg and his colleagues, most delinquents and criminals show a low level of moral reasoning. On the basis of this theory, a number of programs have been designed for use in correctional institutions (for example, in Connecticut, Florida, and Massachusetts) to promote the growth and development of moral reasoning. A series of evaluations of these programs has revealed significant growth in moral development.[17]

In a classic psychology experiment, infant monkeys were given a choice between two wire "mother monkeys." One, made of uncovered wire, dispensed milk. The other, made of wire covered with soft fabric, did not. The infant monkeys gravitated to the warm cloth monkey, which provided comfort and security even though it did not provide food. What does this have to do with criminality? Research has demonstrated that a phenomenon important to social development takes place shortly after the birth of any mammal: the development of an emotional bond, or attachment, between infant and mother. When a child is separated or rejected by its mother, poor attachment results, and the child's capacity to develop close relationships with others is reduced. Habitual criminals, it is claimed, typically have an inability to form close bonds of affection.[18]

Learning. **Social learning theory,** pioneered by Albert Bandura in the 1960s, maintains that delinquent and nondelinquent behavior is learned through the same psychological processes. Behavior is learned when it is reinforced or rewarded, and not learned when it is not reinforced.

Children can learn violence and aggression by modeling their own behavior on what they observe others doing. Their models come from the family, the neighborhood, and the mass media.[19] Another way children learn is from direct experience: what they do and what happens to them. According to social learning theorists, after engaging in a given behavior most of us examine the responses to

psychoanalytic theory
Theory of criminality that attributes delinquent and criminal behavior to a conscience either so overbearing that it arouses excessive feelings of guilt or so weak that it cannot control impulses.

"Is it OK to steal bread for a starving child? Or is it always wrong to steal, no matter what the circumstances?"

moral developmental theory
Theories of moral reasoning in relation to development.

social learning theory
Theory that delinquent behavior is learned through the same psychological processes as nondelinquent behavior, that is, through reinforcement.

• • • • • • • • • • • • • • • • • •

"The consensus among most of the research community is that violence on television does lead to aggressive behavior by children and teenagers who watch the programs."
National Institute of Mental Health, 1982.

"According to one argument, criminals are people who feel a sense of superiority, expect not to be held accountable for their acts, and have a highly inflated self-image."

psychopathy
Condition in which a person has no sense of responsibility; shows disregard for truth; is insincere; and feels no sense of shame, guilt, or humiliation.

Ex law student and serial murderer Ted Bundy, before his execution: "I mean, there are so many people. . . . What's one less person on the face of the earth, anyway?"

our actions and change our future behavior depending on those responses. If we are praised or rewarded for a behavior, we are likely to repeat it. If we are subjected to verbal or physical punishment, we are likely to refrain from such behavior. Moreover, the most meaningful rewards and punishments are those given by groups important in our lives—our peer group, our family, our teachers.[20]

More recently, social learning theorists have been interested in the learning that takes place in front of the television screen or at the movies. Do "successful" gangsters suggest that aggressive behavior is acceptable? The movie industry provides a steady stream of shows about such gangsters: *The Godfather* (I, II, and III); *Goodfellas; Mobsters*. Has the wealthy gangster boss, living a glamorous life, become a folk hero? Research in this area remains inconclusive.

Personality Factors. Whether or not criminals share personality characteristics has long been debated, with no conclusive answers. Are criminals in fact more aggressive and manipulative than noncriminals? Are they more irresponsible? Clearly, many criminals are aggressive; many manipulate situations. But are such personality characteristics common to *all* criminals? In *The Criminal Personality* (1976), a psychiatrist-psychologist team described their experience treating criminals in the Forensic Division of St. Elizabeth's Hospital in Washington, D.C. They claimed criminals share abnormal "thinking patterns" that lead to decisions to commit crime. Criminals are, according to this argument, people who feel a sense of superiority, expect not to be held accountable for their acts, and have a highly inflated self-image.[21]

Much of the work on the association between personality and criminality has been carried out in state and federal prisons. Some has been done by psychologists using personality questionnaires. The evidence from these studies shows that inmates are typically more impulsive, hostile, self-centered, and immature than noncriminals.[22]

Mental Disorders and Crime. Most research on the relationship between mental disorders and crime focuses on a particular type of disorder called **psychopathy.** Estimates are that between 20 and 60 percent of state correctional populations suffer from psychopathy, which in the nineteenth century was described by

an English physician as "moral insanity." Psychopathy, or anti-social personality, is characterized by an inability to learn from experience, a lack of warmth, and no sense of guilt. Psychopaths lie and cheat without hesitation and engage in verbal as well as physical abuse without provocation.[23] Theodore "Ted" Bundy is a classic example. Bundy, a former law student and former crime commission staff member, killed between nineteen and thirty-six young women in the northwestern states and Florida. The handsome physical fitness enthusiast often brutally sexually attacked his victims before murdering them. In prison interviews Bundy speculated on what he believed had motivated the murderer in the crime in which he was the suspect:

"What really fascinated him was the hunt, the adventure of searching out his victim," Bundy said. "And, to a degree, possessing them physically as one would possess a potted plant, a painting or a Porsche. Owning, as it were, this individual.

No matter how hard he tried, this hypothetical killer could never fully extinguish his desires to rape and murder. Instead he rationalized.

He would cling to the belief that there would be virtually no furor over it . . . ," Bundy said. "I mean, there are so many people.

It shouldn't be a problem. What's one less person on the face of the earth, anyway?"[24]

Bundy died in the Florida electric chair in 1989.

Biological and Psychological Theory: Practical Applications

An understanding of the relationship between criminal behavior and biological and psychological factors has been helpful to criminal justice agencies in a number of ways. At the police level, results of studies have been used to develop tests to identify perpetrators (for example, DNA tests). Investigators also match psychological profiles with **modus operandi,** the means and method by which a crime is committed.

modus operandi
Means and method by which a crime is committed.

At the judicial level, the court often uses psychological evaluations such as presentence investigation reports as an aid in imposing appropriate sentences. In correctional settings, a number of psychological tests are used to evaluate inmates for placement in rehabilitation programs. On a daily basis, decisions are made by prison psychologists as to where inmates should be housed (classification decisions), whether individuals are in need of psychiatric treatment, and so forth.[25]

Sociology and Criminality

Biological and psychological theories seek to identify the "kind of person" who becomes a criminal and to find the factors that caused the person to engage in criminal behavior. These theories may explain individual cases, but they do not explain why crime rates vary from one neighborhood to the next, from one group to the next, within large urban areas, or within groups of individuals. Why, for example, are there an estimated 130,000 gang members in Los Angeles County alone? Why do preteen youngsters join groups, usually of their own ethnicity, that account for over 18,000 violent felonies in a single year?

Sociological theories attempt to explain criminal behavior in terms of group rather than individual factors. These theories seek the reasons for differences in crime rates in the social environment. In the United States, explanations of criminal behavior have been dominated by sociological theories since the 1920s. These theories can be grouped into three general categories: strain, cultural deviance, and social control.

strain theory
Theory that a gap between culturally approved goals and legitimate means of achieving them causes frustration, which leads to criminal behavior.

Strain Theory. The roots of modern **strain theory** can be traced to the ideas of Emile Durkheim (1858–1917), a French sociologist who had one of the most powerful influences on contemporary criminology. Durkheim argued that when

GANGS OF THE 1990S

The middle-aged man had fled Cambodia to save his family from the genocidal Khmer Rouge. Now, as he paced furiously back and forth across the grimy patio behind a cramped bungalow in the Little Phnom Penh section of Long Beach, he saw a very different threat materializing—within his own family. His 14-year-old son, gang-named Flipper, and another homeboy, Slicc, 18, were bragging to a stranger about a shoot-out.

"I'm on the corner phone with my girlfriend," Slicc recounted. "The Mexican drives up and yells, 'What set you from?' I yell it ain't none of his business, and he busts three caps [shoots three bullets] at me. I take out my gun and bust four back . . . ." At that point, the father began to wave his arms and shout. Friends of Slicc's and Flipper's pushed the man firmly back inside his house. "Parents don't understand," shrugged Flipper.

In the bizarre and bloody world of Southern California gang life, armed and alienated children are guerrilla warriors. Cambodian gangs battling Hispanic gangs is but the newest infection. Ira Reiner, district attorney for Los Angeles County (pop. 8,776,000), estimates that 130,000 gang members operate in his jurisdiction alone. They range from subteen "peewees" to as many as 13,000 hard-core killers. Last year in the county the gangs accounted for 18,059 violent felonies and 690 deaths. Nearly every ethnic group is represented in the mayhem: the highly publicized black Bloods and Crips; multigenerational Hispanic groups that account for nearly two-thirds of all California gangs; whites; Asians; Pacific Islanders; and Jewish and Armenian groups. (1)

Los Angeles County is not alone in its problems with street gangs. In 1961 there were gangs in twenty-three cities nationwide. In 1992, gangs flourished in more than 250 cities (2). Once, gang wars took place over "turf," territory that members claimed. The weapons were knives, rocks, or metal chains. Gang life was romanticized—for example, in the popular musical drama "West Side Story." Now gang wars are over drugs and huge sums of money, and the weapons are assault rifles or semiautomatic guns. Gangs trade in stolen property that includes submachine guns and powerful handguns. Gang members move from one city to another to transport and sell drugs. Los Angeles gang members, for example, migrate to Seattle, Albuquerque, Denver, Omaha, Buffalo, and Kansas City. And violence has become a characteristic of gang life. In the past, gang members who wanted a reputation for toughness would perform certain acts: "One particular biker would catch a bird and then bite off its head, allowing the blood to trickle from his mouth as he yelled 'All right'" (3). Now younger boys waiting to become members of gangs go through initiations that sometimes demand a drive-by murder. It's hard to imagine romanticizing these events.

What accounts for the changes in gang culture and the multiplying numbers of gangs? Some researchers contend that the urban underclass problem is responsible, that continuing problems of racial segregation, unemployment, and poverty make gang life attractive to young male blacks and Hispanics (4). Although Flipper and other 14-year-olds are gang members, the most common age for street gang

members today is 19 or 20, and gang members in their mid to late 20s or even over 30 are not uncommon. These are young men who could be gainfully employed. And gang culture envelopes all ethnic groups today, even traditionally law-abiding peoples such as Asian Americans. In one-third of major U.S. cities there are now gangs of Chinese, Japanese, Koreans, Vietnamese, Filipinos, Samoans, or Cambodians. The growth of Chinese gangs provides an example both of Asian American involvement in gangs and of some contemporary gang-related crime problems.

Chinese gangs became a problem when the Immigration Act of 1965 opened up a new wave of immigration (see Figure 1). American Chinese communities, generally hard-working and law-abiding, had had few problems with teenagers, but these communities were not prepared to handle the huge influx of newcomers. Traditional family life began to break down as newcomers struggled to solve their housing and employment problems, and delinquent activities increased. Gangs appeared in San Francisco, Los Angeles, Boston, Toronto, Vancouver, and New York City. Their numbers are small— there are perhaps 2,000 Chinese gang members in the United States—but the problems they create are not. Chinese gangs engage in lethal gang-related violence and major heroin trafficking. The gangs are typically controlled by Asian organized crime; they form national and international networks; they are influenced greatly by Chinese secret societies (the Triads); and they resemble adult criminal organizations more than street gangs. The gangs get their money from protection of the gambling clubs popular in Chinese communities and from extortion of between 80 and 90 percent of Chinese businesses (5).

Gang control efforts before the 1970s used "street workers" to work directly with gang members, organizing outings, sports events, and dances and providing counseling services. Control efforts today focus on suppression techniques: gang members are kept under close surveillance and frequent arrests are aimed at deterring them from committing more serious crimes. Early efforts at gang control failed; street gangs clearly are an increasing problem. And little is known about the effectiveness of suppression techniques. No research has been done to evaluate the success or failure of street sweeps, gang harassment, and saturation patrols, all of which focus intense police attention on gang neighborhoods. While many researchers and public policy-makers agree that a variety of social problems contribute to the increase in gangs, no one has mapped out a solidly researched program to solve either these underlying problems or the street gang crime problem itself. (6)

SOURCES

1. James Willerth, "From Killing Fields to Mean Streets," *Time,* November 18, 1991, p. 103.
2. *Time,* June 15, 1992, p. 37.
3. Jay S. Albanese and Robert D. Pursley, *Crime in America* (Englewood Cliffs, N.J.: Regents, 1993), p. 205.
4. Malcolm W. Klein, "Street Gangs," in Calhoun and Ritzer, *Introduction to Social Problems* (New York: Primis Database, McGraw-Hill, 1993).
5. Ko-Lin Chin, *Chinese Subculture and Criminality: Non-traditional Crime Groups in America* (New York: Greenwood Press, 1990).
6. James R. David, *Street Gangs* (Dubuque, Ia.: Kendall/Hunt, 1982).

QUESTIONS FOR DISCUSSION

1. Street gang membership apparently provides young males with a sense of status and identity. Suggest alternative sources for these benefits of gang life.
2. Efforts to break up gangs once they are formed have not been successful in most cases. How might gang formation be prevented?
3. It seems that gang members are more likely to commit violent crimes than they would be if they were not members of gangs. Do you think such crimes should be punished more harshly when the offender is a gang member? Defend your position.

FIGURE 1. Time Line of New York City's Chinese Gangs: 1960–1990

(*Source:* Ko-lin Chin, *Chinese Subculture and Criminality* [New York: Greenwood Press, 1990], p. 76.)

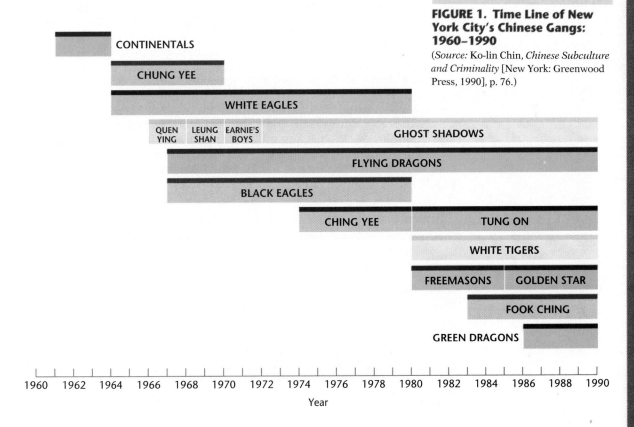

CONTINENTALS

CHUNG YEE

WHITE EAGLES

QUEN YING · LEUNG SHAN · EARNIE'S BOYS · GHOST SHADOWS

FLYING DRAGONS

BLACK EAGLES

CHING YEE · TUNG ON

WHITE TIGERS

FREEMASONS · GOLDEN STAR

FOOK CHING

GREEN DRAGONS

1960 1962 1964 1966 1968 1970 1972 1974 1976 1978 1980 1982 1984 1986 1988 1990

Year

anomie
Societal state marked by "norm-
lessness," in which disintegration
and chaos have replaced social
cohesion.

"In the inner cities, all they have
are the streets or yards, with
nothing in between."
Gary Harris, Newark, N.J.,
councilman, quoted in *The New*
York Times, September 9, 1992.

"It's not black vs. white. It's rich
vs. poor, and we're poor."
Looter shouting into TV cameras, Los Angeles riots, quoted
in *Business Week*, May 18, 1992,
p. 47.

a simple society develops into a modern urbanized one, the intimacy needed to sustain a common set of standards declines. Rules that once guided behavior no longer hold. In the absence of a common set of rules, the actions and expectations of people in some groups may clash with those in others. As behavior becomes unpredictable, the system gradually breaks down, and the society is in a state of **anomie** (defined as the breakdown of the social order as a result of the loss of standards and values).[26]

In the twentieth century, sociologist Robert Merton, like Durkheim, related the crime problem to norms that break down and no longer act as effective guides to behavior.[27] Merton argued that the structure of our society creates the breakdown. According to him, our society holds out the same goals (the American dream) to all members without giving them equal means to achieve them. Very few members of society, especially of the lower classes, have an opportunity to get to the top. Merton emphasized the importance of two elements in any society: (1) cultural aspirations, or goals that people believe are worth striving for; and (2) the accepted ways to attain these goals. A large gap between goals and the means people have to get them fosters frustration, which leads to strain. Strain theory assumes that people are law-abiding, but that under great pressure they will resort to crime; great disparity between goals and means provides that pressure.

Merton suggested that the greatest proportion of crime will be found in the lower classes because lower-class persons have the least opportunity to reach their goals legitimately. Since they have few legitimate means, they design their own ways to get ahead. These may be robbery, burglary, or a host of other crimes.

Merton's theory explains crime in the United States in terms of the wide disparities in income among the various classes. Statistics clearly demonstrate that such disparities exist. Table 3.1 shows that, according to the latest census data, 15 percent of Americans have an annual income under $10,000, 16 percent earn between $25,000 and $34,999, and 10 percent earn over $75,000.[28] Broken down by race, 13 percent of whites, 31 percent of blacks, and 21 percent of Hispanics earn under $10,000 annually. Ten percent of all American families live below the poverty level.[29] It is not, however, solely wealth or income that determines people's position on a social ladder that ranges from the homeless on the streets to penthouse dwellers. Other attributes of social class are education, prestige, power, and even language.

Results of research testing the association between social class and crime rates have been controversial. Some studies report the reason for higher arrest rates among lower-class persons is that the police are more likely to arrest lower-class suspects than middle-class suspects.[30] Others say that there is, in reality, more serious and more frequent delinquency among, for example, lower-class boys.[31]

TABLE 3.1 Income Disparities among American Households, 1990

	Under $10,000	$25,000 to $34,999	$75,000 and Over	Median Income
All households	14.9%	15.8%	9.7%	$29,943
White households	12.8%	16.1%	10.4%	$31,231
Black households	30.8%	13.5%	3.8%	$18,676
Hispanic households	21.1%	16.5%	4.3%	$22,330

"All households" includes other races not shown separately. Hispanic persons may be of any race. Figures in constant (1990) dollars; amounts by race and by Hispanic origin of householder.
SOURCE: *Statistical Abstracts of the United States 1992*, U.S. Department of Commerce, Bureau of the Census (1992), p. 445.

Cultural Deviance Theories. Strain theory attributes criminal behavior in the United States to its citizens' striving to conform with the conventional values of the middle class, primarily financial success. **Cultural deviance theories** attribute crime to a set of values peculiar to the lower class; conformity with the lower-class value system, which determines behavior in slum areas, causes conflict with society's laws. Both strain and cultural deviance theories locate the causes of crime in the disadvantageous position of those at the lowest levels in a class-based society (Figure 3.1).

Scholars who view crime as resulting from cultural values that permit, or even demand, behavior in violation of the law are called cultural deviance theorists. The three major cultural deviance theories are social disorganization, differential association, and culture conflict.

Social disorganization theory focuses on the development of high-crime areas associated with the disintegration of conventional values caused by rapid industrialization, increased immigration, and urbanization. Two researchers, Clifford Shaw and Henry McKay, demonstrated that the highest rates of delinquency persisted in the same areas of Chicago over an extended period from 1900 to 1933, even though the ethnic composition changed (Germans, Irish, and English at the turn of the century; Poles and Italians in the 1920s; increasing numbers of blacks in the 1930s). The evidence indicated to them that delin-

cultural deviance theories
Theories that criminal behavior results from cultural values that permit, or even demand, behavior in violation of the law.

"Damn man, don't you know what would happen to me if I just told my gang I want out? That I'm scared?"
Jimmy T, Chicago gang member, quoted in *Time*, August 17, 1992, p. 38.

social disorganization theory
Theory that criminal behavior is associated with the disintegration of conventional values in neighborhoods characterized by rapid industrialization, increased immigration, and urbanization.

THE PRICE OF POVERTY TODAY

	Billions
Low–income assistance, including food and housing, excluding medical care	**$ 120**
Cost of police and corrections*	**$ 50**
Additional gain to GNP if poor were fully employed	**$ 60**
TOTAL	**$ 230**

*Assumes most crime is linked to poverty

The Growing Disadvantage of the Poor

(a)

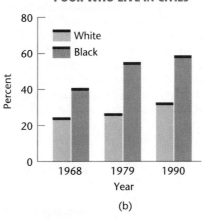

PERCENTAGE OF POOR WHO LIVE IN CITIES

(b)

FIGURE 3.1 *The social costs of poverty and crime: Being poor often means living in a decaying urban center in a single-parent family whose head does not have a job* (*Source: Business Week*, May 18, 1992, pp. 40–41.)

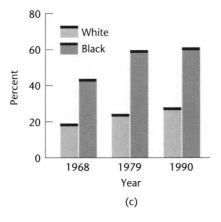

PERCENTAGE OF POOR WHO LIVE IN FAMILIES HEADED BY WOMEN

(c)

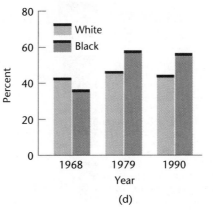

PERCENTAGE OF HEADS OF POOR FAMILIES WITHOUT JOBS

(d)

In building bridges from a delinquent subculture to a conventional one, kids need communication that reflects their way of thinking. This prize-winning newspaper ad, written by youngsters, was a collaborative effort by Bronner Slosberg Humphrey advertising executives and members of the Boys and Girls Clubs of Boston.

cultural transmission
Theory that views delinquency as a socially learned behavior transmitted from one generation to the next in disorganized urban areas.

quency was socially learned behavior, transmitted from one generation to the next in disorganized urban areas. This is called **cultural transmission.**[32]

Studies based on the social disorganization approach have covered a wide range of topics. Douglas Smith, for example, looked at police behavior and characteristics of sixty neighborhoods in three large U.S. cities (Rochester, New York; St. Louis, Missouri; Tampa/St. Petersburg, Florida). His findings suggest that police are less likely to file reports on crime incidents in high-crime (socially disorganized) areas than in low-crime areas, and that they are more likely to assist residents and initiate contacts with suspicious-looking people in low-crime neighborhoods.[33] The cost of disorder in disorganized neighborhoods has been mounting (Figure 3.2).

differential association theory
Theory based on the principle that an individual who learns more definitions favorable to violation of law than unfavorable becomes delinquent.

Differential association theory maintains that people learn to commit crime as a result of contact with antisocial values, attitudes, and criminal behavior patterns. Since Edwin Sutherland introduced the theory in 1939, scholars have tested and reexamined it. Differential association theory explains the processes by which criminal behavior is taught and learned. Sutherland argued that criminal behavior is learned through social interaction. People come into constant contact with "definitions favorable to violations of law" and "definitions unfavorable to violation of law." A definition favorable to crime might be a verbal or

FIGURE 3.2 *The escalating cost of social disorder: The most costly disturbances in modern U.S. history** (Source: *Business Week*, May 18, 1992, p. 43.)

*Estimates in adjusted 1992 dollars.

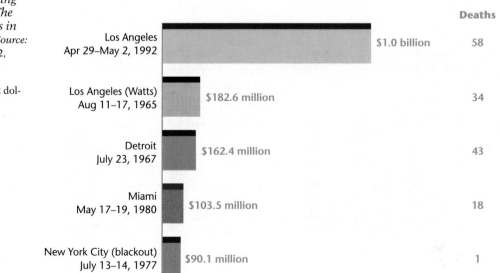

THE ESCALATING COST OF DISORDER

		Deaths
Los Angeles Apr 29–May 2, 1992	$1.0 billion	58
Los Angeles (Watts) Aug 11–17, 1965	$182.6 million	34
Detroit July 23, 1967	$162.4 million	43
Miami May 17–19, 1980	$103.5 million	18
New York City (blackout) July 13–14, 1977	$90.1 million	1

nonverbal message from a parent that some form of antisocial behavior (like cheating on an exam) is acceptable. A definition unfavorable to crime might be taking away a child's allowance for the same behavior.

The ratio of criminal to noncriminal definitions determines whether a person will engage in criminal behavior.[34] The extent to which one's associations/definitions will result in criminality is related to frequency of contact, duration of contact, and meaning to the individual. Despite the many criticisms of differential association—can frequency, duration, and meaning be measured over a lifetime?—the theory has had a profound influence on the search for the causes of criminality.[35]

Culture conflict theory states that different groups learn different conduct norms (standards of right and wrong), and that the conduct norms of some groups may clash with those of others.[36] According to sociologist Thorsten Sellin, individuals may commit crimes by conforming to the norms of their own group if that group's norms conflict with those of the dominant society. According to this argument, the main difference between a criminal and a noncriminal is that each is responding to different sets of **conduct norms.** In the next section, which deals with the formation and operation of subcultures, we will examine the conflict of norms in detail.

culture conflict theory
Theory that two groups may clash when their conduct norms differ.

conduct norms
Norms that regulate the daily lives of people and reflect the attitudes of the groups to which they belong.

Subculture Theories.   A **subculture** is a subdivision within the dominant culture that has its own norms, beliefs, and values. Subcultures typically emerge when people in similar circumstances find themselves isolated from the mainstream and band together for mutual support. Subculture theories in criminology were developed to account for delinquency among lower-class males, especially for one of its most important expressions—the teenage gang. These explanations are based on a combination of strain and cultural deviance theories.

subculture
Subdivision within the dominant culture that has its own norms, beliefs, and values.

According to Albert Cohen, delinquent subcultures emerge in economically deprived areas of larger American cities.[37] He argues that working-class males, frustrated by their inability to compete successfully with middle-class youngsters, set up their own norms by which they define "success" in ways that to them seem attainable. They turn the middle-class standards upside down, making behavior *right* in their subculture because it is *wrong* by the standards of the middle class (for example, pleasure-seeking activities that are malicious and destructive).

"Some kids play sports for identity. Some kids read books to be somebody and some kids steal cars."
Sgt. Henry Alston, Newark, N.J., police auto-theft squad, quoted in *The New York Times*, August 10, 1992, p. A1.

According to Richard Cloward and Lloyd Ohlin's **differential opportunity theory,** the types of delinquent subcultures and of the juvenile gangs that flourish within them depend on the types of neighborhoods in which they develop.[38] Just as means—opportunities—are unequal in the conventional world, so opportunities to reach one's goals in the criminal world are also unequal. A youngster cannot simply decide to join a theft-oriented gang, or even a violence-oriented one. The types of delinquent behavior individuals engage in depend on the illegitimate opportunities available to them—criminal (theft-oriented), conflict (violence-oriented), or retreatist ("dropout") gangs. Since Cloward and Ohlin's description of gangs in the 1950s, "opportunities" to engage in criminal behavior have changed dramatically (see the Criminal Justice in Action box).

differential opportunity theory
Theory that analyzes both legitimate and illegitimate opportunity structures available to individuals and posits that illegitimate opportunities, like legitimate ones, are unequally distributed.

"Opportunity makes the thief.
Italian proverb.

Time and place make the thief."
Dutch proverb.

Marvin Wolfgang and Franco Ferracuti argued that in some subcultures the norms of behavior are dictated by a value system that demands the use of force or violence.[39] Subcultures that adhere to norms conducive to violence are referred to as **subcultures of violence.** Fists rather than words settle disputes. Knives and guns are readily available. When Wolfgang and Ferracuti described population groups that are likely to react violently, they posed a powerful question. How does one go about changing a subcultural norm? This question becomes increasingly important with the merging of the drug subculture and the subculture of violence. Cities across the country have been divided into distinct turfs. Rival drug dealers settle territorial disputes with semiautomatic guns, power struggles

subculture of violence
Subculture with values that demand the overt use of violence in certain social situations.

NATIONS WITH LOW CRIME RATES

Most criminologists devote their efforts to learning why people commit crime and why there is so much crime. A few have looked at the question from the opposite perspective: In places with little crime, what accounts for the low crime rate? Using the United Nations' first World Crime Survey (1970–1975), Freda Adler selected ten countries to study (1): the two countries with the lowest crime rates from each of five general cultural regions of the world (no statistics were available for the sixth region, Africa south of the Sahara). Within each of the five regions, experts from countries other than the ten selected agreed that the countries selected had the reputation of having the lowest crime rates. Here are the countries:

Western Europe: Switzerland and the Republic of Ireland
Eastern Europe: The (former) German Democratic Republic (East Germany) and Bulgaria
Arab countries: Saudi Arabia and Algeria
Asia: Japan and Nepal
Latin America: Costa Rica and Peru (2)

The common factor

This is an odd assortment of countries. They seem to have little in common. Some are democratic, others authoritarian. Some are republics, others are monarchies. Some are ruled by dictators, others by communal councils. Some are rural, others highly urbanized. Some are remote and isolated, others are in the political mainstream. Some are highly religious, some largely atheistic. Some have a very high standard of living, others a very low one. What explains their common characteristic of low crime rates?

The researchers initially compared data from nearly fifty worldwide statistical computer data banks covering a wide variety of information that included gross national product, per capita income, infant mortality, longevity, electricity consumption, available health care, and number of cars, radios, TVs, and telephones. No correlation with low crime rates could be found.

The research then focused on a qualitative analysis of the countries in question, using characteristics of each that are difficult to assess numerically. Investigations in the ten countries slowly revealed one characteristic common to all: Each appeared to have an intact social control system, quite apart from whatever formal control system (law enforcement) it had. No two of these ten countries had exactly the same type of social control system, but they all had one and sometimes more than one.

Western Europe: Switzerland fosters a strong sense of belonging to and participating in the local community (3). The family is still strong in the Republic of Ireland, and it is strengthened by shared religious values.
Eastern Europe: The German Democratic Republic involved all youth in communal activities, organized by groups and aimed at having young people excel for the glory of self and country. In Bulgaria, industrialization focused on regional industry centers so that the workers would not be dislodged from their home towns, which served as continuing social centers.
The Arab countries: Islam continued to be strong as a way of life and exercised a powerful influence on daily activities, especially in Saudi Arabia. Algeria had in addition a powerful commitment to socialism in its post-independence era, involving the citizens in all kinds of commonly shared development activities.
Asia: Nepal retained its strong family and clan ties, augmented by councils of elders that oversee the community and resolve problems. Highly industrialized Japan has lost some of the social controls of family and kinship, but has found a substitute family in the industrial community to which most Japanese belong: Mitsubishi might now be the family that guides your every step.
Latin America: Costa Rica spent all the funds that other governments devote to the military on social services and social development, caring for and strengthening its families. Peru went through a process of urbanization in stages: Village and family cohesion, which marks the lives of people in the countryside, followed the migrants on their way from the Andean villages to smaller towns, and then to the big city, where they would be received by and live surrounded by others from their own home towns.

The effects of change

What happens over time as conditions in low crime countries change, especially conditions imposed from outside and over which the citizens have no control? Will crime rates change? Let us see what this study shows.

Four countries have experienced no significant changes, either from the outside or from within: Switzerland, Ireland, Japan, and Costa Rica. These countries all retained their astonishingly low crime rates. Ireland remains largely unaffected by the strife in Ulster. Switzerland, like all European countries, has felt the impact of narcotic drugs, but has retained a low crime ranking. Costa Rica, despite all the turmoil in neighboring countries, has had no crime wave. Japan has experienced a number of political–white-collar-crime scandals and probably a rise in organized crime, but the street crime rate has remained low.

All the other countries have experienced major turmoil. What has happened to their crime rates? For three of them, although data are not available, it appears that only small increases in crime are occurring. Algeria's political stability is currently in question, and crimes of violence appear to be on the increase. Peru too is in a political crisis. Security has suffered in rural areas, and crime appears to be increasing in Lima, the capital. In Bulgaria, the communist dictator Todor Zhivkov was overthrown in 1989. Crime may have increased, but no major crime wave has been reported.

The other three countries have maintained stable crime rates despite major changes. Saudi Arabia was the heart of Desert Shield and Desert Storm, with over 600,000 foreign soldiers on its territory. The crime rate has not changed. Nepal has undergone a minirevolution against its royal house, with demands for greater democracy.

Crime rates appear unaffected. The most astounding evidence comes from the former East Germany. A major crime wave was expected when the Berlin Wall fell: Without the control exercised by the Communist Party, what was there to stop people from venting their anger, frustration, and despair at thwarted aspirations? The police, their commanders dismissed, were dispirited and hesitant to intervene. But although the fear of crime has increased significantly, no major crime wave has occurred. Some crime types, including hate crimes, increased significantly from a statistical perspective, but nowhere near the extent predicted. The citizens of the old East Germany, now the five new republics of the German Federal Republic, have remained basically law-abiding (4).

What can be concluded from these findings? Once a people have found their own system of social control, whether through family and kinship, the individual family, religion, the community, the factory, or whatever, it appears that crime rates will stay low, even under conditions of stress from within or from outside—at least for a while. Will long-term stress result in increases in crime? Only future research can tell.

SOURCES

1. United Nations, *Report of the Secretary General on Crime Prevention and Control,* A/32/199 (popularly known as the First U.N. World Crime Survey) (New York: United Nations, 1977).
2. Freda Adler, *Nations Not Obsessed with Crime* (Littleton, Colo.: Fred B. Rothman, 1983).
3. Marshall B. Clinard, *Cities with Little Crime: The Case of Switzerland* (Cambridge, Mass.: Cambridge University Press, 1978).
4. Hans Joachim Schneider, ''Crime, Criminological Research, and Criminal Policy in West and East Germany Before and After Their Unification,'' *International Journal of Offender Therapy and Comparative Criminology* 35 (1991):282–295.

QUESTIONS FOR DISCUSSION

1. People in the United States work in factories, live in family groups, go to church, join youth groups. Why do these not function effectively as forms of social control to keep the crime rate low?
2. The data studied here were based on crimes dealt with by the police. What other groups or individuals might deal with crimes in the countries studied? Who besides the police deals with crimes in the United States? How does that affect the crime rate?
3. How could government or community decision-makers use the information presented by this study to help solve crime problems in the United States?

Morning exercises, Japanese workers at a sake distillery

. . . .

focal concerns
*Set of six values passed down
from generation to generation in
lower-class urban slums: trouble,
toughness, smartness, excitement, fate, autonomy.*

*"Nothing stops the bullets like
a job."*
Father Gregory Boyle, quoted in
Newsweek, May 18, 1992, p. 35.

social control theory
*Explanation of criminal behavior
that focuses on control mechanisms, techniques, and strategies
for regulating behavior, and posits that criminality results when
social controls are weakened, so
that individuals are not motivated to conform to them.*

within a single drug enterprise lead to assaults and homicides, one dealer robs another, informers are killed, their associates retaliate, and bystanders, some of them children, get caught in the crossfire.[40]

Besides violence, researchers have found other subcultural values that are passed down from one generation to the next in lower-class urban slums. Walter Miller has identified six (which he refers to as **focal concerns**): trouble (staying out of trouble and getting into trouble are daily preoccupations), toughness (demonstrating masculinity), smartness (meaning outsmarting or conning people), excitement (a search for thrills), fate (life changes with luck), and autonomy ("no one can push me around").[41]

Control Theories.   Strain and cultural deviance theories explain why some people break the law. Social control theories, on the other hand, explain why people do not break the law. Control theorists take for granted that drugs can tempt people; that petty fighting, petty theft, and recreational drinking may be attractive features of adolescence and young adulthood. They ask why people conform in the face of so much temptation and peer pressure. The answer is that juveniles and adults conform to the law in response to certain controlling forces in their lives. They become criminals when the controlling forces are defective or absent.

Social control theory focuses on techniques that regulate behavior and lead to conformity, or obedience to society's rules—the influences of family and school, religious beliefs, moral values, friends, and even beliefs about government (see the Criminal Justice Abroad box). Criminologist Travis Hirschi argues that four social bonds promote conformity: attachment, commitment, involvement, and belief. The stronger these bonds, the less likelihood of delinquency.[42] The first bond, attachment, takes three forms: attachment to parents, to teachers, and to peers. Hirschi's second group of bonds consists of commitment to conventional lines of action that involve high vocational or educational aspirations. The third bond is involvement, or preoccupation with conventional activities (such as homework), rather than with deviant activities. The last of the bonds—belief—consists of respect for the laws and for the people who enforce them.

Social control theory has held a position of prominence among sociological theories of criminal behavior: It has inspired a vast number of studies.[43] It has also emphasized the importance of devising ways to enhance individuals' bonds to society in order to prevent crime.

Sociological Theory: Practical Applications

Sociological theories seek to explain criminal behavior in terms of the social environment—lack of opportunity to attain goals and the learning of criminal values in socially disorganized neighborhoods. They also explain how social bonds promote commitment to conventional behavior in the face of frustration, poor living conditions, and other crime-oriented forces. These theories have been the underpinning for many different types of action programs. In the 1960s, Head Start became part of a major federal antipoverty campaign.[44] The goal of Head Start is to make children of low-income families better equipped to take on later responsibilities. What started as a summer experience for half a million preschool children has expanded into a year-round program that provides educational and social services to millions of young people and their families. Research findings show that the program is modestly successful.

*"The chief problem in any com-
munity cursed with crime is not
the punishment of the criminals,
but the preventing of the young
from being trained to crime."*
W. E. B. DuBois, *The Shields of
Black Folks,* 1903, p. 9.

Opportunity theory was translated into action programs during the 1960s. Both John F. Kennedy and Lyndon Johnson directed that huge sums of money be spent on programs to help move lower-class youths into the social mainstream. The best known, Mobilization for Youth (MFY), provided employment, social services, teacher training, legal aid, and other crime-prevention services to an area on New York's Lower East Side. The cost was over $12 million. MFY ultimately became highly controversial. Many people accused it of being too radical, especially when neighborhood participants became involved in rent strikes, lawsuits charging discrimination, and public demonstrations. The project was eventually abandoned. The political climate had changed, and federal money was no longer available for sweeping social programs. But MFY's failure does not detract from the opportunity theory on which it was based.

If, according to differential association theory, a person can become criminal by learning definitions favorable to violating laws, it follows that programs that expose young people to definitions favorable to conventional behavior should reduce criminality. This theory underlies many treatment programs for young offenders in facilities throughout the country. These programs set up an extended family environment for high-risk youngsters, one that provides positive role models, academic and vocational training, strict rules for behavior, drug treatment, health care, and other services. One such program is the House of Umoja (a Swahili word meaning "unity") in Philadelphia. At any given time, about twenty-five teenage offenders live together as "sons" of the founder, Sister Fattah. Each resident signs a contract with Umoja obligating himself to help in the household, become an active part of the family group, study, and work either in one of the program's businesses (a restaurant, a moving company, a painting shop) or elsewhere.

By many measures, this program is successful. The mayor of the city once threatened, "All gang members have ten days to turn their guns in to the nearest firehouse, after which time we [the police] will kick your door in and take them."[45] Umoja responded by calling a meeting of representatives of all gangs. More than 5,000 youths from seventy-five gangs showed up. The result was a sixty-day truce, during which no one died in gang wars. Programs similar to Umoja exist throughout the country; they include Argus in New York's South Bronx; violent juvenile offender research and development programs in Chicago, Dallas, New Orleans, Los Angeles, and San Diego; and neighborhood anticrime self-help programs in Baltimore, Newark, Cleveland, Boston, Miami, and Washington, D.C. All of these programs have the same mission: to provide a bridge from a delinquent subcultural value system to a conventional one.[46]

The action programs we have been discussing seek to lessen the amount of crime in society by changing the people who commit crime. Recently, some researchers have suggested that to prevent crime we must focus not only on the people who commit crime, but also on the situational factors that influence the commission of crimes (e.g., dark streets, unlocked doors). The approach is particularly important for the development of crime-control policy and of "situational" crime prevention, which consists of changing the conditions and circumstances under which crimes are committed (see the Criminal Justice on Trial box).

ALTERNATIVE EXPLANATIONS FOR CRIME

The 1960s witnessed a movement among students and professors to join advocacy groups and become activists in the social causes that rapidly were gaining popularity across the nation, such as equal rights for minorities, liberation for women, and peace. The generation of the 1960s had become disenchanted with an establishment that seemed to give only lip service to social change. The protests took many forms—demonstrations and rallies, sit-ins, beards and long hair, rock music and marijuana, dropping out of school, burning draft cards.

"The administration here and now declares unconditional war on poverty in America."
Lyndon B. Johnson, 1964.

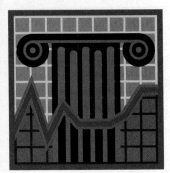

REARRANGING LIVES: THEORIES OF CRIME AND CRIME PREVENTION

A group of scholars has recently begun to focus more on preventing crime than on studying criminals. They study why specific types of crime are increasing, why offenders would choose to commit one offense rather than another at a given time and place, and why criminals sometimes are deterred from committing crimes. These researchers stress the difference between theories of crime and theories of criminality. Theories of criminality, such as strain, cultural deviance, and social control, explain why some people are more likely than others to commit crime. Theories of crime identify conditions under which those persons who are prone to commit crime will in fact do so.

Rational choice, routine activities

Some experts take the position that if crimes are to be prevented and crime control policies developed, the study of criminal behavior must be tied to the decision-making processes of offenders and to the criminal acts themselves. The *rational choice* perspective, developed by Derek Cornish and Ronald Clarke, takes into account the criminal's motivation and the situational factors surrounding the crime (1). In other words, after weighing the benefits against the costs (expertise needed, physical danger, and risk of apprehension, for example), an individual decides whether a crime is worth committing then and there.

Another new theory of crime, *routine activities,* is closely linked to the rational choice perspective. According to Lawrence Cohen and Marcus Felson, there will always be a large group of motivated offenders (2). Crime rates, however, depend on other major factors as well—that targets are suitable (easily transported goods), and that they are unguarded. Over the last few decades the number of suitable targets, such as videocassette recorders and compact disk players, has steadily increased. At the same time, changes in the routine activities of everyday life (greater numbers of women working outside the home, for example) have left those targets unguarded for a good part of the day. People used to do their banking in the relative safety of a bank. Now automated teller machines expose people and their money at all times of day and night—providing attractive, vulnerable, and unguarded targets for criminals (3).

Both the rational choice and the routine activity perspectives demonstrate that the commission of crime is not related solely to the biological and psychological characteristics of individuals or to social and economic factors. Effective crime prevention programs must take into account the other factors that influence the commission of crimes. According to the routine activities idea, crime prevention requires guarding something that is unguarded, hiding something that is exposed, or making an attractive target less attractive.

Rearranging lives

The practical value of this theoretical approach is implicit in people's reactions to crime. Over the last two decades people have been rearranging their lives because of crime—or sometimes just the fear of crime. The new theories of crime can be used to determine the effectiveness of those "rearrangements." Here are some:

- Airports, schools, movie houses, nightclubs, convention centers, libraries, and even department stores have installed electronic detection gates for improved security.
- Security fences patrolled by guards have spread from businesses in high crime areas to wealthy private residential neighborhoods to low-income housing projects.
- Tough "vandal-proof" pay phones are vandalized 175,000 times a year in New York City, and phone companies all over the world are converting to call-on-a-card, coinless telephones.
- Hackers and thieves that charge their calls to others' phones cost cellular telephone companies an estimated $1 million a day, forcing the development of new digital technology to guard against criminal abuse.
- Cash machines have brought with them a rash of robbers forcing customers to make withdrawals or to hand over the cash just withdrawn. The New York City Council passed a measure requiring tough new security measures for the protection of cash machines and their customers.

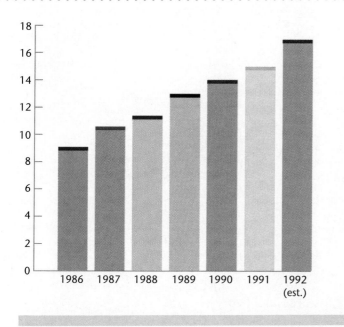

FIGURE 1. Residential Security Systems in Use in the United States, 1986–1992 (in millions)
(*Source: The New York Times,* February 9, 1992, pp. E1,4.)

SOURCES

1. Derek B. Cornish and Ronald V. Clarke, eds., *The Reasoning Criminal* (New York: Springer-Verlag, 1986).
2. Lawrence E. Cohen and Marcus Felson, "Social Changes and Crime Rate Trends: A Routine Activity Approach," *American Sociological Review* 44 (1979):588–608.
3. Michael Gottfredson and Travis Hirschi, "A Propensity-Event Theory of Crime," in *Advances in Criminological Theory,* eds. William S. Laufer and Freda Adler (New Brunswick, N.J.: Transaction, 1989), pp. 57–67.
4. Ronald V. Clarke, ed., *Situational Crime Prevention: Successful Case Studies* (New York: Harrow and Henton, 1992).

QUESTIONS FOR DISCUSSION

1. Have you been a crime victim? What could you have done to avoid victimization? Have you changed your behavior since that event? How has that change inconvenienced you?
2. Assess your current lifestyle. What risks of criminal victimization does it entail? What might you do to minimize those risks?
3. Crime prevention programs that assist homeowners in marking their possessions so that they will be difficult for thieves to sell are making attractive targets less attractive. Can you think of other ways to do this?

- Over 16 million electronic security systems protect American homes, and individual actions aimed at evading criminals also are on the increase (see Figure 1). People don't visit certain neighborhoods, they don't go out at night, they don't park their cars at certain locations, they don't wear jewelry in public, they don't jog where they used to, they go to self-defense training classes, they buy and carry handguns.

Effective crime prevention

Are all these crime evasion techniques worth the cost involved? As the body of research by crime theorists grows, we are learning more and more about appropriate and cost-beneficial crime prevention strategies. When is it necessary to intervene in order to minimize which criminal danger? What targets of criminals need what type of protection (target hardening)? When is the right time, if ever, to build a fence, buy a gun, install an alarm system, change an industrial product, hire more police or private security, install a new lighting system?

Sometimes a change made by only a few people protects many, as researchers found in a study of obscene phone calls in New Jersey. Requests to trace annoyance calls decreased by 25 percent in areas where Caller-ID—a service that provides the phone number of incoming calls—was available, even though only a small number of people had actually subscribed to the service. Apparently just the possibility that they would be identified easily was enough to deter some would-be obscene call makers. As crime theorists develop more ideas and publish more case studies about the factors that contribute to the commission of a crime, they help build a solid foundation for effective crime prevention strategies (4).

Ohio National Guard troops attacking student demonstrators on the Kent State campus in 1970. The killing of students shocked the nation.

Arrests of middle-class youth increased rapidly. Crime was no longer confined to the inner city. People began to ask whether arrests were being made for behavior that was not really criminal. Were the real criminals the legislators and policymakers who pursued war in Vietnam while creating the crime of draft-card burning at home? Were the real criminals the National Guardsmen who in 1970 shot and killed campus demonstrators at Kent State University? Labeling, conflict, and radical theorists provided some answers.

Labeling and conflict theorists turned away from the traditional theories that explained crime by reference to characteristics of the offender or the social environment. They set out to demonstrate that people become criminals because of what others with power, especially those in the criminal justice system, do. Unless an act is made criminal by law, no person who performs that act is a criminal. Alternative explanations of crime begin with this point. Then they ask: Who makes these laws? And why? Are all people who break these laws criminals? What part does the criminal justice system play in creating criminals?

Labeling Theory

Labeling theorists explore how and why certain acts are defined as criminal, or more broadly as deviant behavior, and others are not, and how and why certain people are defined as criminal or deviant. These theorists view criminals not as evil persons engaged in evil acts, but rather as individuals who have had a label attached to them by both the criminal justice system and the community. Viewed from this perspective, the criminal acts themselves are not particularly significant; the social reaction to them, however, is.

Labeling theory argues that society creates criminals through its criminal justice system by passing judgment on some persons as criminals, thereby permanently stigmatizing them. Once it becomes known that a person has engaged in criminal or deviant acts, he or she is segregated from conventional society and is labeled a "thief," "whore," "junkie," and so forth. This process of segregation creates "outsiders" (a term used by Howard Becker), or outcasts from society, who begin to associate with others who have also been cast out.[47] As more people begin to think of these people as criminals, or deviants, and to respond to them accordingly, the labeled individuals react by continuing to engage in the behavior that society now expects of them. Gradually they begin to think of themselves as criminals or deviants.

An important question in labeling theory is: Who makes the rules that define deviant behavior, including crime? Labeling theorists answer that people in high social positions have the power to make and enforce the rules by which all members of a society must live. Certain privileged members of society therefore create the outsiders. The whole process becomes a political one, with some people making the rules that others break.

Critics of labeling theory remind us that, by and large, offenders get into the hands of the criminal justice system because they have broken the law.[48] They question the overly active role labeling theory has assigned to the community and to criminal justice agencies, and the overly passive role it has assigned to offenders. Some suggest that punishment works as a deterrent—and therefore we need formal processing of offenders. Others argue that high rates of recidivism indicate that punishment has little to do with criminality. Moreover, those who are repeatedly arrested, convicted, and incarcerated do tend to live as outsiders in conventional communities. Labeling theorists have made a persuasive argument for more investigations in this area.[49]

> **labeling theory**
> *Explanation of deviance in terms of the way a person acquires a negative identity, such as "addict" or "ex-con," and is forced to suffer the consequences of outcast status.*

> *"The greater the number of laws and enactments, the more thieves and robbers there will be."*
> Lao-tzu (ca. 605–531 B.C.).

Conflict Theory

Like labeling theory, **conflict theory** has its roots in the questioning of values. But while labeling theorists focus on the labeling of the criminal by the system, conflict theorists question the existence of the system itself. Conflict theorists ask: If people agree on the value system, why are there so many crimes, so much threat of punishment, and so many people in prison? The answer: Laws do not exist for the good of all members of society; they represent the interests of specific groups that have the power to get them enacted.[50] Conflict theory holds that the people who have the power work to keep the powerless at a disadvantage. Powerful groups maintain their interests by making illegal any behavior that might be a threat to them. Laws thus become a means of control.

Radical theory, a form of conflict theory, also argues that laws are created by the powerful to protect their own interests.[51] For radical theorists, however, there is only one dominant group, the capitalist ruling class. Radical theory demands the overthrow of capitalism, which is said to perpetuate criminality by keeping workers under the domination of capitalist oppressors. Only true socialism can reduce the crime rate. Opposition to radical theory is primarily concerned with the oversimplifications caused by an exclusive focus on capitalism. Critics also say that radical theory is more political than scientific.[52]

> **conflict theory**
> *Model of crime in which the criminal justice system is seen as being used by the ruling class to control the lower class.*

> **radical theory**
> *Theory that crime is the result of a struggle for power and resources between owners of capital and workers.*

Labeling and Conflict Theory: Practical Application

Labeling and conflict theorists have been instrumental in calling attention to some important questions, particularly about the way defendants are processed through the criminal justice system. Labeling theorists have carried out important scientific investigations of that system. To demonstrate the detrimental consequences of labels, one study found that employers were reluctant to hire anyone with a court record, even though the person was found not guilty.[53]

Radical theorists have encouraged their more traditional colleagues to look with a critical eye at all aspects of the criminal justice system, including the response of the system to both poor and rich offenders.[54] They challenge the system to not ignore population groups that have no share in the making of laws.[55] Such groups include the growing number of homeless people and the increasing numbers of the population that are not working, either because they have lost their jobs or because they have not been equipped with education and working skills.

REVIEW

Explanations of criminal behavior focus on biological, psychological, social, and economic factors. Biological and psychological theories assume that criminal behavior results from underlying physical or mental conditions that distinguish criminals from noncriminals. These theories yield insight into individual cases, but they do not explain why crime rates vary from place to place and from one situation to another. Sociological theories seek to explain criminal behavior in terms of the social environment. Strain and cultural deviance theories focus on the social forces that cause people to engage in criminal behavior. Both theories assume that social class and criminal behavior are related. Strain theorists argue that people commit crime because they are frustrated by not being able to achieve society's goals through legitimate means. Cultural deviance theorists claim that crime is learned in socially disorganized neighborhoods where criminal norms are transmitted from one generation to the next.

In the decade between the mid-1950s and mid-1960s, criminologists began to theorize about the development and content of youth subcultures and the gangs that flourish within them. They suggested that lower-class males, frustrated by their inability to meet middle-class standards, set up their own norms by which they can find status. Often these norms are different from those of the middle class. Social control theorists explain how people remain committed to conventional behavior in the face of frustration, poor living conditions, and other criminogenic factors.

Three quite different theoretical perspectives focus on society's role in creating criminals and defining them as such. Labeling theory, conflict theory, and radical theory offer alternative explanations of crime, in the sense that they do not study individual criminal characteristics or social norms, which all the other theories associate with crime. These three theories examine the impact of the processes of lawmaking and law enforcement on the creation of offenders.

Notes

1. Jay Robert Nash, *Encyclopedia of World Crime*, Vol. vi (Wilmette, Ill.: Crimebooks, 1990).

2. See Jack Altman and Marvin Ziporyn, *Born to Raise Hell: The Untold Story of Richard Speck* (New York: Grove, 1967).

3. Thorsten Sellin, *Slavery and the Penal System* (New York: Elsevier, 1976).

4. Cesare Lombroso, *Crime, Its Causes and Remedies* (Boston: Little, Brown, 1918). See also Marvin Wolfgang, "Cesare Lombroso," in *Pioneers in Criminology*, ed. Hermann Mannheim (Chicago: Quadrangle Books, 1960). On the development of criminological thought in general, see Randy Martin, Robert J. Mutchnik and W. Timothy Austin, *Criminological Thought* (New York: Macmillan Publishing Co., 1990).

5. E. A. Hooten, *The American Criminal* (Cambridge, Mass.: Harvard University Press, 1939), p. 308.

6. William H. Sheldon, *Varieties of Delinquent Youth: An Introduction to Constitutional Psychiatry* (New York: Harper, 1949).

7. Richard J. Dugdale, *The Jukes: A Study in Crime, Pauperism, Disease, and Heredity*, 4th ed. (New York, London: Putnam, 1910).

8. Karl O. Christiansen, "A Preliminary Study of Criminality among Twins," in *Biosocial Bases of Criminal Behavior*, eds. Sarnoff A. Mednick and Karl O. Christiansen (New York: Gardner Press, 1977). For a critique of genetic studies, see G. D. Walters and T. W. White, "Heredity and Crime: Bad Genes or Bad Research?," *Criminology* 27 (1989):455–485. For an overview of the biological approach, see Diana H. Fishbein, "Biological Perspectives in Criminology," *Criminology* 28 (1990):27–72.

9. A. A. Sandberg, G. F. Koepf, and T. Ishihara, "An XYY Human Male," *Lancet* (August 1961):488–489.

10. Travis Hirschi and Michael J. Hindelang, "Intelligence and Delinquency: A Revisionist Review," *American Sociological Review* 42 (1977):571–587.

11. Stephen Schoenthaler, "Diet and Crime: An Empirical Examination of the Value of Nutrition in the Control and Treatment of Incarcerated Juvenile Offenders," *International Journal of Biosocial Research* 4 (1983):25–39.

12. Doris J. Rapp, *Allergies and the Hyperactive Child* (New York: Simon & Schuster, 1981); Diana H. Fishbein and Susan Pease, "The Effects of Diet on Behavior: Implications for Criminology and Corrections," in *Research on Corrections* 1 (1988):1–47.

13. See, for example, Sarnoff A. Mednick, Jan Volavka, William F. Gabrielli, and Turan M. Itil, "EEG as a Predictor of Antisocial Behavior," *Criminology* 19 (1981):219–229.

14. *Regina v. Charlson*, 1 All. E. R. 859 (1955).

15. Sigmund Freud, *A General Introduction to Psychoanalysis* (New York: Boni and Liveright, 1922).

16. Lawrence Kohlberg, "Stage and Sequence: The Cognitive-Development Approach to Socialization," in *Handbook of Socialization Theory and Research*, ed. David A. Goslin (Chicago: Rand McNally, 1969).

17. William S. Jennings, Robert Kilkenny, and Lawrence Kohlberg, "Moral Development Theory and Practice for Youthful Offenders," in *Personality Theory, Moral Development, and Criminal*

Behavior, eds. William S. Laufer and James M. Day (Lexington, Mass.: Lexington Books, 1983); see also Daniel D. Macphail, "The Moral Education Approach in Treating Adult Inmates," *Criminal Justice and Behavior* 16 (1989):81–97; Jack Arbuthnot and Donald A. Gordon, "Crime and Cognition: Community Applications of Sociomoral Reasoning Development," *Criminal Justice and Behavior* 15 (1988):379–393.

18. John Bowlby, *The Making and Breaking of Affectional Bonds* (London: Tavistock, 1979). For longitudinal research on the relationship between family atmosphere and delinquency, see Joan McCord, "Some Child-Rearing Antecedents of Criminal Behavior," *Journal of Personality and Social Psychology* 37 (1979):1477–1486.

19. Albert Bandura, *Aggression: A Social Learning Analysis* (Englewood Cliffs, N.J.: Prentice-Hall, 1973).

20. C. Ray Jeffery, "Criminal Behavior and Learning Theory," *Journal of Criminal Law, Criminology and Police Science* 56 (1965):294–300; Ernest L. Burgess and Ronald L. Akers, "A Differential Association-Reinforcement Theory of Criminal Behavior," *Social Problems* 14 (1966):128–147.

21. Samuel Yochelson and Stanton Samenow, *The Criminal Personality* (New York: Jason Aronson, 1976).

22. William S. Laufer, Dagna K. Skoog, and James M. Day, "Personality and Criminality: A Review of the California Psychological Inventory," *Journal of Clinical Psychology* 38 (1982):562–573; Anne Campbell and John J. Gibbs, eds., *Violent Transactions: The Limits of Personality* (Oxford: Blackwell, 1986); Hans J. Eysenck, "Personality and Criminality: A Dispositional Analysis," in *Advances in Criminological Theory*, eds. William S. Laufer and Freda Adler (New Brunswick, N.J.: Transaction, 1989), vol. 1; William S. Laufer and James M. Day, eds., *Personality Theory, Moral Development, and Criminal Behavior* (Lexington, Mass.: Lexington Books, 1983).

23. Hervey Cleckley, *The Mask of Sanity* (St. Louis: C. V. Mosby, 1976), pp. 56–57.

24. Barry Bearak, "Bundy Is Electrocuted as Crowd of 500 Cheers," *Los Angeles Times*, January 25, 1989, p. 1.

25. Ira Sommers and Deborah R. Baskin, "The Prescription of Psychiatric Medications in Prison: Psychiatric versus Labeling Perspectives," *Justice Quarterly* 7 (1990):739–755.

26. Emile Durkheim, *Suicide* (Glencoe, Ill.: Free Press, 1951).

27. Robert K. Merton, "Social Structure and Anomie," *American Sociological Review* 3 (1938):672–682. Also see Robert Agnew, "Foundation for a General Strain Theory of Crime and Delinquency," *Criminology* 30 (1992):47–87; Robert Agnew and Helene Raskin White, "An Empirical Test of General Strain Theory," *Criminology* 30 (1992):475–499. For a discussion of the relationship between economic opportunities and the urban poor, see Pamela Irving Jackson, "Crime, Youth Gangs, and Urban Transition: The Social Dislocations of Postindustrial Economic Development," *Justice Quarterly* 8 (1991):379–397.

28. *Statistical Abstract of the United States 1991*, U.S. Department of Commerce, Bureau of the Census (1991), p. 449; Mike Neustrom, Jay Jamieson, David Manuel, and Bob Gramling, "Regional Unemployment and Crime Trends: An Empirical Examination," *Journal of Criminal Justice* 16 (1988):395–402.

29. Ibid., p. 465.

30. Belinda R. McCarthy, "Social Structure, Crime, and Social Control: An Examination of Factors Influencing Rates and Probabilities of Arrest," *Journal of Criminal Justice* 19 (1991):19–29.

31. See, for example, Delbert S. Elliott and Suzanne S. Ageton, "Reconciling Race and Class Differences in Self-reported and Official Estimates of Delinquency," *American Sociological Review* 45 (1980):95–110; Donald Clelland and Timothy J. Carter, "The New Myth of Class and Crime," *Criminology* 18 (1980):319–336.

32. Clifford R. Shaw and Henry D. McKay, *Juvenile Delinquency and Urban Areas* (Chicago: University of Chicago Press, 1969).

33. Douglas A. Smith, "The Neighborhood Context of Police Behavior," in *Communities and Crime*, eds. Albert J. Reiss and Michael Tonry (Chicago: University of Chicago Press, 1986), pp. 313–

341; Douglas A. Smith and C. Roger Jarjoura, "Social Structure and Criminal Victimization," *Journal of Research in Crime and Delinquency* 25 (1988):27–52. See also Ralph B. Taylor and Jeanette Covington, "Neighborhood Changes in Ecology and Violence," *Criminology* 26 (1988):553–589; Ralph B. Taylor, "Urban Communities and Crime," in *Urban Life in Transition*, eds. M. Gottdiener and C. G. Pickvance (Newbury Park, Calif.: Sage, 1991); E. Britt Patterson, "Poverty, Income Inequality, and Community Crime Rates," *Criminology* 29 (1991):755–776; Robert J. Sampson and W. Byron Groves, "Community Structure and Crime: Testing Social Disorganization Theory," *American Journal of Sociology* 94 (1989):774–802; James M. Byrne, "Cities, Citizens, and Crime: The Ecological/Nonecological Debate Reconsidered," in *The Social Ecology of Crime*, eds. James M. Byrne and Robert J. Sampson (New York: Springer-Verlag, 1986), pp. 77–101. See also Robert J. Bursik, Jr., "Social Disorganization and Theories of Crime and Delinquency: Problems and Prospects," *Criminology* 26 (1988):519–551. For social disorganization applied to illicit drug use, see Finn-Aage Esbensen and David Huizinga, "Community Structure and Drug Use: From a Social Disorganization Perspective," *Justice Quarterly* 7 (1990):691–709.

34. Edwin H. Sutherland, *Principles of Criminology*, 3d ed. (Philadelphia: Lippincott, 1939).

35. See, for example, Mark Warr and Mark Stafford, "The Influence of Delinquent Peers: What They Think or What They Do?," *Criminology* 29 (1991):851–866; Charles R. Tittle, Mary Jean Burke, and Elton F. Jackson, "Modeling Sutherland's Theory of Differential Association: Toward an Empirical Clarification," *Social Forces* 65 (1986):405–432; R. Matsueda and K. Heimer, "Race, Family Structure, and Delinquency: A Test of Differential Association and Social Control Theories," *American Sociological Review* 52 (1987):826–840. See also James D. Orcutt, "Differential Association and Marijuana Use: A Closer Look at Sutherland (with a Little Help from Becker)," *Criminology* 25 (1987):341–358; Clayton A. Hartjen, *Crime and Criminalization* (New York: Praeger, 1974), p. 51; Gary F. Jensen, "Parents, Peers, and Delinquent Action: A Test of the Differential Association Perspective," *American Journal of Sociology* 78 (1972):562–575.

36. Thorsten Sellin, *Culture Conflict and Crime*, Bulletin 41 (New York: Social Science Research Council, 1938).

37. Albert K. Cohen, *Delinquent Boys: The Culture of the Gang* (Glencoe, Ill.: Free Press, 1955). For a comprehensive examination of Chinese gangs, see Ko-lin Chin, *Chinese Subculture and Criminality* (New York: Greenwood Press, 1990).

38. Richard A. Cloward and Lloyd E. Ohlin, *Delinquency and Opportunity* (Glencoe, Ill.: Free Press, 1960).

39. Marvin E. Wolfgang and Franco Ferracuti, *The Subculture of Violence* (London: Tavistock, 1967). See also Lin Huff-Corzine, Jay Corzine, and David C. Moore, "Deadly Connections: Culture, Poverty, and the Direction of Lethal Violence," *Social Forces* 69 (1991):715–732; Steven F. Messner and Reid M. Golden, "Racial Inequality and Racially Disaggregated Homicide Rates: An Assessment of Alternative Theoretical Explanations," *Criminology* 30 (1992):421–445; Jo Dixon and Alan J. Lizotte, "Gun Ownership and the Southern Subculture of Violence," *American Journal of Sociology* 93 (1987):383–405; Colin Loftin and Robert Hill, "Regional Subculture of Violence: An Examination of the Gastil-Hackney Thesis," *American Sociological Review* 39 (1974):714–724; Judith Blau and Peter Blau, "Cost of Inequality: Metropolitan Structure and Violent Crime," *American Sociological Review* 47 (1982):114–129. For a study that examines the subculture of violence thesis as it relates to three ethnic groups—blacks, Hispanics, and American Indians—see Donald J. Shoemaker and J. Sherwood Williams, "The Subculture of Violence and Ethnicity," *Journal of Criminal Justice* 15 (1987):461–472. See also Neil Alan Weiner and Marvin E. Wolfgang, "The Extent and Character of Violent Crime in America, 1969–1982," in *American Violence and Public Policy*, ed. Lynn Curtis (New Haven, Conn.: Yale University Press, 1985), pp. 17–39; G. David

Curry and Irving A. Spergel, "Gang Homicide, Delinquency, and Community," *Criminology* 26 (1988):381–405.

40. Paul Goldstein, "Drugs and Violent Crime," in *Pathways to Criminal Violence*, eds. Neil Alan Weiner and Marvin E. Wolfgang (Newbury Park, Calif.: Sage, 1989), pp. 16–45.

41. Walter B. Miller, "Lower-Class Culture as a Generating Milieu of Gang Delinquency," *Journal of Social Issues* 14 (1958):5–19.

42. Travis Hirschi, *Causes of Delinquency* (Berkeley: University of California Press, 1969). See also Jackson Toby, "Social Disorganization and Stake in Conformity: Complementary Factors in the Predatory Behavior of Hoodlums," *Journal of Criminal Law, Criminology, and Police Science* 48 (1957):12–17.

43. Marvin D. Krohn and James L. Massey, "Social Control and Delinquent Behavior: An Examination of the Elements of the Social Bond," *Sociological Quarterly* 21 (1980):529–544. For a critique of this study, see Richard L. Amdur, "Testing Causal Models of Delinquency: A Methodological Critique," *Criminal Justice and Behavior* 16 (1989):35–62. See also Merry Morash and Meda Chesney-Lind, "A Reformulation and Partial Test of the Power Control Theory of Delinquency," *Justice Quarterly* 8 (1991):347–377; Michael D. Wiatrowski, David Griswold, and Mary K. Roberts, "Social Control Theory and Delinquency," *American Sociological Review* 46 (1985):525–541; Michael D. Wiatrowski and Kristine L. Anderson, "The Dimensionality of the Bond," *Journal of Quantitative Criminology* 3 (1987):65–81; Jennifer Friedman and Dennis P. Rosenbaum, "Social Control Theory: The Salience of Components by Age, Gender, and Type of Crime," *Journal of Quantitative Criminology* 4 (1988):363–381; James R. Lasley, "Toward a Control Theory of White-Collar Offending," *Journal of Quantitative Criminology* 4 (1988):347–362; Freda Adler, *Nations Not Obsessed with Crime* (Littleton, Colo.: Fred B. Rothman, 1983); Albert J. Reiss, "Delinquency as the Failure of Personal and Social Controls," *American Sociological Review* 16 (1951):196–206. See also Terence P. Thornberry, Rolf Loeber, and David Huizinga, "Symposium on the Causes and Correlates of Juvenile Delinquency," *Journal of Criminal Law and Criminology* 82 (1991):1–155; Robert Agnew, "A Longitudinal Test of Social Control Theory and Delinquency," *Journal of Research in Crime and Delinquency* 28 (1991):126–156. See also L. Edward Wells and Joseph H. Rankin, "Direct Parental Controls and Delinquency," *Criminology* 26 (1988):263–285; Douglas Smith and Raymond Paternoster, "The Gender Gap in Theories of Deviance: Issues and Evidence," *Journal of Research in Crime and Delinquency* 24 (1987):140–172; John Hagan, A. R. Gillis, and John Simpson, "The Class Structure of Gender and Delinquency: Toward a Power-Control Theory of Common Delinquent Behavior," *American Journal of Sociology* 90 (1985):1151–1178. For a discussion of paternal and maternal patterns of control on male and female children, see Gary D. Hill and Maxine P. Atkinson, "Gender, Familial Control, and Delinquency," *Criminology* 26 (1988):127–149; Jill Leslie Rosenbaum, "Family Dysfunction and Female Delinquency," *Crime and Delinquency* 35 (1989):31–44; Walter C. Reckless, Simon Dinitz, and E. Murray, "Self-concept as an Insulator against Delinquency," *American Sociological Review* 21 (1956):744–746. See also Madeline G. Aultman and Charles F. Wellford, "Toward an Integrated Model of Delinquency Causation: An Empirical Analysis," *Sociology and Social Research* 63 (1979):316–327; Charles Fenwick, "Culture, Philosophy and Crime: The Japanese Experience," *International Journal of Comparative and Applied Criminal Justice* 9 (1985):67–81; J. M. Day and William S. Laufer, eds., *Crime, Values, and Religion* (Norwood, N.J.: Ablex, 1987); Freda Adler and William S. Laufer, "Social Control and the Workplace," in *US-USSR Approaches to Urban Crime Prevention*, eds. James Finckenauer and Alexander Yakovlev (Moscow: Soviet Academy of State and Law, 1987).

44. R. H. McKey, L. Condelle, H. Ganson, B. J. Barrett, C. McConkey, and M. C. Planty, *Executive Summary: The Impact of Head Start on Children, Families, and Communities: Final Report of the Head Start Evaluation, Synthesis, and Utilization Project*, for U.S. Department of Health and Human Services, Administration for Children, Youth, and Families (Washington, D.C.: U.S. Government Printing Office, 1985).

45. Quoted in David Fattah, "The House of Umoja as a Case Study for Social Change," *Annals of the American Academy of Political and Social Science* 494 (1987):37–41. See also Charles E. Wellford, "Delinquency Prevention and Labeling," in *From Children to Citizens*, vol. 3, *Families, Schools, and Delinquency Prevention*, eds. James Q. Wilson and Glenn C. Loury (New York: Springer-Verlag, 1987), pp. 257–267; Denise C. Gottfredson, "An Empirical Test of School-Based Environmental and Individual Interventions to Reduce the Risk of Delinquent Behavior," *Criminology* 24 (1986):705–731.

46. Lynn A. Curtis, Preface, "Policies to Prevent Crime: Neighborhood, Family, and Employment Strategies," ed. Lynn A. Curtis, *Annals of the American Academy of Political and Social Science* 494 (1987):9–18.

47. Howard S. Becker, *Outsiders: Studies in the Sociology of Deviance* (London: Freepress of Glencoe, 1963), p. 9. For an excellent discussion of how society controls deviance, see Nicholas N. Kittrie, *The Right to Be Different: Deviance and Enforced Therapy* (Baltimore: Johns Hopkins University Press, 1971). See also Bernard Cohen, *Deviant Street Networks: Prostitution in New York City* (Lexington, Mass.: Lexington Books, 1980).

48. Charles Wellford, "Labelling Theory and Criminology: An Assessment," *Social Problems* 22 (1975):332–345.

49. Charles W. Thomas and Donna M. Bishop, "The Effect of Formal and Informal Sanctions on Delinquency: A Longitudinal Comparison of Labelling and Deterrence Theories," *Journal of Criminal Law and Criminology* 75 (1984):1222–1245; Gordon Bazemore, "Delinquent Reform and the Labeling Perspective," *Criminal Justice and Behavior* 12 (1985):131–169.

50. Austin Turk, *Political Criminality: The Defiance and Defense of Authority* (Beverly Hills, Calif.: Sage, 1982), p. 15. See also William J. Chambliss, "A Sociological Analysis of the Law of Vagrancy," *Social Problems* 12 (1966):67–77. For an opposing view on the historical development of criminal law, see Jeffrey S. Adler, "A Historical Analysis of the Law of Vagrancy," *Criminology* 27 (1989):209–229; and a rejoinder to Adler: William J. Chambliss, "On Trashing Criminology," ibid., pp. 231–238. For the relationship between unemployment and social control from a conflict perspective, see Belinda R. McCarthy, "A Micro-Level Analysis of Social Structure and Social Control: Intrastate Use of Jail and Prison Confinement," *Justice Quarterly* 7 (1990):325–340. See also Stuart Henry and Dragan Milovanovic, "Constitutive Criminology: The Maturation of Critical Theory," *Criminology* 29 (1991):293–315.

51. Richard Quinney, *Class, State, and Crime: On the Theory and Practice of Criminal Justice*, 2d ed. (New York: David McKay, 1977). See also Henry and Milovanovic, "Constitutive Criminology"; Jock Young, "Radical Criminology in Britain: The Emergence of a Competing Paradigm," *British Journal of Criminology* 28 (1988):159–183; William Chambliss and Robert Seidman, *Law, Order and Power* (Reading, Mass.: Addison-Wesley, 1971); Barry Krisberg, *Crime and Privilege: Toward a New Criminology* (Englewood Cliffs, N.J.: Prentice-Hall, 1975); Herman Schwendinger and Julia Schwendinger, "Delinquency and Social Reform: A Radical Perspective," in *Juvenile Justice*, ed. Lamar Empey (Charlottesville: University of Virginia Press, 1979), pp. 246–290.

52. Jackson Toby, "The New Criminology Is the Old Sentimentality," *Criminology* 16 (1979):516–526; Carl B. Klockars, "The Contemporary Crises of Marxist Criminology," *Criminology* 16 (1979):477–515.

53. Richard D. Schwartz and Jerome H. Skolnick, "Two Studies of Legal Stigma," *Social Problems* 10 (1962):133–138.

54. Kathleen Daly, "Neither Conflict nor Labeling nor Paternalism Will Suffice: Intersections of Race, Ethnicity, Gender, and Family in Criminal Court Decisions," *Crime and Delinquency* 35 (January 1989):136–168; Freda Adler, "Socioeconomic Variables Influencing Jury Verdicts," *New York University Review of Law and*

Social Change 3 (1973):16–36. See also Martha A. Myers, "Social Background and the Sentencing Behavior of Judges," *Criminology* 26 (November 1988):649–675; Celesta A. Albonetti, Robert M. Hauser, John Hagan, and Ilene H. Nagel, "Criminal Justice Decision-Making as a Stratification Process: The Role of Race and Stratification Resources in Pretrial Release," *Journal of Quantitative Criminology* 5 (1989):57–82. For a compilation of recent tests of the conflict model, see John Hagan, *Structural Criminology* (New Brunswick, N.J.: Rutgers University Press, 1989).

55. David Greenberg and Drew Humphries, "The Cooptation of Fixed Sentencing Reform," *Crime and Delinquency* 26 (1980):206–225; Lance H. Selva and Robert M. Bohm, "A Critical Examination of the Informalism Experiment in the Administration of Justice," *Crime and Social Justice* 29 (1987):43–57.

CHAPTER 4

CRIMINAL LAW

The Minneapolis newspaper the Star Tribune *had
a curious headline on its front page November 20,
1991: "Who Killed Gary Wall? Jury Clears Man Who
Stabbed Him, Blames His Doctor." It appears that
Daniel Guevara had stuck a kitchen knife into the
stomach of his drunken roommate Gary Wall. Although Daniel was indicted on a second-degree murder charge, a Kandiyohi, Minnesota, jury found him
guilty only of the lesser charge of first-degree assault.
His defense attorney had argued that the doctor who
treated Gary was to blame for his death. He had
stitched up what appeared to be a superficial stab wound. Had he made a thorough
examination, he would have found that the knife had penetrated Gary's liver. Gary
died three days after the stabbing, from internal bleeding. So it was not Daniel who
had caused Gary's death, but the surgeon. And if Daniel had not caused Gary's
death, he could not be guilty of murder.*[1] ∎

Under the law, a person must cause a crime to be found guilty of it. Causation is one of the seven basic principles that determine what we call criminal law and define what we call crime. In this chapter we will explore the criminal law, first by examining these basic principles and then by examining the defenses, or patterned answers, created by courts and legislatures over the centuries to deal with common and frequently occurring situations.

SEVEN BASIC PRINCIPLES

All crimes have something in common, something that distinguishes them from noncrimes, or acts not recognized by the law as criminal. Some of these commonalities may be called principles of criminal law. Criminal law scholar Jerome Hall analyzed the relevant law and found that seven principles mark every crime—or should mark every crime.[2] These principles are so much a part of what we call crime that if you were to ask us for a general definition of crime, we would have to say that we cannot define crime until we have put the seven principles, or definitional ingredients, before you. Together they define crime.

We hasten to add that sometimes legislatures (or courts) have skipped one or even two of the definitional ingredients. We refer to some of these problem cases later in the chapter. First we examine criminal law according to the seven basic principles, beginning with the one that is at the very source of the law—the principle of legality.

1. Legality: Is There a Law that Makes Something Criminal?

It would seem obvious that there must *be* a law before it can be applied. In terms of criminal law, there must be a criminal law before somebody can be charged with having violated it. An old maxim says: no crime without criminal law *(Nulum crimen sine lege)*. Where do these laws come from? Today, for the most part, it is legislatures that make them. But this was not always the case. The common law, as our law is still called, for the most part did not come to us through legislation. (In fact, the principles behind it still are not normally contained in legislation.)

"No crime without criminal law." Latin maxim.

Origin of the Common Law of Crimes. Let us see what common law is and where it comes from. Following William's conquest of England in 1066, the Norman kings established themselves as rulers and began to govern the country under a unitary rule. Henry II, who ruled from 1154 to 1189, became concerned that there was no law common to all the people of his kingdom. He thus established a permanent tribunal of five judges who traveled around the country, administering what was to be the beginning of a common or unified law. Whenever the judges found conflicting local laws or customs, they were to decide which should prevail as the law of the land. They

selected what was good, rejected what was bad, and created out of it all a system of law for the nation which was distinctly new, though based on the customs of the past and grounded on fundamental principles of legal concepts which in most cases can be traced back to the Anglo-Saxon period, in other cases to Roman law.[3]

However, despite the efforts of Henry's judges, there remained enormous differences in the law in various parts of Henry's realm. Help came from an unlikely source. Henry III (ruled 1234–1258) appointed as a clerk and later justice a young priest named Henry de Bracton (died 1268) who had studied the recently rediscovered Roman law at the University of Bologna in Italy. Bracton knew the beauty of the ancient Roman law, how well organized it was, how it covered all potential problems, and how clearly it was stated. To King Henry, Bracton seemed the right person to travel around the country and record everything that was common to the law of England. Bracton did just that, and ultimately published his work (in Latin) as *Treatise on the Laws of England*. He did, in fact, discover what was common to the law of England, and is therefore regarded as a principal source of the "common law." But whenever he found no solution, or conflicting solutions, Bracton "borrowed" liberally from the Roman law he had learned in Bologna. For example, he found nothing but confusion as to what constituted a theft, or larceny. So he simply reported as English law the Roman law concept of larceny.[4]

In formulating the "common" law, both Henry II's judges and Bracton relied heavily on the reported decisions of courts. That was to remain the hallmark of the common law: **Common law** was what the courts of England decided, and the law was always being developed by new cases that elaborated on or extended the law of preceding cases. As far as the criminal law was concerned, however, the king's courts became increasingly reluctant to make new laws or to extend the scope of what had previously been defined as criminal. The last major decision about the coverage of criminal law occurred in 1473, in the famous *Carrier's Case*, which broadened the law of larceny.[5] This reluctance of courts to extend the law, the preference to stick to previous decisions, is one of the hallmarks of common law. It is called the rule of *stare decisis* (to adhere to decided cases).

common law
Law as developed in England and later in the United States on the basis of court decisions (precedents) and as supplemented by legislation.

Parliament and Legislatures Extend the Common Law. More and more, whenever the need for further criminal law protection was felt, it was the English Parliament that had to legislate such protection (create a "new" crime). After American independence, the state legislatures and the Congress took the place of Parliament in creating new or codifying old crimes. In the twentieth century the American process of codification of the criminal law was aided by a gigantic effort by the American Law Institute, an elite group of outstanding lawyers and law professors. Between 1954 and 1962 this group, led by Professor Herbert Wechsler of Columbia University, drafted the Model Penal Code.

In effect, this group did what Bracton had done for England 700 years earlier—defined and selected what was best and most common in the criminal law of the fifty American states (and the various federal jurisdictions), and decided the best ways of organizing and formulating this information. The effort was largely successful. New Jersey and Pennsylvania adopted the Model Penal Code virtually in its entirety, and more than thirty other states used the Model Penal Code to make or improve their own criminal codes (see the Criminal Justice on Trial box).

Still, many states have left general propositions of the criminal law for development by the courts. These propositions, usually called the *General Part of Criminal Law*, cover such matters as the defenses to crime, the definition of criminal relationships (*accessoryship*), limits to the courts' rights to act (**jurisdiction**), and so on. Unless legislatures act to fill the gaps, courts have been free to fashion the law on these general propositions. The defense of insanity is an example. On the insanity issue, the various federal courts of appeal were extremely active in inventing every new law until Congress stepped in and legislated the issue in 1982 (see p. 91). For that matter, Gary Wall's "defense" still is not covered by legislation in many states, so that courts in these jurisdictions are free to fashion common law.

"Unless legislatures act to fill the gaps, courts have been free to fashion the law on . . . general propositions."

jurisdiction
Authority of the court to adjudicate a matter within its competence and territory.

The principle of **legality** is firmly established in America today: Only legislatures can make laws that prohibit an act under threat of punishment. Moreover, the principle of legality also requires that the legislatures have made the law prior to the commission of the act. Human beings can be expected to act in a given manner only if there is a clear and intelligible law telling them what is expected of them, and what will happen if they do not follow the law.

legality
Principle that every crime must be clearly defined by common law or legislation prior to its commission.

CREATION OF LAW: ALWAYS A RATIONAL EFFORT?

We often describe the penal codes of a society as the outcome of rational efforts to deal with crime and criminals. To be considered a crime, an act should meet the seven requirements discussed in the text of this chapter. Legislators are responsible for translating these requirements into laws, and they, as society's representatives, are also responsible for creating laws that safeguard their constituents.

But in our society there appears to be a universe of many more or less powerful interest groups, or lobbies, who influence legislators while they are in the process of writing new laws. Whether an act is a crime or not may depend on who lobbies hardest as much as anything else. Gambling, and the laws affecting it, is an obvious example.

Since civilization began—and maybe before—people have risked their fortunes on all kinds of chances. They still do in the stock market and in commerce generally. That kind of chance-taking is legal in most parts of the world, although it was certainly illegal in the formerly Communist countries of Eastern Europe: Free enterprise was a capital offense in these societies. But other kinds of risk-taking— what we call "games of chance," like betting on cards, dice, and horse races, for example—have long been considered immoral and prohibited by law.

In England in the early days of the common law, gambling was not illegal. Later statutes made "gaming," including playing billiards or tennis, illegal. In the eighteenth century, the keeping of a gaming house became a "criminal nuisance." But in the American colonies, lotteries, another form of gambling, were perfectly legal. [They were used, in fact, to fund Columbia University (then King's College), Harvard, Yale, Dartmouth, and Williams College.] But in the nineteenth century, gambling became less and less acceptable, until finally it was prohibited in almost every state (1).

What is the situation in the United States today? All American states except Nevada prohibit gambling in general, but there are many legal exceptions. States have legalized certain forms—for example, dog racing, horse racing, or (in Nevada, New Jersey, and Puerto Rico) casino gambling—and state lottery programs and church-sponsored Bingo are also defined as legal gambling in many jurisdictions.

Why is gambling sometimes legal and sometimes not? The great English jurist Sir James Fitzjames Stephen wrote in 1877: "Unlawful gaming means gaming carried on in such a manner, or for such a length of time or for such stakes (regard being had to the circumstances of the players) that it is likely to be injurious to the morals of those who game" (2). It appears, then, that the harm in gambling is the threat to gamblers' morals—the idea that the gambler who wins receives an undeserved, unearned reward.

One of the problems in the question of the legality of gambling seems to have economic roots: Gambling is extremely profitable for the operators of games. The 1976 Federal Commission on Gambling reported a turnover of $75 billion per year for American gambling activities; organized crime netted an estimated $7 billion. By now the figures are certainly much higher. So it is possible that states and localities hungry for money and facing budget cuts and the end of subsidies want some of the vast sums that now are siphoned off into illegal channels. Government, in other words, wants a piece of the action. Anti-gambling laws may seek less to protect the morals of gamblers, then, than to keep organized crime out of an extremely lucrative business.

Proposed laws prohibiting or allowing certain forms of gambling may be opposed or promoted by such diverse interest groups as churches, horsebreeders, travel agents, hotels, and citizens' groups. They all bring pressure to bear on lawmakers, who then must fashion laws that balance these competing interests with the public interest. The result may be statutes that are the product not of rational debate and careful thought, but of a long process of compromise and negotiation that focuses more on social, political and economic power than on what may in fact be right or wrong for that particular time and circumstance (3).

Sometimes the pressures on legislators may result in corruption. In West Virginia, for example, legislators accepted large bribes from lobbyists to influence legislation— essentially criminal law—that raised the amount of the take for the state's dog tracks. A South Carolina sting operation by the FBI netted a group of legislators and lobbyists who accepted money to influence a parimutuel betting bill (4). In Arizona, seven legislators were indicted for selling their votes (to a sting operator) on a bill that would have legalized casino gambling.

Let's ask again: Why is gambling sometimes legal and sometimes illegal?

- Is it because lawmakers are concerned about the morals of gamblers?
- Is it because lawmakers are listening to those who would profit most from making gambling legal?
- Is it because some decision-makers feel that organized crime can be controlled by making gambling illegal?
- Is it because sometimes gambling is profitable to governments, communities, churches, or citizens' groups?

Making criminal laws is a complex social process—and one that is not always free of corruption.

SOURCES
1. Gresham M. Sykes, *Criminology* (New York, Harcourt Brace Jovanovich, 1978), pp. 192–193.
2. Sir James Fitzjames Stephen, *A Digest of the Criminal Law* (London: Macmillan, 1877, 5th ed. 1894), p. 143.
3. M. Cherif Bassiouni, *Substantive Criminal Law* (Springfield, Ill.: Charles C. Thomas, 1978), pp. 355–397.
4. Thomas B. Edsall, "South Carolina Capital Girds for Sting Arrests; Vote-Buying May Hasten Power Shift," *The Washington Post,* August 12, 1990, p. A9; "S.C. Lawmakers Convicted," *The Washington Post,* March 10, 1991, p. A12.

Legal gambling: a state lottery

QUESTIONS FOR DISCUSSION

1. Why is the gamble you take when you place your money with a Wall Street futures trader on next year's coffee crop—which depends on the weather, on war and peace, on labor union action, and a host of other factors—a legal investment, but not the off-track gamble on the outcome of a horserace?
2. Is there a parallel between the way legislatures define what is illegal and the way universities do? Could legislatures learn anything from the universities' ways of making codes of conduct for students and professors?
3. Do you think gambling should be legal throughout the United States, illegal throughout the United States, or decided on a state-by-state basis? Defend your position.

Article 63, French Penal Code

Any person who, by his immediate action and without danger to himself or others, could have prevented either a felonious act or a misdemeanor against the person, willfully fails to do so, shall be punished by jailing for no less than three months nor more than five years and by fine from 36,000 to 1,500,000 francs, or either punishment, unless more severe punishments are provided by this Code or special law.

SOURCE: The cartoon is from an edition of the French Penal Code with crime cartoons by the French caricaturist Sinè, *Code Pénal—Texte Officiel*, Illustrations de Sinè, Paris: Maurice Gonon Éditeur, 1959, p. 35. English text from Jean F. Moreau and Gerhard O.W. Mueller, *The French Penal Code*, Vol. 1, American Series of Foreign Penal Codes, South Hackensack, NJ: Fred B. Rothman & Co., London: Sweet and Maxwell, 1960, p. 39.

2. Conduct: Only the Acts of Persons Can Be Covered by Criminal Law

Modern criminal law directs itself only at human action. It is only humans, acting singly or in groups (or even as corporations), who are being alerted by the criminal law: Don't do this or that, or else (see the Criminal Justice in Action box). Make a test: Look at any of the many crimes specified in the penal laws (criminal code) of your state. All prohibit *persons* from *acting* in a given manner. The verb *act* implies some degree of rationality or voluntariness in choosing to do or to accomplish something. A sleepwalker does not act from choice, does not act rationally. Consequently, under the criminal law a sleepwalker does not act, and any conduct of a sleepwalker is not criminal conduct. Likewise, a convulsion or a reflex does not amount to action.

Sometimes under the law *inaction* may amount to action. A parent who fails to rescue a drowning child, a law enforcement officer who fails to stop a violent criminal, a firefighter who fails to put out a fire, a babysitter who fails to prevent an infant from strangling itself at the playground, or a person who under law must register but does not, can be found guilty of a crime for not acting. The crime consists of inaction when there is a legal duty to act.

It follows that a person without a special legal duty to act is not obligated to come to the assistance of a person in trouble. Here law and morality differ: The biblical Good Samaritan came to the rescue even without legal obligation. This is but one of many instances where law and morality differ: Not everything immoral is illegal, and not everything illegal is immoral.

3. Harm: Protecting a Legally Recognized Value

With every criminal prohibition, the legislature seeks to protect a value, presumably one dear to all citizens. The threat to or destruction of a given value is the harm of a particular crime. Homicide legislation seeks to protect the value of human life. In the case of larceny, the harm obviously is the loss of property. In the case of treason, it is the threat to the security of the state.

The concept of harm is vital to an understanding of crime. First of all, it permits us to determine whether a crime has in fact taken place. If the legislatively prohibited harm has not been caused, then no crime has been committed. Second, harm is the evil the legislature wished to prevent, and this evil ultimately determines the punishment for committing it.

Legislators and criminal justice specialists have grouped all crimes into categories distinguished by the harm the crimes entail. Crimes against the person can be subdivided into those against life and those against physical integrity. Crimes against property include larceny, burglary, arson, fraud. Crimes against national security include treason, and crimes against humankind include genocide.

In describing the concept, or principle, of harm as a fundamental ingredient of every crime, what is most important is this premise: A crime is not constituted, a crime is not complete, until the perpetrator has indeed brought about the harm. Murder is not complete until the victim is dead. However, if the perpetrator has tried but has not succeeded in bringing about the harm, there may still be criminal liability for an *attempt* or an *assault* (see p. 99). Thus, even endangerment of the legally protected interest may be a punishable harm.

To the politically astute observer, it is extremely interesting to see what is regarded as harm by different types of societies. How they identify and order groups of offenses in their penal codes tells us much about their political orientation. In Figure 4.1, the liberal-democratic state (in this case Sweden) appears most concerned with harm to life, then to property; offenses against public order and the security of the state appear toward the end of the list. The totalitarian penal code of Communist Romania starts with harm to the state, followed by

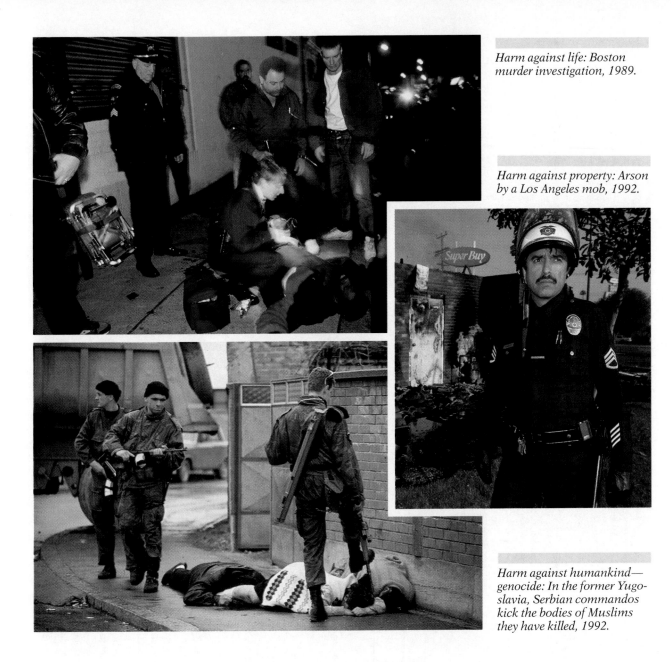

Harm against life: Boston murder investigation, 1989.

Harm against property: Arson by a Los Angeles mob, 1992.

Harm against humankind—genocide: In the former Yugoslavia, Serbian commandos kick the bodies of Muslims they have killed, 1992.

harms to the system—economic, social, political, and military. The American Model Penal Code omits all references to harm to state security because this is a federal concern. It rank-orders harm in the traditional manner of the common law, in descending order from harm to life, person, property, and family and only then turns to harm affecting public and governmental operations, ending with public indecency (which includes prostitution).

4. Causation: Bringing About the Harm

We now return to the case of Gary Wall, with which we began this chapter. At whose hands did Gary Wall really die? Was it Daniel Guevara who knifed him? Or was it the physician who sewed up the wound without noticing the extent of the injury? The jury rightly concluded that Guevara did not cause the death, though

Liberal-Democratic Society (Sweden)

- Ch. 3 Of Crimes against Life and Health
- Ch. 4 Of Crimes against Liberty and Peace
- Ch. 5 Of Defamation
- Ch. 6 Of Crimes against Morals
- Ch. 7 Of Crimes against Family
- Ch. 8 Of Theft, Robbery, and Other Crimes of Stealing
- Ch. 9 Of Fraud and Other Dishonesty
- Ch. 10 Of Embezzlement and Other Breaches of Trust
- Ch. 11 Of Crimes in Connection with Debts
- Ch. 12 Of Crimes Inflicting Damage
- Ch. 13 Of Crimes Involving Public Danger
- Ch. 14 Of Crimes of Falsification
- Ch. 15 Of Perjury, False Prosecution, and Other Untrue Statements
- Ch. 16 Of Crimes against Public Order
- Ch. 17 Of Crimes against Public Activity
- Ch. 18 Of Crimes of Lese-Majesty
- Ch. 19 Of Crimes against the Security of the Realm
- Ch. 20 Of Crimes in Office
- Ch. 21 Of Crimes of Members of the Armed Services
- Ch. 22 Articles of War

Totalitarian/Communist Society (Romania)

- Title I Offenses against State Security
- Title II Offenses against the Person
  1. Offenses against life, bodily integrity, and health
     - Section I: Homicide
     - Section II: Battery
     - Section III: Abortion
  2. Offenses against individual liberty
  3. Sexual offenses
  4. Offenses against dignity
- Title III Offenses against Personal or Private Property
- Title IV Offenses against Social Property
- Title V Offenses against Authority
- Title VI Offenses Which Threaten the Activities of State Organizations, or Other Activities Regulated by Law
  1. In-service or service-related offenses
  2. Offenses impeding the administration of justice
  3. Offenses against the safety of rail transportation
  4. Offenses concerning the principles established for certain activities regulated by law
- Title VII Offenses Related to Falsification
  1. Counterfeiting of money, stamps, or other items of value
  2. Counterfeiting of authentication or marking instrument
  3. Falsification of written documents
- Title VIII Offenses against Principles Established for Certain Economic Activities
- Title IX Offenses Which Threaten Certain Relations of Common Social Life
  1. Offenses against the family
  2. Offenses against public health
  3. Offenses concerning the assistance of persons in danger
  4. Offenses which threaten relations concerning common social life
- Title X Offenses against the Defense Capacity of the Socialist Republic of Romania
  1. Offenses committed by members of the armed forces
  2. Offenses committed by members of the armed forces or civilians
  3. Offenses committed by civilians
- Title XI Offenses against Peace and Mankind

U.S. Model Penal Code (States)
Part II. DEFINITION OF SPECIFIC CRIMES

Offenses Involving Danger to the Person
- Art. 210 Criminal homicide
- Art. 211 Assault; reckless endangering; threats
- Art. 212 Kidnapping and related offenses; coercion
- Art. 213 Sexual offense

Offenses against Property
- Art. 220 Arson, criminal mischief, other property destruction
- Art. 221 Burglary and other criminal intrusion
- Art. 222 Robbery
- Art. 223 Theft and other related offenses
- Art. 224 Forgery and fraudulent practices
- Art. 230 Offenses against the family

Offenses against Public Administration
- Art. 240 Bribery and corrupt influence
- Art. 241 Perjury and other falsification in official matters
- Art. 242 Obstructing governmental operations: escapes
- Art. 243 Abuse of office

Offenses against Public Order and Decency
- Art. 250 Riot, disorderly conduct, and related offenses
- Art. 251 Public indecency

Key/Legend
- Crimes against the person (violent crime)
- Crimes against property
- Crimes against the state, administration
- Vice crimes (drugs, alcohol, morals)

FIGURE 4.1 *Criminal harm: Rank-ordering of offenses, by penal code and social system* (*Sources:* Sweden: Thorsten Sellin and Jerome L. Getz, trans., *The Penal Code of Sweden*, Vol. 17, *American Series of Foreign Penal Codes* [South Hackensack, N.J.: Fred B. Rothman; London: Sweet & Maxwell, 1972], p. vii. Romania: Simone-Marie Vabriescu Kleckner, trans., *The Penal Code of the Romanian Socialist Republic*, Vol. 20, *American Series of Foreign Penal Codes* [South Hackensack, N.J.: Fred B. Rothman; London: Sweet & Maxwell, 1976]. United States: The American Law Institute, Model Penal Code, proposed official draft [as adopted], 1962, pp. xiii–xviii.)

he surely assaulted his victim. Rather, the surgeon caused Gary's death, perhaps through gross criminal negligence.

The law demands that a defendant's *act* must have *caused* the *harm*. If somebody else intervened and caused the harm, the defendant may be guilty for *trying* to cause the harm (we call this an attempt), but cannot be blamed for the harm. In most criminal cases, attribution of the harm to the defendant's act is not a problem. Indeed, we are normally not even compelled to ask the question. When we say A killed B, we are expressing the act-causation-harm sequence in a single word. To *rape*, to *steal*, to *speed*, to *defraud*—all imply a unified concept: act, causation, harm. But at times, as in the Gary Wall case, it becomes important to examine the action word (in this case "kill") in terms of the three parts.

The Model Penal Code codifies the common law principle that there must be a causal link between the defendant's act and the requisite harm. In Section 2.03 it provides: "Conduct is the cause of a result when . . . it is an antecedent but for which the result in question would not have occurred . . . ." That definition is not totally clear. Consider Ben Franklin's famous passage from *Poor Richard's Almanac,* to which we added three lines:

For want of a nail the shoe is lost,
for want of a shoe the horse is lost,
for want of a horse the rider is lost.
 —Poor Richard's Almanac, 1757[6]
For want of a rider the message is lost,
for want of a message the battle is lost—
the war is lost—the fatherland is lost.[7]

The lost horseshoe nail caused the loss of the country. But surely there must be some limitation on how far back courts should go in the causal chain. So courts and judges have tried to shorten the causal chain by requiring that, to be a cause in the legal sense, the event in question must not be too remote; it must be "proximate." The lost horseshoe nail might therefore not be regarded as the proximate cause of the loss of the country. But what is proximate and what is remote? Judges tend to use the simple test: Was the result (harm) the natural and probable consequence of the act? The Gary Wall case gives us some indication: True, without Daniel Guevara's stabbing, Gary would not have wound up in the hospital, and therefore he would not have been exposed to a negligent doctor. But, so the court ruled, the negligent doctor was an "intervening cause" that broke the original causal chain. The doctor had started a new causal chain, and therefore, he was the cause of Gary Wall's death.

5. Mens Rea (Guilty Mind): Criminal Intent

Nothing is as well established in all legal systems as the principle that no conduct can be considered criminal unless there is a guilty mind—an intent to commit a crime or to do harm. In law this "guilty mind" is referred to by its Latin term: **mens rea** (evil mind). It has sometimes been said that it is the intention to do the prohibited thing that is the mens rea: the intention to kill (in murder), the intention to deprive the owner of property (in larceny). But that cannot be so entirely. If it were, then the soldier who kills an enemy in wartime or the executioner who carries out the death sentence would have the mens rea for murder. The police officer who seizes the murder weapon would have the mens rea for larceny.

Mens rea, then, is more than just intent; it is intent coupled with the knowledge or awareness that one has no right to do the act.[8] This becomes apparent when we examine how defenses work: A person who takes another's raincoat from a restaurant rack has the intention to take the coat; but if the person believes he is taking his own coat he is not guilty of larceny, because he lacks the awareness of wrongdoing. (We will return to this issue in our discussion of various defenses.)

"Guilt matters. Guilt must always matter. Unless guilt matters the whole world is meaningless." Archibald MacLeish: JB.

mens rea (Latin)
Guilty mind; awareness of wrongdoing. Intention to commit a criminal act, or recklessness.

THE HUMAN CONDUCT REQUIREMENT

Ancient French court records reveal that when swarms of grasshoppers invaded the countryside and were gobbling up crops, a summons was issued to all grasshoppers to appear in court promptly on charges of devastating the harvest. In medieval Germany, goats or geese that had committed criminal mischief on a neighbor's property could be hanged as a punishment for their crimes. In 1386, a sow that had killed a child in Falaise, France, was tried, found guilty of homicide, and executed by hanging.

Punishment for status

Today human conduct is one of the seven criteria that define a crime. Although animals have been tried, convicted, and punished for crimes in the past, we now reserve blame, responsibility, and liability for *human* action only. After all, only human beings can act responsibly. Acting, conducting oneself, doing something is intrinsically human. It involves the human capacity to reason, to choose among various courses of conduct. And blame can be imposed only if there was an appeal to human reason and a corresponding failure to act in accordance with the appeal.

No lawgiver can command animals to respond to reason, for they have none. Nor can a lawgiver expect mountains to move on command, or any condition of nature to change under threat of punishment. Unfortunately, we have not always recognized this truth. History records many examples of punishment for conditions of nature, status, and relationships. Under Stalin's penal code, for example, any relative of a deserter from the Red Army could be punished by ten years of exile to Siberia, simply for the family relationship—even if the person had not seen the relative in twenty years. Under Hitler's racial and martial laws, all Jews were to be executed, all Gypsies, all relatives of any general officer who had surrendered. In such laws there was no appeal to reason; the punishment for being Jewish could not possibly change Jews into non-Jews (1).

Robinson v. California

Our own law, too, from time to time has imposed punishment for a status rather than for failure to respond to an appeal to reason. Until 1964 it was possible in New York for a woman to be sent to jail for a year for being a prostitute, without regard to whether she was currently soliciting or engaging in sex for hire. She had a status: Once a prostitute, always a prostitute. This law no longer exists. But a similar law reached the Supreme Court in 1962: California had made it a misdemeanor to be a drug addict, and a drug addict, Robinson, was convicted under the statute. How could an addict have evaded the impact of this law? Drug addiction is a condition, a status. The law can say what it wants; it can make unreasoned demands; but it can no more expect people to alter their status or condition than it can expect animals to abide by its commands. The Supreme Court declared the statute unconstitutional, reasoning that one may be a drug addict through no fault of one's own, for example, by being born to an addict mother. To punish people for being this or that kind of person violates the Constitution's (Eighth Amendment) prohibition of cruel and unusual punishment (2). The upshot is this: Only human *action* can be prohibited under threat of punishment. Justice Fortas of the Supreme Court provided this summary:

Robinson stands upon a principle which, despite its subtlety, must be simply stated and respectfully applied because it is the foundation of individual liberty and the cornerstone of the relations between a civilized state and its citizens: Criminal penalties may not be inflicted upon a person for being in a condition he is powerless to change (3).

The principle finally settled in *Robinson v. California* is clear: Only *human conduct* can be made criminal; every crime involves *human conduct* as a basic ingredient.

SOURCES

1. Rudolf His, *Deutsches Strafrecht bis zur Karolina* (Munich: Oldenbourg, 1928), p. 18.
2. *Robinson v. California,* 370 U.S. 660 (1962).
3. Justice Fortas, dissenting in *Powell v. Texas,* 392 U.S. 514, 567 (1968).

Execution of a Sow.

Fresco on a church wall in Falaise, France, depicting a 1386 execution of a sow

QUESTIONS FOR DISCUSSION

1. In Texas it was criminal "to be drunk in public." In *Powell v. Texas,* the U.S. Supreme Court upheld the validity of the statute. How can this be reconciled with the conduct requirement?

2. Sometimes criminal liability is based on (or increased by) a status. For example, under 8 U.S.C. § 1726 it is unlawful, "being a postmaster," to demand unauthorized rates or gratuities. Is that reconcilable with the conduct requirement?

3. Is there a difference between the way lawyers and psychologists define conduct? Explain.

The mens rea requirement raises difficult ethical and moral questions. Think of the sincere, honest pacifist who objects to war, burns his draft card (when these existed), and refuses to enter military service. Does he have an evil intent? Hardly, from a moral perspective. But here law and morality differ once again. The law regards his action as bad and so his intention is bad, because he knows that draft-card burning is a legal offense. No matter how morally praiseworthy this person's inner convictions may be, legally he acts with mens rea. Another example is the recent case of the mother who killed her drug-addicted daughter to end the daughter's suffering. "May God forgive me," the mother said. But again, inner considerations or praiseworthy motives are beyond the recognition of the law. Heaven may forgive, such actors and judges may impose minimal sentences, but a crime has been committed. Generally speaking, the blameworthiness mens rea implies is simply a conscious nonconformity with a standard imposed by law.

"It is not always the case that the law . . . requires an intention to do the illegal act."

It is not always the case that the law, for purposes of imposing criminal liability, requires an intention (coupled with awareness of wrongdoing) to do an illegal act. Sometimes the law imposes criminal liability for a reckless (or grossly negligent) causing of harm. Suppose you drive your souped-up car at high speed down a narrow, rain-slicked street and a child jumps into the road. You slam on the brakes, but the car cannot be stopped and it hits and kills the child. You are guilty of a form of criminal homicide called involuntary manslaughter (reckless killing). There was no intention to kill, but there was a grave, conscious (and therefore blameworthy) disregard of a substantial risk of injury or death. On that basis, you have incurred liability for homicide.

In one area of the law criminal liability may be imposed without any proof of mens rea. This is strict, or absolute, liability. Most offenses in this area are regulatory or public welfare offenses and include violations of laws governing traffic, selling food, dispensing medicine, and operating licensed businesses. In these cases, anyone who technically violates the law, even without the slightest fault on his or her part, incurs criminal liability. The grocer who sells adulterated milk without knowledge that the milk was tampered with at the farm is guilty of a regulatory offense.

mala prohibita (Latin)
Wrongs that are merely prohibited.

mala in se (Latin)
Offenses deemed inherently evil.

Lawyers have called the group of offenses for which absolute criminal liability is frequently imposed **mala prohibita,** meaning wrongs that are merely prohibited. They distinguish these from offenses called **mala in se,** or offenses that are inherently bad, such as murder, rape, and robbery. The differentiation between the two has led to interminable discussions and disputes. For example, is violation of a banking regulation, for which the banker may get a ten-year prison sentence, merely prohibited or inherently bad? And what difference does it make whether you attach one label or another? Mala prohibita are not necessarily offenses not requiring a criminal intent. Moreover, society's views as to what is particularly bad, and what is merely prohibited, change constantly.

"Some legal scholars believe that if the law punishes the innocent and guilty alike, it will frustrate those who suffer punishment without any fault on their part."

Various justifications have been given for the imposition of criminal liability and punishment without fault on the part of the actor—for example, that it would be harder to get a conviction if criminal intent had to be proved, that the penalty usually is small, or that absolute criminal liability has great deterrent value. But some legal scholars believe that if the law punishes the careful and the careless, the innocent and the guilty, alike, it will frustrate those who suffer punishment without any fault on their part.[9]

6. The Concurrence Requirement

The concurrence requirement means that the criminal act must be accompanied by an equally criminal mind. Suppose a striker throws a stone at an office window and a piece of broken glass pierces the throat of a secretary, who then bleeds to death. Property damage deserves condemnation, but far less than murder. In this case, act and intent did not concur. The striker should not be found guilty of murder.

The principle of concurrence is particularly significant in some of the doctrines of the criminal law, e.g., somnambulism (sleepwalking) . . . . A person who retires to rest with the deliberate purpose of rising during the night to take the life of another inmate of the same house and who does so in a state of somnambulism, clearly established, is no more guilty of murder than if he had never entertained such an unlawful purpose. There was, to be quite sure, an original evil intent and overt act of homicide, but they did not concur or coexist.[10]

The law has created a number of exceptions to the concurrence requirement— for example, in considering the impact of intoxication on criminal liability or in the application of the felony murder rule. Again, those are deviations from the general proposition that each act requires all seven basic principles to be considered a crime.

7. The Punishment Requirement

The seventh and last ingredient needed to constitute a crime is punishment. An illegal harmful act coupled with criminal intent still does not constitute a crime unless the law subjects the act to a punishment. If a sign is posted in the park saying "Do not step on the grass" and you do it anyway, have you committed a criminal offense? Not unless a law subjects that particular act to punishment. Otherwise it is simply improper or inconsiderate, no more (Figure 4.2). The punishment requirement, more than any other, also helps us differentiate between crimes (which are subject to punishment) and **torts,** civil wrongs for which the law does not prescribe punishment but merely grants the injured party the right to recover damages.

The nature and severity of the punishment also help us to differentiate grades of crime. Most penal codes recognize three degrees of severity: **felonies** (severe crimes subject to punishments of a year or more in prison or to capital punishment); **misdemeanors** (less severe crimes, subject to a maximum of one year in jail); and **violations,** infractions of the law for which normally only fines can be imposed. Fines can also be imposed as punishments for felonies and misdemeanors.

Quite apart from the amount of punishment imposable for felonies on the one hand and misdemeanors on the other, a number of legal consequences flow from the difference between these two categories of crime. Table 4.1 presents a summary. There is much more to know about punishment, and we shall return to the subject in the chapter on sentencing (Chapter 13) and in Part IV of this book, which is devoted to corrections.

tort
Wrong committed by one person against another, other than mere violation of a contract, which entitles the victim to compensation.

felony
Serious crime, subject to punishment of one year or more in prison, or to capital punishment.

misdemeanor
Crime less serious than a felony and subject to a maximum sentence of one year in jail or a fine.

violation
Infraction of the law for which normally only a fine can be imposed.

Having completed our survey of the seven basic principles, or seven basic ingredients, of every crime, we can finally provide the promised definition, one that incorporates all of the principles:

A crime is:	*Principles:*
legally prohibited	legality
human conduct	conduct (actus reus)
that causes	causation
a stated harm,	harm
committed with	concurrence
the requisite criminal intent	criminal intent (mens rea)
and subject to punishment.	punishment

FIGURE 4.2 *Has a crime been committed? Is walking on the grass prohibited by law, subject to punishment?*
© 1962 *The Saturday Evening Post*

TABLE 4.1 Differences in Legal Consequences for Felonies and Misdemeanors

Felonies	Misdemeanors
• capital punishment possible (in some states)	
• imprisonment in state prison	• stay in county jail
• sentence of a year or more	• sentence of less than a year
• considered serious crime	• considered minor crime
• conviction usually bars person from certain employments or professions	
• spouse of convicted person entitled to divorce or annulment of marriage (in some states)	• normally no such consequence
• convicted person may be deported if an alien	
• arrest may occur at any time	• arrest may occur only if act committed in presence of officer
• usually triable only in court of "general (unlimited) jurisdiction"	• triable in court of limited jurisdiction
• may require an indictment for trial	• normally is triable on an information

THE PRINCIPLES APPLIED: DEFENSES

An ancient lawyers' wisdom says that "general principles do not decide concrete cases." If that is so, why have we discussed the general principles? We had to, because it is impossible to remember the decisions made in millions of concrete cases, but it is possible to identify and learn the few principles that are applied in all of these cases. It is the principles, then, that make sense out of the criminal law, and they help us understand it.

In practice, the principles are rarely referred to by the courts. Instead, courts use legal rules and propositions that they, and the legislatures, have developed over the centuries. These propositions (also called doctrines) provide the answers to frequently occurring situations like these: What is a court to do when a child or a mentally ill person is charged with a crime? What is a court to do when somebody has been forced against his or her will to do an illegal act? And so on. For these situations the law has created patterned answers. The most frequently applicable of such patterned answers are the so-called defenses to crime. Let us start with these.

There are two types of defenses, excuses and justifications. We will explain the differences between the two after we have explained excuses.

Excuses

Infancy. Suppose a 3-year-old pushes her baby brother down the stairs, and the baby dies. Could we try the 3-year-old for murder? Did the 3-year-old commit the act of killing? Did she have the requisite criminal intent (mens rea)? In fact, a 3-year-old does not even know the meaning of life and death. To prevent silly inquiries into whether an infant committed a criminal act with the requisite criminal intent, the common law rules flatly that all children under age 7 (infants) are incapable of engaging in any kind of rational act or forming the requisite criminal intent. That is the common-law defense of infancy. (For details see Chapter 17.)

Insanity. When an adult charged with a crime pleads insanity as a defense—which happens very infrequently—he or she, in effect, asserts: "The normal rule that all adults are presumed legally capable of committing a crime does not apply in my case, because I am so severely mentally ill that I am incapable of committing crime. Thus, what looks like a crime in my case really was not a crime at all." Under common law, the so-called M'Naghten Rules (1843) made this defense concrete. It was an interesting case, worth remembering. Daniel M'Naghten (he actually spelled his name McNaughten, but nowadays his name is customarily spelled differently[11]) was obsessed by the idea that Sir Robert Peel, by creating the Metropolitan Police in London (see Chapter 6), wanted to destroy the liberties of Englishmen. He stalked Sir Robert to kill him, but mistakenly shot and killed his secretary. M'Naghten was acquitted of the murder charge by virtue of insanity.

The Trial of Daniel M'Naughten. Daniel M'Naughten, obsessed with the idea that Sir Robert Peel was destroying the liberty of individual Englishmen by creating a police force, stalked Peel but murdered his secretary by mistake. He was acquitted of murder by reason of insanity.

This acquittal aroused so much controversy that the House of Lords was called on to clarify the defense of insanity for future cases (1843). It did so, and the ruling became known as the M'Naghten Rules. Simply stated, they provide: A defendant is not guilty of crime if, at the time of the act, due to severe mental illness, (1) the defendant did not know the nature and quality of his or her act (in other words, did not appreciate what he was doing so that the "act requirement" was not fulfilled), or (2) the defendant did not know the wrongfulness of his or her act (in other words, could not form the requisite mens rea).[12]

This test was widely used in England and America, yet it was frequently misunderstood. In fact, some courts, emphasizing the second part of the test, simply inquired whether the defendant knew the difference between right and wrong. This interpretation produced many miscarriages of justice, so that courts constantly changed and reshaped their tests of insanity. Among these (usually short-lived) insanity tests were:

• The *irresistible impulse addition* to the M'Naghten test: A defendant may be acquitted if he or she was unable to control the action due to mental illness.
• The *Durham Rule, or "product test"* (1954): The defendant must be acquitted if the crime was the product of mental disease or defect.
• The *Currens Test* (1961): The defendant must be acquitted if he or she "lacked substantial capacity to conform his conduct to the requirements of the law . . . as a result of mental disease or defect."

In 1982 Congress settled the issue, at least as far as federal law is concerned, by providing for an acquittal by reason of insanity if "at the time of the commission of the act the defendant, as a result of severe mental disease or defect, was unable to appreciate the nature and quality or wrongfulness of his act."[13] This text is a modern version of the old M'Naghten formula. Several states have similar tests, but the majority have adopted the version codified in the American Law Institute's Model Penal Code and known as the ALI test:

A person is not responsible for criminal conduct if at the time of such conduct as a result of mental disease or defect he lacks substantial capacity either to appreciate the criminality (wrongfulness) of his conduct or to conform his conduct to the requirements of law.[14]

This test focuses on the defendant's capacity to form the necessary criminal intent by asking whether the defendant appreciated the wrongfulness of the act. It also emphasizes, as part of the mens rea, the defendant's volitional capacity: Could the defendant really intend to commit the wrongful act? Did he have the "(substantial) capacity" "to conform his conduct to the requirements of law"?

Whenever a particularly notorious crime has been committed by someone who then pleads insanity, there is public clamor for revenge by toughening the insanity test. That was as true when Daniel M'Naghten attempted to assassinate

"Whenever a particularly notorious crime has been committed by someone who then pleads insanity, there is an immediate public clamor to toughen the insanity test."

John W. Hinckley's acquittal by reason of insanity of the attempted assassination of President Reagan in March 1981 caused federal and state legislative changes in the insanity defense. Defendant's exhibit: Note written by Hinckley to the actress Jodie Foster (shown at right).

Sir Robert Peel as it was when John W. Hinckley, Jr., attempted to assassinate President Ronald Reagan in 1981. The Hinckley case prompted several states to pass legislation providing for an alternative disposition, that of "guilty but mentally ill." This novel verdict is meant to cover defendants not mentally ill enough to qualify for an outright acquittal "by reason of insanity," yet not well enough to be found fully accountable and "guilty." It is therefore an in-between solution. Unhappily, the sentence that may be imposed on an in-between defendant can be the same as that received by a normal "guilty" defendant, and while some states offer special "treatment" for such convicts, there is no constitutional obligation that they do so.[15]

Intoxication. Perhaps no type of deviance causes police officers more wasted time and effort than public intoxication. The law has not been sympathetic to public drunkenness, as Leroy Powell's case demonstrates. Leroy was found guilty in Austin, Texas, of having been "found in a state of intoxication in [a] public place." Leroy, as the Supreme Court put it, conjures up "the picture of the penniless drunk propelled aimlessly and endlessly through the law's 'revolving' door of arrest, incarceration, release and rearrest."[16] The Powell case ultimately reached the Supreme Court of the United States. Should Powell, a chronic alcoholic, not have been treated like Robinson, the drug addict, whose case was discussed in the Criminal Justice in Action box? Both were afflicted with a status—alcoholism in one case, drug addiction in the other. And status does not qualify for a crime. Crime requires conduct. No, said the Supreme Court, there was conduct in Powell's case, namely *being in public*—and being drunk. Had Leroy Powell chosen to get drunk at his home, he could not have been found guilty. However, many chronic alcoholics, quite apart from suffering the disease of alcoholism, are homeless as well. The only place they can be found, drunk or sober, is in public. Had there been proof that Leroy Powell was a homeless person, one of the concurring justices would have voted for reversal of Powell's conviction. In that case the majority of the Court would have reversed the conviction, and Powell would have been treated like Robinson. As it was, Powell's conviction was affirmed.

American law is and always has been tough on the issue of intoxication. Most state penal codes state flatly that intoxication is no defense. Actually, that is not true. Involuntary intoxication, for example, because of prescription medication, can constitute a defense. Moreover, most courts have held that even voluntary intoxication, when severe, may render a person incapable of forming certain types of criminal intent. For example, murder in the first degree requires, among other things, premeditation and deliberation. Many courts have held that if a defendant was so grossly intoxicated that he or she could not premeditate and deliberate, he or she can at best be found guilty of murder in the second degree. To that extent, the law on intoxication conforms to the mens rea principle. But American law does not absolve intoxicated perpetrators of all criminal liability: Gross voluntary intoxication may simply lower the degree of the crime committed. It is as if the law has retained its Puritan imprint: Drunkenness is bad, and people who drink and violate the law do not deserve much leniency, even though alcohol has lowered their resistance, removed their inhibitions, and stimulated their aggressiveness.

The problems intoxication poses to the criminal justice system, and to law enforcement in particular, are enormous, considering that a majority of all persons arrested have recently (within seventy-two hours before arrest) used alcohol (Figure 4.3) or drugs, and between one-third and three-quarters of arrestees test positive for cocaine use.[17] Drug addiction and alcoholism remain two of the foremost unsolved problems confronting the criminal justice system. To hold perpetrators responsible for crimes committed under the influence of either may not be a solution, but may have the minimal advantage of making treatment services accessible for them.

Mistake of Fact. Let us go back to the coat rack situation. A restaurant patron goes to the coat rack to retrieve his raincoat. He verifies the manufacturer's label, takes the coat, and begins to depart. Another patron, obviously agitated, jumps up and grabs the coat-taker. "You stole my coat!" The first man is greatly embarrassed. It turns out that the coat is not his. But is he a thief?

To be a thief, as we have seen, one has to intend to deprive someone of his or her property. That is the mens rea requirement. In this instance the first patron is *not* a thief, because, thinking the coat to be his, he had no awareness of wrongdoing. That is the essence of the defense of mistake of fact: If there is no mens rea, there is no crime. When an honest mistake of fact negates the mens rea requirement, no crime is committed.[18]

"If there is no mens rea, there is no crime."

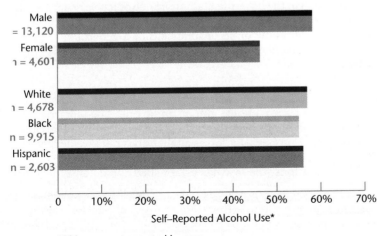

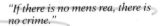

FIGURE 4.3 *Self-reports of recent alcohol use by arrestees** (*Source:* National Institute of Justice/Drug Use Forecasting Program.)

*Data based on self-reported use of alcohol in the past seventy-two hours. April through December 1989.

Male = 13,120
Female n = 4,601
White n = 4,678
Black n = 9,915
Hispanic n = 2,603

Self-Reported Alcohol Use*

*521 cases not reported by race

Mistake-of-fact problems usually are easily resolved in pretrial proceedings or at trial, but they can be troublesome to law enforcement officers. Many suspects, caught redhanded by the police, will immediately offer some excuse, often based on mistake of fact: "Gee, officer, I thought . . . ." Suppose that in the case of the mistaken raincoat the proprietor had summoned a police officer. What is the officer to do? Should he or she make an arrest and let the court worry about defenses? Or should he or she ascertain the facts, conclude that there was probable cause a theft had been committed, but that there also was the defense of mistake of fact? Police officers must know enough law to make on-the-spot decisions within the discretion vested in them. If a suspect's explanation seems reasonable (there was a "reasonable mistake"), and especially if the victim agrees, the officer probably would not make an arrest. But if the facts are complex and unclear, the officer has no choice but to let the courts adjudicate the question of whether there was a reasonable mistake that nullifies the defendant's mens rea.

Mistake or Ignorance of Law. Every law enforcement officer quickly learns through practical experience that the law does not recognize a mistake of law: If an officer thinks he has a right to make an arrest, but the law is otherwise, the arrest is illegal. Similarly, if a banker believes that a given money transaction is legal, but the law says it is not, the banker has committed an offense. Everybody is supposed to know and understand the law. Obviously, however, that is impossible. Even trial judges frequently do not know the law properly or misunderstand it, so that appeals courts later reverse decisions.

To legal scholars the maxim that ignorance or mistake of law does not excuse made sense in ancient times, when the number of crimes was limited to serious felonies that everybody knew: murder, arson, robbery, rape, burglary, and so on. But today, they argue, when there are thousands of crimes on the statute books, the rule no longer makes sense, because it violates the mens rea principle: a person who acts in ignorance of a legal prohibition simply has no mens rea.

"My ignorance of the law was simply appalling."

SOURCE: *The New Yorker*, July 20, 1992, p. 28.

"The potential of blame that follows a choice to commit a crime is meant to be a powerful incentive to do the right thing."

Let us examine the case of Ms. Lambert. She was convicted in Los Angeles of an offense created by city ordinance: living in the city without registering with the police as a person previously convicted of a crime. Ms. Lambert had no idea that Los Angeles had such a registration requirement. Nor could she possibly have known that she was required to register. She appealed all the way to the U.S. Supreme Court, and she won. Said the Court: "Where a person did not know [of the prohibition] (s)he may not be convicted consistent with due process."[19]

The potential of blame that follows a choice to commit a crime is meant to be a powerful incentive to do the right thing and avoid doing the wrong thing. No blame can attach when the law's command did not reach the person expected to follow it. The Supreme Court reversed Ms. Lambert's conviction only grudgingly. It could have said: We abolish the doctrine that ignorance of law is no excuse. But it did not go that far. The court grants ignorance of the law only when the defendant did not, and could not, know of an ordinance (not a general law) that requires the doing of something, like registering. As for the rest, ignorance of law remains no defense.

Duress. A robber approaches a bank teller with the following demand: "Your money or you're dead!" Not a fun choice, but a simple one. The teller probably reaches into the drawer and hands over the cash. Is the teller guilty of larceny or embezzlement? It is not her money. Her job as a teller does not give her the right to steal, to embezzle, or to give away funds entrusted to her.

To deal with such situations, the law has established the defense of duress:

It is . . . [a] defense that the actor engaged in the conduct charged to constitute an offense because he was coerced to do so by the use of, or a threat to use, unlawful force against his person or the person of another, which a person of reasonable firmness in his situation would have been unable to resist.[20]

This defense applies when the actor has done something the law prohibits. The bank teller has taken money entrusted to her and given it to someone else, without authorization. All the elements of the crime of embezzlement are there. But the teller had no choice. The law recognizes that we cannot be expected to yield our lives, our limbs, the safety of our relatives, our houses, or our property when confronted by a criminal threat that forces us to violate a law. In the defense of duress it may be said that the actor acted not of his or her own free will. Thus, the element of the required voluntary action (conduct) is not there. There is, however, a general requirement that the evil that threatens the actor ("Your money or you're dead") and the evil created by the actor (handing over cash out of the till) not be out of proportion.

Necessity. The rule is similar for the defense of necessity. Here the threat to the actor comes from nature. It is sometimes called an "act of God," and it may be a fire, a storm, an earthquake, or a shipwreck that compels the actor to do something that otherwise would be illegal. Suppose two hikers are surprised by a snowstorm. They stumble upon an unoccupied vacation cottage. Under the rule of necessity, they may break into and enter the cottage and use its provisions to stay alive. But here, as in cases of duress, the actor must not act out of proportion to the need. The stranded hikers may seek shelter in the cottage and use necessary provisions. They cannot feast on the owner's caviar, champagne, and cigars.

The defense of necessity is not available whenever there are legal means in existence to avert the threat: A starving person should seek public welfare rather than steal for his or her survival. This is a harsh rule. The welfare office may be miles away, and its processes may take weeks. Should the hungry, homeless person choose to die rather than steal a pretzel from a vendor's cart? This limit on the defense of necessity opens up an inquiry into the overall justness of society and its laws.

"Should the hungry, homeless person choose to die rather than steal a pretzel from a vendor's cart?"

Justifications

The preceding defenses all rest, basically, on a claim that either the necessary mens rea or the necessary voluntary act was missing so that there was no crime. These defenses are commonly called excuses. There is a second set of defenses called **justifications.** *Jus* is Latin for law. The law itself provides a counter-law to the prohibitory law. The prohibitory law says: You must not kill. But the counter-law says: If you are a soldier in combat, you must kill. That is the justification.[21]

justifications
Defenses in which the law authorizes the violation of another law within limits of proportionality.

Public Duty. Justification is nowhere applied more appropriately than in conjunction with the defense of public duty, particularly when force has to be used by an officer of the law. The law prohibits an act, such as restraining a person, but the counter-law commands an officer of the law to restrain a person for purposes of effecting an arrest. There is a limit: The officer must use no more force than necessary. The use of deadly force by law enforcement officers is subject to exacting restrictions (see Chapter 8). Law enforcement officers who use more force than necessary to achieve legitimate objectives are likely to be committing a criminal offense, such as assault and battery or even criminal homicide.

Few situations arouse as much public passion as the use of excessive force by law enforcement officers in the otherwise lawful execution of their duties. Obviously, when officers abuse their authority, the law must hold them accountable and charge them for the excess, whether it be an assault and battery, an unlawful imprisonment, or a trespass. But many situations of excessive force can best be understood by viewing two of our doctrines in conjunction: Public duty is the doctrine that requires officers to take appropriate measures. But there is also the doctrine of (reasonable) mistake of fact. Law enforcement officers, like all human beings, can only be expected to act reasonably under the circumstances

CRIMINAL LAW IN AN AGE OF ETHNIC DIVERSITY

On January 1, 1992, the once-mighty Soviet Union ceased to exist. It had been the largest country in the world—2.5 times the size of the United States—with nearly 300 million people of over 100 nationalities. The three Baltic nations, Lithuania, Latvia, and Estonia, which had been annexed by the U.S.S.R. in 1939, regained their independence in 1991. The remaining thirteen republics declared their independence, but agreed to remain in a loose-knit commonwealth. In Yugoslavia, the Balkan state with six major ethnic groups, a civil war has resulted in independence for Croatia and Slovenia. Czechoslovakia broke up on January 1, 1993, and now consists of two ethnic republics, one inhabited by Czechs and the other by Slovaks. In Iraq the Kurds, an ethnic group living in parts of Iraq, Iran, Turkey, and the former U.S.S.R., are fighting for independence.

There is hardly a region in the world that is free from ethnic conflict: we live in an age of ethnicity and of a drive, often by force of arms, to break up nation-states into ethnic states. What does this have to do with criminal law? A great deal.

Everywhere in the world, ethnic groups are fighting for greater autonomy; they want to be governed by laws of their own making, compatible with their own customs and traditions:

- Basques and Catalonians in Spain
- Tamils in Sri Lanka
- Sikhs in India
- Tibetans in China
- Kurds in Iraq

It has been the practice of nation-states to adopt a single penal code that governs everyone, regardless of ethnic group. But such a policy can lead to problems for law enforcement and criminal justice: A penal code written and imposed by a distant "central authority" which is itself of one particular ethnic group may not be effective with another group far from the seat of government. The former Soviet Union is one example; the United States and its Native American peoples is another.

The breakup of the U.S.S.R.

To some extent, the central authorities have made allowances for ethnic diversity. The Soviet Penal Code of 1953 imposed only its General Part on the entire U.S.S.R., with provisions on jurisdiction, the various defenses, accessoryship. The Special Part, which defined the various crimes and punishments, was reserved for variations among the republics. For example, Chapter 11 of the Russian criminal code outlaws such customs as blood feuds, sale of brides, and polygamy. These crimes have no counterpart in the codes of the other republics. Compelling another to be a co-author or co-inventor is not a crime in Ukraine, Kyrgyzstan, and Turkmenistan, but it is in the other republics (1). But such regional deviations were minor, as Moscow wanted as much conformity as possible.

So what happens now that the various republics are independent? The three newly independent Baltic states, Lithuania, Latvia, and Estonia (whose populations are not Slavic), are in the process of resurrecting their pre-1939 national penal codes. The predominantly Islamic republics, Kazakhstan, Uzbekistan, Turkmenistan, and Kyrgyzstan, had long been unhappy with a Russian-inspired penal code and are now searching for something more compatible with their Islamic traditions. Nearby countries, including Turkey, Iran, Iraq, and Saudi Arabia, are competing for intellectual impact in the formulation of new penal codes for these new republics. The new independent countries with predominantly Christian traditions, including Ukraine, Moldova, Georgia, and Armenia, also want to shed the Russian imprint. Russia itself is rapidly discarding the Soviet features of its penal code. A law of 1961 had made it criminal for persons to "avoid socially useful work, derive unearned income from the exploitation of land plots, automobiles or housing, or commit other antisocial acts which enable them to lead a parasitic way of life" (2). What was a vice and crime has now become a virtue: Today people are encouraged to exploit land plots, automobiles or housing, and derive "unearned income" from investments.

The Native American experience in the United States

The United States has its own share of ethnic diversity affecting criminal justice. The federal government recognizes that it has a special trust responsibility for 307 federally recognized Indian (Native American) entities in the continental United States, plus some 200 tribal entities in Alaska. ''Entities'' includes nations or tribes, bands, villages, groups, pueblos, Eskimos (Inuits), and Aleuts. This is not just a domestic problem; it is an international problem because of the treaty obligations of the U.S. government vis-à-vis Indian nations. In the beginning Native American nations enjoyed their own jurisdiction in all matters, including what we term criminal justice. By now, all Native Americans, even those living in ''Indian country'' (18 U.S. 1151) are subject to federal (or state) criminal law:

18 U.S. C. § 1153. Offenses committed within Indian country

(a) Any Indian who commits against the person or property of another Indian or other person any of the following offenses, namely, murder, manslaughter, kidnapping, maiming, a felony under chapter 109A, incest, assault with intent to commit murder, assault with a dangerous weapon, assault resulting in serious bodily injury, arson, burglary, robbery, and a felony under section 661 of this title within the Indian country, shall be subject to the same law and penalties as all other persons committing any of the above offenses, within the exclusive jurisdiction of the United States.

(b) Any offense referred to in subsection (a) of this section that is not defined and punished by Federal law in force within the exclusive jurisdiction of the United States shall be defined and punished in accordance with the laws of the State in which such offense was committed as are in force at the time of such offense. (1992 Amendment.) (3)

There is not much Native American law left. As Chief Heinmoot Tooyalaket (Chief Joseph) of the Nez Percé put it many years ago:

Say to us if you can say it, that you were sent by the Creative Power to talk to us. Perhaps you think the Creator sent you here to dispose of us as you see fit. If I thought you were sent by the Creator I might be induced to think you had a right to dispose of me. Do not misunderstand me, but understand me fully with reference to my affection for the land. I never said the land was mine to do with it as I chose. The one who has the right to dispose of it is the one who has created it. I claim a right to live on my land, and accord you the privilege to live on yours. (4)

Penal codes, to be respected, must conform to the cultural norms of the people; otherwise those addressed will not comply readily, and the police and courts will have a difficult time enforcing them.

SOURCES

1. Harold J. Berman and James W. Spindler, *Soviet Criminal Law and Procedure* (Cambridge, Mass.: Harvard University Press, 1966), pp. 15–16.
2. Edict of the Presidium of the Supreme Soviet of the RSFSR of May 4, 1961, as quoted in Berman and Spindler, p. 9.
3. Paul S. Volk, ''The Legal Trail of Tears: Supreme Court Removal of Tribal Court Jurisdiction over Crimes by and Against Reservation Indians,'' *New England Law Review* 20 (1984/5):247–283.
4. Dee Brown, *Bury My Heart at Wounded Knee* (New York: H. Holt & Co., 1971), p. 300.

QUESTIONS FOR DISCUSSION

1. Some crimes, like murder, robbery, or arson, seem to be so universal that they should be included in all penal codes. Right or wrong? Or does it depend on how we define them?
2. What makes for the severity of the various crimes defined in a penal code? Is there agreement on severity within a country, or between countries?
3. To what extent should a dominant government (like that of the former U.S.S.R., or of the U.S.A.) have the right to impose penal codes on ethnically diverse groups?

that appear to them. If they make a reasonable mistake in the assessment of the facts, they too are entitled to be excused. If an officer orders a fleeing felony suspect to stop and the suspect twirls around and produces a metallic object that the officer reasonably mistakes for a gun, inducing her to shoot, the officer should be cleared of an assault or homicide charge, but not because the officer acted lawfully in the execution of public duty. Objectively, public duty did not permit her to shoot. But she is to be cleared under the doctrine of mistake of fact, which made it reasonably appear that she had a right to shoot. That, of course, leads directly to the discussion of self-defense.

"When you are surrounded by four people, one of them smiling, taunting, terrorizing, you don't have a complete grasp or perfect vision."
Bernhard Goetz, quoted in *Newsweek*, March 11, 1985.

Self-Defense, Defense of Others, and Defense of Property. On the Saturday before Christmas in 1984, Bernhard H. Goetz entered a subway car at the IRT station at Seventh Avenue and Fourteenth Street in Manhattan. He sat down close to four young men in their late teens. One of them offered a "How are ya," then approached Goetz and asked for 5 dollars. At that point Goetz pulled out a .38-caliber revolver and shot all four youths (one in the back).[22]

Few cases have ignited so much controversy. Some people saw Goetz as the avenger of the city dweller, who suffers constantly from crime and the fear of crime. Others labeled him a vigilante. Or was he simply the meek underdog, as his appearance suggested, trying to defend himself against yet another attack on the subway? He could have been any of these. Goetz was charged with attempted murder, assault, and illegal possession of a weapon. In legal terms, the case simply raised the question of the right to use force, even deadly force, in self-defense, and the extent to which the defense exists if the actor is mistaken about the actual threat that confronts him.

It is safe to say that in most states a person can use as much force as is reasonably necessary to defend against what appears to be an immediate threat of violence by another as long as the following four elements are present:

• The person must have an "honest and reasonable belief" that the force is necessary.
• The person must believe that the harm threatened will be immediately forthcoming.
• The harm threatened must be unlawful.
• The force used must be reasonable—only so much as appears necessary under the circumstances.

Let us return to the Goetz case. Did Goetz find himself in a life-threatening situation? We shall never know. As it turned out, some of the victims had criminal records. They carried no firearms, only screwdrivers, which they said they used to pilfer vending machines. Objectively, it appears that Goetz was in no immediate physical danger. What, then, went on in his mind? He had experienced a prior brutal mugging in similar circumstances. Like many other subway riders, he feared the predators who seemed to be ever present beneath the streets. The defense made a strong case that Goetz was in fear of his life. The legal question was whether he should be judged by a subjective standard—whether *he* felt in fear of his life—or by an objective standard: whether a reasonable person in his situation would have been in fear of his or her life. The jury resolved this issue by acquitting him of all charges except one: illegal possession of a handgun.

The right to use reasonable force, and if necessary deadly force, extends to the defense of others. In most jurisdictions, a defender can use as much force on behalf of another as he or she could have used in self-defense. Of course, such defenders must reasonably believe that if they were in the other person's position they would have the right to defend themselves, and the amount of force used must be reasonable. But some states require in addition that the person being assisted must actually have the right to use force, regardless of the defender's perception.

The law views the protection of property and of human life differently. With few exceptions, the right of self-defense is far more extensive than the right of defense of property. The general rule in this area is that nondeadly force may be used, typically after some request has been made to desist, when it is necessary to thwart an intrusion. When there is some indication that the intruder intends to commit a felony on the premises, and a warning to desist has been issued and ignored, deadly force may be used.

Other Defenses

A few other defenses normally covered in textbooks on criminal law deserve mention, though not discussion. Some of them are of limited, others are of broader reach. Among them are:

- the doctrine of crime commission by innocent agent, where a perpetrator abuses the ignorance or innocence of another to commit a crime
- the doctrine of superior orders, where a subordinate follows orders of a superior officer, thinking such orders to be legal
- the doctrine of entrapment, where a law enforcement officer induces an originally unwilling person to violate the law (see Chapter 7)
- the doctrine of vicarious criminal liability, where a person is held liable for the criminal act of another to whom he or she stands in a certain relationship
- the doctrine of corporate criminal liability, under which corporations bear responsibility for the acts of corporate officers or agents
- the defense of diplomatic or legislative immunity
- the defense of the statute of limitations, when the time for instituting proceedings has passed

THE ARITHMETIC OF CRIME

The patterned propositions pertaining to defenses are not the only doctrines of criminal law used to assess criminal charges. There is a whole set of doctrines concerned with the arithmetic of crime. How do we deal with a situation in which only a fraction of a crime has been committed, for example an attempted but incomplete crime? How do we deal with a crime in which several persons collaborate?

Attempt

Foremost among these doctrines of the arithmetic of crime is the one pertaining to attempted crimes. What should the law do to someone who tries to commit a crime but does not succeed? Under early common law, attempts to commit crimes were not considered crimes, because the criminal act (*actus reus*) was not completed. But a person who tries to complete a crime surely has the same mens rea and thus the same culpability as one who succeeds in creating harm. Should the would-be perpetrator be treated differently just because he or she did not succeed? In 1784 in England, it was decided that an attempt to commit a felony was indeed a crime.[23] That case laid the foundation for our present conceptualization of **criminal attempt,** as contained in the Model Penal Code: "an act or omission constituting a substantial step in a course of conduct planned to culminate in the commission of a crime."[24]

This definition is overly elastic: What is a substantial step? What is a course of conduct? What is planned to culminate? Would it be an attempted bank robbery to enter a bank with a prepared note that says "Hand over the money or I'll blow your brains out"? Courts have said that this is not yet a substantial step. (Handing the note to the teller, however, would be). To make criminal dangerous acts

"The person who tries to complete a crime surely has the same evil intent and thus the same culpability as the one who succeeds."

criminal attempt
Act or omission constituting a substantial step in a course of conduct planned to culminate in the commission of a crime.

intended to culminate in a crime, but not yet constituting a "substantial step," legislatures have often made mere preparatory actions criminal. Entering a federally insured bank for a criminal purpose, or possessing explosives, have become criminal offenses. Ultimately it is left to the courts, on a case-by-case basis (in typical common-law fashion), to define such concepts as "substantial step."

There is less difficulty in defining the end of an attempt: the end is either withdrawal from an attempt (which, in most cases, leaves the attempter guilty of an attempt), or completion of the crime, in which case the attempt disappears (merges) in the completed crime, and the perpetrator is guilty of the completed crime. The attempted murder is over when the victim dies; the attempted arson of a dwelling is over when even the smallest part of the house catches fire. Oddly enough, the laws of most states and countries permit the same punishment to be imposed for an attempted as for a completed crime. In practice, however, lesser sentences are imposed for an attempt.

Accessoryship

accessoryship
Criminal liability of all those who aid the perpetrator of an offense.

principal
Perpetrator of a criminal act.

accomplice
Person who helps another to commit a crime.

"He who holds the ladder is as bad as the thief."
German proverb.

conspiracy
Agreement among two or more persons to commit a crime, making each guilty of conspiracy and all other crimes committed in furtherance of the conspiracy.

The common law also created a sophisticated system for determining the liability of all persons involved in the commission of a crime. Here we have an arithmetical situation of additions—of persons. **Accessoryship** refers to the criminal liability of all those who aid the perpetrator(s) of an offense.

Today most states recognize only **principals** (all persons who commit an offense by their own conduct) and **accomplices** (all those who aid the perpetrator). That system has not solved all problems, because the line between committing a crime and aiding in its commission is a fine one. Though principals and accomplices are usually considered equally at fault, in practice judges often impose lighter sentences on accomplices.

Conspiracy

Conspiracy is a concept in some ways similar to accessoryship, but with a far broader reach. A **conspiracy** is an agreement among two or more persons to commit a specified crime. As soon as these parties have committed any act (even a legitimate one) in furtherance of the conspiracy, they are guilty of the crime of conspiracy. Thus, if Rob, Pim, Jill, and Nanci agree to hold up a bank teller and Pim rents a car for getaway purposes, all four are guilty of the crime of conspiracy to commit robbery. But, unlike accessoryship, in conspiracy all of the conspirators are guilty of all crimes committed by any one of them in furtherance of the conspiracy. Thus, if Pim had not rented a car but instead had taken Victor's automobile by killing him, all four would now additionally be guilty of murder. If any of them then commits the planned robbery, they are all guilty of robbery as well.

The history of the law of conspiracy has been full of abuses. Most notorious was its use during the McCarthy era (1950s) of persecution and prosecution of persons suspected of Communist leanings. The Smith Act of 1940 made anybody criminally liable who "knowingly or willfully advocates, abets, advises, or teaches the duty, necessity, desirability, or propriety of overthrowing or destroying the government of the United States. . . . If two or more persons *conspire* to commit any offense named in this section, each shall be . . . imprisoned not more than twenty years . . . ."[25] This conspiracy provision was widely used to find members of suspect organizations (for example, the Communist Party) guilty of conspiracy, on the basis of mere membership.

The conspiracy concept has been in disrepute as a law enforcement tool throughout history. It has been called "the lazy prosecutor's tool," because it has been easier to obtain convictions for conspiracy, with its minimal elements, than for substantive crimes, which require proof of substantial activity and harm. Today, prosecutors tend to throw in a conspiracy charge for good measure when two or more perpetrators are indicted, especially as a means of inducing a plea bargain. No doubt, in organized crime prosecutions there have been some successful and proper convictions, and perhaps that is conspiracy's remaining utility (see the Criminal Justice Abroad box).

REVIEW

Seven principles, or definitional ingredients, mark every crime. Foremost among these is the principle of legality: no crime without criminal law. Where does criminal law come from? Much comes from court decisions, known as common law. Legislatures also create criminal laws when the public demands protection against "new" crimes and to meet new situations. The unifying influence in shaping American criminal law has been the Model Penal Code of the American Law Institute. The other principles that mark every crime are the harm requirement, the causation requirement, the mens rea requirement, the concurrence requirement, and the punishment requirement.

General principles do not decide concrete cases, though they help us greatly in understanding the criminal law. In their everyday business, criminal court judges rarely refer to principles. Instead they use patterned formulas to solve frequently recurring problems. Most notable among these are the defenses. Most of the defenses are based on the alleged absence of one of the basic principles. A mistake of fact alleges that the defendant had no criminal intent; the defense of necessity alleges that there was no voluntary act on the part of the defendant; and the justification of public duty alleges that a law demanded that a law enforcement officer do something that normally is illegal (for example, use force against a suspect).

The law also has formulas to deal with situations when only a part of the crime has been committed (attempt), or when crimes are committed by several persons acting jointly (conspiracy).

The broad propositions discussed in this chapter (called the general part of the criminal law) are not arbitrary. They can be explained largely as the result of logical reasoning heavily influenced by experience, history, and political expedience. Together they are applicable to all crimes, and in that sense they are useful, necessary, and vital to the administration of the criminal law, from the street level up to the Supreme Court.

Notes

1. Richard Meryhew, "Who Killed Gary Wall? Jury Clears Man Who Stabbed Him, Blames His Doctor." Minneapolis *Star Tribune*, November 20, 1991, pp. 1, 11.

2. Jerome Hall, *General Principles of Criminal Law*, 2d ed. (Indianapolis: Bobbs-Merrill, 1960); Gerhard O. W. Mueller, "The Law of Public Wrongs—Its Concepts in the World of Reality," *Journal of Public Law* 10 (1962):203–260, 1962.

3. William F. Walsh, *A History of Anglo-American Law*, 2d ed. (Indianapolis: The Bobbs-Merrill Co., 1932, 1950), pp. 63–64.

4. Theodore T. F. Plucknett, *A Concise History of the Common Law*, 2d ed. (Rochester, N.Y.: The Lawyer's Co-operative Publ. Co., 1936), p. 396.

5. *Carrier's Case*, Y.B. 13 Edw. IV, f.9, pl.5. See Jerome Hall, *Theft, Law and Society*, 2d ed. (Indianapolis: Bobbs-Merrill Co., 1952).

6. Benjamin Franklin took the quote for *Poor Richard's Almanac* from George Herbert, *Jacula Prudentum*.

7. Gerhard O. W. Mueller, "Causing Criminal Harm," in *Essays in Criminal Science*, ed. G. O. W. Mueller, (South Hackensack, N.J.: F. B. Rothman, 1961), pp. 167–214, at 169.

8. G. O. W. Mueller, "On Common Law Mens Rea," *Minnesota Law Review* 42 (1958):1043–1104; see also Paul H. Robinson and Jane A. Grall, "Element Analysis in Defining Criminal Liability: The Model Penal Code and Beyond," *Stanford Law Review* 35(1983):681–762.

9. Wayne R. LaFave and Austin W. Scott, Jr., *Criminal Law* (St. Paul, Minn.: West, 1983), p. 222.

10. Adapted from Gerhard O. W. Mueller, "The Public Law of Wrongs—Its Concepts in the World of Reality," *Journal of Public Law* 10 (2) (1962):203–260, at 242.

11. See Richard Moran, *Knowing Right from Wrong: The Insanity Defense of Daniel McNaughten* (New York: Free Press; London: Collier Macmillan, 1981). Moran proved that McNaughten spelled his name McNaughten, though in American legal usage the spelling M'Naghten gained favor.

12. *Daniel M'Naghten's Case*, 8 Eng. Rep. 718, 722–723 (1843), 10 C.F. 200, 210–211 (1843).

13. 18 U.S.C. § 17.

14. American Law Institute, Model Penal Code, sec. 4.01.

15. Debra T. Landis, "'Guilty But Mentally Ill' Statutes: Validity and Construction," *American Law Reports*, 71 ALR 4th 702 (1991).

16. *Powell v. Texas*, 392 U.S. 514 (1968).

17. U.S. Department of Justice, Bureau of Justice Statistics, *Profile of State Prison Inmates, 1986*, Special Report NCJ-109926 (Washington, D.C.: U.S. Government Printing Office, January 1988), p. 6, Table 12.

18. Paul H. Robinson, *Fundamentals of Criminal Law* (Boston: Little, Brown, 1988), pp. 287ff.

19. *Lambert v. California*, 355 U.S. 225 (1957).

20. Basically, the defense is not available if the actor was at fault by placing himself or herself in the situation: Model Penal Code, sec. 2.09(1).

21. There is much dispute as to where to draw the line between justifications and excuses. Volumes have been written on the subject. The fact is that our law is fuzzy in this respect. Yet much hinges on the difference. Thus, a third party may intervene to stop somebody who acts under an excuse, but may not do so with respect to somebody who acts under justification. In general, see Albin Eser and George P. Fletcher, eds., *Justification and Excuse Comparative Perspectives*, (Freiburg, Germany: Max-Planck Institut, 1987), 2 vols.

22. For a legal and factual analysis of the case, see George P. Fletcher, *A Crime of Self-Defense: Bernhard Goetz and the Law on Trial* (New York: Free Press; London: Collier Macmillan 1988).

23. *Rex v. Scofield*, 1784 Cald. 402.

24. Model Penal Code, sec. 5.01(1) (c).

25. 18 U.S.C. § 2385 (our emphasis).

CHAPTER 5

THE CRIMINAL JUSTICE SYSTEM

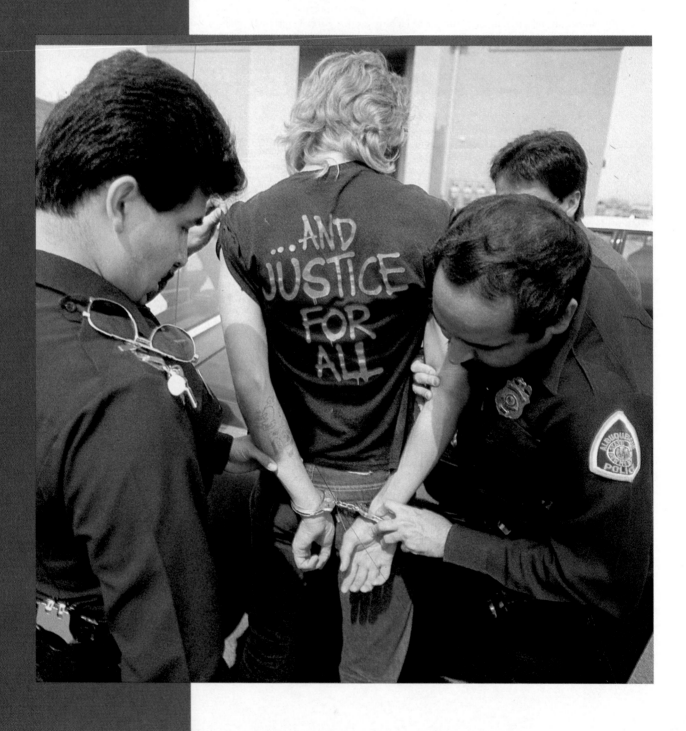

"*In dark and dirty courtrooms one young man after another describes to a tired judge how the only job available to him is peddling pills and pot. A parade of prostitutes plead guilty, only to return directly to the streets to work harder so that their new pimp, the City of New York, can be paid the fine it will demand in 30 days. Frustrated victims of burglaries, muggings and rapes seethe when they must appear for the fourth time, only to be told that they must again arrange a day off from work to return for a fifth.*

"*It is doubtful, under these conditions, that the Criminal Court is in fact a court of justice. What can be done? How can confidence in the Criminal Court be restored?*

"*These questions are important because the Criminal Court is the judicial institution closest to the lives of the people of the city. Routinely, the court adjudicates cases ranging from serious assault to turnstile jumping. Accordingly, the perception of justice, or lack of it, that the court conveys to the public is as important a function as the actual dispensing of justice.*

"*The fundamental problem is that we have asked this court to do too much. Instead of assessing culpability for crimes, the criminal court has been asked to address and indeed reverse many aspects of the decline in the quality of life in New York City.*

"*But crimes such as car abandonment, building violations, prostitution, three-card monte and even small drug sales are not effectively, or even appropriately, addressed by the traditional criminal justice process in the Criminal Court. When the court is asked to give each of these smaller offenses the full judicial treatment—a complaint, presentation of evidence and sentencing—the system clogs up. These crimes have more to do with the condition of life in New York than its crime problem. They are therefore poor candidates for the formal judicial process.[1]*" ■

But the judicial process cannot choose which criminal acts will come to it; police make these decisions. Correctional authorities cannot choose which defendants will end up serving a sentence—that is for the courts to decide. If this illustrates anything, it is the interconnectedness of the various stages of the criminal justice system. When we say system, we really mean it! Law enforcement efforts feed into the court system. The court system feeds into the correctional system.

This is not to say that all parts of the criminal justice system are in perfect harmony. There is great conflict, fierce competition over resources, and vast differences in occupational culture. Some scholars go so far as to call it a nonsystem. But this probably goes too far. After all, each and every decision made at each and every stage has consequences for later stages. The more people arrested, the more defendants in court. The more defendants in court, the more inmates in prison.

In this chapter we will first discuss different ideas of the criminal justice system, focusing on the goals and corresponding means. Next we will present the various stages of the system, from entry to exit. Throughout we will be concerned with the kinds of decisions made by criminal justice professionals—decisions that have significant consequences for the accused and the victim, as well as for the allocation of scarce resources.

MODELS OF THE CRIMINAL JUSTICE SYSTEM

The Goals

An influential group of criminal justice thinkers has argued that just as a society must maintain armed forces to defend itself against foreign aggressors, it must maintain a force of internal peacekeepers to defend itself against aggression from within. "Social defense" demands a criminal justice system, whose purpose, goal, or end is to defend society.[2] These thinkers formed an International Society for Social Defense, and their views were so influential that the first United Nations unit charged with criminal justice functions was called the Social Defence Section.[3] But there were second thoughts, and a desire for greater precision. In a worldwide debate, the thinkers finally identified two, competing or complementary goals: crime prevention and criminal justice. The United Nations unit soon took the name Crime Prevention and Criminal Justice Branch.

The prevention of crime—and of repeated crime—has been presented as an end or goal of all criminal justice systems. When a law enforcement officer separates a quarreling couple, when a probation officer guides a client away from a tavern, when a judge orders confiscation of a smuggling vessel or the arrest of a drug dealer, each acts to prevent crime. It is easy to conclude, then, that the criminal justice system is dedicated to preventing crime. But critics will immediately counter with statistics proving that the system does a poor job of this, and that it even fosters crime in a variety of ways: by criminalizing conduct in the first place, by raising the statistics, by labeling individuals as criminal (thus creating criminal careers), by making convicts unfit for life in a free society, and so on. This is not the place to argue how well the system works. Nor is it the place to point to other options for the prevention of crime, like better secondary schools, economic opportunities, and intact family units. Here we simply note that crime prevention is a recognized, although sometimes disputed, goal or end of the criminal justice system.

The other major goal or end is said to be criminal justice itself. That sounds a bit like the chicken and the egg: The end of criminal justice is criminal justice. Yet this is what proponents argue: The criminal justice system can do no more

"The 'social defense' approach demands a criminal justice system whose purpose, goal, or end is to defend society."

"It is a very easy thing to devise good laws; the difficulty is to make them effective."
Henry St. John Bolingbrooke.

"The law is not an end in itself, nor does it provide ends. It is pre-eminently a means to serve what we think is right."
Justice William J. Brennan, Jr.,
Roth v. U.S., 1957.

than deliver criminal justice. The end product must be justice (done justice, perceived justice, etc.), and at each stage of the process justice must also be applied and delivered.

But the two goals are not mutually exclusive; in fact, they complement each other. Of course we do not want to increase crime; crime prevention and control are a primary goal. (See Chapter 3, on theories of crime.) But we also do not want our criminal justice system to promote or deliver injustice. Obviously, the two goals may come into conflict, especially when it comes to prevention of repeated crime by sentencing individuals to prison.

The Means

Herbert Packer, in *The Limits of the Criminal Sanction,*[4] has made an important contribution to identifying the methods by which criminal justice seeks to achieve its goals. He presents two approaches for the criminal justice process: the due process model and the crime control model. The due process model requires strict adherence to the Constitution. The focus is squarely on the accused and on his or her rights. The focus is also on providing some balance to the power and authority of the state. Quite simply, due process protections under the Constitution force the state to fulfill its burden of proving its case against the accused. The crime control model focuses on the efficiency and effectiveness of the process. The criminal process exists to investigate crimes, screen suspects, detain dangerous defendants, and secure convictions of guilty parties. This should be done with speed and finality. Each agency at every stage of the process assumes the responsibility for dealing efficiently with the criminal case.

Packer describes the due process model as an obstacle course: Each stage creates barriers to the successful prosecution of an accused. The crime control model resembles an assembly line: Efficiency, productivity, and reliability are its hallmarks. Constitutional rights take second place to the desirability of processing offenders quickly and successfully.

This identification of two different approaches explains many of the differences in policymakers' views. The two models are the practical and theoretical extremes of how the process can be conducted. They neither explain the goals at the end of the criminal justice system nor pinpoint the operational ideal, which is to operate a criminal justice system under the rule of law.

Other objectives have been proposed for criminal justice. Wayne R. LaFave and Jerold H. Israel have articulated the following eight goals for the ideal criminal justice system[5]:

"Swift justice demands more than just swiftness."
U.S. Supreme Court Associate Justice Potter Stewart, *Time,* October 20, 1958.

• Establishing an adversarial system of adjudication. Neutral decision-makers must make decisions in a forum where opponents present interpretations of facts and law in a light most favorable to their case.

• Establishing an accusatorial system of prosecution. In such a system the state bears the burden of proving the guilt of the accused.

• Minimizing erroneous convictions. Protecting an accused from erroneous conviction is an important goal of the process.

• Minimizing the burdens of accusation and litigation. The process must reduce the likelihood that innocent people will be accused of crimes.

• Providing lay participation. The criminal justice process must not be left entirely to government officials. Lay participation can ensure objectivity and independence.

• Respecting the dignity of the individual. The criminal process must ensure respect for privacy and autonomy, as well as freedom from physical and emotional abuse.

• Maintaining the appearance of fairness. Ensuring fairness in the process is not enough. There must also be an appearance of justice and fairness to the participants and the public.

"Ensuring fairness in the process is not enough: There must also be an appearance of justice and fairness to the participants and the public."

• Achieving equality in the application of the process. Ensuring the just treatment of an accused is not enough. The criminal justice process must also ensure that like cases are treated alike.

Some of these eight goals deal with broad policy issues; others focus on tactics. In the past, the Anglo-American criminal process was purely adversarial: prosecutor and defendant were regarded as two equal adversaries whose arguments would establish the truth before the jury. Some features of the adversarial process survive: The judge sits as an umpire over two parties seeking to establish guilt or innocence. But many features have been lost, so that the process has become much more accusatorial. The state accuses, and it has the burden of proving the defendant guilty. Some of the eight goals are universally accepted (minimizing accusation or conviction of innocent people, for example); others are hotly debated. The idea of equal treatment of like cases is controversial. Cases may seem alike, yet critics assert that like cases may involve individuals of totally different character, motivation, or capacity.

The two complementary goals or ends of the criminal justice process have not yet been harmonized in practice. They continue to compete at the operational level, especially in sentencing. The means of achieving either or both goals through the criminal justice process promote even greater conflict. Insistence on due process, for example, may seem inconsistent with efficiency. Research in criminal justice may eventually resolve some of this conflict. But as Kevin N. Wright has argued, conflict over the ends and means of the criminal justice system may be desirable. This is so because competing or even antagonistic interests promote a balanced set of goals. Further, competing interests and goals encourage adaptation and change (see the Criminal Justice in Action box).[6]

FIGURE 5.1 *The paths of the criminal justice system* (*Source:* Adapted from the President's Commission on Law Enforcement and Administration of Justice, *The Challenge of Crime in a Free Society* [Washington, D.C.: U.S. Government Printing Office, 1967], pp. 8–9; in U.S. Department of Justice, Bureau of Justice Statistics, *Report to the Nation on Crime and Justice,* 2d ed. [Washington, D.C.: U.S. Government Printing Office, 1988].)

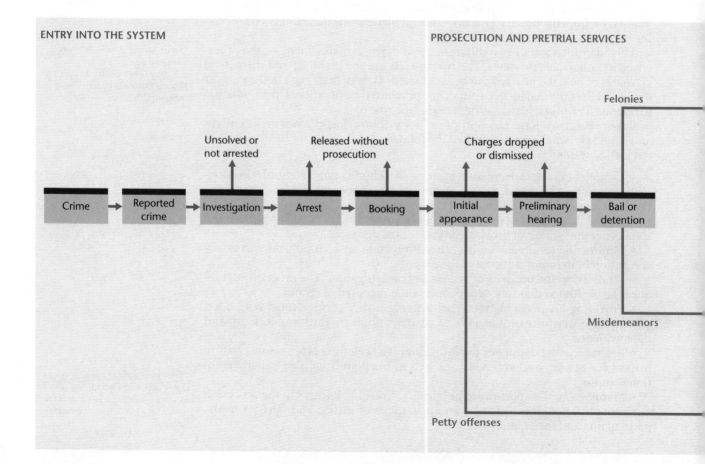

ENTRY INTO THE SYSTEM

PROSECUTION AND PRETRIAL SERVICES

Felonies

Unsolved or not arrested

Released without prosecution

Charges dropped or dismissed

Crime → Reported crime → Investigation → Arrest → Booking → Initial appearance → Preliminary hearing → Bail or detention

Misdemeanors

Petty offenses

STAGES OF THE CRIMINAL JUSTICE PROCESS

Until the 1960s, criminal justice procedures from arrest to conviction were generally not seen as an orderly process like that of a manufacturer's production line. The various procedures seemed to exist in isolation. But in 1967 the President's Commission on Law Enforcement and Criminal Justice showed the criminal justice system as an orderly process by which a product is produced.[7] Some people regard the symbolic "product" of this system as justice, others as crime control, and still others as a combination of both.

The President's Commission depicted the criminal justice system as comprising five interrelated phases with four paths (Figure 5.1). Every criminal case may potentially flow through all the phases, though most do not. In the first phase, called entry into the system, citizens play an important role by bringing criminal events to the attention of the police. The police investigate the case and identify a suspect. The judiciary issues search and arrest warrants.

The second phase, prosecution and pretrial services, is dominated by prosecutors, who prepare the charges; grand juries, who indict defendants; and judges, who conduct a series of hearings, including the initial appearance of an arrested person at court and a preliminary hearing.

The third phase, adjudication, begins with an arraignment, at which the officially accused person pleads to (answers) the formal charges (indictment or information) against him or her, and ends with a judgment of guilty or not guilty. This phase is conducted by a judge, with or without a jury. The prosecutor, representing the state and people, and the defense lawyer play the most active roles.

"Some people see the product of the system as justice, others as crime control, and still others as a combination of both."

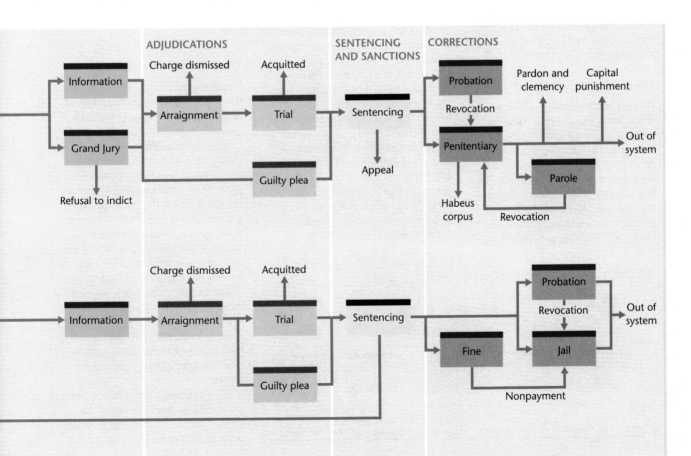

THE SYSTEM OF THE CRIMINAL JUSTICE SYSTEM

The term "criminal justice system" is so familiar that you have probably never questioned whether or not there is in fact a "system." The various components of a system form a unified whole. The steps and processes of a system are interdependent, and its agencies and actors serve a common purpose. Are these characteristics of the criminal justice system? Do the police, courts, and corrections operate this way? Are their actions interactive, interdependent, and unified?

The production process model

These questions have challenged researchers and policy analysts for years. Some see the criminal justice system as a production process—a process where "raw materials" are screened and refined (see Figure 1). The raw material of the criminal justice process is the criminal suspect. Specialists from three segments of the system are involved actively in processing this raw material: police, courts, and corrections. As the raw material moves along in the production line, it changes in character. A suspect becomes an accused, an accused becomes a defendant, a defendant becomes a convicted offender, and a convicted offender becomes a probationer or inmate. Finally, in almost every case, an inmate becomes an ex-convict.

But the criminal justice "production process" differs from a commercial process in a number of important respects. First, while in industrial production all component units are closely interconnected and subject to overall supervision and direction, the criminal justice process lacks overall coordination. There is no equivalent to a manufacturer's board of directors or a top management team.

Second, the raw material in criminal justice is human, typically reluctant to participate, and experiencing feelings of helplessness or loss of control and perhaps even anger. Because this is not the processing of inanimate raw materials, criminal justice must use forms of social control (coercive processes, including physical detention) to ensure that the processing of human beings will be efficient, orderly, and ultimately just and effective.

Third, the criminal justice system must maintain legitimacy in the community. Law enforcement officers, judges, and correction officials must have standing in the community. The criminal justice process is open to public inspection, criticism, and reform. Commercial processes are rarely open to public scrutiny except for their end products— "the market" ultimately judges the product.

Fourth, the "dropout" rate in the criminal justice system is much higher than in commercial processes. There are many diversion points along the line; very few of the original raw materials reach the end.

The wedding cake model

The one-dimensional structure of the production line analogy has prompted some researchers to propose innovative multidimensional models. Samuel Walker argues that the straight-line production analogy fails to consider that cases receive differential treatment, both in the press and in the criminal justice system. He depicts criminal justice processes (see Figure 2) in the shape of a wedding cake (1). At the top are the celebrated cases that receive disproportionate press coverage and public scrutiny. As we move down the layers of the cake, the seriousness of the crimes decreases, as do the penalties. At the lowest layer, misdemeanors, there is much less concern for procedural rights.

The wedding cake model is not an alternative explanation of the system. Rather, it shows that we are dealing with perhaps three distinct

FIGURE 1. The Production Process Model

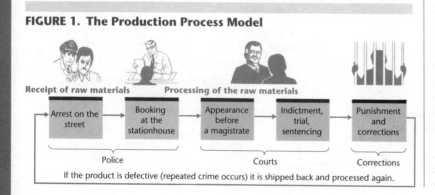

Receipt of raw materials   Processing of the raw materials

Arrest on the street → Booking at the stationhouse → Appearance before a magistrate → Indictment, trial, sentencing → Punishment and corrections

Police   Courts   Corrections

If the product is defective (repeated crime occurs) it is shipped back and processed again.

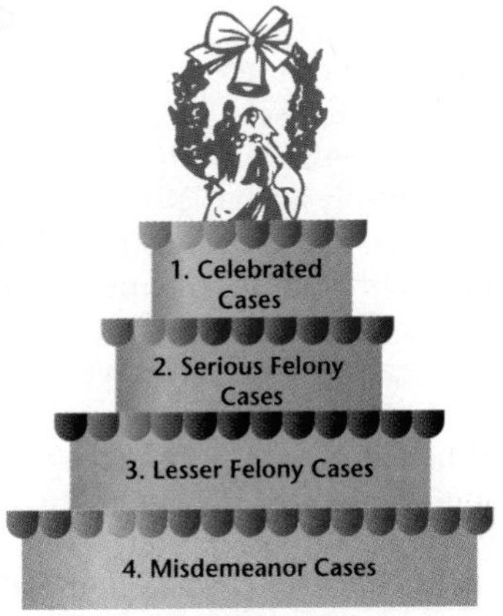
1. Celebrated Cases
2. Serious Felony Cases
3. Lesser Felony Cases
4. Misdemeanor Cases

FIGURE 2. The Wedding Cake Model

processes: the most refined and ideal one is found at the top of the cake (dispositions of highly visible cases); the least refined and most hurried one lies at the bottom (misdemeanor dispositions).

Diversion

Let us return to the high attrition rate in the criminal justice system. If we were to measure the effectiveness and efficiency of the criminal justice production process by the same standards we use for a commercial manufacturing enterprise, we would be likely to include an appearance before a bankruptcy judge. To extend the assembly line analogy, much of the raw material that starts through the process is diverted. One recent study analyzed the processing of criminal cases in Los Angeles Superior Court. In the initial screening, over 50 percent of the cases were rejected or reduced to lesser charges. From the original sample, only some 40 percent survived a preliminary hearing, 31 percent made it to the arraignment stage, and 26 percent got as far as sentencing. Only 8.4 percent of the total number of cases resulted in prison sentences. Over 67 percent of the cases (see Figure 3) were filtered out of the criminal justice process entirely (2). Imagine a business where over two-thirds of the raw materials being processed are disposed of prior to completion; then consider the rates of re-offense and re-arrest in our society. No business engaged in commercial production could operate successfully with such an enormous product return rate.

One final difference between assembly line production and the criminal justice process: Raw materials or semi-finished products do not ride through the criminal justice system on a conveyor belt, guided by the magic hand of a robot. Rather, at every stage of the criminal justice process a human being makes a decision that affects the fate of another human being.

SOURCES

1. Samuel Walker, *Sense and Nonsense about Crime* (Belmont, Calif.: Wadsworth, 1985).
2. Huey-tsyh Chen, "Dropping In and Dropping Out: Judicial Decisionmaking in the Disposition of Felony Arrests," *Journal of Criminal Justice* 19 (1991):1–17.

QUESTIONS FOR DISCUSSION

1. Is the criminal justice system really a system? Defend your opinion.
2. If you were arrested, would you rather go through a system in which humans made the decisions at each step or one in which a computer program made the decisions? Explain.
3. Walker's wedding cake model suggests that "exciting" cases are more likely to be handled carefully and properly. Suggest some reforms.

FIGURE 3. Case Flow: Los Angeles Superior Court

(*Source:* Huey-tsyh Chen, "Dropping In and Dropping Out: Judicial Decisionmaking in the Disposition of Felony Arrests," *Journal of Criminal Justice* 19 [1991], pp. 1–17.)

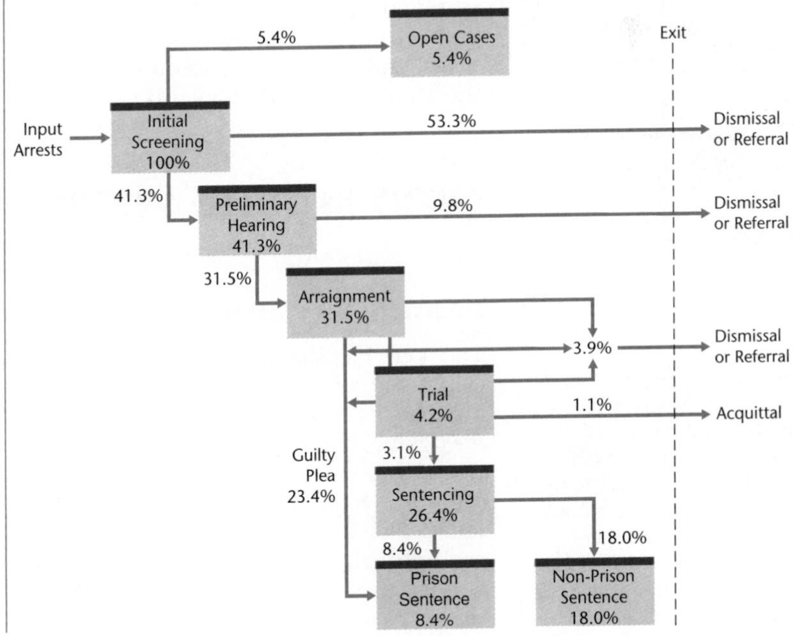
5.4%
Open Cases 5.4%
Exit
Input Arrests
Initial Screening 100%
53.3%
Dismissal or Referral
41.3%
Preliminary Hearing 41.3%
9.8%
Dismissal or Referral
31.5%
Arraignment 31.5%
3.9%
Dismissal or Referral
Trial 4.2%
1.1%
Acquittal
Guilty Plea 23.4%
3.1%
Sentencing 26.4%
8.4%
18.0%
Prison Sentence 8.4%
Non-Prison Sentence 18.0%

The fourth phase consists of sentencing and sanctions. In most cases, in most states, jurors do not participate in sentencing. The judge imposes the sentence, usually after hearing a presentence investigation (PSI) report prepared by a probation officer. Prosecutors, defense lawyers, and defendants have their say, and in some states victims do as well.

The fifth and final phase, corrections, is in the hands of the executive branch of government. Its Department of Corrections executes the sentence imposed by the court. Even though courts defer to correction officials in matters of inmate care, custody, and control, courts require them to comply with the law.

The flowchart devised by the President's Commission shows four different paths through the system (Figure 5.1). The first path is for major crimes, or felonies (top layers of Walker's wedding cake [see the Criminal Justice in Action box]); the second is for minor crimes, or misdemeanors (bottom layer of the cake). The paths differ. Misdemeanors normally require no grand jury indictment and no trial by jury, and the sanctions imposed are jail sentences of one year or less or fines, rather than imprisonment (meaning confinement in a prison for more than a year). A third path is for petty offenses, with summary proceedings resulting in minor sanctions, usually fines. (A fourth path, described in Chapter 17, is for juveniles. It resembles the paths for adults in many respects, except that the proceedings are less formal and rarely include juries.)

If the President's Commission had worked three decades later, it would have added at least three more paths. One of these would depict the process used for the growing mass of violators of regulatory legislation affecting business, banking, commerce, and the environment. Such offenders travel a rather distinct and novel route. The police investigating these offenders do not generally wear a uniform; they are federal and state bureaucrats sitting in office buildings, just like the offenders. Hearings are held before administrative tribunals—rarely before criminal courts—and the conclusion of the case may be a consent decree; a civil fine; sometimes even imprisonment, perhaps in a minimum security federal facility, a "club fed," a "country-club prison."

Yet another path would show the now more clearly recognized distinct route of crime victims through the criminal justice system (we deal with that in Chapter 18). Finally, there is an incipient separate path for international criminals (see Chapter 19).

As the flowchart indicates, the traditional paths through the criminal justice system do not end at a single exit; they lead to many exits. An accused person's path through the system is not fixed or predestined. The direction that path takes, and its end, depend on the actions of several decision-makers, including the accused. Let's see how this works.

"An accused person's path through the system is not fixed or predestined."

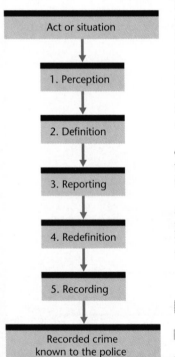

FIGURE 5.2 *The process of bringing crime to the attention of police* (*Source:* R. F. Sparks, H. G. Genn, and D. J. Dodd, *Surveying Victims: A Study of the Measurement of Criminal Victimization, Perceptions of Crime, and Attitudes to Criminal Justice* [Chichester, England: Wiley, 1977], p. 6.)

ENTRY INTO THE SYSTEM

Decisions by Victims

The mere fact that a crime has taken place does not, in and of itself, activate the criminal justice system. A series of decisions—some complex, others simple—must be made to begin the machinery turning. For a criminal act to be *known to the police*, initiating the process, the act must first be *perceived* by an individual (the car is not in the garage where I left it). The act must then be *defined* or *classified* as one that places it within the jurisdiction of the criminal justice system (a theft has taken place), and it must be *reported* to the police. Once the police are notified, they classify it and often *redefine* what may have taken place (a youngster has taken the car out without parental permission) before *recording* the act as a *crime known to the police* (Figure 5.2).

Victims of criminal acts have been called the "most influential" of all the decision-makers, or "principal gatekeepers," of the entire criminal justice process.[8] For many offenses, except for the victim's report of the crime to the police the system would never be involved. Early studies of the role of victim reporting reveal that approximately 95 percent of all crime known to the police comes from victim initiatives.[9]

But surveys also reveal that victims often do not report offenses to the police. Some researchers attribute failure to report to the victims' concern for their present and future safety.[10] Others have found that feelings of self-blame and loss of personal control may inhibit reporting. One recent study suggested that much of the nonreporting of minor criminal victimization may be accounted for by efforts on the part of the victim to engage in self-help, that is, ignoring it, talking it out, engaging in interpersonal violence, or receiving insurance proceeds.[11] The literature on victim reporting is certainly clear on one issue—reasons for reporting or not reporting vary according to the crime committed. Consider why victims of rape may fail to report. Recent victimization surveys reveal that 35 percent of victims consider it a "private/personal matter," 18 percent are of the opinion that nothing can be done because they cannot prove they have been victimized, and 16 percent fear reprisals.[12]

Decisions by the Police

Once information about a possible crime has come to the attention of the police, a decision has to be made whether to investigate the case. The police cannot possibly investigate every complaint. Because of heavy case loads, they emphasize the investigation of major crimes. Petty larcenies are rarely investigated because of the sheer bulk of the cases and the shortage of investigators.

Other factors are also on the minds of police when they decide whether to make an arrest or to seek an arrest warrant, or to drop an investigation entirely. They consider, for example, public ambivalence about the significance of a given criminal law, the probability that a witness will or will not cooperate, and whether an arrest is too harsh a response to a particular act. The police may choose from a series of alternatives to arrest ranging from outright release to release with a citation to release of a youngster into the custody of parents or guardians.[13] As Anthony Amsterdam has noted: "The criminal justice process, particularly in its early stages, is honey-combed with police and prosecutorial discretion."[14] It is worth considering that (1) not all those known to have committed a crime are arrested; (2) after arrest a "desk officer" may change the charge or go so far as to reject the arrest; and (3) investigating officers may, at any point in their investigation, consider the arrest too weak, and reject it.

"Victims of criminal acts have been called the 'most influential' of all the decision-makers, or 'principal gatekeepers,' of the entire criminal justice process."

"Justice is a machine that, when someone has given it a starting push, rolls on of itself."
John Galsworthy.

"The criminal justice process, particularly in its early stages, is honey-combed with police and prosecutorial discretion."
Anthony Amsterdam, *Trial Manual for the Defense of Criminal Cases*, 1988.

Upon receiving a report of a serious crime, police will make an on-the-scene investigation, like that shown here of a murder scene. The investigation starts the criminal justice process.

Legal Standards

What legal criteria determine when and whether a suspect can be brought into the criminal justice system? When may the system do something to or about a suspect? As we will see in Chapter 8, the Constitution, as interpreted by the Supreme Court, provides some of these criteria.

The Constitution states that nobody may be "seized" (taken into the criminal justice process) except on a warrant issued on the basis of probable cause of having committed a crime. For almost two centuries, the **probable cause** requirement was deemed to establish the point at which potential guilt is clear enough to take a person into custody. Ideally this determination is made by a judge or magistrate on the basis of the testimony of witnesses (including the police) delivered under oath that a given suspect has committed a given crime. In practice, the probable cause decision is frequently made by a law enforcement officer at the scene of the crime. Neither magistrates who issue warrants of arrest nor police officers who make an arrest without a warrant are guided by any precise standard of probable cause: The Supreme Court has ruled that the police have probable cause to take a suspect into custody when "the facts and circumstances within their knowledge and of which they [have] reasonable trustworthy information [are] sufficient to warrant a prudent man in believing that the [suspect] had committed or was committing an offence."[15]

This definition relies on vague terms—"reasonable trustworthy information" and "prudent man." Nevertheless, arrests made without probable cause, or not resting on a warrant issued on sworn testimony before a judge and based on a determination of probable cause, are considered unreasonable seizures of the person and in violation of the Fourth Amendment. Evidence taken in the course of such an arrest may be ruled inadmissible and barred from use at a trial.

probable cause
Set of facts that would induce a reasonable person to believe that the accused committed the offense in question; the minimum evidence requirement for an arrest, according to the Fourth Amendment.

A heroin-crack bust by a tactical narcotics team in Brooklyn, New York. This procedure is a search and seizure, requiring officers to comply with the Fourth Amendment's reasonableness and warrant requirements in obtaining evidence.

The practice of finding inadmissible evidence that is illegally obtained is called the **exclusionary rule.** As we will see in Chapter 8, the rule is a judicially created rule of law designed to deter the police from engaging in illegal practices and to keep the courts from condoning such conduct. The Supreme Court ruled in 1969, in *Mapp v. Ohio,* that all state courts in the country must apply the exclusionary rule as a matter of constitutional law.[16] The ruling has been hailed by civil libertarians, who view it as a necessary safeguard against police misconduct, and strongly attacked by conservatives, who argue that now an arbitrary measure "handcuffs" the police.

exclusionary rule
Rule prohibiting use of illegally obtained evidence in a court of law.

These two positions illustrate the fundamental issues in a Fourth Amendment analysis—that is, the need for effective law enforcement versus the need to protect individual rights and liberties. Conservatives call for unhampered law enforcement and liberals ask for the protection of rights. Research, as we will see in Chapter 8, suggests that law enforcement has not been seriously hindered by the exclusionary rule.

"The exclusionary rule is viewed as a necessary safeguard by civil libertarians and by conservatives as an arbitrary measure that 'handcuffs' the police."

Recent Supreme Court decisions have strengthened police powers. Faced with mounting public concern over street crime in the 1960s, the Supreme Court was under pressure to legitimize prudent police action for the purpose of preventing a specific crime about to be committed, even when an officer had no probable cause to make an arrest. In 1968 the Supreme Court acknowledged the propriety of police intervention when evidence against a suspect fell short of probable cause. If a police officer has **reasonable suspicion** that a person might be engaged in the commission of a crime, the officer is authorized to stop the person, ask questions, and frisk him or her to make sure that the suspect is not armed and dangerous.[17]

reasonable suspicion
Warranted suspicion (short of probable cause) that a person may be engaged in the commission of a crime.

In some circumstances law enforcement officers can intervene even short of reasonable suspicion. The highest court of New York, the New York Court of Appeals, stated in the case of *People v. de Bour* (1967) that police officers have the right and duty to approach a person for purposes of making an inquiry on the basis of "articulable facts" that "crime is afoot."[18]

The Right to Counsel

Assume that a police officer or a magistrate has made the decision to arrest a suspect, and a suspect has in fact been arrested. What happens now?

Immediately after the arrest, when the person is in custody, the arresting officer must recite the ***Miranda* warning** explaining the rights of an arrestee. The *Miranda* warning derives from one of the Supreme Court's most important rulings, which laid down the standards of procedural fairness mandated by the Fourth, Fifth, and Sixth Amendments to the Constitution (1966; see Chapter 8).[19] If the warning is not given, a judge may exclude from evidence presented at trial any incriminating statement the arrestee may have made, as well as any evidence that resulted from it.[20] Once the suspect has been taken into custody, the processing of the event and of the offender begins with booking, the taking of fingerprints and mug shots (identifying photographs), the filling out of forms, and detention in holding pens.

***Miranda* warning**
Warning that explains the rights of an arrestee, and that police recite at the time of the arrest or prior to interrogation.

In the case of *Gideon v. Wainwright* (1963), the Supreme Court laid down the rule that every person charged with a crime that may lead to incarceration has the right to an attorney, and that the state must pay for that service if the defendant cannot afford to do so.[21] This case, which involved an indigent Florida defendant, established the universal right to free defense counsel for the poor. It has been implemented nationwide by the provision of assigned counsel, public defenders, contract counsel, or legal aid. As we will see in Chapter 11, however, these defense lawyers, under tremendous case load pressures, often suggest plea bargains.[22] So their decisions, too, have a considerable impact on the direction and outcome of the process.

"Every person charged with a crime that may lead to incarceration has the right to an attorney, and the state must pay for that service if the defendant cannot afford to do so."

WHAT HAPPENS WHEN THERE ARE NO POLICE?

. . . it is incumbent upon the Nuer to avenge the death of a kinsperson. If a man kills someone, by accident or intent, he immediately seeks sanctuary in the home of a leopard-skin chief. A leopard-skin chief holds no formal political power; he is simply a man whom people respect and would not directly challenge or attack. His home is inviolate. In homicide cases, the leopard-skin chief acts as an intermediary between the murderer and the victim's kin, trying to persuade the latter to accept compensation (perhaps forty or fifty head of cattle) in lieu of blood vengeance. He has no way of *forcing* the injured parties to accept a settlement, but in most cases they do. The leopard-skin chief is successful because he enables both sides to avoid a blood feud neither really wants without losing face. Typically, the kin of the dead person refuse to accept payment for several months, but eventually concede—not because they forgive the murderer, but out of respect for the chief. The chief's intervention gives them an excuse not to fight. (1)

All peoples have shared ideas about proper behavior—and all peoples have formal or informal methods of settling disputes and ending conflicts. Social control is maintained by a variety of mechanisms, of which police forces are only a recent invention. Although they have no police, lawyers, courts, or prisons, the Nuer, a tribal society of the Sudan, have a way to deal with homicide.

When there are no police

The Nuer are a relatively small, rural, agricultural, and sometimes nomadic society in which people live in small groups. In such societies, designated police officers make their appearance only when many clans or bands come together for a ceremony or for some other social occasion. One example in North America was the annual buffalo hunt among American Plains Indians, when warriors would be appointed to serve as police officers for the duration of the hunt, until the groups dispersed again to their home grounds.

Standing police forces are a feature of urbanization, and by now almost all the world's societies are urbanized and so used to the presence of police forces that life without them probably seems unimaginable. What would happen if there suddenly were no police in a society long accustomed to having an appointed force to deal with disputes and maintain law and order? Let us look at two examples in Europe half a century ago.

When there are suddenly no police

Nearly fifty years ago in Denmark during World War II

. . . the Germans arrested the entire Danish police force in September of 1944. During the remainder of the occupation, police duties were carried out by an improvised and unarmed defense-guard which, practically speaking, was incapable of doing anything unless the offender was caught in the act. The Danish District Attorney, Jorgen Trolle,

chief of public prosecution in Copenhagen, has described the development during this time in the extraordinarily interesting book *Syv Maaneder uden Politi (Seven Months without Police)* (Copenhagen, 1945). Criminality increased immensely, but there was a great difference in the various types of offenses. While in 1939 only ten robberies were reported to the Copenhagen police, the figure by 1943 had increased to ten per month as a result of wartime conditions. After the action against the police, the figure rose rapidly to over 100 per month, and it continued to increase. (2)

Another instance of a country suddenly deprived of its police shows that new attempts to control crime may result from the deprivation. In Germany at the end of World War II, the country found itself without a police force. The old police, tainted by affiliation with the Nazi regime, had vanished. The military police forces of the occupying powers had more important things to do than watch over the civilians, and they were slow and cautious in organizing a more democratic police. With cities and towns plagued by armed robberies and burglaries, the citizens formed watchgroups that patrolled neighborhoods, armed only with canes and bats. These were soon augmented by civilian watchmen, appointed by the towns, and soon thereafter civilian, unarmed police forces were established by military and civilian authorities. These were then uniformed and, gradually, armed. Here, compressed into the span of just a few years, was the entire evolution of policing.

SOURCES

1. Fred Plog, Clifford J. Jolly, and Daniel G. Bates, *Anthropology: Decisions, Adaptation, and Evolution* (New York: Alfred A. Knopf, 1976), p. 439.
2. Johannes Andenaes, *The General Part of the Criminal Law of Norway* (South Hackensack, N.J.: Fred B. Rothman, 1965), pp. 70–71.

QUESTIONS FOR DISCUSSION

Imagine that the police of your community suddenly disappeared.

1. Would a major crime wave occur instantly? Why or why not?
2. Would police duties be taken over by other law enforcement agencies such as the sheriff's force, the state police, or federal law enforcement agencies? What problems might such action cause?
3. Would citizens or citizen groups form civilian self-defense forces? How effective do you think these would be in preventing or fighting crime?

A German soldier directs traffic in occupied Copenhagen, which had no police force for seven months in 1944–1945.

PROSECUTION AND PRETRIAL SERVICES

During the prosecution and pretrial services phase, prosecutors and judges make the decisions. Far fewer persons go through this phase than enter the system. Many arrested persons have already been diverted out of the system; others will be diverted at this stage, when charges are dropped or cases dismissed. Charges may be dropped for many reasons. Perhaps the evidence is not strong enough to support probable cause. Perhaps the arrested person is a juvenile who should be dealt with by the juvenile justice system, or a mentally disturbed person who requires hospitalization. Perhaps the judge believes that justice is best served by compassion.

The Judicial Decision to Release

An arrested person must promptly be taken before a magistrate, a judge at the lowest level of the judicial hierarchy, who makes a determination that probable cause exists. The magistrate will use a standard of probable cause a bit tougher than the police officer's. For one thing, the magistrate has more time to view the evidence, to reflect, and then to decide, than the police officer had at the scene of the crime. The magistrate must also repeat the *Miranda* warning and then decide whether to permit the defendant to be released on bail or on percentage bail (the defendant deposits with the court only a certain percentage of the bail set); to release on recognizance (ROR; no bail required on condition that the defendant appear for trial and remain law-abiding in the meantime); to release the defendant into someone's custody; or to detain the defendant in jail pending further proceedings.

In making the decision to release, judges or magistrates are strongly influenced by prosecutors' views as to whether a given defendant is a safe risk for release. In most states, release criteria have been enacted into law. Historically, however, the only criterion for release on bail has been whether the defendant can be relied on to be present for the next court appearance. In practice, judges tend to rely on such factors as the gravity of the charge and the probability that the defendant may commit a crime or harass victims if released.[23] The District of Columbia and a few other jurisdictions permit "preventive detention" when there is a high probability that the defendant may commit a crime if released. Despite the difficulty of predicting human behavior, the Supreme Court has ruled that it is constitutional to deny bail to a person who is considered dangerous.[24]

"Historically, the only criterion for release on bail has been whether the defendant can be relied on to be present for the next court appearance."

The Preliminary Hearing

preliminary hearing
Preview of a trial held in court before a judge, in which the prosecution must produce sufficient evidence for the case to proceed to trial.

The next step in the process in many states is the **preliminary hearing,** a preview of the trial in court before a judge, in which the prosecution must produce enough evidence to convince the judge that the case should proceed to trial or to the grand jury. In many jurisdictions the preliminary hearing is officially considered another probable cause hearing, but what emerges is more than probable cause. In this proceeding, conducted with some of the rights given the accused at trials—cross-examination of witnesses and the introduction of evidence under stringent rules—enough evidence must be produced to *bind the defendant over* to the grand jury, in other words, to constitute reasonable inference of guilt or reasonable grounds to believe the defendant is guilty. In the preliminary hearing, in which the defense presents no evidence, the defendant (and the defense attorney) have the advantage of finding out how the prosecution is developing its case. The defense attorney's decision—whether to enter a plea or to engage in plea negotiations—depends very much on what happens during the preliminary hearing.

The Decision to Charge and to Indict

No matter what the result of the preliminary hearing, the decision to charge the defendant with a crime rests with the prosecutor. Even in states where a grand jury must determine whether a defendant is to be indicted for a felony, it is the prosecutor who decides in the first place whether to place a case before the grand jury. The prosecutor also decides what evidence to present to the grand jury and how to present it.

In one study, researchers found that the prosecutor's reasons not to proceed after an arrest vary by offense. Of all reasons given for not proceeding with robbery cases, 43 percent were "witness problem(s);" 35 percent were "insufficiency of evidence;" and 22 percent were "other." For nonviolent property offenses, the reasons were 25 percent "witness problems;" 37 percent "insufficiency of evidence;" and 36 percent "other."[25]

The **grand jury** is one of the oldest institutions of the Anglo-American criminal justice system. It has been abolished in Britain, but in most American states it has been retained for serious (felony) cases to screen the prosecution's evidence, in secret hearings, and decide whether the defendant should be formally charged with a crime.

Federal grand juries are composed of 16 to 23 citizens, and an indictment in the federal criminal process requires the concurrence of at least twelve grand jurors.[26] State rules are similar. The indictment must rest on evidence indicating a prima facie case against the defendant. A **prima facie case** exists when there seems to be sufficient evidence to convict the defendant. The case may still be defeated by evidence at trial that raises reasonable doubt or constitutes a legal excuse. Since that is a strong requirement, most indicted defendants are inclined to make a plea bargain at this point. The conviction rate of persons who stand trial is high. Of every sixteen persons indicted, ten plead guilty (usually in a plea bargain) and four go to trial. Three of the four are convicted; only one is acquitted, dismissed by the judge, or dismissed by the prosecutor.[27]

"No matter what the result of a preliminary hearing, the decision to charge the defendant with a crime rests with the prosecutor."

grand jury
Panel of sixteen to twenty-three citizens who screen the prosecution's evidence, in secret hearings, to decide whether someone should be formally charged with a crime.

prima facie case
Case in which there is evidence that would warrant the conviction of the defendant unless otherwise contradicted; a case that meets evidentiary requirements for grand jury indictment.

Serial murderer Jeffrey Dahmer arrives in a Milwaukee courtroom in January 1992 for a pretrial or preliminary hearing at which the prosecution must present enough evidence to convince the judge there are reasonable grounds to believe the defendant is guilty.

As soon as the grand jury has indicted, or the prosecutor has made a decision to charge the defendant and has informed defense counsel accordingly, the stage is set for plea bargaining. This process is part of the Anglo-American system, under which a trial always proceeds in accordance with the prosecution's charge and the defendant's response to it: a plea of not guilty.

Plea-Bargaining

"Every criminal defendant exercises some power over the way the case is to be conducted."

indictment
Accusation against a criminal defendant rendered by a grand jury on the basis of evidence constituting a prima facie case.

information
Accusation against a defendant prepared by a prosecuting attorney.

Every criminal defendant exercises some power over the way the case is to be conducted. A defendant who pleads guilty admits all the facts alleged in the accusation, whether it is an **indictment** or an **information,** and all the legal implications of those facts. He or she admits to being guilty as charged, and no trial is needed. A defendant who pleads not guilty denies all the facts and their legal implications and forces the government (the prosecutor) to prove guilt in a criminal trial.

The idea arose centuries ago that both prosecution and defense could benefit if they were to agree on a plea that would save the government the expense of a trial and the defendant the risk of severe punishment if he or she were found guilty. By the mid-twentieth century it had become common practice in the United States for prosecutors and defense attorneys to discuss the charges against criminal defendants and to agree on a reduced or modified plea that would spare the state the cost of a trial and guarantee the defendant a sentence more lenient than the original charge warranted.

At first such plea negotiations were quite clandestine and officially denied. In fact, when accepting a plea, the judge would always inquire whether the plea was freely made, and the defendant always answered yes, when in fact the plea was the result of a bargain in which the defendant and the prosecutor manipulated each other into a deal. Contemporary legislation, federal and state, fully recognizes guarantees that no one be coerced and that all pleas are voluntarily entered, with full awareness of the consequences.

The practice of plea-bargaining today is widespread. A Bureau of Justice Statistics report has estimated that in urban areas guilty pleas outnumbered trial by about 17 to 1, and nearly all of those guilty pleas were negotiated.[28]

Nevertheless, the process of plea-bargaining invites injustices. Defendants who are legally not guilty, for example, may feel inclined to accept a plea bargain in the face of strong evidence. Other defendants may plead guilty to a lesser charge even though the evidence was obtained in violation of constitutional guarantees. In some cases, by "overcharging" (charging murder instead of manslaughter, for example), a prosecutor may coerce a defendant into pleading guilty to the lower charge, in effect forcing him or her to relinquish the right to a jury trial.

As we will see in Chapter 12, research on why defendants accept plea bargains and on the factors that weigh heavily in the decisions is inconclusive.[29] Nevertheless, abolishing plea-bargaining would require significant changes and reforms in criminal law and procedure and thus in the entire criminal justice system. Until such changes and reforms are achieved, if ever, the system will continue to rely on the decisions of prosecutors and defense counsels to agree on a plea.

"Abolishing plea-bargaining would require significant changes and reforms in criminal law and procedure, and thus in the entire criminal justice system."

If prosecutor and defense counsel have agreed on a plea bargain, for example, reducing the charge from murder to manslaughter or reducing the number of charges from four counts of larceny to one, the judge will have to decide whether that bargain is in the interest of justice. Before accepting the bargained plea, the judge must:

- inform the defendant of the implications of the plea (that the defendant can now be sentenced),
  - ascertain that the facts support the plea,
  - accept the plea,[30]
  - impose sentence.

The second of these requirements is particularly important, as it requires the judge to adjudicate the facts of the case to determine whether the plea of guilty is warranted. This determination of fact may amount to a miniature trial.

If no plea bargain is agreed on, the case will be set for trial.

ADJUDICATION AND SENTENCING

Defendants may choose to be tried by a judge (a bench trial) or by a jury (consisting usually of twelve citizens, but as few as six in some states for lesser offenses).[31] In a jury trial the judge rules on matters of law, instructs the jurors about relevant legal questions and definitions, and tells them how to apply the law to the facts of the case.

A defendant may prefer a jury trial or a bench trial for any number of reasons. When a defense is based largely on the application and interpretation of technical legal propositions, a judge is likely to be the preferable choice. If the defense appeals more to sympathy and emotion, a jury is likely to be the better choice. Much research has been done on the functions and functioning of judges and juries, beginning with the University of Chicago Jury Project in the 1950s.[32] Much of that research focused on whether jurors often differ widely and fail to reach decisions. Apparently they do not; most juries come to a unanimous verdict. That was believed to be the general requirement under American law. In a surprise decision in 1972, however, the Supreme Court ruled that a conviction decided on by fewer than all twelve jurors is constitutionally acceptable.[33]

If a defendant has not been diverted out of the system, has pleaded guilty, or, after a plea of not guilty, has been tried and convicted, the next step in the process is the imposition of a sentence. In some states, with respect to some crimes, the statute leaves the sentencing judge no choice: A mandatory sentence is imposed by law. But in most states judges still have some choice. The judge must decide whether to place the defendant on probation and, if so, on what type of probation; whether to impose a sentence of incarceration, and for what length of time; whether to impose a minimum or maximum term (or both), or to leave the sentence open-ended (indeterminate) within statutory limits; whether to impose a fine, and how much; whether to order compensation for the victims; whether to impose court costs; and so on. Criminologists Don Gottfredson and Bridget Stecher conducted research on what factors judges take into consideration when they select an "appropriate" sentence. In studying seventeen judges who sentenced 982 adult offenders, they found that the main objective in 36 percent of the cases was rehabilitation, followed by 34 percent "other purposes including general deterrence," 17 percent retribution, 9 percent special deterrence, and 4 percent incapacitation.[34]

In making sentencing decisions, judges consider the offenders' personal characteristics, their past, their problems, and their needs. The principal guidance and advice comes from probation departments. These are part of the court system, and they operate under the court's supervision. To help the court find the most appropriate sentencing decision, the probation department supplies the judge with a presentence investigation report on every convicted offender.

To avoid bias that results in different sentences for more or less similar offenses and offenders, policymakers and researchers have developed **sentencing guidelines.** These guidelines assign specific values to the important sentencing criteria—principally the seriousness of the offense and possibly prior record and other factors. Such guidelines are meant to assist judges in selecting the length and type of punishment.

"If criminals wanted to grind justice to a halt, they could do it by banding together and all pleading not guilty."
Dorothy Wright Wilson, Dean UCLA Law Center, quoted in *LA Times,* August 11, 1974.

sentencing guidelines
Scheme to limit the discretion of judges in imposing sentences, requiring them to give specific weight to a limited number of factors.

"THE LOST AND SOMETIMES FOUND"

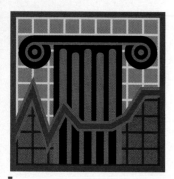

If you find the criminal justice system complex and unwieldy, you will be in good company in the Baltimore City Jail. The jail was once well known for its overcrowding, escapes, and organizational disarray. Now it is better known for its "lost" inmates.

When in July 1991 the state of Maryland took control of the beleaguered jail, state investigators found more than 100 lost inmates—inmates who once were charged with a crime or assigned a court date but forgotten, as well as inmates everyone thought had been released but were still imprisoned. The examples are hair-raising:

- A man charged with shoplifting was held for more than 500 days without a trial date (1).
- A man was held for thirteen months on arson charges without a scheduled court appearance because jailers thought he had been released.
- A man was held five months on traffic charges without a scheduled court date.
- A woman was held for 1,210 days thinking that she was there awaiting trial for theft, when she was actually serving an indefinite term for contempt of court in a child custody case.
- A man who jail administrators thought was awaiting trial on robbery and assault charges for over two years was actually not in the jail at all; he was living in a mental hospital over twenty miles away.

After an in-depth investigation, Commissioner LaMont W. Flanagan announced the discovery of a total of 114 forgotten inmates (2).

The problem of warrants outstanding

"Clients" of the criminal justice system are not lost only in city jails. Every year hundreds of thousands of defendants fail to show up at a scheduled court date, and many of these are eventually all but forgotten. A 1983 news story reported that the courts had issued 312,000 arrest warrants for people who had jumped bail or otherwise failed to make their court appearances in New York City; 31,000 of these were for felony charges, many of which were violent crimes (3). Over 500 new arrest warrants are issued daily for defendants who fail to show in New York.

The problem of failure to appear in court is nationwide. In San Diego municipal courts, there are over 700,000 outstanding arrest warrants. In Cook County Court, Chicago, nearly 35 percent of all defendants do not appear for scheduled court dates. For the 120,000 outstanding arrest warrants, there are only twenty-six officers in the Cook County Sheriff's Warrant Section to follow up on them.

Former New York City Police Commissioner Robert J. McGuire has summed up a prevailing view: "The number of warrants outstanding is horrendous" (3). Some see serious implications in the backlog: "In short, 'minor crimes' have been decriminalized," notes sociologist and political commentator Ernest van den Haag. "The system is too busy with major ones" (4). New York County District Attorney Robert Morgenthau has stated, "The problem is extraordinarily large. We need a different attitude toward fleeing—that is, that the courts won't tolerate it" (3).

Washington's Failure to Appear Unit

But is the large number of "no-shows" indicative of defendants "fleeing"? The director of an innovative program in Washington, D.C., doesn't think so. Mohammed Chaudhari heads the Pretrial Services Agency's Failure to Appear Unit in the D.C. Superior Court. With twelve years of research and experience to back him up, Chaudhari says that defendants often fail to appear in court because of system-related problems over which defendants have no control (see Table 1). Chaudhari's office tracks down defendants and verifies their excuses, and he says many more miss their court appearances due to incompetence in the criminal justice system than because they are lazy or irresponsible. Defendants frequently fail to receive a notice of the proceeding, are sent to the wrong courtroom, or are detained elsewhere by the system at the time of their trials. Other "no-shows" have been found by his office to have been killed on city streets before their court date arrived (5).

Chaudhari's work saves the system—and the taxpayer—lots of money. Defendants can surrender to his unit, and very few are then prosecuted for their initial failure to appear in court. The surrender costs the city approximately $25, com-

TABLE 1 Excuses Offered by Defendants for Missed D.C. Superior Court Dates, 1989	
System-related	
Incarcerated	180
Notification problem	177
Court problem	62
Transfer failure	31
Attorney problem	28
Subtotal	478
Defendant-related	
Forgot/confused	197
Sick	129
Transportation problem	86
Family emergency	68
Subtotal	480
Other	
Hospitalized	359
Miscellaneous	195
Inpatient drug/alcohol	69
Dead	17
Subtotal	640
Total	1,598

SOURCE: Daniel Klaidman, "Bureaucracy That Works; 'Mr. Lost and Found' Woos Court's No-Shows," *Legal Times,* February 25, 1991, p. 1.

pared with $1,200 for each defendant arrested, booked, and jailed for failure to appear. A different approach to clear warrant backlogs was tried in San Diego, where an amnesty program offered traffic crime offenders an opportunity to pay off their fines without further prosecution (6).

Losing clients in the criminal justice system frustrates police, court, and corrections officials. Police arrest and re-arrest. Courts waste time and money on no-shows and resulting dismissals. Correctional institutions expend unnecessary resources on inmates who should be released. But programs like Chaudhari's offer hope. While Washington's arrest rate has more than doubled in ten years, its no-show rate is one of the lowest in the country. New York City, Portland,

Boulder, and other cities are trying similar programs; perhaps fewer "lost" defendants will be the result.

SOURCES

1. Paul W. Valentine, "Inmate Forgotten in Baltimore Jail; Shoplifting Suspect Was Held 500 Days Awaiting Trial Date," *The Washington Post,* August 24, 1991, p. B3.
2. ArLynn Leiber Presser, "Lost and Found: Baltimore Jail Officials Find Forgotten Inmates," *ABA Journal,* November 1991, p. 42.
3. Marcia Chambers, "Thousands Ignore New York City Court Date," *The New York Times,* December 4, 1983, p. 1.
4. Ernest van den Haag, "Worse Than a Crime: The Blunders of Our Political System Have Made Crime a Virtually Risk-Free Enterprise," *National Review,* January 20, 1992, p. 48.
5. Daniel Klaidman, "Bureaucracy That Works; 'Mr. Lost and Found' Woos Court's No-Shows," *Legal Times,* February 25, 1991, p. 1.
6. Leonard Bernstein, "Court Will Offer Scofflaws a Bargain Deal," *Los Angeles Times,* January 29, 1992, p. B3.

QUESTIONS FOR DISCUSSION

1. If it is true that America's criminal justice system is overburdened, would you support decriminalization of minor crimes so that more serious crimes could be dealt with more effectively? Where would you draw the line between "minor" and "serious"?
2. Mohammed Chaudhari found that very few of the defendants who fail to show up for trials have just plain "forgotten." What accounts for the public perception that no-shows are criminals evading the law?
3. What compensation, if any, should be given to inmates who serve more time than they should have because of an "administrative error"?

LaMont W. Flanagan, who discovered 114 forgotten inmates

CORRECTIONS

The correctional sector of the criminal justice system is composed of institutions of varying degrees of security, with varying programs, and of quasi-institutional as well as community-based programs. In making its placement decision, the correctional staff takes into consideration such factors as security requirements, availability of treatment and rehabilitation programs, and organizational needs. All inmates are placed into categories for the purpose of cell placement. In some institutions, this is done in accordance with the placements that are available.[35] In others, factors such as offense severity and psychopathology are considered.

Let us look now at what sentencing options are available to the court, and what correctional implications the court's judgment may have.

Community Decisions

probation
Serving a sentence in the community in lieu of a prison term, on condition of good conduct, compliance with conditions, and under supervision.

If the offense is not serious and the offender is a good candidate for reform, the judge may decide on a *community* sentence. The judge may place the convict on **probation,** the release of a prison-bound convict into the community, usually with specified conditions: that the convict not commit another offense, not leave the county without permission, make payments to the victim, attend meetings of Alcoholics Anonymous, and so on.

alternative sanctions
Punishments or other dispositions imposed instead of the principal sanctions currently in use, such as imprisonment or probation.

More recently states have experimented with a variety of additional options, called **alternative sanctions.** Among them are placement in restitution programs, intensive supervision programs (ISP), shock incarceration, and regimented discipline programs (RDP, also called boot camp). While much research has been done on the success or failure of traditional probation among various types of offenders, the newer programs have not been in existence long enough to permit reliable evaluation. Initial research (discussed in Chapter 16) indicates that some alternative sanctions may be cost beneficial and somewhat successful in lowering **recidivism** rates.[36]

recidivism
Repeat offending on the part of a given offender.

Institutional Decisions

Suppose the court has decided a defendant's crime is too serious to allow for a sentence to be served in the community. In that case, an institutional sentence will be imposed. But while the judge may express his or her preferences, it is now entirely up to the executive department of government, the Department of Corrections, to decide on the placement of the convict.

These decisions may be very difficult and have far-reaching consequences, yet they are often made with little information. Classifications of security level or status, for example, may have to be made on the basis of little more than the offense of which the person stands convicted. Predicting the success of educational programs, vocational training, or any other treatment program is also difficult. It is often easier to place inmates in the jobs that keep an institution running. Here inmates do clerical and classification work; they work in the library, the infirmary, the laundry, the kitchen. But even these placement decisions require considering other factors, especially safety. A host of objective classification measures have been devised that offer some hope for increasing the predictive validity of inmate classification (see Chapter 15).

Release and Parole Decisions

"One of the most important decisions in the entire criminal justice process is when to release a convict from an institution."

One of the most important decisions in the entire criminal justice process is when to release an inmate from an institution. There are two types of release from the correctional system. One is release at the expiration of a sentence. Cor-

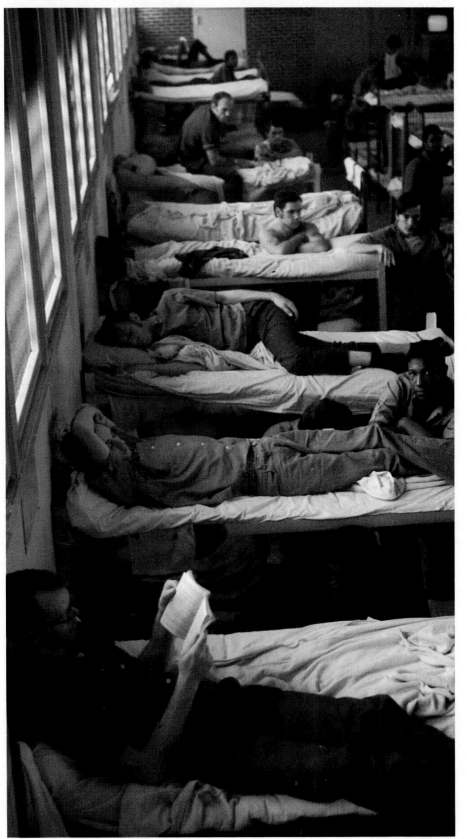

*Even the best inmate classifi-
cation systems break down
when prisons are hopelessly
overcrowded.*

parole
Release of a prisoner into the community during the last part of a prison term, on promise of good conduct and under supervision.

rectional administrators have little choice in this case, although the expiration point depends to some degree on administrative decisions. In the course of disciplinary proceedings, for example, correctional administrators must decide whether an inmate will lose "good-time" benefits because of violations of the institution's rules. Good-time benefits, which have the effect of reducing prison sentence lengths, are given to inmates for institutional behavior that conforms to rules and regulations. An inmate who violates the rules loses the benefit of the early release that comes with good behavior. Today, release decisions are further complicated by policy decisions made at higher governmental levels or by judges, who frequently order prisoners released to make space for new ones in an effort to relieve prison overcrowding.

The second way an inmate may be released is through **parole.** In its original and ideal form, parole was a benefit bestowed on a prisoner for good behavior in prison and a promise of good conduct after discharge. Success on parole was to be achieved with the aid of a parole officer. As parole officers' case loads increased in the 1960s, however, that ideal faded, until today parole is simply an early release from prison, based on the decision of a parole board. Parole boards make these decisions with very little information. Conduct in the institution, however, has been demonstrated to relate to behavior outside it.[37] Some progress has been made in the development of devices to predict success on parole (see Chapter 16).[38] Nevertheless, the decision remains difficult. Statistics show that re-arrest rates of released inmates are very high, as are rates of reconviction and reincarceration.[39] Variations in these rates depend on number of previous incarcerations, types of crimes committed, ethnic background, education, length of prison term served, time elapsed since release, and other factors. Some states have abolished parole, and others are using it with steadily declining frequency. (Several special forms of parole, such as intensive supervision parole with and without electronic monitoring, are discussed in subsequent chapters.)

DIVERSION

attrition (mortality) rate
Rate at which the numbers decrease in the course of the criminal process because persons are diverted out of the system.

Throughout the criminal justice process, the number of persons within the system steadily decreases. This decrease is usually reported as the **attrition rate,** or the **mortality rate.** The report of the President's Commission on Law Enforcement and the Administration of Justice published in 1967 depicted the criminal justice system as a funnel. In the mid-1960s, 727,000 defendants entered the wide opening at the top of the funnel—roughly one for every four of the 2.78 million index crimes reported. Slightly more than one in five of those arrested were convicted.[40] Two decades later, by the mid-1980s, the 1965 numbers

FIGURE 5.3 *Funnel effect: Reported crimes through prison sentence, 1965 and 1987* (*Source:* President's Commission on Law Enforcement and the Administration of Justice, *Task Force Report on Science and Technology* [Washington, D.C.: U.S. Government Printing Office, 1967], p. 61; and compiled from the U.S. Department of Justice, *Sourcebook of Criminal Justice Statistics, 1988* [Washington, D.C.: U.S. Government Printing Office, 1989].)

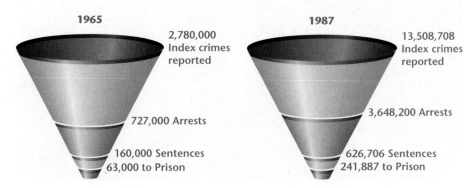

1965

2,780,000
Index crimes
reported

727,000 Arrests

160,000 Sentences
63,000 to Prison

1987

13,508,708
Index crimes
reported

3,648,200 Arrests

626,706 Sentences
241,887 to Prison

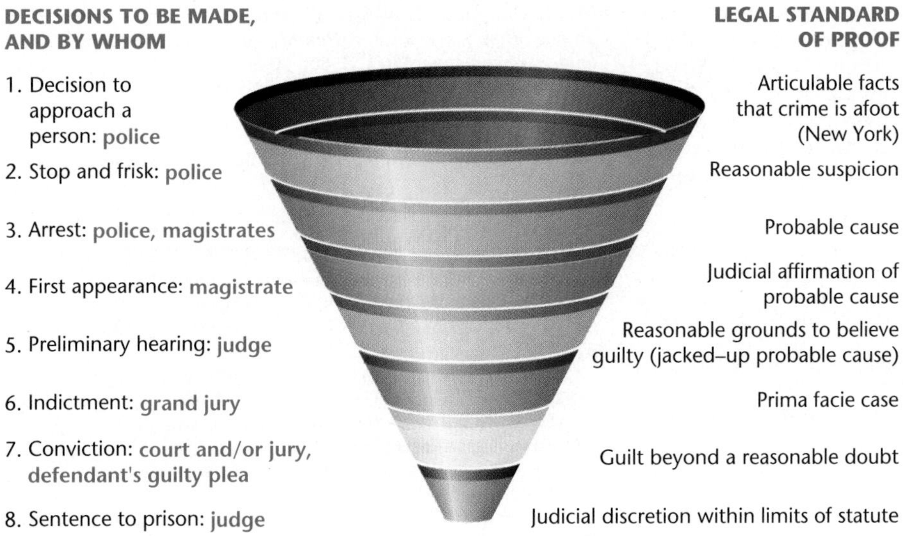

DECISIONS TO BE MADE, AND BY WHOM

1. Decision to approach a person: police
2. Stop and frisk: police
3. Arrest: police, magistrates
4. First appearance: magistrate
5. Preliminary hearing: judge
6. Indictment: grand jury
7. Conviction: court and/or jury, defendant's guilty plea
8. Sentence to prison: judge

LEGAL STANDARD OF PROOF

Articulable facts that crime is afoot (New York)

Reasonable suspicion

Probable cause

Judicial affirmation of probable cause

Reasonable grounds to believe guilty (jacked–up probable cause)

Prima facie case

Guilt beyond a reasonable doubt

Judicial discretion within limits of statute

FIGURE 5.4 *The funnel effect of the standard of proof*

had quadrupled or quintupled, yet the proportions remained essentially the same (Figure 5.3).

As we have seen, there are three reasons for the enormous amount of diversion from the system at various stages. First, decision-makers may, for a variety of reasons, deem a case inappropriate for further processing. If they did not do this, the system would become clogged, dispositions would be unreasonably delayed, and the flow would stop. Moreover, this exercise of discretion keeps an already punitive system from becoming overly punitive. Second, in many situations decision-makers have no choice but to dismiss a case. At each stage of the process the authorities must meet a legal standard of proof. When that standard is not met, the case leaves the criminal justice process. These standards become progressively stricter as the case (and the person) proceeds through the various stages. And third, many cases are simply lost, for example, by failure of the accused to appear at a selected court date (see the Criminal Justice on Trial box).

A very broad standard of proof—reasonable suspicion—permits a large intake into the system. A very tight standard of proof—guilt beyond a reasonable doubt—permits individuals ultimately to be convicted and retained. Various intermediate standards determine whether a defendant should be processed to the next stage (Figure 5.4).

REVIEW

The criminal justice system, like any other system, is made up of related and interdependent components. Its processes begin with the perception that a crime has been committed. After the crime has been reported, the authorities follow procedures developed for the arrest of suspects and for the presentation of the case to the courts. When the facts warrant a grand jury indictment or a prosecutor's information, the case moves to trial. At this stage a plea agreement may be reached under which the defendant avoids trial and receives a reduced sentence in return for a plea of guilty to a lesser charge or to fewer charges. The conviction rate of defendants who do go to trial is high.

The ends or goals of the criminal justice system (the products of the criminal justice process) are generally recognized to be "justice" or "crime prevention," or a combination of the two. Dispute continues as to the nature of the process, crystallized at the two polar positions of the due process approach and the effectiveness-efficiency approach. The prevailing view is that effectiveness and efficiency are important, but these must be subjugated to due process. Likewise in dispute is the question of whether adherence to the due process model decreases the effectiveness of the process. Recent research indicates that fear of decreased efficiency as a result of due process may be exaggerated.

Movement through the criminal justice system is not automatic and inevitable. At each stage of the process it is dependent on decisions made by criminal justice officials and by the defendant. These decisions may lead to the diversion of the defendant out of the system at any stage. Multiple exits explain the high attrition rate: Only a fraction of the offenders who enter the criminal justice system wind up in corrections.

Notes

1. Richard Emory, "Courts Can't Do It All," *The New York Times,* July 16, 1983, p. 23, col. 1.

2. Marc Ancel, *Social Defense* (Thorsten Sellin, transl.), (Littleton, Colo.: Fred B. Rothman & Co., 1987).

3. See Torsten Eriksson, *The Reformers* (New York: Elsevier 1976), pp. 241–244.

4. Herbert Packer, *The Limits of the Criminal Sanction* (Stanford, Calif.: Stanford University Press, 1968).

5. Wayne R. LaFave and Jerold H. Israel, *Criminal Procedure,* 1992 ed. (St. Paul, Minn.: West Publishing Co., 1991).

6. Kevin N. Wright, "The Desirability of Goal Conflict within the Criminal Justice System," *Journal of Criminal Justice* 9 (1981):209–218.

7. President's Commission on Law Enforcement and the Administration of Justice, *The Challenge of Crime in a Free Society* (Washington, D.C.: U.S. Government Printing Office, 1967).

8. Michael R. Gottfredson & Don M. Gottfredson, *Decision Making in Criminal Justice,* 2d ed. (New York: Plenum Press, 1988), pp. 21–22.

9. Ibid., p. 22.

10. Robert F. Kidd and Ellen F. Chayet, "Why Do Victims Fail to Report? The Psychology of Crime Victimization," *Journal of Social Issues* 40 (1984):39–50.

11. Leslie W. Kennedy, "Going It Alone: Unreported Crime and Individual Self-Help," *Journal of Criminal Justice* 16 (1988):403–412.

12. Ibid., Chapter 2.

13. Ibid., Chapter 3.

14. Anthony Amsterdam, *Trial Manual for the Defense of Criminal Cases* (Philadelphia: American Law Institute, 1988).

15. *Beck v. Ohio,* 379 U.S. 89 (1964).

16. *Mapp v. Ohio,* 367 U.S. 643 (1961).

17. *Terry v. Ohio,* 392 U.S. 1 (1968).

18. *People v. de Bour,* 40 N.Y. 2d 210 (1967).

19. *Miranda v. Arizona,* 384 U.S. 436 (1966). Miranda warnings are not always recited at the time of arrest and may, depending on the jurisdiction, be recited when the suspect is booked or prior to any custodial interrogation.

20. But there is an exception to this rule: When public safety is at risk, the warning may be postponed. See *New York v. Quarles,* 467 U.S. 649 (1984).

21. *Gideon v. Wainwright,* 372 U.S. 335 (1963), as amplified by, among others, *Argersinger v. Hamlin,* 407 U.S. 25 (1972) and *Strickland v. Washington,* 466 U.S. 668 (1984) (counsel must be competent). See also Anthony Lewis, *Gideon's Trumpet* (New York: Random House, 1974).

22. Robert Hermann, Eric Single, and John Boston, *Counsel for the Poor* (Lexington, Mass.: Lexington Books, 1977), especially page 153.

23. Gottfredson & Gottfredson, *Decision Making in Criminal Justice,* Chapter 4.

24. *United States v. Salerno,* 481 U.S. 739 (1987).

25. Brian Forst, Judith Lucianovic, and Sara J. Cox, *What Happens after Arrest?,* Institute for Law and Social Research Publication No. 4 (Washington, D.C.: U.S. Government Printing Office, 1978), p. 67.

26. Federal Rules of Criminal Procedure, Rule 6.

27. Forst, Lucianovic, and Cox, *What Happens after Arrest,* p. 17.

28. "Only 3 of every 100 Arrests Went to Trial in 1986, Whereas 52 Resulted in a Guilty Plea," U.S. Department of Justice, Bureau of Justice Statistics, *Annual Report, Fiscal 1988* (Washington, D.C.: U.S. Government Printing Office, 1989), p. 49.

29. For a critique on the inducements to plead guilty, see David Brereton and Jonathan D. Casper, "Does It Pay to Plead Guilty? Differential Sentencing and the Functioning of Criminal Costs," *Law and Society Review* 16 (1981):45–70.

30. Federal Rules of Criminal Procedure, Rule 11.

31. Held constitutional in *Williams v. Florida,* 399 U.S. 25 (1972).

32. See Harry Kalven, Jr., and Hans Zeisel with collaboration of Thomas Callahan and Philip Ennis, *The American Jury* (Boston: Little, Brown, 1966).

33. *Apodaca v. Oregon,* 406 U.S. 404 (1972). The case involved a homicide less than first-degree murder.

34. Don Gottfredson and Bridget Stecher, "Sentencing Policy Models," manuscript, School of Criminal Justice, Rutgers University, New Brunswick, N.J., 1979.

35. Hans Toch, contributions by John Gibbs, John Seymour, Daniel Lockwood, *Living in Prison* (New York: Free Press, 1977).

36. Joan Petersilia, *Expanding Options for Criminal Sentencing* (Santa Monica, Calif.: Rand Corporation, 1987).

37. Michael R. Gottfredson and K. Adams, "Prison Behavior and Release Performance: Empirical Reality and Public Policy," *Law and Policy Quarterly* 4 (1982):373–391.

38. Gottfredson and Gottfredson, *Decision Making in Criminal Justice,* Chapter 8.

39. Allen J. Beck and Bernard E. Shipley, *Recidivism of Young Parolees: Special Report,* U.S. Department of Justice, Bureau of Justice Statistics (Washington, D.C.: U.S. Government Printing Office, 1987).

40. For a discussion of this study see Charles Silberman, *Criminal Violence, Criminal Justice* (New York: Random House, 1978), pp. 257–261.

THE POLICE

This part of the book is concerned with police, or law enforcement in general. The police are the first criminal justice agents contacted by victims of crime. Their actions determine all subsequent steps of the criminal process. The police, moreover, constitute by far the largest of the three sectors of criminal justice.

Chapter 6 provides an overview of the history of policing and describes the various types of law enforcement agencies, their typical structure and functioning, and their organizational responses to societal stresses and changing demands.

Chapter 7 analyzes the types of activities in which police departments engage to fulfill the three functions assigned to them: the service function, the order maintenance function, and the law enforcement function. The emphasis today is on community policing, a distinct shift from the paramilitary style that prevailed until recently.

Chapter 8 explains the constitutional framework within which all police must conduct their activities, from arrest to arraignment. Although the Bill of Rights is two centuries old, it was only during the last forty years that the U.S. Supreme Court has made most of its provisions binding on the actions of state and local police.

In our final police chapter, Chapter 9, we look at police officers as human beings, and also members of their own distinct subculture. Selection processes and training, peer pressure and shared dangers, common temptations and joint griefs, are a common mold for all police officers. At one time, such officers were exclusively white and male. As we demonstrate, this stereotype has changed significantly, with growing numbers of women and minorities now serving as line officers as well as in command posts. ■

CHAPTER 6

HISTORY AND ORGANIZATION OF THE POLICE

Crime is everywhere. Pickpockets and purse snatchers lurk on every street. To protect their money from muggers, people carry their wallets on a leather strap around their necks. Just the other day a noted wit said: "Only a fool would go out to dinner without having made his will."[1] The police are sparse in the neighborhoods. The city has even installed dummy police officers at intersections and school crossings. Citizens buy padlocks to protect their homes. You have never seen so many "Beware of Dog" signs! The more affluent hire private security agencies to protect their premises. It has become common practice for people to carry charms in their bags and pouches to protect them from muggers. Others simply pray to be safe from attack. At home all valuables are locked in strongboxes. Those who can afford it put their jewelry in bank safe deposit boxes. But nothing is safe from burglars, not the homes, not the banks, not even the gilding that covers public monuments. Merchants are putting chains around merchandise on display. Most shop owners have security guards. At the end of the business day they bar their doors with heavy boards and bolts. Homeowners have installed double doors for protection. More and more people take classes on self-defense techniques and carry knives not outlawed by the weapons laws. Public officials don't even ride around in public anymore without security agents in front, in back, and on the sides. Neighborhoods have formed citizens' watch groups. And everybody is upset about the lack of police presence.[2] ■

Although it could be a description of many cities in the United States today, this was the situation reported about the Rome of 2,000 years ago. Crime and policing have always been problems, especially in urban areas.

No society is capable of ensuring an orderly, secure life for its members unless it polices itself. In the ancient world, citizen-organized watchmen performed police functions, as we know, for example, from the Old Testament. Police forces, in the sense of a government-controlled, uniformed corps, on the other hand, were found mainly in large urbanized states with centralized governments, strong rulers, and the perception of a crime problem, for instance, Egypt, Greece, and Rome.

This chapter deals with the ever-changing yet often similar challenges faced by law enforcement agencies. We begin by tracing the emergence of contemporary law enforcement agencies.

THE HISTORY OF THE POLICE

During the Middle Ages, a long period of turmoil and lawlessness in Europe without strong rulers or centralized governments, policing was done by citizens. Change came with the establishment of absolute monarchies beginning in the fourteenth century. Louis XIV (ruled 1643–1715), the most absolute of absolute monarchs, strengthened the French police force (composed of members of the nobility serving the king) as an instrument of crime control and oppression by appointing a lieutenant (later general) of police to be head of a national, uniformed police corps. Other continental European monarchies and principalities followed the French example. The English, however, did not (see the Criminal Justice in Action box).

Fearful of giving the state the power to intrude into citizens' everyday lives and of the loss of individual liberty, the English resisted the idea of a police force. When finally industrialization and the growth of cities made policing necessary, the English developed a system different from the continental European one. As a British colony, the United States inherited this system along with other institutions.

The English Model

From at least the time of Kings Edward and Ethelred in England (tenth century),[3] the citizens of the realm (above age 12)[4] were grouped into **tythings.** Ten tythings formed a larger group, called the **hundred.** A territory composed of many hundreds constituted the **shire.** Within these groupings, the people were supposed to take care of their own law enforcement. (A similar system, called **frankpledge,** existed in the Danelaw parts of England.) After the conquest of 1066 A.D., the new Norman kings relied heavily on this communal system, but with strengthened royal supervision. Overall responsibility for maintaining peace within the shire was given to the **shire reeve** (the "sheriff"), who had the power to muster the **posse comitatus,** the entire force of the shire, in the event of an emergency. Similarly, all men were obliged to respond to the **hue and cry,** a call for assistance in the pursuit of felons.

The Statute of Winchester   Toward the end of the twelfth century, the feudal lords assumed the role formerly held by the tything, and the manorial court took over the responsibilities of the sheriff's court. The most important officer now was the **constable,** who was recognized by the Crown as responsible for keeping the king's peace.

By the Statute of Winchester (1285 A.D.), Edward I introduced the **watch and ward** system. The gates of walled towns were ordered shut from sunset to sunrise

tythings
In Anglo-Saxon law, an association of ten families bound together by a frankpledge.

hundred
Group of ten tythings.

shire
Territory composing many hundreds.

frankpledge
Ancient system whereby every male member of the community over the age of 12 was bound by a mutual pledge to keep the peace.

shire reeve
Person responsible for maintaining peace within the shire *(term from which the word "sheriff" is derived).*

posse comitatus
Latin for "power of the county" or the entire force of the shire.

hue and cry
Old English call for assistance in the pursuit of felons.

constable
Official charged with enforcing the law at the township level.

watch and ward
System (established in 1285 A.D.) of townspeople standing guard at the gates of walled towns.

and a watch of up to sixteen men, drawn from the householders on a rotating basis, was stationed at each gate. Those who served on the watch were required to be armed with their own battle-axes and halberds. The statute also contained a provision, called the "assize of arms," that required any male aged 15 to 60 to keep arms in his house. The statute strengthened the office of constable, which was to be filled on a rotating basis by qualified residents of the parish (the people of a neighborhood defined by a common church congregation and later in history, forming a political unit such as a village or district). It was the constable who was responsible for setting the nightly watch, taking charge of prisoners from the watchmen, and initiating the hue and cry. In addition to constables and watchmen, from the twelfth century on policing was done by **justices of the peace** appointed by the king. This position combined judicial, administrative, and police authority.

justice of the peace
Originally (est. 1326) an untrained man, usually of the lower nobility, assigned to investigate and try minor cases. Today a judge of a lower court, local or municipal, with limited jurisdiction.

Constables and justices of the peace were to be the primary officers of policing in England until modern times, but their effectiveness did not survive much beyond the seventeenth century. The office of constable, once regarded as prestigious, was gradually degraded to an obligation. The result was that the office was often held by men who were clearly incompetent. Over time the justices, too, became increasingly corrupt. Because they were paid for each act performed and each conviction obtained, justices often found they could do better by blackmailing or extorting money from suspects than by performing their duties.

The Bow Street Runners. The constable and justice-of-the-peace system, coupled with the tradition of collective citizen responsibility for keeping the peace, proved inadequate to deal with the disorder and crime brought by the growth of cities and the spread of industrialization in England. The population of both England and its capital, London, doubled during the eighteenth century. The sheer numbers of people placed a serious strain on the informal and formal means of social control on which English society had until then relied.

The voluntary citizen watch of Amsterdam, as depicted by Rembrandt in Nightwatch, *1642. The Rijksmuseum, Amsterdam.*

MILESTONES IN THE HISTORY OF POLICING

Time Frame	Event
Earliest recorded history, biblical times	Watchmen, police appointed for towns, cities in ancient Middle East
Ca. 1340 B.C.	Egypt: Nile River Police established
Ca. 1000–300 B.C.	Greece: The *polis,* which meant all municipal government activities, including police
Ca. 510 B.C.–A.D. 375	Rome: Various kinds of public and private police forces, including Praetorian Guard (like a state police) and Lictors (who protected officials)
Ca. 400–1200	England: Communal policing at various levels—tything, hundred, shire. After the Norman Conquest of 1066, centralized royal control
1285	England: Statute of Winchester sets up watch-and-ward system for towns, with citizen police, constables, justices of the peace
1300s	France: Charles V (1364–80) establishes national police (*gens d'armes*)
17th–18th centuries	France: Louis XIV (1643–1715) establishes standing, uniformed police with "Lieutenant" of police; other European countries follow
	England: period of general lawlessness

Time Frame	Event
1750–1798	England, 1750: Henry Fielding organizes official "thief-takers"; brother John Fielding creates Bow Street Runners, first salaried police in England
	England, 1798: Marine Police Establishment (Thames River Police) established
19th century	England: Sir Robert Peel establishes (London) Metropolitan Police, known as Peelers or Bobbies (1829)
	Similar police forces established all over England (1856)
17th–early 19th centuries	North America: Colonists follow English model—town watchmen, constables, sheriffs, marshals
1790	United States: Alexander Hamilton establishes first federal police force—U.S. Coast Guard (Marine Revenue Cutter Service)
19th century	United States: Politically dominated municipal police forces established (1838 Boston, 1845 New York, 1855 Milwaukee)
1890s–1920s	United States: Progressive period—International Association of Chiefs of Police founded; Leonhard Fuld publishes first police textbook; reformers Raymond Fosdick, August Vollmer
1930s–1960s	United States: Wickersham Commission documents American police as incompetent, ineffective, brutal. Reformers: professionalization (O. W. Wilson), crime fighter (J. Edgar Hoover, FBI)
1960s	United States: Crime fighter/ professional police style backfires: unrest and riots. Civil libertarians call for new approach
Since 1970	United States: Police democratization, equal employment opportunity, community relations, better recruitment & training; search for new management models

"The London of 1752 was so dangerous a place that Horace Walpole wrote: 'One is forced to travel, even at noon, as if one were going to battle.'"

Bow Street Runners
Earliest salaried police force in England.

"There is no qualification more indispensable to a police officer than a perfect command of temper. . . ."
Metropolitan Police Force Instruction Book, 1829.

The London of the early 1700s was a city of frequent riots, a place where thieves and highwaymen moved freely. Residents were in such fear that, as Horace Walpole wrote in 1752, "One is forced to travel, even at noon, as if one were going to battle."[5] The career of Jonathan Wild illustrates the freedom with which criminals of the day were able to operate. Wild managed to gain control over most of the criminals operating in London. Having set up an office in the city as a self-advertised "Thief-taker General," Wild would order his men to commit a burglary and then wait for the victims to present themselves at his office to ask for assistance in tracking down their stolen property. Restoring the goods to their owners was of course a simple matter for him, and the grateful victims were glad to provide a reward, which he would then share with the thieves. Wild was ultimately sentenced to death and hanged in 1725, but the open operation of his criminal enterprise was a clear indicator of how ineffectual the system of law enforcement had become.[6]

By the middle of the eighteenth century, a reform movement had begun. Among the earliest reformers was Henry Fielding (1707–1754), author of the novel *Tom Jones*. Appointed to the post of chief magistrate of Bow Street, the principal magistrate of London, Fielding instituted an innovation that would provide a foundation on which to build a new system of police. In 1750 he organized six citizens into a small band of "thief-takers," who were successful at breaking up some gangs. Henry Fielding's successor, his half-brother John, continued the new system. The small band of paid thief-takers evolved into the **Bow Street Runners,** the earliest salaried police force in England. Nevertheless, it took nearly another three-quarters of a century before the idea of a formal, paid police force was accepted.

The Metropolitan Police. The only model of police most English citizens knew was that used in France. The French had created a strong national police force (called the *Sûreté*) that was military in style and made extensive use of undercover agents. This was not the sort of institution that fit the English fear of military institutions or England's self-image as a land of liberty.[7] At this point, Patrick Colquhoun, another notable metropolitan magistrate, came up with an idea for solving another problem: London and its port suffered extremely high losses from crime. Colquhoun estimated them at over half a million pounds a year. His idea, which appealed to those involved in trade, was the Marine Police Establishment. It was created in 1798, with sixty salaried officers and Colquhoun as its superintending magistrate. Four-fifths of the cost was borne by West Indian merchants. By 1800, following its success, this private force had been converted into the first professional police force in London. It exists to this day as the Thames River Police.

By 1828, the city of London had approximately 450 police officers, including the Bow Street patrols and the Thames River Police. London also still had 4,500 watchmen. It was at this point that Home Secretary (later Prime Minister) Sir Robert Peel (1788–1850) successfully steered his "Bill for Improving the Police In and Near the Metropolis" through Parliament. This Metropolitan Police Act, enacted in 1829, created the Metropolitan Police, whose officers have ever since been known as "the little Roberts," or *bobbies*. The first bobbies patrolled a seven-mile radius from the center of London. The handbook issued to the new recruits emphasized crime prevention and the importance of civility in dealing with the public.[8] Concern about the potential for use of force against citizens led to the decision to arm the police only with a short wooden baton, a tradition that continues today.

The Metropolitan Police proved successful, and by 1856 professional police forces had been established in all the counties and boroughs of England. Unlike the national police forces of some European countries, however, the system remained decentralized and the smaller forces were under local control.

The London bobby on his beat on a snowy London night, 1872.

The American Experience

The linked concepts of local control and decentralization are two of the most important characteristics of the English system as adopted by the new nation that grew from British colonies in North America.[9]

Colonial America.   The English colonists brought with them English institutions, including systems of law enforcement. In towns like Boston, Philadelphia, and Charleston, constables were appointed and watches created. Counties elected sheriffs to enforce the law. These officials, however, played a mostly reactive role, since prevailing notions of law enforcement still emphasized citizen initiative. Political entities offered rewards to the public for the apprehension of felons, and citizens could be called on to form posses in pursuit of criminals.[10] The victim of a crime had to initiate action against the offender by going to court to swear out a warrant and by requesting the assistance of the constable in serving the warrant and making the arrest.

Constables performed a variety of duties, including law enforcement functions like serving warrants, making arrests, and testifying in court, as well as generally preserving order. As was the case in England, residents had an obligation to serve as constables or watchmen.[11] When the tasks associated with these offices became unwelcome and sometimes dangerous,[12] the colonies tried various solutions to persuade citizens to fulfill their obligations. Boston and Philadelphia, for example, imposed large fines for failure to serve.[13] New York held popular elections for its constables in 1800,[14] while Boston made the position an appointive one. In 1802 the position became a full-time and sought-after occupation, largely because of the payment of fees for services.[15]

Outside the cities, the chief law enforcement officer was the county sheriff. The position was considered one of considerable prestige and power, and typically was given to a member of the local elite. As a law enforcement officer, the sheriff responded to formal complaints lodged by members of the community,

"Law enforcement in colonial America consisted of a variety of strategies, most of them tailored to the needs of the particular communities in which they were established."

made arrests, and served subpoenas. To him also fell the political tasks of supervising elections and collecting taxes. Paid by fees for services rendered, the sheriff could earn more for tax collection than for law enforcement. One consequence of this arrangement was widespread corruption of the sheriff's office.[16]

Law enforcement in colonial America thus consisted of a variety of strategies, most of them tailored to the needs of the particular communities in which they were established. Viewing this period of American history, Samuel Walker, historian of the police, depicts colonial law enforcement as "inefficient, corrupt, and subject to political interference."[17] There was virtually no crime prevention, while limitations on personnel and resources resulted in largely ineffective fulfillment of both the crime investigation and order maintenance functions.

Expansion and Urbanization. The problems that arose as towns grew into cities and as the social and economic order became more complex required solutions that went beyond the weak system in use throughout the early years of the nation. In the nineteenth century, and especially in the post–Civil War years, paid professional police forces were finally introduced in the United States.

As the nation expanded, social disorder increased. Expansion created settlements in the West without well-developed local governments to maintain order or enforce law. Tensions between the various ethnic groups that moved west, as well as between competing economic groups such as cattlemen and sheepherders, contributed to violence and disorder.[18] In the East, settlements that had started as small towns grew into large, impersonal cities with increasingly complex demands on the governing structure. The transition from a local to a national market created boom and bust cycles that affected most workers.[19] Increasing specialization threatened job security and lowered the status of many jobs.[20] Antagonisms between ethnic groups were sharpened by the arrival of new immigrants. The different problems faced by the two regions, the expanding West and the settled East, gave rise to different solutions for enforcing the law and maintaining order.

The Expanding West. The absence of effective government in many of the newly settled parts of the West created a vacuum that was often filled by private citizens taking the law into their own hands. **Vigilante groups,** which typically consisted of a few hundred people led by the town elite, would track down criminals or people creating disorder in the settlement and administer "justice" to them. At some "trials" the captured outlaws were given a chance to present a defense. Determination of guilt most often resulted in the execution of the "defendant," usually by hanging. Vigilante groups were generally well organized along military lines, and had written manifestos or constitutions to which the members would subscribe.[21]

Law enforcement of the lawful variety also existed in the West. In federal territories, United States **marshals** were the principal law enforcement officers. Like their counterparts in the eastern constabularies, marshals were paid for the services they performed, so low-paying criminal matters tended to be neglected in favor of more lucrative civil duties.

Once an area became a state, law enforcement became the responsibility of state and local officials. In the counties, sheriffs were the chief peace officers. Cities and towns settled in the latter part of the nineteenth century created police forces like those that had by then developed in the eastern cities. The sheriffs were much like those of colonial times: important political figures drawn from the dominant power group, with duties such as tax collection, inspection of cattle brands, and the serving of civil processes, in addition to law enforcement. Even famous personalities like James "Wild Bill" Hickok and William B. "Bat" Masterson, who were known as hired gunmen, were willing to serve as sheriffs.[22]

Private police were used in the West along with official and citizen forces. In the 1860s, the ambitious effort to create a transcontinental railroad provided

vigilante group
Group of private citizens taking the law into their own hands by tracking down criminals and punishing them.

marshal
Federal law enforcement officer of the U.S. Marshal Service. Formerly, federal law enforcement officer in territories.

"William B. (Bat) Masterson, a famous gunman and personality in the West, actually served as a law enforcement officer, as did James (Wild Bill) Hickok."

new opportunities for crime. As trains passed through unsettled areas, they became easy targets for robbers who would "hold up" the train (the source of the
term *holdup* for robbery), remove its freight or rob its passengers, and escape
without fear of immediate pursuit. To provide increased protection, a number of
railroad companies engaged the services of Allan Pinkerton, founder of the most
famous private detective agency in America, or of hired guns like Bat Masterson
and Wyatt Earp.[23] Together with the other informal and formal law enforcement
groups operating in the West, private police provided a form of "frontier justice."

The East: Urban Riots.   In the growing urban centers of the East, the stress
caused by social dislocation frequently erupted into riots, a phenomenon historian Roger Lane considers the most important precipitating factor in the creation of professional police forces.[24] Riots in Boston, Philadelphia, and Louisville
in the first half of the century were attributable to tensions between different
immigrant groups. Racial prejudice against blacks living in northern cities and
opposition to abolition also resulted in riots: There were five major race riots in
Philadelphia between 1829 and 1850, each requiring military intervention.[25]
Some riots were economic, such as those in which depositors stormed banks
during times of economic crisis.[26] The system of constables and watchmen simply could not deal with this kind of social turmoil. Pressure mounted for finding
an alternative means of maintaining order and enforcing the law.

*"The urban system of constables
and watchmen could not deal
with the riots, both economic
and racial, that swept American
cities in the first part of the nineteenth century."*

London's newly created Metropolitan Police provided what many Americans
considered the appropriate model. The earliest attempt to create such a force
was short-lived: Philadelphia in 1833 established a day police force of 24 men to
supplement the night watch of 120 men, but it was disbanded two years later. In
1838, Boston appointed a force of nine police officers to deal with riots, while
maintaining the night watch system already in place; the two forces were consolidated in 1854. New York City commissioned a police force in 1845. Philadelphia
followed suit in 1854 and Chicago and Milwaukee in 1855.

The early urban forces adopted features of the London police. Crime prevention was stressed and twenty-four-hour patrol beats were instituted. There was a
two-platoon system in which officers alternated between long shifts on patrol
and "reserve" duty, when they sat in the station house waiting to be called in if
necessary.[27] In addition to crime prevention, the police assumed social welfare
duties such as providing housing in the precinct stations for the homeless, operating soup kitchens, and returning lost children to their homes.[28]

Like the style favored by Sir Robert Peel for the London bobbies, American
forces patterned themselves after the military. Ranks and titles such as sergeant,
lieutenant, and captain were used and officers had to participate in morning roll
calls and drills. Although the earliest forces did not use firearms, American police eventually did carry guns, unlike their English counterparts. The police and
the public were generally receptive to these practices, but the notion of wearing
uniforms was one aspect of the military model to which people objected. Officers
themselves worried not only about the ability of "toughs looking for trouble"[29] to
identify them but also the ease with which their beat supervisors (called
"roundsmen") would be able to spot them passing time in billiard halls or taverns
instead of on patrol. Moreover, the image of a uniformed force on the streets
made the public fearful that the police might become a sort of standing army
in their midst.[30] Eventually, however, uniforms were adopted by all the forces.

The Problem of Political Control

From the outset, American police forces were beset with problems, many of
which can be traced to one source: political control. Unlike the London bobbies,
whose existence was mandated by an act of Parliament, police in the United
States derived their authority and obtained their jobs largely from local politicians.[31] Consequently, these grateful recipients of political patronage were loyal

*"From the outset, American po-
lice forces were plagued by the
problem of political control."*

to the politicians, not the people and the government. The police had a vested interest in keeping in office the politicians to whom they owed their jobs. Since the police had the duty of supervising polling places, officeholders had a distinct advantage in elections. Political control was facilitated by the decentralized structure of most urban forces. This type of arrangement began in New York City, where each political ward had a separate patrol precinct. Each precinct remained under the authority of a precinct captain, who usually worked closely with the ward politicians. Police chiefs exercised little control over officers working at the precinct level. All these practices meant that the police were decidedly not a professional force.

Effective policing was hampered by other factors as well. Moral reformers wanted strict enforcement of laws dealing with prostitution, gambling, and liquor, while many working-class people and those in the liquor business opposed attempts to enforce these laws. The police were caught between the two, and enforcement became a source of chronic tension between the public and the police as well as the occasion for bribes, protection money, and corruption.[32]

Crime detection was another area that created the image of an unprofessional force. Before the establishment of uniformed police departments, "thief-taking" had been considered a private enterprise in which a reward would be paid for the return of stolen property. Detectives continued this practice even after the formation of police departments. To recover stolen goods, detectives had to rely on contacts with criminals who could lead them to the proper sources. On occasion, this meant that criminals were hired as detectives.[33] The combination of fees paid for work and association with criminals resulted in a detective force with a lax attitude toward law enforcement.

Finally, the crime prevention function of the police was severely hindered by the absence of a communications system and the lack of supervision of patrol officers. Without an effective means of communication, the police could not be notified that a crime had occurred and respond promptly. Moreover, the lack of supervision left patrol officers free to pass their time in saloons, barber shops, or other gathering places.[34]

The Progressive Movement.   Serious efforts at social reform were undertaken at the end of the nineteenth century in the context of the Progressive movement, a campaign to restore honesty and efficiency to government. To separate politics from the police and to transform policing into a profession, reformers advocated centralizing police departments through the consolidation or closure of many precinct houses. As part of this process, they recommended the development of special units to deal with such matters as vice, charges of police misconduct, and crime detection. Personnel were to be upgraded by the use of rigorous selection criteria, including intelligence tests. Appointed jobs were to become civil service positions to make them immune from political manipulation. Finally, reformers proposed that the police function should be narrowed, with unrelated duties such as poll watching, providing lodging to the homeless, operating soup kitchens, and inspection of the markets turned over to other public officials.[35]

Early Reformers: Vollmer.   Reform was supported by many of the nation's early police chiefs. The International Association of Chiefs of Police (IACP), founded in 1893 and given its present name in 1900, was the first professional association in law enforcement. The IACP spearheaded the movement for reform under the direction of Richard Sylvester, superintendent of the Washington, D.C. police, who served as president from 1901 to 1916. Other important reformers included Leonhard Fuld, author of the first textbook on the subject of police administration; Arthur Woods, commissioner of the New York City police; and Raymond B. Fosdick, who documented American policing in a book entitled *American Police Systems*.[36] The single most important reformer of this period, and the one who would prove to have the most profound influence on the development of the police, was August Vollmer.

"The single most important reformer of the early period was August Vollmer, who began his career as the town marshal of Berkeley, California, in 1905."

Vollmer's career in law enforcement began with his election as town marshal of Berkeley, California, in 1905. He went on to head the Berkeley police as chief until 1932. His approach to policing emphasized professionalism among the ranks, a goal he attempted to achieve in part by selecting college students as recruits and devising a set of entrance tests. He also established a police school to ensure proper training. Vollmer believed the primary function of the police should be crime fighting and that they should be aided in this mission by the scientific methods utilized in the crime lab he created. He was also concerned with the social dimensions of police work and established a crime prevention division as well as delinquency prevention programs.[37] Vollmer's book *The Police and Modern Society* (1936) remained a guide for police professionals for decades. The American Society of Criminology gave his name to its most prestigious award for outstanding achievement in law enforcement and criminal justice.

The Wickersham Report.   The early reformers made limited progress in the first decades of the twentieth century. A survey conducted in the 1920s found that only two out of three officers had finished elementary school and that only 10 percent were high-school graduates. Training programs were not up to the standards proposed by Vollmer, and politicians still managed to exert some control. In 1929 the United States National Commission on Law Observance and Enforcement, under the direction of Attorney General George W. Wickersham (and therefore commonly referred to as the Wickersham Commission), was given a mandate to investigate the criminal justice system.

"The great majority of the police are not suited either by temperament, training, or education for their position."
National Commission on Law Observance and Enforcement Report, 1931.

Its findings painted a dismal picture of the police at that time, noting inadequacies in many areas, including recruitment, training, standards, communications, statistics, and fulfillment of the crime prevention mission. Having discovered evidence of extensive use of the **third degree**—which it labeled a "flagrant violation of the law by the officers of the law"[38]—and other forms of police brutality, the commission chose to devote an entire volume of its report to the subject of lawlessness in law enforcement.

third degree
Torturing a suspect to gain information.

The New Wave of Reform: Crime-Fighters.   The Wickersham report shocked the nation and provided additional impetus to reform. The most prominent leader of this new wave of reform was O. W. Wilson, a protégé of August Vollmer. Wilson was chief of police in Wichita, Kansas, from 1928 to 1935, where he fought a vigorous campaign for reform within his own department. He became a professor of police administration at the University of California and helped to create Berkeley's School of Criminology, the first of its kind in the country; from 1950 to 1960 he served as its dean. While at Berkeley, Wilson wrote a book entitled *Police Administration* (1950), which became the standard text on the subject.

The renewed reform effort focused on professionalism, with the objective of creating a well-disciplined and highly trained police force, immune to the corrupting influence of politics. Crime control was to be its primary function. The image of law enforcement officers as crime-fighters was advanced especially by J. Edgar Hoover, who had been appointed director of the Federal Bureau of Investigation in 1924. The highly publicized exploits of Hoover's morally irreproachable FBI agents against the notorious criminals of the 1930s helped to foster public perception of police as dedicated crime-fighters.

Technological advances also nurtured this image. Patrol cars were introduced just before World War I and were in widespread use by the end of the 1920s. Wilson was a strong advocate of automobile patrol, believing that the presence of distinctively marked police cars in a neighborhood would be a significant anticrime technique.[39] The advent of two-way radios in patrol cars in the late 1930s meant not only that officers could respond quickly to calls for assistance, but also that supervisors could remain in touch with those on patrol. This "quick response" ability helped to promote the idea that criminals would face an increased probability of being caught thereby reinforcing the crime-fighting image.

"Automobile patrol, believed O. W. Wilson, would be a significant anticrime technique."

The technological progress in policing is demonstrated by the prowl car of the late 1930s, equipped with a two-way radio and loudspeaker public address system, and a computer-equipped police cruiser of the 1990s.

The reforms that were undertaken in earnest during the 1930s had a far more profound effect than merely changing the image of the police. Departments were reorganized along functional lines. Entities such as patrol, traffic, detectives, morals, and crime prevention bureaus replaced in importance the old precinct houses. Hiring guidelines raised the educational requirements for new recruits. By 1968, no large city police department would accept an applicant without a high-school diploma. Psychological testing and extensive background checks were used, with the result that numerous candidates were rejected. In New York, for example, roughly five out of six applicants were rejected during the 1950s and 1960s, while in Los Angeles and Dallas the figure went as high as nineteen out of twenty.[40] Improved training was provided to those who were appointed. Civilians began to perform some tasks within departments, freeing the police to concentrate on those duties that only well-trained professionals with special skills were able to accomplish.

The Sixties: Protests and Confrontations. By the mid-1960s, the professional model of the well-trained, highly disciplined, crime-fighting police force had taken hold across the nation. Certain features of this model, however, created tensions between the police and the public as well as within departments. In their efforts to professionalize, the police had turned themselves into a bureaucratic operation, governed by a rigid chain of command. Rank-and-file officers resented their relatively lowly status within the departments and the strict internal control exercised by commanding officers. Belief in the power of technology led to almost exclusive use of patrol cars and the near abandonment of foot patrols. Without face-to-face contact between foot-patrol officers and the community, officers became increasingly isolated from the neighborhoods they policed.

"In their efforts to professionalize, the police turned themselves into a bureaucratic organization governed by a rigid chain of command."

Many departments instituted new forms of preventive patrols, known as "stop-and-search" or "stop-and-frisk" (see Chapter 8), which typically would be deployed in high-crime areas. People viewed by the police as potential offenders would be rounded up on the street, frisked, and interrogated. San Francisco's Operation S, for example, stopped 20,000 people in its first year, yet only 1,000 of these people were arrested.[41] Aggressive crime-control tactics were a source of antagonism between the police and the public, especially young black males who were often the target of these patrols. As the tumultuous decade of the 1960s got under way, the professional crime-fighter model was being challenged in ways totally unanticipated by those who had struggled to bring it into existence.[42]

The civil rights movement, opposition to the unpopular war in Vietnam, college students seeking refuge in drug use, increased television coverage of confrontations—all stressed police–community relations. At the same time, police unions became stronger and stressed the administration.[43] The fiscal crisis led to increasing "civilianization," the employment of lower-paid civilians to perform some of the functions previously performed by uniformed officers.[44] That led to intradepartmental confrontations. Aggressive policing was under attack.

"What benefit is there to a society in becoming the sole remaining superpower on the planet if it cannot guarantee safe streets at home?"
Hubert Williams, President, Police Foundation, 1993.

In this atmosphere of rising crime rates, civil disorder, and internal pressures, several national studies evaluated the police, together with other criminal justice agencies. Among the most prominent was the President's Commission on Law Enforcement and Administration of Justice, whose members were appointed by President Lyndon Johnson in 1965 to investigate and report on crime and the criminal justice system. The commission issued its findings in 1967 in a report entitled *The Challenge of Crime in a Free Society*. The report called for many of the same reforms that had been advocated before, such as higher standards for police personnel, better training for recruits, and improved management practices. However, the report also spoke of the need for better police–community relations, recommended the hiring of minority police officers, acknowledged the need for civilian grievance procedures, and recognized the need for explicit policies to deal with issues related to the exercise of police discretion.[45]

Another significant outcome of the commission's work was the stimulus it gave to social science research in the area of the police. During its two-year investigation, the commission funded many research efforts that provided empirical information about the performance of the police. After the commission finished its work, the commitment to research was continued through the newly created Law Enforcement Assistance Administration (LEAA). LEAA-funded research provided new insight into the workings of the police. Other important sources of research sponsorship were established when the Ford Foundation created the Police Foundation in 1970, which in turn helped to found the Police Executive Research Forum (PERF).

As a result of these developments, American policing in the 1980s and 1990s differs radically from that of preceding decades. We turn now to contemporary American police forces, their structures and functions.

POLICE SYSTEMS IN THE UNITED STATES

"From its tentative beginnings a mere 150 years ago, American policing has become a formidable enterprise."

Policing in the United States is the responsibility of a combination of federal, state, and local agencies. From its tentative beginnings a mere 150 years ago, policing has become a formidable enterprise. Law enforcement agencies employed approximately 800,459 people in 1990, nearly half the total number of people employed in the nation's criminal justice system. Expenditures on police protection totaled nearly $32 billion that year, or 1.4 percent of all government spending.[46] Furthermore, private security and citizen crime prevention programs are now a growing and important part of the system. To understand that system, it is necessary first to examine the police as a bureaucracy, a governmental institution, and then to survey the many types of police forces in America.[47]

Chain of Command

"Police departments are not democratic organizations."

All but the smallest police departments in the United States are bureaucracies, marked by hierarchical structures with a clearly delineated chain of command from the top down, a division of labor among various bureaus, and a set of rules and regulations to which all officers must adhere.[48] Police departments are not democratic organizations. They function largely along the lines of a military command structure, with military ranks and insignia. Patrol officers are responsible to their sergeants, sergeants to lieutenants, lieutenants to captains, captains to inspectors, inspectors to their chief or director.

span of control
Number of subordinates reporting to a superior officer.

unity of command
Principle that each person should be accountable to only one superior.

levels of authority
Organizational structure within a police department in which all officers of equal authority are headed by superior officers of equal rank.

Two important principles related to structuring the chain of command are span of control and unity of command. **Span of control** refers to the number of subordinates reporting to a superior. The **unity of command** principle holds that each person should be accountable to only one superior.[49] A sergeant's span of control might consist of six to ten patrol officers, but the unity of command principle dictates that each officer take orders only from the sergeant. This chain of command structure is normally coupled with **levels of authority.**[50] Under this concept, there will always be officers of different ranks within a department, and each level of a department will have officers of equal rank. Thus, for example, all section heads may be captains, while all unit heads may be lieutenants.

This type of hierarchical chain of command affords superiors control of subordinates and provides clear communication channels both downward and upward through the organization. The structure is also intended to ensure that orders are passed down and followed. Chain of command is not without its critics, who charge that such an arrangement is overly rigid, leads to inefficiency, and creates obstacles to innovation.

Division of Labor

operations bureau
Unit of a police department responsible for the functions associated with the primary law enforcement mission.

line functions
Law enforcement functions of a police department.

Within a police department organization, the division of labor is based on needs, expertise, and experience. The division of labor is reflected in the overall responsibilities assigned to various bureaus (Figure 6.1). The **operations bureau** of a department performs the functions associated with the primary law enforcement mission of the department. These are referred to as **line functions,** and the police involved in them are called line officers. Nearly three-quarters (73.4%) of all police personnel in large municipal departments work in "operations," including 88 percent of all sworn officers.[51] In larger forces, line activities are assigned to bureaus or divisions, which typically include patrol, traffic, detective, juvenile, and vice units. Among these the patrol division is the largest, as it delivers the bulk of crime prevention and law enforcement services.

Among the line functions, those of the detective (or investigations) bureau are regarded as particularly desirable assignments. Specialized training and expertise are required for work in the various units of the detective bureaus of larger municipal departments, such as homicide, burglary, art theft (a rapidly growing problem worldwide), or the "bias" unit, the youngest specialized unit in larger departments.[52]

The **services bureau** (or bureaus) provides technical services to assist in the execution of line functions, such as keeping records and maintaining a crime laboratory. Services provided in the **administration bureau** include those that relate to the running of the department as an organization: personnel, finance, and research and development.

Figure 6.1 also shows a separate division called **internal affairs,** which is responsible for receiving and investigating charges against the police. Such charges may relate to violations of the criminal law or to procedural issues. Among the most frequent complaints are those of police brutality and abuse of power. The internal investigation (internal affairs) unit is typically responsible for investigating complaints filed by citizens and incidents reported by police officers themselves. It can also initiate its own investigations of possible corruption (see Chapter 9).

Another unit shown in Figure 6.1 is the Bureau of Community Services. The gulf that by the 1960s separated the police and many segments of the community they were supposed to be serving called attention to the need for better relations between police and community. Many departments established a special division for this purpose.

While dividing the labor of a police force into specialized units provides benefits, such as a reduced (because targeted) need for training, more effective means of administrative control, and enhanced job proficiency, there are some disadvantages to this structure. Staffing a large number of specialized units may result in a decrease in the number of officers available for patrol. Moreover, the tasks that are considered the most interesting in police work are delegated to specialists, resulting in job dissatisfaction among patrol officers. Finally, the job of coordinating all police services is made more complex by the presence of a large number of specialized units.

The Eight-Hour Shift

Police labor is divided on the basis of time and place. Since police are on call twenty-four hours a day, the work of most departments is carried out during three eight-hour shifts. Although the most efficient way to organize officers on the basis of time may be to assign them permanently to one of these three shifts, low morale typically results because of resentment at being continuously placed on duty during an undesirable shift. Most officers serve on a rotating schedule.

To provide coverage of all areas within a jurisdiction, a city may be divided into districts, precincts, or sectors, with patrol officers assigned to specific **beats** (area covered by a police officer on a patrol) within these geographic divisions. Districts or precincts usually have their own station houses in which some officers from different specialized functional units may also be housed. For example, detectives who report to the head of a functional unit at central headquarters may have their own offices in a precinct station.

Rules and Regulations

O. W. Wilson recommended that departments create a "formal directive system" of rules and regulations.[53] More recently, the Commission on Accreditation of Law Enforcement Agencies (CALEA) underscored the importance of written policy directives by requiring agencies that wish to be accredited to have a "written directives system that includes, at a minimum, statements of agency policy, procedures for carrying out agency activities, and rules and regulations."[54] Written directives not only set forth the rules and regulations that govern police work, but also define the policy and principles of the department and establish proce-

services bureau
Unit of a police department which provides technical services to assist in the execution of line functions, *such as keeping records.*

administration bureau
Unit of a police department responsible for the management of the department as an organization; includes personnel, finance, research, and planning.

internal affairs
Department responsible for receiving and investigating charges against the police.

beat
Territory covered by a police officer on patrol; derived from hunters' "beating" the bushes for game.

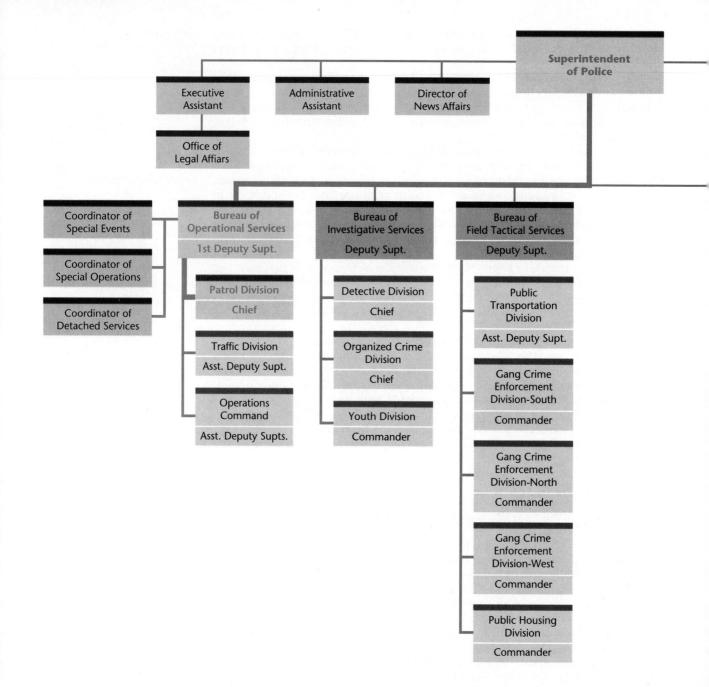

Superintendent of Police

- Executive Assistant
  - Office of Legal Affiars
- Administrative Assistant
- Director of News Affairs

- Coordinator of Special Events
- Coordinator of Special Operations
- Coordinator of Detached Services

Bureau of Operational Services
1st Deputy Supt.
- Patrol Division — Chief
- Traffic Division — Asst. Deputy Supt.
- Operations Command — Asst. Deputy Supts.

Bureau of Investigative Services
Deputy Supt.
- Detective Division — Chief
- Organized Crime Division — Chief
- Youth Division — Commander

Bureau of Field Tactical Services
Deputy Supt.
- Public Transportation Division — Asst. Deputy Supt.
- Gang Crime Enforcement Division-South — Commander
- Gang Crime Enforcement Division-North — Commander
- Gang Crime Enforcement Division-West — Commander
- Public Housing Division — Commander

standard operating procedure (SOP) manual
Collection of departmental directives governing the performance of duties.

dures for the numerous tasks in which officers engage. Collected and issued as a **standard operating procedure (SOP) manual,** these policies and rules have become a key tool in contemporary police management.

Although written rules have their limitations, one of their most important benefits is the role they can play in the control of discretion in the execution of duties. Many departments have in recent years issued rules about the use of deadly force that explicitly set forth the circumstances under which a police officer may shoot at a suspect. Others have adopted written policies about high-speed pursuits, spelling out the situations in which such pursuits may be undertaken and those in which a pursuit must be terminated. Other examples of such administrative rules include policies concerning mandatory arrests in cases of domestic violence and the handling of chronic alcoholics or the homeless. Some

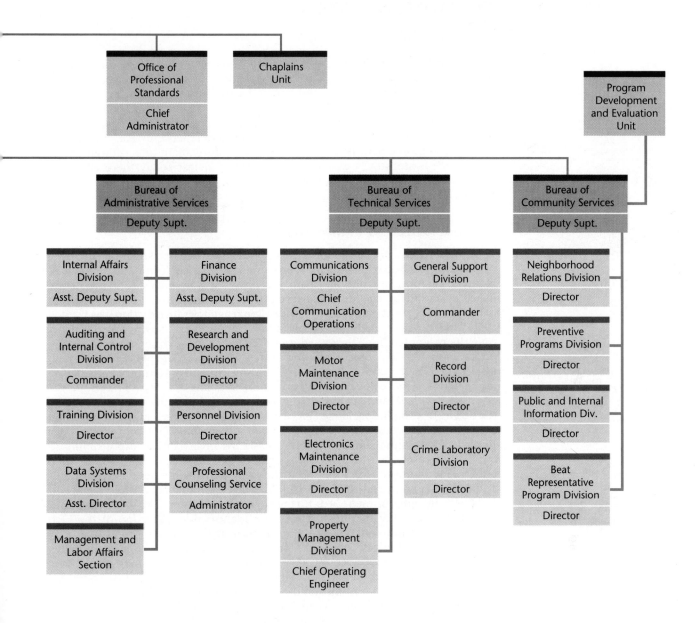

FIGURE 6.1 *Organization for command: The Chicago Police Department* (*Source:* Larry K. Gaines, Mittie D. Southerland, and John E. Angell, *Police Administration* [New York: McGraw-Hill, 1991], p. 82.)

research evidence suggests that written rules restricting the use of deadly force in New York City have helped to reduce considerably the number of police shootings and injuries to both citizens and officers.[55] There is also evidence that even written rules concerning matters such as hot pursuits and mandatory arrest policies in cases of domestic violence may be ignored by individual officers.[56]

Having discussed the police as a governmental, bureaucratic, institution, we turn now to the different types of police forces in the United States. We start with the federal police forces, and end up at the local level. Keep in mind, however, that it is at the local level where most police officers serve and where most policing takes place. This is the result of historical circumstances: After independence, the states assumed most governmental functions. The federal structure was created afterward to perform functions specifically assigned to it.

THE FEDERAL SYSTEM

Policing at the federal level can be dated to 1790, when Congress established a revenue marine force, subsequently called the Revenue Cutter Service and long since known as the U.S. Coast Guard, to police the nation's coasts and to enforce the revenue laws of the country. In the two centuries since then, the number of federal police forces has grown immensely. Although only 8.2 percent of all American law enforcement officers are employed in federal services, the federal role in law enforcement is an important one. Enforcement of certain laws and regulations is statutorily assigned to specific agencies. Today there are some sixty federal law enforcement agencies; here we will discuss only some of the largest.

The Federal Bureau of Investigation

The largest federal police agency is the Federal Bureau of Investigation (FBI), the principal investigative arm of the Department of Justice. While the FBI is now regarded as a powerful national agency, its original mandate was narrow. Established by President Theodore Roosevelt in 1908 as the Bureau of Investigation and given its current name in 1935, the original agency's jurisdiction was limited to just five offenses, including bankruptcy fraud and antitrust violations. Over time, its responsibilities expanded and the agency grew from 35 agents to approximately 23,000 people, including some 9,500 special agents in fifty-six field offices nationwide and sixteen foreign liaison posts. Its statutory jurisdiction now extends to more than 260 violations of federal laws.[57]

Passage of the Mann Act in 1910 marked the first step in the transformation of the FBI from a small, specialized force into a law enforcement agency that would be seen as a national crime-fighting arm of government. This act (named after Illinois Congressman James R. Mann) assigned investigative responsibility to the FBI for cases involving the transportation of women over national or state borders for "immoral purposes." But the early bureau was beset by charges of political corruption and abuses of civil liberties. That image began to change in 1924 with the appointment of J. Edgar Hoover as director. The same year Congress authorized the establishment of the Identification Division of the FBI, which became a national repository for fingerprints.

"With the appointment of J. Edgar Hoover as director in 1924, the image of the FBI began to change from a corrupt federal agency to that of a crack crime-fighting force."

Hoover instituted new standards for agents: they had to be college graduates with a degree in law or accounting and had to undergo a training course in a special school created for the FBI. Hoover's early tenure at the FBI coincided with the heyday of Prohibition and the growth of organized crime. Frustrated by the inability of local and state agencies to deal with the violent and highly publicized exploits of gangsters, many citizens began to call for the creation of a national police force. Hoover argued instead for legislation to give the bureau jurisdiction over criminals who crossed state lines, a technique many used to avoid being caught. In 1934 the Fugitive Felon Act made escape over a state line for the purpose of avoiding prosecution a federal crime. This legislation opened the way for the FBI to polish its image as a crack crime-fighting force. Its agents played key roles in the investigation and capture of such notorious criminals of the 1930s as John Dillinger, Clyde Barrow and Bonnie Parker, Baby Face Nelson, Pretty Boy Floyd, and Al Capone. Designation of the agency as the collector and disseminator of crime statistics nationwide through the Uniform Crime Reports (UCR) further secured the FBI's place at the head of the nation's law enforcement community. For decades, the UCR—and, by extension, the FBI—were considered the sole authoritative source of crime statistics.

While the well-publicized efforts of the FBI burnished its image in the public eye, less savory investigative work was being done behind closed doors in the

Federal agents emptying liquor bottles during Prohibition, early 1930s. (A bystander tries to save some liquor in his straw hat.)

name of national security. In 1939, President Franklin D. Roosevelt gave the FBI responsibility for matters related to espionage, sabotage, and violation of neutrality laws. This new responsibility led to the arrest of some spies working on behalf of the German government during World War II. It also provided Hoover with what he considered a mandate to investigate people and groups he deemed subversive. These investigations continued for years,[58] though the targets shifted from Nazis to Communists and eventually to both left-wing and civil rights groups. Techniques such as illegal wiretaps, opening of private citizens' mail, burglarizing of offices of targeted groups, forging of documents, and dissemination of rumors were used to discredit people and groups.[59] When many of these covert activities were revealed in the 1970s, the public was stunned to learn that the FBI had attempted to discredit not only left-wing groups such as the Black Panthers, but also such esteemed national leaders as Martin Luther King, Jr.[60] Hoover remained head of the FBI until his death in 1972. Since then, revelations of political surveillance of opponents of U.S. foreign policy, the maintenance of secret files on respected American authors, and charges of internal racial harassment of agents have surfaced periodically and caused renewed public concern about the FBI's activities.[61] (See the Criminal Justice Abroad box.)

New leadership has done much to restore the image of the agency. In recent years, the FBI has reordered its priorities and focused on areas such as white-collar crime, public corruption, organized crime, terrorism, drugs, and violent crime. It has conducted several well-known and successful investigations in these areas, such as the Walker spy case; the international "pizza connection" heroin ring investigation; Operation Greylord, an investigation of public corruption in Cook County, Illinois, that resulted in the conviction of thirteen county judges, eight police officers, and ten deputy sheriffs, among others; and ILLWIND, an investigation into fraud and bribery in the procurement process at the Department of Defense that has resulted in the conviction of thirty-three defendants thus far.[62] With the collapse of the Soviet Union and the consequent end of the Cold War, several hundred FBI agents have been reassigned from counterintelligence to enforcing organized crime laws against street gangs and drug groups.[63]

THE KGB—CONTROLLING INTELLIGENCE

(In 1940) the N.K.V.D., the Soviet secret police that was the forerunner of the K.G.B., was instructed to carry out "the supreme punishment—execution by a firing squad" against "14,700 former Polish officers, officials, landowners, policemen and gendarmes, held in camps for prisoners of war," as well as another 11,000 "members of different subversion and espionage organizations, former land- and factory owners, former Polish officers, former officials and former clergymen, arrested and held in jails in the western regions of Ukraine and Belarus." (1)

In October of 1992, Russia released secret documents detailing the Soviet massacre of 20,000 Poles in 1940. Although the bodies had been unearthed in 1943 in a mass grave in the Katyn forests west of Moscow, Soviet officials had asserted that Nazis were responsible for the deaths. In 1990, then-president of the USSR Mikhael Gorbachev admitted Soviet guilt in the Katyn massacre, but the 1992 release of secret files provided all the information that had been a mystery for fifty years.

Police forces serve to keep social order. As we pointed out at the beginning of this chapter, policing a society ensures an orderly, secure life for its members. Police forces protect the state and themselves, and not infrequently they function to protect a particular regime as well, through illegal as well as legal means. When a society undergoes some sort of upheaval, previously secret activities are exposed to view. The KGB activities that were exposed after the dissolution of the Soviet Union provide a perfect example.

Going public: The KGB

The Soviet Union's KGB (Komitet Gosudarstvennoy Bezpasnosti, or Committee of State Security) was probably the most notorious of all intelligence agencies. Undoubtedly the world's largest such organization, in 1985 the KGB had 400,000 officers inside the Soviet Union, 200,000 border troops, and a vast network of informers and agents at home and abroad.

The KGB no longer exists in its old form. It lost its components in all of the newly independent republics, which formed their own intelligence services. According to Eduard Shevardnaze, chairman of the Georgia State Counsel, the KGB has been replaced by the Information and Intelligence Bureau, a "totally new structure that . . . objectively informs the leadership and public opinion about home and world developments" (2). In Russia itself the new Agency for Federal Security, which replaces the KGB in that republic, has been scaled down to 40,000 personnel.

The Katyn massacre is not the only KGB-related "mystery" that has been made public. Once the USSR collapsed, any number of top-secret files began making their way into the light. Former KGB operatives began selling their memoirs. Many former officers started lecture tours in Western countries for hard-currency honoraria. Spy satellite photographs, too, were for sale; the once "ultrasecret" spy photos were more detailed than those that any nation had made public, according to experts (3). The old KGB headquarters were opened to Western visitors for a thirty-dollar admission charge. And new government officials in the former Soviet Union made public a variety of previously secret files.

While historians were not shocked by the information that came to light after the dissolution of the USSR, American citizens learned a great deal about the KGB in a few short months of newspaper reading. Among KGB files stamped "Top Secret" acquired in 1992 by the *Boston Globe* are those pertaining to Soviet involvement in

- the funding of Palestinian terrorists in the 1970s
- the bugging of foreign journalists
- financial support for Indian Prime Minister Indira Ghandi
- "a document from Andropov dated August 1969 offering to set up a demonstration outside the U.S. Embassy in New Delhi . . . (by) 'not less than 20,000 Muslims' at the bargain price of 5,000 rupees—about $500 at that time"
- the funding of the decaying Polish Communist Party
- recent arms shipments to the now-fallen government of Afghanistan (4)

Some of the files indicated the extent to which the KGB violated human rights. It appears that a KGB team in 1971 unsuccessfully tried to poison the dissident novelist Alexander Solzhenitsyn, who developed severe burns after the attempt and suffered the aftereffects for three months (5).

Standards of conduct for intelligence agencies?

Attempts have been made to provide standards of conduct for all police forces, including intelligence agencies. The member states of the United Nations unanimously adopted the *U.N. Code of Conduct for Law Enforcement Officials* in the General Assembly of 1979. They made it clear that

In countries where police powers are exercised by military authorities, whether uniformed or not, or by state security forces, the definition of law enforcement officials shall be regarded as including officers of such services. (6)

In other words, the officers of intelligence services are held to the same professional standards and obligations to respect human rights as the officers of civilian police forces. As yet, there is a big gap between standards and their realization—a fact that offending countries rarely acknowledge. In 1979 two of the authors of this textbook had the extraordinary experience of being invited, under United Nations auspices, to present lectures at the KGB senior officers' academy in Moscow. The 200 bemedaled officers in the audience listened intently to the presentations—on the U.N. Code of Conduct for Law Enforcement Officials and Human Rights in Criminal Justice—and applauded politely. In concluding remarks, the KGB general in charge assured the lecturers that, of course, the lectures simply confirmed the standards by which the KGB had always been guided.

The Russian people apparently have a different view. They have toppled the statue of Dherzhinsky, the founder of the KGB, on Moscow's Dzerzhinsky Square in front of the old KGB headquarters. Memorial, the Russian human rights organization, has erected in its place a monument dedicated to the victims of Stalin's and Dherzhinsky's secret police, the KGB (7).

SOURCES

1. Celestine Bohlen, "Russian Files Show Stalin Ordered Massacre of 20,000 Poles in 1940," *The New York Times,* October 15, 1992, p. 1.
2. David Molivani, "K.G.B. Liquidated," *Soviet Press Report,* May 26, 1992.
3. William J. Broad, "Russia Is Now Selling Spy Photos from Space," *The New York Times,* October 4, 1992, p. 8.
4. Paul Quinn-Judge, "Files Show K.G.B. Ties to Terrorism," *The Boston Globe,* May 29, 1992, p. 1.
5. David Remmisck, "KGB Plot to Assassinate Solzhenitsyn Reported," *The Washington Post,* April 21, 1992, p. D1.
6. U.N. General Assembly Resolution 34/169, of 17 December 1979.
7. Nancy Adler, *Memorial* (New York: Praeger, 1993).

QUESTIONS FOR DISCUSSION

1. Is it realistic to hold the officers of intelligence services to the same standards that govern civilian police officers?
2. Should exceptions be made in (a) wiretapping, (b) arrest, (c) search and seizure, (d) the taking of human life?
3. How should the U.N.'s code of conduct be enforced, and by whom?

Monument to the victims of the KGB, Moscow

"Chemists employed by the police can do remarkable things with blood. They can weave it into a rope to hang a man."
Margery Allingham, *The Tiger in the Smoke*, Doubleday, 1952.

genetic fingerprinting
Use of DNA as a technique for identifying suspects.

The FBI also develops and maintains advanced forensic research capabilities, training facilities, and extensive data bases of information on crime and criminals. The Laboratory Division collects and analyzes evidence for its own investigations as well as for other federal, state, and local law enforcement agencies. In 1982 the laboratory conducted nearly 800,000 scientific investigations; by 1985 that number had almost doubled.[64] The Forensic Science Research and Training Center provides advanced forensic training to FBI staff and other law enforcement personnel, including a technical training course in the implementation of new DNA technology (sometimes referred to as **genetic fingerprinting**) in criminal investigations.

Fingerprints are still maintained in the Identification Division that was established in 1924. Today, the bureau's files contain more than 181 million fingerprint cards, including more than 96 million that contain criminal history data on some 24 million people. Approximately 31,000 additional fingerprint cards arrive at the Identification Division every day. The FBI also maintains the National Crime Information Center (NCIC), a nationwide network of criminal justice information available to law enforcement agencies in all fifty states that contains records on stolen property, wanted persons with outstanding arrest warrants, criminal histories on persons arrested for serious offenses, and records of certain missing persons. More than 900,000 transactions are processed per day at the NCIC.[65]

In 1985, the bureau established the National Center for the Analysis of Violent Crime (NCAVC), a research and training center that provides assistance to law enforcement agencies faced with violent crimes that are unusual and/or particularly vicious or repetitive in nature, such as sexually oriented serial murders or child molestation cases involving multiple victims. Finally, the FBI National Academy, located at Quantico, Virginia, provides training free of charge to state, local, and foreign law enforcement officials. These courses are given to more than 1,000 state and local law enforcement administrators annually.

The Drug Enforcement Administration

Established in 1973, the Drug Enforcement Administration (DEA) is the primary federal agency responsible for enforcement of federal laws concerning the use, sale, and distribution of narcotics and other controlled substances in the United States. Of DEA's over 6,000 staff members, nearly half are special agents. The agency is headquartered in New York; its agents are stationed throughout the United States in nineteen divisional offices and fourteen strike forces in major cities. Some agents are posted overseas. Since 1982 the DEA has shared concurrent jurisdiction with the FBI for investigations of federal drug violations. Inasmuch as drug offenders frequently violate other laws as well, the DEA also cooperates with the Bureau of Alcohol, Tobacco and Firearms (ATF) and the Immigration and Naturalization Service. Cooperation also extends to law enforcement agencies at the state and local levels.

In support of its investigative endeavors, the agency maintains a narcotics intelligence system that collects, analyzes, and disseminates data. At the international level, the DEA assists foreign governments with programs intended to reduce the availability of illicit drugs, such as the eradication of crops like coca and poppies from which drugs are derived, crop substitutions, and the training of foreign officials. Other responsibilities include the investigation of drug seizures by U.S. Customs agents at border points and regulation of the distribution of legal narcotics and drugs.

The Bureau of Alcohol, Tobacco and Firearms

Although less well known than the FBI, ATF is a federal police agency with considerable success in law enforcement, ever since Elliot Ness—one of its most famous agents—battled bootleggers and gamblers during Prohibition days. Originally part of the Internal Revenue Service, the Bureau of Alcohol, Tobacco and Firearms was created to enforce the ban on alcohol that was mandated by the Volstead Act and ratified as the Eighteenth Amendment to the Constitution in 1919. ATF became an independent bureau under the Department of the Treasury in 1972.

Since the repeal of the Eighteenth Amendment in 1933, the suppression of the illegal manufacture and sale of alcoholic beverages has become a less important part of the duties of ATF, although as recently as 1983 it seized sixty illegal stills.[66] Today's ATF is primarily concerned with firearms; its mission is to reduce the illegal use of firearms and enforce federal firearms laws. As part of this charge, ATF maintains the National Firearms Tracing Center, which completes hundreds of thousands of trace requests annually, the majority of them for other law enforcement agencies. ATF is also responsible for issuance of federal firearms licenses and permits for the import and export of firearms. Additional duties include reducing criminal use of explosives, combating arson-for-profit schemes, and ensuring voluntary compliance with federal alcohol and tobacco taxes. A staff of more than 2,900 employees, including 1,200 criminal investigators, carries out the many responsibilities of this agency all across the nation.

Among the agency's recent law enforcement successes, two stand out: Operation Intercept (1990–1992), run by ATF jointly with other federal and local law enforcement agencies, netted 647 illegal firearms and 32,000 rounds of ammunition[67]; and Project Triggerlock (1989–1991), a joint operation with DEA and the Internal Revenue Service, resulted in fifty-four arrests and seventy-nine federal and state indictments on drug-and-gun trafficking charges, and the confiscation of 400 weapons (including machine guns), 21 properties, and 80 vehicles. This operation dealt a major blow to Chicago West Side gang activities.[68] ATF has also come under recent attack when on February 28, 1993, in an operation against a heavily armed cult headquarters near Waco, Texas, four ATF agents lost their lives in the initial assault. Operational control was then transferred to the attorney general and to the FBI. On the fifty-first day of the siege, April 19, 1993, the FBI commenced an assault on the heavily fortified compound with a tank and disabling gas. The result was an inferno in which 86 persons died, including 24 children.

Immigration and Naturalization Service

The Immigration and Naturalization Service (INS) has the responsibility of overseeing the admission, naturalization, exclusion, and deportation of aliens. It is also authorized to conduct investigations of aliens who are residing illegally in the United States or who have engaged in activities prohibited by law and to investigate people who attempt to import aliens illegally into the country. In this age of global mobility, the Immigration and Naturalization Service's work load has increased significantly. Just as legitimate business people and tourists travel at vastly increased rates, so do illegal entrepreneurs, from swindlers to drug dealers and terrorists. The immigration laws are calculated to interdict their activities. INS agents are posted at every U.S. point of entry, including ports, airports, and border crossings. Their activities include checking entrants by means of electronic data and profile, as well as actually searching baggage and travelers themselves.

The uniformed enforcement division of the INS is known as the Border Patrol (BP), established in 1924. Today the BP patrols approximately 8,000 miles of international borders using motor vehicles, boats, aircraft, horses, and foot patrols. Their objective is to prevent the illegal entry of aliens through official points of entry and to apprehend others at nondesignated areas. With a force of approximately 3,700 agents, the BP apprehended approximately 855,000 aliens in 1989.[69]

"The Bureau of Alcohol, Tobacco and Firearms' most famous agent may well be Elliot Ness, who battled bootleggers and gamblers during Prohibition in the 1920s."

"Just as legitimate business people and tourists travel at vastly increased rates today, so do illegal entrepreneurs, from swindlers to drug dealers and terrorists, vastly increasing the work of the INS."

The U.S. Secret Service

In July 1992, a federal grand jury in Boston indicted Charles Dwaine Hitt of Riddle, Oregon, for making threats to kill the president of the United States. Hitt was arrested when he tried to gain entrance to the Baltimore Medical Center—dressed in white, like medical staff—where then President George Bush was making a scheduled appearance. The arrest was the result of a successful investigation by the U.S. Secret Service.[70]

Although the Secret Service is best known as the agency responsible for protection of the president, its original purpose when it was created in 1865 was to investigate counterfeiting, under the direction of the Congress. Protection of the president became its responsibility following the assassination of President McKinley in 1901. The Secret Service is now part of the U.S. Department of the Treasury and is responsible for protecting not only the president but also the vice president, their families, presidential candidates, visiting heads of state, and executive buildings. The White House police force is part of the Secret Service. In 1983 there were approximately 2,800 Secret Service agents and uniformed officers.

Other Federal Law Enforcement Agencies

Many other agencies within the federal government perform law enforcement functions. Among the largest is the U.S. Customs Service, part of the Department of the Treasury. The Internal Revenue Service, another Treasury Department agency, has agents to enforce laws relating to taxes and their collection. The Department of Justice maintains the U.S. Marshal Service, which fulfills a number of court-related and law enforcement duties. The Supreme Court of the United States has its own police force of some 200 people. Several other agencies, such as the Federal Trade Commission (FTC), the Securities and Exchange Commission (SEC), the United States Postal Service, and the Environmental Protection Agency (EPA), maintain their own law enforcement agencies to ensure compliance with the laws and regulations within their jurisdiction.

"As of October 1990, 65,490 persons were employed by federal law enforcement agencies; 120,504 were employed in state law enforcement, and 614,465 in county and municipal forces."

As of 1990, 65,490 (full-time equivalent) persons were employed by federal law enforcement agencies, a considerable number indeed. Yet more were employed in state law enforcement (120,504), and vastly more in county and municipal police forces (614,465).[71]

STATE AND LOCAL SYSTEMS

In contrast to federal law enforcement agencies, all others could be loosely referred to as the law enforcement systems of the various states, since all of them are enforcing principally state laws. However, by virtue of their territorially defined jurisdictions, and their affiliation, we must distinguish between those that operate state wide, those that operate countywide, and those that operate within the limits of cities and municipalities.

The U.S. Coast Guard is the oldest police force in the United States. This Coast Guard vessel is rescuing Cuban rafters off Florida.

State Police

State police forces are a relatively modern creation. The advent of the automobile and the highway system, with the concomitant need to regulate traffic on the highways, was a significant impetus for the creation of state police agencies across the country. Since highways may cross the jurisdictional boundaries of local police forces, some agency with statewide authority was required.

The Texas Rangers were the first statewide police force, but they were dis-

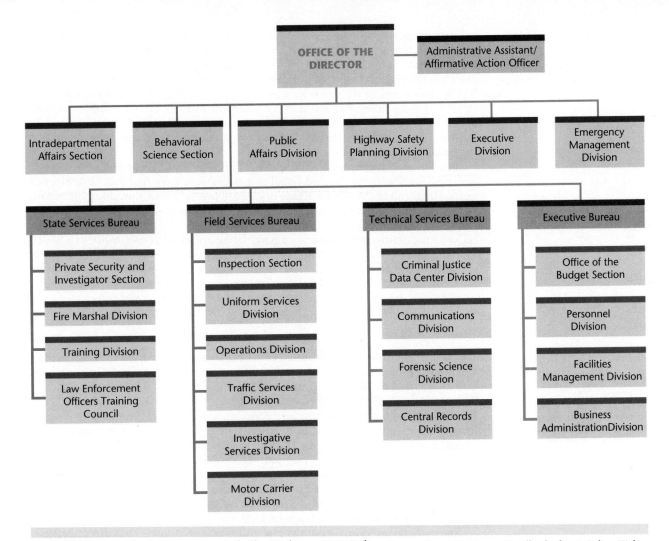

FIGURE 6.2 *Organization for command: The Michigan State Police* (*Source:* Donald A. Torres, *Handbook of State Police, Highway Patrols, and Investigative Agencies* [Westport, Conn.: Greenwood Press, 1987], p. 171.)

tinctly different from contemporary state police forces. The agency that would become the model for many state police forces throughout the country was Pennsylvania's, which was formed in 1905 in response to violence caused by conflicts between labor and management in the coal mines of western Pennsylvania. The Pennsylvania State Constabulary was a highly centralized force inspired by foreign quasi-military units such as the Royal Irish Constabulary. Although it was criticized for its rough treatment of immigrants and accused of acting on behalf of big business interests,[72] Pennsylvania's state police nevertheless inspired fourteen other states to organize similar forces by 1923.

"Pennsylvania's state police inspired fourteen other states to organize similar forces by 1923."

Today there are three types of state law enforcement agencies: state police, highway patrols, and state investigative agencies. While some states have several agencies, like Oklahoma, which has a separate highway patrol, narcotics bureau, and investigation bureau, others, like Michigan's State Police, consolidate all the duties typically associated with the state police into a single agency.[73] (Figure 6.2) Every state but Hawaii now has some form of state police agency. Over a third of those employed by state police agencies are civilians who work in technical support positions, such as dispatching, data processing, and recordkeeping.

Belief in the principle that law enforcement should remain primarily a local responsibility has meant that the role of the state police has been somewhat circumscribed. Nevertheless, they perform several functions in addition to their highly visible role in the enforcement of highway traffic laws. A recent survey of state police agencies showed that, in addition to their enforcement activities, nearly 90 percent of them also perform accident investigations, conduct public information campaigns about traffic safety, and manage accident scenes involving hazardous materials.

All state police agencies also conduct criminal investigations and make arrests in connection with them, and in all but two states they maintain intelligence units. Nearly all of these investigate organized crime, fraud, narcotics violations, violent crime, arson, and motor vehicle theft. Investigative services and information gathered by intelligence units are provided to local agencies without charge. Most states maintain their own forensic laboratories with capabilities in ballistics, analysis of physical and biological evidence, and fingerprint analysis. Forensic services are also made available to local police agencies within the state.[75] A majority (78%) of state police agencies operate training academies, and many provide civil defense and emergency medical services.[76]

County Police

Law enforcement in most counties is the responsibility of a sheriff's agency, although some counties maintain police departments, such as those in Honolulu, Baltimore, and St. Louis counties, and in the populous suburban counties of Nassau and Suffolk on Long Island, New York.[77]

"The county sheriff's position is unique among law enforcement personnel: It is an elected office in all but two states, and has considerable political power."

The county sheriff's position is unique among law enforcement personnel: It is an elected office in all but two states, where the sheriff is appointed.[78] The sheriff holds a considerable amount of political power; in some counties, the sheriff is the most important political figure. Most sheriff departments are responsible for regular law enforcement duties, such as patrol, criminal investigations, traffic enforcement, and accident investigations, as well as civil functions like serving civil processes and providing court security. Furthermore, 89 percent of sheriff departments maintain a jail.[79]

The most recent data on county law enforcement indicate that there are 2,894 rural and suburban county agencies employing approximately 275,000 people. Nearly two-thirds (66%) of county law enforcement personnel are sworn officers and one-third (34%) are civilians.[80] The largest sheriff department is that of Los Angeles County in California, with a force of some 6,500 full-time sworn officers (making it larger than most city police departments).[81] A sizable majority (67%) of sheriff departments, however, employ fewer than twenty-five sworn officers.[82]

Municipal Police Forces

In urbanized modern America, as in urbanized ancient Greece, the city is the societal unit with which most people identify. The city's most visible government representatives are the municipal police. Citizens rely on the police for advice, service, and protection around the clock. No wonder, then, that municipal police forces are one of the largest governmental employers and consume one of the biggest slices of revenue. Local police forces account for more than three-quarters (76.8%) of the total employment in police agencies at all levels of government.[83] A recent survey estimated that 11,989 local police agencies employed approximately 494,000 people, including 376,000 sworn officers.[84] The distribution of personnel is very lopsided, however, ranging from departments with merely one or two employees to the New York City Police Department, with a force of 36,227 law enforcement employees in 1991, the largest in the country. Ninety-one percent of all police departments employ fewer than fifty people and

"In America's cities, citizens rely on the police for advice, service, and protection around the clock and every day of the year."

more than half employ fewer than ten. As a result, a large number of people are
employed by a disproportionately small number of departments.

Big-city departments account for less than 1 percent of the total number of
agencies, but their employees constitute approximately 23 percent of total police
employment at the local level.[85] The sheer size of some of the larger departments
is intimidating. New York City has a police payroll of over $144 million, Chicago
of over $40 million, and Los Angeles of $37 million.[86] Yet fiscal management,
with its constant crises, revenue shortfalls, and budget-cutting exercises, is only
one of the many challenges facing a police department. Controlling crime, controlling officers, and facing constant pressures from all segments of society make
the management of large urban departments one of the most difficult governmental tasks.

The limited size of small-town departments means that they differ from their
big-city counterparts in several respects. Officers who work in small departments usually work as generalists, and there is a much less formal chain of command than that found in the highly bureaucratized structure of large municipal
departments. The chief of police might be found on patrol, and a detective might
be making traffic stops. These departments also usually have a smaller proportion of civilian employees than those in cities.[87] City residents would probably be
surprised to realize that the continuous presence and round-the-clock availability of police officers to which they are accustomed are not the norm in many
departments. Agencies staffed by as few as one or two officers simply cannot
provide service twenty-four hours a day, seven days a week.[88]

The small-town police officer at times has been depicted in popular culture as
a good-natured figure whom nobody takes very seriously as a law enforcement
officer. Some recent research, however, suggests that in fact investigative effectiveness, as measured by clearance rates, is greater in smaller departments than
in larger ones.[89] Additional research will be required before we conclude that
small-town police are more effective than those in large cities or, if they are, what
factors account for the difference.

Special Purpose Police

Throughout the country, police agencies that are not part of the local department
possess police powers within specified jurisdictional limits that may cut across
political boundaries. Special police forces include transit police, public housing
police, airport police, public school police, and park police. In popular conception, special police forces are often regarded as inferior to general municipal
police forces. Indeed, some of them started out as guard services. By now, however, most of the special forces are as well recruited and trained as their municipal counterparts. Some have superior standards of training, given the nature of
their often highly specialized duties. The New York–New Jersey Port Authority
Police, for example, has reached some of the highest standards of recruitment,
training, and performance.

The force most familiar to college students is probably campus security. Campus police originated with a small force at Yale University in 1894 as a result of
frequent confrontations between students and New Haven police precipitated by
strained relationships between students and town residents. The New Haven police decided to assign two officers to the campus to improve relations between
the school and the police. Apparently, past encounters with the students had
been so troublesome that the police had difficulty in recruiting volunteers to
serve in this "hardship" position. When two officers finally came forward, concern about their safety was such that as they "walked across the New Haven
Green each morning and disappeared behind the walls of Yale, their brother
officers wondered at first if they would ever see the pair again."[90] Since then,
campus security forces have become common at schools and universities across
the country. The typical arrangement on today's campus is one in which the

*"Controlling crime, controlling
officers, and facing constant
pressures from all segments of
society make the management of
large urban police departments
one of the most difficult government jobs."*

155

college or university maintains a proprietary security department. The officers in this department often have full police powers, wear uniforms, and may even carry firearms.

Several of the special police forces are quite large. America's five largest special police forces operate in the New York metropolitan area, with over 10,000 sworn officers (Table 6.1). The New York City Transit Authority Police, for instance, has 3,900 officers who patrol approximately 250 miles of subways used by more than three-million riders daily. The size of this force makes it not only the largest special police force in the United States, but also one of the ten largest police departments of any kind (Figure 6.3).

TABLE 6.1 The Ten Largest Special Police Agencies, 1987

City or Metropolitan Area	Jurisdiction	Full-Time Sworn Officers
New York City	Transit system	3,900
New York City	Public schools	2,275
New York City	Public housing	2,171
New York City	Transportation centers*	1,433
New York City	Fire investigation	400
Washington, D.C.	Transit system	242
Philadelphia	Public housing	151
San Francisco	Airport	140
San Francisco	Transit system	132
Boston	Transit system	131

*Include airports, bus terminals, passenger and shipping ports, bridges and tunnels, and industrial parks.
SOURCE: Brian A. Reaves, *Police Departments in Large Cities, 1987* (Washington, D.C.: Bureau of Justice Statistics, 1989), p. 8.

The proliferation of police departments operating within the same jurisdiction, usually a municipality, poses a dilemma. While the need for special skills and often for extended mobility is recognized, the problems associated with overlapping authority and thus conflict loom large. Cities have tried to solve this problem by creating liaisons and, especially during special events, joint commands or task forces. There is a drive to consolidate all local police forces operating within one jurisdiction. Consolidation drives are supported by those who expect higher pay scales. They are opposed by officers of special forces who enjoy their jurisdictional independence and separate status (see the Criminal Justice on Trial box).

Private Police

"Whether at work, at home, or at leisure, Americans are now the object of surveillance or protection furnished by the private security industry more often than at any previous time."

Security guards, alarms, closed-circuit surveillance systems, and antitheft devices are ubiquitous in American life today. Whether at work, at home, or at leisure, Americans are now the object of surveillance or protection furnished by the private security industry more often than at any previous time. Clifford Shearing and Philip Stenning, who have written extensively on the subject, note that the widespread acceptance of private police, or private security, has significantly extended the reach of social control.[91] Given the extent and significance of this phenomenon, any discussion of policing in the United States would be incomplete without reference to private security forces, even though they are not part of the publicly financed system of law enforcement.

While the public is quick to rail against police excesses, most of us willingly

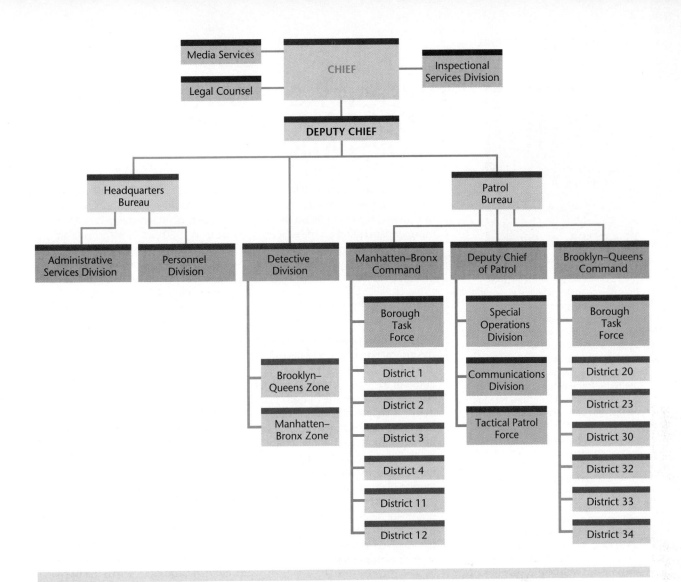

FIGURE 6.3 *Organization for command: The New York City Transit Police Department* (*Source:* New York City Transit Police Department, *Annual Report,* 1987.)

and readily submit to intrusions on our privacy by private police. Surrendering packages to a security guard at the door of a store, allowing shopping bags to be searched, and being watched on camera both inside and outside a building, and even in elevators, are activities citizens accept without complaint.

The notion of private policing is older than the concept of public policing, and the legitimacy of private policing is rooted in the common-law tradition of the right to protect private property.[92] Legislation passed in the nineteenth century in Pennsylvania was an extreme example. In 1865, lawmakers conferred on private corporations the authority to maintain peace by allowing mine owners to create the Iron and Coal Police, a force intended to protect their interests against striking miners.[93] Today's private security companies also have their origins in the nineteenth century. Companies like the American Express Company, founded in 1850 by Henry Wells and Walter Fargo (who later created the Wells Fargo Company), and Brink's (1859) were started for the purpose of protecting valuables in transit and became the predecessors of modern armored guard services. In 1855 Allan Pinkerton established a private investigation agency that became the prototype for private detective agencies and guard services.[94]

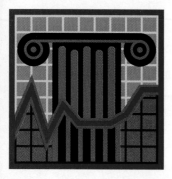

DIVERSITY OF POLICE FORCES—FROM CONFLICT TO COOPERATION

[L]et a crime be committed which promises to make headline news, and all pretense at cooperative relationships may be cast to the winds. In unusual cases, two or three federal agencies and a state police force, as well as the usual police units of the county and of the city, town, or village, will all descend upon the scene of the crime. Each may enter into quick and informal arrangements with one or more of the other forces interested in the case. These are in the nature of temporary alliances, or agreements to exchange pertinent information. The end and aim of such devices is to monopolize the investigation in so far as possible, and to prevent other agencies from sharing in the information and evidence so accumulated. Sometimes the whole affair smacks of conspiracy. Witnesses are spirited away and held incommunicado, rival forces are provided with false leads, while inspired complaints and countercharges of inefficiency arise on every hand. (1)

Police reformer Bruce Smith wrote this half a century ago. Today, cooperation is more likely to prevail than the competition he describes, but the huge number of local, state, and federal law enforcement agencies in the United States makes that cooperation a challenge. While the existence of approximately 14,000 local police departments in the nation may point to an inefficient system, Americans' fears of "big government" make it likely that a highly decentralized system will be the rule for some time to come. Add to 14,000 local departments the 51 state police and highway patrol agencies and the 50 to 200 federal agencies involved in law enforcement (experts differ on the number depending on the exact definition of law enforcement used), and it is easy to see how jurisdictional conflicts can arise.

Crime problems that cross jurisdictions

Some crime problems are clearly the jurisdiction of a local police department. Others, such as treason, abuse of the mail system, and illegal entry of aliens into the United States, are clearly the jurisdiction of federal law enforcement agencies. But what about car theft when the car is driven across state lines? Or local sales of imported drugs? Examples of crime problems falling into a number of jurisdictional categories are nearly endless. Indeed, the number of agencies that could get involved in any one crime also seems nearly endless:

A federal park police official . . . suggested that, at the right kind of criminal event in Washington, D.C.—say, international narcoterrorism directed at the vice-president and a foreign dignitary on the grounds of a national monument—twenty-six separate federal and local law enforcement agencies could plausibly claim entitlement to investigate the incident. (2)

Task forces

As Smith reported in 1949, police forces in the past tended to fight one another rather than crime. Fortunately, much has changed in recent years. It is now a common practice for police forces of various jurisdictional levels, and of differing duties or specializations, to create task forces, joint operations, and consolidated commands. The serial murders of fifteen children in Atlanta in 1980 and 1981 provide an example. Intense public pressure had built up to solve these homicides. Success came through the cooperation of federal, state, county, and city law enforcement agencies advised by "investigative consultants," experienced homicide detectives from five other cities (3).

The nation's "war on drugs" likewise has fostered greater collaboration by potentially competing law enforcement agencies (4). In the early 1980s the South Florida Task Force was established to fight the importation of drugs, with the cooperation of virtually all federal, state, and local police agencies operating in southern Florida (5). The Florida venture was the first of a number of organized crime drug enforcement task forces now operating in large cities across the nation. These task forces are staffed by personnel from as many as nine separate federal law enforcement agencies. A number of interagency approaches to fighting the drug problem have taken on a permanent character. For example, the El Paso Intelligence Center (EPIC) was established to pool all relevant law enforcement intelligence of the Drug Enforcement Administration, the U.S. Customs Service, the U.S. Coast Guard, the Federal Aviation Administration, and the Bureau of Alcohol, Tobacco, and Firearms. Operating as an information clearinghouse, EPIC makes this intelligence available to units operating on land, at sea, or in the air (6).

Number of Employees (1991) in Three of the Largest Federal Law Enforcement Agencies	
FBI	22,932 employees; 10,036 sworn agents
DEA	6,286 employees; 3,312 special agents
U.S. Marshals Service	3,300 employees; 2,300 marshals and deputy marshals

SOURCE: William A. Geller and Norval Morris, "Relations between Federal and Local Police," in *Modern Policing*, eds. Michael Tonry and Norval Morris (Chicago: University of Chicago Press, 1992), p. 245.

Joint training programs

The extension of interagency cooperation to joint training programs helps to maintain the professionalism of law enforcement forces, to foster a spirit of cooperation among officers of different jurisdictions, and to educate law enforcement officials about which agencies have jurisdiction over which types of crimes. The FBI Academy at Quantico, Virginia, trains not only its own agents but also officers from state and local jurisdictions in various investigatory skills. The FBI also provides training via satellite teleconferencing and field training programs for police officers in small departments throughout the country. The Treasury Department operates another training program, the Federal Law Enforcement Training Center (FLETC), with sites in Georgia, Arizona, and New Mexico. FLETC is an interagency training facility for the federal criminal investigators and uniformed police officers of all federal agencies apart from the FBI and for state and local law enforcement personnel (7). FLETC trains approximately 20,000 students each year and provides experts from federal agencies to teach specialized subject matter including fraud, financial crime, forest fire arson, courtroom security, drug law en-

forcement, and forgery. Serving sixty-eight different federal agencies, FLETC was founded in 1970 to improve communication and collaboration among the wide variety of law enforcement officials it trains.

Sharing intelligence, pooling resources, and participating in joint training programs are strategies that are likely to increase police operational efficiency in the United States without raising the fear of the police state that has kept the nation from consolidating its many law enforcement agencies.

SOURCES

1. Bruce Smith, *Police Systems in the United States* (New York: Harper & Brothers, 1949), p. 26.
2. William A. Geller and Norval Morris, "Relations between Federal and Local Police," in *Modern Policing*, eds. Michael Tonry and Norval Morris (Chicago: University of Chicago Press, 1992), p. 247.
3. Pierce R. Brooks, "The Investigative Consultant Team: A New Approach for Law Enforcement Cooperation" (Washington, D.C.: Police Executive Research Forum, 1982).
4. Gwen A. Holden and Susan Keitges, "Intergovernmental Cooperation: Its Role in Law Enforcement," in *State Laws and Procedures Affecting Drug Trafficking Control: A National View*, eds. John T. Bentivoglio et al. (Washington, D.C.: National Governors Association and National Criminal Justice Association, 1985), pp. 217–243; Geller and Morris, "Relations between Federal and Local Police," pp. 231–348.
5. G. O. W. Mueller and Freda Adler, *Outlaws of the Ocean—The Complete Book of Contemporary Crime on the High Seas* (New York: Hearst Marine Books, 1985), pp. 29–30.
6. Geller and Morris, "Relations between Federal and Local Police," pp. 231–348.
7. Charles R. Rinkevich, "Federal Law Enforcement Training Center (FLETC)," in *The Encyclopedia of Police Science*, ed. William G. Bailey (New York: Garland Publishing, 1989), pp. 201–203; Charles Godroe, "Federal Training for State and Local Police Agencies," *Law and Order* (March 1985):22–24.

QUESTIONS FOR DISCUSSION

1. What benefits might there be to having the highly decentralized law enforcement system that exists in the United States?
2. What incentives are there for local, state, and federal law enforcement agencies to cooperate in fighting crime?
3. If you were to opt for law enforcement as a career, which police force would you prefer? Why? Would your answer be different if all police forces had the same entrance and promotion requirements as well as equally high training standards and equal pay scales?

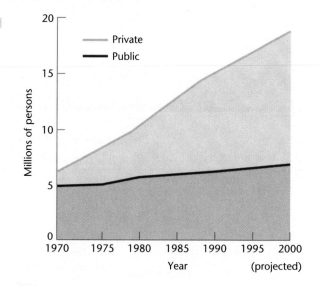

FIGURE 6.4 *The growth of private and public police, 1970–2000* (*Source:* Robert J. Fisher and Gion Green, *Introduction to Security,* 5th ed. [Stoneham, Mass.: Butterworth-Heinemann, 1992].)

Private security today includes guard and patrol services, private investigators, alarm companies, armored car and courier services, and security consulting services for loss prevention strategies, computer security systems, and executive protection strategies. Private security forces even provide protection to entire communities, and some compare very favorably with the public police in surrounding neighborhoods in terms of crime prevention and lower levels of fear of crime.[95] The costs of private security were approximately $52 billion in 1990,[96] while the most recent (1988) expenditure figures for police protection at all levels of governmental spending amounted to only about $32 billion.[97] Estimates for 1990 indicated that 1.5 million people worked in private security, approximately twice as many as were employed by public law enforcement agencies[98] (Figure 6.4). Many of those employed in private security have a background in public law enforcement. In fact, research conducted for the National Institute of Justice indicated that almost one-quarter (24%) of public police personnel also work off-duty in private security.[99]

The widespread use of private security forces has raised a number of issues. One area of concern is the fitness of security personnel, especially of guards. Training is usually minimal, and few states had standards until recently. Worldwide concern about the quality of private policing was expressed in 1975, when the Fifth United Nations Congress on the Prevention of Crime and the Treatment of Offenders called for "public controls" in the nature of "licensing, screening and the requirement of basic qualifications."[100] Another concern is the question of equity. Is it fair for those who can afford it to have more protection than those who cannot? One reason for public police is to provide equal protection to all; the idea that the wealthy can buy added services seems to violate this principle and raises troubling questions about the willingness of the wealthy to support tax-financed public police.[101] The employment of off-duty police officers (an estimated 166,000) by private security companies also raises a number of issues, including questions of police department liability for the actions of its officers while engaged in private duty, potential tarnishing of the image of police if officers give the appearance of serving private interests only, and the possibility of conflicts of interest.[102]

During the 1980s the privatization of criminal justice services, especially policing, was a major political agenda item. Budgetary constraints affected the growth of public policing.[103] It was natural, therefore, that private policing increased during this decade. Yet its numerical growth has not been matched by an expansion of standards and controls.

REVIEW

American policing has its historical roots in Anglo-Saxon law and custom. Over a thousand years ago there originated the strong sense of community self-help that is still with us today. But there also developed the tradition of entrusting the peacekeeping function to leaders within the community, notably the sheriff, an officer who until this day is the principal peace officer at the county level.

In 1829 a standing police force was formed in London, and a generation later American cities followed this example and created police forces performing patrol duty in uniform. Well into the twentieth century, in the United States these forces were dependent on political patronage. Progressive reformers sought to change this, but real professionalization (through recruitment and training) did not occur until the second half of this century.

All but the smallest police departments in the United States are bureaucracies, marked by hierarchical structures with a clearly delineated chain of command, a division of labor among a number of bureaus, and a set of rules and regulations. Two important principles that govern the structure of the chain of command are span of control and unity of command; these, along with levels of authority, ensure control of subordinates and clear communication channels both downward and upward throughout the organization. Orders are passed down and followed.

The contemporary structure of American police organizations is a result of two competing forces: police professionalization within a rigid, bureaucratic, military command structure, on the one hand, and a reaction against that structure by the civil rights movement, and also by many officers and even administrators. Today's police forces have developed strategies for more cooperative and above all more community-related management styles.

Professional police forces can be found at every level of government. Several such forces are empowered to enforce federal laws, among them the Federal Bureau of Investigation (FBI), the Drug Enforcement Administration (DEA), the Bureau of Alcohol, Tobacco and Firearms (ATF), the Immigration and Naturalization Service (INS), the U.S. Secret Service, and many others. At the state level, police forces—often originating as highway patrols—were established in the first half of the twentieth century. State police forces play a vital role in policing the areas of the state outside the jurisdiction of municipal police forces, assisting the cities and counties when needed, and maintaining statewide identification systems, laboratories, and training facilities. Municipal police forces employ by far the largest number of personnel among all public police forces. They bear the brunt of law enforcement and crime prevention activities entrusted to the public police. Increasingly in recent decades, however, Americans have turned to private policing, contracted for through private security firms. These employ twice as many personnel as public police agencies. The protection provided by private policing is much appreciated by many sectors of society, especially industry, but the quality of these services has not yet achieved a uniformly high level.

Notes

1. The quote is from Juvenal (A.D. 40–120), as quoted in William Durant, *The Story of Civilization*, vol. III, *Caesar and Christ* (New York: Simon and Schuster, 1935), p. 341.

2. Written by the authors and based on Martin A. Kelly, "Citizen Survival in Ancient Rome," *Police Studies* 11 (1988):195–201. For more on the origins of police in ancient civilizations, see R. W. Davies, "Augustus Caesar: A Police System in the Ancient World," in *Pioneers in Policing*, ed. Philip John Stead (Montclair, N.J.: Patterson Smith, 1977), pp. 12–32; Patrick B. Adamson, "Some Comments on the Origin of the Police," *Police Studies* 14 (1991):1–2; Martin A. Kelly, "Western Civilization's First Detectives," *Police Studies* 10 (1987):36–41.

3. Charles Reith, *The Blind Eye of History: A Study of the Origins of the Present Police Era* (Montclair, N.J.: Patterson Smith, 1975) (reprint of 1952 edition).

4. T. A. Critchley, *A History of Police in England and Wales*, 2d ed. (Montclair, N.J.: Patterson Smith, 1972).

5. Quoted in Critchley, *A History of the Police*, p. 21.

6. See Reith, *The Blind Eye of History.*

7. Clive Emsley, *Policing and Its Context, 1750–1870* (New York: Schocken Books, 1984), p. 21.

8. Metropolitan Police Force, *Instruction Book* (London, 1829).

9. Samuel Walker, *The Police in America: An Introduction*, 2d ed. (New York: McGraw-Hill, 1992). For further information on the history of policing, see W. L. Melville Lee, *A History of Police in England* (Montclair, N.J.: Patterson Smith, 1971) (reprint of 1901 edition); Emsley, *Policing and Its Context;* Allan Silver, "The Demand for Order in Civil Society: A Review of Some Themes in the History of Urban Crime, Police, and Riots," in *The Police: Six Sociological Essays*, ed. David J. Bordua (New York: Wiley, 1967), pp. 1–24.

10. See Roger Lane, "Urban Police and Crime in Nineteenth-Century America," in *Crime and Justice: A Review of Research*, Vol. 15, eds. Michael Tonry and Norval Morris (Chicago: University of Chicago Press, 1992), pp. 1–50.

11. David R. Johnson, *American Law Enforcement: A History* (St. Louis, Mo.: Forum Press, 1981).

12. Douglas Greenberg, "The Effectiveness of Law Enforcement in Eighteenth-Century New York," *American Journal of Legal History* 19 (July 1975):173–207.

13. Johnson, *American Law Enforcement.*

14. Samuel Walker, *Popular Justice: A History of American Criminal Justice* (New York: Oxford University Press, 1980).

15. Roger Lane, *Policing the City: Boston, 1822–1885* (Cambridge: Harvard University Press, 1967).

16. Walker, *Popular Justice;* and see Julian P. Boyd, "The Sheriff in Colonial North Carolina," *North Carolina Historical Review* 5 (April 1928):151–180.

17. Walker, *The Police in America*, p. 6.

18. Johnson, *American Law Enforcement.*

19. Lane, "Urban Police and Crime in Nineteenth-Century America."

20. James F. Richardson, *Urban Police in the United States* (Port Washington, New York: Kennikat Press, 1974).

21. Richard Maxwell Brown, "The American Vigilante Tradition," in *Violence in America: Historical and Comparative Perspectives*, eds. Hugh Davis Graham and Ted Robert Gurr (Beverly Hills, CA: Sage, 1979), pp. 154–226.

22. Johnson, *American Law Enforcement.*

23. Dorothy M. Schulz, "Holdups, Hobos, and the Homeless: A Brief History of Railroad Police in North America," *Police Studies* 10 (Summer 1987):90–95.

24. Roger Lane, "Urban Police and Crime in Nineteenth-Century America." For a discussion of other historical interpretations of factors that precipitated the creation of the police see Robert Liebman and Michael Polen, "Perspectives on Policing in Nineteenth-Century America," *Social Science History* 2 (1978):346–360;

Eric H. Monkkonen, *Police in Urban America, 1860–1920* (New York: Cambridge University Press, 1981); Brendan Maguire, "The Police in the 1800s: A Three City Analysis," *Journal of Crime and Justice* 13 (1990):103–132. See also Jack Kuykendall, "The Municipal Police Detective: An Historical Analysis," *Criminology* 24 (1986):175–201.

25. Johnson, *American Law Enforcement*.

26. Walker, *The Police in America*.

27. Walker, *Popular Justice*.

28. See Monkkonen, *Police in Urban America*, for a discussion and analysis of the services the police provided to the homeless and to children.

29. Lane, "Urban Police and Crime in Nineteenth-Century America," p. 12.

30. Monkkonen, *Police in Urban America*.

31. See Wilbur R. Miller, "Police Authority in London and New York City, 1830–1870," *Journal of Social History* 8 (Winter 1975):81–101, for an examination of consequences of the differing mandates for English and American police authority.

32. See Lane, "Urban Police and Crime in the Nineteenth-Century," and Monkkonen, *Police in Urban America*.

33. Lane, *Policing the City*.

34. Walker, *The Police in America*.

35. Robert M. Fogelson, *Big-City Police* (Cambridge, Mass.: Harvard University Press, 1977). For a complete discussion of Theodore Roosevelt as police commissioner and reformer see Jay Stuart Berman, *Police Administration and Progressive Reform: Theodore Roosevelt as Police Commissioner of New York* (New York: Greenwood, 1987).

36. Walker, *Popular Justice*.

37. Nathan Douthit, "August Vollmer, Berkeley's First Chief of Police, and the Emergence of Police Professionalism," *California Historical Quarterly* 54 (Summer 1975):101–124.

38. See National Commission on Law Observance and Enforcement, *Report on Lawlessness in Law Enforcement*, No. 11 (Washington, D.C.: United States Government Printing Office, 1931), p. 5.

39. O. W. Wilson and Roy Clinton McLaren, *Police Administration*, 4th ed. (New York: McGraw-Hill, 1977).

40. Fogelson, *Big-City Police*.

41. Ibid.

42. Walker, *The Police in America*.

43. George L. Kelling and Mark H. Moore, "The Evolving Strategy of Policing," *Perspectives on Policing*, No. 4 (Washington, D.C.: National Institute of Justice and Harvard University, November 1988).

44. U.S. Department of Justice, Federal Bureau of Investigation, *Crime in the United States, 1990* (Washington, D.C.: U.S. Government Printing Office, 1991); hereafter cited as *Uniform Crime Reports*.

45. President's Commission on Law Enforcement and Administration of Justice, *The Challenge of Crime in a Free Society* (Washington, D.C.: U.S. Government Printing Office, 1967).

46. Sue A. Lindgren, *Justice Expenditure and Employment, 1990* (Washington, D.C.: U.S. Department of Justice, Bureau of Justice Statistics, 1992).

47. For an excellent overview of the police organization see Albert J. Reiss, "Police Organization in the Twentieth Century," in *Crime and Justice*, eds. Tonry and Morris, pp. 51–97.

48. See Walker, *The Police in America*; Larry K. Gaines, Mittie D. Southerland, and John E. Angell, *Police Administration* (New York: McGraw-Hill, 1991); John Crank and L. Edward Wells, "The Effects of Size and Urbanism on Structure among Illinois Police Departments," *Justice Quarterly* 8 (1991):169–185.

49. Gaines, Southerland, and Angell, *Police Administration*.

50. Wilson and McLaren, *Police Administration*.

51. Brian Reaves, *Profile of State and Local Law Enforcement Agencies, 1987* (Washington, D.C.: Department of Justice, Bureau of Justice Statistics, 1989).

52. Alison Mitchell, "Police Find Bias Crimes Are Often Wrapped in Ambiguity," *The New York Times*, January 27, 1992, p. B1, quoting New York Police Department regulation.

53. Wilson and McLaren, *Police Administration*, p. 136.

54. Walker, *The Police in America*, p. 210.

55. Walker, *The Police in America*.

56. See, for example, James J. Fyfe, "Controlling Police Vehicle Pursuits," in *Police Practice in the '90s: Key Management Issues*, ed. James J. Fyfe (Washington, D.C.: International City Management Association, 1989), pp. 114–123; Kathleen J. Ferraro, "Policing Woman Battering," *Social Problems* 36 (1989):61–74.

57. *FBI: Facts and History* (Washington, D.C.: U.S. Department of Justice, Federal Bureau of Investigation, 1990).

58. See Athan G. Theoharis, "The FBI and the Politics of Surveillance, 1908–1985," *Criminal Justice Review* 15 (1990):221–230; Tony G. Poveda, *Lawlessness and Reform: The FBI in Transition* (Pacific Grove, Calif.: Brooks/Cole, 1990), updated.

59. See Ward Churchill and Jim Vander Wall, *The Cointelpro Papers: Documents from the FBI's Secret Wars against Dissent in the United States* (Boston: South End Press, 1990).

60. See Walker, *Popular Justice*; M. David Ermann and R. J. Lundman, *Corporate and Governmental Deviance: Problems of Organizational Behavior in Contemporary Society* (New York: Oxford University Press, 1978).

61. For journalistic accounts of FBI activities in these areas, see Richard Lacayo, "Bad Habits Die Hard," *Time*, February 8, 1988, pp. 33–34; Natalie S. Robins, "Hoover and American Lit: The Defiling of Writers," *The Nation*, October 10, 1987, pp. 367–372; "A Black-and-White Issue for the FBI," *U.S. News and World Report*, July 18, 1988, p. 9. See also Herbert N. Foerstel, *Surveillance in the Stacks: The FBI's Library Awareness Program* (New York: Greenwood Press, 1991).

62. *FBI: Facts and History*.

63. Sharon LaFraniere, "FBI Reassigning 300 Counter-spies to Crime-Fighting," *The Washington Post*, January 9, 1992, p. 19.

64. Donald A. Torres, *Handbook of Federal Police and Investigative Agencies* (Westport, Conn.: Greenwood Press, 1985).

65. *FBI: Facts and History*.

66. Torres, *Handbook of Federal Police and Investigative Agencies*.

67. Dan Jacobson, "Task Force Cracks Down on Gun Running," United Press International, March 25, 1992, BC Cycle.

68. Lauren Ina, "Chicago Gun, Drug Sweep Brings in 54; 3-Year Probe Targeted West Side Street Gang," *The Washington Post*, October 19, 1991, p. 3.

69. *Annual Report of the Attorney General of the United States, 1989* (Washington, D.C.: U.S. Government Printing Office, 1990).

70. "Oregon Man Indicted for Threatening to Kill President," P.R. Newswire Association, July 7, 1992.

71. Lindgren, *Justice Expenditure and Employment, 1990*, p. 6.

72. See Walker, *Popular Justice*.

73. Donald A. Torres, *Handbook of State Police, Highway Patrols, and Investigative Agencies* (Westport, Conn.: Greenwood Press, 1987).

74. Reaves, *Profile of State and Local Law Enforcement Agencies*.

75. Peter Finn and Daniel McGillis, "Public Safety at the State Level: A Survey of Major Services," *Journal of Police Science and Administration* 17 (1990):133–146.

76. Reaves, *Profile of State and Local Law Enforcement Agencies*.

77. Brian Reaves, *Police Departments in Large Cities, 1987* (Washington, D.C.: U.S. Department of Justice, Bureau of Justice Statistics, 1989).

78. Walker, *The Police in America*.

79. Reaves, *Profile of State and Local Law Enforcement Agencies*.

80. *Uniform Crime Reports*, p. 242.

81. Reaves, *Police Departments in Large Cities*.

82. Reaves, *Profile of State and Local Law Enforcement Agencies*.

83. Lindgren, *Justice Expenditure and Employment, 1990*.

84. Reaves, *Profile of State and Local Law Enforcement Agencies.*

85. *Uniform Crime Reports.*

86. U.S. Department of Justice, *Justice Expenditure and Employment 1988*, Table 20.

87. See John P. Crank, "Civilianization in Small and Medium Police Departments in Illinois, 1973–1986," *Journal of Criminal Justice* 17 (1989):167–177.

88. Victor H. Sims, *Small Town and Rural Police* (Springfield, Ill.: Charles C. Thomas, 1988).

89. Gary W. Cordner, "Police Agency Size and Investigative Effectiveness," *Journal of Criminal Justice* 17 (1989):145–155.

90. John W. Powell, *Campus Security and Law Enforcement* (Boston: Butterworth, 1981), p. 4.

91. Clifford D. Shearing and Philip C. Stenning, "Private Security: Implications for Social Control," *Social Problems* 30 (1983):493–506.

92. Clifford D. Shearing, "The Relation between Public and Private Policing," in *Crime and Justice*, eds. Tonry and Morris, pp. 395–424.

93. Johnson, *American Law Enforcement*, p. 159.

94. For a brief history of the private security industry, see Milton Lipson, *On Guard—The Business of Private Security* (New York: Quadrangle, 1975); "Private Security: A Retrospective," *Annals of the American Academy of Political and Social Science* 498 (1988):11–22; Robert D. McCrie, "The Development of the U.S. Security Industry," *Annals of the American Academy of Political and Social Science* 498 (1988):23–33.

95. William F. Walsh and Edwin J. Donovan, "Private Security and Community Policing: Evaluation and Comment," *Journal of Criminal Justice* 17 (1989):187–197.

96. William C. Cunningham, John J. Strauchs, and Clifford W. Van Meter, *Private Security Trends 1970 to the Year 2000: The Hallcrest Report II* (Boston: Butterworth Heinemann, 1990).

97. Lindgren, *Justice Expenditure and Employment, 1990*, p. 3.

98. Cunningham, Strauchs, and Van Meter, *Private Security Trends.*

99. William C. Cunningham and Todd H. Taylor, *Crime and Protection in America: A Study of Private Security and Law Enforcement Resources and Relationships—Executive Summary* (Washington, D.C.: National Institute of Justice, 1985); Charles P. Nemeth, *Private Security and the Investigative Process* (Cincinnati: Anderson, 1992).

100. Fifth United Nations Congress on the Prevention of Crime and the Treatment of Offenders, *Report Prepared by the Secretariat*, A/CONF. 56/10 (New York: United Nations, 1976), p. 29.

101. See Hubert Williams, "Trends in American Policing: Implications for Executives," *American Journal of Police* 9 (1990):139–149.

102. Albert J. Reiss, Jr., "Private Employment of Public Police," *NIJ Reports, No. 210* (Washington, D.C.: National Institute of Justice, 1988), pp. 2–6.

103. See Steven Spitzer and Andrew T. Scull, "Social Control in Historical Perspective: From Private to Public Responses to Crime," in *Corrections and Punishment*, ed. David F. Greenberg (Beverly Hills, Calif.: Sage, 1977), pp. 265–286; Mahesh Nalla and Graeme Newman, *A Primer in Private Security* (New York: Harrow and Heston, 1990).

CHAPTER 7

POLICE FUNCTIONS

"*T*he American city dweller's repertoire of methods for handling problems includes one known as 'calling the cops.' The practice to which the idiom refers is enormously widespread. Though it is more frequent in some segments of society than in others, there are very few people who do not or would not resort to it under suitable circumstances. A few illustrations will furnish the background for an explanation of what 'calling the cops' means. . . .*

• *In a tenement, patrolmen were met by a public health nurse who took them through an abysmally deteriorated apartment inhabited by four young children in the care of an elderly woman. The babysitter resisted the nurse's earlier attempts to remove the children. The patrolmen packed the children in the squad car and took them to Juvenile Hall, over the continuing protests of the elderly woman. . . .*

• *In a middle-class neighborhood, patrolmen found a partly disassembled car, tools, a loudly blaring radio, and five beer-drinking youths at the curb in front of a single-family home. The homeowner complained that this had been going on for several days and the men had refused to take their activities elsewhere. The patrolmen ordered the youths to pack up and leave. When one sassed them they threw him into the squad car, drove him to the precinct station, from where he was released after receiving a severe tongue lashing from the desk sergeant.*

• *In the apartment of a quarreling couple, patrolmen were told by the wife, whose nose was bleeding, that the husband stole her purse containing money she earned. The patrolmen told the man they would 'take him in,' whereupon he returned the purse and they left.[1]* " ■

"It is the citizens, not the police, who determine in large part the types of activities in which the police will become involved."

Most encounters between the police and the public are initiated by citizens through the 911 system. This has two important consequences for the police. First, it is the citizens, not the police, who determine in large part the types of activities in which the police will become involved. Second, the police often find themselves in the reactive mode of simply responding to requests from the public.

At one time all city functions were regarded as police functions, from welfare to waste disposal, and to some extent this is still true. The police are the most visible representatives of local government: They wear distinctive uniforms, their vehicles have distinctive markings, they are usually present in the neighborhood, the station house is always open, and they are easily reached by dialing 911. It is the police whom people call when the cat ends up on top of a tall tree, the neighbor's TV is too loud, someone's car is parked across the driveway, the local teenagers are whooping it up at 3 A.M., or a tornado strikes.

The urban police we watch in endless TV series are not typical. But although the problems of urban policing are special, particularly in our largest cities, they are becoming problems of size more than anything else, as drugs, street crime, homelessness, child abuse, and other social disorders spread to every corner of the country.

"These detective series on TV always end at precisely the right moment—after the criminal is arrested and before the court turns him loose."
Robert Orben, quoted in Laurence J. Peter, *Peter's Quotations: Ideas for Our Time*, Bantam, 1979, p. 288.

Police work is much different from the way it is portrayed in TV series. It is not just cops pursuing robbers, high-speed auto chases, big drug busts, wild shootouts, and controlling mobs of demonstrators throwing bricks and bottles. It involves handling the growing demands of drug abuse, homelessness, illegal weapons use, domestic violence, and other social problems. Much of the cop-on-the-beat work is boring and routine.

Police functions are traditionally grouped into three categories: service, order maintenance, and law enforcement. These categories are somewhat arbitrary because of the considerable overlap among them. Think of this situation: A state highway patrol car moves down the turnpike to survey the orderly flow of traffic (order maintenance). The officers spot a two-car collision, with one car ablaze. Through quick action they extricate four injured occupants, three of them children (service). They then arrest the grossly intoxicated driver of the other car (law enforcement). Moreover, the methods used to perform any of the funcions may be identical. Saturation patrol, for example, may be effective in deterring robberies at automated teller machines, in rounding up drug dealers, or in collecting the homeless during a blizzard. All these functions have to be "managed," and police bureaucracies (discussed in Chapter 6) have developed various management styles and approaches. So we preface our discussion of the three major functions with an overview of management styles and approaches.

MANAGING POLICE FUNCTIONS

The Politics of Policing

Their central role in municipal government gives the police political significance. Roman police chiefs frequently ended up becoming senators. Two-thousand years later, in 1897, Theodore ("Teddy") Roosevelt used his position as a police commissioner of New York to gain the New York governorship and ultimately the presidency of the United States. The Progressive reformers of the twentieth century—of whom Teddy Roosevelt was one—demanded that the police get out of politics and take politics out of the police. Nevertheless, even the highly regarded and reform-minded Chief O. W. Wilson acknowledged that departments need support from external forces to achieve their objectives.

While strictly partisan politics, with their potential for corruption, are supposed to be avoided, police executives work with other city officials such as the mayor, city manager, or city council, as well as with business and community leaders, to press for decisions favorable to the department.[2] They must fight for their "turf"—their share of the overall budget, their voice in the political decision-making process. Competing demands are especially acute in many cities and towns in the 1990s, as local governments try to deal with shrinking revenues and increasing demands for service. So these lobbying activities, which have been called "administrative politics," can be considered a legitimate part of police work.[3]

Police executives (with the exception of county sheriffs) are not elected officials; they are appointed by elected top administrators such as a mayor, city manager, or governing council. These same officials typically have the power to terminate the police executive's employment, and they often do so when unpopular police practices result in public opposition to police initiatives. Even though, at the time of the Rodney King beating incident in 1991, Los Angeles was an exception to the rule—its police chief could not be removed by elected officials— the city council and the mayor were instrumental in encouraging Chief Darryl Gates to resign.

Thus, although not directly subject to the same considerations as politicians, police officials must respond to community needs or risk erosion of support. Furthermore, regardless of political considerations, the police mission includes serving the public: Community concerns necessarily shape the role of the police. For example, if the community is concerned about drug dealers or bars featuring topless dancers having moved into the neighborhood, it is likely to put the pressure on the police—and the city government in general—to "do something about it." The pressures may focus on the conduct of individual officers or community groups, or the police force in general. It is the highly decentralized structure of policing in America (every state, city, and town has its own independent police force) that allows individual departments to establish mandates based on local concerns.[4]

"Police officials must respond to community needs or risk erosion of support."

"There are not enough jails, not enough policemen, not enough courts to enforce a law not supported by the people."
Hubert Humphrey, speech, Williamsburg, Virginia, May 1, 1965.

Management Styles

Communities across America differ from each other in many ways, including the strategies defined by their police administrators. James Q. Wilson first demonstrated the differences in styles of policing in his 1968 work, *Varieties of Police Behavior.*[5] Through close observation and analysis of police departments in eight communities (six in New York State: Albany, Amsterdam, Brighton, Nassau County, Newburgh, and Syracuse; plus Highland Park, Illinois, and Oakland, California), Wilson delineated three different styles: watchman, legalistic, and service. Each, he believed, reflected not only how police make decisions, but also the special interests of the police chief, the style of government, and expectations in the particular community.

Watchman-style departments are characterized by a concentration on the order maintenance function of policing. Police administrators allow officers to ignore minor infractions of the law, provided that order is maintained in the community. For example, someone acting in a disorderly manner may be told to "leave the area," "get out of town," or "go home"; private disputes may be settled informally; and many vice and gambling offenses are tolerated.[6] Only when the peace has been breached and order cannot be restored are arrests made. **Legalistic-style** departments, by contrast, are those in which police work is marked by a professional orientation with an emphasis on law enforcement. Officers are expected to issue large numbers of traffic tickets, to arrest juvenile offenders, and to take action against illicit enterprises. Administrators often encourage this policing style not only because it is considered right to obey all laws, but also to protect themselves from any suspicion of corruption or criticism that they are not doing a good job.[7] The **service style** is typically true of police departments in suburban middle-class communities where residents expect and receive a high

watchman style
Style characteristic of police departments that concentrate on the order maintenance function.

legalistic style
Style characteristic of police departments where work is marked by a professional orientation with an emphasis on law enforcement.

service style
Style characteristic of police departments in suburban communities where residents expect and receive a high level of service from local government.

level of personal service from local government. Given the low rate of serious crimes in these communities, police officers have the time to respond to community needs. Administrators of service-style departments tend to be highly sensitive to local personalities and politics.

Since the appearance of *Varieties of Police Behavior,* other researchers have examined potential sources of influence on styles of policing and identified other factors related not only to individual communities (degree of urbanization, community resources, racial composition), but also to the police organization itself (department size, span of control, and degree of specialization and centralization).[8] Yet no matter what style they preferred—watchman, legalistic, or service—most police departments in the past implemented that style using quasi-military bureaucracies. While this structure is convenient for administrators because of such factors as clear lines of responsibility and ability to exert control, it has become equally unpopular with the community, which does not want an occupation army, and with police officers themselves, who resent regimentation and autocracy.

"The community does not want a police force that is set up to function like an army of occupation."

Alternatives to Traditional Management Styles

The civil rights movement of the 1960s may have laid the basis for reform, yet changes in policing actually occurred as a result of pressure from within the ranks. They viewed the traditional style as "authoritarian, hierarchical, rigid, pyramidal, para-military, and impersonal in its dealings with its police workers."[9] Surprisingly, many police executives agreed that traditional police bureaucracies were inflexible and rigid, and often failed to adapt to rapid social change and community expectations.[10] What alternatives did the critics propose? Some of the more important innovations of recent years are team policing, management by objective, quality circles, and participatory management.

team policing
Strategy where teams of police officers are assigned to a particular neighborhood, and are responsible for all police services in that area.

Team policing was the first major attempt to create an alternative organization. Intended to make police more responsive to the community, to enhance the morale of police officers, and to overcome fragmentation due to specialization, team policing incorporated a decentralized structure and a neighborhood focus. Teams of officers were assigned to a particular neighborhood where they were responsible for all police services in the area. In contrast to the typical top-down decision-making characteristic of the bureaucratic model, decisions about operations were made by team members, with input from community members.

The concept appealed to many observers and practitioners, but in practice it failed.[11] Poor planning, failure to integrate team policing into the rest of the department, attempts by middle-management officers to undermine the programs, and failure to collect data for evaluation are among the reasons. Nevertheless, some experts argue, team policing helped to better police–community relations,[12] and most agree that it laid the foundation for community policing.

Management by objectives (MBO), pioneered over thirty years ago by Peter Drucker, is a technique that seeks to improve performance through self-motivation. A typical MBO process has managers identify specific, measurable objectives for their units, along with strategies for achieving these goals. Studies of police department utilization of MBO programs reveal that most have not yet realized MBO's full potential. Better definition of objectives, more feedback and training, and involvement of lower-level officers are among the recommendations for effective MBO programs.[13]

A more recent attempt at management innovation is the use of quality circles. Like MBO, the quality circle is a motivational strategy rather than an attempt to restructure the organization. A quality circle consists of a small group of workers from the same unit who meet voluntarily on a regular basis to identify problems within their units and to propose solutions. Participants are usually nonsupervisory personnel who have been given training in group interaction and problem-solving; the circle leader is usually the first line supervisor for the work unit. Studies of quality circles in police departments have shown mixed results.[14]

Participatory management, also known as theory Z management, encourages all employees to participate in decision-making and planning. They are encouraged to suggest improvements and evaluate practices. Participatory management is used in departments that are experimenting with problem-oriented policing. There appears to be widespread support among police personnel for the participatory management concept.[15]

Improving Productivity

Productivity in policing refers to both the work of the individual officer and the work of the department itself: Both are expected to create a product that is in some sense measurable. The officer's product might be number of calls answered, number of citizen contacts, number of arrests, or the overall health of the community. In the case of the department, the product might be law enforcement, order maintenance, and provision of other services the community demands.

To improve productivity, adequate measures of performance must first be devised. For officers, this usually takes the form of a performance appraisal that measures such subjective traits as dependability, cooperation, and decision-making. Better measures, it has been proposed, include the amount of time spent at work, arrest rates and citations issued, the percentage of arrests that lead to conviction, and the number of citizen complaints against the officer. Indicators of departmental productivity include the number of police officers per 1,000 population, crime rates, apprehension rates, response time to calls for service, citizen perceptions of security, and citizen satisfaction with the police.[16] The last may be difficult to gauge, but it may be the best indicator yet of the success of an organization that is not engaged in the production of a commercial product. It is to the community that the police force must look to ascertain how well it is doing.

Community Policing

It may be difficult for the students of the 1990s to visualize the American police of the 1960s. Their style of policing and their very professionalism had isolated them from the community. Minorities, who were not represented among the police, viewed them as occupation troops. A legalistic response like an arrest could ignite a whole neighborhood and lead to a riot—and still does in communities where reform programs have not been thoroughly implemented.

"A legalistic response like an arrest, in a neighborhood that views the police as occupation troops, can ignite a riot."

Only after riots leveled Watts in Los Angeles and Newark, New Jersey, did it occur to government in general, and the police in particular, that a totally new approach was needed, one that reached out and made the police part of the community. Community policing was invented, and large-scale efforts to recruit minorities into the police resulted (see Chapter 9).

Although no single definition exists, the term **community policing** is generally considered to mean programs and policies based on a commitment to a partnership between the police and the community they serve. Some have used the term "community wellness" to describe the philosophy behind this kind of policing.[17] The emphasis is on working in collaboration with residents to determine community needs and how best to address them, and to involve citizens as "co-producers of public safety."[18] Among the goals of community policing are a reduction in fear of crime, the development of closer ties with the community, engagement of residents in a joint effort to prevent crime and maintain order, and an increase in the level of public satisfaction with police services. Many types of programs have been described as community policing, including increased use of foot patrol, storefront police stations, community surveys, police-sponsored youth activities, and Neighborhood Watch programs.[19] (See the Criminal Justice in Action box.)

community policing
Strategy that relies on public confidence and citizen cooperation to help prevent crime and make the residents of a community feel more secure.

THE EMERGENCE OF COMMUNITY POLICING

In 1970, the city of Los Angeles restructured its police department to establish "a sense of territorial responsibility" (1). Patrol officers were to stay in a specific geographic location, and a "senior lead officer" was responsible for establishing and maintaining communication with the citizens served. In 1973, the department went to team policing, in which police lieutenants were "minichiefs" of seventy geographic territories and were judged only on whether conditions improved in those territories. Other cities followed suit, and the programs were popular with police and citizens. More important, they seemed to result in lower crime rates and improved conditions in city neighborhoods.

Broken windows

Despite the apparent success of these community policing efforts, by the end of the 1970s the programs had folded. Reasons offered ranged from decreasing resources to police department politics. But the concept of community policing was given considerable support again after the appearance in 1982 of an *Atlantic Monthly* article entitled "Broken Windows" (2). The authors, James Q. Wilson and George Kelling, criticized the prevailing style of policing in which officers rode inside patrol cars, insulated and isolated from the community. They argued that citizen fear leads to increased crime and to neighborhood degradation. Signs of physical neglect—the "broken windows" of the article's title—together with visible symbols of a breakdown in order, such as drunks in the street or gangs hanging out on corners, further contributed to fear among residents. The atmosphere of fear, Wilson and Kelling contended, increased the likelihood that the community would become a target for criminals, perpetuating the cycle.

The solution, as these social scientists saw it, was to involve the community in efforts to prevent neighborhood deterioration and to reinforce informal controls. Police officers were supposed to get out of their cars and back on the beat and to provide a formal means of helping residents take charge of their streets.

Experimental programs: Newark and Houston

When Wilson and Kelling put forth these ideas about the vicious cycle of deterioration, disorder, and rising fear and crime, little empirical evidence supported the idea that the cycle actually exists. Case studies since then support their argument for the value of community policing (3). In 1982, the National Institute of Justice sponsored experimental programs in Newark and Houston. In both cities, different tactics were used in the various neighborhoods that were part of the study. Strategies included a police community newsletter, a storefront police station, a cleanup program for youngsters, and an effort to establish contacts with neighborhood residents to identify community problems and concerns. Houston police established a program to recontact crime victims in an effort to provide assistance and also helped set up neighborhood organizations. In Newark, a program to reduce the so-called signs of crime, such as physical deterioration and disorder, was instituted. With the exception of the victim recontact program, the newsletter, and the "signs of crime" program, these strategies were considered a success. Overall, they appeared to reduce somewhat the level of fear in the communities (4).

New York and Portland, Oregon: CPO and Safety Action Teams

New York City undertook a large-scale community policing effort beginning in 1984. Dissatisfied with the traditional bureaucratic functioning of its law enforcement agencies, the city established the Community Patrol Officers (CPO) program. Individual officers were taken out of their routine line duties and appointed CPOs. A CPO was to make his or her own rounds, on foot, and "to function as a planner, problem solver, community organizer, and information link between the community and the police" (5). As in Newark and Houston, evaluation of the CPO program has been generally favorable, with reported improvements in police–community relations, efforts to attack street-level drug problems, and increased job satisfaction among officers.

In 1989, Portland, Oregon, assigned a Safety Action Team to a housing project plagued by violence, gangs, drugs, and drive-by shootings. The experiment specified that officers would talk with a minimum of five residents per shift, train residents in crime prevention techniques, establish an athletic program, organize the project's parking lot so that only residents could park there, and identify truants, outsiders "importing" problems, and criminal elements within the housing project. Evaluation of the program showed that fear of crime was reduced, actual criminal activity decreased, and residents were able to "reclaim" their neighborhood (6).

In 1992, the New York Police Department started an experimental Cops on Bikes program, adding bicycle-mounted officers to regular beats. Some 400 other jurisdictions in the United States now use officers on bicycles, including Seattle's Narcotics Squad. Using bicycles keeps officers visible and available in high-crime neighborhoods, and an evaluation of programs in Phoenix and Seattle has shown that bicycle patrol officers make as many as five times the number of arrests as officers on other patrols (7).

Resident Officer programs

The police can't get much closer to the communities they serve than by living in them, and that's what a Resident Officer program facilitates in Elgin, Illinois (8). A similar project in Newark, New Jersey, was described in a 1992 New York Times article:

Residents of the Central Ward were skeptical when police officers and state troopers moved into a dilapidated apartment in a small building there 13 months ago, saying they would work with tenants to drive out drug dealers.

But not any more. Now, some of those same skeptics have embraced their new neighbors.

"Before, we lived in fear for our lives," said Mikki Parker, a 23-year-old with a 5-year-old son, who grew up in the Central Ward of Newark.

Street shootings were part of our daily routine. Before, we didn't communicate, didn't know our neighbors. But once we began talking and working together, we were able to pull together and take back our community. (9)

SOURCES

1. Mark Harrison Moore, "Problem-Solving and Community Policing," in *Modern Policing,* eds. Michael Tonry and Norval Morris (Chicago: University of Chicago Press, 1992), pp. 132–133.
2. James Q. Wilson and George Kelling, "Broken Windows," *Atlantic Monthly* (March 1982):29–38.
3. Robert Trojanowicz and Hazel Hardin, *The Status of Contemporary Community Policing Programs* (Ann Arbor, Mich.: National Neighborhood Foot Patrol Center, Michigan State University, 1985)
4. *The Effects of Police Fear Reduction Studies: A Summary of Findings from Houston and Newark* (Washington, D.C.: Police Foundation, 1986).
5. David Weisburd, Jerome McElroy, and Patricia Hardyman, "Challenges to Supervision in Community Policing: Observations on a Pilot Project," *American Journal of Police* 7 (1988):29–50.
6. Rod Englert, "Safety Action Team," *FBI Law Enforcement Bulletin,* October 1990, pp. 2–5.
7. Carl Ent and James E. Hendricks, "Bicycle Patrol: A Community Policing Alternative," *The Police Chief,* November 1991, pp. 58–59; James Rutenberg, "Pedal Pushing Police on the Upper West Side," *Manhattan Spirit* 8(24) (June 1992):4; Gersh Kuntzman, "Biking the Beat," *The Upper West Side Resident* 3(15) (June 15, 1992):7.
8. Jon Ward, "Community Policing on the Home Front," *CJ The Americas: A Criminal Justice Newsletter* 5(2) (April–May 1992):1, 7, 10.
9. Kathleen Teltsch, "Meeting the Neighbors, Old and New," *The New York Times,* February 6, 1992, p. B5.

QUESTIONS FOR DISCUSSION

1. Is community policing appropriate for all jurisdictions? What factors might affect its usefulness?
2. In the 1960s many college students called police officers "pigs" and viewed them as members of the establishment, not to be trusted. What is your attitude toward police officers? Has a police officer ever helped you in any way? What factors have shaped your view?
3. Some critics maintain that the more closely police work with communities, the more they will find themselves doing work not directly related to arresting crime suspects. Do you think the police should get involved in such activities (helping get cats off roofs, assisting a citizen who has locked himself out of his car, etc.)? What purpose does such work serve?

New York City neighborhood police patrol, 1992: part of the community policing effort

"The consensus of expert opinion is that community policing holds great promise for the future."

The consensus of expert opinion is that community policing holds great promise for the future. Researchers Robert Trojanowicz and Hazel Hardin report that across the country over 140 communities have adopted community policing in one form or another.[20] The mere awareness of the role citizens play in exerting control over their communities and the fact that they can forge a partnership with the police in working to overcome problems is a significant step forward. Reducing the fear of crime, restoring a sense of control over a neighborhood, and improved police–community relations are all important benefits that may be realized from these innovative approaches. Nevertheless, questions about community policing remain. One of the most important is how to implement these new techniques within existing police structures.[21] Police management as well as rank-and-file officers will need to be committed to this new philosophy if programs are to work. New York City, for example, found that many police officers were resistant to the idea of community policing. The city therefore undertook a public relations campaign to sell its benefits to the department.[22]

"The administrative boundaries of districts and precincts may have little to do with the cultural-ethnological conglomerations that mark a community."

Another question concerns the definition or the demarcation of a community. As criminologist Jack Greene has demonstrated, administrative boundaries of districts and precincts may have little to do with the cultural-ecological conglomerations that mark a community.[23] What may seem desirable to one group of residents may in fact have a dubious legal basis and may cause the police to unfairly represent one group's interests over those of another. Some worry that it may even encourage vigilantism.[24] In New York, one frightening example was the black community's perception that in their shared Brooklyn community the police were favoring the Hasidic residents. After the accidental death of a child in January 1992, there were confrontations, riots, and homicide before calmer heads prevailed and a sense of community was restored.[25]

"In the face of nearly a century of false hopes and false promises the need and desire of the public and its press to believe that police can fight crime remains strong."
Carl Klockars in *Police Leadership in America*, 1985, p. 320.

This example poses the larger question of whether the police can be expected to solve a community's social problems.[26] Criminologist Carl Klockars doubts the police will give high priority to such functions: "Although the police are miscast in the crime-fighting role, we in the audience insist that they play the part. In the face of nearly a century of false hopes and false promises the need and desire of the public and its press to believe that police can fight crime remains strong."[27]

Police–Community Relations Programs

police–community relations (PCR) programs
All initiatives, whether from the police or the community, to bridge the gap between law enforcement professionals and the people they serve.

Unlike community policing, **police–community relations (PCR) programs** attempt to enhance the community's perception of the police, not to change the basic method of policing a community. The tangible results of effective PCR efforts include:

- Increased likelihood of citizen cooperation in providing information to assist in law enforcement
- More voluntary compliance with the law
- Improved relations with minority groups[28]
- Community support for budget appropriations in an environment of competing demands[29]

A recent inventory of programs in different jurisdictions showed that department-sponsored activities include "ride-along" programs in which citizens accompany the police on patrols, citizenship awards, citizen citation programs to recognize meritorious acts, liaison programs with the clergy, police headquarters' tours, and public speaking programs.[30]

Maintaining good relations with the media is a key component in shaping public opinion of police performance.[31] Many departments now employ public information specialists to deal with journalists and reporters. Some even have extensive media relations programs as part of an overall effort to achieve the goals of crime prevention and reducing fear of crime.[32]

PCR units often sponsor delinquency prevention programs. One of the best known is the Police Athletic League (PAL), a recreation program in which youngsters get to know police officers in a supportive team environment. Other outreach programs include police-youth discussion groups, law enforcement scholarship programs, gun safety programs, summer camping trips, drug education programs, and youth councils composed of high-school students who meet at police headquarters to advise police on matters of concern to young people.[33] Despite these efforts, at least one observer, George Kelling, believes that "PAL-like programs . . . have largely fallen out of favor and are now outside the mainstream of American policing."[34]

Many students may recall visits to their schools from "Officer Friendly," a uniformed police officer who came to speak to them about safety issues. Officer

"These kids have no respect for authority," said Police Officer David Pitchon, whose ankle was shattered by a bullet as he patrolled outside a school in the Bedford-Stuyvesant section of Brooklyn. A 15-year-old youth, Rasheem Smith, has been arrested in the shooting. The New York Times, January 29, 1992, p. B4.

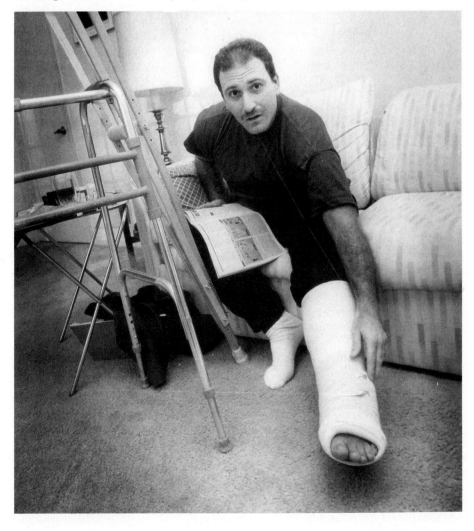

· · · · · · · · · · · · · · · · · ·

*"Drugs and violence have altered
the role police play in schools. In
some inner-city areas, 'Officer
Friendly' is likely to be engaged in
frisking teenagers for weapons
and in danger of being shot by an
aggressive student."*

Friendly is one component of police-school liaison programs intended to increase understanding of the police role. Elementary school programs commonly focus on traffic and bicycle safety and instruction about avoiding potentially dangerous circumstances. In some junior and senior high schools, police team up with teachers to provide instruction about law enforcement.[35]

Drugs and violence have altered the role police play in schools. In some inner-city areas, Officer Friendly is more likely to be engaged in frisking teenagers for weapons and in danger of being shot by an aggressive student. Recent findings from the National Crime Survey indicate that, in one year, nearly 2 million students (9% of all students) had been victims of crime at school.[36] Police officers are now routinely assigned to schools for law enforcement duties, especially in high-crime, drug-infested neighborhoods in large urban centers. They have increasingly been deployed in drug education programs in the schools. The best-known police-sponsored program is called "DARE" (for Drug Abuse Resistance Education). It originated in Los Angeles and has now been adopted by 2,000 localities in forty-nine states and reaches approximately 3 million students per year.[37]

Citizen Involvement

In recent years the police have encouraged citizens to take a more active role in policing their communities.[38] Some citizen crime prevention efforts merely affect personal behavior, such as locking doors, learning self-defense, marking personal property for identification, participating in police-sponsored security surveys of one's home, or buying weapons for self-protection. Other efforts take place at the community level. Neighborhood Watch programs are among the most popular.[39] Neighbors participate by watching out for suspicious activities or people and reporting them to the police if necessary. The programs are usually organized under the sponsorship of a jurisdiction-wide agency, such as the police, that works closely with residents by providing training, speakers, and liaison officers. The purpose is twofold: to reduce crime through techniques such as surveillance, and to create an enhanced sense of community, thereby fostering informal social control, which should lead to less crime. Surveillance tactics are usually fairly unstructured, relying on simple observation by residents during their regular activities. Neighborhood Watch participants call on the police to handle anything suspicious; they do not intervene themselves.

Civilian patrols also offer residents of a community an opportunity to participate in crime prevention. Citizens walk or drive around a neighborhood to provide added surveillance.[40] In some communities, local police departments recruit private citizens who serve as an unarmed auxiliary police and help to patrol the streets for a few hours a week.[41] Other patrols are organized by neighborhood residents on a local basis, with the assistance of the police.

Unlike most citizen crime prevention initiatives, the Guardian Angels, a national civilian patrol group operating in many local chapters, do not work with police. Founded in 1979 by Curtis Sliwa, this band of young people began by patrolling subway trains in New York City. They then spread out to other metropolitan areas. The concept is simple enough: A small platoon of youths, distinguishable by their red berets, make their presence felt in various places considered unsafe (such as subway trains), and through their presence deter crime or aid in apprehending offenders.[42] The National Institute of Justice has recognized the Guardian Angels as a worthy form of crime prevention but cautioned that they must increase their interaction with the police, adhere to state laws and regulations, standardize their training, and meet with community leaders before setting up new patrols.

Television has provided a new means for citizens to become involved in law enforcement. "Crime Stoppers," a program aired nationwide, typically offers rewards for information (the average reward is $77) about crimes. Interestingly, the majority of tips come from the criminals themselves or from so-called fringe players, people who associate with criminals. An estimated 213,000 felony cases have been solved through 570 different "Crime Stoppers" programs, with $1.3 billion worth of stolen property recovered and narcotics seized.[43]

More recent efforts to publicize unsolved crimes or solicit public assistance in the apprehension of fugitives are the popular television series "America's Most Wanted," which shows actual mug shots, and "Unsolved Mysteries," in which actors re-create actual crimes. With the ability to reach millions of people across America, these shows have become powerful sources of information for law enforcement officials. In its first year and a half of broadcasting, "America's Most Wanted" featured more than 166 wanted fugitives and received more than 100,000 tips. The result was that seventy-eight FBI fugitives were taken into custody, including nine on the "Ten Most Wanted" list at the time of their arrest. Thus, as the executive producer of "America's Most Wanted" has noted, television has organized citizens into a national neighborhood watch program.[44]

> *"Television has organized citizens into a national neighborhood watch program."*
> Attributed to an executive producer of "America's Most Wanted."

THE SERVICE FUNCTION

As local government's front-line response to social problems and emergencies, the police are called on to provide service to those members of the community who, by reason of personal, economic, social, or other circumstances, are in need of immediate aid.[45] They deal with people no one else will even talk to. Their duties bring them in contact with knife and gunshot wounds, drug overdoses, alcoholic delirium, and medical problems from childbirth to heart attacks to diabetic comas. They return runaway children to their parents and remove cats from trees.[46] They are the front-line troops in dealing with the homeless and the mentally ill. Research conducted in a city of 400,000 found, in fact, that social service and administrative tasks accounted for 55 percent of officers' time; crime-fighting accounted for 17 percent.[47] Similar analyses in other cities have likewise found that the police spend significantly more time providing service to the community and maintaining order than in fighting crime.[48] Here's how a Canadian officer described his job:

> *"Guys die down here on a regular basis—that's the reality. They die here for a nickel. They are killed for a piece of change or because somebody looks at somebody wrong."*
> Mark Holthaus, social worker with the Los Angeles homeless, in *The New York Times*, November 3, 1986.

Tom Flanagan spins the tale with a practised ease and his deputies just as easily adopt the patient air of having heard a story, oh, maybe two dozen times too often.

Shortly after he started out as a constable, recalls Ottawa's chief of police, he was patrolling on Dalhousie when a man came up and said he wanted to ask a question. Should he get a divorce, the man asked.

Flanagan wasn't sure he should answer. He'd joined the police force to catch crooks, he thought, and wasn't trained for social work. But here was someone who had come to him for help.

"So I told him, 'Why don't you go back home and try harder, that's what I'd suggest.' And he thanked me and left."

A year or so later, Flanagan was in a patrol car on Rideau Street when a man banged on the window. "I'm the fellow who asked you about the divorce," he said.

And then he turned to a woman with him and told her that I was the policeman who saved their marriage. It was his wife and she was pushing a baby carriage.

"So I've always known since then that being a policeman isn't about catching crooks, it's about helping people."[49]

Coping with Injury and Illness

Police are often summoned to the scene when medical emergencies occur, and sometimes they must provide first-aid services. A new health concern has arisen with the advent of the acquired immune deficiency syndrome (AIDS). The AIDS virus is transmitted through sexual contact or by contact with tainted blood. Since police often deal with people who may be infected with AIDS, such as intravenous drug users who share needles, police departments across the country are concerned about officers' exposure to the virus. Crime scene investigators who frequently have to collect samples of tissue, blood, and other body fluids are especially concerned about the risks in handling virus-carrying materials. To lessen the danger, many departments have now issued guidelines for minimizing exposure.[50] Some evidence from a recent survey of crime scene investigators and evidence technicians indicates that the guidelines work. They also help to allay officers' fear of contracting AIDS through on-the-job exposure.[51]

Coping with the Mentally Ill

Responding to calls involving mentally ill persons poses a special challenge for police officers. In the 1960s a series of lawsuits forced the mental health community into a policy under which, in all but the most severe cases, mentally ill people are released into the community rather than kept in an institution. In addition, the law made it more difficult to commit a person to an institution involuntarily.[52] As a result, the number of mentally ill people living on the streets increased considerably (see the Criminal Justice on Trial box).

In the absence of psychiatric intervention, there has to be some alternative way to deal with people who sometimes engage in behavior that others find bizarre or bothersome or that actually poses a threat to themselves or others. It is typically the police who are called on to intervene in such cases. The Los Angeles Police Department has estimated that their officers spend approximately 20,000 hours monthly on such calls. In 1991 alone, over 30,000 calls were received by the LAPD's mental evaluation unit (Figure 7.1).[53] Most cases result in an informal disposition. Arrest is the second most common response.[54] But the police are caught in the middle of a policy dispute over which they have no control. Here is how one enterprising police officer dealt with the problem.

The Smith brothers are two men in their middle 50s who have spent at least the past decade of their lives on skid row. They are familiar figures to the police, who refer to them as "10-81s," the police code for the mentally ill.

Among the Smith brothers problems, as they see them, is that from time to time they are pursued by invisible agents from outer space. These agents have powers that are literally unbelievable. Among them is the ability to insert fine wires into a person's head, through which they can then control him.

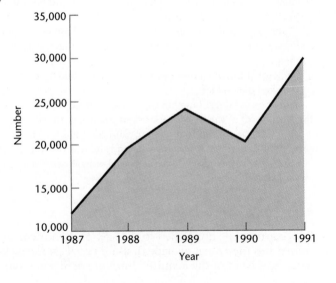

FIGURE 7.1 *Number of calls to the mental evaluation unit of the Los Angeles Police Department, 1987–1991* (*Source:* Irene Wielawski, "Mental Patients Overload Emergency System," *Los Angeles Times,* March 12, 1992.)

The Smith brothers have managed to avoid this victimization largely through the efforts of a sympathetic police sergeant. The sergeant had the good sense to report the invasion to Washington, which immediately responded to his report by dispatching a squad of equally invisible investigators who were especially trained—and armed—to deal with just such intruders. Needless to say, this operation is highly confidential and outside of the Smith brothers, the sergeant, and a handful of persons in Washington with the highest of security clearances, no one knows about it.[55]

ORDER MAINTENANCE

Several researchers have studied police work, usually by observing police on duty or by reviewing and categorizing the nature of the incidents with which police officers deal, based on the calls they receive and the incident reports they file. Specific numbers may vary, but analyses of the types of incidents reveal that the majority usually do not involve law enforcement (Table 7.1). Egon Bittner, for instance, found that patrol officers average about one arrest per month.[56] Many of the calls relate to what has been called order maintenance, peacekeeping, or conflict management (for example, dispersing a group of rowdy teenagers or warning an aggressive panhandler to move on).[57]

"It's 90 percent boredom and 10 percent sheer terror."
John Avery, New York City police officer, in *The New York Times*, February 11, 1985.

Patrol: The Basic Technique

Preventive patrol, the backbone of a municipal department's activities, consists of officers driving or walking through a designated geographic area of responsibility in a varied pattern so that their presence is not predictable. Officers on patrol fulfill several important functions in addition to order maintenance: They enforce the law, and they provide service to the community. They deter crime or catch criminals in the act; they also deal with lost children, rabid dogs, trucks that lose a barrel filled with chemicals, a broken traffic light, or a big pothole.

preventive patrol
Police officers driving or walking through a designated geographic area of responsibilty in a varied pattern so that their presence is not predictable.

Patrol can be fairly boring, with many hours of uncommitted or free time when an officer is not responding to a call for service or performing other identifiable activities. What do officers do with this time? According to one researcher, "the preponderance of patrol work involves not doing anything very specific, but rather taking breaks, meeting with other officers, and engaging in preventive patrolling."[58] Time is also spent on administrative duties at the police station, making court appearances, and on police-initiated activities, especially traffic law enforcement.

Types of Patrol

There are any number of modes of patrolling in addition to the most traditional and familiar—car, foot, and bicycle. Depending on the terrain to be covered, the number of police officers, and the typical problems, officers may patrol on horseback (mounted patrol); by boat (water and harbor patrols); by air (including seaplane and helicopter patrol); by off-road vehicle (motorcycle patrol, jeep patrol). Patrol areas may range from a few congested city blocks to miles and miles of desert or open water. In this discussion we will focus on the most-used mode, car patrol, and on some traditional modes that are being revived, like foot and bicycle patrol.

Car Patrol.   O. W. Wilson was extremely influential in persuading police throughout the country to make extensive use of the automobile for patrol. A car, he reasoned, creates a sense that the police are omnipresent in the community, provides a means of responding more rapidly to calls, and enables officers to

POLICE AND THE HOMELESS

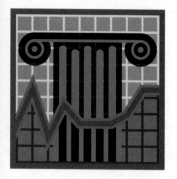

[We] enter an unventilated atmosphere of foulest pollution, and we see more clearly the frowzy, ragged garments of unclean men, and have glimpses here and there of caking filth on a naked limb. . . . Not a square foot of the dark, concrete floor is visible. The space is packed with men all lying on their right sides with their legs drawn up, and each man's legs pressed close behind those of the man in front. (1)

This sounds like a description of the treatment of slaves waiting to be sold or prisoners in a country with no standards of decency. Instead it is how one man who spent a night in a Chicago police station in 1891 described his experience. In those times, people without homes, those often labeled "tramps," "vagabonds," "bums," or "hobos," could seek refuge in a police station when they had nowhere else to turn. The quarters may not have been luxurious, but they probably were better than the freezing streets. Traditionally the police operated soup kitchens for the needy as well.

Today's police departments do not have the resources to offer food and shelter to the growing population of homeless people, but officers find themselves increasingly faced with problems caused by homelessness—and increasingly limited in their ability to respond. While concerned citizens lobby legislators and donate money to charities, "the responsibility of dealing

with the homeless on a day-to-day level ultimately falls on the police department" (2). The homeless of the nineteenth century were men, the "tramps" and "vagabonds" who rode the freight trains. Today's homeless include women and entire families, often with very young children. Recent reports put the number of homeless persons at 6,000 in Miami (3) and the number of homeless families in New York City shelters at 5,400 (4). Growing numbers of mentally ill individuals, who prior to the 1960s were institutionalized, are now living on the streets. Relief workers on New York's Upper West Side report twice as many mentally ill homeless as at any time in the past.

The police dilemma

The police are caught in a dilemma. Many citizens, offended by the presence of homeless men and women on city streets or frightened by aggressive panhandling, call the police for help. The homeless, however, have a legitimate right to be in public places, and in many jurisdictions asking people for money is not illegal. The police have to try to satisfy the public's demand for the appearance of public order without abridging the rights of homeless persons, who also are part of the public.

Recent court decisions and changes in regulations have changed police responsibilities and limited their range of responses to homeless people. In 1992, a New York state law prohibiting begging on the streets was declared unconstitutional by Federal District Court Judge Robert W. Sweet. Judge Sweet banned the issuance of summonses to beggars and explicitly ordered the police not to order

New York City Transit Police outreach unit encourages "Frankenstein" to leave a subway tunnel for shelter, 1991

beggars to "move along" (5).

In Miami, Federal District Court Judge C. Clyde Atkins in 1992 ordered the city to create "safe zones" where homeless people can sleep, bathe, prepare food, and eat without being arrested. Judge Atkins noted in his ruling that "arresting the homeless for harmless, involuntary, life-sustaining acts" violated the Constitution (6). The lawsuit had originated in complaints by three homeless men that the city was using ordinances on disorderly conduct, curfew, vagrancy, and loitering to keep homeless people out of public areas.

In cities where the mercury drops below the freezing point for much of the winter, the problems are exacerbated. Many homeless people claim they prefer to stay out on the cold streets rather than enter a homeless shelter. But many municipalities require the police to take homeless people to shelters when the temperature falls below a certain point.

Crime problems among the homeless

While police department policies with respect to the homeless have become more compassionate and individual officers have switched from law enforcement to service roles, a new problem has surfaced that threatens a reversal: the increasing involvement of the homeless in serious felonies, both as perpetrators and as victims. In Santa Monica, a study showed that approximately half of all serious felonies in the first half of 1990 were committed by homeless people—often against other homeless people (Figure 1).

Recent city and police department decisions may help resolve the difficulties of the homeless. For example, Santa Monica has moved its food programs to the front lawn of City Hall to lessen the mealtime attractions of Palisades Park. Other city programs are being implemented as well. The police department has begun a Homeless Enforcement Liaison Program—HELP—in which two experienced officers are assigned to work only with transient-related crimes. Plans include identifying the most conspicuous criminals among the homeless and arresting them, adding more officers to HELP, and working closely with the city attorney's office. Santa Monica Police Lieutenant Barney Melekian sums up the problems they face:

Unlike drugs, there is no clearly defined public consensus as to whether a law enforcement problem truly exists concerning the homeless, and assuming that it might, what ought to be done about it. The idea of using police force to drive the homeless out of town is emotionally appealing to some segments of the resident population, but it ultimately presents grave moral and constitutional conflicts (7).

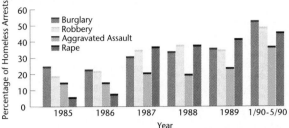

Year	Total Felony Arrests	Homeless Arrests	Homeless Percentage
Burglary			
1985	394	98	25%
1986	389	89	23
1987	307	94	31
1988	336	113	34
1989	420	153	36
1990-5/90	123	65	53
Robbery			
1985	207	39	19%
1986	219	49	22
1987	198	70	35
1988	259	98	38
1989	236	83	35
1990-5/90	94	46	49
Aggravated Assault			
1985	204	31	15%
1986	284	44	15
1987	251	52	21
1988	315	63	20
1989	289	69	24
1990-5/90	98	36	37
Rape			
1985	33	2	6%
1986	38	3	8
1987	38	14	37
1988	37	14	38
1989	26	11	42
1990-5/90	13	6	46

FIGURE 1 The Number of Homeless Suspects Arrested for Serious Felonies in Santa Monica, California

(*Source:* Barney Melekian, "Police and the Homeless," *FBI Law Enforcement Bulletin* 59 [November 1990]:4.)

SOURCES

1. Eric H. Monkkonen, *Police in Urban America, 1860–1920* (Cambridge: Cambridge University Press, 1981), p. 90, quoting Walter Wykoff, *The Workers of the West* (New York: Scribner's, 1898), pp. 36–37.
2. Barney Melekian, "Police and the Homeless," *FBI Law Enforcement Bulletin* 59 (November 1990):1–7.
3. Larry Rohter, "Judge Orders 'Safe Zones' for Homeless," *The New York Times,* November 18, 1992, p. A10.
4. Michael Winerip, "Refusing to Overlook the Homeless," *The New York Times,* November 15, 1992, p. 23.
5. Douglas Martin, "Speech Is Just One Part of Begging," *The New York Times,* October 4, 1992, p. 21.
6. Rohter, "Judge Orders 'Safe Zones' for Homeless."
7. Melekian, "Police and the Homeless."

QUESTIONS FOR DISCUSSION

1. Should the police take a more active role in providing accommodations for homeless people?
2. What should police do with homeless persons who wish to remain on the streets when the temperature falls to dangerously low levels?
3. How should police respond to the increasing role of the homeless as both crime victims and offenders?

TABLE 7.1 Police Workload in Wilmington, Delaware, Unit Activity File

Type of Complaint	Total Hours	% Hours	Collapsed Code*
Officer in trouble	17	0.02	C
Suspicious person/vehicle	1,732	2.46	C
Crime in progress	1,783	2.53	C
Order maintenance—in progress	5,678	8.07	O
Alarm	2,430	3.45	C
Investigate—not in progress	10,625	15.09	C
Animal complaint	41	0.06	O
Noise complaint	426	0.61	O
Service-related	2,977	4.23	S
Service warrant/subpoena	1,805	2.58	C
Assist other police	157	0.22	C
Park and walk	71	0.10	F
Traffic accident investigation	3,787	5.38	T
Parking problems	786	1.12	T
Motor vehicle driving problems	2,887	4.10	T
Traffic control	31	0.04	T
Fire emergency	467	0.68	T
Medical emergency	1,394	1.98	M
Clear	20,860	29.35	F
Unavailable	3,614	5.13	U
Meal break	4,569	6.49	A
Report writing	15	0.02	A
Firearms training	1	0.00	A
Police vehicle maintenance	873	1.24	A
At headquarters	2,386	3.39	A
Court-related	814	1.16	A
At corrections institution/other police agency			
At local hospital	253	0.38	M
At state hospital/medical examiner			
Total UAF district car time	70,396	100.00	

*Classifications:

A = administrative activity   O = order-maintenance activity
C = crime-related activity   S = service activity
F = free patrol   T = traffic-related activity
M = medical-related activity   U = unavailable for assignment

SOURCE: Jack R. Greene and Carl B. Klockars, "What Police Do," in *Thinking About Police*, eds. Carl B. Klockars and Stephen D. Mastrofski, 2d ed. (New York: McGraw-Hill, 1991), pp. 273–284, 279.

"At the core of the argument over one- or two-person patrol cars is the issue of safety versus the budget crunch."

patrol in a less predictable pattern. Today patrol is almost exclusively done in cars. A recent survey of the police in large cities showed that almost 94 percent of patrol time is taken up by motorized patrol.[59]

Few issues have been as hotly debated among police officers as whether to staff patrol cars with one or two officers. At the core of the argument is safety versus the budget crunch. Most research findings have shown that two-officer units provide at best only a slim margin of added safety, but some findings suggest that, in a one-person car, an officer stands a slightly greater chance of being injured if assaulted.[60] However, other variables must be considered: the crime rate and population density of the area to be patrolled, the time of day, the experience of the officers to be deployed, how the officer is armed, and the department's operating procedures (backup units, first-on-the-scene rules).

Theoretically it is possible to devise cost-beneficial plans for the deployment of one-officer patrol cars, at certain times, in certain areas, under certain conditions, without compromising officer safety. The issue is a highly emotional one. It takes the loss of a single life to block the continuation of one-officer patrols, as it did in New York City in the late 1970s when officer Cecil Sledge was killed while on patrol alone shortly after institution of the solo program.[61] Yet one-person cars have now become the national norm: A 1991 survey of large cities shows that 70 percent of patrol cars are staffed by one officer. There is considerable variation in this pattern by city. For example, one-officer cars account for half the patrol units in Los Angeles during the day, but only 9 percent at night. Until recently—and for about a decade—New York City used two-officer units only, whereas Philadelphia uses only one-officer units.[62]

Foot Patrol.   The time-honored tradition of walking the beat now accounts for only a small percentage of patrol work. Limitations of motorized patrol (for example, less contact with citizens) led to suggestions that foot patrol might have more advantages than motorized patrol. Experiments were undertaken in Newark, New Jersey, and Flint, Michigan, to evaluate the effects of foot patrol. In Newark there was no apparent effect on the amount of reported crime, but citizens seemed to be less fearful and more satisfied with police service.[63] Flint reported similar consequences with respect to fear of crime and satisfaction with police service, and in addition found decreases in reported crime.[64]

Foot patrol has proved to be a cost-effective alternative in many situations. It is, however, appropriate only in high-density urban areas such as those found mostly in the Northeast and parts of the Midwest. Foot patrol in many of the younger, lower-density cities of the South and Southwest would be difficult.

Bicycle Patrol.   Before Henry Ford motorized America and put cars at the disposition of criminals and police alike, police used bicycles to respond rapidly to crimes in progress. A century later, the bicycle is once again being pressed into service. Phoenix, Arizona; Seattle, Washington; and other cities find that bicycle patrols are an ideal combination of the popular touch of foot patrols and the mobility of car patrols.[65] The success of bicycle patrols depends on special bikes, special equipment for the officer, special training, and the appropriate area or terrain.

Evaluating Traditional Techniques

The ability to respond as quickly as possible to citizen-initiated calls to the police has been considered one of the more important police techniques. Undoubtedly, a swift response can save lives in many fire and medical situations. This appears to be less true with respect to order maintenance or law enforcement calls. Studies in several cities conducted within the last fifteen years demonstrate that rapid response has very little likelihood of increasing the probability of arrest.

The reason has to do with the nature of most crimes and the time it takes to report a crime. Crimes like murders and burglaries often occur long before they are discovered. Quick arrival on the scene by the police does not improve the probability of finding the perpetrator. Even with index crimes such as rape and robbery, any delay in reporting the crime significantly reduces the probability of arrest. For example, in one four-city study published in 1981, the police had only a 10 percent chance of making an arrest if the crime was reported even one

"When faced with trouble, Americans expect quick police response; when victimized, they want—and expect—the services of a professional."
National Advisory Commission on Criminal Justice Standards and Goals: Report on the Police.

Police officers on the beat: foot patrol, a time-honored tradition, is making a limited comeback in high-density urban areas.

Police on mountain bikes patrol Hollywood's Sunset Boulevard. Bike patrol requires special training and equipment as well as appropriate terrain.

minute after it occurred. Arrest probabilities were highest for crimes reported while in progress, but even then the probability of an arrest was only 35 percent.[66]

To test the effectiveness of traditional police techniques, George Kelling and his associates in Kansas City, Missouri, conducted an experiment between October 1972 and September 1973, funded by the Police Foundation. The Kansas City Preventive Patrol Experiment measured the effectiveness of different levels of patrol presence on crime. With the cooperation of the Kansas City police, various strategies were tried in different sections of the city. Police presence was (1) increased through intensified patrol, (2) reduced by limiting it to responses to citizen calls, or (3) left unchanged. The results were surprising. Crime did not go down in areas of intensified patrol, nor did reduced patrol result in an increase of either crime or fear among residents.[67] The Kansas City experiment led to a reassessment of policing, especially with respect to the most productive use of a patrol officer's time. Administrators began to question the use of traditional preventive patrol as a crime deterrent. The findings of the study, though subject to methodological criticism, have played a major role in the shift in focus from fighting crime to maintaining order and providing service to the community on the part of many departments.[68]

New Patrol Techniques

Taken together, the findings of many studies have highlighted the limitations of traditional techniques. It is clear that new strategies can benefit both the police and the public. Moreover, tightened police budgets have prompted a search for more cost-effective responses.

Differential Response. Some alternatives to rapid response were tried in a field experiment conducted in three cities (Garden Grove, California; Greensboro, North Carolina; Toledo, Ohio) in the early 1980s. The tests involved both the creation of a new means of classifying calls and the implementation of **differential responses.** Among the possible means of responding to calls were these:

differential response
Response strategy that involves classifying calls for service and using various responses.

- taking reports by phone
- delaying the mobile response for thirty to sixty minutes
- referring calls to other agencies
- scheduling appointments for report-taking
- asking the caller to come into the station to make a report or to mail in a report form provided by the police

The results were very encouraging: Proper screening of calls allowed the police to respond quickly when needed, and the use of mobile units to respond to nonemergencies was reduced significantly. In one city, one-fifth of all calls were handled with a nonpatrol response, usually with a telephone report. Another 27 percent of calls were eligible for a delayed response. The use of the alternative responses enabled the patrol units to devote more time to crime prevention activities and to other patrol strategies. More than 90 percent of the citizens involved in the test were satisfied with the alternative responses[69] (Figure 7.2). Cities around the country are now considering ways to implement differential response strategies in their police operations.

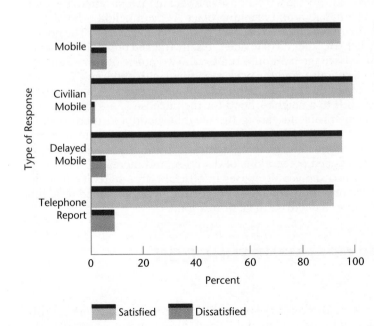

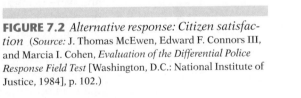

FIGURE 7.2 *Alternative response: Citizen satisfaction* (*Source:* J. Thomas McEwen, Edward F. Connors III, and Marcia I. Cohen, *Evaluation of the Differential Police Response Field Test* [Washington, D.C.: National Institute of Justice, 1984], p. 102.)

Other Kinds of Patrol. In addition to alternate forms of response, other techniques can optimize the use of patrol time. One is **directed patrol.** Patrol officers are assigned to specific activities chosen after an analysis of crime patterns. For example, an officer may be directed to spend a certain amount of time in particular high-crime areas known as "hot spots." Hot spots were discovered as a result of an analysis of the distribution of 911 calls for police assistance in Minneapolis by Lawrence Sherman and his associates. They discovered that 3 percent of the addresses and intersections in the city were the subject of 50 percent of the calls received.[70] Hot spots, then, are a natural target for directed patrol. But although some evidence indicates that directed patrol may reduce the incidence of certain targeted crimes in target areas, further study is required to determine whether crimes are actually being prevented or merely displaced to another location where the police are less in evidence.[71]

Saturation patrol involves increasing the number of units patrolling a particular area, sometimes to target a particular type of offense such as burglary or subway crime. Evaluations of saturation patrols indicate that some reduction in crime may be achieved through this technique. Saturation patrol, however, is not equally effective at all times of the day.[72]

Another technique, **aggressive patrol,** involves the more frequent intervention of patrol officers in what they consider suspicious circumstances. They do this, for example, by increased traffic checks or stopping and interrogating people on the street. Research indicates that crime rates may be reduced by aggressive patrol, but the level of citizen dissatisfaction may rise.[73]

Problem-Oriented Policing. **Problem-oriented policing** is a concept first proposed by Herman Goldstein in a 1979 article.[74] It seeks to identify the underlying problems within a community that create the specific problems police are called on to solve. Once the problems are identified, the police and the community together plan and implement solutions. Problem-oriented policing has been tried in only a few locations. The best known programs are those in Baltimore, Maryland, and Newport News, Virginia.[75] In 1982 the Baltimore County Police Department created three teams of officers to solve recurring problems. The teams, called COPE (Citizen-Oriented Police Enforcement), worked with local patrol officers to pinpoint conditions that appeared to be creating problems. For example, a neighborhood park was not being used by community residents. The reason: rowdy youths had erected a treehouse in a vacant lot adjacent to the park and were using it as a hangout and drinking place. Fearful neighborhood residents did not want their own children exposed to the treehouse boys. The police, unable to enlist the help of other city agencies, finally tracked down the owner of the lot, who agreed to have the treehouse removed. Two police officers went out and demolished the treehouse, and the park soon filled with children.[76]

Another experiment in Baltimore combined foot patrol and a police ombudsman, an officer assigned to a neighborhood for the purpose of asking residents about the most serious problems facing the neighborhood and then working with them to find solutions. Evaluation of the program showed that the problem-oriented approach of ombudsman policing significantly improved evaluations of police effectiveness, reduced perceptions of disorder, and increased feelings of safety. This program also showed decreases in official crime statistics. The decrease may, however, represent changes in reporting behavior, since residents themselves did not report a decrease in victimization.[77]

THE LAW ENFORCEMENT FUNCTION

Police officers are sworn to enforce the law.[78] This aspect of police work is probably the best known and most widely publicized, although not necessarily the

---

directed patrol
Patrol officers assigned to specific activities, such as patrolling a high-crime area, chosen after an analysis of crime patterns.

saturation patrol
Increasing the number of units patrolling a particular area, sometimes to target a particular type of offense, such as burglary or subway crime.

aggressive patrol
More frequent intervention of patrol officers in what are considered suspicious circumstances.

problem-oriented policing
Strategy that seeks to identify the underlying problems within a community so that community and police can work together to solve them.

task to which most police time is devoted. The primary object in law enforcement is the apprehension of law breakers and the collection of evidence that will lead to conviction in a court proceeding.

Criminal Investigation

Criminal investigation conjures up the image of pipe-smoking Sherlock Holmes, deer-stalker hat on his head and magnifying glass in his hand. Television has done much to perpetuate a romanticized version of the detective. Their counterparts do exist in real life, but the modern detective may easily be someone who sits at a computer screening hundreds of MO's (*modus operandi*—characteristic methods used in commission of a crime) or who tests saliva samples for DNA identification. Most detectives are trained in modern investigative techniques and in the laws of evidence and criminal procedure.[79] They spend most of their time on routine chores involving lots of paperwork, hours of interviewing, and not much excitement.

The Initial Investigation.   When a crime is reported to the police, patrol officers are usually the first to arrive on the scene. That scene may be a shopping mall where a store security officer has just caught a person shoplifting, or a remote area in the woods where a body has been found. Patrol officers perform the initial investigation; fill out the forms, such as the complaint; interview witnesses; make an arrest if there is a suspect; and appear in court with the arrestee. If a crime is not "cleared by arrest" by the patrol officer, or requires expert investigation, detectives are called in. One analysis showed that, with the exception of rape, at least two-thirds of all arrests were made by the patrol division.[80]

The detectives' first task usually is to examine the facts in order to determine whether a crime has actually been committed and whether further investigation is warranted. If a full investigation is initiated, detectives collect evidence, interview witnesses and victims, contact informants, and follow up on new leads, all with the purpose of making an arrest, securing evidence, and, where appropriate, recovering stolen property.

Not all cases receive equal attention. Detectives know that there is little probability of finding a suspect in many cases, especially if there are no witnesses. Cases are therefore screened to sort out those worthy of investigation, either because they seem likely to be solved or because of the seriousness of the crime. Case screening is often done in an informal manner,[81] but efforts have been made to develop structured models to assist in the decision-making process.[82] Increasing case loads have made it impossible for urban police forces to investigate property crime complaints involving less than a certain amount of loss, for example, 1,000 dollars—or even 5,000 dollars. Even in cases that are investigated, involvement by detectives usually does not last very long. A study by the Police Executive Research Forum (PERF) published in the early 1980s showed that the vast majority of burglary and robbery investigations are concluded (not necessarily by making an arrest) by the third day of investigation.[83]

Clearing the Case.   The Rand Corporation has made a study of how efficient detectives are at clearing cases. Data from 153 large detective bureaus demonstrated that detectives lacked effective expertise and spent too much time on paperwork.[84] Another analysis of 5,336 cases reported to suburban police departments reached a similar conclusion: The solution of most crimes does not require detective work.[85] But the PERF study had contradictory findings: Data on 3,360 burglaries and 320 robberies in De Kalb County, Georgia; St. Petersburg, Florida; and Wichita, Kansas, show that both initial investigation by patrol officers and follow-up work by detectives are necessary to find suspects.[86] The PERF study concluded that it is important to differentiate among three types of cases when discussing the effectiveness of detective work: (1) cases that cannot be solved, even with investigation; (2) cases that basically solve themselves

"A detective sees death in all the various forms at least five times a week."
Ed McBain, *Ten Plus One.*

through the circumstances of the crime; and (3) cases that can be solved with some investigative effort but would not be solved without it.[87]

After an arrest is made, investigative work is extremely important to the outcome of a court case. It is the principal means by which evidence is gathered in preparation for prosecution.[88] The investigator gathers all the evidence and appears in court to testify to its legality.[89] Case preparation includes reviewing and evaluating all evidence and reports on the case; determining whether physical evidence was properly obtained, transported, and safeguarded; reinterviewing witnesses and assisting in their preparation for court appearances; and preparing the final report.[90]

Case Attrition. Many factors enter into the arrest decision. The decision appears to be based at least in part on an assessment of whether the case can be won in court. Having decided to pursue a case, detectives want the suspect to be prosecuted, convicted, and sentenced.[91] Having a case dismissed on what detectives may consider a technicality, especially rules of evidence, is particularly disturbing.[92] A Rand Corporation study of case processing in two prosecutorial jurisdictions in California found that the thoroughness of the police case preparation had a significant association with the case outcome. Twenty-three percent of cases in the jurisdiction where preparation was consistently less thorough were dismissed, compared with no cases in the other.[93]

Various reforms have been implemented in an attempt to deal with the problem of *case attrition* in the investigatory stage (the dropping out of cases as they

SOURCE: Gary Larson, *The Far Side Gallery 2*, Kansas City: Andrews and McMeel, 1984, p. 167.

"Notice all the computations, theoretical scribblings, and lab equipment, Norm. ... Yes, curiosity killed these cats."

move through the criminal justice process). Reforms include providing checklists of the items of evidence needed before a case is filed with the court; making a single officer in the department responsible for the filing of all cases; and providing better training and more prosecutorial support service to detectives. None of these reforms has yet reduced case attrition significantly.[94]

Law Enforcement Priorities Today

Each era has its own law enforcement concerns and priorities. Four priority areas of the 1980s and 1990s demonstrate an aggressive approach to policing. These areas are

- narcotics
- domestic violence
- drunk-driving
- repeat offenders

Narcotics: Aggressive Enforcement. Illegal drugs have been a major focus of law enforcement for years. The current federal "war on drugs" continues the tradition established by previous administrations of mounting or at least attempting to mount a strong criminal justice response to the problem.[95] The recent rapid spread of crack cocaine in urban areas and the violence associated with the drug trade have lent a new urgency to calls for government to "do something" about the drug problem. As a result, arrests for drug-related offenses increased 126 percent through the decade of the 1980s, a far bigger increase than for any other type of offense during the same period.[96]

"With the proliferation of crack and the proliferation of guns, it's commonplace in every command that a police officer is being shot regularly."
Anthony Garvey, president, Lieutenants Benevolent Association, quoted in *The New York Times*, September 19, 1991.

Policymakers at all levels of government have designed and implemented a variety of strategies intended to control the availability of illegal substances. One approach is to reduce the supply of drugs; the other is to reduce the demand.[97] Controlling supply begins at the international level and follows the production-shipment-distribution path to the local level. Activities related to the importation of drugs from abroad are typically the responsibility of federal law enforcement agencies such as the Drug Enforcement Administration (DEA), the U.S. Coast Guard, and the Customs service; they involve local law enforcement resources only occasionally.[98] (See the Criminal Justice Abroad box.)

Eradication of foreign crops is a U.S. foreign policy priority, and considerable effort has been expended to prompt foreign governments to control the production of narcotics. U.S. military and intelligence assistance is being provided to foreign governments. However, increasing American cultivation has forced domestic police forces to engage in drug eradication programs as well.[99] In 1991, more than 128 million marijuana plants were destroyed as part of this effort. During this year there were over 8,700 arrests, and $48 million in assets were seized. While little is known about the effectiveness of such efforts in reducing supply, a recent evaluation in Kentucky suggested that the program had the opposite effect. Instead of curbing the problem, the eradication program simply forced growers to adopt new strategies. Cultivation was spread out to many smaller, less accessible plots, and the quality and potency of the plants increased. Furthermore, there is evidence that what was a loose confederation of independent growers has been transformed into a "marijuana cartel," in the words of the Kentucky Justice Cabinet.[100]

At the street level, police officers use many tactics to reduce local availability.[101] Among the most common is the buy-and-bust, in which police simply buy some drugs from a dealer and then make an arrest. A recent variation on this technique is sell-and-bust. Working undercover, police pretend to be dealers and then arrest those who buy from them. Other tactics available include undercover operations, electronic surveillance, the use of informants to obtain information about large-scale dealers from smaller dealers in exchange for leniency in case of

INTERPOL: THE INTERNATIONAL CRIMINAL POLICE ORGANIZATION

At the beginning of this century Europe experienced an increase in crime. International commerce was expanding. Vast steamship fleets were plying the oceans. Railroads were criss-crossing Europe. Telegraph and telephone provided instant communication. Border crossings were eased. And as legitimate business expanded throughout Europe, so did illegitimate business.

Against this backdrop, in 1914 Prince Albert I of Monaco organized the First International Criminal Police Congress, held in his principality. The Congress recommended the establishment of an international police force, and in 1923 the International Criminal Police Commission was founded and headquartered in Vienna, Austria.

The German occupation of Austria and World War II suspended the work of the organization, but in 1946 the Commission was revived. The headquarters were moved to St. Cloud, near Paris. In 1956, by then representing some fifty member states, the Commission revised its constitution and became the International Criminal Police Organization, called INTERPOL after its telegraph address.

Since 1989 the organization has been located in Lyons, France. Today, after the collapse of East European dictatorships, membership stands at 158 states, with the newest members including Mongolia, Vietnam, Albania, and Lithuania.

INTERPOL's structure and goals

As a police organization, INTERPOL is unique in that it has no police officers. It is, in fact, a complex communications network. It provides information on criminals and handles requests for wanted criminals. Each member state has a police department that serves as the country's National Central Bureau (NCB) for INTERPOL. The NCB replies to requests from other NCBs and from the INTERPOL General Secretariat and coordinates large-scale police actions when necessary. In the United States, the U.S. National Central Bureau (USNCB), located in the Department of Justice in Washington, D.C., handles all INTERPOL requests. The bureau may be asked to locate a fugitive, check a license, or supply a criminal record (1).

The goals of INTERPOL are carefully defined:

According to the terms of Article 2 of the Organization's Constitution, INTERPOL's aims are:

(a) To ensure and promote the widest possible mutual assistance between all criminal police authorities, within the limits of the laws existing in the different countries and in the spirit of the Declaration of Human Rights;

(b) To establish and develop all institutions likely to contribute effectively to the prevention and suppression of ordinary law crimes.

The limits of INTERPOL's actions are laid down in Article 3: "It is strictly forbidden for the Organization to undertake any intervention or activities of a political, military, religious or racial character." (2)

It is not always easy to separate "ordinary law crimes," with which INTERPOL may deal, from political crimes, with which it may not deal. Drug criminality provides an example. Drug crimes are regarded as "ordinary law crimes," and in fact the control of drug-related criminality is one of INTERPOL's major activities. But the traffic in narcotic drugs can be a highly political affair as well: It destabilizes or even topples governments, and its proceeds have supported armed rebellions, the arms trade, and terrorism. INTERPOL's annual general assemblies of member states help to draw the boundaries between ordinary and political criminality.

INTERPOL's prime targets

Approximately 60 percent of the operational activities of INTERPOL's General Secretariat are devoted to drug-related criminality. The remaining 40 percent of activities recently have included such mandates as assisting member states in efforts to prevent the exploitation of children and devising measures to deal with international organized crime. Other work includes dealing with assets derived from criminal activities, the firearms and explosives trade, antiterrorist measures, the traffic in human beings, missing persons, disaster victim identification, and counterfeiting.

Perhaps one of INTERPOL's most important functions is its continuing activity in the criminal intelligence area—receiving, processing, and disseminating international notices and messages that may lead to crime clearance and arrest of wanted persons in any member state. With computerization, INTERPOL has the ability to respond to requests for assistance and informa-

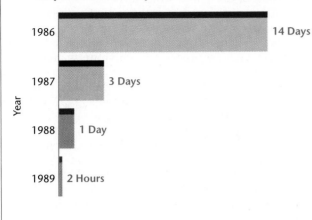

Response time to requests from member states

Year	Response time
1986	14 Days
1987	3 Days
1988	1 Day
1989	2 Hours

FIGURE 1 Response Time to Requests from Member States

(*Source:* Raymond E. Kendall, "Computerization in the General Secretariat," *International Criminal Police Review*, No. 421, November–December 1989, pp. 9–16.)

tion in approximately two hours. Similar requests took two weeks to respond to in 1986 and weeks or months in decades past. Computerization has increased INTERPOL's effectiveness immensely (Figure 1).

Maintaining effectiveness

INTERPOL maintains its effectiveness by holding annual meetings of member governments, by jointly devising crime prevention strategies, by doing research into crime developments, and by maintaining a sophisticated system of tracing firearms. The organization conducts training programs and scientific information exchanges. INTERPOL also publishes crime statistics compiled from the reports of member states.

INTERPOL's work is accomplished with a staff of fewer than 300 people, of whom about 100 are provided by the governments of member states. The remainder work under contract. Thirty-six countries are represented among the staff. While contributions from member states keep INTERPOL going, assistance to members is not based on how much they contribute.

INTERPOL's new headquarters in Lyons, France, are beautiful, but the organization maintains no precinct houses at which a citizen could file a complaint. Its functions are different from those of any other police organization: It works solely at the intergovernmental level, providing information to member states, and its beneficiaries are the citizens of the world.

SOURCES

1. From the Parc Monceau to the Parc de la Tete d'Or," *International Criminal Police Review*, No. 421, November–December 1989, pp. 6–8.
2. Richard Bell, "The History of Drug Prohibition and Legislation," *International Criminal Police Review*, No. 432, September–October 1991, pp. 2–6.

QUESTIONS FOR DISCUSSION

1. Why should ordinary citizens not have the right to file a complaint with INTERPOL if the crime they wish to report has international dimensions and they cannot get any satisfaction from their local or national police?
2. What stands in the way of INTERPOL having its own sworn officers, with power to arrest an international criminal anywhere in the world?
3. What would be the most important job skills for INTERPOL employees?

prosecution, and community-based intelligence gathering, which includes hotlines for reporting drug dealing and collaboration with community groups to identify drug problems. Some narcotics units may decide to target large-scale dealers, whereas others may go after users and street-level dealers, sometimes through street sweeps, which utilize a large police presence on the street to drive dealers away. Another strategy is to mount a focused crackdown on a particular area or type of drug.[102] These tactics can be used alone or combined in different strategies, depending on the needs and resources of the community and the police.

How successful have the police been in their effort to curtail drug abuse?[103] Given the considerable expenditure of resources devoted to drug law enforcement nationwide, surprisingly few evaluations have been made of the effectiveness of different strategies. One major problem in assessing any enforcement effort is determining what the measure of effectiveness will be. If the purpose of the war on drugs is to reduce the use of drugs, then accurate statistics on the amount of drug use are a necessity. Unfortunately, measuring change that results from enforcement activities is extremely difficult; evaluations must rely on reasonable proxies, such as surveys of drug use, statistics on the number of drug arrests, and prison sentences for drug offenders.

The evaluations that have been made show mixed results.[104] New York City's Operation Pressure Point, a crackdown focused on one area of the city, boasts some success in making significant reductions in street-level dealing and in recorded rates of arrests for burglary and robbery, assuming that these property crimes are directly related to drug use. Considerable improvement in the quality of life in several neighborhoods was also achieved. However, the lower-income neighborhoods within the target area did not record significant decreases in drug traffic; dealers simply changed their methods.[105]

Aggressive drug law enforcement at the street level has clogged the nation's courts and resulted in severe overcrowding of jails and prisons, while drug abuse in some jurisdictions appears unaffected.[106] Police officials around the country acknowledge the limits of their efforts at controlling the problem. In the words of

A neighborhood demonstration against drug dealers in Detroit. Community-based intelligence-gathering and targeting is one tactic in the "war on drugs" at the local level.

the chief of police of Shreveport, Louisiana, testifying at a recent congressional hearing: "For all our policing, we understand that law enforcement is not the solution to the problem of drugs in our society."[107] Some observers believe that community and problem-oriented policing offer some hope of making a long-term impact on the seemingly intractable problems associated with drug abuse, but thus far little empirical evidence supports that belief.[108]

Policing Domestic Violence. Tracey Thurman had repeatedly requested police assistance because she feared her estranged husband. Even after he threatened to shoot her and her son, the police merely told her to get a restraining order. Eventually, the husband attacked Thurman, inflicting multiple stab wounds that caused paralysis from the neck down and permanent disfigurement. The police had delayed in responding to her call on that occasion and the city of Torrington, Connecticut, was held liable for having failed to provide her with equal protection of the laws. In the suit that followed, Ms. Thurman was awarded $2.3 million in damages.[109] That 1985 case helped to change the American pattern of policing domestic violence.

The traditional response in the past had been nonintervention: Police often refused to make an arrest even when the victim appeared to be in danger and requested that the assailant be arrested.[110] An arrest usually was made only if the assailant was drunk, had caused serious injury, and/or assaulted the officers.[111] The arrest typically was classified as a misdemeanor unless it was for infliction of serious injury.[112] There are many reasons for the reluctance of police to treat domestic violence as a criminal matter. First, police often look on domestic problems as requiring "social work" skills rather than policing. Second, they may feel an arrest will be futile because the case will never be prosecuted or, if it is, that a conviction is unlikely. Finally, police do not like to become involved in domestic disputes because of the perceived danger to themselves associated with responding to such calls. Recent analyses of FBI and police data, however, demonstrate that responding to domestic violence calls does not carry with it a disproportionately high risk.[113]

Today in the 1990s we view domestic violence as a major social problem. Family disturbance calls now represent the largest single category of calls received by the police.[114] The police response began to change during the 1980s for several reasons. First, feminists successfully pressed their case that domestic violence must be seen as a criminal matter. Second, the huge damage award in *Thurman v. Torrington* sent a clear message: If law enforcement agencies fail to protect victims of domestic violence, the cost will be high. In addition, studies conducted in the late 1970s had shown a relationship between domestic-related homicides (and assaults) and calls for police intervention in disputes. In a Kansas City study of these domestic violence cases, researchers found that the police had been previously called to the address at least once in 85 percent of the cases, and at least five times in 50 percent of the cases. Furthermore, threats preceded physical violence in nearly 80 percent of cases.[115] Similar findings about threats as predictors of violence were made in Detroit.[116]

The change in response to domestic violence was given significant impetus by the highly publicized findings of an experiment conducted in Minneapolis in 1981 and 1982. The purpose of the Minneapolis Domestic Violence Experiment was to assess the deterrent effect of different police interventions on future incidents of domestic violence. Police were randomly assigned one of three possible actions to take when responding to domestic disturbances: (1) arrest, (2) separate the parties, or (3) give advice to the parties, including mediation between them. Following the intervention, follow-up interviews were conducted with the victims over a six-month period. Recidivism was measured by official police records and by victim accounts. Analysis provided consistent evidence that those who had been arrested had the lowest rates of recidivism.[117] Although a 1991

"For all our policing, we understand that law enforcement is not the solution to the problem of drugs in our society." Chief of police, Shreveport, Louisiana, testifying before Congress, quoted in *The New York Times,* December 28, 1989.

"There are a lot of scared and abused women out there." Gregory J. Kollke, bodyguard agency, quoted in *The New York Times,* April 3, 1992.

study revealed that neither short-custody arrests for domestic violence in inner-city areas nor longer-term arrests are effective in curbing domestic violence, especially in the long run,[118] the original Minneapolis findings had an enormous effect on the public and the law enforcement community.[119] In 1984 the Attorney General's Task Force on Family Violence recommended that "[c]onsistent with state law, the chief executive of every law enforcement agency should establish arrest as the preferred response in cases of family violence."[120] By 1986, forty-seven large cities had adopted a policy of presumptive (make an arrest unless there are clear reasons why an arrest would be counterproductive) or mandatory arrests for family fights.[121]

Drunk-Driving: Aggressive Enforcement.   Concern over drunk driving has increased markedly during the last several years, with groups like Mothers Against Drunk Driving (MADD) making the public aware of the seriousness of the problem. The result has been an enhanced police effort to combat drunk driving, coupled with legislatively mandated increased penalties for those convicted of the offense. The various techniques used to catch and deter drunk drivers include increasing the number of officers assigned to the traffic unit, creating incentives for making more arrests, launching media campaigns, and using roadblocks and checkpoints to stop and question all drivers.

Crackdowns targeting drunk driving have been utilized worldwide. A recent study in England found that traffic fatality rates declined 25 percent following an intensification of police enforcement of drunk-driving laws. Within two years, however, fatalities had returned to their previous levels. Apparently, people return to old habits once the effect of a newly announced policy has worn off and they begin to realize that the risk of arrest is, once again, extremely low.[122]

Scandinavian countries impose punishment when a driver's blood level exceeds a statutory level; sanctions are severe and include imprisonment, heavy fines, and temporary or permanent loss of license. This approach is credited with having significantly reduced the frequency of drunk driving, with a lesser impact on drunk-driving accidents. For several countries it has been shown that cultural factors, including social disapproval and publicity, are more effective in controlling drunk driving than police-enforced deterrence.[123]

Policing Career Criminals.   In Chapter 2 we pointed out that a small percentage of offenders, called career criminals, commit a disproportionately large amount of crime. Prosecutors have long used this information to ensure that frequent offenders are prosecuted to the fullest extent. Recently police have undertaken similar efforts, for the same reason.

Career-criminal programs in police departments do not generally require any new techniques. Rather, the same techniques, only in more concentrated form, are used by designated officers in a career-criminal unit. Their case load is reduced so that they can focus their attention on frequent offenders.[124] William Gay and Robert Bowers have identified three types of career-criminal programs in current use by law enforcement agencies.[125] The first is post-arrest case enhancement. This involves special handling of a case after the arrest of a suspect who has been identified as a career criminal. The detective works closely with the prosecutor to prepare the case for court, ensuring that the evidence developed meets the most stringent standards.

Targeted-warrant service, another program, affords a greater opportunity for officers of the career-criminal unit to identify warrants for repeat offenders. Locating and serving such warrants, however, is often difficult because offenders in this category frequently move from place to place to avoid apprehension. Pre-arrest targeting, the third type of program, is the most complicated and time-consuming strategy. It is aimed at apprehending a suspect during the commission of a crime. To accomplish this, criminal investigators make extensive use of informants and surveillance techniques. Since it is hard to predict when and where a crime will occur, it is difficult to evaluate the success of pre-arrest targeting—or of any of the approaches to dealing with career criminals.[126] For the time being, practitioners are convinced that these techniques are worthwhile.

Controversial Law Enforcement Techniques

Some aggressive law enforcement activities, such as crackdowns, roadblocks, decoys, undercover work, and reliance on informants, have generated controversy and raised legal and ethical problems.

Crackdowns are an intensified effort by the police to deal with a problem in a particular area or to reduce the incidence of a particular crime. Targets include drunk driving, drug dealing, prostitution, and even illegal parking or bicycle riding. Research on the results of crackdowns indicates that they may result in an initial decrease in crime, but that the effect may be short-lived. The question is whether such a short-term benefit outweighs the risk of violations of civil liberties that are inherent in any operation that arbitrarily stops people in a targeted area. Philadelphia's "Operation Cold Turkey," for example, stopped 1,000 people over a four-day period, yet only eighty narcotics arrests were made. The public outcry—and a lawsuit—forced the department to stop the operation abruptly.[127]

Another police strategy—the use of roadblocks and sobriety checkpoints to catch drunk drivers—has also been challenged. When the police stop drivers without any suspicion that the particular person has committed an offense, it may well be argued that such a stop is an unreasonable—though very temporary—search and seizure. Yet, in several cases the Supreme Court has upheld the right of states to conduct roadblocks and sobriety checkpoints.[128]

In a number of cities the police have deployed **decoys** (officers disguised as potential victims) in an effort to attract and then arrest criminals thought to be responsible for crime problems in a given area.[129]

Sting operations, in which the police pretend to be involved in illegal activities to trap a suspect, have become highly controversial because of their resemblance to entrapment.[130] **Entrapment,** by which the police actually prompt an originally unwilling person to commit a crime, has been held to be an illegal police practice.[131]

Detectives are also called on to do undercover surveillance work, often to investigate crimes between consenting parties where there is no "victim" to notify the police that a crime has taken place. Examples include gambling and drug dealing. In recent years the use of surveillance by federal and local law enforcement agencies has risen steadily. Between 1977 and 1984, the FBI's use of undercover agents rose from 53 to 350 cases and budget requests for surveillance operations rose from $1 million to $12 million. Also, the targets and nature of undercover investigations appear to be changing, with the government casting an ever wider net in search of wrongdoers. Undercover operations used to focus on vice; today's targets include white-collar crimes like corruption, labor racketeering, and customs law violations.

A number of concerns have been raised in connection with undercover work. Extensive reliance on undercover techniques that involve deception and coercion raises questions about the ethics of their use even if they are technically legal. Another issue pertains to the isolation in which undercover officers work. The close associations developed with criminals might lead the officer into criminality. Such fears are not without foundation: An officer in Chicago became a pimp after infiltrating a prostitution ring.

The police feel strongly that, to conduct effective investigations of crimes that are not likely to be reported because they involve consensual transactions, they must rely on informants. These people frequently are criminals themselves. But the practice is not new: Investigators have always had to rely on criminals as sources of information.[132] Typically the police use criminals to obtain information in exchange for some form of lenient treatment, such as reduced charges for

crackdown
Intensified effort by the police to deal with a problem in a particular area, or to reduce the incidence of a particular crime.

decoy
Police officer disguised as a potential crime victim to attract criminal attacks precipitating an arrest.

sting operation
Deceitful but lawful technique in which police pretend to be involved in illegal activities to trap a suspect.

entrapment
Illegal police practice of persuading an initially unwilling party to commit an offense.

a crime. In some cases police will even pay for the information.

Many ethical and legal problems arise in connection with the use of informants. Since informants often face stiff penalties for their own crimes, the incentive to lie in exchange for lenient treatment is strong. Using informants also raises the possibility of police corruption. In the 1970s, for instance, the New York City police provided their informants with narcotics in exchange for information. In effect, they themselves became dealers.[133] Questions also arise about the ethics of rewarding people for selling information. Payment to informants is justified on the grounds that the informer deserves compensation in exchange for the information provided as well as for the risk he or she takes. The practice has become quite lucrative. Federal law enforcement agencies paid out $63 million in 1989, nearly double what they had paid two years before. Local law enforcement agencies paid out an additional $60 million.[134]

REVIEW

The division of police functions into four distinct categories is somewhat arbitrary, since these categories are intertwined, mutually supportive, and often identical. The bureaucratic function includes the politics of bureaucratic existence and relationships with other departments of the government. Since police forces are relatively rigidly constructed hierarchies, following the military model, police departments have been criticized for separating themselves from the community. During the last two decades, administrators have been searching for more effective and acceptable forms of organizational functioning. Such innovations as team policing, management by objectives, and participative management have been tried. The service function is as old as American policing itself. The soup kitchens and night shelters that the police operated a century or more ago have their modern counterparts. The police, as government's uniformed front-line service, are called on by people in trouble—the homeless, the injured, the sick, and the mentally ill.

The order maintenance function is traditionally performed through patrolling, and more recently by innovative improvements in, and substitutes for, traditional patrols. These include preventive patrol, differential response techniques, directed patrol, saturation patrol, and aggressive patrol. Not all of these have proved effective, and some raise civil liberties issues. To counteract community objections, community policing and problem-oriented policing were instituted.

The best-known police function is law enforcement. Responding to a crime call and readying a case for prosecution are the most traditional law enforcement functions. They are reactive, a response to a crime having been observed or reported. Modern law enforcement functions, however, include a variety of proactive or aggressive means of dealing with crime that reflect current law enforcement priorities: drug law enforcement, policing domestic violence, drunk-driving law enforcement, and dealing with career criminals. The new approaches, while enthusiastically embraced by some departments, are not necessarily cost beneficial. Some are particularly controversial: the use of crackdowns, roadblocks (and sobriety checkpoints), decoys, sting operations, undercover work, and the reliance on informants.

Notes

1. Egon Bittner, "The Functions of Police in Modern Society," in *Thinking about Police*, eds. Carl B. Klockars and Stephen D. Mastrofski (New York: McGraw-Hill, 1991), pp. 44, 45; Eric J. Scott, *Calls for Service: Citizen Demand and Initial Police Response* (Washington, D.C.: U.S. Government Printing Office, 1981); James F. Gilsinan, "They Is Clowning Tough: 911 and the Social Construction of Reality," *Criminology* 27 (1989):329–344.

2. See O. W. Wilson and Roy Clinton McLaren, *Police Administration*, 4th ed. (New York: McGraw-Hill, 1977).

3. Louis A. Radelet, *The Police and the Community* (Beverly Hills, Calif.: Glencoe Press, 1973).

4. Albert J. Reiss, Jr., "Shaping and Serving the Community: The Role of the Police Chief Executive," in *Police Leadership in America: Crisis and Opportunity*, ed. William A. Geller (Chicago and New York: American Bar Foundation and Praeger Publishers, 1985), pp. 3–19. For descriptions of alternative, more centralized systems found in other countries, see David H. Bayley, *Patterns of Policing: A Comparative International Analysis* (New Brunswick, N.J.: Rutgers University Press, 1985); Ronald D. Hunter, "Three Models of Policing," *Police Studies* 13 (1990):118–124. See also James J. Fyfe, ed., *Police Practices in the 90s: Key Management Issues* (Washington, D.C.: International City Management Association, 1989). For a more recent analysis see Dennis Jay Kenney, "Strategic Approaches in Police Management: Issues and Perspectives," ed. L. Hoover (Washington, D.C.: Police Executive Research Forum, 1992). See also John P. Crank and Robert Langworthy, "An Institutional Perspective of Policing," *Journal of Criminal Law and Criminology* 83(2) (1992):338–363; David John Farmer, *Crime Control: The Use and Misuse of Police Resources* (New York: Plenum, 1984).

5. James Q. Wilson, *Varieties of Police Behavior: The Management of Law and Order in Eight Communities* (Cambridge, Mass.: Harvard University Press, 1968).

6. Ibid., p. 142.

7. Ibid., p. 180.

8. See, for example, John P. Crank, "The Influence of Environmental and Organizational Factors on Police Style in Urban and Rural Environments," *Journal of Research in Crime and Delinquency* 27 (1990):166–189; Jeffrey S. Slovak, *Styles of Urban Policing: Organization, Environment, and Police Styles in Selected American Cities* (New York: New York University Press, 1986); M. Steven Meagher, "Police Patrol Styles: How Pervasive Is Community Variation?," *Journal of Police Science and Administration* 13 (1985):36–45.

9. William G. Archambeault and Charles R. Fenwick, "A Comparative Analysis of Japanese and American Police Organizational Management Models: The Evolution of a Military Bureaucracy to a Theory Z Organization," in *Police and Law Enforcement*, vol. 4, eds. Daniel B. Kennedy and Robert J. Homant (New York: AMS Press, 1987), p. 151. See also Verl Franz and David M. Jones, "Perceptions of Organizational Performance in Suburban Police Departments: A Critique of the Military Model," *Journal of Police Science and Ad-*

ministration 15 (1987):153–161; Richard M. Ayres and George S. Flanagan, *Preventing Law Enforcement Stress: The Organization's Role* (Alexandria, Va.: The National Sheriffs' Association, 1990). Larry T. Hoover and Edward T. Mader, "Attitudes of Police Chiefs toward Private Sector Management Principles," *American Journal of Police* 9 (1990):25–37.

10. Samuel Walker, *The Police in America: An Introduction*, 2d ed. (New York: McGraw-Hill, 1992), p. 359.

11. Lawrence W. Sherman, Catherine H. Milton, and Thomas V. Kelly, *Team Policing: Seven Case Studies* (Washington, D.C.: Police Foundation, 1973).

12. John P. Kenney, *Police Administration* (Springfield, Ill.: Charles C. Thomas, 1972).

13. Harry P. Hatry and John M. Greiner, *How Can Police Departments Better Apply Management-by-Objectives and Quality Circle Programs?* (Washington, D.C.: The Urban Institute, 1984).

14. Ibid. See also Larry K. Gaines, Mittie D. Southerland, John E. Angell, *Police Administration* (New York: McGraw-Hill, 1991).

15. Jeffrey H. Witte, Lawrence F. Travis III, and Robert H. Langworthy, "Participatory Management in Law Enforcement: Police Officer, Supervisor and Administrator Perceptions," *American Journal of Police* 9 (1990):1–23.

16. Gaines, Southerland, and Angell, *Police Administration*, pp. 420–430. For an informative discussion of police productivity, see Julia Vernon and Dorothy Bracey, *Police Resources and Effectiveness* (Phillip, Australia: *Australian Institute of Criminology*, 1989). See also National Commission on Productivity, *Opportunities for Improving Productivity in Police Services* (Washington, D.C.: National Commission on Productivity, 1977). On the role which high technology can play in improving police effectiveness and productivity, see Charles W. Clark and Diane Maus, "Selection and Installation of a Mobile Digital Communications System," *Police Chief* 55 (1988):34–40.

17. Robert C. Wadman and Robert K. Olson, *Community Wellness: A New Theory of Policing* (Washington, D.C.: Police Executive Research Forum, 1990). See also Mark H. Moore, "Problem-Solving and Community Policing," in *Crime and Justice: A Review of Research*, vol. 15, eds. M. Tonry and N. Morris (Chicago: University of Chicago Press, 1992), pp. 99–158; Patrick V. Murphy, "Organizing for Community Policing," in *Issues in Policing: New Perspectives*, ed. John W. Bizzack (Lexington, Ky.: Autumn Press, 1992), pp. 113–128.

18. Gary W. Cordner and Robert C. Trojanowicz, "Patrol," in *What Works in Policing? Operations and Administration Examined*, eds. Gary W. Cordner and Donna C. Hale (Highland Heights, Ky., and Cincinnati, Ohio: Academy of Criminal Justice Sciences and Anderson, 1992), p. 11.

19. Jerome H. Skolnick and David H. Bayley, *Community Policing: Issues and Practices around the World* (Washington, D.C.: National Institute of Justice, May 1988). See also David Weisburd, Jerome McElroy, and Patricia Hardyman, "Challenges to Supervision in Community Policing: Observations on a Pilot Project," *American Journal of Police* 7 (1988):29–50; Jerome E. McElroy, Colleen A. Cosgrove, and Susan Sadd, *CPOP: The Research: An Evaluative Study of the New York City Community Patrol Officer Program* (New York: Vera Institute of Justice, 1990).

20. Robert Trojanowicz and Hazel Hardin, *The Status of Contemporary Community Policing Programs* (Ann Arbor, Mich.: National Neighborhood Foot Patrol Center, Michigan State University, 1985).

21. See Lisa M. Reichers and Roy R. Roberg, "Community Policing: A Critical Review of Underlying Assumptions," *Journal of Police Science and Administration* 17 (1990):105–114; Jerome H. Skolnick and David H. Bayley, *The New Blue Line: Police Innovation in Six American Cities* (New York: The Free Press, 1986); Lee P. Brown, "Neighborhood-Oriented Policing," *American Journal of Police* 9 (1990):197–207; Michael E. Buerger, "Problems of Redefining Police and Community," in *Police Innovation and Control of the Police*, eds. David Weisburd and Craig Uchida (Springer-Verlag,

1993). For ways to assess community policing, see Robert Trojanowicz and Bonnie Bucqueroux, *Toward Development of Meaningful and Effective Performance* (National Center for Community Policing, Michigan State University: East Lansing, Mich., Community Policing Series No. 22, 1992).

22. George James, "Having to Sell as New an Old Idea: The Cop on the Beat, "*The New York Times*, October 10, 1991, pp. B1, B7.

23. Jack R. Greene, "The Effects of Community Policing on American Law Enforcement: A Look at the Evidence," paper presented at the International Congress on Criminology, Hamburg, Germany, 1980; Jack Greene and Ralph Taylor, "Community-Based Policing and Foot Patrol: Issues of Theory and Evaluation, in *Community Policing, Rhetoric or Reality*, eds. Jack R. Greene and Stephen Mastrofski (New York: Praeger, 1988); see also Roger G. Dunham and Geoffrey P. Alpert, "Neighborhood Differences in Attitudes toward Policing: Evidence for a Mixed-Strategy Model of Policing in a Multi-Ethnic Setting," *Journal of Criminal Law and Criminology* 79 (1988):504–523; Kenneth W. Findley and Robert W. Taylor, "Rethinking Neighborhood Policing," in *Journal of Contemporary Criminal Justice* 6 (1990):70–78.

24. See David H. Bayley, "Community Policing: A Report from the Devil's Advocate," in *Community Policing*, eds. Greene and Mastrofski, pp. 225–237.

25. N. R. Kleinfeld, "Bias Crimes Hold Steady, but Leave Many Scars," *The New York Times*, January 27, 1992, pp. 1, B2.

26. See, for example, Stephen D. Mastrofski, "Community Policing as Reform," in *Community Policing*, eds. Greene and Mastrofski, pp. 47–67; Robert R. Friedmann, "Community Policing: Promises and Challenges," *Journal of Contemporary Criminal Justice* 6 (1990):79–88; Carl B. Klockars, "The Rhetoric of Community Policing," in *Community Policing*, eds. Greene and Mastrofski, pp. 239–258.

27. Carl B. Klockars, "Order Maintenance, the Quality of Urban Life and Police: A Different Line of Argument," in *Police Leadership in America*, ed. Geller, p. 320.

28. For recent surveys of attitudes of minority group members toward the police, see James R. Davis, "A Comparison of Attitudes toward the New York City Police," *Journal of Police Science and Administration* 17 (1990):233–243; Komanduri S. Murty, Julian B. Roebuck, and Joann D. Smith, "The Image of the Police in Black Atlanta Communities," *Journal of Police Science and Administration* 17 (1990):250–257.

29. See Earl M. Sweeney, *The Public and the Police: A Partnership in Protection* (Springfield, Ill.: Charles C. Thomas, 1982); Radelet, *The Police and the Community*.

30. Thomas A. Johnson, Gordon E. Misner, and Lee P. Brown, *The Police and Society: An Environment for Collaboration and Confrontation* (Englewood Cliffs, N.J.: Prentice-Hall, 1981). See also Fred I. Klyman and Joanna Kruckenberg, "A National Survey of Police-Community Relations Units," *Journal of Police Science and Administration* 7 (1979):72–79. For the importance of municipal police organization to police community relations, see Thomas A. Johnson, *A Study of Police Resistance to Police Community Relations in a Municipal Police Department* (Ann Arbor, Mich.: University Microfilms, 1971).

31. For an analysis of media contribution to the fear of crime, see Mary Holland Baker, Barbara C. Nienstedt, Ronald S. Everett, and Richard McCleary, "The Impact of a Crime Wave: Perceptions, Fear, and Confidence in the Police," *Law and Society Review* 17 (1983):319–335. See also Jerome H. Skolnick and Candace McCoy, "Police Accountability and the Media," in *Police Leadership in America*, ed. Geller, pp. 102–135.

32. Skolnick and McCoy, "Police Accountability and the Media." See also Gerald W. Garner, *The Police Meet the Press* (Springfield, Ill.: Charles C. Thomas, 1984).

33. Roslyn Muraskin, "Police Work and Juveniles," in *Juvenile Justice: Policies, Programs and Services*, ed. Albert R. Roberts (Chicago: Dorsey Press, 1989), pp. 93–109.

34. George L. Kelling, "Juveniles and Police: The End of the Nightstick," in *From Children to Citizens, vol. II. The Role of the Juvenile Court*, ed. Francis X. Hartmann (New York: Springer-Verlag, 1987).

35. John P. Kenney and Dan G. Pursuit, *Police Work with Juveniles and the Administration of Juvenile Justice*, 5th ed. (Springfield, Ill.: Charles C. Thomas, 1975).

36. Lisa D. Bastian and Bruce M. Taylor, *School Crime: A National Crime Victimization Survey Report* (Washington, D.C.: Bureau of Justice Statistics, 1991).

37. For the full evaluation of DARE, see Evaluation and Training Institute, *DARE Longitudinal Evaluation Annual Report, 1987–88* (Los Angeles: Evaluation and Training Institute, 1988). For the implications of DARE on policing, see Malcolm K. Sparrow, Mark H. Moore, and David M. Kennedy, *Beyond 911: A New Era for Policing* (New York: Basic Books, 1990).

38. Gary T. Marx, "Commentary: Some Trends and Issues in Citizen Involvement in the Law Enforcement Process," *Crime and Delinquency* 35 (1989):500–519. See Dennis P. Rosenbaum, "Community Crime Prevention: A Review and Synthesis of the Literature," *Justice Quarterly* 5 (1988):323–395; Dennis P. Rosenbaum, ed., *Community Crime Prevention: Does It Work?* (Beverly Hills, Calif.: Sage Publications, 1986); Trevor Bennett, *Evaluating Neighbourhood Watch* (Hants, England: Gower, 1990).

39. James Garofalo and Maureen McLeod, "The Structure and Operations of Neighborhood Watch Programs in the United States," *Crime and Delinquency* 35 (1989):326–344.

40. Martin Alan Greenberg, "Volunteer Police: The People's Choice," *The Police Chief* 58 (1991):42–44.

41. See Georgia Smith and Steven P. Lab, "Urban and Rural Attitudes toward Participating in an Auxiliary Policing Crime Prevention Program," *Criminal Justice and Behavior* 18 (1991):202–216.

42. See Joseph B. Perry, Jr., and M. D. Pugh, "Public Support of the Guardian Angels: Vigilante Protection against Crime, Toledo, Ohio, 1984," *Sociology and Social Research* 73 (1989):129–131; see also Susan Pennell, Christine Curtis, Joel Henderson, and Jeff Tayman, "Guardian Angels: A Unique Approach to Crime Prevention," *Crime and Delinquency* 35 (1989):378–400.

43. Dennis P. Rosenbaum, Arthur J. Lurigio, and Paul J. Lavrakas, "Enhancing Citizen Participation and Solving Serious Crime: A National Evaluation of Crime Stoppers Programs," *Crime and Delinquency* 35 (1989):401–420.

44. Scott A. Nelson, "Crime-Time Television," *FBI Law Enforcement Bulletin* 58 (1989):1–9.

45. Albert J. Reiss, Jr., *The Police and the Public* (New Haven, Conn.: Yale University Press, 1971), pp. 70–72. For a discussion of the homeless, see Candace McCoy, "Policing the Homeless," *Criminal Law Bulletin* 22 (1986):263–274; Barney Melekian, "Police and the Homeless," *FBI Law Enforcement Bulletin* 59 (1990):1–7.

46. For a discussion of the law enforcement response to runaway and missing children, see *Missing Children: The Law Enforcement Response*, ed. Martin L. Forst (Springfield, Ill.: Charles C. Thomas, 1990); Cheryl L. Maxson, Margaret A. Little, and Malcolm W. Klein, "Police Response to Runaway and Missing Children: A Conceptual Framework for Research and Policy," *Crime and Delinquency* 34 (1988):84–102.

47. John A. Webster, "Police Task and Time Study," *Journal of Criminal Law, Criminology, and Police Science* 61 (1970):94–100.

48. See, e.g., J. Robert Lilly, "What Are the Police Now Doing?," *Journal of Police Science and Administration* 6 (1978):51–60; Wilson, *Varieties of Police Behavior*; Reiss, *Police and the Public*; Bittner, *The Functions of Police in Modern Society* (Cambridge, Mass.: Oelgeschlager, Gunn and Hain, 1980).

49. Peter Calamai, "Here's to a More Personable, More Effective Police Service," *The Ottawa Citizen*, January 18, 1992, p. 36.

50. Theodore M. Hammett, *AIDS and the Law Enforcement Officer: Concerns and Policy Responses* (Washington, D.C.: U.S. Department of Justice, 1987). See also Marilyn B. Ayres, "AIDS/HIV Carriers: An Organizational Response," *FBI Law Enforcement Bulletin* 58 (1989):6–12.

51. Daniel B. Kennedy, Robert J. Homant, and George L. Emery, "AIDS Concerns among Crime Scene Investigators," *Journal of Police Science and Administration* 17 (1990):12–19. See also articles focusing on police and infectious diseases in *Police Chief* 56 (December 1989):19–29.

52. See Kevin M. Gilmartin, "The Effects of Psychiatric Deinstitutionalization on Community Policing," *The Police Chief* 53 (December 1986):37–39. See also Freda Adler, "From Hospital to Jail: New Challenges to the Law-Enforcement Process," *Criminal Law Bulletin* 17 (1981):319–333.

53. Peter Finn, "Coordinating Services for the Mentally Ill Misdemeanor Offender," *Social Service Review* 63 (1989):127–141. See also Paulette M. Gillig, Marian Dumaine, Jacqueline Widish Stammer, James R. Hillard, and Paula Grubb, "What Do Police Officers Really Want from the Mental Health System?," *Hospital and Community Psychiatry* 41 (1990):663–665.

54. See Finn, "Coordinating Services." Also see Egon Bittner, "Police Discretion in Emergency Apprehension of Mentally Ill Persons," *Social Problems* 14 (1967):278–292; Peter E. Finn and Monique Sullivan, *Police Response to Special Populations: Handling the Mentally Ill, Public Inebriate, and the Homeless* (Washington, D.C.: National Institute of Justice, 1988); Janet M. Ruane and Karen A. Cerulo, "The Police and CMHCs: The Transition from Penal to Therapeutic Control," *Law and Policy* 12 (1990):137–154; J. Michael Olivero, "Police Linkage with Community Mental Health Centers in the Management of Criminal Justice-Mental Health Emergencies," *Journal of Police and Criminal Psychology* 6 (1990):8–13.

55. Carl B. Klockars, "Blue Lies and Police Placebos: The Moralities of Police Lying," in *Thinking about Police*, eds. Klockars and Mastrofski, pp. 424–432, 426–427.

56. Bittner, "The Functions of Police in Modern Society."

57. See, for example, Wilson, *Varieties of Police Behavior*; Eric J. Scott, *Calls for Service: Citizen Demand and Initial Police Response* (Washington, D.C.: U.S. Government Printing Office, 1981); Steven P. Lab, "Police Productivity: The Other Eighty Percent," *Journal of Police Science and Administration* 12 (1984):297–302; Reiss, Jr., *The Police and the Public*. See also David H. Bayley and James Garofalo, "The Management of Violence by Police Patrol Officers," *Criminology* 27 (1989):1–25.

58. Gary W. Cordner, "Police on Patrol," in *Police and Policing: Contemporary Issues*, ed. Dennis J. Kenney, (New York: Praeger, 1989), pp. 60–71.

59. Brian A. Reaves, *Police Departments in Large Cities, 1987* (Washington, D.C.: Bureau of Justice Statistics, 1989). On the dangers associated with the most dangerous extension of car patrols, see Daniel B. Kennedy, Robert J. Homant, and John F. Kennedy, "A Comparative Analysis of Police Vehicle Pursuit Policies," *Justice Quarterly* 9 (1992):227–246.

60. Laura Ann Wilson, Gregory G. Brunk, and C. Kenneth Meyer, "Situational Effects in Police Officer Assaults: The Case of Patrol Unit Size," *Police Journal* 63 (1990):260–271.

61. Lee A. Daniels, "How Many Does It Take to Staff a Squad Car," *The New York Times*, December 8, 1991, p. 18; George James, "Police to Put Lone Officers in Patrol Cars," *The New York Times*, September 19, 1991, pp. B1, 9; Nick Ravo, "One Officer Cars: A Plan Tried Before," *The New York Times*, September 19, 1991, p. B9.

62. Anthony Pate and Edwin E. Hamilton, *The Big Six: Policing America's Largest Cities* (Washington, D.C.: Police Foundation, 1991).

63. See Police Foundation, *The Newark Foot Patrol Experiment* (Washington, D.C.: Police Foundation, 1981); Anthony M. Pate, "Experimenting with Foot Patrol: The Newark Experience," in *Community Crime Prevention*, ed. Rosenbaum, pp. 137–156.

64. See Robert C. Trojanowicz, "An Evaluation of a Neighborhood Foot Patrol Program," *Journal of Police Science and Administration* 11 (1983):410–419. See also Anthony Michael Pate, "Community-Oriented Policing in Baltimore," in *Police and Policing*, ed. Kenney, pp. 112–135; Dennis M. Payne and Robert C. Trojanowicz, *Performance Profiles of Foot Versus Motor Officers* (Lansing, Mich.: National Neighborhood Foot Patrol Center, 1985).

65. Carl Ent, "Bicycle Patrol: A Community Policing Alternative," *The Police Chief* 58 (1991):58–59.

66. William Spelman and Dale K. Brown, *Calling the Police: Citizen Reporting of Serious Crime* (Washington, D.C.: National Institute of Justice, 1984). See also Kansas City, Missouri, Police Department, *Response Time Analysis—Executive Summary* (Washington, D.C.: U.S. Department of Justice, 1978).

67. See George L. Kelling, Tony Pate, Duane Dieckman, and Charles E. Brown, *The Kansas City Preventive Patrol Experiment: A Summary Report* (Washington, D.C.: Police Foundation, 1974).

68. See Richard C. Larson, "What Happened to Patrol Operations in Kansas City? A Review of the Kansas City Preventive Patrol Experiment," *Journal of Criminal Justice* 3 (1975):267–297.

69. J. Thomas McEwen, Edward F. Connors III, and Marcia I. Cohen, *Evaluation of the Differential Police Response Field Test* (Alexandria, Va.: Research Management Associates, 1984).

70. Lawrence W. Sherman, "Repeat Calls for Service: Policing the 'Hot Spots,'" in *Police and Policing*, ed. Kenney, pp. 150–165. See also Lawrence W. Sherman, Patrick R. Gartin, and Michael E. Buerger, "Hot Spots of Predatory Crime: Routine Activities and the Criminology of Place," *Criminology* 27 (1989):27–55.

71. Cordner and Trojanowicz, "Patrol."

72. See, for example, John F. Schnelle, Robert E. Kirchner, Jr., Joe D. Casey, Paul H. Uselton, Jr., and M. Patrick McNees, "Patrol Evaluation Research: A Multiple-Baseline Analysis of Saturation Police Patrolling during Day and Night Hours," *Journal of Applied Behavior Analysis* 10 (1977):33–40.

73. Cordner and Trojanowicz, "Patrol."

74. Herman Goldstein, "Improving Policing: A Problem-Oriented Approach," *Crime and Delinquency* 25 (1979):236–258. See also Herman Goldstein, *Problem-Oriented Policing* (Philadelphia: Temple University Press, 1990).

75. John E. Eck and William Spelman, *Problem-Solving: Problem-Oriented Policing in Newport News* (Washington, D.C.: National Institute of Justice, 1988).

76. See Gary Cordner, "A Problem-Oriented Approach to Community-Oriented Policing," in *Community Policing*, eds. Greene and Mastrofski, pp. 135–152; John E. Eck and William Spelman, "Who Ya Gonna Call? The Police as Problem-Busters," *Crime and Delinquency* 33 (1987):31–52.

77. Anthony Michael Pate and Sampson O. Annan, *The Baltimore Community Policing Experiment: Summary Report* (Washington, D.C.: Police Foundation, 1989); Anthony Michael Pate, "Community-Oriented Policing in Baltimore," in *Police and Policing*, ed. Kenney, pp. 112–135.

78. See Lawrence W. Sherman, "Attacking Crime: Police and Crime Control," in *Crime and Justice*, eds. Tonry and Morris, pp. 159–230.

79. See Elizabeth M. Watson and William A. Young, "Criminal Investigation Trends," in *Issues in Policing*, ed. Bizzack.

80. Reiss, *The Police and the Public*, p. 104.

81. For a description of how detectives handle cases, see William B. Waegel, "Patterns of Police Investigation of Urban Crimes," *Journal of Police Science and Administration* 10 (1982):452–465.

82. For an example of one such model, see Bernard Greenberg, Carola V. Elliott, Lois P. Kraft, and H. Steven Proctor, *Felony Investigation Decision Model—An Analysis of Investigative Elements of Information* (Washington, D.C.: U.S. Government Printing Office, 1977); John E. Eck, *Managing Case Assignments: The Burglary Investigation Decision Model Replication* (Washington, D.C.: Police Executive Research Forum, 1979).

83. John E. Eck, *Solving Crimes: The Investigation of Burglary and Robbery* (Washington, D.C.: Police Executive Research Forum, 1983).

84. Peter Greenwood and Joan Petersilia, *The Criminal Justice Investigation Process, vol. 1. Summary and Policy Implications* (Santa Monica, Calif.: Rand Corporation, 1975).

85. Mark T. Willman and John R. Snortum, "Detective Work: The Criminal Investigation Process in a Medium-Sized Police Department," *Criminal Justice Review* 9 (1984):33–39.

86. Eck, *Solving Crimes*.

87. See John E. Eck, "Criminal Investigation," in *What Works in Policing?* eds. Cordner and Hale, pp. 19–34.

88. For an example of the importance of the police report in the success of prosecutions, see John R. Snortum, Paul R. Riva, Dale E. Berger, and Thomas W. Mangione, "Police Documentation of Drunk-Driving Arrests: Jury Verdicts and Guilty Pleas as a Function of Quantity and Quality of Evidence," *Journal of Criminal Justice* 18 (1990):99–116.

89. Peter W. Greenwood, Jan M. Chaiken, Joan Petersilia, and Linda Prusoff, *The Criminal Justice Investigation Process, vol. 3: Observation and Analysis* (Santa Monica, Calif.: Rand Corporation, 1975).

90. Wayne W. Bennett and Karen M. Hess, *Criminal Investigation* (St. Paul, Minn.: West Publishing Company, 1981).

91. W. Boyd Littrell, *Bureaucratic Justice: Police, Prosecutors, and Plea Bargaining* (Beverly Hills, Calif.: Sage Publications, 1979).

92. William F. McDonald, "Prosecutors, Courts, and Police: Some Constraints on the Police Chief Executive," in *Police Leadership in America*, ed. Geller, pp. 203–215.

93. Greenwood, Chaiken, Petersilia, and Prusoff, *The Criminal Justice Investigation Process*.

94. Joan Petersilia, Allan Abrahamse, and James Q. Wilson, "The Relationship between Police Practice, Community Characteristics, and Case Attrition," *Policing and Society* 1 (1990):23–38.

95. Some commentators have questioned the integrity of the administration's commitment to this war. Others have discussed the war in political terms, questioning the motivations of its supporters.

96. Kathleen Maguire and Timothy J. Flanagan, eds., *Sourcebook of Criminal Justice Statistics—1990* (Washington, D.C.: U.S. Department of Justice, Bureau of Justice Statistics, 1991), p. 419.

97. See Jan Chaiken, Marcia Chaiken, and Clifford Karchmer, *Multijurisdictional Drug Law Enforcement Strategies: Reducing Supply and Demand* (Washington, D.C.: National Institute of Justice, 1990).

98. See Mark H. Moore, "Supply Reduction and Drug Law Enforcement," in *Drugs and Crime*, eds. Michael Tonry and James Q. Wilson, (vol 13. of *Crime and Justice*, eds. Tonry and Morris) (Chicago: University of Chicago Press, 1990), pp. 109–157.

99. Ralph Weisheit, "The Intangible Rewards from Crime: The Case of Domestic Marijuana Cultivation," *Crime and Delinquency* 37 (1991):506–527. For the role of the military on the war on drugs, see Harry L. Marsh, "Law Enforcement, The Military and the War on Drugs: Is the Military Involvement in the War on Drugs Ethical?," *American Journal of Police* 10 (1991):61–75.

100. Gary Potter, Larry Gaines, and Beth Holbrook, "Blowing Smoke: An Evaluation of Marijuana Eradication in Kentucky," *American Journal of Police* 9 (1990):97–116.

101. See Mark A. R. Kleiman and Kerry D. Smith, "State and Local Drug Enforcement: In Search of a Strategy," in *Drugs and Crime*, eds. Tonry and Wilson, pp. 69–108; Mark H. Moore, *The Police and Drugs* (Washington, D.C.: National Institute of Justice, 1989).

102. Mark A. R. Kleiman, "Crackdowns: The Effects of Intensive Enforcement of Retail Heroin Dealing," in *Street-Level Drug Enforcement: Examining the Issues*, ed. Marcia R. Chaiken (Washington, D.C.: National Institute of Justice, 1988), pp. 3–34. In the same collection see Arnold Barnett, "Drug Crackdowns and Crime Rates: A Comment on the Kleiman Report," pp. 35–42, for another view of the outcome of the Massachusetts crackdowns.

103. Peter Reuter, John Haaga, Patrick Murphy, and Amy Praskac, *Drug Use and Drug Programs in the Washington Metropolitan Area* (Santa Monica, Calif.: Rand Corporation, 1988).

104. For a review of evaluations, see David W. Hayeslip, Jr., and Deborah L. Weisel, "Local Level Drug Enforcement," in *What Works in Policing?* eds. Cordner and Hale, pp. 35–48.

105. Lynn Zimmer, "Proactive Policing against Street-Level Drug Trafficking," *American Journal of Police* 9 (1990):43–74.

106. For discussions of police activities and drug law enforce-

ment within the context of the entire criminal justice system, see Thomas C. Castellano and Craig D. Uchida, "Local Drug Enforcement, Prosecutors and Case Attrition: Theoretical Perspectives for the Drug War," *American Journal of Police* 9 (1990):133–162. For examples of police-prosecutor cooperation in drug cases, see John Buchanan, "Police-Prosecutor Drug Enforcement Teams: Innovations in Three Jurisdictions," *American Journal of Police* 9 (1990):117–131.

107. Quoted in Robert Reinhold, "Police, Hard Pressed in Drug War, Are Turning to Preventive Efforts," *The New York Times*, December 28, 1989, pp. A1, B8.

108. See Deborah Lamm Weisel, "Playing the Home Field: A Problem-Oriented Approach to Drug Control," *American Journal of Police* 9 (1990):75–95; Hayeslip and Weisel, "Local Level Drug Enforcement."

109. *Thurman v. Torrington*, 596 F. Supp. 1521 (1985).

110. Eve S. Buzawa and Carl G. Buzawa, *Domestic Violence: The Criminal Justice Response* (Newbury Park, Calif.: Sage, 1990); Eve S. Buzawa and Carl G. Buzawa, "Changing the Police Response to Domestic Violence: The Continuing Controversy," in *Issues in Policing*, ed. Bizzack. For an overview, see J. David Hirschel, Ira W. Hutchison, Charles W. Dean, and Anne-Marie Mills, "Review Essay on the Law Enforcement Response to Spouse Abuse: Past, Present, and Future," *Justice Quarterly* 9 (1992):247–283. See also Sarah F. Berk and Donileen R. Loseke, "'Handling' Family Violence: Situational Determinants of Police Arrest in Domestic Disturbances," *Law and Society Review* (1981):317–346; Donald Black, *The Manners and Customs of the Police* (New York: Academic Press, 1980); Philip W. Davis, "Restoring the Semblance of Order: Police Strategies in the Domestic Disturbance," *Symbolic Interaction* 6 (1983):216–274.

111. Richard A. Berk, Sarah Fenstermaker Berk, and Phyllis J. Newton, "An Empirical Analysis of Police Responses to Incidents of Wife Battery," paper presented at the Second National Conference of Family Violence Researchers, University of New Hampshire, Durham, July 1984; Robert E. Worden and A. A. Pollitz, "Police Arrests in Domestic Disturbances: A Further Look," *Law and Society Review* 18 (1984):105–119; R. Tong, *Women, Sex, and the Law* (Totowa, N.J.: Rowman & Allanheld, 1984); Edward W. Gondolf and J. Richard McFerron, "Handling Battering Men: Police Action in Wife Abuse Cases," *Criminal Justice and Behavior* 16 (1989):429–439; J. David Herschel and Ira W. Hutchinson III, "Female Spouse Abuse and the Police Response: The Charlotte, North Carolina Experiment," *Journal of Criminal Law and Criminology* 83 (1992):73–119; Cynthia Grant Bowman, "The Arrest Experiments: A Feminist Critique," *Journal of Criminal Law and Criminology* 83 (1992):201–208. For a discussion of batterers, see Albert R. Roberts, "Psychosocial Characteristics of Batterers: A Study of 234 Men Charged with Domestic Violence Offenses," *Journal of Family Violence* 2 (1987):81–93.

112. G. A. Goolkasian, *Confronting Domestic Violence: A Guide for Criminal Justice Agencies*, for U.S. Department of Justice (Washington, D.C.: U.S. Government Printing Office, 1986). See also Elizabeth A. Stanko, "Missing the Mark? Police Battering," in *Women, Policing, and Male Violence: International Perspectives*, eds. Jalna Hanmer, Jill Radford, and Elizabeth A. Stanko (New York: Routledge, 1989), pp. 46–69; Lawrence W. Sherman, Janell D. Schmidt, Dennis P. Rogan, Douglas A. Smith, Patrick R. Gartin, Ellen G. Cohn, Dean J. Collins, and Anthony R. Bacich, "The Variable Effects of Arrest on Criminal Careers: The Milwaukee Domestic Violence Experiment," *Journal of Criminal Law and Criminology* 83 (1992):137–169.

113. See Joel Garner and Elizabeth Clemmer, "Danger to Police in Domestic Disturbances: A New Look," in *National Institute of Justice: Research in Brief* (Washington, D.C.: National Institute of Justice, 1986); Rose Mary Stanford and Bonney Lee Mowry, "Domestic Disturbance Danger Rate," *Journal of Police Science and Administration* 17 (1990):244–249; Buzawa and Buzawa, *Domestic Violence*; David B. Mitchell, "Contemporary Police Practices in Domestic Violence Cases: Arresting the Abuser: Is It Enough?" *Journal of Criminal Law and Criminology* 83 (1992):241–249.

114. Delbert S. Elliott, "Criminal Justice Procedures in Family Violence Crimes," in *Crime and Justice: An Annual Review of Research*, vol. 11, eds. Michael Tonry and Norval Morris (Chicago: University of Chicago Press, 1989), pp. 427–480.

115. Ronald K. Breedlove, John W. Kennish, Donald M. Sandker, and Robert K. Sawtell, *Domestic Violence and the Police: Studies in Detroit and Kansas City* (Washington, D.C.: Police Foundation, 1977), pp. 22–33.

116. G. Marie Wilt and James D. Bannon, "Conflict-Motivated Homicides and Assaults in Detroit," in *Domestic Violence and the Police*, pp. 34–44.

117. Lawrence W. Sherman and Richard A. Berk, "The Specific Deterrent Effects of Arrest for Domestic Assault," in *American Sociological Review* 49 (1984):261–272; Lisa G. Lerman, "The Decontextualization of Domestic Violence," *Journal of Criminal Law and Criminology* 83 (1992):217–240.

118. Lawrence W. Sherman, Janell D. Schmidt, Dennis P. Rogan, Patrick R. Gartlin, Ellen G. Cohn, Dean J. Collins, and Anthony R. Bacich, "From Initial Deterrence to Long-Term Escalation: Short Custody Arrest for Poverty Ghetto Domestic Violence," *Criminology* 29 (1991):821–850. See also James Meeker and Arnold Binder, "Experiments as Reforms: The Impact of the 'Minneapolis Experiment' on Police Policy," *Journal of Police Science and Administration* 17 (1990):147–153; Michael Steinman, "Lowering Recidivism among Men Who Batter Women," *Journal of Police Science and Administration* 17 (1990):124–132.

119. See Meeker and Binder, "Experiments as Reforms."

120. William L. Hart, John Ashcroft, Ann Burgess, Newman Flanagan, Ursula Meese, Catherine Milton, Clyde Narramore, Ruben Ortega, and Frances Seward, *Attorney General's Task Force on Family Violence—Final Report* (Washington, D.C.: U.S. Department of Justice, 1984), p. 17.

121. Kathleen J. Ferraro, "Policing Woman Battering," *Social Problems* 36 (1989):61–74. For a discussion of possible unintended consequences of policies favoring arrests in domestic violence cases, see Susan L. Miller, "Unintended Side Effects of Pro-Arrest Policies and Their Race and Class Implications for Battered Women: A Cautionary Note," *Criminal Justice Policy Review* 3 (1989):299–317. For a discussion of restraining orders in domestic violence cases, see Judy Hails Kaci, "A Study of Protective Orders Issued Under California's Domestic Violence Prevention Act," *Criminal Justice Review* 17 (1992):61–76. See also literature on child abuse and policing: Susan E. Martin and Edwin E. Hamilton, "Police Handling of Child Abuse Cases: Policies, Procedures, and Issues," *American Journal of Police* 9 (1990):1–24; Cecil L. Willis and Richard H. Wells, "The Police and Child Abuse: An Analysis of Police Decisions to Report Illegal Behavior," *Criminology* 26 (1988):695–716; Linda Meyer Williams, "Defining Child Sexual Abuse as Criminal Behavior: The Extent of Police Response to Child Sexual Abuse in Day Care Settings," paper presented at the annual meeting of the American Society of Criminology, Montreal, 1987; and Lisa A. Frisch, "Research That Succeeds, Policies That Fail," *Journal of Criminal Law and Criminology* 83 (1992): 209–216.

122. Walker, *Police in America*. See also James B. Jacobs, *Drunk Driving: An American Dilemma* (Chicago: University of Chicago Press, 1989); H. Laurence Ross, "Law, Science, and Accidents: The British Road Safety Act of 1967," *Journal of Legal Studies* 2 (1973):1–78; H. Laurence Ross, *Deterring the Drinking Driver: Legal Policy and Social Control* (Lexington, Mass.: Lexington Books, 1984).

123. See articles in Michael D. Laurence, John R. Snortum, and Franklin E. Zimring, eds., *Social Control of the Drinking Driver* (Chicago: University of Chicago Press, 1988).

124. For guidelines on chronic offender programs, see William Spelman, *Repeat Offender Programs for Law Enforcement* (Washington, D.C.: Police Executive Research Forum, 1990), and Allan F. Abrahamse, Patricia A. Ebner, Peter W. Greenwood, Nora Fitzger-

ald, and Thomas E. Kosin, "An Experimental Evaluation of the Phoenix Repeat Offender Program," *Justice Quarterly* 8 (June 1991):141–168.

125. William G. Gay and Robert A. Bowers, "Police Targeting of Career Criminals: Issues, Strategies, and Tactics," in *Police and Law Enforcement*, vol. 4, eds. Robert J. Homant and Daniel B. Kennedy (New York, AMS Press, 1987), pp. 219–251.

126. Susan E. Martin and Lawrence W. Sherman, *Catching Career Criminals: The Washington, D.C. Repeat Offender Project* (Washington, D.C.: Police Foundation, 1986); Susan E. Martin, "Policing Career Criminals: An Examination of an Innovative Crime Control Program," *Journal of Criminal Law and Criminology* 77 (1986):1159–1182. For a description of a more recent program in Dade County, Florida, see John S. Farrell and Joseph J. Vince, Jr., "Cost-Effective Pursuit of the Career Criminal," *The Police Chief* 58 (March 1991):39–40.

127. Mark A. R. Kleiman, "Crackdowns."

128. *Michigan v. Sitz*, 110 S. Ct. 2481 (1990); *Delaware v. Prousse*, 440 U.S. 648 (1979). See also Joseph M. Pellicciotti, "The Law and Administration of Sobriety Checkpoints," *Journal of Police Science and Administration* 16 (1988):84–90; Bryan Scott Blade, "Fourth Amendment—The Constitutionality of a Sobriety Checkpoint Program: Michigan Department of State Police v. Sitz, 110 S. Ct. 2481," *Journal of Criminal Law and Criminology* 81 (1991):800–818; Tom Christoffel, "Using Roadblocks to Reduce Drunk Driving: Public Health or Law and Order?," *American Journal of Public Health* 74 (1984):1028–1030; Robert F. Stone, "Roadside Sobriety Checkpoints: A Synopsis of Current Case Law," *The Police Chief* 52 (1985):61–63.

129. Gary T. Marx, "The New Police Undercover Work," *Urban Life* 8 (January 1990):399–446, reprinted in *Thinking About Police*, eds. Klockars and Mastrofski, pp. 242–243.

130. C. Cotter and J. Burrows, *Property Crime Program, A Special Report: Overview of the STING Program and Project Summaries*, for U.S. Department of Justice (Washington, D.C.: U.S. Government Printing Office, 1981); Gary Marx, "The New Police Undercover Work," *Urban Life* 8 (1980):399–446; Carl B. Klockars, "Jonathan Wild and the Modern Sting," in *History and Crime: Implications for Criminal Justice Policy*, eds. James A. Inciardi and Charles Faupel (Beverly Hills, Calif.: Sage, 1980), pp. 225–260; Henry W. Prunckun, "It's Your Money They're After: Sting Operations in Consumer Fraud Investigations," *Police Studies* 11 (1988):190–194; Clarence Dickson, "Drug Stings in Miami," *FBI Law Enforcement Bulletin* 57 (January 1988):1–6; Robert H. Langworthy, "Do Stings Control Crime? An Evaluation of a Police Fencing Operation," *Justice Quarterly* 6 (1989):27–45; Robert H. Langworthy and James L. LeBeau, "Temporal Evolution of a Sting Clientele," *American Journal of Police* 9 (1990):101–114; Kenneth Weiner, Kenneth Chelst, and William Hart, "Stinging the Detroit Criminal: A Total System Perspective," in *Police and Law Enforcement*, vol. 4, eds. Kennedy and Homant, pp. 281–296; Robert A. Bowers and Jack W. McCullough, *Assessing the "Sting": An Evaluation of LEAA's Property Crime Program* (Washington, D.C.: University City Science Center, 1983).

131. *Sherman v. United States*, 356 U.S. 369 (1958).

132. For an historical account, see Jack Kuykendall, "The Municipal Police Detective: An Historical Analysis," *Criminology* 24 (1986):175–201. For a contemporary account of police work with informants, see Jerome Skolnick, *Justice Without Trial: Law Enforcement in Democratic Society*, 2d ed. (New York: Wiley, 1975); Peter K. Manning, *The Narcs' Game: Organizational and Informational Limits on Drug Law Enforcement* (Cambridge, Mass.: MIT Press, 1980).

133. Walker, *Police in America*.

134. Mark Curriden, "Making Crime Pay: What's the Cost of Using Paid Informers?," *ABA Journal* 77 (1991):43–46.

THE RULE OF LAW IN LAW ENFORCEMENT

BILL OF RIGHTS

FREEDOM of SPEECH

FREEDOM of ASSEMBLY

FREEDOM of RELIGION

FREEDOM of The PRESS

In June of 1987, Theodore Genovese, a supervisor in the Radiology Department of Yale–New Haven Hospital, was found dead in his Connecticut home. He had been strangled with an electric cord. Later that summer, David Mooney, 41 years old, was picked up for questioning by New Haven Police. Mr. Mooney was homeless and living in a makeshift cardboard shelter beneath Interstate 91. His girlfriend led the police to him. A search of the box revealed a 38-inch belt matching the waist size of the victim. In a duffel bag, police found a pair of bloody trousers. Mr. Mooney was convicted of felony murder and robbery.[1]

The case against Mr. Mooney did not end with his conviction. On appeal, the Connecticut State Supreme Court ruled that the police violated Mr. Mooney's rights under the Fourth Amendment to the U.S. Constitution—the right of individuals "to be secure in their persons, houses, papers, and effects, against unreasonable searches and seizures." Quite simply, the police had neglected to obtain a search warrant before examining the contents of the cardboard shelter. Mr. Mooney, who was scheduled to serve a minimum of twenty-seven years in state prison, will now be released.[2] ■

The case of Mr. Mooney is far from typical. Most searches and seizures do not amount to unreasonable invasions of privacy; just as most confessions elicited by police interrogation are not coerced and therefore not found by courts to have been involuntary. But the Mooney case is important because it demonstrates the limits on police conduct. It reminds us that there is indeed a rule of law and that it binds everyone, including those sworn to enforce it. Law is enforced within a context that sets boundaries and standards for every participant in the system (see the Criminal Justice Abroad box). In this chapter we will focus on the police role in the law enforcement process. It is their job to uphold and enforce the law by preventing law-breaking if possible and by apprehending law-breakers and bringing them into the system so that the other actors (lawyers, judges, juries, corrections officers) can perform their roles. But this does not mean that police can use any means they wish to fight or solve crime. The Bill of Rights, part of the federal Constitution, curbs the police power of the state at all levels of government. We will see first how this came about. Then we will examine how interpretations of the Bill of Rights by courts of law have influenced and shaped how police fulfill their law enforcement function.

CRIMINAL JUSTICE UNDER THE CONSTITUTION

"Most of the revolutions that have changed the world have been fought for the rule of law."

Most of the revolutions that have changed the world have been fought for the rule of law. When the French rebelled in 1789 against Louis XVI and his aristocracy, they fought for abolition of secret trials, for jury trials and legal guarantees. So did the people of the central European countries in 1848, and so did the Eastern Europeans in 1989 when they turned against their oppressors and established the rule of law.

The American revolution was no exception. The colonists demanded rights the King of England either withheld or threatened, such as the right to jury trial in revenue cases or the right to be free from arbitrary searches and seizures. A great deal of myth surrounds the conduct of arbitrary searches and seizures in the colonies. Painstaking historical research demonstrates quite clearly that the colonists themselves generally were not targets of abuse. So-called general warrants, issued by executive authority without judicial supervision (and usually authorizing searches for libelous publications), were not in common use in the colonies. But they were very much in use in England, and the colonists feared such warrants would be used against them. The colonists also felt threatened by the use of so-called writs of assistance, which allowed customs officers to request the participation of local officials in conducting searches for suspected violations of revenue laws. Writs were used in England, and occasionally in Massachusetts and New York, but they were not common everywhere. It was the fear that they would be widely used that worried Americans, not actual instances of use.[3]

These concerns explain why the representatives of the thirteen former colonies wrote such a strong Bill of Rights into the federal Constitution, with guarantees to be observed by the central government. But the Bill of Rights imposed no restrictions on the states; what the founders of the new nation feared was centralized power. Virginia's James Madison knew that the states' powers had to be curbed as well, and he proposed an additional amendment: "The equal rights of conscience, the freedom of speech or of the press, and the right of trial by jury in criminal cases shall not be infringed by any State."[4] But this amendment did not pass (Figure 8.1).

The story of how American criminal procedure was shaped by the Constitution is the focus of this chapter. It is an exciting story that shows the power of the courts to fashion and direct criminal justice procedures. It also shows how the courts can influence and shape the role the police play in carrying out criminal justice procedures.

<figure>**FIGURE 8.1** *Facsimile of the first draft of the Bill of Rights, 1789, containing twelve amendments, of which ten were adopted in 1791*</figure>

Federal Criminal Justice: The Bill of Rights

The Bill of Rights was passed in 1791, but it had to wait a century to be awakened. What finally brought it to life was the U.S. Supreme Court. For over a hundred years, federal courts exercised little control over the procedures used in federal cases.[5] But this changed in 1897. In a case in which a confession had been extorted (*Bram v. United States*), the U.S. Supreme Court ruled that extorting a confession violates the Fifth Amendment's privilege against self-incrimination.[6] From then on, the Bill of Rights set the outer limits of permissible (federal) police conduct in the *federal* criminal process.

Of course, other issues affected federal criminal procedure. Imagine yourself a U.S. marshal somewhere out West, with little if any salary, your earnings dependent largely on fees for services performed. To transport a prisoner to the federal court (or magistrate), for example, you earn 10 cents a mile. If the U.S. court is twenty miles away, that amounts to 2 dollars. But if you pretend that hostile native tribes sit between the point of departure and the U.S. Courthouse, you may be justified in traveling a wide circle, say, of 100 miles, around the danger area. Now your earnings are 10 dollars, instead of 2. Congress became aware of the cheating on mileage fees, and in 1893 and 1894 passed legislation requiring marshals to bring arrestees to the nearest available magistrate without unreasonable delay.[7] That bit of legislation was to play a major role in reshaping federal criminal procedure. The Federal Rules of Criminal Procedure *later* included this law as Rule 5(a). But now the courts interpreted it differently: Left to their own devices, police may mistreat those they arrest. Arrested persons thus may not be held indefinitely in custody, but must be brought to a judge as soon as possible.[8]

Until the early 1920s federal law enforcement procedures were subject to the Bill of Rights, the Federal Rules of Criminal Procedure, and the common law of evidence. The states, however, still went their own ways.

"The Bill of Rights was passed in 1791, but it had to wait a century to be awakened."

THE BATTLE AGAINST LAWLESSNESS IN ITALY

On May 23, 1992, 750 pounds of dynamite exploded under a roadbed in Palermo, Italy, at precisely the moment that Prosecutor Giovanni Falcone's motorcade of armored cars passed. Mr. Falcone, the head of a national anti-Mafia task force, died instantly. So did his wife, also a prosecutor, and three bodyguards.

On July 20, 1992, 170 pounds of Semtex plastic explosives blew up when Prosecutor Paolo Borsellino approached his mother's home in Palermo. Mr. Borsellino died instantly. He had been the designated successor of Mr. Falcone.

These recent incidents in Italy's war against organized crime and organized terrorism certainly make it seem that law and order are on the losing side. As a reporter in Palermo commented, ''By killing Falcone, the Mafia seemed to be making a statement about being willing and able to eliminate anyone who stood in its way'' (1).

Confronting organized crime

What do Italian police officers confront in their work to fight organized crime?

The Mafia's numerous henchmen . . . have given Italy the highest murder rate in the European Community. They were responsible for 718 killings [in 1991] alone. The Mafia's stranglehold on Italy's political system makes all the rest of its crimes possible. By some estimates the mob has gained control over many hundreds of elected officials and other political figures. . . . With the law looking the other way, the Mafia and its lesser-known imitators . . . can go about their numerous businesses— construction scams, drugs, extortion, robberies, illegal betting, fraud and contraband—with impunity. According to most estimates, the Italian Mafia probably earned enough last year to cover Italy's 1991 $125 billion national deficit. (2)

In countries with less commitment to the rule of law than Italy— the mother country of law—such a situation would produce calls to introduce martial law and to get tough against criminals by emergency measures. In Italy, although citizens are unquestionably concerned about the Mafia, almost the opposite has happened. In 1989 a new code of criminal procedure granting more rights to the accused was adopted by Italy's Parliament. For sixty years the country had had a criminal justice system in which the defendant had virtually no right to counsel; a judge directed the prosecution; the prosecution could arrest, search, and seize with few restrictions; and the trial proceeded almost exclusively on evidence gathered before trial, verifying the prosecution's case.

The new code of criminal procedure: strengthening the rule of law

Italy's new code of criminal procedure instituted changes at every stage of the process. Provisions that relate to police include a requirement for judicial warrants for arrest, search and seizure, and electronic eavesdropping and the immediate right to counsel for arrested persons. Despite the limits these requirements may place on police activity, the legislators who drafted the new code stressed the importance of combatting organized crime. One change provides for an increased role for the police in that battle:

[T]he public prosecutor has . . . become the directing element of the inquiries, [and] he will be in direct, continuous and cohesive contact with the police. The latter will no longer have a servile role, but a driving one which was unknown under the former Code. (3)

Other new measures were designed to ensure coordination among police forces and to prevent jurisdictional conflicts among public prosecutors' offices:

. . . the new Code allows several different public prosecutors' offices to work together on facts which are related to each other, but come under the jurisdiction of different courts. The Code now requires the circulation of sources of evidence and, in short, makes certain that each public prosecutor will have full knowledge of all the facts. It is well known that organized crime groups could count on the former highly compartmentalized system to obtain favourable verdicts. (4)

How does the new criminal procedure translate into ''live action'' for Italian police forces? In mid-November 1992, a ''dragnet'' of 2,000 law officers arrested more than seventy-five suspects in a coordinated crackdown, the largest since 1984. Two hundred arrest warrants had been issued for 120 suspects at large and for another 80 already in jail on other charges. Another 100 persons were told that they were under investigation for

Mafia-related crimes. The arrestees included businessmen, local politicians such as mayors and deputy mayors, and the son of a top mobster (5). In early December, investigators issued ninety-six new arrest warrants for Mafia-linked activities in a small seaside town in Sicily (6). In actions aimed at ending political corruption, hundreds of politicians and businessmen suspected of taking bribes in return for business contracts have been investigated or arrested (7). In a country where top officials are "eliminated" with dynamite, such police activities are courageous indeed.

Winning the battle: reform and revolution

It is the Mafia's infiltration into the fabric of life in Italy that makes the battle so difficult. A priest actively engaged in challenging the Mafia says that they are held in "an ambivalent light. For some, it is prestige and money. For others, it is violence and fear" (8). Another local source explained the situation to reporters this way:

There are two social blocs against one another. On the one hand, there are efficient magistrates; on the other there are inefficient magistrates in collusion with the Mafia. You have people who want a civil society and who want to rebel against the Mafia, and then there's a polluted civil society that works with the Mafia. It's the same for the police and the politicians. This is the fight. (9).

So despite the new criminal procedure code, the protests of the people, and the recent arrests both of corrupt politicians and top Mafiosi, the fight is far from over. The rule of law provides a framework within which the police can work to apprehend lawbreakers, but much more will be needed to break the grip of the Mafia. A professor of law in Sicily expressed the feelings of many:

It's going to be a long process, because it's not something you can achieve only through the judicial system. It needs a powerful reform of politics and intervention on an economic level. At the same time, you need a cultural revolution. (10)

SOURCES

1. Pia Hinckle, "The Grip of the Octopus: Italy's Top Mafia-Fighter Is Blown Up as a Growing National Movement Says 'Basta' to the Mob," *Newsweek,* June 8, 1992, pp. 32–33, 36.
2. Ibid.
3. Loris d'Ambrosio, "The New Italian Code of Criminal Procedure," *International Criminal Police Review,* No. 434, January–February 1992, pp. 8–16, at p. 14.
4. Ibid.
5. Alan Cowell, "Italy Arrests 75 in Mafia Roundup: Politicians and Businessmen Are among Suspects Named in Warrants," *The New York Times,* November 18, 1992, p. A3.
6. Alan Cowell, "Italy Aide Accused of Mafia Ties Found Dead," *The New York Times,* December 4, 1992, p. A5.
7. Alan Cowell, "Italy Looks to End of the Old Politics," *The New York Times,* November 22, 1992, p. A6.
8. Alan Cowell, "Sicilians Try to Combat the Mafia's Pervasive Taint," *The New York Times,* October 26, 1992, p. A3.
9. Ibid.
10. Ibid.

QUESTIONS FOR DISCUSSION

1. Italian organized crime groups and terrorists have assassinated dozens of judges, prosecutors, and law enforcement officials. This has not happened in the United States, but could it? Why or why not?
2. Many of the features of the Italian code of criminal procedure were derived from the American process. Reviewing what you have learned since Chapter 6, which of our rule-of-law ideas would you recommend for other countries? What rule-of-law ideas from other countries would you like to see implemented in our own system?
3. What would you have to do to ensure compatibility before undertaking any rule-of-law transplant?

Coffins of Giovanni Falcone and his wife being carried out of the Church of San Domenico in Palermo, Italy, May 25, 1992.

TABLE 8.1 The Process of Selective Incorporation

	Year	Right	Case
TAFT Court	1925	Freedom of speech	*Gitlow v. New York*, 268 U.S. 652, 45 S. Ct. 625
	1931	Freedom of the press	*Near v. Minnesota*, 283 U.S. 697, 51 S. Ct. 625
HUGHES Court	1932	Fair trial	*Powell v. Alabama*, 287 U.S. 45, 53 S. Ct. 55
	1934	Free exercise of religion	*Hamilton v. Regents of the University of California*, 293 U.S. 245, 55 S. Ct. 197
STONE Court	1937	Freedom of assembly	*D. Jonge v. Oregon*, 299 U.S. 353, 57 S. Ct. 255
	1942	Right to counsel in capital cases	*Betts v. Brady*, 316 U.S. 455, 62 S. Ct. 1252
VINSON Court	1947	Separation of church and state: right against the establishment of religion	*Everson v. Board of Education*, 330 U.S. 1, 67 S. Ct. 594
	1948	Public trial	*In re Oliver*, 333 U.S. 257, 68 S. Ct. 499
	1949	Right against unreasonable searches and seizures	*Wolf v. Colorado*, 338 U.S. 25, 69 S. Ct. 1359
WARREN Court	1961	Exclusionary rule as a deterrent to unreasonable searches and seizures	*Mapp v. Ohio*, 367 U.S. 643, 81 S. Ct. 1684
	1962	Right against cruel and unusual punishments	*Robinson v. California*, 370 U.S. 660, 82 S. Ct. 1417
	1963	Right to counsel in felony cases	*Gideon v. Wainwright*, 372 U.S. 335, 83 S. Ct. 792
	1964	Right against self-incrimination	*Malloy v. Hogan*, 378 U.S. 1, 84 S. Ct. 1489; *Murphy v. Waterfront Com'n of New York Harbor*, 378 U.S. 52, 84 S. Ct. 1594
	1965	Confrontation of witnesses	*Pointer v. Texas*, 380 U.S. 300, 85 S. Ct. 1065 *Griswold v. Connecticut*, 381 U.S. 479, 85 S. Ct. 1678
	1967	Right to speedy trial	*Klopfer v. North Carolina*, 386 U.S. 213, 87 S. Ct. 988
		Compulsory process to obtain witnesses	*Washington v. Texas*, 388 U.S. 14, 87 S. Ct. 1920
	1968	Jury trial for all serious crimes	*Duncan v. Louisiana*, 391 U.S. 145, 88 S. Ct. 1444
BURGER Court	1969	Right against double jeopardy	*Benton v. Maryland*, 395 U.S. 784, 89 S. Ct. 2056
	1972	Right to counsel for all crimes involving a jail term.	*Argersinger v. Hamlin*, 407 U.S. 25, 92 S. Ct. 2006

SOURCE: Adapted from Craig R. Ducat and Harold W. Chase, *Constitutional Interpretation* (St. Paul, Minn: West, 1982), p. 264.

State Criminal Justice: Selective Incorporation of the Bill of Rights

The Bill of Rights limited only the federal government. But the Fourteenth Amendment provides that no *state* shall "deprive any person of life, liberty, or property without due process of law." Many defense attorneys argued that **due process** includes such rights as protection against unreasonable searches and seizures (Fourth Amendment), freedom from self-incrimination (Fifth Amendment), or right to counsel (Sixth Amendment). The U.S. Supreme Court rejected these arguments until 1925. In that year, in the landmark case *Gitlow v. New York,*[9] the Supreme Court ruled that the First Amendment rights to freedom of speech and of the press are fundamental personal rights and liberties and are guaranteed by the due process clause of the Fourteenth Amendment to the U.S. Constitution.[10] This was an epochal ruling: Due process, guaranteed by the Fourteenth Amendment to all citizens in both state and federal cases, *does* include some of the guarantees of the Bill of Rights. The implications were far-reaching: Potentially all of the due process guarantees in criminal justice that heretofore had obligated only the federal government might now also obligate the states.

Twelve years after *Gitlow,* in *Palko v. Connecticut* (1937),[11] the Supreme Court ruled that the Fourteenth Amendment prohibits all state action that "offends some principle of justice so rooted in the traditions and conscience of our people as to be ranked as fundamental."[12] With this case, the Court agreed to incorporate the Bill of Rights selectively by identifying federal rights that were "implicit in the concept of ordered liberty" and applying them to the states through the Fourteenth Amendment's due process clause. This was called the doctrine of **selective incorporation.** As Table 8.1 illustrates, most of the provisions in the Bill of Rights have by now been made applicable to the states under the Fourteenth Amendment. The practical effect is that all of us now enjoy a host of additional protections against the actions of *both* federal and state law enforcement officials.

The impact of all of these Supreme Court rulings has been immense. In effect, the criminal procedures of the fifty states have been unified to conform to the Bill of Rights, as interpreted by the U.S. Supreme Court. We call this the American criminal justice revolution. It is the legacy of the Warren Court—the U.S. Supreme Court under the leadership of Chief Justice Earl Warren, 1953 to 1969.[13]

due process of law
According to the Fourteenth Amendment, a fundamental mandate that a person should not be deprived of life, liberty, or property without reasonable and lawful procedures.

selective incorporation
Supreme Court practice of incorporating the Bill of Rights selectively, by identifying federal rights that are "implicit in the concept of ordered liberty" and applying them to states through the Fourteenth Amendment's due process clause.

"The American criminal justice revolution, which unified the criminal procedures of all fifty states, is a legacy of the Warren Court."

FOURTH AMENDMENT: UNREASONABLE SEARCHES AND SEIZURES

Let us look next at how the U.S. Supreme Court used the Fourteenth Amendment to incorporate the provisions of the Bill of Rights and to fashion criminal justice procedures for all the states. We start with the Fourth Amendment and the all-important police power to arrest persons and to search them and their premises.

Search and Seizure

The right of the people to be secure in their persons, houses, papers, and effects, against unreasonable searches and seizures, shall not be violated; and no Warrants shall issue but upon probable cause, supported by oath or affirmation, and particularly describing the place to be searched, and the persons or things to be seized.

In the seventeenth and eighteenth centuries, homeowners throughout England had the right to defend their "castles" against any unlawful entry—including by agents of the King. Even a cardboard box in which a homeless person lives is a castle in that sense: It is inviolable. Yet until 1949, this limitation bound only

"Even a cardboard box in which a homeless person lives is a home, and thus inviolable, in the constitutional sense."

federal police forces and courts in the United States. The states were left to fashion their own procedures. In 1949 the Supreme Court handed down its decision in *Wolf v. Colorado*.[14] It held that the Fourth Amendment protection against unreasonable searches and seizures is a fundamental right implicit in the concept of ordered liberty, and therefore covered by the Fourteenth Amendment due process clause and binding on the states.

search
Any governmental intrusion upon a person's reasonable expectation of privacy.

seizure
Exercise of control by a government official over a person or thing.

The Right to Privacy.   What do we mean by the terms "search" and "seizure"? A **search** is any governmental intrusion upon a person's reasonable expectation of privacy. A **seizure** is the exercise of control by a government official over a person or thing. The Fourth Amendment simply requires that both searches and seizures be "reasonable."

The Warrant Requirement.   So far we have been describing searches and seizures without a warrant. But the Fourth Amendment requires, with the exceptions noted below, that searches be conducted according to the terms of a warrant issued by a neutral and detached magistrate or judicial officer (see the Criminal Justice in Action box). The warrant must be based on probable cause, and describe with reasonable certainty the place to be searched and the items to be seized. As we noted earlier, probable cause simply means a reasonable belief that certain pieces of evidence connected with a crime that has been or is being committed may be found on a particular person or in a particular place. The warrant requirement shifts the decision (regarding the reliability of an informant's affidavit, the extent of probable cause, and ultimately whether to engage in the search) from the law enforcement officer, who has a definite interest, to the disinterested judge. As a result, searches conducted with a warrant find easy acceptance at trial and offer far greater protection for officers against civil and/or criminal liability.[15] Whenever possible, therefore, law enforcement officers must obtain a judicial warrant to search and seize, with the following specific exceptions.

"Searches conducted with a warrant find easy acceptance at trial and offer far greater protection for officers against civil and/or criminal liability."

Warrantless Searches

There are eight exceptions to the general rule that a warrant is required to conduct a search. With each it should be clear that the willingness of courts to pass on the need for a warrant reflects their perception of a diminished expectation of privacy, due perhaps to the timing of the search (conducted during the "hot pursuit" of a suspect), the location of the search (conducted in an automobile that has been stopped on the side of a public highway), or the social relationships involved in the search (conducted in a shared bedroom after consent is given by a roommate).

Regular Fourth Amendment protections do not apply to persons crossing U.S. borders: Here customs agents in Miami check the baggage of incoming international passengers.

1. Border Searches.   Fourth Amendment rights are severely restricted at international borders or their "functional equivalent," such as international airports. Customs agents and immigration officials have significant discretion at borders to conduct searches that range from superficial to invasive, without probable cause or a search warrant and with perhaps no reason other than mere suspicion. This was precisely the case in *United States v. Montoya de Hernandez* (1985). The defendant, who arrived at Los Angeles Airport from Bogotá, Colombia, fit a drug courier profile. Customs agents suspected that she had swallowed balloons filled with drugs, which were concealed in her alimentary canal. Reasonable suspicion was sufficient to justify a thorough search and sixteen-hour detention.[16]

2. Automobile Searches.   The U.S. Supreme Court has repeatedly held that there is a diminished expectation of privacy in automobiles. Three reasons have been given: (1) The mobility of cars creates circumstances that make a warrant requirement impractical; (2) automobiles are regulated, licensed, and inspected on a regular basis by the government, resulting in a lesser expectation of privacy;

and (3) cars move on public roads and highways, where the contents of the automobile as well as the occupants are in plain view. Even so, police officers must have probable cause to search a vehicle—but they can develop the belief that the car contains incriminating evidence while they question the driver! In the case of *Colorado v. Bannister* (1980),[17] a police officer, while writing a speeding ticket, noticed tools and steel parts on the back seat of the car. The driver and other occupant fit the description of suspects wanted for the theft of auto parts. A full search of the car was upheld by the U.S. Supreme Court.

3. Consent Searches. A warrantless search may be conducted where the party to the search provides "voluntary and intelligent consent." The ultimate test of the **consent search** is voluntariness. As one Supreme Court decision states: "Two competing concerns must be accommodated . . . —the legitimate need for such searches and the equally important requirement of assuring the absence of coercion."[18] Police may seek consent for a variety of reasons. Perhaps they have little evidence and could not get a search warrant. Perhaps they feel there may be insufficient time to get the warrant, given the nature of the criminal activity. Often they will ask the suspect to sign a consent form.

> **consent search**
> *Warrantless search conducted when the party to the search provides "voluntary and intelligent consent" to police.*

Police may also attempt to gain consent from a "third party," a person who has the right to consent but is not the suspect or object of the search. Third-party consent has been upheld by the Supreme Court where it is demonstrated that: (1) the third party had mutual use or joint access and control over property or premises (called "common authority") and (2) the object of the search (the target) assumed the risk that the co-occupant, for example, might permit the search.[19] This means, for example, that spouses or roommates can give consent for each other; it also means that employers can give consent for employees.[20]

4. Hot Pursuit. Police are permitted to engage in a warrantless search and seizure when they are in **hot pursuit** of a suspect believed to be dangerous. Police may enter a suspect's house without a warrant if they are in hot pursuit and have reason to believe that he or she is on the premises. The scope of the search can be as extensive as necessary to prevent escape or apprehend the suspect.[21]

> **hot pursuit**
> *Exception to the rule requiring police to have a warrant to conduct a search; applies to cases of pursuit of vehicles and of suspects on foot.*

5. Plain View. Police need not obtain a warrant where the fruits or instrumentalities of a crime are in **plain view.** Such warrantless searches and seizures are upheld so long as the police are lawfully on the premises and they inadvertently see objects in plain view.[22] Consider what might happen if campus police arrive at a friend's door during a loud party and, when the door is opened, see illegal substances or objects on the dining room table. Would the police need a warrant? If they remove the substances from the table, would that be an unconstitutional seizure? Because of the plain view exception to the warrant requirement, the answer in both cases is no!

> **plain view**
> *No warrant is needed to conduct a search when the fruits or instrumentalities of a crime are in plain view.*

6. Stop and Frisk. Police do not need probable cause to stop a person who is reasonably suspected of criminal activity, whether in a car or on foot. Moreover, they do not need a warrant to engage in a search of that person. They must, however, have a **reasonable suspicion** that the suspect is armed and presently dangerous in order to **frisk,** or pat down the outer clothing, for concealed weapons.[23] This reasonable suspicion may be based on the "totality of the circumstances," a consideration of the whole picture.[24] (See Chapter 5.)

> **stop and frisk**
> *Technique used by police to "pat down" a person suspected of being armed or in possession of the instrumentalities of a crime.*

> **reasonable suspicion**
> *Suspicion (short of probable cause) that a person has been or may be engaged in the commission of a crime.*

Short of a stop and frisk, police have the right to stop a person and ask for identification or perhaps ask if assistance is needed.[25] In such cases, all that is required is "articulable suspicion"—the police must be able to say why they stopped the person (see Chapter 5). But the standard situation is that of an *arrest*, for which police must have probable cause to believe that a crime has been committed (Table 8.2).

> **frisk**
> *Patting down a suspect's clothing to search for concealed weapons, under reasonable suspicion.*

GREAT EXPECTATIONS OF PRIVACY

Until the 1960s, courts that considered search and seizure cases had been principally concerned with physical intrusions into houses, clothing, luggage, automobiles, and other so-called "constitutionally protected areas" (1). But with *Katz v. United States* (1967) a dramatic change occurred.

Katz's phone booth business

Charles Katz was a bookie, and he ran his betting business out of a public telephone booth. The FBI knew this and attached a "bug" to the outside of the booth. At Katz's trial, the government introduced into evidence recordings of phone

conversations in which Katz and others discussed the placing of bets. The Supreme Court had to decide whether the government's recording of conversations constituted an unreasonable search and seizure in violation of the Fourth Amendment.

In *Katz v. United States,* the majority found that such recording did in fact violate Katz's Fourth Amendment rights, because the Fourth Amendment "protects people—and not simply 'areas'" (2). Katz thus had a legitimate and reasonable expectation of privacy, whether or not the public telephone booth was a constitutionally protected area. In effect, Charles Katz had bought himself a dime's worth of privacy in a public phone booth. After the Katz case, search and seizure questions could no longer be decided solely on the basis of the place or area that was searched; decisions would rest on the reasonableness of the privacy expectation held by the person searched. The real legacy of this case is found in a two-part opinion written by Supreme Court Justice John M. Harlan. The following words from Justice Harlan's opinion have appeared in hundreds of state and federal search and seizure decisions since *Katz:*

My understanding of the rule that has emerged from prior decisions is that there is a twofold requirement, first that a person have exhibited an actual (subjective) expectation of privacy and, second, that the expectation be one that society is prepared to recognize as "reasonable." (3)

Deciding what is reasonable

How do courts evaluate whether a privacy expectation is a "reason-able" one? The justices appear to rely on their own perceptions, disposing of controversies on a case-by-case basis. Courts must judge the "reasonableness" of searches of bedrooms, living rooms, dorm rooms, backyards, cars, boats, and even motor homes. The questions for the court to resolve in each case are whether the suspect expected privacy *and* whether society would view that expectation of privacy as reasonable.

Let's compare your views on how society conceives of privacy with the Supreme Court's view. The following Supreme Court cases were decided over the past ten years. Predict whether the justices ruled that the search was reasonable or unreasonable.

California v. Greenwood

In 1984, Laguna Beach, California, police investigating a person suspected of narcotics trafficking first tried surveillance of the suspect's home. To get additional incriminating evidence, officers looked through the contents of the suspect's trash. The garbage that police examined had been left in plastic bags on the curb in front of the suspect's home. Items recovered in the trash bags were used to support the issuance of a search warrant (*California v. Greenwood,* 108 S. Ct. 1625, 1988).

Was the search of the suspect's trash "reasonable"? In other words, was the suspect's expectation of privacy one that society is prepared to recognize as reasonable? Why or why not?

California v. Carney

In 1979, Drug Enforcement Agency officers received uncorroborated information that a person was using a "mini motor home" parked in downtown San Diego for the purpose of exchanging marijuana for sex. Officers stopped a person as he was leaving the motor home and were told that those activities were in fact taking place. They then asked that person to knock on the door of the motor home. The suspect came out of the motor home, apparently in response to the knocking, and officers immediately searched the rooms inside the motor home and found marijuana (*California v. Carney,* 105 S. Ct. 2066, 1985).

Was the search of the suspect's motor home reasonable? Explain your position.

Winston v. Lee

In July of 1982, a Richmond, Virginia, storekeeper was locking up his store at 1 A.M. when he was approached by someone with a gun who yelled "Freeze!" This person shot at the storekeeper, who shot back, and the assailant ran off. Eight blocks away a wounded person was found by police and sent to a hospital in an ambulance. This suspect was wounded in his left side, with a bullet lodged "just beneath the skin." Police needed the bullet to make out a case of attempted rob-

bery, but that required surgery under local anesthesia (*Winston v. Lee,* 105 S. Ct. 1611, 1985).

Would the surgical removal of the bullet violate the suspect's reasonable expectation of privacy? In other words, would it be a reasonable search and seizure? Why or why not?

What the Court decided

Do the court decisions match yours? In the first case, *California v. Greenwood,* the justices ruled that the Fourth Amendment does *not* prohibit the warrantless search and seizure of garbage left for collection outside. The Court held:

Since respondents voluntarily left their trash for collection in an area particularly suited for public inspection, their claimed expectation of privacy . . . was not objectively reasonable. It is common knowledge that plastic garbage bags left along a public street are readily accessible to animals, children, scavengers, snoops, and other members of the public. . . . The police cannot reasonably be expected to avert their eyes from evidence of criminal activity that could have been observed by any member of the public.

In the second case, *California v. Carney,* the search also was ruled

not in violation of the Fourth Amendment. Here the justices reasoned as follows:

When a vehicle is being used on the highways or is capable of such use and is found stationary in a place not regularly used for residential purposes, the two justifications for the vehicle exception come into play. First, the vehicle is readily mobile, and, second, there is a reduced expectation of privacy stemming from the pervasive regulations of vehicles capable of traveling on highways.

In the third case, *Winston v. Lee,* the Supreme Court ruled that the search was *not* reasonable and did constitute a violation of the suspect's Fourth Amendment rights. Surgery to recover a bullet, the justices felt, would violate an individual's legitimate right to expect to be left alone. The court held: "The proposed surgery would violate respondent's rights to be secure in his person and the search would be 'unreasonable' under the Fourth Amendment."

SOURCES
1. *Silverman v. United States,* 365 U.S. 505 (1961).
2. *Katz v. United States,* 389 U.S. 347 at 353 (1967).
3. Ibid., at 360–361.

TABLE 8.2

	"Stop and Frisk"	"Arrest"
1. Degree of certainty	"Reasonable suspicion"	"Probable cause"
2. Scope	Very limited—only pat down for weapons	Full body search
3. Purpose	Stop—to prevent criminal activity	To take person into custody
4. Warrant	Not needed	May or may not need warrant

SOURCE: Rolando del Carmen, *Criminal Procedure: Law and Practice* (Pacific Grove, Calif.: Brooks Cole, 1991), p. 109.

exigent circumstances
Certain emergencies that call for immediate action and therefore do not allow time for a search warrant to be obtained.

7. Exigent Circumstances. Certain emergencies that call for immediate action do not allow time to obtain a search warrant; they are **exigent circumstances.** Two different kinds of emergencies qualify: (1) an ongoing physical event, such as a fire or the taking of hostages,[26] and (2) cases where physical evidence would disappear (e.g., due to the disposal of the substance) well before officers could obtain a warrant.[27]

8. Incident to an Arrest. There is no need for police to secure a warrant for a search incident to (part of) an arrest. For the safety of the officers and to prevent the concealment or destruction of evidence, police can conduct a full search of a person once that person has been lawfully arrested. This search includes the areas within his or her immediate control, such as furniture within reach of the arrestee.[28]

Arrests

arrest
Seizure of the person; the taking of a person into custody.

probable cause
Set of facts that would lead a reasonable person to believe that an accused person committed the offense in question; the minimum evidence requirement for an arrest, according to the Fourth Amendment.

arrest warrant
Written order from a court directing the police to effect an arrest.

"*Most street arrests take place without a warrant, although under federal law and the law of some states, a judicial warrant must later be issued.*"

The Bill of Rights does not use the term "arrest", but when it speaks of seizures, it includes seizures of the person, or what we call arrest. Consequently, the Fourth Amendment is largely applicable to arrest as well, with some exceptions.

An **arrest** is the act of taking a person into custody by restricting that person's right to leave.[29] The grounds for a lawful arrest are straightforward—police must have probable cause. In this context, **probable cause** amounts to facts that would lead a reasonable person to believe that the suspect had committed or was committing a crime. Common law placed certain limitations on the ability of police to act without an **arrest warrant**—an order from a court directing the police to effect an arrest. The person arrested must have committed a felony in the presence of the officer or there must be knowledge that a felony has been committed and probable cause to believe that the suspect committed it. Arrests for misdemeanors were limited to a breach of the peace committed in the presence of the officer.

Most arrests take place without a warrant, and here is one of the legal differences between seizures of property and seizures of the person. While, as we have just noted, law enforcement officers must obtain a warrant to search unless the situation allows for no delay (our eight categories above), when it comes to seizure of the person police need not obtain a warrant,[30] although warrantless arrests in a home can be made only when there is danger in delay.[31] Most street arrests take place without a warrant, although under federal law and the law of some states, a judicial warrant must later be issued.[32]

FIFTH AMENDMENT: SELF-INCRIMINATION

The relevant part of the Fifth Amendment reads: "nor shall any person . . . be compelled in any criminal case to be a witness against himself . . . ."

The Self-Incrimination Privilege

The source of the Fifth Amendment's privilege against self-incrimination is the ancient Latin maxim of the common law, *nemo tenetur prodere seipsum* (nobody is bound to accuse him/or herself). The specific right against self-incrimination originated in sixteenth-century England in reaction to government-sponsored inquisitions against political and religious dissidents. Once this right was achieved, suspects were no longer forced or coerced into making incriminating statements, they were spared torture as a means of extracting a confession, and they were not required to answer questions under oath. On the other hand, they were interrogated by justices of the peace without the benefit of counsel.[33]

Historical accounts and documents show that the Americans setting up a new nation were concerned that without a constitutional prohibition on self-incrimination, the federal government might resort to torture and coercion to extract confessions. Over 200 years ago, at Virginia's ratification convention, a strong argument was made for a bill of rights that included provisions prohibiting self-incrimination:

Congress may introduce the practice of the civil law, in preference to that of the common law. They may introduce the practice of France, Spain, and Germany—of torturing, to extort a confession of the crime. They will say that they might as well draw examples from those countries as from Great Britain, and they will tell you that there is such a necessity of strengthening the arm of government, that they must have a criminal equity, and extract confession by torture, in order to punish with still more relentless severity.[34]

But it was not until well over a century after the promulgation of the Bill of Rights that the U.S. Supreme Court invoked the Fifth Amendment in a federal case.[35] And in the century since, the Court has seldom applied this Amendment against the states. The process of broadening the use of the Fifth Amendment started with a case that truly shocked the conscience of the Court and of the nation: Three young black men were arrested in Mississippi and charged with murder. They were beaten, brutalized, and tortured into a confession of having committed a crime for which there was no other evidence. The Mississippi trial court hurriedly convicted them. A shocked Supreme Court in 1936 reversed the conviction as "revolting to the sense of justice."[36] But it did not rest its reversal on the Fifth Amendment's self-incrimination privilege; rather, it ruled that the brutalization of the defendants violated their entitlement to "due process of law" (in general), under the Fourteenth Amendment.

In the years that followed, state convictions resting on a claim of violation of due process were generally based on psychological pressure rather than physical torture. In 1957 the Supreme Court, after reviewing some thirty of its own previous decisions, invented the "totality of the circumstances test."[37] Suppose a suspect, member of an ethnic minority, confessed after a prolonged interrogation by relays of officers using psychological pressure (or even deceit) and withholding food, drink, and sleep. The "totality of the circumstances" may be deemed to have broken down the suspect's power to resist. Any confession obtained in such a manner will be deemed involuntary,[38] and thus in violation of Fourteenth Amendment due process, just as if it had been beaten out of the suspect.

Next, the Supreme Court was to find help in its own "right to counsel" decisions (see Chapter 5). In 1963, in the famous *Gideon v. Wainwright* case, the

Ernesto Miranda, at right, with his lawyer, in 1967. In 1966 the Supreme Court overturned his rape conviction and made constitutional history by instituting the so-called Miranda *warnings. (Miranda was later stabbed to death in a Phoenix bar.)*

Court had made the Sixth Amendment's right to counsel applicable to state criminal proceedings (again by the process of incorporation through the Fourteenth Amendment).[39] It was then logical for the Court to find that when defendants are made to incriminate themselves while being deprived of right to counsel, any such statements or confessions also violate the Sixth Amendment.[40] The link to the Fifth Amendment came with the *Miranda* case.

The *Miranda* Warnings

Miranda v. Arizona (1966) is the one Supreme Court decision every law enforcement officer remembers by name. Ernesto Miranda, an indigent with an eighth-grade education and a history of psychological problems, had confessed to a kidnap and rape after interrogation in police custody for less than two hours. The Court "did not find the defendant's statements to have been involuntary in the traditional sense," but found them to have been induced in a "menacing police interrogation procedure," in violation of the defendant's Fifth Amendment self-incrimination privilege. The Supreme Court was quick to add that Miranda's Sixth Amendment right to counsel was also violated.[41] If an attorney had been brought in, either the defendant would not have incriminated himself, or at least the "menacing police interrogation procedure" would not have taken place. The Court took one additional step by requiring that from here on, as soon as a suspect is taken into custody, the officer must advise the arrestee of his or her rights under the Constitution—the officer must read the *Miranda* warnings (see Figure 8.2).

"Legislatures make law wholesale. Courts make law retail." Statement attributed to Justice Frankfurter when he was a law school professor. In Claude R. Sowle, ed., *Police Power and Individual Freedom* (Chicago, Aldine, 1960), p. 226.

The *Miranda* decision was truly a first. Never before had the Supreme Court provided such a clear rule in the area of law enforcement or influenced the criminal justice system so significantly. And never before had the Supreme Court created so much controversy in the field of criminal justice. Before reviewing the impact of *Miranda*, we need to consider the ways in which courts have interpreted this landmark case. When does *Miranda* apply? And when are the warnings not required?

custody
Suspect under arrest or deprived of freedom in a significant way.

interrogation
Explicit questioning or actions that may elicit an incriminating statement.

Miranda warnings must be given whenever a suspect is taken into **custody** (when the suspect is placed under arrest or is deprived of freedom in a significant way) and may be subjected to **interrogation** (explicit questioning or actions that may elicit an incriminating statement). Generally, *Miranda* warnings are given when there is: (1) questioning of a suspect at a police station, (2) questioning of a suspect in a police car, (3) questioning of a suspect who is not free to leave, and (4) questioning of a defendant who is in custody for another offense.[42] On the other hand, *Miranda* warnings may not be necessary: (1) with roadside questioning of a motorist during a routine traffic stop; (2) when police do not intend to ask the suspect questions; (3) with nonspecific on-the-scene questioning by the police; (4) when a statement is actually volunteered by the suspect.[43]

The Evolution of *Miranda*

Much has happened in the aftermath of *Miranda*. Empirical studies appeared within a year of the decision,[44] most of them reporting some reduction in the number of confessions.[45] In 1967 Congress held hearings on the "*Miranda* problem." Legislation was enacted that was intended to defeat or overrule *Miranda*. This legislation (18 U.S.C. § 3501) directed federal courts to admit confessions into evidence under the voluntariness standard that prevailed prior to *Miranda*. The Senate committee report that accompanied this bill summed up the intensity of the resistance to the *Miranda* rules: "[C]rime will not be effectively abated so long as criminals who have voluntarily confessed their crimes are released on mere technicalities. The traditional right of the people to have their prosecuting attorneys place in evidence before juries the voluntary confessions and incriminating statements made by defendants simply must be restored."[46]

MIRANDA WARNINGS

1. You have the right to remain silent.
2. Anything you say can and will be used against you in a court of law.
3. You have the right to talk to a lawyer and have him present with you while you are being questioned.
4. If you cannot afford to hire a lawyer, one will be appointed to represent you before any questioning, if you wish one.
5. You may stop answering questions at any time.
6. Do you understand each of these rights I have explained to you?
7. Having these rights in mind, do you wish to talk to us now?

FIGURE 8.2 *The Miranda warning*

Miranda still stands, but as Table 8.3 reveals, the strength of the *Miranda* decision has been undercut by a series of Supreme Court cases that allow the use of confessions after some defect in the administration of the warnings,[47] and that limit *Miranda*'s reach to custodial interrogations only. Moreover, several decisions allow pretrial statements obtained in violation of *Miranda* to be used to impeach or discredit subsequent testimony. Cases supporting *Miranda* have a more narrow focus. Typically, these cases concern attempts to continue questioning once counsel has been requested.

> *"The idea that the police cannot ask questions of the person that knows most about the crime is an infamous decision."*
> Edwin Meese 3rd, U.S. Attorney General, in *The New York Times*, September 1, 1985, commenting on *Miranda*.

ENFORCING CONSTITUTIONAL RIGHTS: THE EXCLUSIONARY RULE

Throughout the 1960s and 1970s, the Supreme Court continued to expand the reach of the Fourth, Fifth, and Sixth Amendments to the states in offering protection to the accused. The landmark decision that started this criminal justice revolution was *Mapp v. Ohio,* which extended the exclusionary rule to state criminal proceedings.

Mapp v. Ohio (1961)

Dolree Mapp was a Cleveland landlady. On May 23, 1957, police officers knocked at her door and demanded entry. When entrance was denied, they entered forcefully, waving a piece of paper they claimed was a search warrant. Dolree grabbed the paper and shoved it down her bosom. A struggle ensued and the officers retrieved it. (In all probability, so the courts noted, it was not a search warrant.) They then searched the house, including her dresser drawers and a boarder's locked suitcase in the basement. In it they found "incriminating evidence"— obscene magazines. It appears that neither Mrs. Mapp nor the police knew of the presence of these magazines; the police apparently had been looking for something else.

Mrs. Mapp was convicted of the crime of possession of obscene publications. Her case wound its way through the Ohio appeals process until it reached the Supreme Court of the United States. Most observers were expecting a decision to

TABLE 8.3 Cases Affirming and Eroding *Miranda*

Cases affirming *Miranda:* evidence ruled not admissible

	Factual Situation
1. *U.S. v. Henry* (1979)	Questioning of defendant without a lawyer after indictment
2. *Edwards v. Arizona* (1981)	No valid waiver of right to counsel
3. *Smith v. Illinois* (1985)	After invocation of right to counsel during questioning
4. *Michigan v. Jackson* (1986)	Right to counsel invoked at arraignment
5. *Arizona v. Roberson* (1988)	Invoking *Miranda* for one offense, admissible for second offense?
6. *Minnick v. Mississippi* (1990)	When counsel is requested the suspect has the right to have an attorney present during the interrogation

Cases eroding *Miranda:* evidence ruled admissible

	Factual Situation
1. *Harris v. New York* (1971)	Impeachment of credibility
2. *Michigan v. Tucker* (1974)	Collateral derivative evidence
3. *Michigan v. Mosley* (1975)	Questioning on an unrelated offense
4. *New York v. Quarles* (1984)	Threat to public safety
5. *Berkemer v. McCarty* (1984)	Roadside questioning of a motorist pursuant to routine traffic stop
6. *Oregon v. Elstad* (1985)	Confession obtained after warnings given following earlier voluntary but unwarned admission
7. *Moran v. Burbine* (1986)	Failure of police to inform suspect of attorney retained for him
8. *Colorado v. Connelly* (1986)	Confession following advice of God
9. *Connecticut v. Barrett* (1987)	Oral confession
10. *Colorado v. Spring* (1987)	Shift to another crime
11. *Arizona v. Mauro* (1987)	Officer recorded conversation with defendant's wife
12. *Pennsylvania v. Bruder* (1988)	Curbside stop for traffic violation
13. *Duckworth v. Eagan* (1989)	Variation in warning
14. *Michigan v. Harvey* (1990)	Impeachment of testimony
15. *Illinois v. Perkins* (1990)	Officer posing as inmate
16. *Pennsylvania v. Muniz* (1990)	Routine questions and videotaping DWI
17. *Mc Neil v. Wisconsin* (1991)	Invoking a suspect's Sixth Amendment right to counsel does not amount to an invocation of the right to counsel derived by *Miranda*

SOURCE: Adapted from Rolando del Carmen, *Criminal Procedure: Law and Practice* (Pacific Grove, Calif.: Brooks Cole, 1991), p. 307.

the effect that the states cannot punish innocent people—Mrs. Mapp did not possess obscene publications (they were her boarder's), nor did she have any criminal intent (mens rea) to possess "obscene" publications. But the Supreme Court ignored that substantive issue and decided the case on a procedural question: The search was unreasonable and therefore illegal. The Court did not stop there. It delivered the constitutional bombshell that became the **exclusionary rule:** "We hold that all evidence obtained by searches and seizures in violation of the Constitution is, by that same authority, inadmissible in a state court."[48]

Let us examine the decision. Until that time every state had been left free to devise its own means of enforcing constitutional rights, including those of the Fourth, Fifth and Sixth Amendments. Theoretically, the state systems had at their disposition:

- criminal law remedies against police officers violating the law (criminal trespass, assault and battery)
- civil remedies against offending officers and their employers, such as city and state governments
- administrative remedies, such as departmental disciplinary proceedings
- "bonding" law enforcement officers and forfeiting the bond for the benefit of aggrieved parties

and possibly other remedies.[49]

The fact is, as the Supreme Court noted, none of these remedies had ever been seriously tried, and in any case, they did not work. The Court noted that by then (1961), most of the states had switched to the one remedy the federal courts had used since the *Weeks* case of 1914: exclusion of evidence obtained by unconstitutional methods.[50] "Other means of protection," said the Court in *Mapp*, have not worked. It felt compelled "to close the only courtroom door remaining open to evidence secured by official lawlessness in flagrant abuse" of the Constitution.

More particularly, there were two considerations. First, courts should not "dirty" their hands by making decisions on the basis of dirty evidence, procured in violation of law. Second, excluding illegally obtained evidence, reasoned the Court, punishes the police for violating the law by depriving them of their victory (a conviction). To avoid such punishments police will abide by the law, just as potential criminals will not offend for fear of punishment. This is the deterrence argument, and it involves a big assumption: that deterrence works to stop people from committing offenses. Yet to this day we know only that some would-be offenders are deterred from committing some types of crime, under some circumstances (see Chapter 13). Even less is known about the effect of the exclusionary rule on the conduct of individual police officers.[51] Studies have shown inconclusive results.[52] One thing is certain: By forcing the exclusion of illegally obtained evidence, the Supreme Court shocked the law enforcement community into setting up intensified training programs for law enforcement officers. In the

---

CHAPTER 8: The Rule of Law in Law Enforcement

exclusionary rule
Rule prohibiting use of illegally obtained evidence in a court of law.

"We hold that all evidence obtained by searches and seizures in violation of the Constitution is, by that same authority, inadmissible in a state court."
Mapp v. Ohio, 367 U.S. 643 (1961).

"I think it is a lesser evil that some criminals should escape than that the government should play an ignoble part."
Justice Oliver Wendell Holmes, Jr., *Olmstead v. United States, 277 U.S. 438 (1928).*

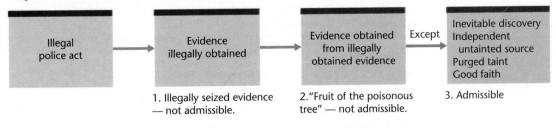

FIGURE 8.3 *How evidence becomes inadmissible and the exceptions that make it admissible* (*Source:* Adapted from Rolando del Carmen, *Criminal Procedure: Law and Practice* [Pacific Grove, Calif.: Brooks Cole, 1991] p. 61.)

long run, improved training may have led to greater adherence to the law on the part of the police.

The exclusionary rule typically comes into play prior to trial, when the attorney for the accused makes a motion to suppress or exclude illegally obtained evidence, such as an illegally obtained confession, or the instruments of a crime (the tools used by a burglar or an auto thief) or other evidence suggesting the defendant's guilt (blood-stained clothing). If a court fails to exclude illegally obtained evidence and the evidence is used at trial, its use may constitute an error and require reversal of a conviction.

But the reach of the exclusionary rule does not stop there. Any additional evidence that police acquire, directly or indirectly, as a result of the illegal search, arrest or confession, also may be excluded (see Figure 8.3). Courts have called this additional or secondary evidence "fruit" and the illegal search or arrest "the poisonous tree." Thus, in legal terms, evidence that is obtained from illegally obtained evidence is excluded from trial because it is tainted—it is **fruit of the poisonous tree.**[53]

fruit of the poisonous tree
Evidence obtained through other, illegally obtained evidence, inadmissible because it is tainted by the illegality of the initial search, arrest, or confession.

inevitable discovery exception
Exception to the exclusionary rule in cases where it is inevitable that police would have discovered the evidence regardless of an illegally obtained confession.

independent untainted source exception
Exception to the exclusionary rule in which evidence is admissible if police obtained it from a source that is sufficiently independent of the illegally obtained evidence.

purged taint exception
Exception to the exclusionary rule in which a voluntary act by the defendant removes the taint of prior illegal evidence-gathering by the police.

good faith exception
Exception to the exclusionary rule in which evidence obtained by police acting in good faith with a search warrant issued by a neutral and detached magistrate is admissible, even though the warrant is ultimately found to be invalid.

Exceptions to the Rule

But not all evidence that comes from an illegal search or seizure is ultimately excluded by courts. Evidence that ordinarily would be inadmissible may be introduced at trial if it is established that the taint has been removed, for example, if the police would have discovered the evidence regardless of the illegally obtained confession known as the **inevitable discovery exception**[54]; if the police obtained the additional evidence from a source that is sufficiently independent of the illegally obtained evidence, called the **independent untainted source rule**[55]; or if the defendant engaged in a voluntary act that broke the causal chain between the illegal police conduct and the tainted evidence. For example, an accused may make a voluntary statement to police that is wholly unaffected by the prior illegality.[56] This is known as the **purged taint exception.**

Recently, the U.S. Supreme Court added a new exception to the exclusionary rule. In the 1984 cases of *Massachusetts v. Sheppard*[57] and *United States v. Leon*,[58] the Court ruled that evidence obtained by police acting in good faith with a search warrant issued by a neutral and detached magistrate, but ultimately found to be invalid, may be used at trial. This has been called the **good faith exception.**[59]

The Demise of *Mapp v. Ohio*?

The increasing number of exceptions to the exclusionary rule may signal that the rule itself is on its way out, at the hands of a far more conservative Supreme Court. The battle lines have been drawn and the arguments on both sides of the issue have been marshalled along political and ideological lines.[60] Proponents argue that the exclusionary rule:

- effectively deters violations of constitutional rights by police officers
- promotes the notion that no one is above the law
- does not result in a significant number of lost prosecutions
- increases the level of professionalism within police departments
- preserves the integrity and legitimacy of the judicial system
- prevents the government from profiting from illegal police practices
- ensures the right to privacy

Opponents counter by arguing that the exclusionary rule:

- releases dangerous criminals through a legal technicality
- encourages plea bargains and reduced charges through the perception by prosecutors that a case may be lost due to suppressed evidence

- excludes reliable evidence and thus undermines the "truth seeking" function of the judiciary
  - diminishes respect for and perception of legitimacy of the system of justice
  - vindicates the rights of the accused, but provides no remedy for the victims of crime
  - fails to deter police misconduct and may actually promote other tactics of questionable constitutional validity, such as raids and sting operations
  - distorts the allocation of criminal justice resources given the time and money necessary to dispose of the many efforts to suppress evidence.[61]

On whatever arguments the Supreme Court may eventually base its potential abandonment of the exclusionary rule, it cannot be claimed that the rule has severely handicapped the police. Nor has it resulted in the wholesale discharge of obviously guilty parties. Indeed, several studies found that only between 0.5 and 0.8 percent of felony cases resulted in nonconviction due to the exclusionary rule.[62]

Alternatives to the Rule

Should the exclusionary rule be abandoned, some alternatives have surfaced from the heated debate over its benefits and drawbacks.[63] There have been proposals for police-civilian review boards to examine allegations of police illegality.[64] Other proposals have suggested that the evidence in question should be allowed in at trial, but that a separate hearing on the police officer's conduct should take place as well. And then there are the old standbys that have not worked before: criminal actions, civil suits, and administrative sanctions against offending officers.[65]

In considering the reasonableness of these alternatives, it is worth noting that the United States is the only nation with a common law tradition to have a mandatory exclusionary rule for illegally obtained evidence. In England, for example, illegally seized evidence is almost always allowed in at trial. Judges have the discretion to exclude it, especially in instances where inclusion would result in a "hardship on the accused" or where evidence is very unreliable. But such cases are rare, and police seem to comply with established procedure out of fear of internal disciplinary procedures.[66] This is similar to the criminal procedure of Canada and Germany, where exclusion is a last resort for some types of evidence, for example, coerced confessions, that are considered significantly unreliable. In both of these countries, judges have the discretion to balance the importance of the evidence against the alleged privacy intrusion.[67]

"The United States is the only nation with a common law tradition to have a mandatory exclusionary rule for illegally obtained evidence."

Illegally Seized Persons

We cannot end the discussion of the exclusionary rule without describing a significant oddity in the law. Illegally seized evidence (mostly personal property) may be excluded at trial, but an illegally seized person may not be excluded. This results from a Supreme Court decision well over a century old, and never overturned. In 1883 an agent of the U.S. government (Henry G. Julian) went to Lima, Peru; kidnapped Frederick Ker, a thief and embezzler under indictment in Illinois; and brought him back to Illinois for trial.

The U.S. Supreme Court ruled that it makes no difference how a defendant's presence at trial is secured (in this case by kidnapping); the court has jurisdiction, no matter what. In other words, an illegally seized person cannot be "excluded" from trial.[68] This rule was applied in subsequent cases. The Supreme Court of Israel relied on the U.S. Supreme Court ruling when it found that its courts had jurisdiction over the infamous Nazi mass murderer Adolf Eichmann, who had been kidnapped by Israeli agents in Argentina.[69] Most recently, a Mexican resident was forcibly taken from his home, flown to Texas, and arrested for

Police officer Mark Hoppe displaying evidence in a New York court during the September 1992 trial of a 17-year-old accused of the fatal stabbing of a Hasidic scholar.

WATCHING BIG BROTHER: THE ADVENT OF THE CAMCORDER

When it premiered last March, CamNet—America's first all-camcorder network—became a sort of nonestablishment C-SPAN. While cable-supported C-SPAN covers power in Washington, CamNet's army of unpaid photographers serves up raw, and often fascinating, scenes from the fringe that the traditional news media frequently ignore. And that, in turn, gives clout to people who don't hobnob with the elite. . . . It's difficult to keep secrets when everyone has a camera. . . . As the Rodney King video showed, even government officials can't fight the power that ordinary citizens can wield with a tiny camcorder. (1)

The amateur eye

The 1991 videotaping of the Los Angeles Police Department officers' brutalization of Rodney King may not have been the first time private citizens caught police on camera, but it certainly was the one that shook the country and the world. There have been other such video recordings since then, and there will be more. Several million camcorders—videotape camera recorders—are in the hands of ordinary Americans, and they record everything from weddings and puppet plays at kids' birthday parties to brutalities and illegalities committed by "Big Brother" government, especially its police.

Sometimes it is a television network whose camera catches an event on tape. Police departments now often and readily grant permis-

sion to the news media to ride shotgun in squad cars and capture police events on tape, and shows featuring those sorts of "live action" segments are popular with the public.

Some law enforcement officers and agencies, such as the Coast Guard, are taping their own law enforcement efforts to forestall claims of illegal activity. These recordings can be tragic, as in the case of Constable Darryll Lunsford of Garrison, Texas. Lunsford started his personal video camera as he left his patrol car for a routine traffic stop. The camera recorded two individuals jumping him and killing him with his own gun.

But the most significant impact of videotaping on policing is the prevalence of video cameras in amateur hands. The more cameras there are, the more likely it is that someone with such a camera will be around when law enforcement officers themselves are violating the law. Video cameras in private hands are a new and totally unforeseen answer to the age-old question: *quis enim custodiet custodes*—who watches the watchmen?

The limits of effectiveness

We should not think, however, that with the advent of video cameras all problems of illegal police actions can be solved. These cameras record only what the operator zeros in on. They do not catch what is outside the range of the lens or the microphone, nor do they necessarily catch what is outside the reach of the law. The difficulties in using videotapes were shown in the aftermath of the Los Angeles riots in 1992, as recorded by a reporter for *The New York Times:*

A joint local-Federal team . . . spent weeks poring over hundreds of feet of videotape and hundreds of photographs.

The pictures show hordes of people running amok, but only a few prosecutions have resulted. (2)

Despite the "miles" of videotape available to police for identifying suspects, most of it recorded by trained camera operators for news agencies, there were significant problems in using it effectively. Recorded images may be of deceptive or baffling angles; shades and shadows may be hard to interpret. Three-dimensional human faces, caught in the middle of an active expression and made two-dimensional, may be hard to recognize. Prodded by persuasive lawyers, juries may disregard a videotape entirely (3). Problems in interpreting recorded images and demonstrating their validity as evidence may be even worse when the camera operators are private citizens with no training in videotaping. And one further problem: There is the chance that, guided by the hand of law-violating officers, the camera may drop "accidentally" to the ground and be smashed, destroying all potential evidence.

Do the police have privacy rights?

But camcorders are around, and the "watchmen"—our police officers—rightfully are concerned about being watched. Dave Forman, the executive producer and host of "On Scene: Emergency Response," says that both the New York and Los Angeles Police Departments have allowed the show's cameras to patrol with them. He speculates that the surveillance provided by the prevalence of camcorders may help to prevent police brutality and other illegal activities:

In all the months with official organizations across the USA and in Canada and Mexico, we've never encountered anything like the Rodney King affair. We have never witnessed any police brutality. Is it because our cameras are there? Maybe.

But if the horror stories we've been seeing and hearing are widespread, I can't believe we'd be given such free access to patrol with them, on vice raids, with gang task forces, even SWAT teams.

For the most part, it seems that the Rodney King affair represents the way it was—and it probably was widespread—the corruption, the brutality, back when Big Brother was camera-shy. (4)

There remains the argument about the right to privacy. Private citizens in their private lives have a right to be free from intrusion by prying eyes and prying cameras. But law enforcement officers are not private citizens when acting in the course of duty. Their acts are public acts and subject to public scrutiny. And they should know that their acts are being scrutinized—and recorded—by the public they serve.

SOURCES

1. "Video Power to the People: CamNet, America's First All-Camcorder Channel, Shows Life on the Fringe," *TV Guide,* November 28, 1992, p. 19.
2. Seth Mydans, "Wheels of Justice Lurch after Los Angeles Riots," *The New York Times,* October 13, 1992, p. A8.
3. "Videos of LA Riots Useful in Investigation," National Public Radio's Weekend Edition, May 23, 1992, 53rd story.
4. Dave Foreman, "Orwell Couldn't Have Predicted the Home Video Camera," *USA Today,* February 3, 1992.

QUESTIONS FOR DISCUSSION

1. Because the use of camcorders is relatively new, we are only guessing that camcorders in private hands have a positive impact on police practice. How would you go about testing this hypothesis?
2. Should it be made a special offense for a law enforcement officer to destroy a camcorder or its tape?
3. What other ways are there to curb police abuses in citizen encounters?

Videotape of the Rodney King beating, March 3, 1991

his participation in the murder and kidnapping of a DEA agent. He subsequently challenged the abduction on the grounds that it violated international law. The U.S. Supreme Court did not agree. In an opinion by Chief Justice Rehnquist, the Court ruled that international law does not prohibit forcible abductions for the purposes of securing a person accused of violating U.S. law.[70] You may recall as well that the United States invaded Panama in 1989 and arrested General Manuel Noriega on U.S. drug charges. He was recently convicted in federal court in Miami and is now serving his sentence in federal prison.[71] (See Chapter 19.)

THE USE AND ABUSE OF FORCE

In 1829, Sir Robert Peel gave officers of the first police in England the advice that we here quote from the Metropolitan Police Force *Instruction Book* (1829) as still valid: "Remember, that there is no qualification more indispensable to a police officer than a perfect command of temper, never suffering himself to be moved in the slightest degree, by any language or threats that may be used." (See Chapter 6.) But when force becomes necessary, how do police officers regulate its use and avoid its abuse? We examine two current issues in law enforcement: the use of deadly force, and the abuse of nondeadly force.

The Ultimate Seizure of the Person: Deadly Force

In *Tennessee v. Garner* (1985), the Supreme Court decided a case in which a father sued a Memphis police officer, as well as governmental agencies, for the loss of life of his 17-year-old son. The son, according to undisputed facts, had burglarized a home, and the police had responded instantly to the homeowner's call. An officer spotted the suspect fleeing across the backyard and ordered him to stop. The officer saw that the suspect was unarmed. The youngster made an effort to jump over a high fence. The officer shot and killed him. The common-law rule of England and the United States, as well as the law of Tennessee, had always been that the police may use deadly force to stop a fleeing felon whether or not he or she is in possession of a weapon. The officer had acted properly when he shot and killed the suspect; the Supreme Court found that the officer could not be sued for wrongful death.

The Court reached a different conclusion, however, with respect to governmental liability. The Court reasoned that in England when all felonies were capital crimes, perhaps such a rule on the use of deadly force made sense, because an offender found guilty of a felony could be sentenced to death. But taking the life of a suspect who, if convicted, might receive only a relatively short prison sentence makes no sense and constitutes an unreasonable seizure of the person in violation of the Fourth Amendment.

"The shoot-to-kill rule for fleeing felons does not prevent crime or enhance the protection of police officers, and thus is unreasonable as a law enforcement tool."

The Police Foundation was allowed to file an *amicus curiae* (friend of the court) brief in which it supported abandonment of the harsh common-law rule. The brief demonstrated through research that the shoot-to-kill rule for fleeing felons does not prevent crime or enhance the protection of police officers, and thus is unreasonable as a law enforcement tool. The Supreme Court therefore overturned the common-law rule as violating the due process clause of the Fourteenth Amendment. Deadly force may not be used unless it is necessary to prevent the escape of a suspect who, the officer has probable cause to believe, poses a significant threat of death or serious injury to the officer or others.[72]

"As most police recruits learn in the academy, the cop on the street . . . carries in his holster more power than has been granted the Chief Justice of the Supreme Court."
James J. Fyfe, *Justice Quarterly* 5 (June 1988).

Use of deadly force by police officers has been a major issue in police-minority relations. James J. Fyfe writes, "As most police recruits learn in the academy, the cop on the street . . . carries in his holster more power than has been granted the Chief Justice of the Supreme Court."[73] Used improperly, this power can lead to riots, more deaths, litigation against the police, and the downfall of entire city administrations. During and after the upheavals of the 1960s, the issue was confronted by two presidential commissions, the Commission on Civil Disorders (1968) and the President's Commission on Law Enforcement and the Administration of Justice (1967). Both suggested that use of deadly force was the immediate cause of urban riots.

Before the work of these commissions, little had been done in the way of empirical research.[74] Since then, a number of social scientists have studied the issue. John Goldkamp poses two conflicting perspectives. One is that the disproportionately high number of minority persons shot and killed by police can be explained by irresponsible use of deadly force by some police officers and differential law enforcement toward minorities. Another is that the disproportion can be explained by disproportionately high arrest rates among minorities for crimes of violence.[75]

There is evidence to support both claims. Catherine Milton and her associates point out that 70 percent of the people shot by police in the seven cities they studied were black, although blacks made up only 39 percent of the population.[76] Betty Jenkins and Adrienne Faison showed that 52 percent of the persons killed by police in New York City over a three-year period were black and 21 percent were Hispanic.[77] Paul Takagi sums up this side of the controversy: "The news gets around the community when someone is killed by police. It is part of a history—a very long history of extralegal justice that included whippings and lynchings."[78] The other side of the argument—that larger proportions of minorities are shot by police because they live in high-crime areas and are more likely to own guns also finds support. James Fyfe's study of New York City shootings, for example, shows that in many incidents in which a shooting took place, police officers themselves were killed or wounded. He also found that minorities were more likely than whites to be involved in incidents in which guns were used.[79]

Official inquiries and empirical studies of police use of deadly force continue to be made. Lawrence Sherman maintains that there have been some positive developments. Data obtained from surveys of killings of civilians by police in fifty-nine cities between 1970 and 1984 show that such killings have decreased by 50 percent as a result of higher standards, including those restricting the use of firearms, and better training of officers.[80]

Of course, even with improved training, controversial incidents will still happen, often polarizing an entire county or city. For example, on April 10, 1990, a black teenager, Phillip Pannell, was shot and killed by a white Teaneck, New Jersey, police officer. The shooting resulted in riots throughout Teaneck and polarized Bergen County, New Jersey, for nearly two years.[81]

Abuse of Force

The use of overwhelming force against persons, frequently suspects, who are deemed not to respect the power of the police is what we call **police brutality.** Who can forget the image of Rodney King being beaten mercilessly, without any apparent reason, by four Los Angeles police officers?[82] But Los Angeles is not an exception. A similar amateur videotape recorded a beating inflicted by a Trenton, New Jersey, police officer on Thomas Downing, who simply inquired why his stepson was being arrested.[83] (See the Criminal Justice on Trial box.)

Force must be used in law enforcement, but democracies always put limits on that use. In this chapter we have examined the constitutional restrictions on the abuse of force. The best-known abuse historically was probably the "third degree"—torture for the purpose of extracting a confession. Torture by police may be rare in the United States today, but it remains a significant problem in many countries around the world (Chapter 19) even with the adoption of the United Nations Code of Conduct for Law Enforcement Officials, which prohibits all police abuses.[84] We have a long way to go before the ideals found in the Code guide police practices in every nation.

Rodney King's lawyer during a press conference in Los Angeles in March 1991, holding a photo of King showing the injuries inflicted on him by police. Both criminal and civil cases resulted from the beating incident made famous by an amateur videotape.

"The news gets around the community when someone is killed by police. It is part of a history— a very long history of extralegal justice. . . ."
Paul Takagi, "Death by Police Intervention," in *A Community Concern: Police Use of Deadly Force.*

police brutality
Use of excessive physical force against another person (usually a suspect) by law enforcement officers.

REVIEW

The Bill of Rights of 1791, as interpreted by the Supreme Court of the United States, determines the powers of law enforcement at both the federal and the state levels. But it took a century until the federal courts subjected the federal criminal process to the Bill of Rights, and it took more than another half century until the Supreme Court, by a process of selective incorporation, made the principal provisions of the Bill of Rights binding on the states: the Fourth Amendment's protection against unreasonable searches and seizures and the Fifth Amendment's privilege against self-incrimination. In doing so, the Supreme Court engaged in judicial legislation by requiring police officers to give the *Miranda* warnings to arrested persons and by mandating the exclusion of all evidence obtained illegally.

A growing number of exceptions to the original rulings could signal a change: The Supreme Court may abandon its insistence on the exclusionary rule as a "constitutional" requirement. Empirical evidence seems to indicate that constitutional restraints have not handicapped law enforcement—but they have led to improved police training. A troubling issue remains, that of the abuse of force by law enforcement officers. Although the Supreme Court has laid down definite limits on the use of deadly force by such officers, instances of abuse continue to occur.

Notes

1. This excerpt is based on "Homeless Man Convicted of Murder Is to Be Freed," *The New York Times*, January 8, 1992, p. B5.

2. Recently the U.S. Supreme Court refused to hear the state's appeal. Ibid.

3. John Phillip Reid, *Constitutional History of the American Revolution: The Authority of Rights* (Madison Wis.: University of Wisconsin Press, 1986), pp. 193–198.

4. *Annals of Congress*, vol. 1 (August 17, 1789), p. 755.

5. See *Hopt v. Utah*, 110 U.S. 574 (1884). B. James George, *Constitutional Limitations on Evidence in Criminal Cases* (New York: Practicing Law Institute, 1969), pp. 257–258.

6. *Bram v. United States*, 168 U.S. 532 (1897).

7. See Lester B. Orfield, *Criminal Procedure under the Federal Rules*, vol. 1 (Rochester, N.Y.: Lawyer's Cooperative Publishing Co., 1966), p. 235.

8. *Wan v. United States*, 266 U.S. 1 (1924).

9. *Gitlow v. New York*, 268 U.S. 652 (1925).

10. See, e.g., Raoul Berger, *Government by Judiciary: The Transformation of the Fourteenth Amendment* (Cambridge, Mass.: Harvard University Press, 1977).

11. *Palko v. Connecticut*, 302 U.S. 319 (1937).

12. Ibid., at 325.

13. See *The Criminal Law Revolution and Its Aftermath (1960–1977)* by the editors of *Criminal Law Reporter* (Washington: Bureau of National Affairs, 1972).

14. *Wolf v. Colorado*, 338 U.S. 25 (1949).

15. See John N. Ferdico, *Criminal Procedure for the Criminal Justice Professional* (St. Paul, Minn.: West, 1985), p. 139.

16. *United States v. Montoya de Hernandez*, 473 U.S. 531 (1985).

17. *Colorado v. Bannister*, 449 U.S. 1 (1980).

18. *Schneckloth v. Bustamente*, 412 U.S. 218 (1973).

19. *United States v. Matlock*, 415 U.S. 164 (1974); see also Dorothy Kagehiro and William S. Laufer, "The Assumption of Risk Doctrine in Third Party Consent Searches," *Criminal Law Bulletin* 26 (1990):195; Dorothy Kagehiro and William S. Laufer, "*Illinois v. Rodriguez* and the Social Psychology of Consent," *Criminal Law Bulletin* 27 (1991):42.

20. See Wayne R. LaFave and Jerold H. Israel, *Criminal Procedure* (St. Paul, Minn.: West, 1985), p. 213.

21. See *Warden v. Hayden*, 387 U.S. 294 (1967).

22. *Coolidge v. New Hampshire*, 403 U.S. 443 (1971); *Texas v. Brown*, 460 U.S. 730 (1983).

23. *Terry v. Ohio*, 392 U.S. 1 (1968).

24. See *United States v. Cortez*, 449 U.S. 411 (1981).

25. See *Kolender v. Lawson*, 461 U.S. 352 (1983).

26. See, e.g., *Michigan v. Tyler*, 436 U.S. 499 (1978).

27. See, e.g., *Schmerber v. California*, 384 U.S. 757 (1966). Max DeBerry and G. O. W. Mueller, "Pending Peril and the Right to Search Dwellings," *West Virginia Law Review* 58 (1956):219–240.

28. See *Chimel v. California*, 395 U.S. 752 (1969).

29. See *Dunaway v. New York*, 442 U.S. 200 (1979).

30. *Carroll v. United States*, 267 U.S. 132 (1925).

31. *Payton v. New York*, 445 U.S. 573 (1980).

32. See *Welsh v. Wisconsin*, 466 U.S. 740 (1984); *Payton v. New York*, 445 U.S. 573 (1980).

33. See Glanville Williams, *Proof of Guilt* (London: Stevens and Sons, 1955); Leonard W. Levy, *Origins of the Fifth Amendment: The Right Against Self-Incrimination* (New York: Oxford University Press, 1968).

34. *Elliots Debates*, vol. III, p. 658, as quoted in *Report to the Attorney General on the Law of Pre-Trial Interrogation* (Washington, D.C.: Office of Legal Policy, 1986), p. 11.

35. *Bram v. United States*, 168 U.S. 532 (1897).

36. *Brown v. Mississippi*, 297 U.S. 278 (1936).

37. *Fikes v. Alabama*, 352 U.S. 191 (1957).

38. *Rogers v. Richmond*, 365 U.S. 534 (1961).

39. *Gideon v. Wainwright*, 372 U.S. 335 (1963).

40. *Spano v. New York*, 360 U.S. 315 (1959); *Massiah v. United States*, 377 U.S. 201 (1964); *McLeod v. Ohio*, 381 U.S. 356 (1965).

41. *Miranda v. Arizona*, 384 U.S. 436 (1966).

42. These categories are found in Rolando del Carmen, *Criminal Procedure: Law and Practice*, 2d ed (Pacific Grove, Calif.: Brooks Cole, 1991). See Table 8.3.

43. Ibid.

44. See, e.g., Richard H. Seeburger and R. Stanton Wettick "*Miranda* in Pittsburgh—A Statistical Study," *University of Pittsburgh Law Review* 29 (1967):1.

45. See *Report to the Attorney General*, pp. 62–64.

46. Senate Report No. 1097, 90th Congress 2nd Session.

47. See Jill Adler, "The U.S. Supreme Court's 'Harmless Error': An Essay on *Arizona v. Fulminante*," *Tilburg Foreign Law Review* 1 (1991):15.

48. *Mapp v. Ohio*, 367 U.S. 643 (1961).

49. See B. James George, Jr., *Constitutional Limitations on Evidence in Criminal Cases* (New York: Practicing Law Institute, 1969), pp. 119–132.

50. *Weeks v. United States*, 232 U.S. 383 (1914).

51. See Yale Kamisar, "Does (Did) (Should) the Exclusionary Rule Rest on a 'Principled Basis' Rather Than an 'Empirical Proposition'?" *Creighton Law Review* 16 (1983):565.

52. Thomas Y. Davies, "On the Limitations of Empirical Evaluations of the Exclusionary Rule: A Critique of the Spiotto Research and *United States v. Calandra*," *Northwestern University Law Review* 69 (1974):740. See also Charles H. Whitebread and Christopher Slobogin, *Criminal Procedure*, 2d ed. (Mineola, N.Y.: The Foundation Press, 1986), pp. 44–45; Craig D. Uchida and Timothy S. Bynum, "Search Warrants, Motions to Suppress and 'Lost Cases': The Effects of the Exclusionary Rule in Seven Jurisdictions," *Journal of Criminal Law and Criminology* 81 (1991):1034–1066. William C. Heffernan and Richard W. Lovely, "Evaluating the Fourth Amendment Exclusionary Rule: The Problem of Police Compliance with the Law," *University of Michigan Journal of Law Reform* 24 (2) (1991):311–369, finding the exclusionary rule to be a

weak deterrent. For an innovative study on what really determines attitudes of the police toward "the rule of law" and specific rights and procedures, see Thomas E. Reed and William D. Beckerman, "The Value of Equality in the Rule of Law," *International Journal of Criminology and Penology* 6(4) (1978):363–371.

53. See *Nardone v. United States*, 308 U.S. 338 (1939); *Wong Sun v. United States*, 371 U.S. 471 (1963).

54. See *Nix v. Williams*, 467 U.S. 431 (1984).

55. *United States v. Crews*, 445 U.S. 463 (1980).

56. *Wong Sun v. United States*, 371 U.S. 471 (1963).

57. 468 U.S. 981 (1984).

58. 468 U.S. 897 (1984).

59. See, e.g., Wayne LaFave, "The Seductive Call of Expediency: *United States v. Leon*, Its Rationale and Ramifications," *University of Illinois Law Review* (1984):896; William J. Mertens & Silas Wasserstrom, "The Good Faith Exception to the Exclusionary Rule: Deregulating the Police and Derailing the Law," *Georgetown Law Journal* 70 (1981):365. In addition to this good faith exception, Congress has made attempts to legislate an exception. See, e.g., Senate Report No. 350, S. 1764, Exclusionary Rule Limitation Act of 1983, 98th Congress 2nd Session 3 (1984).

60. See K. E. Goodpaster, "An Essay on Ending the Exclusionary Rule," *Hastings Law Journal* 33 (1984):1065; Dale H. Oaks, "Studying the Exclusionary Rule in Search and Seizure," *University of Chicago Law Review* 37 (1970):665.

61. These arguments are based on those presented in *Report to the Attorney General: Search and Seizure—Exclusionary Rule* (Washington, D.C.: Department of Justice, 1986) and found in Rolando del Carmen, *Criminal Procedure: Law and Practice* (Pacific Grove, Calif.: Brooks Cole Publishing Company, 1991).

62. Peter Nardulli, "The Societal Cost of the Exclusionary Rule: An Empirical Assessment," *American Bar Foundation Journal* (1983):585. *Report of the Comptroller General*, April 19, 1979 (Washington, D.C.: U.S. Government Printing Office, 1979); National Institute of Justice, *The Effects of the Exclusionary Rule* (Washington, D.C., 1982); Thomas Y. Davies, "A Hard Look at What We Know (and Still Need to Learn) about the 'Costs' of the Exclusionary Rule: The N.I.J. Study and Other Studies of 'Lost' Arrests," *American Bar Foundation Journal* (1983):611.

63. The alternatives include, of course, the abolition of the exclusionary rule. See *Report to the Attorney General* at pp. 50–54. But another remedy is stepped-up remedial police officer training. See Indy Hails Keci, "Improving the Exclusionary Rule: A Remedial Education Model," *American Journal of Criminal Justice* 12 (1988):147–166.

64. See James Hudson, "Police Review Boards and Police Accountability," *Law and Contemporary Problems* 36 (1971):515.

65. For a discussion of criminal prosecutions and civil damage suits, see *Report to the Attorney General*. See also William A. Schroeder, "Deterring Fourth Amendment Violations: Alternatives to the Exclusionary Rule," *Georgetown Law Journal* 69 (1981):1361; Potter Stewart, "The Road to *Mapp v. Ohio* and Beyond: The Origins, Development and Future of the Exclusionary Rule in Search and Seizure Cases," *Columbia Law Review* 83 (1983):1365.

66. See Comment, Barry F. Shanks "Comparative Analysis of the Exclusionary Rule and Its Alternatives," 57 *Tulane Law Review* (1983):648–681.

67. See Craig M. Bradley "The Exclusionary Rule in Germany," *Harvard Law Review* 96 (1983):1032.

68. *Ker v. Illinois*, 119 U.S. 436 (1886).

69. See Michael H. Cardozo, "When Extradition Fails, Is Abduction the Solution?," in *International Criminal Law*, eds. G. O. W. Mueller and Edward M. Wise (South Hackensack, N.J.: Fred B. Rothman, 1965), pp. 465–475.

70. *United States v. Humberto Alvarez-Machain*, 112 S. Ct. 2188 (1992).

71. See Sam Vincent Meddis, "Noriega Defense Team Chips Away," *USA Today*, February 17, 1992, p. 2.

72. *Tennessee v. Garner*, 471 U.S. 1 (1985). For an examination of police shootings subsequent to *Tennessee v. Garner*, see Terry R. Sparger and David J. Giacopassi, "Memphis Revisited: A Reexamination of Police Shootings after the Gainer Decision," *Justice Quarterly* 9(2) (1992):211–225.

73. James J. Fyfe, "Police Use of Deadly Force: Research and Reform," *Justice Quarterly* 5 (June 1988):165–205; see also Geoffrey P. Alpert and Lorie A. Fridell, *Police Vehicles and Firearms: Instruments of Deadly Force* (Prospect Heights, Ill.: Waveland Press, 1992). Deadly force does not necessarily imply use of a firearm. See Terry C. Cox, Jerry S. Faughn, and William M. Nixon, "Police Use of Metal Flashlights as Weapons: An Analysis of Relevant Problems," *Journal of Police Science and Administration* 13(3) (1985):244–250. And see Geoffrey P. Alpert and Lorie A. Fridell, *Police Vehicles and Firearms: Instruments of Deadly Force.* (Prospect Heights, Ill.: Waveland, 1992).

74. With the exception of, for example, Gerald D. Robin, "Justifiable Homicide by Police Officers," *Journal of Criminal Law, Criminology, and Police Science* 54 (1963):225–231.

75. John S. Goldkamp, "Minorities as Victims of Police Shootings: Interpretations of Racial Disproportionality and Police Use of Deadly Force," *Justice System Journal* 2 (1976):169–183.

76. Catherine Milton, J. W. Halleck, J. Lardner, and G. L. Albrecht, *Police Use of Deadly Force* (Washington, D.C.: Police Foundation, 1977).

77. Betty Jenkins and Adrienne Faison, *An Analysis of 248 Persons Killed by New York City Policemen* (New York: Metropolitan Applied Research Center, 1974).

78. Paul Takagi, "Death by Police Intervention," in *A Community Concern: Police Use of Deadly Force*, eds. R. N. Brenner and M. Kravitz (Washington, D.C.: U.S. Government Printing Office, 1979), p. 34.

79. James J. Fyfe, "Race and Extreme Police-Citizen Violence," in *Race, Crime, and Criminal Justice*, eds. R. L. McNeely and C. E. Pope (Beverly Hills, Calif.: Sage, 1981), pp. 89–108. After extensive analysis, Prof. Fyfe and Mark Blumberg concluded that the defense-of-life standard is not a feasible means of controlling police use of deadly force, and that control of force is best left in the hands of police chiefs. James J. Fyfe and Mark Blumberg, "Response to Griswold: A More Valid Test of the Justifiability of Police Actions," *American Journal of Police* 4(2) (1985):110–132. See also Arnold Binder and Peter Scharf, "Deadly Force in Law Enforcement," *Crime and Delinquency* 28 (1982):1–23; Albert J. Reiss, Jr., *Police and the Public* (New Haven, Conn.: Yale University Press, 1971).

80. Lawrence W. Sherman, *Citizens Killed by Big City Police, 1970–1984* (Washington, D.C.: Crime Control Institute, Crime Control Research Corporation, 1986). On the difficulty of assessing the relationship between justifiable homicide rates and rates of police use of deadly force, see Lorie Fridell, "Justifiable Use of Measures in Research on Deadly Force," *Journal of Criminal Justice* 17(3) (1989):157–165.

81. Anthony Destefano et al., "NJ Cop Innocent: Slain Teen's Mom Falters after Verdict," *Newsday*, July 12, 1992, p. 3; John Kifner, "Evidence Shows Youth's Hands Up when Teaneck Officer Killed Him," *The New York Times*, August 2, 1990, p. 1.

82. The four officers whom a videotape showed beating the black driver were acquitted. Thereupon the Los Angeles riots occurred, resulting in over 50 deaths and the destruction of nearly $1 billion worth of property. Subsequently, the officers were federally indicted for civil rights violations. Two were convicted, two acquitted; Carl E. Pope and Lee E. Ross, "Race, Crime and Justice: The Aftermath of Rodney King," *The Criminologist* 17 (1992): 1–10.

83. Jerry Gray, "In Police Brutality Case, One Videotape but Two Ways to View It," *The New York Times*, December 13, 1991, p. B7. A jury subsequently found the police officer not guilty of official misconduct; see "Videotape Discounted in Beating," *The New York Times*, February 20, 1993, p. A25.

84. U.N. General Assembly Resolution 34/169, December 17, 1979.

CHAPTER 9

POLICE OFFICERS AND THEIR LIFESTYLES

"**E**ven before we were married, we learned how traumatically the police department could disrupt a marriage. Significant dates stand out. Arthur joined the New York City Police Department in June 1940. We set our wedding day for the first Sunday in March 1943. Three weeks before, Arthur approached the commanding officer of the precinct and requested a day off for that Sunday, to get married. Dispassionately, the captain told him that he would have to choose another day because he could not spare him on the weekend. Why so indispensable? At that time, Arthur was assigned to the Central Park precinct, guarding half-frozen lakes and half-thawed lawns from the encursions of pedestrians. But having been a police officer for almost three years, Arthur had fatalistically expected the negative response. In those days, captains automatically refused any request from young patrolmen. Perhaps this was because the department believed implicitly that until a patrolman had five years of experience and abrasion, he was not a real cop and, therefore, not entitled to respect.

Daily, Arthur pleaded with him. Finally, the captain relented to the extent that he switched Art's scheduled day off, which was Monday, to Sunday. And thankfully, we were permitted to marry on the prearranged date and to enjoy a honeymoon from 2 A.M. when the celebration ended until 6 A.M., when Arthur had to leave bed and bride to rush to work at lake and lawn."[1] ■

This story of the unusual marriage is from *The Police Family,* by Arthur Nieder-hoffer, a police officer and professor, and his wife Elaine. What, in the Nieder-hoffers' terms, constitutes a "real cop"? That is the question we try to answer in this chapter. We begin by examining the recruitment process and the selection criteria used by police departments in their search for good applicants. Have those criteria changed over the years? If so, what factors have caused the change? Once an applicant is accepted, how does he or she become a "real cop"? How much of policing is learned at the academy and how much on the street? We will analyze how new officers are socialized into the police subculture and how a "police personality" develops. We will also demonstrate how police have tried to fight for their interests through collective bargaining. Finally, we will look at the darker side of policing: the problem of corruption.

SELECTING POLICE OFFICERS

Recruiting and selecting police officers is an extremely important part of the administrative duties of a police department. Many officers spend their entire career at one department. Thus, when a particular officer is selected for employ-ment, the department is making a long-term investment in that individual.

Recruitment entails identifying the appropriate labor market and seeking out and attracting qualified candidates. Police work appeals to applicants for a num-ber of reasons. It offers job security, competitive pay, good benefits, an opportu-nity for adventure, and a chance to serve the community in a responsible and meaningful way (Table 9.1).

Since the early 1980s, the number of applicants has been increasing. Among the several factors that account for this are the difficulty in finding jobs, the need for security in uncertain times, and the lesser importance of the armed forces. Moreover, with the passage of Title VII of the Civil Rights Act of 1972, which made it illegal to discriminate in employment decisions on the basis of gender, race, religion, or national origin, many departments began actively to recruit women and minority groups.

Various screening criteria are used to select those who will become police officers. Over the last twenty years, police departments have adopted new meth-ods and standards of selection. They rely less on such standards as minimum and maximum height and weight and more on various types of tests, including psy-chological, and on educational requirements.

Qualifications

Police work involves danger, stress, temptations, challenges to integrity, discre-tion in the use of force, and constant interaction with people who are often hos-tile or indifferent. Clearly, not everyone is equipped to handle these demands. Until the last twenty years, however, selection techniques did not differ very much from those used in the nineteenth century. The 1829 selection criteria in England, were a character check, a medical examination, and a personal inter-view.[2] The criteria in this country were about the same. According to one expert, "If you asked the mayor of a city employing police officers, the answer might have been that a 'good' officer was one who was dependable, did what he was told, and stayed sober on duty."[3]

New Selection Criteria.   Over the last two decades many departments have insti-tuted more objective selection procedures. Most departments require that new recruits be in good physical condition, have no criminal record, and have a high-

Only their gloves are still all white: Every police depart-ment in the United States has been integrated. Police Academy graduation, Boston, May 1990.

TABLE 9.1 Reasons for Choosing Police Work as a Career

	Male	Female	Total
Variety	62.2%	92.1%	69.4%
	(74)	(35)	(109)
Responsibility	50.4%	55.3%	51.6%
	(60)	(21)	(81)
Serve public	48.7%	50%	49%
	(58)	(19)	(77)
Adventure	49.6%	39.5%	47.1%
	(59)	(15)	(74)
Security	46.2%	34.2%	43.3%
	(55)	(13)	(68)
Pay	43.7%	42.1%	43.3%
	(52)	(16)	(68)
Benefits	36.1%	31.6%	35%
	(43)	(12)	(55)
Advancement	31.9%	34.2%	32.5%
	(38)	(13)	(51)
Retirement	27.7%	5.3%	22.3%
	(33)	(2)	(35)
Prestige	16%	13.2%	15.3%
	(19)	(5)	(24)

SOURCE: Harold P. Slater and Martin Reiser, "A Comparative Study of Factors Influencing Police Recruitment," *Journal of Police Science and Administration* 16 (1988):170.

school diploma. Other criteria for selection, used to varying degrees by different departments, are a written exam (78%); an interview (97%); a background check (99%); physical strength and agility tests (80%); psychiatric examinations (over 50%); situational tests, that is, exercises simulating real-life experience (60%); and lie detector tests (40%).[4]

Since 1982, the number of police departments appointing only candidates that live within their jurisdictions has been rising. Even without an absolute requirement, departments have various ways of encouraging their personnel to reside where they work. A New York City Mayor's Advisory Committee, for example, recommends that city residents be given extra credit on entrance examinations. The argument is that police officers are better able to understand their communities if they have first-hand experience as residents. A counterargument to the residency requirement is that it limits the pool of eligible candidates.[5]

Before enactment of Title VII, physical requirements were based on standards of height and weight. Since enactment, so as not to discriminate against the hiring of women and some ethnic groups, height and weight requirements are used by only a handful of departments (e.g., 3.5% have minimum height standards). Departments do require, however, that weight be reasonably related to height. Close to 3 percent of departments do not accept smokers.[6]

Psychological Testing. On September 27, 1972, Susan Place, 17, and Georgia Jessup, 16, disappeared after leaving their homes in Oakland Park, Florida, to spend the day at the beach. Seven months later their beheaded battered bodies were discovered in a shallow grave on Hutchinson Island. Martin County Deputy

Sheriff Gerard Schafer was found guilty of first-degree murder. Authorities also linked him to the murders and disappearances of two dozen other women. Schafer, dubbed by newspapers "the Bluebeard of the Beach," received two concurrent life sentences. In pretrial evaluations, the six-foot-tall law enforcement officer told psychiatrists that "all indecent women should be destroyed for the good of society."[7] Within one year after Schafer's conviction, Florida's Police Standards Commission proposed that a statewide psychological testing program be instituted. Today, most large departments use psychological testing as a screening device. The two most popular personality assessment tests are the Minnesota Multiphasic Personality Inventory (MMPI) and the California Psychological Inventory (CPI).[8] They measure such personality dimensions as responsibility, interpersonal maturity, and extent of socialization.

The issue of psychological testing has given rise to a considerable amount of research.[9] Such testing is used to screen out people who are believed to be unsuited to police work. This assumes that the psychological characteristics of a good police officer are well defined and that the available tests can validly measure such characteristics and predict future performance. Some critics believe that neither of these requirements has been met satisfactorily by the available tests, so their usefulness for police screening is questionable.[10] In summarizing the problem, Dennis Kenney and Steuart Watson argue that

". . . it would seem that due to the varied nature of police work and the diverse demands placed upon officers, there is no 'ideal' police profile upon which to pick and choose applicants."
Dennis Kenney and Steuart Watson, *American Journal of Police* 9 (1990).

questions should be addressed more fully in future research before any meaning can be placed on the differences in personality as measured by traditional paper-and-pencil tests. Until then, it would seem that due to the varied nature of police work and the diverse demands placed upon officers, there is no 'ideal' police profile upon which to pick and choose applicants.[11]

Nevertheless, the question of liability is so serious that departments usually have no choice but to use psychological tests to screen out those who may have emotional problems.[12]

Education. In 1973, the National Advisory Commission on Criminal Justice Standards and Goals recommended:

Every police agency should, no later than 1982, require as a condition of initial employment, the completion of at least 4 years of education (120 semester hours or a baccalaureate degree) at an accredited college or university.[13]

FIGURE 9.1 *Police profile: College education of all sworn officers* (*Source:* David L. Carter, Allen D. Sapp, and Darrel W. Stephens, *The State of Police Education: Policy Direction for the 21st century* [Washington, D.C.: Police Executive Research Forum, 1989], p. 45.)

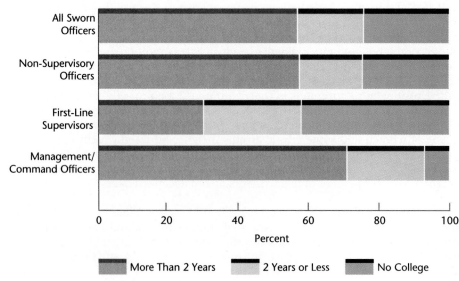

To help meet this standard, the Law Enforcement Education Program (LEEP), a major part of the Law Enforcement Assistance Administration (LEAA) program, provided grants and loans to as many as 100,000 students per year in law-enforcement-related college programs. Since the termination of LEAA (April 1982), these funds are no longer available. Nevertheless, a growing number of applicants have more than a high-school diploma. By 1988, 65.2 percent of all sworn officers had one or more years of college [14] (Figure 9.1).

The question of whether police officers should have a college degree, although this educational standard has been recommended by national commissions since 1931, is still controversial. In a 1988 survey of law enforcement agencies conducted by the Police Executive Research Forum, some consistent themes emerged. Those in favor of higher education argued that college-educated officers

- communicate better with the public
- show more initiative
- write better reports
- are more effective
- have greater sensitivity to minorities
- in general, are more professional [15]

Those who questioned higher education requirements for police officers argued that college-educated officers

- might leave police work
- are more prone to question orders
- expect preferential treatment
- cause animosity within the ranks
- feel dissatisfied with the job [16]

Who Makes a Good Officer?

Experts disagree on the best way to predict which applicants will make effective officers. A great deal of research has been done in this area. For example, in a major study of 1,608 New York City officers, Bernard Cohen and Jan Chaiken related background variables such as age, race, IQ, civil service examination scores, and personal history to performance measures that included termination of employment, absenteeism, and disciplinary actions against officers. Among those factors not related to performance were civil service exam scores, IQ, and arrest records for petty crimes. The recruit training score and probationary rating were the best predictors of later successful job performance. [17]

CHANGING COMPOSITION OF THE POLICE FORCE

The political and social crises of the 1960s challenged Americans to reaffirm their commitment to equality before the law. Title VII of the Civil Rights Act of 1964 prohibited the private sector from discrimination in employment on the basis of race, gender, religion, or national origin. In 1972, the Equal Employment Opportunity Act amended the Civil Rights Act to include the public sector. The 1972 Act also required that federal agencies develop affirmative action programs. Besides federal legislation, state and local laws prohibit discrimination on the basis of race, national origin, religion, and gender. Two states and over sixty cities go even further by prohibiting discrimination on the basis of sexual preference. [18]

These social and legal changes have had a major impact on the composition of

AFFIRMATIVE RECRUITMENT AND PROMOTION OF MINORITIES

Although blacks reportedly served as police officers in the United States as early as 1861, it is only very recently that minority groups have been hired at rates approaching their proportions of the population.

The evolutionary 1980s

In the mid-1970s, recruitment drives to hire minorities began in most major metropolitan police departments amid significant controversy. Today, minority officers serve in police departments in proportions reflecting their share of the general population. Several major cities, including Los Angeles; Newark, New Jersey; Philadelphia; Detroit; Washington, D.C.; and New York, now have or have recently had black police chiefs. In 1992, for example, Los Angeles appointed Willie Williams, a highly regarded and reform-oriented black police chief. Many community leaders believe that the hiring of a black chief to run the department may increase the sensitivity of the L.A. Police Department to the concerns of the black community.

According to the research of Samuel Walker a number of changes occurred between 1983 and 1988 in the police departments of the fifty largest cities in the United States:

- Nearly half made significant progress in the employment of black officers, and only 17 percent showed a decrease in the percentage of black officers on the force.
- Over 40 percent made significant progress in the employment of Hispanic officers, with 11 percent showing a decrease in the percentage of Hispanic officers.
- Two-thirds had affirmative action plans (most of them court-ordered).
- In some departments (e.g., Detroit, Atlanta, El Paso, and Miami) officers from minority groups represented the majority of officers (1).

Recruitment problems

Recruitment of minority officers has been a difficult task for a number of reasons. Minority communities may view the police as "the enemy" or "the oppressors," and friends and relatives may discourage would-be applicants with arguments that minority officers will be treated unfairly. In Hispanic communities with residents who emigrated from countries in which the police were used for political repression, the image of the police may be particularly bad.

On the other hand, minority recruits may regard a job on the police force as a route to success. As one black Atlanta lieutenant put it in 1986: "There were two ways to get out of my neighborhood and not end up dead or in prison. [You] either become a minister or a cop. I always fell asleep in church so I decided to become a cop" (2).

Entrance requirements have been criticized as barriers to minority recruits. A height requirement may exclude large numbers of otherwise qualified Hispanics, Asians, and women of all races, who are on average smaller than white men in the United States. Written examinations have been criticized as testing applicants' abilities to use standard English but not their actual abilities to communicate.

Some of these issues have made it to the U.S. Supreme Court: A ruling on the impermissibility of both height and weight requirements unless they can be proved to be "business necessities" was upheld by the Supreme Court, and the Court also has ruled that if strength or physical agility is a job-related occupational requirement, the state must adopt a validated test that can measure strength directly. A 1971 case resulted in the ruling that when employee screening procedures cannot be shown to be related to successful job performance but can be shown to have adverse effects on minority hiring, they are in violation of the Equal Employment Opportunity Act.

Court-ordered affirmative action programs and the changing of entrance requirements have created a great deal of controversy (3). Concerns about new standards for accepting recruits are that unqualified individuals will be hired and police departments will be weakened. Those supporting the changes counter that many of the requirements had no demonstrated relationship to performance of police officers. Advocates of quotas for hiring and promotion argue that this system is an essential remedy for changing the composition of a police force with a history of systematic discrimination. Critics of affirmative action programs claim that quota systems represent reverse discrimination against white men. The U.S. Supreme Court has answered critics and advocates alike by determining that all affirmative action programs must (a) be tailored to accomplish a legitimate objective, (b) be flexible, (c) not impose an undue burden on the majority, and (d) not trample on the rights of the majority.

Problems in uniform

Unfortunately, problems for minorities are far from over once they're in uniform. Dr. Elsyee Scott, a former Rutgers professor and past executive director of the National Organization for Black Law Enforcement Executives (NOBLE) and now Deputy Police Commissioner of New York City, recalls that when she was growing up in a Louisiana town in the 1950s black police officers drove squad cars labeled "Colored People" and were permitted to arrest only "colored" people [4]. Although there have been changes since then, many problems faced by minorities once they are hired have not yet been resolved.

A 1986 study of the L.A. Police Department showed that minority academy graduates were fired or resigned, before they even completed their probationary periods, at twice the rate for whites. In the New York City Police Department, seen by many as racially liberal, a 1984 study showed that choice assignments such as anticrime and undercover patrols were given more often to white officers than to blacks. In four predominantly black or mixed precincts there were no black anticrime cops at all, and of 186 special anticrime officers assigned to eighteen precincts only 12 percent were black, compared with 17 percent of the department as a whole. Promotions, too, seem to be out of reach for most minorities, who are severely underrepresented above the level of patrol officer. In general, departments with the best records for promoting minorities are those of big cities with large minority populations.

Promotion problems

In April 1991, 300 black FBI agents threatened to file a class-action suit against the bureau, which they accused of discriminating in promotion, assignments, and transfers. One year later a settlement was reached. The bureau agreed to changes in selection and promotion procedures and to increase the number of blacks assigned to prestige units like the Hostage Rescue Team and the SWAT units [5]. Promotion issues reached the U.S. Supreme Court in a case concerning the Alabama State Police (*United States v. Paradise,* 107 S. Ct. 1053, 1987). After twenty years of lower court action, the Supreme Court laid down its one-on-one mandate: Out of a pool containing qualified black and white candidates, whether for initial appointment or promotion, the state must pick one black candidate for each white candidate until racial balance on the force is achieved. For that purpose, the ranking of individual candidates within the qualified pool can be ignored. This decision was seen as protecting more than 100 other affirmative action cases involving quotas and timetables and as providing minority groups with the support of the law to require minority hiring, deployment, and promotion in police departments.

* * *

The drive to get individuals from minority groups hired as police officers, given equitable duties, and promoted into positions of authority will continue, and successes could result in more effective police forces in the United States. As Hubert Williams, president of the Police Foundation, said in 1993, "A police force that reflects the divergent racial and ethnic mix of the community it serves is the cornerstone of modern crime control strategies" [6].

SOURCES

1. Samuel Walker, *The Police in America,* 2d ed. (New York: McGraw-Hill, 1992), p. 247.
2. As quoted in Peggy S. Sullivan, "Minority Officers: Current Issues," in *Central Issues in Policing,* eds. Roger G. Dunham and Geoffrey P. Alpert (Prospect Heights, Ill.: Waveland Press, 1989), p. 338.
3. See George T. Felkenes and Peter C. Unsinger, eds., *Diversity, Affirmative Action, and Law Enforcement* (Springfield, Ill.: Charles C. Thomas, 1992), for an excellent summary of the issues and problems relating to affirmative action of police; Herman Goldstein, *Problem-Oriented Policing* (Philadelphia: Temple University, 1990), p. 166. See also Candace McCoy, "Affirmative Action in Police Organizations," in *Police Management Today,* ed. James J. Fyfe (Washington, D.C.: International City Management Association, 1985), pp. 149–161.
4. Sullivan, "Minority Officers: Current Issues," p. 331.
5. David Johnston, "FBI Promises Gains to Blacks in a Settlement," *The New York Times,* April 22, 1992, pp. A1, A22. See also Ellen Hochstedler, "Impediments to Hiring Minorities in Public Police Agencies," *Journal of Police Science and Administration* 12 (1984):227–240.
6. Hubert Williams, statement to the authors.

QUESTIONS FOR DISCUSSION

1. Do you think setting racial quotas for the purposes of remedying past discrimination in police departments is necessary?
2. What sorts of recruitment strategies might be effective to get more minority group members to apply for police work?
3. Do you agree that a racial and ethnic mix within the police force is crucial to modern crime control?

Over the past twenty years, most of the largest police departments in the country have been sued.

the police force (Figure 9.2). First, the law made it easier for individuals to bring employer discrimination suits against police agencies. Many did. In fact, over the last twenty years, most of the largest police departments in the country have been sued. Second, to comply with federal guidelines, police departments had to make an effort to attract minority and female applicants.[19] And third, the community has continued to put pressure on the police administration to make policy changes.

Minority Groups in Policing

The first minority police officer was hired in Washington, D.C., in 1861.[20] In 1940, only 1 percent of all sworn police officers in the United States came from minority groups; in 1950, only 2 percent. The percentage increased to 3.6 in 1960 and to 6.5 in 1973. By the late 1980s the figure had risen to between 12 and 14 percent.[21] Civil unrest in the 1960s showed that if police officers were recruited from only a limited segment of the population, there was a risk of alienating groups that were not represented in law enforcement.[22] The contention was that officers from different backgrounds would have different attitudes and therefore would behave differently in their contact with the public.[23] (See the Criminal Justice in Action box.) In 1973, the National Advisory Commission on Criminal Justice Standards and Goals adopted the following standard:

> Every police agency shall engage in positive efforts to employ ethnic minority group members. When a substantial ethnic minority population resides within the jurisdiction, the police agency should take affirmative action to achieve a ratio of minority group employees in approximate proportion to the makeup of the population.[24]

Women in Policing

Black and Hispanic officers are not the only "minorities" in policing. In many ways, women have had parallel experiences. Despite the increasing acceptance of women in law enforcement, there are still problems concerning their number and duties. For example, in 1985 Lucille Burrascano, one of the first women in the New York City Police Department, reported the following incident:

> During training, I rode as the third person with two men. We're on a robbery run, the siren's blaring, and we pull up right in front of the door. We're supposed to come out with guns drawn but, instead, one of the cops jumps out and opens the door for me. I said, "What are you doing? This is not a date."[25]

The first American woman to serve as a sworn police officer was Lola Baldwin, who joined the Portland, Oregon, Police Department in 1905. Like the police matrons of the nineteenth century, she dealt primarily with women and children. In fact, she was originally granted police power so that she could take care of children at the Ohio State Exposition. Five years later, in Los Angeles in 1910, Alice Stebbin Wells became the first officially classified policewoman, assigned to "supervising and enforcing laws concerning dance halls, skating rinks, and theaters; monitoring billboard displays; locating missing persons; and maintaining a general bureau for women seeking advice on matters within the scope of the police department."[26] In 1915 she founded the International Policewomen's Association. This organization is now called the International Association of Women Police. There are 1,500 members.

Recruitment of Women. More than 60 police departments had women on their staffs by 1919; 145 had women by 1925. But the police roles of the women remained restricted; women did not attain patrol officer status until the 1960s. There were no female sergeants until 1965, after a successful lawsuit against New York City.[27] With the resurgent drive for women's rights in the late 1960s and early 1970s and the passage of the 1972 Equal Employment Opportunity Act, many departments began to recruit women.[28] Others resisted. Serious obstacles and stereotypes had to be overcome: that women were physically weak, irrational, and illogical; that they lacked the toughness to work on the streets. Some critics argued that the association of female with male officers would cause complications in both job and family life.

By 1980 the number of policewomen was still low—under 4 percent of all officers. By 1990 that proportion had more than doubled, to 8.6 percent.[29] Most recent surveys of personnel practices have found that eligibility criteria and mechanisms used to recruit, screen, and select candidates have changed dramatically, thus enlarging the pool of eligible women. For example, in a national survey done by the Police Foundation, Susan Martin found that some departments have been actively recruiting women with strategies such as "prehire" programs, in which otherwise qualified applicants can get into physical condition. Martin also found that women have made few gains in achieving supervisory ranks, have more nonpatrol assignments than men, and still encounter problems regarding acceptance by their male peers.[30]

Relationships with Male Peers. Women are still not fully accepted by their male colleagues or the public, despite high performance on the job. Most of the resistance stems from the belief that women do not have the physical strength to perform well in violent situations. Responding to these concerns, many police departments continue to assign women to clerical duties or specific types of problems, such as domestic disputes and runaways. Research has demonstrated, however, that these fears are unfounded. Eight out of nine major evaluations of women in policing (Pennsylvania; Washington, D.C.; St. Louis; California; Denver; Newton, Massachusetts; New York City; Philadelphia I; and Philadelphia II) found that despite some gender differences, female and male officers are equally capable (Philadelphia II was the exception).[31] Female officers make almost as

Operation Take Back, July-August 1990, Jamaica, Queens. In many departments, women now share the risks and dangers associated with policing.

FIGURE 9.2 *The changing profile of the American police officer* (*Source:* Samuel Walker, *The Police in America,* 2d ed. [New York: McGraw-Hill, 1992], p. 303.)

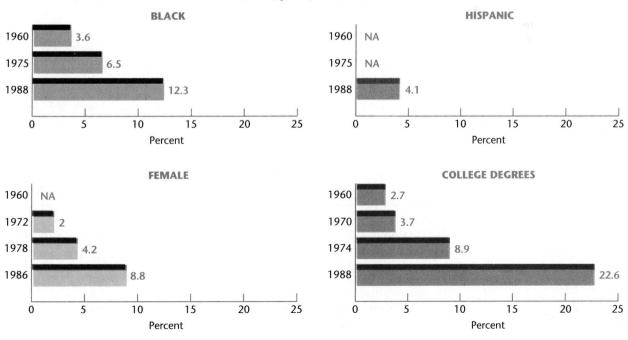

many successful arrests as male officers, their overall work performance has been rated extremely satisfactory by superiors, their level of strength is well within the acceptable range for the profession, and they may be more pleasant and respectful with the public than their male counterparts. As regards the way policewomen perceive themselves, it appears that they enter the force self-confident and a bit idealistic, but gradually become disillusioned by others' beliefs that they are flirtatious and ineffective.[32]

The first women assigned to units that have been exclusively male usually experience a difficult adjustment period. A study of a West Coast police department found a number of expressions used by male officers to describe their female counterparts: "runt," "wimp woman" and "pencilneck." One woman found a dead rat in her mailbox and another found an application for a job at a fast food restaurant.[33]

According to Barbara Price, the slow integration of women into policing stems from a number of factors: the police's sharing the traditional belief that policing is a male occupation, the exclusion of women from police duties that lead to promotions, and the general ideology of male dominance and superiority.[34] But as increasing numbers of women join police forces, they are gradually gaining acceptance. While there continue to be problems (even if they are subtle) between female and male officers, one they both have in common is job-related stress. On the job, they rely heavily on each other as partners. They both belong to what is called the police subculture.

THE POLICE SUBCULTURE

police subculture
Set of norms and values that govern police behavior, brought about by stressful working conditions plus daily interaction with an often hostile public.

In a 1950 study of the police in Gary, Indiana, William Westley described how police officers stick together when they work the streets because of the constant stress and anxiety that goes with the job. These working conditions, plus daily interaction with an often hostile public, combine to produce a set of norms and values that govern police behavior. This is called a **police subculture.**[35]

Socialization of New Recruits

Recruits learn the norms of the subculture during training and in the field. According to Jonathan Rubenstein,

> On his first day as a policeman a rookie may capture an armed felon, be cracked on the head with a rock, be offered sexual favors, free food, or money; he may be confronted by a naked woman, screaming hysterically, or a belligerent drunk who outweighs him by fifty pounds; or if he begins on 'last out,' he may spend the entire tour trying to fight off the desire to sleep. He has no control over what he will learn first, and when he will learn it. . . . Regardless of what occurs, he is obliged to be immediately what he has chosen to become, although his colleagues know he has only the vaguest appreciation of what that is."[36]

Rubenstein describes the world of the "rookie" police officer. "Bits and pieces of knowledge, information, and experience" are passed on initially during a period of formal training. All states have a Police Officer Standards and Training (POST) Commission that sets mandatory minimum requirements for training, although there is a great deal of difference among the states. Some states mandate sixteen weeks of training; others mandate three weeks. Depending on the length of the time, training programs range from basic training (handling of weapons) to academic courses.[37]

"Rookies learn very quickly that loyalty—the obligation to support another officer—is the first priority."

The process of socialization into the culture begins as soon as new recruits enter the academy. They get to know not only the formal rules of policing but also the informal norms a person must observe to be accepted into the group. They learn very quickly that loyalty—the obligation to support another officer—is the first priority. Respect for police authority, honor, individualism, and group solidarity also rank high. But there is much more to policing than what is learned at the academy.

In 1972 a police recruit from the San Jose, California, Police Department negligently operated a police car, causing an accident in which a passenger in the car was killed and the officer received serious injuries. A follow-up investigation demonstrated serious inadequacies in the department's training program. In 1972—the year of the accident—San Jose initiated what appears to be the earliest Field Training Program.[38] After graduation from the police academy, field training officers teach rookies that police work on the street may be quite different from police work learned in the classroom. According to one Illinois police department commander: "It was not unheard of for the experienced officers to tell the rookie, 'Forget what you learned in the academy, kid. I'll show you how it's done on the street.'"[39]

The Police Personality

In *Justice without Trial*, sociologist Jerome Skolnick argued that in the same way doctors, janitors, lawyers, and industrial workers develop unique ways of looking at, and responding to, their work environment, so too do police officers. This effect of work on a person's outlook on the world he calls the **working personality.**[40] The working personality of the police officer is molded by two elements of the police role: danger and authority.

Danger and Authority. Police officers are often viewed as suspicious and authoritative. Police work is potentially dangerous, so officers need to be constantly aware of what is happening around them. At the academy they are warned about what happens to officers who are too trusting. They learn about the many officers who have died in the line of duty because they did not exercise proper caution. On the street they need to stay alert for signals that crimes may be in progress: an unfamiliar noise, someone "checking into" an alleyway, a secret exchange of goods. Under these conditions, it would be surprising if officers did *not* become suspicious. As George Kirkham, police officer and professor, argues: "Chronic suspiciousness is something that a good cop cultivates in the interest of going home to his family each evening."[41]

The working environment also demands that officers gain immediate control of potentially dangerous situations. They are routinely called on to demonstrate authority. Uniforms, badges, nightsticks, and guns signify authority—but officers soon learn that this authority is often challenged by a hostile public. Public hostility, coupled with other factors—a belief that courts are too lenient on criminals, the realization that it is often wiser to "look the other way" if they become aware of corrupt practices by their peers, the part that favoritism may play in promotions—leads to yet another trait that characterizes the police officer's "working personality": cynicism.

Cynicism. In a study of 220 New York City police officers, Professor Arthur Niederhoffer, himself a former police officer, found that 80 percent of the new recruits believed that the department was a smoothly operating, effective organization. Within a couple of months on the job, fewer than one-third still held that belief. They had become cynical about police work, supervisors, and the operating policies of the department. Moreover, cynicism increased with length of service and among the more highly educated who were not promoted.[42] Robert Regoli and Eric Poole argue that cynicism increases police officers' desire to exert authority over ordinary citizens. As the use of authority increases, citizens become more hostile. Police feel even more threatened, and the cycle continues.[43]

Scholars have long debated whether there is something unique about the per-

working personality
Effect of police work on an officer's outlook on the world. Danger and authority are important factors.

"Chronic suspiciousness is something that a good cop cultivates in the interest of going home to his family each evening." George Kirkham, police officer and professor, in *Order under Law* (1981).

Officers are routinely required to exercise authority, often under difficult conditions. Here police arrest New York demonstrators protesting the Rodney King verdict, May 1992.

POLICE STRESS

The First Amendment guarantees freedom of speech—even for those who describe lawlessness against law enforcement officers, as Ice-T did in the song "Cop Killer." But hearing oneself maligned in a popular song is probably the least of most police officers' problems. The risk of being killed—or of having to kill someone—is high. Close to 100 police officers die annually in the line of duty, and American police officers lawfully kill between 3,000 and 4,000 persons annually (1). It's not a job that brings a lot of love from the public, either. Police work subjects officers to the temptation of corruption, and although only a small percentage become corrupt, widespread publicity taints all officers. The abuse of force on the part of a few police officers likewise tarnishes the reputation of entire departments.

The impact of such problems can be summed up in one word: stress. Having to shoot a suspect may cause an officer to have nightmares for years, accompanied by elevated blood pressure, heart palpitations, cold sweats, flashbacks, guilt, remorse, and anger. Some officers become alcoholics. Others commit suicide: Twenty did so in Chicago in 1978 and 1979, ten in New York in 1990.

Stress results in accidents, absenteeism, inability to solve problems, pessimism, chronic fatigue, social withdrawal, and complete burnout. A study of 2,300 officers in twenty departments found that 37 percent had serious marital problems, 36 percent suffered physical ailments, 23 percent abused alcohol, 20 percent indicated problems among their children, and 10 percent abused drugs (2). Top police executives view the growing use of illegal drugs by officers as a major problem facing the law enforcement community.

A police officer under stress takes the problems home. Policing is not just a job, it is a way of life. Officers need to control situations at all times on the job; often they transfer patterned responses from the job to the home. As a sixteen-year veteran of the Virginia State Police explained:

Take, for example, the day my wife was trying to get our son to wash the dishes. They were locked in a battle of wills. After I walked into the kitchen, I evaluated the situation and immediately took control. I admonished my wife for being bossy, talked to my son about responsibility, and told everyone else to leave the room so that the job could get done.

In less than 5 minutes, I issued a warning, dispersed the participants in the dispute, and got the job done. I acted like a good trooper. The problem was I still had to live with these people. I could not get into my patrol car and drive away. Predictably, my wife and I argued, my daughter defended her mother, my son sulked, and I justified my actions like a good trooper. Everyone was upset, all because I took control. (3)

The most extreme response to stress, of course, is suicide. Although claims often are made that suicide rates among officers are high, studies are inconclusive. Researchers argue that it is extremely difficult to study suicides among officers. Death certificates do not indicate occupation, and even when death-by-suicide figures can be collected for police officers, those figures may be artificially low. A police officer found dead at home with the barrel of a gun in his mouth and his finger on the trigger was listed as an accidental death; officers investigating the death knew that the family would receive higher insurance benefits for accidental death (4). In an Arizona case, a medical examiner could not determine whether an officer found shot by his own gun was murdered or took his own life. A massive search by fellow officers using helicopters and dogs never turned up a suspect. The autopsy did report that the officer had terminal cancer, and there was a large insurance policy on his life (5).

Stressed police officers who continue working can cause real problems. An officer who loses efficiency is sometimes labeled "an empty suit" or is said to have "retired in place." Such officers create problems for their peers on the street, who depend on a backup in life-threatening situations. They also create major problems for their departments. Recent court decisions in suits by citizens harmed by inadequate police action hold that law enforcement agencies are responsible for the behavior of their officers (see Chapter 8). Departments can be held liable for not taking action after indications that officers demonstrated poor performance. Settlements for these cases have ranged from $222,000 to $3 million.

Private industry has been concerned with job-related stress for some time. Now criminal justice authorities have begun to address the problem. Many departments, especially the larger ones, are trying to provide medical attention, psy-

25 Most Stressful Law Enforcement Critical Life Events

1. Violent death of a partner in the line of duty.
2. Dismissal.
3. Taking a life in the line of duty.
4. Shooting someone in the line of duty.
5. Suicide of an officer who is a close friend.
6. Violent death of another officer in the line of duty.
7. Murder committed by a police officer.
8. Duty-related violent injury (shooting).
9. Violent job-related injury to another officer.
10. Suspension.
11. Passed over for promotion.
12. Pursuit of an armed suspect.
13. Answering a call to a scene involving violent nonaccidental death of a child.
14. Assignment away from family for a long period of time.
15. Personal involvement in a shooting incident.
16. Reduction in pay.
17. Observing an act of police corruption.
18. Accepting a bribe.
19. Participating in an act of police corruption.
20. Hostage situation resulting from aborted criminal action.
21. Response to a scene involving the accidental death of a child.
22. Promotion of inexperienced/incompetent officer over you.
23. Internal affairs investigation against self.
24. Barricaded suspect.
25. Hostage situation resulting from domestic disturbance.

SOURCE: James D. Sewell, "Police Stress," *FBI Law Enforcement Bulletin*, April 1981, p. 9.

chological counseling, and a greater range of disability and retirement benefits. Stress reduction programs that include exercise, meditation, biofeedback, and diet control have been introduced. Better shift patterns—rotating fifteen to twenty times per year rather than fifty to sixty times, for example—also may help. When suicides among New York City police officers reached a record of ten in 1987, the department initiated a confidential hot line and posted announcements that counseling was available for troubled officers. As departments give higher priority to community-oriented policing, which lessens tensions between police and citizens, experts believe that levels of job satisfaction may increase, reducing tension and frustration among officers.

SOURCES

1. Lawrence W. Sherman and Robert H. Longworthy, "Measuring Homicide by Police Officers," in *Readings on Police Use of Deadly Force*, ed. James J. Fyfe (Washington, D.C.: Police Foundation, 1982), pp. 12–41.
2. John Blackmore, "Are Police Allowed to Have Problems of Their Own?," *Police Magazine* 1 (1978):47–55.
3. Harry W. More, *Special Topics in Policing* (Cincinnati, Ohio: Anderson, 1992), p. 199.
4. William H. Kroes, *Society's Victim—The Police: An Analysis of Job Stress in Policing*, 2d ed. (Springfield, Ill.: Charles C. Thomas, 1985), pp. 27–34.
5. Richard N. Southworth, "Taking the Job Home," *FBI Law Enforcement Bulletin*, U.S. Department of Justice, 59 (November 1990):21.

QUESTIONS FOR DISCUSSION

1. What could police departments do to reduce stress affecting officers?
2. What can individual officers do to reduce stress affecting their personal lives and their police performance?
3. Police work may attract people with certain personality traits. What characteristics might help an officer cope with the kinds of stressors listed in the table of "critical life events"?

- MY TAXES ARE DOUBLED.
- MY WIFE'S GOING TO HAVE TWINS.
- MY WATCH COMMANDER IS GOING TO . . ., WHEN HE SEES THIS CAR.
- WHEN I SHOOT BACK I'VE GOT TO ACCOUNT FOR EVERY BULLET IN TRIPLICATE.
- IF I HIT AN INNOCENT PERSON MY ASS IS IN THE FIRE.
- IF I HIT THE SUSPECT THE CITIZENS WILL SPIT ON ME.
- IF I MISS AND THEY GET AWAY, OH MAN...
- IF I CATCH 'EM SOME HIGH PRICED LAWYER WILL GET 'EM OFF—
- IF I LIVE THROUGH THIS I THINK I'LL BECOME A CHICKENFARMER

Source: William H. Kroes, *Society's Victims—The Police*, 2d ed. (Springfield, Ill.: Charles C. Thomas, 1976), p. 18.

sonality of police officers that differentiates them from other citizens.[44] A survey of the literature on police personality concludes that officers "may be rather ordinary people, not greatly unlike other middle-Americans. We cannot even be sure that there is such a thing as a police personality, however loosely we define it."[45]

Styles of Policing

There are many styles of policing. One expert, Susan White, presents four types: the "tough cop," the "problem solver," the "rule applier," and the "crime fighter."[46] Another distinguishes between "street cops" (who are attracted to job security and benefits, good salary, and so forth), "action seekers" (who focus on the excitement of crime-fighting), and "middle-class mobiles" (who enjoy the professional status of policing and the opportunity for upward mobility).[47]

Styles of policing are classifications based on officers' particular approaches. Some officers adhere strictly to departmental rules to make arrests; others use a variety of nonconformist means. The criminologist Carl Klockars suggests that the nonconformists suffer from the Dirty Harry problem (from the popular movie hero Dirty Harry, played by Clint Eastwood). These officers are glorified for their bravado, invulnerability, charisma, resourcefulness, and sheer arrogance in defying the rules of good police work.[48]

Whatever style police officers may prefer, experts agree that officers should be "generalists" who can readily adapt to all aspects of their role as a police officer. Their responses vary between situations and, in like situations, at different times.[49]

styles of policing
Classifications based on officers' particular approaches to the job (for example, "problem solver," "tough cop").

"Some nonconformist police officers suffer from the "Dirty Harry" problem: They are glorified for bravado, charisma, resourcefulness, and sheer arrogance in defying the rules of good police work."

Stress

Crime and crime-fighting have always captured the imagination, and the media have always capitalized on the heroic crime-fighter. In the fall of 1992, the TV networks opened with seven reality-based police shows in prime time, including

FIGURE 9.3 *Law enforcement officers killed, 1980–1989* (*Source:* Victoria L. Major, "Law Enforcement Officers Killed, 1980–89," *FBI Law Enforcement Bulletin,* 60 [1991]:2–5).

Law Enforcement Officers Killed 1980-1989

801 feloniously killed in line of duty

104, highest annual total, killed in 1980

66, lowest annual total, killed in both 1986 and 1989

783 male

18 female

515 aged 25 to 40

327 attempting an arrest when killed

735 killed by firearms

120 killed with their own weapons

157 of those killed by firearms were wearing protective armor

7 of every 10 were in uniform when killed

2 of every 3 were patrol officers

"Cops," "Rescue 911," "American Detective," "Top Cops," and "Secret Service." The emphasis in these shows is on reality, action, excitement, and good guys and bad.

Flying bullets are in fact a rare event during the ordinary shift. But other stresses are more pervasive: hours of boredom, negative attitudes of citizens, unfavorable press, threats of civil suits, departmental rules, perceived leniency of the courts, anger over early release of offenders, and daily exposure to a range of human tragedy.[50] Police officers' personal lives are disrupted by irregular working hours and regular rotation through different shifts. These days, officers fear increasing exposure to serious diseases, such as hepatitis B, tuberculosis, and acquired immune deficiency syndrome (AIDS). Encounters with broken glass, the jagged metal of wrecked cars, knives, razor blades, hypodermic needles, and attacks (including bites) from angry suspects are not uncommon at crime scenes. Though a National Institute of Justice study on AIDS reported that no police officers have contracted the disease on the job, officers remain very wary.[51] For example, at a Washington, D.C., demonstration, officers used yellow gloves to handle demonstrators, claiming that they were taking precautions in case the protest became violent.[52]

Among the many factors contributing to stress among officers none is as important as the constant threat of danger. Despite the decreasing number of officers killed in the line of duty, from a high of 134 in 1973 to 69 in 1991 (attributed to policies limiting use of deadly force, thereby diminishing citizens' use of firearms against officers; the wearing of bulletproof vests; and a decrease in the incidence of robbery, a crime that often ends in confrontation), police work involves high risk (Figure 9.3). Not all officers can withstand the pressure. (See the Criminal Justice on Trial box.)

Behind the Blue Curtain

Two other characteristics of the police subculture are solidarity and isolation.

Hackensack, N.J., Jan. 31—The manslaughter trial of a Teaneck police officer was thrown into an uproar today for the second time in two weeks when a former New York City officer who was paralyzed by a 15-year-old gunman's bullet was wheeled into the courtroom while the defendant was being cross-examined.[53]

Officer Gary Spath, 31, was on trial for the manslaughter (by recklessness) of 16-year-old Phillip Pannell. Spath testified that he had shot and killed the boy as he reached into his jacket pocket. In a show of solidarity for Officer Spath, Steven McDonald, paralyzed from the neck down, was brought into the courtroom in an elaborate wheelchair equipped with a life-support system and chin-operated controls. McDonald, a 34-year-old former New York City officer, was shot in the neck in Central Park in 1986 by a teenager he believed was stealing a bike.

One of the primary reasons for the existence of a subculture that is characterized by very strong in-group ties, loyalty, secrecy, and isolation is the nature of police work.[54] Officers often view the external community as hostile and threatening.[55] They are caught in a bind: The job calls for them to discipline the people they serve, and they are allowed to use force to do it. Given the nature of their assignment, citizen complaints about threats to their civil liberties are often perceived by police as a challenge to their authority.[56]

The uniform also isolates officers. Easily recognizable, they are constantly approached on the beat by people who know what is going on (doormen, bartenders, waitresses) or who want to complain. When they are off duty, police officers also tend to isolate themselves from the community: they spend most of their time with other officers and their families.

Oddly enough, isolation does not occur when two police officers are married to each other. Police couples tend to help each other maintain nonpolice friend-

"Many cops retire after sterling careers never having drawn their gun."
Time, February 17, 1992, p. 70.

"Encounters with broken glass, jagged metal, knives, razor blades, hypodermic needles, and attacks (including bites) from angry suspects are not uncommon at crime scenes."

"Policing is not just a job—it is a way of life."

Police solidarity: Former officer Stephen McDonald, paralyzed by a gunshot received on the job, with New York Governor Mario Cuomo after the signing of legislation to help police victims. McDonald also appeared in court at the 1992 trial of Teaneck, N.J., officer Gary Spath for the fatal shooting of a black youth.

"There is something that separates the society of the police from the rest of the community—something called the blue curtain.*"*

blue curtain
Screen that separates police from civilians in society; isolation of police who spend time only with other police officers and their families.

ships and avoid the clannishness typical of police. Of course, as yet there are few police couples in America, due to the newness of women serving as line officers on the force. But already, among the 2,300-member Dallas Police Department, there are fifty police marriages. In contrast is the situation in the Netherlands, where 65 percent of women officers were found to date, live with, or be married to fellow officers.[57] Shared life among fellow officers has many advantages, including good communication, mutual support and respect, and shared pride. Nevertheless, all in all there is something that separates the society of the police from the rest of the community. William Westley has called this separating screen the **blue curtain.**[58]

Several experts contend that the concept of a police subculture does not take into account major changes that have taken place in policing over the last two decades. Susan Martin found that the introduction of women changed the traditional solidarity of the police force. Officers no longer shared like interests in cars, fishing, and hunting.[59] Or perhaps Joseph Wambaugh, former officer and author of best-selling books on the police, would have to change his description of "choir practice," a term used to describe officers getting together after shifts to "hoist a few" (drinks) and trade war stories.[60]

Samuel Walker contends that the police subculture may have changed as a result of various Supreme Court decisions. Since the 1960s, he suggests, tensions between police norms (getting the job done) and the rule of law have lessened. With the progressive acceptance by the police of Supreme Court decisions delimiting police practices, police–community relations are likely to improve over time, and so will the police subculture.[61]

We have demonstrated that police officers are extremely loyal to each other. Now let us look at whether this loyalty extends to covering up co-workers' illegal practices.

CORRUPTION

In the early 1970s, in the course of their work, a New York City police lieutenant, David Durk, and his partner, Detective Frank Serpico, discovered massive corruption among fellow officers and superiors. Durk and Serpico collected the evidence and reported it to higher authorities within the department. Neither there nor at the highest level of the department was any action taken. They ultimately reported their findings directly to the mayor. Still nothing happened. In frustration, they released the information to the press. Durk and Serpico were attacked by other officers for "dirtying their own nest," "washing dirty laundry in public," and "tarnishing their shields." The result of their revelations was the creation by the mayor of New York City of the Knapp Commission (1969–1972), which unraveled the existing police corruption in the city and recommended measures to avoid it in the future.[62]

"The rookie who comes into the Department is faced with the situation where it is easier for him to become corrupt than to remain honest."
Knapp Commission Report on Police Corruption, New York, 1973, p. 4.

The Range of Corrupt Activities

The term "corruption" covers a wide range of conduct. The Knapp Commission itself distinguished (in typical police jargon) between **meat eaters,** who solicit bribes or actually cooperate with criminals for personal gain, and **grass eaters,** who accept payoffs for rendering police services or for looking the other way when action is called for. The commission found a distinct pattern of corrupt activities. Officers assigned to enforce gambling and vice laws routinely collected graft payments of up to $3,500 a month from each location. Officers received shares of $300 to $1,500 a month. Those higher in rank—supervisors, sergeants, and lieutenants—received more. New officers had to wait two months before their payoffs could begin.[63] Uniformed officers received much less than plainclothes officers. The payoffs came from bars, construction sites, grocery stores, after-hour clubs, motorists (for traffic violations), prostitutes, parking lot operators, and others.[64]

In addition to "meat eating" and "grass eating," subsequent empirical and analytical studies have provided other classifications and descriptions of police misconduct, including dereliction of duty and street crime offenses such as larceny, embezzlement, and coercion.[65] Samuel Walker has identified four distinct types: gratuities, bribes, theft and burglary, and illegal administrative actions (including internal corruption).[66]

The most frequent corrupt activity involves receiving gratuities, such as free meals, goods, or services. Business owners often offer gratuities in return for favors, such as extra patrol coverage of the premises. While the practice may appear harmless, it can lead to active solicitation of favors on the part of the officer for his/her service (extortion).

Bribes involve offering money to police to ensure that they do not enforce the law. Drivers, for instance, may use this technique to avoid getting traffic violations. Business owners may bribe officers to "overlook" double-parked delivery trucks. More serious corruption stems from bribes offered on a regular basis—guarantees that police ignore various gambling, narcotics, or prostitution offenses. Some bribes are given for selling information about criminal investigations, for destroying evidence, or for altering testimony of witnesses.

Acts of theft and burglary may be isolated acts by lone officers (e.g., taking money from someone, an arrestee who is drunk) or well-planned acts by groups of officers. In Chicago, Denver, and Omaha, several officers formed burglary rings comprised of those who committed the burglaries and those who patrolled the neighborhood to cover for them. Another not uncommon corrupt practice is stealing money or property from departmental property rooms.

Occasionally, promotions to higher rank can be bought from supervisors. In the nineteenth century buying one's promotion was so customary in New York City police departments that there was a printed "price list" for each rank. Recently, in Mexico City, police officers claimed that they had to solicit bribes from citizens in order to pay up to $50 a day—from a salary of about $233 per month—extorted by their supervisors. Said one officer: "If we don't comply, we end up guarding banks or cleaning bathrooms!"[67] (See the Criminal Justice Abroad box.)

meat eaters
Officers who solicit bribes or cooperate with criminals for personal gain.

grass eaters
Officers who accept payoffs for rendering police services or for looking the other way when action is called for.

bribes
Offers of money or goods to police to ensure that they do not enforce the law.

POLICE CORRUPTION

There are countries in the world where the police provide no service unless a special gratuity is paid. Widespread corruption usually requires the connivance or active participation of the heads of government. Such corrupt governments are routinely toppled by would-be reformers, who frequently become corrupt themselves, and rely on corrupt police forces for protection and support. Uganda, Nigeria, and other countries in Africa, as well as a number of Caribbean and Latin American countries, have served as examples. Let's look at police corruption—and the fight against it—in three countries.

Government initiative: Uganda

Sometimes attempts to end police corruption are started by the government. In Uganda in 1988, the Minister of Internal Affairs, Ibrahim Mukiibi, initiated an ambitious plan to recruit a new, professional—and uncorrupted—police force (1). In 1986, a massive screening exercise had been undertaken to remove discredited officers from the force. Previous recruiting for the Uganda Police Forces had been based on tribal affiliations, religion, or region of the country; the new effort was to select officers based on competence and to subject candidates to rigorous training. In addition, the government planned to establish police courts to help eradicate corruption (2). Thousands of new offi-

cers have already gone through the training academy, and a force of 20,000 incorruptible officers is the ultimate goal.

Change from below: Mexico

Where government itself is part of the corrupt system, change may have to be initiated by the lowest ranks. In Mexico, where police forces have been much maligned in the past, officers are now demonstrating publicly against corruption. In 1992, two former officers erected a tent outside the U.S. Embassy in Mexico City and flew the red-green-white Mexican flag (3). They were on a hunger strike to denounce the practice of superior officers forcing line officers to pay between eight and twenty dollars a day in bribes to keep their jobs. Officers have claimed they have to pay superiors "rent and maintenance fees" for the use of patrol cars and tow trucks and that superior officers offer to improve their performance records in exchange for money.

Patrol officers pass the cost to citizens. As a *Los Angeles Times* report explained, "Mexico City motorists, vendors and other residents have long accused their police of demanding bribes, called *mordida*—a bite" (4). Now the officers are saying they have to do that in order to meet the demands of their bosses.

The corruption is apparently deeply rooted. Officers protesting the bribe system have been fired, transferred, and reprimanded. "In each case, the government has gone to great lengths to discredit the demonstrators and insists that there was no connection between the protest and job changes," reported the *Los Angeles Times* writer. "One former Mexico City police officer says he was abducted for three

days, blindfolded, beaten, and dumped by a roadside after he organized a police protest."

The Inspector Jobic case: France

Is police corruption endemic only in the developing countries of the Third World? The form and extent of bribery may differ, but police officers everywhere are tempted by schemes to enhance their salaries. In 1988 the reputation of the French police was damaged when a chief inspector was accused of pimping and running a protection racket. A 1988 news report gave the details:

The controversial "Inspector Jobic" case, with its allegations of police corruption and bitter rivalry between the police and the gendarmes—the country's two forces of law and order—has scandalised the French public.

Yves Jobic, a 30-year-old police inspector with a brilliant record, was arrested last November by a team of gendarmes and charged with pimping, theft and running a protection racket.

His arrest was based on evidence given by a group of North African prostitutes and a pimp operating on the Rue de Budapest, a well-known red light district near Saint-Lazare railway station.

The prostitutes claimed Jobic was a well-known figure among the peepshows and sex-shops, demanding money from prostitutes and pimps in return for police protection as well as running his own prostitution racket.

Jobic was arrested after gendarmes taped several conversations between the police inspector and a cabaret owner who agreed to turn informer after being pulled in on drugs charges. (5)

The chief inspector pleaded innocent and said that "close contacts with the Paris underworld" were a necessary part of police work. If Jobic were innocent, the case can be seen as an example of another form of corruption—one police force attacking another. In France, gendarmes patrol the countryside and police officers the cities, but overlapping jurisdictions have led to clashes between the two forces. Some saw the Jobic case as this kind of internal issue, with the gendarmes trying to "humiliate and discredit" the police.

The U.N. effort to curb corruption

International attempts to curb police corruption around the world received a boost when in 1979 the United Nations General Assembly drafted the U.N. Code of Conduct for Law Enforcement Officials (6). Article 7 provides: "Law enforcement officials shall not commit any act of corruption. They shall also rigorously oppose and combat all such acts."

No government had any problems with this mandate. But there were problems in agreeing on how police officers should "oppose and combat" corruption. Experience in the United States had shown that if officials in the police or city hierarchy do not listen to "whistle blowers," the media may provide the only remedy. A compromise was found between balancing the need for internal discipline (reporting misconduct within the chain of command) and the need to expose corruption to the appropriate authorities. Commentary (d) of Article 8 of the Code reads:

In some countries, the mass media may be regarded as performing complaint review functions. . . . Law enforcement officials may, therefore, be justified if, as a last resort and in accordance with the laws and customs of their own countries and with the provisions of article 4 of the present Code, they bring violations to the attention of public opinion through the mass media.

At that time, the Socialist (Communist) countries had no free press. Today they have, and the press in countries such as Russia and Romania is working to report on past and current police corruption and abuses.

SOURCES

1. "Uganda Interior Minister Denounces Police Corruption," The British Broadcasting Corporation, *Summary of World News*, No. 16, 1988, p. ME/0310/B/1.
2. "Uganda Government to Move against Police Corruption," The British Broadcasting Corporation, *Summary of World News*, 1990, p. ME/0715/B/1.
3. "Ex-Cops Stage Hunger Strike against Mexico Police Corruption," *Agence France Press*, March 12, 1992; Nancy Cleeland, "Mexico City Cop Attacks System Built on Bribes," *San Diego Union Tribune*, March 8, 1992, p. 1.
4. Marjorie Miller, "Mexico City Police Complain of Extortion," *Los Angeles Times*, March 8, 1992, p. 5.
5. Michela Wrong, "French Police Traumatized by Lurid 'Inspector Jobic' Case," *Reuters Library Report*, July 3, 1988, AM cycle.
6. General Assembly Resolution 34/169 of 17 December 1979.

QUESTIONS FOR DISCUSSION

1. What are some of the characteristics of police work that make officers susceptible to corruption? Do those characteristics differ in different countries, or are they universal?
2. Do you think police work is more likely to lead employees into corruption than most other types of work? Defend your position.
3. Should other countries get involved in "cleaning up" corrupt police forces when the home government seems to be involved in and supportive of the corruption? Why or why not?

Ex-policemen José Angel Perez and Ricardo Chaires during hunger strike outside the U.S. Embassy to protest police corruption in Mexico City.

Miami police officer Armando Garcia, accused of acting in concert with other officers to "rip off" drug dealers, steal two 400-kilogram shipments of cocaine, and then push the drug dealers overboard. FBI Ten Most Wanted poster, September 1990. As of November 1992, Garcia was still at large.

civilian police review boards
External control mechanism composed of persons usually from outside the police department.

"Except for your paycheck, there is no such thing as a clean buck." "Patrick Murphy, New York City Police Commissioner, as quoted in The New York Times, October 29, 1970, p. 1.

Despite the efforts of the Knapp Commission in 1972 and the National Advisory Commission on Criminal Justice Standards and Goals in 1973, corruption continues. According to experts, corruption may be even more serious now than it was in the 1970s.[68]

One of the more remarkable aspects of the expansion of the drug trade has been its effect on criminal justice officials. The illicit drug market poses a potential for corruption among officers, in general, and especially among those officers who abuse drugs. Many police departments have instituted drug-testing programs. In a 1986 survey of thirty-three large police departments across the country, the National Institute of Justice found that most departments have written procedures to test officers who are suspected of drug abuse. Seventy-three percent of the departments tested applicants, and 21 percent were considering testing all officers.[69]

The issue of drug testing is complex, and cases are still being resolved in the courts. In *Turner v. Fraternal Order of Police* (1985), drug testing, based on a reasonable suspicion that drug use is occurring, was supported by the D.C. Court of Appeals. In 1986 the New York State Supreme Court banned random drug testing in *Caruso v. Benjamin Ward, Police Commissioner*. Of major consideration in the drug-testing issue is the intrusion on the personal rights and dignity of individuals.[70]

Controlling Corruption

Modern policing relies on internal and external controls to maintain its professionalism and its integrity. The court system, and above all the Supreme Court, plays a role in policing the police by holding law enforcement activities to strict constitutional standards. Another external control mechanism is the **civilian police review boards** established in the 1960s to fulfill a review function. From the outset, however, they were opposed both by police unions (such as the Fraternal Order of Police) and by management organizations (such as the International Association of Chiefs of Police). The boards were short-lived in Philadelphia and New York. Voters in other cities defeated proposals to establish such boards, and both the 1967 President's Commission on Law Enforcement and the Administration of Justice and the 1973 National Advisory Commission on Criminal Justice Standards and Goals opposed them as being unworkable and detrimental to morale. Nevertheless, by 1993, 33 of the nation's 50 largest cities had established civilian review boards, and New York City activated its civilian review board in the spring of 1993.[71]

Although civilian police review boards function well in some municipalities, police departments rely primarily on internal controls to police themselves. If internal controls are to be effective, experts argue, law enforcement professionals need to change their thinking about self-policing. In the past, departmental whistleblowers were regarded with derision. The claim is made that this attitude needs to be replaced by intolerance toward those who abuse the public trust and the power of the shield by engaging in abuses, corruption, and other forms of criminality. Studies indicate, however, that officers are usually unwilling to report misconduct by fellow officers. Robert Daley's *Prince of the City* describes the emotional struggle New York City Detective Robert Leuci went through when he had to testify against his corrupt partners.[72]

Half a century ago, O. W. Wilson argued that even a free cup of coffee could put police officers in a compromising position. Several decades later, Patrick Murphy, former police commissioner of New York City, made it clear to his officers: "Except for your paycheck there is no such thing as a clean buck."[73]

Experts predict that by the beginning of the twenty-first century increased professionalism of police forces will become the major factor in corruption control.[74]

UNIONIZATION

In 1889, five Ithaca, New York, police officers went on strike after the mayor cut their paychecks by three dollars a week. The strike was called off a few days later when the wages went back up to twelve dollars per week.[75] It was not until the Boston police strike of 1919 that major questions arose regarding police unionization. Shortly after World War I, the police joined other workers in the fight for better wages, benefits, and working conditions.[76] This marks the beginning of the movement toward unionization.

Growth of Police Unions

The American Federation of Labor issued union charters to thirty-seven police groups, among them the Boston Organizations of Police. Legal and administrative restrictions, however, did not allow unionization of police. Police chiefs challenged the move. They argued that police officers had as little right as armed forces personnel to join a union. But many officers believed they had good reasons to need union backing: annual salaries of $1,400 had not changed in twenty years, work weeks were on average eighty-seven hours, and most promotions depended on political connections.

Shortly after the granting of their charter, Boston officers had a dispute with management over working conditions. Nineteen officers were suspended for union activity. Angry over the suspension of their colleagues, the Boston police voted to strike. At 5:45 P.M. on Tuesday, September 9, 1919, they walked away from their jobs. On the first night of the strike mobs rioted—15,000 people in one square alone. They looted, they killed. Governor Calvin Coolidge brought in the National Guard. Seven-thousand militia and 825 civilian volunteers took over the law enforcement functions of the city of Boston.[77] When the striking patrolmen voted to go back to work, the governor fired them and hired a new police force. And that ended the action President Woodrow Wilson termed "a crime against civilization."[78] Coolidge's forceful action helped him gain the presidency of the United States.

Police Unions Today

Police management and the public remained antiunion for several decades after the Boston strike. In the 1960s, police efforts to unionize began once again. The police union movement developed at that time for a number of reasons: Courts took the position that police and other public employees had the right to form unions; police, too, were becoming activists in a period of civil rights struggles; officers were increasingly dissatisfied that their salaries and benefits had not kept pace with those offered in other jobs; and there was general disillusion with what the police perceived as unlimited power of police chiefs.[79]

There is no one national union of officers comparable, for example, to the Teamsters (representing all truck drivers). Police unions may be local unions with no national affiliations, or they may be part of national federations. The International Conference of Police Associations (ICPA) is the largest, with 100 local and state units representing over 200,000 officers. The International Union of Police Associations represents about 20,000 officers. The Fraternal Order of Police is the oldest national organization. These national organizations function as legislative lobbies, assist officers in employment conflicts, and work for the general improvement of the working conditions of police officers. Organizations such as the Patrolman's Benevolent Association (PBA) are concerned more with local problems than with the general struggles that characterize affiliated national organizations.

Police officers demonstrating against an unpopular action by New York City's mayor, September 1992.

Police unions have become active in collective bargaining; in hiring, firing, and promotion decisions; and in introducing grievance procedures. In most states it is illegal for police officers to strike. Intermittently there are other types of "job actions": "blue flu" epidemics (officers calling in sick), "ticket droughts" (not writing up violations), and short-term walk-outs. And despite restraining orders (a court order prohibiting a strike), fines, and dismissals, several departments, including those in New Orleans, San Francisco, and Youngstown, Ohio, have gone on strike.

"Three quarters of the police officers in the United States belong to police unions that have a powerful impact on all aspects of the lifestyles of police officers."

Three-quarters of the police officers in the United States belong to police unions. These unions have a powerful impact on all aspects of the lifestyles of police officers: recruitment and training, the composition of the police force, morale (through improvement of working conditions), and police corruption.

REVIEW

How does one become a police officer? What qualifications are typically required for the job? Until the 1960s, policing had been a largely male occupation. The equal rights movement opened police careers to minorities and women. Their numbers have been increasing steadily, yet the battle for full acceptance has not yet been won.

The police have developed and live in their own subculture, marked by loyalty to each other, respect for police authority, honor, and group solidarity. The police subculture is separated from the general culture by what some have called the "blue curtain." All officers have their own style of policing: "tough cop," "problem solver," "rule applier," "crime fighter." Officers are constantly subjected to levels of stress not experienced in other professions. Such stress produces personal and family problems, which many departments now try to meet with consulting and other services. The authority and power of police officers subject them to the temptation of abuse of power through corruption. Some officers yield, especially those assigned to drug law enforcement. Effective control of police corruption remains a problem.

Police unions, at one time nonexistent, indeed outlawed, now have become important in collective bargaining, criminal justice legislation, and improving the lot of those in this very difficult profession.

Notes

1. Arthur Niederhoffer and Elaine Niederhoffer, *The Police Family: From Station House to Ranch House* (Lexington, Mass.: Lexington Books, 1978), pp. 4–5.

2. Philip Ash, Karen B. Slora, and Cynthia F. Britton, "Police Agency Officer Selection Practices," *Journal of Police Science and Administration* 17 (1990):258–269.

3. Alan W. Benner, "Psychological Screening of Police Applicants," in *Critical Issues in Policing*, eds. Roger J. Dunham and Geoffrey P. Alpert (Prospect Heights, Ill.: Waveland Press, 1989), p. 5.

4. These figures come from Jack Aylward, "Psychological Testing and Police Selection," *Journal of Police Science and Administration* 13 (1985):201–210, and Ash, Slora, and Britton, "Policy Agency Officer Selection Practices." See also Elizabeth Burbeck and Adrian Furnham, "Police Officer Selection: A Critical Review of the Literature," *Journal of Police Science and Administration* 13 (1985):58–69; L. E. Prior, "Polygraph Testing of Vermont State Police Officers,"

Polygraph 14 (1985):256–257. Kenneth T. Moran, "Pathways Toward a Nondiscriminatory Recruitment Policy," *Journal of Police Science and Administration* 16 (1988):274–287. As to vision standards, see Richard N. Holden and Lisa Lotte Gammeltoft, *"Toonen v. Brown County:* The Legality of Police Vision Standards," *American Journal of Police* 10 (1991):59–66.

5. Mayor's Advisory Committee on Police Management and Personnel Policy, *Preliminary Report* (New York: 1986, unpublished), pp. 17–18. James J. Fyfe, *Police Personnel Practices*, Baseline Data Reports 18: 1–11 (Washington, D.C.: International City Management Associates, 1986).

6. For a discussion of the relationship between height and the potential for aggression, see K. R. Willoughby and William R. Blount, "The Relationship between Law Enforcement, Officer Height, Aggression, and Job Performance," *Journal of Police Science and Administration* 13 (1985):225–229.

7. *The Miami News*, December 26, 1979, p. 5A.

8. George Pugh, "The California Psychological Inventory and Police Selection," *Journal of Police Science and Administration* 13 (1985):172–177; George Hargrave and Deirdre Hiatt, "Law Enforcement Selection with the Interview, MMPI and CPI: A Study of Reliability and Validity," *Journal of Police Science and Administration* 15 (1987):110–114.

9. See, for example, Robin E. Inwald, Hilary F. Knatz, and Elizabeth J. Shusman, *Inwald Personality Inventory Manual* (New York: Hilson Research, 1983).

10. See Robert D. Meier, Richard E. Farmer, and David Maxwell, "Psychological Screening of Police Candidates: Current Perspectives," *Journal of Police Science and Administration* 15 (1987):210–215; Joyce I. McQuilkin, Vickey L. Russell, Alan G. Frost, and Wayne R. Faust, "Psychological Test Validity for Selecting Law Enforcement Officers," *Journal of Police Science and Administration* 17 (1990):289–294; Benjamin S. Wright, William G. Doerner, and John C. Speir, "Pre-Employment Psychological Testing as a Predictor of Police Performance During an FTO Program," *American Journal of Police* 9 (1990):65–84; William O. Dwyer, Erich P. Prien, and J. L. Bernard, "Psychological Screening of Law Enforcement Officers: A Case for Job Relatedness," *Journal of Police Science and Administration* 17 (1990):176–182; Vesta S. Gettys and Joseph D. Elam, "Validation Demystified: Personnel Selection Techniques That Work," *Police Chief* 52 (1985):41–43; Robin E. Inwald, "Administrative Legal and Ethical Practices in the Psychological Testing of Law Enforcement Officers," *Journal of Criminal Justice* 13 (1985):367–372; Nathaniel J. Pallone."The MMPI in Police Officer Selection: Legal Constraints, Case Law, Empirical Data," *Journal of Offender Rehabilitation* 17 (1992):171–188.

11. Dennis Jay Kenney and Steuart Watson, "Intelligence and the Selection of Police Recruits," *American Journal of Police* 9 (1990):39–64.

12. Larry K. Gaines and Victoria E. Kappeler, "Selection and Testing," in *What Works in Policing? Operations and Administration Examined*, eds. Gary W. Cordner and Donna C. Hale (Highland

Heights, Ky. and Cincinnati: Academy of Criminal Justice Sciences and Anderson Publishing Co., 1992), pp. 107–123. Danny E. Bradley and Robert D. Pursley, "Behaviorally anchored rating scales for patrol officer performance appraisal: development and evaluation," *Journal of Police Science and Administration* 15 (1987):37–45.

13. National Advisory Commission on Criminal Justice Standards and Goals, *Report on the Police* (Washington, D.C.: U.S. Government Printing Office, 1973), p. 369.

14. David L. Carter, Allen D. Sapp, and Darrel W. Stephens, *The State of Police Education: Policy Direction for the 21st Century* (Washington, D.C.: Police Executive Research Forum, 1989), p. 38. See also James J. Fyfe, "Police Personnel Practices," *Baseline Data Reports 15*, No. 1 (Washington, D.C.: International City Management Association, 1983). For a discussion of a New York City Police Department program (the Police Cadet Corps) designed to attract college students to careers as police officers, see Antony M. Pate and Edwin E. Hamilton, *The New York City Police Cadet Corps: Final Evaluation Report* (Washington, D.C.: Police Foundation, 1991).

15. Carter, Sapp, and Stephens, *The State of Police Education*, p. 47. See also Lee H. Bowker, "A Theory of Educational Needs of Law Enforcement Officers," *Journal of Contemporary Criminal Justice* 1 (1980):17–24. For a discussion of the best type of college education for law enforcement officers, see Lawrence W. Sherman and Warren Bennis, "Higher Education for Police Officers: The Central Issues," *Police Chief* 44 (August 1977):32. See also Lawrence W. Sherman and the National Advisory Commission on Higher Education for Police Officers, *The Quality of Police Education* (San Francisco: Jossey-Bass, 1978).

16. Elizabeth Burbeck and Adrian Furnham, "Police Officer Selection: A Critical Review of the Literature," *Journal of Police Science and Administration* 13 (1985):58–69. See also Robert E. Worden, "A Badge and a Baccalaureate: Policies, Hypotheses and Further Evidence" *Justice Quarterly* 7 (1990):565–592; Robert Fisher, Kathryn Golden, and Bruce Heininger, "Issues in Higher Education for Law Enforcement Officers: An Illinois Study," *Journal of Criminal Justice* 13 (1985):329–338.

17. Bernard Cohen and Jan M. Chaiken, *Police Background Characteristics* (New York: Rand Institute, 1972). For selection of investigators, see Bernard Cohen and Jan Chaiken, *Investigators Who Perform Well* (Washington, D.C.: National Institute of Justice, 1987).

18. Samuel Walker, *The Police in America*, 2d ed. (New York: McGraw-Hill, 1992), p. 313.

19. Candice McCoy, "Affirmative Action in Police Organizations: Checklist for Supporting a Compelling State Interest," *Criminal Law Bulletin* 20 (1984):245–254; Timothy Stroup, "Affirmative Action and the Police," in *Police Ethics: Hard Choices in Law Enforcement*, eds. W. C. Heffernan and Timothy Stroup (New York: John Jay, 1985). See also Isaac C. Hunt, Jr., and Bernard Cohen, *Minority Recruiting in the New York City Police Department* (New York: Rand Institute, 1971).

20. Jack L. Kuykendall and David E. Burns, "The Black Police Officer: An Historical Perspective," *Journal of Contemporary Criminal Justice* 1 (1986):4–12.

21. Walker, *The Police in America*, p. 246; James J. Fyfe, *Police Personnel Practices*; Ellen Hochstedler, Robert M. Regoli, and Eric D. Poole, "Changing the Guard in American Cities: A Current Empirical Assessment of Integration in 20 Municipal Police Departments," *Criminal Justice Review* 9 (1984):8–14.

22. Bruce L. Berg, Edmond J. True, and Marc G. Gertz, "Police, Riots, and Alienation," *Journal of Police Science and Administration* 12 (1984):186–190.

23. Samuel Walker, "Paths to Police Reform–Reflections on Twenty-five Years of Change," in *Police and Policing: Contemporary Issues*, ed. Dennis Jay Kenney (New York: Praeger, 1989), pp. 271–284. According to James J. Fyfe, there is, however, little evidence to support the contention that different attitudes of black officers result in different behavior. See James J. Fyfe, "Who Shoots? A Look at Officer Race and Police Shooting," *Journal of Police Science and Administration* 9 (1981):373.

24. National Advisory Commission on Criminal Justice Standards and Goals, *Report of the Commission* (Washington, D.C.: U.S. Government Printing Office, 1973), p. 329.

25. As quoted in Tom Seligson, "How Good Are Women Cops?," *Parade*, March 31, 1985, pp. 4–7.

26. Daniel J. Bell, "Policewomen: Myths and Reality," *Journal of Police Science and Administration* 10 (1982):112–120.

27. Samuel S. Janus, Cynthia Janus, Leslie K. Lord, and Thomas Power, "Women in Police Work—Annie Oakley or Little Orphan Annie?" *Police Studies* 11 (1988):124–127; Susan E. Martin, *Women on the Move? A Report on the Status of Women in Policing* (Washington, D.C.: Police Foundation, 1989).

28. See, for example, Lee W. Potts, "Equal Employment Opportunity and Female Employment in Public Agencies," *Journal of Criminal Justice* (1983):505–523; Susan E. Martin, "The Effectiveness of Affirmative Action: The Case of Women in Policing," *Justice Quarterly* 8 (1991):489–504; Barbara Raffel Price, "Police Community Relations—Sex Conscious Hiring and Professionalism," *Journal of Crime and Justice* 4 (1981):48–53; Barbara Raffel Price and Susan Gavin, "A Century of Women in Policing," in *The Criminal Justice System and Women: Women Offenders, Victims, Workers*, eds. Barbara Raffel Price and Natalie J. Sokoloff (New York: Clark Boardman, 1982), pp. 339–412; Roi Dianne Townsey, "Black Women in American Policing: An Advancement Display," *Journal of Criminal Justice* 10 (1982):455–468; Harold R. Slater and Martin Reiser, "A Comparative Study of Factors Influencing Police Recruitment," *Journal of Police Science and Administration* 16 (1988):168–176.

29. Uniform Crime Reports, Federal Bureau of Investigation, *Uniform Crime Reports for the United States, 1990* (Washington, D.C.: U.S. Government Printing Office, 1991), p. 242.

30. Susan E. Martin, *The Status of Women in Policing* (Washington, D.C.: Police Foundation, 1990), pp. xi–xvii. For changes worldwide see United Nations Report A/Conf. 121/17, July 1, 1985, with a comprehensive analysis of women in law enforcement by Edith Flynn, who served as U.N. consultant on the topic. See also Carole G. Garrison, Nancy Grant, and Kenneth McCormick, "Utilization of Police Women," *The Police Chief* (1988):32–35, 69–73; Marc Pogrebin, "The Changing Role of Women: Female Police Officers' Occupational Problems," *The Police Journal* 59 (1986):127–133; Kenneth W. Kerber, Steven M. Andes, and Michele B. Mittler, "Citizen Attitudes Regarding the Competence of Female Police Officers," *Journal of Police Science and Administration* 5 (1977):337–347.

31. Merry Morash and Jack Greene, "Evaluating Women on Patrol: A Critique of Contemporary Wisdom," *Evaluation Review* 10 (1986):230–255. A study of patrol teams in New York City found policewomen less likely to injure citizens or to be injured. See Sean Grennan, "Findings on the Role of Officer Gender in Violent Encounters with Citizens," *Journal of Police Science and Administration* 15 (1988):78–85. Texas and Oklahoma study found arrest rates of male and female officers almost alike. See James A. Davis, "Perspectives of Policewomen in Texas and Oklahoma," *Journal of Police Science and Administration* 12 (1984):395–403. See also Robert J. Homant and Daniel B. Kennedy, "Police Perceptions of Spouse Abuse: A Comparison of Male and Female Officers," *Journal of Criminal Justice* 13 (1985):29–47; Michael T. Charles, "Women in Policing: The Physical Aspects," *Journal of Police Science and Administration* 10 (1982):194–205; James A. Davis, "Perspectives of Policewomen in Texas and Oklahoma," *Journal of Criminal Justice* 13 (1985):49–64; Peter Bloch and Deborah Anderson, *Policewomen on Patrol: Final Report* (Washington, D.C.: Urban Institute, 1974).

32. Sally Gross, "Women Becoming Cops: Developmental Issues and Solutions," *Police Chief* 51 (1) (1984):32–35; M. L. West, "Sexual Harassment Complaints: A Growing Concern for Police Management," *Journal of California Law Enforcement* 20 (1986):55–58. See also Eric D. Poole and Mark R. Pogrebin, "Factors Affecting the Decision to Remain in Policing: A Study of Women Officers," *Journal of Police Science and Administration* 16 (1988):49–55.

33. Harry W. More, *Special Topics in Policing* (Cincinnati: Anderson, 1992), p. 127. See also Douglas S. Drummond, "Law En-

forcement: The Cultural Impact of an Occupation (Santa Ana, Calif.: Vollmer University, 1988).

34. Barbara Raffel Price, "Sexual Integration in American Law Enforcement," in *Police Ethics: Hard Choices in Law Enforcement,* eds. William C. Heffernan and Timothy Stroup (New York: John Jay Press, 1985). See also Ralph A. Weisheit, "Women in the State Police: Concerns of Male and Female Officers," *Journal of Police Science and Administration* 15 (1987):137–144; Bruce Berg and Kimberly Budnick, "Defeminization of Women in Law Enforcement: A New Twist in the Traditional Police Personality," *Journal of Police Science and Administration* 14 (1986):314–319; John R. Snortum and John C. Beyers, "Patrol Activities with Male and Female Officers as a Function of Work Experience," *Journal of Police Studies* 6 (1983):36–42; Judie Gaffin Wexler and DeAna Dorman Logan, "Sources of Stress among Women Police Officers," *Journal of Police Science and Administration* 11 (1983):46–55.

35. William A. Westley, *Violence and the Police: A Sociological Study of Law, Custom, and Morality* (Cambridge, Mass.: MIT Press, 1970), p. 11; Michael K. Brown, *Working the Street* (New York: Russell Sage, 1981).

36. Jonathan Rubenstein, *City Police* (New York: Farrar, Straus, and Giroux), pp. 127–128.

37. Kenneth E. Christian and Steven M. Edwards, "Law Enforcement Standards and Training Councils: A Human Resource Planning Force in the Future," *Journal of Police Science and Administration* 13 (1985):1–9. For changes over time in police training, see Thomas M. Frost and Magnus J. Seng, "Police Recruit Training in Urban Departments: A Look at Instructors," *Journal of Police Science and Administration* 11 (1983):296–302. For a methodology of police training evaluation, see Richard A. Talley, "A New Methodology for Evaluating the Curricula Relevancy of Police Academy Training," *Journal of Police Science Administration* 14 (1986):112–120. For a discussion of police academy instructors currently teaching in America, see Bruce L. Berg, "Who Should Teach Police: A Typology and Assessment of Police Academy Instructors," *American Journal of Police* 9 (1990):79–100.

38. Michael S. McCampbell, "Field Training for Police Officers: State of the Art," in *Critical Issues in Policing,* eds. Dunham and Alpert, p. 111. See also William C. Smith and Geoffrey P. Alpert, "A Critical and Constructive Look at the Defensibility of Police Pursuit Training," ibid., pp. 172–194.

39. See James T. Haider, *Field Training Police Recruits: Developing, Improving and Operating a Field Training Program* (Springfield, Ill.: Charles C. Thomas, 1990), p. 3. For a study of attitudes of new recruits see Robert J. Meadows, "Police Training Strategies and the Role Perceptions of Police Recruits," *Journal of Police Science and Administration* 13 (1985):195–200; John Van Maanen, "Observations on the Making of a Policeman," in *Order Under Law,* eds. R. Culbertson and M. Tezak (Prospect Heights, Ill.: Waveland Press, 1981), p. 111–126. For a discussion of law expectations of rookie officers as different from reality, see M. Steven Meagher and Nancy Yentis, "Choosing a Career in Policing: A Comparison of Male and Female Perceptions," *Journal of Police Science and Administration* 14 (1986):320–327.

40. Jerome H. Skolnick, *Justice without Trial: Law Enforcement in Democratic Society* (New York: Wiley, 1966), p. 42.

41. George Kirkham, "A Professor's Street Lessons," in *Order under Law,* eds. Robert G. Culbertson and M. Tezak, p. 81.

42. Arthur Niederhoffer, *Behind the Shield* (Garden City, New York: Doubleday (1967), pp. 216–220. See also Robert Langworthy, "Police Cynicism: What We Know from the Niederhoffer Scale," *Journal of Criminal Justice* 15 (1987):17–35; Richard Anson, J. Dale Mann, and Dale Sherman, "Niederhoffer's Cynicism Scale: Reliability and Beyond," *Journal of Criminal Justice* 14 (1986):295–307. For changes over time attributed to occupational socialization, see Jesse L. Maghan, "The 21st Century Cop: Police Recruit Perceptions as a Function of Occupational Socialization" (Ph.D. dissertation, City University of New York, 1988). See also Edward E. Peoples, "The impact of the criminal justice system upon its personnel," *Criminology* 13 (1975):118–120.

43. Robert M. Regoli and Eric D. Poole, "Measurement of Police Cynicism: A Factor Scaling Approach," *Journal of Criminal Justice* 7 (1979):37–52. See also John P. Crank, Robert M. Regoli, Eric D. Poole, and Robert G. Culbertson, "Cynicism among Police Chiefs," *Justice Quarterly* 3 (1986):343–352; and Robert M. Regoli, John P. Crank, and Robert G. Culbertson, "Rejoinder-Police Cynicism: Theory Development and Reconstruction," *Justice Quarterly* 4 (1987):281–286.

44. Some people believe police work attracts individuals with unique characteristics. See Milton Rokeach, Martin Miller, and John Snyder, "The Value Gap between Police and Policed," *Journal of Social Research* 27 (1971):155–171; James Teevan and Bernard Dolnick, "The Values of the Police: A Reconsideration and Interpretation," *Journal of Police Science and Administration* 1 (1973):366–369; Richard Lundman, *Police and Policing* (New York: Holt, Rinehart, and Winston, 1980); Bruce Carpenter and Susan Raza, "Personality Characteristics of Police Applicants: Comparison across Subgroups and with Other Populations," *Journal of Police Science and Administration* 15 (1987):10–17.

45. Harry W. More, Jr., *The American Police, Text and Readings* (St. Paul, Minn.: West, 1976), p. 125.

46. Susan O. White, "A Perspective on Police Professionalism," *Law and Society Review* 7 (1972):61–85. Similarly, Muir has identified "professionals," "reciprocators," "enforcers," and "avoiders." See William Ker Muir, Jr., *Police: Street Corner Politicians* (Chicago: University of Chicago Press, 1977).

47. James Leo Walsh, "Career Styles and Police Behavior," in *Police and Society,* ed. David H. Bayley (Beverly Hills, Calif.: Sage, 1977), pp. 149–167. See also David H. Bayley and Egon Bittner, "Learning the Skills of Policing," in *Critical Issues in Policing,* eds. Dunham and Alpert, p. 97.

48. Carl Klockars, "The Dirty Harry Problem," *Annals of the American Academy of Social and Political Science* 452 (1980):33–47.

49. Ellen Hochstedler, "'Testing Types,' A Review and Test of Police Types," *Journal of Criminal Behavior* 9 (1981):451–466. Kathryn Golden found that pre-law-enforcement students do not enter policing experience to be "Dirty Harry" (Kathryn Golden, "The Police Role: Perceptions and Preferences," *Journal of Police Science and Administration* 10 [1982]:108–111). See also William F. Walsh, "Patrol Officer Arrest Rates: A Study of the Social Organization of Police Work," *Justice Quarterly* 3 (1986):271–290; Jack Kuykendall, "Police managerial styles: A grid analysis," *American Journal of Police* 4 (1985):38–70; and Jack Kuykendall & Roy R. Roberg, "Police Managers' Perceptions of Employee Types: A Conceptual Model," *Journal of Criminal Justice* 16 (1988):131–137.

50. Joseph Victor, "Police Stress: Is Anybody There Listening?," *New York Law Enforcement Journal* (June 1986):19–20; Mark L. Dantzker, "A View into Police Stress," *Journal of Police and Criminal Psychology* 2 (1986):36–43; John M. Violanti, "Stress Patterns in Police Work: A Longitudinal Study," *Journal of Police Science and Administration* 11 (1983):211–216. See also Francis Cullen, Terrence Lemming, Bruce Link, and John Wozniak, "The Impact of Social Supports on Police Stress," *Criminology* 23 (1985):503–522; Nancy Nowell, Dale Belles, and Holly Hills, "Perceived Stress Levels and Physical Symptoms in Supervisory Law Enforcement Personnel," *Journal of Police Science and Administration* 16 (1988):75–79; W. Clinton Terry III, "Police Stress: The Empirical Evidence," *Journal of Police Science and Administration* 9 (1981):61–65; Richard Lawrence, "Police Stress and Personality Factors: A Conceptual Model," *Journal of Criminal Justice* 12 (1984):247–263; Dennis L. Conroy and Karen M. Hess, *Officers at Risk* (Placerville, Calif.: Custom, 1992). Civilian employees are also under stress: see Roy Roberg, David Hayhurst, and Harry Allen, "Job Burnout in Law Enforcement Dispatches: A Comparative Analysis," *Journal of Criminal Justice* 16 (1988):384–394. See also Clement Mihanovich, "The Blue Pressure Cooker," *Police Chief* 47(2) (1980):20–21; Mary Hageman, "Occupational Stress and Marital and Family Relationships," *Journal of Police Science and Administration* 6 (1978):402–416; Francis T. Cullen, Terrence Lemming, Bruce G. Link, and John F. Wozniak, "The Impact of Social Supports on Police Stress," *Crim-*

inology 23 (1985):503–522; T. E. Malloy and G. L. Mays, "The Police Stress Hypothesis: A Critical Evaluation," *Criminal Justice and Behavior* 11 (1984):197–226; B. A. Vulcano, G. E. Barnes, and L. J. Breen, "The Prevalence and Predictors of Psychosomatic Symptoms and Conditions among Police Officers," *Psychosomatic Medicine* 45 (1983):277–293; Robert C. Trojanowicz, *The Environment of the First-Line Police Supervisor* (Englewood Cliffs, N.J.: Prentice-Hall, 1980); W. Clinton Terry III, "Police Stress as a Professional Self-Image," *Journal of Criminal Justice* 13 (1985):501–512; Katherine W. Ellison and John L. Genz, *Stress and the Police Officer* (Springfield, Ill.: Charles C. Thomas, 1983); William H. Kroes, *Society's Victims—The Police*, 2d ed. (Springfield, Ill.: Charles C. Thomas, 1985). An entire organization devoted to the study of police stress (the International Law Enforcement Stress Association) has been founded; it publishes its own journal, *Police Stress*. See also Vivian B. Lord, Denis O. Gray, and Samuel B. Pond III, "The Police Stress Inventory: Does It Measure Stress?," *Journal of Criminal Justice* 19 (1991):139–149.

51. Theodore M. Hammett, "AIDS and the Law Enforcement Officer: Concerns and Policy Responses," National Institute of Justice Report, (Washington, D.C.: U.S. Government Printing Office, 1987).

52. *Newsweek*, June 1987, p. 60.

53. Robert Hanley, "Officer's Trial in Teaneck is Disrupted," *The New York Times*, February 1, 1992, p. 23. Mr. McDonald's entrance into the courtroom apparently violated the presiding judge's order barring admission of spectators during testimony. The case was a complex one involving the state's contention that the victim was shot in the back with his hands raised. The victim was black and the officer was white.

54. Michael K. Brown, *Working the Street* (New York: Russell Sage, 1981), p. 82; Westley, *Violence and the Police*.

55. Albert Reiss, *The Police and the Public* (New Haven, Conn.: Yale University Press, 1971), p. 51; David H. Bayley and James Garofalo, "The Management of Violence by Police Patrol Officers," *Criminology* 27 (1989):7–25.

56. See Stan K. Shernock, "The Effects of Patrol Officers' Defensiveness toward the Outside World on Their Ethical Orientations," *Criminal Justice Ethics* (1990)7–9:24–42; Charles Bahn, "Police Socialization in the Eighties: Strains in the Forging of an Occupational Identity," *Journal of Police Science and Administration* 12 (1984):390–394; Barbara Raffel Price, *Police Professionalism* (Lexington, Mass.: Lexington Books, 1977).

57. Patricia W. Lunneborg, *Women Police Officers—Current Career Profile* (Springfield, Ill.: C. C. Thomas, 1989), pp. 39–40.

58. Westley, *Violence and the Police*, p. 226. See also the research of a sociologist who spent three years as a participant observer with the police at work and at leisure: Claude L. Vincent, *Police Officer* (Ottawa, Canada: Carleton University, 1990), pp. 102–103.

59. Susan Ehrlich Martin, *Breaking and Entering: Police Women on Patrol* (Berkeley: University of California Press, 1980), pp. 79–108.

60. Joseph Wambaugh, *The Choirboys* (New York: Dell, 1975).

61. Walker, *The Police in America*, p. 335. See also Samuel Walker, "Historical Roots of Legal Control of Police Behavior," in *Police Innovation and Control of the Police*, eds. David Weisburd and Craig Uchida (New York: Springer, 1993).

62. Commission to Investigate Allegations of Police Corruption and the City's Anticorruption Procedures (New York City; Whitman Knapp, chairman), *Commission Report* (1972); *Knapp Commission Report on Police Corruption* (New York: George Braziller, 1973).

63. Harry W. More, *Special Topics in Policing* (Cincinnati: Anderson, 1992), p. 257.

64. Ibid., p. 258.

65. Herman Goldstein, *Police Corruption: A Perspective on Its Nature and Control* (Washington, D.C.: Police Foundation, 1975); Lawrence Sherman, *Police Corruption: A Sociological Perspective* (Garden City, N.Y.: Doubleday, 1974); Ellwyn Stoddard, "Blue Coat Crime," in *Thinking about Police: Contemporary Readings*, ed. Carl Klockars (New York: McGraw-Hill, 1983), pp. 338–349; Michael Johnston, *Political Corruption and Public Policy in America* (Monterey, Calif.: Brooks/Cole 1982), p. 75.

66. Walker, *The Police in America*, pp. 263–265.

67. As quoted in Marjorie Miller, "Mexico City Police Complain of Extortion," *Los Angeles Times*, March 8, 1982, p. 5.

68. Robert J. McCormack, "Confronting Police Corruption: Organizational Initiatives for Internal Control," in *Managing Police Corruption: International Perspectives*, eds. Richard H. Ward and Robert McCormack (Chicago: Office of International Criminal Justice, University of Illinois at Chicago, 1987), pp. 151–165.

69. "Employee Drug Testing Policies in Police Departments," National Institute of Justice Research (Washington, D.C.: Department of Justice, 1986).

70. *Turner v. Fraternal Order of Police*, No. 83–1213, D.C. Court of Appeals, November 13, 1985; *Caruso, President of P.B.A. v. Benjamin Ward, Police Commissioner*, New York State Supreme Court, Pat. 37, Index No. 12632-86, 1986.

71. Maria Newman, "Report Details Variations in Police Review Boards," *The New York Times*, January 10, 1993, p. 26. On the question of the relationship between the type of civilian oversight and community satisfaction, see Samuel Walker and Vic Bumphus, *A National Survey of Civilian Oversight of the Police* (Omaha: University of Nebraska at Omaha, 1991). See also Andrew J. Goldsmith, *Complaints against the Police* (Oxford, England: Clarendon Press, 1991).

72. Robert Daley, *Prince of the City: The Story of a Cop Who Knew Too Much* (Boston: Houghton Mifflin, 1978). See also Paul Chevigny, *Police Power: Police Abuses in New York City* (New York: Pantheon Books, 1969); Lawrence W. Sherman, *Police Corruption* (Garden City, N.Y.: Anchor, 1974).

73. Herman Goldstein, *Police Corruption*, p. 29.

74. Harry W. More, "The Delphi Analysis of Police Corruption," *Journal of Police Science and Administration* 8 (1980):107–115.

75. Robert O'Block, "The Movement for Police Unionization," *The Police Chief* XLV (1978).

76. Anthony V. Bouza, "Police Unions: Paper Tigers or Roaring Lions?," in *Police Leadership in America: Crisis and Opportunity*, ed. William A. Geller (New York and Chicago: Praeger and American Bar Association, 1985), pp. 241–280.

77. O'Block, "The Movement for Police Unionization"; More, *Special Topics in Policing*, pp. 86–87.

78. Francis Russell, *A City in Terror* (New York: Viking, 1975), p. 170.

79. Walker, *The Police in America*, p. 371.

PART 3

THE COURTS

Courts, the heart of the criminal justice system, have had the same function for thousands of years. The American court system grew out of the English system, which in turn grew out of earlier systems. In Chapter 10 we discuss the contemporary American judicial system and its origins, noting the diversity of federal and state courts, their hierarchical structure (trial and appellate courts), and their interrelationships (especially when federal constitutional issues arise). Chapter 11 makes clear that there is much more to courts than judges. Prosecutors and defense attorneys, too, are officers of the court, as are the many administrators and officials who ensure the day-to-day functioning of the judicial machinery. Prosecutors, representing the people of a particular jurisdiction, seek convictions of criminal suspects; defense attorneys stand in opposition, and ensure that the rights of the accused are protected. Trial judges make sure that the trial is fair, that it follows the rules of law, procedure, and evidence. The functionaries of the court system have distinct, though interrelated, careers, with a common background in legal education.

Chapter 12 focuses on the judicial process. Only a small fraction of criminal charges lead to trial; most others are disposed of by diversion of various sorts and by guilty pleas—usually as the result of a plea bargain. Judges, prosecutors, and defense attorneys are involved in all phases of the judicial process, from first appearance before a judge through bail decisions, arraignment, and trial. In this chapter we consider the participation of lay people, the grand and petit jurors, in the trial process, as well as the rights of appeal.

The final chapter of this part, Chapter 13, deals with sentencing—with the many considerations that go into a judicial decision to impose a sentence, the options available, and the limitations on judicial discretion. Sentencing guidelines, which are one kind of limit, are an outgrowth of the just-deserts movement that has shaped sentencing goals and practices during the last two decades. ∎

CHAPTER 10

THE ORIGIN AND ROLE OF THE COURTS

England, 1632

The hall in which the King's Great Council met during the fifteenth, sixteenth, and seventeenth centuries was called the "Starred Chamber" because the ceiling was painted with stars. But the court itself was anything but a "star" in the history of English law: It ignored the guarantees of the common law. There were only informants, not witnesses. Proceedings were inquisitorial and secret; torture of defendants—all charged with crimes deemed dangerous to the established order—was common. The Long Parliament abolished the Court of Star Chamber in 1641.

Germany, 1942

If you had walked into a courthouse in Germany during the Nazi era, say in 1942, you would have found the proceedings in one wing of the building to be totally proper. There were old-fashioned judges, applying old-fashioned criminal law, according to old-fashioned procedural standards. Three months for chicken theft, suspended sentence for assault during a brawl. But in the other wing of the building, young prosecutors and judges, wearing the eagle and swastika on their robes, were adjudicating "political criminals" on such charges as having tuned their radios to the BBC. A summary proceeding usually ended with a ten-year sentence to a concentration camp. These were the Sondergerichte, *or* Volksgerichte *(Special, or People's courts), set up to deal with political offenses.*

Jamaica, 1978

The door to this facility has an entrance, but no exit. Prisoners are led into a courtroom where walls, ceiling, judge's bench, all the benches are painted scarlet. The prime minister is reported to have quipped, "It's red because it's dread." The color scheme was purportedly recommended by an American psychologist who thought that total red best served to drive home the message to those brought here: Anyone found in the possession of a gun was to be tried, instantly convicted, and sentenced to life without parole, such sentence to be served in red hot cages on the premises of the "Gun Court"—Jamaica's answer to the violence of the 1970s. The violence has subsided, but the Gun Court still exists. ◼

A cartoonist's depiction of an English trial as a tennis match.

SOURCE: *The Comic Blackstone,* Gilbert Abbott à Beckett, Chicago: Callaghan & Cockcroft, 1869, Illustrations by George Cruikshank, facing page 12.

In medieval England, subjecting accused to cruel procedures to reveal God's judgment of the person's guilt or innocence.

These three courts are the exception, not the rule. In most societies, including our own, the process for resolving disputes and judging guilt or innocence is governed by laws that spell out the rules of the process and the limits of the court's power. These rules are known to everyone and are applied to everyone equally. In this chapter we discuss the emergence of the American court structure—regular standing courts dedicated to the rule of law. We also examine their composition and function.

ORIGIN OF AMERICA'S COURTS

Throughout history, emperors, kings, dukes, and other nobles had estates or castles that were referred to as "courts"—the court of the king of England, the court of the queen of Spain, and so on. Important business was conducted at the court, including the business of resolving disputes and adjudging the guilt or innocence of persons accused of crime by means of a trial. Trial was a game at the court, very much like games played on basketball courts and tennis courts.

What all these court games had in common was the fact that they were played in established public places in accordance with established rules, and were judged by referees or judges in the presence of the public. Some changes have been made in our criminal procedure over the centuries, but the basic idea still holds: A criminal trial is a game played in court by competitors; it is an adversarial contest in which combatants defend opposing positions.

The British Model

The basic premises of this adversarial system evolved slowly over the centuries in England. With Magna Carta (1215) came lay participation in the form of grand and petit juries, and rational guilt determination on the basis of facts. The judge became an umpire. In the seventeenth century, judicial independence was established; the writ of habeas corpus—to test the legality of imprisonment—was guaranteed (1679); fines were sharply limited; and cruel and unusual punishments were prohibited.

In medieval times, England was divided into units called "shires" within which there were groupings of citizens called "hundreds" (Chapter 6). Both the hundreds and the shires had their own communal courts, presided over by a hundred reeve and a shire reeve, respectively. Their role, however, was simply to lead the court proceedings, not to decide questions of law. That task was left to lay persons known as "suitors," who made decisions based on their knowledge of local customs and norms. While the hundred court heard some criminal cases, the shire court was more important because it had a wider jurisdiction and drew both its suitors and the parties to a case from among the most influential people in the area. The findings of both courts were final unless a litigant believed an error of procedure had occurred. In such cases, an appeal could be made directly to the king and his council. (See the Criminal Justice in Action box.)

The tradition of a trial by jury originated in this early court system. The earliest juries were composed of twelve men from each hundred and four from each vill (village), who appeared voluntarily at the communal courts to place charges against suspects. These were the forerunner of the grand jury. Many of the accused were subjected to **trial by ordeal,** a cruel practice that was thought to reveal God's judgment of guilt or innocence. An accused might be forced to plunge his hands into a pot of boiling water to retrieve a hot stone, or might be made to carry a piece of hot iron down the aisle of a church and then drop it into a water bucket. The defendant's wounds would then be bandaged. If, after three days, the wounds were free from infection, pus, or blistering, God had proved the defendant innocent.[1] These brutal practices ceased when in 1215 the pope forbade the clergy to celebrate mass during such trials.

Gradually shires lost power to the royal councils, and by the thirteenth century the jurisdiction of the communal courts was limited to minor cases. A centralized system under the king developed, and royal courts, governed by common law, soon prevailed throughout England. Four of these courts became particularly powerful and ultimately influenced the development of the court system in the American colonies: the High Court of Parliament, the Court of King's Bench, the courts of assize, and the courts of quarter sessions.[2]

Medieval duel between a man and a woman. The man's feet are suspended in a hole; the woman stands free.

High Court of Parliament was the judicial body where decisions made by the King's Bench could be reviewed. Only appeals that related to procedural matters were reviewed by the High Court.

Court of King's Bench was the court through which the king is said to have rendered justice directly. It had almost unlimited jurisdiction in criminal matters, ranging from treason to minor misdemeanors, and also the authority to review decisions of inferior courts.

Courts of assize were the main trial courts for serious crimes, including capital offenses (crimes punishable by death). Courts of assize had jurisdiction in so many criminal matters that their judges traveled around the English countryside twice a year to facilitate the hearing of cases. This was called "riding the circuit."

Quarter sessions courts met four times a year and were considered the "judicial workhorse"[3] of the court system because they handled a large number of cases, including felonies and capital cases. The more serious cases, however, had to be tried in the presence of a justice of either the King's Bench or the assize court. Quarter sessions courts were presided over by justices of the peace.

Colonial Courts

Colonial courts started modestly. Perhaps Thomas Olive, the governor of the colony of West Jersey, summed up the prevailing view: He said that he was "in the habit of dispensing justice sitting on a stump in his meadow."[4] As the population of the colonies grew, however, formal courts of law appeared in Virginia, Plymouth, Massachusetts Bay, Maryland, Rhode Island, Connecticut, and New Haven. Drawing on the example set by the English Parliament, the colonial legislatures became the highest courts.[5] The Massachusetts Bay Colony established a powerful body known as the General Court that acted as both a legislature and the highest court of the colony.[6]

"Thomas Olive, governor of West Jersey, was 'in the habit of dispensing justice sitting on a stump in his meadow.'"

"County courts played a key role in both the government and the social life of the colonies."

Beneath the legislatures were the superior courts, which had the same jurisdiction as the Kings Bench and the courts of assize. Examples were the Court of Assistants in the Massachusetts Bay Colony, the General Court in Virginia, and the Court of Tryals in Rhode Island. These courts heard both civil and criminal cases (Table 10.1). Over time, some colonies established trial courts headed by a chief justice and several associate justices. Appeals from the trial courts were heard by the governor and his council in what were often called "courts of appeals."[7]

Courts established at the county level played a key role in both the government and the social life of the colonies. In addition to having jurisdiction in both civil and criminal cases, county courts fulfilled many administrative duties: setting and collecting taxes, supervising the building of roads, and licensing taverns.

The Trial of George Jacobs, August 5, 1692, by J. H. Matteson, 1855. George Jacobs, a patriarch of Salem, Massachusetts, was accused, tried, and executed as a witch.

Courts for a New Nation

The founders of the new republic had profound concerns about the distribution of power between courts and legislatures, and between the states and the federal

MILESTONES IN THE HISTORY OF THE COURTS

Time Frame	Event	
Prehistoric times, preliterate societies, clans, tribes	Justice achieved by communal consensus, compensation, appeasing deities. Administered by councils, tribal groups, elders	
Middle East city-states after 3500 B.C.	Justice dispensed by powerful rulers, alone or with councils	
Since 1965	Greece, Rome: Regular court systems, many with lay participation (jurors); lawyers; as well as judges	
400–1200	Europe, the Dark Ages: proceedings before popular or royal tribunals, city courts, peasant courts. No professionals; only primitive written law	
13th–18th centuries	Europe: Roman law revived; professional lawyers, judges; city, state, and royal courts. With coming of Age of Enlightenment, inquisitorial and secret proceedings abandoned	
1215	England: Nobles force King John to sign Magna Carta, granting jury trials	
	Rome: Pope Innocent III forbids clergy to officiate at trials by ordeal	

Time Frame	Event
17th century	England: Lord Chief Justice Coke establishes judicial independence. Rule of law firmly established by Petition of Right (1628), Habeas Corpus Act (1679), Bill of Rights (1687–88), Act of Settlement (1700)
17th–18th century	North America: English common law administered by common law courts in the colonies
18th century	United States: creation of independent judicial system, under the rule of law 1776 Declaration of Independence 1787 Constitution 1789 Bill of Rights
19th–20th century	United States: 1868 Fourteenth Amendment 1946 Federal Rules of Criminal Procedure adopted
	1953–69 Due-process revolution, led by Warren Court
Since 1965	United States: judicial education for trial judges at National Judicial College, Reno, Nevada
	1967: first African-American Supreme Court Justice, Thurgood Marshall
	1981: first woman Supreme Court Justice, Sandra Day O'Connor
Late 20th century	United States: Court system in crisis; case overload

TABLE 10.1 Business in Colonial Superior Courts by Class of Crime*

	Virginia General Court 1622–29 (67 items)	Plymouth Particular & General Court 1633–60 (260 items)	Massachusetts Assistants Court 1630–43 (290 items)	Maryland Provincial Court 1630–60 (100 items)	Connecticut Particular Court 1639–60 (193 items)
Homicide	7.4%	1.1%	2.4%	13%	2.6%
Theft	10.4	10.3	13.1	9	8.8
Drunkenness	16.4	11.6	26.9		11.9
Slander	12.0	3.0	1.4	21	22.3
Fornication	6.0	11.0	6.9	2	2.6
Other sex crimes	9.0	3.0	2.4	7	2.1
Sexual behavior[†]	1.4	8.8	9.7	7	7.8
Sedition	3.0	1.6	3.5	11	.5
Contempt	18.0	5.0	9.7	12	6.9
Religion[**]	3.0	21.9	1.4	5	5.2
Witchcraft	1.5			1	2.6
Servant[‡]	3.0	2.7	9.7	5	2.6
Lying		1.9	1.0	1	2.6
Assault and battery	6.0	8.6	2.4	5	5.7
Swearing		2.7	7.2	5	2.1
Disorderly living	3.0	6.6	2.0		12.4
Arson			.3		1.0
Piracy				2	

*All incidents are recorded, whether they resulted in conviction, acquittal, or dismissal. Figures are percent of total.
†Actions described variously as lewd behavior, filthy dalliance, unclean carriage, and lascivious conduct.
**Nonchurch attendance, working on Sabbath, blasphemy, scoffing, or reviling church or ministers.
‡Mostly runaways or court discipline of unruly servants.
SOURCE: Bradley Chapin, *Criminal Justice in Colonial America* (Athens: University of Georgia, 1983), p. 77.

"There are two legal systems in America, one implemented by the state courts, and the other created by Congress and implemented by the federal courts."

government. For good and obvious reasons they feared the tyranny that flows from the concentration of governmental power. After all, they were living in the shadow of their experience with English rule. On the other hand, they were also living with the problems associated with a weak centralized government. This conflict prompted the delegates to the Constitutional Convention (1787) to create a separate federal judiciary. As a result, there are two legal systems in America, one implemented by the state courts (inherited directly from the Crown of England) and another artificially created by the Congress and entrusted to the federal courts.

The Federal Judiciary

In one long sentence, Article III of the United States Constitution created a new branch of government and a new federal court system: "The judicial Power of the United States, shall be vested in one supreme Court, and in such inferior Courts as the Congress may from time to time ordain and establish."[8] Judges were to be appointed by the president with the advice and consent of the Senate; they were to hold office "during good behavior," which meant virtual lifetime tenure.

During the debates over ratification of the Constitution, many delegates expressed concern about Article III, fearing that it would mean an overly powerful judiciary. Congress acted swiftly and passed the Judiciary Act of 1789, which created a system of lower federal courts.

The Judiciary Act of 1789 divided the country into thirteen districts, whose boundaries generally coincided with the borders of the states. Each federal district had a **district court** and a district judge. District courts served mainly as courts of admiralty, although they also had jurisdiction in certain petty federal criminal cases. With the exception of the new states of Kentucky and Maine, the districts were grouped into three circuits: an eastern, a middle, and a southern. Two Supreme Court justices and one district judge constituted a circuit court, to be convened twice a year in each district. Supreme Court justices traveled hundreds and sometimes thousands of miles "riding the circuit."

district courts
Trial courts in the federal and in some state systems.

The Judiciary Act set the number of Supreme Court justices at six: one chief justice and five associates. George Washington, the only president who was able to appoint all the justices to the Supreme Court, established a tradition of choosing politically compatible justices. The beginnings of the court were nothing short of disappointing. Only three justices attended the first session (all three wearing robes and one wearing a wig), which opened on February 1, 1790, in the First Merchant Exchange in the Wall Street area of New York City. It lasted a mere nine days, since the court had no cases to hear. In fact, the court decided no cases in its first three years, and a total of only fifty during its first decade.[9]

"The first sitting of the U.S. Supreme Court in 1790 lasted only nine days and heard no cases."

The federal court system was restructured throughout the early 1800s. But major changes did not take place until 1891, with passage of the Circuit Court of Appeals Act, popularly called the Evarts Act, after the senator who headed the Senate Judiciary Committee. The Evarts Act created a new court known as the circuit court of appeals, with one court for each of eleven circuits. This made the old circuit courts obsolete; in 1911 Congress passed legislation that abolished them (Figure 10.1).

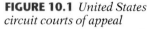

FIGURE 10.1 *United States circuit courts of appeal*

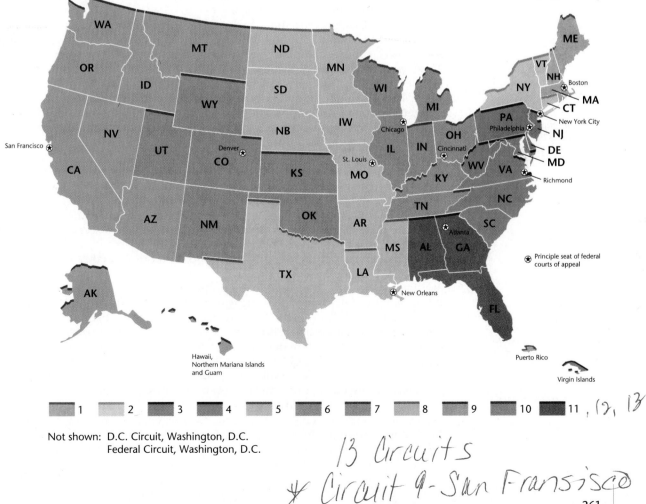

Not shown: D.C. Circuit, Washington, D.C.
Federal Circuit, Washington, D.C.

261

The new federal system was now in place: a three-level structure with a trial court (district court) at the bottom, an intermediate appellate court (court of appeals) in the middle, and the Supreme Court, the court of last resort, at the top. This three-level system has remained the basic structure of the federal judiciary, although the size of the system has grown to accommodate changes in case loads and population.

State Courts

The colonial courts, though successors to the common-law courts of England, were characterized by a lack of separation of powers among the different branches of government. In fact, colonial legislatures were viewed as the highest courts. The U.S. Constitution remedied this at the federal level by mandating a definite division between the executive, legislative, and judicial branches and by providing a system of checks and balances to ensure that all would share power equally. At the state level, however, the adoption of such a separation was slow, perhaps because of the long tradition of shared judicial functions between legislature and executive. New Jersey's constitution of 1776 provided that the governor would hold the post of chancellor. In this post he, together with his council, would constitute the "Court of Appeals," in the last resort. New York's highest court consisted of the senate president along with the senators, the chancellor, and the state supreme court justices.[10]

The slow pace at which the states embraced the concept of separation of powers was also attributable to the colonists' longstanding distrust of the courts and the common law.[11] Only during the nineteenth century did the states begin to confer judicial power exclusively on the judiciary, with the highest court in the state being given final judicial authority.

By the late 1800s, many states had established new trial and appellate courts to hear both civil and criminal cases.[12] Some states established intermediate-level courts, called circuit courts, superior courts, or courts of common pleas. These were trial courts, but some also heard appeals from lower courts. At the lowest level of the system, many courts were presided over by justices of the peace. One feature of the state systems that differentiated them from the federal was the election of judges. Traditionally, judges had been appointed by the executive, but the citizens of the new nation wanted public control of government officials. Electing judges, usually for a fixed term, was the way to assert this power. Vermont's constitution of 1777 gave the "freemen" of the state the right to choose the judges of the lower court of common pleas, the justices of the peace, and the probate judges.[13] Popular election of trial judges had become common by the 1820s, but the states resisted electing appellate judges. In 1832 Mississippi became the first state to elect all state judges for limited terms. After 1846, every new state that entered the union provided for the election of some or all judges. By 1885, 73 percent of all state judges were elected.[14]

As state courts developed, they tended to be more specialized than federal courts, with separate tribunals for probate, juvenile, small claims, and domestic relations cases. This specialization contributed to what is aptly called a "confusing array"[15] of state courts, or **court fragmentation.** Roscoe Pound, an eminent legal scholar and dean of the Harvard Law School from 1916 to 1936, was a strong advocate of **court unification,** suggesting that the various specialized courts be consolidated into one or two courts of broader jurisdiction. The standard state court system, he charged, was "a hierarchy of distinct courts, involving waste of judicial power, waste of time and money in elaborate proceedings to get from one tribunal to another, and elaborate appellate procedure."[16]

But reform has been difficult to achieve. Arthur T. Vanderbilt, the eminent legal scholar and later chief justice of the New Jersey Supreme Court, devoted a lifetime to achieving reform of the New Jersey court structure between 1937 and 1957. His success in New Jersey provided the model for the entire country.[17]

"In state systems, unlike the federal system, judges are elected: the citizens of the new nation wanted public control of government officials."

court fragmentation
The specialization of state courts into separate tribunals for probate, juvenile, small claims, domestic relations cases, and others.

court unification
Term used to describe reform efforts to consolidate various specialized state courts into one or two courts of broader jurisdiction.

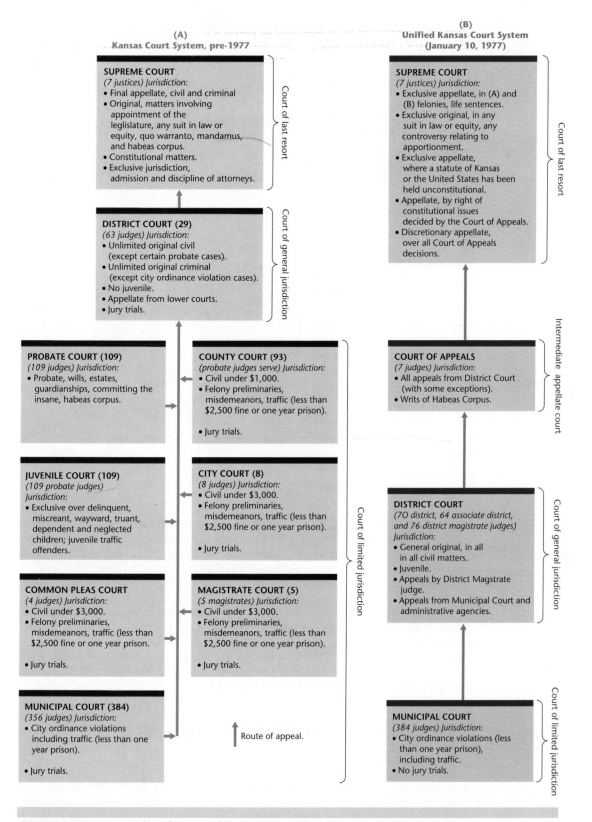

SUPREME COURT
(7 justices) Jurisdiction:
• Final appellate, civil and criminal
• Original, matters involving
  appointment of the
  legislature, any suit in law or
  equity, quo warranto, mandamus,
  and habeas corpus.
• Constitutional matters.
• Exclusive jurisdiction,
  admission and discipline of attorneys.

Court of last resort

DISTRICT COURT (29)
(63 judges) Jurisdiction:
• Unlimited original civil
  (except certain probate cases).
• Unlimited original criminal
  (except city ordinance violation cases).
• No juvenile.
• Appellate from lower courts.
• Jury trials.

Court of general jurisdiction

PROBATE COURT (109)
(109 judges) Jurisdiction:
• Probate, wills, estates,
  guardianships, committing the
  insane, habeas corpus.

COUNTY COURT (93)
(probate judges serve) Jurisdiction:
• Civil under $1,000.
• Felony preliminaries,
  misdemeanors, traffic (less than
  $2,500 fine or one year prison).

• Jury trials.

JUVENILE COURT (109)
(109 probate judges)
Jurisdiction:
• Exclusive over delinquent,
  miscreant, wayward, truant,
  dependent and neglected
  children; juvenile traffic
  offenders.

CITY COURT (8)
(8 judges) Jurisdiction:
• Civil under $3,000.
• Felony preliminaries,
  misdemeanors, traffic (less than
  $2,500 fine or one year prison).

• Jury trials.

COMMON PLEAS COURT
(4 judges) Jurisdiction:
• Civil under $3,000.
• Felony preliminaries,
  misdemeanors, traffic (less than
  $2,500 fine or one year prison.

• Jury trials.

MAGISTRATE COURT (5)
(5 magistrates) Jurisdiction:
• Civil under $3,000.
• Felony preliminaries,
  misdemeanors, traffic (less than
  $2,500 fine or one year prison).

• Jury trials.

Court of limited jurisdiction

MUNICIPAL COURT (384)
(356 judges) Jurisdiction:
• City ordinance violations
  including traffic (less than one
  year prison).

• Jury trials.

Route of appeal.

SUPREME COURT
(7 justices) Jurisdiction:
• Exclusive appellate, in (A) and
  (B) felonies, life sentences.
• Exclusive original, in any
  suit in law or equity, any
  controversy relating to
  apportionment.
• Exclusive appellate,
  where a statute of Kansas
  or the United States has been
  held unconstitutional.
• Appellate, by right of
  constitutional issues
  decided by the Court of Appeals.
• Discretionary appellate,
  over all Court of Appeals
  decisions.

Court of last resort

COURT OF APPEALS
(7 judges) Jurisdiction:
• All appeals from District Court
  (with some exceptions).
• Writs of Habeas Corpus.

Intermediate appellate court

DISTRICT COURT
*(70 district, 64 associate district,
and 76 district magistrate judges)
Jurisdiction:*
• General original, in all
  in all civil matters.
• Juvenile.
• Appeals by District Magstrate
  judge.
• Appeals from Municipal Court and
  administrative agencies.

Court of general jurisdiction

MUNICIPAL COURT
(384 judges) Jurisdiction:
• City ordinance violations (less
  than one year prison),
  including traffic.
• No jury trials.

Court of limited jurisdiction

FIGURE 10.2 *Structural unification of the Kansas courts, 1977* (*Source:* William E. Hewitt, *Courts That Succeed: Six Profiles of Successful Courts* [Williamsburg Va.: National Center for State Courts, 1990], p. 133.)

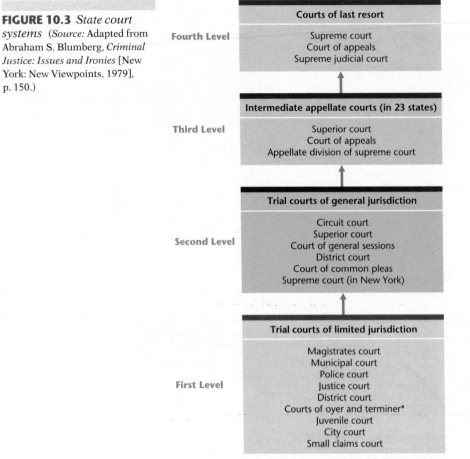

FIGURE 10.3 *State court systems* (*Source:* Adapted from Abraham S. Blumberg, *Criminal Justice: Issues and Ironies* [New York: New Viewpoints, 1979], p. 150.)

Courts of last resort

Fourth Level

Supreme court
Court of appeals
Supreme judicial court

Intermediate appellate courts (in 23 states)

Third Level

Superior court
Court of appeals
Appellate division of supreme court

Trial courts of general jurisdiction

Second Level

Circuit court
Superior court
Court of general sessions
District court
Court of common pleas
Supreme court (in New York)

Trial courts of limited jurisdiction

First Level

Magistrates court
Municipal court
Police court
Justice court
District court
Courts of oyer and terminer*
Juvenile court
City court
Small claims court

*As limited jurisdiction courts are called in some states

By the 1970s, as Figure 10.2(A) shows, Kansas too had an elaborate system: Under the state supreme court there were eight inferior courts, each with a different jurisdiction. In an effort to cut back on delay, increase communication, and maintain accountability, Kansas moved to a more centralized and unified system with just three inferior courts [Figure 10.2(B)]. The result was significantly less delay.

Yet many state court systems are still characterized by overlapping jurisdictional boundaries, a lack of supervision of lower courts, and decentralized budgeting and personnel systems. Reformers generally believe a unified system could eliminate many of the problems and inefficiencies associated with fragmentation.[18] Opponents fear that unification will take away control from local courts and impose a centralized bureaucracy.

STATE COURTS: ORGANIZATION AND ROLE

We begin our detailed examination of the two court structures with the state court system, since it began at the moment of independence and simply continued the prerevolutionary (royal) system but under republican auspices. Moreover, there is far more activity in the state courts than in federal courts. In 1990, for example, 100,555,147 cases were filed in the trial courts of the fifty states, the

District of Columbia, and Puerto Rico, including 13,074,146 criminal and 18,382,137 civil cases. Juvenile cases accounted for an additional 1,543,667 cases, but the great majority concerned traffic and other local law violations, which numbered 67,555,197.[19]

Most states have a three-tier system of courts: courts of limited or special jurisdiction, courts of general jurisdiction, and a double tier of appellate courts (Figure 10.3). We will start our description at the lowest level.

Courts of Limited or Special Jurisdiction

Dimmit County, Texas, has been called "an easy target" and "the land that law forgot," because the judge who presides over the local court has had no trials in fourteen years. According to friends, the former service-station clerk is simply "nervous" about the trial process. As a nonlawyer, he may feel at a distinct disadvantage.[20]

But if nonlawyer judges feel disadvantaged, at least they are not alone. Most every town or city has a court with a **justice of the peace,** magistrate, or judge, who is not necessarily trained in law, who handles minor criminal cases (misdemeanors or violations), less serious civil suits (involving small sums of money), traffic and parking violations, and health law violations. These courts are variously called municipal courts, justice of the peace courts, and magistrate's courts. They are known more generally as **courts of limited jurisdiction.**

Courts of limited jurisdiction have been called the "workhorses of the state judiciary." This is a well-deserved name. As of 1989 there were 14,126 courts of limited jurisdiction in forty-four states, with 18,738 magistrates, district judges, and justices of the peace. Courts of limited jurisdiction tried approximately 62 percent of all the cases tried in state courts. Criminal cases accounted for 13 percent, civil cases for 12 percent, and juvenile cases for 1.5 percent of the trials carried out in courts of limited jurisdiction in 1989. The balance of the cases were traffic and local law violations.[21] **Courts of special jurisdiction** include courts that specialize in certain areas of law: family courts, juvenile courts, and probate courts (which deal with the transfer of property and money of a deceased).

Keeping pace with the growing number of cases filed has been difficult for most trial courts. A survey of twenty-four states in 1989 showed that only two of them were able to dispose of more pending cases than the number of new cases filed. The remaining twenty-two states ended the year with more cases on their dockets than when they started.[22]

Courts of General Jurisdiction

At the next level are the major trial courts—**courts of general jurisdiction.** Such courts have regular jurisdiction over all cases and controversies involving civil law and criminal law. Courts of general jurisdiction are typically county courts but, in less populated states, may be courts of a region that includes several counties. They may be called superior courts or district courts, and their judges are law-school graduates, often with extensive experience at the bar. They are either elected or appointed.

The 2,449 state courts of general jurisdiction in the United States, consisting of 9,250 judges, heard approximately 28 percent of the trial court cases in 1989. In six states (Idaho, Illinois, Iowa, Massachusetts, Minnesota, and South Dakota) and the District of Columbia, the court of general jurisdiction is the lowest level court because there are no courts of limited jurisdiction. Traffic and other ordinance violations still account for the majority (52%) of the cases heard in the courts of general jurisdiction, but the proportion of such cases is much lower than in the courts of limited jurisdiction. Civil cases represent the next largest (31%) category of cases heard, followed by criminal (13%) and juvenile (4%)

justice of the peace
Originally a judicial officer, normally not learned in the law, assigned to investigate and try minor cases. Presently, a judge of a lower local or municipal court with limited jurisdiction.

courts of limited jurisdiction
Courts (with a justice of the peace, magistrate, or judge presiding) that handle minor criminal cases, less serious civil suits, traffic and parking violations, and health law violations.

courts of special jurisdiction
Courts that specialize in certain areas of law: family courts, juvenile courts, probate courts (transfer of property and money of deceased).

have been called the 'workhorses' of the state judiciary."

courts of general jurisdiction
Major trial courts that have regular, unlimited jurisdictions over all cases and controversies involving civil and criminal law.

cases.[23] Like the lower trial courts, the general jurisdiction courts were unable to keep pace with the rate of new cases filed in 1989. A survey of forty states showed that thirty-five began 1990 with bigger case loads than they had at the start of 1989.[24]

Appellate Courts

James Cecil Law, Jr., decided to purchase a thirty-nine-dollar shotgun. Why? He and his wife had recently moved into a new neighborhood and were burglarized within two weeks of their arrival. The shotgun, along with special locks on the windows, would protect the home. Several weeks after the purchase of the shotgun, a neighbor of Law's called police to investigate a strange light that appeared to come from Law's home. The police arrived and first checked all doors. They started looking at the condition of the windows and found a broken pane of glass on a door. An officer removed the pane and stuck his hand through the opening to see whether he could open the door. As the officer reached inside, Law, suspecting another burglary, fired his shotgun through the door, killing the officer.

A jury found Law guilty of second-degree murder and assault with intent to murder. He was sentenced to two concurrent ten-year prison sentences. Law appealed: He asked the Maryland Court of Appeals to consider if (1) there was sufficient evidence to sustain a conviction, (2) the trial court's instructions to the jury unfairly shifted the burden of proof, and (3) the degree of force used by Law was justifiable in light of the circumstances. You may be disappointed to learn that Judge Lowe of the Maryland Court of Appeals affirmed Law's conviction, ruling that he had failed to establish the necessity of his conduct.[25]

Maryland, like all other states, has developed elaborate procedures of appeal for parties who are unsuccessful at trial. In criminal cases this refers exclusively to those claiming to be unjustly convicted. In some states the only **appellate court** is the state's supreme court; others provide an intermediate court of appeals. A person convicted of a crime has the right to appeal to an appellate court and ultimately to the court of last resort, usually the state supreme court, whenever the trial court is alleged to have erred on a point of law. Some appeals are mandatory—the appellate court is required to hear the case (death sentences

"The fair and efficient administration of the law in trial court is the cornerstone of justice."
American Bar Association Commission on Standards of Judicial Administration, 1975.

appellate court
Court with the power to review the judgment of a trial court, examining errors of law.

General jurisdiction courtroom: Lawyers argue a point before the judge as the jury listens.

often result in mandatory appeals). States can also permit their appellate courts to choose which appeals they will hear in certain categories of cases. These are known as discretionary appeals.

Intermediate Appellate Courts and Supreme Courts

The majority (thirty-two) of states have one intermediate appellate court and a single court of last resort, which is usually called the **state supreme court** but in some states is known as the supreme judicial court or the court of appeals. Texas and Oklahoma have two separate courts of last resort, one for civil and one for criminal appeals. Supreme courts consist of five to nine justices, usually sitting together (*en banc*) to hear a case, although in some states they will divide into panels for certain cases.

In most states with intermediate appellate courts, appeals from trial courts automatically go to that court before going to the state's court of last resort (Figure 10.4). Only a small proportion of intermediate appeals decisions are reviewed by the courts of last resort, thus making the intermediate appellate court the final arbiter in many cases.[26] And what are the chances of a successful appeal? In reviewing the work of a sample of state supreme courts over a 100-year period, Stanton Wheeler and his colleagues found that an average of 60 percent of lower-court rulings were affirmed by the supreme courts. Of the criminal appeals filed during this time frame, the government has become far more successful than individuals in their appeals: The government was successful in 68 percent of the criminal appeals filed between 1935 and 1970, the latest period Wheeler examined.[27]

The intermediate appellate courts handle the majority of appeals filed at the state level. Of the 238,007 appeals filed in these courts in the fifty states and the District of Columbia in 1990, 70.5 percent were heard in the intermediate courts. Of the more than 167,000 appeals filed in the intermediate appellate courts, 88.7 percent were mandatory appeals. Only 36 percent of the 70,235 appeals to the state supreme courts, on the other hand, were mandatory.[28]

State appellate courts have fared somewhat better than the trial courts in keeping pace with the rate of new filings. In 1989, intermediate appellate courts in thirteen of thirty states reduced their case load of cases pending during the year, while fourteen of thirty-one state supreme courts did so.[29]

state supreme court
State court of last resort (except in certain jurisdictions, where the supreme court is a trial court of unlimited jurisdiction).

Can go to U.S. Sup. Ct.

"Justice is truth in action."
Benjamin Disraeli, speech, February 11, 1851.

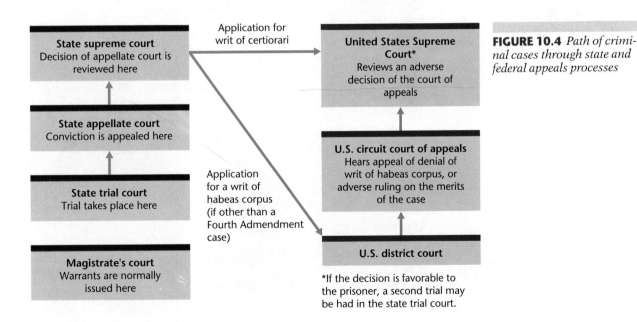

FIGURE 10.4 *Path of criminal cases through state and federal appeals processes*

State supreme court — Decision of appellate court is reviewed here

State appellate court — Conviction is appealed here

State trial court — Trial takes place here

Magistrate's court — Warrants are normally issued here

Application for writ of certiorari

Application for a writ of habeas corpus (if other than a Fourth Admendment case)

United States Supreme Court* — Reviews an adverse decision of the court of appeals

U.S. circuit court of appeals — Hears appeal of denial of writ of habeas corpus, or adverse ruling on the merits of the case

U.S. district court

*If the decision is favorable to the prisoner, a second trial may be had in the state trial court.

THE SHAPE OF THE COURTS

Nearly all courts, everywhere in the world, are the same: a rectangular room, boxlike, with several boxes placed inside it for the judge (or judges), for the jury, for the prosecutor, for the defendant and defense counsel, and for the spectators (Figure 1). The boxes may simply be represented by tables, benches, or railings, or there may be actual "cages" in which the defendant sits or stands, as is the case in Russia.

In other countries, including France, Germany, and the United States, the judge's bench is elevated above all the other "boxes," with the psychological effect of dwarfing the defendant (Figure 2).

How did the world end up with box-shaped courts? The word "court" is derived from the Latin *co-hortus* (later contracted to *cohort* or *court*), meaning "being together in the same garden"—the garden of a medieval castle, or its courtyard.

The castles, and their garden-yards, belonged to feudal rulers. In these yards contests were held, such as jousting, jumping, and dancing, and also contests of a more serious sort—contests for the truth of an accusation, or criminal trials. At that time criminal trials were conducted just like mock combats among knights: Accuser and accused would battle each other, personally or using a more capable substitute fighter. The feudal ruler observed the fighters from the cas-

tle steps or the balcony, making sure the combatants played by the rules, and ultimately pronounced the winner.

Much later, rulers conducted criminal trials in special houses established for the purpose: the house of the ruler's court, or the "court house." Many courts have retained the two prominent features of the medieval court: the idea that trial is a battle between two opposing parties, and the square battleground, or court. Like the criminal trials held in the medieval rulers' courtyards, the place, the time, and the rules of the game are established.

Criminal trials have not always been this way. Among the ancient Germanic peoples, trial was conducted by an *Umstand,* a gathering around of all the tribesmen, with accuser and accused standing in the middle. The tribesmen would listen to the evidence and announce their judgment by clanging spears and shields together.

Many of the peoples whom some call primitive conduct their trials in the same manner to this day, with those sitting in judgment forming a circle. Some industrialized nations also use circular courts. Sweden recently has returned to

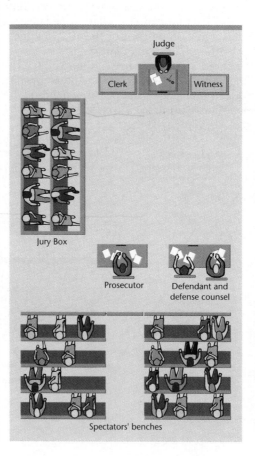

Judge

Clerk **Witness**

Jury Box

Prosecutor **Defendant and defense counsel**

Spectators' benches

FIGURE 1. The Standard Rectangular Courtroom
(*Source:* Freda Adler, Gerhard O. W. Mueller, and William S. Laufer, *Criminology* [New York: McGraw-Hill, 1991], p. 422.)

FIGURE 2. A Prisoner's Perspective of a Judge

the circular approach to trying criminal cases, as this depiction of a criminal trial shows (Figure 3).

A criminal trial is held when one person is alleged to have violated the communal rules, and it is convened to determine how the communal peace can be restored. Does the shape of the court affect the way in which this is accomplished? A circular court is very different from an array of confronting boxes in a rectangular structure. Opposing boxes signify opposition and amplify the idea of a contest, of a battle. The circle is the opposite of the confrontation model; it signifies a getting together, a unity of purpose in resolving a problem with which all are faced. It is a conflict-resolution model.

Several American courtrooms recently have been constructed on the circular model. As contemporary courtrooms of both styles are used, we may discover whether outcomes depend on the shape of the courts or on the people within them (Figure 4).

QUESTIONS FOR DISCUSSION

1. The boxlike courtroom shape and structure has lasted for centuries; perhaps it has some benefits. What might these be?
2. Does the circular model lend itself more to some types of cases than to others? Give some examples of cases in which "communal problem-solving" might be more appropriate than a battle between opposing forces.
3. Would rules of procedure, evidence, and so on have to change for the United States to use the circular courtroom model instead of the rectangular model?

FIGURE 3. A Swedish Criminal Trial, in a Circular Courtroom
(*Source:* Brochure, the National Courts Administration, Sweden.)

FIGURE 4. Round courtroom, Rockville, MD, 1990

FEDERAL COURTS: ORGANIZATION AND ROLE

Imagine traveling with a friend to Barbados on a scuba-diving trip. After working hard all semester, this is a needed vacation. You pack your wet suit, fins, snorkel, and compass in a suitcase and place your fishing knife (5 1/2-inch blade) in an overnight bag, which is carried over your shoulder. Walking through the metal detector at the airport, you realize that the overnight bag is in the process of being examined because an x-ray machine has disclosed the presence of the knife—a deadly weapon.

Are you liable? Have you suddenly been transformed into a federal offender? The answer is "yes" to both questions:

[W]hoever—(a) while aboard or attempting to board any such aircraft has on or about his person or his property a concealed deadly or dangerous weapon which is, or could be, accessible to such person in flight; shall be fined not more than $10,000 or imprisoned not more than one year, or both.[30]

This law, part of the Federal Aviation Act of 1958, was passed by Congress to deter would-be skyjackers. You have become an unfortunate victim of federal legislation designed to deter anyone from committing air piracy.

The primary function of the **federal courts** is to apply and enforce all federal laws created by Congress, such as the Federal Aviation Act of 1958. These laws, in the form of statutes or codified law, include a large body of federal criminal laws, which range from violations of the Migratory Bird Act to treason and piracy. Most of the federal criminal laws can be found in one title or chapter (Title 18) in the comprehensive collection of federal statutes called the U.S. Code. But there are more than 1,700 non-Title-18 federal statutes that have criminal penalties. All of these crimes have been created to protect the powers of the federal government to carry out both domestic and foreign policy.

The federal courts have a second and perhaps even more important function: They are continually called on to test the constitutionality of federal and state legislation and of court decisions. Let us begin with an example. Can a state pass and enforce a statute making it a criminal offense for black and white citizens to intermarry? In *Loving v. Virginia* (1967), the Supreme Court of the United States resoundingly said no.[31] The states cannot create such a crime because it violates the equal protection clause of the Fourteenth Amendment to the Constitution. In other words, the United States Supreme Court (a federal court) has the power to hold as a matter of law that a state cannot enact a statute that violates the United States Constitution. Consider another example, this time from the realm of criminal procedure. Can a state court receive in evidence at trial an object seized by state or local law enforcement officers in violation of the Fourth Amendment, which protects citizens against unreasonable searches and seizures? No, said the Supreme Court in *Mapp v. Ohio*, the Fourth Amendment, under the due process guarantee of the Fourteenth Amendment, protects all people in the United States.[32]

Federal Magistrates

At the lowest level of jurisdiction are the federal magistrates, formerly called United States Commissioners. The magistrates not only have trial jurisdiction over minor federal offenses, but they also have the important task of issuing warrants of arrest or search warrants to federal law enforcement officers, such as agents of the Federal Bureau of Investigation and the Drug Enforcement Administration. (See Chapter 6.) Congress recently expanded the power of the federal magistrates by allowing them to "undertake virtually any task performed by district judges, except for felony trials and sentencing."[33]

federal courts
Courts of the federal system, applying federal law, with power to test the constitutionality of state law and adjudicate controversies arising between residents of two or more states.

"Federal courts are continually called on to test the constitutionality of federal and state legislation and of court decisions."

United States District Courts

94

The trial courts in the federal system, called United States district courts, have both civil and criminal jurisdiction. There are ninety-four federal district courts, including those in Guam, the Virgin Islands, the northern Marianas, and Puerto Rico. Every state has at least one such court, and the populous states have more than one. As of 1990, a total of 649 presidentially appointed judges were sitting in these courts.

During 1990, 258,961 civil and criminal cases were filed in the district courts, of which 47,335 (18.3%) were criminal cases involving 67,188 defendants. The total number of cases filed declined for the second year in a row, although criminal cases continued to increase, albeit at a slower rate than they had in recent years. While the total case load of the district courts grew 27 percent in the decade from 1980 to 1990, the number of criminal cases filed increased nearly 64 percent during the same period. As a result of this increase in filings, the number of pending criminal cases has also increased, by 46 percent since 1986.[34]

Drug cases represent the single largest category of criminal cases filed (26% of all criminal filings in 1990). These figures probably fail to reveal the full extent of drug-related cases brought before the district courts. The Anti-Drug Abuse Act of 1988 designated drug crimes as "crimes of violence" and enabled the United States to wage a "war on drugs" with weapons of war and immigration laws. In 1991, the attorney general announced "Operation Triggerlock," an enforcement effort aimed at finding and prosecuting individuals and drug gangs that violate federal weapons laws.[35] The result: in one year, a 15-percent increase in immigration cases and a 20-percent increase in weapons and firearms cases. Another "hidden" area of drug-related cases is civil suits filed to seize assets in criminal drug cases. In 1990 alone, these suits increased 180 percent.

"Drug cases represent the single largest category of criminal cases filed."

In 1974, Congress passed the Speedy Trial Act, which requires that all criminal cases be brought to trial within 100 days or be dismissed. Quite obviously, criminal cases are now given priority over civil cases in the district courts. But this has resulted in civil suits having to wait years to be heard. In 1990, the number of civil cases pending three or more years in the district courts increased from 25,222 to 27,204. District Court Judge Charles Richey lamented: "I'm a drug judge five days a week and a civil judge at night and on the weekend."[36]

"In all criminal prosecutions, the accused shall enjoy the right to a speedy and public trial, by an impartial jury of the State and district wherein the crime shall have been committed."
U.S. Constitution, Amendment VI.

United States Circuit Courts of Appeal

An appeal of a conviction in a federal district court is heard by a United States **circuit court of appeal.** There are thirteen appeals courts: one in each of eleven circuits, plus one in the District of Columbia and another (since 1982), also in Washington, D.C., called the Federal Circuit. The last handles appeals that originate anywhere in the country when they pertain to such matters as patents and copyrights, some tax disputes, and suits against the federal government. There are 167 federal appeals court judges (see Figure 10.1).

circuit courts of appeal
Federal appellate courts with the power to review judgments of federal district courts (see appellate court).

The original designation of states included within the federal circuits was made when most of the business of the federal courts was on the heavily populated East Coast and in the Midwest. Because the West Coast has since become very populous, the Ninth Circuit, which covers a vast area, has more business than any of the other courts.

In 1965, 6,766 cases were filed in the courts of appeal.[37] Twenty-five years later the number had increased more than 500 percent, to 40,982. Analysis of the circuit court case loads reveals the diversity of cases heard. In 1984, criminal cases constituted 31.3 percent of the cases heard in the Eleventh Circuit and only 5.2 percent of the cases in the District of Columbia Circuit. There are also variations in the rates of reversal and dismissal of the cases heard by the courts of appeal. Nearly one-third of prisoners' civil rights petitions were dismissed in 1984, compared with only 10 percent of social security cases.[38]

The Supreme Court of the United States

In 1982, Heath Wilkins was 16 years old when he, and his accomplice Patrick Stevens, walked into a convenience store in Avondale, Missouri. Wilkins' plan was to "rob the store" and murder "whoever was behind the counter." In Wilkins' own words, "a dead person can't talk." That evening, Nancy Allen was behind the counter. She was 26 years old, the mother of two children. Stevens held Allen as Wilkins stabbed her repeatedly. Allen begged for her life, which prompted Wilkins to stab her four more times. Wilkins and his accomplice helped themselves to $450 in cash and checks, liquor, cigarettes, and rolling papers. They then left the store as Allen bled to death on the floor.

Due to the nature of the crime, the juvenile court approved the transfer of the case to superior court, where Wilkins was tried as an adult for first-degree murder. He was convicted and sentenced to death. After an appeal to the supreme court of Missouri failed, Wilkins sought review by the U.S. Supreme Court. He wanted the Court to resolve a question of great constitutional importance: Does the imposition of the death penalty on a 16-year-old violate the Eighth Amendment to the Constitution? In other words, is it cruel and unusual punishment to use the death penalty on juveniles? Wilkins asked the Court to draw the line (according to chronological age) below which the death penalty would violate our evolving standards of decency—and that age should be 16 and younger. The Court did not agree. In 1989 Justice Scalia, writing for the Court, concluded: "We discern neither a historical nor a modern societal consensus forbidding the imposition of capital punishment on any person who murders at 16 or 17 years of age. Accordingly, we conclude that such punishment does not offend the Eighth Amendment's prohibition against cruel and unusual punishment."[39]

"The power of the U.S. Supreme Court is not equaled by the courts of any other country."

The Supreme Court of the United States occupies a unique position in our system of government. It represents the highest echelon of the third branch of government, the judiciary. The power of the Court is not equaled by courts of any other country. The chief justice is not just the chief justice of the Supreme Court but the chief justice of the United States. The chief justice and the eight associate justices are appointed by the president of the United States, with the advice and consent of the Senate (Figure 10.5).

"What has once been settled by a precedent will not be unsettled overnight. . . . "
Benjamin Cardozo, *The Paradoxes of Legal Science.*

Each year approximately 5,000 cases are filed in the Supreme Court asking for review. The justices agree to hear only a few hundred of them and have time to issue only about 150 written opinions per year. As in the *Wilkins* case, these deal with significant areas of the law and interpretations of the Constitution. Over the years, the Court has focused on specific areas. Earlier this century, for example, the Court issued an extensive number of rulings that dealt with economic regulation. Beginning at mid-century, the Court's attention shifted to civil rights, an area in which the Court has led the way for the other branches of government in instituting important social changes.

United States Supreme Court
Federal court that has ultimate authority in interpreting the Constitution as it applies to federal and state law; final authority in interpreting federal law.

The **United States Supreme Court** is the ultimate authority in interpreting the Constitution as it applies to both federal and state law. It also is the final authority in interpreting federal law. Thus, both federal and state cases may reach the Supreme Court.

INTERACTION BETWEEN STATE COURTS AND FEDERAL COURTS

It is important not to view the state and the federal court systems as wholly independent or mutually exclusive. A legal controversy that arises in a state court may raise federal constitutional questions. In such a case, a federal court may be asked to resolve the federal constitutional question, as it did in *Loving v. Virginia* and *Mapp v. Ohio.* (See the Criminal Justice on Trial box.)

Suppose, for example, that on the tip of an anonymous informer, with no corroborating evidence, a local magistrate issues a search warrant authorizing the search of a college dormitory room for marijuana. Suppose further that several joints are found in the drawer of a desk that is used by two students. Both are arrested, tried in a local court, and convicted of the crime of possession of a controlled substance. Defense counsel claims that the search warrant was illegally issued, because it was not based on the constitutionally required "probable cause" that a crime was committed. Therefore, the evidence—the joints—should never have been admitted in court. Suppose the state trial judge does not agree with this defense.

Appeal and the Writ of Certiorari. The students decide to appeal their conviction, claiming that the trial judge committed a legal error by not excluding the evidence. Suppose the state court of appeals (if there is one) rules against the students. They next appeal to the state supreme court. If the state supreme court rejects the argument as well, the next option is to appeal to the United States Supreme Court. The basis of this appeal is the violation of a federal constitutional right, under the Fourth Amendment, to be free from unreasonable searches and seizures. This option is exercised by an application for a **writ of certiorari,** a document issued by a higher court (in this case the United States Supreme Court) directing a lower court (the state supreme court) to send to it the records of the case.

The Supreme Court may accept this case because it has established the rule that a search warrant issued on the basis of an unreliable informant's tip does not meet the reasonableness test and probable cause requirements of the Fourth Amendment.[40] But, as we noted earlier, the Supreme Court receives thousands of appeals and applications for writs of certiorari every year; it can consider only very few. Normally the Court chooses to review a case only if the case involves a substantial unresolved constitutional question, particularly one on which the findings of the various federal courts of appeals have diverged.

writ of certiorari
Document issued by a higher court directing a lower court to prepare the record of a case and send it to the higher court for review.

COURTROOM SEATING OF THE JUSTICES, MARSHAL, CLERK AND COUNSEL

THE SUPREME COURT OF THE UNITED STATES

```
      8  6  4    2  1  3    5  7  9
 10                                        11
                    12
```

1. Chief Justice Rehnquist

2. Justice White	3. Justice Blackmun
4. Justice Stevens	5. Justice O'Connor
6. Justice Scalia	7. Justice Kennedy
8. Justice Souter	9. Justice Thomas
10. Clerk of the Court	11. Marshal of the Court

12. Counsel

FIGURE 10.5 *The Supreme Court of the United States, 1992–1993 term. Justice White retired in 1993; Ruth Bader Ginsburg was confirmed to succeed Justice White in August 1993.*

Rehnquist	White	Blackmun	Stevens	O'Connor	Scalia	Kennedy	Souter	Thomas

THE SUPREME COURT AND PUBLIC OPINION

Should young offenders receive the death penalty?

Should retarded people who commit murder be executed?

Do sobriety checkpoints constitute an unreasonable search and thus violate the Constitution?

Should flag burning be allowed?

It is nearly impossible for many Americans to avoid taking a position every time the Supreme Court decides a case, and public opinion polls conducted by Roper, Gallup, Harris, the Eagleton Institute (Rutgers University), and various news media often include questions about Supreme Court decisions. Over the last decade, the court has grown increasingly conservative. Do citizen views match those of the justices? Let us compare your opinions with court decisions and with public opinion poll data for seven recent Supreme Court cases ranging from death penalty decisions to decisions on abortion.

Performing drug tests

THE CASE: *National Treasury Employees Union v. Von Raab,* 489 U.S. 656 (March 21, 1989).

THE SUPREME COURT: Upheld the right to perform reasonable drug tests.

PUBLIC OPINION: "Would you favor (drug testing) for those responsible for the safety of others, such as surgeons, airplane pilots, and police

officers, or would that be an unfair invasion of privacy?"

    Yes, favor—83 percent
    No, unfair—11 percent
    Depends—3 percent
    No opinion—3 percent

(CBS, *The New York Times poll,* August 18–21, 1986)

Using checkpoints

THE CASE: *Michigan Department of State Police v. Stitz,* 496 U.S. 444 (June 14, 1990)

THE SUPREME COURT: Upheld the right to use checkpoints to stop cars and check for drunk drivers.

PUBLIC OPINION: "Do you favor or oppose the use of random police checks at toll booths to check drivers for signs of alcohol and drug intoxication?"

    Yes, favor—74 percent
    No, oppose—25 percent
    Not sure—1 percent

(Harris poll, January 11–February 11, 1990)

Raising the drinking age

THE CASE: *South Dakota v. Dole,* 483 U.S. 203 (June 23, 1987)

THE SUPREME COURT: Upheld the power of Congress to raise the drinking age to 21 across the country, but indirectly, under Congress's spending powers.

PUBLIC OPINION: "Would you favor or oppose having the federal government start withholding funds from these states if they fail to raise their drinking age to 21 by October first?"

    Yes, favor—64 percent
    No, oppose—32 percent
    No opinion—4 percent

(Gallup poll, June 9–16, 1988)

No abortions in public hospitals

THE CASE: *Webster v. Reproductive Health Services,* 492 U.S. 490 (July 3, 1989)

THE SUPREME COURT: Gave any state the right to prohibit public employees or public hospitals from performing abortions except to save the mother's life.

PUBLIC OPINION: "Are you in favor of that part of the decision, or are you opposed to it?"

    Yes, favor—56 percent
    No, oppose—40 percent
    Not sure—4 percent

(*Los Angeles Times* poll, July 3, 1989)

Executing 16-Year-Olds

THE CASES: *Wilkins v. Missouri* and *Stanford v. Kentucky,* 106 L. Ed. 2d 306 (June 26, 1989)

THE SUPREME COURT: Upheld the right to execute 16-year-olds.

PUBLIC OPINION: "In many states, one of the criminal punishments that is available is the death penalty. Some people think that persons convicted of murder committed when they are under 18 years old should never be executed, while other people think it is right to execute those who are under the age of 18 at the time the crime was committed. Which is closer to the way you think, that young people who are convicted of murder committed when they are under 18 years old should never be executed, or is it right to execute young people for a murder they committed before they were 18?"

    Never execute—49 percent
    Right to execute—44 percent
    Not sure—7 percent

(Harris poll, June 3–September 12, 1988)

Reverse discrimination

THE CASE: *Johnson v. Transportation Agency of Santa Clara County,* 480 U.S. 616 (March 25, 1987)

THE SUPREME COURT: Ruled that employers may sometimes favor women and minorities over better qualified men and whites in hiring and promoting to achieve better balance in their work forces.

PUBLIC OPINION: "Do you approve or disapprove of this decision?"
Yes, approve—29 percent
No, disapprove—63 percent
No opinion—8 percent

(Gallup poll, April 10–13, 1987)

Executing retarded defendants

THE CASE: *Penry v. Lynaugh,* 492 U.S. 302 (June 26, 1989)

THE SUPREME COURT: Upheld the right to execute retarded defendants.

PUBLIC OPINION: "Some people think that persons convicted of murder who have a mental age of less than 18 (or the 'retarded') should not be executed. Other people think that 'retarded' persons should be subject to the death penalty like anyone else. Which is closer to the way you feel, that 'retarded' persons should not be executed, or that 'retarded' persons should be subject to the death penalty like anyone else?"
Should not be executed—71 percent
Should be executed—21 percent
Depends—4 percent
Not sure—3 percent

(Harris poll, June 3–September 12, 1988)

SOURCE

Thomas R. Marshall, "Public Opinion and the Rehnquist Court," *Judicature* 74 (6): 324–325 (April/May 1991).

QUESTIONS FOR DISCUSSION

1. Would you expect the Supreme Court rulings to be consistent with public opinion?
2. Do you think that the nomination process for Supreme Court justices should include an examination of the political or ideological orientation of the nominee?
3. Is there any consistency in the unpopular versus popular decisions?

FIGURE 1. Popular and Unpopular Rulings by the Rehnquist Court, from Public Opinion Polls. Plus and Minus Ratings (in Percentages) Show Preponderance of Opinion on a Given Decision.
(*Source:* Adapted from Thomas R. Marshall, "Public Opinion and the Rehnquist Court," *Judicature* 74 [6] [April–May 1991]:323.)

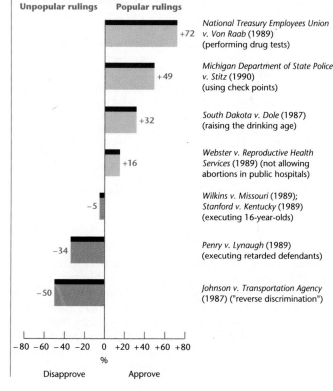

Unpopular rulings	Popular rulings	
	+72	*National Treasury Employees Union v. Von Raab* (1989) (performing drug tests)
	+49	*Michigan Department of State Police v. Stitz* (1990) (using check points)
	+32	*South Dakota v. Dole* (1987) (raising the drinking age)
	+16	*Webster v. Reproductive Health Services* (1989) (not allowing abortions in public hospitals)
−5		*Wilkins v. Missouri* (1989); *Stanford v. Kentucky* (1989) (executing 16-year-olds)
−34		*Penry v. Lynaugh* (1989) (executing retarded defendants)
−50		*Johnson v. Transportation Agency* (1987) ("reverse discrimination")

−80 −60 −40 −20   0   +20 +40 +60 +80
%
Disapprove   Approve

habeas corpus
Writ requesting that a person or institution detaining a named prisoner bring him or her before a judicial officer and give reasons for the detention.

Habeas Corpus. Having been denied a writ of certiorari by the Supreme Court, the students may apply for a writ of **habeas corpus** at the federal district court. Historically, under the common law of England, a prisoner's detention could be tested by a judicial writ (command) to a jailer for an inquiry. Written in Latin, the writ contained the crucial words *habeas corpus,* which means "you have the body (person) of . . . ." The text of the writ concluded with a request to produce the prisoner before the reviewing judge, and to explain by what lawful authority the prisoner is being detained. Used in Anglo-American law since the seventeenth century, such inquiries still determine whether the Constitution was violated during the trial that resulted in the conviction that led to imprisonment.

In our hypothetical case, until 1976 the student could indeed have applied to the federal district court for a writ of habeas corpus. But in that year the United States Supreme Court held that the writ was no longer available in Fourth Amendment search-and-seizure cases because the federal courts were so flooded with applications they could not manage the case load.[41] Whenever the alleged constitutional violation pertains to issues other than search and seizure, the writ is still legally available. If the district court denies the writ of habeas corpus, the prisoner can appeal that decision to a United States court of appeal. If that court does not overrule the district court, the prisoner can appeal again to the United States Supreme Court (Figure 10.4).

THE FUTURE OF THE COURTS: ISSUES

In 1992 Chief Justice Benjamin K. Miller of the Illinois state supreme court called a meeting of lawyers, judges, and academics to reflect on how America's court system should evolve in the twenty-first century. According to Miller, "The conference mission is to identify the forces and trends that can be discerned and to begin building the type of judicial system we will want to have 30 years from now."[42] To some, the conference seemed to fall short of expectations: There were no magic cures, no simple answers, just many questions and concerns, and much anxiety.

"The single most significant issue for federal and state judiciary is mushrooming case loads."

If you were to ask judicial leaders what single issue has most affected the judiciary at both the federal and the state levels in recent years, they would say: case loads. For example, at the federal level, the number of cases filed in the district courts tripled between 1958 and 1988; ten times more appeals were filed in 1988 than in 1958.[43] At the state level, cases filed at the trial level increased 62 percent in the six years from 1984 to 1990; appeals in state courts grew by a more modest 36 percent during the same period, but this slowed growth followed three decades in which the number of appeals filed in state appellate courts doubled every ten years.[44] The increases far outpaced the growth in population during the same period. The Administrative Office of the United States courts predicts that filings in the federal district courts will certainly triple in the next twenty-five years, and case loads in the courts of appeal will nearly triple during this time.[45]

Federal Issues

The chief justice of the United States, William Rehnquist, recently characterized the federal courts as "an exhaustible resource."[46] The supply of judges has not kept up with the demand. Between 1958 and 1988, Congress more than doubled the number of federal district and appellate judgeships. Yet there has been a sixfold increase in the case load of appellate judges since 1945. The problem is exacerbated by the fact that the president has run into difficulties making judicial appointments. The situation in the Southern District of New York demonstrates the point. There, as of August 1991, of twenty-eight seats on the bench, seven were vacant. The reasons for the shortage: delays in screening, selection, and confirmation; inadequate salaries; and an increased scrutiny of a candidate's political orientation. According to Conrad Harper, president of the New York City Bar Association: "It is simply unconscionable for us to have this number of vacancies, and it needs prompt remedy . . . . It has a decisive and terrible influence upon the prompt dispatch of justice."[47]

In 1988 Congress authorized the creation of the Federal Courts Study Committee to assess the federal judiciary and its relationship to the states, analyze the federal court structure, and develop a long-range plan, including legislative recommendations. The final report of this committee was issued in 1990 with a series of recommendations, including

- shifting some drug-related cases currently being filed in federal courts to the state courts. Drug cases in the federal courts should be limited to those arising from large drug ring operations on a multistate or multinational basis. Reason: From 1980 to 1990, drug case filings in the federal district courts increased 280 percent. In 1990, they accounted for 26 percent of all federal criminal trials and 60 percent of all pending federal criminal appeals[48]
- placing new requirements for the filing of civil rights petitions by state prison inmates seeking remedies for infringements of their civil rights due to the conditions of their imprisonment. The committee's plan would require that prisoners exhaust all remedies available under state law before being allowed to turn to the federal courts. The reason: Civil rights suits are civil suits and now constitute 11 percent of all civil suits filed in the federal district courts, up from 1 percent in 1958[49]
- recodifying federal criminal laws. The reason: The existing code has become

hard to find, hard to understand, redundant, and conflicting . . . . Important offenses, such as murder and kidnapping, are commingled with trivial offenses like reproducing the image of "Smokey the Bear" without permission (18 U.S. C. § 711) and taking false teeth into a state without the approval of a local dentist (18 U.S. C. § 1821)[50]

- reviewing Federal Rules of Criminal Procedure to determine if revisions are needed to assist in complex criminal trials. The reason: The Federal Rules of Criminal Procedure of 1946, originally designed to streamline federal criminal procedure, have become complicated and confusing

State Issues

State courts face similar pressures as they look toward the twenty-first century. A few states, such as Virginia, Arizona, Michigan, Utah, Maine, and Colorado, have appointed commissions to study and plan for the future of the courts. The recommendations issued thus far show diversity in their approaches to handling existing and emerging problems. Arizona's commission, for example, recommended the creation of a three-level court system, while Virginia's advocated reorganizing its courts into a single-level system with divisions.[51]

The federal "war on drugs" has had a significant impact on state court case loads. New York's courts, for instance, saw a 270 percent increase in drug cases between 1985 and 1989. Nearly half the 15,000 felony cases pending in the Cook County, Illinois, criminal courts involve drug offenses. Some courts have been so overwhelmed that they have had to institute special case-processing procedures to deal with drug cases. New York City, Jersey City, New Jersey, and Cook County, Illinois, have created "drug courts" as part of the regular court structure, but designated to deal solely with drug offenses. Some states, like New Jersey, have reassigned trial court judges to do nothing but dispose of drug cases.[52]

Despite the vast number of cases added to the courts by the onslaught of drug arrests, the effect on court delay is still unclear. A recent study examined the case loads of twenty-six urban trial courts from 1983 to 1987 and found that most had experienced increases in the numbers of drug cases filed. Boston had the largest increase: Its case load of drug cases rose 175 percent over a four-year period. The courts with the largest increases and the largest total percentage of drug-related cases tended to be the slowest in terms of the average length of time it took them to process a case from indictment to disposition. These same courts also tended to be the slowest in overall handling of all types of cases. It is possible, therefore, that delays may simply be the result of a particular court's case-load management, and not necessarily of the infusion of additional drug cases.[53]

"Courts will continue to be affected by shifting social and political currents as groups continue to use them as an arena in which to air problems or make policy."

Courts will continue to be affected by shifting social and political currents as more and more groups use them as the arena in which to air their grievances or enforce their policies. Technology is also a likely source of change. Increasingly, courts conduct their business through such innovations as fax machines to file court papers, satellite and closed circuit television hookups to conduct various court proceedings with people not present in the courtroom, or videotape cameras to replace the traditional court stenographer as the recorder of what happens in the courtroom.[54]

REVIEW

Since earliest times society has had processes to resolve disputes arising under its rules, or laws. With the emergence of centralized government under strong rulers, the establishment of courts became a sovereign prerogative. In colonial times there was a definite shift away from the use of legislatures as courts. Local and state-level courts were created according to English models. With the achievement of their independence, state courts simply took over the powers of the courts of the Crown of England. Soon thereafter, the Congress established a system of federal courts.

In the United States, criminal cases are tried in state courts when the crime is a violation of state law, and in federal courts when it is a violation of federal law. Each state has its own court system, with courts of limited and special jurisdiction, courts of general jurisdiction, an intermediate appellate court (in most states), and courts of last resort. In the federal system the trial courts are called district courts, the appellate courts are courts of appeal, and the highest court is the Supreme Court. Both state and federal convictions may be appealed within their respective system. Federal review of state cases may take place when federal constitutional issues are raised.

Both state and federal courts face many challenges. The most significant are related to case loads. Drug cases, in particular, have had a significant impact on state and federal court case loads.

Notes

1. Christopher Hibbert, *The Roots of Evil: A Social History of Crime and Punishment* (Boston: Little, Brown, 1963).

2. Bradley Chapin, *Criminal Justice in Colonial America, 1606–1660* (Athens: University of Georgia Press, 1983).

3. Ibid., p. 68.

4. Erwin C. Surrency, "The Courts in the American Colonies," *American Journal of Legal History* 11 (1967):258.

5. Kermit L. Hall, *The Magic Mirror: Law in American History* (New York: Oxford University Press, 1989).

6. Lawrence M. Friedman, *A History of American Law* (New York: Simon and Schuster, 1973).

7. Surrency, "Courts in the American Colonies."

8. For a complete history of the federal judicial system, see Erwin C. Surrency, *History of the Federal Courts* (New York: Oceana Publications, 1987).

9. Robert A. Carp and Ronald Stidham, *Judicial Process in America* (Washington, D.C.: CQ Press, 1990).

10. Friedman, *A History of American Law*, p. 122.

11. Carp and Stidham, *Judicial Process in America*.

12. Hall, *The Magic Mirror*.

13. Friedman, *A History of American Law*.

14. Samuel Walker, *Popular Justice: A History of American Criminal Justice.* (New York: Oxford University, 1980).

15. Carp and Stidham, *Judicial Process in America*, p. 51.

16. Roscoe Pound, *Criminal Justice in America* (Cambridge, Mass.: Harvard University, 1930), p. 189. See also Roscoe Pound, "The Causes of Popular Dissatisfaction with the Administration of Justice," *Journal of the American Judicature Society* 20 (1937):178–187.

17. Fannie J. Klein and Joel S. Lee, eds. *Selected Writings of Arthur T. Vanderbilt*, 2 vols. (Dobbs Ferry, N.Y.: Oceana Publications, 1965).

18. For discussions of court reform and court unification, see Malcolm H. Feeley, *Court Reform on Trial: Why Simple Solutions Fail* (New York: Basic Books, 1983); Herbert Jacob, *Justice in America: Courts, Lawyers and the Judicial Process*, 4th ed. (Boston: Little, Brown, 1984); H. Ted Rubin, *The Courts: Fulcrum of the Justice System*, 2d ed. (New York: Random House, 1984); Geoff Gallas, "The Conventional Wisdom of State Court Administration: A Critical Assessment and an Alternative Approach," *Justice System Journal* 2 (1976):35; Larry Berkson and Susan Carbon, *Court Unification: History, Politics and Implementation*, National Institute of Law Enforcement and Criminal Justice (Washington, D.C.: U.S. Government Printing Office, 1978).

19. National Center for State Courts, *State Court Caseload Statistics: Annual Report 1990* (Williamsburg, Va.: National Center for State Courts, 1992).

20. Robert Elder, Jr., "The Land That Law Forgot; With No Trials for 14 Years, Court May Break Streak," *Texas Lawyer*, November 18, 1991, p. 1.

21. National Center for State Courts, *State Court Caseload Statistics: Annual Report 1989* (Williamsburg, Va.: National Center for State Courts, 1991).

22. David B. Rottman and Brian J. Ostrom, "Caseloads in the State Courts: Volume, Composition, and Growth," *State Court Journal* 15(2) (Spring 1991):4–20.

23. National Center for State Courts, *State Court Caseload Statistics: Annual Report 1989.*

24. Rottman and Ostrom, "Caseloads in the State Courts."

25. *Law v. State,* 318 A.2d 859 (Maryland, 1974).

26. National Center for State Courts, *Intermediate Appellate Courts: Improving Case Processing* (Williamsburg, Va.: National Center for State Courts, 1990).

27. Stanton Wheeler, Bliss Cartwright, Robert A. Kagan, and Lawrence M. Friedman, "Do the 'Haves' Come Out Ahead? Winning and Losing in State Supreme Courts, 1870–1970," *Law and Society Review* 21 (1987):403–445.

28. National Center for State Courts, *State Court Caseload Statistics: Annual Report, 1990.*

29. Rottman and Ostrom, "Caseloads in the State Courts."

30. 49 U.S. C. § 1472 (1) (1992).

31. *Loving v. Virginia,* 388 U.S. 1 (1967).

32. *Mapp v. Ohio,* 367 U.S. 643 (1961).

33. Christopher E. Smith, *United States Magistrates in the Federal Courts: Subordinate Judges* (New York: Praeger, 1990).

34. Case-load figures are from Administrative Office of the United States Courts, *Federal Judicial Workload Statistics, 1990.* (Washington, D.C.: U.S. Government Printing Office, n.d.).

35. See Michael deCourcy Hinds, "Bush's Aides Push Gun-Related Cases on Federal Courts," *The New York Times,* May 17, 1991, pp. A1, B16.

36. Garry Sturgess, "Another Clash over Criminal Caseload," *Legal Times,* April 1, 1991, p. 7.

37. Carp and Stidham, *Judicial Process in America.*

38. Sue Davis and Donald R. Songer, "The Changing Role of the United States Courts of Appeals: The Flow of Litigation Revisited," *Justice System Journal* 13 (1988–89):323–340. See also J. Woodford Howard, Jr., *Courts of Appeal in the Federal Judicial System: A Study of the Second, Fifth, and District of Columbia Circuits* (Princeton: Princeton University Press, 1981).

39. *Stanford v. Kentucky & Wilkins v. Missouri,* 492 U.S. 361 (1989).

40. See, e.g., *Illinois v. Gates,* 462 U.S. 213 (1983).

41. See *Stone v. Powell,* 428 U.S. 465 (1976).

42. Randall Samborn, "Court-Future Forum Airs Current Peeves," *National Law Journal,* April 20, 1992, p. 3.

43. U.S. Federal Courts Study Committee, *Report of the Federal Courts Study Committee, April 2, 1990* (Philadelphia, PA).

44. National Center for State Courts, *State Court Caseload Statistics: Annual Report, 1989, 1990.*

45. *Report of the Federal Courts Study Committee.*

46. William K. Slate II, "Congress Needs to Get to Work on Judicial Workloads; Courts Have Already Reached Outer Limits of Their Capacity," *Connecticut Law Tribune,* March 2, 1992, p. 21.

47. Constance L. Hays, "Shortage of Judges Slows Cases," *The New York Times,* August 6, 1991, p. B1.

48. Administrative Office of the United States Courts, *Federal Judicial Workload Statistics—December 31, 1990* (Washington, D.C.: U.S. Government Printing Office, n.d.).

49. A study of prisoners' civil rights petitions revealed, however, that only 4 percent ever went to trial, the majority being dismissed. See William Bennett Turner, "When Prisoners Sue: A Study of Prisoner Section 1983 Suits in the Federal Courts," *Harvard Law Review* 92 (1979):618.

50. *Report of the Federal Courts Study Committee,* p. 106.

51. National Center for State Courts Information Service, "Special Report: Trends in the State Courts," *State Court Journal* 15(1) (Winter 1991):4–12.

52. Ibid.

53. John A. Goerdt and John A. Martin, "The Impact of Drug Cases on Case Processing in Urban Trial Courts," *State Court Journal* 13(4) (Fall 1989):4–12.

54. See, for example, Selwyn Raab, "New York City Plans a TV Network to Link Jails and Courts," *The New York Times,* September 15, 1991, p. A33. See also National Center for State Courts Information Service, "Special Report."

CHAPTER 11

LAWYERS AND JUDGES

"**L**ong *before the coaches jarred to a halt in the shadow of the Langtry water tank, the greenhorns in the smoking car would have full information, some of it true, about the law West of the Pecos, as Roy Bean called himself. With their curiosity already on edge they would take in the handful of adobe buildings which was Langtry, the little station and the big water tank, and finally the small frame shack twenty steps north of the tracks with a covered porch in front and signs plastered over it: THE JERSEY LILLY: JUDGE ROY BEAN NOTARY PUBLIC. LAW WEST OF THE PECOS.*

"Someone would say, 'There he is!' And there he would be—a sturdy, gray-bearded figure with a Mexican sombrero on his head and a portly stomach mushrooming out over his belt, waiting on his porch for the swirl of business and excitement which always came at train time. You could see at a glance that he was as rough as a sand burr and tough as a boiled owl, but you realized also that he was a genuine character with plenty of salt in him.

"For a while he lived the epic he imagined. He really was the Law in those parts for a few years. It was two hundred miles to the nearest justice court and naturally he had things his own way. Before long civilization and lawyers moved in on him, but by that time his saga was started and his position was assured. He became in the minds of other men a sort of Ulysses of West Texas—a man of craft and action combined—a figure of colorful peculiarities and great resourcefulness. His fame was no surprise to him, though it was to a great many other people, for he had been convinced all along that he was no ordinary citizen. He probably thought his recognition was, if anything, considerably overdue.

"And so when the train pulled into Langtry, there he was on his porch. He always exposed himself at train time so people could see him. He was sure they would want to.[1]" ■

Judge Roy Bean and his courthouse in Langtry, Texas, 1900

"The prosecutor has more control over life, liberty, and reputation than any other person in America."
Robert H. Jackson, attorney general and Supreme Court justice.

Texas and the rest of the country have come a long way since Roy Bean held court in Langtry 100 years ago. During the twentieth century "the law" has covered the countryside. In fact, over the last forty years alone, the number of lawyers has more than tripled: from 221,605 in 1951 to 723,189 in 1988.[2] Today the United States has nearly 40 percent of all of the world's practicing and nonpracticing lawyers. There are also thousands of state and federal judges, supported by court administrators, clerks, and administrative staff.

In this chapter we examine the professional and social roles of attorneys and judges and the many organizational and personal constraints that defense and prosecuting attorneys experience in providing representation. We then consider the qualifications and selection of judges. Finally, we discuss the other key players in the courtroom, including court administrators, court clerks, and court personnel.

Throughout the chapter we will be describing personnel in both state and federal courts. As we discovered in Chapter 10, the state and federal courts differ considerably. These differences include

- the law that governs (federal law in federal courts and state law in state courts)
- the jurisdiction of the courts (the power of state and federal courts to hear certain kinds of cases differs)
- the procedure followed in the courts (in federal courts there are uniform rules of procedure and evidence, while procedures vary among state courts)
- the case load of the courts (state courts hear a vast majority of court cases)

So it is not surprising that the tasks and roles of state and federal court functionaries differ as well. Let us begin with a discussion of the government's attorney, the prosecutor. Attorney General Robert H. Jackson, who later became a United States Supreme Court justice, once said: "The prosecutor has more control over life, liberty, and reputation than any other person in America."[3]

PROSECUTION

Some prosecutors become well-known figures. For example, District Attorney Michael Bradbury has become an outspoken symbol of law and order in Ventura County, California.[4] Other district attorneys, such as Robert Morgenthau (New York County), maintain a less visible public image but act aggressively and decisively in the prosecution of violent, property, and white-collar offenders. But most prosecutors do not have the high profile or prominent reputation of Bradbury or Morgenthau, even though they have considerable decision-making powers within their county or district.

Roles and Duties

prosecutor
Attorney and government official who represents the people against persons accused of committing criminal acts.

Prosecutors are government lawyers, public officials, who represent the people of a particular jurisdiction (county, city, state, or federal district) in a criminal case. When a crime is committed the "people of the state," acting through the prosecutor, proceed in court against the suspected criminal. Today prosecution is almost exclusively the responsibility of an elected or appointed prosecutor.[5] More than 8,000 state and local government agencies are involved in prosecution, as is the federal government.[6]

Prosecutors have many duties. Once an arrest has been made, the prosecutor

- screens cases to determine which should be accepted for further processing
- decides with what specific offenses to charge a suspect

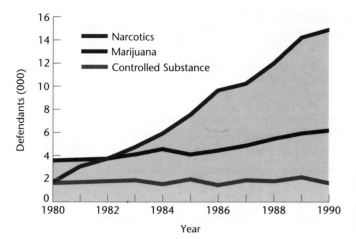

FIGURE 11.2 *Drug filings: marijuana, narcotics, controlled substances* (*Source: Federal Offenders in the U.S. Courts, 1986 through 1990* [Washington, D.C.: Administrative Office of the Courts, 1991], pp. 12–13.)

Federal Prosecutors

Prosecutions at the federal level are carried out by **United States attorneys.** Each federal judicial district has one U.S. attorney with a large staff of assistant attorneys, who carry out most of the day-to-day work of the office. United States attorneys are appointed by the president, subject to Senate confirmation. Assistant U.S. attorneys are formally appointed by the **United States Attorney General,** the highest ranking official in the U.S. Department of Justice (Figure 11.1). Usually the U.S. attorneys select their own assistants and pass the names on to the attorney general for official appointment. In practice, most U.S. attorneys are from the same political party as the president, who may use this appointment as a reward for political support. The position of U.S. attorney can be a highly visible one that some see as a stepping stone to a prominent political office. In the 1980s, the local law enforcement hero in Manhattan was Rudolph W. Giuliani, the U.S. attorney for the Southern District of New York. Giuliani's much publicized prosecutions of organized crime figures earned him great praise, some controversy, and mayoral aspirations.

While federal criminal law spans a wide range of offenses, all of which U.S. attorneys have the power to prosecute, the focus of investigations changes frequently. Antitrust violations were the focus at one time, organized crime at another. Today, national policy, as interpreted by the attorney general, has called for an emphasis on prosecuting narcotic drug traffickers and fraudsters (Figure 11.2).

United States attorney
Attorney and government official who prosecutes cases at the federal level.

United States attorney general
Highest ranking official in the United States Department of Justice.

State Prosecutors

The State Attorneys General. The state counterpart to the attorney general of the United States is the **state attorney general.** Like the U.S. attorney general, the state attorneys general are the chief legal officers of their jurisdictions. But here the analogy ends. State attorneys general are, for the most part, elected officials. They normally do not have the same power over the local prosecutors in their state that the U.S. attorney general has over the federal prosecutors (Figure 11.3).

State attorneys general, assisted by staff, are not concerned with local criminal prosecutions. Most of the work of this office concerns civil cases; most violations of the state criminal code are handled at the local level. State attorneys general, however, often play an important role in the investigation of statewide criminal activities (e.g., consumer, medicaid, and financial fraud). They may work closely with federal and local prosecutors to prepare the criminal cases resulting from such investigations.

state attorney general
Chief legal officer of the state; state counterpart to the U.S. attorney general.

"In cities, where the vast majority of arrests occur, the D.A.'s office may be one of the city's largest employers of lawyers."

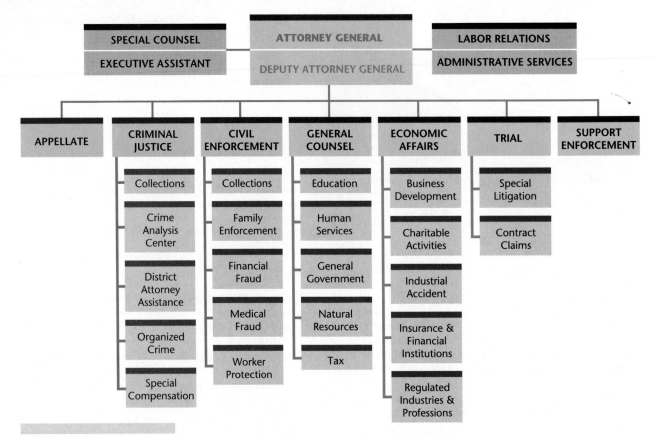

| SPECIAL COUNSEL | ATTORNEY GENERAL | LABOR RELATIONS |
| EXECUTIVE ASSISTANT | DEPUTY ATTORNEY GENERAL | ADMINISTRATIVE SERVICES |

APPELLATE	CRIMINAL JUSTICE	CIVIL ENFORCEMENT	GENERAL COUNSEL	ECONOMIC AFFAIRS	TRIAL	SUPPORT ENFORCEMENT
	Collections	Collections	Education	Business Development	Special Litigation	
	Crime Analysis Center	Family Enforcement	Human Services	Charitable Activities	Contract Claims	
	District Attorney Assistance	Financial Fraud	General Government	Industrial Accident		
	Organized Crime	Medical Fraud	Natural Resources	Insurance & Financial Institutions		
	Special Compensation	Worker Protection	Tax	Regulated Industries & Professions		

FIGURE 11.3 *Oregon attorney general's organizational structure* (*Source:* Lynne M. Ross, *State Attorneys General: Powers and Responsibilities* [Washington, D.C.: BNA, 1990], p. 351.)

District Attorney E. Michael McCann prosecuting serial murderer Jeffrey Dahmer, Milwaukee, 1992.

Local Prosecutors.   Most criminal cases arising under state law are handled by a local prosecutor, who is given different titles in different states: state's attorney, district attorney, county prosecutor. In most jurisdictions the office of the prosecutor is filled by the winner of local partisan elections, often young attorneys aiming for a political career. Let us examine the role of this all-important functionary in the criminal justice system more closely.

In rural areas, where crime is less frequent, the prosecutor may be a local attorney with a part-time appointment, working without staff. In cities, where the vast majority of arrests occur, the district attorney's office may be one of the city's largest employers of lawyers, hiring a battery of assistant DA's—often recent graduates of law school. For example, the Los Angeles County district attorney's office, the largest in the country, employs more than 800 attorneys in twenty-three offices around the county. The New York County district attorney's office employs nearly 450 lawyers and the Dallas County district attorney's office 175.

Organization of District Attorney's Offices.   It would be misleading to suggest that all urban DA's offices are as large and diversified. But it is fair to say that three organizational models characterize the structure of most such offices. Smaller jurisdictions with a limited case load will frequently use a *vertical model* in which a single assistant district attorney will be responsible for a given case from the time it is initially filed until its final disposition. Offices in jurisdictions with large case loads, on the other hand, often use a *horizontal model* (or zone model). Assistants are assigned to handle different steps in the process, rather than overseeing a case from start to finish. One assistant may do nothing but screen cases to determine which to accept for prosecution; another may handle only a particular type of court hearing, such as preliminary hearings; and yet another may be assigned to trial duty. A third type of arrangement, the *mixed model*, incorporates features of the other two: Routine cases may be processed through a horizontal model, special cases through a vertical model. For example, some offices may have units or bureaus that deal with organized crime, gang activities, or bias crimes[8]:

- *Organized Crime/Narcotics Task Force* (Multnomah County, Oregon). A team of twelve investigators and two prosecutors target narcotics organizations and seize assets of traffickers
- *Oriental Gang Unit* (New York City). Six assistant district attorneys and five New York Police Department detectives target violent crimes committed by Asian gangs
- *Civil Rights Unit* (Norfolk County, Massachusetts). Two prosecutors prosecute bias crimes and other violations of criminal provisions of the Massachusetts State Civil Rights Act[9]

Politics and Policy

"We are going to make the streets hot in Teaneck," said the Reverend Al Sharpton in February, 1992. "The process has not been completely fair and thorough," said Keith Jones, president of the New Jersey Chapter of the NAACP.[10] Earlier, Sharpton and Jones, along with other community leaders, had joined the U.S. attorney for New Jersey in calling for federal charges to be brought against Officer Gary Spath in the Teaneck Police Department. Spath, a white police officer, had just been acquitted of manslaughter in the killing of Phillip Pannell, a 16-year-old black youth whom the officer was chasing. Spath testified at trial that he fired in self-defense. Medical experts testified that Pannell had his hands raised in surrender at the time he was shot to death. An all-white jury acquitted Spath.[11]

"We are going to make the streets hot in Teaneck."
Reverend Al Sharpton, after the acquittal of Officer Gary Spath in the killing of Philip Pannell in 1992.

The Pannell case, like countless others, suggests the obvious—that prosecutors' offices face significant political pressures from the community. But these pressures may be minor or insignificant compared with pressures brought to bear from other sources. Prosecutors function within a larger system with many other "players." They interact constantly with police, judges, and defense attorneys and must be ready to work in a cooperative way to achieve the goals of the office. This is not an easy task given the many roles that prosecutors play.[12]

"Prosecutors function within a larger system with many other players: police, judges, defense attorneys, the local government, the media."

Prosecutors can have a major impact on policy by targeting particular types of crime. In 1992 the Department of Justice reported that Rockwell International Corporation agreed to pay $18.5 million in fines for violations of environmental statutes. U.S. Attorney William P. Barr commented:

Our criminal enforcement efforts have increased to record levels over each of the last three years. By painstakingly developing solid criminal cases such as this, and demanding appropriate fines against corporations, such as today's action against Rockwell, the Department of Justice is making it quite clear that environmental crimes do not pay.[13]

Prosecutors play a number of roles not necessarily made explicit by law. In smaller communities they may collect and dispense money to cover debts, such as those due to missing family support payments or from the issuing of bad checks, or arising from fraud. They also dispense justice by weighing the available penalties provided for certain crimes and then using their discretion to "do justice," perhaps by not prosecuting (See Criminal Justice in Action box).

As "political enforcers," prosecutors may aggressively prosecute or fail to prosecute a case for reasons and purposes other than a desire to achieve justice—perhaps to make a political point, to deter certain conduct, or to damage a reputation. To get the conviction of General Manuel Antonio Noriega on eight of ten counts of cocaine trafficking, racketeering, and money-laundering charges in

April 1992, three prosecutors spent over two years exclusively preparing and presenting this case (see Chapter 19). Was this case more of a political statement than an attempt to "do justice?" Critics have strongly debated this point.[14]

Prosecutors can also take on the role of "overseer of police" when they monitor the work of a department.[15] They influence law enforcement by focusing on certain types of criminals. To target a particular type of offender, such as a "career criminal," the prosecutor needs the cooperation of the police. In many cities around the United States, special police-prosecutor teams work together toward such common goals.[16]

Political Styles. A prosecutor also exists in a political environment that demands a particular style. A recent study by Roy Flemming of prosecutors' offices in nine midwestern jurisdictions led to the identification of three distinct political styles that influenced the policies of each office. "Courthouse insurgents" were dissatisfied with the status of their office, and fought to change it, even at the cost of alienating judges and defense attorneys. "Policy reformers" shared the insurgents' dissatisfaction with the status of the office but were willing to compromise to achieve their goals. "Office conservators" simply accepted the status quo and worked within the system.[17]

The Media Influence. The media and political party leaders also contribute to the politicization of prosecutors' offices by scrutinizing prosecutors and making demands on the way in which work is carried out.[18] Most prosecutors campaign on a tough "law and order" platform in response to the perceived public demand for such a position. Moreover, there is at times pressure to prosecute certain cases that may generate publicity and public reaction even if the evidence in the case is not as strong as normally desired for prosecution.[19] With the advent of "court TV" and other live broadcasts of courtroom proceedings, political pressure on local prosecutors is likely to increase.

Political pressure on prosecutors is just as great at the federal level. The U.S. attorneys are part of the executive branch and may be called on to carry out the administration's policies in the battleground of the courts. And U.S. attorneys are tied to local constituencies as well, that is, the local bar, press, and federal judges. As one U.S. attorney explained:

There are so many kinds of pressures. I mean, from the two-bit attorney who says, just remember you will be on the outside some day and you will need a favor, to somebody calling you up and just, you know, I don't want to interfere but I've heard this and it disturbs me. What is the picture on this? You get calls from Washington, from congressmen, and even a judge. There are a lot of pressures from people seeking to influence your decisions and a great deal of it is appropriate and proper.[20]

"With the advent of 'court TV' and live broadcasts of courtroom procedures, political pressure on local prosecutors is likely to increase."

Attorney Roy Black making a statement to the press during jury selection at the William Kennedy Smith rape trial, Palm Beach, Florida, Oct. 30-Nov. 1, 1991.

Discretion

On paper, the rules for the administration of the criminal law provide that all offenders should be treated equally—no defendant should receive more or less punishment than another who committed a similar offense and the rich and powerful should be prosecuted as vigorously as the poor and weak. Actually, however, . . . whether or not a particular offender is prosecuted depends very largely upon the personal reactions (or judgment) of the prosecutor.[21]

These are the words of Newman Baker, author of a series of classic articles in the 1930s about the American prosecutor, at a time when the public was first learning about the role that prosecutorial discretion plays in the administration of criminal justice. Of course, there is nothing inherently bad about discretion, properly used: Charles Breitel, then a justice of the New York Supreme Court (later chief judge of the New York Court of Appeals), noted some years ago that (i)f every policeman, every prosecutor, every court, and every post-sentence agency performed his or its responsibility in strict accordance with rules of law, precisely and narrowly laid down, the criminal law would be ordered but intolerable. . . . [T]he presence and expansion of discretion in crime control is both desirable and inevitable in a modern democratic society.[22]

"[T]he presence and expansion of discretion in crime control is both desirable and inevitable in a modern democratic society." Charles Breitel, chief judge of the New York Court of Appeals, 1960.

Prosecutors cannot pursue every case. Decisions have to be made—and most often these decisions are guided by the strength of the evidence. After all, a weak case is less likely to result in a conviction. But, as we shall see, strength of evidence is not the *sole* criterion.

Extent of Discretion. At each stage in the processing of a case, discretion is used in arriving at a decision. Among the most important decisions are the following:

- Does a case warrant further action beyond the arrest? Should it be rejected for prosecution?
  - If a decision is made to file charges, what specific charges should they be?
  - What recommendations should be made regarding bail?
  - Should the case be resolved through a plea bargain or a trial?

Figure 11.4 shows the effects of discretion at different stages in the criminal process. It illustrates the typical outcome of 100 felony arrests, based on an analysis of cases in thirty-five jurisdictions across the country. Only 55 of every 100 felony arrests are actually carried forward to the point where a determination of guilt will be made.[23] Those that are not prosecuted are rejected by the prosecutor before charges are filed, dismissed in court after charges have been filed, or diverted or referred to another agency for processing. Similar results are obtained in studies of U.S. attorneys' offices: Only 55.8 percent of all offenses investigated in 1989 resulted in prosecution.[24]

Of course, discretion varies significantly from jurisdiction to jurisdiction and from district attorney to district attorney. Some prosecutors attempt to eliminate weak cases before charges are even filed; others file charges and then have cases weeded out at later stages. For example, in New York County, only 2 percent of all cases presented by the police are rejected before the filing of criminal charges, whereas Los Angeles County rejects 35 percent of cases before charges are filed. However, 40 percent of New York's cases are dismissed following the filing of charges, compared with only 10 percent of Los Angeles' cases.[25] Another

FIGURE 11.4 *Typical outcome of 100 felony arrests brought by police for prosecution* (*Source:* Barbara Boland et al. *The Prosecution of Felony Arrests, 1988* [Washington, D.C.: Bureau of Justice Statistics, 3 1992].)

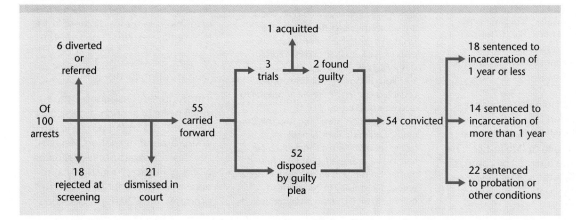

A DAY IN THE LIFE OF A ROOKIE D.A.

At age 28, John F. Kennedy, Jr., was one of sixty-four rookie prosecutors hired in 1989 by the New York County District Attorney's office, one of the nation's most prestigious prosecutors offices. Perhaps it was Kennedy who took the place of David Heilbroner, an assistant district attorney who had retired in 1988 after a three-year stint. Heilbroner's recollections of his work reveal some of the frustrations and realities of the life of a rookie district attorney.

Doing justice

Heilbroner retired after only three years because he lacked the zeal that seemed to fuel his colleagues' efforts—the zeal for "locking up the scum" who prey on innocent New Yorkers. Heilbroner reports about the people with whom he worked:

Questions about social injustice or the fact that jails only made defendants more deeply embittered brought unencouraging answers: "The slimeballs shouldn't have been there in the first place." "You know what they say: 'Don't do the crime if you can't do the time.'"(1, p. 76)

Oliver W. Holmes, Jr., once remarked, "I don't do justice. I merely apply the law." Heilbroner, however, had hoped to "do justice"; he soon became disabled by compassion and disillusioned by the never-ending constraints on the system.

Some of these feelings are recorded in his descriptions of courtroom interactions:

David Middleton, a sixteen-year-old felon with three aliases, had been arrested for beating the subway fare. *Manipulating a turnstyle.* $24.00. The case, like all farebeats, was probably a winner. When Middleton's name was run through a computer, a bench warrant "dropped." It had been issued in a shoplifting case when Middleton skipped out. Judges usually gave teenagers the benefit of every doubt, since the more time kids spend inside, the less likely they are to reform. But Middleton had worn out his welcome. In only three years, he had amassed a felony conviction for robbery and two drug-related misdemeanors, not to mention the open shoplift case. He wasn't old enough to drink legally, yet he probably knew the arraignment process better than I did.

Middleton had served first fifteen and then forty-five days on his two drug convictions and he was still on probation for the robbery. He faced up to one year or a one-thousand-dollar fine on the farebeat alone. Our class had recently been instructed that, as a matter of policy, sentences should increase with every new arrest. Sixty days, therefore, seemed about right.

One of the court officers announced, "The people versus David Middleton, Docket Number 5N078546," and Middleton, a handsome, well-built youth, got up off the defendant's bench and strutted over to the defense table. Expensive basketball sneakers. Padded leather jacket. The usual.

"Your honor," said Middleton's Legal Aid lawyer, "may we approach to discuss a disposition?"

"Gentlemen, step up," said the Honorable Louis Friedland. Friedland, a heavy-set man with a shock of black hair, was a seasoned jurist who prided himself on running a tight ship. Cases proceeded quickly in his court, so quickly, in fact, that he often requested that overflow cases from secondary arraignment parts be added to the day's work. He was known as the Tsar of Arraignments.

"Mr. D.A.," he asked the moment I arrived at the bench, "what are you looking for to cover the farebeat?"

"Well, Judge," I answered nervously, "the defendant got fifteen days for his first misdemeanor and forty-five days for his last offense. It seems to me the penalties should go up with each subsequent—"

"Cut the crap, Mr. D.A., just tell me what you're looking for to cover the farebeat." I should have known I didn't have to explain sentencing policy to a judge with twenty years on the bench.

"Sixty days," I answered.

Friedland froze for a moment. Then he pounced: "Sixty days for a farebeat? Listen, Mister, you better get it together or you'll be practicing law in Poughkeepsie. You don't give two months to a sixteen year old kid for beating unless you're out of your fucking mind. Who the hell told you a kid should go to jail for two months over a one-dollar token? You're lucky I don't call your bureau chief."

"Sir." Friedland turned to the tired looking Legal Aid lawyer, who, decently enough, had stepped back, "tell Mr. Middleton that the offer is thirty days—to cover the shoplifting case as well."

As I turned to the prosecution table, I felt as if I had just committed an unpardonable error in judgment. For the rest of the morning the word echoed in my ears: "Poughkeepsie."(1, pp. 41–42)

Doing rough justice

These interactions expose only a small piece of a much larger, complex, and disturbing puzzle in urban courts around the nation. Heilbroner describes the administration of a "rough justice," a justice that reflects accommodations and compromises in the name of case-load management or system efficiency. It was not the kind of justice he felt comfortable with.

And in every direction innumerable aspects of the justice system cried out for reform: police misconduct, defense attorneys' delays, meaningless paperwork, the rubber-stamp grand jury, rigid strictures on sentencing, incarceration of psychiatric patients, insufficient numbers of judges and courtrooms, to name just a few of the egregious problems. "The crisis of the courts," itself the result of too many cases, was also the product of broader social injustices: the inequitable distribution of wealth, the legacy of racism, bleak opportunities for minori-

ties and the poor. None of these were any less a problem for my having spent three years as an agent of the system."(1, pp. 284–285)

Looking back

In the end, Heilbroner looked back at the system of criminal justice with some concrete suggestions:

- rookies should be encouraged to dismiss more marginal cases, e.g., prostitution and marijuana possession;
- the distinction between felonies and misdemeanors should be reformed so that sentencing deci-

sions are not hampered by artificial distinctions;
- the grand jury should be abolished—it is a waste of resources and accomplishes little;
- police officers should be fined every time they engage in illegal searches and arrests; and
- lawyers should be disciplined for delays and misrepresentations.

Heilbroner admits, however, that the work associated with prosecution does not "lend itself" to reform or analysis. All energy is expended on keeping pace and maintaining some degree of perspective. And Heilbroner's energy? He is now expending it on writing about the system.

SOURCE

1. David Heilbroner, *Rough Justice: Days and Nights of a Young D.A.* (New York: Pantheon, 1990), p. 76.

QUESTIONS FOR DISCUSSION

1. Why do you think law students are interested in working as prosecutors?
2. What changes to the criminal justice system would allow rookie prosecutors to remain idealistic and committed to "justice"?
3. Perhaps lawyers becoming disillusioned as they begin work in "the real world" is just a normal part of gaining experience. Do you think they should remain idealistic, or is it better that they fit into the system?

Jacket design and illustration by Janet Perr. Courtesy of Pantheon Books © 1990 Random House, Inc.

study of Los Angeles prosecutors asked about the standards of proof used in deciding whether to file a criminal complaint against a suspect. One-fifth of the prosecutors said they would file a complaint even if they thought the case would go no further than a preliminary hearing, while another 30 percent said they would file the complaint even though they thought the case would be lost at trial. Half said they would file the complaint only if they thought the case would probably be won at trial.[26]

Decision to Prosecute. Among the most important of the case-related factors that affect the decision to prosecute are the seriousness of the offense and the amount of harm that may have resulted, in terms of injury to a victim or loss involved in property offenses.[27] The strength and amount of evidence against a suspect,[28] whether a weapon was used in the commission of the offense,[29] whether a suspect has confessed,[30] and the prior criminal record of the suspect[31] have been identified as additional factors that are taken into account in the decision to file charges, reduce charges, or continue prosecution after the initial charges have been filed.

These case-related factors seem like perfectly appropriate criteria to use in prosecutorial decisions. But consider some of the other factors that have been identified as determinants of prosecutors' decisions. Prosecutors must consider whether the victim wants prosecution to proceed. A recent study that examined 200 domestic assault cases in which charges were not filed against the offender found that "victim wishes" accounted for nearly half the decisions not to file charges.[32]

"One factor that determines a prosecutor's decision to go ahead is whether or not the victim wants prosecution to proceed."

Victims have been shown to have an effect on the prosecutor's decision-making in other ways as well (see Chapter 18). A study of New York County prosecutors found that district attorneys often judge the victim's credibility and use this assessment in weighing prosecution decisions. Less-than-credible victims may have their cases rejected, since prosecutors are always interested in maximizing the number of convictions obtained.[33]

Factors such as the relationship between the victim and the accused, whether the victim took action that might be considered provocation, and whether the victim participated in the crime may also play a role. Victim provocation and participation in the crime appear to decrease the likelihood that a case will be prosecuted, perhaps because the prosecutor believes that the victim is more blameworthy in such cases and less likely to be believed.[34]

Many personal characteristics are used by prosecutors to evaluate whether to prosecute a suspect. Women suspects, for example, are less likely to be prosecuted than men.[35] Surprisingly, some studies have shown that blacks and other minorities are less likely to be prosecuted than whites,[36] and that charges against blacks are more likely to be reduced than those against whites.[37] Research examining prosecutorial discretion in requesting the death penalty, on the other hand, has consistently shown that prosecutors are more likely to request the death penalty in cases where the murder victim is white.[38]

Factors that have little or nothing to do with the offender or victim also appear to affect prosecutorial decision-making. Among the most common are[39]

"Some of the factors that appear to affect prosecutorial decision-making may have little or nothing to do with the offender or the victim."

• *Case-load Considerations*—Every prosecutor's office has limited resources to deal with all the cases presented to it. Prosecutors therefore use a selection process to keep case loads to a manageable size. Similarly, concerns about overcrowding on court dockets and in prisons are thought to affect prosecutor's decision-making[40]

• *Community Factors*—Outrage in the community about a particular crime or types of crime, public opinion, and media attention may exert some pressure on the prosecutor's choice of the course of action to pursue in certain cases

• *Law Enforcement Concerns*—In the interest of obtaining valuable information that may assist law enforcement agencies in apprehending a suspect, prosecutors may be willing to reduce charges, decline prosecution, or reduce already imposed prison sentences, in exchange for such information

- *Availability of Alternatives to Prosecution*—In some instances, alternatives to prosecution such as diversion to special programs may be available. In Chapter 12 we will examine these programs in detail[41]

Controlling Discretion. Concerns about discretion are magnified by the fact that prosecutorial decisions are rarely subjected to review. Courts simply give great deference to prosecutors.[42] Advocates of discretion argue that a trial effectively serves as a review of the prosecutor's actions. If the prosecutor has acted improperly or brought charges without justification, the defendant will be acquitted. But this is small consolation to the innocent person who has been charged with a crime and possibly placed in a detention facility while awaiting trial.

"Courts simply give great deference to prosecutors."

Calls for the control of discretion have prompted proposals such as

- Decision-making guidelines—Written guidelines that would provide specific criteria for decision-making[43]
- Intraoffice reviews—The simple practice of having a superior check the work of those under his or her supervision can be an effective means of oversight
- Limiting the number of decision-makers—The horizontal model of prosecution that assigns specific duties to experienced prosecutors may help control discretion. Seemingly arbitrary variations among prosecutors are also minimized by this method
- Periodic review of charging policies and decisions

Of course, discretion is not likely to be eliminated. The real issue of concern is not how to "do away" with discretion but rather, in the words of Justice Charles Breitel, "how to control it so as to avoid the unequal, the arbitrary, the discriminatory, and the oppressive."[44]

DEFENSE COUNSEL

The typical TV image of the defense lawyer is Perry Mason—a brilliant legal detective, strategist, and orator, whose clients are never guilty and who always succeeds in making the prosecutor look silly. Scripts call for flamboyant, publicity-seeking, and often unscrupulous attorneys who may well use legal technicalities to help their clients go free. Yet another image is the idealistic and bumbling public defender who, due to time and budgetary constraints, can barely afford to become acquainted with each impoverished defendant prior to trial. Yet, as we shall see, none of these popular images is a fair representation of the defense attorney.

Defense attorneys occupy a critical place in our adversarial system of justice. They ensure that the legal rights of an accused person are fully protected at every stage in the criminal justice process, and that those accused of crime receive zealous representation. Fewer than 5 percent of all lawyers today practice criminal law on a regular basis, and only 1.2 percent of all practicing lawyers may be found in legal aid or public defender offices. The number of single-practitioner defense lawyers is also declining—they have been properly called an "endangered species," a "dying breed."[45]

Roles and Duties

Manhattan Criminal Court Judge Harold J. Rothwax, formerly a Legal Aid attorney, once described the "typical day" in his court:

The Prosecutor and the Legal Aid attorney, respectively and hurriedly, begin to look through the large pile of papers in front of them; the judge sits and waits; having found the paper they begin their preparation by glancing at it quickly; the judge waits; the prosecutor then turns to his witnesses, ascertains who they are, and discusses the case with them; the Legal Aid attorney turns to the defendant, introduces himself if they have not previously met, and discusses the case with him; the judge waits, reads or shouts for quiet in the court room; having concluded their preparation the prosecutor and the Legal Aid attorney begin to negotiate with each other to see if they can agree upon a disposition; the judge waits. The case is then either disposed or adjourned.[46]

But there is more. The complaint that the defendant has received reveals little information, other than the charge and its alleged time and place of occurrence. Thus, the defendant is often ill-informed and sometimes lacks an appreciation of the nature and consequences of the proceedings that are taking place.

In considering the roles and duties of defense lawyers, it is important to remember the distinction between theory and practice. Much of what is presented here is theoretical. In many urban criminal courts around the United States, theory is overridden by limited budgets and resources, overcrowded dockets, and inadequately trained personnel. In fact, the New York State Judicial Commission on Minorities recently reported that the state's court system is "infested with racism," and that it doles out "basement justice."[47] According to its final report, there are two systems of justice in New York, one for whites and one for blacks and the poor. One important recommendation for change is the proposed requirement of attorney certification (above and beyond the admission to the bar) for all Legal Aid and contract attorneys, to ensure minimal levels of competence.[48]

defense attorney (in criminal cases)

Lawyer retained by an individual accused of committing a crime, or assigned by the court if the individual is unable to pay.

"Defense attorneys are there to ensure that the interests of an accused are fully protected."

Defense Attorney Roles.   All persons accused of a crime for which jail or prison is the possible penalty have a right to counsel under the Sixth Amendment to the United States Constitution.[49] The person who represents the accused is called a **defense attorney.** In theory, defense attorneys fulfill three roles.[50] First, they are advocates for the accused. It is important to remember that an accused is presumed innocent until such time as guilt may be proven in a court of law. Even if an accused admits guilt, the person is still entitled to the full protection of the law, that is, advice and representation of counsel. Defense attorneys are there to ensure that the interests of an accused are fully protected.

A second role is that of an intermediary. The language used in criminal court may be confusing to those not educated in law. Many criminal defendants are poorly educated and may be intimidated by the nature of criminal proceedings. They may be unable to fully or adequately express themselves or to assist in the presentation of their own defense. The defense attorney becomes a spokesperson for the accused.

A third function is that of a learned friend. The defense attorney is also a counselor, offering advice and assistance in explaining the risks and benefits of alternative courses of action. Together, attorney and client formulate an agreement as to the best steps to take at each juncture of the process.

Defense Attorney Duties.   The defense attorney has duties to perform at the various stages in the criminal process. For example, defendants have a right to have an attorney present at police interrogations, lineups, preliminary hearings, and probation and parole revocation proceedings. The defense attorney's first and foremost duty in the proceedings is to protect the accused. This includes informing the client of the rights guaranteed by law and determining what procedural steps should be taken to ensure those rights. These may include

- seeking the pretrial release of the accused
- filing motions to suppress evidence illegally obtained

- moving to have the client's case separated from others' if several people have been jointly accused of the same offense
- seeking to have the charges dismissed

One of the first duties of a defense attorney on agreeing to represent a client is to investigate the circumstances of the case by securing information held by the prosecutor or police, and interviewing witnesses. On conclusion of an investigation, the attorney advises the accused about all aspects of the case and provides an assessment of the probable outcome. This consultation allows both the attorney and the accused to make three important decisions about the case:

- what plea to enter in response to the charges filed
- whether to waive the right to a jury trial
- whether the accused should testify in his or her own behalf

If the defense attorney concludes that a conviction is probable, the accused may be asked to consider entering a discussion with the prosecutor about a negotiated plea, or plea bargain. If the defendant chooses to go to trial, the defense attorney, together with the prosecutor, is responsible for *voir dire,* or selection of the jury members (see Chapter 12). During the trial, the defense counsel and the prosecutor perform essentially the same duties: presentation of evidence, examination of witnesses, and raising of objections to any questions or evidence by the other side considered inadmissible. If the defendant is convicted, the defense counsel has an important role to play in sentencing.[51]

Private Defense Counsel

Famous celebrity defense lawyers, like Alan Dershowitz, Melvin Belli, William Kunstler, and F. Lee Bailey, thrive on cases that generate a lot of publicity. They command high fees for their professional expertise, often with the justification that such fees will allow them to represent clients with lesser means. Not surprisingly, the number of criminal defendants who can afford the services of attorneys like these is very small.[52]

Besides "celebrity lawyers," private criminal lawyers can be grouped into three other categories: First, those who represent frequently arrested clients, such as gamblers, drug dealers, and prostitutes. Among them are also lawyers who serve as "in house counsel" on a regular basis to members of organized crime. This group is quite small. "Occasionals" are attorneys who, from time to time, agree to handle a criminal case.[53] The experience of representing a defendant charged with a criminal offense may represent a diversion from their regular practice. Their livelihood is not dependent on these cases, and concerns about fees and the cost of time consumed while waiting for a case to be called in the courtroom will not cause them to modify their style of representation or strategy. "Regulars," by contrast, depend on criminal cases for a sizable portion of their income. Most of the defendants they work with, however, are able to pay only small fees. Thus the regulars must carefully monitor their time to be sure they are adequately compensated for the services they perform.[54]

Public Defenders

Life in the fast lane of the law can be observed on the fourth floor of the municipal court building each morning beginning at 9.

Columbus defense attorney Madelon Rosenfeld was at work only 15 minutes one recent Monday morning and she already had a standing-room-only string of clients.

She would confer with one client, move down a long table to talk with another, hurry to comfort a third, pause for a minute to consult with a legal colleague, then return to the first client ready to make a careful legal recommendation.

"At sentencing, the defense counsel 'is put in the position of being a social worker, investigator, resource center, diagnostician, and adviser.'"
Benson D. Weintraub, criminal lawyer, 1987.

"And, if by any chance we lose your case, we specialize in sentence reduction, parole eligibility, and locating community service that isn't too onerous."

Source: *The New Yorker,* Dec. 31, 1990, p. 29.

Public defender counseling 3 of more than 14,000 people arrested in the Los Angeles riots, May 1992. Los Angeles Municipal Court.

"[L]awyers in criminal courts are necessities, not luxuries."
Gideon v. Wainwright, 1963.

About 100 Columbus men and women would seek Rosenfeld's legal skills that Monday, not an unusual daily workload for her.

Rosenfeld is a public defender, one of 17 attorneys assigned to the Municipal Court division of the Franklin County Office—the largest criminal defense law office in the state.[55]

After reading this, it may come as a surprise that the poor—at least in theory—are entitled to the same legal rights as the rich.

The Constitutional Right to Counsel.   In 1932, the Supreme Court ruled that the Fourteenth Amendment of the Constitution required that defense counsel be provided for poor defendants on trial for a capital offense.[56] Six years later, the right of indigent defendants to be represented in all criminal proceedings in federal courts was established.[57] Not until the landmark case of *Gideon v. Wainwright* was decided in 1963 did the court extend the right to appointed counsel to indigent defendants charged with felonies in state courts, ruling that "lawyers in criminal courts are necessities, not luxuries."[58] Nine years later, the Supreme Court's decision in *Argersinger v. Hamlin* expanded the right to counsel to include all cases, including misdemeanors, that may result in sentences of imprisonment.[59]

Types of Public Defense.   Once the Supreme Court had ruled that indigents were entitled to be represented by counsel in criminal proceedings, the bar had to find the means of providing this service. The first response came from law schools. The New York University Law School started a crash program to train specialized criminal law professors who in turn would train young lawyers at their universities in the special skills required of the criminal defense bar. In a very short time, hundreds of criminal law practitioners were created to provide the defense necessitated by the Supreme Court. These specialists now work in three types of arrangements for the defense of persons charged with crime: public defenders, assigned counsel, and contract systems. These systems are funded primarily by state and county governments and have become a significant resource in, and burden on, the justice system. Counties have the sole responsibility for providing indigent defense systems in twenty-four states, while seventeen states have statewide systems. Other states use a district-based system or apportion the responsibility among more than one system. Spending on public defense reached nearly $1.4 billion in 1988, more than double the amount spent just six years earlier.[60] In 1986, counsel was provided for approximately 4.4 million cases. Estimates of the number of people who qualify for indigent defense counsel vary widely, from 48 percent of all defendants charged with felonies nationwide to 90 percent in some counties in Michigan.[61]

Each state and county may utilize more than one type of system, although within each jurisdiction there is a primary system. **Assigned counsel systems** are the most frequently used. Here the judge appoints a private lawyer selected from a list of attorneys. Assigned counsel systems are favored in rural areas, so even though 52 percent of counties use this type of system, assigned counsel programs actually serve less than one-third of the population. **Public defender systems,** consisting of public or nonprofit organizations with staff that provide defense services, are used by all but seven of the fifty largest counties in the country, which by themselves account for one-third of the nation's population.[62] There is considerable regional variation in the types of programs (Figure 11.5). In the Northeast, for example, nearly four-fifths (78.8%) of the counties use public defender systems, whereas in the South almost 70 percent of the counties use assigned counsel systems.[63] Finally, **contract systems,** under which private attorneys from law firms or local bar associations contract to provide defense services, are used in 11 percent of all counties.

assigned counsel system
Judge appoints a private lawyer selected from a list of attorneys to represent indigent defendants in criminal proceedings.

public defender system
Public or nonprofit organizations (with staff) provide defense services to indigent defendants.

contract system
Private attorneys from law firms or local bar associations provide defense services to indigent defendants.

Evaluations of Public Defense. Federal District Judge Ann Williams does not mince words. For the second time in a month, in November 1986, Judge Williams overturned a conviction in Cook County Court due to attorney incompetence—the first time by a states attorney, the second by a Cook County public defender. In her words: "This case teaches the lesson that sloppy lawyering can undermine individual rights and drain judicial resources. The inferior counseling of a defendant means that the efforts of many participants in the judicial process have been wasted and may mean that an individual has been unjustly incarcerated for eight years."[64]

Defense attorneys, both private and public, have frequently been the targets of accusations of incompetence. One observer of the courts remarked that "incompetence is more the rule than the exception. . . . Whether public defender, court-appointed attorney, or counsel retained by the defendant, defense lawyers frequently are inexperienced, incompetent, unprepared, and uninterested in their clients' interests and needs."[65] Defendants—the clients of the indigent defense bar—sometimes share a dim appraisal of the effectiveness of the assistance they receive. Their views are perhaps best summed up by the oft-quoted remark recorded by Jonathan Casper:

> "Did you have a lawyer when you went to court?"
> "No, I had a public defender."[66]

This remark is troubling because the public defender office was once viewed as a solution to the problems associated with the private defense bar.[67] The defendants discussed in Casper's study, however, felt that they would have been better represented by private attorneys than by public defenders. Much of their dissatisfaction with public defenders stemmed from the perception that any attorney who is paid by the state, in effect, works for the state, not the defendant. Some depictions of the way in which public defenders operate have tended to confirm this view of the defender as negotiator and conciliator, interested in helping the system to dispose of cases rather than being a zealous and rigorous advocate for the defendant.[68]

"[S]loppy lawyering can undermine individual rights and drain judicial resources."
Federal District Judge Ann Williams, Cook County, Illinois.

"Did you have a lawyer when you went to court?"
"No, I had a public defender."
Yale Review of Law and Social Action, 1971

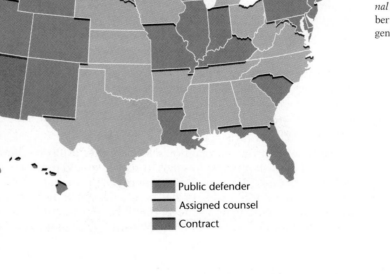

FIGURE 11.5 *Predominant system for defense of the indigent in the fifty states* (*Source:* Robert L. Spangenberg et al. of Abt Associates, Inc., Bureau of Justice Statistics, *National Criminal Defense Systems Study,* October 1986, updated by the Spangenberg Group, March 1987.)

- Public defender
- Assigned counsel
- Contract

Courts have held that defendants are entitled to more than cursory representation by an attorney. In the case of _McMann v. Richardson_ (1970), the Supreme Court ruled that "defendants facing felony charges are entitled to the effective assistance of _competent_ counsel."[69] Courts have reversed convictions in some cases because of ineffective assistance of counsel. Among these cases are those where the attorney has failed to put forth a valid and viable defense, to file motions that would have requested suppression of evidence illegally obtained, to participate effectively in jury selection, or to conduct a proper cross-examination of prosecution witnesses that would have permitted an examination of contradictory statements made by the witnesses.[70]

Several guidelines attempt to specify competence standards for the criminal defense bar.[71] However, guidelines do not ensure that defense attorneys will provide competent assistance in the face of the realities of the criminal courtroom. Studies of indigent defense systems over the last several years have concluded that the poor are not always well served by the private or public defense bar. Generally, these studies found that the systems are underfunded and understaffed and, as a result, there is enormous pressure to simply get the defendant to "cop a plea," that is, accept a plea bargain.[72] Defendants in some jurisdictions are treated to a sort of "assembly line justice," in which they may not meet their defense attorney until they arrive at the courtroom, only to find the attorney suggesting that they plead guilty.[73]

Studies of prisoners' perceptions reveal that, in general, they have a more positive assessment of private attorneys than of public defenders.[74] With some inmates this should not be at all surprising. Consider that of the twenty-six death-row inmates in Kentucky, for example, six had lawyers who subsequently were disbarred or suspended from practicing law.[75] But systematic research comparing the effectiveness of private and public counsel has shown mixed results: In some cases, private counsel seems to do better, whereas in others public defenders are more effective. Studies that control for factors such as the prior record of the defendant and offense seriousness indicate generally that there is little difference in terms of case outcome.[76] Thus, some commentators may have portrayed public defenders in an overly critical light.[77]

> "Studies of indigent defense systems over the last several years have concluded that the poor are not always well served by the private or public defense bar."

Ethical Issues

Zealous Representation. When defense lawyers attend social functions they are invariably asked: "How can you defend people who you know are guilty?" To most people, it seems that lawyers who defend a criminal must have to compromise their own values. However, most members of the criminal defense bar will respond with a little lesson in civics, explaining that under the United States Constitution every person is entitled to a fair trial, that every person is to be presumed innocent until proven guilty, and that everyone is entitled to be represented by counsel. Defense attorneys see themselves as performing a function that is a fundamental part of our Constitution. As one veteran public defender put it:

> "Defense attorneys see themselves as performing a function that is a fundamental part of our Constitution."

> Representing an indigent criminal defendant is all about duty. When a case is assigned, that duty arises, and it remains until the defendant is sentenced after a plea of guilty, he is freed after a successful trial, or his case is appealed after an unsuccessful one. Because your client is poor and can't afford anyone else, the duty owed him is the highest duty a lawyer can have.[78]

> "To some lawyers all facts are created equal."
> Justice Felix Frankfurter

The American Bar Association's Model Code of Professional Responsibility contains a provision that states that "a lawyer should represent a client zealously within the bounds of the law."[79] That does not mean that a defense attorney must go beyond the limits of his or her own conscience, nor does it mean that the attorney has license to do whatever might be necessary to win a case. As with the prosecutor, the defense counsel's paramount obligation is to the administration of justice. But he or she is also an advocate who must make sure that all legal mechanisms available to the defense are utilized. Sometimes this may result in attacks based on seeming technicalities, which can create anger on the part of the public, especially if a client ends up "getting off" on a technicality. It can also lead defense attorneys to cross-examinations of victims and witnesses that may make these persons feel as though they are the ones who are on trial.

The bounds of "zealous representation" are not clearly articulated, although the ABA's Standards, along with its Model Code of Professional Responsibility and Model Rules of Professional Conduct, attempt to provide guidance to defense attorneys by defining specific behaviors as unprofessional conduct. Examples include counseling a client to engage in conduct the lawyer knows to be illegal, using illegal means to obtain evidence, paying a witness (other than an expert witness) for testimony, and knowingly entering false evidence.

One of the most troubling issues arises when a defendant wishes to testify in court and the defense attorney knows that the defendant is going to lie, or commit perjury. The ABA's rules are not totally clear on this matter, suggesting on the one hand that a lawyer would have a duty to reveal the perjury but acknowledging that concerns about the right to counsel and other constitutional guarantees may qualify this requirement.[80] The dilemma that faces a defense attorney can have harsh consequences—as Ellis Rubin learned. While representing an accused murderer, Rubin was told by his client that he planned to lie on the witness stand. Rubin's reaction: "I could not live with myself knowing that I'm deceiving a jury, with or without the court approval."[81] When Rubin refused to continue representing his client, the trial judge sentenced him to serve thirty days in Dade County Jail for contempt of court.

Case-load Issues.   Case loads are another ethical issue. Programs for the defense of the indigent are chronically underfunded.[82] The result is that they suffer from staff shortages, which in turn means that each attorney has to carry a large case load, particularly in urban areas. The problem of carrying too many cases has been recognized for some time. In 1973, the National Advisory Commission on Criminal Justice Standards and Goals estimated that the maximum felony case load should be 150 cases per attorney annually.[83] The reality appears to be significantly different from the ideal. Albert Alschuler reported in 1975 that in New York City, the average case load per defender was 922 cases, and Philadelphia's defenders were carrying case loads of 600 to 800 per year.[84] In the last decade, indigent defense systems have been hard hit by growing court case loads. In Minneapolis, for example, the average felony and misdemeanor case load increased 100 percent between 1981 and 1989, and in San Francisco County the average case load of public defenders increased 35 percent in just one year, from 1983 to 1984.[85]

Heavy case loads have a detrimental effect on the provision of effective assistance in several ways. First, an attorney with an excessive case load simply does not have the time to investigate each case and make adequate preparations for it. Inadequate preparation can result in critical deficiencies that can affect each subsequent stage in a case. Attorneys faced with an excessive number of cases to handle simply do not have the time to visit the scene of the crime, locate and interview witnesses, or consult experts to testify during a trial.

Time constraints created by case loads also mean that a defense attorney usually has little time to consult with the client. The problem is particularly acute with public defenders, who can rarely find time to visit their clients in jail.[86] Hurried consultations conducted in a courthouse hallway or even inside the courtroom mean that the defense attorney does not get adequate information about the case and that there is virtually no time to build a relationship of trust between attorney and client. This contributes to the perception that indigent defendants are poorly represented by public defenders.

JUDGES

At 5 A.M., he wakes to down a bowl of cold cereal in an otherwise sleeping house in the remote northern suburbs. By 6:05 he is on the Metro-North train, another harried commuter balancing legal briefs and statute books on his lap.

A little more than an hour later he is waiting on the Grand Central subway platform for a No. 4 or No. 5 express to Brooklyn Bridge, and by 7:30 he is at his desk on the fifth floor of the columned United States Courthouse on Foley Square, sipping from a container of steaming tea.

So begins another work day for Louis J. Freeh, the newest Federal District Judge in the Southern District of New York, another day of juggling accident claims, prisoner lawsuits and criminal charges—another day in the making of a judge.[87]

What do judges do besides sit in court? What roles do they assume? What duties do they perform? Who are they? How are they selected? We will address these questions next.

Roles and Duties

Judges are the supreme officers of the court. They preside over courtroom proceedings, interpret and decide questions of law. In doing so they play a prominent role in ensuring that justice is served—sometimes at great expense. As decision-makers and arbiters, judges exert control over criminal cases at each stage of the criminal process. Judges are called on to decide questions presented to the court. While each side in a case may present arguments asking for a ruling in their favor, the judge must weigh both sides and make a decision. Rulings are required about whether to detain a defendant pending trial. If the defendant is to be released, the judge must determine if bail is required or if the defendant can be released on his own recognizance. The judge also sets the dollar amount of bail required. Defense attorneys may file pretrial motions requesting, for example, the suppression of evidence that allegedly has been obtained illegally. The judge must rule on all pretrial motions. Before setting a case for trial, the judge may be called on to rule on the competence of a defendant to stand trial. If the defense attorney and prosecutor negotiate an agreement in which the defendant will plead guilty, the judge still has to decide whether to accept that agreement. (See the Criminal Justice Abroad box.)

Trials. If a case does proceed to trial and the defendant opts to have the case heard before a jury, the judge oversees the jury selection and controls the presentation of evidence. During the trial, the judge must maintain the decorum of the courtroom and rule on any motions and objections. Avoiding legal errors during a trial is extremely important because such errors can form the basis of an appeal that may result in reversing the decision. At the conclusion of the presentation of evidence and arguments, the judge must formulate instructions that will advise jurors of the law to be applied to the facts presented to them.

In cases where the defendant chooses to waive the right to a jury trial, the judge becomes the trier of facts and decides the guilt or innocence of the defendant. If a defendant is found guilty by a judge or jury, the judge determines the sentence given to the defendant (see Chapter 13).

Other Judicial and Nonjudicial Functions. Of course, judges perform many other duties besides their critical trial role. Judges are responsible for the functioning of their courts. Fewer than half preside at a trial on an average day, but nearly three-quarters report that they spend time on administrative duties.

The administrative functions of the judge include responsibility for support staff, lending assistance in the preparation of the budget, and management of the

---

judge
Public officer lawfully instituted (by appointment or election) to decide litigated questions according to law, presiding in a court of law.

"Judges play a prominent role in ensuring that justice is served—sometimes at great expense."

"Our judges are not monks or scientists, but participants in the living stream of our national life, steering the law between the dangers of rigidity on the one hand and formlessness on the other."
Chief Justice Earl Warren, *Fortune*, 1955.

"In cases where the defendant chooses to waive the right to a jury trial, the judge becomes the trier of facts and decides the guilt or innocence of the defendant."

case flow within the court. Case-flow management, extremely important because of concerns over backlogs, has been given added importance because of the passage of "speedy trial laws" at the federal and state levels. These laws require that a defendant in a criminal case be brought to trial within a specified time, usually within four to six months.

Management of case flow involves control over what is called the court calendar. Each case that is filed in a court is entered into the records and is then placed on the court calendar for a hearing. In jurisdictions with many judges, courts may organize themselves in different ways for calendar management. Two primary methods of calendar management are used. In the individual calendar system, a case is randomly assigned to whichever judge is free. That judge is then responsible for the case from beginning to end. In the master calendar system, judges are assigned to hear particular kinds of cases. Thus, one judge may hear all the pretrial issues of a case while another judge may be responsible only for trials. Not surprisingly, some courts also utilize a modification of these systems.

Types of Judges

In federal courts, there are four different types of judges:

- *Magistrates*, whose responsibility is to hear such matters as pretrial motions and whose duties may include the trial and disposition of minor federal offenses
- *District judges*, who are the trial judges of the federal courts
- *Judges of the court of appeal*, who hear appeals from district courts
- *Justices of the Supreme Court*, who review a small number of cases and render definitive opinions binding all federal courts and, in constitutional matters, all state courts as well

In addition to these, the federal system also has nearly 300 bankruptcy court judges. Moreover, a variety of administrative law judges, tax court judges, and judges of other specialized courts deal primarily with matters of administrative law.

In state courts, justices of the peace and magistrates are found at the lowest level of the state court systems, typically in courts of limited jurisdiction and often at the municipal level. Trial judges are found in both courts of general jurisdiction and courts of limited jurisdiction. Appellate court judges and the justices of a state's court of last resort hear appeals on points of law and render final judgments.

Approximately 60 percent of the nation's trial court judges have general assignments in which they handle all types of cases that come before them, while 13 percent handle only criminal cases. About one-quarter of trial judges are assigned to hear only civil cases. Depending on the operation of the court in which they serve, judges may also be assigned to handle a particular aspect of cases, such as bail hearings or preliminary hearings.

Qualifications and Background

What are the formal requirements for a person who wishes to become, say, a U.S. Supreme Court justice? There are none! The Constitution, which authorizes the establishment of the Supreme Court, confers on the president the power to appoint judges to the highest court, subject to approval by the Senate. Congress has established the same selection process for lower court federal judges. However, there is no mention in the Constitution or elsewhere of any particular qualifications for federal judgeships. Candidates need have no special educational backgrounds, meet no minimum age requirements, or even be lawyers. There is no stipulation that a judge be a citizen of the United States or a legal resident. Interestingly, qualifications for U.S. magistrates have been set forth: a full-time magistrate must be a lawyer and a member of the state bar.

"There are no formal requirements for a person who wishes to become a U.S. Supreme Court justice."

THE FACE OF THE JUDICIARY

If we were to ask judges across the world what they regard as the essential characteristics of a judge, they would all answer independence, legitimacy, integrity, and impartiality. Yet the preparation judges receive for their work varies a great deal. Judges are molded by their culture, especially their legal culture, and they are different despite these common characteristics.

In some countries, Saudi Arabia for example, judges are religious men, with years of learning in the Sharia—the religious law of Islam—and its application. In other countries, England and the United States for example, judges simply are people learned in the law: graduates of law schools, with experience at the bar, who then move on to become judges. In England, for the upper echelon of the courts, this requires a royal appointment on the advice of the lord chancellor, and these judges are addressed as "your lordship." Lower court judges (lay judges or magistrates) are appointed by the lord chancellor, and legal education is not required. In the United States, most judges win their posts in partisan elections. All federal judges are appointed by the chief executive (the president, with the advice and consent of the Senate), and in some states the governor has similar power.

Judicial education

How to bridge the gap between having a trial lawyer's experience and becoming a good judge is a hotly debated topic among American lawyers (1). The famous American trial lawyer of the 1950s, Sam Liebowitz, described his elevation to a judgeship as simply taking the elevator in the courthouse that was marked "Judges Only." But attitudes have changed since then. In 1965 the National Judicial College was founded. Now located on the campus of the University of Nevada at Reno, it has undertaken to educate freshman judges to develop special skills and competence. Some of the courses aim at a deepened knowledge of law and procedure. Others emphasize decision-making, dispute resolution, sentencing and corrections, psychology, or court management. By now some 30,000 trial judges have gone through the program.

Other systems

This "judicial education" in the United States is a far cry from the type of training career judges obtain in other legal cultures, however. The countries whose laws are based on the system of the Roman law (civil law countries) nearly all have a career judiciary. Becoming a judge in Portugal, France, or Japan, for example, requires graduating at the top of the law school class and then passing a rigorous examination for entry into the judiciary. There follows a training course of several months' duration at the Center for the Training of the Judiciary in Lisbon, or at the Judicial

Training Academy in Tokyo for Japanese candidates. More difficult exams follow. Then comes training in the field, during which the student judge renders nonbinding decisions in the presence of senior judges who actually decide the case. These decisions are evaluated. If the candidate has not flunked out by now, he or she goes back to the Center or the Academy for further training, more examinations, and ultimately an appointment to a small court somewhere in the countryside. The goal of most judges in Portugal is to wind up in Lisbon, the capital, as a judge of the Supreme Court (2).

The Italian system is similar, although it relies less on judicial education. There an applicant for the judiciary takes a very difficult exam after four years of law school. The candidate must be under 30 years of age, a requirement that, for the most part, prevents experienced lawyers from switching over to the judiciary. At a recent annual exam 6,000 candidates competed for 200 openings. The ratio is even lower in Japan. The successful Italian candidates serve for six months as auditor judges, and then they are on their own. At any time during their career they may be outposted to the executive branch of the government—for example, the prison service or the police. After thirty years of service, or earlier if they are very good and very lucky, they may reach the highest level of the judiciary and ultimately retire with an ample pension (3).

Some commonalities

The processes of selection, training, cultural molding, and careerism make for the differences in the nature, outlook, and standing of judges. In the civil law countries, judges tend to resemble the upper echelon of the civil service, the top government administrators. In common law countries, especially the United States, judges resemble their colleagues of the bar in independence of spirit and in their practical approach to the issues before them.

All judges have more that is common than that separates them. Judges in all systems must be fearless in their decision-making. That always has been so, but it is particularly true today, when seventeen judges have been assassinated in Columbia and many judges have been shot by organized criminals and terrorists in Italy, Germany, the United States, Bolivia, Peru, and elsewhere (4). In Peru the situation has gotten so bad that judges con-

duct the trials of terrorists inside prison, hidden behind a one-way mirror, with their voices scrambled to avoid being identified (5).

In all systems, judges earn far less than practicing lawyers. What makes a person choose the bench over the bar? In the English-speaking world it may be the honor ("your honor") of being a judge, and in the civil law countries it is probably the security and independence from outside interference that attracts many to a judicial career. For all judges there is probably more than a little satisfaction in being in a profession known for independence, legitimacy, integrity, and impartiality.

SOURCES

1. Thomas B. Russell, "Bridging the Gap," *The Judges' Journal* 27(4) (1988):16–17, 56–57.
2. John J. Philipsborn, "'A Visit from the Colonies': California Judges and Lawyers Teach and Learn in Portugal," *Judicature* 74 (1990):163–164.
3. Mary L. Volcansek, "The Judicial Role in Italy: Independence, Impartiality, Legiti-
macy," *Judicature* 76 (1990):322.
4. Richard L. Fricker, "A Judiciary under Fire," *A.B.A. Journal,* February 1990, pp. 58–60.
5. Nathaniel C. Nash, "Peru's Invisible Judges: A Faceless Tyranny?" *The New York Times,* September 27, 1992, p. 8.

QUESTIONS FOR DISCUSSION

1. Judges who have been trial lawyers for years before becoming judges have a great deal of experience. How might those years of experience negatively affect their ability to be good judges?
2. The Criminal Justice on Trial box discusses the low numbers of minorities who become judges. Would instituting a judicial education system similar to Portugal's increase the number of minority judges in the United States? Defend your position.
3. In Europe and Japan most trial judges are in their twenties and thirties; in the United States they are much older. Do you think that an age gap between judge and defendant is important?

TABLE 11.1 Characteristics of Supreme Court Justices, 1992–1993 Term

Justice	Political Party	Year Appointed	Major Prior Experience	Law School Attended
Byron White	Democrat	1962	Deputy U.S. Attorney General	Yale
Harry Blackmun	Republican	1970	Federal Court of Appeals judge	Harvard
William Rehnquist	Republican	1971	Assistant U.S. Attorney General	Stanford
John P. Stevens	Republican	1975	Federal Court of Appeals judge	Northwestern
Sandra D. O'Connor	Republican	1981	State judge; state legislator	Stanford
Antonin Scalia	Republican	1986	Federal Court of Appeals judge; law professor at University of Chicago	Harvard
Anthony M. Kennedy	Republican	1987	Federal Court of Appeals judge	Harvard
David H. Souter	Republican	1990	State judge; recent Federal Court of Appeals judge	Harvard
Clarence Thomas	Republican	1991	Federal Court of Appeals judge; Chairman, EEOC	Yale

SOURCE: Henry R. Glick, *Courts, Politics, and Justice,* 3d ed. (New York: McGraw-Hill, 1993), p. 150 (Table 4.4).

Federal Judges. In practice, of course, qualifications for federal judges exist by custom. Most important is professional competence (Table 11.1).[88] Despite the lack of a requirement that judges be lawyers, virtually all appointments are of distinguished attorneys. Virtually all of the nominees of recent presidential administrations have come directly from another level of the judiciary, the practice of law, or the teaching of law. From two-thirds to three-quarters have had prior judicial or prosecutorial experience.[89] It is worth noting that the extent of prior prosecutorial experience has disturbed some members of the defense bar. William M. Kunstler has gone so far as to say: "It is a little short of infantile to expect that any former prosecutor could possibly, by exchanging a dress or business suit for a black robe, suddenly become an impartial adminstrator of the law."[90]

A second factor is political affiliation. With the exception of President Ford, at least 90 percent of every president's judicial nominees in the last thirty years have been in the same political party as the president who made the appointment.[91] Political affiliation does not mean that a nominee has been especially active in politics, but, in the words of one commentator, "partisan political activism has always been considered to be a great boon to a judgeship candidacy."[92]

"Partisan political activism has always been considered to be a great boon to a judgeship candidacy."
Elliot E. Slotnick, *Judicature* 67 (1984):378.

State Judges. At the state level, qualifications are more clearly articulated. With the exception of New Hampshire, every state stipulates minimum requirements for judges of the appellate courts and the courts of general jurisdiction. Criteria vary from state to state, but most require (1) a minimum age, (2) a number of years of residence within the state, and (3) membership in the state bar.[93] Most states do not require that magistrates or justices of the peace have law degrees or bar membership.

TABLE 11.2 Characteristics of State Supreme Court Judges and Federal Appeals Court Judges

	State Supreme Court Judges 1980–81 (N = 300)	Federal Appeals Court Judges (Carter Appointees) (N = 56)
Race and sex		
Female	3.1%	19.6%
Black	0.6	16.1
Religious affiliation		
Protestant	60.2	60.7
Catholic	23.9	23.2
Jewish	11.6	16.1
Other	4.2	—
Government career experience		
Prosecutor	21.5	32.1
Previous judicial	62.9	53.6
Type of undergraduate school		
State	55.2	30.4
Private	34.0	50.0
Prestigious	10.8	19.6
Type of law school		
State	66.0	39.3
Private	12.6	19.6
Prestigious	16.2	41.1
Proprietary	5.2	0.0
Type of law practice		
Solo	26.1	1.8
2–4 partners	54.0	3.6
Larger firm	19.9	26.9
Average age on reaching court	53.0 yrs	51.9 yrs

SOURCES: David A. Neubauer, *America's Courts and the Criminal Justice System*, 3d ed. (Pacific Grove, Calif.: Brooks/Cole, 1988), p. 171; Henry Glick and Craig Emmert, "Stability and Change: Characteristics of State Supreme Court Judges," *Judicature* 70 (1986):107, 109; Sheldon Goldman, "Reorganizing the Judiciary: The First Term Appointments," *Judicature* 68 (1985):313, 324–325.

Typical Judges. Who then serves on the nation's benches? At both federal and state levels, the answer is—an older, white male, born and educated in the jurisdiction where he serves, from a background of relatively high socioeconomic status (Table 11.2).[94] For example, in 1977 only 22 nonwhites and 6 women were among the 500 sitting federal judges. (See the Criminal Justice on Trial box.) President Carter pledged to take steps to change the face of the federal judiciary. With the passage of the Omnibus Judgeship Act of 1978, which created 152 new federal judgeships, the president was able to make an unusually large number of judicial appointments. Including new and replacement nominees, Carter appointed 258 district and appeals court judges, of whom 40 were women and 54 were nonwhite. By the end of Carter's administration, women's representation on the federal bench had risen from 1 percent to 7 percent and blacks from 4 percent to 9 percent.[95] More recent administrations have appointed far fewer minorities.

A recent survey of black judges at the state level found that a majority (59%) serve at the lowest level of the judiciary, either in courts of limited jurisdiction or in quasi-judicial positions. At the higher court levels, blacks account for approximately 3.5 percent of the judges.[96] When considering these figures it is important to keep in mind that the pool of possible candidates is effectively limited to those

"Who serves on the nation's benches? An older white male, born and educated in the jurisdiction where he serves, from a relatively high socioeconomic background."

BLACK ROBES AND WHITE JUSTICE

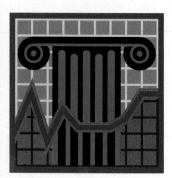

Not one black judge sat on the bench in any of the federal courts—district courts, courts of appeal, and the U.S. Supreme Court—for the first 145 years of our nation's history. The first, William H. Hastie, was appointed by President Harry S. Truman in 1949 (1).

Until only recently there have been policies of racial discrimination in the United States that prevented blacks from attending most of the nation's law schools. In addition, many blacks have been deprived of the high-school education that would afford them a chance to go on to college and then to law school. Others have been discouraged by the strong sense that justice in America is distributed along racial lines—that black lawyers and judges would bear an extra burden in all-white courts.

Times have changed—but not enough for most, and for many, not much at all. Today 2.7 percent of all practicing lawyers in the United States are black. Of the 24,000 judges nationwide, 840 are black. In 1993, more than half of the black judges who sit on the courts of appeal in the United States will be eligible for retirement.

Who will replace them? More than likely, it will be nonblacks. Of the 115 appointments to the courts of appeal during the last twelve years, only two have been African Americans. Even South Africa has a better record: In the last three years of President F. W. de Klerk's term, one of his thirty-one appointments

to South African courts has been black.

And the fear that black judges would "bear an extra burden" in America's courts is well founded. In a recent report of the New York State Judicial Commission on Minorities, white judges and nonwhite judges rated the extent to which the treatment of judges is affected by racial and ethnic differences (2). Essentially, white judges do not think judges are treated any differently if they are not white, but minority judges feel that other judges, attorneys, and courtroom personnel treat white judges one way and minority judges another (Table 1). These differences appear in judges' perceptions of the importance of

TABLE 1 Judge's Ratings: Extent to Which Treatment of Judges and Courtroom Personnel Is Affected by Racial/Ethnic Differences (Numbers in parentheses are percentages)

	White Judges			Minority Judges			Total Judges		
	Not at all	Some-what	Great-ly	Not at all	Some-what	Great-ly	Not at all	Some-what	Great-ly
Treatment of judges by other judges is affected	462 (85.6)	72 (13.3)	6 (1.1)	20 (26.7)	47 (62.7)	8 (10.7)	482 (78.4)	119 (19.3)	14 (2.3)
Treatment of judges by attorneys is affected	417 (77.8)	109 (20.3)	10 (1.9)	18 (24.0)	43 (57.3)	14 (18.7)	435 (71.2)	152 (24.9)	24 (3.9)
Treatment of judges by courtroom personnel is affected	442 (84.2)	79 (15.0)	4 (.8)	27 (37.0)	37 (50.7)	9 (12.3)	469 (78.4)	116 (19.4)	13 (2.2)

SOURCE: *Report of the New York State Judicial Commission on Minorities,* Vol. 4 (1991).

TABLE 2 Judges' Ratings: Importance of Training on Cross-Cultural Sensitivity for Judges (Number in parentheses are percentages)

White Judges				Minority Judges				Total Judges			
Very Impor-tant	Impor-tant	Some-what Impor.	Unim-por-tant	Very Impor-tant	Impor-tant	Some-what Impor.	Unim-por-tant	Very Impor-tant	Impor-tant	Some-what Impor.	Unim-por-tant
143 (27.4)	220 (42.1)	114 (21.8)	45 (8.6)	47 (68.1)	13 (18.8)	5 (7.2)	4 (5.8)	190 (32.1)	233 (39.4)	119 (20.1)	49 (8.3)

SOURCE: *Report of the New York State Judicial Commission on Minorities,* Vol. 4 (1991).

cross-cultural sensitivity training for judges as well (Table 2). Minority judges feel that it is more important than do white judges.

Commission conclusions

The New York commission listed a host of conclusions, including the following four:

1. There is a perception that minorities are underrepresented in the state judiciary in comparison with the available pool of qualified attorneys. Moreover, minorities are underrepresented on the bench in comparison with their share of the overall population.
2. There is a particular need for more minority judges in upstate districts.
3. There is a pool of minority applicants for judgeships who were rated as qualified but who were not appointed.
4. By any measure, minorities are grossly underrepresented in supervisory and other high-level administrative positions within the judiciary.

Justice Wright's experience

The plight of the black judge has been chronicled by New York State Supreme Court Justice Bruce McM.

Wright. Justice Wright, once a judge in the Manhattan Criminal Court and the New York Civil Court, has felt the pain associated with rejection by colleagues, ridicule by the press, and harassment from the public. According to Justice Wright, the differential treatment of black judges—by white defendants, judges, and politicians—reflects the racism found within the structure of American society. As Judge Wright wrote:

Racism inside the courts is but a reflection of what goes on in society in general. This was brought home forcefully to me with a kind of grim humor in 1974. At that time I was teaching a course at The New School for Social Research in the evenings, as well as an early morning one at Staten Island Community College. This called for some tense traveling in order not to be late in reporting to court. After leaving Staten Island, I would speed across the Verrazano Bridge to be in my courtroom by 10 a.m.

One afternoon, during a trial, I felt so faint and weak I could not carry on. The clerks, with affectionate concern, feared that I was having a heart attack. I was taken out of the courthouse lashed to a stretcher. It was an embarrassment to be so helpless and publicly exhibited.

In the emergency room of the hospital, I was placed in a curtained-off area where there was two beds some distance apart. On one was a white man, obviously one of the poor derelicts now

and then brought in from the Bowery. He appeared to be in a state of joyous alcoholic bewilderment. He needed a shave; neither his soiled sneakers nor his socks matched; he drooled a bit and sang softly in garbled syllables.

As I watched him from my bed, I felt pangs of pity. He seemed much worse off than I. I felt guilty for being dressed in a three-piece suit and clean shirt.

I heard a nurse outside the curtained area say, "Hurry, doctor, we have a judge who is ill." A white doctor parted the curtains, paused at the entrance, looked at me and then at the white derelict. He hurried to the side of the white man, lifted his wrist as though to test his pulse, and said, "Judge, what seems to be the matter?"

It was a bracing experience, wholly therapeutic, and I began to recover without delay.

The most remarkable aspect of the hospital experience was the reinforcement of my view that whites almost automatically have a "place" reaction to the color of dark skin. Compared with a poor, ragged, homeless white unfortunate, unshaven and drooling, a well-dressed black simply could not be the judge. What a sadness, I thought, and how appropriate was the observation of an unknown wit who had said that America was the only country in the world to suffer a decline and fall in its civilization without first becoming civilized (3).

SOURCES

1. Franklin Edwards, *The Negro Professional Class* (Glencoe, Ill.: Free Press, 1959), p. 155.
2. New York State Judicial Commission on Minorities, *Report of the New York State Judicial Commission on Minorities,* Vol. 4 (New York: The Commission, 1991).
3. Bruce Wright, *Black Robes, White Justice* (Secaucus, N.J.: Lyle Stuart, 1987), pp. 24–25.

QUESTIONS FOR DISCUSSION

1. How does the lack of minority judges affect American justice?
2. Devise a strategy to increase the representation of blacks and Hispanics on our nation's courts.
3. How would you go about ensuring equal and fair treatment for all judges, regardless of race?

Judge Wright outside Manhattan Criminal Court in 1979, with supporters.

"The disproportionately small representation of women and minorities in the pool of judicial candidates is the result of historical patterns of systematic exclusion."

The process of nominating a potential Supreme Court Justice has become increasingly political. Nominee Bork was not confirmed; nominees Kennedy and Thomas were. Top to bottom: Robert Bork, Arthur Kennedy, Clarence Thomas

who are lawyers. Thus, while a disparity may appear to be extremely large compared with a group's proportional representation in the general population, the same may not be true when we look at the pool of potential judges. For example, blacks constitute 2.7 percent of all lawyers.[97] The disproportionately small representation of women and minorities in the pool of candidates is the result of historical patterns in which these groups were systematically excluded from careers in law.

Several researchers have questioned whether women and blacks on the judiciary rule differently from their white male counterparts. John Gruhl and his colleagues compared the sentencing decisions of male and female judges and found that women were not more lenient in convicting defendants or in sentencing them to periods of incarceration. However, they were more willing than men to sentence women to prison.[98] Cassia Spohn recently examined the sentencing decisions of black and white judges and found that judges' race appears to have little effect on their decision-making.[99] Susan Welch and her associates, however, found that black judges were significantly more likely than white judges to sentence white defendants to prison. However, in keeping with expectations, they found that this reflects the fact that black judges were actually treating whites the same as blacks, while white judges had a tendency to sentence black defendants more harshly than white.[100] Some believe that the relative lack of differences between black and women judges and white male judges may be attributable to the fact that all judges, regardless of gender or race, simply become socialized into the culture of the judiciary. All tend to place value on similar legal considerations, and all come to see themselves first as judges upholding the law, rather than as representatives of a group.

Selection

Federal Judges. Under the Constitution, the president of the United States has the responsibility of selecting nominees for judges at all levels of the federal judiciary. After selection, their names are presented to the Senate for confirmation or approval. Most presidents have traditionally taken a good deal more interest in personally selecting the nominees to the U.S. Supreme Court than to the lower courts. This may be due to the importance of the court, and the fact that a tradition has been established regarding district court appointments: Senators from the president's party tend to exercise virtual veto power over nominees to district judgeships in their state. Should the home-state senator object to the nominee, the members of the Senate Judiciary Committee, who review and make recommendations about all judicial nominees, will simply not recommend the nomination to the full Senate. In view of this tradition, presidents tend to leave the selection of district judges to members of the White House staff and high-ranking officials of the Department of Justice.[101] The great majority of a president's nominees are approved by the Senate.

One important factor in the selection of federal judges has been the rating given to them by the American Bar Association's Committee on the Federal Judiciary. This committee, composed of members from each of the federal circuits, carefully evaluates all potential candidates for the federal bench and gives them one of four possible ratings: "exceptionally well qualified," "well qualified," "qualified," or "not qualified." A rating of "not qualified" by the ABA Committee makes appointment extremely unlikely.[102] But clearly, the most important criterion for selection is political party affiliation.

State Judges. State judiciaries use one of five methods to choose their judges: partisan elections (in which judges' party affiliations appear on the ballot), nonpartisan elections, merit selection, gubernatorial appointment, and appointment by the legislature. Partisan elections are used in nine states, and another thirteen states use nonpartisan elections. This makes the elective process the most popular form of selection at the state level.[103]

Research has shown that voters are often unfamiliar with judicial candidates and therefore do not make informed choices when they vote. In Lubbock, Texas, for example, only 14.2 percent of all voters in a 1979 general election could identify the judicial candidate that they had just voted for. In the 1980 elections for Wyoming Supreme Court, 23.8 percent of all voters did not know why they voted for their candidate.[104]

One alternative to elections that has become extremely popular is merit selection. First adopted in Missouri in 1940, and known ever since as "the Missouri Plan," merit selection is intended to provide a means of selecting well-qualified candidates untainted by political influence. Under the typical plan, a state nominating commission will select several candidates and submit their names to the governor, who then appoints one from among them. After a short period, the judge must stand for election, which usually takes the form of a question on the ballot that asks "Shall Judge X be retained in office?" As in other judicial elections, the voters tend to vote "yes" even though they may know nothing about the judge. Merit selection has grown steadily in popularity and is now used in twenty-one states.

Other Court Personnel

It would be a mistake to assume that judges manage the entire operation of the courts. It would be a mistake as well to assume that courts run by themselves. They are complex organizations requiring day-to-day management, administrative assistance, and support. Figure 11.6 depicts the continuum of administrative-judicial action, revealing the full range of activities that transcend the adjudicatory function.

Most state court systems today use the services of a **court administrator** to execute the many nonjudicial, administrative duties. The court administrator is usually appointed by the state court of last resort, the chief justice of the court of last resort, or a judicial council. Despite the presence of the court administrator, the judges retain the primary responsibility for the way in which the court func-

court administrator
Chief administrative officer of the court, usually appointed by the state court of last resort, the chief justice of the court of last resort, or a judicial council.

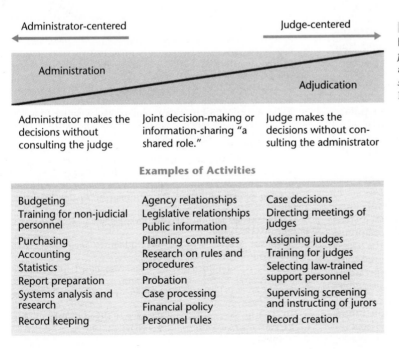

FIGURE 11.6 *Continuum of administrative-judicial activities* (*Source:* Charles R. Swanson and Surette M. Tularico, *Court Administration: Issues and Responses* [Athens: University of Georgia Press, 1987], p. 26.)

Administrator-centered | Judge-centered

Administration

Adjudication

| Administrator makes the decisions without consulting the judge | Joint decision-making or information-sharing "a shared role." | Judge makes the decisions without consulting the administrator |

Examples of Activities

Budgeting	Agency relationships	Case decisions
Training for non-judicial personnel	Legislative relationships	Directing meetings of judges
Purchasing	Public information	Assigning judges
Accounting	Planning committees	Training for judges
Statistics	Research on rules and procedures	Selecting law-trained support personnel
Report preparation	Probation	Supervising screening and instructing of jurors
Systems analysis and research	Case processing	
Record keeping	Financial policy	Record creation
	Personnel rules	

tions. The court administrator may be properly considered the chief operating officer of the court, and the chief judge its executive officer.

The day-to-day affairs of all federal courts are the responsibility of the Administrative Office of the U.S. Courts. The Administrative Office, created by Congress in 1939, serves as the management arm of the federal courts. It also collects and disseminates statistics and information on federal cases. More recently, the Administrative Office has served as an advocate for the federal judiciary before Congress, the White House, professional groups, and the general public.[105]

The same office in smaller, local state courts is clerk of the court—sometimes called registers of probate or prothonotaries. Clerks docket cases, collect fees and court costs, maintain records, and manage jury selection. Their position and role should not be confused with those of the law clerks. Law clerks, both in the state and federal courts, are graduates of law school who spend one or two years in an apprenticeship position to a judge. Law clerks review motions and draft legal memoranda and judicial opinions.

Many other court employees perform useful tasks, including:

- **court officers and marshals,** who provide courtroom security and maintain order
- **bailiffs,** who administer formal procedures, keep order in court, announce a judge's arrival, and administer oaths
- deputy clerks, who, along with secretaries, maintain records and legal documents, type, and duplicate[106]

court officers and marshals
Persons who provide courtroom security and maintain order. See also bailiff.

bailiff
Officer of the court who administers formal procedures, keeps order, announces a judge's arrival, and administers oaths.

REVIEW

Lawyers and judges play different roles, carry out different duties, and operate under different constraints. Prosecutors are government attorneys who represent the people of their jurisdiction. They are responsible for some of the most important initial responses to crime, such as deciding what offenses to charge a suspect with, obtaining an indictment or filing an information against a defendant, and trying the criminal case. The different types of prosecutors include district attorneys, state attorneys general, and United States attorneys. Prosecutors are elected at the local and state level, and are appointed at the federal level.

Both private defense counsel and public defenders represent the interests of those accused of crimes. They are advocates for their clients, and act as intermediaries and as counselors. Defense attorneys, whether private or public, may face significant ethical dilemmas in their attempt to provide zealous representation for those who cannot afford to retain private counsel. Case-load pressures add to the problem.

Judges are the supreme officers of the court. They preside over proceedings, interpret and decide questions of law, and ensure that justice is served. In the federal courts there are four different kinds of judges: magistrates, district judges, judges of the Court of Appeals, and U.S. Supreme Court judges. In state courts there are justices of the peace, trial judges, appellate court judges, and justices of the court of last resort. Federal judges are nominated by the president and appointed by the Senate. At the state level, most judges are elected.

Other court personnel include court administrators, who execute nonjudicial administrative duties; clerks of the court, who collect fees and maintain records; law clerks, who occupy an apprenticeship position to a judge; and court officers, marshals, and bailiffs, who manage the day-to-day operations of a particular courtroom.

Notes

1. C. L. Sonnichsen, *Roy Bean: Law West of the Pecos* (New York: Macmillan, 1934).

2. American Bar Foundation, *Supplement to the Lawyer Statistical Report: The U.S. Legal Profession in 1988* (1989).

3. John Jay Douglass, *Ethical Issues in Prosecution* (Houston: National College of District Attorneys, 1988), p. 9.

4. American Bar Foundation, *Supplement to the Lawyer Statistical Report.*

5. For a view of the historical evolution of prosecution from private to public responsibility, see Joan E. Jacoby, *The American Prosecutor: A Search for Identity* (Lexington, Mass.: Lexington Books, 1980); Allen Steinberg, "From Private Prosecution to Plea Bargaining: Criminal Prosecution, the District Attorney, and American Legal History," *Crime and Delinquency* 30 (1984):568–592.

6. Marianne W. Zawitz, ed., *Report to the Nation on Crime and Justice,* 2d ed. (Washington, D.C.: Bureau of Justice Statistics, 1988).

7. "Financial Institution Prosecution Updated," *U.S. Attorneys' Bulletin* 40 (1992):147.

8. Robert A. Carp and Ronald Stidham, *Judicial Process in America* (Washington, D.C.: CQ Press, 1990).

9. See, e.g., John Buchanan, "Police-Prosecutor Teams: Innovations in Several Jurisdictions," *The Prosecutor* 23 (1988):31–36; Peter Finn, "Bias Crime: A Special Target for Prosecutors," *The Prosecutor* 21 (1986):9–15.

10. Charles Strum, "Federal Prosecutor Urged to Take up Teaneck Case," *The New York Times,* February 14, 1992, p. B7.

11. Ibid.

12. Martin H. Belsky, "On Becoming a Prosecutor," *The Prosecutor* 12 (1981):22–39, p. 22.

13. "Rockwell Pleads Guilty to Environmental Crimes at Rocky Flats," *U.S. Newswire,* March 26, 1992.

14. Larry Rohter, "Victory in Noriega Case Stunned Even Prosecutors," *The New York Times,* April 17, 1992, p. B16.

15. Abraham S. Blumberg, *Criminal Justice: Issues and Ironies* (New York: New Viewpoints, 1979), p. 123.

16. See, for example, J. Buchanan, "Police-Prosecutor Teams: Innovations in Several Jurisdictions," *National Institute of Justice Reports No. 214* (Washington, D.C.: National Institute of Justice, 1989).

17. See Roy B. Flemming, "The Political Styles and Organizational Strategies of American Prosecutors: Examples from Nine Courthouse Communities," *Law and Policy* 12 (1990):25–50; Peter F. Nardulli, James Eisenstein, and Roy B. Flemming, *The Tenor of Justice: Criminal Courts and the Guilty Plea Process* (Urbana and Chicago: University of Illinois Press, 1988).

18. See James Eisenstein and Herbert Jacob, *Felony Justice: An Organizational Analysis of Criminal Courts* (Boston: Little, Brown, 1977).

19. See George F. Cole, "The Decision to Prosecute," *Law and Society Review* 4 (1970):331–343.

20. James Eisenstein. *Counsel for the United States: U.S. Attorneys in the Political and Legal Systems* (Baltimore: Johns Hopkins University Press, 1978).

21. Newman F. Baker, "The Prosecutor-Initiation of Prosecution," *Journal of Criminal Law and Criminology* 23 (1933):770.

22. Charles D. Breitel, "Controls in Criminal Law Enforcement," *University of Chicago Law Review* 27 (1960):427–435.

23. Barbara Boland, Catherine H. Conly, Paul Mahanna, Lynn Warner, and Ronald Sones, *The Prosecution of Felony Arrests, 1987* (Washington, D.C.: Bureau of Justice Statistics, 1990).

24. Bureau of Justice Statistics, *Federal Criminal Case Processing, 1980–89, with Preliminary Data for 1990* (Washington, D.C.: Bureau of Justice Statistics, 1991).

25. Boland et al., *The Prosecution of Felony Arrests, 1987.*

26. Comment, "Prosecutorial Discretion in the Initiation of Criminal Complaints," *Southern California Law Review* 42 (1969):519–545.

27. See, for example, Janell Schmidt and Ellen Hochstedler Steury, "Prosecutorial Discretion in Filing Charges in Domestic Violence Cases," *Criminology* 27 (1989):487–510; Huey-Tsyh Chen, "Dropping In and Dropping Out: Judicial Decisionmaking in the Disposition of Felony Arrests," *Journal of Criminal Justice* 19 (1991):1–17; Martha A. Myers and John Hagan, "Private and Public Trouble: Prosecutors and the Allocation of Court Resources," *Social Problems* 26 (1979):439–451; Celesta A. Albonetti, "Criminality, Prosecutorial Screening, and Uncertainty: Toward a Theory of Discretionary Decision Making in Felony Case Processings," *Criminology* 24 (1986):623–644.

28. See David W. Neubauer, "After the Arrest: The Charging Decision in Prairie City," *Law and Society Review* 8 (1974):495–517; Albonetti, "Criminality, Prosecutorial Screening, and Uncertainty"; and Myers and Hagan, "Private and Public Trouble."

29. See Malcolm D. Holmes, Howard C. Daudistel, and Ronald Farrell, "Determinants of Charge Reductions and Final Dispositions in Cases of Burglary and Robbery," *Journal of Research in Crime and Delinquency* 24 (1987):233–254; Chen, "Dropping In and Dropping Out."

30. See Holmes, Daudistel, and Farrell, "Determinants of Charge Reductions"; Myers and Hagan, "Private and Public Trouble."

31. See, e.g., Albonetti, "Criminality, Prosecutorial Screening, and Uncertainty"; Chen, "Dropping In and Dropping Out."

32. Schmidt and Steury, "Prosecutorial Discretion." See, e.g., Maureen McLeod, "Victim Noncooperation in the Prosecution of Domestic Assault," *Criminology* 21 (1983):395–416; Albert J. Reiss, Jr., "Public Prosecutors and Criminal Prosecution in the United States of America," in *The Criminal Justice System: Materials on the Administration and Reform of the Criminal Law,* eds. Franklin Zimring and Richard S. Frase, (Boston: Little, Brown, 1980), pp. 396–401; Frank W. Miller, *Prosecution: The Decision to Charge a Suspect with a Crime* (Boston: Little, Brown, 1969).

33. Elizabeth Anne Stanko, "The Impact of Victim Assessment on Prosecutors' Screening Decisions: The Case of the New York County District Attorney's Office," *Law and Society Review* 16 (1981–82):225–239. Other research has shown that some victim characteristics that might influence a prosecutor's evaluation are decidedly not "legally relevant," while others reflect at least some dynamics of the case that might represent either aggravating or mitigating circumstances. In the former category are factors such as the victim's age, gender, race, and employment status. In many cases, complaints by older, white, employed men seem to be given more credibility than complaints by other categories of victims. Drug or alcohol abuse by the victim or a history of arrests of the victim may lower the prosecutor's assessment of the victim's credibility. See, e.g., Kristen M. Williams, "The Effects of Victim Characteristics on the Disposition of Violent Crimes," in *Criminal Justice and the Victim,* ed. William F. McDonald (Beverly Hills, Calif.: Sage, 1976), pp. 177–213; Myers and Hagan, "Private and Public Trouble"; McLeod, "Victim Noncooperation." Victim characteristics have even been found to play a role in the prosecution of white-collar crimes: Analysis of prosecutions undertaken by one economic crime unit in a prosecutor's office revealed that cases where a corporation was victimized were more likely to be accepted for prosecution than those where the victim was an individual.

34. See Williams, "The Effects of Victim Characteristics."

35. See Albonetti, "Criminality, Prosecutorial Screening, and Uncertainty"; Chen, "Dropping In and Dropping Out."

36. See Chen, "Dropping In and Dropping Out."

37. See Holmes, Daudistel, and Farrell, "Determinants of Charge Reductions."

38. For examples, see Thomas J. Keil and Gennaro F. Vito, "Race, Homicide Severity, and Application of the Death Penalty: A Consideration of the Barnett Scale," *Criminology* 27 (1989):511–535; Raymond Paternoster, "Prosecutorial Discretion in Requesting the Death Penalty: A Case of Victim-Based Racial Discrimination," *Law and Society Review* 18 (1984):437–478; William J. Bowers, "The Pervasiveness of Arbitrariness and Discrimination under Post-*Furman* Capital Statutes," *Journal of Criminal Law and Criminology* 74 (1983):1067–1083; Michael L. Radelet and Glenn L. Pierce, "Race and Prosecutorial Discretion in Homicide Cases," *Law and Society Review* 19 (1985):587–621; David C. Baldus, Charles Pulaski, and George Woodworth, "Comparative Review of Death Sentences: An Empirical Study of the Georgia Experience," *Journal of Criminal Law and Criminology* 74 (1983):661–753.

39. For discussions of external factors, see Miller, *Prosecution.* See also Cole, "The Decision to Prosecute."

40. Margaret Farnsworth, James Golden, and Kimberly Tester, "Felony Court Processing in an Urban County: Coping with a 'Limited Capacity to Punish'," *Journal of Criminal Justice* 19 (1991):421–438.

41. Although empirical research on decision-making has provided some evidence of the factors that influence prosecutors, there are probably many other variables that need to be examined more closely. Most of the empirical research is based on a single prosecutor's office, thereby limiting the generalizability of the results. Furthermore, statistical analysis of the data used in the research tends to explain only a small amount of the variance in decision-making. One exception to this is a nationwide study of 855 chief and assistant prosecutors in fifteen jurisdictions conducted by Joan Jacoby and her associates. These researchers found an overwhelming consistency among the prosecutors. Three factors play a significant role at almost every stage of decision-making: the seriousness of the offense, the criminality of the defendant, and the strength of the evidence in the case. While this is encouraging news to those concerned about the arbitrary application of discretion, the study was based on test cases, not on records that would show how the prosecutors actually handle cases. Furthermore, many of the personal

factors shown by other research to affect decision-making were not explored in this study. Joan E. Jacoby, Leonard R. Mellon, Edward C. Ratledge, and Stanley H. Turner, *Prosecutorial Decisionmaking: A National Study* (Washington, D.C.: National Institute of Justice, 1982).

42. *Oyler v. Boles*, 368 U.S. 448 (1962). See Cox, "Prosecutorial Discretion."

43. See Charles W. Thomas and W. Anthony Fitch, "Prosecutorial Decision Making," *American Criminal Law Review* 13 (1976):507–559; Kenneth Culp Davis, *Discretionary Justice: A Preliminary Inquiry* (Baton Rouge: Louisiana State University Press, 1969).

44. Charles D. Breitel, "Controls in Criminal Law Enforcement."

45. Paul B. Wise, *Criminal Lawyers: An Endangered Species* (Beverly Hills, Calif.: Sage, 1978).

46. Harold J. Rothwax, "The Criminal Court: Problems and Proposals," unpublished manuscript, Biddle Law Library, University of Pennsylvania, 1970.

47. Edward A. Adams, "State Commission Finds Racism in Courts; 70 Suggestions Proposed to Eliminate 2-Tier System," *New York Law Journal*, June 5, 1991, p. 1.

48. Ibid.

49. *Gideon v. Wainwright*, 372 U.S. 335 (1963); *Argersinger v. Hamlin*, 407 U.S. 25 (1972).

50. American Bar Association Project on Standards for Criminal Justice, *Standards Relating to the Prosecution Function and the Defense Function* (New York: American Bar Association, 1970).

51. Benson B. Weintraub, "The Role of Defense Counsel at Sentencing," *Federal Probation* 51 (March 1987):27.

52. Paul B. Wise, *Chaos in the Courthouse: The Inner Workings of the Urban Criminal Courts* (New York: Praeger, 1985).

53. James Eisenstein and Herbert Jacob, *Felony Justice*.

54. The white-collar-crime defense attorney differs significantly from the courthouse regulars just described. Kenneth Mann's study of white-collar criminal defense attorneys in New York City provides valuable insights into how this new breed of defense counsel operates. In white-collar criminal practices, attorneys handle a small number of cases to which they devote substantial amounts of time. Much time is spent in the early parts of the investigation, with the objective of trying to prevent the formal filing of charges against the client. The white-collar-crime defender may believe that the client is guilty, but does not assume that the government has sufficient evidence for a conviction. The strategy then becomes one of trying to keep inculpatory evidence from the prosecutor by controlling access to information needed to file charges. This strategy typically involves vigorous and uncompromising advocacy on behalf of the client. Mann has pointed out that this style of defense is quite different from the typical conciliatory style of most criminal cases, the vast majority of which end with a negotiated plea. See Kenneth Mann, *Defending White Collar Crime: A Portrait of Attorneys at Work* (New Haven: Yale University Press, 1985).

55. Dick Kimmins, "Public Defenders—Shock Troops of the Legal Profession," *Business First-Columbus* 2 (33, Sec. 1) (May 19, 1986):1.

56. *Powell v. Alabama*, 287 U.S. 45 (1932).

57. *Johnson v. Zerbst*, 304 U.S. 458 (1938).

58. *Gideon v. Wainwright*, 372 U.S. 335 (1963).

59. *Argersinger v. Hamlin*, 407 U.S. 25 (1972).

60. Sue A. Lindgren, *Justice Expenditure and Employment, 1988* (Washington, D.C.: Bureau of Justice Statistics, 1990).

61. Robert L. Spangenberg, Beverly Lee, Michael Battaglia, Patricia Smith, and A. David Davis, *National Criminal Defense Systems Study: Final Report* (Washington, D.C.: Bureau of Justice Statistics, NCJ-94702, 1986); Alissa Pollitz Worden, "Privatizing Due Process: Issues in the Comparison of Assigned Counsel, Public Defender, and Contracted Indigent Defense Systems," *Justice System Journal* 14(3) and 15(1) (1991):390–418.

62. Spangenberg et al., *National Criminal Defense Systems Study*.

63. Bureau of Justice Statistics, *Criminal Defense for the Poor, 1986* (Washington, D.C.: Bureau of Justice Statistics, 1988).

64. "Lawyers Fumble, but Citizens Pay," *Chicago Tribune*, November 11, 1986, Business Section, p. 1.

65. Charles E. Silberman, *Criminal Justice, Criminal Violence* (New York: Vintage Books, 1980), p. 410.

66. Jonathan D. Casper, "Did You Have a Lawyer When You Went to Court? No, I Had a Public Defender," *Yale Review of Law and Social Action* 1 (1971):4–9.

67. See, e.g., Robert Wayne Gordon, "Defense of Indigents in Texas: A Mockery of Justice," *Baylor Law Review* 30 (1978):739–764.

68. See, in particular, David Sudnow, "Normal Crimes: Sociological Features of the Penal Code in a Public Defender Office," *Social Problems* 12 (1965):255–276.

69. *McMann v. Richardson*, 397 U.S. 765, 771 (1970) (emphasis added).

70. Richard Klein, "The Emperor *Gideon* Has No Clothes: The Empty Promise of the Constitutional Right to Effective Assistance of Counsel," *Hastings Constitutional Law Quarterly* 13 (1986):625–693.

71. See, for example, American Bar Association, *Standards Relating to the Defense Function, Model Code of Professional Responsibility*, and *Model Rules of Professional Conduct*.

72. For a summary of these studies, see Richard Klein, "The Emperor *Gideon* Has No Clothes." See also Norman Lefstein, *Criminal Defense Services for the Poor: Methods and Programs for Providing Legal Representation and the Need for Adequate Financing* (American Bar Association Standing Committee on Legal Aid and Indigent Defendants, 1982).

73. Casper, "Did You Have a Lawyer."

74. See Geoffrey P. Alpert and C. Ronald Huff, "Defending the Accused: Counsel Effectiveness and Strategies," in William F. McDonald, *The Defense Counsel* (Beverly Hills, Calif.: Sage, 1983), pp. 247–271.

75. Stephanie Saul, "When Death Is the Penalty: Attorneys for Poor Defendants Often Lack Experience and Skill," *Newsday*, November 25, 1991, p. 8.

76. For examples, see Joyce S. Sterling, "Retained Counsel versus the Public Defender: The Impact of Type of Counsel on Charge Bargaining," in McDonald, *The Defense Counsel*, pp. 151–170; R. Stover and D. Eckart, "A Systematic Comparison of Public Defenders and Private Attorneys," *American Journal of Criminal Law* 3 (1975):265–300; Peter F. Nardulli, "'Insider' Justice: Defense Attorneys and the Handling of Felony Cases," *Journal of Criminal Law and Criminology* 77 (1986):379–417; Dean J. Champion, "Private Counsels and Public Defenders: A Look at Weak Cases, Prior Records, and Leniency in Plea Bargaining," *Journal of Criminal Justice* 17 (1989):253–263; Holmes, Daudistel, and Farrell, "Determinants of Charge Reductions."

77. See Alissa Pollitz Wordin, "Privatizing Due Process."

78. Milton Chivizzani, "A Former Public Defender Proudly States His Case," *Seattle Times*, March 23, 1992, p. A7.

79. American Bar Association, *Model Code of Professional Responsibility* (1979).

80. Terence F. MacCarthy and Kathy Morris Mejia, "The Perjurious Client Question: Putting Criminal Defense Lawyers between a Rock and a Hard Place," *Journal of Criminal Law and Criminology* 75 (1984):1197–1221.

81. Marilyn Moore, "The Law of Lying Clients: Dilemma for the Defense," *U.S. News and World Report*, June 8, 1987, p. 24.

82. See Lefstein, *Criminal Defense Services for the Poor*.

83. Joe Margulies, "Resource Deprivation and the Right to Counsel," *Journal of Criminal Law and Criminology* 80 (1989):673–725.

84. Albert W. Alschuler, "The Defense Attorney's Role in Plea Bargaining," *Yale Law Journal* 84 (1975):1179.

85. Margulies, "Resource Deprivation."

86. See Casper, "Did You Have a Lawyer When You Went to Court?"

87. Ralph Blumenthal, "The View from the Bench: Once a Pros-

ecutor, Now a Federal Judge: A Harried but Happy Life in the Law," *The New York Times*, March 11, 1992, p. B1.

88. Carp and Stidham, *Judicial Process in America*.

89. Kathleen Maguire and Timothy Flanagan, *Sourcebook of Criminal Justice Statistics—1990* (Washington, D.C.: Bureau of Justice Statistics, 1991), pp. 53–54.

90. William M. Kunstler, "The Prosecutor-Judge," *New York Law Journal*, March 31, 1992, p. 2.

91. Ibid.

92. Elliot E. Slotnick, "The Paths to the Federal Bench: Gender, Race and Judicial Recruitment Variation," *Judicature* 67 (1984):378; Glen T. Broach, Phillip D. Jackson, & Victor H. Ascolillo "State Political Culture and Sentence Severity in Federal District Courts," *Criminology* 16 (1978):373–392.

93. Ibid., p. 61.

94. See, e.g., Carp and Stidham, *Judicial Process in America*. See also Elliot E. Slotnick, "Federal Trial and Appellate Judges: How Do They Differ?," *Western Political Quarterly* 36 (1983):570–578.

95. Slotnick, "The Paths to the Federal Bench."

96. Barbara Luck Graham, "Judicial Recruitment and Racial Diversity on State Courts: An Overview," *Judicature* 74 (June–July 1990):28–34.

97. See Nicholas O. Alozie, "Black Representation on State Judiciaries," *Social Science Quarterly* 69 (1988):979–986.

98. John Gruhl, Cassia Spohn, and Susan Welch, "Women as Policymakers: The Case of Trial Judges," *American Journal of Political Science* 25 (1981):308–322.

99. Cassia Spohn, "The Sentencing Decisions of Black and White Judges: Expected and Unexpected Similarities," *Law and Society Review* 24 (1990):1197–2016. See also Thomas M. Uhlman, "Black Elite Decision Making: The Case of Trial Judges," *American Journal of Political Science* 22 (1978):884–895; Thomas G. Walker and Deborah J. Barrow, "The Diversification of the Federal Bench: Policy and Process Ramifications," *Journal of Politics* 47 (1985):596–617; Jon Gottschall, "Carter's Judicial Appointments: The Influence of Affirmative Action and Merit Selection on Voting on the U.S. Courts of Appeals," *Judicature* 67 (1983):164–173.

100. Susan Welch, Michael Combs, and John Gruhl, "Do Black Judges Make a Difference?," *American Journal of Political Science* 32 (1988):126–136. See also Martha A. Myers, "Social Background and the Sentencing Behavior of Judges," *Criminology* 26 (1988):649–675, for comments about the investigation of the social characteristics of judges; see also William Eich, "Gender Bias in the Courtroom: Some Participants Are More Equal Than Others," *Judicature* 6 (1986):339–343.

101. Carp and Stidham, *Judicial Process in America*.

102. See Henry J. Abraham, *Justices and Presidents: A Political History of Appointments to the Supreme Court* (New York: Oxford University Press, 1974).

103. Maguire and Flanagan, *Sourcebook of Criminal Justice Statistics*.

104. Ibid., p. 17. See also Anthony Champagne and Greg Thielemann, "Awareness of Trial Court Judges," *Judicature* 74 (1991):271–276; Lawrence Baum, "Voters' Information in Judicial Elections: The 1986 Contests for the Ohio Supreme Court," *Kentucky Law Journal* 77 (1988–89):645–670; Kenyon N. Griffin and Michael J. Horan, "Patterns of Voting Behavior in Judicial Retention Elections for Supreme Court Justices in Wyoming," *Judicature* 67 (1983):68–77; Elliot E. Slotnick, "Review Essay on Judicial Recruitment and Selection," *The Justice System Journal* 13 (1988):109–124.

105. Robert A. Carp and Ronald Stidham, *The Federal Courts* (Washington, D.C.: CQ Press, 1985).

106. Ibid.

CHAPTER 12

PROSECUTION AND ADJUDICATION

The trial of William Kennedy Smith in December of 1991 has been called "the most celebrated of all trials" in the history of the United States. The media attended in droves. Court-watchers waited for hours just to get a glimpse of the defendant. Americans were glued to their television sets, watching forty-five witnesses during a ten-day trial. It was better than a daytime soap. After Smith was found not guilty, he smiled, hugged his lawyer, and as he was leaving the courthouse, said: "I have an enormous debt to the system and to God and I have terrific faith in both of them. I'm just really, really happy."[1]

To an ordinary citizen charged with a crime, the experience of going to court is vastly different. Trials are rarely well-attended media events. Only a select few attract even local attention. An accused may find a trial confusing, frightening, and often frustrating. Courts follow legal rules and procedures that only lawyers and judges fully understand. Without a legal education it is difficult to grasp the subtleties of the proceedings. Defendants may be frightened because they experience a loss of control over their own destiny. The experience can be frustrating because courts seldom function as effectively or efficiently as they should. Delay is inevitable. Bargains and deals made by prosecutor and defense counsel are common. So are charges of bias, discrimination, and arbitrariness. ■

In this chapter we examine the key decisions made during the process that begins after a person is brought into the court system, from the first stages through postconviction procedures. But first we consider the ways in which some defendants avoid going to trial.

NO TRIAL

Policies about charging decisions vary by jurisdiction. Some prosecutors prefer to screen cases carefully before deciding whether to file charges against a suspect. Others make such decisions after charges have been filed. In any event, many of those arrested are never charged. Of those charged, many do not proceed to trial: The prosecutor may reject a case in which the quality of the evidence is poor or witnesses are reluctant to cooperate. Other cases may be dismissed in court either before or after indictment. After all decisions are made, what percentage of all cases are actually dropped? A recent survey of thirty large urban jurisdictions revealed that 45 percent of all felony arrests do not go past the indictment phase.[2] Figures for the federal courts are similar: In 1989, U.S. attorneys chose to prosecute in only 55.8 percent of the cases that were investigated.[3] Let us see how and why so many cases leave the system at an early stage.

Diversion

William Douglas Teisher's crime was minor compared with the many drive-by shootings, muggings, and drug-related homicides in Washington, D.C. In May of 1991, the young college student went on a one-man drunken rampage through the Mount Zion United Methodist Church in Georgetown, soaking the sanctuary with a fire extinguisher and nearly destroying the church basement. The property damage amounted to nearly $7,000. As a first-time offender, Teisher was given a nontrial option: He agreed to apologize directly to the congregation, perform forty hours of community service, and repay the church for the cost of repairing the damage.[4]

Nearly 5 percent of all criminal cases that are not prosecuted in the United States are referred to **diversion** programs like the D.C. Superior Court program. Such programs remove an accused like Teisher from the court system in order to address a special problem, such as a drug or alcohol addiction. The value of diversion programs was recognized in the report of the President's Commission on Law Enforcement and Criminal Justice (1967). The Commission found that many defendants were in need of treatment or supervision, and that the criminal justice system was too harsh a means of providing such services. It endorsed the establishment of programs to which prosecutors might divert certain offenders in order to avoid formal prosecution.

Today, diversion programs attempt to deal with the problems that may have led to criminal behavior, with the goal of preventing future involvement in crime. Those arrested for public intoxication or certain drug offenses, for example, may be diverted to an alcohol or drug abuse treatment program. Others may be sent to programs like the Manhattan Court Employment Project in New York and Project Crossroads in Washington, D.C., which provide vocational and educational training.[5] Some programs arrange and oversee community service and restitution to victims.

Diversion can occur before or after charges are filed.[6] But once a decision to divert is made and an accused has agreed to participate in the diversionary program, formal prosecution is suspended pending program completion. If the offender completes all program requirements, the charges are usually dismissed. Noncompliance can result in the resumption of formal prosecution.

diversion
Removal of the defendant from the normal path of the criminal justice process to an alternative path (for example a treatment program).

Evaluation of Diversion Programs

Diversion programs appear to benefit the offender, the criminal justice system, and the community. The offender avoids the stigma of being labeled a criminal, as well as the harshness of incarceration. Treatment or assistance focuses on the problem that led to the criminal behavior in the first place. The system benefits by avoiding the costs associated with prosecution, detention, trial, probation, incarceration, and parole. Diversion also relieves pressures on court case loads and jail or prison populations. Finally, the community may benefit when offenders learn the job skills necessary for gainful employment.

Evaluations of diversion programs show that offenders who go through such programs generally have very low rates of subsequent offending. The question is: Are these low rates due to the selection of particular offenders or to the effects of the program? Critics argue that the highly selective process used to choose participants may in fact result in the selection of people who are unlikely to commit new offenses under any circumstances. Moreover, they claim that since many of the cases might have been dismissed if no diversion programs existed, the benefit in terms of cost reduction to the criminal justice system is unclear.[7] In terms of the offender, the programs may even be harmful, because people who would not have been prosecuted anyway are processed by the system.

"Diversion programs appear to benefit the offender, the criminal justice system, and the community."

PRETRIAL

If a case is not diverted, a number of important decisions have to be made. Should an accused be detained or released prior to trial? At what level should bail be set? Should the defendant plead guilty or not guilty? Should the prosecutor and defense attorney engage in plea negotiations? If there is a plea bargain, should the court accept it as having been voluntarily made?

Pretrial Release

Following an arrest, an accused makes an appearance before a magistrate, where a decision is made about whether he or she will be released pending final disposition of the case. The consequences of this decision are obvious. A released defendant can live with, and support, a family; maintain ties to the community; and prepare or assist in the preparation of the defense. A pretrial prisoner, on the other hand, lives in the squalor of jail, perhaps for a crime never to be proved; others may spend a lengthy period there before trial, only to be found guilty and released on probation.[8]

How does an accused end up back on the street pending trial? In this section we will examine the traditional forms of pretrial release, including bail and release on personal recognizance, and the risks associated with release.

Right to Bail. The word **bail** refers to a court-imposed requirement for the posting of a security to obtain release of a defendant pending disposition of a criminal case. Until fairly recently, bail meant posting of cash or a secured bond, but today there are several alternatives. In fact, in 1988 slightly more than half (53%) of the defendants released pending trial did not have to post any money to secure release from custody.[9] For those whose bail requires the posting of cash or a bond, failure to appear in court can result in the forfeiture of the monies posted. Thus, bail serves as a kind of insurance policy against the defendant's failure to appear.

The U.S. Constitution does not grant a specific right to bail, but the Eighth Amendment prohibits excessive bail. What is excessive? Years of experience have shown that excessive is, indeed, a relative word. What might seem like an insig-

bail
Security given to ensure the reappearance of a defendant, in order to obtain his or her release from imprisonment.

"Bail serves as a kind of insurance policy against the defendant's failure to appear."

nificant amount of bail to some may be well beyond the reach of others. Studies have repeatedly demonstrated that a significant number of defendants whose bail is set at amounts of $500 or less are unable to post it.[10]

The U.S. Supreme Court dealt with the question of what constitutes "excessive" bail in 1951 in *Stack v. Boyle*.[11] Bail must be set at an amount no greater than would reasonably ensure the presence of the defendant at required court proceedings, said the Court. This, of course, is the underlying purpose of bail. Rather than establishing specific amounts, the Court left that determination to individual judges, based on their evaluation of the risk of flight. Each defendant's case is to be judged individually, taking into account such factors as the defendant's character, the weight of evidence against her or him, the nature and circumstances of the offense, and the person's financial ability to pay cash bail.[12]

bondsmen
Private business operators, paid by the defendant, who post the amount required by the court to secure the release of the defendant.

Bondsmen. Many states retain a commercial bail system that uses **bondsmen,** private business operators who act as a type of insurance agent for defendants. In exchange for a fee paid by the defendant—usually 10 percent of the bail amount—the bondsman posts the amount required to secure the defendant's release and therefore guarantees to the court that the defendant will appear as required. Should the defendant fail to appear, the bondsman may have to forfeit the bond.[13]

Commercial bonding systems have been criticized over the years, especially since the bail reform movements of the 1960s. Some of the major criticisms are

- freedom of an accused defendant becomes contingent on a business decision made by a bondsman
- kickbacks, bribery, and payoffs are prevalent in the bail bond industry
- bondsmen have used unscrupulous means to apprehend "bail jumpers"[14]

Critiques of the commercial bail bonding system, coupled with the unsavory reputation of some bondsmen, have led a number of states to eliminate bonding.

A Houston, Texas, bail bond office, open for business around the clock.

Bail Reform. The movement to ensure fairness in bail decisions that began in the early 1960s emerged in response to perceptions of racial or other discrimination in the decision-making process. The Manhattan Bail Project, sponsored by the Vera Institute of Justice (a privately funded criminal justice research and reform organization), was an important catalyst in this movement. It demonstrated that it is possible to minimize "no-shows" and to predict with reasonable accuracy whether an accused will return to court on the basis of that person's history, family and community ties, and employment record. The project's early findings revealed a surprisingly low default rate.

Another promising attempt to limit judicial discretion may be credited to the criminologist John Goldkamp who, with his colleague Michael Gottfredson, designed uniform guidelines for bail decision-makers[15] (Figure 12.1). By creating a two-dimensional grid on which they could plot the severity of the offense against a series of variables, such as type of crime, number of arrests, age, and community ties, the researchers enabled judges to minimize the disparities in decisions regarding bail.[16]

"Options for pretrial release now include bail, ROR, conditional release, third-party custody, and citation release."

release on recognizance
Release of a defendant on his or her promise to return to court as required.

In 1966, the federal government enacted the first statute since 1789 that significantly modified bail procedures in federal courts. The Bail Reform Act of 1966 was notable for creating a presumption in favor of releasing defendants simply on their promise that they would return to court as required, a practice known as **release on recognizance (ROR).** It also emphasized that courts should release defendants under the least restrictive conditions needed to ensure their return to court. Another feature of the Act was the authorization of a cash deposit with the court of 10 percent of the bail amount, returnable upon the defendant's appearance in court. Since the enactment of this legislation, many states have adopted similar statutes.[17] As a result, a wide variety of options for pretrial release now exist (Table 12.1).

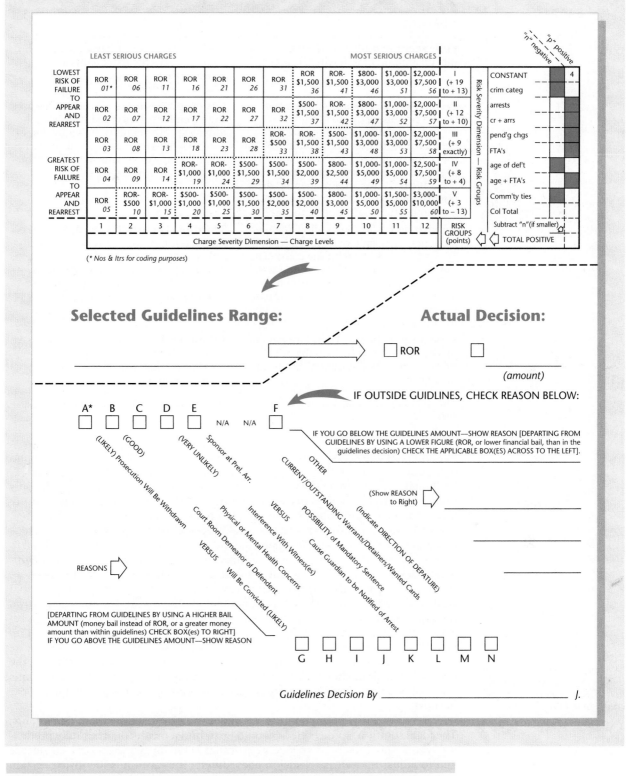

FIGURE 12.1 *Guidelines for bail decision-makers* (*Source:* John Goldkamp and Michael Gottfredson, *Judicial Decision Guidelines for Bail: The Philadelphia Experiment* [Washington, D.C.: National Institute of Justice, 1983].)

TABLE 12.1 Current Pretrial Release Options

Financial Bond	Alternative Release Options
Fully secured bail: The defendant posts the full amount of bail with the court.	**Release on recognizance (ROR):** The court releases the defendant on the promise that he or she will appear in court as required.
Privately secured bail: A bondsman signs a promissory note to the court for the bail amount and charges the defendant a fee for the service (usually 10% of the bail amount). If the defendant fails to appear the bondsman must pay the court the full amount. Frequently, the bondsman requires the defendant to post collateral in addition to the fee.	**Conditional release:** The court releases the defendant subject to his or her following specific conditions set by the court, such as attendance at drug treatment therapy or staying away from the complaining witness.
Deposit bail: The courts allow the defendant to deposit a percentage (usually 10%) of the full bail with the court. The full amount of the bail is required if the defendant fails to appear. The percentage bail is returned after disposition of the case but the court often retains 1% for administrative costs.	**Third-party custody:** The defendant is released into the custody of an individual or agency that promises to assure his or her appearance in court. No monetary transactions are involved in this type of release.
Unsecured bail: The defendant pays no money to the court but is liable for the full amount of bail should he or she fail to appear.	**Citation release:** Arrestees are released pending their first court appearance on a written order issued by law enforcement personnel.

SOURCE: *Report to the Nation on Crime and Justice*, 2d ed. (Washington, D.C.: Department of Justice, 1988), p. 58.

Risk of Pretrial Release.　How do judges determine the risk of releasing a defendant pending trial? In the case of *United States v. Patriarca* (1991), Judge Mark L. Wolf made a decision on the basis of a single statement by the accused: "The only thing I have to give you is my word as a man."[18] Not surprisingly, the accused, former reputed Mafia boss Raymond J. (Junior) Patriarca, was denied bail.

Judge Wolf, and other magistrates and judges who hear bail applications, face two major problems about releasing defendants: the risk that (1) they will fail to appear for subsequent court proceedings (historically this was the sole legitimate question), and (2) they will commit crimes while on release (a question, permissible or not, that judges will always examine). The most recent national study revealed that approximately 18 percent of all felony defendants on pretrial release were re-arrested for a felony offense committed while they were on release. About one-quarter (24%) of the released defendants failed to make all required court appearances.[19] Another recent study suggests that many of those who fail to appear do so because of faulty or nonexistent notification by the courts.[20] The data show, then, that a relatively small proportion of defendants released pending disposition of their cases commit new crimes or fail to appear in court.

"A relatively small proportion of those released pending disposition of their cases commit new crimes or fail to appear in court."

Judges share the public's concern about the risks posed by these defendants. The ideal solution, some believe, would be to find a means of accurately predicting who is most likely to engage in criminal behavior while on pretrial release and to adjust the release decision accordingly. Research has identified certain factors associated with the risk: the length of time the defendant is at liberty between release and case disposition; the defendant's age, employment status, and prior criminal record; and whether the defendant is supervised during release.[21] Unfortunately, statistical "models" based on factors such as criminal history and demographic characteristics have not proved to be reliable predictors of who actually fails to appear in court or who commits another crime.[22]

In the 1980s, a series of studies demonstrated that drug use was related to new arrests of persons on pretrial release.[23] Prompted by these research findings, the District of Columbia undertook a pilot program to test arrestees prior to release on bail. Those who tested positive were required to report for further urinalysis as a condition of release. Failure to comply with this requirement led to more restrictive conditions and revocation of the release. Research findings from the District of Columbia program concluded that there was a relationship between positive drug test results and pretrial flight and re-arrest, and that the testing program increased the likelihood of court appearances and decreased the rate of recidivism during release.[24]

Experts do not agree on the utility of drug testing. Results from Arizona show that drug monitoring during pretrial release appears to have no effect on reducing the risks of flight or pretrial arrest.[25] Studies conducted in Washington, D.C., and Miami conclude that those who test positive for drugs are at a significantly higher risk of being re-arrested than those who test negative,[26] but the risk of flight does not appear to be significantly related to positive drug test results.[27]

Pretrial Detention

In view of the conflicting scientific evidence on the use of bail as an alternative to jail, and with the return of the country to a more punitive approach to crime and justice, both practice and law on the use of bail have become more conservative. Thus, as the Philadelphia data in Figure 12.2 show, in 1990 approximately half of all persons held in jails were those who had not been convicted but were merely awaiting trial or arraignment.[28] The cases of about three-quarters of inmates on pretrial detention are adjudicated within three months. Most of the remaining defendants may spend as much as a year in jail before final disposition of their cases, and a small proportion (4%) remain jailed for more than a year.[29] Those

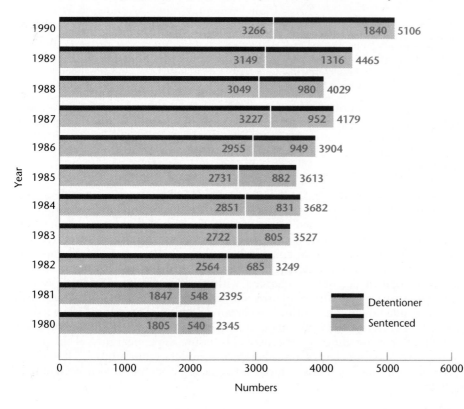

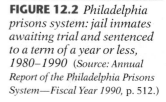

"Experts do not agree on the utility of drug testing during pretrial release."

FIGURE 12.2 *Philadelphia prisons system: jail inmates awaiting trial and sentenced to a term of a year or less, 1980–1990* (*Source: Annual Report of the Philadelphia Prisons System—Fiscal Year 1990*, p. 512.)

321

TABLE 12.2 States That Have One or More Provisions to Ensure Community Safety in Pretrial Release

Type of Provision	States That Have Enacted the Provision
Exclusion of certain crimes from automatic bail eligibility	Colorado, District of Columbia, Florida, Georgia, Michigan, Nebraska, Wisconsin
Definition of the purpose of bail to ensure appearance and safety	Alaska, Arizona, California, Delaware, District of Columbia, Florida, Hawaii, Minnesota, South Carolina, South Dakota, Vermont, Virginia, Wisconsin
Inclusion of crime control factors in the release decision	Alabama, California, Florida, Georgia, Minnesota, South Dakota, Wisconsin
Inclusion of release conditions related to crime control	Alaska, Arkansas, Colorado, Delaware, District of Columbia, Florida, Hawaii, Illinois, Iowa, Minnesota, New Mexico, North Carolina, South Carolina, South Dakota, Vermont, Virginia, Washington, Wisconsin
Limitations on the right to bail for those previously convicted	Colorado, District of Columbia, Florida, Georgia, Hawaii, Indiana, Michigan, New Mexico, Texas, Utah, Wisconsin
Revocation of pretrial release when there is evidence that the accused committed a new crime	Arizona, Arkansas, Colorado, District of Columbia, Georgia, Hawaii, Illinois, Indiana, Maryland, Massachusetts, Michigan, Nevada, New Mexico, New York, Rhode Island, Texas, Utah, Vermont, Wisconsin
Limitations on the right to bail for crimes alleged to have been committed while on release	Arizona, Arkansas, Colorado, District of Columbia, Florida, Georgia, Illinois, Indiana, Maryland, Massachusetts, Michigan, Minnesota, Nevada, New Mexico, New York, Rhode Island, Tennessee, Texas, Utah, Vermont, Wisconsin
Provisions for pretrial detention to ensure safety	Arizona, Arkansas, California, Colorado, District of Columbia, Florida, Georgia, Hawaii, Illinois, Indiana, Maryland, Massachusetts, Michigan, Nebraska, Nevada, New Mexico, New York, Rhode Island, South Dakota, Texas, Utah, Vermont, Virginia, Washington, Wisconsin

Source: Elizabeth Gaynes, *Typology of State Laws Which Permit Consideration of Danger in the Pretrial Release Decision* (Washington, D.C.: Pretrial Services Resource Center, 1982), and updated from Barbara Gottlieb, *Public Danger as a Factor in Pretrial Release: A Comparative Analysis of State Laws*, for National Institute of Justice (Washington, D.C.: U.S. Government Printing Office, July 1985); also in U.S. Department of Justice, Bureau of Justice Statistics, *Report to the Nation on Crime and Justice*, 2d ed. (Washington, D.C.: U.S. Government Printing Office, 1988), p. 77.

convicted of violent offenses are more likely to spend longer periods of time in jail than any other type of offender (Table 12.2). Most significantly, the legislative pendulum has swung against bail. Many states now place significant restrictions on pretrial release decisions and make provision for greater use of preventive detention.

Preventive Detention. In *Stack v. Boyle*, the U.S. Supreme Court underscored the notion that the purpose of bail is to ensure the subsequent appearance in court of a defendant released from custody. The risk of flight posed by a defendant has been the only official basis of pretrial release decisions. Recently, however, twenty-five states have enacted laws that allow for the consideration of danger to others in these decisions and permit **preventive detention** and the denial of bail to defendants charged with certain serious offenses.[30] Among states that have a constitutional provision guaranteeing a right to bail, ten states have amended their constitutions to permit detention of arrestees.[31] The federal Bail Reform Act of 1984 permits preventive detention where "no condition or combination of conditions will reasonably assure the appearance of the person as required and the safety of any other person, and the community."[32] It may well be argued that such new laws simply have enacted what had always been judicial practice.

preventive detention
Pretrial incarceration of an accused deemed dangerous.

Preventive detention has been harshly criticized because it is a deprivation of liberty for those whose guilt has not been proved. Proponents counter that the interests of the community far outweigh those of the individual defendant. In *United States v. Salerno* (1987),[33] the Supreme Court upheld the constitutionality of the preventive detention provisions of the Bail Reform Act of 1984. This decision was based at least in part on the understanding that preventive detention was intended not as punishment but rather as a legitimate means of attempting to prevent harm to the community.

"Preventive detention has been harshly criticized because it is a deprivation of liberty for those whose guilt has not been proved."

"The Supreme Court considered preventive detention to be intended not as punishment but as a legitimate means of attempting to prevent harm to the community."

Impact of Preventive Detention. Preventive detention appears to have had an impact on the patterns of pretrial release. The federal figures demonstrate the point. In a U.S. Department of Justice study comparing the detention of defendants before and after enactment of the Bail Reform Act of 1984, a 21-percent increase in the number of defendants detained between 1983 and 1985 was detected. Furthermore, nearly two-thirds (63%) of those detained were held without bail after the Act, compared with only 7 percent before.[34] Studies by the Administrative Office of the United States Courts and the U.S. General Accounting Office also confirm that detentions are being ordered with greater frequency than ever since passage of the Act.[35]

What effect does preventive detention have on defendants? Defendants held in jail are suddenly cut off from families and friends at a time when social support is critical. They may face the loss of a job, a situation that has severe financial consequences, and their standing in the community may be jeopardized. Added to this is the fact that detainees have a distinct disadvantage with respect to the ultimate disposition of their case. In one study, 79 percent of detained felony defendants in the nation's largest jurisdictions were ultimately convicted, compared with 66 percent of those who were released before the disposition of their case. Of those who were convicted, sentences of incarceration were given to half the released defendants and to 83 percent of the detainees.[36]

"Seventy-nine percent of detained felony defendants in the nation's largest jurisdictions were ultimately convicted."

An obvious explanation for this sort of disparity is that those who commit the most serious offenses are those who are most likely both to be detained before case disposition and to receive the harshest sentence. However, it is important to remember that nearly 90 percent of the defendants detained in the largest jurisdictions were held because they were unable to pay their bail. In other words, had they been better off financially, they would have been able to secure their release. Research that has taken into account a number of other factors that could explain differences in the disposition of cases also shows that pretrial detention exerts a significant influence on case outcome.[37]

"Pretrial detention exerts a significant influence on case outcome."

How does detention affect outcome? First, defendants in jail have limited access to their attorneys and cannot effectively assist in the preparation of their defense through such means as contacting witnesses and gathering evidence. Second, jailed defendants are often less able to strike a plea bargain because of the increased psychological vulnerability resulting from detention.[38] Third, if a detainee loses his or her job while in jail, the judge may view this in an unfavorable light.

The Plea

Defendants in jail or on bail are willingly or unwillingly participating in a process that ultimately leads them before the trial judge. A preliminary hearing may be conducted, various motions may be made by defense counsel, and the prosecutor will ready the case for trial, either on the basis of an **information** (accusation by the prosecutor) or of an **indictment** (accusation by the grand jury). The further proceedings depend entirely on the defendant's response to the accusation, known as the **plea.** No matter how serious the alleged crime, all defendants must enter a plea.

In May 1990, Michael R. Milken appeared before U.S. District Court Judge

information
Accusation against a criminal defendant prepared by a prosecuting attorney.

indictment
Accusation against a criminal defendant rendered by a grand jury on the basis of evidence constituting a prima facie case.

plea
Response to a criminal charge. Traditional pleas are guilty, not guilty, nolo contendere, and not guilty by reason of insanity.

Kimba M. Wood in New York on charges of racketeering, insider trading, and fraud. Judge Wood quizzed the defendant: "Is your mind clear today?" Milken replied, "Yes." "Mr. Milken, how do you plead to the charges set forth?" asked the Judge. "Guilty, your honor," replied the ex-financier.[39] Matthew Barkoff, a 28-year-old resident in medicine from Queens, appeared before Justice Benjamin Mehlmann of the Ocean Beach Village Court, in Fire Island, New York, in August 1991. Barkoff's crime? Making too much noise while he was sitting at a friend's house, singing and playing Bruce Springsteen's "Jungle Land" on the piano. Judge Mehlmann said to the defendant, "You are charged with violating Section 112.5 of the Village Code, unreasonable noise. How do you plead?"[40] "Not guilty," replied Dr. Barkoff. Both Milken and Barkoff appeared at the procedural stage known as the **arraignment,** a proceeding where a person named in the indictment or information is asked to plead to the charge. Milken pleaded "guilty"; Barkoff maintained his innocence by pleading "not guilty." These are two of the four pleas available to all defendants.

arraignment
First stage of the trial process, at which the indictment or information is read in open court and the defendant is requested to respond thereto.

Guilty.   When Milken pleaded guilty, he admitted all the facts alleged to have occurred, as well as their legal implications. Of course, such a plea means that no trial need take place. The trial judge must make sure that the plea has been voluntarily entered, that the defendant understands the implications of the plea, and that, indeed, there is a factual basis for the plea. Such a determination could amount to a mini-minitrial. The judge then accepts the plea of guilty and, as did Judge Wood, schedules a date for sentencing.

"The overwhelming majority of convictions result from guilty pleas."

As we have seen, the overwhelming majority of convictions result from guilty pleas. Typically, people assume that these pleas are the result of a negotiation in which the prosecutor offers leniency to the defendant in return for a guilty plea, an exchange referred to as plea-bargaining. (We will examine plea-bargaining in detail in the next section.) Not all observers agree that the prevalence of guilty pleas is the result of "bargained justice." The facts and evidence of most cases make it obvious to both sides that going to trial would serve no purpose, and both often agree on the plea.

Not Guilty.   The defendant may plead not guilty, like Barkoff, denying the allegations and placing on the prosecution the burden of proving beyond a reasonable doubt all the facts alleged in the indictment. If the defendant enters a plea of not guilty, the judge will set a date for trial. In some cases, a defendant may enter a not guilty plea at the arraignment but later arrange to plead guilty in exchange for some leniency offered by the prosecution.

"Although each citizen accused of a crime has the right to a trial by jury, few defendants choose to exercise that right."

Despite the importance we attach to the idea that each citizen accused of a crime has the right to a trial by jury, few defendants choose to exercise that right. A recent survey revealed that only 6 percent of all felony arrests that led to a misdemeanor or felony charge went to trial. The balance resulted in diversion or referral elsewhere (6%), dismissal (21%), or a guilty plea (67%).[41] Pleas of not guilty are more common among defendants charged with serious violent crimes such as murder or rape than among those charged with less serious property or drug offenses.

nolo contendere
Defendant pleads no contest (admits criminal liability for purposes of this proceeding only).

Nolo Contendere.   In many jurisdictions the defendant may plead no contest, or **nolo contendere,** with the approval of the court and, in some jurisdictions, the prosecution. By this plea the defendant admits criminal liability for purposes of this proceeding only. Such a plea has the practical advantage of avoiding implications of guilt in other proceedings (a civil suit for damages, for example). It also provides the defendant with a face-saving mechanism because he or she can claim that there was no guilty verdict, even though a nolo plea does result in a conviction and the defendant can be given the same sentence that would have resulted from a guilty plea.

For some types of crimes, no contest pleas are quite common. They constitute over half of the pleas for charges of driving while intoxicated. In Georgia, for example, of the 61,622 charges of drunk driving, more than 50 percent (34,642) resulted in a plea of nolo contendere.[42] Despite its widespread use, the legal community is divided over the usefulness of the nolo plea. In fact, nolo pleas are not accepted in about half the states. After evaluating the pros and cons of the plea, the American Bar Association's *Standards Relating to Pleas of Guilty* concluded that its benefits were not sufficient to justify supporting its use. But it did not recommend that the plea be prohibited, largely because the option of pleading nolo contendere might avoid unnecessary trials.[43]

Not Guilty by Reason of Insanity. Psychiatrists who evaluated Milwaukee serial murderer Jeffrey Dahmer in 1992 gave many reasons for his bizarre behavior: "The drugging [was done] to satisfy his sexual need for a not-fully cooperative partner." "Death was an unintended by-product of his efforts to create a zombie." "Dismembering was a disposal problem. . . ." But it was Dahmer who summed it up best, "I carried it too far, that's for sure."[44]

Defendants who enter a plea of not guilty by reason of insanity are claiming that they cannot be held criminally responsible for their acts. The issue in the insanity defense is whether an event that looks like a crime can be attributed to the defendant as his or her (rational) act, and whether the defendant had the requisite guilty mind—or whether it was obliterated by mental illness. (See Chapter 4.) Defendants found not guilty by reason of insanity are, with few exceptions, committed to a psychiatric facility for treatment for an indefinite period. In some jurisdictions they can be discharged upon certification of fitness for release; in others, the trial judge must approve any motion for discharge.

As Chapter 4 shows, opposition to the insanity defense has grown so strong in recent years that three states have even eliminated the defense. Others, led by Michigan in 1975, have added an alternative disposition, "guilty but mentally ill." That verdict usually results in a sentence to a correctional facility, with mandatory mental health treatment. Legislatures that enacted such laws hoped to reduce the number of insanity acquittals and prevent what was perceived as premature release of individuals acquitted by reason of insanity. Research in Michigan has yet to show a reduction in insanity acquittals since the guilty-but-mentally-ill plea was adopted.[45] Like the insanity defense itself, the plea is seldom used.[46]

Plea-Bargaining

"Punch $200 into the machine or I'll blow you away." With these words Curtis K. Taylor would approach customers at automated teller machines throughout California. Taylor was prolific, perhaps the most prolific of all teller-machine bandits in the United States. When apprehended in 1988, he pleaded guilty to thirty-seven robbery and attempted robbery charges. Taylor faced over sixty-five years in prison if convicted on all charges. Under a plea-bargain agreement, the district attorney recommended twenty-eight years.[47]

The idea arose centuries ago that both sides of a criminal case—the prosecution and the defense—could benefit if they were to agree on a plea. This would save the government the expense of a trial and the defendant the risk of a very stiff sentence. Certainly it has always been clear that trial could take place only "if the issues were joined," meaning that both prosecution and defense agreed on the precise nature of the issues before the court. The prosecution presented its views in the indictment, the defense in its response to the indictment, the plea. That necessitated a discussion of what was contained in the indictment, with the resulting need for a trial only on issues not agreed upon. If, for example, the defendant pleads guilty to one count of larceny and not guilty to a second count, trial need be had only on the second count.

By the mid-twentieth century it became an openly recognized (and not just

Amy Fisher, 17, in Nassau County Court, July 1992, entering a plea of not guilty to charges of attempted murder for the shooting of her alleged lover's wife.

"The idea that both sides of a criminal case could benefit if they were to agree on a plea is centuries old."

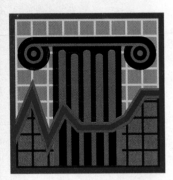

SHOULD PLEA-BARGAINING BE ABOLISHED?

Plea-bargaining has become so common in the United States that we tend to think it is somehow "required" by the criminal justice system. Conventional wisdom is that plea bargains:

- are necessary devices to keep the courts from getting hopelessly clogged with criminal cases;
- are desirable means of compensating for the harshness of the sanctions provided by the penal codes;
- reduce the negative effect of "net-widening"—that is, the tendency of our society to include more and more offenders within the sweep of the criminal justice system;
- allow for consideration of legally irrelevant but socially important factors, ranging from poverty and despair to intense emotional distress.

The National Advisory Commission Recommendations, 1971

Is "conventional wisdom" true? The National Advisory Commission on Criminal Justice Standards and Goals recommended as long ago as 1971 that the practice of plea-bargaining be abolished no later than 1978 (1). Many American citizens favor abolition too. According to the Commission, abolishing plea-bargaining would

- remove the incentive for prosecutors to charge an offender with a crime more serious than they expect to be able to prove, called "overcharging," or with all conceivable crimes, called "bed-sheeting";
- increase the number of trials only insignificantly;
- increase the rationality and fairness of the criminal trial process;
- restore the constitutional right to a trial by jury, which defendants now often are manipulated to give up;
- prevent the prosecution from achieving victory on the basis of insufficient or even illegally obtained evidence, which it currently can hide in a plea bargain.

Many responded to the Commission's proposals with skepticism, especially because one popular explanation for the prevalence of plea-bargaining is related to case-load pressures (2). This theory asserts that case-load pressures are precisely the reason so many prosecutors and defense attorneys are willing to negotiate. They want to reduce the overload on the system caused by time-consuming and expensive trials. Suppose for a moment that plea-bargaining were to be banned throughout the nation's courts. The effect of such a ban is widely assumed to be a significant increase in trials and thus in case-load pressure. Only a 10-percent increase in trials, some experts claim, might cause the court apparatus to stop functioning.

What happens when plea-bargaining is banned?

Would the elimination of plea-bargaining have only an insignifi-

cant effect on the case loads of judges, juries, prosecutors, and defense counsel as the Advisory Commission suggested? Some argue that, if plea-bargaining were prohibited, most defendants who consider themselves guilty would plead guilty anyway in the hope that they might receive a lighter sentence. Others predict an onslaught of trials that would simply overwhelm the system. The evidence from two jurisdictions that have banned plea-bargaining indicates that neither view is fully justified.

Alaska was one of the first jurisdictions to eliminate plea-bargaining, prohibiting both charge and sentence negotiations statewide in 1975 (3). Early evaluations of the ban indicated that the rate of trials did increase substantially, doubling in one year in Anchorage, for example. However, the absolute number of trials remained low, and the state was able to maintain the trend of decreasing case processing time that had preceded the ban. Sentences for some offenses were more severe following the ban, and those who went to trial were more likely to receive harsher sentences than those who pleaded guilty in various categories of offenses. A more recent assessment of the effects of the ban supported the early findings: Trial rates did increase over the long term, although trials still account for only about 10 percent of convictions statewide, and those who went to trial were penalized more severely.

Plea-bargaining was also prohibited in El Paso County, Texas, in 1975. Evaluation of that ban revealed widespread implementation of the policy, with sentence negotiations virtually eliminated. Charge

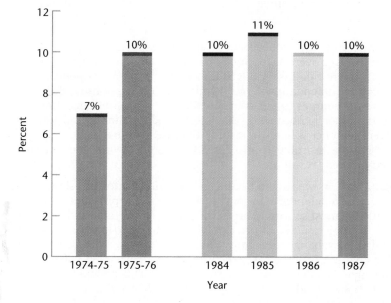

FIGURE 1. Percentage of Filings for Trial Before and After Abolition of Plea-Bargaining (1975): Anchorage, Fairbanks, Juneau
(*Source:* Teresa White Carns and John Kruse, *Alaska's Plea Bargaining Ban Re-Evaluated* [Anchorage: Alaska Judicial Council, 1991].)

reductions, however, did increase. A significant increase in the proportion of cases disposed of by trials occurred in the first two years following the prohibition. In fact, more cases were disposed of by trial than by guilty plea, although approximately one-third of all defendants continue to plead guilty. This increase in trials created considerable backlogs in the trial courts, causing the system to expand the number of courts with trial jurisdiction. Once that happened, erosion of the plea-bargaining ban began, with judges and prosecutors generally more willing to negotiate. As in Alaska, those who went to trial apparently suffered a penalty in the form of harsher sentences.

Prohibition vs. regulation

The experiences of these two jurisdictions indicate that prohibitions on plea-bargaining are difficult to sustain, although the effects of such bans when fully implemented are not necessarily disastrous. Comparisons of jurisdictions with varying levels of controls on plea-bargaining indicate that restrictions on charging concessions can lead to significant increases in sentence differences. Where charge bargaining is restricted, sentences for those convicted at trial are on average 80 percent longer than for those who plead guilty. Eliminating charge bargaining resulted in as much as a 334-percent increase in sentence length for those who were sentenced following a trial. Such increases are thought to be all that is needed to discourage people from going to trial when bargaining over their charges is no longer an option.

Most jurisdictions have made plea-bargaining more open, regulated, and fair instead of abolishing it. The U.S. Supreme Court has insisted that the voluntariness of the plea and an understanding of its implications must be demonstrated in open court and that the prosecution must stick to its part of the bargain. In federal courts the plea-bargaining process has been turned into a minitrial, consisting of such an "inquiry as shall satisfy (the court) that there is a factual basis for the plea" (4).

SOURCES

1. National Advisory Commission on Criminal Justice Standards and Goals, *A National Strategy to Reduce Crime* (Washington, D.C.: U.S. Government Printing Office, 1971), p. 43.
2. Barbara Boland, *Prosecution of Felony Arrests*. Bureau of Justice Statistics (Washington, D.C.: U.S. Government Printing Office, 1986).
3. Theresa White Carns and John Kruse, *Alaska's Plea Bargaining Ban Re-Evaluated* (Anchorage: Alaska Judicial Council, 1991).
4. Rule 11(f), Federal Rules of Criminal Procedure.

QUESTIONS FOR DISCUSSION

1. Should plea-bargaining be banned throughout the United States? Defend your position.
2. One argument for plea-bargaining is that it saves the courts from being hopelessly overwhelmed with cases. Suggest other remedies for that problem.
3. Who is placed more at risk by the practice of plea-bargaining, the public or the accused? Explain.

plea-bargaining
Agreement made between defense and prosecution for certain leniencies in return for a guilty plea.

secretly tolerated) practice in the United States for prosecutors and defense attorneys to engage in **plea-bargaining**—to discuss the criminal charges against defendants and to agree on a reduced or modified sentence that would spare the state the cost of a trial and guarantee the defendant a reduced term of imprisonment.

Types. Plea-bargaining, or plea negotiation, may be explicit or implicit.[48] Explicit bargaining involves overt negotiations between two or more parties in the case (prosecutor, defense counsel, judge) that result in an agreement on the terms under which the defendant will plead guilty. The concessions made by the state can relate to the charges against the defendant or to the sentence. Implicit bargaining, on the other hand, means that the defendant simply understands that a more severe sentence is likely to result if the case goes to trial.

Plea bargains may be desirable, from a defendant's point of view, for a number of reasons. A bargain may result in

- Charge reduction. As we saw in Chapter 11, the prosecutor has significant discretion in charging a defendant. In some jurisdictions, the prosecutor's office may choose to file the most serious charges warranted by the facts and evidence of the case. A prosecutor can then afford to lower the charge to one that carries a less severe penalty, in exchange for a guilty plea.
- Removal of charges. In some cases the prosecutor may agree to drop other charges pending against a defendant who pleads guilty. This typically occurs in one of two ways. If an offender is charged with a number of different offenses arising from the same incident, he or she may plead guilty to one of the lesser offenses in exchange for dropping the more serious ones. For example, a person using a stolen credit card might be charged with theft, forgery, and possession of a stolen credit card. The prosecutor might be willing to drop the theft and forgery charges if the defendant pleads guilty to possession of a stolen credit card. The second type of bargain occurs when there are a number of indictments pending for the same type of crime, committed on different occasions. For instance, a person arrested on a burglary charge may have a number of other burglary charges pending. Should the defendant agree to plead guilty to one of these burglary charges, the other outstanding charges will be dropped by the prosecutor.
- Sentence negotiation. Negotiations about sentences typically involve an agreement by the prosecutor to recommend a lighter sentence in consideration for a guilty plea. The agreement is not binding on the judge. In practice, however, the judge will usually accept the recommendation.

Extent. In New York State in 1829, for example, 22 percent of convictions were the result of guilty pleas. By 1869 that proportion had grown to 70 percent, and by 1920 almost nine out of ten convictions were obtained by guilty pleas.[49] This significant increase in guilty pleas has been attributed to an increased use of plea bargains. Recent studies of state courts show that today's figures remain about the same.[50] Exactly how many of these pleas are the result of plea bargains is not known, but it is widely assumed that most people who decline to exercise their right to a trial do so as a result of some explicit or implicit bargain. (The Criminal Justice on Trial box discusses and evaluates the use and the pros and cons of the plea bargain.)

"It is widely assumed that most people who decline their right to a trial do so as a result of some explicit or implicit bargain."

TRIAL

It is the function of the trial court to find and express the communal judgment, under law, as to the guilt or innocence of an accused person. The public in whose name the judgment is rendered participates actively in the process. Indictments read "The People of the State of . . . versus John Doe (or Jane Roe)." What specifically is meant by "the people"? One answer is that the judge, who is elected by the people or appointed by somebody who was elected by the people, represents the people of the community. Furthermore, when an indictment is handed down and a trial is held, the people are directly represented by a cross section of the community participating in the grand jury that indicts the defendant, and the **trial jury** that tries the defendant. The public is allowed into the courtroom to witness the proceedings. Indeed, in pioneer days, trial day at the county seat was a major social event. Everybody would be there to see justice administered.

Voir Dire

After a plea of not guilty, the first step is the impaneling of the jury (which is called the *petit* or *petty jury* in contrast to the grand jury). Twelve is the traditional number of trial jurors. Some states use fewer than twelve for trials involving crimes of lesser seriousness. Ordinarily, several alternate jurors are selected to take the place of any jurors who might become disabled during the trial. The process of selecting the jury is called **voir dire,** Norman French for "to see and to speak," meaning a visual-oral process for qualifying summoned citizens to serve as jurors in a particular case.

Jury Selection: Objectives. Jury selection is usually guided by three objectives. Attorneys have to

- determine whether prospective jurors meet the minimum qualifications to sit as jurors (e.g., age and residency requirements)
- determine the impartiality of prospective jurors
- obtain sufficient information on prospective jurors to enable them to exclude "for cause" any who may be prejudiced for or against the defendant

The process by which lawyers and the judge examine a prospective juror to determine acceptability extends further. Counsel for both the defense and the prosecution have certain strategic considerations. Attorneys for each side attempt to pick jurors who might be just a little more understanding or sympathetic to their arguments. They can exclude people they think will be unsympathetic by means of **peremptory challenges,** or objections for which no explanation is required. Each side has a certain number of such challenges; usually the defense has more than the prosecution. Either side may use an unlimited number of **challenges for cause,** which are intended to keep persons with a conflict of interest or bias off the jury. A person related by birth or by marriage to any of the parties connected with the case, for example, would almost certainly be challenged for cause.

Jury Selection: Issues. Jury selection has been the subject of controversy. The expectation is that a defendant is to be tried by an impartial jury of peers, although this does not mean that the jurors must be like the defendant in all characteristics. The representativeness of juries has been called into question because most jurisdictions rely on voter registration rolls for their juror pool and such rolls are not representative of the total population. As a result, juror pools tend to have a disproportionately high number of middle-class, employed, educated persons. Racial and ethnic minorities tend to be underrepresented in some areas.

Critics of peremptory challenges have maintained that attorneys have used such challenges to exclude minorities from juries. In 1986, the Supreme Court held that the prosecution's use of peremptory challenges to exclude blacks from a jury solely on the basis of race constituted a violation of the equal protection clause of the Fourteenth Amendment.[51] Peremptory challenges are thought by

trial jury
Body of persons legally selected and sworn to inquire into any matter of fact and to give their verdict according to the evidence.

"In pioneer days, trial day at the county seat was a major social event."

voir dire
Process in which lawyers and a judge question potential jurors to select those who are acceptable.

peremptory challenges
Challenges (limited in number) by which a potential juror may be dismissed by either the prosecution or the defense without assignment of reason. See also challenge for cause; voir dire.

challenge for cause
Challenge to remove a potential juror because of his or her inability to render a fair and impartial decision in a case. See also peremptory challenges; voir dire.

"A fox should not be on the jury at a goose's trial."
Thomas Fuller, 1608–1661.

their very nature to make a mockery of the notion of an impartial jury, since attorneys for both sides use these challenges to try to get a jury that will be partial to their side.[52] In an interesting experiment, Hans Zeisel and Shari Diamond determined that peremptory challenges can have a major effect on the outcome of a trial. In five of twelve jury trials studied, many more jurors who were excluded as a result of peremptory challenges would have voted for a guilty verdict than jurors who actually served on the cases.[53]

"Peremptory challenges can have a major effect on the outcome of a trial."

Opening Statements

Once a jury has been chosen, or the defendant has waived a jury trial and consented to a trial by the judge alone, the trial proceedings begin. The prosecution makes an opening statement, outlining the case and previewing what it proposes to prove and how. The defense may then make or postpone its opening statement. Long opening statements are more common in jury trials, where prosecution and defense know that they will be presenting their cases before people unfamiliar with the law. Both sides hope that well-presented and clear opening statements will make it easier for the jury to follow what happens during the trial and to remain focused on the important points they hope to prove, rather than on the technicalities of the legal process.

The Prosecution's Case

After the opening statements, the prosecution introduces the evidence against the defendant. There are two types of evidence. Physical evidence includes such things as guns, knives, bullets, pieces of clothing, confiscated drugs, fingerprints, blood specimens, and urine analyses. Such evidence is used to establish proof that the crime was committed by the defendant. DNA tests, which attempt to show a sort of genetic fingerprint, are the latest innovation in forensic evidence available to law enforcement. Testimony by witnesses is the other principal form of evidence presented at trial. The prosecution calls a number of people to testify about their knowledge of the crime and the defendant's role in it. Their testimony is elicited by questions posed by the prosecutor. After each prosecution witness

"For a plot hatched in hell, don't expect angels for witnesses." Robert Perry, prosecutor, conspiracy trial of John De Lorean, August 6, 1984.

Public defender Wil Smith addresses the jury, Portland, Oregon.

testifies, the defense has an opportunity to question the witness in a process called cross-examination. The defense hopes to cast doubt on the witness's testimony, either by raising questions about the person's credibility or by demonstrating some alternative interpretation of the events that does not implicate the defendant. Once cross-examination has been completed, the prosecution may question the witness again in a redirect examination. This examination allows the prosecution to clarify or correct statements made by the witness, which can help to counter points made by the defense during cross-examination of the witness.

All evidence necessary to prove the case must be introduced in court directly and in compliance with the laws and rules of evidence. One prominent rule requires that certain out-of-court statements, known as hearsay, not be used. This rule is based on the fact that when information is repeated, relayed from person to person, it tends to become distorted. The authenticity of such information is doubtful if the person who made the statement or the source of the information cannot be examined under oath in court. Thus, it is unsafe to trust secondhand or thirdhand renditions of out-of-court statements.

Over the centuries hundreds of rules of evidence (and exceptions thereto, and exceptions to exceptions) have been developed in the practice of the courts. All are calculated

- to make certain that the parties present their proof in an orderly manner
- to avoid waste of time and confusion, by confining the proof to issues before the court
- to guarantee that all proof before the jury has a certain amount of authenticity, thus avoiding speculation
- to protect the confidentiality of privileged communications among persons standing in a certain relationship to each other (for example, doctor and patient, priest and penitent)

In modern times the exclusionary rule has also been used for public policy purposes. As explained in Chapter 8, the U.S. Supreme Court has used the exclusionary rule for a century to prohibit law enforcement from introducing at trial evidence obtained in violation of the Constitution.[54] Thus, for example, if a suspect is not given the *Miranda* warning, any evidence obtained through police-initiated questioning after arrest may be excluded from trial. The exclusionary rule for unconstitutionally obtained evidence has become a standard of constitutional law that binds not only the federal courts but all state courts as well.[55]

During the entire evidentiary stage of the trial, the defense listens and watches carefully; the defense objects immediately when it appears that one of the rules of evidence may have been violated to the detriment of the defendant. If the breach of the rule is so grave that the defendant's chance of a fair trial has been prejudiced, the defense may even move for a mistrial. A mistrial is an invalid trial, one in which a fundamental requirement of justice is lacking, such as lack of jurisdiction or an error in the selection of jurors. If the defense's **motion** is granted, the prosecution has the option of starting over again before a new jury. The judge rules on all motions and objections. If the judge rules against the defense, defense counsel will have the ruling placed on record as a potential cause to appeal a verdict and judgment of guilty. After presentation of all the evidence, the prosecution rests its case.

The Defense's Case

When the prosecution has completed its case, the defense has several options. If the evidence against the defendant is so weak that there can only be one verdict as a matter of law, the defense may move for a directed verdict of **acquittal** or a motion to dismiss. A directed verdict will be pronounced by the judge if the evi-

Deputy Sheriff John Bonnevier testifying at the murder trial of Aileen Wuornos in early 1991 on charges of shooting a Clearwater, Florida, businessman named Richard Mallory. Bonnevier found Mallory's body.

"A lawyer has no business with the justice or injustice of the cause which he undertakes . . . ."
Samuel Johnson, 1709–1784.

motion
Oral or written request to a judge, asking the court to make a specified ruling, finding, decision, or order; may be presented at any appropriate moment from arrest until the end of the trial.

acquittal
Judicial finding or jury verdict finding the defendant not guilty of the crime charged.

JUDGING AT THE WORLD LEVEL

The International Court of Justice, commonly known as the World Court, is housed in a palace—the Peace Palace—at The Hague, donated by an American philanthropist, Andrew Carnegie. Its labyrinthine halls, cavernous judges' chambers, and imposing courtroom make the World Court look like the Supreme Court of Mankind, which many of its founders intended it to be. Its judges wear somber robes of authority and listen to arguments by eminent counsel, much like their counterparts in the highest national courts. The disputes that come before them are about money, or violence, or contracts (treaties), or real estate (territory), much like those heard in national courts. But the litigants behind the lawyers are not doctors and patients, engineers and real estate operators, buyers and sellers. They are entire nations. And the law that the judges apply is not state or national, but international law. (1)

In the nearly fifty years of the existence of the International Court of Justice, more than 115 decisions have been handed down in cases and advisory proceedings. Established by the Charter of the United Nations (Article 92) of June 26, 1945, the International Court of Justice hears cases ranging from the disposition of a Belgian-Canadian electricity franchise in Barcelona to United States/Nicaraguan relations. All member states of the United Nations are automatically parties to the Court, but states seeking to litigate do not need to be U.N. members if they have accepted the

World Court's jurisdiction in general or for a particular case.

The structure of the Court

The World Court is able to resolve conflicts only when the parties involved agree to abide by its decisions. States are bound to the Court's jurisdiction only in specific instances:

- when they have specially accepted the Court's compulsory jurisdiction, or
- when they have agreed with the other state-party to the dispute to be bound, or
- when they have agreed to be bound when signing a specific international agreement (treaty, convention) that binds the signatories to have any disagreements under such a treaty adjudicated by the Court.

The fifteen judges of the World Court are elected by the General Assembly of the United Nations and the Security Council. No two judges come from the same country, and the bench as a whole is to represent "the main forms of civilization and . . . the principal legal systems of the world (1). The judges serve nine-year terms, with elections for five judges held every three years. All World Court judges must be and are outstanding jurists in their own countries and learned in international law. In cases where neither litigant has a judge on the bench, each may make an ad hoc appointment; if one litigant state has a judge on the bench who does not choose to step down, the other state in the dispute may name a temporary judge from its country to participate in hearing the case.

The World Court presides over a wide variety of cases. It has dealt with disputes over titles to territories between Holland and Belgium, Switzerland and France, Thailand and Cambodia, and countries in West Africa. It has ruled on arguments about ocean floor resources and fishing grounds off Maine, Iceland, and Norway. It has heard cases dealing with ships blown up by mines in public waters and with diplomats taken hostage.

How the World Court operates

Let's take a closer look at how the World Court operates by detailing a specific case. On the morning of September 12, 1992, some Salvadorans woke up and found themselves living in Honduras, while some Hondurans discovered themselves to be living in El Salvador. It was the successful end to a long struggle over the El Salvador-Honduras border. The countries had fought a bloody border war in 1969, each claiming the same territory, including the Gulf of Fonseca. Thousands died in the border war, and the countries agreed in 1986 to submit their dispute to the World Court and to be bound by its decision. The Court made an equitable reapportionment of territory, based on years of deliberation, fifty court sessions, reviews of precedents in other border disputes, and analysis of relevant documents and other evidence. The five-judge panel responsible for the decision represented Britain, Japan, Brazil, Honduras, and El Salvador (2).

The decisions of the World Court are not always accepted by the parties involved. In 1984, the then legitimate government of Nicaragua, the Sandinistas, fought a war against the Contras, who were supported militarily and financially by the United States. Nicaragua sued the United States before the World Court, seeking protection against U.S. interference and as much as $400 million in damages (3). The United States, which had previously signed a treaty with Nicaragua committing itself to friendship and free navigation, became a respondent in the case under compulsory jurisdiction because of the treaty. But on January 18, 1985, the U.S. government announced that it would no longer accept the mandatory jurisdiction of the Court.

Despite this renouncement, the decision of the Court was handed down in 1986, and it went against the United States. The World Court did not convict the United States of any war crimes; it has no power to do so. But in finding the United States liable for damages, it had to find that the United States had committed war crimes. Since the ruling, the Nicaraguans have voted the Contras into office and the Sandinistas out in a democratic election. The Contras—whom the United States had been supporting—have no interest in pursuing the judgment.

Rulings without teeth?

If countries can reject decisions, do the World Court's rulings have no teeth? In 1992, the Court ruled that Libya must extradite accused air terrorists (see Chapter 19). The Security Council ruled that it would impose economic sanctions against Libya unless the ruling was complied with, and such sanctions were finally imposed. In a way, the U.N. Security Council acts as a marshal, with the power to enforce the Court's judgments. But in general, a very significant problem with international law is the question of who enforces court rulings—and how. It is likely that there will never be a truly effective world court unless there is a world government.

The cases the World Court deals with, whether small or large, are difficult because of the very nature of settling international disputes. As Thomas M. Franck, law professor, notes in his book on the World Court,

. . . even "little" cases are important because they come before the World Court as disputes between leviathans— between totalitarian and democratic, socialist and free market, developed and underdeveloped states. And, paradoxically, the World Court, while operating in such a charged political environment, must constantly confront the exaggerated expectation that judges will replace armies in resolving the world's conflicts. (1)

SOURCES

1. Thomas M. Franck, *Judging the World Court* (New York: Priority Press, 1986).
2. "World Court Settles a Latin Border Dispute," *The New York Times*, September 13, 1992, p. 10.
3. *Nicaraqua v. United States of America*, 1986 ICJ Rep. 14.

QUESTIONS FOR DISCUSSION

1. What would be required to bind the United States to adjudications by the World Court?
2. How is the World Court like our state and federal courts? How is it different?
3. What would public order in the United States be like if criminal courts operated as the World Court does?

International Court of Justice in session at The Hague.

"The jury will disregard the witness's last remarks."

dence, before a reasonable jury, could not possibly lead to a verdict of guilty. Here the judge simply takes the case away from the jury by directing the verdict in favor of the defendant. A motion to dismiss is a request that the proceedings be terminated. Most cases are not dismissed or terminated at this stage. More likely the defense will now present its own evidence—alibi witnesses, expert witnesses, and character witnesses. The defendant, however, is under no obligation to testify. Of course, if the defendant does testify, he or she is subject to cross-examination by the prosecution just as any other witness is.

After the defense has rested its case, the prosecution has another opportunity to present evidence to refute the case presented by the defense. This part of the trial is known as a rebuttal. Following a rebuttal, both sides make their closing arguments.

Closing Arguments and Instructions

In their closing arguments, the two opposing lawyers present a summary of their case to the jury, emphasizing the evidence that is most favorable to their side. New evidence may not be presented during this phase of the trial. Closing arguments are usually an occasion for lawyers to display whatever oratorical skills they possess as they try to impress the jury with the cogency of their arguments. The prosecution will normally stress that it has demonstrated the guilt of the defendant beyond a reasonable doubt and will call on the jury to return a verdict of guilty. The defense will take the opposite position, pointing out weaknesses in the case that call the defendant's guilt into doubt. If there seems to be little room for doubt about the defendant's involvement, the defense may attempt to sway the jury toward a lenient verdict.

"The judge's instructions amount to a minicourse in criminal law."

"No free man shall be taken or imprisoned or dispossessed, or outlawed or exiled, or in any way destroyed, . . . except by the lawful judgment of his peers or by the law of the land."
Magna Carta, 1215.

burden of proof
In criminal cases, the legal obligation of the prosecution to prove the charges against the defendant beyond a reasonable doubt.

After the closing arguments, the jurors must apply the law to the facts they have heard and determine whether the prosecution has fulfilled its task of proving guilt beyond a reasonable doubt. To ensure that they do so responsibly, the judge presents the law to the jury in the form of instructions. Often both prosecution and defense will propose instructions to the judge. If the defense counsel objects to the proposed instructions, these objections are noted for a potential appeal.

The judge's instructions amount to a minicourse in criminal law. After all, jurors are usually not familiar with the law they are called on to apply. The crime of which the defendant is accused must be defined for the jury, along with any other legal concepts relevant to the case, such as **burden of proof.** The judge reminds the jury that the defendant is considered not guilty and must be acquitted unless the state has proved its case beyond a reasonable doubt. Finally, the judge will provide the jury with procedural instructions about such matters as contacting the judge during deliberations if they have any questions, or the order in which they must consider charges if the accusation includes more than one charge. Once the jury has been instructed, it retires to a private room to begin its deliberations.[56]

Jury Deliberations

Deliberations inside the jury room are guided by a foreman—a juror selected (or elected) to preside over the deliberations. The jurors may look at items that were entered into evidence during the trial and ask to review portions of the transcript. Beyond that, however, they receive no assistance. They remain in the jury room in complete privacy. If they do not reach a verdict by the end of the day, they go home, with an admonition from the judge not to discuss the case with anyone and not to read anything about it. In cases that have attracted a good deal of media attention, the judge may order the jury to be sequestered, which means they will be kept apart from family, friends, and the general public, until the end of the trial. Instead they will spend the night (or a series of nights) in a hotel at state expense, where they can be shielded from outside influences and kept under guard. (See the Criminal Justice in Action box.)

A significant body of research has evaluated the process of juror decision-making, and whether extralegal issues influence jurors when they grapple with the facts of a case. Studies have demonstrated that jurors are sometimes influenced by their own personal characteristics (age, race, gender, occupation) and by the characteristics of the defendant and the victim, such as the defendant's social attractiveness. In fact, mock jurors who evaluated the culpability of attractive versus unattractive defendants charged with identical crimes attributed greater blame to the unattractive ones.[57] Other studies that considered the character of the victim found that such variables as marital status, unorthodox lifestyle, and past sexual experience can play a role in jurors' decision-making.[58]

Once the jurors have reached a decision, they will return to the courtroom where their verdict will be announced. Occasionally, the defense or prosecution will ask that the jury be polled—that jurors be asked if they agree with the verdict. This process is intended to ensure that all jurors know and agree with the verdict. If the polling reveals that a juror does not agree with the verdict, the jury may be sent back for further deliberations or a mistrial might be called. In that case, a new trial would be required.

Sentencing

After the verdict is pronounced, the proceedings enter the penalty phase where the sentence is determined. In most states and in federal cases, the sentence is decided by the judge alone. Before delivery of the sentence, posttrial motions may be filed and a presentence investigation may be conducted. This investigation is carried out by a probation officer who examines the defendant's record and background and prepares a report making a recommendation of a sentence. In Chapter 13 we will examine sentencing in detail.

POSTTRIAL

An appeal to a higher court from a conviction obtained in a lower court is a relatively recent right in Anglo-American law. Even though the Constitution does not guarantee the right to an appeal in a criminal case, the right exists.

Rights to Appeal

Every state and the federal government have now provided some form of review to convicted defendants. Although all defendants have this right, in reality most do not exercise it. A voluntary guilty plea eliminates most grounds upon which a defendant could base an appeal. Since a large portion of all convictions are the result of guilty pleas, the vast majority of cases will not be appealed.

It is a fundamental concept of our system of justice that the prosecution has no right to appeal an adverse ruling in a criminal case unless the legislature has specifically authorized it by statute. The Supreme Court has stated that appeals by the Government in criminal cases are something unusual, exceptional, not favored.[59] The reasoning was given by the Court in the nineteenth century, in *United States v. Sanges* (1892). The opinion stated:

"It is a fundamental concept of our system of justice that the prosecution has no right to appeal an adverse criminal ruling unless authorized to do so by statute."

[T]he defendant, having been once put upon his trial and discharged by the court, is not to be again vexed for the same cause, unless the legislature, acting within its constitutional authority, has made express provision for a review of the judgment at the instance of the government.[60]

JURORS AND THEIR STORIES

In the words of legal scholar Harry Kalvin, Jr., and sociologist Hans Zeisel, the Anglo-American jury is a "remarkable institution." It recruits a group of twelve laypeople, chosen at random from the population; it convenes them for the purpose of the particular trial; it entrusts them with great official powers of decision; it permits them to carry on deliberations in secret and to report out their final judgment without giving reasons for it; and, after their momentary service to the state has been completed, it orders them to disband and return to private life (1). And for the most part, this "remarkable institution" performs its work very capably.

The story model

The jury is a remarkable institution both for what is known about it and for what is being discovered. Social scientists still are uncovering the influences that move jurors to vote the way they do. For example, research suggests that jurors are influenced by "extralegal" factors. Although extraevidentiary information is not admissible as legal proof, jurors are affected by everything they see and hear at a trial—a witness's refusal to testify, the attorneys' opening and closing statements, testimony presented but declared inadmissible, and the defendant's personal appearance and prior criminal record (2).

Jurors also apparently are affected by what they do *not* see or hear in the courtroom. As they listen to the evidence, they fill in gaps and create a continuing story that is modified as new information is received. Listening to each piece of evidence as it is presented and saving analysis for the deliberation period might be the ideal picture of how jurors work, but in practice jurors are just like all people; they incorporate each piece of information, as they hear it, into an overall framework of their own creation, based on their own experiences and expectations of how the world works.

Psychologists call this explanation of a juror's cognitive processing the "story model" and suggest that it is a necessary part of a juror's work:

. . . Evidence is comprehended and organized into one or more plausible accounts describing "what happened" at the time of events testified to during the trial . . . stories organize information in ways that help the juror perform. . . . (3)

Filling the gaps

The continuing reinterpretation of the evidence as it is presented is the juror's effort to make sense of the evidence, to make it credible and logical, and to make it consistent with their own experiences. A case presented to a mock jury provides an example of the "gap-filling" that jurors do:

In the case, the defendant, Frank Johnson, had quarreled in a bar with the victim, Alan Caldwell, who threatened him with a razor. Later that evening they went outside, got into a fight, and Johnson knifed Caldwell, who died. Disputed points included whether or not Caldwell was a bully who had started the first quarrel when his girlfriend had asked Johnson for a ride to the racetrack, whether Johnson had stabbed Caldwell or merely held his knife out to protect himself, and whether Johnson had gone home to get a knife. (4)

The mock jurors were asked to reach a verdict and then were interviewed about the case and the verdict. Researchers found that 45 percent of the references jurors made were to information that had not been presented in the testimony; these statements were based on inferences and assumptions about the men's psychological states and motives. While some of the jurors pieced the evidence together in a way that led to a not guilty verdict, just as many "created a story" that led to a verdict of first-degree murder. Social class explained some of the difference: Researchers found that middle-class jurors considered the presence of a knife as lending support to Johnson's criminal intentions. Working-class jurors, on the other hand, were more likely to assume that the presence of a knife was necessary for protection and that it did not point to a plan to stab someone.

Mock jury research

Both prosecutors and defense attorneys can challenge potential jurors "for cause," presenting evidence that an individual is likely to be biased in a specific case. Under the system of peremptory challenges, both sides also can strike a certain number of jurors without giving any reason. The fact that different jurors hear evidence in different ways has not been lost on the legal community, and consulting firms offer assistance both in selecting jurors and in presenting evidence. William Kennedy Smith paid $200,000 for

An experimental simulation of a murder case as presented to a jury can lead to opposite verdicts, depending on how the jurors recount the evidence to themselves and fill in blanks with situations, events and motives not presented to them as evidence.

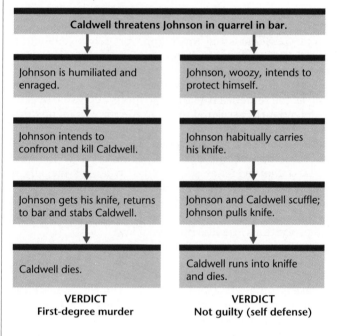

Caldwell threatens Johnson in quarrel in bar.

Johnson is humiliated and enraged.	Johnson, woozy, intends to protect himself.
Johnson intends to confront and kill Caldwell.	Johnson habitually carries his knife.
Johnson gets his knife, returns to bar and stabs Caldwell.	Johnson and Caldwell scuffle; Johnson pulls knife.
Caldwell dies.	Caldwell runs into kniffe and dies.

VERDICT
First-degree murder

VERDICT
Not guilty (self defense)

FIGURE 1. The Story in the Juror's Mind: How the Same Evidence Can Result in Opposite Verdicts
(*Source:* Adapted and excerpted from *Cardozo Law Review;* Daniel Coleman, "Jurors Hear Evidence and Turn It into Stories," *The New York Times,* May 12, 1992, p. C11.)

consulting aid to help select the jury that acquitted him of rape, and consultants can present evidence to mock juries before a trial begins to help attorneys see how jurors are likely to react to methods of questioning witnesses or presenting evidence. (5) In a recent report on patent litigation, the authors—the directors of research and of trial consulting for a litigation consulting firm—claim that mock jury research can be used to predict the "perfect juror" for a particular case:

It is possible, through pretrial research using surrogate jurors, to identify which legal, moral and psychological issues are most likely to be key in the decision-making process of the various types of jurors on a specific case. It is also possible to evaluate witnesses, evaluate the impact of documents and specific exhibits, and develop profiles of "ideal" or "dangerous" jurors. (6)

A key element in the way juries operate is that jurors have to work together to reach a verdict. A study of more than 700 jurors found that individual jurors remember only about 60 percent of the evidence presented and 44 percent of the judge's instructions, while the jury as a whole is able to recall 93 percent of the evidence and 82 percent of the instructions (4). This necessary combining of memories—and of "stories"—helps to prevent verdicts from being based on any one interpretation of the evidence.

SOURCES

1. Harry Kalvin, Jr., and Hans Zeisel, *The American Jury* (Chicago, Ill.: University of Chicago Press, 1966), p. 3.
2. "Incriminating Evidence: How Juries Reach a Verdict," *Psychology Today* 25(5) (September 1992):9.
3. Reid Hastie, Steven D. Penrod, and Nancy Pennington, *Inside the Jury* (Cambridge, Mass.: Harvard University Press, 1983), pp. 22–23. See also Valerie P. Hans, "Jury Decision Making," in D. K. Kagehiro and W. S. Laufer (eds.), *Handbook of Psychology and Law* (New York: Springer-Verlag, 1992).
4. Daniel Coleman, "Jurors Hear Evidence and Turn It Into Stories," *The New York Times,* May 12, 1992, p. C1.
5. Ted Gest and Constance Johnson, "The Justice System: Getting a Fair Trial," *U.S. News and World Report* 112(20) (May 25, 1992):36, 38.
6. Ellen L. Leggett and Dan R. Gallipeau, "Computer Litigation: Jurors' Perceptions and Reactions," *The Computer Lawyer* 9(8) (August 1992):18.

QUESTIONS FOR DISCUSSION

1. Supreme Court Justice Thurgood Marshall proposed in 1986 that all peremptory challenges be eliminated. Do you agree? Why or why not?
2. What modifications to the jury system might make it better?
3. The requirement that jury lists represent a "fair cross-section" of the communities from which they are drawn does not extend to the jury actually seated. Do you think it should? Why or why not?

Virtually all of the states and the federal government now have provisions that do allow appeals by the prosecutor, but they generally contain restrictions as to the conditions under which the prosecution may exercise this option, and generally appeals are not allowed when a defendant has been acquitted.

Appellate Review

Reviews by appeals courts are restricted to procedural questions and questions of law (Chapter 10). Examples include questions concerning the adequacy of a judge's instructions to a jury; evidence that was inappropriately revealed to the jury; failure by the prosecution to disclose material evidence favorable to the defendant. Appellate review rarely considers facts relating to a defendant's guilt or innocence. In most states, the length of a defendant's sentence is also not subject to appeal, as long as the sentence is within the limits allowable by law.[61] In filing an appeal, the defendant is asserting that some error was made during the process by which the conviction was obtained. To be a successful appeal, the alleged error must be reversible—an error that affected the outcome of the case. (An error that had no effect on the outcome is called a harmless error.) For example, a defendant may assert that evidence presented at trial was illegally obtained, that the jury selection process was such that the trial was decided by a biased jury, or that the judge's instructions to the jury were faulty in some way and liable to influence the jurors to decide on a conviction. These are matters related to constitutional protections and due process of law.

Appellate Process

An appeal in a criminal case is initiated by the losing side, which becomes known as the appellant; the opposing side is referred to as the appellee. The first step in the process is to file a notice of appeal with the trial court that heard the original case. This normally must be done within a month or two of the trial. The court then sends a copy of the notice to the appellee. During the next several weeks, the appellant is responsible for getting all the records of the trial court, including a transcript of the trial, to the appeals court. The appellant's lawyer must submit a legal brief setting forth the reasons for the appeal. The appellee prepares a brief that responds to the appellant's arguments, normally asking that the lower-court

Attorney William Kunstler addressing the Court of Appeals in the notorious Central Park jogger case, 1990.

decision be upheld. In some cases the court will allow the two sides to make an oral presentation. After the presentation of the arguments, the court decides the case and issues a written opinion.

Appellate courts have at least five options in deciding an appeal. They may

- affirm, or uphold, the lower-court ruling
- modify the lower-court ruling (change a part of the ruling but not reverse it)
- reverse the lower-court ruling (the trial decision is set aside and no further court action is required)
- remand the case, or send it back down to the lower court without overturning the original ruling. (In such cases, the appellate court will often instruct the lower court to conduct a new trial)
- reverse and remand the case (overturn the lower-court ruling while at the same time require further action by the lower court, such as conducting a new trial)

In most cases, lower-court rulings are not simply reversed. Even a successful appeal usually does not mean that the defendant goes free. More often, the case is remanded to the lower court and the prosecution must then decide whether to pursue the case in a second trial. If the appeal has not been successful, the defendant can request review in the state supreme court (or highest court in the state) and, if a federal constitutional question is involved, in the federal courts.

"Even a successful appeal usually does not mean that the defendant goes free."

REVIEW

The trial segment of the criminal justice process has pretrial, trial, and posttrial stages. For all cases that are not diverted, a host of critical decisions must be made concerning the detention of the defendant, the amount of bail to be imposed (if any), what plea to enter, whether to plea bargain, what jurors to choose, what evidence to present, what motions to file, what instructions to recommend, what kind of closing argument to make, whether to file an appeal, and whether to seek a retrial.

The process is complex, and research on it is still in its early stages. Preliminary findings reveal that persons sent to diversion programs show low rates of recidivism, that bail guidelines may be effective in minimizing judicial discretion, and that certain factors—such as age, drug use, and employment status—are associated with pretrial flight or misconduct.

Significant problems exist at virtually every stage of the criminal process. Inequities in the setting of bail, the pretrial detention of indigents, and the composition of juries are but a few of the challenges facing criminal justice professionals.

Notes

1. Carolyn Pesce, "Smith Has 'Faith' in System: Jury Votes to Acquit in Just 77 Minutes," *U.S.A. Today*, December 12, 1991, p. 1.

2. Barbara Boland, Paul Mahanna, and Ronald Stones, *The Prosecution of Felony Arrests, 1988* (Washington, D.C.: Bureau of Justice Statistics, NCJ-130914, 1992).

3. Bureau of Justice Statistics, *Federal Criminal Case Processing, 1980–89, with Preliminary Data for 1990* (Washington, D.C.: Bureau of Justice Statistics, NCJ-130526, 1991).

4. Alison Howard, "A Vandal Finds Forgiveness at the Scene of the Crime: A N.J. Man Apologizes to D.C. Church for $7,000 Rampage," *Washington Post*, October 7, 1991, p. B3.

5. Roberta Rovner-Pieczenik, *Pretrial Intervention Strategies: An Evaluation of Policy-Related Research and Policymaker Perceptions* (Chicago: American Bar Association, 1974).

6. Peter Zablotsky, "An Analysis of State Pretrial Diversion Statutes," *Columbia Journal of Law and Social Problems* 15 (1979):1–32.

7. Franklin Zimring, "Measuring the Impact of Pretrial Diversion from the Criminal Justice System," *University of Chicago Law Review* 41 (1974):224–241.

8. President's Commission on Law Enforcement and Administration of Justice, *Task Force Report: Courts* (Washington, D.C.: U.S. Government Printing Office, 1967).

9. Brian A. Reaves, *Pretrial Release of Felony Defendants, 1988* (Washington, D.C.: Bureau of Justice Statistics, 1991).

10. See Chris W. Eskridge, *Pretrial Release Programming: Issues and Trends* (New York: Clark Boardman, 1983).

11. *Stack v. Boyle*, 342 U.S. 1 (1951).

12. See Ilene H. Nagel, "The Legal/Extra-legal Controversy: Judicial Decisions in Pretrial Release," *Law and Society Review* 17 (1983):481–515. Bail is not considered excessive simply because a defendant cannot afford to pay it. An analysis of the factors that influence release decisions indicates that those specified in *Stack* are among the most important that judges use in their decision-making. A defendant's employment status, community and family ties, prior record of criminal convictions, history of court appearances, and the possible sentence the person faces also figure into the equation when release decisions are made.

13. Forrest Dill, "Discretion, Exchange and Social Control: Bail Bondsmen in Criminal Courts," *Law and Society Review* 9 (1975):639–674.

14. Andy Hall, *Pretrial Release Program Options* (Washington, D.C.: National Institute of Justice, 1984).

15. John S. Goldkamp, *Two Classes of Accused: A Study of Bail and Detention in American Justice* (Cambridge, Mass.: Ballinger, 1979).

16. Peter R. Jones and John S. Goldkamp, "The Bail Guidelines Experiment in Dade County, Miami: A Case Study in the Development and Implementation of a Policy Innovation," *Justice System Journal* 14 and 15 (1991):445–476.

17. Michele Sviridoff, "Bail Bonds and Cash Alternatives: The

Influence of 'Discounts' on Bail-Making in New York City," *Justice System Journal* 11 (1986):131–147. See also Douglas Martin, "Bail Bondsmen Decline as Clientele Shifts," *The New York Times*, May 9, 1987, pp. 33, 35.

18. John H. Kennedy, "Patriarca Pledges Honor for his Freedom on Bail," *Boston Globe*, May 14, 1991, p. 19.

19. Reaves, *Pretrial Release of Felony Defendants*.

20. D. Alan Henry, "Pretrial Services: Today and Yesterday," *Federal Probation* 55 (June 1991):54–62.

21. Christy A. Visher and Richard L. Linster, "A Survival Model of Pretrial Failure," *Journal of Quantitative Criminology* 6 (1990):153–184. See also James Austin, Barry Krisberg, and Paul Litsky, "The Effectiveness of Supervised Pretrial Release," *Crime and Delinquency* 31 (1985):519–537. For a revealing study of gender bias in pretrial release, see Ellen Hochstedler Stevry and Nancy Frank, "Gender Bias and Pretrial Release: More Pieces of the Puzzle," *Journal of Criminal Justice* 18 (1990):417–432.

22. See Michael R. Gottfredson and Don M. Gottfredson, *Decision Making in Criminal Justice: Toward the Rational Exercise of Discretion* 2d ed. (New York: Plenum, 1988).

23. See, e.g., Mary A. Toborg and Michael B. Kirby, *Drug Use and Pretrial Crime in the District of Columbia—Research Brief* (Washington, D.C.: National Institute of Justice, 1984); D. Smith, E. Wish, and R. Jarjoura, "Drug Use and Pretrial Misconduct in New York City," *Journal of Quantitative Criminology* 5 (1989):101–126; Jeffrey Roth and Paul Wice, *Pretrial Release and Misconduct in the District of Columbia Promis Research Project*, Publication 16 (Washington, D.C.: Institute for Law and Social Research, 1980).

24. For a summary of findings, see Cathryn Jo Rosen and John S. Goldkamp, "The Constitutionality of Drug Testing at the Bail Stage," *Journal of Criminal Law and Criminology* 80 (1989):114–176. Recently, the National Institute of Justice has funded the Drug Use Forecasting (DUF) Program, which tests arrestees anonymously in certain cities to determine the extent of drug use among those arrested and the types of drugs being used.

25. Chester L. Britt, III, Michael R. Gottfredson, and John S. Goldkamp, "Drug Testing and Pretrial Misconduct: An Experiment on the Specific Deterrent Effects of Drug Monitoring Defendants on Pretrial Release," *Journal of Research in Crime and Delinquency* 29 (1992):62–78.

26. See John S. Goldkamp, Michael R. Gottfredson, and Doris Weiland, "Pretrial Drug Testing and Defendant Risk," *Journal of Criminal Law and Criminology* 81 (1990):585–652; Visher and Linster, "A Survival Model of Pretrial Failure."

27. See Goldkamp, Gottfredson, and Weiland, "Pretrial Drug Testing."

28. James J. Stephan and Louis W. Jankowski, *Jail Inmates, 1990* (Washington, D.C.: Bureau of Justice Statistics, 1991).

29. Reaves, *Pretrial Release of Felony Defendants*.

30. Barbara Gottlieb, *Public Danger as a Factor in Pretrial Release: A Comparative Analysis of State Laws* (Washington, D.C.: National Institute of Justice, 1985).

31. Marc Miller and Martin Guggenheim, "Pretrial Detention and Punishment," *Minnesota Law Review* 75 (1990):335–426.

32. Bail Reform Act of 1984, 18 U.S.C. §§ 3141–3150 (1984).

33. *United States v. Salerno*, 481 U.S. 739 (1987).

34. Bureau of Justice Statistics, *Pretrial Release and Detention: The Bail Reform Act of 1984* (Washington, D.C.: Bureau of Justice Statistics, 1988).

35. See Thomas E. Scott, "Pretrial Detention under the Bail Reform Act of 1984: An Empirical Analysis," *American Criminal Law Review* 27 (1989):1–51.

36. Reaves, *Pretrial Release of Felony Defendants*.

37. For example, see Alan J. Lizotte, "Extra-legal Factors in Chicago's Criminal Courts: Testing the Conflict Model of Criminal Justice," *Social Problems* 25 (1978):564–580; James D. Unnever, "Direct and Organizational Discrimination in the Sentencing of Drug Offenders," *Social Problems* 30 (1982):212–225; Charles Ares, Anne Rankin, and Herbert Sturz, "The Manhattan Bail Project: An In-terim Report on the Use of Pre-Trial Parole," *New York University Law Review* 38 (1963):67–95.

Because unconvicted defendants are often housed with convicted inmates, in addition to the fact the jails are overcrowded, electronic monitoring of defendants at home has been used as an alternative to jail detention. See Timothy P. Cadigan, "Electronic Monitoring in Federal Pretrial Release," *Federal Probation* 55 (March 1991):26–30. See also Michael G. Maxfield and Terry L. Baumer, "Home Detention with Electronic Monitoring: Comparing Pretrial and Postconviction Programs," *Crime and Delinquency* 36 (1990):521–536; Keith W. Cooprider and Judith Kerby, "A Practical Application of Electronic Monitoring at the Pretrial Stage," *Federal Probation* 54 (March 1990):28–55.

38. See Malcolm D. Holmes, Howard C. Daudistel, and Ronald A. Farrell, "Determinants of Charge Reductions and Final Dispositions in Cases of Burglary and Robbery," *Journal of Research in Crime and Delinquency* 24 (1987):233–254.

39. Michele Galen, "Guilty, Your Honor," *Business Week*, May 7, 1990, p. 33.

40. Roni Rabin, "Meting out Justice in the 'Land of No,'" *Newsday*, August 16, 1991, p. 3.

41. Barbara Boland, Paul Mahanna, and Ronald Sones, *The Prosecution of Felony Arrests*.

42. Adam Gelb, "Georgia's DUI Scandal," *Atlanta Journal and Constitution*, November 4, 1991, p. E1.

43. American Bar Association Project on Minimum Standards for Criminal Justice, *Standards Relating to Pleas of Guilty* (New York: American Bar Association, 1968).

44. Joan Ullman, "I Carried It Too Far, That's For Sure; Report from Jeffrey Dahmer Trial," *Psychology Today* 25 (May 1992):28.

45. Henry J. Steadman, "Empirical Research on the Insanity Defense," *Annals of the American Academy of Political and Social Science* 477 (1985):58–71; Lisa A. Callahan, Henry J. Steadman, Margaret A. McGreevy, and Pamela Clark Robbins, "The Volume and Characteristics of Insanity Defense Pleas: An Eight-State Study," *Bulletin of the American Academy of Psychiatry and Law* 29 (1991):331–338. See also Pedro R. Portes, Dennis E. Wagner, and Eleanor Love, "How Just Is the Guilty but Mentally Ill Verdict? An Exploration into Personality and Intellectual Factors," *Journal of Criminal Justice* 19 (1991):471–479.

46. Lisa A. Callahan et al., "Volume and Characteristics of Insanity Defense Pleas"; Hugh McGinley and Richard A. Pasework, "National Survey of the Frequency and Success of the Insanity Plea and Alternate Pleas," *Journal of Psychiatry and Law* 17 (1989):205–221; Jeffrey S. Janofsky, Michael B. Vandewalle, and Jonas R. Rappeport, "Defendants Pleading Insanity: An Analysis of Outcome," *Bulletin of the American Academy of Psychiatry and Law* 17 (1989):203–211.

47. Josh Meyer, "Prolific ATM Robber Scheduled to Get Prison Term," *Los Angeles Times*, January 29, 1991, p. 3.

48. See Robert A. Weninger, "The Abolition of Plea Bargaining: A Case Study of El Paso County, Texas," *UCLA Law Review* 35 (1987):265–313.

49. William F. McDonald, *Plea Bargaining: Critical Issues and Common Practices* (Washington, D.C.: National Institute of Justice, 1985). For historical views of plea bargaining see Albert W. Alschuler, "Plea Bargaining and Its History," *Law and Society Review* 13 (1979):211–245; Lawrence M. Friedman, "Plea Bargaining in Historical Perspective," *Law and Society Review* 13 (1979):247–259.

50. Patrick A. Langan and John M. Dawson, *Felony Sentences in State Courts, 1988* (Washington, D.C.: Bureau of Justice Statistics, 1990).

51. *Batson v. Kentucky*, 476 U.S. 79 (1986). For selection of more representative juries, see Hiroshi Fukurai, Edgar W. Butler, and Richard Krooth, "Cross-sectional Jury Representation or Systematic Jury Representation? Simple Random and Cluster Sampling Strategies in Jury Selection," *Journal of Criminal Justice* 19 (1991):31–48.

52. See Marvin B. Steinberg, "The Case for Eliminating Peremptory Challenges," *Criminal Law Bulletin* 27 (1991):216–229; James J. Gobert, "In Search of the Impartial Jury," *Journal of Criminal Law and Criminology* 79 (1988):269–327.

53. Hans Zeisel and Shari Seidman Diamond, "The Effect of Peremptory Challenges on Jury and Verdict: An Experiment in a Federal District Court," *Stanford Law Review* 30 (1978):491–531.

54. *Mapp v. Ohio*, 367 U.S. 643 (1969).

55. The *Mapp* decision made the Fourth Amendment's exclusionary rule applicable to the states through the Fourteenth Amendment's due process clause.

56. See Geoffrey P. Kramer and Dorean M. Koenig, "Do Jurors Understand Criminal Jury Instructions? Analyzing the Results of the Michigan Juror Comprehension Project," *University of Michigan Journal of Law Reform* 23 (1990):401–437.

57. Christy A. Visher, "Juror Decision-Making: The Importance of Evidence," *Law and Human Behavior* 11 (1987):1–17.

58. For a review of extralegal factors affecting jurors, see Marilyn Chandler Ford, "The Role of Extralegal Factors in Jury Verdicts," *Justice System Journal* 11 (1986):16–39. See also John Guinther, *The Jury in America* (New York: Facts on File Publications, 1988).

59. *Carroll v. United States*, 354 U.S. 394 (1957).

60. *United States v. Sanges*, 144 U.S. 310 (1892).

61. G. O. W. Mueller, "Penology on Appeal: Appellate Review of Legal but Excessive Sentences," *Vanderbilt Law Review* 15 (1962):671–697.

CHAPTER 13

SENTENCING

"Gary Fannon, the son of a hard-working single mother who makes her living as a waitress, had finished high school and was on his way to becoming an auto-mechanic. But now Gary is doing life without parole in a Michigan penitentiary. What happened? A friend had asked him to get him some cocaine. Gary did. Then some more, and more. But he chickened out when the deal got too big, $32,000.00 for 2.2 pounds. The friend turned out to be an undercover cop, since fired for drug use.

"Gary is serving a life-without-parole sentence under Michigan's fixed sentencing statute which commits anybody to life imprisonment without parole for dealing in drugs (or conspiring to do so) of 1.4 pounds or more.

"Said he: 'I deserve to do some time. But I don't deserve to die here. I'm no Jeffrey Dahmer!'

"Said his mother: 'Why didn't they bust my son on the first deal?'

"Said State Representative William Bryant (R): 'We gave prosecutors a powerful tool and prayed like hell they wouldn't abuse it. We were wrong.'"[1]

With the controversy that surrounds mandatory sentences, sentencing guidelines, new and novel sentences such as home confinement, and the enduring debate over capital punishment, it is no wonder that sentencing is regarded as the most controversial of all the stages in the criminal justice process. At earlier stages of the administration of justice the defendant benefits from the presumption of innocence, and certain safeguards are built into the adversarial system: notions of due process, fundamental fairness, and impartiality. Once the defendant is convicted, however, the focus shifts away from these concerns to the task of imposing a sentence. The sanctioning decision can mean the difference between imprisonment or the freedom to remain in the community under supervision. In some cases it can mean the difference between life and death. ■

The selection of a criminal sanction, such as the death penalty, is often shaped by the purpose the sanction is supposed to fulfill. For example, a sentence given for the purpose of rehabilitating an offender may differ from one intended to deter other persons from committing similar crimes. Understanding the philosophies that provide a justification for different sanctions is critical. We will therefore start this chapter with a review of the most prominent philosophies of punishment.

PURPOSES AND GOALS OF THE CRIMINAL SANCTION

Four traditional philosophies have molded the types of sentences in use today: retribution, deterrence, incapacitation, and rehabilitation. Another—mixed goals—combines elements of several philosophies.

Retribution

Three elements—a proportionate penalty, a penalty that is deserved, and a penalty that expresses the moral condemnation of society—capture the essence of the conception of retribution. The case of Colin Stuart McCoy is a good illustration.

In May 1992, Colin Stuart McCoy of Beaverton, Oregon, disturbed by demands of the Internal Revenue Service for the payment of "unpaid taxes," decided to commit an act of civil disobedience. McCoy entered the First Interstate Bank and passed a note to a teller demanding money. The teller handed over $1,500, whereupon McCoy handed a note back indicating that this robbery had been staged to get the Internal Revenue Service's attention. McCoy left the bank and immediately set the money on fire in a barbecue grill that he had placed in the bank's parking lot. Two of McCoy's friends recorded the entire incident on videotape, as proof that it was truly an act of civil disobedience. McCoy was arrested and convicted of robbery in federal court.[2] U.S. District Court Judge James Redden sentenced him to a two-year prison term. Such a sentence represents the consensus of the community that bank robbery is wrong, whether it is committed for reasons of civil disobedience or profit.

History.   It may be surmised, although evidence is scarce, that some of the earliest tribal societies reacted quite fiercely to wrongs that threatened the continued existence of the tribe. In the laws of early literate societies we find a limit commonly imposed on unbridled vengeance. The Mosaic laws (about 1200 b.c.) are a prime example: Punishment should be comparable to the harm inflicted, no more, no less ("an eye for an eye"). This distinct advance in civilization is called the "law of retaliation." The same idea is expressed by the term **retribution,** from the Latin "to give back," to respond in kind.[3] The concept of retribution has been with us ever since. (See the Criminal Justice on Trial box.)

In the age of Enlightenment (the late eighteenth century) it became the hallmark of criminal legislation. In determining the punishments in their penal codes, legislatures were to take into account the perceived gravity or seriousness of each offense; and punishments no longer had to be in kind. Murder commanded a more severe punishment than robbery, and robbery a more severe punishment than larceny, yet blinding of a person (felonious assault) no longer required blinding of the offender. Alternate sanctions (especially imprisonment) had taken the place of in-kind sanctions.

"Eye for eye, tooth for tooth, hand for hand, foot for foot."
Deuteronomy XIX:31.

retribution
"Eye for an eye" philosophy of justice.

Just Deserts. In the early part of this century, attitudes began to change. This was a period of great expectations, of advances in medicine and in psychology. Especially in the United States, anything seemed possible, even **rehabilitation,** or the use of education, and vocational and psychological counseling to transform criminals into law-abiding citizens. In this climate, the classic retributive idea seemed to be inherently flawed. Retribution was based on the assumption that all offenders who violate the same provision of the penal law deserve the same punishment. But behavioral scientists pointed out that no two offenders who commit the same crime are completely alike in motivation, personality, intelligence, and potential for rehabilitation. As a result, rehabilitation was the dominant influence on sanctions, until the late 1970s. At that time dissatisfaction with some of the practices associated with the rehabilitative ideal, as well as disappointment with the results of rehabilitative programs, led scholars such as Andrew von Hirsch, Richard Singer, and others to promote a return to retribution.[4] Yet their conception of retribution was different and perhaps more elaborate than earlier models. It focused on the notion of desert, and is thus called **just deserts.**

Underlying the concept of just deserts is the proposition that the punishment must be based on the gravity of the offense and the culpability or blameworthiness of the perpetrator. Just-deserts advocates argue that courts simply do not have the capacity to determine who can be successfully deterred or reformed and who cannot. Parole boards are not prepared to make sound decisions as to which offenders are good risks for release and which are not. Finally, the notion of rehabilitation was premised on the ability of prisons—"correctional" institutions—to correct or rehabilitate; but they fail to do so in most cases. Therefore, it is argued, there are few choices but to return to a system of retribution, which at the bare minimum guarantees like sentences for like crimes. Any rehabilitative efforts in prisons should be made only within the terms of a proportionate sentence, and with the full consent of the inmate.[5]

The just-deserts approach has been successful in minimizing disparities in sentences and in curbing judicial arbitrariness. But it has problems as well. It has been blamed for prison overcrowding. It has been attacked for its insensitivity to the social problems that lead a large proportion of offenders to crime. It has been criticized for its refusal to acknowledge the fact that education or re-education, in the broadest sense, can affect values, attitudes, and behavior. It also has been called unscientific because of its rejection of scientific efforts to identify and selectively incapacitate habitual or chronic offenders. Critics have characterized the concept as superficial for its rejection of the rehabilitative ideal, and for ignoring the fact that rehabilitation has been condemned on the basis of inadequate or flawed evaluations.

Just-deserts theorists have reasonable answers to these criticisms. They are not insensitive to the social problems that promote crime, but feel strongly that defendants should be sentenced on the basis of the crime they have committed, rather than their social background. They are not insensitive to the utility of education, but contend that a defendant's ability to grow intellectually should not influence the sentencing decision. Why should judges be forward-looking in fashioning a sanction, when the sentence must reflect a crime that was committed in the past? Finally, theorists have not condemned rehabilitation on the basis of flawed evaluations. Rather, they have dismissed rehabilitation on the basis of its irrelevance to the nature of the crime that was committed, and the culpability of the offender at the time of the crime.[6]

Deterrence

What would happen if there were no costs associated with illegal activity? According to some scholars, if we disbanded all law enforcement agencies and removed all sanctions from the penal laws, the result would be "a crime wave of

rehabilitation
Reformation of an offender through interventions such as educational and vocational programs and psychotherapy.

just deserts
Philosophy of justice that asserts that the punishment should fit the crime and the culpability of the offender.

"According to some scholars, if we disbanded all law enforcement agencies . . . the result would be 'a crime wave of unprecedented proportion.'"

JUSTITIA: GODDESS OF JUSTICE

The corrections department prison van that ferries prisoners from courthouse to jail displays the service's symbol: the goddess of justice, blindfolded, holding the scales of justice in her left hand and a sword in her right hand. And so the goddess of justice shuttles back and forth between conviction for crime and service of sentence, seemingly forever.

Justice in the ancient world

How did we get this idea of a goddess of justice who weighs crime and punishment, which she then executes with her sword? It appears that all ancient states had a goddess of justice among their many deities. For the Egyptians she was Maat. Egyptians seem to have been the first people to depict the scales of justice—and they were used to weigh hearts. Maat withheld judgment until people had completed their lives; then she weighed their hearts on her scales. If the life value of the heart tipped the scale, she would guarantee a pleasurable afterlife. If not, the jackal—watching the scales of justice—would get the heart as a meal.

The Greeks revered Dike (pronounced Deeke) as their goddess of justice. Daughter of the chief god Zeus and the goddess Themis, Dike was given a place right next to Zeus. The Romans named her Justitia (Justice) and depicted her holding the scales of justice, a staff symbolizing authority, and an olive branch and horn of plenty. In Rome's early days Justitia was as interested in handing out peace and rewards as she was in weighing crime and punishment. But the later Romans dropped the horn of plenty and olive branch and left her holding only the scales and the sword. Later, Justitia appears blindfolded, so that she may not be biased by seeing the person before her—the origin of the term "blind justice."

Gulliver reported a whole different notion of justice among the Liliputians. Their goddess of justice was far from blind; in fact, she had six eyes: two in front, two in back, and one on each side. She held a sword in her left hand, not the strong right hand; in the right hand she held a bag of gold to give out rewards.

The ancient Germans had a kind of goddess of justice, too: Aunt Holly. Nowadays she can be found in the company of Santa Claus, handing out presents to children at Christmas. But in the ancient fairy tale "Aunt Holly," she tars and feathers the delinquents and showers gold on the good.

With the advent of Christianity, the goddess of justice was demoted to a saint, Santa Justitia, and people became a bit suspicious about her ability or willingness to deal out justice in an evenhanded manner. A medieval woodcut shows Santa Justitia without blindfold and with her scales uneven—one justice for the rich, one for the poor. In Western civilization, Justitia has come to symbolize penal justice in the sense of distributive justice, in which punishment is meted out in accordance with the gravity of the crime.

The Egyptian goddess Maat, tomb relief, reign of Ramses VI (1151–1143 B.C.).

But today we shy away from the word "punishment." American criminal justice practitioners have switched from "punishment" to "corrections." This may be little more than a change in labels, well-meaning but misleading: The prison van, meantime, with the goddess Justitia painted on its side, still shuttles between courthouse and jail house.

Contemporary justice

Crowned justice, center, with commutative justice at her left and distributive justice at her right. Detail of Lorenzetti's fresco Allegory of Good Government, *Siena, 1338–40.*

QUESTIONS FOR DISCUSSION

1. The idea that Justitia should not be able to see those whom she judges is an old one. Should it be applied to modern-day courtrooms—should the judge and jury not be able to see the defendant whose fate they are determining?
2. In some cultures and periods of history the person who meted out punishment also handed out rewards. Would there be any benefit to incorporating rewards distribution into the criminal justice system today?
3. The change from using the word "punishment" to the word "corrections" suggests a change in attitude about dealing with criminal offenders. Can you provide any examples of such a changed attitude?

unprecedented proportions."[7] The very existence of the criminal justice system, it has been argued, has a strong general deterrent effect, ensuring obedience in those who otherwise would resort to crime. Thus, the basic principle underlying **deterrence** theory is that people will refrain from engaging in criminal activity because of the consequences associated with detection.

Contemporary notions of the deterrent effect of the criminal law and sanctions grew out of the philosophies of Cesare Beccaria in Italy and Jeremy Bentham in England. They emphasized the importance of making punishment certain, swift, and sufficiently severe to be a deterrent.[8] Deterrence could be best achieved if the laws and the potential sanctions associated with violations were made known to the public, by public reading of the law in the legislature, the distribution of printed copies, publicity by the media, or even by town criers in the villages.

Types of Deterrence. A distinction is often made between two types of deterrence. **General deterrence** refers to the effect that the criminal law with its punishments has on people in general. Those considering whether to commit a crime will be deterred by knowing that a law prohibits certain behavior and that those who have broken the law have paid a penalty for it. **Special deterrence,** sometimes called specific deterrence, reflects punishment that deters an offender from engaging in additional criminal behavior, because of the disagreeable experience of a past punishment.

Effectiveness. If the advocates of deterrence are correct, potential offenders should be affected by the relative certainty that punishment will result from the commission of a crime. Indeed, research has shown that certainty of punishment is more important than either the severity or swiftness of a sanction in achieving the goal of deterrence.[9] For punishment to be certain, however, the criminal must first be caught. For common street crimes, then, a police presence increases the chances of capture and supplies an important component of deterrence. A would-be burglar might decide not to break into a house on a block where a patrol officer is stationed. (Of course, the burglar may then decide to move to another block without police presence, which means that the crime has merely been displaced.) One way to evaluate the effectiveness of deterrence, therefore, is to examine the degree to which a police presence affects the extent of crime. Research on the effect of police strikes in the 1970s on the crime rates of eleven American cities provided very little support for the hypothesis that removal of the police presence raises crime rates.[10] The evidence on the effects of intensified policing is no clearer. In 1982, New York City's transit police force was strengthened to combat subway crime. Additional officers were posted in subway stations and on virtually all trains between 8 P.M. and 4 A.M. The results were inconclusive.[11]

What about the deterrent effect of criminal sanctions? Researchers have studied the effects of increasing the threatened punishments for some crimes. Massachusetts mandated a minimum prison term of one year for carrying a firearm without a permit. This law had a measurable deterrent effect,[12] although studies in both Detroit and Florida, which likewise imposed mandatory sentences for firearm law violations, indicate that such penalties did not lead to declining incidences of the violent crimes measured, such as homicide or robbery.[13] The severity of possible sanctions also does not appear to deter people from drinking and driving. In recent years, several jurisdictions have enacted statutes calling for mandatory jail sentences for those convicted of drinking and driving offenses. Evaluations of the effect of these laws reveal that drivers are not deterred by the threat of jail,[14] although the threat of a lesser formal sanction, such as license suspension,[15] or even moral disapproval[16] may deter some people from drinking and driving.

In a study of deterrence by the Criminal Law Education and Research Center

---

deterrence
Theory of punishment that holds that potential offenders will refrain from committing crimes for fear of punishment (sometimes called general prevention).

general deterrence
Threat of punishment intended to induce the general public not to engage in criminal acts.

special deterrence
Threat of punishment that deters an offender from engaging in any additional criminal behavior, based on the disagreeable experience with a past punishment.

"Certainty of punishment is more important than either the severity or swiftness of a sanction in achieving deterrence."

at New York University, three types of warning stickers were attached to parking meters in three comparable areas. One sticker threatened a $50 fine for the use of slugs in parking meters. The second threatened a $250 fine and three months' imprisonment. The third threatened a $1,000 fine and one year in prison. Slug use decreased substantially where the threatened sanction was lowest and thus realistic. The highest sanction appeared so unrealistic that slug use actually increased, although only slightly. In another area, where new parking meters equipped with slug rejection devices and coin-view windows that revealed what had been inserted into the meter had been installed, slug use decreased substantially.[17] These meters made it fairly easy to determine who had used a slug: it was likely to be the person whose car was parked at the meter. A recent experiment with cable television subscribers who had tampered with their cable service in order to receive cable channels they had not paid for showed similar results. A threat of legal sanctions conveyed by a warning letter was sufficient to deter offenders from tampering with their service again after the company removed the illegal devices.[18]

Overall, research results are still inconclusive, largely because the opportunities for making controlled studies are extremely limited. Early studies tended to support the hypothesis that crime rates will be lower in places where the threat of punishment is great. Subsequent work, which focused on individuals' perceptions of the risk of sanctions, found that certainty is more important than severity of punishment in people's decision-making about engaging in criminal acts.

The methodology of most of the early research was thought to present problems that made the conclusions questionable.[19] Most recently, studies considered by some to be methodologically more sophisticated have revealed that in fact informal sanctions are more influential than formal penalties in shaping individual behavior. Factors such as the disapproval of relatives and friends, jeopardizing of past accomplishments and future achievements like educational or employment goals, personal moral beliefs, and community condemnation have more of a deterrent effect than the threat of arrest or subsequent punishment,[20] but obviously only when and where community standards and norms are shared.

"In fact, informal sanctions are more influential than formal penalties in shaping individual behavior."

Incapacitation

How many times have you heard the expression, "Lock 'em up and throw away the key"? It captures the frustration law-abiding people feel about the problem of crime in America. It reflects a belief that society is best off when criminals are housed in prisons, or **incapacitated,** for long periods. This strategy has an obvious appeal—locking up offenders prevents them from committing additional crimes in the community, at least during the course of their confinement. Yet, according to some scholars, long sentences imposed for the purpose of incapacitation may be unjust, unnecessary, counterproductive, and inappropriate:

incapacitation
Preventing persons from committing crime by physical restraint, for example, incarceration.

"Long sentences imposed for the purpose of incapacitation may be unjust, unnecessary, counterproductive, and inappropriate."

- Unjust if other offenders who have committed the same crime receive shorter sentences
- Unnecessary if the offender is not likely to offend again
- Counterproductive whenever prison increases the risk of subsequent or habitual criminal behavior
- Inappropriate if the offender has committed an offense entailing insignificant harm to the community

Studies examining the effects of incapacitation have come to differing conclusions. Some researchers, for example, suggest that the crime rate could be reduced by as much as 15 percent if every convicted felon were imprisoned for one year.[21] Others project between a 4-percent and an 80-percent reduction in violent crime rates if everyone convicted of a violent crime served five years in prison.[22]

collective incapacitation
Imprisonment of many offenders for long periods.

"Some argue that prosecutors should identify chronic offenders and prosecute them vigorously, and courts should sentence them to long prison terms."

selective incapacitation
Targeting of high-risk and recidivistic offenders for rigorous prosecution and incarceration.

Strategies. The best interpretation of these studies is that a **collective incapacitation** policy—in which many offenders would be imprisoned for long periods—would achieve only modest reductions in the crime rate, while fostering an enormous increase in the size of the prison population.[23] Between 1973 and 1982, the U.S. prison population nearly doubled, while the crime rate rose 28 percent.[24] How many cells would we need to make a dent in this rising crime rate?

Some researchers have concluded that a more rational strategy would call for the incapacitation of only the most serious offenders, those who account for a disproportionately large amount of crime. As we saw in Chapter 2, Marvin Wolfgang and his associates determined that only 6 percent of the nearly 10,000 boys in their study were responsible for over half of all offenses committed. This evidence, in conjunction with research findings that frequent offenders often manage to stay out of prison by plea-bargaining, has led some to argue that prosecutors should identify (or select) chronic offenders and prosecute them vigorously, and that courts should then sentence them to long prison terms.

Some believe that a policy of **selective incapacitation,** or the targeting of high-risk, repeat offenders for rigorous prosecution and incarceration, may be worth pursuing.[25] Researchers at the Rand Corporation used self-report data from inmates to identify characteristics of serious repeat offenders. They then devised a scale composed of seven items (including prior convictions, history of drug use, and history of employment) to predict future offending. This scale could be used at sentencing to identify those who should be selectively incapacitated for longer or shorter periods.[26]

Effectiveness. Use of this predictive scale was intended to result in shorter prison terms for low-rate and medium-rate offenders and longer terms for high-rate offenders. If implemented, such a strategy should, according to researchers, reduce California's robbery rate by 15 percent while lowering its prison population by 5 percent. When these estimates were made, they stirred controversy among policymakers and researchers. Critics charged that

- the scale resulted in a number of "false positives": as many as 55 to 60 percent of those predicted to be high-rate offenders on the basis of the scale turned out not to be. The opposite problem—predicting low rates of crime for people who subsequently offended at high rates—was less pronounced but still occurred.
- the scale used information on several factors, such as employment data and juvenile delinquency history, that may be obtainable through self-reports but generally is not available at the time of sentencing, thereby reducing its usefulness.
- the calculations of the reduction in crime rates have been criticized on methodological grounds and may be much lower than claimed.
- the imposition of different sentences for the same offense violates the notion of just deserts.
- a selective incapacitation policy punishes people not just for past behavior but for anticipated future behavior.[27]

Rehabilitation

The retribution philosophy dominated the practice of punishment, in America and elsewhere, up to the late nineteenth century. But in the late nineteenth and early twentieth centuries, positivist theories about the causes of crime became popular and influential. Theorists and practitioners alike moved away from retribution and toward rehabilitation. Some have called this a move from crime-based to offender-based punishment.

As a sentencing rationale, rehabilitation is based on the notion that through a correctional intervention (educational and vocational training and psychotherapeutic programs), an offender may be changed. This change should result in the

"I think I can get you off with a lighter sentence, but it might screw up your movie deal."

The New Yorker, October 26, 1992, p. 71.

offender's ability to return to society in some productive, meaningful capacity. Consequently, sentences must be individualized. A judge might select a sentence that includes probation or imprisonment of indeterminate length. The parole board decides when the convict should be released and under what conditions.

In the 1970s, rehabilitation came under attack. The dramatic rise in crime rates at the end of the 1960s led conservatives to point to rehabilitation as a failed policy that treated offenders too leniently and did nothing to deter them. Liberals objected to a coercive treatment strategy intended to "habilitate" people so that they would conform to the dominant culture's values and norms. Researchers attacked the rehabilitative ideal as a colossal practical failure. An examination of some 400 evaluations of treatment programs, published in an article entitled "What Works?," concluded that "with few and isolated exceptions, the rehabilitative efforts that have been reported so far have had no appreciable effect on recidivism."[28] In short, the answer to the question, "What works?," was "Nothing." After this devastating analysis of rehabilitation, other scholars published similar findings and conclusions, although the picture they painted was a bit less bleak.[29]

There is still no agreement on the effectiveness of rehabilitation, but more recent analyses of treatment evaluations conclude that some programs do in fact work—if only for a select number of offenders. But successful programs require a careful matching of individual needs and program attributes, and that is very difficult to achieve in practice.[30]

Mixed Goals

Judges often employ a combination or mix of sentencing philosophies in justifying their selection of a sanction. When Judge Kimba M. Wood sentenced legendary junk-bond trader Michael R. Milken in November 1990, she turned the courtroom into a classroom.[31] Judge Wood defended her choice of a ten-year prison sentence, significant fines, and a sentence of community service by explaining a series of goals that would be achieved by this sentence:

- *Special deterrence*—Achieved by barring Mr. Milken from working in the securities industry and by the significant fines imposed
- *General deterrence*—Achieved by the imposition of a long prison term
- *Retribution*—Achieved by the combination of a prison term and a fine
- *Rehabilitation*—Achieved by requiring community service

Judge Wood's sentence, which she later reduced to two years, was a well-crafted effort. It is fair to say that most sentences are not nearly as well tailored, for lack of time and talent. (See the Criminal Justice in Action box.) Of course, the goals of deterrence, retribution, and rehabilitation, integrated by Judge Wood, are not necessarily compatible. For example, a long prison term may be proportional to the crime committed (retribution), but incompatible with the goal of rehabilitation. The problem of integrating the goals of punishment has concerned theoreticians and researchers alike.[32] Some researchers have suggested that judges employ a two-stage approach. If the intention is both to punish and to rehabilitate, a defendant might be sentenced to a term of incarceration followed by a term in a community-based correctional setting.[33]

Most state legislatures, unconcerned with theoretical considerations, simply enacted the mixed sentencing goals of the Model Penal Code into legislation, letting judges worry about how to reconcile potential conflicts. The code mandates the following sentencing goals:

1. To prevent and condemn the commission of offenses
2. To promote the correction and rehabilitation of offenders
3. To ensure the public safety by preventing the commission of the offenses through the deterrent influence of sentences imposed and the confinement of offenders when required in the interest of public protection

"The dramatic rise in crime rates at the end of the 1960s led conservatives to target rehabilitation as a failed policy and the ideal as a colossal practical failure."

"The answer to the question, 'What works?' was 'Nothing.'" Robert Martinson, *Public Interest* 35 (Spring 1974).

"Successful rehabilitation programs require careful monitoring of individual needs and program attributes."

Charles Keating, center, a major figure in the S&L scandal, on the last day of his trial, Superior Court, Los Angeles, November 1991.

CRIME AND PUNISHMENT: OF CHOCOLATE BARS AND PRISON BARS

Judge Chocolate Bar

It was sentencing day in the court for young adult offenders at Darmstadt, Germany, with the Honorable Judge Karl Holzschuh presiding. The courtroom was filled to capacity. The press was there en masse, and representatives of old age homes, hospitals, social welfare groups, and civic organizations crowded the aisles. Everyone was wondering eagerly whom Judge Holzschuh would benefit with his sentences this week.

- First case: A young woman thief who stole largely to satisfy her insatiable appetite for chocolate. Her sentence: For the next three months she was to deliver chocolate bars, purchased with half her weekly wages, to an orphanage.
- Second case: A serious traffic law violator. His sentence: Suspended motorcycle license and participation in the weekend excursions of a hiking club.
- Third case: Arson in a forest. The arsonist's sentence: To spend his entire annual vacation with the forest club, planting pine tree seedlings.

And so it went all day. Judge Holzschuh had quickly acquired the name "Judge Chocolate Bar." His unorthodox sentences rested on the philosophy that evil deeds should be compensated for by good deeds, and he reasoned that

any sanction not prohibited by the code was allowed—at least within the framework of probation. But ultimately his judicial superiors, annoyed by the notoriety of his sentences, reassigned him to probate court where he had to adjudicate last wills and testaments. As he commented, "I was a judge for the living—now I am a judge for the dead" (1).

Some recent innovations

Judge Holzschuh himself is now long dead. But innovative sentences are very much alive. Many judges fashion sentences, usually within the framework of probation, that stretch from handing out candy bars to onerous conditions just short of prison bars. Consider these recent American sentences:

- Florida Circuit Court Judge Harry Lee Coe III ordered a person convicted of trying to "ram" a friend with her car to stay home for a year (2).
- The same judge sentenced a drug offender to one year in college without the right to leave campus (2).
- Tennessee Judge Joseph Brown, Jr., invites the victims of a burglary to enter the homes of their burglars and take equivalent loot. According to Judge Brown, "The victims really get into it. They stalk the house, really look around." The burglars' reactions? "Their mouths just drop" (3).
- Houston District Court Judge Michael McSpadden agreed to a request from an accused rapist that surgical castration be substituted for facing trial and the pos-

sibility of a thirty-five-year prison term. (McSpadden later withdrew his support for the plea and the rapist was sentenced to life in prison.) (4)
- A Tulane County superior court (California) judge ordered a convicted child abuser to have an innovative birth control device implanted in her arm as a condition of probation (5).
- The same judge ordered a man who had stolen beer to wear a T-shirt proclaiming "on felony probation" (5).
- A federal judge (New York) banished a reputed organized crime figure from entering into the eastern and southern districts of New York State during the time of his probation (6).
- A Duval County circuit court judge (Florida) sentenced a 17-year-old woman convicted of smothering her newborn daughter to death to two years in prison and a ten-year probation term that would include finishing high school, receiving psychological and birth control counseling, and using birth control (7).
- A superior court judge in Arizona sentenced a 17-year-old mother convicted of child abuse to a lifetime use of contraception (7).
- A 30-year-old woman who pleaded guilty to felony child neglect agreed to be sterilized as part of a plea agreement (7).
- A Suffolk County superior court judge (Massachusetts) ordered a teenager convicted of robbery, assault, and car theft to finish high school, maintain a job, and stay out of trouble for five years (8).
- An Alexandria (Virginia) judge

sentenced a drunk driver to witness an autopsy (9).

- A circuit court judge in Tennessee confined a man convicted of voluntary manslaughter to his home or yard for five years except for going to work each day and to the grocery store with his mother once a week (10).

Cruel and unusual punishment?

Are there any boundaries constraining a judge's sentencing practices? The Eighth Amendment to the U.S. Constitution does prohibit cruel and unusual punishment. Most of the innovative sentences are probation conditions and are not particularly cruel—but they are certainly unusual. For this reason alone, many such sentences have been overthrown on appeal.

But it is not a desire to be "unusual" that drives most judges to mete out such punishments as finishing high school, going to college, watching an autopsy, or staying home. Motives vary from case to case and from judge to judge. For some, cost is an important consideration. The teenager who was ordered to finish high school and get a job would have cost the state $80,000 had he been imprisoned for two years. Overcrowding in prisons motivates others to come up with innovative sentences.

The safety of a defendant can be a factor as well; there are times when a prison sentence is, in effect, a death sentence, as with the organized crime figure exiled from New York State. "He just knows too much," said the judge in that case, explaining that he was certain the defendant would have died at his own hands or someone else's in prison. Other judges are attempting to make more of an impact on a serious problem than can be made with fines or jail terms; the judge who sentenced the drunk driver to view an autopsy also has considered forcing convicted drunk drivers to ride with rescue squads or sit in emergency rooms so that they can see firsthand the problems that driving "under the influence" cause.

Innovative sentences reflect a movement to reform the criminal justice system from the inside. Perhaps underlying most such sentences is the belief that sending an offender to jail pushes people toward a permanent life of crime. Innovative sentencing gives them a chance to change their lives outside prison.

SOURCES

1. Wolf Middendorff, *Jugendkriminologie* (Ratingen, Germany: A. Henn Verlag, 1956), p. 221. The quote is a personal communication.
2. Rhonda Cook, "Judges," *United Press International,* March 8, 1981.
3. *Life Magazine,* April 4, 1992, p. 20.
4. Richard Lacayo, "Sentences Inscribed in Flesh," *Time Magazine,* March 23, 1992, p. 54.
5. Michael Lev, "Judge Is Firm on Forced Contraception, but Welcomes an Appeal," *The New York Times,* January 11, 1991, p. 17.
6. Leonard Buder, "Crime Figure Given Exile, Not Prison," *The New York Times,* February 5, 1988, p. A1.
7. Felicity Barringer, "Sentence for Killing Newborn: Jail Term, Then Birth Control," *The New York Times,* November 18, 1990, p. A1.
8. "Judge Sentences Convicted Robber to School," *United Press International,* September 8, 1989.
9. "Woman Appealing Judge's Order to View Autopsy," *The Washington Post,* March 7, 1984, p. C8.
10. "Man Convicted of Manslaughter Gets Home-Bound Sentence," *United Press International,* November 6, 1985.

QUESTIONS FOR DISCUSSION

1. The surgical castration sentence for a convicted rapist was criticized because castration would not necessarily prevent the offender from sexually molesting victims in the future. What other problems might castration have as a sentence for sexual assault?
2. Is required contraception a reasonable sentence for a convicted child abuser? Defend your position.
3. The German judge who sentenced a thief to deliver chocolate bars wanted to see evil deeds compensated for by good deeds. What other benefits might his sentences have had?

4. To safeguard offenders against excessive, disproportionate, or arbitrary punishment

5. To give fair warning of the nature of the sentences that may be imposed upon conviction of an offense

6. To differentiate among offenders with a view to a just individualization in their treatment

7. To advance the use of generally accepted scientific methods and knowledge in sentencing offenders.[34]

THE CHOICE OF A SANCTION

"The forms of criminal sanctions at the disposition of the sentencing judge are specified by legislation."

incarceration
Sanction that requires a defendant to serve a term in a local jail, state prison, or federal prison.

split sentence
Sentence that requires the convicted criminal to serve time in jail followed by probation.

restitution
Sanction that requires an offender to cover the cost of a victim's losses.

community service
Sanction that requires an offender to spend a period of time performing public service work.

fine
Sum of money paid as a penalty and/or as an alternative to or in conjunction with incarceration.

"Judges often subscribe to different philosophies for different offenders."

"The most important factors affecting a judge's sentencing decisions are the severity of the offense and the criminal history of the offender."

In all jurisdictions, the forms of criminal sanctions at the disposition of the sentencing judge are specified by legislation. These forms include institutional sanctions—time to be served in prison or jail; and noninstitutional sanctions—fines and forfeiture of the proceeds of crime, service of the sentence in the community in the form of probation or parole. Recently the arsenal of punishments has been considerably enlarged by the creation of mixed sanctions and of alternatives to either institutional or noninstitutional sanctions. Judges now have a variety of options:

• *Death penalty.* In thirty-six states (as well as the federal courts), courts may impose a sentence of death for any offense designated a capital crime, for example, first-degree murder.

• *Incarceration.* The defendant may be sentenced to serve a term in a local jail, state prison, or federal prison.

• *Probation.* The defendant may be sentenced to a period of probationary supervision within the community (Chapter 16).

• *Split sentence.* A judge may split the sentence between a period of incarceration and a period of probation.

• *Restitution.* An offender may be required to provide financial reimbursement to cover the cost of a victim's losses.

• *Community service.* An offender may be required to spend a period of time performing public service work.

• *Fine.* An offender may be required to pay a certain sum of money as a penalty and/or as an alternative to or in conjunction with incarceration. (See the Criminal Justice Abroad box.)

What factors determine the choice of a sanction? Within the range of options imposed by the legislature, judges are given discretion guided by their preference for one or more of the sentencing philosophies discussed earlier.[35] But judges often subscribe to different philosophies for different offenders. Faced with an offender who has a long record of felony arrests and convictions, a judge may place greater emphasis on the incapacitative function of punishment and sentence the offender to a long period of incarceration. The same judge may decide that an offender with no prior record may very well succeed in being "rehabilitated," and therefore order a sentence that involves some type of treatment program.

Research has shown that the most important factors affecting a judge's sentencing decisions are the severity of the offense and the criminal history of the offender.[36] Offense severity is usually measured not only by the statutory classification (for instance, classes of felonies) but also by nonstatutory aspects of the crime, such as the amount of harm inflicted, the value of property lost or damaged, the motive of the offender, and whether a deadly weapon was used in the commission of the crime. A first-time offender who has committed a relatively minor offense is likely to get a more lenient sentence than a repeat offender.

Judges receive information about the nature of the offense and the offender in a **presentence investigation report** prepared by a probation officer.[37] In this report, a probation officer will provide details of the crime and information about the offender, including a history of any prior offenses. The presentence investigation report may also contain a recommendation of an appropriate sentence.[38]

A recent innovation growing out of the victims' rights movement in the sentencing process is the consideration of statements by the victim, known as "victim impact statements" (VIS). Twenty-six states have mandated the use of VIS in criminal cases, while another twenty-two states have adopted so-called "victim bills of rights" that include recognition of the right of a victim to present a VIS. In the VIS, the victim provides a statement about the extent of economic, physical, or psychological harm suffered as a result of the victimization. The victim also can make a recommendation about the type of sentence an offender should receive. Usually the VIS is incorporated into the presentence investigation report written by the probation officer. Research has revealed that a judge's choice of a sentence is influenced much more by legal considerations than by victim preferences in cases where VIS were presented.[39]

presentence investigation report
Report prepared by the probation department for a judge; contains information about the offense, the offender, and the history of prior offenses and may include a recommendation of a sentence.

STRUCTURING SENTENCES

Legislators have devised a number of different methods to structure sentencing decisions. Strategies differ from state to state, and some states even have different sentencing structures to cover different types of offenses.

Indeterminate Sentences

In 1977, Johnny Arafiles fatally stabbed Eddie Leroy Anderson, a witness who had testified against his brother in a drug case. He was convicted of murder in a California court and received a term of seven years to life in prison. With such a sentence, Arafiles could have served as little as seven years (minus time off for good behavior) or an entire life sentence. Thirteen years after his conviction, Arafiles appeared before the state Board of Prison Terms (the parole board) and convinced them that he was a changed man. He had taken educational courses, enlisted in vocational training programs, and participated in psychological therapy. Moreover, he had turned to religion. The Board granted Arafiles parole in March 1990.[40]

Arafiles' **indeterminate sentence** had a fixed minimum (seven years), but no fixed or predetermined end. However, indeterminate sentence statutes may allow the judge to fix a maximum or both a minimum and a maximum. The important aspect of the indeterminate sentence is that the prisoner's actual prison term is undetermined above the minimum and below the maximum, and depends entirely on the discretion of the correctional authorities, especially the parole board. Members of a parole board periodically review the record of an offender's behavior while the offender is under correctional supervision to decide if, in their opinion, release is appropriate.

indeterminate sentence
Sentence for which the legislature allows the judge to impose a minimum and/or a maximum term, the actual length of service depending on the discretion of corrections officials.

While indeterminate sentences may accommodate goals of retribution, deterrence, and incapacitation, the guiding principle behind them is rehabilitation: The indeterminance of a sentence provides flexibility for the offender to demonstrate that he or she has been rehabilitated, at which time the parole board will, at least in theory, authorize a release. Rather than the sentence being the same for every offender, indeterminate sentencing is said to have the advantage of allowing for individualized sentencing on the basis of the offender's background, the circumstances of the crime, and the offender's behavior while incarcerated.

"The guiding principle behind indeterminate sentences is rehabilitation."

Indeterminate sentences were subjected to extensive criticism during the

1970s, fueled by prisoner uprisings that demonstrated their discontent with the conditions of their imprisonment, and particularly the widely varying length of sentences for like crimes. In 1970 the American Friends Service Committee published a report entitled *Struggle for Justice*[41] that galvanized opposition to indeterminate sentences and led eventually to a reconsideration of sentencing practices that had been used throughout the country.[42] Chief among the complaints were the following:

• Individualized sentences based on the characteristics of the offender instead of the crime have led to variations in sanctions that many believe are attributable to extralegal factors such as the offender's sex, ethnic origin, or socioeconomic status.

• Indeterminate sentences represent a particularly cruel injustice to prisoners, suspending them in a nether world of uncertainty, dependent on what many believed were the arbitrary decisions of parole boards. The uncertain release date was depicted not as an incentive to reform, but as a technique to frustrate inmates.

• The emerging research on rehabilitation programs indicated that they were ineffective in achieving their goals. Furthermore, the underlying assumption behind rehabilitation—that criminals are "sick" and need "treatment"—was ill-conceived and arrogant, especially since correctional officials had no effective means of treating the supposed sickness.

• Indeterminate sentencing in many cases meant that sentences were really given not by judges but by parole boards, a questionable shifting of authority.[43]

"Indeterminate sentencing in many cases meant that sentences were really not given by judges but by parole boards."

The solution, as many saw it, was to switch to definite, or determinate, sentences based on the amount of harm inflicted by the offense. The result was widespread change in sentencing structures. In fact, between 1975 and 1985, all fifty states and the District of Columbia considered legislation to change their existing indeterminate sentencing structures.[44] Some states sought to limit indeterminate sentences by giving parole boards guidelines to follow in making release decisions. Others turned to determinate sentences.

Determinate Sentences

determinate sentence
Sentence to prison that has a fixed term; also called a flat sentence.

In 1975 Maine became the first state to abolish its parole board, thereby removing the support for indeterminate sentencing.[45] For nearly twenty years, judges in Maine have sentenced offenders to prison terms of fixed length, called **determinate** (or **flat**) **sentences.** All offenders sentenced under such a scheme must serve the entire length of sentence, less any "good time" accrued while in prison. Early release on parole is unavailable. Since Maine replaced its indeterminate system, at least nine other states—California, Connecticut, Florida, Illinois, Indiana, Minnesota, New Mexico, North Carolina, and Washington—have adopted plans where all or most sentences are determinate.[46] Other states have seriously considered the practice. In New York, for example, the move to a determinate system has been a perennial campaign issue in district attorney election contests. "The certain knowledge that conviction on a given charge will result in a nonnegotiable jail term," argued one candidate, "will serve as a warning and a potential deterrent to anyone contemplating a criminal act. It will not bring crime to a halt, but it will eradicate the notion, encouraging some criminals, that a sentence is open to endless reconsideration."[47] In response, another candidate for the district attorney's office claimed that such a proposal "would double the state prison population in two years."[48]

"The certain knowledge that conviction on a given charge will result in a non-negotiable jail term will serve as a warning and a potential deterrent . . . ."
Candidate for district attorney, New York City, 1989.

"Nonnegotiable jail terms 'would double the state prison population in two years.'"
Candidate for district attorney, New York City, 1989.

Determinate sentencing plans vary from state to state. In Maine, as stated, the legislature simply eliminated parole. The result: Judges resorted to what has been referred to as "judicial parole," a practice in which an offender is given a split sentence consisting of a period of incarceration followed by probationary supervision upon release. Revocation of probation rests with the judge, who thus fulfills the role previously held by the parole board.[49] Other states, such as California and North Carolina, have specific standards for sentences set by the legislature, including aggravating and mitigating factors that must be taken into account in sentencing.[50]

Mandatory Sentences

Determinate sentences should be distinguished from **mandatory sentences,** meaning sentences for given crimes that are fixed by the legislature, from which the judge may not deviate. Laws that require mandatory sentences for certain offenses have been passed in forty-nine states. Most commonly they are used for violent and serious offenses; crimes involving the use of a firearm; violations of drinking and driving statutes; and increasingly, certain drug offenses. Most mandatory sentencing statutes prescribe a minimum period of incarceration for offenders whose crimes and prior record fall within specific categories (although some require incarceration even for first-time offenders).

Mandatory sentences have been justified on the basis of their deterrence value. But such sentences do not appear to have a significant deterrent effect. Furthermore, the severity of the sentences is such that police, judges, and prosecutors have been found to alter their practices to avoid the possibility of a mandatory sentence in cases where they believed the sentence would be too harsh for the crime involved.[51] Finally, new evidence suggests that mandatory sentences may disproportionately affect minorities.

mandatory sentence
Sentence prescribed by the legislature, which a judge has no choice but to impose.

"Mandatory sentences are used for violent and serious offenses in forty-nine states."

Sentencing Guidelines

Sentencing guidelines provide a relatively fixed punishment that corresponds with prevailing notions of harm and allows for upward or downward adjustment of the sentence on the basis of specific aggravating or mitigating circumstances.[52] In the United States, the movement toward sentencing guidelines began with a plea by Federal District Judge Marvin E. Frankel in 1972 for an independent sentencing commission to study sentences and assist in the formulation and enactment of detailed guidelines for use by judges.[53] Since then a number of states have adopted guidelines and several have created sentencing commissions, independent agencies authorized by state legislatures to create guidelines. The best-known state sentencing commissions are those of Minnesota, Washington, and Pennsylvania. In 1984 the United States Sentencing Commission was established by Congress, and in 1987 it delivered its guidelines for the sentencing of individual defendants. In November 1991, Congress adopted guidelines proposed by the Sentencing Commission for organizations, especially for corporations.[54]

At the crux of all guidelines is a sentencing grid, most often in the form of a matrix, in which a ranking of the severity of the offense is combined with a defendant's criminal history or other characteristics to arrive at a recommended sentence or sentence range (Figure 13.1). Guidelines usually allow for mitigating or aggravating circumstances associated with the specific offense. They typically indicate which offenses should be sanctioned by a prison term (the "in/out" decision) and the length of the sentence. A judge simply calculates a defendant's history and the severity of the offense, plus or minus mitigating or aggravating circumstances (where allowed), and, with the exactness of a computer, has a sentence to impose. In practice, some guidelines can be fairly complicated to use because of the number of factors that must be included in calculating the sentence. Every U.S. probation office and U.S. attorney's office has been provided with a computer program to assist in calculating recommended sentences in accordance with the federal sentencing guidelines.[55]

sentencing guidelines
System for the judicial determination of a relatively firm sentence based on specific aggravating or mitigating circumstances.

If mandatory sentences are to have a significant deterrent effect, they must be widely known. This California billboard advertises mandatory sentences for use of a gun in the commission of a crime.

CHOOSING BETWEEN HARD TIME AND HARD CURRENCY

Like nearly everyone else in the world, for many years after World War II West Germany relied on jail sentences as a critical part of its criminal justice system. Although criminological research had established beyond doubt that jail terms deterred few, reformed none, and socialized offenders even more into the criminal subculture, hard time for thieves, batterers, street drug dealers, drunken drivers, and those guilty of traffic manslaughter was thought to be the just and appropriate sentence.

By the end of the 1960s, however, a serious problem began to surface. The West German rate of imprisonment had reached 100 per 100,000 population, and all jails and prisons in the country were filled to capacity. A choice had to be made: build more prisons or reduce the number of prisoners. Money, the West German Deutschmark or DM, was the determining factor. The Germans decided not to build more prisons, and the experiment in depopulating prisons began. The process took a number of years; we will describe three different stages in the changes that took place.

Stage 1: Abolishing short-term jail terms

In 1969 the West German parliament amended the penal code by abolishing all jail terms of up to thirty days and practically abolishing jail terms of up to six months. In all cases where such terms had been imposed, now only fines could be levied. By 1971—only two years later—the proportion of those convicted who were sent to prison had dropped from 23 percent to 7 percent. The rate of imprisonment had declined from 100 per 100,000 population to 66 per 100,000.

Stage 2: The day fine system

Because of criticism that fines hurt the poor more than the rich, Germany took a lesson from its Scandinavian neighbors and introduced the day fine system. Article 40 of the Penal Code spelled out the details:

1. The fine has to be fixed as *day fines*. The minimum number of day fines is 5, the maximum number is, if statutes do not require a higher number, 360 day fines.
2. The amount of one fine day is determined by the court, which has to consider the personal and economic circumstances of the offender. As a rule, the day fine has to be based on the average net income the defendant actually has per day or the defendant could have per day. The minimum amount of one day fine is 2 DM; the maximum amount is 10,000 DM.
3. The income of the defendant, his or her means, as well as other sources of income that seem to be relevant for determination of the amount of one day fine, may be estimates.
4. In the judgment the number as well as the amount of the day fines have to be mentioned.

Judges had some initial problems with determining "rates" of earnings—and thus the amounts of fines—for offenders and offender groups, but acceptable patterns soon developed. An offender from a marginalized population group is as affected, and perhaps deterred, by a 2-DM day fine (the cost of a pack of cigarettes) as an affluent citizen is by a 10,000-DM day fine. Any offender may pay fines in installments.

The benefits of the new system became apparent immediately:

- Seventy-eight percent of the population regarded the new day fine system as a "reasonable and effective punishment."
- Judges liked the new system because they regarded it as more equitable. They also liked the fact that, unless the defendant objects, no trial is needed, resulting in a mail-order criminal justice procedure.
- Hard currency poured into the public coffers and didn't flow out for prison construction or prisoner maintenance.
- The reconviction rate of fined offenders was considerably lower than that of imprisoned offenders.

Stage 3: Community service

By the end of the 1970s unemployment was rising rapidly in Germany, and the number of convicted persons defaulting on fine installments also rose. To avoid resorting to imprisonment for the defaulters, the West Germans borrowed ideas again—this time from the British, who had experimented successfully with community service. Germany

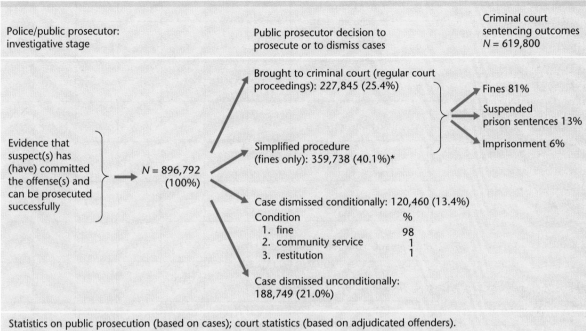

Decision and sentencing structure, West German States

Police/public prosecutor: investigative stage

Public prosecutor decision to prosecute or to dismiss cases

Criminal court sentencing outcomes
N = 619,800

Evidence that suspect(s) has (have) committed the offense(s) and can be prosecuted successfully

N = 896,792 (100%)

Brought to criminal court (regular court proceedings): 227,845 (25.4%)

Simplified procedure (fines only): 359,738 (40.1%)*

Case dismissed conditionally: 120,460 (13.4%)

Condition	%
1. fine	98
2. community service	1
3. restitution	1

Case dismissed unconditionally: 188,749 (21.0%)

Fines 81%

Suspended prison sentences 13%

Imprisonment 6%

Statistics on public prosecution (based on cases); court statistics (based on adjudicated offenders).
*Payment of the fine has to be made to a charitable organization named by the public prosecutor.

FIGURE 1. Decision and Sentencing Structure, West Germany
(*Sources:* Statistics on public prosecution [based on cases]; court statistics [based on adjudicated offenders]. Based on Hans-Jorg Albrecht, "Fines in the Criminal Justice System," in Klaus Sessar and Hans-Jurgen Kerner, *Developments in Crime and Crime Control Research* [New York: Springer-Verlag, 1991], pp. 150–169.)

introduced community service for defaulters at the rate of six hours of service for each fine day. Implementing the community service system cost the government very little and yielded profits in terms of service to hospitals, old-age homes, orphanages, and road-cleaning projects. As in other European countries where community service is in use, the failure rate was low: about 10 to 20 percent.

With about 40 percent of all criminal cases that come to the attention of the public prosecutor resulting in mail-order fines in Germany, and with 81 percent of those convicted in criminal court paying hard currency rather than costing

the public money by doing hard time, the German criminal justice system is both efficient and effective. The researcher who analyzed the German experiment concluded: "The fine experiment in the criminal justice system of the Federal Republic of Germany seems to show that societies can rely on alternatives to prison without affecting the system's performance" (1).

SOURCE

1. Hans-Jorg Albrecht, "Fines in the Criminal Justice System." In *Developments in Crime and Crime Control Research,* eds. Klaus Sessar and Hans-Jurgen Kerner (New York: Springer-Verlag, 1991), pp. 150–169.

QUESTIONS FOR DISCUSSION

1. Of course the Deutschmark is not one of the world's strongest currencies simply because Germany abandoned short-term imprisonment, but money entering the public coffers instead of being drained from them must be a benefit to the government. Why couldn't the United States start with budget considerations in the formulation of correctional policies?
2. Would the day fine system be constitutional in the United States?
3. What are the limits to expanding community service programs?

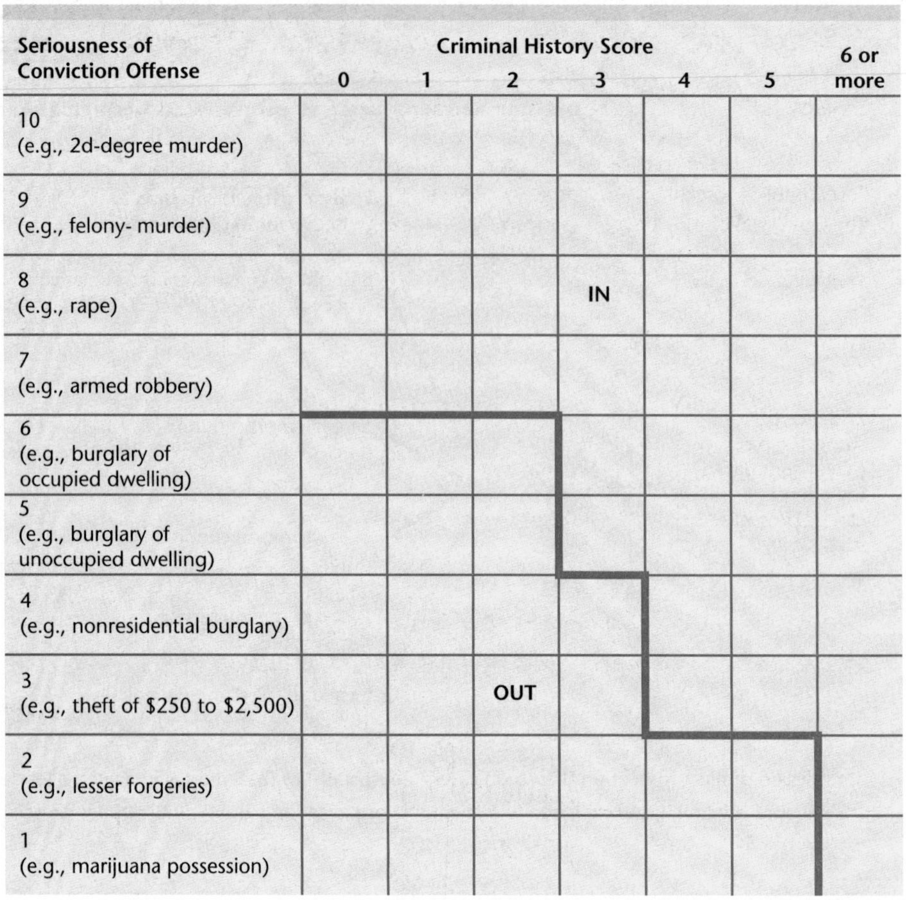

FIGURE 13.1 *The dispositional line on Minnesota's sentencing grid* (*Source:* Andrew von Hirsch, Kay A. Knapp, and Michael Tonry, *The Sentencing Commission and Its Guidelines* [Boston: Northeastern University Press, 1987], p. 91.)

[Opposite page] Sentencing table: Federal courts (in months of imprisonment) (*Source:* United States Sentencing Commission, *Guidelines Manual* [Washington D.C.: U.S. Government Printing Office, 1991].)

Seriousness of Conviction Offense	Criminal History Score						6 or more
	0	1	2	3	4	5	
10 (e.g., 2d-degree murder)							
9 (e.g., felony- murder)							
8 (e.g., rape)				IN			
7 (e.g., armed robbery)							
6 (e.g., burglary of occupied dwelling)							
5 (e.g., burglary of unoccupied dwelling)							
4 (e.g., nonresidential burglary)							
3 (e.g., theft of $250 to $2,500)			OUT				
2 (e.g., lesser forgeries)							
1 (e.g., marijuana possession)							

Types of guidelines.   There are two types of sentencing guidelines: voluntary and presumptive. Voluntary guidelines are created by the judiciary rather than mandated by the legislature. They are sometimes referred to as descriptive guidelines because they describe, rather than prescribe, recommended sentences. A voluntary system was first developed in Denver in 1976 and tried subsequently in other cities, such as Newark, Chicago, and Phoenix. Michigan, Massachusetts, and New Jersey pioneered their use on a statewide basis. Since then they have been tried either at the state or local level in almost every state. However, evaluations have shown that they have had little effect on the sentencing patterns of judges, and interest in them seems to have diminished.[56]

The other form of sentencing guideline is referred to as presumptive because the appropriate sentence for an offender is presumed to fall within the range of sentences specified by the guidelines. Judges are expected to choose from a range of available sentences, and all deviations from the guidelines must be documented in writing. The federal sentencing guidelines and those of Minnesota, Pennsylvania, and Washington are all considered presumptive schemes. Pennsylvania's system, unlike the others, still allows for indeterminate sentences because the sentencing commission sought to incorporate a rehabilitative philosophy into its guidelines, along with goals related to deterrence, incapacitation, and just deserts. For prisoners in Pennsylvania who are to be incarcerated, the judge must specify a minimum and maximum sentence chosen from a wide range allowed in the guidelines. The parole board then decides the actual release date. Minnesota and Washington emphasized a retributive approach and made the range for a given offense narrower than in Pennsylvania.[57]

Criminal History Category (Criminal History Points)

Offense Level	I (0 or 1)	II (2 or 3)	III (4, 5, 6)	IV (7, 8, 9)	V (10, 11, 12)	VI (13 or more)
1	0–6	0–6	0–6	0–6	0–6	0–6
2	0–6	0–6	0–6	0–6	0–6	1–7
3	0–6	0–6	0–6	0–6	2–8	3–9
4	0–6	0–6	0–6	2–8	4–10	6–12
5	0–6	0–6	1–7	4–10	6–12	9–15
6	0–6	1–7	2–8	6–12	9–15	12–18
7	1–7	2–8	4–10	8–14	12–18	15–21
8	2–8	4–10	6–12	10–16	15–21	18–24
9	4–10	6–12	8–14	12–18	18–24	21–27
10	6–12	8–14	10–16	15–21	21–27	24–30
11	8–14	10–16	12–18	18–24	24–30	27–33
12	10–16	12–18	15–21	21–27	27–33	30–37
13	12–18	15–21	18–24	24–30	30–37	33–41
14	15–21	18–24	21–27	27–33	33–41	37–46
15	18–24	21–27	24–30	30–37	37–46	41–51
16	21–27	24–30	27–33	33–41	41–51	46–57
17	24–30	27–33	30–37	37–46	46–57	51–63
18	27–33	30–37	33–41	41–51	51–63	57–71
19	30–37	33–41	37–46	46–57	57–71	63–78
20	33–41	37–46	41–51	51–63	63–78	70–87
21	37–46	41–51	46–57	57–71	70–87	77–96
22	41–51	46–57	51–63	63–78	77–96	84–105
23	46–57	51–63	57–71	70–87	84–105	92–115
24	51–63	57–71	63–78	77–96	92–115	100–125
25	57–71	63–78	70–87	84–105	100–125	110–137
26	63–78	70–87	78–97	92–115	110–137	120–150
27	70–87	78–97	87–108	100–125	120–150	130–162
28	78–97	87–108	97–121	110–137	130–162	140–175
29	87–108	97–121	108–135	121–151	140–175	151–188
30	97–121	108–135	121–151	135–168	151–188	168–210
31	108–135	121–151	135–168	151–188	168–210	188–235
32	121–151	135–168	151–188	168–210	188–235	210–262
33	135–168	151–188	168–210	188–235	210–262	235–293
34	151–188	168–210	188–235	210–262	235–293	262–327
35	168–210	188–235	210–262	235–293	262–327	292–365
36	188–235	210–262	235–293	262–327	292–365	324–405
37	210–262	235–293	262–327	292–365	324–405	360–life
38	235–293	262–327	292–365	324–405	360–life	360–life
39	262–327	292–365	324–405	360–life	360–life	360–life
40	292–365	324–405	360–life	360–life	360–life	360–life
41	324–405	360–life	360–life	360–life	360–life	360–life
42	360–life	360–life	360–life	360–life	360–life	360–life
43	life	life	life	life	life	life

A — Offense levels 1–6
B — Offense levels 7–10
C — Offense levels 7–12

KEY

A – Probation available.

B – Probation with conditions of confinement available.

C – New "split sentence" available.

Criticisms. Sentencing commissions and sentencing guidelines both have met with significant resistance, perhaps because the state sentencing commissions are independent of the judicial and the legislative branches. Some proposed guidelines or recommendations were simply rejected by the legislatures.[58] The Connecticut commission developed a guidelines system but went on record as strongly opposed to its adoption and instead recommended statutory determinate sentences.[59] At the federal level, opposition to individual guidelines came chiefly from the judges themselves. The guidelines for individuals took effect on November 1, 1987, but many judges found them unconstitutional. They reasoned that, since the U.S. Sentencing Commission was created by Congress, the guidelines represented a violation of the separation of powers between the judicial and legislative branches of government. In January 1989, the United States Supreme Court upheld the constitutionality of the U.S. Sentencing Commission and the guidelines.[60] Between the time the guidelines went into effect and this Supreme Court decision, more than 150 federal district judges refused to use the guidelines on the grounds that they might be unconstitutional. An evaluation of the initial implementation of the guidelines at the federal level showed that lawyers also opposed them. Only probation officers, who are responsible for preparing presentence investigation reports, seemed to have mastered the intricacies of the system.[61]

Like statutory determinate sentencing schemes, guidelines represent an attempt to overcome the inequities and uncertainties associated with indeterminate sentences. Critics of presumptive sentencing guidelines, however, fear that their implementation will lead to harsher sentences, and make the already serious problem of prison overcrowding worse. Others suggest that discretion in sentencing will simply move from the judge to the prosecutor. Defendants will seek charge bargains that move their charges to the "out" side of the "in/out" line or to a location on the sentencing grid that carries a more lenient sentence. The pressure to bargain will also lead defendants to avoid trials. Finally, some are concerned that judges will simply ignore the guidelines as compromising their discretion and as inappropriate.

Are critics and skeptics being fair? An answer to this question may be gleaned from the results of a series of studies on the effects of guidelines (Table 13.1).

Special Statutory Schemes

Emmanuel Lucious was first convicted of rape in 1977, at age 17. He was tried as an adult, was convicted, and spent four years in a California prison. In 1982, Lucious was convicted of sexually assaulting several schoolteachers and was sentenced to twenty years in prison, later reduced to fourteen years. In July 1989, Lucious was paroled. Six weeks later he raped two women and committed a series of robberies and burglaries. At his trial for rape, robbery, and burglary, the district attorney's office revealed that since age 17, Lucious had not spent more than two months outside of prison. This revelation prompted Superior Court Judge Laura Palmer to conclude: "In captivity, Mr. Lucious seems to function well."[62] Judge Palmer sentenced him to seventy-one years in prison. But that was not the end of it. In consideration of his habitual offending, Judge Palmer also sentenced Lucious to a separate sentence of twenty years to life in prison, to run consecutive to his other sentence.

Many states, like California, have enacted statutes that allow for enhanced or additional punishment for habitual or persistent offenders. Depending on the statute, offenders like Lucious may face either a mandatory prison sentence or a further term added to their regular sentence, known as a sentence enhancement. In some states, sentence enhancements are left to the discretion of the judge, who has the option of using them. In others, the district attorney is given discretion to decide whether to prosecute under the habitual offender statute. Sentence enhancements are also allowed in many states for specific acts committed during a crime, such as carrying a firearm or dangerous weapon.

The effect of prosecution under habitual offender statutes can be significant, in some cases even resulting in a sentence of life imprisonment, regardless of the severity of the crime.[63] Consider the case of *Rummel v. Estelle:* William James Rummel was sentenced to life imprisonment after committing three felonies over a period of nine years. His three convictions were for use of a credit card with intent to defraud (for $80 worth of goods and services), passing a forged

"Critics of presumptive guidelines fear that they will lead to harsher sentences and make the already serious problem of prison overcrowding worse."

"Many states have enacted statutes that allow for enhanced or additional punishment for habitual or persistent offenders."

*"My object all sublime
I shall achieve in time—
To let the punishment fit the crime."*
    The Mikado (Gilbert & Sullivan)

TABLE 13.1 Effects of Sentencing Guidelines

- *On prison overcrowding*
  In Minnesota and Washington, the sentencing commissions explicitly took into consideration the impact their guidelines would have on prison populations. Presumptive sentences were structured to avoid increasing prison populations above their capacity, an approach adopted by Oregon as well when it recently created guidelines. In Minnesota, during initial implementation of the guidelines, prison populations fell from nearly 100% of capacity to 95%, largely because the number of less serious property offenders sentenced to prison fell even though the number of violent offenders incarcerated increased. After this, the number of prison sentences began to rise and, in 1983, the guidelines had to be modified and legislation passed to avert a crisis in the prison population.

  At the federal level, the impact on prison population has not been determined, although members of the Sentencing Commission assert that the guidelines will have little overall impact on demand for prison space. Anticipated increases in the federal prison population are instead attributed to the impact of federal drug laws and career offender provisions of recent legislation.

- *On sentence severity*
  Sentence severity, measured both by incarceration rates and length of incarceration, appears to have increased in Pennsylvania and, to a lesser extent, in Minnesota.

- *On plea-bargaining*
  At the state level, prosecutors appear to have changed bargaining practices, but the effect has been simply to change the nature of the negotiations that occurred before the guidelines. In Minnesota, bargaining over charges increased, while sentence bargains decreased. In Washington, charge bargaining plays a prominent role.

- *On compliance with guidelines*
  Compliance in Minnesota and Washington has generally been high. In Pennsylvania, however, compliance seems more modest and departures from the guidelines are more likely for more serious offenses because the presumptive sentences are so high. Departures from the guidelines have been increasing in Minnesota over time.

Sources: Kathleen M. Bogan, "Constructing Felony Sentencing Guidelines in an Already Crowded State: Oregon Breaks New Ground," *Crime and Delinquency* 36 (1990):467–487; Kay A. Knapp, "Implementation of the Minnesota Guidelines: Can the Innovative Spirit Be Preserved?," in *The Sentencing Commission and Its Guidelines*, eds. Andrew von Hirsch, Kay A. Knapp, and Michael Tonry (Boston: Northeastern University Press, 1987), pp. 127–141; Michael K. Block and William M. Rhodes, "Forecasting the Impact of the Federal Sentencing Guidelines," *Behavioral Sciences and the Law* 7 (1989):51–71; Andrew von Hirsch, "Federal Sentencing Guidelines: Do They Provide Principled Guidance?," *American Criminal Law Review* 27 (1989):367–390; John H. Kramer and Robin L. Lubitz, "Pennsylvania's Sentencing Reform: The Impact of Commission-Established Guidelines," *Crime and Delinquency* 31 (1985):481–500.

check (in the amount of $28.36), and obtaining money under false pretenses by accepting payment for repairing an air conditioner without performing the repair ($120.75). His total take from these crimes? $229.11. In a 1980 opinion written by Justice William Rehnquist, the United States Supreme Court upheld his life sentence.[64]

CAPITAL PUNISHMENT

A judge's most awesome sentencing alternative for those convicted of a capital crime is the imposition of the death sentence. Capital punishment is a controversial issue, and one that poses particular challenges to the judiciary. After all, it is the only sentence that is irreversible and final: It deprives the convicted person of an ultimate appeal.

Daniel Frank's execution in 1622 was the first on record in America. He was executed in the colony of Virginia for the crime of theft.[65] Scholars have estimated that since that year, between 18,000 and 20,000 people in America have suffered state-sanctioned execution for crimes including train wrecking, aggravated murder, and rape[66] (although the latest estimate puts the total at 14,570).[67] Countless others have died at the hands of lynch mobs.[68] During the last century, Western countries have employed six methods of execution: firing squad, lethal gas, hanging, decapitation by ax or guillotine, electrocution, and lethal injection. Decapitation is the only one of these methods that has never been used in the United States.

"Since 1976, when the death penalty was reinstated in the United States after a short moratorium, more than 201 convicted criminals have been executed."

Since 1976, when the death penalty was reinstated in the United States after a short moratorium, more than 201 convicted criminals have been executed (Figure 13.2). Thirty-six states and the federal government now have death penalty laws in effect (Table 13.2).

The arguments surrounding capital punishment are deceptively simple. What makes them deceptive is that abolitionist or retentionist views of the death penalty often influence assessments of the penalty's utility and effectiveness. Abolitionists find little empirical evidence of a deterrent effect, and retentionists claim

TABLE 13.2 Capital Offenses, by State

Alabama. Murder during kidnaping, robbery, rape, sodomy, burglary, sexual assault, or arson; murder of a peace officer, correctional officer, or public official; murder while under a life sentence; murder for pecuniary gain or contract; aircraft piracy; murder by a defendant with a previous murder conviction; murder of a witness to a crime.

Arizona. First-degree murder.

Arkansas. Capital murder as defined by Arkansas statute. Felony murder; arson causing death; intentional murder of a law enforcement officer; murder of prison, jail, court, or correctional personnel or of military personnel acting in line of duty; multiple murders; intentional murder of a public officeholder or candidate; intentional murder while under life sentence; contract murder.

California. Treason; homicide by a prisoner serving a life term; first-degree murder with special circumstances; train wrecking; perjury causing execution.

Colorado. First-degree murder; kidnaping with death of victim; felony murder.

Connecticut. Murder of a public safety or correctional officer; murder for pecuniary gain; murder in the course of a felony; murder by a defendant with a previous conviction for intentional murder; murder while under a life sentence; murder during a kidnaping; illegal sale of cocaine, methadone, or heroin to a person who dies from using these drugs; murder during first-degree sexual assault; multiple murders.

Delaware. First-degree murder with aggravating circumstances.

Florida. First-degree murder.

Georgia. Murder; kidnaping with bodily injury when the victim dies; aircraft hijacking; treason; kidnaping for ransom when the victim dies.

Idaho. First-degree murder; aggravated kidnaping.

Illinois. Murder accompanied by at least 1 of 11 aggravating factors.

Indiana. Murder with 12 aggravating circumstances.

Kentucky. Aggravated murder; kidnaping when victim is killed.

Louisiana. First-degree murder; treason.

Maryland. First-degree murder, either premeditated or during the commission of a felony.

Mississippi. Capital murder includes murder of a peace officer or correctional officer, murder while under a life sentence, murder by bomb or explosive, contract murder, murder committed during specific felonies (rape, burglary, kidnaping, arson, robbery, sexual battery, unnatural intercourse with a child, nonconsensual unnatural intercourse), and murder of an elected official. Capital rape is the forcible rape of a child under 14 years old by a person 18 years or older. Aircraft piracy.

Missouri. First-degree murder.

Montana. Deliberate homicide; aggravated kidnaping when victim or rescuer dies; attempted deliberate homicide, aggravated assault, or aggravated kidnaping by a state prison inmate who has a prior conviction for deliberate homicide or who has been previously declared a persistent felony offender.

that sophisticated studies can be conducted only after executions have been resumed at a steady pace. They argue, in other words, that it is impossible to tell whether deterrence is fact or fiction until we execute, as a matter of course, all inmates sentenced to death.

"In 1990, more than 2,000 convicted individuals were waiting on death rows across the country."

The Deterrence Argument

Social scientists have long debated whether and to what extent executions deter murder. The debate focuses on two questions: Do would-be murderers decide not to kill out of fear of being put to death? If the threat of execution is in fact a deterrent, would the threat of life imprisonment be just as effective?

The results of studies designed to answer these questions are inconclusive. Thorsten Sellin, Hans Zeisel, William C. Bailey, and Ruth D. Peterson, for example, have found little evidence that homicide rates are affected by executions.[69] On the other hand, Isaac Ehrlich, an economist, has found what does appear to be a deterrent effect; specifically, that each execution prevents between eight and twenty murders.[70] His study, however, has been criticized on a number of methodological grounds. Recent research on the deterrent effect of the death penalty has focused on the relationship between publicity about executions and homicide rates. If deterrence works, the argument goes, then publicized executions should result in lower numbers of murders because of heightened perception of

"If the threat of execution is in fact a deterrent, would the threat of life imprisonment be just as effective?"

TABLE 13.2 Capital Offenses, by State (continued)

Nebraska. First-degree murder.

Nevada. First-degree murder.

New Hampshire. Contract murder; murder of a law enforcement officer; murder of a kidnaping victim; killing another after being sentenced to life imprisonment without parole.

New Jersey. Purposeful or knowing murder; contract murder.

New Mexico. First-degree murder; felony murder with aggravating circumstances.

North Carolina. First-degree murder.

Ohio. Assassination; contract murder; murder during escape; murder while in a correctional facility; murder after conviction for a prior purposeful killing or prior attempted murder; murder of a peace officer; murder arising from specified felonies (rape, kidnaping, arson, robbery, burglary); murder of a witness to prevent testimony in a criminal proceeding or in retaliation.

Oklahoma. Murder with malice aforethought; murder arising from specified felonies (forcible rape, robbery with a dangerous weapon, kidnaping, escape from lawful custody, first-degree burglary, arson); murder when the victim is a child who has been injured, tortured, or maimed.

Oregon. Aggravated murder.

Pennsylvania. First-degree murder.

South Carolina. Murder with statutory aggravating circumstances.

South Dakota. First-degree murder; kidnaping with gross permanent physical injury inflicted on the victim; felony murder.

Tennessee. First-degree murder.

Texas. Murder of a public safety officer, fireman, or correctional employee; murder during the commission of specified felonies (kidnaping, burglary, robbery, aggravated rape, arson); murder for remuneration; multiple murders; murder during prison escape; murder by a state prison inmate.

Utah. Aggravated murder.

Virginia. Murder during the commission or attempts to commit specified felonies (abduction, armed robbery, rape, sodomy); contract murder; murder by a prisoner while in custody; murder of a law enforcement officer; multiple murders; murder of a child under 12 years during an abduction; murder arising from drug violations.

Washington. Aggravated first-degree premeditated murder.

Wyoming. First-degree murder, including felony murder.

SOURCE: U.S. Department of Justice, Office of Justice Programs, *Bureau of Justice Statistics Bulletin, Capital Punishment 1991*, p. 6.

365

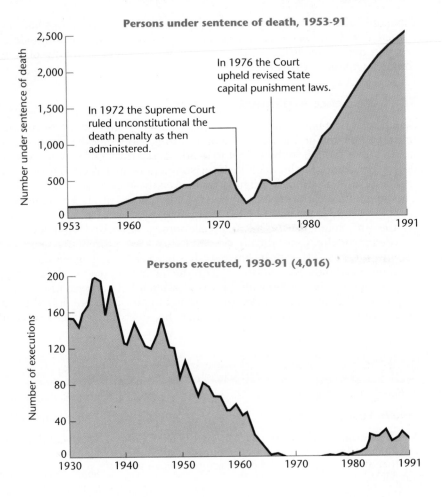

FIGURE 13.2 *Death sentences and executions in the United States, 1930–1991* (*Source: Capital Punishment 1991,* Bureau of Justice Statistics Bulletin [Washington D.C.: U.S. Government Printing Office, September 1991, NCJ-121648], pp. 2, 12, figs. 2,3.)

Persons under sentence of death, 1953-91

In 1972 the Supreme Court ruled unconstitutional the death penalty as then administered.

In 1976 the Court upheld revised State capital punishment laws.

Persons executed, 1930-91 (4,016)

Ronald Monroe on death row in Louisiana. After 21 lawyers from a prestigious law firm demonstrated considerable doubt about his guilt, Monroe's sentence was commuted to life in prison.

the risks of being sentenced to death. Here again, the results of research are equivocal, with some showing that publicity does have some deterrent effect (albeit much weaker than other factors associated with the homicide rate),[71] and others concluding that neither newspaper nor television coverage of executions has had any deterrent effect.[72]

The legal scholar Charles L. Black has noted that it is extremely difficult to design methodologically sound deterrence studies. How can one estimate the number of people who did not commit murder in a jurisdiction with a death penalty or in one without a death penalty? How can we know that a would-be killer decided against the act of murder? According to Black,

After all possible inquiry, we do not know, and for systematic and easily visible reasons cannot know, what the truth about this "deterrent" effect may be . . . . A "scientific"—that is to say, a soundly based—conclusion is simply impossible, and no methodological path out of this tangle suggests itself.[73]

The Discrimination Argument

In the early 1970s Marvin Wolfgang and Mark Riedel identified an anomaly in the use of the death penalty. Since the 1950s it had become clear that death sentences in some southern states fell disproportionately on blacks who had been convicted of the rape of white women. Wolfgang and Riedel noted, "Of the

3,859 persons executed for all crimes since 1930, 54.6 percent have been black or members of other racial minority groups. Of the 455 executed for rape alone, 89.5 percent have been non-white."[74]

Though the discrimination question has been at the core of legal challenges to the constitutionality of many death sentences, it remained in the background until the legal scholar David Baldus and his colleagues conducted a comprehensive and methodologically sound analysis of discrimination in capital sentencing in Fulton County, Georgia.[75] This study, which clearly and unequivocally demonstrated that a black defendant is eleven times more likely to be sentenced to death for killing a white person than a white for killing a black, was presented to the United States Supreme Court in _McKlesky v. Kemp_ (1985).[76] Warren McKlesky asked the Supreme Court to invalidate the Georgia capital punishment statute because of this proven discrimination. The Court refused to do so because defense attorneys had not shown that McKlesky himself had been discriminated against. Further, the Court ruled that if there is such racial bias, it is at a tolerable level. But a level that is tolerable is difficult to specify. For over fifty years research on sentencing disparity has found racial discrimination in both capital and noncapital cases. This is not to suggest that all judges discriminate. Rather, as it has been said, some judges discriminate and some do not.[77] Furthermore, differences based on race are not solely the result of judicial decision-making. Research has found evidence that prosecutors are more likely to request the death penalty for black killers of white people.[78]

"Our procedure has been always haunted by the ghost of the innocent man convicted. It is an unreal dream."
Judge Learned Hand, *United States v. Garsson*, 1923.

"Of the world's major industrialized nations, only the United States, Japan, and South Africa retain the death penalty."

Other Arguments

Other arguments have been advanced for and against the death penalty. They are based on everything from religious concerns to a calculation of the cost of imprisonment. Table 13.3 lists these arguments and gives the rationale for them.

The Future of the Death Penalty

The number of people sentenced to death grew more than three times between 1980 and 1990. In 1990, 2 percent of offenders convicted of homicide were given sentences of death. Given the public support for the death penalty and the increasing calls for politicians to "get tough" on crime, the death penalty in America is likely to continue for the foreseeable future.[79] Furthermore, recent Supreme Court decisions indicate a growing impatience with the number of appellate reviews traditionally granted a death-row inmate, perhaps presaging a willingness to consider restrictions on the number of such appeals. Legislation has been introduced in Congress to limit the number of appeals available for a death sentence.

Of the world's major industrialized nations, only the United States, Japan, and South Africa retain the death penalty. Much of the rest of the world has shown the opposite trend. Between 1965 and 1990, twenty-five countries abolished the death penalty altogether and ten abolished it for "ordinary crimes" (i.e., crimes other than those under military codes or those enforced in time of war). The only country in the region of Western Europe that retains the death penalty in practice is Turkey (Belgium, Ireland, and Greece also retain the death penalty but do not use it in practice), and the trend in the Eastern European countries is toward abolition.[80] The lessons learned from those countries where capital punishment has been abolished might be useful in this country when the future of the death penalty is discussed. The deterrence argument would hold that homicide rates should go up when the death penalty is abolished. An analysis of murder rates in fourteen abolitionist nations showed that homicide rates actually declined more often than not after abolition.[81]

The use of capital punishment is an emotional issue in the United States. This anti-death penalty demonstration is being held outside a prison where an execution is about to take place.

TABLE 13.3 Arguments Against and For the Death Penalty

Arguments	Rationale
AGAINST	
Arbitrary Use Argument	With over 2,600 inmates on death row, the process by which an inmate is selected to die is entirely arbitrary; it is not determined by the seriousness of the crime committed or any other objective measure.
Mistakes Argument	Studies have documented cases in which individuals were wrongly convicted and thus executed in error.[*] It is impossible to be entirely certain that a person is truly guilty. Are we willing to permit mistakes?
Religious Argument	Organizations representing most of the major religions have called for an end to the death penalty. Interreligious task forces have voiced concern over issues of ethics and guilt in the putting to death of fellow human beings.
Cost-Benefit Argument	The cost of appeals and maintenance of a person on death row is higher than the cost of maintaining a prisoner sentenced to life imprisonment—approximately $3 million.
Risk Argument	Convicted murderers behave well in prison and, if paroled, rarely commit violent offenses.
Morality Argument	Examinations of the relation between moral development and attitudes toward capital punishment show that the more developed one's sense of morality, the less likely one is to favor the death penalty.
FOR	
Economic Argument	The cost of maintaining an inmate in prison for life places an unfair burden on taxpayers and the state.[†]
Retribution Argument	Any individual who kills another human being must pay for the crime.
Community Protection Argument	It is always possible that a person on death row may escape and kill again, or may kill another inmate or correctional officer. Thus the community cannot be fully protected unless the person is executed.[**]
Public Opinion Argument	Standards of decency, the criteria by which courts judge the humaneness of a punishment, are continually evolving. Two decades ago public opinion was not in favor of the death penalty. Today three-quarters of Americans favor capital punishment.

[*] Hugo Adam Bedau and Michael L. Radelet, "Miscarriages of Justice in Potentially Capital Cases," *Stanford Law Review* 40(1) (1987):21–129.

[†] Actually, the cost of appeals and maintenance of a person on death row is far higher than the cost of maintaining a prisoner sentenced to life imprisonment—approximately $3 million. See Andrew H. Malcolm, "Capital Punishment Is Popular, but So Are Its Alternatives," *The New York Times*, September 10, 1989, p. E4.

[**] Thorsten Sellin research demonstrated that this argument is specious. Convicted murderers behave exceedingly well in prison, and if released have very good parole records. Repeat homicides are statistically rare. See Sellin, *Death Penalty*, pp. 69–79.

REVIEW

Criminal sanctions are shaped by four philosophical traditions: retribution, deterrence, incapacitation, and rehabilitation. Three elements capture the essence of the modern conception of retribution—a proportionate penalty, a penalty that is deserved, and a penalty that expresses the moral condemnation of society. The basic principle underlying deterrence is that people will refrain from engaging in criminal activity because of the consequences of detection. Collective and selective incapacitative strategies require the use of imprisonment to remove offenders from the community. Rehabilitation promises meaningful changes in offenders following appropriate correctional interventions. Finally, a mixed-goals approach allows for a combination of different philosophical rationales.

Legislative and judicial policies in sentencing convicted offenders are in a state of turmoil. Evidence of disproportionate sentences for comparable offenders has led to a large-scale abandonment of the rehabilitative ideal and a return to retributive and incapacitative approaches. But sentencing continues to be in a state of flux, with some signs of a rebirth of the rehabilitative goal. At the moment, many states operate sentencing guidelines that seek to curb abuses of judicial discretion, incorporate just-desert ideals, and allow some degree of flexibility for considering aggravating and mitigating circumstances.

Capital punishment as a sentencing option preoccupies the thinking of policymakers and the general public. The United States is the last major democratic country to have retained capital punishment without any clear evidence that it promotes public safety.

Notes

1. Dennis Cavchon, "Michigan Drug Law: No Exceptions—No Mercy," *U.S.A. Today*, April 7, 1992, p. 3A.

2. "Bank Robber Who Burned His Loot Sentenced," *Reuters*, May 27, 1992.

3. Immanuel Kant, *Critique of Pure Reason* (1781).

4. Andrew von Hirsch, *Doing Justice: The Choice of Punishment* (New York: Hill & Wang, 1976). And see Andrew von Hirsch, *Past or Future Crimes: Deservedness and Dangerousness in the Sentencing of Criminals* (New Brunswick, N.J.: Rutgers University Press, 1985), and Andrew von Hirsch and Andrew Ashworth, eds., *Principled Sentencing* (Boston: Northeastern University Press, 1992). For an application of just desert theory to corporate and white collar crime, see Kip Schlegel, *Just Deserts for Corporate Criminals* (Boston, Mass.: Northeastern University Press, 1990); Kip Schlegel and David Weisburd, eds., *White Collar Crime Reconsidered* (Boston, Mass: Northeastern University Press, 1992).

5. Norval Morris, *The Future of Imprisonment* (Chicago: University of Chicago Press, 1974).

6. See von Hirsch, *Doing Justice*.

7. Philip Cook, "The Demand and Supply of Criminal Opportunities," in *Crime and Justice: An Annual Review of Research*, eds. Michael Tonry and Norval Morris, vol. 7 (Chicago, Ill.: University of Chicago Press, 1986).

8. Cesare Beccaria, *On Crimes and Punishment*, trans. Edward D. Ingraham, 2d ed. (Philadelphia: Philip H. Nicklin, 1819); Jeremy Bentham, *An Introduction to the Principles of Morals and Legislation* (1780), ed. Laurence J. LaFleur (New York: Hafner, 1948).

9. See, for example, Franklin E. Zimring and Gordon J. Hawkins, *Deterrence: The Legal Threat in Crime Control* (Chicago: University of Chicago Press, 1973); J. L. Miller and Andy B. Anderson, "Updating the Deterrence Doctrine," *Journal of Criminal Law and Criminology* 77 (1986):418–438; Scott H. Decker and Carol W. Kohfeld, "Certainty, Severity, and the Probability of Crime: A Logistic Analysis," *Policy Studies Journal* 19 (1990):2–21.

10. Edwin H. Pfuhl, Jr., "Police Strikes and Conventional Crime," *Criminology* 21 (1983):489–503.

11. Ari L. Goldman, "In Spite of Dip, Subway Crime Nears a Record," *The New York Times*, November 20, 1982, pp. 1, 26.

12. James A. Beha II, "And Nobody Can Get You Out: The Impact of a Mandatory Prison Sentence for the Illegal Carrying of a Firearm on the Administration of Criminal Justice in Boston," *Boston University Law Review* 57 (March 1977):96–146.

13. See Colin Loftin and David McDowall, "'One with a Gun Gets You Two': Mandatory Sentencing and Firearms Violence in Detroit," *Annals of the American Academy of Political and Social Science* 455 (1981):150–167; Colin Loftin and David McDowall, "The Deterrent Effects of the Florida Felony Firearm Law," *Journal of Criminal Law and Criminology* 75 (1984):250–259.

14. See H. Laurence Ross, Richard McCleary, and Gary LaFree, "Can Mandatory Jail Laws Deter Drunk Driving? The Arizona Case," *Journal of Criminal Law and Criminology* 81 (1990):156–170; H. Laurence Ross and Robert B. Voas, "The New Philadelphia Story: The Effects of Severe Punishment for Drunk Driving," *Law & Policy* 12 (1990):51–79; Rodney F. Kingsnorth, "The Gunther Special: Deterrence and the DUI Offender," *Criminal Justice and Behavior* 18 (1991):251–266.

15. See Dennis M. Donovan, "Driving While Intoxicated: Different Roads to and from the Problem," *Criminal Justice and Behavior* 16 (1989):270–298.

16. Lonn Lanza-Kaduce, "Perceptual Deterrence and Drinking and Driving among College Students," *Criminology* 26 (1988):321–341.

17. Robert P. Barry, "To Slug a Meter: A Study of Coin Fraud," *Criminology* 4(4) (1969):40–47; John F. Decker, "Curbside Deterrence," *Criminology* 10 (1972):127–142, also published in *Situational Crime Prevention*, ed. Ronald V. Clarke (New York: Harrow and Herton, 1992), pp. 39–51.

18. Gary S. Green, "General Deterrence and Television Cable Crime: A Field Experiment in Social Control," *Criminology* 23 (1985):629–645.

19. See Alfred Blumstein, Jacqueline Cohen, and Daniel Nagin, eds., *Deterrence and Incapacitation: Estimating the Effects of Criminal Sanctions on Crime Rates* (Washington, D.C.: National Academy of Sciences, 1978).

20. For examples, see Raymond Paternoster, Linda E. Saltzman, Gordon P. Waldo, and Theodore G. Chiricos, "Perceived Risk and Social Control: Do Sanctions Really Deter?," *Law and Society Review* 17 (1983):457–479; Irving Piliavin, Rosemary Gartner, Craig Thornton, and Ross L. Matsueda, "Crime, Deterrence, and Rational Choice," *American Sociological Review* 51 (1986):101–119; Raymond Paternoster, "Decisions to Participate in and Desist from Four Types of Common Delinquency: Deterrence and the Rational Choice Perspective," *Law and Society Review* 23 (1989):7–40. See also Kirk R. Williams and Richard Hawkins, "Perceptual Research on General Deterrence: A Critical Review," *Law and Society Review* 20 (1986):545–572; Daniel S. Nagin and Raymond Paternoster, "The Preventive Effects of the Perceived Risk of Arrest: Testing an Expanded Conception of Deterrence," *Criminology* 29 (1991):561–585.

21. See, for example, Joan Petersilia, Peter Greenwood, and Marvin Lavin, *Criminal Careers of Habitual Felons*, for Law Enforcement Assistance Administration (Washington, D.C.: U.S. Government Printing Office, 1978).

22. Reuel Shinnar and Shlomo Shinnar, "The Effects of the Criminal Justice System on the Control of Crime: A Quantitative Approach," *Law and Society Review* 9 (1975):581–611.

23. Jacqueline Cohen, "Incapacitation as a Strategy for Crime

Control: Possibilities and Pitfalls," in *Crime and Justice: An Annual Review of Research*, eds. Michael Tonry and Norval Morris, vol. 5 (Chicago: University of Chicago Press, 1983), pp. 1–84.

24. Sheldon L. Messinger and Richard A. Berk, "Review Essay: Dangerous People," *Criminology* 25 (1987):767–781.

25. See, for example, Peter Greenwood with Allan Abrahamse, *Selective Incapacitation* (Santa Monica, Calif.: Rand Corporation, 1982).

26. Ibid.

27. For reviews of the critiques of incapacitation policies, see Jacqueline Cohen, "Incapacitation as a Strategy for Crime Control"; Stephen D. Gottfredson and Don M. Gottfredson, "Selective Incapacitation?," *Annals of the American Academy of Political and Social Science* 478 (1985):135–149; Andrew von Hirsch, "Selective Incapacitation Reexamined: The National Academy of Sciences' Report on Criminal Careers and 'Career Criminals'," *Criminal Justice Ethics* 7 (1988):19–35; Alfred Blumstein, "Selective Incapacitation as a Means of Crime Control," *American Behavioral Scientist* 27 (1983):87–108. Ethical concerns about incapacitation are discussed in Andrew von Hirsch, "The Ethics of Selective Incapacitation: Observations on the Contemporary Debate," *Crime and Delinquency* 30 (1984):175–194.

28. Robert Martinson, "What Works? Questions and Answers about Prison Reform," *Public Interest* 35 (Spring 1974):25. For the complete report, see Douglas R. Lipton, Robert Martinson, and Judith Wilks, *The Effectiveness of Correctional Treatment: A Survey of Treatment Evaluation Studies* (New York: Praeger, 1975). See also James Q. Wilson, "'What Works?' Revisited: New Findings on Criminal Rehabilitation," *Public Interest* 61 (Fall 1980):3–17.

29. The National Research Council, for example, appointed a Panel on Research on Rehabilitative Techniques, which extended the work of Lipton and his colleagues and published its findings in 1979. Commenting on the "What Works?" evaluation, the panel noted that the earlier studies

were reasonably accurate and fair in their appraisal of the rehabilitation literature . . . however, . . . there are suggestions to be found concerning successful rehabilitation efforts that qualify the conclusion that "nothing works." Although the data are far from consistent, there may be some treatments that are effective for certain subgroups of offenders.

Lee Sechrest, Susan O. White, and Elizabeth D. Brown, eds., *The Rehabilitation of Criminal Offenders: Problems and Prospects* (Washington, D.C.: National Academy of Sciences, 1979), pp. 5–6.

30. See Ted Palmer, "The Effectiveness of Intervention: Recent Trends and Current Issues," *Crime and Delinquency* 37 (1991):330–346. See also Paul Gendreau and Robert R. Ross, "Revivification of Rehabilitation: Evidence from the 1980s," *Justice Quarterly* 4 (1987):349–407; D. A. Andrews, Ivan Zinger, Robert D. Hoge, James Bonta, Paul Gendreau, and Francis T. Cullen, "Does Correctional Treatment Work? A Clinically Relevant and Psychologically Informed Meta-analysis," *Criminology* 28 (1990):369–404; John T. Whitehead and Steven P. Lab, "A Meta-analysis of Juvenile Correctional Treatment," *Journal of Research in Crime and Delinquency* 26 (1989):276–295.

31. "The Milken Sentence: Excerpts from Judge Wood's Explanation of the Milken Sentencing," *The New York Times*, November 22, 1990, p. 1.

32. Gerhard O. W. Mueller, *Sentencing: Process and Purpose* (Springfield, Ill.: Charles C. Thomas, 1977), pp. 32–66.

33. H. R. DeLuca, Thomas J. Miller, and Carl F. Wiedemann, "Punishment v. Rehabilitation: A Proposal for Revising Sentencing Practices," *Federal Probation* 55(3) (1991):37–45.

34. American Law Institute, *Model Penal Code*, Section 1.02b.

35. Gottfredson and Gottfredson, "Selective Incapacitation?"

36. See Alfred Blumstein, Jacqueline Cohen, Susan E. Martin, and Michael H. Tonry, eds., *Research on Sentencing: The Search for Reform*, vol. 1 (Washington, D.C.: National Academy Press, 1983).

37. See Robert O. Dawson, *Sentencing: The Decision as to Type, Length, and Conditions of Sentence* (Boston: Little, Brown, 1969).

38. See Anthony Walsh, "The Role of the Probation Officer in the Sentencing Process: Independent Professional or Judicial Hack?," *Criminal Justice and Behavior* 12 (1985):289–303.

39. Edna Erez and Pamela Tontodonato, "The Effect of Victim Participation in Sentencing on Sentence Outcome," *Criminology* 28 (1990):451–474. See also Edna Erez, "Victim Participation in Sentencing: Rhetoric and Reality," *Journal of Criminal Justice* 18 (1990):19–31; Maureen McLeod, "Victim Participation in Sentencing," *Criminal Law Bulletin* 22 (1986):501–517; William E. Hellerstein, "The Victim Impact Statement: Reform or Reprisal," *American Criminal Law Review* 27 (1989):391–430.

40. California Governor Pete Wilson overturned the Board's decision. See Philip Hager, "High Court Asked to Void Wilson Veto of Parole for Killer," *Los Angeles Times*, July 4, 1991, p. 3.

41. American Friends Service Committee, *Struggle for Justice: A Report on Crime and Punishment in America* (New York: Hill and Wang, 1971).

42. See also Marvin E. Frankel, *Criminal Sentences: Law without Order* (New York: Hill and Wang, 1972); Norval Morris, *The Future of Imprisonment* (Chicago: University of Chicago Press, 1974); Andrew von Hirsch, *Doing Justice*.

43. American Friends Service Committee, *Struggle for Justice*. For a recent study of race disparities in sentencing, see Cassia Spohn and Jerry Cederblom, "Race and Disparities in Sentencing: A Test of the Liberation Hypothesis," *Justice Quarterly* 8 (1991):305–327.

44. Sandra Shane-DuBow, Alice P. Brown, and Erik Olsen, *Sentencing Reform in the United States: History, Content, and Effect* (Washington, D.C.: National Institute of Justice, 1985).

45. See Andrew von Hirsch and Kathleen Hanrahan, "Determinate Penalty Systems in America: An Overview," *Crime and Delinquency* 27 (1981):289–316.

46. Marianne W. Zawitz, *Report to the Nation on Crime and Justice*, 2d ed. (Washington, D.C.: Bureau of Justice Statistics, 1988); Lynne Goodstein and John Hepburn, "Determinate Sentencing in Illinois: An Assessment of Its Development and Implementation," *Criminal Justice Policy Review* 1 (1986):305–327.

47. Joshua Quittner, "DA Candidate Seeks to End Parole Board," *Newsday*, October 4, 1989, p. 24.

48. Ibid.

49. See Donald F. Anspach and S. Henry Monsen, "Determinate Sentencing, Formal Rationality, and Khadi Justice in Maine: An Application of Weber's Typology," *Journal of Criminal Justice* 17 (1989):471–485.

50. See von Hirsch and Hanrahan, "Determinate Penalty Systems in America."

51. See Michael Tonry, "Structuring Sentencing," *Crime and Justice: A Review of Research v. 10* (Chicago: University of Chicago, 1988), p. 267.

52. Contemporary sentencing guidelines are neither novel nor unique. Mosaic law (Exodus 21) (*lex talionis*) graded the punishment in accordance with the harm done. The Germanic Codes (*Leges Barbarorum*, 500–1100 A.D.) had similar provisions. Nineteenth- and twentieth-century penal codes (starting with the French of 1810), have more or less binding guidelines or postulates adjusting the severity of the punishment to the harm done (e.g., loss of a limb, an eye, etc.). Most notable is the current Spanish Penal Code (of December 23, 1944), which provides in article 9 for a list of mitigating circumstances, in article 10 for aggravating circumstances, and in articles 58 through 67 for the interrelation between aggravating and mitigating circumstances.

53. Frankel, *Criminal Sentences*.

54. Sally S. Simpson and Christopher S. Koper, "Deterring Corporate Crime," *Criminology* 30 (1992):347–373; see Andrew von Hirsch, Kay A. Knapp, and Michael Tonry, *The Sentencing Commission and Its Guidelines* (Boston: Northeastern University Press, 1987); William S. Laufer, "Culpability and the Sentencing of Corporations," *Nebraska Law Review* 71 (1992):1049–1094.

55. See Eric Simon, Gerry Gaes, and William Rhodes, "AS-

SYST—The Design and Implementation of Computer-Assisted Sentencing," *Federal Probation* 55(3) (1991):46–55.

56. See Michael Tonry, "The Politics and Processes of Sentencing Commissions," *Crime and Delinquency* 37 (1991):307–329. See also Alfred Blumstein, Jacqueline Cohen, Susan E. Martin, and Michael H. Tonry, *Research on Sentencing: The Search for Reform* (Washington, D.C.: National Academy Press, 1983); Joann L. Miller, Peter H. Rossi, and Jon E. Simpson, "Felony Punishments: A Factorial Survey of Perceived Justice in Criminal Sentencing," *Journal of Criminal Law and Criminology* 82 (1991):396–422.

57. See John H. Kramer, Robin L. Lubitz, and Cynthia A. Kempinen, "Sentencing Guidelines: A Quantitative Comparison of Sentencing Policies in Minnesota, Pennsylvania, and Washington," *Justice Quarterly* 6 (1989):565–587.

58. For a complete account of the fate of New York's sentencing commission, see Pamala L. Griset, *Determinate Sentencing: The Promise and the Reality of Retributive Justice* (Albany, N.Y.: State University of New York Press, 1991).

59. Michael Tonry, "Sentencing Guidelines and Their Effects," in *The Sentencing Commission*, eds. von Hirsch, K. Knapp, and M. Tonry, pp. 16–43; Laura Lein, Robert Rickards, and Tony Fabelo, "The Attitudes of Criminal Justice Practitioners toward Sentencing Issues," *Crime and Delinquency* 38 (1992):189–203.

60. *Mistretta v. U.S.*, 488 U.S. 361 (1989).

61. Stephen J. Schulhofer and Ilene H. Nagel, "Negotiated Pleas under the Federal Sentencing Guidelines: The First Fifteen Months," *American Criminal Law Review* 27 (1989):231–288.

62. "Habitual Offender Gets 71-Year Sentence for Sexual Assaults," *Los Angeles Times*, March 28, 1991, p. 2.

63. For a discussion of the implications of habitual offender statutes, see Markus Dirk Dubber, "The Unprincipled Punishment of Repeat Offenders: A Critique of California's Habitual Criminal Statute," *Stanford Law Review* 43 (1990):193–240.

64. *Rummel v. Estelle*, 445 U.S. 263 (1980).

65. Sara T. Dike, "Capital Punishment in the United States. Part I: Observations on the Use and Interpretation of the Law," *Criminal Justice Abstracts* 13 (1981):283–311; Hugo A. Bedau, *The Death Penalty in America* (New York: Oxford University Press, 1984).

66. William Bowers, *Executions in America* (Lexington, Mass.: Lexington Books, 1974).

67. Victoria Schneider and John Ortiz Smykla, "A Summary Analysis of *Executions in the United States: 1608–1987: The Espy File*, in *The Death Penalty in America: Current Research*, ed. Robert M. Bohm (Cincinnati, and Highland Heights, Ky.: Anderson Publishing and Academy of Criminal Justice Sciences, 1991), pp. 1–20.

68. Sandra Nicolai, Karen Riley, Rhonda Christensen, Patrice Stych, and Leslie Greunke, *The Question of Capital Punishment* (Lincoln, Neb.: Contact, 1980).

69. Thorsten Sellin, *The Death Penalty* (Philadelphia: American Law Institute, 1959); Thorsten Sellin, *Capital Punishment* (New York: Harper and Row, 1967); Thorsten Sellin, *The Penalty of Death* (Beverly Hills, Calif.: Sage, 1980); Hans Zeisel, "The Deterrent Effect of the Death Penalty: Facts v. Faith," in *The Supreme Court Review*, ed. P. E. Kurland (Chicago: University of Chicago Press, 1976), pp. 317–343; William C. Bailey, "A Multivariate Cross-sectional Analysis of the Deterrent Effect of the Death Penalty," *Sociology and Social Research* 64 (1980):183–207; Ruth D. Peterson and William C. Bailey, "Murder and Capital Punishment in the Evolving Context of the Post-*Furman* Era," *Social Forces* 66 (1988):774–807.

70. Isaac Ehrlich, "The Deterrent Effect of Capital Punishment: A Question of Life and Death," *American Economic Review* 65 (1975):397–417. For discussions demonstrating that convicted murderers, if paroled, rarely commit violent offenses, see Thorsten Sellin, *The Death Penalty* (Philadelphia, Pa.: American Law Institute, 1959), pp. 69–79; Gennaro F. Vito, Pat Koester, and Deborah G. Wilson, "Return of the Dead: An Update on the Status of *Furman*-Commuted Death Row Inmates," in *The Death Penalty in*

America: Current Research, ed. Robert M. Bohm (Cincinnati, Ohio, and Highland Heights, Ky.: Anderson Publishing, 1991), pp. 89–99; James W. Marquant and Jonathan R. Sorensen, "Institutional and Post-Release Behavior of *Furman*-Commuted Inmates in Texas," *Criminology* 26 (1988):677–693. See also Thomas J. Keil and Gennaro F. Vito, "Fear of Crime and Attitudes Toward Capital Punishment: A Structures Equation Model," *Justice Quarterly* 8 (1991):447–464.

71. See Steven Stack, "Publicized Executions and Homicide, 1950–1980," *American Sociological Review* 52 (1987):532–540; David J. Phillips, "The Deterrent Effect of Capital Punishment: New Evidence on an Old Controversy," *American Journal of Sociology* 86 (1980):139–148.

72. See William C. Bailey and Ruth D. Peterson, "Murder and Capital Punishment: A Monthly Time-Series Analysis of Execution Publicity," *American Sociological Review* 54 (1989):722–743; William C. Bailey, "Murder, Capital Punishment, and Television: Execution Publicity and Homicide Rates," *American Sociological Review* 55 (1990):628–633; Ruth D. Peterson and William C. Bailey, "Felony Murder and Capital Punishment: An Examination of the Deterrence Question," *Criminology* 29 (1991):367–395.

73. Charles L. Black, *Capital Punishment: The Inevitability of Caprice and Mistake* (New Haven, Conn.: Yale University Press, 1984).

74. Marvin Wolfgang and Mark Riedel, "Race, Judicial Discretion, and the Death Penalty," *Annals of the American Academy of Political and Social Sciences* 407 (1973):119–133. See also Joseph E. Jacoby and Raymond Paternoster, "Sentencing Disparity and Jury Packing: Further Challenges to the Death Penalty," *Journal of Criminal Law and Criminology* 73 (1982):379–387; Joseph E. Jacoby, "The Deterrence and Brutalizing Effects of the Death Penalty," in *The Death Penalty in South Carolina*, ed. Bruce L. Pearson (Columbia, S.C.: Acluse Press, 1981).

75. David Baldus, Charles Pulaski, and George Woodworth, "Comparative Review of Death Sentences: An Empirical Study of the Georgia Experience," *Journal of Criminal Law and Criminology* 74 (1983):661–678.

76. *McKlesky v. Kemp*, 478 U.S. 109 (1985). For a recent study, see Thomas J. Keil and Gennaro F. Vito, "Race and the Death Penalty in Kentucky Murder Trials: An Analysis of Post-*Gregg* Outcomes," *Justice Quarterly* 7 (1990):189–207. On the overall use of social science data by the Supreme Court in capital cases, see James R. Acker, "Social Science in Supreme Court Death Penalty Cases: Citation Practices and Their Implications," *Justice Quarterly* 8 (1991):422–446.

77. Abraham S. Blumberg, *Criminal Justice: Issues and Ironies* (New York: New Viewpoints, 1979).

78. See Raymond Paternoster, "Prosecutorial Discretion in Requesting the Death Penalty: A Case of Victim-Based Racial Discrimination," *Law and Society Review* 18 (1984):437–478; Michael L. Radelet and Glenn L. Pierce, "Race and Prosecutorial Discretion in Homicide Cases," *Law and Society Review* 19 (1985):587–621; Thomas J. Keil and Gennaro F. Vito, "Race, Homicide Severity, and Application of the Death Penalty: A Consideration of the Barnett Scale," *Criminology* 27 (1989):511–535; Paige H. Ralph, Jonathan R. Sorensen, and James W. Marquart, "A Comparison of Death-Sentenced and Incarcerated Murderers in Pre-Furman Texas," *Justice Quarterly* 9 (1992):185–209.

79. Robert M. Bohm, Louise J. Clark, and Adrian F. Aveni, "The Influence of Knowledge on Reasons for Death Penalty Opinions: An Experimental Test," *Justice Quarterly* 7 (1990):175–188.

80. Roger Hood, *The Death Penalty: A World-Wide Perspective* (New York: Oxford University Press, 1989).

81. See Dane Archer, Rosemary Gartner, and Marc Beittel, "Homicide and the Death Penalty: A Cross-National Test of a Deterrence Hypothesis," *Journal of Criminal Law and Criminology* 74 (1983):991–1013.

PART 4

CORRECTIONS

Burdened by a history of inhumanity and brutality, corrections acquired its name less than a century ago, when it was believed that offenders should and could be corrected. Chapter 14 focuses on the history of corrections in the United States, with special attention to efforts at reform, and on the prisoners' rights movement and the Supreme Court's subsequent recognition of constitutional guarantees for prisoners. The chapter also describes the variety of contemporary correctional facilities, and the variety of problems the system faces at all levels.

Chapter 15 is devoted to contemporary American institutional corrections, how it deals with its clients, how these clients (prisoners) behave in prison, how they interact with corrections personnel, and how these officers perceive and fulfill their functions. The chapter examines special problems, like the increasing number of women prisoners and of violent and addict offenders in confinement, as well as contemporary prison health problems such as AIDS and TB. It also examines the contemporary state of rehabilitation, education, and vocational training programs.

Chapter 16 focuses on the topic of noninstitutional corrections, which has been and continues to be shaped by imaginative reformers. Probation and parole, a century and a half old, are now being supplemented by other alternatives to incarceration, among them the increased use of fines, restitution to victims, intensive supervision programs, halfway houses, shock programs (boot camps), house arrest, and particularly community service. All of these are meant to assist in relieving prison overcrowding, yet they may actually widen the net of societal control over wrongdoers. ■

CHAPTER 14

CORRECTIONS: YESTERDAY AND TODAY

In 1584 Balthazar Geraerts assassinated King Willem of Orange (Holland). His punishment, inflicted before a cheering multitude, consisted of unspeakable cruelties and finally decapitation.[1] These atrocities took place at a time of great advances: the worldwide voyages of discovery; the expansion of scientific knowledge; the flourishing of art, literature, and music. Human life, however, was still cheap. Cruelty was a way of life and death was usually early and sudden, whether from marauding armies, from disease, or from an executioner's ax.

Today we pride ourselves on the progress we have made and the barbarities we no longer practice. We pride ourselves on our extraordinary advances in many fields: the exploration of space, great leaps in technology, the conquest of many diseases. And yet human life is still cheap. The inner-city ghettoes are hard cruel places where life is often cut short suddenly and violently. We still execute prisoners. And to some, going to jail is regarded as a rite of passage. Tattoos acquired in prison are badges of honor, and the returning offender may be a hero in the community. The prospect of prison, far from being a deterrent, has turned into the opposite—an acceptable alternative, a respite for street warriors, time to build muscles and connections, a period of rest and preparation for the next battle.[2] ■

Institutional corrections has a long history, from the workhouses (or houses of corrections) of Holland, England, and colonial Pennsylvania through the penitentiary movement, the reformatory movement, and the medical model of confinement to the contemporary prison and jail. As we will see, treatment of prisoners has also evolved from a rule of terror and brutality to a rule of law.

In this chapter we focus on the evolution and contemporary state of the system that currently bears the name "corrections." In the early twentieth century, Americans adopted this term with the expectation that offenders could be corrected by the system, just as nearsightedness is corrected by eyeglasses. The personnel who run this system consist of corrections officers, corrections administrators (superintendents and wardens), and administrative staff.

THE HISTORY OF INSTITUTIONAL CORRECTIONS

"There can be no humane penology as long as punishment masquerades as 'correction.' No person or group has the right to 'correct' a human being; only God does."
Thomas D. Szasz, MD, in *Leaves* (Connecticut Department of Corrections, 1977).

Imprisonment as a punishment was rarely used before the end of the Middle Ages. Before then, most of the Western world was dominated by the notion that prisons should be used to contain people, not to punish them. It was the Dutch who in the mid-sixteenth century constructed the first prisons to be used for the purpose of "correcting" wrongdoers[3] in "work houses."

The Workhouse Movement

Amsterdam built one workhouse (*tuchthuis*, literally "house of compulsory reformation") for men and one for women. The men ground wood into sawdust; the women spun yarn. Two purposes were foremost in the minds of the reformers who created the workhouses: Useful labor was more humane and less degrading than barbaric punishments, and it was also more beneficial for the common good to put offenders to work. (See the Criminal Justice in Action box.)

The English, with their close commercial and intellectual ties to Holland, established their first workhouse at about the same time at the old Bridewell Castle in London. Many other Bridewells were subsequently opened in England.[4] As social scientists George Rusche and Otto Kirchheimer have demonstrated, the profit motive always played a significant role in devising punishments; witness the Romans who put prisoners to work in mines and rowing on galleys.[5]

Early houses of correction did not replace other punishments entirely. Brutal public executions, a mark of the Middle Ages, continued to exist. Persons sentenced to death were hanged, burned at the stake, drawn and quartered, disemboweled, boiled, broken on the wheel, stoned to death, impaled, drowned, pressed to death in spiked containers, and torn by red-hot tongs. Noncapital punishments were also marked by extreme cruelty: Prisoners were branded, dismembered, flogged, and tortured by specially designed instruments. By those standards, the Dutch and English houses of correction were humane alternatives.

During the reign of Queen Elizabeth I (1558–1603), the English began to experiment with additional forms of punishment which the Queen characterized as "more merciful."[6] In 1598, galley slavery (the ancient Roman punishment) was introduced.[7] Slave galleys were also maintained by France, Spain, Denmark, and other European countries well into the eighteenth century. Conditions on the galleys were anything but merciful. Chained to crowded benches, exposed to all kinds of weather, whipped by brutal overseers, and fed on harsh rations, galley slaves often welcomed death. Nor did the Bridewells measure up to expectations. Designed to accommodate, "repress," and reform "the idle and sturdy vagabond and common strumpet,"[8] they could not handle the armies of social failures assigned to them. Soon these institutions turned into overcrowded slave-

Brutal public executions, like this drawing and quartering, were the rule until relatively recent times.

labor camps in which convict labor contributed to the wealth of the rulers of the countries.

To deal with the overflow of prisoners, the English introduced **prison hulks,** decommissioned and deteriorated warships that were converted into prisons, most of which were docked in the River Thames. By the 1840s, the British government had about twelve hulks that housed up to 4,000 inmates.[9] These hulks were overcrowded, unsanitary places of confinement, with high death rates due to communicable diseases. When prison ships were used during times of war (American War of Independence, Civil War, World War II) and emergency (Northern Ireland), these terrible conditions led the world to outlaw imprisonment on ships for prisoners of war—but not for convicts.[10] Recently, in fact, New York City has commissioned a fleet of five ships to house convicts.

England (and France) devised yet another form of punishment that was important to the development of the New World. In the eighteenth century, English convicts were sentenced to be "transported" to the colonies. Virginia, Georgia, and other southern colonies received many convicts who labored to develop towns and plantations. After the American colonies won their independence, England transported convicts to Australia.[11]

prison hulks
Decommissioned ships converted into prisons.

The Penitentiary Movement

Jails for the detention of persons pending trial or execution of sentence are an ancient institution, in England dating at least to 1166, when Henry II ordered their construction. By the seventeenth century, English jails increasingly housed convicted offenders and drunks. It was that institution which the early settlers brought with them to the northern and southern colonies. The jails at York Village, Maine (1653), and Williamsburg, Virginia (1701), are still in place and may be visited.

Philadelphia's Walnut Street Jail played a crucial role in the history of corrections. William Penn's "Great Law" of December 4, 1682, provided for the establishment of houses of correction as an alternative to corporal and capital punishment in Pennsylvania.[12] (Penn's law retained capital punishment and whipping for the more serious offenses.[13]) After independence, Pennsylvania continued to follow the liberal ideas of William Penn. In Philadelphia, the physician William Rush took up the cause of penal reform with his work, *An Enquiry into the Effects*

"Philadelphia's Walnut Street Jail, built in the late seventeenth century, played a crucial role in the history of corrections in the United States."

MILESTONES IN THE HISTORY OF CORRECTIONS

Time Frame	Response to Wrongdoing
Prehistoric times, preliterate societies, clans, tribes	Sacrifices to spirits of animals and birds (a tradition which lived on in the later practice of tarring and feathering)
3500–500 B.C.	Early civilizations: Conciliation and victim compensation (Code of Hammurabi, 1750 B.C.); confinement of wrongdoer (slavery); exile and outlawry (declaring wrongdoer a wolf); private/tribal vengeance; capital punishment. (The wolf-outlaw lives on in fairy tales like "Little Red Riding Hood")
	Ancient empires Egypt, Greece, Rome: Emergence of idea of a goddess of justice who weighs the crime and the punishment
ca 1200 B.C.	Ancient Israel: Mosaic law limits punishment to the amount of harm done: an eye for an eye
500 B.C.–A.D. 375	Rome: Forced labor (mining, galley slavery), public executions (the Christians to the lions)
A.D. 400–1500	Middle Ages, Europe: Blood feuds (Germanic law), capital punishment, corporal punishment (branding), compensation (fines); ever-increasing severity of these punishments
14th–17th centuries	Europe: Galley slavery reintroduced; landlocked cities sell prisoners to port cities as galley slaves
Late 16th–19th centuries	Holland and England create first houses of correction (Amsterdam; Bridewell, England); imprisonment becomes principal form of punishment; capital and corporal punishment continue, esp. flogging

Time Frame	Response to Wrongdoing
18th–19th centuries	British Empire: England uses deportation of convicts to America (and later Australia); in England itself, prisoners incarcerated in "prison hulks"
	Prison reform: Italy and France: Enlightenment reformers like Cesare Beccaria press for humanization of punishment England: Jeremy Bentham invents panopticon prison (central control of all cells) United States: "Penitentiary wing" is built in Philadelphia's Walnut Street Jail
Mid-19th century	United States: John Augustus, Boston cobbler, invents practice of probation Britain: Alexander Maconochie, governor of a penal colony in Norfolk Islands in the Pacific, invents practice of parole
Late 19th century	United States: Reformatory movement 1870: First Prison Administrators meeting, Cincinnati. National Prison Association founded 1876: Elmira, New York: Penitentiary built according to reformatory principles: lockstep, isolation, parole for "deserving"
Mid-20th century	United States: post 1945: Medical treatment model, but rigid and disciplinary practice; prison riots 1960s: Beginnings of humane approach; well-meaning treatment methods; only superficial change Prisoners' rights movement begins Supreme Court begins to involve itself in protecting inmate rights
Late 20th century	United States: 1975: Just deserts approach; fixed sentences; prison construction, overcrowding; prison ships used again in New York City 1980s–1990s: Cost-beneficial but tough alternatives

379

penitentiary
Prison or place of confinement and correction for persons convicted of criminal acts; originally a place where convicts did penance.

of Public Punishment upon Criminals (1787). Rush helped organize the Pennsylvania Society for the Abolition of Slavery and was instrumental in the creation of the Philadelphia Society for Alleviating the Miseries of Public Prisons (1787). As a result of Rush's work, and consistent with the Quaker idea of "redemption through penitence," a small extension called the penitentiary wing was added to the Walnut Street Jail. The penitentiary was born.

The idea of the **penitentiary** was simple enough: Like medieval monks in their monastery cells, convicts were to do penance in places designed for that purpose. The penitentiary wing was used to house prisoners in solitary confinement, for even at work prisoners were not allowed to communicate with each other.

The Quaker idea of redemption through labor and religious reflection, instead of capital and corporal punishment, seemed persuasive. Moreover, for a few years after the Walnut Street penitentiary wing was opened, the crime rate in Philadelphia appeared to drop. New York (1791), New Jersey (1798), Virginia (1800), Kentucky (1800), and later other states adopted the penitentiary concept and reduced the use of capital punishment.[14]

But on Walnut Street in Philadelphia reality looked different. Barely a decade after the penitentiary wing had been inaugurated, the visiting committee of the Philadelphia Society for Alleviating the Miseries of Public Prisons reported "idleness, dirt, and wretchedness" in the facility.[15] Prisoners were not at all penitent, useful labor could not be provided, and the authorities were unable to maintain the institution in a condition conducive to the improvement of prisoners. Dr. Rush, convinced that the idea of the penitentiary was basically sound, began to campaign for better conditions and better management. After much lobbying by Dr. Rush and the Pennsylvania Society, the state legislature approved the construction of two new penitentiaries, the Western in Pittsburgh and the Eastern in Philadelphia. They received their first inmates in 1826 and 1829.

"Bentham's 'panopticon' prison was designed to maximize surveillance and minimize the cost of guarding prisoners."

The Pennsylvania System. The Western Penitentiary was designed in 1818 according to plans drawn by the great English lawyer and philosopher Jeremy Bentham. Bentham had invented the "panopticon" prison, which was laid out to maximize surveillance and minimize the cost of guarding prisoners. All the cells in this circular prison faced the guard station, strategically placed in the center. Each small tomblike cell could be seen and the movements of prisoners monitored. Prisoners had to work in their cells and were permitted only one hour of exercise daily. They were not allowed to communicate with each other. The impact of this type of confinement was disastrous: physical and emotional illness, anxiety and depression. The prison had to be rebuilt at great cost to allow sunlight into the cells.

The Eastern Penitentiary (designed 1821) operated along similar lines: solitary confinement, work in the cells, religious instruction, and penitence.[16]

The Auburn System. A similar approach to imprisonment developed in New York at the Auburn Penitentiary. Here the rule of silence was so profound and so pervasive that it became the most striking feature of these fortresslike prisons. About their tour through Auburn in the nineteenth century, the French reformers de Beaumont and de Tocqueville wrote: "We felt as if we traversed catacombs; there were a thousand living beings, and yet it was a desert solitude."[17]

"The lockstep, a silent shuffle in which prisoners were required to walk, was considered therapeutic in nineteenth-century prisons."

To maintain the silence and order in the movement of large numbers of inmates about the prison, Auburn devised the lockstep, a silent shuffle. Inmates stood in line, each with the right foot slightly behind the left and the right arm outstretched with the hand on the right shoulder of the man in front of him. They moved in a shuffle, sliding the left foot forward, then bringing the right foot to its position just behind the left, then the left again, then the right. This awkward locomotion, coupled with the wearing of striped uniforms, was considered therapeutic.

The only innovation added by the Auburn system was congregate (group) labor. Younger offenders were permitted to work and eat in groups. But they still were not allowed to talk to or glance at one another. Allowing prisoners to work outside their cells was much more cost-effective than the Pennsylvania system; Auburn even made a profit in the early years of its existence. Most other states adopted the cheaper Auburn system.

In New York, as one prison became overcrowded, another was built, always on the Auburn principle. In 1825 Sing Sing was built along the Hudson River north of New York City by 100 inmates from Auburn who were transported down the Hudson by boat, shackled in irons.[18] The ultimate penitentiary, which opened in 1931, was Attica.

Attica. Attica was designed to counteract the rioting that had been experienced in Auburn-style prisons, with their bunk beds and mess-hall locksteps. Besides the usual workshops, a cafeteria was added. There were recreation rooms, and sunlight streamed into the cells. No other prison since Auburn had created such interest. Attica's wall, enclosing fifty-five acres, was thirty feet high, extended twelve feet into the ground, and cost $1,275,000 to erect. The prison contained four separated cell blocks, each of which could house some 500 men in individual cells. The total cost of the prison eventually reached the then astronomical sum of $9 million. Because Attica's construction coincided with the Great Depression, however, many of the planned extras were never completed. Still, Attica became the model for the prisons of the future: escape-proof, riot-proof, (so it was thought), with unbreakable toilets and fixtures, a vast system for locking up cells and other rooms, yet without the enforced silence and the lockstep of the past.

"In the 1930s, Attica became a model for the prisons of the future: It was considered escape-proof and riot-proof."

The Reformatory Movement

As early as the 1860s, while many of the country's politicians and prison administrators, as well as the public, held high hopes for the penitentiary, a group of reformers had abandoned the idea. They found that penitence rarely resulted from a period of incarceration in a penitentiary. Costs were high, prison labor did not yield the expected profit, brutality continued, and corruption was common. In 1870, a world prison congress was summoned by Dr. Enoch C. Wines, then secretary of the Prison Association of New York, and his friend and collaborator Theodore Dwight, to meet in Cincinnati. All the leaders of American prison reform (including Gaylord Hubbel, New York; Franklin Sanborn, Massachusetts; and Zebulon R. Brockway, Michigan) and guests from abroad (including Sir Walter Crofton, Ireland; Bonneville de Marsagny, France; and Mary Carpenter, England) met and organized the National Prison Association. The Congress culminated in a Declaration of Principles, which advocated reformation rather than punishment. Included in the program were a system for early release of prisoners, the indeterminate sentence, and the cultivation of inmates' self-respect.[19] The reformers called for an end to the penitentiary, and its replacement by the **reformatory**. The model was to be Brockway's Elmira Reformatory in New York, which provided individualized treatment, grade-school education, lectures by professors from nearby Elmira College, and vocational training. Yet the institution was run with military discipline, on the theory that, above all, inmates lacked discipline.

reformatory
Institution designed to reform criminals through individualized treatment, education, and vocational training.

The new reform spirit was kept alive by the National Prison Association (now called the American Correctional Association). Reformatories were built in many states, often alongside old-style penitentiaries. But it soon became apparent that, just as houses of correction did not correct and penitentiaries did not produce penitence, so reformatories did not reform. The search for a better system continued.

"We use prisons as the solutions for everything. It doesn't work."
Pennsylvania Corrections Commissioner Joseph D. Lehman, September 1992.

The Rehabilitation Model

The rehabilitation model that emerged from houses of corrections, penitentiaries, and reformatories was based on indeterminate sentencing, careful classification, and treatment. Advocates argued that all offenders, independent of the nature of their offense, should be sentenced for a term ranging from a very short period to life in prison. Release would depend on when the criminality was cured. Classification was an elaborate, systematic diagnosis and prescription. On classification, inmates would be assigned to programs involving psychotherapy, vocational training, and education.[20] Offenders would be retrained, resocialized, rehabilitated, and reintegrated as socially skilled citizens.

The medical approach to dealing with criminality flourished until the 1970s. California was the leader in the therapeutic approach, but nearly all states instituted group and individual therapy programs, counseling services, and behavior modification programs of various sorts. Conditions in the prisons, however, actually changed very little. Prisoners were permitted to leave their cells only for exercise, group work, religious services, therapy, and meals. Underfunded and inadequately staffed rehabilitative programs reached only a small number of inmates. The results of most programs were disappointing.

Some of the treatment methods—the coercive nature of treatment more generally, as well as the absence of treatment when mandated by a sentence—caused concern among civil libertarians. More important, ramifications of a conviction as well as the conditions of confinement seemed to be at odds with constitutional rights. In most states, after a felony conviction the prisoner was considered civilly dead. He or she lost the right to vote, and in some states the spouse was entitled to have the marriage annulled. All this suggested that, despite an outward commitment to a rehabilitation or treatment model of corrections, very little had changed inside the prison world. Yet the world outside was changing rapidly: the emphasis shifted to the protection of individual rights.

MAJOR DEVELOPMENTS IN AMERICAN CORRECTIONS

The Prisoners' Rights Movement

Under the U.S. doctrine of the separation of powers, legislatures make laws, courts adjudicate controversies arising under these laws, and the executive executes the laws. Oddly enough, until the 1960s courts were quite willing to test laws made by the legislatures but were unwilling to supervise or review the execution of these laws by the executive branch of government. In corrections, the executive branch is the correctional administration. The courts were unwilling to examine how the executive branch carried out the sentences imposed by the judiciary. This was called the "hands-off" doctrine. As late as 1958, Justice Felix Frankfurter, in *Gore v. United States*, held that "in effect, we are asked to enter the domain of penology. . . . [T]his Court has no such power."[21]

But in the 1960s, society experienced rapid social change. In the United States, minority groups demanded equality in voting rights, housing, education, and employment. Women strove for equal treatment in public and private domains. Students rebelled against complacent and conservative political and social systems. The young rebelled against the old. Prisoners, too, demanded their rights. During these years the National Prison Project of the American Civil Liberties Union, the NAACP Legal Defense and Educational Fund, the legal services branch of the federal government's Office of Economic Opportunity, public defenders and legal aid lawyers, as well as countless volunteers from the legal

"For years, courts followed a 'hands-off' doctrine with respect to the administration of corrections."

profession and hundreds of self-trained jailhouse lawyers, succeeded in overturning the traditional hands-off doctrine. But it took some very dramatic events to get the prisoners' rights movement under way.

"I looked around the yard and there were people working together as a unit. . . . I saw black and white inmates holding hands as if they were brothers, which they were then, brothers fighting for a common cause."
Che Nieves, former Attica prisoner, quoted in *Newsday*, September 1991.

Riots in Attica. On September 9, 1971, a riot broke out in New York's Attica prison, an institution then holding 2,200 inmates. Prisoners took over most of the facility and held corrections officers hostage. Governor Nelson Rockefeller ordered an attack by the state police. State police helicopters then dropped bombs and tear gas canisters in an attempt to end the uprising. After four days and forty-three lives lost, "peace" was restored.[22]

The prisoners of Attica rioted for basic rights guaranteed them under the Constitution and the United Nations Standard Minimum Rules for the Treatment of Prisoners. G. O. W. Mueller and Douglas J. Besharov compared the list of demands by the Attica prisoners with the United Nations Standard Minimum Rules for the Treatment of Prisoners to which all countries, including the United States, had agreed. They concluded that most of the demands were in conformity with these minimum standards. The standards pertain to diet, the handling of complaints, hygiene, religious freedom, contact with the outside world, treatment, education, legal assistance, recreation, medical treatment, inmate funds, parole, and discipline.[23]

Attica was only the most publicized of the riots in demand of prisoners' rights. There were many others. These riots opened the floodgates to lawsuits by prisoners testing not only the right of access to the courts, but also the particular conditions of their confinement (Table 14.1).[24]

The Role of the Supreme Court. Any analysis of the prisoners' rights movement must acknowledge the crucial role of the United States Supreme Court. James Jacobs, law professor and corrections scholar, suggests that, to begin with, the prisoners' rights movement required a symbolic "shot in the arm from the Supreme Court."[25] *Cooper v. Pate* (1964) was the opening.[26] Ninety-three years after passage of the Civil Rights Act (1871), prisoners could finally sue a warden for a violation of their civil rights. The old "hands-off" doctrine was dead.

Many legal victories followed *Cooper v. Pate*, and each contributed to the strength, self-confidence, and momentum of the prisoners' rights movement.

Attica in the aftermath of the 1971 uprising: Inmates ordered to lie down in A yard, prior to a skin search. As the area became crowded, they were made to crawl away from the door on their bellies, hands locked behind their heads, to make room for more.

TABLE 14.1 Benchmarks in Rights for Prisoners

Year	Case	Ruling
1958	*Gore v. United States*, 357 U.S. 386	The "hands-off" doctrine. The court has no right to enter the domain of penology.
1964	*Cooper v. Pate*, 378 U.S. 546	End of the "hands-off" doctrine. Prisoners may bring civil action for violation of their civil rights under the Civil Rights Act of 1871.
1964	*Rouse v. Cameron*, 373 F.2d 452 (D.C. Cir.)	Right to treatment. A person imprisoned for "treatment" has a right to such treatment; otherwise he or she must be discharged.
1968	*Lee v. Washington*, 390 U.S. 333	Equal protection (Fourteenth Amendment). Racial discrimination in prison is unconstitutional.
1969	*Johnson v. Avery*, 393 U.S. 499	Right to legal defense. Prisoners have a right to assistance from jailhouse lawyers.
1970	*Goldberg v. Kelly*, 397 U.S. 254	Due process rights (Fourteenth Amendment). Prisoners have a right to due process when threatened with a loss resulting from arbitrary or erroneous official decisions.
1972	*Cruz v. Beto*, 405 U.S. 319	Freedom of religion (First Amendment). Religious freedom must be granted equally to inmates of all faiths.
1974	*Wolff v. McDonnell*, 418 U.S. 539	Due process in disciplinary proceedings. When faced with serious disciplinary action, prisoners are entitled to procedural due process.
1974	*Procunier v. Martinez*, 416 U.S. 396	Freedom of speech (First Amendment). Prisoners' mail may be opened only by "legitimate," "least restrictive" means. Relative freedom from censorship.
1976	*Estelle v. Gamble,* 429 U.S. 97	Medical treatment. Deliberate indifference to prisoners' serious medical needs is cruel and unusual punishment.
1977	*Bounds v. Smith*, 430 U.S. 817	Legal assistance. Prison law libraries must be adequately staffed to provide legal assistance to inmates in need.
1978	*Hutto v. Finney*, 437 U.S. 678	Prohibition of cruel and unusual punishment (Eighth Amendment). Confinement in a segregation cell for 30 days is cruel and unusual punishment. (Totality of circumstances test.)
1992	*Hudson v. McMillian*, 112 S. Ct. 995, 117 L. Ed. 2d 156	Use of excessive force. Beating of a prisoner by guards, or use of excessive force, may constitute cruel and unusual punishment even if not resulting in serious injury.

SOURCE: Based on Geoffrey P. Albert, ed., *Legal Rights of Prisoners* (Beverly Hills, Calif.: Sage, 1980).

(See the Criminal Justice on Trial box.) A high-water mark was reached in 1974 with *Wolff v. McDonnell*,[27] a case that resolved issues about the procedural protections to which prisoners are entitled at disciplinary hearings. In *Wolff*, the Supreme Court provided the statement that served as a rallying call for prisoners' rights advocates. Speaking for the Court, Justice White said:

[The State of Nebraska] asserts that the procedure for disciplining prison inmates for serious misconduct is a matter of policy raising no constitutional issue. If the position implies that prisoners in state institutions are wholly without the protections of the Constitution and the Due Process Clause, it is plainly untenable. Lawful imprisonment necessarily makes unavailable many rights and privileges of the ordinary citizen, a "retraction justified by the considerations underlying our penal system." But though his rights may be diminished by the needs and exigencies of the institutional environment, a prisoner is not wholly stripped of constitutional protections when he is imprisoned for crime. There is no iron curtain drawn between the Constitution and the prisons of this country.[28]

Since *Wolff*, prisoners have won several important victories in the Supreme Court.[29] For example, the Court in *Estelle v. Gamble* (1976) found that "deliberate indifference to serious medical needs" constitutes cruel and unusual punishment.[30] In *Hutto v. Finney* (1978) it approved a wide-ranging structural injunction against certain practices and conditions in the Arkansas prisons.[31]

"There is no iron curtain . . . between the Constitution and the prisons of this country."
Justice White, *Wolff v. McDonnell*, 1974.

Constitutional Rights of Inmates

First Amendment: Freedom of Speech and Religion. Since 1970, the federal and state courts have extended the rights of freedom of speech and religion to prisoners and have required correctional administrators to show why restrictions on these rights were imposed. Some of the landmark cases applying First Amendment rights to prisoners include *Procunier v. Martinez* (1974), where the court said that censorship of mail could be allowed only where there is a substantial government interest in maintaining security.[32] In *Fulwood v. Clemmer* (1962), the U.S. District Court of the District of Columbia declared that the Muslim faith must be recognized as a religion and officials may not restrict members from holding services.[33] In *Cruz v. Beto* (1972), the Supreme Court ruled that it was discriminatory and a violation of the First Amendment right under the Constitution for Buddhist prisoners to be denied opportunities to practice their faith comparable to those accorded to prisoners who belonged to more "conventional" religions.[34]

Fourth Amendment: Protection against Arbitrary Search and Seizure. The courts have not been equally active in extending Fourth Amendment rights to prisoners to protect them against unreasonable searches and seizures. Generally, it is fair to say that inmates have very few legitimate privacy expectations. For example, in *Hudson v. Palmer* (1984), the Court upheld the right of officials to search cells and confiscate any contraband found.[35] With respect to body searches, the courts are a little more restrictive. Thus, in *Lee v. Downs* (1981), the Court ruled that staff members may not supervise inmates of the opposite sex during bathing or use of the toilet or carry out strip searches of the opposite sex.[36]

Eighth Amendment: Protection against Cruel and Unusual Punishment. The courts had been reluctant to apply this constitutional provision to the execution of sentences, but ultimately had to. Prison overcrowding was the issue. Many cases have reached the courts, and new standards have evolved.

Crowding alone does not amount to cruelty in violation of the Eighth Amendment. Courts must, in each case, determine whether and to what extent crowding has caused "deprivation of basic human needs," before they can order relief from the offending conditions. "Basic needs" are needs that, if not met, result in "wanton pain." Courts must consider the quality and amount of medical and mental health services, the extent of violence, the quality of food, and the availability of recreational opportunities.

In determining the extent to which deficiencies in these areas are the consequence of crowding—as distinct from inadequate funding, poor administration, or sheer indifference—the lower courts hear a wide range of evidence, including testimony from corrections officials, inmates, and experts. Not surprisingly, corrections administrators themselves often blame any failures to meet minimum standards of humane treatment on crowded conditions.

Expert witnesses in the fields of corrections, public health, psychology, and

"NOR CRUEL AND UNUSUAL PUNISHMENT INFLICTED"

Is the unprovoked and unjustifiable beating of an inmate by two corrections officers a violation of the Eighth Amendment to the U.S. Constitution? Even if the inmate did not suffer a serious or permanent injury, is the beating still cruel and unusual punishment?

The circumstances of the case

In 1991 Keith Hudson, an inmate of the state penitentiary in Angola, Louisiana, asked the U.S. Supreme Court to answer these questions. The Court heard evidence that on October 30, 1983, Hudson had an argument with a corrections officer, Jack McMillian. This argument led to the issuance of two disciplinary reports and a decision to place Hudson in administrative lockdown. The beating occurred on the way to lockdown:

Assisted by Woods [a corrections officer], McMillian placed Hudson in handcuffs and shackles, took the prisoner out of his cell, and walked him toward the penitentiary's "administrative lockdown" area. Hudson testified that, on the way there, McMillian punched Hudson in the mouth, eyes, chest, and stomach while Woods held the inmate in place and kicked and punched him from behind. He further testified that Mezo, the supervisor on duty, watched the beating but merely told the officers "not to have too much fun." As a result of this episode, Hudson suffered minor bruises and swelling of his face, mouth, and lip. The blows also loosened Hud-

son's teeth and cracked his partial dental plate, rendering it unusable for several months." (1)

When Hudson first sued the three corrections officers (McMillian, Woods, and Mezo), a magistrate concluded that there was no need to use force and awarded Hudson $800 in damages. The Court of Appeals for the Fifth Circuit, in New Orleans, reversed the magistrate's ruling, finding that the use of force was unreasonable—but that the minor injuries that resulted did not rise to the level of an Eighth Amendment violation.

The majority opinion

The U.S. Supreme Court, then, had to determine whether a beating that did not cause "significant injury" still violated the Eighth Amendment's prohibition of cruel and unusual punishment. In a 7 to 2 decision, the Court sided with Hudson. Justice Sandra Day O'Connor wrote the majority opinion:

When prison officials maliciously and sadistically use force to cause harm, contemporary standards of decency always are violated. This is true whether or not significant injury is evident. Otherwise, the Eighth Amendment would permit any physical punishment, no matter how diabolic or inhuman, inflicting less than some arbitrary quantity of injury. Such a result would have been as unacceptable to the drafters of the Eighth Amendment as it is today. (1, at 1000)

That is not to say that every malevolent touch by a prison guard gives rise to a federal cause of action. The Eighth Amendment's prohibition of "cruel and unusual" punishment necessarily excludes from constitutional recognition *de*

minimis (minimal) uses of physical force, provided that the use of force is not of a sort "'repugnant to the conscience of mankind.'" Justice O'Connor concluded that Hudson's injuries were not *de minimis* and thus reversed the judgment of the Court of Appeals.

The dissenting opinion

This case would have been no more than a footnote in the continuing saga of prisoners' rights litigation but for a well-publicized dissenting opinion, authored by Justice Clarence Thomas and signed also by Justice Antonin Scalia. In one of the first opinions written by the newly appointed Justice Thomas, he wrote:

In my view, a use of force that causes only insignificant harm to a prisoner may be immoral, it may be tortuous, it may be criminal, and it may even be remediable under other provisions of the Federal Constitution, but it is not "cruel and unusual punishment." In concluding to the contrary, the Court today goes far beyond our precedents.

Today's expansion of the Cruel and Unusual Punishment Clause beyond all bounds of history and precedent is, I suspect, yet another manifestation of the pervasive view that the Federal Constitution must address all ills of our society. Abusive behavior by prison guards is deplorable conduct that properly evokes outrage and contempt. But that does not mean that it is invariably unconstitutional. The Eighth Amendment is not, and should not be turned into, a National Code of Prison Regulation. To reject the notion that the infliction of concededly "minor" injuries can be considered either "cruel" or "unusual" "punishment" (much less cruel *and* unusual punishment) is not to say that it amounts to acceptable conduct. Rather, it is to recognize that primary responsi-

Petitions Filed in U.S. District Courts by State and Federal Prisoners

Type of Petition	1977	1978	1979	1980	1981	1982	1983	1984	1985	1986	1987	1988	1989
Total	19,537	21,924	23,001	23,287	27,711	29,303	30,775	31,107	33,468	33,765	37,316	38,839	41,481
Petitions by federal prisoners	4,691	4,955	4,499	3,713	4,104	4,328	4,354	4,526	6,262	4,432	4,519	5,130	5,577
Petitions by state prisoners	14,846	16,969	18,502	19,574	23,607	24,975	26,421	26,581	27,206	29,333	32,797	33,709	35,895

SOURCE: *Sourcebook of Criminal Justice Statistics, 1991*, U.S. Dept. of Justice, Bureau of Justice Statistics, Table 5.69, p. 555.

bility for preventing and punishing such conduct rests not with the Federal Constitution but with the laws and regulations of the various states. (1, at 1010)

The first application of the Eighth Amendment to prison conditions beyond the actual sentence was in 1976 in a Supreme Court decision that Justice Thomas referred to as having "cut the Eighth Amendment loose from its historical moorings" (2). The opinion by Justice Thomas reflects a conservative view of the prohibition of cruel and unusual punishment. He argued that the Eighth Amendment requires a more significant injury than Hudson was able to demonstrate. But Justice O'Connor, in expressing the majority opinion, took a different view:

. . . we hold that whenever prison officials stand accused of using excessive physical force in violation of the Cruel and Unusual Punishment Clause, the core judicial inquiry is . . . whether force was applied in a good-faith effort to maintain or restore discipline, or maliciously and sadistically to cause harm. . . . The absence of serious injury is . . . relevant to the Eighth Amendment inquiry, but does not end it. (1, at 999)

Some argue that Justice Thomas's dissenting opinion in *Hudson v. McMillian* reflects frustration with state inmates' use of the federal courts to pursue claims of constitutional violations. The table shows the number of petitions filed in U.S. district courts by state and federal prisoners over a twelve-year period.

SOURCES

1. *Hudson v. McMillian*, 112 S.Ct. 995, at 997 (1992).
2. Linda Greenhouse, "High Court Defines New Limit on Force by a Prison Guard," *The New York Times*, February 26, 1992, p. 1.

QUESTIONS FOR DISCUSSION

1. Do you agree with Justice Thomas that the Cruel and Unusual Punishment Clause should apply only to the sentence itself and not to prison conditions? Why or why not?
2. What are some punishments that prison officials could use against inmates, either male or female, that would not cause "significant injury" and therefore not be cruel and unusual punishment according to Justice Thomas's opinion?
3. Do you think the Supreme Court should be deciding matters of prison discipline and inmate treatment?

AND YOU THOUGHT RODNEY KING HAD PROBLEMS....

Paul Conrad © 1992, Los Angeles Times. Reprinted with permission.

medicine testify about the connection between overcrowding and a facility's ability to meet basic needs. Inmates testify about the misery of cramped cells, sleeping on cement floors, clogged toilets, overtaxed medical facilities, lack of recreational services, and inability to protect themselves from other inmates.

Four factors must be taken into consideration before overcrowding can be held to amount to cruel and unusual punishment:

1. The actual level of crowding, that is, the cubic footage of living space designated for each inmate
2. The location of the inmates' beds, for example whether mattresses are placed on the floors of cells, dayrooms, corridors, or elsewhere
3. How much time away from their sleeping quarters inmates are afforded on a daily basis, and how much space these other areas provide
4. In the case of pretrial confinement, its duration

If crowding is extreme, if the sleeping arrangements are unsanitary, and if deprivations endure for many weeks, a finding of unconstitutional crowding is likely.[37]

"Correctional administrators had long been free to dispense administrative punishments for disciplinary infractions."

Due Process in Disciplinary Proceedings. Corrections administrators had long been at liberty to dispense administrative punishments (punishments within punishment) to prisoners for disciplinary infractions. Now the Supreme Court has introduced due-process guarantees: Inmates are entitled to (1) notice of the charges brought against them, (2) the chance to prepare a defense, (3) an impartial hearing, and (4) the opportunity to present witnesses and evidence on their behalf.[38] The inmate also has to be provided with a written statement of a hearing board's statement.[39] (More recently, in the case of *Ponte v. Real* [1985], the Supreme Court held that prison officials must provide an explanation to inmates who are denied the opportunity to have a desired witness at their hearing.[40]) The case of *Vitek v. Jones* (1980) extended the requirement of due process to inmates about to be transferred from prisons to mental hospitals.[41]

Sixth Amendment: Legal Services in Prison.[42] Nothing can be as frustrating to a prisoner as the helplessness confinement entails. In the past, prisoners were barred from access to legal services after confinement. Such access became one of the principal demands during the riots of the 1960s and 1970s, of which Attica was the most symbolic and costly.

In 1968, the Supreme Court ruled in the case of *Johnson v. Avery* that prisoners have a right to consult "jail house lawyers" for advice when assistance from trained professionals is not available.[43] Building on this precedent, a number of other standards have since been established to enhance legal assistance to prisoners. *In re Harrell* (1970) gave prisoners the right to meet with counsel for reasonable lengths of time.[44] In *Taylor v. Sterrett* (1976), a prisoner's right to correspond with his or her attorney was recognized, although the court allowed attorney–client letters to be opened for contraband checks, but not to be read.[45] In 1977, in *Bounds v. Smith*, the Supreme Court imposed on the states the duty of assisting inmates in the preparation and filing of legal papers.[46] Such assistance can be provided through trained personnel knowledgeable in the law, or via law libraries in each institution. In *Guajardo v. Estelle* (1977), the Court ruled that indigent defendants must be provided with stamps for the purpose of legal correspondence.[47]

Some of the decisions, while recognizing the prisoners' right to legal assistance, have nevertheless delimited them. Thus, in *O'Brien v. United States* (1967) and *Weatherford v. Bursey* (1977), the Court decided that conversations between inmates and their lawyers could be monitored, although any evidence obtained through such a process could not be used in court.[48] And in *United States v. Gouveia* (1984), the Court held that indigent inmates do not have the right to an appointed lawyer unless judicial proceedings have been initiated.[49] While this may put a damper on excessive litigation, it impedes an inmate's capacity to initiate judicial proceedings in the first place when there is just cause.

The Impact of the Prisoners' Rights Movement

The prisoners' rights movement has had an enormous impact on American corrections. The developmental stage in which it was necessary for the U.S. Supreme Court to set policy for correctional institutions is over; now federal district courts are busy implementing these mandates. As of January 1, 1992, forty states, plus the District of Columbia, Puerto Rico, and the U.S. Virgin Islands, are under court order (or consent decree) to limit populations and/or improve conditions of confinement. Some of these court orders are applicable to the entire correctional system, others to major institutions.[50] In many states the federal courts have appointed special masters or monitors who supervise the management of institutions as they move toward compliance with court orders. Only five states have not been under court order with respect to prison conditions.

"As of January 1, 1992, forty states plus the District of Columbia, Puerto Rico, and the Virgin Islands are under court order to limit prison populations."

Unfortunately, conditions in jails have been even worse than those in prisons. As Table 14.2 indicates, 142 jail systems were under court order in 1990 to limit jail populations, and 128 were ordered to correct specific conditions. The impact of these orders has been immense.

According to James Jacobs, the prisoners' rights movement has

- contributed to the bureaucratization of the prison
- produced a new generation of administrators
- expanded the procedural protections available to prisoners
- heightened public awareness of prison conditions
- politicized prisoners and heightened their expectations
- demoralized prison staff
- made it more difficult to maintain control over prisoners
- contributed to a professional movement within corrections to establish national standards[51]
- vastly increased prison construction by attacking prison overcrowding

The Rebirth of Retribution Philosophy

The prisoners' rights movement was one of two factors that changed the nature of American corrections. The other was the rebirth in the mid-1970s of retribution in the form of the just-deserts model (see Chapter 13). As sentencing became oriented toward proportionate prison sentences, corrections became more punitive and custodial. Most rehabilitative programs in prisons, already discredited, were abandoned. Prisoners were "doing time" in proportion to the seriousness of their crime; they were not there to be rehabilitated or to be reformed. This more punitive attitude had an unfortunate consequence: Legislators passed more punitive sentencing laws, and parole boards became more reluctant to grant parole or were abolished altogether. The result was a steep increase in prison populations, filling the prisons that had been constructed as a consequence of prisoners' rights suits.

INSTITUTIONAL CORRECTIONS TODAY

Today there are two categories of prison facilities—detention and correctional. **Detention facilities** normally do not house convicted inmates and are not tech-

detention facility
Facility that houses persons arrested and undergoing processing, awaiting trial, or awaiting transfer to a correctional facility.

TABLE 14.2 Jurisdictions under Court Order to Reduce Population or to Improve Conditions of Confinement, 1989 and 1990

| | Number of Jurisdictions with Large Jail Populations | | | | | |
| | Total | | Ordered to limit population | | Not Ordered to limit population | |
	1989	1990	1989	1990	1989	1990
Total	508	508	134	142	374	366
Jurisdictions under Court Order Citing Specific Conditions of Confinement	156	152	125	128	31	24
Subject of court order:						
Crowded living units	127	128	115	119	12	9
Recreational facilities	71	67	55	56	18	11
Medical facilities or services	60	50	45	41	15	9
Visitation practices or policies	51	42	40	37	11	5
Disciplinary procedures or policies	49	32	39	25	10	7
Food service	36	36	29	30	7	6
Administrative segregation procedures or policies	40	26	33	23	7	3
Staffing patterns	57	51	47	43	10	8
Grievance procedures or policies	44	34	35	28	9	6
Education or training programs	27	16	20	14	7	2
Fire hazards	27	14	24	11	3	3
Counseling programs	24	20	17	17	7	3
Inmate classification	47	37	38	32	9	5
Library services	51	50	36	41	15	9
Other	14	14	10	11	4	3
Totality of conditions	38	37	33	34	5	3

SOURCE: Bureau of Justice Statistics, *Jail Inmates, 1990* (Washington, D.C.: Bureau of Justice Statistics, 1991), p. 3.

correctional facility
Facility where convicted offenders serve their sentence; includes county jails and state and federal prisons.

nically correctional facilities. They house persons arrested and undergoing processing, awaiting trial, or awaiting transfer to a correctional facility after conviction. **Correctional facilities,** where convicted offenders serve their sentence, include county jails and state and federal prisons. Those convicted of misdemeanors normally serve sentences of not more than one year in county jails. But there are exceptions to the rule. Many jails operated by counties and cities serve two purposes. They house those awaiting trial or transfer, and also hold convicts serving misdemeanor sentences. Moreover, because of overcrowding in state prisons, many states have found it necessary to house inmates sentenced for felony offenses in county jails. Local variations cloud the distinction even further. Riker's Island in New York City serves not only as the jail for all the boroughs of the city, but also as a prison for those serving longer state sentences. A few states call some of their prisons "houses of detention," but the basic differences remain: County jails are intended for the temporary detention of prisoners and for persons serving sentences for misdemeanors; federal and state prisons are intended for felons, whose sentences are for longer than one year.

"County jails are intended for those undergoing temporary detention or serving misdemeanor sentences; federal and state prisons are intended for felons."

Jails

jail
Place of confinement administered by local officials and designed to hold persons for more than 48 hours but usually less than one year.

Jails are generally defined as facilities administered by local officials and designed to hold persons for more than forty-eight hours but usually less than one year. There are over 3,000 jails of various sizes in the United States. A jail in one state may be as large as the entire prison system of another state. The men's central jail of Los Angeles has a rated capacity of 5,136 inmates, and the Cook County Jail in Chicago has a rated capacity of 4,600 inmates. Many jails in rural counties, by contrast, house but a few prisoners and operate with a fee system, under which the county government pays a modest amount of money for each prisoner per day. (Other jails operate on regular and fixed budgets.)

Criminal justice specialists generally consider the conditions in jails to be inferior to those in prisons, since county governments have comparatively fewer resources than state governments. Most jails are overcrowded, underfunded, and unsanitary; have few services or programs for inmates; and rarely separate dangerous from nondangerous offenders.[52]

At mid-year 1991, local jails in the United States held an estimated 426,479 persons, a 5.2-percent increase from 1990. The average daily jail population for the year ending June 28, 1991, was 422,609, a 3.6-percent increase since 1990. A survey of jails conducted by the Bureau of Justice Statistics found that

- during the year ending June 28, 1991, there were nearly 20 million jail admissions and releases
- men constituted 91 percent and women 9 percent of all jail inmates. Whites were 41 percent of the local jail population, blacks were 43 percent; Hispanics were 14.2 percent
- unconvicted inmates (those on trial or awaiting arraignment or trial) were 51 percent of the adults being held in jails; convicted inmates (those awaiting or serving a sentence or those returned to jail for violating probation or parole) were 49 percent
- jails were operating at 101 percent of capacity in 1991, down from 104 percent in 1990
- there were 505 jurisdictions with at least 100 jail inmates as an average daily population in the most recent census (1988). In 1991, these jurisdictions operated 823 jails, which held a total 343,702 inmates or about 81 percent of all jail inmates in the country

In the 505 jurisdictions with at least 100 jail inmates, 546 inmate deaths were reported for the year ending June 28, 1991. Deaths resulted from (1) natural causes other than AIDS (51%); (2) suicide (34%); and (3) diseases related to AIDS (15%).[53]

The movement to deinstitutionalize mental patients, begun in the 1960s, created an additional burden for the criminal justice system, especially for jails. It was demonstrated in a study of county jails in New Jersey in the 1980s that 10.9 percent of inmates had a history of mental hospitalization. That figure did not include inmates who were confined on special tiers reserved for those exhibiting grossly bizarre, irrational, or violent behavior patterns.[54] The inmates on these segregated tiers were even more likely to have some history of mental institutionalization.

Jail staff, whether law enforcement or corrections employees, cannot be expected to have the expertise to deal with such significant mental health problems.[55] Experts argue that if public policy requires jail administrators to address the problems of emotionally disturbed and mentally ill offenders, a far better program of identification, diagnosis, treatment, and case management at release is necessary.

Prisons

Prisons are federal or state penal institutions in which offenders serve sentences in excess of one year. For the most part, both state and federal prisons have been blessed with better management than jails and often with better education, recreation, and employment training programs.[56] But this is not too surprising. After all, prisons are larger, have many more inmates, and thus have much bigger budgets. A prison normally has three distinct custody levels for inmates, based on an assessment of their perceived dangerousness: maximum danger, medium danger, and minimum danger. Maximum security prisons are designed to hold the most violent, dangerous, and aggressive inmates. They have high concrete walls or double-perimeter razor wire fences, gun towers with armed officers, and strategically placed electronic monitors. Every state has one or several maxi-

"There is no emergency. There is, rather, an ongoing condition that must be recognized by the state. County jails are bursting at their seams . . . ."
Judge William A. Dreier, *The New York Times*, April 30, 1992, p. B7.

prison
Federal or state penal institution in which offenders serve sentences longer than one year.

mum security prisons. The Illinois State Penitentiary near Joliet, Illinois, is typical of a state institution; the United States Penitentiary at Marion, Illinois, typifies a maximum security federal prison.

Medium security prisons house inmates who are considered less dangerous or escape prone than those in maximum security facilities. These structures typically have no high outside wall, only a series of fences. Many medium security inmates are housed in large dormitories rather than cells.

Minimum security prisons hold inmates who are considered the lowest security risks. Very often these institutions operate without armed officers and without perimeter walls or fences. The typical inmate in such an institution has proved trustworthy in the correctional setting, is nonviolent, and/or is serving a short prison sentence.

Federal Prison System

The federal correctional system is operated by the Federal Bureau of Prisons. Its institutions house prisoners convicted of federal crimes. It became a professionally run system in 1929, when Sanford Bates, a Massachusetts corrections official, was appointed its director (he served until 1937). He was charged with reorganizing an institutional system long troubled by political domination, official incompetence, and corruption. The federal correctional system was reconstituted as the Federal Bureau of Prisons in 1930. At that time there were only five federal institutions: three penitentiaries and two reformatories, one for men and one for women. Today there is a federal system of more than thirty diversified institutions and facilities containing over 71,000 adults and youths, of which most are classified as medium or minimum security. All personnel working for the Bureau of Prisons are under civil service, salaries are competitive, and tenure and promotion are based on merit.[57]

Due to the nature of federal criminal law, prisoners in most federal prisons have different profiles from those in state institutions. Federal prisons contain more white-collar offenders than state facilities. Over the last decade, the number and percentage of drug offenders in federal prisons have been increasing. In 1980, drug law violators made up 27 percent of all federal admissions. In 1990, it was 47 percent. The typical federal drug law offender is (1) male, (2) about age 30, (3) most likely to be white, and (4) has a 7-percent chance of opiate use or addiction and a 14-percent chance of current or past abuse of other drugs.[58]

State Prison Systems

State correctional institutions for adult inmates include a wide variety of prisons, penitentiaries, reformatories, industrial institutions, prison farms, and halfway houses. Over half of the nation's inmates are in institutions with average daily populations of more than 1,000 prisoners.

As a rule, felony offenders serve only in state facilities, but at the end of 1991, nineteen states reported a total of 12,225 state prisoners held in local jails or other facilities because of crowding in state facilities. Three states—Louisiana, New Jersey, and Tennessee—accounted for more than half of the prisoners sentenced to prison but incarcerated locally. Overall, 1.5 percent of the state prison population was confined in local jails on December 31, 1991, because of prison overcrowding.[59]

In 1991, persons sentenced for drug offenses made up 22 percent of state prison inmates with no known prior sentence to probation or incarceration. This was a larger percentage than for any other offense.[60]

Institutions for Women

"The women's prison is not merely a version of prisons for men."

Until the early nineteenth century, women convicts were imprisoned in institutions designed primarily for male prisoners. In some prisons they were housed in separate quarters. The initial step toward the establishment of a system of separate prisons for women was taken in 1835, when New York founded the Mount Pleasant Female Prison (closed in 1865), which was administratively attached to neighboring Sing Sing, a prison for men. This was the first and only penal institution for women established before the great era of prison construction of the late nineteenth century. The first women's prison to be built in that era was the Women's Prison of Indiana (1873).

During the twentieth century, women inmates have been incarcerated exclusively in women's prisons. These institutions have tended to be smaller and less threatening in appearance and operation than male prisons (no high walls and guard towers, and less regimentation). Yet, being smaller, they also lack many of the facilities of male institutions.

Until recently, women's institutions and their inmates had received little attention in the scholarly literature. In a review of the research on women's prisons, Nicole Hahn Rafter examines the differences between men's and women's prisons. She attributes the historical neglect of women's prisons in part to the fact that over time women have comprised only a small fraction of the total prison population. However, this lack of attention is also the product of two commonly held assumptions: that the development of the women's prison system and the experiences of women inmates closely resemble those of men; and that, if different, the evolution of the women's prison system and female experience of incarceration are irrelevant to mainstream corrections because they can shed little light on the prison system as a whole. Rafter proposes that neither assumption is correct.

She points out that during the first stage in the development of the women's system (1790–1870), female penal units outwardly resembled male penitentiaries, but in some respects their inmates received inferior care. During the second stage (1870–1935), strenuous and often successful efforts were made to establish an entirely new type of prison, the women's reformatory, in which women would receive care more appropriate to their "feminine" nature. Yet by institutionalizing differential treatment, the reformatories legitimized a tradition of care that was inherently unequal. In the third stage (1935 to present), the women's prison system continued to evolve in ways that perpetuated the older traditions of differential treatment. The women's prison is not merely a version of prisons for men. Nor is the history of incarceration of women irrelevant to an understanding of the prison system as a whole.[61]

While still very small in comparison with the male rate of imprisonment,[62] female imprisonment has been increasing at a fast pace. From 1980 to 1989, the male prison population increased by 112 percent, the female by 202 percent.[63] In 1990, for the first time since 1981, the number of male inmates increased at a faster rate than the number of female inmates.[64] In total, 43,845 women were imprisoned in state and federal correctional institutions throughout the United States at year-end 1990.

Comparable increases were experienced in the female jail incarceration rates. The number of women in jails increased from 15,652 in 1983 to 37,253 in 1990. The number of violent female offenders had declined by 8 percent. One in three women was jailed for drug-related offenses in 1989, compared with one in eight in 1983.[65] Both in jail and in prison, about two-thirds of women had children under age 18, and four out of five imprisoned mothers had their children with them at the time of their arrest.

The issues and challenges facing women's prisons are complex. Institutions for women need to receive funding for starting or expanding educational, vocational, and psychological programs. Experts argue that women's prisons must devise classification systems and institutional practices and procedures that are appropriate for female offenders. Prison policies for such institutions should be gender-specific and not simply "borrowed" from male institutions.[66] Yet, advances in female corrections may have implications for male corrections.

(Top) Minimum security prisons like this one in Pleasanton, California, often do not even have armed officers. (Middle) Medium-security prisons, like this one at LaGrange, Kentucky, have more relaxed dormitory-style living arrangements. (Bottom) Maximum-security prisons like this one emphasize control, even inside the buildings.

TORTURE AND ABUSE IN PRISONS AROUND THE WORLD

A detailed report of one country's human rights abuses in prisons included this list of recommendations:

1. The use of physical restraints should be abolished.
2. Outdoor exercise should be allowed at least once a day.
3. Prison administration has an obligation to protect inmates from violence by other inmates.
4. Incarceration of illegal aliens for periods often exceeding a year in duration, when no crime has been committed, should end.
5. Denial of access to reading matter as a disciplinary measure should end. (1)

Which country allows physical restraints, denies access to reading matter, restricts inmate privilege to exercise, and incarcerates aliens for over a year just because they are aliens? If your guess was the United States, you're right. As we travel the world and note the wretched conditions in other country's prisons, it is worth remembering that the conditions in our own state and federal institutions often leave a great deal to be desired. Approximately forty state prison systems in the United States are under some form of court order regarding prison conditions.

But no matter how bad U.S. conditions may seem, a look at the rest of the world can humble even the most ardent American prison reformer. Amnesty International, a human rights organization, has re-

ported that nearly 3,200 prisoners of conscience—political prisoners—remain in custody in sixty-five countries. And prisoners are being tortured in more than 100 countries (2). In Asia, inmates are subjected to severe psychological abuse and whipped with bamboo sticks; women prisoners are raped in many cases. African prisoners are reportedly beaten on the bottoms of the feet. In Latin America, it is not uncommon for prison inmates to be forced to eat and drink excrement (3). Here are some other human rights abuses that have been documented:

China

In China, Asia Watch has documented the use of electric shock, beatings, and solitary confinement in the case of political prisoners. Malnutrition and denial of access to medical treatment appear common. Wei Jingsheng, a student activist in 1978–1979, has spent the last thirteen years in solitary confinement. A more recent example is Wang Juntao, who was sentenced to thirteen years for his role in the 1989 Tiananmen Square protests. In 1992 he charged that prison officials had illegally confiscated his notebooks, tape recorder, and money, and that the hepatitis he contracted in prison was not being treated (4).

Iraq

The treatment prisoners receive and the conditions in detention centers and prisons in Iraq are inconsistent with any notion of human rights. Iraq holds thousands of political prisoners, most of whom were detained and imprisoned without

charges or trial. Reports of inmate torture are widespread.

Iran

Tales of daily torture of prisoners held in pretrial detention in Iran continue. Inmates are beaten on the slightest pretext. One political prisoner described being strapped to a bed face down and beaten with whips and cables. An interrogator would hold a pistol to his neck while a guard fired shots in the air. Hundreds of political prisoners remain in prison, held indefinitely without charge or trial.

Malawi

In the former British colony, prisoners are reported to be housed in unimaginable conditions. Inmates are kept in leg irons, and there is evidence of severe beatings and use of electric shock. Reports have been made of gross violations of minimal standards of human dignity, such as cramming 285 prisoners into one cell and using electric cattle prods against women prisoners (5).

Mexico

In Mexico, torture of detainees appears to be a common practice of state and federal judicial police in an effort to extract confessions. Techniques include psychological torture, beatings, electric shock, forcing carbonated water and chili pepper into the nose, and near suffocation, either in water or by placing a plastic bag containing ammonia or another irritant over the head of the suspect. Prison conditions are reported to be harsh, with severe overcrowding and inadequate sanitary facilities. In an armed confrontation between prison gangs, eighteen people were killed—and prison officials had allowed the arms to be smuggled in (6).

Venezuela

Venezuela's Justice Minister Jose Mendoza admitted in 1992 that prisoners "are constantly mistreated and tortured" in prisons. The prison system has a capacity of 15,000 inmates and a population of 31,000, only 30 percent of whom actually have been sentenced. The severe overcrowding contributes to outbreaks of cholera, yellow fever, and malaria (7).

India

A student volunteer at a human rights documentation center was arrested in 1991 and held without bail or charges for a year. Friends testify that he was tortured very badly. A *New York Times* report noted: "Torturing suspects has become part of the police's daily routine throughout India, where hundreds if not thousands of people have died from beatings in recent years and women are regularly raped in jail cells" (8).

Brazil

In October 1992, the "worst prison violence in Brazil's history" occurred when a fight between two inmates escalated into a riot. Some 340 police officers were sent in to control the riot. They attacked with shotguns and machine guns; police dogs savagely attacked inmates as well. At least 111 prisoners died, and a Human Rights Watch worker on the scene said that many of the deaths were the result of "deliberate and systematic executions" (9).

Amnesty International was founded in 1961 and has worked for more than thirty years to document cases of torture, executions, "disappearances," and unfair trials around the world. Other national and international groups do similar work. But they face many problems, and not all of the problems are at the government level. In some countries, one barrier to effective reform is the lack of support from citizens. In one example of citizen attitudes toward prisoners, a Brazilian press assertion that animals in Brazil's zoos get better care than prisoners in Brazil's jails was challenged by a São Paulo resident. She wrote to the magazine: "We should not forget that the animals in the zoo are not criminals" (10).

SOURCES

1. Human Rights Watch, *Prison Conditions in the United States* (New York: Human Rights Watch, 1991), pp. 12–15.
2. Amnesty International, *Amnesty International Report: 1991* (New York: Amnesty International, 1991).
3. Anita Parlow, "Doctor's Role in Combating Torture: U.S. Physicians Being Called Upon to Help Stop Violence around the World," *The Washington Post,* August 25, 1992, p. Z9.
4. David R. Schweisberg, "Dissident's Wife Appeals to Human Rights Groups," *United Press International,* August 15, 1992.
5. "Malawi Rejects Amnesty Torture Reports," The Reuters Library Report, September 3, 1992.
6. "Torture a Common Practice in Mexico; Official Measures Failing to Prevent Abuses, Says Amnesty," Latin American Newsletters, Ltd., 1992.
7. "Venezuela: Justice Minister Admits to Torture in Prisons," International Press Service, July 22, 1992.
8. Edward A. Gargan, "India Rights Group's Cry: Police Rape and Torture," *The New York Times,* October 14, 1992, p. A3.
9. James Brooke, "After Prison Riot, Brazilians Hear of Police Atrocities," *The New York Times,* October 5, 1992, p. A3.
10. James Brooke, "Brazil's Police Enforce Popular Punishment: Death," *The New York Times,* November 4, 1992, p. A6.
11. United Nations Economic and Social Council Resolution 663 (XXIV), 1957.

QUESTIONS FOR DISCUSSION

1. Many countries have bound themselves morally to abide by

AUNG SAN SUU KYI
MYANMAR
Under house arrest because of her non-violent political beliefs

MULUGETTA MOSISSA
ETHIOPIA
Jailed for over 10 years because of his ethnic origin

REVEREND LAWFORD IMUNDE
KENYA
Six years' imprisonment for writing opinions in his diary

MOHAMED SRIFI
MOROCCO
Sentenced to 30 years in jail for his peaceful political views

VERA CHIRWA
MALAWI
Jailed for believing that her country should be run differently

ERHAN TUSKAN
TURKEY
Imprisoned for publishing political writings in his magazine

Victims of human rights abuse: some of the real faces behind the stories.

the standards of humane confinement contained in the United Nations *Standard Minimum Rules for the Treatment of Prisoners* (11). How active should the United Nations become in ensuring compliance with its international standards?
2. What role, if any, should the United States play in leading the effort to humanize the world's prison systems?
3. Has the United States ever held political prisoners? Cite examples.

Co-correctional Facilities

It seemed like a step backward when, in 1971, the Federal Correctional Institute (Fort Worth, Texas) became the first co-correctional institution. But in this institution men and women were not haphazardly thrown together; a structured program had been worked out. Men and women, segregated at night, participated in joint daytime programs of work, education, recreation, and meals. Infraction of the rules led to transfer to a separate institution. Observers have credited co-correctional institutions with creating an atmosphere more like the one to which the inmates will return upon release. Yet, most of the state co-correctional institutions have now been closed. Both custodial and treatment staff have had difficulty creating and administering rules. Ensuring reasonable restraints on physical contacts has been a consistent problem. Notwithstanding the problems, the federal prison system continues to play a leading role in operating co-correctional institutions. Most women inmates in the federal system serve their sentences in such facilities.[67]

THE SIZE AND COST OF THE CORRECTIONS ENTERPRISE

When politicians and citizens call for longer prison sentences to control the "crime epidemic," they rarely consider the resulting burden on the taxpayer. Yet it is precisely this burden that has made the American correctional system an incredibly costly enterprise.

The Size of the System

America's correctional system is a vast enterprise, in terms of the number of people it processes and services; the number of employees required for inmate care, custody, and control; the cost of outside contracting required to maintain and constantly enlarge facilities; and the burden to the taxpayer.

"If we continue to incarcerate people at our present rate, there will be more of us in than out by the year 2053. That is simple arithmetic . . . ."
Warren I. Cikins, The Brookings Institution, June 14, 1992.

The Incarcerated Population.   The number of people incarcerated in America's jails and prisons has steadily increased. Over a century ago, in 1880, the imprisonment rate in state institutions was 61 per 100,000 citizens.[68] Today over 500 persons per 100,000 citizens are incarcerated at any moment. That means that about 1 in every 200 Americans is incarcerated at any particular point in time (see Table 14.3).

During the decade from 1980 to 1990, per capita incarceration rates grew most rapidly in the Northeast, increasing by 167 percent, and in the West, up by nearly 163 percent. The per capita incarceration rates climbed 119 percent in the Midwest and 68 percent in the South.[69]

California has the largest prison population in the United States, and accounted for more than 17 percent of the increase nationwide during 1990.[70] At the end of 1990, about one in eight prisoners nationwide was confined in a California institution. California officials project that by 1995 the adult prison population will exceed 110,000. Another 100,000 will be held in jails and juvenile facilities. Nevada, which has the highest rate of imprisonment in the nation (420 prisoners in the state system per 100,000 population), is expected to double its prison population by 1995, at which time Nevada's imprisonment rate will approach 700 per 100,000.[71]

"The challenge of this decade is going to be moving corrections beyond bricks and bars."
Joseph D. Lehman, Pennsylvania commissioner of corrections, June 14, 1992.

The Nonincarcerated Population.   In addition to the offenders in correctional institutions, a far larger number of offenders are sentenced to noninstitutional or

TABLE 14.3 Number of Persons Incarcerated in the United States[*]

Prison Population	Number	Source
Federal prisons	71,608	(year-end count 1991) Bureau of Justice Statistics, *Prisoners in 1991*, (Washington, D.C., 1991)
State prisons	751,806	(year-end count 1991) Bureau of Justice Statistics, *Prisoners in 1991*, (Washington, D.C., 1991)
Jails	426,479	(one-day count mid-1991) Bureau of Justice Statistics, *National Update*, (Washington, D.C., 1992)
Children in custody	99,617	(mid-1990 one-day count) National Council on Crime and Delinquency, *Juveniles Taken Into Custody* 1990 Report (San Francisco: NCCD, 1991)
Total	1,349,510	

[*]These figures do not include the 37,842 persons on average arrested daily for index crimes and the many more arrested for misdemeanors and disorderly charges, most of whom are being detained on any given day (usually for several days) in the country's 13,500 police lockups or holding pens. Todd Clear and George Cole, *American Corrections* (Monterey, Calif.: Brooks/Cole, 1986), p. 198

community corrections. With 2,670,234 people on probation and 531,407 on parole at the end of 1990 over 4 million adult men and women were estimated as being serviced by the correctional system. This means one in fifty-two U.S. adult residents.[72]

Incarceration Rates Worldwide. Columnist Tom Wicker of *The New York Times* bestowed on the United States the "Iron Medal" for being the world's leader in rates of imprisonment.[73] With 426 Americans imprisoned per 100,000 of our population (1991), the American imprisonment rate has far outstripped that of South Africa (333) and of the former Soviet Union (268 prisoners and work-camp inmates). The rate of incarceration in the Netherlands is only 8 percent that of the United States (40 per 100,000) (Figure 14.1). Our rate of incarceration is far higher than the rates of other comparable Western countries. In the United States, 25.8 people per 100,000 of the population are incarcerated for robbery; Canada incarcerates 15.5, and England only 4.3. For burglary and theft, the rates are similar (see Figure 14.1).[74]

These comparisons may make the United States look bad. Bud if we were to base comparative prison rates not on population (per capita), but rather on the volume of crime (measured by arrest rates), we may not deserve the "Iron Medal" after all for then our imprisonment rate is more or less on a par with those of the comparable Western countries like Canada and England (Figure 14.2).

"The United States now incarcerates a greater percentage of its population than any other country in the world."
Marc Mauer, *Americans Behind Bars* (Washington, D.C.: The Sentencing Project, 1991).

The Cost of the System

The correctional system requires nearly one-third of all the resources allocated to the criminal justice system, in terms of employment (450,000 staff = 32% of total criminal justice employment)[75] and expenditures (31% of total criminal justice cost).[76] Annually, it costs over $15 billion to operate the correctional systems of the fifty states, the District of Columbia, and the federal government. To this we must add another $2.6 billion reported to have been spent by forty-two correctional agencies for capital expenditures. The grand total for fiscal year 1991 stands at $18.1 billion.[77] This is a very large public expenditure. But keep in mind that this sum amounts to only 1 percent of all government spending.

FIGURE 14.1 *International and U.S. incarceration rates* (*Source: Americans behind Bars: A Comparison of International Rates of Incarceration* [Washington, D.C.: The Sentencing Project, 1991]. Reprinted with permission.)

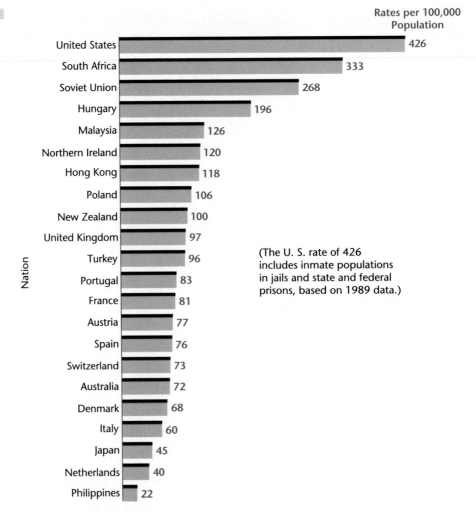

(The U. S. rate of 426 includes inmate populations in jails and state and federal prisons, based on 1989 data.)

Costs per Prisoner.   While there is considerable variation among the states, on average prison officials report that it costs about $20,000 per year to house, feed, clothe, and supervise a prisoner. Because this estimate does not include indirect costs, the true annual expenditure probably exceeds $30,000 per prisoner. The other significant cost is construction. We divide the total construction cost of any one institution by the number of prisoners it houses to get the cost per "bed." This cost may be as low as $7,000 per year for a minimum security prisoner to as high as $155,000 for a maximum security prisoner. (The comparable cost fifty years ago was between $4,000 and $6,000.) Of course, the annual cost of incarcerating just one offender varies from state to state. In 1985, the cost of housing one prisoner in Nevada was $10,873, while a New Mexico prisoner cost an average of $24,700.[78]

"The annual cost of keeping someone in prison is . . . more than twice what it costs to send a student to Harvard for a year." National Commission on Crime and Delinquency, *Crime,* 1987."

During 1990, sixty-two new institutions were opened, and a total of 36,373 beds were added as a result of this new construction: Of these 15,330 were maximum security, 14,811 were medium security, and 6,232 were minimum security. The average construction cost per bed was $47,531.[79]

"It's amazing what we spend to make people worse, but no one will listen much until the budgetary implications start to sink in and the soft on crime political attacks dry up." Jerome Miller, National Center on Institutions and Alternatives, 1990.

Impact on State Budgets.   The enormous cost of imprisonment is just beginning to be felt by the states. For example, Florida recently completed the construction of a 336-person death row and two 900-inmate prisons—yet it has no operating budget to run these facilities.[80] In California, a $300 million state deficit, caused

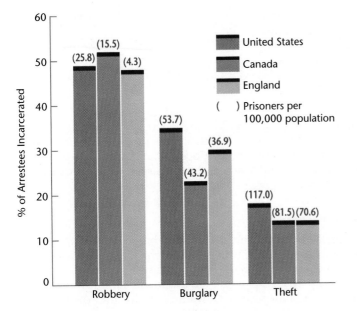

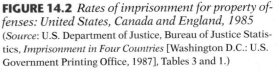

FIGURE 14.2 *Rates of imprisonment for property offenses: United States, Canada and England, 1985* (*Source*: U.S. Department of Justice, Bureau of Justice Statistics, *Imprisonment in Four Countries* [Washington D.C.: U.S. Government Printing Office, 1987], Tables 3 and 1.)

in part by uncontrolled rising costs of the prison system, resulted in a cutback in funds for public education and medical services for the poor. Budgetary battles have begun in which important state services for children, the elderly, the sick, and the poor are being cut back to pay for prisons.[81] While it may be too early to discern any particular trends, it is notable that in some states new political alliances have been formed between liberal and conservative legislators. Liberal legislators, in general, support humane correctional policies and have been less punitive. Conservative legislators, on the whole, have supported more punitive imprisonment policies. Yet with the enormous budget increases required for new prison construction and prisoner maintenance, conservative legislators, ever intent on cutting costs, have joined their liberal colleagues in opposing new prison construction. The result has been a search for cost-beneficial alternatives (see Chapter 16), and the privatization of corrections.

"This is the first time in my career that institutions are built and there is no money to operate them."
Deputy Corrections Secretary Bill Thurber, quoted in *Newsweek*, May 18, 1992, p. 63.

PRIVATIZATION OF CORRECTIONS

Frustration over high rates of recidivism and spiraling prison maintenance costs have prompted policymakers to search for alternatives to government-operated prisons. One such alternative is to contract with private firms that administer "for profit" prisons.[82]

This is a rather revolutionary concept if you consider that, since the Middle Ages, the punishment of offenders has been viewed as the sole prerogative of the sovereign, or the people, whose laws the offender has violated. In modern times the sovereign (the state) exercises this prerogative through the correctional system (the executive branch of government). Can the sovereign (the state) delegate any of its functions to private enterprise? The state can let private entrepreneurs sell postage stamps and deliver mail. It can, and does, let private security perform functions that heretofore were the prerogative of the government police force—always subject to a certain amount of control or supervision by government.[83] And now privatization has entered corrections.[84]

At this point, the private sector is performing a series of functions in the correctional sector:

- financing and constructing prisons
- operating facilities for juveniles
- operating facilities for adults
- providing work for prisoners
- providing specific contractual services to prisons, for example health care and vocational education for the inmates and training for the staff.[85]

The first private "for profit" prison was established in 1975 when RCA, under contract with the Commonwealth of Pennsylvania, opened a training school for delinquents in Weaversville. When James O. Finckenauer evaluated this facility, he found it "better staffed, organized, and equipped than any other program of its size."[86] In 1987, approximately 3,000 adults were incarcerated in privately run prisons. Private juvenile facilities were in operation in twelve states.[87]

Effectiveness of Privatization

"The move toward privatization of adult correctional facilities in America is more than a passing fad."
David K. Burright, *FBI Law Enforcement Bulletin*, February 1990.

A report prepared for the National Institute of Justice, based on a survey of private-sector corrections in all states, is optimistic about the future of private prisons. It was found that idleness is reduced, prison administration has access to private-sector economic expertise, the prison environment is improved, prisoners may earn real wages and obtain vocational training useful after their release, taxpayers benefit because the wages of prisoners help offset the cost of incarceration, and victims have a better chance of obtaining compensation from prisoners' earnings.[88]

A study of the issue of privatization by Samuel Jan Brakel explored how inmates perceived the effectiveness of one private institution in Tennessee. He found that, by and large, prisoners do not care who runs the institution. Their paramount interest is in the quality of conditions and decent treatment of prisoners.[89]

Trends in Privatization

In recent years there has been a growth in correctional contracting to private agencies. A study conducted by Camp and Camp in 1985 for the National Institute of Corrections included responses from fifty-two agencies, representing fifty-four jurisdictions. They found twenty-nine juvenile and thirty-seven adult agencies purchasing thirty-three types of services and/or programs from the private sector. The management of prisons was not in the top ten most frequently used services or programs. Rather, human services were ranked first among those most frequently purchased from private sources. Physicians, health, mental health, community treatment centers, education, drug treatment, college programs, staff training, vocational training, and counseling ranked from two to eleven. Construction of correctional facilities ranked number five for private contracting. Most highly rated for private sector growth in the future are food services, canteen and commissary, vocational training, drug treatment, health services, and recreational therapy.[90]

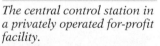

The central control station in a privately operated for-profit facility.

The trend is clearly toward more contracting for correctional services. New Jersey is an example. For the four-year period (end of fiscal year 1984 to end of fiscal year 1987), the State Department of Corrections reported a steady growth in contracted halfway-house services. There were five contracted halfway houses in 1984, seven in 1985 and in 1986, and eight in 1987. New Jersey's correctional agency also contracts for other services: A fifty-bed unit was purchased from an acute care general hospital; psychological testing, urine testing, and data processing are among the other contracted services.[91]

The move toward privatization of corrections raises some troubling questions that to date have not been entirely resolved. Experts agree that the most disturbing and basic question is whether the sovereign right of the people, as represented by their government, to punish those found guilty of violating laws should ever be transferred to private hands. The question is whether the authority to deprive others of their liberty and to coerce them ought to be delegated to non-governmental entities, not whether such persons or groups ought to profit financially from their services. Thus, in the unlikely event that private prison firms were to offer their services free, the ethical case against privatization would not be affected in the least.[92]

Other troubling questions include those asked by Ira P. Robbins[93]:

- What standards will govern the operation of the institution?
- Who will monitor the implementation of the standards?
- Will the public have access to the facility?
- Who will be responsible for maintaining security if the private personnel go on strike?
- Where will the responsibility for prison disciplinary procedures lie?
- Will the company be able to refuse servicing certain inmates, such as those who have contracted AIDS?
- What options will be available to the government if the corporation substantially increases its fees?
- What will happen if the company declares bankruptcy or simply goes out of business because there is not enough profit?

The general reluctance to accept the concept of private correctional institutions may perhaps be offset by a reminder that American corrections, institutional and noninstitutional, owe their origin largely to private entrepreneurship, private concern for convicts, and community action in caring for convicted offenders.

REVIEW

Institutional corrections is only 450 years old. It was meant to be a humane alternative to the brutal punishments of old. The first institutions were the houses of correction (workhouses) of Holland, England, and Pennsylvania. But it was soon apparent that houses of correction did not correct. Penitentiaries were invented, but it was clear that these did not produce penitence. Reformitories replaced penitentiaries, but reformatories did not reform. Nor did the medical-therapeutic model prove to be a cure for the crime problem. Thus, in the 1970s punishment returned to the classic form of being a just desert—retribution.

The bright light in the history of American corrections is the extension of due process guarantees to inmates by the Supreme Court, a result of the prisoners' rights movement.

American corrections today is a vast enterprise. One in every 200 Americans is incarcerated on any given day, and one in fifty-two adult residents is under some form of correctional control. No other country has a system of this scope and size. The staggering cost of maintaining such a pervasive apparatus has put pressure on political leaders to search for more cost-beneficial ways of dealing with the corrections problem.

Notes

1. John Lothrop Motley, *Rise of the Dutch Republic*, vol. III (New York: Harpers, 1880), pp. 612–613. See also Harry Elmer Barnes and Negley K. Teeters, *New Horizons in Criminology*, 2d ed. (Englewood Cliffs, N.J.: Prentice-Hall, 1951), p. 344.

2. Don Terry, "Prisons as Usual," *The New York Times*, September 13, 1992, Section A, p. 1.

3. Thorsten Sellin, *Pioneers in Penology: The Amsterdam Houses of Correction in the 16th and 17th Centuries* (Philadelphia: University of Pennsylvania Press, 1944).

4. Barnes and Teeters, *New Horizons in Criminology*, p. 385.

5. Georg Rusche and Otto Kirchheimer, *Punishment and Social Structure* (New York: Columbia University Press, 1939).

6. George Ives, *A History of Penal Method* (1914); (Montclair, N.J.: Patterson Smith, 1970), p. 104.

7. Thorsten Sellin, "Two Myths in the History of Capital Punishment," *Journal of Criminal Law and Criminology* 50 (1959):114–117.

8. Thorsten Sellin, *Slavery and the Penal System* (New York: Elseiver, 1976), p. 71.

9. Thorsten Sellin, *Slavery and the Penal System*, pp. 77, 101.

10. Geneva Convention Relative to the Treatment of Prisoners of War, August 12, 1949, Art. 22.

11. It is estimated that 100,000 convicts were transported from England to the American colonies and Australia over a period of nearly 200 years. See, for example, J. J. Tobias, *Nineteenth-Century Crime: Prevention and Punishment* (Newton, Mass.: David and Charles, 1972); C. R. Henderson, *Penal and Reformatory Institutions* (New York: Charities, 1910).

12. David Rothman, *The Discovery of the Asylum* (Boston: Little, Brown, 1971), p. 48.

13. Graeme R. Newman, *The Punishment Response* (Philadelphia: Lippincott, 1978), p. 121.

14. See also Dario Melossi and Massimo Pavarini, *The Prison and the Factory: Origins of the Penitentiary System* (Totowa, N.J.: Barnes and Noble, 1981), for a discussion of the U.S. development of penitentiaries in the context of parallel European trends.

15. Harry Elmer Barnes and Negley K. Teeters, *New Horizons in*

Criminology, rev. ed. (New York: Prentice-Hall, 1945), p. 505.

16. See Harry Elmer Barnes, *The Evolution of Penology in Pennsylvania: A Study in American Social History* (Montclair, N.J.: Patterson Smith, 1968).

17. G. A. de Beaumont and A. de Tocqueville, *On the Penitentiary System in the United States and Its Application in France* (1833) (Carbondale, Ill.: Southern Illinois University Press, 1964), p. 59.

18. The New York State Special Commission on Attica, 1972, *Official Report of the New York State Special Commission* (New York: Praeger, 1972), p. 11.

19. Barnes and Teeters, *New Horizons in Criminology*, pp. 523–526. See also Blake McKelvey, *American Prisons: A History of Good Intentions* (Montclair, N.J.: Patterson Smith, 1977), for an historical discussion of American prisons; Alexander W. Pisciotta, "A House Divided: Penal Reform at the Illinois State Reformatory, 1891–1915," *Crime & Delinquency* 37 (1991):165–185; Alexander W. Pisciotta, "Scientific Reform: The 'New Penology' at Elmira, 1876–1900," *Crime and Delinquency* 29(4) (October 1983):613–630.

20. J. Michael Oliverio and James B. Roberts, "The United States Federal Penitentiary at Marion, Illinois: Alcatraz Revisited," *New England Journal on Criminal and Civil Confinement* 16(1) (1990): 21–51. For an effort made to deal with rehabilitating alcoholic recidivists (historical), see Beverly A. Smith, Dennis J. Palumbo, Steven Maynard-Moody, and James P. Levine, "Ireland's Ennis Inebriates' Reformatory: A 19th Century Example of Failed Institutional Reform," *Federal Probation* 53 (1989):53–64.

21. *Gore v. United States*, 357 U.S. 386 (1958), at 393.

22. *Attica: The Official Report of the New York Special Commission on Attica* (McKay Commission Report) (New York: Bantam, 1972); Herman Badillo and Milton Haynes, *Bill of No Rights: Attica and the American Prison System* (New York: Outerbridge and Lazard, 1972). For an astute analysis of conditions leading to prison riots and management proposals for the future, see Edith E. Flynn, "From Conflict Theory to Conflict Resolution: Controlling Collective Violence in Prisons," *American Behavioral Scientist* 23 (1980):745–776. For an overall account of prison riots, see Bert Useem and Peter Kimball, *States of Siege: U.S. Prison Riots, 1971–1986* (New York: Oxford University Press, 1989).

23. "United Nations Standard Minimum Rules for the Treatment of Prisoners," in Center for Human Rights, *Human Rights: A Compilation of International Instruments* (New York: United Nations, 1988), pp. 190–209; Gerhard O. W. Mueller, and Douglas J. Besharov, "The Demands of the Inmates of Attica State Prison and the United Nations Standard Minimum Rules for the Treatment of Prisoners: A Comparison," *Buffalo Law Review* 21 (1972):839–854.

24. See Useem and Kimball, *States of Siege*, for a discussion of prison riots starting with the Attica riots in 1971.

25. James B. Jacobs, "The Prisoners' Rights Movement and Its Impacts, 1960–80," in *Crime and Justice: An Annual Review of Research*, eds. Norval Morris and Michael Tonry, vol. 2. (Chicago: The University of Chicago Press, 1980).

26. *Cooper v. Pate*, 378 U.S. 546 (1964).

27. *Wolff v. McDonnell*, 418 U.S. 539 (1974).

28. See *Wolff v. McDonnell*, at 555.

29. For the impact of the Supreme Court decisions, see Jacobs, "The Prisoners' Rights Movement."

30. *Estelle v. Gamble*, 429 U.S. 97 (1976).

31. *Hutto v. Finney*, 437 U.S. 678 (1978).

32. *Procunier v. Martinez*, 416 U.S. 396 (1974).

33. *Fulwood v. Clemmer*, 206 F. Supp. 370 (1962).

34. *Cruz v. Beto*, 405 U.S. 319 (1972).

35. *Hudson v. Palmer*, 468 U.S. 517 (1984).

36. *Lee v. Downs*, 641 F.2d 1117 (4th Cir., 1981).

37. Claudia Angelos and James B. Jacobs, "Prison Overcrowding and The Law," *Annals*, 478 (1985):100–112. An even more important Eighth Amendment decision dealt with abuse of force. In 1992, Justice Sandra Day O'Connor's opinion for the court in *Hudson v. McMillian* noted: "Beating or other use of excessive force by a prison guard may violate the Constitution even if it does not result in serious injury to the prisoner." *Hudson v. McMillian*, 112 S. Ct. 995 (1992).

38. Frank Schmalleger, *Criminal Justice Today* (Englewood Cliffs, N.J.: Prentice-Hall, 1991).

39. *Wolff v. McDonnell*.

40. *Ponte v. Real*, 471 U.S. 491 (1985).

41. *Vitek v. Jones*, 445 U.S. 480 (1980).

42. See Geoffrey P. Alpert and Neal Miller, "Legal Delivery Systems to Prisoners: A Preliminary Evaluation," in *The Justice System Journal* 4 (1978):9–25 for a review of the cases having an impact on legal services delivery to prisoners while in prison.

43. *Johnson v. Avery*, 393 U.S. 483 (1968); see Dragan Milovanovic and Jim Thomas, "Overcoming the Absurd: Prisoner Litigation as Primitive Rebellion," *Social Problems* (1989): 48–60, for a discussion of the role of jail house lawyers.

44. *In re Harrell*, 87 Cal. Rptr. 504, 470 P.2d 640 (1970).

45. *Taylor v. Sterrett*, 532 F.2d 462 (5th Cir. 1976).

46. *Bounds v. Smith*, 430 U.S. 817, 821 (1977).

47. *Guajardo v. Estelle*, 432 F. Supp. 1373 (S.D. Texas, 1977).

48. *O'Brien v. United States*, 386 U.S. 345 (1967); *Weatherford v. Bursey*, 429 U.S. 545 (1977).

49. *United States v. Gouveia*, 467 U.S. 180 (1984).

50. The National Prison Project, "Status Report: State Prisons and the Courts," *Corrections Digest*, March 19, 1992, pp. 3–9; April 1, 1992, pp. 2–6.

51. James B. Jacobs, "The Prisoners' Rights Movement"; Alfred Blumstein, "American Prisons in a Time of Crisis," in *The American Prison: Issues in Research and Policy*, eds. Lynne Goodstein and Doris Layton MacKenzie (New York: Plenum Press, 1989).

52. Michael T. Charles, Sesha Kethineni, and Jeffrey L. Thompson, "The State of Jails in America," *Federal Probation* 56 (1992):56–62. See also Wayne N. Welsh, Henry N. Pontell, Matthew C. Leone, and Patrick Kinkade, "Jail Overcrowding: An Analysis of Policy Makers' Perceptions," *Justice Quarterly* 7 (1990):339–370. For an historical description, see Lois A. Guyon and Helen Fay Greer, "Calaboose: Small Town Lockup," *Federal Probation* 54 (1990): 58–62.

53. Bureau of Justice Statistics, *Jail Inmates, 1991* (Washington, D.C.: U.S. Department of Justice, June 1992).

54. Freda Adler, "Jails as a Repository for Former Mental Patients," *International Journal of Offender Therapy and Comparative Criminology* 30 (1986):225–236.

55. See John J. Gibbs, "Symptoms of Psychopathology among Jail Prisoners: The Effects of Exposure to the Jail Environment," *Criminal Justice and Behavior* 14 (1987):288–310.

56. See Richard Hawkins and Geoffrey P. Alpert, *American Prison Systems: Punishment and Justice* (Englewood Cliffs, N.J.: Prentice-Hall, 1989).

57. Austin MacCormick, "Adult Correctional Institutions in the United States," *President's Commission on Law Enforcement and Administration of Justice: Consultant's Paper*, 1967, pp. 36–53.

58. Bureau of Justice Statistics, *National Update* (Washington, D.C.: U.S. Department of Justice, January 1992), p. 6.

59. Bureau of Justice Statistics, *Prisoners in 1990* (Washington, D.C.: Bureau of Justice Statistics, May 1991).

60. Bureau of Justice Statistics, *Prisons and Prisoners in the United States* (Washington, D.C.: Bureau of Justice Statistics, 1992), p. 14.

61. Nicole Hahn Rafter, "Prisons for Women, 1790–1980," in *Crime and Justice: An Annual Review of Research*, vol 5, eds. Norval Morris and Michael Tonry (Chicago: University of Chicago Press, 1983).

62. At year-end 1959, 549 men per 100,000 men in the resident population, and 31 women per 100,000 women, were serving a prison sentence of more than one year. Lawrence A. Greenfield and Stephanie Minor-Harper, *Women in Prison*, Bureau of Justice Statistics Special Report (Washington, D.C.: Bureau of Justice Statistics, 1991).

63. Ibid.

64. Bureau of Justice Statistics, *Prisoners in 1990*.

65. Corrections Compendium, August 1992, p. 6.

66. See Elaine DeCostanzo and Janet Valente, "Designing a Corrections Continuum for Female Offenders: One State's Experience," *Prison Journal* 64 (1984):120–128; Susan M. Hunter, "Issues and Challenges Facing Women's Prisons in the 1980's," *Prison Journal* 64 (1984):129–135. For the situation in the United Kingdom, see Joycelin M. Pollock-Byrne, *Women, Prison, and Crime* (Pacific Grove, Calif.: Brooks/Cole, 1990); Phyllis Jo Baunach, "Critical Problems of Women in Prison," in *The Changing Roles of Women in the Criminal Justice System*, 2d ed., ed. Imogene L. Moyer (Prospect Heights, Ill: Waveland Press, 1992), pp. 99–112.

67. For fiscal year 1990, the Federal Bureau of Prisons reported 5,853 women incarcerated in federal institutions for both men and women, and 800 inmates in institutions for women. Kathleen Maguire and Timothy J. Flanagan, eds., *Sourcebook on Criminal Justice Statistics* (Washington, D.C.: Government Printing Office, 1991), Table 1.87, pp. 107–108.

68. U.S. Department of Justice, *Correctional Populations in the United States* (Washington, D.C.: U.S. Department of Justice, 1991); see also John Irwin and James Austin, "It's About Time: Solving America's Prison Crowding Crisis," *The National Council on Crime and Delinquency* (1987), p. 7.

69. Bureau of Justice Statistics, *Prisoners in 1990*.

70. Ibid.

71. Irwin and Austin, "It's About Time."

72. Bureau of Justice Statistics, *Prisoners in 1988* (Washington, D.C.: U.S. Government Printing Office, 1989).

73. Tom Wicker, "The Iron Medal," *The New York Times*, January 9, 1991, A21.

74. William Raspberry, "Prison Costs More Than Harvard: We Could Learn from Europe's Example," *The Washington Post*, May 13, 1991, p. 11.

75. Bureau of Justice Statistics, *Justice Expenditure and Employment, 1988* (Washington, D.C.: U.S. Department of Justice, July 1990).

76. Ibid.

77. George Camp and Camille Camp, *The Corrections Yearbook, 1991: Adult Corrections* (South Salem, N.Y.: Criminal Justice Institute, 1991); see also Chiquita A. Sipos, "The Corrections Workforce: Professionalism in a Thankless Profession," *Vital Statistics in Corrections* (Laurel, Md.: American Correctional Association, 1991).

78. Bureau of Justice Statistics, *Report to the Nation on Crime and Justice*, 2d ed. (Washington, D.C.: U.S. Government Printing Office, 1988), p. 124.

79. Camp and Camp, *The Corrections Yearbook*.

80. Peter Katel, "New Walls, No Inmates," *Newsweek*, May 18, 1992, p. 63.

81. Irwin and Austin, "It's About Time."

82. For a discussion of the need for caution in establishing private prisons, see Alexis M. Durham III, "Origins of Interest in the Privatization of Punishment: The Nineteenth and Twentieth Century American Experience," *Criminology* 27 (1989):107–139.

83. Harold W. Demone, Jr., and Margaret Gibelman, "Privatizing the Treatment of Criminal Offenders," *Clinical Treatment of the Criminal Offender* 15 (1990):7–26.

84. For a general overview, see "Privatization of Corrections," *Corrections Today* 50 (special issue) (1988). See also Byron R. Johnson and Paul P. Ross, "The Privatization of Correctional Management: A Review," *Journal of Criminal Justice* 18 (1990):351–358.

85. E. S. Savas, "Privatization and Prisons," *Vanderbilt Law Review* 40 (1987).

86. Quoted in Kevin Krajick, "Punishment for Profit," *Across the Road* 21 (1984):25.

87. J. C. Hackett, H. P. Hatry, R. B. Levinson, J. Allen, K. Chi, and E. D. Feigenbaum, *Issues in Contracting for the Operation of Prisons and Jails*, for National Institute of Justice (Washington, D.C.: U.S. Government Printing Office, 1986).

88. Barbara J. Auerbach, et al., *Work in American Prisons: The Private Sector Gets Involved*, for National Institute of Justice (Washington, D.C.: U.S. Government Printing Office, 1988).

89. Samuel Jan Brakel, "Prison Management, Private Enterprise Style: The Inmates' Evaluation," *New England Journal on Criminal and Civil Confinement* 14 (1988):175–244; B. A. Bakeman, B. Jennings, and L. Smith, "Contracting for Medical Services in Selected Texas State Institutions and Agencies," in *Contracting Selected State Government Functions: Issues and Next Steps*, eds. T. Blodgett and J. Chapman, Policy Research Project Report No. 75 (Austin: Lyndon B. Johnson School of Public Affairs, University of Texas, 1986).

90. C. Camp and G. Camp, "Correctional Privatization in Perspective," *The Prison Journal* (1985):14–31.

91. New Jersey Department of Corrections, *Admissions, Releases and Residents* (Trenton, N.J.: New Jersey Department of Corrections, 1988).

92. See, for example, John Dilulio, Jr., "Prisons, Profits and the Public Good: The Privatization of Corrections," *Criminal Justice Research Bulletin* No. 1, Sam Houston State University, 1986.

93. Ira P. Robbins, "Privatization of Corrections: Defining the Issues," *Federal Probation* 50 (1986):24–30.

CHAPTER 15

INSTITUTIONAL CORRECTIONS

"On December 16, 1937, the second escape attempt [from Alcatraz] ended in the death of two inmates . . . at the merciless hands of the swift, icy, turbulent, racing waters of the Bay. Theodore Cole (AZ258) was serving fifty years for kidnapping, and Ralph Roe (AZ260) ninety-nine years for bank robbery. On this cold and extremely foggy day, with a strong 8 mph outgoing tide, Cole and Roe engaged in what they had considered their well-planned escape. . . .

"After the guard had left at 1:00 p.m., Roe and Cole wrenched loose the cut bars, dropped to the ground below and proceeded to a locked gate in the fence. This particular gate was used to dump useless parts of tires from the mat shop into the Bay. Here, they used a wrench to break the gate lock, after which they climbed down to a ledge twenty feet below. They were now at the water's edge. Each inmate carried a sealed five gallon can with straps attached to act as a life preserver, and a knife. Not taken into account in all their well-laid plans were the treacherous, menacing waters on which they depended for transportation to freedom.

"Shortly after entering these waters, the two men were grabbed by the swift, moving current and swept outward toward the ocean. As they approached "Little Alcatraz," a tiny island off the end of Alcatraz, they were torn loose from their supportive cans. They both disappeared beneath the surface of the water—first Roe, then Cole—never to be seen again. Their cans raced away to vanish in the now heavy fog."[1]

*　　*　　*

"Alcatraz juts out of the sea about a mile and a quarter from shore and is swept by treacherous currents and enveloped by a soupy fog most of the time. Guards are forced to wear overcoats many days throughout the summer. This old establishment was renovated and turned into the most scientific prison in the world. It had for its objectives: maximum security, minimum privileges, complete isolation of dangerous convicts from the outside world, and 100 percent 'humane' treatment. . . . From the moment the convict enters he becomes victim to all the mechanical gadgets that science has perfected to depersonalize not only him but the administrative officers as well. He is frisked at the entrance by a steel detector, known by the convicts as a 'mechanical stool pigeon' or 'snitch box.' In the dining room, the inmate is ever conscious of the large metal cylinders above him filled with tear gas and ready upon a moment's notice to be opened to hurl down upon him this terrible punishment."[2] ■

"When rehabilitation was abandoned in the late 1970s, the 'lock 'em up' philosophy made a near-complete comeback."

"The vilest deeds like poison weeds
Bloom well in prison air;
It is only what is good in man
That wastes and withers there."
Oscar Wilde, "The Balad of Reading Gaol."

maximum security prison
Penal institution designed and operated with the principal goal of preventing escape and avoiding violence on the part of prisoners, virtually to the exclusion of rehabilitation or other programs.

medium security prison
Penal institution with emphasis on control and custody, but not to the exclusion of rehabilitative or other programs.

minimum security prison
Penal institution allowing inmates and visitors internal freedom of movement and program participation consistent with incarceration.

San Francisco's Alcatraz penitentiary, the "Rock," epitomized the American preoccupation with security. On March 21, 1963, twenty-nine years after Alcatraz opened in 1934, it was abandoned. To optimists, the closing was a sign of a new direction in American corrections. The aim would now be to socialize convicts rather than "asocialize" them by totally withdrawing them from society. The President's Commission on Law Enforcement and Administration of Justice (1967) emphasized such innovations as small-unit institutions for community-based treatment, rehabilitation programs administered jointly by staff and inmates, the upgrading of education and vocational training for inmates, the improvement of prison industries, and gradual release and furlough programs.[3] Just a few years later, in 1973, the National Advisory Commission on Criminal Justice Standards and Goals focused on the rights of prisoners. Its report included plans for education, recreation, counseling, and other prison reforms.[4]

During the 1960s and early 1970s, the rehabilitative approach dictated the direction of American corrections. But the "lock 'em up" philosophy was never totally replaced, and when rehabilitation was abandoned in the late 1970s, it made a near-complete comeback. The spirit of Alcatraz was resurrected in the 1980s with the opening of the super-maximum security Marion (Illinois) Federal Penitentiary. At Marion there are, in addition to the general population units, two less restrictive units, one high-control unit, and a special basement unit for high-profile inmates, among them a spy, Jonathon Pollard, and the former head of the Gambino crime family, John Gotti. A federal court described conditions at Marion as "horrible":

[E]ach inmate at Marion is confined to a one-man cell (there are no female inmates in the prison) round the clock, except for brief periods outside the cell for recreation (between 7 and 11 hours a week), for a shower, for a visit to the infirmary, to the law library, etc. (Some inmates have more time outside the cell, ...) Recreation means pacing in a small enclosure—sometimes just in the corridor between the rows of cells. The inmate is fed in his cell, on a tray shoved in between the bars. The cells are modern and roomy and contain a television set as well as a bed, toilet, and sink, but there is no other furniture and when an inmate is outside his cell he is handcuffed and a box is placed over the handcuffs to prevent the lock from being picked; his legs may also be shackled. Inmates are forbidden to socialize with each other or to participate in group religious services. Inmates who throw food or otherwise misbehave in their cells are sometimes tied spread-eagled on their beds, often for hours at a stretch, while inmates returning to their cells are often (inmates of the control unit, always) subjected to a rectal search. . . . [5]

Human Rights Watch recently investigated the state equivalents of federal super-maximum security prisons and found that here, too, prisoners spend nearly all of their time in locked cells that are usually badly ventilated. They cannot participate in classes, outdoor exercises, or recreation. The super-maximum prisons or units in prisons in 36 states are the source of the most troubling abuses.[6]

Given the high priority of custody/security in institutional corrections, we focus first on institutional control and on the corrections officers charged with maintaining orderly and safe jails and prisons. Then we describe prison life and how that life has changed since the 1960s with the influx of a younger, more heterogeneous population that often forms racial and ethnic power blocks. We examine rehabilitation and the intervention strategies used in various institutions. Last, we look at programs aimed at the well-being of prisoners.

CUSTODY/SECURITY

Nearly all correctional institutions have security as their first priority. This includes not only **maximum security** but also **medium security** and **minimum**

security prisons. In 1990, only 2,583 prisoners escaped from locked institutions, from among a population of about 1 million.[7] Critics claim that officials regard an escape as an incredible blemish on the whole system, a far bigger blemish than the many crimes committed by those discharged after serving their time. European administrators see their American counterparts as too little concerned with the reintegration of convicts into the community, and overly concerned with security. (See the Criminal Justice Abroad box.)

The focus on security is evident not only from the construction of prisons, with their security perimeters, high walls, guard towers, TV scanners, and electronic signals and alarms, but also from internal, management-designed procedures ranging from classification to examination of mail (or anything or anybody entering the security perimeter) to constant inmate counts, cell-locks, passes, and the harsh communal punishment of lockdowns for all inmates whenever an escape has been rumored or has taken place. This concern with security also appears in the training of correctional officers, which is devoted more to security than to long-range prevention through socialization. Look at Standard 2-4092 of the *Standards for Adult Correctional Institutions* of the American Correctional Association and the Commission on Accreditation for Corrections:

2-4092—Written policy and procedure provide that all new correctional officers receive an additional 120 hours of training during their first year of employment and an additional 40 hours of training each subsequent year of employment. At a minimum this training covers the following areas:

Alcatraz, "the Rock," once America's most secure and most dreaded prison, now sits abandoned in San Francisco Bay.

> Security procedures
> Supervision of inmates
> Use of force regulations and tactics
> Report writing
> Inmate rules and regulations
> Rights and responsibilities of inmates
> Fire and emergency procedures
> Firearms training
> Key control
> Interpersonal relations
> Social/cultural life styles of the inmate population
> Communications skills
> First aid.[8]

Body search at Marion, Illinois, the most secure federal penitentiary. Prisoners are searched even when moving from one part of the prison to another.

Rules and Regulations

Prisons were and are run by the rule, within a strictly hierarchical system. Corrections officers are expected to apply the rules, and prisoners are expected to obey them. Every state system has its own set of rules, incorporating state law and directives from the governor and/or the state correctional administration, as well as staff directives from the chief executive officer, usually the warden or superintendent. To comply with the standards of the American Correctional Association, institutions must inform all incoming inmates of the rules and the penalties imposed for violations.[9] The rule book for the State of Kansas, for example, opens with this instruction: "You should read well this entire book and keep it available for quick reference."[10] Rules dictate all aspects of daily life:

- *44-12-101.* Inmate clothing. (a) Turn-in and issuance. Inmate will turn in all personal clothing upon admission to an institution. Clothing furnished by the state facility shall be worn by all inmates unless exception is granted by the principal administrator with the approval of the secretary of corrections.
- *44-12-102.* Personal cleanliness. Inmates shall shower or bathe a minimum of once a week. Inmates shall brush their teeth a minimum of once a day.
- *44-12-103.* Tattoos and body markings. Inmates shall not place on or remove from, or allow to be placed on or removed from their body any tattoo or body marking, nor shall

THE *ULTIMA RATIO* (LAST RESORT) THEORY OF IMPRISONMENT: COOL THINKING IN NORTHERN CLIMATES

The sentence of imprisonment remains the backbone of the system of penal sanctions—in spite of the repeated proclamations at international congresses and in resolutions of the United Nations and the Council of Europe that it should be seen solely as an *ultima ratio.* (1)

Greenland's punishments

Kalaallit Nunaat is probably the only country in the world that truly considers a punishment involving custody as the *ultima ratio,* the last resort—the ultimate tool in society's arsenal for dealing with offenders who have committed grave violations of society's standards as embodied in the criminal code (2). The population of Kalaallit Nunaat, once known as Greenland, lives under home rule, granted by Denmark. In 1954 the Danish authorities codified existing customary law in the Greenland Criminal Code. That codification, together with increasing Europeanization of the country, increased the crime rate threefold, and for the first time the need for a tiny prison was felt. But prison sentences still are rare. In practically all cases of conviction under the Greenland Penal Code, the sanction imposed is:

- a warning
- a fine
- restrictions as to residence and visiting of particular places
- compulsory labor
- medical treatment
- limitations on freedom of action
- confiscation

Some of these sentences are considered very harsh. Kalaallit Nunaat is a country as big as Alaska and Texas, the two largest American states, combined, and it is also the world's largest island. Yet only about 55,000 people live there, mostly on the southern coast, for much of the rest of the country—89 percent—is covered by a sheet of ice 1,000 feet thick. Not to be able to visit a community center, or to have to work with hunters or fishers in the isolated wilds, or not to have access to alcohol, may be severe deprivations in a country of harsh climate and great distances.

Denmark's depenalization

Among other countries that mean to be serious about prison as the *ultima ratio* are the other Nordic countries. In Denmark, if a prison sentence is imposed at all, it is served in an open institution to which the prisoner reports after being informed by mail of an available room. Prisoners are given keys to their rooms. The institutions are locked from the outside to keep trespassers out rather than prisoners in. Only offenders classified as dangerous, or walk-aways, are placed in one of the few locked institutions. In Denmark, as in Norway, Sweden, Finland, and Iceland, institutions are tiny. Corrections officers wear blazers; prisoners work or undergo training. Compulsory therapy has been abandoned, and the United Nations or Council of Europe Standard Minimum Rules for the Treatment of Prisoners are complied with strictly. Civil rights are not lost and contacts with family and community are maintained.

Despite increases in crime rates, drug addiction, and alcoholism, the Danes have not increased their prison population, relying instead on fines and community service. In 1973 Denmark's prison population was rising, and several changes were made to Danish penal law (3). A "depenalization" law resulted in new policies: Shorter sentences were given to property offenders, and more people were placed on probation. The Danish probation administration was placed under the same management as the prison system, with a transfer of penal institution resources to probation. Another change in the system was the elimination of indeterminate sentences, which had been shown to result in periods of imprisonment disproportionate to the crime committed—and burdensome on the system.

Avoiding the *ultima ratio*: benefits

The result of all these changes? Fewer people in prison. The general director of the Danish Prison and Probation Administration lists four reasons for avoiding the *ultima ratio,* prison:

- General humanitarian concerns. "The harm caused by confinement often extends beyond the deprivation of liberty itself to broken family life, loss of work, and stigmatization."
- "The findings . . . do not support deprivation of freedom as a suitable means of resocialization. . . . It . . . strengthens feelings of insecurity, apathy, and aggressiveness toward the community . . . and promotes identification with those who display patterns of criminal behavior."
- "Offenses against property . . . are looked upon totally differently than was the case in the past. The general growth in wealth and the prevalence of theft insurance mean that this offense is not as burdensome for the victim as in previous years . . . consequently not necessarily requiring such serious sanctions."
- "Incarceration is a costly measure" (3, pp. 188–189).

The decrease in Denmark's prison population has not been accompanied by a decline in the crime rate, but the Danes have been successful in working toward two of the goals of a criminal justice system proposed in a white paper on crime policy issued by the Danish government in 1978: "complying with fundamental principles of justice and humanity and maintaining a balance between the cost of criminal justice policy and the benefits to society of that policy" (3, p.

Prisoners per 100,000 Population (1988 and 1989)			
Countries Committed to the *Ultima Ratio* Approach		Countries Not Committed to the *Ultima Ratio* Approach	
Greenland (Kalaallit Nunaat)	Too small to measure	United States	426+
Norway	48.4	South Africa	333
Sweden	56.0	Former U.S.S.R.	268
Denmark	68.0	Hungary	196

SOURCE: Frieder Dünkel and Dirk van Zyl Smit, "Conclusion," in *Imprisonment Today and Tomorrow*, eds. Dirk van Zyl Smit and Frieder Dünkel (Deventer, Netherlands: Kluwer Law and Taxation Publishers, 1991), p. 715, and Table 14:4, infra.

185). About the problem of combating crime, the general director says, " . . . a more lenient—and more flexible—penal policy affords more genuine possibilities for avoiding an outbreak of serious crimes than does a stricter system" (3, p. 185).

SOURCES

1. Frieder Dunkel and Dirk van Zyl Smit, "Conclusion," in *Imprisonment Today and Tomorrow: International Perspectives on Prisoners' Rights and Prison Conditions*, eds. Dirk van Zyl Smit and Frieder Dunkel (Deventer, Netherlands: Kluwer Law and Taxation Publishers, 1991), p. 714.
2. *The Greenland Criminal Code*, translated at the Center for Studies in Criminal Justice, University of Chicago Law School, with an introduction by Dr. Verner Goldschmidt [South Hackensack, N.J.: Fred B. Rothman (Vol. 16, American Series of Foreign Penal Codes), 1970].
3. H. H. Brydensholt, "Crime Policy in Denmark: How We Managed to Reduce the Prison Population," in *Prisons Around the World*, eds. Michael K. Carlie and Kevin I. Minor (Dubuque, Ia.: William C. Brown, 1992), p. 188.

QUESTIONS FOR DISCUSSION

1. Both the United Nations and the Council of Europe support prison as the *ultima ratio*. Why do more countries of the world not put this theory into practice?
2. Would you favor instituting any of Denmark's depenalization policies in the United States? If so, which ones?
3. It is obvious from the table presenting imprisonment rates that the United States, South Africa, the former Soviet Union, and Hungary imprison far more people than do Norway, Sweden, Denmark, and Kalaallit Nunaat. What accounts for these differences?

"Prison rules dictate every aspect of daily life, even the most trivial."

they place on or remove from the body of another inmate any tattoo or body marking.

- *44-12-202.* Radios, T.V.'s, musical instruments or other sound equipment. All personal radios, T.V.'s, and other electronic sound equipment shall by played only with the use of earphones worn on the person so that no sound will be emitted from the equipment itself.

- *44-12-301.* Fighting. Fighting or other activity which constitutes violence, or which is likely to lead to violence is prohibited, unless such activity is in self-defense.

- *44-12-302.* Noise. Inappropriate booing, whistling, shouting, or other loud and disturbing noises are not permitted.

- *44-12-303.* Lying. Every inmate shall speak the truth. No inmate shall lie, misrepresent the facts, mislead, or give false or misleading information to an officer, employee, or any other person assigned to supervise inmates or others having a right to know. No inmate shall make any false allegations against any officer, employee, inmate, or other person.

- *44-12-315.* Lewd acts. No inmate, while on premises of a correctional or contract facility, shall engage in a lewd or lascivious manner in any acts of kissing, fondling, touching, or embracing, whether they be with a person of the same or opposite sex.

- *44-12-316.* Aggravated sodomy or aggravated sexual act. No inmate shall force, or intimidate another person, or solicit or arrange for another person to apply force or intimidation to another person, in order to commit any kind of sexual act or sodomy.

- *44-12-325.* Religious activity; limitations. (a) No proselytizing of religious faiths or beliefs shall be allowed in the facilities. By proselytizing is meant the active effort to persuade one to convert to a religious belief without such person's prior consent. However, nothing herein shall prohibit one to one conversation about religious matters.[11]

If inmates commit acts covered by criminal law, their cases are referred to law enforcement or prosecutorial agencies. Prosecution by the outside agency does not preclude a disciplinary charge and proceeding by the institution for the infraction of its own rule. If inmates believe they have been treated unfairly they may file grievances using official procedures.[12]

Classification

Perhaps more important than rules and regulations in the smooth functioning of a correctional institution is a classification system that permits organization of inmates into cohesive, manageable units. The **classification** process consists of regular procedures through which the custodial, treatment, vocational, and educational needs of each individual are determined. While program classifications are important, security classifications are the number-one priority. Security requirements are necessary for the protection of the inmates themselves, for the safety of other persons within the institution, and for the protection of the public. Custodial classification is based on the inmate's behavior, mental health, attitude, and likelihood of attempting escape.

All new prisoners pass through a diagnostic or reception center where specialized personnel such as social workers, psychologists, and physicians make decisions about treatment and custodial needs.[13] Decisions on placement are made by classification committees, typically comprising the warden or deputy warden and the heads of various prison departments, including chaplains, vocational and recreational supervisors, medical officers, and others. Information from the diagnostic process, the presentence investigation report, police records, and an interview with the inmate help to determine placement.

Throughout the course of an inmate's correctional stay, he or she may be reclassified as needs change. Some classification systems today rely on **objective classification,** a process that uses a narrow set of well-defined legal factors (such as severity of offense, number of prior convictions and prior incarcerations) and personal characteristics (such as age, length of residence, and employment history) to guide decision-making.[14] These factors are incorporated into a

classification
Process that consists of regular procedures through which the custodial, treatment, vocational, and educational needs of each prisoner are determined.

objective classification
Process that uses a standardized form with well-defined legal factors and personal characteristics to assess every inmate's custody and program needs.

standardized form or checklist used to assess every inmate's custody and program needs. Some administrators believe that objective classification procedures result in more equal treatment of offenders, ensure that inmates are assigned to proper supervision, and provide information that can be used for program planning.[15]

Classification of prisoners is an idea dating back to the reformatory movement of the 1800s. It has been a useful technique for matching the prisoner to the prison. The problem is that often placement decisions are determined on the basis of institutional constraints rather than individual needs.

Corrections Officers

In West Virginia the story is told that, shortly after statehood (1863), there was a heated argument over the site of the university and the site of the state prison. Moundsville and Morgantown were the choices. Morgantown lost—it got the university. Moundsville won—it got the state prison, and with it vast employment opportunities requiring no skills.

In the past, state prisons (like the one in West Virginia), located in little towns far from crime-prone urban centers, provided employment for generations of local youth. They needed no education past public schooling, and they filled the jobs their fathers had occupied. These civil service careers offered security (if the person played it right) and a pension to start a second career in town after retirement.[16] During the 1970s, however, changes began to take place in the correctional employment field. With the vast increase in correctional facilities, many states adopted proactive recruitment policies emphasizing education and qualifications. Salary levels began to go up, and officer training was somewhat upgraded. New affirmative action goals resulted in recruitment of minorities and women (Figure 15.1). Women officers now work in both men's and women's prisons.[17] There has also been a rise in membership of prison employee unions.

"In the past, state prisons, located in little towns far from crime-prone urban centers, provided employment for generations of local youths, who filled the jobs their fathers had occupied."

Despite the somewhat improved situation of the corrections officer, the job still has little prestige. Officers spend long hours in hostile surroundings with few contacts outside the walls. While they may move to higher ranks within the corrections hierarchy, they generally do not move into administrative positions. Turnover rates are high (28% nationally), salaries are still relatively low (Figure 15.2), and absenteeism reaches 15 percent at any one time in many prisons.[18]

"Harshness, silence, twilight, discipline holds true, not only for the prisoner, but also for the keeper." Frank Tannenbaum, *Wall Shadows*, 1922, p. 24.

The Corrections Officer Role. The popular perception of the corrections officer is that he or she controls prisoners by brute force. Yet officers rarely carry weapons inside the prison (because inmates would likely take them away). Officers survive by earning respect and resorting, whenever necessary, to unarmed coercion, or the granting of rewards.[19]

"Corrections officers survive by earning respect, by resorting to unarmed coercion, and by granting informal rewards."

Criminologist Lucien Lombardo has classified officers' assignments into seven categories: block officers, work detail, supervisors, industrial shop and school officers, yard officers and administration building assignments. Block officers have the most demanding assignments.

Let [the inmates] in and out on time, make regular counts. Let those in coming from work. Give out medication. Lock them in and count again. Then let them out into the yard. All the while I have to handle all kinds of problems, personal, plumbing or electrical. I hand out newspapers and mail. I make check rounds to make sure there's no two in a cell. Let some in at seven o'clock and after eight o'clock let those in from the yard. Then I make the final count. There's call-outs and everything else in between. Anything can happen and always does.[20]

Several studies have identified different types of officers. One divides new officers into three groups on the basis of their attitudes toward inmates and other officers: "Pollyanas" (positive to both groups), "white hats" (positive to inmates, negative toward other officers), and "hard asses" (negative toward in-

FIGURE 15.1 *Percent of women and nonwhites hired as corrections officers, 1987–1990* (*Source:* George M. and Camille Graham Camp, *The Corrections Yearbook, 1991* [South Salem, N.Y.: Criminal Justice Institute, 1991], p. 3.)

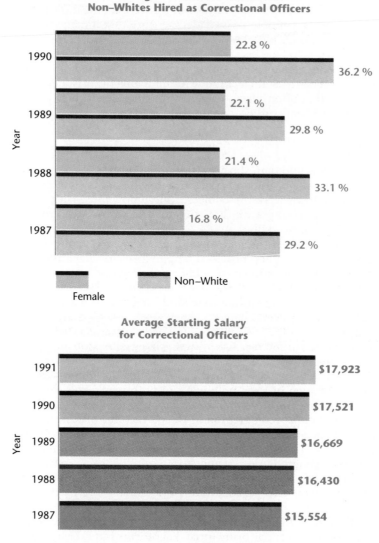

Average Percent of Females and Non–Whites Hired as Correctional Officers

- 1990: 22.8 % / 36.2 %
- 1989: 22.1 % / 29.8 %
- 1988: 21.4 % / 33.1 %
- 1987: 16.8 % / 29.2 %

Year

Female — Non–White

Average Starting Salary for Correctional Officers

- 1991: $17,923
- 1990: $17,521
- 1989: $16,669
- 1988: $16,430
- 1987: $15,554

Year

FIGURE 15.2 *Average starting salary for corrections officers, 1987–1991* (*Source:* George M. and Camille Graham Camp, *The Corrections Yearbook, 1991* [South Salem, N.Y.: Criminal Justice Institute, 1991], p. 75.)

mates, positive toward fellow officers). With time, most officers become either "burnouts" (negative to both groups) or "functionaries" (indifferent to both groups).[21] Another study describes "John Waynes" (disciplinarians), "wishy-washies" (appear afraid of inmates), "lazy-laid-backs" (don't care), "all rights" (usually old-timers who accept their rules), and "dirty cops" (who do illegal favors for prisoners).

Job Satisfaction among Officers. Most corrections officers choose the job for security, for civil service benefits, or because it may be the only work available in the small towns and farm areas where most prisons are located. There are several negative factors associated with the work. According to one officer: "[The worst thing about the job] is the fear there might be a riot. That you might be dead, that you might not come out. It's there every day, but you just wonder if it will happen today."[22] In addition to their concern with danger, officers resent the "hostile" attitudes of inmates, their isolation behind walls, and the little input that they have into decisions that affect assignments and working conditions.[23] A recent study shows that the level of corrections officer job satisfaction is lower than that of any other occupational category.[24]

"A career officer in effect commits himself to a life sentence in prison."
James Jacobs and Norma Crotty, *Guard Unions and the Failure of Prisons*, 1978, p. 2.

412

LIVING WITH CONVICTS

Corrections officers and administrators work with people whose lives are marked by poverty, lack of education, and violence, and who live by very different rules in a very different kind of society.

Who Are the Inmates?

Most state and federal prison inmates are men (91.5%); their average age is 30 years.[25] Women make up 8.5 percent with a mean age of 31. Only 5 percent of the inmate population is 50 years old or older.[26] In Chapter 2, we noted that while there is controversy among researchers as to whether social class is related to the commission of crime, there is no controversy among them about the social class of inmates.

The probability that people such as New York hotel queen Leona Helmsley and Wall Street trader Ivan Boesky will be punished with imprisonment is extremely low. They do not fit the typical profile of the hundreds of thousands of inmates in our nation's jails and prisons:

They are educated, whereas only 25 percent of prison inmates have completed high school.[27]

Their income was in the millions. Prior to their imprisonment, sixty percent of prison inmates had an annual income of less than $10,000 (40% were unemployed or had part-time jobs).[28]

They had white-collar jobs; 85 percent of prison inmates were blue-collar workers.

They committed white-collar offenses. Only 18 percent of persons convicted of such offenses go to prison for more than one year, whereas 39 percent of violent offenders and 26 percent of the property offenders do.[29]

"Prior to their imprisonment, 60 percent of prison inmates had an annual income of less than $10,000; 40 percent were unemployed or worked only part-time."

The likelihood that a male will serve time in jail or prison is estimated to be 18 percent for blacks and 3 percent for whites.[30] Over the decade of the 1980s, the percentage of persons admitted to state prisons who were drug addicts went from 7.7 percent to 29.5 percent. In fact, the increase in prisoners admitted for drug offenses accounted for over half the growth in total admissions.[31] Inmate W. is a good example:

W. is a forty-year-old black man raised by his mother in San Francisco. He has been a heroin addict for the last fifteen years. During this period he has been arrested at least twenty-two times. These arrests have resulted in two county jail sentences, a prison term, and several trips to the California Rehabilitation Center, which is the drug treatment prison in California. The present arrest occurred in a motor hotel in a relatively nice residential section of San Francisco. He was seen by police in the halls of the hotel and stopped. When he was searched, they found jewelry and a screwdriver and charged him with burglary. His fingerprints matched those from another burglary. He was eventually charged with three different burglaries. . . . He was sentenced to the state prison for three years.[32]

Nationwide statistics show a wide range in number of prisoners per 100,000 population among the states.[33] Nevada has the highest rate (473), followed by South Carolina (419), Louisiana (395), Alaska (363), Oklahoma (355), Arizona (354), and Delaware (344). At the other end of the spectrum there is North Dakota (61), Minnesota (71), and West Virginia (83).[34] Thirty-seven percent of prison inmates report that family members have also been incarcerated—7 percent, a parent; 32 percent, a brother or sister.[35]

The Deprivation Model

Inmates constitute a unique social group. They live together, but not voluntarily. They live in extremely close quarters, often sharing all space other than a bed. They must stay in the group even if they fear for their personal safety.

For over half a century social scientists have studied the prison as a social entity. Some experts argue that the traditions, norms, language, and roles that develop in prison result from the deprivations of prison life (the **deprivation model**).[36] Donald Clemmer, who has described the prison subculture and how inmates adapt to it, uses the term **prisonization** to describe the complex process by which new inmates learn the ways of the prison society and what is expected of them. Inmates are first reduced in status from civilians to anonymous figures, numbers in a common uniform, subject to institutional rules and the prison's rigid hierarchy. After a while they begin to accept the inferior role; to take on new habits of eating, sleeping, and working; and to learn that they do not owe anything to anybody for their subsistence.[37]

Building on Clemmer's work, Gresham Sykes has described how people respond to the deprivations they experience as inmates. According to him, a "society of captives" emerges as a response to imprisonment.[38] To cope with the "pains of imprisonment" that new inmates suffer, they become part of a society that has an **inmate code** (a set of rules that tell the inmate how to behave toward other inmates and toward custodial officers) and a set of social roles defined in terms of **prison argot** (a unique vocabulary used by prisoners).

The Pains of Imprisonment. First, inmates are deprived of liberty and are cut off from friends and family. The results are lost emotional relationships, boredom, and loneliness.[39] Second, inmates are deprived of goods and services. While it is true that an inmate will get "three squares and clean sheets," the standard of living inside a jail or prison is very low. Prisoners have no chance to keep or to obtain material possessions. **Hustling,** obtaining goods and services that are unavailable through legitimate channels, is a basic inmate activity. The informal economy can supply drugs, alcohol, food, and sex. Cigarettes are a valued commodity. They are permitted in the institution, and they are popularly used for trading purposes.[40]

The third "pain of imprisonment" is the deprivation of heterosexual relations. Criminologists have identified a number of psychological problems that result from this deprivation. The worst of these expresses itself in the homosexual enslavement of younger prisoners by aggressive older inmates. Few studies have been more shocking and revealing than an investigation of local corrections facilities by the Philadelphia district attorney's office and police department conducted nearly twenty years ago. It revealed that over a twenty-six-month period there were 2,000 sexual assaults involving 3,500 perpetrators and 1,500 victims. Furthermore, they found that almost all "slightly built" young men were sexually approached almost immediately upon admission. Many were raped repeatedly by gangs of inmates.[41]

For heterosexual inmates the deprivation of a partner of the opposite sex is one of the worst forms of punishment. Precisely for that reason, eight correctional systems—California, Connecticut, Minnesota, Mississippi, New Mexico, New York, Washington, and Wyoming—have instituted programs of conjugal visits. At the Eastern Correctional Facility in Napanoch, New York, for example, inmates are given the opportunity to stay with their spouse for forty-four hours every three or four months.[42] Conjugal visits help to maintain family relationships and reduce sexual frustration. There are no comparable programs for unmarried inmates.

The fourth pain of imprisonment is deprivation of personal autonomy. Inmates' lives are regulated and controlled twenty-four hours a day. Yet the control by corrections staff is selective. Staff are likely to look the other way when prison-

---

"Inmates are a unique group, because they are people who do not choose to live together."

deprivation model
Explanation of prison subculture that suggests norms, language, roles, and traditions are developed in the prison to help prisoners adjust to the pains of imprisonment.

prisonization
Socialization process in which new prisoners learn the ways of prison society, including rules, hierarchy, customs, and culture.

inmate code
Informal set of rules that reflect the values of the prison society.

prison argot
Unique vocabulary used by prisoners.

hustling
Inmate activity that involves obtaining goods and services that are unavailable through legitimate channels.

"According to Gresham Sykes, a 'society of captives' emerges as a response to imprisonment."

Inmates socializing in a Georgia prison. Prison life often mirrors the racial divisions and tensions of the outside world.

ers enforce, often brutally, their own code of conduct among themselves. The fifth pain of imprisonment is the deprivation of security. When a prisoner shares a small space with other inmates, some of whom are likely to be violent, aggression, violence, and sexual exploitation are inevitable. Inmates who are attacked and do not fight back suffer the contempt of the prison community and open themselves to further victimization.

The Convict Social System. To cope with these pains of imprisonment, an inmate needs to live by the inmate code. "Don't inform on another convict" and "do your own time" are the two basic rules of the code. Among the others are "don't interfere with inmate interests," "don't quarrel with fellow inmates," "don't weaken," and "don't trust the guards or the things they stand for."[43]

The prison social system also defines various social rules in terms of prison argot. Some roles undermine group solidarity. There are "rats" and "snitches" who get inmates into trouble, "merchants" who deal in stolen goods (usually from the prison supply store), "gorillas" who use violence to get what they want, "wolves" who coerce other inmates into homosexual relations, and "centermen" who take the side of the custodians. The "real man," on the other hand, is loyal, maintains dignity, shares possessions, yet remains tough. The characteristics of the "real man" build a cohesive inmate society that provides the prisoner with a social group with which to identify—one that will support him in his struggle with captivity.[44]

"When a prisoner shares a small space with other inmates, some of whom are likely to be violent, aggression, violence, and sexual exploitation are inevitable."

"The inmate code: 'Don't inform on another convict'; 'Do your own time.'"

The Importation Model

Clarence Schrag has offered an opposing explanation of prison cultures. In his view, the values one finds within the prison are precisely those found on the streets from which the offenders come.[45] The **importation model** suggests that the inmate subculture is brought in from the outside. Schrag identified four major roles within the prison community—"square John," "right guy," "con politician," and "outlaw"—and argued that these roles correspond to the life experiences of those brought into the institution. John Irwin and Donald Cressey developed this idea further. To them, the prison subculture represents a combination of the "convict" subculture (those who spend most of their lives in foster homes, reform schools, jails, and prisons), the "straight" subculture (those—usually one-time offenders—who live by conventional social rules and want to avoid trouble in prison), and the "thief" subculture (professional criminals who keep to themselves). Only the convict subculture is unique to the prison; the others are imported from outside the walls.[46]

importation model
Explanation of prison subculture that suggests norms, language, roles, and traditions are brought into the prison from outside the walls.

"Schrag holds that the values found in prison are precisely those found on the streets from which the offenders come."

A New Prison Society

Changes in the prison population since the 1960s have created a new prison society. Contemporary prisons now house a more heterogeneous group of inmates, and it appears that a single inmate code for the whole population no longer exists. Race plays the dominant role in inmate relationships.[47] In many state prison systems competition among black, Hispanic, Native American, and white power blocks often leads to alliances that resemble international treaties among nations. Robert G. Leger concludes:

Whites, who represent the dominant race outside prison, find themselves [to be] a distinct minority group on the inside. Whites' apparent realization of their minority position seems to affect their perception of their living space, levels of aggression, and attitudes towards the dominant racial group—blacks.[48]

Leo Carroll's *Hacks, Blacks, and Cons* also identified race as a crucial factor in inmate social relationships.[49] In 1980, John Irwin's study *Prisons in Turmoil* showed how the social structure of California prisons was divided into white,

• • • • • • • • • • • • • • • • •

black, and Hispanic groups. Hostile racial gangs emerged with links to their old gangs outside the walls.[50]

A number of other changes occurred: More persons were convicted on drug-related crimes; the mean age of prisoners went down; and inmates became more politically active. Unlike members of groups like the armed forces, prisoners do not believe in the legitimacy of their captors. There is often open hostility between prisoners and guards, and the reactions and solutions vary. For example:

Problem inmates who throw food at guards at Louisiana State Penitentiary in Angola may soon be served splatter-proof meals. Under a plan submitted by state officials to a federal judge, all ingredients in meals at the prison's discipline camp would be mixed together and baked into a loaf.[51]

"But I ain't scared. . . . My brothers are there."
Mario Gray, first-time inmate, quoted in *The New York Times,* September 13, 1992, p. 1.

The modern prison, according to James Jacobs, can be understood only in terms of the interaction between the institution and the larger society. He claims that there are still unique conditions in the prison environment that require special adaptation (as described by Clemmer, Sykes, Schrag, and Irwin), but that the isolation of inmates from the world outside the prison walls is decreasing. Television, radio, newspapers, more visitation, and increased legal representation account for the changes. Jacobs says the idea that "prison subculture" means a group that is "isolated, separate, and opposed to the dominant culture" may no longer be true.[52]

Prison Violence and Overcrowding

The new prison society is also characterized by more violence. On February 2, 1980, the New Mexico Penitentiary in Santa Fe exploded in the most violent and destructive riot since forty-three inmates and hostages were killed at Attica in 1971. In Attica, the disturbance was tightly controlled by a small group of powerful inmates. By contrast, the New Mexico inmates were leaderless and out of control. Fourteen guards were held hostage while hundreds of prisoners roamed the prison smashing and burning everything in sight. At least seven of the hostages were severely beaten and several were repeatedly raped. But the inmates reserved the brunt of their rage for each other: Thirty-three inmates were killed, some after being brutally tortured and mutilated. As many as 200 other inmates were beaten and raped. The terror was so pervasive and uncontrolled that the majority of the 1,136 inmates fled and sought safety among the state police and National Guard personnel ringing the penitentiary. The level of inmate-to-inmate violence was unprecedented. (See the Criminal Justice on Trial box.)

"In the New Mexico prison riot in February 1980, the inmates reserved the brunt of their rage for each other."

When the riot was over, officials acknowledged that the New Mexico corrections system had long been neglected. Maximum-custody inmates, including some labeled psychotic, were mixed together with young and vulnerable first offenders, often in dormitories holding as many as ninety men each.[53]

The increasing violence in prisons has been attributed to the younger age of inmates, warring racial groups, and the transfer of the subculture of violence from the streets into the prison.[54] Lee Bowker adds the easy availability of deadly weapons, the mixing of violence-prone with nonviolent inmates, the level of tension, and inadequate supervision.[55]

"The overriding problem in American prisons today is overcrowding."

Overriding many of the factors related to violent behavior is the problem of overcrowding.[56] In a review of the literature, Gerald Gaes reports that the major findings about prison overcrowding are that (1) prisoners housed in large dormitories are more likely to visit clinics and have high blood pressure than are prisoners in other housing arrangements such as single-bunked cells and small dormitories; (2) prisons that use dormitories have higher assault rates than those with cells; and (3) prisons housing significantly more inmates than design capacity based on sixty feet per inmate have higher assault rates than other prisons.[57] A study of four Virginia institutions found a prison assault rate of 9.96 attacks per 100 inmates each year.[58] Hans Toch has commented that many inmates "spend years in fear of harm. Some inmates request segregation, others lock themselves in and some are hermits by choice."[59]

As the prison population grows, violence continues to escalate. Is violent behavior among inmates inevitable when thousands of persons, many with histories of violent behavior, live in close quarters? How can we protect both the custodians and their charges? Not all experts agree that inmates inevitably become "unmanageable."[60] They contend that "good administration" can overcome many difficulties. "Good administration" refers not only to a military-style discipline, but also to the availability of recreational, educational, and vocational programs.[61]

"We have no elbow room and no activities. Anybody who works in corrections will tell you that's a recipe for disaster."
Maine Corrections Commissioner Donald Allen, in *The Washington Post*, February 21, 1992, p. A1.

Life in a Women's Prison

The road to the Alderson Federal Reformatory for Women snakes its way for hours through the rugged mountains of West Virginia, until its travelers finally reach a small town deep in the heart of the Appalachian poverty belt. The road takes one final half-mile curve along an ancient railroad and opens to a broad expanse of red-brick buildings bounded on all sides by mountains. The first, and perhaps the most lasting, impression of Alderson is that of its absolute isolation.

That isolation must be understood in the context of the philosophy of female corrections. . . . As with Devil's Island, Alcatraz, and Siberia, the physical distance which was routinely put between prisons and population centers was a measure of the social distance which society wished to maintain from its criminals. . . .

Now, wardens at institutions such as Alderson must spend a good deal of their time struggling with the vocational and rehabilitative impediments that such isolation causes. For one thing, Alderson's out-of-the-way location virtually ensures that the husbands, children, and other relatives of an inmate will have a difficult, if not impossible, time getting to the prison for a visit. It helps little that the institution itself sprawls across five hundred rolling acres of woodland, or that its buildings are generously spaced and the areas between them well carpeted with close clipped lawns and clusters of park benches.[62]

Like Alderson, most facilities for women have better physical surroundings than institutions for men. Fortresslike walls and gun towers restrain male inmates who have little freedom of movement. Women are usually free to roam the grounds of their institutions. But, despite the more pleasant surroundings, according to many experts, the frustration of incarcerated women may be even greater than that of men. Because women represent only 8.5 percent of the state inmate population, women's facilities have been assigned a low priority.[63] Money spent for women's education, job training, or counseling would reach too few of the total prison population. Women are therefore offered little more than inexpensive programs that emphasize stereotypes of "women's work": cooking, sewing, cosmetology, and office work, to which more recently computer languages and programming have been added.

The populations in women's prisons generally share many socioeconomic characteristics:

- They are disproportionately black (36%) and Hispanic (15%).
- They are in their late twenties and early thirties.
- They tend to have few work skills. Their employment histories show a predominance of service-related jobs.
- Many come from broken homes where drug abuse, mental illness, and child abuse were common.
- About one-third have completed high school or have an equivalence degree.
- Most are unmarried, divorced, or separated.[64]

The Women's Subculture. In *Society of Women,* Rose Giallombardo compared the subculture of male and female prisons.[65] Her findings are consistent with the

"Women in prison often come from broken homes, are young, and have few work skills; more than 76% are mothers."

Riker's Island, New York: cosmetology is one of the few skills taught at women's prisons.

ORGANIZED PRISON GANGS

When a battle erupted in 1986 in an exercise yard at Arizona State Prison,

. . . one inmate was stabbed to death and two others were critically injured before guards brought the melee under control.

About 200 of the unit's 598 inmates reportedly were involved in the disturbance.

. . . the melee began after a black inmate was stabbed outside the Ira Hayes Dormitory. The fighting escalated when whites on one side of an exercise yard charged a group of blacks on the other side.

Corrections Director Sam Lewis arrived at the prison during the morning . . . but Lewis is leaving it up to leaders of race-based prison gangs to stop the bloodshed.

Officials said the fighting Friday was in retaliation for the death of Paul Engle, 26, of Phoenix, whose throat was slashed Thursday. Engle was a member of the Aryan Brotherhood, a white supremacist prison gang. (1)

Over the past thirty years prison gangs have evolved from small groups of inmates associated for mutual protection into self-perpetuating criminal gangs with the characteristics of organized crime syndicates. The first prison gang, the Gypsy Jakers, started at Washington State Penitentiary, Walla Walla, in 1950. In the 1960s, racial turmoil in American society spilled into the prisons, sometimes resulting in inmate race wars. Gangs provided protection for their members. At

San Quentin, for example, there were the Aryan Brotherhood, supposedly created to protect white inmates; the Black Guerrilla Family, a militant gang associated with the Black Panther Party; the Mexican Mafia, with members from East Los Angeles; and their bitter rivals, the Nuestra Familia, consisting of rural Chicanos. Gangs developed in Illinois in the late 1960s, and by the 1970s and 1980s prison gangs had spread throughout the country. A recent report indicates that there are prison gangs in the federal system and in thirty-two state jurisdictions (2). Most gang members are in Illinois (5,300), Pennsylvania (2,400), and California (2,050).

The Texas experience

Some argue that court decisions on prisoners' rights, while improving the treatment of inmates, may have limited prison administrators' recourse to punitive sanctions, thus allowing gangs to strengthen their power base. Texas, for example, had few gang problems during the time of its "building tender" system, a system using inmates as guards. Administrators chose inmates to serve as "tenders," who performed various staff functions including maintaining order and gathering information. The system was declared unconstitutional in *Ruiz v. Estelle* (1980). Chaos followed the June 1982 court order eliminating building tenders, and the chaos was attributed to the lack of inmate informants and a shortage of security staff to take the place of inmate guards.

Until 1983 Texas had had only one known prison gang—the Texas Syndicate, a gang that had been closely watched by the tenders. But during the organizational crisis fol-

lowing the elimination of the building tender system, "inmates began actively to organize themselves to fill this power vacuum" (3). Among gangs that formed at this time were the Texas Mafia, the Nuestro Carneles, and the Mandango Warriors. By 1985 there were 1,400 gang members, violence had escalated dramatically (25 murders and 409 stabbings in one year alone), and there were as many as 3,000 inmates in segregation at a time.

How gangs work

Gangs typically are organized in paramilitary fashion. The Texas Syndicate, for example, has an elected president and vice president, along with unit chairmen, vice chairmen, captains, lieutenants, sergeants of arms, and soldiers. Many gang officials are elected, usually on the basis of their criminal record working for the gang. Prison gangs have codes of conduct ("once a member always a member," for example), and the penalty for violating rules may well be death. New gang members must be brought in by old gang members. The "syndicates" typically have a "blood-in blood-out" rule: An inmate has to kill or assault another inmate or staff member to get into the gang, and his own blood is at stake if he decides to quit the gang (4). Inmates have used mail to communicate with other gang members, and sometimes the letters contain coded assassination orders from gang leaders (5). Members stay in the gang when they get back to their neighborhoods—and continue a liaison with gang members inside the walls. Some gangs even require released inmates to work for them by expanding illegal enterprises and sharing the profits (3).

Youngsters on the street offer their services in return for a place in the prison gang at some point in their lives. Most gangs have written constitutions and by-laws and require new recruits to take an oath of allegiance.

Organized along racial and ethnic lines, gangs serve many purposes. They protect members in a dangerous environment. They provide goods and services. They give psychological support. The Aryan Brothers creed reads:

An Aryan Brother is without a care,
He walks where the weak and heartless
   won't dare,
And if by chance he should stumble and
   lose control,
His brothers will be there, to help reach
   his goal.
For a worthy brother, no need is too
   great,
He need not but ask, fulfillment's his
   fate.

For an Aryan Brother, death holds no
   fear.
Vengeance will be his, through his
   brothers still here,
For the Brotherhood means just what it
   implies,
A brother's a brother, till that brother
   dies.

And if he is loyal, and never lost faith
In each brother's heart, will always be a
   place.

So a brother am I and always will be,
Even after my life is taken from me.
I'll lie down content, knowing I stood,
Head held high, walking proud in the
   Brotherhood. (6)

The problem of organized crime groups

Prison gangs have undergone a major change through the decades. The politically militant gangs of the 1960s became the organized crime groups of the 1980s. The Black Guerrilla Family at San Quentin, for example, was replaced by the drug-trafficking Crips and Bloods.

The President's Commission on Organized Crime (1986) estimated that nine out of ten inmate murders were associated with criminal activities of gang members—extortion, drug trafficking, prostitution, gambling—and their competition for control of illicit markets.

It is estimated that the United States now has about 13,000 prison gang members. While they account for a small proportion of all inmates, they create over half the problems. Among the many problems prison gangs present for prison officials are violence, drug trafficking, gang wars, contract murders, rapes, co-opting of guards, confrontation between gang members and non-members, and the difficulties in gaining information about secret activities. Gang-related problems may increase as more and more street gang members wind up in prison. For example, the Bloods and Crips, two well-publicized Los Angeles-based street gangs, will eventually add many from their ranks to the prison gang population—and to the wars with other dominant prison gangs.

SOURCES

1. "Arizona Prison Racial Conflicts Leave Two Dead," Associated Press, *Los Angeles Times,* October 25, 1986, p. 2.
2. George M. Camp and Camille Graham Camp, *Prison Gangs,* U.S. Department of Justice (South Salem, N.Y.: Criminal Justice Institute, 1985).
3. Robert S. Fong, "The Organizational Structure of Prison Gangs: A Texas Case Study," *Federal Probation* LIV (1990):36–43.
4. *New Mexico Prison Gangs,* The Governor's Organized Crime Prevention Commission, July 1990.
5. Robert Reinhold, "Killings Prompt Texas Prisons to Halt Inmates' Mail," *The New York Times,* January 20, 1986, p. A18.
6. Pete Earley, *The Hot House* (New York: Bantam Books, 1992), p. 81.

QUESTIONS FOR DISCUSSION

1. The article about the Arizona State Prison battle indicated that the director of corrections intended to let the leaders of the prison gangs "stop the bloodshed." Do you think corrections administrators should use inmate power groups to control institutional life?
2. What strategies might lessen the negative impact of gangs on prison life? Would those strategies infringe upon the rights of prisoners in general?
3. Why were prisons free of gangs prior to 1950?

Source: New Mexico Prison Gangs. The Governor's Organized Crime Prevention Commission, July 1990, pp. 7–10.

conclusions of John Irwin and Donald Cressey that inmate norms are imported from the outside. Inmates adapt to prison life by developing roles inside the institution that they played in the free community. Typically they develop pseudo families in which inmates adopt various roles—mother, father, sister, brother.[66] These kinship networks provide mutual support and stable relationships, and help to alleviate the deprivation caused by removal from their real families.

Investigators disagree on the extent and nature of homosexual relationships in women's prisons. Imogene Moyer argues that situations differ depending on factors specific to various institutional settings—separation of prisoners, average time served, and amount of supervision.[67] Argot terms also vary from one institution to another. Giallombardo found that inmates who were gay outside prison usually assumed a male role in prison and planned to continue homosexual liaisons after release. They were labeled "stone butch," "big hard daddy," or "true butch." A woman who played the part of the woman in a homosexual liaison was labeled "true fem." Inmates who "play the field," not making a commitment to one relationship or another, have been called "jive butches" or "jive fems."[68]

Informal social structures in women's prisons differ in a number of ways from those of male prisons. First, Edna Erez argues that an antiauthority inmate code does not appear to exist in women's prisons.[69] Second, unlike those in male prisons, homosexual relationships appear to be voluntary among women. Third, a role resembling the "right guy" does not exist: "Concepts such as 'fair play,' 'courage,' and the like—which are consistent with the concepts of endurance, loyalty, and dignity associated with the 'right guy'—are not meaningful to the female."[70] Argot terms found among women inmates are "square," "the life," and "cool." The "square"—usually a one-time offender—adheres to conventional values and wants to lead a life in prison that is respected by officers and peers. Those in "the life" are habitual offenders who are antisocial both outside and inside prison walls. "Cool" inmates are professional criminals who stay out of trouble, keep busy, and try to do "easy time" with the shortest stay.[71]

Mothers in Prison. More than 76 percent of women prisoners are mothers[72] (Table 15.1). Many give birth in prison. At most institutions mothers may keep their newborns only for a few weeks. At the Federal Correctional Institution in Lexington, Kentucky, the home of approximately 1,400 female offenders, seventy-three babies were born to incarcerated mothers at a local community contract hospital from October 1, 1988, to June 1, 1989. Between the time the mother arrives at the prison and the baby's birth, the staff does extensive preparation. The woman is interviewed to determine her possible due date and her plans for the newborn. When labor begins, she is taken by correctional staff to a local hospital for delivery. Barring complications, the inmate and her baby stay at the hospital for three days. The baby is then transported to the designated family member.

The issue of babies delivered to incarcerated women is extremely complex. The incarcerated mother fears that her infant children will no longer need her nor, in fact, recognize her upon her release.[73] Very few prisons allow mothers to keep their babies incarcerated with them. Some question whether a prison, under any circumstances, can provide safety and the proper emotional environment for a child. There are also those who take a strictly punitive view—a mother who commits a crime has lost the right to nurture and enjoy her baby. But at Bedford Hills, New York, a different philosophy is in evidence:

Tammy Taylor is worried. It's the day before her release from the maximum-security prison here, and the thought of freedom weighs on her mind.

She's been here before. But as Taylor smoothes her green prison-issue skirt and ticks off a list of things to do—reapply for welfare, visit her probation officer—a new item crops up: arrange day care.

"Very few prisons allow mothers to keep their babies with them; New York's Bedford Hills' prison nursery is definitely an exception."

TABLE 15.1 Children of State Prison Inmates, 1986

Characteristic	Percent of State Prison Inmates, 1986	
	Female	Male
Have children		
No	23.6%	40.4%
Yes	76.4	59.6
Under age 18	67.5	54.4
Adult only	8.9	5.5
Number of children under age 18[*]		
1	31.7%	42.2%
2	28.7	27.8
3–4	29.1	21.8
5–6	8.3	5.7
7 or more	2.1	2.4
Lived with child(ren) under 18 before entering prison[*]		
No	22.0%	49.5%
Yes	78.0	50.5
Had legal custody of child(ren) under 18 before entering prison[*]		
No	15.1%	53.1%
Yes	84.9	46.9
Since arrest, court placed child(ren) in custody of others[†]		
Yes	28.3%	17.0%
No	71.7	83.0
Where child(ren) under 18 live(s) now[*,**]		
Child's mother/father	22.1%	88.5%
Maternal grandparents	45.4	5.8
Paternal grandparents	7.7	4.7
Other relative	22.1	2.7
Friends	3.4	.4
Foster home	8.9	1.3
Agency/institution	1.6	.4
Other	4.3	1.8
Plan to live with child(ren) under 18 after release from prison[*]		
Yes	85.2%	51.9%
No	10.9	36.7
Don't know	3.9	11.3

[*] Percents are based on those inmates with children under age 18.

[†] Percents are based on all inmates who had legal custody of their child(ren) under age 18 before entering prison.

[**] Percents add to more than 100% because inmates with more than 1 child may have provided multiple responses.

Source: Bureau of Justice Statistics, *Women in Prison* (Washington, D.C.: Bureau of Justice Statistics, 1991).

"I'm nervous," she says. "I've been here before, but it's different going home with a baby. There's all this responsibility."

Taylor, 24, entered jail alone, but she's not leaving that way. During her prison term, her son, James Carter, was born. Now a chubby 13-month-old gnawing on an Oreo cookie, James is going home to a world he's never known. Except for his birth at a nearby hospital, this smiling toddler has never been outside the razor-ribbon fences of Bedford Hills.

In most states, James would have been taken from his mother's arms within hours after his birth and placed in foster care if there were no relatives to care for him.

Instead, he has been raised in a prison nursery—one of only three such facilities in the United States.

While these programs—all in New York state—are considered by advocates to be models for the rest of the country, corrections officials still get queasy at the thought of allowing babies to be raised behind bars. When Florida closed its nursery in 1981, one legislator applauded the action, saying: "Jail babies never smile."[74]

Phyllis Jo Baunach's study of the effects of separation on 138 inmate mothers in Washington state and Kentucky showed that the women felt guilt and shame. Many of the drug abusers, drug-free in prison, began to realize for the first time the effects of their behavior on the family. Some inmate mothers wanted their experience to serve as an example to their older children of what can happen when you commit a crime; other mothers did not tell their children about their incarceration, fearing that the children would suffer ostracism among friends.[75]

The vast majority of inmate mothers attempt to fulfill their maternal roles in spite of their incarceration. Mothers who are in prison manifest concern about the welfare of their children and generally attempt to maintain contact with them through prison visits, letters, telephone calls, and furloughs. Most inmate mothers lived with their children before their arrest and plan to reunite with them when released from prison.[76]

BEYOND CUSTODY AND CONTROL: OLD AND NEW GOALS

To this point we have discussed the primary goal of prisons, namely custody and control, and the implications of this goal for the lives of inmates. But prisons were designed for more than just custody and control. Workhouse advocates expected that habituation to good work habits would turn the prisoner into a useful citizen (besides cutting down on the cost of imprisonment or even enriching the treasury). Penitentiary advocates expected convicts to become penitent and thus less crime prone. Reformatory advocates hoped to reform inmates, and rehabilitation proponents hoped to rehabilitate or habilitate prisoners to function well in the mainstream society. Of course, accomplishing these goals requires effort by those with skills capable of producing the desired result.

The Rehabilitation Approach

Unlike rehabilitation programs of the 1970s and earlier, nearly all of today's programs are voluntary (except prison labor which, in many jurisdictions, is required). It seems that after a period of nearly twenty years during which the correctional approach was out of favor, the tide may have turned. An increasing number of criminologists and specialists in criminal justice and corrections now support a cost–benefit rehabilitative approach. As Francis T. Cullen and Karen E. Gilbert aptly remark, it is "the only justification of criminal sanctioning that obligates the state to care for an offender's needs or welfare."[77] It is a humanitarian approach. The reform-minded maintain that if we were not trying to change

"Unlike rehabilitation programs of decades past, nearly all of today's programs are voluntary."

offenders into nonoffenders, we would systematically increase the offender population. They regard the principal objective of the correctional system to be **reformation,** the voluntary transformation of an individual lacking in social or vocational skills into a productive, well-socialized citizen. According to proponents, offenders are in need of rehabilitation. They may be psychologically disturbed, addicted to alcohol or drugs, or simply lacking in the basic skills necessary to survive in a complex society.

The cards, however, are generally stacked against rehabilitation for a variety of reasons, including the age-old problem of goal conflict:

- Custodial goals may conflict with rehabilitation goals.
- Punitive goals may conflict with socialization efforts.
- Prison isolation conflicts with the goal of reintegrating offenders into society.[78]

Matching offenders with available treatment programs has been difficult in the past and will continue to be a problem.

Among criminologists, there is a strong and honest split in views. Some have little faith in rehabilitation programs or are opposed to placing the primary emphasis on treating and correcting behavior. Moreover, integration of a treatment approach with the widely accepted just-deserts model seems hard to achieve. But even those who do not support the rehabilitative model would not deny prisoners the right to participate in voluntary programs.

The Fall and Rise of Rehabilitation. **Rehabilitation** has been broadly defined as the result of any social or psychological intervention intended to reduce an offender's potential future criminal activity.[79] By this standard, the true test of success is noninvolvement in crime following participation in an intervention program. Criminologists examine recidivism data for those who have and have not been exposed to intervention programs. **Recidivism** refers to repeated or habitual relapses into criminal behavior; it may be measured by rates of re-arrest, reconviction, or reimprisonment. Supporters of rehabilitation hope to see lower recidivism rates for those who have been in rehabilitation programs. The three types of programs used most frequently are psychological (psychotherapy and behavior therapy), educational, and vocational.

Innovative rehabilitation programs usually start with great enthusiasm, but typically fail to produce results. In 1964 Daniel Glaser found that vocational rehabilitation programs had virtually no effect on postrelease behavior.[80] A 1966 evaluation of 100 correctional treatment programs concluded: "Evidence supporting the efficacy of correctional treatment is slight, inconsistent and of questionable reliability."[81] Roger Hood came to similarly disappointing conclusions in England.[82] In the early 1970s Freda Adler and her colleagues, after evaluating all Pennsylvania prison-based drug treatment programs, concluded that virtually none could claim any significant successes.[83] The most devastating evaluation was that by Douglas Lipton, Robert Martinson, and Judith Wilks, published in 1975, proclaiming that "nothing works."[84] As a result of these studies, the treatment philosophy was discredited, programs were dismantled, and the vacuum in corrections was filled by the just-deserts approach.

Some criminologists who subsequently scrutinized Martinson's evaluations found them methodologically flawed.[85] Martinson himself later confirmed that some programs have had some success in curbing recidivism.[86] After a thorough review of treatment programs initiated between 1981 and 1987, Paul Gendreau and Robert Ross concluded it is downright ridiculous to say nothing works.[87] Their analysis of biomedical, diversion, family intervention, education, get-tough, and work programs gives reason for hope. The expectation that appropriate rehabilitation efforts may yield some success in curbing recidivism rates has thus been rekindled, and the rehabilitation approach has been reborn.[88] Let us look now at some of the current programs.

reformation
Voluntary, self-initiated transformation of an individual lacking in social or vocational skills into a productive, normally functioning citizen.

"The cards are generally stacked against rehabilitation for a variety of reasons."

rehabilitation
Punishment philosophy that asserts that through proper correctional intervention, a criminal can be reformed into a law-abiding citizen.

recidivism
Repeated or habitual relapses into criminal behavior.

"Innovative rehabilitation programs are generally begun with great enthusiasm, but often fail to produce results."

Offender Therapy.   One approach to offender therapy assumes that a large proportion of inmates have failed to develop adequate internal or self controls. Psychologists, social workers, counselors, and teachers assume the task of socialization in correctional institutions. Programs attempt to socialize offenders by instilling in them a sense of responsibility and self-worth. One classic example is the BASICS (Bar Association Support to Improve Correctional Services) program in Georgia, which has an enrollment of 500 volunteer felons, nine instructors, and an annual budget of $130,000. Graduates have a recidivism rate of 7 percent, as contrasted with 35 percent for the Georgia prison population as a whole.[89]

In their recent study of the psychology of criminal behavior, Nathaniel Pallone and James Hennessy conclude that the future of rehabilitation will be found in models of education and reeducation developed for behavior therapy. These approaches seek incremental changes in behavior through incentives and disincentives. They are, therefore, far different from psychoanalytic and psychotherapeutic treatment models of the 1940s to 1970s.[90]

Vocational Training and Prison Industries

"They learn work ethics . . . and lack of work ethics is what puts a lot of them in prison."
Lieutenant Dan Clark, Angel Camp, California, quoted in *The New York Times*, August 23, 1992, p. 20.

It is fair to say that the vast majority of inmates are "economic failures." They do not have the skills and work ethic to perform gainful legitimate employment in a highly competitive society.[91] The aim of vocational training programs, therefore, is to turn these economic failures into successes. Yet vocational training and the instilling of a work ethic have a sad history in American corrections, where the state's profit motive has ranked first and meaningful vocational training for prisoners a distant second.

In the nineteenth century, American convicts were farmed out to private entrepreneurs. In Alabama until 1862, Burrows, Holt & Company used prison labor for the manufacture of "sacks, blinds, doors, russet, brogans, cabinet furniture, wagons, wheat fans, well buckets and kegs."[92] The attitudes of progressive penologists merely reinforced long-standing opposition to prison work. As early as 1801 the New York mechanics had protested the competition from prison labor. The establishment of the successful and widely imitated factory system in Auburn Prison, New York, initiated a century-long struggle culminating in federal legislation—the Hawes-Cooper Act (1929) and the Ashurst-Sumners (1935) and Sumners-Ashurst (1940) acts—and legislation in some thirty states restricting the sale of prison-made goods.[93] This vast array of restrictions crippled prison production and finally forced abandonment of the system.[94] When the lease system was abolished in the 1920s, the legislatures of southern states enacted statutes permitting state highway authorities to use prison labor on the roads.

1920s prison work program: prisoners at a southern work farm doing road work on a chain gang. Guards armed with shotguns stand watch at left and in the background.

The exploitation of prison labor came to a virtual halt in the early 1930s when federal legislation prohibited the interstate sale of prison-made goods.[95] In some states, prison administrators disregarded federal restraints on inmate labor and defiantly maintained their own prison industries. In other states, prison labor was restricted to government services such as the manufacture of license plates and the repair of state vehicles.

During the 1970s prison administrators once again realized the potential profit in prison industries. The U.S. Department of Justice now certifies state prison systems that have met certain standards, authorizing them to ship prison-made goods in interstate commerce. Today, more than thirty private-sector prison industry projects are in operation. Companies such as Best Western International Hotels, Wahlers Company (office furniture), and Utah Printing and Graphics have set up shops in prisons around the United States. Prisoners manufacture such products as disk drives, airplane parts, light metal products, and condensing units. The wages, however, are less than those paid to free workers.[96] Other troublesome issues involve industrial safety, absence of benefits, and labor union objections to competition from prisoners.

Among the states that have experimented with productive prison labor are New York and Florida. New York State created CORCRAFT, a corporation empowered to run its prison industries. It has proved economically beneficial for the state, and jobs displaced in the private sector have been more than offset by new civilian employment opportunities created by CORCRAFT.[97] Florida created PRIDE, Inc. (Prison Rehabilitative and Diversified Enterprises), a nonprofit corporation that since 1982 has operated all prison industries at double the profit made before it took over. The corporation has increased prisoner employment rates by 70 percent and seems to have lowered the recommitment rate for prisoners who participate in the program.[98] However, a study comparing the recidivism rates of former prisoners who had participated in prison industry programs and that of nonparticipants found that when differences among the two groups in regard to other characteristics associated with imprisonment were taken into account, the recidivism rates were virtually identical.[99]

In more general terms, the accepted thesis regarding the importance of work in inmate rehabilitation is that inmates who return to society unprepared for productive work roles in the community and who cannot support themselves and their dependents will, in fact, return into the criminal justice system. Therefore, the correctional system has a responsibility to help inmates become employable, not only as a means of protecting society, but also to save taxpayers' money. Moreover, preparation for employment entails more than development of job-specific talents; equally important is the need to develop positive attitudes and good work habits.[100]

A new organizational strategy for identifying motivated inmate workers in the prison population has been gaining attention nationwide—the Training Industry Education (TIE) concept. With TIE, industries and education are linked in program planning and design. Often, industries provide the training for the workers, while vocational education programs are linked with industrial objectives to ensure that inmate workers possess the necessary educational skills. Not only does the TIE approach help ensure a better quality product, but the inmate, upon release, will be a more well-rounded worker who may be successful in the outside world. The TIE concept has been implemented in the preemployment program at Nebraska State Penitentiary and Lincoln Correctional Center in Nebraska. The program is a joint endeavor between the correctional administration and Cornhusker State Industries. Special areas directly related to prison industries in Nebraska include wood and metal working and blueprint reading skills. There is also a special program in sewing. The curriculum is competence based, with progress measured by performance tests.[101]

One successful correctional program that incorporates both career planning and goal setting in its curriculum is the Vocational Assessment and Evaluation Program (VAE) at the Huron Valley Women's Facility, Ypsilanti, Michigan. The women at this facility are screened and then an individual educational requirement and educational/career plan is developed. In the orientation and counseling components of the program, the women become aware of occupational opportunities, employment trends, and the job market in locations to which they will return upon release. They are made aware of their interests and aptitudes, as well as the requirements and descriptions of a variety of jobs that have been traditionally seen as occupations for both men and women. The women have opportunities to explore career options and to become familiar with career ladders.[102]

Educational Programs

It has been argued that education for inmates will improve their chances of staying out of prison. One study found that only a third of prisoners had completed high school, contrasted with 85 percent of a cohort of 20- to 29-year-old nonprisoners.[103] Educational programs are promoted with great fervor in most prisons,

> *"I've been troubled for years by the public perception that inmates sit around all day watching TV, while the average guy is trying hard to make ends meet."* Thomas A. Coughlin, Commissioner, New York State Department of Correctional Services, quoted in *The New York Times*, January 27, 1992, p. B1.

"We have a basic responsibility to teach inmates to read and write." Thomas A. Coughlin, Commissioner, New York State Department of Correctional Services, quoted in *The New York Times*, January 27, 1992, p. B1.

1990s prison work program: inmates learn to work with computers.

yet there are continuous problems. Educational efforts in prison are far more difficult than providing public school education. Many prisoner-students have disciplinary problems, learning disabilities, adjustment problems, and a history of failure. It is not easy to find devoted and courageous teachers. Most prison educational programs must be at the elementary-school level, yet elementary-school texts are hardly fit for teaching adults. Moreover, prison education programs are dogged by Daniel Glaser's thirty-year-old finding that such programs have no impact on recidivism rates.[104]

Still, there is a great need to provide prisoners with a basic education to make them functional in society, and such programs are very much alive. Most correctional facilities currently offer academic programs with courses for which inmates are credited in accordance with state requirements. In fact, all states offer some form of academic education. Recently some 20,000 inmates were in literacy programs; some 50,000 in adult basic education; over 18,000 completed their GED (general equivalency diploma); and about 25,000 attended college classes.[105] Academic education means adult basic education (ABE), general educational development, special education, and life skills education. ABE is typically developed with two tracks—lower and upper. While these tracks are usually measured by competence in basic skills and in applied life and work skills and knowledge, the first of these tracks is developmentally equivalent to grade levels 0 through 6 in most states. Mastery of skills necessary for an acceptable level of functioning in society is an important task for this first track. The second level is generally equivalent to grades 7 and 8. To be able to compete successfully and to complete vocational training for specific trades, in most instances a minimum of an eighth-grade education is essential.[106]

Special education programs are designed to meet the needs of handicapped individuals in prisons. In fact, under federal Public Law 94-142, special education services are mandated for handicapped individuals. Life skills education encompasses developmental areas essential for effective functioning in society, on the job, in the community, in prison, and in prison industries. Life skills courses typically include health and hygiene, money management, personal economics, civic and social responsibilities, family and child development, drug education, and information about HIV and other sexually transmitted diseases. Life skills also include job-related areas such as attitudes, work habits, job seeking, and job keeping.[107] A recent review of research examining the relationship between education in prison and recidivism rates contradicts Glaser's work by finding that basic education has a positive impact on recidivism. Table 15.2 summarizes these findings.

Prison administrators have long recognized the value of rehabilitative programs for the overall prison culture. They help to maintain a more peaceful atmosphere and a certain comfort level in prison. Other programs are specifically aimed at the well-being of prisoners. These are recreational and health programs.

Recreation

Social life in prison is unimaginable without recreational programs. Prisoners need recreation to interrupt a dull routine. Recreation in prison may take many forms. At one time restricted to an hour's circular walk in the yard, then enhanced by music or individual radios, recreation now extends to television, handicrafts (and their sale), rap music, and hobby and interest sessions on any imaginable subject. Prisoners may use the skills other inmates have to start new programs, and administrators generally favor any recreational program that does not create security risks. As in normal life, sports are of paramount interest to prisoners. His fellow-inmates welcomed ex-heavyweight champion Mike Tyson to the Indiana Youth Center and wanted his autograph. For them, Tyson is

TABLE 15.2 Studies of Adult Offenders in Basic Education Programs

Study	Setting	Number of Offenders	Follow-up Period (Months)	Recidivism Effect	Recidivism Rates (%) (Participants: Nonparticipants)
Glaser, 1964	5 U.S. federal institutions	2,908	48	No	39:33
Ingalls, 1978	Canadian federal pen., Drumheller	89	60	No	81:62
Mace, 1978	West Va., state institutions	320	48	Yes	13:26
Mason & Seidler, 1977	Oregon state institutions	405	20–26	No	26:22
Stevens, 1986	18 state of Georgia institutions	3,041	24	Yes	12:19
Walsh, 1985	Adult probation, Ohio	75	42	Yes	16:44
Zink, 1970	New Castle Institution, Delaware	220	60	Yes	40:60

SOURCE: Correctional Service, Canada, "Research in Brief: Education and Recidivism," *Forum on Corrections Research* 3 (1991).

a role model. Most institutions have teams—softball, baseball, boxing, even football and soccer. Administrators like them: they take the steam out of the inmates, and they provide entertainment.[108]

Health Problems: TB and AIDS

Apart from the routine medical problems everyone encounters, prisoners have special and more profound medical problems, caused by close living and confinement. The recent spread of tuberculosis (TB) in the prisons of New York and other states is an example. In early 1992, 23 percent of New York prison inmates and 6 percent of staff tested positive for TB. (The national TB rate is 4%). TB is a typical prison disease, an airborne infection that spreads through repetitious exposure in poorly ventilated spaces.[109] Prisons are challenged to provide isolation wards for those affected and to improve ventilation for all prisoners. There is also the danger of infection for the community at large from released TB-infected convicts.

AIDS (acquired immune deficiency syndrome) poses an even greater danger, and is proving to be a vast drain on prison budgets. According to the National Institute of Justice, there were 5,411 confirmed AIDS cases among inmates in federal, state, and local correctional systems as of October 1, 1989. In New York State alone, 525 prisoners have died of AIDS. Moreover, the New York Department of Correctional Services estimated that between 17 and 20 percent of all prisoners are HIV positive (total population 54,000 inmates).[110] Coping with AIDS patients in prison is a major problem. (See the Criminal Justice in Action box.)

"He's just a kid and he's dying fast . . . trapped inside a cell sick as a dog and made to lay in his own filth. . . . Mass killers get treated better."
Angelo Rizzo, talking of another inmate in AIDS block at Rikers Island, New York. Quoted in *The New York Times*, March 5, 1987.

AIDS IN PRISON

Correctional facilities experience all the problems and controversies related to acquired immune deficiency syndrome, or AIDS, that trouble the community at large, but at a more intense level. The incidence of AIDS in prisons is nearly fourteen times higher than it is in the general population. Because of the higher concentration among inmates of people with histories of high-risk behaviors for contracting the disease, particularly IV drug use, the incidence of AIDS is 202 per 100,000 in correctional facilities versus 14.65 per 100,000 in the general population (1). In some correctional systems AIDS is now the leading cause of death, and management of AIDS-related problems has become a major item in correctional budgets.

Despite the higher AIDS incidence rates, HIV transmission is not a common occurrence within correctional institutions (2). The number of cases in correctional facilities is increasing, but not as quickly as in the general population (3). Prisons have a reputation for male homosexual activity, and that has caused fear that AIDS would spread quickly within them. But it is IV drug use that is the key AIDS risk factor for inmates (3, p. 198). (The validity of current evidence about transmission is doubted by some because of the long incubation period for the disease.) Fears that prisons are or will become "breeding grounds" for AIDS are common (3, p. 196).

With no cure for AIDS and no vaccine to protect against the virus that causes it, long-term health care for infected inmates and long-range plans for minimizing transmission both are important. The fear of contagion is great, both among prison guards and among inmates, raising questions about isolation or quarantine of AIDS-infected prisoners—but civil libertarians are opposed to segregating infected patients unless the patient needs to be protected from the violence of others or has valid medical needs that can be met only through segregation (3, p. 202). There is little risk of HIV infection through assault and none through casual contact, but corrections officers often are afraid of dealing with HIV-infected inmates, and administrators must devise strategies for coping with such fears.

AIDS patients suffer mental as well as physical distress, and their psychological needs can affect other inmates and prison officials. Inmates with HIV infection need psychological help to cope with persistent anxiety and depression. Every cold or skin lesion may signal the onset of serious pneumonia or skin cancer. With little or nothing to do with their time, inmates may become totally preoccupied with the possibility of death. Others who want to regain a sense of power and control may use their diagnosis to manipulate or threaten prison officials or other inmates. They insist on particular medical treatments or institutional privileges to prevent their condition from deteriorating.

The cost of caring for one terminal AIDS patient has been estimated to be $500,000. Most prison systems and about 75 percent of jails provide AZT, an expensive AIDS drug. How should prison officials deal with the financial strain AIDS puts on the entire medical budget? Prison hospitals are not equipped to provide adequate care for AIDS patients, but the placement of such patients in community hospitals poses security risks. In a recent case (*Dow v. State of New York*), $5.4 million in damages were awarded to a 42-year-old nurse who tested positive for HIV after being jabbed by an intravenous needle that came loose while she tried to restrain an AIDS-infected inmate being treated in a community hospital. Nurses testified that they had screamed fifty times for help from corrections officers who were standing in the doorway and did nothing to help (4).

Prison administrators are pursuing a multipronged approach to handle the AIDS problem, an approach that takes into account the needs of the uninfected population as well as the needs of those who are infected. This approach involves health care for the ill, risk reduction for the well, and education and training for both.

The goal of education and training is to decrease transmission behaviors inside and outside the institution, decrease anxieties and fear among staff and inmates, and minimize operational problems surrounding the management of inmates with AIDS. Virtually all correctional systems currently are offering or developing AIDS training sessions or educational materials for staff and inmates. Evaluations of the impact of such programs conclude that while it is possible to change HIV risk behavior, such change is highly unlikely with the current programs (5). What is needed are programs targeted to change specific high-risk behaviors, particularly IV drug use, but researchers say that so little reliable information about AIDS education programs in prisons is available that their effectiveness can't be judged. Further, prison policies may prevent prisoners from adopting lower-risk behaviors, such as using condoms or disinfecting needles with bleach (5, p. 345). Nevertheless, it is crucial to provide accurate information to inmates and staff, if only to reduce fear. And while current information suggests the transmission rate of AIDS to be low inside correctional facilities, there may be other reasons to provide prisoners with education:

. . . many inmates have been deeply involved in high risk behaviors outside of prison, and public health efforts typically have been ineffective in reaching this population. These factors forbode a potentially serious public health hazard as prisoners are released back into the community, and this seems a sufficient justification for aggressive intervention efforts during incarceration. (5, p. 345)

Most issues facing corrections officials are the same as those faced by society in general: Should prisons institute mandatory testing programs? Who should have access to the results of positive HIV tests? Should educational programs emphasize abstinence or "safer sex," stopping drugs, or use of drugs with sterile needles? Should condoms be distributed, or does that encourage sex activity? Should an inmate's family or sex partner be notified if he or she develops AIDS? Researcher Mark Blumberg raises these issues and a more general one: "At the heart of the debate is this question: Should prisons and jails adhere to the practices of the larger society, or is the institutional environment sufficiently unique that deviations from these policies are acceptable?" (2, p. 196)

Thus far, the challenge of handling AIDS in prison has not been met. Administrators need to gear up to a problem that is expected to increase. Short-term "crisis" management has not been successful. Experts argue that long-term plans must be made on issues of housing, medical service, and better education of staff and inmates. But with increasing prison overcrowding and growing budgetary constraints, the AIDS crisis in prison appears to be one that will exist indefinitely.

SOURCES

1. Theodore M. Hammett and Saira Moini, "Update on AIDS in Prisons and Jails," *National Institute of Justice AIDS Bulletin,* September 1990.
2. Mark Blumberg, "The Transmission of HIV: Exploring Some Misconceptions Related to Criminal Justice," *Criminal Justice Policy Review* 4 (1990):288–305.
3. Mark Blumberg, "Issues and Controversies with Respect to the Management of AIDS in Corrections," in *AIDS: The Impact on the Criminal Justice System,* ed. Mark Blumberg (Columbus, Ohio: Merrill, 1990), p. 195.
4. John O'Brien, "Record Award in HIV Needle Case," *New York Law Journal,* July 14, 1992, p. 1.
5. Randy Martin and Sherwood E. Zimmerman, "Adopting Precautions against HIV Infection among Male Prisoners: A Behavioral and Policy Analysis," *Criminal Justice Policy Review* 4 (1990):330–348.

QUESTIONS FOR DISCUSSION

1. The French correctional system has special institutions for the handicapped, those suffering from infectious diseases, and other groups. Should we follow this model in dealing with HIV-positive prisoners?

2. How would you answer Blumberg's question? Should correctional facilities abide by the decisions reached in "the larger society" with respect to AIDS testing, condom distribution, and so on?

3. Do you think condoms and sterile needles should be made available to inmates? Why or why not?

In 1990 AIDS sufferer Patrick McGuire spent his final months in prison after an arrest for breaking and entering when area hospitals refused to treat him because of his past behavior.

Mental Health

Mentally ill offenders pose a special and costly challenge for correctional services. Every state operates one or more facilities for mentally ill offenders. A small part of this population (8%) is made up of persons acquitted by reason of insanity. An even smaller part is made up of sex offenders. Nearly one-third (32%) of the patients are individuals unable to stand trial by virtue of mental illness, and over half (54%) are prisoners who have become mentally ill in prison.[111]

The nation's jails have been swelled by former or would-be mental patients who, under the deinstitutionalization policies in effect since the 1960s, are no longer cared for in mental hospitals. They are forced to live on their own, frequently become homeless, and are often in conflict with the law.[112] Prison and jail inmates often migrate between correctional and mental health facilities.[113] The cost to the public is considerable, and there are no promising cures on the horizon.

Drug and Alcohol Abuse

In addition to AIDS and mental health problems, inmates bring their drug and alcohol problems with them to jails and prisons.[114] A 1987 survey of 1,687 U.S. jails found that only about 7 percent of an average daily population of jail inmates are enrolled in drug treatment programs. Even in jails that have such programs, only about 13 percent receive daily treatment. Further, even among many of the more comprehensive programs, treatment services are not comparable to those provided in community residential or intensive outpatient programs. Only a small fraction, perhaps fewer than 10 percent, of those requiring drug treatment actually receive these services. The costs of operating an in-jail drug treatment program are relatively modest, about $3.50 per day, per inmate, above and beyond the ordinary cost of incarceration. Enhanced treatment services would raise this cost to no more than eight dollars per day.

In 1988, a National Abuse Program Coordinator position was established to oversee the development and implementation of new drug treatment strategies for federal inmates. The multidimensional approach to serving the growing population of drug-abusing inmates includes four types of programs: drug education, drug abuse counseling services, residential drug abuse treatment, and transitional services.[115] Many criminal justice personnel believe that rehabilitative efforts aimed at substance-abusing offenders are relatively ineffective.[116]

Religion in Prison

Religion has been part of prison life since the establishment of prisons 450 years ago. It is surprising, however, that until recently not a single study documented the influence of religious experiences on prisoners.[117] Recent studies have revealed a modest to strong relationship between religiosity, religious commitment, and coping in prison.[118]

Furloughs

To soldiers and prisoners equally, a furlough and thus a break with boredom or stress is one of the most welcome privileges. Furloughs may be granted as a reward for good behavior, or for purposes of participating in some outside program (education, or work-release), or for compassionate reasons such as a death in the family. During the 1970s, furloughs were increasingly granted. Only a very small proportion of prisoners on furlough did not return to the institution, or did not return in a timely fashion.

A 1988 survey of home furlough programs, with a sample of forty-seven state and federal prison directors, showed that such programs were extremely conservative. Alaska, Illinois, Nevada, Washington, and Wyoming reported either inactive or extremely conservative programs. In the first half of 1988, a total of 67,736 furloughs were granted with a low rate (less than 1%) of reported absconding. During the reporting period, about twenty offenders (not including escapees) were involved in criminal activity or were arrested while on furlough. Thirty-eight respondents indicated that home furloughs help rehabilitation efforts; two reported they do not.[119] A recent study examined two types of correctional programs—community-based prison prerelease programs and furloughs—and found them to have a pronounced and consistently positive impact on recidivism.[120]

Furlough programs, like probation and parole, are strongly influenced by public opinion. It takes only one major failure to result in program curtailment or abandonment. The Willie Horton case is an example. Horton, a convicted murderer, committed rape and an assault while on furlough from a Massachusetts state prison. During the 1988 presidential campaign the Horton case became a major issue for liberal Democrats and conservative Republicans. The result was a sharp restriction of the federal furlough program: Whereas 4,610 federal furloughs had been granted in 1987, the number was down to 3,190 by 1991. If we consider that during the same period the federal prison population increased from 44,679 to 63,041, the furlough rate had in fact been decreased by over 50 percent. Still, all prison systems continue to operate furlough programs, in some places, on a reduced scale and often with a change in name, such as work-release.[121]

REVIEW

A very strong concern for security marks the American prison today. Maximum security prisons are dedicated solely to that purpose. Medium security prisons have a somewhat more relaxed attitude but still emphasize security. Only minimum security prisons subordinate security to institutional programs.

Prisoners live "by the rules"; their assignments depend on their "classification" (profile). Corrections officers—predominantly custodial—have a difficult life in an environment that always seems threatening, yet their salaries and social prestige are low. Given the history of prison riots and attacks on officers, this fear is not exaggerated. The majority of inmates are young, black, undereducated, and largely aggressive. Aggressiveness is aggravated by prison overcrowding.

Women's prisons have their own distinct problems. Their subcultures include the formation of pseudo-families. Three-quarters of all imprisoned women are mothers. In some states mothers may keep their newborns with them for a while, but in most states children are placed with relatives in the community.

Correctional goals have changed somewhat over the last thirty years. Rehabilitation programs today are entirely voluntary, there are fewer of them, and enthusiasm has decreased ever since, in the 1970s, researchers demonstrated their overall ineffectiveness. But rehabilitation is making a comeback.

Vocational training and prison labor have likewise been transformed. Some correctional systems have formed their own prison industry organizations, and these are producing profits and creating skills and work discipline for inmates. Educational programs, provided by all federal and state correction systems, cover basic academic subjects as well as life skills.

Contemporary prison health problems are severe, particularly because of AIDS and TB. Programs designed to promote health, including mental health, through hygiene and recreation, are found in all prisons. Furlough programs, despite their positive effect on morale, have been decreasing for security reasons.

Notes

1. Jim Quillan, *Alcatraz from Inside* (San Francisco: Golden Gate National Park Association, 1991). pp. 154, 155.

2. Harry Elmer Barnes and Neagley K. Teeters, *New Horizons in Criminology*, 2d ed. (Englewood Cliffs, N.J.: Prentice-Hall, 1951), p. 456

3. The President's Commission on Law Enforcement and Administration of Justice, *Task Force Report: Corrections* (Washington, D.C.: U.S. Government Printing Office, 1967).

4. National Advisory Commission on Criminal Justice Standards and Goals, *Corrections* (Washington, D.C.: U.S. Government Printing Office, 1973).

5. *Bruscino v. Carlson*, 854 F.2d (7th Cir. 1988).

6. *Prison Conditions in the United States*, Human Rights Watch Report (New York: Human Rights Watch, 1991). p. 43.

7. George M. Camp and Camille Graham Camp, *The Corrections Yearbook, 1991: Adult Prisons and Jails* (South Salem, N.Y.: Criminal Justice Institute, 1991), pp. 23, 24.

8. American Correctional Association and Commission on Accreditation for Corrections, *Standards for Adult Correctional Institutions*, 2d ed. (College Park, Md.: American Correctional Association, 1981), p. 23.

9. *Guidelines for the Development of Policies and Procedures, Adult Correctional Institutions* (College Park, Md.: American Correctional Association, May 1981).

10. *Inmate Rule Book*, State of Kansas, May 1, 1986.

11. Ibid.

12. David R. Eichenthal and James B. Jacobs, "Enforcing the Criminal Law in State Prisons," *Justice Quarterly* 8 (1991):283–303. See also Rebecca L. Bordt and Michael C. Musheno, "Bureaucratic Co-optation of Informal Dispute Processing: Social Control as an Effect of Inmate Grievance Policy," *Journal of Research in Crime and Delinquency* 25 (1988):7–26.

13. Classification, which usually takes three to six weeks, is done either in a central recovery facility that serves the entire system or (in most states) in a reception center within each facility. For important classification factors, see Doris Layton MacKenzie and Robert A. Buchanan, "The Process of Classification in Prisons: A Descriptive Study of Staff Use of the System," *Journal of Crime and Justice* 13 (1990):1–26. For an empirical study of the processing of inmates demonstrating inappropriate classification, see Gary L. Webb, *The Prison Ordeal* (Fayetteville, GA: Coker, 1984). For innovative correctional programs, see Bruce I. Wolford and Pam Lawrenz, *Classification: Innovative Correctional Programs* (Richmond, KY: Department of Correctional Services, Eastern Kentucky University, 1988)—includes historical trends (Michael W. Forcier), classification and managing resources (Carl B. Clements), needs of learning-handicapped (Robert Hoellein and Nancy H. Yauger), a process for development (Karen L. Whitlow and Robert A. Buchanan), effect on social climate (William Carter Smith), effect of direct supervision on classification system (Sandra Denise Thacker), and the Massachusetts system (Michael W. Forcier).

14. For classification in jails, see Terry Wilson, "New System Keeps Track of Inmates," *Chicago Tribune*, January 20, 1992, p. C3.

15. James Austin, "Objective Jail Classification—Screening Jail Inmates: An Effective Tool for Improving Security," *Corrections Today* (July 1991).

16. Lucien X. Lombardo, *Guards Imprisoned* (New York: Elsevier, 1981), p. 21.

17. Nicolette Parisi, "The Female Correctional Officer: Her Progress toward and Prospects for Equality," *Prison Journal* 64 (1984):92–109. See also Kevin N. Wright and William G. Saylor, "Male and Female Employees' Perceptions of Prison Work: Is There a Difference?," *Justice Quarterly* 8 (1991):504–524.

18. Kathleen Maguire and Timothy J. Flanagan, *Sourcebook of Criminal Justice Statistics—1990* (Washington, D.C.: U.S. Government Printing Office, 1991), p. 612. See also Elizabeth L. Grossi and Bruce L. Berg, "Stress and Job Dissatisfaction among Correctional Officers: An Unexpected Finding," *International Journal of Offender Therapy and Comparative Criminology* 35 (1991):73–91.

19. Gresham Sykes, *The Society of Captives: A Study of a Maximum Security Prison* (Princeton, N.J.: Princeton University Press, 1958).

20. Lombardo, *Guards Imprisoned*, p. 39.

21. Kelsey Kauffman, *Prison Officers and Their World* (Cambridge, Mass.: Harvard University Press, 1988).

22. Lombardo, *Guards Imprisoned*, p. 115; Stephen C. Light, "Assaults on Prison Officers: Interactional Themes," *Justice Quarterly* 8 (1991):243–261. See also John R. Hepburn, "The Prison Control Structure and Its Effects on Work Attitudes: The Perceptions and Attitudes of Prison Guards," *Journal of Criminal Justice* 15 (1987):49–64.

23. Lombardo, *Guards Imprisoned*, pp. 113–140.

24. Francis Cullen, Bruce Link, John Cullen, and Nancy Wolfe,

"How Satisfying Is Prison Work? A Comparative Occupational Approach," *Journal of Offender Counseling, Services and Rehabilitation* 14 (1989):89–108. See also William G. Saylor and Kevin N. Wright, "Status, Longevity, and Perceptions of the Work Environment among Federal Prison Employees," *Journal of Offender Rehabilitation* 17 (1992):133–160.

25. George M. Camp and Camille Graham Camp, *The Corrections Yearbook*, pp. 10–12.

26. Ibid., p. 24. On the special problems of older inmates, male and female, see Peter C. Kratcosci and Susan Babb, "Adjustment of Older Inmates: An Analysis by Institutional Structure and Gender," *Journal of Contemporary Criminal Justice* 6 (1990):264–281.

27. Maguire and Flanagan, *Sourcebook of Criminal Justice Statistics*, p. 612.

28. Ibid.

29. Bureau of Justice Statistics, *Annual Report, Fiscal 1986* (Washington, D.C.: U.S. Government Printing Office, April 1987), p. 39.

30. Joan Petersilia, "Racial Disparities in the Criminal Justice System: A Summary," *Crime and Delinquency* 31 (1985):15–34.

31. Tracy L. Snell and Danielle C. Morton, *Prisoners in 1991*, Bureau of Justice Statistics Bulletin (Washington, D.C.: U.S. Department of Justice, May 1992), p. 7.

32. John Irwin, *The Jail: Managing the Underclass in American Society* (Berkeley: University of California Press, 1985), p. 29.

33. Lawrence A. Greenfeld et al., *Prisoners in 1989* (Washington, D.C.: U.S. Department of Justice, Bureau of Justice Statistics), p. 4.

34. Ibid.

35. Bureau of Justice Statistics, *National Update* (Washington, D.C.: U.S. Department of Justice, April 1992), p. 7.

36. Social scientists began to study inmate subcultures in 1934 with the publication of Joseph Fishman's *Sex in Prison* (New York: Padell Book Co., 1934).

37. Donald Clemmer, *The Prison Community* (New York: Holt, Rinehart and Winston, 1940). For adjustment to prison, see Kevin N. Wright, "A Study of Individual, Environmental, and Interactive Effects in Explaining Adjustment to Prison," *Justice Quarterly* 8 (June 1991):216–242.

38. For a full discussion of the "society of captives," the process of imprisonment, the inmate code, and the argot roles, see Gresham M. Sykes, *The Society of Captives*.

39. For a discussion of how prisoners deal with rejection from the free community, see Lloyd W. McCorkle and Richard Korn, "Resocialization within Walls," *Annals of the Academy of Political and Social Science* 293 (1954):88–98.

40. Susan Sheehan, *A Prison and a Prisoner* (Boston: Houghton Mifflin, 1978).

41. Alan J. Davis, "Sexual Assaults in the Philadelphia Prison System," in *Corrections: Problems and Prospects*, eds. David M. Peterson and Charles W. Thomas (Englewood Cliffs, N.J.: Prentice-Hall, 1975), pp. 64–75.

42. Camp and Camp, *Corrections Yearbook* (South Salem, N.Y.: Criminal Justice Institute, 1989), p. 40; J. Q. Burstein, *Conjugal Visits in Prison: Psychological and Social Consequences* (Lexington, Mass.: Lexington Books, 1977); Ann Goetting, "Conjugal Association in Prison: Issues and Perspectives," *Crime and Delinquency* 28 (1982):52–71; Randolph Davis, "Education and the Impact of the Family Reunion Program in a Maximum Security Prison," *Journal of Offender Counseling, Services, and Rehabilitation* 12 (1988):153–159.

43. See Gresham M. Sykes and Sheldon L. Messinger, "The Inmate Social System," in *Theoretical Studies in the Social Organization of the Prison*, eds. Richard A. Cloward, Donald R. Cressey, George H. Gresser, Richard McCleery, Lloyd E. Ohlin, Gresham M. Sykes, and Sheldon L. Messinger (New York: Social Science Research Council, 1960), pp. 6–8. See also Sykes, *Society of Captives*, pp. 63–108.

44. Sykes, *Society of Captives*, p. 107.

45. Clarence Schrag, "Some Foundations for a Theory of Cor-

rections," in *The Prison: Studies in Institutional Organization and Change*, ed. Donald R. Cressey (New York: Holt, Rinehart and Winston, 1961). For a comparative analysis, see William G. Archambeault and Charles Fenwick, "A Comparative Analysis of Culture, Safety, and Organizational Management Factors in Japanese and U.S. Prisons," *Prison Journal* 68 (1988):3–23.

46. John Irwin and Donald R. Cressey, "Thieves, Convicts, and the Inmate Culture," *Social Problems* 10 (1962):142–155.

47. Frank S. Pearson, "Evaluation of New Jersey's Intensive Supervision Program," *Crime and Delinquency* 34 (1988):437–448.

48. R. G. Leger, "Perception of Crowding, Racial Antagonism, and Aggression in a Custodial Prison," *Journal of Criminal Justice* 16 (1988):167–181, p. 178.

49. Leo Carroll, *Hacks, Blacks, and Cons: Race Relations in a Maximum Security Prison* (Lexington, Mass.: Lexington Books, 1974).

50. John Irwin, *Prisons in Turmoil* (Boston: Little, Brown, 1980).

51. "Special Prison Food Designed to Bounce," *Los Angeles Times*, July 6, 1991, p. A21.

52. James B. Jacobs, "Prisons: Prison Subculture," in *Encyclopedia of Crime and Justice*, ed. Sanford H. Kadish (New York: Free Press, 1983), p. 1224; James B. Jacobs, *New Perspectives on Prisons and Imprisonment* (Ithaca, N.Y.: Cornell University, 1983); Robert A. Buchanan, Cindie A. Unger, and Karen L. Whitlow, *Disruptive Maximum Security Inmate Management Guide* (Washington, D.C.: U.S. National Institute of Corrections, 1988).

53. Michael S. Serrill and Peter Katel, "New Mexico: The Anatomy of a Riot," *Corrections Magazine* 6 (1980):6–7. For causes of riots, see Randy Martin and Sherwood Zimmerman, "A Typology of the Causes of Prison Riots and an Analytical Extension to the 1986 West Virginia Riot," *Justice Quarterly* 7 (1990):711–737.

54. Marvin E. Wolfgang and Franco Ferracuti, *The Subculture of Violence* (London: Tavistock, 1967), p. 263.

55. Lee H. Bowker, "Victimizers and Victims in American Correctional Institutions," in *Pains of Imprisonment*, eds. Robert Johnson and Hans Toch (Beverly Hills, Calif.: Sage, 1982), p. 64; Peter Kratcoski, "The Implications of Research Explaining Prison Violence and Disruption," *Federal Probation* 52 (1988):27–32; Randy Martin and Sherwood Zimmerman, "A Typology of the Causes of Prison Riots and an Analytical Extension to the 1986 West Virginia Riot," *Justice Quarterly* 7 (1990):711–737.

56. For a study of violence in female prisons, see Richard H. Anson and Barry W. Hancock, "Crowding, Proximity, Inmate Violence, and the Eighth Amendment," *Journal of Offender Rehabilitation* 17 (1992):123–132; Candace Kruttschnitt and Sharon Krmpotich, "Aggressive Behavior among Female Inmates: An Exploratory Study," *Justice Quarterly* 7 (1990):371–389.

57. Gerald G. Gaes, "The Effects of Overcrowding in Prison," in *Crime and Justice: An Annual Review of Research*, eds. Norval Morris and Michael Tonry (Chicago: University of Chicago Press, 1985).

58. Lee H. Bowker, *Prison Victimization* (New York: Elsevier, 1980), p. 25.

59. Hans Toch, *Peacekeeping: Police, Prisons, and Violence* (Lexington, Mass.: Lexington Books, 1976), pp. 47–48.

60. John J. Di Iulio, Jr., *No Escape: The Future of American Corrections* (New York: Basic Books, 1990), p. 12.

61. Bert Useem and Peter Kimball, *States of Siege: U.S. Prison Riots, 1971–1986* (New York: Oxford University Press, 1989), p. 227.

62. Freda Adler, *Sisters in Crime* (New York: McGraw-Hill, 1975), pp. 180–181.

63. Camp and Camp, *Corrections Yearbook*, 1991, p. 24. For an historical study of the problems of female inmates, see Beverly A. Smith, "The Female Prisoner in Ireland, 1855–1878," *Federal Probation* 54 (1990):69–81; Beverly A. Smith, "Female Admissions and Paroles of the Western House of Refuge in the 1880s: An Historical Example of Community Corrections," *Journal of Research in Crime and Delinquency* 26 (1989):36–66.

64. Joycelyn M. Pollock-Byrne, *Women, Prison, and Crime* (Pacific Grove, Calif.: Brooks/Cole, 1990), pp. 57, 58; see also Ronald Barre Flowers, *Women and Criminality: The Woman as Victim, Offender, and Practitioner* (New York: Greenwood, 1987), p. 152.

65. Rose Giallombardo, *Society of Women: A Study of a Women's Prison* (New York: Wiley, 1966).

66. David A. Ward and Gene G. Kasselbaum, *Women's Prison: Sex and Social Structure* (Chicago: Aldine, 1965).

67. Imogene L. Moyer, "Differential Social Structures and Homosexuality among Women in Prison," *Virginia Social Science Journal* 13 (1978), pp. 13–14, 17–19.

68. Rose Giallombardo, *The Social World of Imprisoned Girls* (New York: Wiley, 1974), pp. 146–147. See also Alice Propper, *Prison Homosexuality: Myth and Reality* (Lexington, Mass.: Lexington Books, 1981).

69. Edna Erez, "The Myth of the New Female Offender: Some Evidence from Attitudes toward Law and Justice," *Journal of Criminal Justice* 16 (1988):499–509.

70. Giallombardo, *Society of Women*, p. 130.

71. Esther Heffernan, *Making It in Prison* (New York: Wiley, 1972), pp. 41–42.

72. Bureau of Justice Statistics, *Women in Prison* (Washington, D.C.: Bureau of Justice Statistics, 1991), p. 6.

73. Joyce Carmouche and Joretta Jones, "Her Children, Their Future: Learning to Parent in Federal Prison," *Federal Prisons Journal* 1 (1989):23, 26, 27.

74. Paul La Rosa, "Babies Behind Bars; In 3 New York Prisons, Inmates Who Give Birth May Keep Their Babies with Them. Dr. Spock Endorsed the Idea, but Critics Are Queasy," *Los Angeles Times*, May 12, 1992, p. E1.

75. Phyllis Jo Baunach, *Mothers in Prison* (New Brunswick, N.J.: Transaction, 1985); Phyllis Jo Baunach, "Critical Problems of Women in Prison," in *The Changing Roles of Women in the Criminal Justice System: Offenders, Victims, and Professionals*, ed. Imogene L. Moyer (Prospect Heights, Ill.: Waveland, 1992), pp. 99–112.

76. See, for example, D. Lundberg, A. Sheekley, and T. Voelker, "An Exploration of the Feelings and Attitudes of Women Separated from Their Children Due to Incarceration," unpublished master's thesis, Portland State University, 1975; B. McGowen and K. Blumenthal, "Children of Women Prisoners: A Forgotten Minority," in *The Female Offender*, ed. L. Crites (Lexington, Mass.: D.C. Heath, 1976); M. Bonfanti, "Enactment and Perception of a Maternal Role of Incarcerated Mothers," unpublished master's thesis, Louisiana State University, 1971.

77. Francis T. Cullen and Karen E. Gilbert, *Reaffirming Rehabilitation* (Cincinnati: Anderson, 1982), p. 247. It appears that wardens had never really given up on the rehabilitative idea. See Francis T. Cullen, Edward J. Latessa, Velmer S. Burton, Jr., and Lucien X. Lombardo, "The Correctional Orientation of Prison Wardens: Is the Rehabilitative Ideal Supported?," *Criminology* 31 (1993):69–92.

78. Michael Lipsky, *Street-Level Bureaucracy: Dilemmas of the Individual in Public Services* (New York: Russell Sage Foundation, 1980).

79. D. Sechrest, S. O. White, and E. D. Brown, eds., *The Rehabilitation of Criminal Offenders: Problems and Prospects* (Washington, D.C.: National Academy of Sciences, 1979).

80. Daniel Glaser, *The Effectiveness of a Prison and Parole System* (Indianapolis: Bobbs-Merrill, 1964).

81. Walter C. Bailey, "Correctional Outcome: An Evaluation of 100 Reports," *Journal of Criminal Law, Criminology, and Police Science* 57 (1966):153–160.

82. Roger Hood, "Research on the Effectiveness of Punishments and Treatments," in *Collected Studies in Criminological Research* (Strasbourg: Council of Europe, European Committee on Crime Problems, 1967).

83. Freda Adler, Arthur D. Moffett, Frederick B. Glaser, John C. Ball, and Diane Horwitz, *A Systems Approach to Drug Treatment* (Philadelphia: Dorrance, 1974).

84. Douglas Lipton, Robert Martinson, and Judith Wilks, *The Effectiveness of Correctional Treatment: A Survey of Treatment Evalu-*

ation Studies (New York: Praeger, 1975); Robert Martinson, "What Works?: Questions and Answers About Prison Reform," *Public Policy* 35 (1974):22–54.

85. Carl B. Klockars, "The True Limits of the Effectiveness of Correctional Treatment," *Prison Journal* 55 (1975):53–64; Ted Palmer, "Martinson Revisited," *Journal of Research in Crime and Delinquency* 12 (1975):133–152.

86. Robert Martinson, "New Findings, New Views: A Note of Caution Regarding Sentencing Reform," *Hofstra Law Review* 7 (1979):254–258.

87. Paul Gendreau and Robert R. Ross, "Revivification of Rehabilitation: Evidence from the 1980's," *Justice Quarterly* 4 (1987):395–407; Francis T. Cullen and Paul Gendreau, "The Effectiveness of Correctional Rehabilitation: Reconsidering the 'Nothing Works' Debate," in *The American Prison: Issues in Research and Policy,* ed. Lynne Goodstein and Doris Layton Mackenzie (New York: Plenum, 1989), pp. 23–44.

88. Carol J. Garrett, "Effects of Residential Treatment on Adjudicated Delinquents: A Meta-analysis," *Journal of Research in Crime and Delinquency* 22 (1985):287–308; Carol J. Garrett, *Treating the Criminal Offender,* 3d ed. (New York: Plenum, 1988). See also D. A. Andrews, Ivan Zinger, Robert D. Hoge, James Bonta, Paul Gendreau, and Francis T. Cullen, "Does Correctional Treatment Work? A Clinically Relevant and Psychologically Informed Meta-Analysis," *Criminology* 28 (1990):369–404; Steven P. Lab and John T. Whitehead, "From 'Nothing Works' to 'The Appropriate Works': The Latest Stop on the Search for the Secular Grail," *Criminology* 28 (1990):405–417.

89. Chris Drake, "Back to Basics," *American Bar Association Journal* (1991):64–67.

90. Nathaniel J. Pallone and James J. Hennessy, *Criminal Behavior—A Process Psychology Analysis* (New Brunswick, N.J.: Transaction Publishers, 1992), pp. 362–363.

91. G. O. W. Mueller, "Economic Failures in the Iron Womb: The Birth of Rational Alternatives to Imprisonment," in *Sentencing: Process and Purpose,* Ch. 6 (Springfield, Ill.: Charles C. Thomas, 1977), pp. 110–143. See also William S. Laufer, "Vocational Interests of Criminal Offenders: A Typological and Demographic Investigation," *Psychological Reports* 46 (1980):315–324.

92. Thorsten Sellin, *Slavery and the Penal System* (New York: Elsevier, 1976), p. 143.

93. Hawes-Cooper Act (1929), 49 U.S.C. Art. 60; Ashurst-Sumners (1935) and Sumners-Ashurst (1940) Acts, 18 U.S.C. 1761, 49 Stat. 494 and 54 Stat. 1134.

94. Gordon Hawkins, "Prison Labor and Prison Industries," in *Crime and Justice: An Annual Review of Research,* ed. Norval Morris and Michael Tonry, vol. 5 (Chicago: University of Chicago Press, 1983). See also Frank Flynn, "Employment and Labor," *Contemporary Correction,* ed. Paul Tappan (New York: McGraw-Hill, 1951).

95. Barnes and Teeters, *New Horizons in Criminology,* p. 702.

96. Todd Clear and George F. Cole, *American Corrections* (Pacific Grove, Calif.: Brooks/Cole, 1990), pp. 348–354.

97. Institute for Economic and Policy Studies, *The Economic Impact of Corcraft Correctional Industries in New York State* (Alexandria, Va.: Institute for Economic and Policy Studies, 1988).

98. Florida House of Representatives, Committee on Corrections, Probation, and Parole, *Oversight Report on PRIDE* (Tallahassee, Fla., 1988).

99. Kathleen Maguire, Timothy J. Flanagan, and Terence P. Thornberry, "Prison Labor and Recidivism," *Journal of Quantitative Criminology* 4 (1988):3–18.

100. American Correctional Association, *Perspectives on Inmate Work Programs* (Washington, D.C.: St. Mary's Press, 1990); Dianne Carter, "The Status of Education and Training in Corrections," *Federal Probation* 55 (1991):17–23.

101. American Correctional Association, *Perspectives on Inmate Work Programs.*

102. Ibid.

103. Bureau of Justice Statistics, *Report to the Nation on Crime and Justice: The Data,* 2d ed. (Washington, D.C.: U.S. Government Printing Office, 1989), p. 37.

104. Daniel Glaser, *The Effectiveness of a Prison and Parole System;* Daniel Glaser, "The Effectiveness of Correctional Education," *American Journal of Corrections* 28 (1966):4–9.

105. William Timmins, "Prison Education in Utah: From 'The Penwiper' to the 'South Park Academy,'" *Journal of Offender Counseling, Services and Rehabilitation* 14 (1989):61–76.

106. American Correctional Association, *Perspectives on Inmate Work Programs;* Robert B. Rutherford, C. Michael Nelson, and Bruce I. Wolford, "Special Education in the Most Restrictive Environment: Correctional/Special Education," *Journal of Special Education* 19 (1985):59–71.

107. Ibid.

108. Rick Telander, "Sports behind the Walls," *Sports Illustrated,* October 17, 1988, p. 82.

109. Lisa Belkin, "23% of State Prisoners Test Positive for TB," *The New York Times,* March 31, 1992, p. B4; Mireya Navairro, "As Suspects Wait, the Fear of Tuberculosis Rises," *The New York Times,* January 30, 1992, pp. B1, 2.

110. National Commission on AIDS, *Report: HIV Disease in Correctional Facilities* (Washington, D.C.: National Commission on AIDS, 1991). See also Sherwood E. Zimmerman and Randy Martin, "AIDS Knowledge and Risk Perceptions among Pennsylvania Prisoners," *Journal of Criminal Justice* 19 (1991):239–256.

111. Bureau of Justice Statistics, *Report to the Nation on Crime and Justice* (Washington, D.C.: U.S. Government Printing Office, 1983), p. 68. On the extent of psychopathology in prison, as related to violence, see Deborah R. Baskin, Ira Sommers, and Henry H. Steadman, "Assessing the Impact of Psychiatric Impairment on Prison Violence," *Journal of Criminal Justice* 19 (1991):271–280. For the implications arising out of the need to provide medication for psychiatrically impaired prisoners, see Ira Sommers and Deborah Baskin, "Assessing the Appropriateness of the Prescription of Psychiatric Medications in Prison," *Journal of Nervous and Mental Disease* 179(5) (1991):267–273; Ira Sommers and Deborah Baskin, "The Prescription of Psychiatric Medications in Prison: Psychiatric Versus Labeling Perspectives," *Justice Quarterly* 7 (1990):739–755.

112. Freda Adler, "Jail as a Repository for Former Mental Patients," *International Journal of Offender Therapy and Comparative Criminology* 30 (1986):225–236.

113. Henry J. Steadman and Joseph J. Cocozza, *Careers of the Criminally Insane* (Lexington, Mass.: Lexington Books, 1974), p. 17.

114. There is the additional problem of controlling drug and alcohol abuse inside prison. See Gerald Vigdal and Donald Stadler, "Controlling Inmate Drug Use: Cut Consumption by Reducing Demand," *Corrections Today* (June 1989).

115. Susan Wallace, "Beyond 'Nothing Works': History and Current Initiatives in BOP Drug Treatment," *Federal Prisons* 1 (1990):22–26. For an overview of other substance abuse programs in prison, see "Substance Abuse: Responding to the Crisis," in the special edition of *Corrections Today* 51 (1989):28–106; Faye Taxman, "Jail Based Drug Treatment Programs," Montgomery County Criminal Justice Coordinating Commission (Montgomery County, Maryland, 1992).

116. M. Douglas Anglin and Yih-Ing Hser, "Treatment of Drug Abuse," in *Drugs and Crime: A Review of Research,* eds. Michael Tonry and James Q. Wilson, vol. 13 (Chicago: University of Chicago Press, 1990).

117. See James M. Day and William S. Laufer, eds., *Crime, Values and Religion* (Norwood, N.J.: Ablex, 1987); Byron R. Johnson, "Religious Commitment within the Corrections Environment: An Empirical Assessment," in *Crime, Values and Religion,* eds. Day and Laufer. See also Harry Dammer III, *Prisoners, Prisons and Religion,* Ph.D. dissertation, Rutgers University, 1992.

118. See Day and Laufer, *Crime, Values and Religion.* For a discussion of prison chaplains, see Bruce D. Stout and Todd Clear, "Federal Prison Chaplains: Satisfied in Ministry but Often Undervalued," *Federal Prisons Journal* 2 (1992):8–10.

119. Robert Smith and David Sabatino, "American Prisoner Home Furloughs," *Journal of Offender Counseling* 10 (1990):18–25.

120. Daniel LeClair and Susan Guarino-Ghezzi, "Does Incapacitation Guarantee Public Safety? Lessons from Massachusetts' Furlough and Pre-release Programs," *Justice Quarterly* 8 (1990):9–36.

121. Michael Isikoff, "Debate Rises on Prison Furlough Cuts; Critics Quizz Reasons Behind the Crackdown," *The Houston Chronicle,* March 15, 1992, Star Edition, p. 2. See also Gordon Waldo and Theodore Chiricos, "Work Release and Recidivism," *Evaluation Quarterly* 1 (1977):87–106.

CHAPTER 16

ALTERNATIVES: COMMUNITY CORRECTIONS

"In the month of August, 1841, I was in court one morning, when the door communicating with the lock-room was opened and an officer entered, followed by a ragged and wretched looking man, who took his seat upon the bench allotted to prisoners. I imagined from the man's appearance, that his offence was that of yielding to his appetite for intoxicating drinks, and in a few moments I found that my suspicions were correct, for the clerk read the complaint, in which the man was charged with being a common drunkard. The case was clearly made out, but before sentence had been passed, I conversed with him for a few moments, and found that he was not yet past all hope of reformation, although his appearance and his looks precluded a belief in the minds of others that he would ever become a man again. He told me that if he could be saved from the House of Correction, he never again would taste intoxicating liquors; there was such an earnestness in that tone, and a look expressive of firm resolve, that I determined to aid him; I bailed him, by permission of the Court. He was ordered to appear for sentence in three weeks from that time. He signed the pledge and became a sober man; at the expiration of this period of probation, I accompanied him into the court room; his whole appearance was changed and no one, not even the scrutinizing officers, could have believed that he was the same person who less than a month before, had stood trembling on the prisoner's stand.—The Judge expressed himself much pleased with the account we gave of the man, and instead of the usual penalty,—imprisonment in the House of Correction,—he fined him one cent and costs, amounting in all to $3.76, which was immediately paid. The man continued industrious and sober, and without doubt has been by this treatment, saved from a drunkard's grave.

"This was truly encouraging, and before January, 1842, I had bailed seventeen persons for a similar offence, and they had severally been sentenced in the same manner, which in all amounted to $60.87. Eleven of this number paid the fine, but the other six being too poor to raise the amount, I paid it for them."[1] ■

Plaque commemorating the centennial of the founding of the probation movement in 1841 by a Boston shoemaker named John Augustus (1785-1859). School of Criminal Justice N.C.C.D. Library, Rutgers University, Newark, New Jersey.

It was not a behavioral scientist, nor a famous philosopher or jurist, who invented the great humanitarian alternative to imprisonment. It was a shoemaker, John Augustus, the author of this 1852 report, to whom we owe the practice of community corrections. In this chapter we examine the alternatives to incarceration, most—but not all—of which are forms of correction in the community. We begin our discussion with the alternatives created during the first wave of community corrections, in the middle of the nineteenth century. We then turn to alternatives created in the second wave of community corrections, in the 1960s.

The community corrections movement of the 1960s emerged simultaneously with the growing concern for the rights of the accused in the criminal justice system. It was not coincidental that the decisions of the United States Supreme Court of the 1960s, notably cases that resulted in an expansion of the due process rights of defendants, had an effect on the corrections system. The use of alternatives to incarceration was consistent with the demand for more humane and effective methods of dealing with offenders who do not require imprisonment. More recently, a major challenge to the criminal justice system—prison overcrowding—has been the significant factor in rapid and politically motivated changes in corrections.[2] Probation, parole, and fines have always been regarded as cost-beneficial alternatives to imprisonment.[3] However, in an era when violent crime is increasing, policymakers and the public sometimes view these sanctions as inadequate solutions to the problem of prison overcrowding. Conservative legislators generally have been willing to fund the construction of new prisons, but construction costs and the frequency with which new facilities have to be built have put such a strain on state budgets that many conservatives have joined their liberal colleagues in opposing the expansion of the prison system. These circumstances have prompted the search for correctional alternatives consistent with the public demand for security, lower costs, and punishment (retribution). There are some promising possibilities, among them intensive supervision programs, shock programs, residential programs, home confinement, electronic monitoring, the use of volunteers in probation, and community service orders. We begin with the traditional alternative sanctions—probation and parole.

PROBATION

John Augustus was born in Woburn, Massachusetts, in 1784. He moved to Lexington at the age of 21, learned the shoemaking trade, and by 1827 had become a successful craftsman in Boston. Appalled by what he saw on his frequent visits to the courts—petty criminals jailed simply because they could not pay their fines—Augustus stepped forward and paid the fines himself. Nearly a century later, Sheldon Glueck described how John Augustus worked:

His method was to bail the offender after conviction, to utilize this favor as an entering wedge to the convict's confidence and friendship, and through such evidence of friendliness as helping the offender to obtain a job and aiding his family in various ways, to drive the wedge home. When the defendant was later brought into court for sentence, Augustus would report on his progress toward reformation, and the judge would usually fine the convict one cent and costs, instead of committing him to an institution.[4]

John Augustus promoted this new approach through his Washington Total Abstinence Society, and the Boston courts endorsed the idea. Thus was born the idea of **probation,** the release of a prison-bound convict into the community under the supervision of a trustworthy person and bound by certain conditions, such as not to violate the law, not to leave the jurisdiction, and to maintain employment.[5] Probation was a welcome alternative to prisons in the mid-nine-

probation
Alternative to imprisonment, allowing a person found guilty of an offense to stay in the community, under conditions and with supervision.

TABLE 16.1 Significant Events in the Development of Probation

Year	Event
1841	John Augustus becomes the "father of probation."
1869	Massachusetts develops the visiting probation agent system.
1875	Society for the Prevention of Cruelty to Children established in New York, paving way for the juvenile court.
1878	Massachusetts passes first juvenile probation law.
1899	First juvenile court in the United States is established in Cook County (Chicago), Illinois.
1925	Congress authorizes probation at the federal level.
1927	All states but Wyoming have juvenile probation laws.
1954	Last state enacts juvenile probation law.
1956	Mississippi becomes the last state to pass authorizing legislation to establish adult probation.
1967	*In re Gault* decided by U.S. Supreme Court.
1973	National Advisory Commission on Criminal Justice Standards and Goals endorses more extensive use of probation.
1980	American Bar Association Institute issues restrictive guidelines to limit use of preadjudication detention.
1982	Mulvey and Saunders develop prototype criteria for limiting preadjudicative detention, with feedback loops for comparing outcomes.*

SOURCE: Harry Allen, Chris Eskridge, Edward Latessa, and Gennaro Vito, *Probation and Parole in America* (N.Y.: Free Press, 1985), p. 44.

teenth century, when the demand for prison space was greater than the supply, the first disenchantment about the capacity of penitentiaries to make inmates "penitent" had set in, and the exorbitant cost of imprisonment was first perceived (Table 16.1).

The Benefits of Probation

The purpose of probation has always been to integrate offenders, under supervision, into law-abiding society.[6] By 1956 all states had a probation system. Most systems operate on the county level, but some are statewide.[7] Probation is now one of the most widely used correctional dispositions. In fact, approximately four times as many offenders are placed on probation as are sent to prison. Probation serves the dual purpose of protecting the community through continued court supervision and of attempting to rehabilitate the offender.

"Approximately four times as many offenders are placed on probation as are sent to prison."

Some judges attach community service to probation sentences. For example:

A brush with the law in Niles, Mich., can put petty offenders into a dirt-filled plot rather than behind bars—growing vegetables to feed the needy and the homeless.

Through a novel gardening project that doesn't cost taxpayers a penny, non-violent petty offenders are placed on probation and ordered to spend time weeding and hoeing a 3-acre plot that yielded 2,500 bushels of fresh vegetables for community food banks last year.

Some of the produce also helps feed prisoners at the county jail and a juvenile hall, relieving a portion of the grocery tab for taxpayers.[8]

The benefits of probation are great: (1) Not all types of offenses are serious enough to require incarceration; (2) probationers can obtain or maintain employment and pay taxes; and (3) offenders can care for their families and meet their other financial responsibilities without becoming burdens on the state.

The Bureau of Justice Statistics (BJS) collects information annually from all federal, state, and local adult probation agencies in the United States. This includes information on the number of offenders on probation, their race, and their gender and ethnicity. As of January 1, 1990 *(p. 442)*:

VOLUNTEERS IN PROBATION: THE JAPANESE RESPONSE

Over 48,000 Japanese proudly wear this little medal:

These are the voluntary probation officers, or *hogoshi,* who donate their time and energy to assisting probationers. The idea of probation was unknown to the Japanese until the American occupation after World War II. During the administration of General Douglas MacArthur as military governor of Japan (1945–1951), several features of the American criminal justice system were introduced into Japan. Foremost among them was probation, which was established by the Offender Rehabilitation Law of 1949. For the first five years probation was used for juvenile offenders only. But success in juvenile cases persuaded the Japanese to extend probation to adult offenders.

It was easy for General MacArthur to order the creation of a probation system. It was not so easy to implement the enabling legislation. There was no probation tradition in Japan, no probation training, no profession, no professionals. A probation system required probation

officers. For that reason the idea of volunteers as an integral part of the system was anticipated from the very beginning. Article I of the Offender Rehabilitation Law states:

The objective of this law is to protect society and promote individual and public welfare by aiding the reformation and rehabilitation of offenders . . . and facilitating the activities of crime prevention. All the people are required to render help according to their position and ability, to accomplish the objective mentioned. . . . (1)

Since then, parole and probation have come to occupy an important position in the Japanese criminal justice system. Mitsugu Nishinsukama, a special assistant in the Rehabilitation Bureau of Japan's Ministry of Justice, explains:

Offenders' rehabilitation services occupy the final position in the current criminal justice system . . . the parole and probation systems have the fundamental characteristic that the offenders are supervised actively and their rehabilitation is strongly promoted. The Japanese parole and probation systems aim at the offenders' rehabilitation and reintegration into society. We call that system *kosei-hogo* in Japanese. (2)

The *kosei-hogo* system

The volunteers for "offender rehabilitation," recruited from all walks of life, were 80,000 strong when the system began. Now, because of low crime rates in Japan and more professionals, the number of volunteer probation officers has leveled off at approximately 48,000. Each leaves home for a weekend day or an evening or two to visit the probationers assigned to him or her. While many volunteer probation

officers are retired and have time to devote to their volunteer work, others take leave from offices or factories. Visits and interviews typically take place twice a month, and the volunteers may assist their probationers with housing problems, employment, medical care, adjustment to living with their families, and other aspects of life. Volunteers will open their doors at any time of the day or night for a troubled probationer who needs guidance. They invite probationers for lunch or dinner, take them to baseball games, and socialize with them in other ways.

By now the country has about 620 professional probation officers, who work out of fifty district offices. Each officer has a case load of about 150 probationers, a number totally beyond the capacity of the officers. Only the willingness of so many volunteers makes it possible to provide the supervision, care, and attention that John Augustus, the father of probation, deemed essential for success. Most services are in fact provided by the volunteers, with professional officers responsible for supervision of volunteers and for tough cases.

"Volunteer probation officer" is an honorable position in Japan, and not everyone is accepted. Eligibility depends on patience, intelligence, kindness, and a good reputation. In some respects, the problems of the Japanese volunteers in the field are similar to those faced by American probation officers: assisting the court in determining eligibility for probation; finding appropriate, individualized means of intervention and assistance; struggling with the police officer–social worker conflict that is common in the probation

Number of Japanese Probationers and Parolees over a Five-Year Period

	1983		1984		1985		1986		1987	
	Placed under Supervision in 1983	Case Load as of Dec. 31 1983	Placed under Supervision in 1984	Case Load as of Dec. 31 1984	Placed under Supervision in 1985	Case Load as of Dec. 31 1985	Placed under Supervision in 1986	Case Load as of Dec. 31 1986	Placed under Supervision in 1987	Case Load as of Dec. 31 1987
(The first type) Juvenile probationers	70,385	55,824	70,758	54,938	71,411	55,941	72,268	55,840	70,747	51,695
(The second type) Training school parolees	4,945	5,879	5,569	6,665	5,585	7,202	5,580	7,473	5,313	7,119
(The third type) Prison parolees	16,890	6,898	18,718	8,000	17,795	8,393	18,130	8,693	17,603	8,931
(The fourth type) Adult probationers	7,798	22,756	7,692	22,215	7,180	21,430	6,456	20,279	6,477	19,372
(The fifth type) Guidance home parolees	1	—	—	—	—	—	—	—	—	—
Total	100,019	91,357	102,737	91,818	101,971	92,966	102,434	92,285	100,140	87,117

SOURCE: Mitsugu Nishinsukama, "The Development of Non-institutional Treatment for Criminal Offenders in Japan." *UNAFEI Resource Material Series,* Fuchu, Tokyo, Japan, 36 (1989):124–130; and personal observations.

service; meeting the incessant demands for paperwork. But in other ways the lot of Japanese volunteers is easier than that of their American counterparts. Japan is a high employment country, which makes it much easier to find jobs for probationers. Public health services are far more accessible in Japan than in the United States. And the fact that the whole country is served by the same criminal justice organization also helps the Japanese volunteers. Probation and parole are handled by the same service.

Private citizens can get involved in "offender rehabilitation" in another way in Japan. When probationers have no home to return to because their families have rejected them, they can live in rehabilitation aid hostels, which are run by the private sector in Japan. The first such hostel was established in 1888 to provide private "aftercare" for discharged offenders who had nowhere else to turn. Now Japan has 100 rehabilitation aid hostels for

adults and juveniles, all run by the private sector and authorized by the Ministry of Justice.

Japan's use of volunteers is not without problems. Because many of the volunteers are retired, there is often a significant age gap between the offenders being supervised and the volunteer officers. Recruitment of younger volunteers is difficult, however, because employed people have so little spare time. Training in social work for volunteers also is felt to be inadequate. But as criminologist William Clifford noted,

. . . the system has stood the test of time, and even the surge of affluence that would have permitted the appointment of far more full-time staff did not induce the government to change its voluntary probation officer system that facilitates a nation-wide and community-deep pattern of aid and guidance for those placed on probation by the courts. (1, p. 107)

SOURCES

1. William Clifford, *Crime Control in Japan* (Lexington, Mass.: Lexington Books, 1976), pp. 100–107.
2. Mitsugu Nishinsukama, "The Development of Non-institutional Treatment for Criminal Offenders in Japan," *UNAFEI Resource Material Series,* Fuchu, Tokyo, Japan, 36 (1989):124–130.

QUESTIONS FOR DISCUSSION

1. What stands in the way of combining probation and parole in the same service in the United States as the Japanese have done in Japan?
2. What complications might arise in the United States if the probation system were to switch to using more volunteer probation officers than professionals?
3. Japan's probation system originated during a period of American occupation, but it has evolved since then. How would you go about determining which system—Japan's or the United States'—is more successful?

- There were 2,670,234 offenders on probation nationwide.
- There were 1,443 adults on probation for every 100,000 adults in the population.
- Of the probation population, 68 percent were white, 31 percent were black, and 1 percent were of other races.
- Of the probation population, 82 percent were males; 18 percent were females.
- Of the probation population, 48 percent had been convicted of a felony.
- Eighty-seven percent of probationers were sentenced directly to probation without jail, 8 percent had a sentence of probation with jail, and 5 percent had probation of other types.
- Among those discharged from probation, 69 percent exited by successful completion of their term.[9]

Revocation of Probation

Probation was often regarded as a favor bestowed by the judge on worthy prisoners. The court retained jurisdiction over probationers, reserving the right to revoke probation or to change probation conditions. With few restrictions on the court, judges used their discretion as to when and how to revoke or modify the original probation order. There was little concern for the normal due-process guarantees defendants enjoyed at their original trials. This situation began to change in 1967, when the Supreme Court ruled in *Mempa v. Rhay* that probationers are entitled to counsel at revocation proceedings.[10] *Gagnon v. Scarpelli* (1973) mandated the right to probation and parole revocation hearings, due-process guarantees during the probable-cause hearing, and a trial-like determination of the charges.[11]

The grounds for revocation have been somewhat softened over the years. Technical violations—including, in many cases, alcohol consumption—no longer routinely lead to revocation. Normally, revocations are based on the commission of another offense.

"Judges used their discretion as to when and how to modify an original probation order."

Probation Officers

probation officer
Officer attached to the trial court who is responsible for administering the court's probation program.

Probation officers are responsible for monitoring probationers' activities in the community. Treatment programs in general and probation programs in particular depend heavily on the personality and style of the person providing the service. The relative success of probation programs may be attributable to the professionals who have joined the probation service. An evaluation of the Massachusetts probation system found the quality of probation staff to be outstanding, officers having a strong and common desire to ensure public safety while providing rehabilitative support for offenders.[12] Generally they liked what they were doing, except for the endless administrative procedures.[13]

More than 80 percent of all probation departments in the United States require at least a bachelor's degree for initial appointment. In addition, many require specific courses of study (for example, criminal justice, sociology, or psychology), as well as varying levels of training and experience. Continuous in-service training is used in the majority of probation agencies to maintain and improve the skills of their personnel.

What Probation Officers Do. Probation officers are employment agents, vocational counselors, marital counselors, school counselors, psychoanalysts, sheriffs, and moralists.[14] In short, probation officers are expected to help their clients comply with court orders, and this help calls for control/law enforcement functions and treatment/social service functions.[15] Because case loads now include an increasing number of high-risk probationers, the control/law enforcement function has become dominant.[16] Other risk factors also have been changing the duties of probation officers, as this California example shows:

Growing fears that violent crime is out of control in East Palo Alto have prompted San Mateo County to bar probation officers from making unannounced visits to the homes of clients in the beleaguered city.

"We're trying to reduce our exposure to the volatile situation there," Rick Jones, deputy chief probation officer, said yesterday. . . .

Jones said the probation department has been told that trouble between two street gangs has increased in recent weeks and that there have been reports of as many as 30 recent gunfire exchanges involving the gangs.[17]

"I don't scold. I talk and I send to jail. There's no need to be ugly. It just makes people get an attitude."
Probation officer Mary Williams, quoted in *Atlanta Journal and Constitution*, January 4, 1992, p. B2.

Presentence Investigations.

The trial judge, in order to determine a convicted defendant's eligibility for probation, requests a presentence investigation (PSI) report (Chapter 12).[18] This report is prepared by a probation officer, who focuses on such factors as the nature of the offense (violent or nonviolent), the defendant's version of the offense, previous criminal record, employment history, family background, financial situation, health, religious involvement, length of current residence, and community ties.[19] On the basis of the report, the judge decides whether to impose a prison sentence or probation.

The PSI report is a basic working document in judicial and correctional administration: (1) It aids the court in determining the appropriate sentence; (2) it aids the probation officer's rehabilitative efforts during probation supervision; (3) it assists prison staff in classification and in planning of treatment programs; (4) it furnishes the Board of Parole with pertinent information; and (5) it serves as a source of information for systematic criminal justice research.[20]

"The PSI report is a basic working document in judicial and correctional administration."

Some researchers have found that probation officer recommendations have a substantial effect on actual sentences.[21] Key factors used to make decisions about the perceived risk of probationers are information about previous record, seriousness of the offense, and negative attitudes about the consequences of the offense.[22] Some argue that the reason PSI reports have an impact on actual sentences is precisely because probation officers try to classify offenders according to the usual judicial considerations of offense and prior record. Moreover, even though other data, such as defendant's attitudes and social history, are collected and included in the report, critics suggest probation officers give them much less weight in order to satisfy judicial expectations.[23]

The preparation of the presentence report is a complex process. Where appropriate, the information is verified through other sources. The massive amount of information that results from the investigatory process is then sorted, analyzed, and condensed into a written report. The investigator often encounters resistance, unclear leads, ambiguous information, and even misinformation. It takes a considerable amount of skill and experience to translate the mass of information into meaningful recommendations.[24]

Volunteers in Probation

In 1960, Judge Keith Leenhouts of the Royal Oak, Michigan, Municipal Court, resurrected John Augustus' original concept of volunteers in probation. Since that time volunteer programs have grown rapidly. Volunteer projects operate on the premise that certain probationers can be helped by the services that a volunteer can offer and that such services can be provided at a minimal direct tax-dollar cost. In general, the principal function of the volunteer is to supplement, not replace, probation officer efforts, including the provision of specialized services.[25] (See the Criminal Justice Abroad box.)

Project Jaguar began in July 1973 in Philadelphia and used ex-offenders as probation officer aides. A study was conducted to compare the success of the

"Volunteer programs are at least as effective as professionally staffed programs in reducing recidivism and improving self-concept."

offender-supervised cases with the regular probation officer-supervised cases. The results show that Jaguar aides appeared to be as capable of supervision as their professional counterparts, measured by rates of recidivism among their probationers.[26] Similarly, in a comparison of major findings on formal methods of rehabilitation in the courts and corrections and the informal method of using volunteers, researchers found that volunteer programs were at least as effective as professionally staffed programs in accomplishing the objectives of reducing recidivism and improving self-concept.[27]

Effectiveness of Probation

Probation as it works in practice has two major flaws.

1. Judges generally do not have the time, the information, or the ability to determine whether a given person is a good prospect for probation. They frequently view probation simply as a means to control the prison population by keeping less serious offenders out of prison or jail.

2. The probationer does not have the assistance and guidance that John Augustus considered essential for the success of probation.

There are 30,606 probation officers in the United States, each with an average case load of 115 probationers at any given moment.[28] Some officers supervise many more. The Metro West probation office in Atlanta supervises 4,800 probationers with sixteen officers. Many probationers, including "maxes"—violent or repeat offenders—are seen only twice a month in the office and twice quarterly on the outside.[29] The cases are constantly changing. Under such circumstances, the officer has no chance to provide meaningful guidance and assistance. One would expect very high failure rates. But this is not the case: A seventeen-state Bureau of Justice survey of felons sentenced to probation in 1986 shows that within three years, only 20 percent were re-arrested for violent crimes.[30]

The relatively high success rate of probation poses several challenges:

"Probation in fact has a relatively high success rate, despite the well-publicized cases of people who have been released and committed new crimes."

1. If the success rate is as high as it is despite the lack of close supervision, what is the use of subjecting these offenders to probation in the first place? Perhaps other sanctions (like fines or community service) might be better.

2. Given the relatively high success rate, perhaps we are not taking enough chances with probation; perhaps more convicts should be sentenced to probation instead of confinement.

3. What should we do about the 20 percent of probation violators who constitute a danger to the public?

Research evidence is tentative and limited.

What is in store for the future of probation? In 1980 criminologists Harry Allen and Edward Latessa predicted that by the year 2000:

1. The American prison population would reach 1.2 million.

2. This would put pressure on the system to increase the use of probation, so as to decrease the prison population.

3. New forms of tougher types of probation would gain popularity.[31]

These predictions were largely accurate:

1. The American prison population exceeded the 1.2-million mark, but almost a decade earlier than predicted.

2. The prison population already has put pressure on the system, and the use of probation has increased.

3. Tough new probation programs have been developed and are being used increasingly.

But the use of both old and new probation programs is not keeping up with the rising prison population, even now. By the year 2000 the situation may well be

TABLE 16.2 Probation vs. Parole

Probation	Parole
A convict is sentenced to a period of probation *in lieu of prison.*	A prisoner is *released from prison* and placed on parole.
Probation is a front-end measure.	Parole is a tail-end measure.
The court imposes the sentence of probation.	A parole board grants release on parole.
The court retains jurisdiction.	A parole board retains jurisdiction.
A probation officer is an officer of the court and is employed by a county or district.	A parole officer is a state officer employed by the state government.
Probation is an alternative sentence for less serious cases.	Originally serious offenders earn parole through good conduct in prison.
Eligibility depends on a favorable PSI report.	Eligibility depends on successful service of a specific part of the prison sentence.

worse, as most specialists deem community-based corrections inadequate for the young, aggressive, male offender whose numbers consistently rise. There are scholars, however, who argue for the abolition of prisons for all offenders. (See the Criminal Justice on Trial box.)

PAROLE

Parole (from the French for "word" [of honor]) is a prisoner's conditional release under supervision after a portion of a sentence has been served. On the surface, parole may appear to be similar to probation. Both programs provide periods in which an offender lives in the community instead of serving time in a prison. Both programs require that the convict be under supervision to ensure good conduct. When the condition is violated, confinement results. But here the similarity ends (see Table 16.2).

parole
Supervised conditional release of a convicted prisoner before expiration of the sentence of imprisonment.

Origins of Parole

The concept of parole was introduced about the same time as that of probation. In the 1840s, Captain Alexander Maconochie of the Royal Navy administered an English penal colony on Norfolk Island, a speck of land in the Pacific Ocean 900 miles east of Australia. He observed that

A man under a time sentence thinks only how he is to cheat that time and while it away; he evades labor, because he has no interest in it whatsoever, and he has no desire to please the officers under whom he is placed, because they cannot . . . in any way promote his liberation.[32]

Maconochie's solution was to create a "scheme of marks awarded for industry, labor, and good conduct, [which] gave prisoners an opportunity to earn their way out of confinement."[33] Tickets of leave (documents issued to prisoners enabling them to work for wages and to choose their own employers) were given on the basis of these good-conduct marks.

The idea of parole was introduced in the United States at the first National Prison Association Congress in Cincinnati in 1870. Warden Zebulon Brockway of the Elmira Reformatory in New York began using parole in 1876. Promising convicts were released into the care of private reform groups before their terms

"The idea of parole was first introduced in the United States in 1870; today all jurisdictions use parole."

445

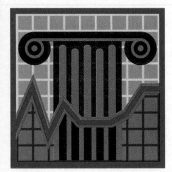

"LET'S GET RID OF THE CRIMINAL JUSTICE SYSTEM!": THE EUROPEAN ABOLITIONIST MOVEMENT

One group of criminal justice scholars in Europe proposes to abolish the criminal justice system. Rather than help to resolve social problems, they argue, the criminal justice system itself is a social problem. They contend that the system "can never provide for a humane and sensible way of dealing with problems generally referred to as 'crime'" (1). This view, termed the "abolitionist perspective," is held by a number of European researchers, including Louk Hulsman, John Blad, Hans van Mastrijt, Niels Uildriks, and Sebastian Scheerer of the Netherlands and Nils Christie and Thomas Mathiesen of Norway.

The system itself is the problem

According to this perspective, there are four major reasons for considering the criminal justice system itself as a social problem:

- "First of all, the criminal justice system inflicts suffering. . . . It therefore furthers the existing inequality and hardship in society."
- "Secondly, the criminal justice system does not work in terms of its own declared aims. . . . It would seem at present that it is widely accepted that the criminal justice system does not work, or at least not to any satisfactory degree."
- "A third criticism . . . is its fundamental uncontrollability, . . . [because the system comprises] a number of organizations that work quite independently from each other and which have their own—informal—aims to achieve."
- Fourth, "the criminal justice approach is fundamentally flawed" because there is no longer any consensus in our "pluriformic" society whose constituent parts (including ethnic groups, professions, age groups, neighborhoods) hold divergent views as to how social problems should be solved. (1)

The abolitionists further explain: "Professor Hulsman has replaced the Holy Trinity of 'crime,' 'criminal,' and 'punishment' by the concepts of 'problematic situation,' 'directly involved,' and 'styles of social control/structural change'" (1). From the abolitionist perspective, a mugging or an insurance fraud would be a "problematic situation" (not a crime) in which the perpetrators are those "directly involved" (not criminals), and there should be no punishment, but varying "styles of social control/structural change." These might include social changes that would make it unnecessary for people to commit muggings or to engage in insurance fraud, or structural changes to provide for the compensation of victims. There could be therapy or, if necessary, restraint for those "directly involved."

Alternatives to punishment

Above all, abolitionists argue, it is essential to get rid of punishment, especially imprisonment. All this may sound impractical, but abolitionists claim that we are well on the way to this goal already:

- The cruel punishments of the eighteenth century have been abolished.
- Capital punishment has been abolished in all but three major industrialized nations (the United States, Japan, and South Africa).
- Imprisonment for life has been abolished in many countries.
- Long-term prison sentences have been virtually abolished in Scandinavia, where a "lifer" serves ten years.
- Short-term prison sentences have been virtually abolished in some countries.

The abolitionists know that there are at least 10 million people in prison in the world. What would happen if we were to release them all tomorrow? No great crime wave would result, they argue, but they also say it is not necessary to close all prisons tomorrow. They only want all prisons, everywhere, to be closed eventually. According to abolitionist Sergio Politoff,

The great changeover through the abolitionist way of thinking does not mean that the prisons will suddenly be closed and the criminal code sent to the museum of antiquities. What is proposed is the dissolution of the closed universe of the penal system and its systematic dismantling based on the recognition of the specific nature of each conflict. (2)

The abolitionists are interested in alternatives to prison, and they point out that many such alternatives are already in place. In fact, far more "convicts" are doing community service, are making reparations, are on probation, or are subject to conflict resolution with their victims than are in prison.

Socioeconomic and cultural reform

Will there not always be persons of such demonstrated dangerousness that we must retain places of safe confinement? The abolitionists don't want a substitute prison system based on the fear of dangerous individuals rather than on punishment, and they acknowledge that some alternatives to the current system could be worse. Politoff notes, "The consequences for freedom would be much more serious yet if the alternative to the penal system had to be a system of social control of a psychiatric, curative, indemnifying, re-education model, based on notions such as 'dangerous' or 'anti-social' people" (2). One of the solutions the abolitionists propose is a return to people solving their own problems without the interference of an enormous governmental machinery.

But the abolitionists have not come up with a plan for a future without criminal justice and imprisonment. Three proponents explain:

The abolitionist perspective . . . does not believe in the possibility of improvement through reform, since the system is thought to suffer from irreparable *structural faults* . . . abolitionism basically involves a *negative perspective:* abolishing what has been found to be unsatisfactory without immediately offering a detailed blueprint as to how various social phenomena should be reacted to instead. Within the abolitionist perspective, abolishing the old *makes room* for new forms of reaction which do not have the same negative social consequences . . . abolitionism should be looked upon in terms of a *continual process and struggle* in the course of which the developed alternatives will continuously need to be scrutinized from a sceptical and critical point of view. (1)

The heart of the abolitionist perspective is the argument that prisons cannot control the crime rate but that socioeconomic and cultural reforms can. Abolitionists propose that we try such reforms, and they predict that crime rates will drop and prison will become unnecessary. The complaint of a Japanese prison official supports their view: "The situation is getting to be very serious. With the drop in crime and imprisonment in Japan, our jobs are seriously in jeopardy."

SOURCES

1. John Blad, Hans van Mastrijt, and Niels Uildriks, "Hulsman's Abolitionist Perspective: The Criminal Justice System as a Social Problem," in *The Criminal Justice System as a Social Problem: An Abolitionist Perspective,* eds. John Blad, Hans van Mastrijt, and Niels Uildriks (Rotterdam: Erasmus University, 1987), pp. 5–17.
2. Sergio Politoff, "Giving Chances to the 'Impossible,'" in *The Criminal Justice System as a Social Problem,* eds. Blad et al., pp. 87–93.

QUESTIONS FOR DISCUSSION

1. The American criminal justice system stands in sharp contrast to the trends abolitionists say prevail in other industrialized nations; the United States is moving to more capital punishment and more and longer prison sentences. What accounts for that difference?
2. Can nations and their peoples get rid of crime problems through socioeconomic and cultural reform? Defend your position.
3. Suppose we were to resort to such alternatives to prison as community service and letting people solve their own problems without government intervention. What would happen?

TABLE 16.3 Significant Developments in Parole

Year	Events
1840	Alexander Maconochie devises mark system for release of prisoners in Australian penal colony, a forerunner of parole.
1853	Sir Walter Crofton in Ireland establishes system under which prisoners can earn conditional freedom.
1869	New York State legislature passes enabling legislation and establishes indeterminate sentencing.
1870	American Prison Association endorses expanded use of parole.
1876	Parole release adopted at Elmira Reformatory, New York.
1931	Wickersham Commission criticizes laxity in use of early parole.
1944	Last state passes enabling legislation for parole.
1980s	Parole comes under attack as inconsistent with the just-deserts model of sanctions. Twenty-nine states and the federal government abolish parole altogether or modify it severely by guidelines.
1993	Abolition and modifications have not created a decline in the number of parolees.

had expired. Later on, corrections officers were assigned to supervise the parolees. By 1900, twenty states and the federal government had parole systems in place. Ultimately all jurisdictions instituted parole (see Table 16.3).

The Bureau of Justice Statistics collects information annually on the number of parolees by jurisdiction, race, sex, and ethnicity. As of January 1, 1990:

- Over 531,407 adults were under the supervision of parole agencies nationwide.
- For every 100,000 adults in the population, 287 adults were on parole.
- Of the parole population, 45 percent was white, 40 percent black, and 15 percent of other races.
- Of the parole population, 93 percent was male.[34]

The Decision to Parole

parole board
Group of citizens, usually appointed by the governor of a state, who determine the eligibility of prisoners for release from prison and the dates for their release from prison and from parole.

The authority to release a prisoner on parole is usually vested in a **parole board** made up of respected citizens, usually appointed by the governor of the state. To provide professional input, governors have favored doctors, lawyers, educators, and psychologists in their appointments. Yet the boards do not present themselves as professional decision-makers; they are there to represent the people of the state.

Members of the parole board serve for terms that range from two years to life. The average term is six years.[35] In some jurisdictions, the terms of the board members are staggered. Traditionally it has been the function of parole boards

1. to determine the eligibility of prisoners for parole, and to place them on parole at their discretion
2. to aid, supervise, and provide continuing control of parolees in the community
3. to determine when the parole term is completed and to discharge a person from parole
4. if violation of conditions of parole occurs, to determine whether parole revocation should take place[36]

Over a thirteen-year period, the process by which offenders have been discharged from prison and placed on conditional supervision in the community has undergone radical change. In 1977, nearly 72 percent of the 115,000 persons discharged from state prisons nationwide were released as a result of parole board decisions. In contrast, of those prisoners placed on parole among the 358,820 discharged from prisons in 1990, 53 percent were released by a discretionary parole board decision, 37 percent were released in accordance with terms of the original sentence (mandatory release), and nearly 10 percent were released by special procedures established to cope with prison crowding.[37]

Parole Hearings. Members of the parole board meet to decide which prisoners will be granted parole at a **parole hearing.** Hearings are held in camera, meaning they are closed to the public, usually at penitentiaries, with only prisoners, attorneys, and witnesses in attendance. At the hearing, the board reviews information from many sources. In a recent hearing, for example:

parole hearing
Meeting held by members of the parole board to decide whether prisoners will be granted parole.

The videotape of an Oprah Winfrey show, a prosecutor's empassioned letter and a public television documentary will be introduced as evidence today at a parole hearing for Michelle Mann, whose 5-year-old son was beaten to death in 1990.

The tapes were submitted in an effort to block Mann's release from Bedford Hills prison, where she has served nearly two years of a 2-to-6-year sentence after pleading guilty to two counts of assault in connection with her son Adam's death.[38]

The Board thoroughly reviews the prisoner's file, which includes work reports from corrections officers, psychiatrists' reports on the "readiness" of the prisoner for release into the community, remarks the judge made at the time of sentencing, and, in some jurisdictions, statements submitted by victims of the crime. The prisoner may then be summoned to the hearing to argue why he or she is ready for release.

Parole boards are often faced with the difficulty of preferring to keep an inmate imprisoned, even though the individual is eligible for parole. Such a case may attract nationwide publicity because of the notoriety of the crime, such as that of Arthur Jackson, who attempted to kill the actress Theresa Saldana; or of Sirhan Sirhan, the assassin of Robert F. Kennedy; or of Charles Manson (and his followers) who massacred actress Sharon Tate and others. In many cases parole is strongly opposed by victims or victims' families, or by police groups, which routinely oppose the paroling of murderers of police officers.

"Parole boards are often faced with the difficulty of preferring to keep an inmate imprisoned, even though the person is eligible for parole."

The actress Theresa Saldana demonstrating outside the Santa Monica courthouse on November 10, 1983, to demand the maximum sentence for the convicted killer of actress Dominique Dunne. Saldana herself was repeatedly stabbed by an assailant in March 1982; he was convicted of attempted murder.

Rights of Parole Applicants. The inmate's legal rights at parole hearings differ from jurisdiction to jurisdiction. The inmate is permitted counsel in twenty-one states and allowed to present witnesses in twenty states.[39] The United States Supreme Court dealt with the issue of the right to due process at parole board hearings in two important cases. In *Greenholtz v. Inmates of the Nebraska Penal and Correctional Complex* (1979), the Court ruled that early release on parole is a privilege, not a right, and that this act of "grace" does not entitle inmates to all of the due-process rights at a parole hearing.[40] This decision was reinforced by *Connecticut Board of Pardons v. Dumschat* (1981), where the Supreme Court ruled that an inmate has only "mere hope" of pardon or parole and therefore need not be accorded the full range of due-process rights.[41]

Conditions of Parole. Inmates granted parole are released into the community under supervision. As a prerequisite to release, the inmate must sign an agreement to adhere to the parole conditions—rules that prohibit, demand, or encourage certain behavior on the part of the parolee. The rules are meant to prevent the person from getting into trouble. Common conditions include abstinence from alcohol and drugs, restrictions on the people with whom the parolee can associate, curfew restrictions, and the prohibition against frequenting places the parole board deem a threat to the parolee's lawful behavior. Usually, the parolee is required to report at frequent intervals to a parole officer and to notify the officer of any changes in place of residence or employment.

- - - - - - - - - - - - - - - - - -

revocation of parole
Return of an offender to prison for the violation of parole conditions.

Revocation of Parole

Technically still under the control of the corrections department while living in the community under "contract," parolees traditionally were returned to prison with few formalities when they violated the conditions of their contract. But since 1972, procedures for **revocation of parole** (the return of the offender to prison for violating the conditions of parole) have undergone major changes. In a landmark decision (*Morrissey v. Brewer*) that changed parole agency procedures nationwide, the Supreme Court mandated that the Fourteenth Amendment requirement of due process of law applies to parole revocation proceedings.[42] While the Court did not call for the full range of rights due a defendant in a criminal proceeding, it set up procedural guidelines that states must follow before revoking an offender's parole.

Violations of parole conditions can be of two types: (1) commission of another crime, or (2) technical violation of a condition, such as breaking a curfew, leaving the jurisdiction, frequenting an off-limits place, or drinking alcohol. While commission of another crime may appear to be the major factor influencing decisions to revoke parole, results of a study by Michael Gottfredson and his colleagues show that two-thirds of all parolees released by decisions of the parole board, along with one-half of the mandatory releases, were returned to prison for technical violations (such as missing a curfew or a meeting with the parole officer) of the conditions of their release. These investigators maintain that the parole-revocation process cannot be fully understood without examining the strong influence of technical violations.[43]

A California study undertaken by the National Council on Crime and Delinquency (NCCD) tried to determine why the percentage of parolees failing to complete their period of parole supervision rose from 23 percent in 1975 to 53 percent in 1985. The increase was attributed primarily to technical violations rather than the commission of new felonies. The research also found that the dramatic increases in technical revocations were due to (1) declining levels of financial assistance, especially for narcotic treatment of parolees; (2) increases in parole supervision caseloads; (3) hardening of public law enforcement attitudes regarding parolees and law violators in general; and (4) jail and prison overcrowding leading to early release.[44]

Parole Officers

parole officer
Officer of the executive branch of government responsible for the supervision of convicts released from prison on parole.

At the time of release, the parolee is assigned to a **parole officer** who is responsible for monitoring the parolee's activities and for providing him or her with help in readjusting to life in the community. This dual role makes the parole officer both a cop and a social worker. In the police officer's role the parole officer has the duty to restrict the parolee's activities, to detect violations, to make an arrest, and to initiate revocation proceedings. As a social worker the parole officer has to assist the parolee with adjustment and lend a helping hand when he or she is about to stumble. It is not easy to play both roles. A considerable body of research has tried to unravel the conflict between the roles to find practical solutions to the parole officer's predicament.[45] Georgia has experimented with assigning two officers to each case—one taking the role of the cop, the other the role of the social worker.[46]

"A parole officer is both a cop and a social worker."

And who are these officers of which society expects virtual magic in the management of human behavior? For the most part they are college graduates with majors in relevant fields. A master's degree is frequently required for a supervisory position. Starting salary can be as low as $14,712 (in Tennessee) or as high as $37,714 (in California), depending on education and experience.[47]

An analysis of the work load allocation of parole officers, undertaken by the Adult Probation and Parole Services of Virginia, found that 36.4 percent of a parole officer's time was spent on supervising clients, 26.2 percent on investigations for courts and for the parole board, 11.2 percent on travel, 10.9 percent on administrative tasks, and the rest on training, public relations, and waiting.[48] The study also noted that time spent on investigatory activities had increased in recent years because of policy changes requiring a formal report on all persons entering supervision. Supervisory time had declined as a result of the increase in investigation activities.[49]

Effectiveness of Parole

Just two weeks after he was paroled from an Illinois state prison, police allege that Burl Mason crossed the narrow gravel road in front of his mother's Spring Grove cottage, forced his way into a neighbor's home, tied her to a bed and strangled her.

Police said physical evidence, including duct tape found inside Mason's mother's cottage that matched tape found on Pauly's bed, link Mason to the crime. Investigators also said Mason was seen by acquaintances Friday behind the wheel of Pauly's stolen silver Chevy Blazer.

As they search for Mason, officials on Monday expressed anger that Mason—described by police as a "career criminal"—was free after serving less than half of a six-year term for burglary. . . . He has a criminal record dating to 1978, records show.

"He didn't belong on the street," said Lake County Undersheriff, Willie Smith. Lake County Sheriff Clinton Grinnell said, "I think we have to rethink this early release, and these paroles. We didn't even known he was out on the street."[50]

Parole success rates have never been great. Perhaps parole is granted too late. Don M. Gottfredson and his colleagues at the National Council on Crime and Delinquency found that success on parole diminishes as the length of time served in prison increases.[51] In 1990 only 45 percent of parolees had completed their terms successfully.[52]

"Parole success rates have never been great; perhaps parole is granted too late."

The high failure rate is not the only reason parole has come under attack in recent years. First, parole is supposed to be a reward for rehabilitation in prison, yet prisons are generally not known for rehabilitating inmates. Thus prisoners are denied a reward because of the prison's failure. Second, the parole system has long been plagued by questions about the validity of the criteria used by parole boards in making parole decisions. Though nineteen jurisdictions have had guidelines for such decisions since federal guidelines were introduced in 1973, parole decision-making nevertheless remains a mysterious and seemingly arbitrary process. Moreover, the system is subject to political manipulation and lobbying. For example, the governor may pressure the parole board to grant more releases when prisons are overcrowded. Lobbyists may exert pressure against a parole decision when a notorious inmate comes up for parole. Parole, like probation, depends for its success on assistance and supervision. Yet case loads are so great that such assistance is usually not available.[53] There is also the problem of changing release criteria every time the composition of the parole board changes.

In *The Question of Parole*, Andrew von Hirsch and Kathleen J. Hanrahan argue persuasively for the abolition of parole. The decision to release an offender, they argue, should not be based on questions of treatment or likelihood of offending again; rather, prison time should be correlated with degree of responsibility for the current offense. Parole supervision and the potential for revocation particularly disturb von Hirsch and Hanrahan on grounds of fairness and appropriateness. They propose instead a fixed release date, rather than one that can change after a large portion of a sentence has been served.[54]

"The Question of Parole argues persuasively that parole should be abolished."

These criticisms have led some jurisdictions to terminate discretionary releases by parole boards and substitute mandatory release, either through determinate sentencing (Alaska, Arizona, Colorado, Indiana, Maine, Missouri, New Jersey, New Mexico, North Carolina, Tennessee) or parole guidelines (Florida, Georgia, Hawaii, Louisiana, Maryland, Michigan, New York, Ohio, Oregon,

good time system
System under which time is deducted from a prison sentence for good behavior within the institution.

Rhode Island, South Carolina, Virginia, Washington, West Virginia, Wisconsin, and the federal system). Some jurisdictions use both methods (California, Minnesota, Pennsylvania), and some have returned to the "good time" system.[55]

The **good time system** entails a procedure by which the length of the sentence is shortened by specific periods if the prisoner performs in accordance with the expectations of prison authorities. There may be many risks, especially to public safety, in the good time system, and much has to be learned about it before it can be considered an effective mechanism for alleviating prison overcrowding.[56] One survey from the 1980s found strong public approval for the use of good time and community-based corrections. Construction of more prisons received only moderate support, and shortening sentences and increasing parole boards' authority were disapproved.[57]

PARDONS AND MONETARY SANCTIONS

Probation and parole came into existence about 150 years ago. Before we survey some new alternatives to imprisonment, we need to touch briefly on two alternatives that have been in use for almost 4,000 years: pardons and fines.

Pardons

pardon
Release from the legal penalties of an offense.

conditional pardon
Pardon that depends on the fulfillment of specified conditions.

Mechanisms resembling pardons existed in ancient legal systems, and exist in all legal systems today. A **pardon** is the release from the legal penalties of an offense. Pardons are either full (absolute) or conditional. A pardon is **conditional** when its effectiveness depends on the fulfillment of a condition (for example, serving a lesser sentence). A conditional pardon may be revoked for violation of the conditions imposed; a full pardon cannot be revoked. In 1867 the Supreme Court decreed that a pardon makes the offender "as innocent as if he had never committed the offense" (*Ex parte Garland*),[58] but in some states and for some purposes, a pardoned conviction may count as a previous offense.[59]

The power to pardon is exercised by the chief executive officer—the president of the United States in federal cases and the governor in state cases. In 1974 President Ford, for example, granted a pardon to ex-President Nixon, thereby sparing Nixon criminal prosecution. In 1992 President Bush granted Caspar Weinberger a pardon for his role in the Iran-Contra affair. In state cases, pardons may be issued by the governor, usually acting through a state board of pardons, which is sometimes the parole board.

"The pardoning power was originally seen as a method of righting legal wrongs, of freeing the innocent."

The pardoning power was originally seen as a method of righting legal wrongs, of freeing the innocent. Following this, a commutation of sentence, in the form of a pardon, became an acceptable way to correct unduly severe sentences, or to recognize mitigating circumstances that were not taken into consideration at the trial. When pardons are granted to an entire group of defendants, we speak of an amnesty. Although frequently used in other (especially Latin American) countries, and particularly in the case of political prisoners, neither pardons nor amnesties have played a significant role in the American criminal justice system. Nevertheless, the pardoning power remains important in individual cases, because it is the only available remedy—short of an act of the legislature—in the case of convicted persons whose innocence is discovered after all rights of appeal have expired.

Fines

Forced labor to pay the treasury and fines to enrich the government and to reimburse it for its trouble in dealing with or punishing an offender have been part of legal systems since ancient times. The Code of Hammurabi (about 1750 B.C.), for example, decreed that anyone stealing royal property must pay thirty times the value of the article (ox, sheep, ass, pig, boat) stolen. Medieval codes had a scale of fines, adjusted to whether the victim lost an arm, a leg, a nose, or an ear.[60] Today state penal codes have many provisions for fines as punishments for crime, either alone, in conjunction with, or instead of some other punishment like imprisonment.

Until recently fines were not used much in the American legal system, largely because it was felt that most offenders were unable to pay. Now the use of fines is increasing. A National Institute of Corrections report suggests that the increase has been prompted by financial pressure on the criminal justice system to demonstrate to the public that the "user" of the system must pay. Monetary sanctions include fines and also the payment of court costs and various types of fees including those for bail, public defender services, alcohol or drug assessment, urinalysis, and out-of-state transfers.[61] In traffic courts, fines are used almost exclusively. In courts that handle serious felony offenses, fines are much less common.[62] There appear to be significant gender differences in the assessment of fines. In cases of violence against the person, for example, fines are imposed in 40 percent of cases with male defendants but only 25 percent of cases with female defendants. But for indictable traffic offenses, 73 percent of cases with females result in fines compared with 53 percent of male cases.[63]

As fines become more important as sanctions in the United States, court administrators' success in monitoring, encouraging, and compelling payment becomes a significant factor in their successful use. Research in both American and Western European courts indicates that many court administrators are doing a better collecting job than most people realize. However, performance can be substantially improved if administrators systematically apply the collection and enforcement techniques and strategies used by businesses, such as private collection agencies.[64]

Although monetary sanctions may seem an effective and cost-beneficial alternative to incarceration, many offenders are too poor to pay fines. A fixed sum of money has different meanings for people in high, medium, and low income brackets. To compensate for income differentials among offenders, the Nordic countries (Sweden, Denmark, Norway, Finland, and Iceland) have long used the "day fine" system: the amount of the fine is measured in days of earnings. For a drunk-driving offense, the fine may be ten days' earnings. For the corporate executive, the fine may amount to ten times $500, or $5,000. For a factory worker, it may amount to ten times $50, or $500. This scheme, which is like the graduated income tax, helps the treasury as well. The offender stays in the community and is able to meet other obligations, such as supporting a family and making the car payments.

Restitution to Victims

The concept of restitution by offenders to their victims is as old as that of punishment. In ancient legal systems we find the two side by side, either as sole or as alternative sanctions. In theory, victims of crime have always had some recourse against victimizers. Modern legal systems have permitted a civil suit by the victim against the offender, and in some European countries the crime victim may join the criminal prosecution and obtain a damage award in case of conviction.

Restitution is different from victim compensation. **Restitution** binds the offender to pay the victim; in victim compensation schemes it is the state that compensates crime victims (see Chapter 18). In recent years victim advocates have endorsed restitution as part of the sentence imposed on the convict. The purpose of restitution is to make up for some of the victim's financial losses and to begin the process of healing and recovery.[65] (Restitution programs will be discussed fully in Chapter 18.)

"Medieval codes had a scale of fines, adjusted to the injury suffered by the victim—so much for an arm, so much for a leg, a nose, an ear."

restitution
Compensation (normally court ordered) on the part of an offender to the victim, or a victim substitute, for any losses or harm inflicted, usually in money or services.

INTENSIVE SUPERVISION PROGRAMS

intensive supervision probation (ISP)
Alternative to prison for convicted nonviolent offenders who do not qualify for routine probation; probation subject to stringent supervision.

As originally conceived, probation programs were aimed at prison-bound convicts for whom it was thought that safety considerations did not require imprisonment and for whom association with other prisoners in confinement would do more harm than good. Traditional probation requires intensive supervision, and such supervision has become impossible because the number of probationers is so enormous.[66] Some states continue to use token or routine probation for low-risk cases, but many have also introduced **intensive supervision probation** (ISP) for convicts who do not qualify for routine probation.

The New Jersey Experience

The experience of the New Jersey ISP program has been particularly encouraging. This program, directed by the Administrative Office of the Courts since 1983, is designed to handle 500 convicts, the equivalent of the population of one prison. Since only nonviolent offenders are eligible, the program excludes armed robbers, murderers, and all sex offenders. Inmates who want to be considered must apply between the first and second month of imprisonment. (This period is considered a desirable shock incarceration period.)

The Offender's ISP Plan.
Each applicant must develop a personal plan describing his or her own problems, available community resources, and contacts. A community sponsor must be identified with whom the offender will live during the early months after release and who will help the offender fulfill the program's objectives. Applicants must also identify several other people in the community who can be relied on for help. These people are called the "network team."

The offender's ISP plan and the persons identified in it are closely checked. All information is placed before the ISP screening board, which includes the ISP director, corrections staff, and community representatives. If the screening board's decision is positive, the application goes to a three-judge resentencing panel. A positive decision by this panel results in a ninety-day placement in the ISP program; the placement is renewable after ninety days. Each ISP participant must serve a minimum of one year in the program, including time on parole after release, during which period he or she is on a bench-warrant status (subject to immediate arrest should a violation occur).

"ISP programs, which focus on employment and hard work, are punitive and onerous, and their success rate is disputed."

Program Conditions.
The program conditions, focusing on employment and hard work, are punitive and onerous. They include the following:

- At least sixteen hours of community service per week
- Multiple weekly contacts with the ISP officer and the community sponsor
- Maintenance of a daily diary detailing accomplishments
- Immediate notification of the ISP officer of any police contact or arrest
- Participation in weekly counseling activities, if ordered
- Maintenance of employment or participation in a vocational training program
- Participation in any treatment program (drug, alcohol) designated by the ISP officer
- Adherence to curfew (normally 10 P.M. to 6 A.M.)
- Electronic monitoring, if ordered
- Payment of all obligations, such as the cost of electronic monitoring ($5 to $18 daily), court costs, fines, victim compensation, and child support, to the extent ordered by the court

Evaluation. The failure rate in the New Jersey ISP program has been far lower than anybody expected. As of 1987, of the 600 participants accepted into the program, 27 percent had been expelled, most for technical violations, for use of drugs or alcohol, or for disorderly conduct. Only 5 percent committed a felony during the average eighteen months in the program.

Among the program's greatest benefits are these:

• Rather than costing the state $17,000 per year for incarceration, ISP costs $7,000, thus saving the state $10,000 yearly per convict.

• The offender earns a living, pays taxes and pays the cost of electronic monitoring, fines, fees, and other obligations.

• There is significant evidence that ISP participants do better after discharge than prison inmates.[67]

ISP Nationwide

New Jersey's program is particularly strict and demanding, and thus more costly than that of any other state. Yet by saving prison space it is cost effective.[68] The program in Illinois targets offenders who constitute a lesser risk and costs only $2,500 per convict. ISP programs in some other jurisdictions have proved to be similarly cost effective. In Georgia, ISP proved to be an effective alternative to prison with little risk to the public. On the basis of numbers of offenders diverted from prison to the program, it is estimated that the program saved $20 million.[69] The ISP program in Montgomery County (Dayton), Ohio, was also found to be cost effective.[70]

But not all research supports the use of ISP. A recent scathing attack suggests that ISP does not reduce recidivism rates, is not cost effective, and does not reduce rates of imprisonment.[71] It is not surprising, then, that some states seem reluctant to experiment with it. In fact, James Byrne estimated that less than 5 percent of the total corrections population was under intensive supervision in 1989.[72]

Intensive Supervision of Parolees

Intensive supervision appears to be effective and cost beneficial for convicts who are eligible for parole but who might pose undue risks and are therefore denied release on routine parole. Release into an intensive supervision parole program, structured along the same lines as front-end programs, frees prison bed space and provides the same financial rewards to the community as front-end programs. New Jersey's Intensive Supervision and Surveillance Program (ISSP), operated by the Bureau of Parole, assigns high-risk offenders to ISSP for ninety days. Following a case evaluation, the parolee may be assigned to standard parole. As of 1991, 46,586 parolees around the United States were under intensive supervision.[73] Judgment on the effectiveness of these types of programs awaits further research.

"The question is not should we invent new alternatives in the community, but should we increase the amount of supervision of people in existing programs." James Q. Wilson, professor, University of California, quoted in *The New York Times*, August 7, 1992.

SHOCK PROGRAMS

Shock probation is probation granted after a short period of incarceration. Some corrections specialists believe that punishment should be measured not by time alone, but also by the punitiveness and severity of the experience. A short, sharp shock incarceration may be as intense as a longer, "easy-time" confinement in a prison. Moreover, the shorter incarceration may avoid the "prisonization effects" that longer prison sentences entail.

shock probation
Sentence that allows for brief incarceration followed by probation, in an effort to induce law abidance by shocking the offender.

Shock incarceration attempts to "shock" offenders out of criminal behavior by subjecting them to short periods (90 to 180 days) of intense drills, hard work, and character-building exercises. Similar to Marine Corps or Army training, these shock programs are sometimes referred to as "boot camp."

shock incarceration
Short term of incarceration that subjects offenders to hard work, intense drills, and other character-building exercises.

Shock Incarceration

There are many types of shock incarceration (SI) programs. They operate either inside prison or in separate facilities and focus on young prison-bound convicts, many with histories of alcohol and drug abuse. The first SI program, Oklahoma's Regimented Inmate Discipline (RID) program, was established in 1983. Inmates who meet the criteria for eligibility (no previous prison term) may volunteer. Along with the usual strict discipline and drill of all SI programs, inmates of RID spend several hours daily in educational, vocational, drug-abuse, and counseling programs. After completing the 120-day program, the Oklahoma Department of Corrections recommends that judges resentence the inmates to probation, or in some cases to a halfway house.[74]

The inmates of Georgia's Special Alternative Incarceration (SAI) programs spend eight hours a day at hard labor in addition to the usual boot camp activities. Except for drug abuse education, SAI participants get little counseling or treatment. The "shock" component of the program is primary. After completion of the program, inmates are released to regular probation supervision.[75] Recent SI programs have more innovative goals than the older ones. The New York program, for example, created in 1987, features more extensive therapy programs; Connecticut's program includes community service as part of the incarceration program.[76]

Evaluation of SI Programs

The Oklahoma RID program, with carefully selected participants, has a success rate (participant is crime-free twelve months after discharge) of 85 percent. Georgia's program has a success rate of 90 percent. The cost of such programs, at $26.43 per day in Georgia, is lower than the cost of secure incarceration. Graduates of the Louisiana SI program have been found to have more positive attitudes toward society, greater self-esteem, and more prosocial attitudes than regular prison inmates.[77]

Boot camp programs are politically attractive because they are cost effective and they demonstrate to the public that offenders are undergoing an intense disciplinary experience. Their popularity has spread across the country.[78] The programs have been used only for young (under age 30) male offenders, but these traditionally constitute two-thirds of all inmates. It may be too early to assess the value of boot camps to the correctional system, but the legislatures of several states, including Mississippi, Louisiana, Michigan, Florida, Colorado, and Nevada, have been willing to experiment with this alternative form of confinement.[79] It remains to be seen whether American boot camps will produce disciplined and productive members of the community.[80] In several European countries, similar treatment programs have had little success and have therefore been discontinued.[81]

Alternative programs: (Top) Huntsville, TX: Goree boot camp, an intensive supervision program. (Bottom) Stillwater, MN: Native American ritual drum therapy for offenders.

RESIDENTIAL AND COMMUNITY SERVICE PROGRAMS

Mexico's Toluca Federal Prison has a number of cottages right outside the prison wall where inmates may spend the last portion of their sentence in relative freedom. They lead their own lives, they are not locked up, and they are bused to town for work. The prison wall behind the cottages reminds them of what will happen if they fail. At the same time, the social workers at the penitentiary are close enough to provide counseling and assistance. Toluca's cottages illustrate the worldwide search for a correctional strategy somewhere between prison and the community.

Halfway Houses

In the United States, residential programs take a variety of forms, so that it is difficult to classify them. The most common form is the **halfway house.** Halfway houses are located in the community, have resident staff (social workers, clergy), typically offer drug and alcohol treatment, and are most often operated by private organizations under contract with the state. The average capacity of halfway houses is twenty-five residents, and individuals stay for an average of eight to sixteen weeks.[82]

Halfway houses often face objections from the community: No one wants "ex-cons" in their neighborhood. This is called the Nimby attitude, short for "not in my back yard." To overcome this problem, a variation on the standard halfway house has been developed. For want of a better name one could call this variation the "economic opportunity group home." The group home leaders are social activists who want to change former inmates from economic failures to economic successes. Leading examples are House of Umoja in Philadelphia; Achievement Place in Lawrence, Kansas; Pyramid House in Newark, New Jersey; and the Delancy Street Foundation in San Francisco. Some of these group homes accept mostly juveniles (often violent and drug addicted); others target primarily adults. In the adult halfway houses, all types of offenders live together—those who have committed street crimes and those involved in white-collar crimes. (Baseball hero Pete Rose recently spent three months in a halfway house in the same city where a street is named after him.)

Halfway houses rely on group therapy, education, training, and jobs to help the "ex-cons" adjust to life outside prison. Yet another and more recent version of halfway houses are restitution centers, designed to provide a basis for convicts to meet their financial obligations, including restitution.

Home Confinement and Electronic Monitoring

House Arrest. In 1985, Federal District Court Judge Jack Weinstein imposed an unusual sentence on Maureen Murphy, who had been convicted of a large insurance fraud. Instead of being confined to prison, she was confined to her own home. The judge explained his departure from the traditional sentence as an effort to balance the competing aims of public safety, humaneness, and accountability against a backdrop of seriously crowded prisons. Probation did not seem severe enough; on the other hand, prison for a person with no previous criminal record seemed too severe.[83] Since then, some 50,000 Americans have been sentenced to what has become known as **house arrest.**

House arrest is a sentence imposed by the court whereby offenders are legally ordered to remain confined in their own residences for the duration of their sentence. House arrestees may be allowed to leave their homes for medical reasons, employment, and approved religious services. They may also be required to perform community service and to pay victim restitution and probation supervising fees. In selected instances, electronic monitoring equipment may be used to monitor an offender's presence in a residence where he or she is required to remain.[84]

The selection criteria for house arrest offenders are similar across all jurisdictions. Offenders are disqualified if they have *(text continues on p. 460)*

halfway house
Residential correctional facility in which an offender may have to serve the last portion of his or her sentence outside prison, but not yet in the community.

"Halfway houses often face objections from the community; no one wants 'ex-cons' in their neighborhood."

Good News Regeneration House, Brooklyn, New York. A refurbished tenement in Bedford-Stuyvesant, one of Brooklyn's poorest neighborhoods, has become a halfway house for criminals and addicts. It is the work of prison chaplain the Rev. Roberto Rodriguez, right, shown here with four residents.

house arrest
Sentence in which convicts are confined to their own residence in lieu of imprisonment in an institution.

"Since 1985, some 50,000 Americans have been sentenced to what has become known as house arrest."

THE VAGARIES OF NET-WIDENING

America's criminal justice system has not been working very well. According to official estimates, crime continues to increase despite massive efforts to improve law enforcement, the courts, and correction. . . . Some critics complain that the criminal justice net reaps an unnecessarily abundant catch of deviants. Too often people are arrested, prosecuted, sentenced, and punished (corrected) for behaviors that do not warrant such severe intervention. For some . . . the specter of the widening net is nightmarish.

Other critics of the criminal justice system agree with the first group that things have been getting worse for some time. [But for them] the failure of criminal justice is traced to the growing impotence of the state to intervene in and punish criminal activity swiftly. The net has been made too small and too weak to catch criminals. Reforms are needed both to strengthen and to expand the net to preserve social order. (1)

Crime researchers James Austin and Barry Krisberg presented this paradox in a 1981 research paper: How is it that "widening the net" can be seen as both the path to salvation for and a fundamental flaw of the criminal justice system? In criminal justice, the idea of a net or a series of nets brings to mind the regulation and control of deviant and criminal behavior—in other words, state-sanctioned social control. For most theorists, social control is conceptualized as a response to deviance and crime. For others, it is that which the government offers

in order to direct or guide social change. Social control also is often seen as ensuring conformity to law through strong social bonds, investment and participation in conventional activities, and the maintenance of a value system.

Social control and net-widening

When we think of nets and net-widening, a full range of social control comes to mind: conscious attempts by powerful segments of society to control constituents; the social and economic planning undertaken by governmental agencies and agents; the legitimate use of influence and power in society. Different reactions to criminal justice nets can be attributed to this wide range of possibilities for social control.

To some criminal justice specialists, social control is an effort by those in power to obtain norm and rule conformity by oppressive, restrictive, or corrupt control. Here the idea of wider, stronger, or new nets is frightening. As Austin and Krisberg put it, "'widening the net' describes the nightmare of the benevolent state gone haywire. This horror has already been vividly portrayed in Orwell's *1984,* Solzhenitsyn's *Cancer Ward,* Kesey's *One Flew Over the Cuckoo's Nest,* and Burgess's *Clockwork Orange*" (1, p. 188). From this perspective, the nets are too wide and unnecessarily strong already, catching far too many people. Many arrests, prosecutions, sentences, and terms of incarceration are seen as unnecessary. Crime control is overused and overrated.

To others, social control and net-widening is the legitimate and necessary use of state-sanctioned

force, power, or coercion to control and punish criminals. Criminal justice specialists who support this view see the net as too small and weak to deal effectively with crime. For them, net-widening is good—it is a healthy expansion of an effective criminal justice system.

Reform efforts: More radical remedies?

These two "camps" have tried to implement a series of reform strategies that reflect their views on net-widening. For those who condemn the effort to expand the social control of deviance, diversion, decarceration, decriminalization, and due process have been shared goals. For those who support an expansion of social control—a strengthening of crime control efforts—deterrence, just deserts, and certainty of punishment are advocated.

But reform efforts have produced some unintended results. Diversionary programs, aimed at reducing the reach of the criminal justice net through the "filtering out" of offenders, have not succeeded in reducing court congestion and prison populations. Such programs actually have created new nets and strengthened old ones. As new diversionary agencies and programs were established, researchers soon realized that the competition and conflict between and among criminal justice agencies produced greater social control, not less.

Efforts to decarcerate produced similar findings. Incarceration rates often were reduced, at least initially, with corresponding increases in temporary facilities or innovative programs. Over time, however, rates often returned to preintervention levels. If the rates remained low, new "nets" were observed to capture those who were displaced by decarceration policies. Again, one's perspective on social control colors the picture. Home electronic monitoring, for example, can be seen as an effort to decarcerate or to increase the reach of the criminal justice net. It may provide an alternative to prison for offenders who would otherwise serve a sentence, or it may have the effect of containing many offenders who would ordinarily escape any kind of correctional intervention.

Due-process reforms and decriminalization both strengthened and increased the size of the criminal justice net. *Miranda* and *In re Gault* prompted needed reforms—but the development of new policies and procedures counteracted their effects. Elaborate exceptions and countermoves to both rulings typify the limits of due-process reform. Decriminalization of laws relating to marijuana use, abortion, and homosexuality have met a similar fate. Enforcement efforts decreased for certain offenses while increasing for others, with little change overall.

While reforms intended to reduce the size and strength of the criminal justice net seem to have failed to do so, Austin and Krisberg argue that net-widening reforms such as just deserts and deterrence also have failed to deal effectively with the problems of crime in the United States. The apparent failure of diversion, decarceration, decriminalization, and due-process reforms reveals how difficult it is to make lasting changes in a highly complex and dynamic system. As Austin and Krisberg note, "To respond in so-

A still photo of a scene from A Clockwork Orange: *social control gone haywire.*

cially constructive ways to crime without widening the net is a dilemma" (1, p. 189). It is a dilemma that is limited by strong—and often countervailing—political and economic forces. What is needed, they suggest, is "more radical remedies than the current menu of criminal justice reforms" (1, p. 189).

SOURCES

1. James Austin and Barry Krisberg, "Wider, Stronger, and Different Nets: The Dialectics of Criminal Justice Reform," *Journal of Research in Crime and Delinquency* 18 (1981):165–196. See also Maeve McMahon, "Net-Widening: Vagaries in the Use of a Concept," *British Journal of Criminology* 30 (1990):121–149.

QUESTIONS FOR DISCUSSION

1. Do you side with those who think the criminal justice net is already too wide, or with those who think it should be wider and stronger? Why?
2. Should concerns about increasing the reach of criminal justice nets inhibit the development of new and innovative community-based programs?
3. What sorts of "more radical remedies" can you suggest for improving the criminal justice system in the United States?

- a history of violence
- chronic drug or alcohol problems
- unstable interpersonal relationships at home
- immigration problems
- a prior criminal history, including a history of failure to appear
- an unstable employment history

In general, probation officers and judges look at the whole picture of prior record, age, health, substance abuse, circumstances of the current offense, home life, employment, and the attitude of the offender to decide if home confinement is a "good bet."[85]

Michigan, Nevada, and Oklahoma have experimented with residential confinement programs with participants drawn from the prison population. Most states with such programs use them for front-end diversion from prison. In the Maryland program, which has operated successfully for several years, the sentencing judge and the Department of Corrections jointly make the decision to use the defendant's home rather than a prison cell as the place of confinement. This twofold approval is designed to ensure that dangerous or high-risk offenders are not placed in the program.

electronic monitoring
Computer-assisted checks on offender's movement to ensure that he or she is not going to places in violation of restrictions.

Electronic Monitoring. Most house arrest programs incorporate a level of **electronic monitoring.** Electronic devices provide for computer-assisted checks on an offender to ensure that he or she is not moving about in the community in violation of restrictions ordered by the court.[86] Electronic monitoring is used in conjunction with both home detention and intensive supervision programs. About 8,300 adults are now on probation under electronic monitoring[87] (Figure 16.1).

There are two types of electronic monitoring systems—active and passive. Active systems (sometimes called "continuous signal systems") provide constant monitoring. A transmitting device strapped to the offender continuously signals either a central tracking computer or a portable receiver carried in the supervisor's vehicle. The transmitter signals a receiver-dialer. The receiver-dialer receives the signal and dials the central office computer when the transmitter is within a predetermined geographic range, indicating that the offender is at home. Passive systems (sometimes called "programmed contact systems") include less sophisticated techniques such as telephone verification. The offender must respond to a telephone call within a prescribed time period, or a failure reading is recorded.[88] Although the technology gets more sophisticated every year, there have been technical problems with the transmitting devices. Among the early electronic monitoring devices, ankle and wrist bracelets were easy to tamper with. Defective telephone equipment was often the cause of violation recordings.[89]

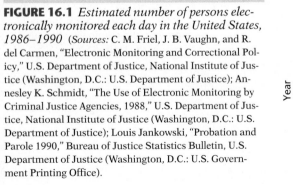

FIGURE 16.1 *Estimated number of persons electronically monitored each day in the United States, 1986–1990* (*Sources:* C. M. Friel, J. B. Vaughn, and R. del Carmen, "Electronic Monitoring and Correctional Policy," U.S. Department of Justice, National Institute of Justice (Washington, D.C.: U.S. Department of Justice); Annesley K. Schmidt, "The Use of Electronic Monitoring by Criminal Justice Agencies, 1988," U.S. Department of Justice, National Institute of Justice (Washington, D.C.: U.S. Department of Justice); Louis Jankowski, "Probation and Parole 1990," Bureau of Justice Statistics Bulletin, U.S. Department of Justice (Washington, D.C.: U.S. Government Printing Office).

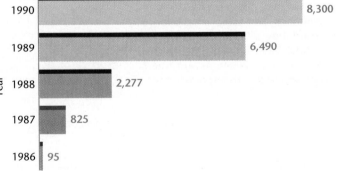

Estimated Daily Monitored Population in the United States, 1986–1990

Year	
1990	8,300
1989	6,490
1988	2,277
1987	825
1986	95

House Arrest and Monitoring of Juveniles. There has been widespread hesitation in using house arrest and electronic monitoring as a sanction for juveniles for fear youngsters will be stigmatized by the wrist and ankle bracelets. The system is also regarded as an intrusion on the juvenile's family, and some argue that juveniles are harder to keep confined to the home. The concern is that juveniles will be bound to a home in which there is no parental supervision.

The first known program for juveniles began in North Carolina in 1986, and since then at least eleven electronic monitoring systems for juveniles have been implemented. An overview of juvenile electronic monitoring systems found that the average length of monitoring ranged from sixteen to ninety days. Failure rates ranged from 4.5 percent to 30 percent, although program administrators claimed that the majority of unsuccessful cases resulted from technical violations rather than from new offenses.[90]

Cost-Benefit Analysis of House Arrest/Electronic Monitoring. House arrest/electronic monitoring sentences have come under criticism. The National Association of Probation Officers (NAPO) argues that the people selected for release subject to electronic monitoring are those who probably would normally be placed on bail.[91] The value of the deterrent component of the electronic monitoring of offenders is minimized when clients learn that there is a low certainty of detection and no swift response with more serious sanctions.[92] But, a study that compared the frequency of success among offenders who would otherwise have had their liberty revoked with that among those who have more successfully adapted to community control found that electronic monitoring is an effective method for reducing revocations in community corrections populations.[93]

Many researchers agree on the cost effectiveness of house arrest. The total cost of the Prince Georges County, Maryland, home detention program, including staff, transportation, and equipment, is seven dollars per day per prisoner, contrasted with the forty-five dollars it costs to maintain a prisoner in the County Detention Center for a day. In the first two years of this program, 188 convicts successfully completed their period of confinement on home detention, at a savings to the county of well over $1 million. A Florida home arrest cost-benefit evaluation found that offenders sentenced to house arrest were not only able to keep their jobs, but were able to pay in excess of $9 million in fees associated with home detention.[94]

Joan Petersilia's cost-benefit analysis of house arrest programs, however, suggests that when electronic monitoring is used, the cost of equipment makes this technique less attractive (Figure 16.2). For instance, $30,000 was spent to purchase twelve electronic monitors in Kentucky. The six-month house arrest program in Kentucky cost the county $10,000 to $20,000 more than it would have if the twenty-three persons in the study had been sent to prison.[95] A one-year evaluation of a South Carolina electronic monitoring pilot program also found that there were no savings within the criminal justice system, mainly due to the low number of participants and the low utilization rate of the monitoring equipment.

To some critics, the question whether electronic monitoring and house arrest are effective ignores the central question of their constitutionality. They suggest that house arrest and electronic monitoring interfere with First Amendment (freedom of speech and assembly) and Fourth Amendment (unreasonable search and seizure) rights.[96] These critics suggest that the law, having failed to keep pace with technological changes in punishment alternatives, does not provide adequate protection for offenders.[97] Others see the introduction of electronic monitoring as destroying the notion that one's home is the ultimate refuge from state authority.[98]

In contrast, advocates of house arrest programs using electronic monitoring devices argue that these do not infringe upon First or Fourth Amendment rights because the devices do not record any conversations or actions within the home. Additionally, advocates point out that the people who enter house arrest and

"Many researchers agree on the cost effectiveness of house arrest; offenders are able to keep their jobs, support their families, and pay their fines."

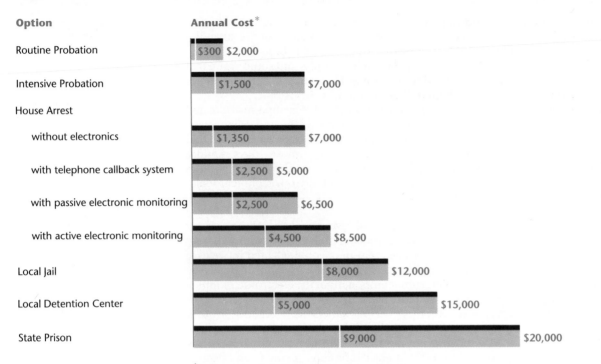

Option	Annual Cost*		
Routine Probation	$300	$2,000	
Intensive Probation	$1,500	$7,000	
House Arrest			
without electronics	$1,350	$7,000	
with telephone callback system	$2,500	$5,000	
with passive electronic monitoring	$2,500	$6,500	
with active electronic monitoring	$4,500	$8,500	
Local Jail	$8,000	$12,000	
Local Detention Center	$5,000	$15,000	
State Prison	$9,000	$20,000	

*Dollar amounts indicate range of annual costs.

FIGURE 16.2 *Annual cost of sentencing options, exclusive of construction costs* (*Source:* Joan Petersilia, *Expanding Options for Criminal Sentencing* [Santa Monica, Calif.: Rand Corporation, 1987], p. 32.)

electronic monitoring programs do so on a voluntary basis.[99] Home confinement is seen as punitive; the retribution and deterrence goals of punishment are satisfied; and the offender is still allowed to maintain employment as well as close family ties, which can be particularly important when the family includes young children who need the offender at home. But it is too early to claim that such programs are a total success.[100]

Community Service

The Vera Institute of Justice, in New York, has pioneered many improvements in corrections. In the 1960s it began experimenting with a novel alternative to incarceration in cases where imprisonment is not called for, because neither the offense nor the offender justifies its use, and where a fine is not appropriate, usually because the offender would have to commit another offense to get the money to pay it. The answer: the **community service order.** The sentencing judge orders the convict to perform any of a range of services to the community: driving a bus for the handicapped, serving meals to the elderly, building a playground for kids, or landscaping a highway.[101]

One of the first jurisdictions in the United States to use community service orders was Alameda County, California. In October 1966 the Alameda County Court agreed to permit those convicted of misdemeanors to serve their sentences as volunteers for community organizations. Thereafter community service programs proliferated around the country. Such programs promised that

- offenders will have opportunities to engage in constructive activities
- offenders will likely undergo a change of attitude through the experience of volunteer work
- community service is a sentence uniquely appropriate to indigent offenders
- community service also can be an appropriate sentence for persons in higher income brackets whose offenses merit publicity and public shaming

But some researchers think that these are largely "unmet promises."[102]

community service order
Sanction in which sentencing judge orders the convict to perform any of a range of services to the community.

"These programs are clearly the right thing to do, no question. But I want to know what it will take to sell these programs because they might leave you open to political pot shots from people who would say you're soft on crime."
Governor Bruce Sundlun, Rhode Island, in *The New York Times*, August 7, 1992, p. A17.

EVALUATION OF ALTERNATIVE PROGRAMS

In recent years, both liberal and conservative legislators have challenged criminologists to devise alternatives to incarceration. Some notable liberal thinkers argued that it is inhumane to house offenders in overcrowded jails and prisons. Some conservative thinkers could no longer justify spending ever-increasing portions of state budgets to build new jails and prisons for low-risk offenders. Since the late 1970s, the programs described in this chapter have proliferated throughout the United States and also abroad. Many were readily implemented because of their political appeal. An extensive assessment of the entire body of evaluation research undertaken on these alternative programs concludes that traditional probation and some community corrections programs are cost effective.[103] The assessment also found that intensive supervision programs do not significantly reduce the risk of recidivism and that house arrest programs have not yet been shown to be successful. The argument is made that before more alternative programs are implemented, already existing programs should be rigorously evaluated.

REVIEW

The first set of alternatives to imprisonment, probation and parole, were intended to humanize corrections. Probation and parole were the innovations of practical people, not scholars or jurists. John Augustus, who invented probation, was a cobbler, and Alexander Maconochie, who invented parole, was a naval officer. These two alternatives to prison (or continued prison confinement), now a century and a half old, are still widely in use, servicing a convict population three times the size of that incarcerated. Both sanctions are more cost beneficial than prison. The effectiveness of probation is considerable: Only 20 percent of probationers are re-arrested for violent crime within three years. With parole, the failure rate is over 50 percent. While predicting success of probationers and parolees is difficult (and failure has led to a movement to abolish or curtail parole), it is generally agreed that if officers' case loads were reduced, the success rate would rise.

Because of rising crime rates and an increasingly punitive public attitude, we have recently witnessed the emergence of tough new programs designed to control and penalize even some of the more severe offenders by sanctions short of traditional imprisonment, yet more severe than traditional probation. Among them are intensive supervision programs which, in effect, were part of the original idea of probation and parole; shock programs in the form of Marine Corps-type boot camps emphasizing discipline and re-education; and residential programs in the community aimed at teaching self-respect and the capacity to survive economically. Some of these programs rely on various forms of electronic monitoring, and all are meant to be tough alternatives, so as not to detract from the perceived severity of a sentence. Additional recent alternatives are volunteers in probation programs, restitution to victims (some programs with residential requirements), community service programs, and greater use of fines.

The effectiveness of these innovative programs is not yet fully established. Some have proved cheaper than imprisonment and not less effective, as measured by recidivism rates. The danger is that they can be used to "widen the net" by subjecting more persons to control by the criminal justice system. All the new programs have political appeal. Whether they are an improvement over past penal practice, only evaluation research and time will tell.

Notes

1. *John Augustus—First Probation Officer* (1852). John Augustus' original Report of his Labors (1852), with an introduction by Sheldon Glueck (Montclair, N.J.: Patterson Smith, 1972), pp. 4–5.

2. Steven Dillingham and Lawrence Greenfield, "An Overview of National Corrections Statistics," *Federal Probation* 55 (1991): 27–34.

3. This section is based on Kevin Krajick and Steven Gettinger, *Overcrowded Time: Why Prisons Are So Crowded and What Can Be Done* (New York: Edna McConnel Clark Foundation, 1982).

4. Sheldon Glueck, Introduction, *John Augustus, First Probation Officer*, p. xvi.

5. Charles Lindner and Margaret Saverese, "The Evolution of Probation: University Settlement and Its Pioneering Role in Probation Work," *Federal Probation* 68 (1984):3–13.

6. Harry Allen, Chris Eskridge, Edward Latessa and Gennaro Vito, *Probation and Parole in America* (New York: Free Press, 1985); David Fogel, "The Emergence of Probation as a Profession in the Service of Public Safety: The Next Ten Years," *Probation and Justice: Reconsideration of Mission*, ed. Patrick D. McAnany, Doug Thomson, and David Fogel (Cambridge, Mass.: Oelgeschlager Gunnard Hain, 1984).

7. Randall Guynes, "Difficult Clients, Large Caseloads Plague Probation Parole Agencies," *Research in Action* (Washington, D.C.: National Institute of Justice, 1988). See also R. M. Carter and L. T. Wilkins, *Probation and Parole: Selected Readings* (New York: Wiley, 1970).

8. Jane Sutton, "Probation Gardeners Feed the Homeless—Gardening," *United Press International*, March 13, 1989, Monday, BC cycle.

9. Bureau of Justice Statistics, *Corrections Populations in the United States, 1990* (Washington, D.C.: Bureau of Justice Statistics, July 1992), p. 24.

10. *Mempa v. Rhay*, 389 U.S. 128 (1967); Terence D. McCann, "The Impact of *Mempa v. Rhay* on Probation and Parole Revocation Hearings," *Probation and Parole* 3 (1971):54–64.

11. *Gagnon v. Scarpelli*, 411 U.S. 778 (1973).

12. Robert L. Spangenberg, et al., *Assessment of the Massachusetts Probation System* (Newton, Mass.: Spangenberg Group, 1987).

13. Robert L. Thomas, "Stress Perception among Select Federal Probation and Pre-trial Services Officers and Their Supervisors," *Federal Probation* 52 (1988):48–58.

14. See Dale G. Hardman, "The Function of the Probation Officer," *Federal Probation* (1960):3–10; Thomas Ellsworth, "The Goal Orientation of Adult Probation Professionals: A Study of Probation Systems," *Journal of Crime and Justice* 12 (1990):55–76.

15. Lori Colley, Robert Culbertson, and Edward Latessa, "Probation Officer Job Analysis: Rural-Urban Differences," *Federal Probation* 50 (1986):67–71. See also D. Glaser, *The Effectiveness of a Prison and Parole System* (Indianapolis: Bobbs-Merrill, 1964).

16. Charles Lindner, "The Refocused Probation Home Visit: A Subtle but Revolutionary Change," *Journal of Contemporary Criminal Justice* 7 (1991):115–127; Thomas Ellsworth, "Identifying the Actual and Preferred Goals of Adult Probation," *Federal Probation* 54 (1990):10–15. With increased emphasis on the control function there may arise the need to arm probation officers. See Richard D. Sluder, Robert A. Shearer, and Dennis W. Potts, "Probation Officers' Role Perceptions and Attitudes toward Firearms," *Federal Probation* 55(3) (1991):3–11.

17. Bill Workman, "Probation Cops in East Palo Alto Can't Drop In on Their Clients," *The San Francisco Chronicle*, December 18, 1991, p. A15. An additional risk factor for probation officers is the emerging potential of civil liability. See Charles Linder and Norman A. Olch, "The Emergence of Section 1983 Litigation into Probation and Parole Practice," *Journal of Probation and Parole* 14 (1982):17–25. Richard D. Sluder and Rolando V. del Carmen, "Are Probation and Parole Officers Liable for Injuries Caused by Probationers and Parolees?," *Federal Probation* 54 (1990):3–12.

18. Todd Clear, Val Clear and William Burrell, *Offender Assessment and Evaluation: The Pre-Sentence Investigation Report* (Cincinnati: Anderson Publishing, 1989).

19. Gennaro F. Vito, "Developments in Shock Probation: A Review of Research Findings and Policy Implications," *Federal Probation* 48 (1984):22–27.

20. Division of Probation, Administrative Office of the United States Courts, Washington, D.C.: "The Selective Presentence Investigation Report," *Federal Probation* (1974):47–54.

21. Anthony Walsh, "The Role of the Probation Officer in the Sentencing Process: Independent Professional or Judicial Hack?," *Criminal Justice and Behavior* 12 (1985):289–303.

22. Kriss A. Drass and J. William Spencer, "Accounting for Pre-Sentencing Recommendations: Typologies and Probation Officers' Theory of Office," *Social Problems* 34 (1987):277–293.

23. John Rosecrance, "Maintaining the Myth of Individualized Justice: Probation Pre-Sentence Reports," *Justice Quarterly* 5 (1988):235–256. For a direct dissenting opinion about the myth of presentence reports, see Joseph W. Rogers, "The Predisposition Report: Maintaining the Promise of Individualized Juvenile Justice," *Federal Probation* 54 (1990):43–57.

24. Clear, Clear, and Burrell, *Offender Assessment and Evaluation*.

25. Chris Eskridge and Eric Carlson, "The Use of Volunteers in Probation: A National Synthesis," *Journal of Offender Counseling, Services and Rehabilitation* 4 (1979). See also Ivan H. Scheier, "The Professional and the Volunteer in Probation: An Emerging Relationship," *Federal Probation* 34 (1970):12–18; Richard Seiter, Sue Howard, and Harry Allen, *Effectiveness of Volunteers in Court: An Evaluation of the Franklin County Volunteers in Probation Program* (Columbus: Ohio State University, Program for the Study of Crime and Delinquency, 1974).

26. Edward Latessa, Eric Carlson, and Harry Allen, "Paraprofessionals in Probation: A Synthesis of Management Issues and Outcome Studies," *Journal of Offender Counseling, Services and Rehabilitation* 4 (1979):163–173.

27. Frank Scioli and Thomas Cook, "How Effective Are Volunteers? Public Participation in the Criminal Justice System," *Crime and Delinquency* (April 1976). See also Eskridge and Carlson, "The Use of Volunteers in Probation," for concurrence with Scioli and Cook's findings.

28. George M. Camp and Camille Camp, *The Corrections Yearbook 1991: Probation and Parole* (South Salem, N.Y.: Criminal Justice Institute, 1991), p. 9. For a study of the effectiveness of probation with felons, see John T. Whitehead, "The Effectiveness of Felony Probation: Results from an Eastern State," *Justice Quarterly* 8 (1991):525–543.

29. Holly Morris, "Georgia's Busiest Probation Office," *The Atlanta Journal and Constitution*, January 4, 1992, p. B2.

30. "AP, 43% of Probationers Arrested," *The New York Times*, February 11, 1992, p. A16.

31. Harry E. Allen and Edward J. Latessa, "Corrections in the Year 2000 A.D.," *Journal of Contemporary Criminal Justice* 1 (1980):1–3. See also Harry E. Allen, Chris W. Eskridge, Edward J. Latessa, and Gennaro F. Vito, *Probation and Parole in America* (New York: Free Press, 1985), ch. 12.

32. Alexander Maconochie, quoted in Harry Elmer Barnes and Negley K. Teeters, *New Horizons in Criminology* (New York: Prentice-Hall, 1943), p. 548.

33. Ibid.

34. Bureau of Justice Statistics, *Corrections Populations in the United States, 1990*, pp. 117–122. For parole decision-making regarding women, see Edna Erez, "Dangerous Men, Evil Women: Gender and Parole Decision-making," *Justice Quarterly* 9 (1992):105–126.

35. Vincent O'Leary and Joan Nuffield, *The Organization of Parole Systems in the United States* (Hackensack, N.J.: National Council on Crime and Delinquency, 1972).

36. William Parker, *Parole: Origins, Development, Current Practices and Statutes* (College Park, Md.: American Correctional Association, 1975).

37. Bureau of Justice Statistics, *Corrections Populations in the United States, 1990*, p. 119.

38. Nina Bernstein, "Bid to Deny Mom's Parole," *Newsday*, January 28, 1992, p. 8.

39. Vincent O'Leary and Kathleen Hanrahan, *Parole Systems in the United States: A Detailed Description of Their Structure and Procedures*, 3d ed. (Hackensack, N.J.: National Council on Crime and Delinquency, 1976), pp. 42–47.

40. *Greenholtz v. Inmates of Nebraska Penal and Correctional Complex*, 442 U.S. 1 (1979).

42. *Connecticut Board of Pardons v. Dumschat*, 101 S. Ct. 2460 (1981).

42. *Morrissev v. Brewer*, 408 U.S. 471 (1972).

43. Michael Gottfredson, S. Mitchell-Herzfield, and T. Flanagan, "Another Look at the Effectiveness of Parole Supervision," *Journal of Research in Crime* 19 (1982):277–298. See also L. Thomas Winfree, Jr., John Wooldredge, Christine Sellers, and Veronica Smith Ballard, "Parole Survival and Legislated Change: A Before and After Study of Parole Revocation Decision Making," *Justice Quarterly* 7 (1990):151–173.

44. James Austin, *Success and Failure on Parole in California: A Preliminary Evaluation* (San Francisco: National Council on Crime and Delinquency, 1987).

45. See Billie S. Erwin, *Evaluation of Intensive Probation Supervision in Georgia* (Atlanta: Georgia Department of Offender Rehabilitation, February 1985). Daniel Glaser, *The Effectiveness of a*

Prison and Parole System, pp. 292–293; Todd R. Clear and Edward Latessa, "A Study of Role Perception among ISP Officers," paper presented to Academy of Criminal Justice Sciences, Washington, D.C. (March 1989); Elliott Studt, *Surveillance and Service in Parole,* publication of U.S. Department of Justice (Washington, D.C.: U.S. Government Printing Office, 1973); Todd R. Clear and Vincent O'Leary, *Controlling the Offender in the Community* (Lexington, Mass.: Lexington Books, 1982), p. 120.

46. Carl B. Klockars, "A Theory of Probation Supervision," *Journal of Criminal Law, Criminology and Police Science* 63 (1972):550–557.

47. Camp and Camp, *The Corrections Yearbook, 1991,* p. 45.

48. Adult Probation and Parole Services, *Workload Measurement Study* (Richmond, Va.: Department of Corrections, Division of Adult Community Corrections, March 1987).

49. Ibid.

50. Drass and Spencer, "Accounting for Pre-Sentencing Recommendations.

51. Don M. Gottfredson, M. G. Neithercutt, Joan Nuffield, and Vincent O'Leary, *Four Thousand Lifetimes: A Study of Time Served and Parole Outcomes* (Davis, Calif.: National Council on Crime and Delinquency, Research Center, 1973).

52. Bureau of Justice Statistics, *Corrections Populations in the United States, 1990,* p. 120.

53. M. K. Harris, "Disquisition on the Need for a New Model for Criminal Sanctioning Systems," *West Virginia Law Review* 77 (1974):263–326.

54. Andrew von Hirsch and Kathleen J. Hanrahan, *The Question of Parole: Retention, Reform or Abolition?* (Cambridge, Mass.: Ballinger, 1979).

55. Bureau of Justice Statistics, *Parole Today* (Washington, D.C.: U.S. Government Printing Office, 1980), p. 11.

56. Norval Morris and Michael H. Tonry, *Between Prison and Probation* (New York: Oxford University Press, 1990); David Weisburd and Ellen F. Chayet, "Good Time: An Agenda for Research," *Criminal Justice and Behavior* 16 (1989):183–195.

57. Sandra Evans Skovron, Joseph E. Scott, and Francis T. Cullen, "Prison Crowding: Public Attitudes toward Strategies of Population Control," *Journal of Research in Crime and Delinquency* 25 (1988):150–169.

58. *Ex parte Garland,* 71 U.S. 333, 18 L. Ed. 366 (1867).

59. *Burdick v. United States,* 236 U.S. 79, 59 L. Ed. 476 (1915); *People ex rel. Prisament v. Brophy,* 287 N.Y. 132 (1942).

60. G. O. W. Mueller, "Tort, Crime and the Primitive," *Journal of Criminal Law, Criminology and Police Science,* 46 (1955):303–332.

61. Fahy G. Mullaney, *Economic Sanctions in Community Corrections* (Washington, D.C.: U.S. Department of Justice, National Institute of Corrections, August 1988).

62. Ida Zamist, *Fines in Sentencing: An Empirical Study of Fine Use, Collection and Enforcement in New York City Courts* (New York: Vera Institute of Justice, 1981, revised 1986).

63. Pat Carlen and Dee Cook, eds., *Paying for Crime* (Philadelphia: Open University Press, Milton Keynes, 1989).

64. Sally Hillsman and Barry Mahoney, "Collecting and Enforcing Criminal Fines: A Review of Court Processes, Practices and Problems," *Justice System Journal* 13:17–36 (1988). See also Judith Greene, "Structuring Criminal Fines: Making an 'Intermediate Penalty': More Useful and Equitable," *Justice System Journal* 13 (1988):37–50; George Cole, Barry Mahony, Marlene Thornton, and Roger Hanson, *The Practice and Attitudes of Trial Court Judges Regarding Fines as a Criminal Sanction* (Washington, D.C.: U.S. Department of Justice, National Institute of Justice, July 1987).

65. Barbara Smith, Robert Davis, and Susan Hillenbrand, *Improving Enforcement of Court-Ordered Restitution: A Study of the American Bar Association Criminal Justice Victim Witness Project* (Washington, D.C.: American Bar Association, August 1989).

66. James Byrne, A. Lurigio, and S. Baird, "The Effectiveness of the 'New' Intensive Supervision Programs," *Research in Corrections* 5 (1989):2. See also D. E. Jernigan and R. F. Kronick, "Intensive

Parole: The More You Watch, the More You Catch," *Journal of Offender Rehabilitation* 17 (1992):65–76.

67. New Jersey Criminal Disposition Commission, *Report to the Governor and Legislature,* 1987. See also William B. Lawless and Gerhard O. W. Mueller, *Report of the Commission to Advise the Nevada Legislature on the Question of Prison Overcrowding* (Reno: National Judicial College, 1989).

68. Frank S. Pearson, *Research on New Jersey's Intensive Supervision Program: Final Report* (New Brunswick, N.J.: Institute for Criminological Research, Rutgers University, 1987).

69. Joan Petersilia, "Georgia's Intensive Probation: Will the Model Work Elsewhere?," in *Intermediate Punishments: Intensive Supervision, Home Confinement and Electronic Surveillance,* ed. Belinda McCarthy (Monsey, N.Y.: Criminal Justice Press, 1987), p. 21; Joan Petersilia, *Expanding Options for Criminal Sentencing* (Santa Monica, Calif.: Rand Corporation, 1987), pp. 10–32; Billie S. Erwin and Lawrence Bennett, "New Dimensions in Probation: Georgia's Experience with Intensive Probation Supervision," *Research in Brief,* National Institute of Justice (Washington, D.C.: U.S. Government Printing Office, 1987).

70. Susan B. Noonan and Edward J. Latessa, "Intensive Probation: An Examination of Recidivism and Social Adjustment for an Intensive Supervision Program," *American Journal of Criminal Justice* 12 (1987):45–61. The effectiveness of ISP programs in other jurisdictions is inconclusive. See, e.g., *Intensive Supervision Program: Final Evaluation Report Client Characteristics and Supervision Outcomes: A Caseload Comparison* (Richmond, Va.: Department of Corrections, Research and Evaluation Unit, 1988).

71. Michael Tonry, "Stated and Latent Features of ISP," *Crime and Delinquency* 36 (1990):174–191; Joan Petersilia and Susan Turner, "Comparing Intensive and Regular Supervision for High Risk Probationers: Early Results from an Experiment in California," *Crime and Delinquency* 36 (1990):87–111; Joan Petersilia, "When Probation Becomes More Dreaded Than Prison," *Federal Probation* 54 (1990):23–27.

72. James Byrne, "Assessing What Works in the Adult Community Corrections System," paper presented to Academy of Criminal Justice Sciences, Denver, March 1990.

73. Camp and Camp, *The Corrections Yearbook, 1991,* p. 49.

74. Dale Parent, *Shock Incarceration: An Overview of Existing Programs* (Washington, D.C.: National Institute of Justice, 1989), p. 9. See also Jody Klein-Saffran, "Shock Incarceration: Bureau of Prisons Style," *Research Forum,* Federal Bureau of Prisons, Office of Research and Evaluation, July 1992, pp. 1–9.

75. Ibid., p. 7.

76. New York State Division of Parole, Shock Incarceration: One Year Out of 3 (prepared by the New York Office of Policy Analysis and Information, August 1989); *New Haven Register,* November 10, 1989, p. 15.

77. Doris Layton MacKenzie and Dale Parent, "Shock Incarceration and Prison Crowding in Louisiana," *Journal of Criminal Justice* 19 (1991):225–237. See also Doris Layton MacKenzie, Larry Gould, Lisa Riechers, and James Shaw, "Shock Incarceration: Rehabilitation or Retribution?," *Journal of Offender Counseling, Services and Rehabilitation* 14 (1989):25–40; Doris Layton MacKenzie and James W. Shaw, "Inmate Adjustment and Change during Shock Incarceration: The Impact of Correctional Boot Camp Programs," *Justice Quarterly* 7 (March 1990):125–150.

78. Doris MacKenzie, "Boot Camp Prisons: Components, Evaluations and Empirical Issues," *Federal Probation* 54 (1990):44–52.

79. Doris Layton MacKenzie and Deanna Bellew Ballow, "Shock Incarceration Programs in State Correctional Jurisdictions— An Update," *Research in Brief* (Washington, D.C.: National Institute of Justice, 1989). See also Dale Parent, *Shock Incarceration: An Overview of Existing Programs* (Washington, D.C.: U.S. Government Printing Office, 1989).

80. See, for example, Edward Latessa and Gennaro F. Vito, "The Effects of Intensive Supervision on Shock Probationers," *Journal of Criminal Justice* 16 (1988):319–330.

81. See Günther Kaiser, *Kriminologie*, 2d ed. (Heidelberg: C. F. Müller Jur. Verlag, 1988).

82. Edward Latessa and Harry Allen, "Halfway Houses and Parole: A National Assessment," *Journal of Criminal Justice* 10 (1982):156.

83. Joan Petersilia, *Exploring the Option of House Arrest* (Santa Monica, Calif.: Rand Corporation, 1986). See also Judge Jack Weinstein's sentencing memorandum in the Maureen Murphy case (United States District Court, Eastern District of New York, December, 1985).

84. Joan Petersilia, *Expanding Options for Criminal Sentencing*, p. 32; see also Joan Petersilia, *Exploring the Option of House Arrest*.

85. Paul Hofer and Barbara Meierhoefer, *Home Confinement: An Evolving Sanction in the Federal Criminal Justice System* (Washington, D.C.: Federal Judicial Center, 1987), pp. 19–20. For disadvantages of home confinement, see Marie Whittington, *Adult Home Detention as an Alternative to Incarceration*, Orange County Probation Department (Santa Ana, Calif.: June 1986).

86. See Ken Russell and Robert Lilly, eds., *The Electronic Monitoring of Offenders*, monograph (Leister, England: Polytechnic Law School, 1989) for an overview of electronic monitoring. See also Robert Rogers and Annette Jolin, "Electronic Monitoring: A Review of the Empirical Literature," *Journal of Contemporary Criminal Justice* 5 (1989):133–180, for a review of the empirical literature. For a review of electronic monitoring in the federal system, see Timothy P. Cadigan, "Electronic Monitoring in Federal Pretrial Release," *Federal Probation* (March 1991):26–33. See also James Beck, Jody Klein-Saffran, and Harold Wooten, "Home Confinement and the Use of Electronic Monitoring with Federal Parolees," *Federal Probation* 54 (December 1990):22–33.

87. Bureau of Justice Statistics Bulletin, *Probation and Parole 1990* (Washington, D.C.: U.S. Dept. of Justice, November 1991), p. 4. See also Kenneth T. Moran and Charles Lindner, "Probation and the Hi-Technology Revolution: Is a Reconceptualization of the Traditional Probation Officer Role Inevitable?," *Criminal Justice Review* 10 (1985):25–32; Charles M. Friel, Joseph B. Vaughn, and Rolando del Carmen, *Electronic Monitoring and Correctional Policy: The Technology and Its Application* (Washington, D.C.: U.S. Government Printing Office, prepared for the U.S. National Institute of Justice by the Criminal Justice Center, Sam Houston State University, 1987); Charles M. Friel and Joseph B. Vaughn, "A Consumer's Guide to the Electronic Monitoring of Probationers," *Federal Probation* 50 (1986):3–14.

88. Ibid. See also U.S. Department of Justice, *Electronic Monitoring in Intensive Probation and Parole Programs* (Washington, D.C.: Office of Justice Programs, Bureau of Justice Assistance, February 1989); Annesley K. Schmidt, "Electronic Monitoring," *Journal of Contemporary Criminal Justice* 5 (1989):133–180; Annesley K. Schmidt, "Electronic Monitors—Realistically, What Can Be Expected?," *Federal Probation* 55 (1991):47–53.

89. B. Berry and R. Matthews, "Electronic Monitoring and House Arrest," in *Privatizing Criminal Justice*, ed. R. Matthews, (Newbury Park, Calif.: Sage, 1989).

90. Vaughn, 1991. See also Michael T. Charles, "Research Note: Juveniles on Electronic Monitoring," *Journal of Contemporary Criminal Justice* 5(1989):133–180; Michael Charles, "The Development of a Juvenile Electronic Monitoring Program," *Federal Probation* 53 (1989):3–12.

91. J. Muncie, "A Prisoner in My Home: The Politics and Practice of Electronic Monitoring," *Probation Journal* 37(1990):72–77.

92. State of South Carolina State Reorganization Commission, *Evaluation of the Electronic Monitoring Pilot Program, 1988–1989* (March 1990).

93. James Quinn and John Holman, "The Efficacy of Electronically Monitored Home Confinement as a Case Management Device," *Journal of Contemporary Criminal Justice* 7 (1991):128–134. See also Robert Rogers and Annette Jolin, "Electronic Monitoring: A Review of the Empirical Literature," *Journal of Contemporary*

Criminal Justice 5 (1989):141–152; James F. Quinn and John E. Holman, "Electronic Monitoring and Family Control in Probation and Parole," *Journal of Offender Rehabilitation* 17 (1992):77–87; Joseph Vaughn, "Planning for Change: The Use of Electronic Monitoring as a Correctional Alternative," in *Intermediate Punishments: Intensive Supervision, Home Confinement and Electronic Surveillance*, ed. Belinda R. McCarthy (Monsey, N.Y.: Criminal Justice, 1987).

94. Berry and Matthews, "Electronic Monitoring and House Arrest," p. 123.

95. Joan Petersilia, "Exploring the Option of House Arrest," *Federal Probation* 50 (1986):50–55. For another critique, see Ronald Corbett and Gary T. Marx, "Critique: No Soul in the New Machine: Technofallacies in the Electronic Monitoring Movement," *Justice Quarterly* 8 (1991):399–414.

96. R. Ball, R. C. Huff, and J. R. Lilly, *House Arrest and Correctional Policy: Doing Time at Home* (Newbury Park, Calif.: Sage, 1988).

97. Federal Government Information Technology, *Electronic Surveillance and Civil Liberties* (Washington, D.C.: Congress of the United States, Office of Technology Assessment, 1985).

98. See Barton L. Ingraham and Gerald W. Smith, "The Use of Electronics in the Observation and the Control of Human Behavior and Its Possible Use in Rehabilitation and Parole," *Issues in Criminology* 7 (1972):35–53; George E. Rush, "Electronic Surveillance: An Alternative to Incarceration," *American Journal of Criminal Justice* 12 (1989):219–242. For a detailed discussion of the psycholegal effects of home confinement, see Dorothy K. Kagehiro and Ralph Taylor, "A Social Psychological Analysis of Home Electronic Confinement," in *Handbook of Psychology and Law*, eds. D. K. Kagehiro and W. S. Laufer (New York: Springer-Verlag, 1991); see also J. Robert Lilly, "Tagging Reviewed," *The Howard Journal of Criminal Justice* 29 (1990):229–245.

99. M. Renzema and D. Skelton, *The Use of Electronic Monitoring by Criminal Justice Agencies: 1989* (Kutztown, Pa.: Criminal Justice Program, 1990).

100. For a pilot study on a limited number of home confinement offenders, see Paulette Hatchett, *The Home Confinement Program: An Appraisal of the Electronic Monitoring of Offenders in Washtenaw County, Michigan* (Lansing: Community Programs Evaluation Unit, Michigan Department of Corrections, 1987).

101. Mark S. Umbreit, "Community Service Sentencing: Last Alternative or Added Sanction?," *Federal Probation* 45 (1981):3–14.

102. Barry Krisberg and James Austin, *The Unmet Promise of Alternatives to Incarceration* (San Francisco: National Council on Crime and Delinquency, 1981).

103. Byrne, "Assessing What Works in the Adult Community Corrections Systems," p. 10. On the experiences with the Kansas Community Corrections Act, see M. Kay Harris, Peter R. Jones, and Gail S. Funke, *The Kansas Community Corrections Act: An Assessment of a Public Policy Initiative* (Philadelphia, Pa.: Temple University—Edna McConnell Clark Foundation, 1990); Peter R. Jones, "Expanding the Use of Non-Custodial Sentencing Options: An Evaluation of the Kansas Community Corrections Act," *Howard Journal of Criminal Justice* 29 (1990):114–129; Peter R. Jones, "The Risk of Recidivism: Evaluating the Public-Safety Implications of a Community Corrections Program," *Journal of Criminal Justice* 19 (1991):49–66. For an overview of the effectiveness of community corrections, see Thomas Ellsworth, *Contemporary Community Corrections* (Prospect Heights, Ill.: Waveland, 1992). For a discussion of implementation of community corrections, see Michael C. Musheno, "Community Corrections as an Organizational Innovation: What Works and Why," *Journal of Research in Crime and Delinquency* 26 (1989):136–167. For an evaluation of European alternatives, see David Fogel, *On Doing Less Harm: Western European Alternatives to Incarceration* (Chicago, Ill.: Office of International Criminal Justice, University of Illinois, 1988). J. D. Jamieson and William E. Stone, "Predicting DWI Education Success," *Federal Probation* 55 (1991):43–47.

PART 5

COMPLEMENTARY JUSTICE SYSTEMS

The preceding parts of this book have looked at the criminal justice process as it functions in the case of the average felony offender. But in fact, that process covers only some offenders; and it also ignores the victims of crime. There is not just one criminal justice system. There are many, and they are distinct. In this part of the book we examine three systems that complement the main system.

First there is the system designed for juveniles (Chapter 17). The process here begins with an "intake" (not normally an arrest), leads to a "petition" (not an indictment), and may end with an "adjudication" (not a trial) and "disposition" (not a sentence). Constitutional rights for juveniles are only a generation old. In the last decade Americans have opted for a more punitive approach to juvenile offenders, whose numbers are rapidly growing and whose crimes are increasingly violent.

For victims of crime, the criminal justice system looks quite different than it does for offenders. Chapter 18 describes the victim's progress through the criminal justice process, from the trauma of victimization and suffering to the difficult choice of whether or not to report a crime to the burdens of having to participate in the arrest and trial process, often under demeaning conditions, and in sentencing and parole decisions. Recently the system has done much to improve the lot of the victim in the criminal justice process, including providing compensation and restitution for harm suffered. Yet much remains to be done.

In the final chapter of the book (Chapter 19), we discuss the new phenomenon of the massive expansion of crime across international boundaries and its impact on life at home. There is much new international and transnational criminality. To deal with it, a system focused on international and transnational crime is in a formative stage. To understand this system and to participate in developing it, criminal justice specialists must become increasingly familiar with the functioning of foreign criminal justice systems. That is the province of comparative criminal justice, with which this chapter concludes. ■

CHAPTER 17

JUVENILE JUSTICE

"Clarence Mitchell Courthouse, a brooding Beaux Arts monolith in the heart of Baltimore, contains the Baltimore City Juvenile Court. Like the 2,500 similar juvenile courts across the nation, this is where the battles are being fought against some of America's toughest problems: drugs, disintegrating families, household violence. As these problems have grown worse over the past two decades, the judicial system designed to deal with them has crumbled. These courts are an indicator of the country's compassion for families and its commitment to justice, but increasingly they have neither the money nor the personnel to save most of the desperate young souls who pass through their doors. Almost no one seems to care.

"Almost every child at Clarence Mitchell could use an advocate, but there aren't enough to go around. 'It's overwhelming, and nobody really has the time to prepare them for what's happening,' says Diane Baum, who heads Baltimore's more than 160 volunteer advocates. What is needed, says juvenile-court administrative Judge David Mitchell, is 'a fundamental change in the way society views the family and children.' Nothing less than that will make the system work."[1] ■

The historical legacy of juvenile justice supports this pessimistic view. There have been three remarkable revolutions in juvenile justice since the early 1800s, yet positive change still seems all too distant. The first revolution culminated in the creation of separate courts and correctional institutions for juveniles. The second revolution, which began in the 1960s, focused on efforts to divert children from the juvenile justice system, deinstitutionalize juvenile correctional facilities, and ensure the due-process rights of juveniles in court. A third revolution, which began in the late 1970s, involved a new emphasis in juvenile sentencing on the provision of just deserts punishment for and the incapacitation of all serious juvenile offenders.[2]

Some scholars believe that we are still in the midst of the third revolution, at a time when the problem of juvenile delinquency and juvenile crime is overwhelming. Juveniles under age 18 represented 15.6 percent of all persons arrested for index crimes in 1990. If we adopt the age of 21 as our standard—the traditional age of majority—then nearly one-third of all crimes of violence appears to be committed by juveniles.[3] These statistics reflect only part of the tragedy. The juvenile justice system "processes" not only children who have violated criminal laws, but also children in need of supervision, neglected children, and abused children. It often does so with inadequate resources, overburdened courts, and overcrowded and outmoded correctional institutions and reformatories. That it stands in need of reform and refocusing is clear.

In this chapter we trace the development of the justice system specially designed to handle children. Next we consider the many stages in the system: stages that require a full range of decisions concerning custody, detention, disposition, and treatment. Finally we discuss issues in juvenile justice policy and some of the problems we still face.

> *"There are young people in our system who we simply are not prepared to handle."*
> MaryAnn Saar, state youth services secretary, quoted in *The Washington Post*, September 29, 1992, p. C1.

DEVELOPMENT OF THE JUVENILE JUSTICE SYSTEM

The roots of our system of juvenile justice are 2,000 years old, in classical Roman law. There are two roots, one clearly punitive, the other supportive and caring. The punitive root has brought the imposition of adult criminal liability on children. In the Middle Ages, under the law of the Church, the Roman classification of children with respect to criminal liability took definitive shape and was adopted in the common law. This system (shown in Table 17.1) subjected children to adult criminal liability, proceedings, and punishments. It still affects our thinking, and its impact can be seen in the laws of many states. Theoretically, today a ten-year-old can be tried as an adult in Vermont, a 12-year-old in Montana, and a 13-year-old in Georgia, Illinois, and Missouri. Theory became reality recently in Georgia. At age 13, Demale Henry sexually assaulted and then murdered a 7-year-old playmate, Cherida Kinlaw. Kinlaw was found with one end of a cloth belt wrapped around her neck and the other attached to a doorknob.[4] According to DeKalb County Chief Assistant District Attorney John Petrey, "Our juvenile justice system is ill-equipped to handle this. The maximum sentence in the juvenile system is 18 months and this was no 18-month offense."[5] Henry was subsequently convicted of murder.

The second root is that of concern for troubled children. It was very much present in the concept of **parens patriae** (parent of the country) which to the Romans meant that the emperor, and in medieval times the king or queen, could exercise *patria potestas* (parental power) *in loco parentis* (in the place of a parent deemed incapable or unworthy) over children in trouble or in danger of becoming wayward. The power of the monarch was eventually transferred to the people of the state, as represented by the juvenile court judge. We find its traces in the concepts used today in juvenile court proceedings.

> *"Theoretically, today a 10-year-old can be tried as an adult in Vermont, a 12-year-old in Montana, and a 13-year-old in Georgia, Illinois, and Missouri."*

> **parens patriae**
> *(Latin, "parent of the country") Assumption by the state of the role of guardian over children whose parents are deemed incapable or unworthy.*

TABLE 17.1 Age Categories for Criminal Liability under Common Law

Age (years)	Category	Liability and Burden of Proof
0–7	Infantia (infancy)	None
7–10½	Infantia proxima (close to infancy)	Presumed incapable of committing crime but proof of malice makes up for lack of age
10½–14	Pubertate proxima (close to puberty)	Presumed capable of committing crime, but defendant may prove incapacity
14+	Adulthood	Full criminal liability

Early Approaches

Houses of Refuge.   After centuries of a punitive approach to dealing with troubled children, *parens patriae* made its appearance in 1838 with the case of *Ex parte Crouse*. On the petition of her mother, a young girl, Mary Ann Crouse, had been committed by the court to the Philadelphia House of Refuge as wayward and incorrigible. When Mary Ann's father, who was estranged from his wife, learned what had happened, he sought a writ of habeas corpus to secure the release of his daughter, who, so he alleged, had been imprisoned without a jury trial. The Pennsylvania Supreme Court rejected this argument, reasoning that under the *parens patriae* doctrine the state has every right to protect children from improper upbringing.[6]

Houses of refuge were based on an earlier English model and designed to care for the impoverished, "dangerous" street people of the time. In fact, however, these houses were little more than prisons to which one could be sent without trial. The houses of refuge proved a dismal failure: They neither educated nor reformed anybody.

Massachusetts tried a new approach in 1854, with the creation of the Massachusetts Industrial School for Girls. In a cottage-style setting, surrogate families were created, with the goal of reforming girls who were considered "wayward and delinquent." Other states followed Massachusetts' lead. The problem with this approach was the lack of judicial determination that a given child had indeed violated the law and therefore was in need of some remedial placement.

Juvenile Court.   The all-important change occurred in Chicago where Timothy D. Hurley, a judge and former probation officer, and Julia Lathrop, of the Illinois Board of Charities, advocated abandonment of the system that placed child offenders and wayward children in adult jails and prisons and removed children who had been arbitrarily declared wayward from the custody of their parents and placed them in prisonlike institutions. In the late 1890s Hurley and Lathrop lobbied for the creation of a juvenile court, and with the help of the Catholic Visitation and Aid Society and the Chicago Bar Association, they succeeded.

In a report presented to the Illinois legislature, Lathrop reasoned:

There are at the present moment in the state of Illinois, especially in the City of Chicago, thousands of children in need of active intervention for their preservation from physical, mental and moral destruction. Such intervention is demanded, not only by sympathetic consideration for their well-being, but also in the name of the Commonwealth, for the preservation of the State. If the Child is the material out of which men and women are made, the neglected child is the material out of which paupers and criminals are made.[7]

The Illinois legislature created the nation's first juvenile court, in Chicago, in 1899.

The concepts that guided the operation of this and subsequent similar courts were captured by Judge Gustav L. Schramm of the Juvenile Court of Allegheny

"We must enact wholesale reform of the juvenile justice system so that for the vast majority of juvenile offenders, their first brush with the law will be their last." U.S. Attorney General William Barr, *The Toronto Star*, August 30, 1992, p. A16.

"The Illinois legislature created the nation's first juvenile court, in Chicago, in 1899."

County, Pennsylvania, in his 1945 article, "The Judge Meets the Boy and His Family."[8] Judge Schramm described the juvenile court judge as a personification of power, understanding, and interest. His role is to uncover the problems that plague the youthful offender and determine how best to correct them. The judge administers equity to a child in need "of consideration, of guidance and of correction."[9] These principles are in perfect harmony with those underlying the creation of a juvenile court:

• All dependent, neglected, and delinquent children under 16 years of age could be brought under the jurisdiction of the juvenile court.
• The juvenile court did not find youngsters guilty of anything, but simply determined their status as dependent, neglected (in a very broad, sweeping sense), or delinquent.
• The juvenile court judge acted as a surrogate parent, conducting informal proceedings (in contrast to the formal adversarial proceedings in criminal court).
• Exercising much discretion, the juvenile court judge gave first consideration to the best interest of the child.
• Dispositions by the court were not punishments; they might include only friendly probation, in the child's own home, or placement in a suitable foster home or training in an industrial school.[10]

dependent children
Legal status (granting jurisdiction to a juvenile court) reflecting inadequate and/or abusive parents or guardians.

delinquent children
Children who have committed an act that if committed by an adult would be a crime or an act considered deviant in a child (truancy, running away from home) that is not so considered in an adult.

status offenders
Juveniles who engage in behavior that violates the juvenile law but would not be considered a crime if committed by an adult; includes neglected children.

Criticisms of the System.   There were three problems with this approach. First, the definition of behavior that brought a child under the jurisdiction of the juvenile court was still extremely broad. **"Dependency"** and "neglect" are vague terms. Nor are these conditions the youngster's fault; they are the parents' fault. Dependent children are children whose parents are actually unable to provide the care required by law. Neglected children have parents who, although able, fail to provide them with necessary and proper care, guidance, subsistence, and education. Moreover, the concept of **delinquency** included not only acts that would be crimes if an adult committed them, but also behavior that would not be considered deviant in adults, such as truancy or running away from home. When dependency and neglect were included in the definition of delinquency, neglect itself became a **status offense.** A neglected child was by definition delinquent. The problems associated with the definition of delinquency and status offenses were captured by the 1967 report of the President's Commission on Law Enforcement and Administration of Justice. According to the commission, such definitions allowed for great subjectivity with the "imposition of the judge's own code of youthful conduct."[11]

Second, while the motives for using informal proceedings in the juvenile justice system were good, they often led to intolerable abuses. Many police officers, probation officers, and judges ignored the possibility that juveniles were guaranteed federal constitutional rights. Most juvenile court judges did not view their practices as abuses, and sincerely regarded what they did as in the best interests of the child.[12]

Finally, the juvenile court was accused of meting out an inferior brand of assembly-line justice. Judges were found to be poorly qualified for the job and poorly educated. As of 1963, nearly 50 percent of all juvenile court judges had not attended college. And although delay prior to juvenile court hearings was often substantial, the actual time spent before a juvenile court judge rarely exceeded 15 minutes.[13] The image of the juvenile court as a superparent had become tarnished.[14]

"Juvenile judgeships have long been considered . . . 'a hardship post—a heartbreak post.'" Juvenile specialist Barbara J. Ruhe, *Connecticut Law Tribune,* August 3, 1992, p. 19.

Constitutional Reform

This juvenile court system was dominant until 1967, when the United States Supreme Court at last ruled that children too have rights that are protected by the Constitution. The decision in *In re Gault* changed the juvenile justice system forever. It all started on June 8, 1964, in Gila County, Arizona, when a Mrs. Cook complained to Deputy Sheriff Flagg about obscene phone calls she had received. She attributed them to a neighborhood kid, Gerald Francis Gault, aged 15. The deputy sheriff knew Gerry Gault; the boy was on probation, having been found in the company of another youngster who had lifted a wallet from a woman's handbag. (See the Criminal Justice on Trial box.)

Deputy Sheriff Flagg promptly went to Gerry's home, arrested him, and placed him in the juvenile detention facility. When Gerry's mother returned home that night and found him gone, she sent her elder son out to find him. He learned from acquaintances that Gerry was in detention. Gerry's mother promptly went to the detention center, but she did not get to see her son. The deputy told her of Gerry's arrest and informed her that there would be a hearing in juvenile court at 3 P.M. the next day. On that day the deputy filed an application with the court noting that Gerry, as a minor, is "in need of the protection of the honorable court, as he is delinquent." The application contained no reference to Mrs. Cook's complaint. The hearing took place before Judge McGhee of juvenile court. Present were Deputy Sheriff Flagg in his capacity as a probation officer, Gerry, and by chance, his mother and elder brother.

In an informal proceeding, Gerry denied ever having made an obscene phone call. The judge returned Gerry to the detention facility. A second hearing was held one week later. Gerry's mother was informed about this hearing through a handwritten note Deputy Sheriff Flagg left at her door. The second hearing was as formless as the first one: There was no complaining witness, and Judge McGhee ruled that none was necessary. The court declared that Gerry's obscene phone call was proved, and that such an act, if committed by an adult, was a misdemeanor subject to a fine of from five to fifty dollars and a jail term of up to two months. Juveniles, he declared, could not be so punished. Judge McGhee found Gerry to be a juvenile delinquent, therefore not to be punished but to be sent to a juvenile correctional facility for six years, until he reached the age of 21.

Gerry's parents finally contacted a lawyer, and the case got widespread publicity. Everything seemed to have been done wrong, yet all the appeals courts upheld Judge McGhee's disposition. With the help of civil libertarians and members of prestigious law school faculties, the case reached the United States Supreme Court. By this time Gerry had been incarcerated for three years. The Supreme Court's opinion was written by one of the most compassionate men ever to sit on that bench, Justice Abe Fortas. Children, Fortas wrote, have fully as much right as adults to the protection of the Constitution. Never again would a child be sentenced to six years in jail for an act that was never proved, and that if proved against an adult would have warranted a term of two months.

The Court also ruled that virtually all the guarantees of the Fourth, Fifth, and Sixth Amendments, made applicable to the states under the due-process clause of the Fourteenth Amendment, must be extended to juveniles. These guarantees include

- the right to receive adequate and timely notice of the charges
- the right to counsel
- the right to be confronted by and to examine witnesses
- the privilege against self-incrimination[15]

Three years later, in the case of *In re Winship*,[16] the Court ruled that proof of juvenile delinquency, like that of a crime charged to an adult, must be established beyond a reasonable doubt. Only the right to a jury trial need not be accorded to juveniles, perhaps to preserve some of the informality of the juvenile court.[17] These decisions severely curtailed a juvenile court judge's discretion and subjugated *parens patriae* to the rule of law. Justice Fortas put it more clearly: "Under our Constitution, the condition of being a boy does not justify a kangaroo court."[18]

"The Supreme Court's decision in In re Gault *in 1967 changed the juvenile justice system forever: Never again would a child be sentenced to six years of incarceration for an act that was never proved and that if proved against an adult would have warranted a jail term of two months."*

(Top) Patti, a truant suspect, being questioned by police on a Seattle street. (Bottom) Juvenile gang member being taken into custody in Los Angeles.

"In 1970, in In re Winship, *the Court ruled that proof of juvenile delinquency, like that of a crime charged to an adult, must be established beyond a reasonable doubt."*

ABOLISH THE JUVENILE COURT SYSTEM?

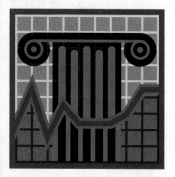

I believe that we should abolish the juvenile court system, give family and welfare courts responsibility for offenders under the age of 14 or 16, and deal with those over 16 in the criminal courts.

Youth should be given all the aid that educational and other helping services can provide, but serious crime should be treated seriously whether the offender is 17, 37, or 67 years old. . . . Humanity, not arbitrary age categories, should be the object of our concern. (1)

A major focus of abolitionist arguments is that the way society perceives adolescents has changed since the juvenile court system began at the turn of the century, making the many differences between juvenile and criminal courts unnecessary and unfair. The juvenile court system was established at a time when children were viewed as having emotional, intellectual, and moral properties completely distinct from those of adults. Psychological and emotional development was seen as dichotomous—people could be categorized as adults or children. Now, argues law professor Janet E. Ainsworth, "the child-adult distinction is a false dichotomy that can no longer support disparate justice systems" (2). The human life cycle has been fragmented into more stages than just "child" and "adult," and it is increasingly difficult to see each stage as distinct. Ainsworth points out that "youth," for example, is now defined as a life stage including per-

sons from their late teens through college and graduate school—sometimes into their early thirties. "Boundaries delineating age-appropriate behavior have blurred," states Ainsworth, "especially among the young, with both younger children and young adults adopting styles, attitudes, and activities that society formerly considered characteristic of adolescence" (2, p. 1102).

Supreme Court rulings that deny juveniles special treatment are used by abolitionists as support for the breakdown in the adult-child dichotomy (2, p. 1116). Marvin Wolfgang cites evidence that children under age 14 vary greatly in their perceptions of the seriousness of crimes, but that by age 14, "their perceptions mirror those of adults." He argues, "There is no convincing evidence that persons between the ages of 16 and 18 differ significantly from those over 18 in their capacity to understand the consequences of their acts. Late adolescence is therefore not a meaningful category when applied to criminal offenders" (1).

Arguments for abolition

Arguments for the abolition of the juvenile court system fall into two general categories: (1) Adolescents should be held responsible for, and face the consequences of, committing crimes in the same way that adults currently are held responsible; and (2) adolescents who are accused of committing crimes should have access to the same services, protections, and rights that adults do currently.

Crime studies lend support to the first rationale. Research conducted by Wolfgang and his col-

leagues at the Sellin Center for Studies in Criminology and Criminal Law at the University of Pennsylvania have established that habitual offending can begin early in life. A small group of juvenile offenders—6 percent of a study group of 10,000 males born in 1945—was responsible for more than half of all the crimes committed by all the boys before they reached the age of 18. These "chronic offenders," each of whom was arrested five or more times before age 18, also committed the most serious crimes: Seventy-one percent of the homicides were attributed to these 627 boys, 73 percent of the rapes, 82 percent of the robberies, and 60 percent of the aggravated assaults. A similar study of 14,000 boys born in 1958 has yielded similar results, with the chronic offenders committing an even higher proportion of the most serious crimes. Wolfgang uses these data to support abolition of the juvenile court system: "A justice system that closes juvenile records to the criminal court, permitting serious recidivists to be reborn with virginal records at the age of 18, is failing to protect society from persons who have already established a criminal career by that age" (1).

The second major argument is that offenders are not given the same rights and protections in juvenile courts as in criminal courts. Juvenile courts, abolitionists contend, are not courts at all. In many states, jury trials are limited or unavailable. Research has shown that juvenile offenders denied a jury trial are more likely to be convicted and, once convicted, are "unlikely to be able to prove an error of law which would allow them to prevail on appeal" (2, p. 1126). In many suburban and rural communities, more than 50 percent of all juveniles fail to retain counsel; the right to counsel, achieved in *In re Gault,* is therefore meaningless. In addition, juvenile court proceedings lack the sense of legitimacy found in adult criminal courts. Children exposed to the juvenile court system often feel as if justice and fairness are far from the primary objectives of the proceedings and lose any faith they may have had in the criminal justice system.

Arguments against abolition

What arguments support maintaining a juvenile court system in the United States? One of the major arguments is that the criminal court system is already overburdened and ineffective. Sociologist Leonard P. Edwards says,

The juvenile court is capable of responding with sufficient authority in most delinquency cases. It can utilize the waiver process for the most serious. What must happen now is the development of a new vision of what the juvenile court can accomplish and how that vision can be realized. Before we turn over these children to a more tragically underresourced and insensitive adult criminal justice system, we should examine whether there are realistic possibilities that resources can be obtained for the delinquency system. As it is, the juvenile justice system has more services for children than the adult criminal justice system has for adults. (3)

Abolitionists say that if juvenile courts were replaced by criminal courts, juveniles would win a right to jury trials and have access to effective legal representation. If juveniles were treated as adults, Wolfgang says, they "would have the protections of the Constitution and all the judicial rights afforded anyone accused of committing serious criminal acts, and both the offender and society would be better protected" (1).

SOURCES

1. Marvin E. Wolfgang, "Abolish the Juvenile Court System," *California Lawyer,* November 1982, pp. 12–13.
2. Janet A. Ainsworth, "Re-Imagining Childhood and Reconstructing the Legal Order: The Case for Abolishing the Juvenile Court," *North Carolina Law Review* 66 (1991):1083–1133, at p. 1104.
3. Leonard P. Edwards, "Alternatives to the Juvenile Court," *Juvenile and Family Court Journal* 43 (1992):1–45, at p. 19.

QUESTIONS FOR DISCUSSION

1. Do you support abolishing or maintaining the juvenile court system? What additional reasons can you give for the position you take?
2. In what ways would both the accused juvenile and the public be protected by the abolition of the juvenile court system?
3. How might the juvenile court system be improved to provide some of the elements abolitionists feel are missing?

• • • • • • • • • • • • • • • • • • •

"Juvenile proceedings are not criminal trials. They are not civil trials. They are simply not adversary proceedings."
Justice Potter Stewart, dissenting, in *In re Gault*.

The Supreme Court decision was not unanimous. In a dissenting opinion, Justice Stewart wrote that the majority opinion had gone too far:

Juvenile proceedings are not criminal trials. They are not civil trials. They are simply not adversary proceedings. Whether dealing with a delinquent child, a neglected child, a defective child, or a dependent child, a juvenile proceeding's whole purpose and mission is the very opposite of the mission and purpose of a criminal court. The object of the one is correction of a condition. The object of the other is conviction and punishment for a criminal act.[19]

There is some evidence that children and parents do not always claim the procedural rights to which they are constitutionally entitled.[20] In a major study of juveniles' waiver of rights, one researcher found that

• during interrogation, after receiving Miranda warnings, 90.6 percent of those juveniles studied chose to talk—and risk incrimination (adults waive their rights in about 60% of cases)
• refusal to waive the right to remain silent was virtually nonexistent below age 15
• nearly 90 percent of juveniles tested revealed a deficient understanding of Miranda warnings
• nearly 30 percent of all juvenile subjects misinterpreted the nature of the attorney–client relationship[21]

These findings resulted in some startling conclusions. First, according to researchers, juveniles under the age of 14 are generally incompetent to waive their rights to silence and legal counsel. And second, juveniles between the ages of 15 and 16 with IQ scores of less than 80 are incompetent to waive their rights.[22]

In response to these problems, courts have considered various safeguards.[23] One court ruled that an additional warning must be given to juveniles: "the right for juveniles to consult their parents and to remain silent until that time [of consultation]."[24] Another court ruled that when administering Miranda warnings to a 7-year-old, they must be "explained in language comprehensible to the minor. . . ."[25]

Waiver and Transfer

In Minnesota in February 1992, Jill Kennedy, age 16, plotted to kill her mother, Kathy, because her mother and her live-in boyfriend had objected to Jill's truancy and use of drugs and alcohol. Jill rejected their attempts at discipline and often ran away. This time she did not run away. Instead, she enlisted the help of a 14-year old friend in a plot to shoot her mother. When Kathy entered the house on April 1, Jill fired a .22-caliber rifle at her mother's head. She narrowly missed. Should Jill be tried as a juvenile? Should she be transferred to a criminal court in Minnesota? Judge Patrice Sutherland of the Dakota County District Court ruled that Jill appeared receptive to treatment and that the public was best served by keeping her out of state prison and thus out of the company of the "most corrupted and maladjusted adult females in the state."[26]

"It used to be the old rock through somebody's window. Now it's carrying a handgun."
Scott County Attorney James Terwedo, Minnesota, quoted in *Minneapolis Star Tribune* (St. Paul Edition), March 23, 1992, p. 1A.

The transformation of juvenile justice proceedings into a junior model of adult criminal justice seemed to have a peculiar result. If juveniles are to have the rights of adults charged with crime, should they not also have the responsibilities? In 1977 an influential joint committee of the Institute of Judicial Administration at New York University and the American Bar Association formulated a set of standards for juvenile justice. The committee proposed that juvenile proceedings be based on the seriousness of the offense committed.[27] In most states today, the juvenile justice system is indeed a junior criminal justice system. Only the offenders are junior, however; the rest of the players are not.

Most states specify an age (16, 17, 18, 21) below which an offender can be brought before a juvenile court. But most states have a provision that permits a

TABLE 17.2 Youngest Age at Which a Juvenile May Be Transferred to Criminal Court by Judicial Waiver in All States, the District of Columbia, and Other Federal Districts

Age (Year)	States
No specific age	Alaska, Arizona, Arkansas, Delaware, Florida, Indiana, Kentucky, Maine, Maryland, New Hampshire, New Jersey, Oklahoma, South Dakota, West Virginia, Wyoming, federal districts
10	Vermont
12	Montana
13	Georgia, Illinois, Mississippi
14	Alabama, Colorado, Connecticut, Idaho, Iowa, Massachusetts, Minnesota, Missouri, North Carolina, North Dakota, Pennsylvania, South Carolina, Tennessee, Utah
15	District of Columbia, Louisiana, Michigan, Nebraska, New Mexico, Ohio, Oregon, Texas, Virginia
16	California, Hawaii, Kansas, Nevada, New York, Rhode Island, Washington, Wisconsin

SOURCE: Adapted from Lina A. Szymanski, *Waiver/Transfer/Certification of Juveniles to Criminal Court: Age Restrictions, Crime Restrictions* (Washington, D.C.: National Center for Juvenile Justice, February, 1987).

juvenile court judge to waive the jurisdiction of the juvenile court and transfer the case to the criminal court. The State of Florida appears to lead the nation in juvenile transfers; in 1991 alone, over 6,000 juveniles were transferred to adult court.[28] Table 17.2 indicates the youngest age at which a juvenile may be transferred to criminal court in various states.

Ever since the Supreme Court decision in *Kent v. United States* (1966), a **waiver hearing** has been a constitutional right.[29] No one appreciates this more than Morris A. Kent, Jr. In September 1961, 16-year-old Morris was arrested and charged with robbery and rape. The juvenile court of the District of Columbia had jurisdiction over cases like this unless a judge ruled, in a waiver hearing, that the child should be tried as an adult. For some reason the judge failed to hold such a hearing for Morris, and instead issued an order that he be tried as an adult. The maximum sentence in adult court was death in the electric chair. No such penalty was or is available in the juvenile justice system. (See the Criminal Justice in Action box.)

In *Kent,* the Court ruled that a waiver hearing is a " 'critically important' action determining vitally important statutory rights of a juvenile."[30] The case was remanded back to juvenile court for a waiver hearing that would consider all relevant factors. In such a hearing the judge would determine if Morris were amenable to treatment and rehabilitation. In addition to factors bearing on an individual's amenability to treatment, after *Kent* judges must consider

* The seriousness of the alleged offense to the community and whether the protection of the community requires waiver.
* Whether the alleged offense was committed in an aggressive, violent, premeditated, or willful manner.
* The prosecutive merit of the complaint, i.e., whether there is evidence upon which a Grand Jury may be expected to return an indictment (to be determined by consultation with a prosecutor).
* The desirability of trial and disposition of the entire offense in one court when the juvenile's associates in the alleged offense are adults who will be charged with a crime in the U.S. District Court for the District of Columbia.

waiver hearing
Hearing in juvenile court that determines whether jurisdiction shall be waived and granted to an adult criminal court.

- The sophistication and maturity of the juvenile as determined by consideration of his home, environmental situation, emotional attitude and pattern of living.
- The record and previous history of the juvenile, including previous contacts with the Youth Aid Division, other law enforcement agencies, juvenile courts in other jurisdictions, prior periods of probation to this court, or prior commitments to juvenile institutions.
- The prospects of adequate protection of the public and the likelihood of reasonable rehabilitation of the juvenile (if he is found to have committed the alleged offense) by the use of procedures, services and facilities currently available to the Juvenile Court.[31]

In most states, fewer than 5 percent of all juvenile cases are in fact waived to criminal court. But recent evidence clearly points to a growing trend in the number of waiver hearings. In one study of teenage felons and waiver hearings in Virginia, Tennessee, Mississippi, and Georgia, a 104.3-percent increase in waiver hearings was found between 1980 (228) and 1988 (466).[32]

legislative exclusion
Elimination of juvenile court jurisdiction for certain serious offenses (e.g., murder and sexual assault) through the passage of legislation.

"New York's Juvenile Offender Law of 1978 abolished juvenile court jurisdiction for a wide range of crimes, from murder in the second degree to burglary and assault, and granted jurisdiction to adult courts."

"Court administrators are constantly frustrated by the inability of the system to handle violent juvenile offenders."

Another noticeable trend is toward the partial elimination of juvenile court jurisdiction through what has been called **legislative exclusion.** New York, for example, passed the Juvenile Offender Law of 1978 that abolishes juvenile court jurisdiction for a wide range of crimes, from murder in the second degree to burglary and assault. Legislative exclusion—or the grant of jurisdiction to an adult court to adjudicate cases against juveniles for specific offenses—is designed to increase the deterrent effect of the law by providing significant terms of confinement (Table 17.3). At least this is its goal. A recent evaluation of the New York Juvenile Offender Law concluded that there was no appreciable reduction in juvenile crime following its passage. The authors of the evaluation concluded that either the terms were too weak or juveniles were not deterred by its provisions.[33]

The apparent failure of these laws reflects a much larger problem: What should be done with children who are violent offenders? This question is raised over and over again as court administrators are frustrated by the inability of the system to handle violent juvenile offenders.

THE JUVENILE JUSTICE PROCESS

In Chapter 5 we considered the criminal process. We discussed the various decisions that comprise the process, from decisions of victims and witnesses to report a crime, to sentencing decisions by judges. Now we consider the juvenile justice process (Figure 17.1). Like the criminal process, the juvenile justice process has its clients (alleged delinquents, status offenders, and dependent or neglected children). There is also a process that results in some distinct products: protected and rehabilitated children, a safe community, and a sense that justice was accomplished.[34] Like the criminal process, the juvenile process begins with a person's entry into the system and ends with diversion from the system or with a correctional program. But there are some notable differences.

First, there are critical differences in the very nature of the proceedings. Criminal courts have adversarial proceedings, while juvenile courts still are guided, to some extent, by the *parens patriae* philosophy. Here are some other critical differences:

1. In criminal proceedings, charges are filed to start the process. Juvenile proceedings begin with a petition.

2. Adults charged with crime may be released by judicial decisions before trial. Most juvenile courts release children to their parents' custody before an adjudicatory hearing.

3. Plea-bargaining practices, common in adult proceedings, are absent in juvenile proceedings.

4. The right to trial by jury exists in criminal but not in juvenile proceedings.

TABLE 17.3 Provisions of New York's Juvenile Offender Law

Acts Covered	Ages Affected	Terms of Confinement
Murder 2, excluding felony murder	13–15	Minimum: 5–9 years; maximum: life
Murder 2	14, 15	Minimum: 5–9 years; maximum: life
Kidnapping 1, Arson 1	14, 15	Minimum: 4–6 years; maximum: 12–15 years
Manslaughter 1, Rape 1, Sodomy 1, Burglary 1, Robbery 1, Arson 2, Attempted murder 2, Attempted kidnapping 1	14, 15	Minimum: $\frac{1}{3}$ of maximum; maximum: 3–10 years
Assault 1, Robbery 2, Burglary 2	14, 15	Minimum: $\frac{1}{3}$ of maximum; maximum: 3–7 years

SOURCE: Simon I. Singer and David McDowall, "Criminalizing Delinquency: The Deterrent Effects of the New York Juvenile Offender Law," *Law and Society Review* 22 (1988):521–535.

5. Criminal proceedings have procedural formality; juvenile court proceedings are informal.

6. Criminal courts are strictly bound by rules of evidence; juvenile courts are not.

7. An adult convicted in criminal court is sentenced. In the case of a juvenile, the juvenile court judge makes a "disposition."

Entry into the System

Perceptions and tolerance levels vary from area to area and neighborhood to neighborhood, but on the whole there appears to be much more tolerance for juvenile misconduct than for adult misconduct.[35] The number of deviant and criminal acts actually committed by juveniles is far greater than those reported to the police. But while this is true, the jurisdictional reach of the juvenile justice system is far greater than that of the adult criminal justice system. The juvenile court hears cases involving (1) delinquent children, (2) children in need of supervision, sometimes called status offenders, (3) neglected children, and (4) dependent children. Juveniles are subject to the criminal law and to laws relating to juvenile conduct. Violations of the former result in a finding of delinquency. And as Table 17.4 suggests, few crimes are outside juvenile court jurisdiction.

What does it mean to be a **person in need of supervision (PINS),** a "juvenile in need of supervision" (JINS), or a "child in need of supervision" (CHINS)? A wide range of conduct falls within these categories, from idleness to disobeying parental orders. In Pennsylvania, need for supervision may be established with evidence of lack of parental care or control, lack of subsistence or education, abandonment by parents, or delinquency below 10 years of age. Incorrigibility statutes are perhaps the best examples of laws that control youthful misbehavior. These laws allow police to take into custody a child who is unruly, unmanageable, or ungovernable. Consider the incredible reach of Georgia's statute: In Georgia, an "unruly child" includes a child who

- is habitually truant from school;
- is habitually disobedient, and ungovernable;
- has committed an offense applicable only to a child;
- deserts his home or place of abode;
- wanders or loiters about the streets of any city, between the hours of 12:00 midnight and 5:00 A.M.[36]

person in need of supervision (PINS)
Juvenile (or adult) requiring supervision but usually not incarceration.

"A wide range of conduct falls within the categories of PINS, JINS, and CHINS."

DEATH PENALTY FOR JUVENILES

In the landmark decision *Gregg v. Georgia* (428 U.S. 153 [1976]), the U.S. Supreme Court reinstated the death penalty. In 1977, executions began: one in 1977, two in 1979, one in 1981, two in 1982. By 1984 the pace picked up—there were twenty-one executions in that year alone. By 1992 more than 190 death row inmates had been executed, by lethal injection, the gas chamber, electrocution, or the firing squad. Of this group, five merit special attention:

Charles Rumbaugh, executed in 1985; Jay Pinkerton and James Roach, put to death in 1986; Dalton Prejean, executed in 1990; and Johnny Garrett, executed in 1992. All five had been under the age of 18 at the time their crimes were committed.

Whether you support the death penalty or not—and according to public opinion polls, the chances are good that you do—you may have qualms about executing children. Some U.S. citizens feel that executing anyone, of any age, is contrary to "the evolving standards of decency" in our society. Others can always imagine a crime so dreadful that it is deserving of the ultimate penalty, no matter if the accused is 50, 25, or 12 years old. What does the Constitution say? Is there an age below which execution is a cruel and unusual punishment?

Eddings v. Oklahoma

This question was evaded by the U.S. Supreme Court in *Eddings v. Oklahoma* (455 U.S. 104 [1982]). Attorneys for 16-year-old Monty Lee Eddings asked the court to rule as a matter of law that any execution of a child under the age of 17 would be cruel and unusual punishment and thus violate the Eighth Amendment to the U.S. Constitution. Eddings had run away from his abusive parents and was stopped by an Oklahoma state police officer while driving away from his home with some friends. As the officer approached the car, Eddings fired one shot from a .410 shotgun, hitting the officer in the chest. The officer died of exsanguination ("bleeding out" as a result of a perforated heart) within a matter of seconds. After killing the officer, Eddings said, "I would rather have shot an officer than go back where I live" (1).

When the *Eddings* case came before the Supreme Court, Justice Lewis Powell, Jr., stopped short of prohibiting the death penalty for Monty and other 16-year-olds. But he found that age, as well as troubled family background, psychological disturbances, substance abuse, indigence, and mental retardation, must be considered seriously as a mitigating circumstance at the time of sentencing. "Youth is more than a chronological fact," he noted in the Court's majority decision. "It is a time of life when a person may be most susceptible to influence and psychological damage. Our history is replete with laws and judicial recognition that minors, especially in their early years, generally are less mature and responsible than adults" (2).

The trial court that had convicted Monty had failed to take his age and his troubled upbringing into consideration, and the case went back for resentencing. Monty Lee Eddings is now in prison for life—but he is off death row.

Thompson v. Oklahoma

At the time of the *Eddings* case, there was no age below which capital punishment was unconstitutional (see Table 1). This changed in 1988 with the case of *Thompson v. Oklahoma* (455 U.S. 104 [1988]). In *Thompson* the Supreme Court ruled that executing a juvenile under the age of 16 *did* violate the evolving standards of decency that mark the progress of a civilized society—the basic test for finding an Eighth Amendment violation. Now 15-year-olds are safe from execution. Older children are safe from execution as well, if they can establish at time of sentencing more mitigating as opposed to aggravating circumstances. But the Court has not indicated clearly what factors, together with youth, are sufficient to block capital punishment.

The requirement to consider mitigating factors in imposing sentences in capital cases may result in a life sentence instead of the death penalty for some young offenders. But mitigating factors are "the most elusive and problematic component of capital sentencing decisions" (3).

In a review of all juveniles sentenced to death between 1974 and 1991, researchers found that "most juvenile offenders sentenced to death in this time frame were multiply and profoundly disadvantaged"—in other words, they had numerous mitigating circumstances

TABLE 1 Minimum Age of Offender Required in Thirty-seven Capital Punishment Jurisdictions

Age at Offense	Jurisdiction	Total
10	Indiana	1
12	Montana	1
13	Mississippi	1
14	Alabama, Arkansas, Idaho, Kentucky, Missouri, New Jersey, North Carolina, Pennsylvania, Utah	9
15	Louisiana, Virginia	2
16	Nevada	1
17	Georgia, New Hampshire, Texas	3
18	California, Colorado, Connecticut, Illinois, Nebraska, New Jersey, New Mexico, Ohio, Oregon, Tennessee	10
No minimum	Arizona, Delaware, Florida, Maryland Oklahoma, South Carolina, South Dakota, Washington, Wyoming	9
Total:		37

SOURCE: Adapted from Victor L. Streib, "The Eighth Amendment and Capital Punishment of Juveniles," *Cleveland State Law Review* 34 (1986):362–399, at p. 378.

SOURCES

1. *Eddings v. Oklahoma,* Brief for the Petitioner, No. 80-5727, p. 17.
2. *Eddings v. Oklahoma,* 455 U.S. 104 (1982), at 115–116.
3. Dinah A. Robinson and Otis H. Stephens, "Patterns of Mitigating Factors in Juvenile Death Penalty Cases," *Criminal Law Bulletin* 23 (1992):246–270.
4. *Safeguards Guaranteeing Protection of the Rights of Those Facing the Death Penalty.* United Nations Economic and Social Council Resolution 1984/50.

QUESTIONS FOR DISCUSSION

1. Do you support the ban on executions of juveniles under the age of 16 years? Where would you draw the line? Defend your answer.
2. Is chronological age the appropriate measure for sentencing purposes, or should courts consider emotional and intellectual age as well?
3. How would you resolve the apparent dilemma between the conflicting U.N. resolution and Supreme Court precedent?

that obviously had not been considered, or had not been considered enough to protect them from a death sentence (3).

One or more mitigating factors was present in sixty-one of the ninety-one cases the researchers reviewed. In forty-five of the cases, defendants had a troubled family history or social background. Psychological disturbances affected twenty-nine of the ninety-one juveniles sentenced to death, and twenty-four were mentally retarded. Substance abuse was a problem for eighteen of the defendants, and in forty-eight cases the defendant was indigent.

Of these ninety-one sentenced juveniles, five have been executed and fifty-six have obtained reduced sentences or remands of their convictions on appeal. In 1992, thirty-three juveniles were on death row. Of the five youths executed, only one was found by these researchers to have no mitigating factors associated with his case. The others had one, three, four, and even five of the five mitigating factors the researchers—and supposedly the courts—considered.

In the United States, the Supreme Court has decided that executing a youth under the age of 16 is unconstitutional. Even if the Court had not found such executions to be "cruel and unusual punishment," thirty-two states specifically prohibit the execution of defendants who were under the age of 16 at the time the crime was committed. But what about the rest of the world? All member states of the United Nations have adopted a resolution by consensus that provides that "persons below 18 years of age at the time of the commission of the crime shall not be sentenced to death . . . " (4). The participation of the United States in this resolution creates an interesting—and disturbing—dilemma. By allowing 16-year-olds to be executed for capital crimes, the U.S. Supreme Court would seem to be violating a commitment that the executive branch of the government has made to the world community.

Wayne Thompson on death row, Oklahoma State Penitentiary, March 1988.

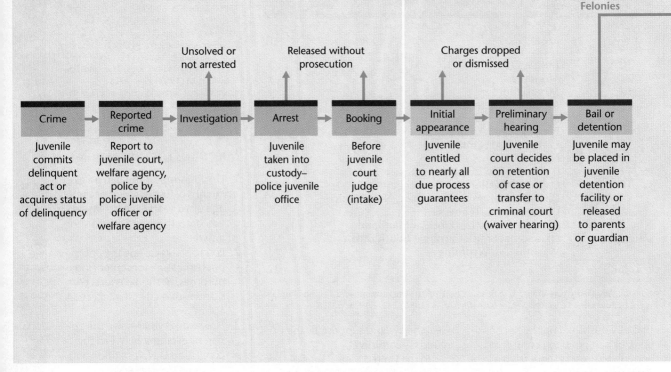

FIGURE 17.1 *The juvenile justice process compared with the adult criminal process.*

The case of *In re Daniel R.* (1969) stands as a testament to the broad reach of juvenile laws.[37] In September 1968, Daniel R. was taken into police custody, without probable cause and without a warrant, for selling marijuana on the campus of Costa Mesa High School in Orange County, California. A juvenile court ordered Daniel to be committed to the Orange Juvenile Home for sixty days because he was "in danger of leading a dissolute life."[38] This was not a delinquency case based on drug possession or sale. Daniel was not adjudicated a ward of the court. Daniel's actions suggested that he was in danger of leading a life that was idle, lewd, and immoral.

"A local official . . . figures, 'What's one night in jail? The kid's detention hearing is in the morning.'"
Margaret Poethig, "Getting Kids Out of Jail," *CJ the Americas,* April–May 1990, p. 13.

Custody

Once juvenile misconduct has been brought to the attention of the authorities, usually the police, the next step is a decision to investigate, to take the juvenile into custody, and to process him or her. There is no uniform standard as to whether the taking of a juvenile into custody is in fact an arrest.[39] In some states it is; in others it is not; in some states the law is not clear. But in all states the taking of a juvenile into custody requires compliance with the constitutional mandates of *In re Gault,* including the probable cause requirement and the administration of the Miranda warning. Generally the police have broad power when a juvenile is taken into custody for reasons other than criminal conduct, such as being in danger, in trouble, or in violation of a juvenile court's order. As Figure 17.2 suggests, the range of possible dispositions subject to police discretion is vast, ranging from a verbal reprimand or warning that settles the incident

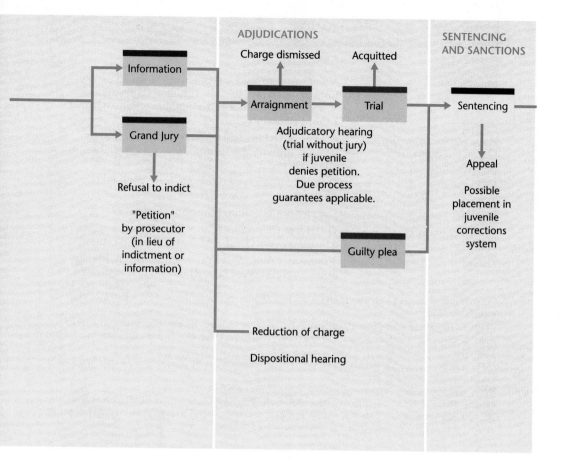

without formal legal action to referral of the youth to an appropriate agency to the processing of the child for juvenile court proceedings. In some states, officers may also give an official reprimand.

The Decision to Release or Retain. After an arrest or detention, usually by a patrol officer, the juvenile ordinarily is handed over to a specially trained member of the police juvenile unit. Such units exercise broader discretion than units that process adult criminal cases. Members may decide to release a juvenile into the custody of parents or otherwise involve parents, who may be called to the station house to discuss the matter. What factors appear to influence the decision to release or detain a juvenile? Many state laws mandate the detention of a child when required to protect persons or property; to prevent flight from a jurisdiction; or in cases where the child has no parent or guardian. Often decisions turn on the seriousness of the alleged offense, any history of previous offenses, and the extent to which both the accused and parents (or guardian) express a willingness to cooperate with a police investigation.

In a study of 2,489 cases drawn from juvenile court records of six New Jersey counties, researchers identified some additional factors that appear to contribute to the detention decision. These include (1) family configuration, (2) gender, and (3) the presence of emotional problems.[40] Specifically, children charged with delinquent acts were more often detained if they lived with only one parent. A significantly lower percentage of boys charged with status offenses were detained than girls. And children who were alleged to have emotional problems were much more likely to be detained.

TABLE 17.4 Offenses Excluded from Juvenile Court Jurisdiction[*]

Excluded Offenses	States[†]
Murder[**]	Arkansas, Connecticut, Delaware, District of Columbia, Idaho, Illinois, Indiana, Louisiana, Nevada, New York, Ohio, Oklahoma, Pennsylvania, Utah, Vermont
Rape (including criminal sexual conduct of penetration)	Arkansas, Delaware, District of Columbia, Idaho, Illinois, Indiana, Louisiana, New York, Oklahoma, Utah, Vermont
Kidnapping	Delaware, Indiana, Louisiana, New York, Oklahoma, Utah
Burglary	District of Columbia, Louisiana, New York
Armed robbery or robbery	District of Columbia, Idaho, Illinois, Indiana, Louisiana, Maryland, Oklahoma, Utah, Vermont
Other[‡]	Arkansas, Colorado, Connecticut, Florida, Idaho, Kansas, Nebraska, Ohio, Rhode Island, Wyoming

[*] Only criminal courts can try for such crimes by juveniles, provided they have reached minimum age (see Table 17.2).

[†] Only twenty-three states plus the District of Columbia legislatively exclude certain offenses from juvenile court jurisdiction. Because of the different offense categories, some states are listed more than once.

[**] This category includes various degrees of criminal homicide including attempted murder in some states (e.g., Nevada and New York).

[‡] This category includes offense categories such as "any offense."
SOURCE: Barry C. Feld, "The Juvenile Court Meets the Principle of the Offense: Legislative Changes in Juvenile Waiver Statutes," *Journal of Criminal Law & Criminology,* 78 (1987):512–514. Reprinted by special permission of Northwestern University, School of Law.

". . . the cop on the street has a right to know that if he is rammed by a juvenile, then that person is going to be accountable to that act of violence."
Union County, New Jersey, Prosecutor Andrew K. Ruotolo, Jr., *The New York Times,* September 1, 1992, p. B5.

"There is clear evidence of a trend in the direction of greater punitiveness toward juvenile offenders."

Facing the juvenile court judge at an intake hearing, the less formal juvenile equivalent of the adult arraignment.

Disposition. Once a juvenile has been taken into custody, the police juvenile unit must also decide, guided by law, whether to process the youngster as an adult offender and take him or her before a magistrate for a first appearance; to choose the juvenile path and take the suspect before a juvenile court judge; or to deal with the case in a less formal manner. Over the years, dispositions of juveniles have tended to become increasingly formal. In 1972, half of all juvenile cases were referred to juvenile court. By 1987, two-thirds of all cases reached the juvenile court. In 1972, 45 percent of all cases were handled informally within the department and the suspect was released; by 1987, only 30.3 percent were handled informally. Referral to a criminal court increased from 1.3 percent in 1972 to 5.2 percent in 1987. This is clear evidence of a trend in the direction of greater punitiveness toward juvenile offenders.[41]

Intake Hearing

If the case is not informally disposed of by the police or the juvenile probation department, it moves before a juvenile court judge for an intake hearing, which is similar to an arraignment in criminal court. In large metropolitan areas the juvenile court judge usually is a specialist in juvenile matters.[42] Perhaps he or she was a juvenile probation officer who went on to obtain a law degree. In the more rural parts of the country the criminal court judge doubles as juvenile court judge.

The juvenile court then decides, on the basis of the report of the intake department, whether the case should be waived to criminal court; whether the juvenile should be transferred to a social agency or placed on probation; whether the case should be dismissed; or whether a petition should be filed. A petition sets forth specific charges or allegations and resembles a criminal complaint. Juvenile court judges have broad discretion in making these decisions.[43]

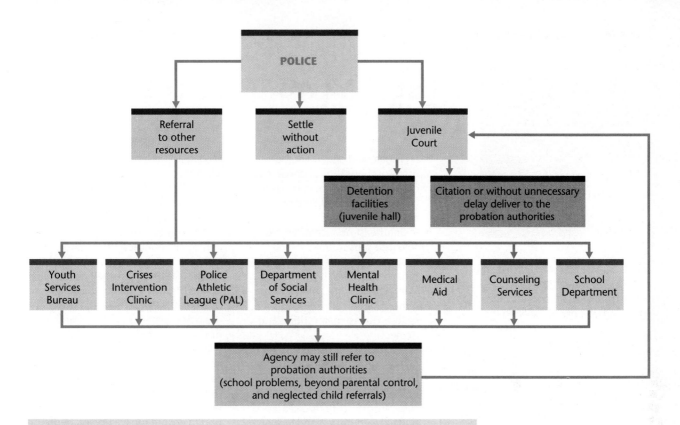

FIGURE 17.2 *Range of police dispositions for juveniles* (*Source:* Edward Eldefurso and Alan R. Coffey, *Process and Impact of the Juvenile Justice System* [Beverly Hills, Calif.: Glencoe, 1975], p. 47.)

Adjudication

If the juvenile court has retained jurisdiction over the alleged delinquent, the case moves into the adjudicatory hearing, which is the equivalent of a trial in criminal court. Under the terms of *In re Gault* the juvenile is entitled to nearly all the procedural guarantees that protect adults charged with crime, as we noted earlier.

In this adjudicatory hearing, the juvenile court judge first hears from a probation officer who recounts details concerning the allegations made in the petition. After a waiver hearing, a judge asks the child to admit or deny the petition (similar to pleading guilty or not guilty). Most often juveniles admit the petition. Such a decision has serious consequences. An admission essentially waives the juvenile's right to confront and cross-examine witnesses, to exercise the privilege against self-incrimination, and to present evidence. Given the importance of the decision, most courts inquire as to whether the admission of the petition is voluntarily, knowingly, and intelligently given. Next a judge must decide whether the facts warrant a decision in accordance with the petition. This is accomplished in a fact-finding hearing presided over by the judge. Only rarely are advisory juries used.[44] The hearing includes testimony from the victim, any witnesses, and often, the juvenile.

If the petition alleges that the juvenile has committed an act which if committed by an adult would be a crime, then he or she will be adjudicated a delinquent. If the juvenile is alleged to be a truant, a runaway, or incorrigible, and if the facts support the petition, the court will adjudicate the juvenile as a PINS, JINS, or CHINS—depending on the jurisdiction. The judge will then proceed to the second stage of the adjudication process, which corresponds to sentencing in criminal court. In many states, the adjudicatory and dispositional hearings are sepa-

"If the petition alleges that the juvenile has committed an act which if committed by an adult would be a crime, he or she will be adjudicated a delinquent."

THE WAR AGAINST THE CHILDREN

Thomas J. Bernard, a juvenile crime specialist, has concluded that the problem of juvenile crime can be solved only by "solving the larger social conditions that gave rise to the problem in the first place" (1). Those conditions, worldwide, stagger the imagination. Indeed, the struggle for survival faced by many of the world's children renders insignificant their participation in "criminal activities." Consider the "larger social conditions" in which countless children live:

• Forty million Africans, the majority of them children, have been displaced by military violence. Many more are fleeing from drought-stricken lands. A million African children have the AIDS virus, as do 3 million women, who can transmit the disease to the children they bear.
• Forty percent of school-age children all over the world have no access to any education. In Cambodia, for example, the schools have been razed and the teachers killed or dispersed.
• A quarter of a million of the world's youngest children are dying every week, and millions more are surviving in a half-life of malnutrition and almost permanent ill health. One-hundred million children the world over are in the process of dying due to malnutrition.
• In the war zones of the former Soviet Union and of Yugoslavia, Kuwait, Iraq, Ethiopia, Somalia,

Sri Lanka, and elsewhere, hundreds of thousands of children are or have been bombed, machine-gunned, napalmed, and orphaned.
• In Southeast Asia, children are sold into prostitution.
• In some Latin American and Caribbean countries, body parts of living children are being sold. Other children are dying in the gutters due to malnutrition and neglect.
• Five million Philippine children have been exposed to war.
• In the Magreb (in Africa just south of the Sahara), 11 million children suffer from infectious diseases due to malnutrition and lack of sanitation and medicine.
• In the United States, the number of children institutionalized every year is close to the 1-million mark.

The survivors of these conditions will join the swelling ranks of the world's street children. In some South American countries, street children are chased down by the police and shot like the rats whose lifestyles they share. Elsewhere street children are delinquents by definition and are likely to grow up to be adult predators—criminals.

Universal strategies

Many countries—but by no means all—have set up systems to deal with their delinquent children in a manner intended to be humane, and to guide them into culturally acceptable life patterns. These countries have pooled their know-how and promulgated model guidelines for dealing with delinquent children. But by the time children are caught in the net of the juvenile justice system, it may be

too late to "reform" them. This realization has spurred the development of a set of additional strategies to prevent juvenile delinquency from occurring in the first place.

The drafting of strategies acceptable to all countries was no easy task. Some governments view their children as they view their economy: The state should not interfere in the natural processes that guide the development of either; somehow the economy and the children will take care of themselves. Other governments feel strongly that in a democracy the collective has the duty to step in. The economy as well as the children need intervention to ensure the well-being of the whole community. Ultimately, however, the view emerged that regardless of government involvement in economic matters, children are helpless by definition and require communal support systems. This is especially true when there are no parents or when parents do not have the capacity to provide nurture, whether because of their own shortcomings or because of circumstances beyond their control such as war or famine.

The U.N. Guidelines

In 1990 the General Assembly of the United Nations unanimously accepted this set of strategies in the form of the United Nations Guidelines for the Prevention of Juvenile Delinquency (Riyadh Guidelines) to "assist Member States in formulating and implementing specialized programmes and policies, emphasizing assistance, care and community involvement" (2).

Many of these guidelines are well known to American criminal justice specialists and supported by research:

- "Youthful behavior or conduct that does not conform to overall social norms and values is often part of the maturation and growth process and tends to disappear spontaneously in most individuals with the transition to adulthood."
- "Labelling a young person as 'deviant,' 'delinquent,' or 'pre-delinquent' often contributes to the development of a consistent pattern of undesirable behaviour by young persons."
- "Young persons should have an active role and partnership within society and should not be considered as mere objects of socialization or control."
- "Criminalizing and penalizing a child for behaviour that does not cause serious damage to the development of the child or harm to others" should be avoided.

The three support systems

The *Guidelines* contain detailed provisions for the coordination of services between governmental and nongovernmental agencies, community involvement, reduction of the opportunity to commit delinquent acts, and research and analysis as part of program design. They place primary emphasis on positive socialization through the family as the responsible unit and stress the provision of such support services as day care and services to families in need, especially indigenous, migrant, and refugee families. When children have no parents, foster care and adoption must be provided.

The second support system—although primary in many circumstances—is the educational system, which must teach basic values and develop respect for the child's own cultural identity. These values include the universal value system, especially that elaborated in the Universal Declaration of Human Rights. Moreover, "schools should serve as resource and referral centres for the medical, counselling and other services to young persons, particularly those with special needs and suffering from abuse, neglect, victimization and exploitation."

The third pillar of support is the community, with its voluntary organizations capable of providing shelter for street children, aid to young drug abusers, and recreational facilities and services to all.

Just another piece of paper?

The United Nations *Guidelines* conclude with recommendations on social policy and legislation suggested for all countries, with such specific recommendations as the following:

- Legislation preventing the victimization, abuse, exploitation, and the use for criminal activities of children and young persons should be enacted and enforced.
- No child or young person should be subjected to harsh or degrading correction or punishment measures at home, in schools, or in any other institutions.
- Legislation and enforcement aimed at restricting and controlling accessibility of weapons of any sort to children and young persons should be pursued.
- To prevent further stigmatization, victimization, and criminalization of young persons, legislation should be enacted to ensure that any conduct not considered an offense or penalized if committed by an adult is not considered an offense or penalized if committed by a young person.
- Consideration should be given to the establishment of an office of ombudsman or similar independent organ that would ensure that the status, rights, and interests of young persons are upheld and that proper referral to available services is made.

Critics have said that these guidelines are "just another piece of paper from the United Nations." But Magna Carta was "just a piece of paper," and so was the U.S. Constitution. It is up to the 179 countries that adopted these *Guidelines* to turn them from paper to practice. There is a war against the world's children, and this "piece of paper" may well be the peace treaty.

SOURCES

1. Thomas J. Bernard, *The Cycle of Juvenile Justice* (New York: Oxford University Press, 1992), p. 186.
2. *Guidelines for the Prevention of Juvenile Delinquency,* U.N. General Assembly Resolution 45/112, 1990.

QUESTIONS FOR DISCUSSION

1. List some of the first steps that would have to be taken to implement the United Nations' *Guidelines* in the United States.
2. What could be done to assist impoverished and war-torn countries such as the former Yugoslavia or Somalia in implementing the *Guidelines* and helping their children?
3. How could the extent to which countries are following the recommendations detailed in the *Guidelines* be monitored?

rate. Separate and distinct hearings protect the child from any prejudice resulting from irrelevant, often damaging evidence raised during the adjudicatory hearing. Even more important, separating them keeps unsavory evidence out of the first stage of the process, while making it available at the dispositional hearing. The separate hearings also give probation officers time to prepare a social history for the presentence investigation report (PSI).

Dispositional Hearing

"People who think punishment should characterize juvenile justice should understand that these youngsters are going to come back into society."
George Napper, head, Department of Children and Youth Services, quoted in *Atlanta Journal and Constitution,* July 10, 1992, p. A10.

In finding an appropriate disposition, the juvenile court is guided by any relevant information, especially that provided in the social history. The court must balance the child's best interests with society's best interests. It must protect society from dangerous and disruptive individuals; guide delinquent children into a socially acceptable path; set an example for other children; make children responsible for their harmful actions.[45] In choosing a disposition, juvenile court judges have broader discretion than criminal court judges. The judge may choose probation, with numerous conditions; commitment to a juvenile correctional facility; restitution; or fines. The judge may also choose placement in a foster home or in a special program.

Scholars have carefully examined three factors in dispositional decisions: race, gender, and social class. Research on the association between race and disposition is clear—black youths are between three and four times more likely than white youths to be committed to correctional facilities.[46] Gender differences also have been observed. For example, white female first offenders tend to be incarcerated less frequently than other first offenders.[47]

"The types of cases that are coming through the system now are so violent and vicious that people are frightened to death. . . . I don't think the juvenile system is able to handle it."
State Attorney Alexander Williams, Jr., Prince George's County, quoted in *The Washington Post,* September 29, 1992, p. B1.

In a few jurisdictions, juveniles may now be committed to adult correctional facilities where they are often placed in the general population. In Texas, for example, juveniles convicted of (1) murder, (2) capital murder, (3) aggravated kidnapping or sexual assault, (4) deadly assault on a law enforcement officer, or (5) attempted capital murder may be referred to the grand jury.[48] With grand jury approval, the juvenile court has the authority to transfer the child to the Texas Department of Corrections for up to thirty years. A variation of the Texas statute was recently passed in Massachusetts. This law allows juveniles who have been adjudicated on charges of first- and second-degree murder to be committed to an adult correctional facility following their twenty-first birthday. Juveniles thus may now serve split sentences—part in a juvenile facility and part in an adult institution.[49]

JUVENILE CORRECTIONS

The juvenile court may decide that the only option is to place the individual in an institution. There has been considerable debate over whether such placement is ever an appropriate response to juvenile wrongdoing. Jerome G. Miller, as head of the Massachusetts juvenile correction system, tried to prove the point by closing down all Massachusetts juvenile detention facilities in the early 1970s.[50] The experiment did not last: Policymakers determined that some juvenile offenders must be segregated to protect the community. Although researchers continue to demonstrate that the jailing of juvenile offenders has no appreciable effect on the juvenile crime rate, all states maintain confinement facilities.[51]

"'I don't think there is any dispute the system is inadequate,' Judge [Robert] Mason said. But 'to take them and dump them into an adult system doesn't seem to me to be the answer.'"
Quoted in *The Washington Post,* September 29, 1992, p. B1.

Most inmates of juvenile facilities (74%) have committed crimes. Only 12 percent are status offenders, but a surprising 14 percent are classed as nonoffenders, including dependent, neglected, and abused children. Even more surprising, the total number of residents in juvenile facilities grows by 6 to 9 percent annually.[52]

A survey revealed that in 1990:

619,181 juveniles were admitted to public detention, correctional, and shelter facilities.

141,463 juveniles were admitted to private facilities.

65,263 juveniles were admitted to adult jails.

9,078 juveniles were admitted to state correctional facilities.

The total was 834,985. The number of residents on an average day, however, amounts to only about 99,617, of which about half are long-term residents.[53] Fifty percent of all admissions to juvenile facilities come from only five states—California, Ohio, Texas, Washington, and Florida—which together have only 5 percent of the entire juvenile population of the United States.[54]

"The total number of residents in juvenile facilities grows by 6 to 9 percent annually."

Juvenile facilities encompass a wide spectrum: detention centers, training schools, reception or diagnostic centers, shelters, ranches, forestry camps and farms, halfway houses, and group homes. Most of the 3,267 facilities in the nation are privately operated. Yet the majority of juvenile offenders are being held in public facilities (619,181), which are far more prisonlike than the private facilities.[55] Juvenile facilities range from serene, campuslike complexes with understanding counselors to sordid prisons. Commentators have argued that incarceration of juveniles will do more harm than good unless the conditions of detention are radically reformed and the population is kept at a minimum.[56]

"Commentators have argued that incarceration of juveniles will do more harm than good unless the conditions of detention are radically reformed...."

DIVERSION OUT OF THE JUVENILE JUSTICE SYSTEM

In Chapter 5 we described the attrition rate or mortality rate of the criminal justice system. There is a significant funneling effect throughout the process, beginning with the number of crimes reported and ending with the number of convicted offenders serving prison terms. There is also significant attrition in the juvenile justice system. More than half the total number of juveniles who appear at intake are diverted through dismissal or informal adjustment. Of those detained and subsequently adjudicated, 12 percent had their cases dismissed and 1 percent were transferred to adult court. Two-thirds of those who remained for disposition hearings were placed on probation, and less than 10 percent were sent to a juvenile correctional facility. A recent depiction of the filtering process separates those cases that are not handled by petition.[57] Of the total number of juveniles charged (1,348,100), slightly more than 20 percent were detained prior to a fact-finding hearing. For cases handled with a petition, nearly 2 percent were waived to criminal court; 26 percent had the petitions dismissed; 34 percent were placed on probation; and nearly 14 percent (85,600) were sent to correctional facilities (Figure 17.3).

Juvenile correctional institutions have a disproportionate number of African American and other minority inmates.

Comparisons of the juvenile and adult attrition rates reveal more significant diversion in the adult criminal justice system. This is remarkable given that the juvenile court was originally designed as a diversion from the adult court. Moreover, literally thousands of diversionary programs were created in the 1970s to filter out juveniles who would "do better" outside the system. Diversion was justified as follows:

- The earlier a youth enters the juvenile justice system, the more likely he or she is to become a career criminal.
- Children who are not diverted miss out on a wide range of community services.
- Juvenile court jurisdiction should be reserved for extraordinary cases.
- Filtering out cases relieves overcrowded juvenile court dockets.
- Programs for juveniles cost less than juvenile court processing.[58]

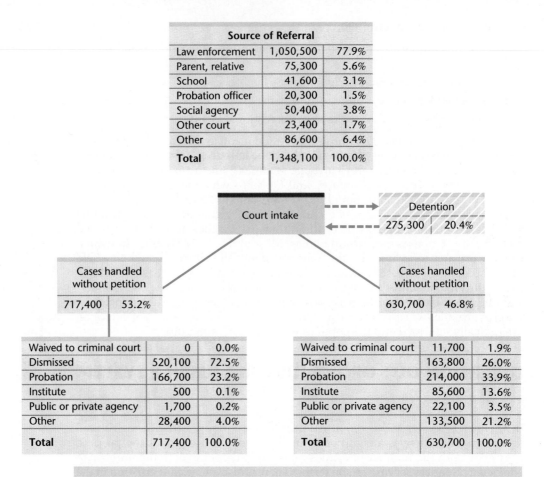

Source of Referral		
Law enforcement	1,050,500	77.9%
Parent, relative	75,300	5.6%
School	41,600	3.1%
Probation officer	20,300	1.5%
Social agency	50,400	3.8%
Other court	23,400	1.7%
Other	86,600	6.4%
Total	1,348,100	100.0%

Court intake

Detention
275,300   20.4%

Cases handled without petition
717,400   53.2%

Cases handled without petition
630,700   46.8%

Waived to criminal court	0	0.0%
Dismissed	520,100	72.5%
Probation	166,700	23.2%
Institute	500	0.1%
Public or private agency	1,700	0.2%
Other	28,400	4.0%
Total	717,400	100.0%

Waived to criminal court	11,700	1.9%
Dismissed	163,800	26.0%
Probation	214,000	33.9%
Institute	85,600	13.6%
Public or private agency	22,100	3.5%
Other	133,500	21.2%
Total	630,700	100.0%

FIGURE 17.3 *Delinquency case characteristics (1981 estimates)* (*Source:* Philip J. Cook and John H. Laub, "Trends in Child Abuse and Juvenile Delinquency," in *From Children to Citizens: The Role of Juvenile Courts,* ed. F. Hartmann [New York: Springer-Verlag, 1987], p. 111.)

Over the last two decades, some have found a wide gap between diversion in theory and diversion in practice. According to some scholars, diversionary programs were originally conceived as alternatives to the formal juvenile justice system—they were to be privately run ("nonlegal"), community-based programs. But most diversionary programs ended up being sponsored by state or local justice agencies. The result seemed to be only a widening of the net of the juvenile justice system—an increase in the reach of state-sponsored social control. Moreover, evidence emerged that diversionary programs were in fact sometimes coercive. Finally, to the extent that diversion programs became government sponsored, the benefit of using such programs so that children would avoid stigmatization was all but lost.[59]

Recent research on the court careers of juvenile offenders makes the issue of diversion all the more complicated. In a major study of 69,504 youths born between 1962 and 1965 and processed in juvenile courts in Arizona and Utah, some startling findings emerged, findings that should force a reevaluation of the role of diversion in the court careers of juveniles. Here are some of the more important findings:

• "Approximately one-third of all youths residing within the courts' jurisdictions were referred to juvenile court for a delinquency or status offense before their eighteenth birthday. More specifically, 46 percent of all males and 21 percent of all females had juvenile court careers.

"The result of most diversion programs seems to be only a widening of the net of the juvenile justice system—more state-sponsored social control, not less."

• The majority of youths referred to court were referred at least once for a delinquency offense (a criminal law violation). Eighty-one percent of all court careers (85% of male careers and 73% of female careers) contained a delinquency referral.

• Over half of all youths with a status offense in their career also were referred for a delinquency offense; one quarter of all youths with a delinquency offense in their career were referred at some time in their career for a status offense.

• Sixteen percent of all youths referred to court, those with four or more referrals, were responsible for over half of all juvenile court cases.

• As the number of referrals in a career increased, the youth was more likely to be referred for an index violent offense."[60]

According to the researchers, the finding of a developmental pattern of offenses in the court careers of juveniles suggests the need for programs that focus on children at the beginning of their career.[61] Of course, these expenditures and the targeting of chronic offenders would also affect the number of diversions, as well as the amount of attrition out of the juvenile justice system.

JUVENILE VIOLENCE AND JUVENILE JUSTICE POLICY

Between 1980 and 1990 the rate of violent juvenile crime increased 27 percent, to a record high of 430 such crimes per 100,000 juveniles. During this decade, the rate of white juvenile violent crime increased 44 percent, compared with a 19-percent increase for blacks. Nevertheless, in 1990, the juvenile violent crime arrest rate hit 1,429 per 100,000 black juveniles. These somewhat startling statistics prompted the following conclusions by the authors of the FBI's 1991 UCR report on crime in the United States: "Nationwide, there is a growing concern over an escalation in juvenile delinquency, a perception supported by the unprecedented level of juvenile violence confronting the nation."[62]

This concern is justified. The percentage of juvenile arrest rates for all violent crimes (except robbery) increased 36.7 percent for forcible rape and 87.3 percent for murder over the last decade. Weapons law violations increased 62.6 percent. And heroin/cocaine arrests increased 713.4 percent. Of course these statistics tell only part of the story. Increases in arrest rates have a profound effect on the functioning of the juvenile courts, as well as on all juvenile correctional facilities. Figure 17.4 shows the upward trend in arrests and custodial commitments throughout the past decade.

In addition to its effect on the juvenile justice system, the apparent increase in murder, rape, weapons use, drug sales, and related street violence has led to a dramatic increase in fear of crime. Public perceptions of crime rates, of safety in walking alone at night and physical safety at home, as well as fear of violent victimization, have all increased over the past decade. What effect do public perceptions of violent juvenile crime have on the juvenile justice system? According to criminologist Thomas J. Bernard, the effect is seen in the cyclical pattern of juvenile justice policies[63] (Figure 17.5): Within the last 200 years we have repeated the same cycle three times. The cycle starts with a public outcry that juvenile crime is out of control. A general agreement develops that only harsh penalties are the answer. Minor offenders are diverted from the system because of lack of resources and concern that exposure to the process of juvenile justice may do more harm than good. Next, consensus is reached that the choice between the harsh penalties and no involvement in the juvenile justice system is actually contributing to the problem. Harsh punishments as well as "doing nothing" may in fact increase crime rates. The solution? Find some middle ground by

"He possessed that gun not for show and tell, but with full knowledge about what he could do with it."
Assistant State Attorney Jon King, *Chicago Tribune*, July 14, 1992, p. C3.

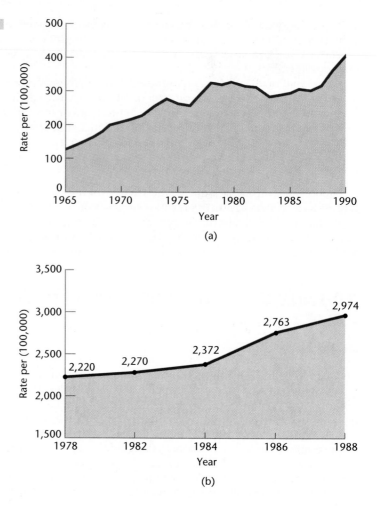

FIGURE 17.4

[A] Juvenile violent crime arrest rates, United States 1965–1990 (*Source: Uniform Crime Reports, 1991* [Washington D.C.: Department of Justice, 1992], p. 280.)

[B] Public and private juvenile facility admission rates, United States 1978–1988 (*Source:* National Council on Crime and Delinquency, *Juveniles Taken into Custody, 1990 Report* [San Francisco: National Council on Crime and Delinquency, 1991], p. 15.)

legislating "lenient treatments" or minor penalties. As crime rates remain high, the public makes an association between the lenient treatments and the crime problem. The response to this is a toughening of policy, so that serious juvenile offenders receive increasingly harsh punishments. This continues until such time as there are no longer any minor penalties. The cycle is complete.

What drives us from one stage to the next? Ideas. At each stage in the cycle, according to Bernard, officials of the juvenile justice system as well as the public subscribe to three ideas that sound all too familiar:

- The level of juvenile violent crime is unprecedented.
- Existing juvenile justice policies contribute to the problem.
- Change in juvenile justice policies will result in a reduction in crime.

Two additional ideas create shifts in juvenile justice policy: ideas of juvenile delinquency and ideas of juvenile justice. The former consists of a person's perception of the causes of delinquency; the latter reflects a person's vision of the juvenile justice mission. Ideas of juvenile justice shape the kinds of policies that appear desirable. Ideas of juvenile delinquency reveal why the policy is expected to work.

The value of Bernard's work rests in his concluding message: Juvenile justice policy will not solve the vast problem of juvenile crime. The introduction of new policies to counteract the perception of a high crime rate will only result, after some period of time, in a countervailing policy. Juvenile crime may be addressed only by "changing the larger social conditions that gave rise to the problem in the first place."[64]

Juvenile crime is thought to be unusually high. There are many harsh punishments and few lenient treatments. Officials often are forced to choose between harshly punishing juvenile offenders and doing nothing at all.	Juvenile crime is thought to be unusually high and is blamed on the "forced choice." That is, both harshly punishing and doing nothing at all are thought at all are thought to increase juvenile crime.
Juvenile crime is thought to be unusually high and is blamed on the lenient treatments. Harsh punishments gradually expand and lenient treatments gradually contract.	A major reform introduces lenient treatment for juvenile offenders. This creates a middle ground between harshly punishing and doing nothing at all.

FIGURE 17.5 *The cycle of juvenile justice* (*Source:* Thomas J. Bernard, *The Cycle of Juvenile Justice* [New York: Oxford University Press, 1992], p. 4.)

REVIEW

The juvenile justice system, like the criminal justice system, has components that are related and interdependent. But the process differs in important respects from its adult counterpart. Criminal courts are adversarial, while juvenile courts are guided, at least in theory, by the *parens patriae* philosophy. In juvenile courts, release decisions, evidentiary considerations, and disposition (sentencing) all differ. In addition, the juvenile law has a broad reach. It is far more inclusive than the criminal law with its strict definitional limitations.

The juvenile process filters out a significant number of those taken into the system. They are diverted into other programs, or out of the system altogether. Yet there is much debate about the benefit of diversionary programs. To some, they appear as a widening of the net of social control. To others, they are coercive. To still others, they are humane alternatives to harsh treatment.

Finally, juvenile justice policy is cyclical. It appears that, over the centuries, one society confronts the same concerns repeatedly, and moves to harsher solutions, followed by more humane and urbane responses. All indications are that the effort to combat juvenile crime by tougher policies is bound to fail. Evidence suggests that underlying social conditions must be changed to achieve a lasting change in juvenile crime.

NOTES

1. Michael Riley Baltimore, "Corridors of Agony: A Rare Look Inside a Juvenile Court Reveals a System Waging a Thankless Struggle to Save Society's Lost Children," *Time*, January 1, 1992, p. 40.

2. Barry Krisberg, *The Juvenile Court: Reclaiming the Vision* (San Francisco: National Council on Crime and Delinquency, 1990).

3. U.S. Department of Justice, Bureau of Justice Statistics, *Criminal Victimization in the United States, 1987* (Washington, D.C.: U.S. Government Printing Office, June 1989), Table 40, p. 47.

4. Beverly Shepard, "Violent Kids: A Dilemma in the Courts," *Atlanta Journal and Constitution*, April 13, 1992, p. D1.

5. Ibid. See also Mark C. Seis and Kenneth L. Elbe, "The Death Penalty for Juveniles: Bridging the Gap between an Evolving Standard of Decency and Legislative Policy," *Justice Quarterly* 8 (1991): 465–487.

6. *Ex parte Crouse*, 4 Wharton, Pa., 9 (1838). See Steve L. Schlossman, *Love and the American Delinquent: The Theory and Practice of "Progressive" Juvenile Justice, 1825–1920* (Chicago: University of Chicago Press, 1977).

7. Robert M. Mennel, *Thorns and Thistles: Juvenile Delinquency in the United States, 1825–1940* (Hanover, N.H.: University Press of New England, 1973), p. 129.

8. Gustav L. Schramm, "The Judge Meets the Boy and His Family," *National Probation Association Yearbook* (New York: National Probation Association, 1945), pp. 182–194.

9. Ibid., p. 183.

10. President's Commission on Law Enforcement and Administration of Justice, *Challenge of Crime in a Free Society* (Washington, D.C.: U.S. Government Printing Office, 1967), p. 25.

11. Ibid.

12. On the problems inherent in the concepts that guide the juvenile justice system, see Sanford Fox, "Juvenile Justice Reform: An Historical Perspective," *Stanford Law Review* 22 (1970):1187–1239; Anthony M. Platt, *The Child Savers: The Invention of Delinquency*, 2d ed. (Chicago: University of Chicago Press, 1977).

13. President's Commission on Law Enforcement and Administration of Justice, *Juvenile Delinquency and Youth Crime* (Washington, D.C.: U.S. Government Printing Office, 1967), p. 7.

14. For an excellent account of the evolution of the juvenile courts, see Lamar T. Empey, *American Delinquency: Its Meaning and Construction* (Chicago: Dorsey, 1982).

15. *In re Gault*, 387 U.S. 1 (1967); Ruth Steinfeldt, Hazel B. Kerper, and Charles M. Friel, "The Impact of the Gault Decision in Texas," *Juvenile Court Journal* 20 (1969):154–158.

16. *In re Winship*, 397 U.S. 358 (1970).

17. *McKeiver v. Pennsylvania*, 403 U.S. 528 (1971). Notably, the public's right of access is limited in juvenile court hearings. Twenty-seven states have statutes that prohibit the general public from attending. Fifteen states allow the court discretion as to whether a hearing shall be open to the public. Finally, five states require that juvenile delinquency hearings be open to the public for certain serious offenses. See Note, "The Public Right of Access to Juvenile Delinquency Hearings," *Michigan Law Review* 81 (1983):1540–1565.

18. *In re Gault*, at 12.

19. Ibid., at 15.

20. Charles F. Reasons, "Procedural Change and Substantive Effect," *Crime and Delinquency* 16 (1970):163–171; Barry Feld, "*In re Gault* Revisited: A Cross-State Comparison of the Right to Counsel in Juvenile Court," *Crime and Delinquency* 34 (1988):23–48; Thomas Grisso, *Juveniles' Waiver of Rights: Legal and Psychological Consequence* (New York: Plenum, 1981); Norman Lefstein, Vaughan Stapleton, and Lee Teitelbaum, "In Search of Juvenile Justice: *Gault* and Its Implementation," *Law and Society Review* 3 (1969):491; H. Ted Rubin, "The Juvenile Court's Search for Identity and Responsibility," *Crime and Delinquency* 23 (1977):1–13.

21. Grisso, *Juveniles' Waiver of Rights.*

22. Ibid.

23. See, e.g., Stephen J. Bogacz, "Juveniles in New York under 'Miranda' Rule 25 Years Later," *New York Law Journal,* March 20, 1992, p. 1

24. *People v. Castro,* 118 Misc. 2d 868 (Supreme Court, Queens County, N.Y., 1983).

25. *In re Julian B.,* 125 A.D. 2d 666 (N.Y., 1986).

26. Dennis Cassano, "Girl Accused of Trying to Kill Mother Will Be Tried in Juvenile Court," *Minneapolis Star Tribune,* June 3, 1992, p. 1B.

27. Institute of Judicial Administration-American Bar Association, *Juvenile Justice Standards: A Summary and Analysis,* 2d ed., ed. Barbara Dansiger Flicker (Cambridge, Mass.: Ballinger, 1982), p. 47.

28. "Former Florida Judge Says Juvenile Courts Need Help," *United Press International,* March 5, 1992.

29. *Kent v. United States,* 383 U.S. 541 (1966). On remand, the district court acted as a juvenile court and upheld the waiver. However, the Court of Appeals (District of Columbia Circuit), in an opinion written by the late Chief Judge Bazelon, reversed the lower court, finding the waiver "inappropriate" due to Mr. Kent's serious mental illness.

30. Ibid., at 556.

31. Ibid., at 567.

32. Dean J. Champion, "Teenage Felons and Waiver Hearings: Some Recent Trends, 1980–1988," *Crime and Delinquency* 35 (1989):590–601. See also Dean J. Champion and G. Larry Mays, *Transferring Juveniles to Criminal Courts: Trends and Implications for Criminal Justice* (New York: Praeger, 1991).

33. Simon I. Singer and David McDowall, "Criminalizing Delinquency: The Deterrent Effects of the New York Juvenile Offender Law," *Law and Society Review* 22 (1988):521–535.

34. Michael W. Oshima and Francis X. Hartman, "Juvenile Justice in Transition: An Industry Note," in *From Children to Citizens: The Role of the Juvenile Court,* ed. F. X. Hartman (New York: Springer-Verlag, 1987), p. 309.

35. Richard J. Lundman, Richard E. Sykes, and John P. Clark, "Police Control of Juveniles: A Replication," in *Police Behavior: A Sociological Perspective,* ed. Richard J. Lundman (New York: Oxford University Press, 1980), pp. 130–151.

36. *Ga. Code Ann.,* § 15-11-2 (12) (1990).

37. *In re Daniel R.,* 274 Cal. App. 2d 749, 79 Cal. Rptr. 247 (1969).

38. Ibid., at 750.

39. For an excellent account of the problems associated with juvenile arrest definitions, see Malcolm W. Klein, Susan Kabin Rosensweig, and Ronald Bates, "The Ambiguous Juvenile Arrest," *Criminology* 13 (1975):78–89.

40. Russell K. Schutt and Dale Dannefer, "Detention Decisions in Juvenile Cases: JINS, JDs, and Gender," *Law and Society Review* 22 (1988):509–520.

41. See Philip J. Cook and John H. Laub, "Trends in Child Abuse and Juvenile Delinquency," in *From Children to Citizens,* ed. Hartman. See also Samuel M. Davis, *Rights of Juveniles: The Juvenile Justice System,* 2d ed. (New York: Clark Boardman, 1980), pp. 3–9.

42. Nancy Lewis, "One Robe, Many Roles for Juvenile Judges," *The Washington Post,* June 29, 1992, p. D1.

43. See, e.g., C. Needleman, "Discrepant Assumptions in Empirical Research: The Case of Juvenile Court Screening," *Social Prob-* *lems* 28 (1981):247–262; L. E. Cohen and J. R. Kluegel, "Selecting Delinquents for Adjudication: An Analysis of Intake Screening Decisions in Two Metropolitan Courts," *Journal of Research in Crime and Delinquency* 16 (1979):143–163; A. C. Meade, "The Labeling Approach to Delinquency: State of the Theory as a Function of Method," *Social Forces* 53 (1974):83–91; C. W. Thomas and C. H. Sieverdes, "An Analysis of Discretionary Decisionmaking," *Criminology* 12 (1975):413–432; T. P. Thornberry, "Race, Socioeconomic Status and Sentencing in the Juvenile Justice System," *Journal of Criminal Law and Criminology* 64 (1973):90–96; Donna B. Towberman, "National Survey of Juvenile Needs Assessment," *Crime and Delinquency* 38 (1992):230–238.

44. *McKeiver v. Pennsylvania,* 403 U.S. 528 (1971); see Joseph B. Sanborn, Jr., "Pleading Guilty in Juvenile Court: Minimal Ado about Something Very Important to Young Defendants," *Justice Quarterly* 9 (1992):127–154.

45. *State ex. rel. D.D.H. v. Dostert,* 165 W. Va 448, 269 S.E.2d 401 (1980). See also Institute of Judicial Administration-American Bar Association, *Juvenile Justice Standards.*

46. See Charles E. Frazier, Donna M. Bishop, and John C. Henretta, "The Social Context of Race Differentials in Juvenile Justice," *Sociological Quarterly* 33 (1992):447–458; J. Fagan, E. Slaughter, and E. Hartstone, "Blind Justice? The Impact of Race on the Juvenile Process," *Crime and Delinquency* 33 (1987):1–23. See also D. M. Bishop and C. S. Frazier, "The Influence of Race in Juvenile Justice Processing," *Journal of Research in Crime and Delinquency* 25 (1987):242–263; B. R. McCarthy and B. L. Smith, "The Conceptualization of Discrimination in the Juvenile Justice Process: The Impact of Administrative Factors and Screening Decisions on Juvenile Court Dispositions," *Criminology* 24 (1986):41–64. For earlier work on this subject, see W. R. Arnold, "Race and Ethnicity Relative to Other Factors in Juvenile Court Dispositions," *American Journal of Sociology* 77 (1971):211–227; T. P. Thornberry, "Race, Socioeconomic Status and Sentencing in the Juvenile Justice System," *Journal of Criminal Law and Criminology* 64 (1973):90–98; T. P. Thornberry, "Sentencing Disparities in the Juvenile Justice System," *Journal of Criminal Law and Criminology* 70 (1979):164–171; G. S. Kowalski and J. P. Rickicki, "Determinants of Juvenile Postadjudication Dispositions," *Journal of Research in Crime and Delinquency* 19 (1982):66–83; C. R. Mann, "Courtroom Observations of Extra-Legal Factors in the Juvenile Court Dispositions of Runaway Boys: A Field Study," *Juvenile and Family Court Journal* 31 (1980):43–52.

47. See Donna M. Bishop and Charles E. Frazier, "Gender Bias in Juvenile Justice Processing: Implications of the JJDP Act," *Journal of Criminal Law and Criminology* 82 (1992):1162–1186; Ruth Horowitz and Anne E. Pottieger, "Gender Bias in Juvenile Justice Handling of Seriously Crime-Involved Youths," *Journal of Research in Crime and Delinquency* 28 (1991):75–100; Rosemary Sarri, "Gender Issues in Juvenile Justice," *Crime and Delinquency* 29 (1983):381–387; Carl Pope and William H. Feyerherm, "Gender Bias in Juvenile Court Dispositions," *Social Science Research* 6 (1982):1–17; Katherine Teilmann and Pierre H. Landry, Jr., "Gender Bias in Juvenile Justice," *Journal of Research in Crime and Delinquency* 18 (1981):47–80; Coramae Mann, "The Differential Treatment between Runaway Boys and Girls in Juvenile Court," *Juvenile and Family Court Journal* 30 (1979):37–48. For a discussion of social class issues, see Timothy J. Carter, "Juvenile Court Dispositions: A Comparison of Status and Nonstatus Offenders," *Criminology* 17 (1979):341–359.

48. *Tex. Fam. Code Ann.,* § 54.054(b) (d) (Supp. 1990).

49. John Ellement, "DYS Head Says New Law on Killers Will Wreak Havoc," *The Boston Globe,* January 10, 1992, p. 28.

50. Jerome G. Miller, *Last One Over the Wall: The Massachusetts Experiment in Closing Reform Schools* (Columbus: Ohio State University Press, 1991). See Lloyd E. Ohlin, Robert B. Coates, and Alden D. Miller, "Radical Correctional Reform: A Case Study of the Massachusetts Youth Correctional System," *Harvard Educational Review* 44 (1974):74–111.

51. Richard Allinson, "There Are No Juveniles in Pennsylvania

Jails," *Corrections Magazine* 9(3) (1983):13–20; Paul W. Keve, *The Consequences of Prohibiting the Jailing of Juveniles* (Richmond: Virginia Commonwealth University, 1984).

52. U.S. Department of Justice, Bureau of Justice Statistics, *Report to the Nation on Crime and Justice*, 2d ed. (Washington, D.C.: U.S. Government Printing Office, 1988), pp. 95, 103, 105.

53. National Council on Crime and Delinquency, *Juveniles Taken into Custody*, 1990 Report (San Francisco: National Council on Crime and Delinquency, 1991), p. 15.

54. Arnold Binder, Gilbert Geis, and Bruce Dickson, *Juvenile Delinquency: Historical, Cultural, Legal Perspectives* (New York: Macmillan, 1988), p. 329.

55. Ibid., p. 110.

56. Steven P. Lab and John T. Whitehead, "An Analysis of Juvenile Correctional Treatment," *Crime and Delinquency* 34 (1988):60–83. Albert R. Roberts, "Wilderness Programs for Juvenile Offenders: A Challenging Alternative," *Juvenile and Family Court Journal* 39 (1988):1–12; Robert J. Mutchnick and Margaret Fawcett, "Group Home Environments and Victimization of Resident Juveniles," *International Journal of Offender Therapy and Comparative Criminology* 35 (1991):126–142; Douglas Lansing, Joseph B. Bogan, and Loren Karacki, "Unit Management: Implementing a Different Correctional Approach," *Federal Probation* 41 (1977):43–49. See also Jospeh B. Vaughn, "A Survey of Juvenile Electronic Monitoring and Home Confinement Programs," *Juvenile and Family Court Journal* 40 (1989): 1–36.

57. See LaMar T. Empey and Mark C. Stafford, *American Delinquency: Its Meaning and Construction.* 3d ed. (Belmont, Calif.: Wadsworth, 1991); Howard N. Snyder, Terrence A. Finnegan, and John L. Hutzler, *Delinquency, 1981* (Pittsburgh: National Center for Juvenile Justice, 1983), citing Philip Cook and John Laub, "Trends in Child Abuse and Juvenile Delinquency," in *From Children to Citizens*, ed. Hartmann.

58. Harjit S. Sandhu and C. Wayne Heasly, *Improving Juvenile Justice: Power Advocacy, Diversion, Decriminalization, and Due Process* (New York: Human Sciences Press, 1981), pp. 100–101.

59. See, e.g., James Austin and Barry Krisberg, "Wider, Stronger and Different Nets: The Dialectics of Criminal Justice Reform," *Journal of Research in Crime and Delinquency* 18 (1981):165–196; Edwin M. Lemert "Diversion in Juvenile Justice: What Hath Been Wrought," *Journal of Research in Crime and Delinquency* 18 (1981):35–46; Malcolm W. Klein, "Deinstitutionalization and Diversion of Juvenile Offenders: A Litany of Impediments," in *Crime and Justice*, eds. N. Morris and M. Tonry (Chicago: University of Chicago Press, 1979), pp. 145–200.

60. Howard N. Snyder, *Court Careers of Juvenile Offenders* (Pittsburgh: National Center for Juvenile Justice, 1988).

61. Ibid.

62. *Uniform Crime Reports, Crime in the United States, 1991* (Washington, D.C.: U.S. Department of Justice, 1992), p. 279.

63. Thomas J. Bernard, *The Cycle of Juvenile Justice* (New York: Oxford University Press, 1992). See also Stephen J. Brodt and Steven J. Smith, "Part I: Public Policy and the Serious Juvenile Offender," *Criminal Justice Policy Review* 2 (1988):70–85.

64. Ibid., at p. 186. Until such time as we address such conditions, states will do their best to balance competing interests. According to Jeffrey L. Bleich, states and even regions differ with respect to the values that underlie their juvenile justice policies. In a state-by-state analysis of policy, as reflected by the contents of state statutes, three main themes appeared:

• Recognition of the importance of individual development, guidance, and protection
• Protection of the community
• Respect for family autonomy

States in the South, Midwest, and Pacific Northwest emphasize public protection. Individual development and family integrity is more often emphasized in the east and northeast. See Jeffrey L. Bleich, "Appendix to Chapter 2: Legislative Trends," in *From Children to Citizens*, ed. Hartmann.

CHAPTER 18

JUSTICE FOR VICTIMS

Alleged Victim

CNN
LIVE

After a night at the theater, Caroline Isenberg headed home alone. The 23-year-old Harvard graduate and aspiring actress entered the darkened lobby of her Upper West Side apartment house in Manhattan. Inside, Emmanuel Torres, son of the building superintendent, lurked in the shadows. At knife point he forced Isenberg into the elevator. On the roof he tried to rape and rob her. When she resisted, Torres stabbed her twenty-three times. She screamed, "He's going to kill me! I'm bleeding to death!" Neighbors called police, who found the victim in a pool of blood. She died five hours later at St. Luke's Hospital.

"Anyone who was near the building in the early hours of Dec. 2, 'still hears Caroline Isenberg screaming frantically and futilely at the hands of this defendant,' said Patrick J. Dugan, the prosecutor, in urging the judge to give Mr. Torres the maximum sentence of 25 years to life. . . .

"Both Mr. Dugan and the judge spoke at length about all the victims in this case—Miss Isenberg, her family, her friends, the community. . . .

"The judge urged the parents, who are now divorced, 'to put your bottomless grief behind you and, out of love for her and to perpetuate her memory, to carry on as you know she would have done'. . . .

"'Because of this defendant's horrible crime,' the prosecutor said, 'those mothers and fathers sleep less peacefully at night, they worry more, and they pray they never hear the voice of a New York City police officer when they pick up the phone. By murdering this woman, Emmanuel Torres has marred the soul of this city.'"[1] ∎

In this chapter we look at the criminal justice system from another perspective—that of the victims, including family members. We concentrate on the plight of victims and their role in the criminal justice system. This focus is relatively new. Until very recently, the criminal justice system, and the legal system in particular, have been primarily offender oriented. All the attention and resources had been focused on the perpetrator. But the perpetrator is only one of several key persons in the criminal justice process. Although often forgotten or ignored in the past, the victim plays a key role at almost every step.

VICTIMS IN THE CRIMINAL JUSTICE SYSTEM

When social scientists view individuals, they regard them not as isolated beings but as persons who interact with each other. In recent decades, a noticeable change has occurred in law: The law too now recognizes that each criminal actor exists within a social context. What brought about this change in thinking?

Hans von Hentig, scholar of criminal law and criminology, told this story:

It was soon after Hitler had assumed power in Germany when I received an invitation to meet with him at the Reich-Chancellory in Berlin. It was an invitation one could not afford to decline, especially in my case. Hitler knew that I detested him. So I went. Hitler received me with seeming cordiality and explained his vision of greatness for Germany and the Aryan race. Then he looked me straight in the eyes and said, "von Hentig, I need you. Ancient nobility, war hero, scholar with great respect in Europe, leader among German professors. If you join our cause, all the other academics will follow. Are you going to follow me? I am going to make you a very important power in the Reich!"

I replied: "Mr. Chancellor, this is an offer hard to refuse. You will know my answer within twenty-four hours."

I left the Chancellory. My wife was waiting in a taxi-cab—with our suitcases. Within minutes we were on a train to Switzerland. Now Hitler knew our answer. We left for America.[2]

For the first time, von Hentig had experienced the role of the victim, and his thinking changed. He saw crime as the "interaction of perpetrator and victim." In 1941 he published his first article on that topic.[3] But as yet this new perspective on crime and criminals did not have a name.

On March 29, 1947, the Romanian lawyer Beniamin Mendelsohn delivered a remarkable lecture before the Romanian Psychiatric Association in Bucharest. It was entitled "New Bio-Psycho-Social Horizons: Victimology."[4] The new science now had a name: **victimology**—the systematic study of the role played by the victim in a criminal incident and in the criminal justice process. With the publication of von Hentig's monumental work, *The Criminal and His Victim* in 1948, the science of victimology was firmly established.[5] Many leading scholars of criminology and criminal justice have contributed to the development of victimology through their research, and in turn have vastly broadened the capacity of the criminal justice system to deal with crime. Stephen Schafer's principal work, *The Victim and His Criminal* (1968), for example, did much to gain acceptance for victimology in the United States.[6]

Now we are beginning to understand the crucial role victims play in the criminal and juvenile justice processes. But, as the Canadian criminologist Ezzat Fattah demonstrated, the search continues for a more perfect victimology.[7]

If victims do not complain, the process will not start. Victims may play an equally significant role at all subsequent stages, as witnesses, and in the last stage, as resource persons at sentencing or even parole hearings.

victimology
Systematic study of the role played by the victim in a criminal incident and in the criminal process.

WHO ARE THE VICTIMS?

One of the greatest contributions of victimology to the functioning of the criminal justice system is the development of victimization surveys. These surveys were first conducted in 1967 by the President's Commission on Law Enforcement and Administration of Justice. By surveying a large and representative sample of the population as to their victimization by crime, these studies provide a measure of the full extent of crime, far more so than police department crime reports (see Chapter 2).[8] They are therefore particularly important to government agency staffs who must devise crime prevention strategies and deploy resources as cost beneficially as possible.

Research has shown that just as we can describe and categorize offenders, we can describe and categorize victims. Victims of violent crimes are typically black males from lower-income families. White, middle-class persons are more likely to be theft victims. Victimization rates are highest among households that are headed by blacks or young people, are renters rather than owners, include six or more persons, and are located in urban rather than in suburban or rural areas.[9]

In 1991, nearly 23 million American households, or 24 percent, were touched by a crime of violence or theft. The likelihood of such victimization has decreased since 1975, when one-third of American households experienced such crimes. Households in the Northeast are least vulnerable to crime (19%) and those in the West most vulnerable (29%). Southern and midwestern households fall in between. The likelihood of car theft is low: It happens to only 1.8 percent of all households. The likelihood of personal theft is the highest (10.4% of households).[10] As people grow older, their fear of crime tends to increase, but the chances of being victimized decrease with every age group after the age of 24.[11] Finally, although violent crimes are typically associated with an attack from behind on an unknown victim, the reality is quite otherwise. In most homicides and assaults, victims know their assailants.[12] And while it is possible to find common denominators among victims of violence and theft, there is some dispute over who the victims of white-collar and environmental crime are.[13] (See the Criminal Justice in Action box.)

"Teenagers were much more likely than adults to be victims of crimes of violence."
National Crime Survey Report, 1991.

"Five out of every six Americans will be victims of violent crime at least once in their lifetimes."

"Of all the tasks of government, the most basic is to protect its citizens against violence."
John Foster Dulles.

THE CRIMINAL JUSTICE PROCESS FOR VICTIMS: UP TO TRIAL

Survey data have focused attention on the impact of crime and demonstrated the importance of the victim's perception of any criminal event and willingness to report it to the authorities. The victim sometimes determines the course of the criminal justice process by his or her willingness to report a victimization and to testify before the authorities, especially at a trial.[14] But Geis, in interviews with victims, reported that many feel their needs have the lowest priority in the criminal justice system:

Crime victims . . . feel that they are, at best, tolerated and then only with ill-humor. Their role, they say, seems much like that of the expectant father in the hospital at delivery time; necessary for things to have gotten underway in the past but at the moment rather superfluous and mildly bothersome.[15]

Victims have several areas of concern: the bail system, which lets the offender out on the street again; police apathy in apprehending and arresting an offender who fails to appear in court; a public defender who vigorously works for the accused and interferes with the person's getting a deserved punishment. Other victims are concerned with the amount of attention the offender receives while

"Justice, though due to the accused, is due to the accusers too."
Justice Benjamin N. Cardozo.

VICTIMS OF THE CRIMINAL JUSTICE SYSTEM

PARIS, Nov. 16, 1992—For generations, if not centuries, the atrocities committed by Gilles de Rais [known to history as "Bluebeard"] before he was simultaneously hanged and burned in 1440 have served to spook children and to draw tourists to his ruined castles near Nantes in western France." (1)

Five hundred and fifty-two years later a court of scholars acquitted him of all original charges, to which he had been made to confess under torture. The reputation of an innocently executed person was restored.

In this century, twenty-three persons believed by many to be innocent have been executed, and twenty-two others were reprieved just prior to execution (Table 1). Researchers Hugo Adam Bedau and Michael L. Radelet describe a total of 350 twentieth-century cases in which defendants convicted of capital, or potentially capital, crimes have later been found to be innocent (2).

The rate of wrongful convictions

Wrongful convictions are daily occurrences. Their exact number is unknown, but estimates of one-half of 1 percent of all convictions are probably conservative (3). This translates to an annual rate in the United States of 6,000 erroneous convictions. When the miscarriage of justice results in an execution, or a close call, the harm associated with being a victim of the criminal justice system is very clear. Loss of liberty for an innocent person also is

a serious consequence of the miscarriage of justice. And there are other problems associated with erroneous convictions, whether for relatively insignificant crimes or for capital crimes. False charges and wrongful convictions

- distort criminal justice statistics;
- unnecessarily increase the workload of criminal justice agencies;
- constitute criminal offenses by themselves ("False Reports to Law Enforcement Authorities" is a crime under state law);
- cause great agony and torment to those falsely accused or processed by the criminal justice system, especially when they are convicted and imprisoned or executed.

Causes of wrongful conviction

Erroneous convictions and execution of sentences result from a variety of errors. Criminologists C. Ronald Huff, Arye Rattner, and Edward Sagarin studied the issue and concluded that eyewitness misidentification is the single most important factor leading to wrongful conviction in the United States. They include in their report a quote from a judge:

Centuries of experience in the administration of criminal justice have shown that convictions based solely on testimony that identifies a defendant previously unknown to the witness is highly suspect. Of the various kinds of evidence it is the least reliable, especially where unsupported by corroborating evidence. (3, p. 524)

The next most important causes of wrongful conviction are cited by these researchers as police and prosecutorial errors resulting from

unprofessional behavior. Plea-bargaining also results in wrongful conviction—studies have shown that innocent people will plead guilty to avoid the severe punishment they might receive if found guilty by a jury. Community pressure for a conviction, inadequacy of counsel, and false accusations also can result in miscarriage of justice. For example, Deborah Ford, age 36, over a period of six years accused thirteen men of rape, robbery, and larceny. One of the accused received a ninety-day jail term; another was arrested and then released. A third is still in jail. A fourth suspect, with a lengthy criminal history, pleaded guilty. All the charges were without any foundation in fact (4).

Other less frequent causes of wrongful conviction include the mental incompetence of the accused; judicial error, bias, or neglect of duty; errors made by medical examiners or forensic science experts; voluntary and deliberate false confessions; and errors in record keeping or in computerized information systems (3, pp. 528–533).

Overturning wrongful convictions

How are wrongful convictions discovered? In none of the 350 cases examined by Bedau and Radelet was the defendant alone responsible for overturning the conviction. In seven of the cases, the supposed murder victim turned up alive and well and was discovered by someone who knew of the conviction. In other cases, the real culprit confessed.

What recourse do victims of the criminal justice system have? They can bring a civil action against their

TABLE 1 Close Calls (N = 22)*		
Year of Conviction	Defendant	Proximity to Execution
1901	J.B. Brown	At gallows
1907	Zajicek	Three days
1907	Sherman	A few days
1915	Stielow	Strapped in chair
1925	Larkman	Ten hours
1925	Reno	Seven hours
1926	Vargas	Head shaved
1927	Cero	Four hours
1927	Weaver	A few days
1931	Hollins	Thirty hours
1932	Langley	Twenty-five minutes
1933	Bernstein	Within minutes
1936	Jones	Five hours
1937	Zimmerman	Two hours
1942	Wellman	Seated in chair
1949	Irvin	Two days
1950	Bailey	Two days
1953	Morris	Three days
1953	Labat & Poret	Three hours
1956	Miller	Seven hours
1957	Bundy	Three days

*Reprieved within 72 hours of execution.
SOURCE: Hugo A. Bedau and Michael L. Radelet, "Miscarriages of Justice in Potentially Capital Cases," *Stanford Law Review* 40(1) (1987):72.

Randall Ayers, laughing with his sisters on his first day of freedom, served eight years in jail after an erroneous rape conviction resting on mistaken identity.

false accusers for harm suffered, but most accusers are judgment-proof—they cannot pay any damage award. On the basis of "newly discovered evidence," wrongly convicted persons can have their convictions overturned, provided the time period for filing such an appeal has not lapsed. If the appeal time frame for a convict has passed, there is no legal recourse. Occasionally governors issue pardons, and sometimes state legislatures pass special laws indemnifying and exonerating a falsely convicted person.

In the United States, only a few states have created compensation programs for the wrongfully convicted: California, Illinois, New York, Tennessee, and Wisconsin. And these monetary awards, while probably better than no compensation at all, often are inadequate. As one judge who reviewed an award noted:

. . . the legislature and the legal system have a responsibility to . . . diligently attempt to make the person as whole as is possible where the person has been deprived of his freedom and forced to live with criminals. Indeed the legal system is capable of creating few errors that have a greater impact upon an individual than to incarcerate him when he has committed no crime. (3, p. 539)

SOURCES

1. Alan Riding, "550 Years Later, a Bluebeard Has His Day in Court: Not Guilty," *The New York Times,* November 17, 1992, p. A8.
2. Hugo Adam Bedau and Michael L. Radelet, "Miscarriages of Justice in Potentially Capital Cases," *Stanford Law Review* 40 (1987):21–179.
3. C. Ronald Huff, Arye Rattner, and Edward Sagarin, "Guilty until Proved Innocent: Wrongful Conviction and Public Policy," *Crime and Delinquency* 32 (1986):518–544, at p. 523.
4. Lynette Holloway, "False Charges by Woman Culminate in Her Arrest," *The New York Times,* October 18, 1992, p. L7.

QUESTIONS FOR DISCUSSION

Suppose we were to enact legislation to compensate victims of the criminal justice system.

1. Should we exempt anyone from the right to compensation? What about habitual offenders, or those who plead guilty to false charges?
2. What compensation could be made for those who have been executed wrongly?
3. Should such a compensation program provide awards to those who are wrongly accused, wrongly convicted, or only to those who serve a prison sentence?

incarcerated compared with the relative lack of attention they or their relatives receive from the criminal justice system. In short, victims of crime feel that the system is designed for offenders, and not for victims. All the attention—and the due-process guarantees—are showered on offenders. Victims are left out.[16]

In fact, as we will see, this is not entirely so. Victims' frustrations are certainly understandable. If we were to refocus the criminal justice system, victim frustration might diminish and victim participation might increase. In this chapter we will follow the same path through the criminal process we followed earlier with the focus on the accused (Chapter 5) and on juvenile offenders (Chapter 17), but this time with the focus on victims. (See Figure 18.1.)

Entry into the System

Reporting to the Police.   In most cases, police officers are the first criminal justice officials with whom victims of a crime come into contact. Victims expect police to respond to their needs quickly: to accept the allegation, conduct a thorough investigation, recover stolen property, make arrests, and gather enough evidence to lead to a conviction. If the police fail to meet these expectations, victims may become bitter and disillusioned. Police, in return, expect victims to report, identify, and testify. Police frequently complain about citizen apathy in reporting crime incidents. They believe that if the victims were able and willing to provide more accurate accounts of crimes, the police could be more effective.[17]

"Police expect victims to report, identify, and testify."

The Bureau of Justice Statistics (BJS) reports that most crimes, in fact, are *not* reported to the police (see Chapter 2). Generally, victims report about 48 percent of violent crimes, which include rape, robbery, and assault; 29 percent of thefts; approximately 51 percent of burglaries; and 75 percent of motor vehicle thefts.[18] Victims are more likely to report a crime that results in an injury, particularly if the injury is serious. Table 18.1 shows the reasons why victims do not report crimes.

The Police Investigation.   Once the victim makes the decision to report a crime to the police and follows through, clearly he or she wants to be believed. However, the police have wide discretion in deciding if there is sufficient evidence to believe a crime has been committed. At the crime scene, the victim and any witnesses are questioned, usually by a patrol officer, who prepares the initial report. At this point victims are considered "presumptive victims," or **complainants,** because it has yet to be established that a law was actually broken or that someone was criminally harmed.

complainant
Person who files an official complaint with the police, a prosecutor, or a court, usually alleging personal damages and possibly a criminal offense.

At the investigation stage there are two sources of possible conflict between the victim and the police officer: (1) The police may not investigate as thoroughly as the victim desires, and (2) the police may conclude that the victim's charges lack credibility and discontinue the investigation. In most larger cities, police departments tend to be bombarded with complaints about incidents that may be considered too minor to justify spending limited resources. In many departments around the country, both large and small, regulations specify cutoff points below which no action will be taken other than formal noting of the complaint. It is difficult to estimate the number of charges judged to be unfounded (claims of victimization rejected by the police). In a study of California police departments, the "unfounded" rate for burglary was 32 percent; for robbery complaints it was 8 percent.[19]

Police officer interviews victims at the scene.

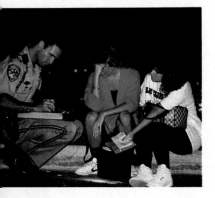

Some scholars have suggested that the police, individually or as a department, may want to downplay the amount of crime. As a result they do not record all reported crimes, even when sufficient evidence is available. For example, an internal investigation in the Chicago Police Department showed that the department discarded as unfounded as many as 40 percent of the rape, robbery, burglary, and theft reports for which there was sufficient evidence that a crime had been committed.[20] Chicago police officers blamed the situation on the depart-

TABLE 18.1 Why Victims Do Not Report Crime, 1990

Reason	Personal Crimes[*]	Household Crimes[*]
Reported to another official	14.7%	3.5%
Private or personal matter	6.8	5.0
Object recovered; offender unsuccessful in crime	24.2	30.5
Not important enough	3.6	3.9
Insurance would not cover	1.7	1.9
Not aware crime occurred until later	4.3	7.4
Unable to recover property; no ID number	6.8	7.9
Lack of proof	10.5	12.4
Police would not want to be bothered	8.0	9.7
Police inefficient, ineffective, or biased	3.3	4.0
Fear of reprisal	1.3	0.6
Too inconvenient or time consuming	4.1	2.6
Other reason	10.7	10.5

[*] Personal crimes N = 14,852,980. Household crimes N = 11,061,260.

Source: Bureau of Justice Statistics, *Criminal Victimization in the United States, 1990* (Washington, D.C.: U.S. Government Printing Office, February 1992), pp. 110–111.

ment, claiming that policies on recording and discarding reported crimes were unclear. They also claimed that unfounded cases were related to "pressure to perform." After departmental policies changed, there was a 25-percent increase in recorded/reported crime.

Generally the police are under no obligation to provide information about the progress of an investigation to the individual crime victim, and the courts are not obligated to provide information about the result of the trial of the accused.[21] Perhaps one of the most disconcerting aspects as far as victims are concerned is that the case may be closed even if it remains unsolved. Police may decide to discontinue any active effort to solve the case when the evidence is insufficient to justify an arrest. To date, victims have no formal means to force the police department to keep a case open.

"To date, victims have no formal means to force the police department to keep a case open."

Victims also expect the police to recover property taken from them. Victims have reason to be dissatisfied and frustrated: The recovery rates for most kinds of theft are low. Only owners of stolen automobiles are likely to get back some or all of what was taken. Throughout the 1980s, the proportion of robbery victims who got some of their property back—either on their own or with police help—was about one in ten.[22]

Even when the police recover stolen property, victims may not have access to it for some time. Both law enforcement officers and prosecutors have the authority to hold seized items as long as they are of value to a continuing investigation or as evidence to be used in the trial. In some cases, property is held until the offender's appeal process is complete.

Prosecution and Pretrial Proceedings

The police are not the only criminal justice officials about whose responsiveness victims voice doubts and concerns. The difficulties, inconveniences, and frustra-

"Victims encounter many difficulties, inconveniences, and frustrations in serving as witnesses for the prosecution."

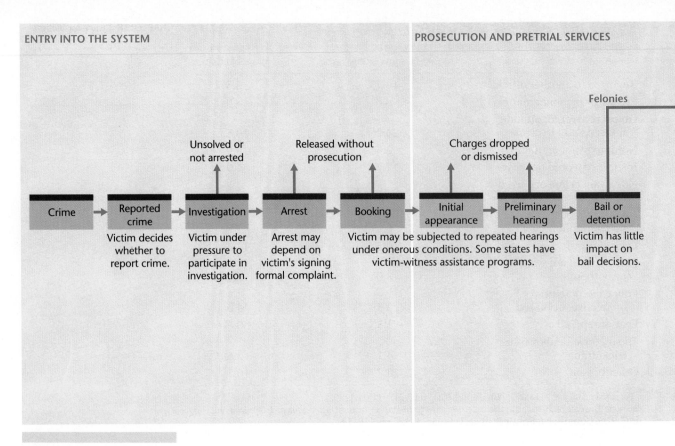

FIGURE 18.1 *The path of the victim through the criminal justice process*

tions faced by victims serving as witnesses for the prosecution have been known for decades, but they have been recorded and publicized only since the emergence of victimology as a science.[23]

There are four general categories of problems victims experience at this stage of their involvement with the criminal justice system:

• Time-related problems: unnecessary trips; long waiting time; time lost from work or school; adjournments; time spent waiting for the case to be handled on the day of the interview contact

• Financial problems: lost income; transportation and parking costs

• Court problems: Difficulties in determining where to go, finding out what to do on arrival; discomfort because of unpleasant waiting conditions; anxiety because of exposure to threatening or unsettling persons

• Personal problems: arranging child care; arranging transportation; having one's property retained as evidence[24]

Involvement with the Prosecutor. Victims may have difficulty in understanding that prosecutors are lawyers for the government who represent the interests of their state, county, or municipality as a whole and not those of individual victims. Prosecutors can become involved in criminal proceedings before an arrest takes place. Some states even require the concurrence of both the judge and the prosecutor to issue an arrest warrant.[25] Statutory requirements like these may involve the victim as a complainant long before the actual decision to prosecute is made. Some victims seek aggressive prosecution; others are ambivalent.

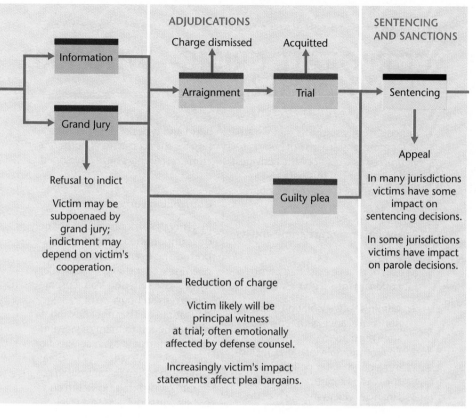

ADJUDICATIONS

SENTENCING AND SANCTIONS

Information

Charge dismissed

Acquitted

Arraignment → Trial → Sentencing

Grand Jury

Refusal to indict

Victim may be subpoenaed by grand jury; indictment may depend on victim's cooperation.

Guilty plea

Appeal

In many jurisdictions victims have some impact on sentencing decisions.

In some jurisdictions victims have impact on parole decisions.

Reduction of charge

Victim likely will be principal witness at trial; often emotionally affected by defense counsel.

Increasingly victim's impact statements affect plea bargains.

Still others try to prevent prosecution by actively discouraging the prosecutor.[26] Reasons for this vary, but most know or have heard about the inconvenience of being a prosecution witness: waiting for hours in dingy corridors; having to return frequently to the same grim surroundings; having to stand around, bewildered and ignored; losing wages in the process or missing school.[27]

Whether a prosecutor will actually seek an indictment or present an information is a matter of considerable discretion (Chapter 11). To some extent, that discretion is influenced by the victims of the crime. The 1982 President's Task Force on Victims of Crime sought to identify several areas of responsibility toward crime victims:

• Keeping victims informed of the status of their case, from initial charges lodged against the defendants to the parole of the convicts
• Bringing to the attention of the appropriate authorities victims' views on bail, pleas, dismissed cases, dropped charges, restitution arrangements
• Protecting victims from harassment, injuries, threats, and other forms of intimidation and retaliation
• Resolving cases as quickly as possible and without unnecessary delays
• Helping victims avoid wasting time and money by notifying them of court appearances and scheduling changes
• Assisting victims in getting back their stolen property recovered by the police[28]

Regardless of their level of participation, victims cannot compel prosecutors to take action against suspects. A number of court decisions have established

CORPORATE CRIME—WHO ARE THE VICTIMS?

- Thirty percent of all employees have personally witnessed violations of criminal or ethics codes by their bosses, including making dangerous products, engaging in criminal activity, practicing discrimination, and/or breaking job safety laws. (1)
- By 1982, it was estimated that price fixing among corporations costs the consumer $60 billion per year. (1, p. 9)
- The Environmental Protection Agency has estimated that 90 percent of the United States' toxic waste is illegally disposed of. (1, p. 10)

We live in a world where savings and loans scandals and hazardous waste dumpsites are in the headlines nearly every day. By most estimates acts by corporations cost us more in human lives and in dollars than does the more highly publicized and more severely punished street crime, with which we are more familiar. For example, it is estimated that 100,000 to 200,000 people die each year from unquestionably job-related illnesses and injuries. That is a rate five times higher than the number of people murdered by all street criminals (1, p. 40). If you add to this the number of people who die each year from causes related to corporate "oversight," marketing, or profiteering, the rate is far higher. "All things considered," concludes sociologist Sandra Walklate, "this evidence strongly suggests that we are at far more physical risk of being victimized as a result of the activities and inactivities of business and industry than by street crime or burglary" (2).

Analyzing corporate crime and its victims

Researchers have classified corporate offenses into six types:

1. Administrative violations, such as noncompliance with federal and state regulations
2. Environmental violations, including air and water pollution and the waste of natural resources
3. Financial violations, such as tax fraud, bribery, and securities violations
4. Labor violations, including unfair labor practices, employment discrimination, and occupational safety and health violations
5. Manufacturing violations, typically involving defective products and cases of consumer fraud
6. Unfair trade practices, such as bid-rigging, price fixing, and misleading or false advertising (3)

Within each of these categories of violations there are victims, and they are victims who rarely, it seems, make their victimization known to authorities—sometimes because they don't even realize they are victims. (3, p. 73).

Criminologist David Shichor distinguishes between direct and indirect victims: Direct victims are those against whom a crime is committed; indirect victims are those who suffer from a violation even though they were not the targets of the offense. Table 1 presents the types of harm and types of direct victimization for the six classes of corporate crime researchers have developed.

Controlling corporate crime

In general, corporate crime not only goes unpunished; it goes unreported and even undetected. As one researcher stated: "The majority of those suffering from corporate crime remain unaware of their victimization—either not knowing it has happened to them or viewing their 'misfortune' as an accident or 'no one's fault'" (4, p. 17). "Clearly a major problem in controlling corporate crime is raising victim and public consciousness to a level where the community desires and supports a policy of more active and effective state control and regulation" (4, p. 66).

"Raising victim and public consciousness" is a problem. When victims are the public-at-large or another corporation, they don't fit our traditional ideas of victims—they are not individuals. And even when the victim is an individual, as in a case of death caused by occupational safety violations, we may not think of him or her as a victim of *crime.* Since we do not know whom to blame (the offender is "depersonalized"), we tend not to blame anyone but to say it was an accident.

According to Shichor, several scholars have suggested that social control of corporations will not occur until public opinion toward "big business" has been changed. A better understanding of corporate victimization could improve efforts to educate the public about corporate crime through publicity, "personalization of the harm," "in-

TABLE 1 Corporate Deviance: Types of Victims, Harms, and Victimization

Corporate Deviance	Victims of Corporate Deviance (Direct)	Type of Harm	Type of Victimization
Administrative	Government	Collective Moral climate	Tertiary Secondary
Environmental	Public	Collective Physical	Tertiary Secondary
Financial			
Payoffs & kickbacks	Government Competitors	Collective Financial	Primary Secondary
Transactions	Consumers Business Partners	Individual Financial	Primary Secondary
Securities	Shareholders Consumers	Individual Financial	Primary
Tax	Government Public	Collective Financial	Tertiary
Accounting	Shareholders	Individual Financial	Primary
Labor			
Discrimination	Public Employees	Individual Financial & moral climate	Primary
Occupational safety	Employees	Individual Physical	Primary
Unfair labor practices	Employees	Individual Financial	Primary Secondary
Wage	Employees	Individual Financial	Primary
Manufacturing	Consumers	Individual Collective Physical & financial	Primary Secondary
Unfair trade	Competitors Business Partners	Individual Collective Financial & moral climate	Primary Secondary

SOURCE: David Shichor, "Corporate Deviance and Corporate Victimization: A Review and Some Elaborations," *International Review of Victimology* 1 (1989):67–88, p. 74.

dividualization of the victim," and "personalization of the offender." The goal, says Shichor, is "to demonstrate to the public and to corporate executives that many corporate actions and business practices are often more harmful than street crimes, victimize a large number of people, undermine public trust in social institutions and deviate from social and legal norms" (3, p. 82).

There is some reason to be optimistic. The United States Sentencing Commission's guidelines for organizations, which became law in November, 1991, significantly raised the level of available penalties (5). Judicial discretion in fashioning a corporate sanction is now far more limited. Over the next several years, it seems clear that corporations will face significant fines and, it is hoped, hear the message of moral condemnation for corporate violators.

SOURCES

1. David R. Simon and D. Stanley Eitzen, *Elite Deviance* (Boston: Allyn and Bacon, 1993), p. 4.
2. Sandra Walklate, *Victimology: The Victim and the Criminal Justice Process* (London: Unwin Hyman, 1989), p. 91.
3. David Shichor, "Corporate Deviance and Corporate Victimization: A Review and Some Elaborations," *International Review of Victimology* 1 (1989):67–88, at p. 72.
4. S. Box, *Power, Crime and Mystification* (London: Tavistock, 1983), p. 31.
5. William S. Laufer, "Culpability and Sentencing the Corporations," *Nebraska Law Review* 71 (1992):1049–1094.

QUESTIONS FOR DISCUSSION

1. Estimates of dollar amounts lost as a result of corporate crime are typically highly speculative. What sorts of practices and violations would you take into account if you were responsible for developing the estimate?
2. Do you think there are any corporate crimes that should be "overlooked" because they are "part of the free enterprise system"?
3. Those injured by corporations are free to sue for damages. Do you think that corporate conduct can be adequately controlled by the threat of a lawsuit, or are more pervasive compensation schemes called for?

Protest at Rocky Flats, near Denver, Colorado, against environmental degradation.

• • • • • • • • • • • • • • • • •

"Victims cannot compel prosecutors to take action against suspects."

presentment
Grand jury's accusation of crime without the application of a prosecutor.

"In most states crime victims have no legal right to participate directly in bail decisions."

"The bullet couldn't kill me, but the judicial system surely will."
Mary Jo Buttafuoco, victim, quoted in *Time*, October 5, 1992, p. 24.

that attorneys general and district attorneys have absolute discretion over whether to charge defendants with crimes and what charges to press or drop. Victims cannot compel prosecutors to act and courts cannot intervene in this decision-making process.[29] However, in some states, but not under federal law, it still is theoretically possible for victims to place a complaint with the grand jury. The grand jury has the traditional right, even without the agreement of the prosecutor, to issue an accusation which, in such a case, is called a **presentment.**[30]

The Bail Process.   Victims, like police officers, resent the granting of bail, or of low bail, to persons charged with crime. The official purpose of bail, however, is the (financial) guarantee of an accused person's appearing for trial. Bail should not be used for other purposes, such as the prevention of crime or retribution. Although bail may be set at any time between arrest and sentencing, the subject of bail is usually introduced during the arraignment. Prosecutor and defense attorney make recommendations to the judge, who makes the final decision.

Currently, in most states crime victims have no legal right to participate directly in bail decisions. However, if a victim does object to a defendant's release from jail pending trial, he or she may ask the prosecutor to advise the judge of those objections. The prosecutor may contact the victim to determine the extent of injury and potential damage to the victim if the defendant were to be released. The prosecutor may then use this information to provide a rationale for seeking a higher bail or for opposing bail completely. Generally, however, victims have no real impact on the bail decision.

The Adjudication Stage

Once a defendant has been formally charged at the arraignment, the ultimate disposition of the case may be settled without trial, through the process known as plea-bargaining. In most criminal proceedings, a plea negotiation takes the place of a criminal trial.

Plea-Bargaining.   Resolving cases by negotiating pleas may be in the best interests of certain crime victims. Besides the certain conviction and vindication that it brings, plea-bargaining may also spare victims the emotional trauma of a trial. But even a victim who generally accepts plea-bargaining may have a strong negative reaction to the plea in his or her particular case. The disposition may be or seem to be much less severe than the disposition a trial might have produced. Some victims may have a difficult time determining whether the plea bargain in their case was reasonable. On the other hand, victims may be satisfied with the results of plea-bargaining.[31]

Victims justify their involvement in the plea-bargaining process by emphasizing their direct involvement in the criminal incident and the personal harm they suffered. Generally, victims are not invited to be present during plea-bargain negotiations with the defense attorney. Prosecutors argue that the victim might want a stronger penalty than what is acceptable to the offender and the defense attorney, and thus help to send to trial a case in which evidence against the accused may be somewhat weak.

Victims traditionally had no right to participate or even be consulted during plea negotiations on the theory that the question of guilt or innocence is to be resolved solely between the two parties to the proceeding, prosecution and defense. But as of 1988 seven states had passed legislation requiring victims to be consulted before acceptance of a plea. Six other states grant victims the right to be consulted, and three grant them the right to be informed of pleas.[32]

In Nevada, judges may interview witnesses, including victims, to inquire if the offenses were more serious than the crimes to which the defendants have pled guilty. In Indiana, judges cannot accept the recommendation of the prosecutor unless victims have been notified of the terms of the plea negotiation and of their right to be present in court when the pleas are considered.[33] The American Bar Association has recently directed prosecuting attorneys to "make every effort to remain advised of the attitudes and sentiments of victims" before reaching a plea agreement.[34] Nevertheless, one researcher established that only one-third of victims chose to participate in the plea-bargaining process, and their participation was minor.[35] Yet another study found victims to be very active in plea-bargaining, as demonstrated by the fact that 46 percent asked for the maximum punishment.[36]

Court Proceedings.   If a case goes to trial, the victim is likely to be called as a witness. Although the defendant, handcuffed and in a holding pen (cell-like locked waiting room), may be less comfortable and more anxious than the victim-witness, the anxiety of the victim and the discomfort of waiting in a courthouse corridor are also painful experiences. During the trial, the victim is subject to rigorous cross-examination by the defense attorney, whose primary purpose may be to damage the victim's credibility as a witness.

Once a case enters the criminal court system, the victim-witness is open to a new type of victimization. In his critical review of the criminal justice system's treatment of witnesses, Michael Ash has labeled these problems "victimization by administrative runaround."[37]

A 1975 Alameda County, California, survey produced the following findings:

"Once a case enters the criminal court system, the victim-witness is open to a new type of victimization."

- Almost 13 percent of the victims and witnesses surveyed were never notified to appear for an interview or for a court session.
- Almost 27 percent of the victims and witnesses surveyed who were called to court were not subsequently called on to give testimony.
- About 95 percent of all witnesses received no compensation for their court appearance.
- Almost 78 percent of those surveyed lost pay due to their court appearance.
- About 45 percent of those surveyed reported that no one explained to them what their court appearance would entail.
- Witnesses waited an average of two hours before taking the stand to testify, and witnesses in sexual assault cases waited an average of seven hours before testifying.
- About 42 percent were never notified of the outcome of the case in which they were involved.
- Almost 30 percent of all victims never got their property back even though the property had been recovered and had been used in court.[38]

While the survey that produced these findings is a modest one, it does seem clear that victims of and witnesses to crime are also victimized by the system.

In the 1980s various organizations contributed to an increasing awareness of the plight of victims. Among them are MADD (Mothers Against Drunk Drivers), SADD (Students Against Drunk Driving), Parents of Murdered Children, and organizations representing women, the elderly, and gays and lesbians. Though not a coalition, they nevertheless make up a victims' rights movement that has spurred the development of legislation and services more responsive to the plight of victims called to testify in court. Several states have increased witness fees from five dollars to as much as thirty dollars a day. Some states have created procedures to notify victims of court proceedings and to guarantee them the right to speedy dispositions of their cases. Nine states and the federal government have enacted comprehensive bills of rights for victims. Thirty-nine states and the U.S. Congress have enacted laws or provided guidelines requiring that victims and witnesses be informed of the scheduling and cancellation of criminal proceedings. These changes have vastly improved the experience of the victim in criminal court proceedings.[39]

GENOCIDE AND POLITICAL MASS MURDER: VICTIMS OF THE STATE

It would be unusual to meet a person who has not heard of the horrors of the holocaust, who did not know about the systematic murder of nearly six million Jews (and countless numbers of Gypsies and political opponents) by the Nazis fifty years ago. Death came by the gas chamber, firing squad, starvation, medical experimentation, torture and disease. Death camps at Auschwitz, Majdanek, Chelmno, Belzec, Treblinka, and Sobibor, among others, engaged in systematic mass exterminations. Inmates also died in huge concentration camps like Bergen-Belsen, Dachau, and Buchenwald. But far fewer people are aware of the extent to which the destruction of ethnic, religious, national, and political groups has occurred in more recent decades. Between 7 and 16 million people have died in genocides and political murders since World War II, a higher death toll than the total number of battle-related fatalities in international and civil wars in the same period (1). At least 10,000 Taiwanese political activists were killed by the Chinese nationalists who took control of Taiwan in 1947. Millions of people have been killed in the former Soviet Union. Some 15,000 Catholics were killed in North Vietnam in the 1950s. The list goes on and on. But more often than not, because those whose lives were ended were so powerless that their destruction was given little

news coverage and little attention, these victims are forgotten.

Victims of political mass murder also have received little attention in criminal justice research, but some scientists are studying the circumstances that lead to the annihilation of groups. Barbara Harff and Ted Robert Gurr have collected data on groups that have suffered genocide and on groups currently subjected to systematic repression or discrimination. The information they have gathered about forty-four cases of genocide or political murder that have occurred since World War II is presented in Table 1. The table is not intended to be all-inclusive; Harff and Gurr considered several factors before listing an episode. The state's complicity in the mass murder had to be firmly established; the episodes had to have lasted for at least six months, excluding brief episodes of mass murder; and, while "body counts" were not as important as the proportion of victims to the total size of the group, very small groups undoubtedly were missed.

Of the episodes of mass murder that appear in Table 1, Harff and Gurr found that five were "pure genocides," in which the victims can be defined primarily in terms of their communal characteristics. Another thirty-one cases were clearly political murders (which they labeled "politicides"), where the victimized group is defined by its social/economic position or by its political opposition to dominant groups. A number of episodes had characteristics of both "politicide" and genocide, which Harff and Gurr coded accordingly.

Prevention

How can these mass murders be prevented? Critical to effective intervention, argue Harff and Gurr, is a reliable database, for which their lists can form a starting point. They conclude: "Detailed monitoring of government actions affecting high-risk minorities should provide the information needed by activists to bring world attention to bear on abusive governments" (1, p. 39). It has been said that "those who cannot remember the past are condemned to repeat it." If the atrocities of World War II are, in fact, remembered, then one must wonder how civilized societies around the world have tolerated the systematic extermination of millions of lives over the past fifty years.

SOURCE

1. Barbara Harff and Ted Robert Gurr, "Victims of the State: Genocides, Politicides and Group Repression since 1945," *International Review of Victimology* 1 (1989):23–41, at p. 30.

QUESTIONS FOR DISCUSSION

1. How are genocide and political mass murder different from deaths caused by military action in war?
2. How can we ensure that international action against genocide and political mass murder is not dependent on the political support of superpowers?
3. Are there groups in the United States possibly at risk of genocide or politicide? If yes, why? If no, what protects them?

TABLE 1 Victims in Forty-four Cases of Genocide and Politicide (Political Mass Murder) since World War II*

Country	Type(†)	Dates of Episode	Communal Victims	Political Victims	Numbers of Victims (in thousands)
USSR	P	1943–47		Repatriated Soviet nationals	500–1100
USSR	G	11/43–1/57	Chechens, Ingushi, Karachai, Balkars		230
USSR	G	5/44–1968	Meskhetians, Crimean Tatars		57–175
China	PG	2–12/47	Taiwanese nationalists		10–40
USSR	P	10/47–?	Ukrainian nationalists		?
Madagascar	P	4/47–12/48	Malagasy nationalists		10–80
Malaya	PG	1948–56	Chinese		5–20
PR China	P	1950–51		Kuomintang cadre, landlords, rich peasants,	800–3000
N. Vietnam	P	1953–54		Catholic landlords, rich and middle peasants	15
Sudan	P	1952–72	Southern nationalists		100–500
Pakistan	PG	1958–74	Baluchi tribesmen		?
PR China	GP	1959	Tibetan Buddhists, landowners		65
Iraq	PG	1959–75	Kurdish nationalists		?
Angola	P	5/61–1962	Kongo	Assimilados	40
Algeria	P	7–12/62		Harkis (French-Muslim troops), OAS supporters	12–60
Paraguay	G	1962–72	Ache Indians		0.9
Rwanda	PG	1963–64	Tutsi ruling class		5–14
Laos	PG	1963–?	Meo tribesmen		18–20
Zaire	P	2/64–1/65	Europeans, missionaries	Educated Congolese	1–10
S. Vietnam	P	1965–72		Civilians in NLF areas	475
Indonesia	GP	10/65–1966	Chinese	Communists	500–1000
Burundi	PG	1965–73	Hutu leaders, peasants		103–205
Nigeria	G	5–10/66	Ibos living in the north		9–30
PR China	P	5/66–1975		Cultural Revol. victims	400–850
Guatemala	P	1966–84	Indians	Leftists	30–63
India	P	1968–82		Naxalites	1–3
Philippines	PG	1968–85	Moro (Muslim) nationalists		10–100
Eq. Guinea	GP	3/69–1979	Bubi tribe, political opponents of Macias		1–50
Uganda	GP	2/71–1979	Karamojong, Acholi, Lango; Catholic clergy	Political opponents of Idi Amin	100–500
Pakistan	PG	3–12/71	Bengali nationalists		1250–3000
Chile	P	9/73–1976		Leftists	5–30
Ethiopia	P	1974–79		Political opposition	30
Kampuchea	GP	1975–79	Muslim Chams	Old regime supporters, urban people, disloyal cadre	800–3000
Indonesia	PG	12/75–pres.	East Timorese nationalists		60–200
Argentina	P	1976–80		Leftists	9–30
Zaire	P	1977–?	Tribal, political opponents of Mobutu		3–4
Burma	G	1978	Muslims in border region		?
Afghanistan	P	1978–pres.		Supporters of old regime, rural supporters of rebels	1000
Uganda	GP	1979–1/86	Karamojong Nilotic tribes, Bagandans	Supporters of Amin regime	50–100
El Salvador	P	1980–pres.		Leftists	20–70
Iran	GP	1981–pres.	Kurds, Baha'is	Mujahedeen	10–20
Syria	P	4/81–2/82		Muslim Brotherhood	5–25
Sri Lanka	PG	1983–8/87	Tamil nationalists		2–10
Ethiopia	PG	1984–85+	Victims of forced resettlement		?

*Episodes of mass murder carried out by or with the complicity of political authorities, directed at distinct communal (ethnic, national, religious) or politically defined groups. Politically organized communal groups, placed in the table between the two column headings, share both kinds of defining traits.

†This code is based on a more precise categorization of types of genocide and politicide:

    G = genocide, victims defined communally   PG = politicides against politically active communal groups

    P = politicide, victims defined politically   GP = episodes with mixed communal and political victims

Source: Barbara Harff and Ted R. Gurr, "Victims of the State: Genocides, Politicides, and Group Repression since 1945," *International Review of Victimology* 1 (1989):23–41, pp. 26–27.

THE VICTIM'S ROLE IN SENTENCING AND CORRECTIONS

". . . victims have tended to be
'forgotten' persons in the post
conviction stages of the criminal
justice process."
Office for Victims of Crime,
Report to Congress, April 1990,
p. xi.

Just as our adversary criminal procedure viewed trial as merely a contest between prosecution and defense, it regarded sentencing and corrections as purely a matter for the judicial and executive arms of government. But here too, changes are occurring, and increasingly victims are becoming participants in sentencing and even release decisions.

Participation in Probation Decisions

In most jurisdictions, victim impact statements are incorporated into the presentence investigation report routinely prepared by the probation officer at the request of a judge. As its name indicates, this statement records the victim's view of the effects of the crime on the victim and the victim's family. Generally recorded by the probation officer after conversation with the victim, the impact statement is an excellent way for the victim to communicate with the sentencing judge.

A sample statement is shown in Figure 18.2. Typically, the probation officer will seek information from the victim concerning personal injury, property loss, the need for restitution, and any other harm the crime has caused the victim. The probation department may also require the victim to file a form indicating the nature and amount of any financial or property loss. Although not specifically required to do so, many probation officers will include the victim's views of the criminal and any sentencing recommendations the victim may wish to make.

Before the invention, adoption, and implementation of the victim impact statement, victims were forced to rely on prosecutors to present their views to the judge. But although victim impact statements and the granting of the allocution privilege (oral testimony given at a sentencing hearing) represent important gains for victims, these practices have not become widespread.

Another more visible and tangible form of victim participation is the order that a defendant released on probation make restitution to the victim. In some states, power to grant probation conditioned on restitution is specifically provided for in statutes.[40]

The Victim's Role in Sentencing

Many policymakers, judges, and scholars fear that allowing victims a role in the sentencing process will interfere with the legislatively mandated aims of punishment, whether these be just deserts, deterrence, incapacitation, or rehabilitation, and might even result in undue delays.[41] But policies are changing rapidly. Victims now have the right to make statements at sentencing hearings in thirty states.[42] While victims' influence is still limited, their views are considered by the sentencing court, either in personal appearances (allocution) or in written statements, and they do have an impact.[43] In capital punishment cases, the Supreme Court has ruled (1987) that such statements are constitutionally permissible and do not create an unacceptable risk of the imposition of the death penalty by juries in an arbitrary and capricious manner.[44]

Crime victims and the general public both share the perception that many judges are too lenient. A study of over 300 victims of felonies in eight jurisdictions indicated that most victims were dissatisfied with the sentences judges handed down in their cases. Eighty-six percent agreed with the statement that "guilty offenders are not punished harshly enough." Only 30 percent agreed that "the court system cares about victims' needs."[45] These views are comparable to those of the population at large. A nationwide poll (1972) asked: "In general, do you think courts in this area deal too harshly or not harshly enough with criminals?" Sixty-six percent answered "not harshly enough." By 1976 this figure had

*Mary Jo Buttafuoco at the
sentencing hearing of Amy
Fisher, who was convicted of
attempting to kill Mary Jo,
December 1992.*

"Crime victims and the general
public both share the perception
that many judges are too lenient."

STATE VS. _____ CASE # _____ SENTENCING DATE _____

To assist the court in its efforts to weigh all factors before imposing sentence, we request your *voluntary* cooperation in completing this form. This statement is intended to be submitted to the judge imposing sentence herein.

_____

NAME OF VICTIM: _____

ADDRESS:

STREET _____ CITY _____ STATE _____ ZIPCODE _____ DATE OF BIRTH: _____

1. Please describe the nature of the incident in which you were involved.

2. As a result of this incident, were you physically injured? If yes, please describe the extent of your injuries.

3. Did you require medical treatment for the injuries sustained? If yes, please describe the treatment received and the length of time treatment was or is required.

4. Amount of expenses incurred to date as a result of medical treatment received: $_____
Anticipated expenses: $_____

5. Were you psychologically injured as a result of this incident? If yes, please describe the psychological impact the incident has had on you.

6. Have you received any counseling or therapy as a result of this incident? If yes, please describe the length of time you have been or will be undergoing counseling or therapy, and the type of treatment you have received.

7. Amount of expenses incurred to date as a result of counseling or therapy received: $_____

8. Has this incident affected your ability to earn a living? If yes, please describe your employment, and specify how and to what extent your ability to earn a living has been affected, days lost from work, etc.

9. Have you incurred any other expenses or losses as a result of this incident? If yes, please describe.

10. Did insurance cover any of the expenses you have incurred as a result of this incident? If yes, please explain.

11. Has this incident in any way affected your lifestyle or your family's lifestyle? If yes, please explain.

12. Are you or members of your family experiencing any other residual effects of this incident?

13. Please describe what being the victim of crime has meant to you and to your family.

14. What are your feelings about the criminal justice system? Have your feelings changed as a result of this incident? Please explain.

15. Do you have any thoughts or suggestions on the sentence the Court should impose herein? Please explain, indicating whether you favor imprisonment.

This form is subscribed and affirmed as true under the penalties of perjury. The information and thoughts you have provided are very much appreciated.

_____   _____
          DATE   SIGNATURE

FIGURE 18.2 *Sample victim impact statement* (*Source:* Washington Legal Foundation, 1981.)

risen to 81 percent, and in 1986 it stood at 85 percent.[46] Because of this documented punitive attitude, politicians and legislators are reluctant to accord greater weight to victim participation at sentencing. But the debate continues.

Victims and the Parole Process

Whether officially or unofficially, the public has always had an impact on the parole decision. Victims and victim interest groups watch these decisions carefully. The police lobby keeps track of convicts who have killed a police officer; national nursing associations attended all of Richard Speck's hearings until his death. Opposition to parole on the part of victims, relatives, or victim interest groups becomes particularly vociferous when it is felt that the sentence was too lenient in the first place. Conflicts also arise when victims have not been adequately notified of a scheduled parole board hearing, or when the victims' wishes are not adequately considered.

Several states have granted victims the specific right to attend parole hearings of convicts who have injured or otherwise harmed them. However, most states restrict these appearances to victims of serious or violent crimes. In California, the victim, or the victim's next of kin, has the right to make a statement, either in person or in writing, to the panel conducting the hearing.[47] But victims and their families are notified of parole hearings only if they request such notification. The statement may contain comments about both the crime and the inmate. A few states require parole boards to notify victims of their right to appear, either through personal letters or through notices in local newspapers.

Because parole hearings are held under tight security within the walls of a medium or maximum security prison, conditions are likely to be quite uncomfortable. Victims who choose to speak at the hearing, like everyone else entering the prison, must undergo a clearance procedure that customarily includes the temporary removal of belts, jewelry, and shoes. Items such as keys may be held in custody until the victim leaves the prison. While waiting for the hearing, the victim is often seated within view of the offender-inmate, who is secured in a nearby holding cell.

Hearings are conducted in a structured manner and last between two and three hours. The victim may speak after the panel members have questioned the inmate, the prosecutor has argued against parole, and the defense attorney has argued in favor. The victim does not speak directly to the inmate; rather, he or she addresses the members of the panel. The victim is not usually subject to cross-examination by the defense attorney and usually is not asked questions by the panel members.

Offender Release or Escape: Victim Protection

Victims may want to keep track of the whereabouts of offenders, especially if they have been threatened with reprisal. Without notification from corrections or parole authorities, victims are unable to take precautions, or at least prepare themselves mentally for possible face-to-face encounters with the offender.[48]

One potential problem related to victim notification of an offender's release is locating victims. A lot of time may elapse between the initial sentencing stage and the offender's release from prison. During that time victims may have moved and not informed the appropriate agency of their current address. For example, the parole board in Illinois reported that over 50 percent of its letter notifications were returned because victims had moved and had not left forwarding addresses.[49]

It is understandable that victims become fearful if their assailants are once again in the community. This anxiety increases when a victimizer has escaped from prison, an event that is frequently highly publicized. It is normal procedure everywhere for law enforcement authorities—including police and corrections—

"My name is Rona Smith. As some of you might know, Wesley Miller killed my sister, Retha. He stabbed her 38 times. And as you might also know, he was mandatorily released from prison and is now living in Wichita Falls." Rona Smith, at meeting of Fort Worth support group Families of Murder Victims, quoted in *The Houston Chronicle,* January 30, 1992, p. 10.

to notify victims if at all possible. Yet this is not a legal requirement except in California, where, in the event of an escape, the Department of Corrections must immediately notify the victim (or next of kin if the crime was a homicide) *if* notice was previously requested. If the inmate is recaptured, notice of this event must also be sent within thirty days.[50]

COMPENSATION AND RESTITUTION

Compensation and restitution are different remedies. Both are intended to provide victims with some reparation for damages. With restitution, the offender is required to make the reparation. With compensation, there is no link between offender and victim. Rather, the state pays the compensation much like an insurance company paying a damage claim.

"Compensation and restitution are different remedies."

In 1957 the English magistrate and social reformer Margery Fry stunned the criminal justice community with a call for "justice for victims" in the form of government payments to compensate victims for their losses.[51] Reactions of the criminal justice community to this challenge were immediate and worldwide.[52] Some scholars responded with surprise. Had the law not always provided victims with the right to sue for damages? Some responded with caution: Why not rely on health and property insurance? Some responded with enthusiasm: Legislation was enacted, first in New Zealand, then all over the world, including, by 1990, in forty-four U.S. states. (Table 18.2). The fact is that the law had always provided the victims of crime the right to sue those who had harmed them. But the victimizers often were and are indigent. Private insurance to cover crime losses is available, but the poor cannot afford insurance. Therefore, legislation was needed to provide equitable relief for all crime victims, either by compensation or by restitution.

Government Compensation Programs

The earliest reference to government compensation for crime victims can be found in the Babylonian Code of Hammurabi (about 1750 B.C.), which is one of the oldest written bodies of criminal law. The code instructed territorial governors to compensate robbery victims. In the case of murder, the governor was to pay the heirs a specific sum in silver from the treasury. But later in history the focus of the law changed: Both Roman and Germanic law used forms of restitution by which offenders had to cover the victim's losses. In the Middle Ages, and indeed until recently, victims had only civil remedies to rely on.

". . . too few victim assistance programs are located in high-crime neighborhoods to serve poor and minority victims." Office for Victims of Crime, *Report to Congress*, April 1990.

Today, government compensation programs for the victims of violent crime are common. However, relatively few eligible victims file claims and receive awards, with rates widely varying among the states.[53] As Table 18.2 shows, there are considerable variations in **victim compensation** programs. However, all share some basic features:

All grant full reimbursements only to innocent victims. If the victim is deemed partially responsible for the crime, he or she receives a significantly reduced award. If the victim was injured by a close relative, he or she usually receives no award.

victim compensation
Scheme, usually based on statute, by which victims of violent crime may receive a limited financial award out of public funds for criminal harm suffered.

Most deal only with serious crimes—those that result in injury or death. With minor exceptions, the victim receives no awards for loss of or damage to property, or for injuries received through violations of traffic laws, or for pain and suffering. Payments can be made for medical expenses as well as for some of the earnings lost because of missed work. If a victim dies as a result of injuries, the family is eligible for assistance to cover funeral and burial costs and, sometimes, a death benefit or pension for surviving dependents.

". . . this modest financial assistance can be the lifeline that preserves not only some modicum of stability, but also life itself." President's Task Force on Victims of Crime, *Final Report*, 1982, p. 38.

TABLE 18.2 Compensation Programs to Help Victims of Violent Crime

State	Victim Compensation Board Location[*]	Financial Award	To Qualify, Victim Must: Show Financial Need	To Qualify, Victim Must: Report to Police Within:	To Qualify, Victim Must: File Claim Within:
Alabama	Alabama Crime Victim Compensation Commission	$0–10,000	No	3 days	12 mos.
Alaska	Department of Public Safety	$0–40,000	Yes	5	24
Arizona	Arizona Criminal Justice Commission	—	Yes	3	—
California	State Board of Control	$100–46,000	Yes	[†]	12
Colorado	Judicial district boards	$25–10,000	No	3	6
Connecticut	Criminal Injuries Compensation Board	$100–10,000	No	5	24
Delaware	Violent Crimes Board	$25–20,000	No	[†]	12
D.C.	Office of Crime Victim Compensation	$100–25,000	Yes	7	6
Florida	Department of Labor and Employment Security, Workmen's Compensation Division	$0–10,000	Yes	3	12
Hawaii	Department of Corrections	$0–10,000	No	[†]	18
Idaho	Industrial Commission	$0–25,000	No	3	12
Illinois	Court of Claims	$0–25,000	No	3	12
Indiana	Industrial Board	$100–10,000	No	2	24
Iowa	Department of Public Safety	$0–20,000	No	1	6
Kansas	Executive Department	$100–10,000	Yes	3	12
Kentucky	Victim Compensation Board	$0–25,000	Yes	2	12
Louisiana	Commission on Law Enforcement	$100–10,000	No	3	12
Maryland	Criminal Injuries Compensation Board	$0–45,000	Yes	2	6
Massachusetts	District Court system	$0–25,000	No	2	12
Michigan	Department of Management and Budget	$200–15,000	Yes	2	12
Minnesota	Crime Victims Reparation Board	$100–50,000	No	5	12
Missouri	Division of Workmen's Compensation	$200–10,000	No	2	12
Montana	Crime Control Division	$0–25,000	No	3	12

[*] If location of the board is not indicated in the state statute, the board itself is noted.
[†] Must report but no time limit specified.
[**] Program administratively established but not funded.
[††] Plus unlimited medical expenses.

State	Victim Compensation Board Location[*]	Financial Award	To Qualify, Victim Must: Show Financial Need	Report to Police Within:	File Claim Within:
Nebraska	Commission on Law Enforcement and Criminal Justice	$0–10,000	Yes	3	24
Nevada	Board of Examiners and Department of Administration	$0–15,000	Yes	5	12
New Jersey	Executive Branch	$0–25,000	NO	90	24
New Mexico	Executive Branch	$0–12,500	No	30	12
New York	Executive Department	$0–30,000[††]	Yes	7	12
North Carolina[**]	Department of Crime Control and Public Safety	$100–20,000		3	24
North Dakota	Workmen's Compensation Bureau	$0–25,000	No	3	12
Ohio	Court of Claims Commissioners	$0–25,000	No	3	12
Oklahoma	Crime Victims Board	$0–10,000	No	3	12
Oregon	Department of Justice Workmen's Compensation Board	$250–23,000	No	3	6
Pennsylvania	Crime Victims Board	$0–35,000	No	3	12
Rhode Island	Superior Court system	$0–25,000	No	10	24
South Carolina	Crime Victims Advisory Board	$100–3,000	No	2	6
Tennessee	Court of Claims Commission	$0–5,000	No	2	12
Texas	Industrial Accident Board	$0–25,000	No	3	6
Utah	Department of Administrative Services	$0–25,000	—	7	12
Virgin Islands	Department of Social Welfare	Up to $25,000	No	1	24
Virginia	Industrial Commission	$0–15,000	No	5	24
Washington	Department of Labor and Industries	$0–15,000[††]	No	3	12
West Virginia	Court of Claims Commissioner	$0–35,000	No	3	24
Wisconsin	Department of Justice	$0–40,000	No	5	12

SOURCE: U.S. Department of Justice, Bureau of Justice Statistics, *Report to the Nation on Crime and Justice,* 2d ed. (Washington, D.C.: U.S. Government Printing Office, March 1988), p. 37.

All state programs prohibit double recoveries. Any money collected from insurance policies or government agencies is deducted from the compensation board's final award. If offenders are apprehended, found guilty, and required to make restitution to their victims, state programs deduct that amount.

The burden of proof that a violent crime did take place falls on the victim. Additionally, the victim must have reported the crime to the police and must cooperate with any investigation and prosecution to remain eligible.

The forty-four state programs also differ significantly in several ways:

- The time period within which victims must report the crime
- The length of time victims can take before applying for reimbursement
- The amount of loss required to be eligible for an award
- The amount of compensation
- The source of compensation
- Whether the program will lend victims money to cover immediate expenses before their case is heard
- Whether victims who are out-of-state visitors or commuters are covered

The funding for most compensation programs is derived from what are called "penalty assessments" or "abusers' taxes." These include fines and surcharges levied on those convicted of traffic violations, misdemeanors, and felonies, plus, in some states, taxes imposed on the earnings of offenders on work release programs, as well as collateral forfeited by defendants who jump bail. Other programs rely on general revenue funds or on taxes. When Congress passed the Victims of Crime Act in 1984, substantial financial assistance became available to state and local crime victim compensation and assistance programs.[54]

To ensure that government funds are available to those most in need, some states deny benefits to victims who have not suffered serious financial hardships. This is commonly called the "means test." Many programs also have a "minimum loss" provision and will not consider claims under $100. Others eliminate small claims under a "deductible clause" that stipulates the victim is responsible for the first $100 or $200 of the loss.[55]

Several trends in victim compensation programs are becoming evident. Many governments are periodically raising the upper limits for awards because of substantial increases in the cost of living. Programs are also more likely to rely on penalties rather than taxes. Minimum loss provisions are being dropped, as is the "means test." Some states have started experimental programs to reimburse victims for pain and suffering, child care, cleaning up at the crime scene, and replacing essential personal property. Other programs are extending eligibility to those injured by drunken drivers. A few programs are compensating incest and sexual assault victims who escape without physical injuries, and others assist parents of missing children.[56]

Restitution from the Offender

In ancient law, restitution, or a payment from the wrongdoer to the victim, was intended not only to make the victim whole again but also to satisfy the victim's desire for vengeance. Restitution was also intended to encourage a lasting peace between the parties.[57] During the last half century, restitution has made a comeback. It has been increasingly sanctioned by statutes and has become a common condition for probation.

"Restitution was also intended to encourage a lasting peace between the parties."

Restitution is based on the idea of the offender's responsibility to his or her victim. Authorized officials of the justice system impose sanctions that require offenders to return stolen goods to their owners, to hand over equivalent amounts of money to cover out-of-pocket expenses, or to provide services to those they have harmed. Four different types of restitution arrangements are possible and may be combined:

- Payments by the offender to the actual victim or through an intermediary (this is the most common definition and actual use of restitution)
- Earnings shared with some community agency or group serving as a "substitute victim"
- Personal services performed by the offender to benefit the victim[58] (an uncommon arrangement)
- Labor donated by the offender for the good of the community (community service), which is frequently ordered in lieu of imprisonment[59]

Restitution amounts and payments must be formally specified and scheduled. Probation officers can include restitution plans and recommendations in their presentence reports. Prosecutors can investigate defendants' financial status and ask for repayments in plea negotiations. Victim impact statements or allocutions can be used by victims to inform the court of costs and losses. Restitution contracts can be administered and supervised by any criminal justice agency. When the burden of supervision is on the court system, the court clerk usually is responsible for seeing that victims actually receive payments.

Restitution may seem to be an underutilized, highly flexible, and viable sanction. Yet, although it may be morally appropriate and theoretically possible, in practice it does not help most victims. Only a small percentage of victims will ever get anything back from those who have harmed them. Just as most criminals escape punishment, most also evade restitution obligations. Of offenders who are apprehended and convicted, or who plead guilty, not all are willing or able to repay their victims. For restitution to succeed as a program and as a sanction, all parties—victims, offenders, and criminal justice decision-makers—must cooperate. A systematic approach is needed to identify appropriate victims and offenders, investigate losses, schedule repayment, monitor compliance, and collect and keep track of all disbursements.[60]

"Only a small percentage of victims will ever get anything from those who have harmed them."

Initial research conducted on a few restitution programs suggests that they are feasible in both juvenile and adult correctional systems. Moreover, victims of crime, and the public generally, support such programs.[61] A 1990 evaluation of a Texas program found it to be cost beneficial and at least as effective as prison and parole in controlling crime. Moreover, the program received considerable support from the community because it brought peace among participants and some restoration of loss.[62]

For a summary of the current status of all victims' rights see Table 18.3.

Victim–Offender Mediation

If the objective is to achieve a lasting peace, perhaps even a reconciliation, between offender and victim, might it not be advisable to bring offender and victim together? These ideas are behind the recent emergence of victim–offender mediation programs.

Mediation programs provide opportunities for citizen participation in the criminal justice process. Mediation programs are intended to facilitate communication between offenders and victims, encourage offenders to assume responsibility for their conduct, and provide better opportunities for social control of offenders than do programs that separate and isolate offenders from their community and those they have harmed.[63]

How mediation works.   In mediation, a neutral person helps the feuding parties arrive at their own settlement. The mediator provides opportunities for discussion, solicits viewpoints, and helps uncover areas of common interest to provide the basis for a mutually acceptable compromise. Hearings are usually held at dispute resolution centers and are scheduled at the convenience of the participants, not the staff. The rules of evidence are minimized; witnesses are not sworn in and mediators do not wear robes or sit on raised seating (as judges normally

TABLE 18.3 Victims' Rights: A Summary

Subject	Right of Victims	Enactment
General rights	To be "read their rights" as soon as a crime is reported, or to be provided with written information about all obligations, services, and opportunities for protection and reimbursement	Many local jurisdictions
Case status	To be kept posted about any progress in their cases; to be advised when arrest warrants are issued or suspects are taken into custody	Many local jurisdictions
Employer intercession	To have the prosecutor explain to the complaining witness's employer that the victim should not be penalized for missing work because of court appearances	35 states
Creditor intercession	To have the prosecutor explain to creditors like banks and landlords that crime-inflicted financial losses necessitate delays in paying bills	10 states
Offender's age	To be assured that juvenile offenders do not escape full responsibility for serious crimes, by having such cases transferred from juvenile court to adult criminal court	50 states
Denial of bail	To be protected from suspects whose pretrial release on bail might endanger them	24 states
Suspect out on bail	To be notified that a suspect arrested for the crime has been released on bail	21 states
Protection from further harm	To be reasonably protected during the pretrial release period from the accused through orders of protection and by increased penalties for acts of harassment and intimidation	46 states
Plea bargaining	To participate or be consulted	13 states
Negotiated plea	To be notified that both sides have agreed to a plea of guilty in return for some consideration	28 states
Court appearances	To be notified in advance of all court proceedings and of changes in required court appearances	41 states
Secure waiting areas	To be provided with courthouse waiting rooms separate from those used by defendants, defense witnesses, and spectators	31 states
Defenses	To be assured that offenders cannot avoid imprisonment by pleading "not guilty by reason of insanity," through the substitution of "guilty and mentally ill," which requires treatment in a mental institution followed by incarceration in prison	16 states

Subject	Right of Victims	Enactment
Counseling	To be assured that statements divulged to counselors remain confidential if requested by the defense during the discovery phase of court proceedings	20 states
Evidence	To be assured that defendants cannot benefit from the exclusion of illegally gathered evidence, by having all evidence obtained by the police in good faith declared admissible in trials	1 state
Sentencing	To make statements orally (allocution) or in writing, at sentencing hearing	30 states
Sentence and final disposition	To be notified of the verdict and sentence after a trial, and the final disposition after appeals	35 states
Appeals	To appeal sentences that seem too lenient	1 state
Work release	To be notified if the convict will be permitted to leave the prison to perform a job during specified hours	29 states
Notoriety for profit	To have any royalties and fees paid to notorious criminals confiscated and used to repay victims or to fund victim services	42 states
Abuser's tax	To have penalty assessments collected from felons, misdemeanants, and traffic law violators to pay for victim services, compensation, and assistance programs	28 states
Parole hearings	To be notified when a prisoner will be appearing before a parole board to seek early release	44 states
Pardon	To be notified if the governor is considering pardoning the convict	27 states
Release of a felon	To be notified when a prisoner is to be released on parole or because the sentence has expired	39 states
Prison escape	To be notified if the convict has escaped from confinement	23 states
Return of stolen property	To have recovered stolen property that has been held as evidence returned expeditiously by the police or prosecution	43 states
Compensation	To be reimbursed for out-of-pocket expenses for medical bills and lost wages arising from injuries inflicted during a violent crime	45 states
Restitution	To receive mandatory repayments from convicts who are put on probation or parole unless a judge explains in writing the reasons for not imposing this obligation	33 states

SOURCE: Based on Andrew Karmen, *Crime Victims*, 2d ed. (Pacific Grove, Calif.: Brooks-Cole, 1990), p. 332, updated.

do in courtrooms). Nontechnical language is used and only limited records of the proceedings are kept.[64]

A typical hearing involves one or two mediators, the disputants, and perhaps a witness. At the outset the disputants are reminded that their participation is voluntary, and that either party can withdraw at any point and pursue the matter with other criminal justice agencies—police, prosecutor, criminal or civil court. Each party tells his or her side of the story without interruption. Then the disputants tell the mediator what arrangements they are willing to accept and what accommodations they are likely to make. When an understanding is reached, a contract is drawn up detailing, in simple language, the terms they have agreed to abide by in the future.[65]

Both parties are given a copy of the agreement and are encouraged to return to the center if the conditions are not fulfilled. While the dispute resolution centers have no authority to enforce the terms of the contracts, the threat of return to the criminal justice system can strongly encourage compliance.

Advantages and Disadvantages of Victim–Offender Mediation.
From a victim's perspective, mediation has several advantages over adjudication in criminal or civil court. Cases are often handled sooner, cost less in terms of time and money, and are heard at times and places convenient to the participants. Victims who do not want to press charges now have another option besides the traditional criminal justice process. Those who dread testifying and being cross-examined in open court can choose to participate in a closed-door hearing. Finally, the agreed-upon settlement can be seen as a vindication if the respondent (offender) takes responsibility for harm caused.

Victim–offender mediation also has its drawbacks. For victims intent on exacting revenge, the greatest disadvantage is that the process is not punishment oriented. Dispute resolution centers are not authorized to convict offenders, label them "criminals," and fine or incarcerate them. To improve the chances of reconciliation, retaliation is not permitted. Obviously, some victims do not want to be reconciled with their offenders.[66] Another drawback is that the complainants' (victims') conduct is more open to scrutiny, especially in the absence of rules of evidence. To reach a compromise, complainants might feel pressured to concede more responsibility (involvement) than they feel they should.

On balance, however, victim–offender mediation programs seem feasible and sensible, and a promising alternative for the future.

VICTIMS AND THE MEDIA

"Sensational media coverage may aggravate the victim's plight."

The media—newspapers, radio, television, magazines—report accounts of crime as front page items and lead stories. These crime stories often include details about the victim, and are justified as "human interest" stories. It is not a revelation that bad news sells. But sensational coverage may aggravate the victim's plight, whether the report is understated or overstated. When a crime story makes the headlines of a local newspaper or is featured as the lead story in a television news broadcast, the victim suffers an invasion of privacy. The victim may also experience a loss of control as others comment on, interpret, and impose judgments on the case.

Victim advocates, editors, and journalists have begun to address questions of ethics concerning media portrayal of crime victims. There appears to be a consensus that media portrayals of the victim's plight are abusive, unethical, and unfair if

• names and exact addresses are needlessly made public, and repeated in subsequent accounts

- the victim's family finds out about the crime from media coverage instead of being personally notified by the victim or the police
- victims are hounded at home or at work by packs of reporters and camera crews
- reporters use deceit or intense pressure to convince victims to participate in interviews
- reporters intrude at private moments of shock and grief
- camera crews shoot pictures in poor taste, such as blood stains at the scene of the crime, dead bodies, or hysterical relatives
- reporters conduct interviews with children who were victimized or who are relatives or eyewitnesses
- editors run headlines and captions that demean the victim and reduce him or her to less than a person, and merely a category, using labels such as "blonde" or "model"
- reporters recklessly spread half-truths, inaccuracies, or unchecked or misinterpreted details[67]

There are several ways to stop or decrease unfair treatment of victims by insensitive journalists. Some have suggested that the media should adopt a code of ethics, part of which involves reading victims their rights at the outset of interviews, just as the police read suspects their Miranda rights.[68]

According to the Reporters Committee for Freedom of the Press, the states of Colorado, Washington, and Oklahoma have all passed or are considering legislation to protect the identity of sexual assault victims. These moves follow the acquittal of William Kennedy Smith, who was accused of rape in Florida. Ironically, Florida was then the only state to have a law prohibiting identification of a rape victim at any age. Several newspapers, including a Florida-based tabloid, *The Globe*, did reveal her name, as did the NBC television network. The State of Florida prosecuted the newspaper and a judge declared the law unconstitutional.

The latest state to consider providing protection to rape victims against having their identities disclosed is New Jersey, where Assemblyperson Lee Solomon introduced a bill on April 30, 1992, that would make it a disorderly persons offense to disclose the name of an adult victim of rape. The offense would be punishable by a sentence of up to six months' imprisonment, a fine of $1,000, or both. There are opponents to the bill. Many people feel that the only way to remove the stigma attached to rape is to treat it like any other violent crime—without secrecy. Others claim that if the government is able to decide what is news and orders restrictions on its dissemination, freedom of the press is destroyed and the public's right to know is lost.

As a recent highly publicized rape trial opened in Queens, New York, in 1992, women demonstrators protested continuing victimization of women by rapists and the inadequacies of the legal process in these cases.

REVIEW

In ancient law, the victim played a role in the criminal event equal to that of the perpetrator. Then for a thousand years, the victim was all but forgotten. Now the pendulum has swung back again with the emergence of "victimology" fifty years ago, with the creation of victim compensation schemes forty years ago, with the invention of victimization surveys thirty years ago, and with the passage of victim advocacy and victim protection legislation less than twenty years ago.

Victims play a significant role in the criminal justice process. There is active victim participation at every juncture of the criminal procedure, from reporting the event, to partici-

pating in identification and arrest, to prosecution and trial. Very recently, largely through victim impact statements, in many jurisdictions victims have begun to exert an influence on sentencing and release as well. Remedies for victims can take various forms: government compensation programs or restitution from the offender, sometimes through institutional restitution programs, and mediation.

Much of the current victims' rights effort is aimed at minimizing the hardships the victims encounter in their involvement with the criminal justice system. Improvements are being made, but the system is still far from providing justice for victims.

Notes

1. Marcia Chambers, "Life Term Imposed in Rooftop Slaying of Aspiring Actress," *The New York Times*, August 6, 1985, p. A1.

2. G. O. W. Mueller in conversation with Hans Ritter von Hentig, August 1961.

3. Hans von Hentig, "Remarks on the Interaction of Perpetrator and Victim," *Journal of Criminal Law and Criminology* 31 (1941):303–309.

4. See Beniamin Mendelsohn, "The Origin of the Doctrine of Victimology," in *Victimology*, eds. Israel Drapkin and Emilio Viano (Lexington, Mass.: Lexington Books, 1974), pp. 3–4. It appears that in America the term "victimology" was first used by the psychiatrist Frederick Wertham in his book, *The Show of Violence* (New York: Doubleday, 1949); see Ezzat A. Fattah, "Victims and Victimology: The Facts and the Rhetoric," *International Review of Victimology* 1 (1989):44–66.

5. Hans von Hentig, *The Criminal and His Victim* (New Haven, Conn.: Yale University Press, 1948).

6. Stephen Schafer, *The Victim and His Criminal, A Study in Functional Responsibility* (New York: Random House, 1968). See also Stephen Schafer, *Victimology: The Victim and His Criminal* (Reston, Va.: Reston Publishing, 1977); Stephen Schafer, *Compensation and Restitution to Victims of Crime* (Montclair, N.J.: Patterson Smith, 1970 [first edition, 1960]).

7. Ezzat A. Fattah, ed., *Towards a Critical Victimology* (New York: St. Martin's Press, 1992).

8. Albert J. Reiss, Jr., *Studies in Crime and Law Enforcement in Major Metropolitan Areas*, The President's Commission on Law Enforcement and Administration of Justice, Field Survey I–III (Washington, D.C.: U.S. Government Printing Office, 1967). R. F. Sparks, H. G. Green, and D. J. Dodd, *Surveying Victims: A Study of the Measurement of Criminal Victimization, Perceptions of Crime and Attitudes to Criminal Justice* (Chichester, England and New York, N.Y.: Wiley, 1977).

9. Bureau of Justice Statistics Bulletin, *Crime and the Nation's Households, 1991* (Washington, D.C.: U.S. Government Printing Office, July 1992).

10. Ibid.

11. For a discussion of fear among the elderly, see Ronald L. Akers, Anthony J. La Greca, Christine Sellers, and John Cochran, "Fear of Crime and Victimization among the Elderly in Different Types of Communities," *Criminology* 25 (1987):487–505. See also Vincent J. Webb and Ineke Hahn Marshall, "Response to Criminal Victimization by Older Americans," *Criminal Justice and Behavior* 16 (1989):239–259. For a discussion of the need to assess level of threat in the environment and the supply of safety in relation to fear of crime, see J. J. Gibbs and K. Hanrahan, "Safety Demand and Supply: An Alternative to Fear of Crime," *Justice Quarterly* (1993). See also Mark Warr, "Fear of Victimization and Sensitivity to Risk," *Journal of Quantitative Criminology* 3 (1987):29–46.

12. Marvin E. Wolfgang, *Patterns in Criminal Homicide* (Philadelphia, Pa.: University of Pennsylvania Press, 1958). See also Robert Lee Pierce and Rosilee Trotta, "Abused Parents: A Hidden Family Problem," *Journal of Family Violence* 1(1986):99–110.

13. Hans Joachim Schneider, "The Present Situation of Victimology in the World," in *The Victim in International Perspective*, ed. Hans Joachim Schneider (Berlin: Walter de Gruyter, 1982), pp. 11–46, at p. 14.

14. Martin S. Greenberg and R. Barry Rubeau, *After the Crime: Victim Decision Making* (New York: Plenum Press, 1992); for the situation worldwide, see Ezzat Fattah, *Understanding Criminal Victimization* (Scarborough, Ontario: Prentice-Hall, 1992); for an English view see Martin Wright, *Justice for Victims and Offenders* (Philadelphia: Open University Press, 1991).

15. Gilbert Geis, "Victims of Crimes of Violence and the Criminal Justice System," in *Perspectives on Crime Victims*, eds. Burt Galaway and Joe Hudson (St. Louis: C.V. Mosby, 1981), p. 64.

16. Eduard Ziegenhagen, "Toward a Theory of Victim-Criminal Justice System Interactions," in *Criminal Justice and the Victim*, ed. W. F. McDonald (Beverly Hills, Calif.: Sage, 1976), pp. 261–280.

17. "Crime Control Needs Citizens to Do Their Part in Helping," *Crime Victims Digest*, August 1985, pp. 1–2.

18. U.S. Department of Justice, Bureau of Justice Statistics, *Criminal Victimization in the United States, 1990* (Washington, D.C.: U.S. Government Printing Office, 1992), p. 102.

19. Jerome H. Skolnick, *Justice without Trial: Law Enforcement in a Democratic Society* (New York: Wiley, 1966).

20. "Burying Crime in Chicago," *Newsweek*, May 16, 1983, p. 63; "Chicago Police Found to Dismiss Cases Erroneously," *The New York Times*, May 2, 1983, p. A20.

21. Ziegenhagen, "Toward a Theory of Victim-Criminal Justice System Interactions."

22. Andrew Karmen, *Crime Victims: An Introduction to Victimology*, 2d ed. (Pacific Grove, Calif.: Brooks/Cole, 1990), p. 176.

23. William F. McDonald, "Criminal Justice and the Victim: An Introduction," in *Criminal Justice and the Victim*, ed. McDonald, pp. 17–56.

24. Mary S. Knudten and Richard D. Knudten, "What Happens to Crime Victims and Witnesses in the Justice System?," in *Perspectives on Crime Victims*, eds. Galaway and Hudson, pp. 52–72.

25. F. Miller, *Prosecution: The Decision to Charge a Suspect with a Crime* (Boston: Little, Brown, 1970), pp. 283–284.

26. Donald J. Hall, "The Role of the Victim in the Prosecution and Disposition of a Criminal Case," in *Perspectives on Crime Victims*, eds. Galaway and Hudson, p. 326.

27. Karmen, *Crime Victims*, p. 178.

28. President's Task Force on Victims of Crime, *Final Report*, (Washington, D.C.: U.S. Government Printing Office, 1982).

29. James H. Stark and Howard W. Goldstein, *The Rights of Crime Victims* (New York: Bantam Books, 1985).

30. Marshall Houtts, *From Arrest to Release* (Springfield, Ill.: Charles C. Thomas, 1958), p. 97.

31. Karmen, *Crime Victims*, pp. 196–198.

32. Robert C. Davis, Madeline Henley, and Barbara Smith, *Victim Impact Statements: Their Effect on Court Outcomes and Victim Satisfaction*, Report (New York: Victim Services Agency, April 1990).

33. James H. Stark and Howard W. Goldstein, *The Rights of Crime Victims* (New York: Bantam Books, 1985).

34. A. M. Heinz and W. A. Kerstetter, "Victim Participation in Plea Bargaining: A Field Experiment," in *Plea Bargaining*, eds. W. F. McDonald and J. A. Cramer (Lexington, Mass.: D.C. Heath, 1979), pp. 167–177.

35. William F. McDonald, "The Victim's Role in the American Administration of Justice: Some Developments and Findings," in *The Victim in International Perspective*, ed. Schneider, pp. 397–407. See also Lis Wieht, "Victim and Sentence: Resetting Justice's Scale," *The New York Times*, September 29, 1989, p. B5.

36. Bureau of Justice Statistics, *Report to the Nation*, U.S. Department of Justice, 2d ed. (Washington, D.C.: U.S. Government Printing Office, 1988), p. 82.

37. Michael Ash, "On Witnesses: A Radical Critique of Criminal Court Procedures," *Notre Dame Lawyer* 48 (1972):397.

38. Richard Lynch, "Improving the Treatment of Victims: Some Guides for Action," in *Criminal Justice and the Victim*, ed. McDonald, pp. 165–176.

39. Hall, "The Role of the Victim."

40. Michigan Statutes Annotated, §§ 28.1133 (1954); see also American Bar Association Project on Standards for Criminal Justice, *Probation*, § 3.2 (1970).

41. William McDonald, "Criminal Justice and the Victim," in *Criminal Justice and the Victim*, ed. McDonald, pp. 17–56.

42. Hall, "The Role of the Victim."

43. Karmen, *Crime Victims*, p. 199; Edna Erez and Pamela Tontodonato, "The Effect of Victim Participation in Sentencing on Sentence Outcome," *Criminology* 28(3) (1990):451–474.

44. *Payne v. Tennessee*, 111 S. Ct. 2597(1991); see J. Triebwasser,

"Victims' Non-impact on Sentence," *Law Enforcement News*, September 29, 1987, p. 5.

45. G. Forst and J. Hernon, *NIJ Research in Brief: The Criminal Justice Response to Victim Harm* (Washington, D.C.: U.S. Department of Justice, 1985).

46. K. Jamieson and T. Flanagan, *Sourcebook of Criminal Justice Statistics, 1986* (Washington, D.C.: U.S. Government Printing Office, 1987).

47. Edwin Villmoare and Jeanne Benvenuti, *California Crime Victims Handbook* (Sacramento, Calif.: McGeorge School of Law, University of the Pacific, 1988), pp. 33–46.

48. President's Task Force on Victims of Crime, *Final Report, 1982*.

49. David Austern, *The Crime Victims' Handbook: Your Rights and Role in the Criminal Justice System* (New York: Viking, 1987).

50. Villmoare and Benvenuti, *California Crime Victims Handbook*, p. 45.

51. Margery Fry, "Justice for Victims," *The Observer (London)*, May 7, 1957, p. 8; see also Margery Fry, *Arms of the Law* (London: Golancz, 1951).

52. See especially Stephen Schafer, *Compensation and Restitution to Victims of Crime*; G. O. W. Mueller, "Compensation for Victims of Crime: Thought before Action," *Minnesota Law Review* 50 (1965):213–221.

53. G. O. W. Mueller, "Tort, Crime and the Primitive," *Journal of Criminal Law, Criminology and Police Science* 46(3) (1955):303–332; Robert J. McCormack, "Compensating Victims of Violent Crime," *Justice Quarterly* 8 (1991):329–346.

54. Dale G. Parent, Barbara Auerbach, and Kenneth E. Carlson, *Compensating Crime Victims: A Summary of Policies and Practices* (Washington, D.C.: Office of Justice Programs, 1992).

55. Leroy Lamborn, "Victim Compensation Programs," in *Perspectives on Crime Victims*, eds. Galaway and Hudson, pp. 418–423.

56. National Organization for Victim Assistance (NOVA), *Victim Rights and Services: A Legislative Directory—1987*, (Washington, D.C.: National Organization for Victim Assistance, 1988; Albert R. Roberts, "Delivery of Services to Crime Victims: A National Survey," *American Journal of Orthopsychiatry* 61 (1991):128–137; Robert C. Sullivan, *Twice Violated: New Hope for the Victims of Criminal Violence* (New York: Vantage Press, 1988).

57. Shafer, *Compensation and Restitution to Victims of Crime*.

58. John Palmer, "The Night Prosecutor," in *Perspectives on Crime Victims*, eds. Galaway and Hudson, pp. 262–265.

59. Burt Galaway, "The Use of Restitution," in ibid., pp. 277–285.

60. Alan Harland, "Restitution Statutes and Cases: Some Substantive and Procedural Restraints," in *Victims, Offenders, and Restitutive Sanctions*, eds. Burt Galaway and Joe Hudson (Lexington, Mass.: Lexington Books, 1979), pp. 151–171.

61. Burt Galaway, "Restitution as Innovation or Unfulfilled Promise?," *Federal Probation* 52(3) (1988):3–14.

62. Richard Lawrence, "Diverting Offenders from Prison to Restitution Center," *Journal of Crime and Justice* 13 (1990):27–41. See also Burt Galaway and Joe Hudson, "Introduction: Towards Restorative Justice," in *Criminal Justice, Restitution, and Reconciliation*, eds. Burt Galaway and Joe Hudson (Monsey, N.Y.: Willow Tree Press, 1990). But the Georgia program was less successful, with a 75-percent reconviction rate within twelve months. See Gerald Flowers, *The Georgia Restitution Shelter Program* (Atlanta: Program Evaluation Section, Georgia Department of Offender Rehabilitation, 1977); James Austin and Barry Krisberg, "The Unmet Promise of Alternatives to Incarceration," *Crime and Delinquency* 28 (July 1982):374–409; see also Joe Hudson and Burt Galaway, "Financial Restitution: Toward an Evaluable Program Model," *Canadian Journal of Criminology* 31 (1989):1–18.

63. Burt Galaway, "Victim-Offender Mediation as the Preferred Response to Property Offenses," in *Crime and Its Victims*, ed. Emilio C. Viano (New York: Hemisphere Publishing, 1989), pp. 101–111.

64. Dorothy (Edmonds) McKnight, "The Victim-Offender Reconciliation Project," in *Perspectives on Crime Victims*, eds. Galaway and Hudson, pp. 292–298.

65. Ibid.

66. J. Garofalo and K. Connelly, "Dispute Resolution Centers. Part 1. Major Features and Processes; Part 2. Outcomes, Issues and Future Directions," *Criminal Justice Abstracts*, September 1980, pp. 416–610; Deborah Baskin, "Community Mediation and the Public/Private Problem," *Social Justice* 15 (1988):98–115.

67. T. Thomason, "The Issue Is Ethics," in *Crime Victims and the News Media*, eds. T. Thomason and A. Babbili (Fort Worth: Texas Christian University, Department of Journalism, 1987), pp. 2–3; J. Greenfield, "TV: The Medium Determines Impact of Crime Stories," in ibid., pp. 19–23; A. Seymour, "Victim Advocate Suggests Code for Journalists," in ibid., pp. 31–33.

68. Sunny von Bulow National Victim Advocacy Center, *Victims Rights and the Media* (Fort Worth, Tex.: 1986); L. Barker, "The Media and Victims of Crime," *NOVA Newsletter*, April 1985, pp. 4–5.

CHAPTER 19

INTERNATIONAL AND COMPARATIVE CRIMINAL JUSTICE

On December 21, 1988, Pan Am flight 103, en route from Frankfurt, Germany, to New York, filled with Americans on their way home to celebrate the holidays, exploded in midair. The debris fell on Lockerbie, Scotland. There were 270 casualties in passengers, crew, and people on the ground. From the outset it was clear that this was no accident. But it took investigators three years to assemble evidence sufficient to satisfy an American grand jury that a crime, or crimes, had been committed.

The dimensions of this case were broad and the details complex: An American airliner, en route from Frankfurt, Germany, explodes over a Scottish (United Kingdom) town. Of those killed, 189 were Americans and the others had a multitude of nationalities, including of course British (those on the ground). Since the impact of the crime was in Scotland, the Scottish police force was the principal agency for investigation. U.S. federal law enforcement agencies joined their Scottish colleagues. But American officers cannot just descend on Scotland. They have no "jurisdiction," no power or authority, there. Such cooperation requires agreement, either preexisting or specially achieved.

The joint Scottish-U.S. investigation quickly spread all over the world. Leads to Iranian-backed Syrian terrorist groups apparently led nowhere. But searches on the ground in Lockerbie revealed fragments of a bomb timer. Photographs obtained in Senegal (Africa) led investigators to intact bomb timers in Togo (Africa). These, it turned out, had been manufactured in Switzerland. Some of them had been sold to Libyans. Further investigation established that the bomb (and its timer) had been placed in a shirt (the fragments of which were found at Lockerbie) that had been purchased in Malta (Mediterranean island nation) by the station agent of the Libyan airlines.

An indictment for murder and conspiracy (193 counts) was issued on Friday, November 15, 1991, against three Libyans—after investigators had conducted 14,000 interviews and extended their investigation to fifty countries (about 25% of the world's countries). ■

"There is no longer any such thing as purely domestic business, . . . all business is international."
From Richard Schaffer, et al.,
International Business Law and its Environment (2nd ed. 1993
Minneapolis, Minn.: West Publishing Co.), p. xxv.

The globalization of life, commerce, and crime has brought in its wake a multitude of new problems. The Pan Am flight 103 investigation is far from atypical; it is a representative sample of law enforcement and criminal justice in the age of the global village. We could add many more examples, covering other types of crime: global insurance fraud; worldwide pollution; overfishing of the oceans; people-smuggling; counterfeiting of money, securities, and products; drug-smuggling. But the Pan Am case exemplifies how difficult it is for the people of today's world to protect themselves. This case does not involve the kinds of problems that the average county court or even federal district court, the average police department or correctional service, can deal with. It challenges us in criminal justice to think globally, even though the impact of the crime is ultimately felt by all of us locally and as individuals.

In the first part of this chapter we introduce the intricacies of the new crimes, and the new forms of old crimes, that criminal justice must deal with at national and international levels. Some of these are transnational crimes (crimes that violate the laws of more than one nation); others are international crimes (crimes that violate international law, as established by the world community).

THE CONCEPT OF JURISDICTION

jurisdiction
Power of a sovereign state to make and enforce its own laws. Also, the power given to a court to adjudicate matters in dispute.

In this book we have operated under the assumption that the power to make criminal laws, and the power to enforce them, rests with a single government—that of any state within the United States, the U.S. federal government, or the government of any country. Every state, every country, has **jurisdiction,** that is, the right and duty to make and enforce its own laws. Jurisdiction is part of its sovereignty, its legitimate right to rule. To put it another way, only sovereign states have the right (the jurisdiction) to make and enforce laws. How did the state get that power? Let us take a look at history.

When human beings lived as clans in hunting and gathering societies, there was no need for a complex system of criminal justice to govern behavior. Patterns were determined by close living: If you were to step out of line, or leave the clan, you would perish. As nearly as we can tell by inference (and by comparison with the few indigenous cultures left on earth), the clan—or its head—had the power of life and death over its members. It had jurisdiction.

Empires: Unitary Systems

"The Romans initiated the diplomatic procedure that today we call extradition."

The early Romans, a cattle-raising people who had migrated to what is now central Italy, were composed of a number of clans, which they called *familias*. The earliest historical records tell us that the head of the clan (the *pater familias*) had the power of life and death over its members. In modern terms, we say that the family was the jurisdictional unit that would make laws and punish offenders for law violations. When an offender and a victim were from different clans, two distinct sovereignties were involved. The Romans did exactly what we do when jurisdictions clash today: They initiated a diplomatic procedure called **extradition,** by which the offender is surrendered to the offended sovereign (clan). The Roman solution to violations of clan law was very practical. For example, in a case of homicide, the victim clan had lost a worker, so the offender clan surrendered the offender to take the victim's place as a worker.

extradition
Process of ancient origin by which an alleged offender is transferred from one sovereign country to another for trial.

When the Roman clans formed a city (Rome, around 753 B.C.), they recognized the need for each clan to give up some of its jurisdiction for the common good. Criminal jurisdiction over treason, including such crimes as putting a hex on the harvest, is a good example. Ancient city-states slowly grew into mighty empires, and as they did the cities had to yield some of their criminal jurisdiction to the empire, again for the common good. The head of the clan still retained some jurisdiction, the city exercised some, and now so did the empire.

Federal Systems

Something along the same lines happened much later in history in America. At the moment of independence, the thirteen new states had all the sovereignty to make (or retain) criminal laws and to enforce them. But for the common good they gave the new, greater entity, the federal government, the right to make and enforce criminal laws for the protection of the Union—laws pertaining to the common defense, foreign relations, interstate commerce, protection of the currency and the postal system, and so on. In the Constitution (Art. I, Sec. 8), they also gave the federal government power "to define and punish . . . offenses against the Law of Nations." (Most of these criminal laws can be found in Title 18 of the United States Code.)

Regional and Worldwide Systems

Today, a new situation has arisen. Due to the easing of frontiers; the development of instant communication exchange; global mass media; jet transport; the interlocking of commercial activities worldwide; and the emergence of environmental, nuclear, and toxic dangers, human beings all over the world have become dependent on the activities of all other human beings. And as all other human endeavors have become global, so has crime. Now the question is: What can we do about it?

We could, of course, do what the Romans (and the inhabitants of other ancient cities) did and have a complex system of extradition proceedings to bring offenders to justice where, or against whom, they have offended. But that is not as easy as it was long ago, when the heads of two clans would meet privately to discuss a solution. At the other extreme, many experts on international criminal law think we could do what people also have always done—give up a slice of sovereignty to form a new criminal jurisdiction, at the next higher level. That level might be found within regional groupings of states, such as the European Economic Community, the Council of Europe, the Organization of American States, or the Organization of African Unity. It might also be found at the world level in the United Nations.

With the emergence of a new criminal jurisdictional level, the jurisdiction of the earlier and smaller units does not cease. All jurisdictional levels, from family through state and nation, retain some criminal jurisdiction, each yields a little to the next higher level. Necessity dictates how much criminal jurisdiction should be given to higher authority. Experience tells us that each jurisdictional level should do only what it can do best, leaving to other units, up or down the ladder, what they can do best. The United Nations cannot run families, nor can families protect the world from international criminals. States cannot protect us against global pollution, nor can regional groupings of states protect us from muggers (at least not yet). What the community of nations, through the United Nations, can do, and can do best, is protect all people from global threats.[1] (See the Criminal Justice on Trial box.)

International crime: Passengers leaving the Achille Lauro after a terrorist hijacking in 1985.

"As all other human endeavors have become global, so has crime."

"We could do what people have always done: Give up a slice of sovereignty to form a new criminal jurisdiction."

"Perhaps little has changed since earliest recorded history: the jurisdictional unit is still the village, except the village is now the world."
G. O. W. Mueller, "Four Decades after Nuremberg," 1987.

INTERNATIONAL AND TRANSNATIONAL CRIMINALITY

At the global level, there are two major categories of crimes: international (violating international law) and transnational (violating the laws of more than one

CRIME AND CRIMINAL JUSTICE AFLOAT: A QUESTION OF JURISDICTION AND ENFORCEMENT

"[The marauders] strike primarily at night in small boats driven by powerful outboard motors. After pulling alongside their prey, they board the victim ship, using ropes with grappling hooks. . . . [P]assengers are robbed of cash, equipment, electronic gear, and even bicycles, and cargo is pilfered" (1). Anybody who resists is shot. None of the tens of thousands of large ships traveling the Malacca Strait between Malaysia and Indonesia is safe from attack, nor any of the thousands of refugee boats in the South China Sea, nor any of the hundreds of ocean vessels approaching West African ports.

The scope of the losses

While no accurate estimates of worldwide losses from modern-day piracy are possible, knowledgeable experts think the total is probably near $250 million a year. The thieves make off with tons of cement, coffee, sugar, tomato paste, ladies' undergarments, steel, and whatever other cargo they think they can fence on shore. Even more common is the direct attack on the safe in the captain's cabin—pirates may be able to collect $50,000 in cash during a fifteen-minute job. Because large ships are so automated, crews are typically too small to try to resist or even to allow for enough guards to be posted on deck. In 1991 more than 120 pirate attacks were reported worldwide, and it is likely that only 40 percent

of the total are reported to authorities (2).

Perhaps more than any other type of transnational or international crime, crimes that occur on the water present vast jurisdictional difficulties: ". . . there is no single authority, nation, or consortium of nations which is responsible for discipline on the high seas" (3).

The Law of the Sea Treaty

But at least the basis for law on the oceans has been laid: In 1982 the United Nations Convention on the Law of the Sea, or the Law of the Sea Treaty, was completed, and it has gone into effect (although the United States has not yet acceded to it). To guarantee rights, and to establish discipline, the treaty has established four zones:

1. From a state's shoreline up to twelve miles out, the country has territorial jurisdiction and control. (But it will not apply its own criminal law for offenses committed aboard foreign vessels unless such crimes threaten the country.)
2. Up to 200 miles out, coastal states enjoy an "exclusive economic zone" where they may fish or mine the ocean bed, or sell such rights to others.
3. Similar but more restricted rights exist beyond the 200-mile zone, to the edge of the continental shelf (where the seabed drops deep down).

4. Beyond these zones is the open high sea, where all states have equal rights, subject to protective provisions of the treaty.

Besides these zones there are also international waters, like straits, canals, and rivers, that are recognized as open to navigation (innocent passage) by all.

The lack of policing

Unhappily, the world does not yet have an international marine enforcement agency to police the oceans. There is no one to spot a vessel dumping nuclear waste into the high seas or into an exclusive economic zone. Who can intercept arms or narcotics smugglers? Even powerful nations, like the United States, have trouble policing their own zones. Some narcotics smuggling vessels are caught by the U.S. Coast Guard, but more go undetected. The problems are much worse for small nations that cannot afford to maintain marine police forces of any size. A look at the Law of the Sea Treaty map indicates that most regions affected by piracy and terrorism are in areas of notoriously underpoliced territorial waters.

The scope of crime on the oceans

All these problems are magnified when we realize that piracy is only one of many crimes committed on the oceans. For example,

- Terrorism has spread beyond the airways. Thirteen oceangoing passenger liners have been victimized in the last thirty years. Our nation's attention was caught in 1985, when the Achille Lauro was attacked by Palestinian guerrillas who killed the wheelchair-bound American passenger Arthur Klinghoffer (4).
- During the 1960s and 1970s competition by jet airliners decreased the profitability of passenger liners. Nineteen such ships were lost in a short span of time because shipping owners, largely from criminal negligence, permitted their ships to fall into disrepair.
- Pollution due to criminal negligence or criminal intent increasingly threatens the oceans. The Exxon Valdez and its widespread contamination of Alaskan waters, and Saddam Hussein's oil pollution of the Persian Gulf, are two examples.
- Frauds in the marine shipping industry have caused severe damage to international trade and threatened the collapse of entire national economies in Africa and Latin America.
- The international drug trade uses the oceans for about half its shipments from the points of origin or manufacture to the points of distribution.
- Currently over 30,000 American boats are listed on the FBI's Stolen Boat File as having been stolen and not recovered.

There are signs of the beginnings of an international maritime system for enforcing treaties and agreements. NATO warships, acting under a U.N. Security Council resolution, are enforcing the arms embargo against the former Yugoslavia and have already seized several vessels engaged in arms smuggling. International conventions to protect whales are being enforced by a group of international inspectors sailing aboard whaling ships. The future looks promising.

SOURCES

1. G. O. W. Mueller and Freda Adler, Outlaws of the Ocean (New York: Hearst Marine Books, 1985, p. 150).
2. Alan Farnham, "Pirates," Fortune, July 15, 1991, pp. 113–118.
3. Roger Villar, Piracy Today (London: Conway Maritime Press, 1985), p. 59.
4. G. O. W. Mueller and Freda Adler, "Terrorism at Sea: Passenger Ship Targets," Violence, Aggression and Terrorism 1(1987):327–342.

QUESTIONS FOR DISCUSSION

1. Much piracy could be prevented if specific precautions were taken: traveling through dangerous areas only in broad daylight, posting a sufficient guard on deck, and so on. Why are such precautions rarely taken?
2. What stands in the way of a United Nations global maritime police force?
3. Propose an alternate mechanism for law enforcement on the oceans.

FIGURE 1. United Nations Law of the Sea Treaty Map

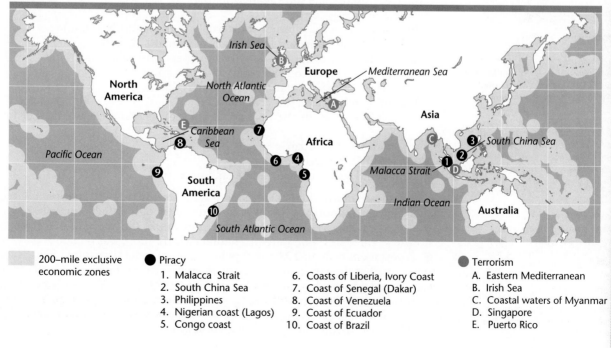

200–mile exclusive economic zones	Piracy		Terrorism
	1. Malacca Strait	6. Coasts of Liberia, Ivory Coast	A. Eastern Mediterranean
	2. South China Sea	7. Coast of Senegal (Dakar)	B. Irish Sea
	3. Philippines	8. Coast of Venezuela	C. Coastal waters of Myanmar
	4. Nigerian coast (Lagos)	9. Coast of Ecuador	D. Singapore
	5. Congo coast	10. Coast of Brazil	E. Puerto Rico

nation). Some crimes are clearly one or the other; others, like Pan Am 103, combine elements of both.

International Crimes

In 1943, the Allies, then in the midst of a world war, agreed that no one nation could ensure the continued existence of the peoples of the world in safety, given the scope of the aggression, and the resulting mass destruction and genocide, unleashed by some nations against the world as a whole (Figure 19.1). The nations in this particular case were Germany and Japan. The remedy created by the Allies (the United States, Great Britain, France, the USSR, and China) was the International Military Tribunal, and in 1945–46, at the end of World War II, at Nuremberg, Germany, the major German war criminals were brought to trial before it for crimes such as these:

- Conspiracy to commit war crimes
- Planning, preparing, initiating, or waging aggressive war
- Violation of the laws and customs of war
- Crimes against humanity[2]

Of the defendants, all leading Nazis, twenty-three were sentenced to death by hanging, seven were sentenced to prison terms ranging from ten years to life, three were acquitted, one was not tried because of ill health, and one committed suicide prior to sentencing. A similar Far Eastern International Military Tribunal was established at Tokyo, and between 1946 and 1948 it tried and convicted Japanese war criminals.

There was a problem with respect to these crimes: They had not previously been defined in written law. But there were enough precedents in history (including the condemnation of Napoleon Bonaparte in 1814–1815, as well as of World War I war criminals in 1920) to conclude that international criminal law existed by virtue of common law, just as Anglo-American criminal law existed as common law long before it was written down.

international crimes
Crimes, established largely by conventions, violative of international law, including but not limited to crimes against the peace and security of mankind.

Today the basic **international crimes** are well recognized and are awaiting codification by the United Nations. They are called "crimes against the peace and security of mankind," and include the following:

- **Aggression** (by one state against another)
- Threat of aggression
- Intervention (in the internal or external affairs of another state)
- Colonial domination and other forms of alien domination
- **Genocide** (destroying a national, ethnic, racial, or religious group)
- Apartheid (suppression of a racial or ethnic group)
- Systematic or mass violations of human rights
- Exceptionally serious war crimes
- Recruitment, use, financing, and training of mercenaries (soldiers of fortune)
- International terrorism
- Illicit traffic in narcotic drugs
- Willful and severe damage to the environment[3]

aggression
Use of armed force by a state against the sovereignty or territory of another state, inconsistent with the Charter of the United Nations. An international crime.

genocide
International crime defined by convention (1948) and consisting of specific acts of violence committed with intent to destroy, in whole or in part, a national, ethnic, racial, or religious group.

conventions
International agreements by which many nations commit themselves to common, legally binding obligations.

"International crimes are defined by international agreements called conventions, or by precedents."

All of these international crimes are based on existing international agreements, called **conventions,** or on precedents, although not all countries recognize all of them as part of their own law. For example, the international crime of genocide, created in 1948 by an international convention, was recognized by the U.S. government only in 1986, and is now part of federal criminal law. These "crimes against the peace and security of mankind" are by no means the only international crimes; they are only the most severe offenses. Many other international crimes have been established by various international agreements. Among these are such offenses as the cutting of undersea cables, the international traffic in women for prostitution, and fisheries offenses.[4]

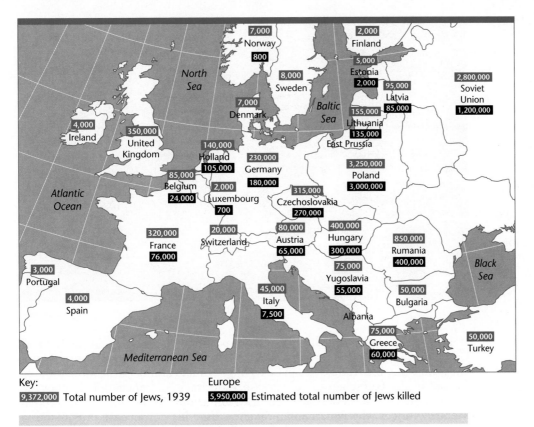

Key:

9,372,000 Total number of Jews, 1939	Europe
	5,950,000 Estimated total number of Jews killed

FIGURE 19.1 *The extermination of European Jews, by country*

Transnational Crimes

Although it has become customary to distinguish between international and transnational crimes,[5] there is by no means agreement on their differentiation, and most experts concede there is considerable overlap between the two. **Transnational crimes** are criminal transactions offending the laws of more than one country, regardless of whether they are also criminal under international law. Think, for example, of dealings in stolen or counterfeit works of art, or of counterfeit stocks and bonds; of fraudulent commercial transactions; or the bribery of foreign officials by businesspeople of other countries. As commercial life becomes increasingly globalized, there is a greater likelihood that fraud schemes will violate the laws of more than one country. These crimes do not necessarily threaten the peace and security of all people, but they are often so complex that one country alone, or even two or three, are at a loss to deal with them. More and more, there are demands for an international criminal justice system to provide protection and to solve these problems.

transnational crimes
Criminal activities extending into, and violating the laws of, several countries.

"Often more than 50 percent of my day is devoted to . . . our international involvement in fighting drug trafficking, money laundering, international organized crime and business fraud, . . . terrorism or espionage."
U.S. Attorney General Richard Thornburgh, August 1989.

International and Transnational Jurisdiction

To test the concepts of international and transnational crime, let us examine four well-known cases: In 1990 military forces commanded by Saddam Hussein, the Iraqi dictator, attacked, occupied, and looted neighboring Kuwait. These were clearly criminal acts under international law. The U.N. Security Council condemned the acts and ordered Iraq to withdraw. When Saddam Hussein refused, a multinational armed force expelled the Iraqis from Kuwait (the Persian Gulf War of 1991). In the following years Iraq continued to violate U.N. sanctions and conditions, prompting the Security Council to authorize a second military strike by multinational forces against Iraq in January 1993.

• • • • • • • • • • • • • • • • •

*The International Military
Tribunal at Nuremberg,
Germany, September 1945:
Generals, admirals, ambassadors, bankers, and cabinet
ministers who held office
under the Nazis being tried
for war crimes committed
during World War II.*

In the second case, in 1988 U.S. Customs agents discovered that the Bank of
Credit and Commerce International (BCCI), which operated in sixty-nine countries and many U.S. states, was in fact a huge scam to launder drug money and to
finance bank fraud schemes. In this case, the crimes are transnational—they are
crimes under the laws of many countries and states. In the third case, General
Manuel Noriega, the Panamanian dictator, used his power base in Panama to
engage in large-scale drug smuggling. His drug dealings violated the laws of
many countries, including those of the United States and Panama. They also
violated a number of international conventions.[6] The fourth case, Pan Am 103,
with which we began the chapter, involves a clear-cut violation of international
criminal law: airplane terrorism. The individual perpetrators are also punishable
under U.S. law and under British law.

All four of these complex cases demonstrate the enormous difficulties any one
or several criminal justice systems have in bringing criminals to justice and adjudicating matters beyond the normal jurisdiction of local courts. To deal with
them, is it necessary to have an international court, perhaps an entire international criminal justice system? The Nuremberg tribunal, of course, was designed
to deal with international crimes. But it was a temporary court, disbanded once
the job was done. As early as 1950, the United Nations tried to create a permanent **international criminal court.** These efforts were stalled during the Cold
War, but have now been vigorously revived.[7]

Once established, a permanent international criminal court would not have
exclusive jurisdiction over all international crimes and criminals. It would serve
as one option among three: (1) governments are always free to try international
criminals in their own courts; (2) governments may want to transfer the case to
another government for trial; or (3) the case may be initiated by or transferred to
the international criminal court. In many situations the international criminal
court might be the most appropriate and even the most effective forum, especially if the case threatens the continued existence of the world. Experts argue
that such a court must be above suspicion, command worldwide respect, and
represent all peoples as a whole. (See the Criminal Justice in Action box.)

There is a model for such a fair and respected worldwide court, the **International Court of Justice** at The Hague, the Netherlands. International criminal
lawyers believe this court might be given criminal jurisdiction. Until that happens, or until the United Nations activates its planned international criminal

international criminal court
*Court created by the Security
Council of the United Nations,
with power to adjudicate charges
of international crimes by states
and individuals, so far restricted
to crimes on the territory of the
former Yugoslavia.*

International Court of Justice
*Court of the United Nations with
jurisdiction to adjudicate disputes among states. Also known
as World Court.*

court, the nations of the world are doing the best they can by using their own national courts and by resorting to various means of international cooperation. Thus, in the case of Saddam Hussein, the government of Kuwait could endeavor to try the defendant(s) for murder under its own laws, or even for war crimes under international law, if it could secure custody of the defendants. In the bank case, American law enforcement agencies and courts brought a few of the offenders to trial but failed to reach the more important offenders. In the Noriega case, again, the United States did it on its own, from military invasion of Panama to arrest of the defendant abroad by U.S. armed forces to trial, in a federal district court in Florida. In the case of the transcontinental terrorists, at least three countries want to try the defendants. But experts believe that using national law enforcement and criminal justice systems leaves something to be desired: It is inadequate, costly, complicated, incomplete, and inefficient. Besides, it is not just the people of one or a few countries who have been victimized; it is the people of the entire world.

INTERNATIONAL/TRANSNATIONAL CRIMINAL PROCEEDINGS

With all the problems and inadequacies in dealing with international and transnational offenders, it is nevertheless possible to identify the movement of such offenders through the emerging international criminal justice process (Figure 19.2).[8]

Entry Into the System

Police Investigation.   There are no U.N. precinct houses where one can report an international or transnational crime, and the closest to a 911 emergency call is a request by a government to convene the U.N. Security Council. The Council is composed of fifteen nations: five permanent members (China, France, Russia, United Kingdom, United States) and ten memberships filled by rotation from among all the other member states. The Council can convene at virtually a moment's notice and make binding decisions affecting any situation (thus any crime) threatening the peace and security of the world.

A typical case in point is the Council's condemnation of Iraq's act of aggression in 1990, its attempt to restore peace by negotiation, and ultimately its launch of the police action that ousted the Iraqis from Kuwait and restored peace. The United Nations has increasingly used peacekeeping forces, for example in Cambodia, Somalia, and the former Yugoslavia, as an international police force, to prevent and end crimes against the peace and security of humankind and to maintain peace. Other international crimes are more likely to be reported to U.N. bodies with specialized functions. For example, human rights violations (including the international crime of torture) are regularly reported to the U.N. Commission on Human Rights; violations of the whaling regulations are reported to the Whaling Conference by the international inspectors aboard whaling vessels; violations of the telecommunications agreements are brought before the International Telecommunications Union. In addition, nongovernmental organizations working with the U.N. Economic and Social Council play a major role in finding facts pertaining to international criminality, especially those involving human rights violations. (Amnesty International, one of the nongovernmental organizations protecting prisoners' rights worldwide, was awarded the Nobel Peace Prize for its activities.)

The situation is more troublesome with respect to transnational crimes. In the BCCI case, the laws of many jurisdictions were violated. Separate investigations

"The people of the world have high expectations for a new world order in which peace is more than the absence of war, and justice more than hollow slogans. . . . an international court, . . . is part of these high expectations."
M. Cherif Bassiouni, Draft Statute, International Criminal Tribunal, Paris, 1992.

"The pressure for an international criminal justice system comes partly from the fact that it is not just the people of one or a few countries who are victimized, it is the people of the entire world."

"The closest to a 911 international emergency call is a request by a government to convene the United Nations Security Council."

AN INTERNATIONAL CRIMINAL COURT: THE LONG ROAD FROM SARAJEVO

In 1914, a Serbian freedom fighter assassinated the heir to the Austro-Hungarian throne, Archduke Franz Ferdinand, and his wife Sophie, who were visiting the city of Sarajevo, then part of the Austro-Hungarian empire. The assassination precipitated war between Austria-Hungary and Serbia and, ultimately, World War I. Four years and 8 million lost lives later, the 1919 Treaty of Versailles called for the creation of an international criminal court to try the German emperor Wilhelm II as the principal war criminal of World War I. But no such court was created, because the emperor had been forced into exile in the Netherlands, and the Dutch refused to extradite him for trial.

Nearly eighty years later, Sarajevo was again at the center of a war. In 1990, Yugoslavia split into a number of republics, and civil war erupted in the spring of 1992. Before the war in Bosnia-Herzegovina was a year old, Serbian nationalists were believed to "have left more than 130,000 Muslims dead or missing and more than a million others homeless." (1) The Serbian "ethnic cleansing" policy was aimed at creating exclusively Serbian territories by killing Muslims or driving them out (2). Hundreds of thousands of Bosnian refugees were held in enclaves surrounded by Serbian forces, who prevented food and other relief supplies from reaching starving and ill people. The international criminal charges in-

cluded massive, systematic rapes of Bosnian Muslim women—perhaps as many as 20,000 (3)—and the elimination through killing, torture, and deportation of non-Serb citizens in occupied areas (3). Such activities amount to genocide under international law, which includes in its definition the destruction of ethnic groups in whole or in part. The government of Bosnia-Herzegovina, located in Sarajevo, appealed to the United Nations Security Council for help. The Council, composed of fifteen countries, debated the question. It had several options: It could appeal to the warring factions to stop fighting; it could send in truce observers and relief for civilian victims; it could impose sanctions against the Serbian aggressors; it could establish a commission of investigation to assemble the facts.

It did all that, to no avail. The facts that the commission of inquiry assembled amounted to massive and widespread international crimes, violations of international humanitarian law, and a "threat to international peace and security" (4). Only one option was left: the establishment of an international criminal court, with the objective of bringing to trial those who could be charged with international crimes, and deterring them from committing further atrocities. There was at least one successful model for war crimes trials: the war crimes tribunals that in 1945–1946 had tried German and Japanese war criminals in Nuremberg and Tokyo, respectively (see text). But these were temporary tribunals and were dis-

banded once the job was done.

The newly established United Nations in 1948 began a half-hearted effort to create an international criminal court and a "code of crimes against the peace and security of mankind." The endeavor languished in the International Law Commission, a subsidiary body of the General Assembly. For twenty-five years the major powers, waging the Cold War, could not even agree on the definition of aggression.

But help was to come from the scholarly community. In the early 1970s, the American Foundation for the Establishment of the International Criminal Court produced valuable draft proposals, and the International Association of Penal Law became active under its president, Professor M. Cherif Bassiouni of Chicago, who prepared a draft statute for the creation of the International Criminal Court and a code of international crimes. The International Law Commission continued to work on its proposal for the international criminal court.

Meantime, wars of aggression had killed millions in all parts of the world. It was the Iraqi aggression against Kuwait, 1990–1991, however, that alerted the world to the lack of an international system to deal with war criminals. At an historic meeting at New York University on March 27, 1991, American scholars of international criminal law met with the few surviving officials of the Nuremberg tribunal and jointly drafted a call for the immediate establishment of the international criminal court. The document was transmitted to the U.S. Senate, which passed a nonbinding resolution urging President Bush to push for the establishment of this Court by the U.N. Security Council. But he did not act.

The scholarly community kept up the momentum. In May 1991 an international conference at the Max Planck Institute for Foreign and International Criminal Law at Freiburg, Germany, made specific proposals and urged governments to act. Then civil war broke out in the wake of Yugoslavia's breakup, and reports of atrocities surfaced. Two more meetings in March and December 1992 saw the scholars united with government leaders and U.N. officials. In quick succession, the permanent Conference on Security and Cooperation in Europe (CSCE), representing the West and East European countries, and the governments of Italy and France, placed before the Security Council detailed draft statutes for the immediate creation of the International Criminal Court to try war criminals in the former Yugoslavia.

Finally, the Security Council was ready to act. At an historic session on February 22, 1993, it determined "to put an end to such crimes and to take effective measures to bring to justice the persons who are responsible for them," and it decided "that an international tribunal shall be established for the prosecution of persons responsible for serious violations of international humanitarian law committed in the territory of the former Yugoslavia since 1992" (3).

There are some limitations: This court has jurisdiction only over crimes committed in the former Yugoslavia, after 1991, under international and Yugoslav criminal law. It is again only a temporary court, and it may suffer from the "Emperor Wilhelm" problem—namely, that it can try only persons who can be brought before the court. While a few potential defendants are in custody, most are as yet guarded by powerful armies. But then, an international indictment, resting on solid evidence, will be a powerful tool for future action. If the tyrants fall, they can be brought to trial. In the meantime, international criminal law scholars and diplomats at the United Nations are at work to turn this temporary international criminal court into a permanent one, with universal jurisdiction.

SOURCES

1. John F. Burns, "Sarajevo Muslims Try to Fathom Hate," *The New York Times*, January 3, 1993, p. 6.
2. John F. Burns, "2 Serbs to Be Shot for Killings and Rapes," *The New York Times*, March 31, 1993, p. A6.
3. European Community investigation into the treatment of Muslim women in the former Yugoslavia, Annex I to letter dated 2 February 1993 from the Permanent Representative of Denmark to the United Nations addressed to the Secretary General, S/25240 of 3 February 1993, and Security Council Resolution S/RES/771 of 13 August 1992.
4. Resolution of the United Nations Security Council S/RES/808 of 22 February 1993.

QUESTIONS FOR DISCUSSION

1. What sorts of problems have prevented the establishment of a permanent international criminal court since the first call for one after World War I?
2. Why did President Bush fail to support the establishment of an international criminal court with power to try Iraqi aggressors?
3. How will such a court deal with accused war criminals who are still under arms?

The Serbian "ethnic cleansing" policy in Bosnia aimed at creating exclusively Serbian territories by killing the Muslim population or driving Muslims out.

"The old-fashioned methods are time consuming, costly, and inefficient in dealing with the new transnational crimes."

"Arresting transnational criminals can be a problem: General Noriega, for example, was not about to arrest himself."

were launched by New York State prosecutors and federal officials. But California, Connecticut, Georgia, and other U.S. states also had jurisdiction; so did the authorities of sixty-eight other countries. This is an investigative nightmare, just like the investigation into the Pan Am disaster. Up to now, police have relied on old-fashioned methods: local investigations, cooperation with the police of other countries (aided by the information network of the International Criminal Police Organization [INTERPOL] in Lyons, France), and officially transmitted requests for assistance (evidence, documents, testimony) from abroad. But the old-fashioned methods are time consuming, costly, and inefficient in dealing with the new transnational crimes. Some scholars argue, therefore, that an international criminal court should be given the power to bring before it and try transnational criminals, at the request of any state that has jurisdiction.

Arrest. It is usually possible to arrest an international or transnational criminal who is in one's country, but it is much more difficult if the wanted person is someone abroad, in high office, or protected by another government. General Noriega held all the power in Panama and was not about to arrest himself, and the German and Japanese war criminals in 1945 could not be arrested until their power had been taken away.

When a wanted person remains abroad but is supposed to stand trial in another jurisdiction, extradition proceedings have traditionally been used to obtain custody. An extradition request, usually made after indictment, is transmitted to the "requested" government by the "requesting" government. Usually a judicial hearing is then held by the requested government, and if the request is found to be proper, the wanted person is extradited (transported) to the requesting coun-

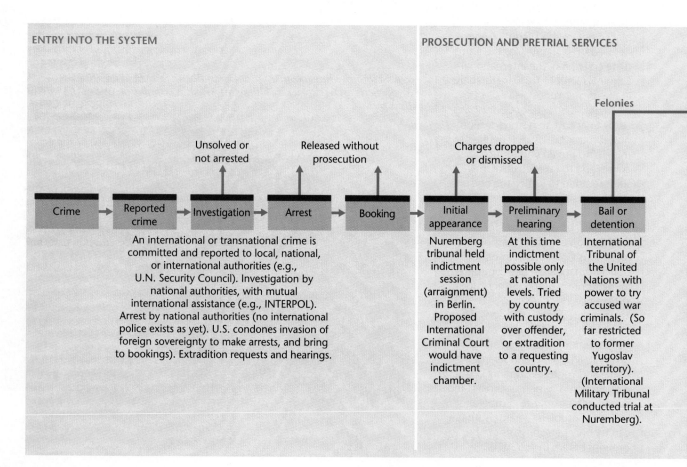

ENTRY INTO THE SYSTEM

PROSECUTION AND PRETRIAL SERVICES

Felonies

Unsolved or not arrested

Released without prosecution

Charges dropped or dismissed

Crime → Reported crime → Investigation → Arrest → Booking → Initial appearance → Preliminary hearing → Bail or detention

An international or transnational crime is committed and reported to local, national, or international authorities (e.g., U.N. Security Council). Investigation by national authorities, with mutual international assistance (e.g., INTERPOL). Arrest by national authorities (no international police exists as yet). U.S. condones invasion of foreign sovereignty to make arrests, and bring to bookings). Extradition requests and hearings.

Nuremberg tribunal held indictment session (arraignment) in Berlin. Proposed International Criminal Court would have indictment chamber.

At this time indictment possible only at national levels. Tried by country with custody over offender, or extradition to a requesting country.

International Tribunal of the United Nations with power to try accused war criminals. (So far restricted to former Yugoslav territory). (International Military Tribunal conducted trial at Nuremberg).

try. Experts agree that this is a cumbersome procedure whose effectiveness is severely limited by four factors:

1. Many countries do not have extradition treaties (agreements) with many other countries.
2. Most governments have a policy of not extraditing their own nationals.
3. Many countries have a "political offense" exception, and do not extradite for crimes they consider political.
4. Many countries without capital punishment refuse to extradite to a country with capital punishment.

The Pan Am flight 103 case demonstrates the point. Libya apparently conducted a hearing following the various extradition requests for the alleged terrorists, but refused to extradite its own nationals. American law has long found ways to get around the frustrating limitations of extradition. Over a century ago, the U.S. Supreme Court decided that an American court has the power to try a criminal defendant even if he or she was brought before the court in an illegal manner (in this case by having been kidnapped by a U.S. federal law enforcement officer in Lima, Peru).[9] Such a kidnapping violates international law and the law of the country where it takes place; the kidnapping country owes an apology and civil compensation to the country whose laws were violated. There is another means of making an arrest overseas that is even worse than kidnapping: military invasion of a foreign country, for example, the U.S. invasion of Panama. This, in itself, constitutes the international crime of aggression. Experts argue that the time has come for the international community to agree on more civilized procedures for taking international/transnational criminals into custody.

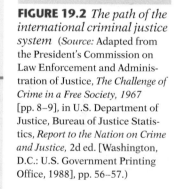

Investigators from many jurisdictions picking through the debris of Pan Am flight 103, destroyed over Lockerbie, Scotland, by a terrorist bomb.

"Experts argue that the time has come for the international community to agree on more civilized procedures for taking international/transnational criminals into custody."

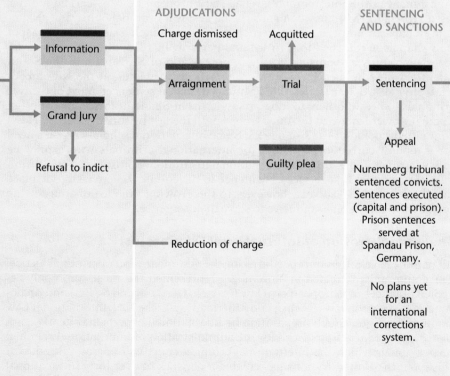

FIGURE 19.2 *The path of the international criminal justice system* (*Source:* Adapted from the President's Commission on Law Enforcement and Administration of Justice, *The Challenge of Crime in a Free Society,* 1967 [pp. 8–9], in U.S. Department of Justice, Bureau of Justice Statistics, *Report to the Nation on Crime and Justice,* 2d ed. [Washington, D.C.: U.S. Government Printing Office, 1988], pp. 56–57.)

ADJUDICATIONS

SENTENCING AND SANCTIONS

Information

Charge dismissed

Acquitted

Arraignment

Trial

Sentencing

Grand Jury

Appeal

Refusal to indict

Guilty plea

Nuremberg tribunal sentenced convicts. Sentences executed (capital and prison). Prison sentences served at Spandau Prison, Germany.

Reduction of charge

No plans yet for an international corrections system.

Pretrial and Adjudication

The classic example of pretrial proceedings for international criminals is the pretrial and indictment session conducted after World War II by the four major Allied powers in Berlin, at the old German parliament building, before their trial as war criminals at Nuremberg. Here the indictments were prepared and presented in open court. Defense counsel made many requests for subpoenaing of witnesses, access to documents, motions, and pleas. In one case, that of Hitler's deputy Rudolph Hess, a plea of insanity was made and an appropriate pretrial examination was conducted.

The permanent international criminal court of the United Nations would have such an indictment chamber, and trial could take place only after an official accusation had been found. Grand-jury-type proceedings have special value in the case of hard-to-reach absent defendants. In such proceedings, just as in grand-jury proceedings, evidence could be assembled to make a prima facie case against the defendant. A warrant of arrest could then be issued to be executed anywhere in the world. If the defendant's country would not extradite, the defendant would be virtually confined to that country, since all other countries might make an arrest and allow extradition.

The International Law Commission of the United Nations has been working on a draft statute for the creation of the United Nations' international criminal court, but progress has been slow. In February 1993, events in the former Yugoslavia acted as a catalyst for drastic change: The Security Council finally decided to create an international criminal court.

Corrections

Historically, incapacitation and retribution have been the primary approaches to punishment in the international arena. The European powers learned a bitter lesson when, in 1814, they banished the biggest war criminal of his time, Napoleon Bonaparte, emperor of the French, to Elba, a French island off the coast of Italy. Napoleon returned to start yet another war. In 1815, after his second defeat, Napoleon was banished to the remote island of St. Helena in the South Atlantic, where he died in 1821. More than a century later, at the Nuremberg trials after World War II, the Allied Military Tribunal sentenced most of the war criminals to death, others to long prison terms at Spandau Prison near Berlin. There they were guarded by Allied troops until the last prisoner (Rudolph Hess) committed suicide in 1987, at age 93. Some international scholars argue a need for a modest correctional system for international criminals who cannot be safely incarcerated within any one national institution. For transnational criminals, they suggest that service of sentence in the country where trial took place may be preferable—subject, however, to the growing practice of transferring prisoners to their home countries to serve their sentence.

"Some scholars argue the need for a modest correctional system for international convicts who cannot be safely incarcerated within any one national institution."

The Administration of International Criminal Justice

All nations have different procedures for the administration of criminal justice. The compromises created at Nuremberg represented the most commonly accepted practices of European civil law (French, German, and Soviet) and Anglo-American common law (English and American law). The U.N. International Law Commission, after much preparation by international experts, has nearly completed a procedural framework for the administration of international criminal justice, under which the international criminal court will operate. Besides, at this point the United Nations has created a network of over forty international standards, norms, guidelines, and models for the administration of national criminal justice systems. These include what U.N. experts agree are the most effective and humane principles of criminal procedure.[10] Inasmuch as the governments of the world have created these standards for their own national criminal justice systems, there is an expectation that they might serve an international system equally well.

Just a few years ago, scholars and policymakers working toward the establishment of a worldwide international criminal justice system were regarded as dreamers.[11] Today they are considered realists, as the need for an equitable and effective system of international criminal justice becomes more and more obvious.

"A few years ago, scholars working for a worldwide criminal justice system were regarded as dreamers; today they are considered realists."

COMPARATIVE CRIMINAL JUSTICE

So far we have dealt with the very practical question of how to protect ourselves against criminality that crosses international boundaries or may span the entire globe. That concern, and the system developing to deal with it, is called **international criminal justice.** We turn now to a different aspect of the globalization of crime: **comparative criminal justice,** or the science of evaluating the features, successes, and failures of various distinct criminal justice systems, to determine which works best under different cultural, social, or economic conditions and what should be held in common by all systems simply because they all deal with human beings. This urgent task requires us to consider a multitude of cultural factors which, more than criminal justice factors, may determine any one country's crime rate.

international criminal justice
Emerging international system for dealing with international and transnational crime.

comparative criminal justice
Science of evaluating the features, successes, and failures of various distinct criminal justice systems.

The Emergence of Different Legal Systems

The Romans, whose example we used before, learned and borrowed heavily from the Greeks and perfected an extraordinarily sophisticated system of justice. This system was extended to the regions of Europe, North Africa, and the Near East that the Romans controlled. Beyond these borders, so the Romans contended, there lived only lions and barbarians. Among these barbarians were the Germanic tribes of Eastern and Northern Europe, who lived by relatively simple and concrete customary or tribal law. These two legal systems, the Roman and the Germanic, have provided the world with its two dominant systems of justice, including criminal justice (see Table 19.1 for an analysis of the systems). In the Middle Ages, Roman law was taught at the European universities, and in its

"Two legal systems, the Roman and the Germanic, have provided the world with its two dominant systems of justice."

TABLE 19.1 Dominant Criminal Justice Systems	
Roman (Civil) Law	Common Law
Law and procedure governed by separate, comprehensive, systematized codes, which are forward-looking, wishing to anticipate all new problems	Law and procedure governed by laws and precedents which, if codified at all, simply organize past experiences
Codes based on scholarly analysis and conceptualizations	Laws reflect experience of practitioners, on a case-by-case basis
Supreme Courts interpret nuances of law	Supreme Courts develop law
Legal proceedings must establish entire truth	Truth-finding strictly limited by pleadings and rules of evidence
Judges free to find and interpret facts	Rules of evidence limit fact-finding process
Very little lay participation	Grand and petit juries play strong role
No presumption of guilt or innocence	Presumption of innocence

THE IMAGINATIVE BEGINNING OF COMPARATIVE CRIMINAL JUSTICE

More than half a century ago there appeared a curious book. In the preface the author addressed his reader with this warning: "Reader! This work is not offered to you as a piece of scientific research, but mainly as a book of informational entertainment." It was a remarkable book in every respect, since it led the reader through reports of trials in all ages, in all parts of the world. But then the author was a remarkable person. He was John Henry Wigmore, one of the founders of modern criminal justice, dean of Northwestern University School of Law (Chicago), founder of the Journal of Criminal Law and Criminology (in 1909) and of the American Institute of Criminal Law and Criminology, and the absolute authority on the law of evidence (1).

The book to which we refer is called *A Kaleidoscope of Justice*. Wigmore himself explained its purpose as follows:

And what is a "kaleidoscope"? It is now only a child's toy, though it was once regarded as a scientific instrument when it was invented a century or more ago. A dictionary definition would be: "An instrument in the shape of a telescopic tube containing colored pieces of glass with reflecting surfaces, so arranged that when it is revolved by hand the same pieces fall at each turn again and again into new symmetrical varicolored forms." And the Kaleidoscope of Justice shows the different peoples of the world in all times and climes perpetually engaged in this perennial process of seeking to administer justice, in one or another fashion. The same recurring elements are found combining again and again in new designs. (2)

And what are these "recurring elements" of justice? As Wigmore saw it, they are:

- a responsible person at the head
- the people exercising the power of justice
- the tribunal
- personnel associated with the tribunal
- the party complaining or prosecuting
- the quest for the wrongdoer
- the opportunity for a hearing
- the kind of proof
- the deliberations of the tribunal
- the judgment that frees or convicts the accused (2, pp. v–vi)

Here are some samples from Wigmore's rich collection:

Scholars believe that the jurymen at the trial of Socrates, in 399 B.C., took an oath something like this:

"I shall vote in conformity with the laws and with the decrees, those of the people of Athens and the Senate of Five Hundred; in cases which the legislature has not foreseen I will do what is just, not guided by fear or authority; I shall vote only on the questions submitted to the Court; I shall listen with attention to accuser and accused, the plaintiff and the defendant; I swear it by Zeus, by Apollo, by Demeter. If I am true to my oath, may my life be long! If I perjure myself, a curse be on me and my family!" (2, p. 675)

An account of a homicide trial among the Mano Tribe of Liberia describes the oath-taking procedure quite differently:

[M]agic drinks played a special part in legal proceedings among these tribes. . . . A substance of this kind which is in general use is *kefu*, the "oath medicine." A bottle of this concoction . . . is administered quite officially to everybody who has a statement to make in court. If his evidence should be false, *kefu* will make him ill until he is brought before the court himself and confesses his lie. . . . Lying is so common and so widely recognized as a habit . . . that no statement in court is taken seriously at all in the absence of the oath magic. (2, p. 418)

From Samoa, Wigmore reports yet another "chemical" method of discovering the truth:

The chief would take a certain plant and chew it, ejecting the juice into the hollow of his right hand. Then extending his arm full length, he would solemnly call over the names of his people; so long as the innocent were named, the fluid in the hollow of his hand would give no sign, but on the mention of the guilty one, the liquor would run over the edge of his hand and up his arm. (2, p. 622)

As late as 1940, a Choctaw chief in Louisiana was acquitted of murder in a white man's court but explained to the judge that he still had to undergo a tribal trial:

If the tribal trial finds him guilty, . . . he will be sentenced to suicide.

"They give me gun. They say: 'Go shoot yo'se'f.' I do."

Choctaw law gives only one defense for killing a human being outside of war, he said; that is accident. "But if you can't prove it was accident, what will you do?," asked Judge Stennis.

"Shoot myself," said Chief Cameron Wesley slowly.

"But if you change your mind and won't shoot yourself," asked Judge Stennis. "What happens then?"

"They give gun to my oldest son, John Wesley," said Chief Cameron Wesley. "He shoot me. Make all clean." (2, p. 474)

We have come a long way in the study of comparative criminal justice since the days when Wigmore's observations permitted him to identify universal commonalities of justice. After Wigmore, the search concentrated—and still does concentrate—much more on the differences. Today's comparatists believe that a study of different approaches to dealing with problems of crime and justice makes it possible to identify what seems to work best and what therefore might be suitable for transplant. Much attention is given to cultural differences. But comparatists are also searching for commonalities, basic standards that should govern all criminal justice systems, simply because all systems involve human beings dealing with other human beings.

Not all of Wigmore's initiatives outlived him. The American Institute of Criminal Law and Criminology existed for only a few decades. But the forces Wigmore mobilized are still powerful: the drive for a humane, effective criminal justice, resting on a scientific criminological basis, and on the experience of all humankind, for the benefit of all humankind. It was Wigmore who mobilized the fields of criminal justice and comparative criminal justice.

A Tuareg chief and his council, Azaouak, Sahel.

SOURCES

1. Gerhard O.W. Mueller, *Crime, Law and the Scholars* (London; Heinemann; Seattle: University of Washington Press, 1969), pp. 78–81.
2. John Henry Wigmore, *A Kaleidoscope of Justice* (Washington, D.C.: Washington Law Book Co., 1941), p. v.

QUESTIONS FOR DISCUSSION

1. Those who work in comparative criminal justice must take into account cultural differences. Using any of the accounts from Wigmore's book, explain how cultural differences affect the differences in criminal justice procedure.
2. Does Wigmore's list of the common elements of criminal justice systems suggest that all societies would eventually develop very similar systems?
3. What are some of the hazards of using anecdotal evidence to draw conclusions about criminal justice systems?

revitalized form spread all over the Continent. Today, all continental European countries have systems of justice that belong to the family of Roman law. As the influence of the European powers spread across the globe through colonialism and trade, the Roman system reached Latin America, Africa (where territory was controlled by continental European countries), and Asia, where China and Japan adopted codes derived from the continental European (Roman) system.

England was the one country that did not adopt the Roman system: The English retained and developed a legal system that was Germanic in origin. The system was founded on the common law. During the era of colonization, England too extended its influence across the globe, and it spread its legal system to America north of Mexico (with the exception of Quebec and Louisiana), to the West Indies, to those parts of Africa it controlled, and to India.

A number of countries have retained or returned to indigenous (native) systems of justice, among them Islamic countries, including Saudi Arabia, Iran, Pakistan, and the Sudan. In these countries, the Koran (Islamic holy book) governs the daily lives of the people. Moreover, in many countries that have adopted "Western" (a term used to describe both Roman law and common law) legal systems, indigenous law is still applied by many people living far from the capitals and the urban centers.

For example, in 1957 Emperor Haile Selassie I of Ethiopia, in an effort to modernize his country, introduced a modern penal code drafted by the highly respected Swiss scholar Jean Graven.[12] This very sophisticated Swiss-style code was completely alien to the customs of the Ethiopians. A few European-trained judges applied it in the courts of the capital, but it was meaningless in the distant provinces. There tribal elders continued to apply established tribal law and, despite a Communist revolution that deposed the emperor and a counterrevolution that deposed the Communists, continue to do so to this day. In other countries— Nigeria, for example—tribal (indigenous) justice was retained for all but the most serious crimes, which are tried in the federal courts according to British-imposed English common law.

"In many countries, tribal or indigenous traditional justice has been retained for all but the most serious crimes."

The Comparative Study of Criminal Law and Justice

The major differences between the two main systems of criminal justice are shown in Table 19.1. Scholars and researchers in comparative criminal justice study these differences and their impact on the day-to-day administration of justice. Most of all, comparative scholars are interested in learning what works best in providing justice and in controlling crime. Which solutions are more humane, more effective, more efficient?[13] Studies attempting to address such questions have proved enormously difficult. There is not only the difference in laws and their enforcement; there is also the difference in culture, historical experience, economic system, and social development.

Moreover, there are major differences in the outlook, orientations, and education of scholars from various countries who study criminal justice problems. Italian criminologists and criminal justice researchers tend to come from a background in medicine (especially psychiatry) or psychology. German and Dutch researchers usually have a legal background. For other countries, the background may be social work or philosophy. American researchers come predominantly from criminal justice and criminology. Their approach is now spreading all over the world because many foreign researchers have been educated in America and take these methods back to their home countries. Thus, American criminal justice research tends to provide the common language or approach for comparative studies in the field.

"From small beginnings, comparative study has grown into a great endeavor, a search for what is culturally transferable, effective, and humane."

The comparative study of criminal law had its antecedents in the nineteenth century, but became scientific only in the second half of the twentieth.[14] From small beginnings, comparative study has grown into a great endeavor, a search for what is culturally transferable, effective, and humane.[15] The empirical study of the functioning of criminal justice systems and their strategies is of even more recent origin. Such studies depend on the availability of accurate information. For many years INTERPOL has collected national crime statistics from as many of its member states as cared to report and has published these biannually.[16] The Secretariat of the United Nations, through its Crime Prevention and Criminal Justice Branch, has completed three world surveys on crime and the operations of criminal justice systems. (A fourth survey is in progress.) Beginning with 1970, these surveys record annual changes over five-year periods. The reports group types of crime in broad categories that include comparable—though not necessarily definitionally identical—types. But the difficulties with gathering world-wide statistics are considerable[17]:

- Response rates are low. Many countries regard crime as a reflection on the national image.
- Many crime types, as statistically reported, have no equivalents in other systems. What is—or was—a serious crime type, for example speculative commerce in the former Soviet Union, may be a totally legitimate activity elsewhere.
- Methods of recording may differ markedly. Attempted crimes may or may not be included in the statistics for completed crimes.
- The capacity to collect and record statistics varies among countries; so does the significance attributed to statistics. Moreover, there are no statisticians to gather data in many countries that have only recently emerged from colonial rule.

Despite these problems, the U.N. world crime surveys have improved over the years and now constitute a valuable initial basis for comparative study. The surveys have become more complete, less complex, and more reliable. Whereas only sixty-four countries participated in the first crime survey, the numbers rose to seventy-two for the second and ninety-three for the third.[18]

What do all the world crime surveys reveal? Broadly speaking, they show a steady increase in crime worldwide. The sharpest increases have been in drug-related crimes and robbery. Incarceration rates have risen, proportionate to the increase in crime (but prison sentences in the United States have risen disproportionately). The crime trend shows that by the year 2000 the world crime rate may be four times as high as it was in 1975.

One of the shortcomings of the U.N. surveys has been their dependence on official government statistics. Victim surveys to validate such statistics have been rare. The first major international (sixteen European and non-European countries) victimization study was undertaken in 1989. It revealed what American victimization studies indicate: There is divergence between police statistics and the results of victimization surveys:

"The crime trend shows that by the year 2000, the world crime rate may be four times as high as it was in 1975."

There is far from close correspondence between the two measures, but similarity on various fronts. The closest association was between the two measures of thefts of cars, an offense particularly likely to be reported to the police. Burglary levels were moderately associated. For robbery, assault and sexual offenses, there was poor correspondence. However, correspondence was fairly strong when only survey crimes reported to the police were considered.

These results suggest that for comparative purposes survey victimization rates may well be a more valid measure of the burden of crime upon the public than police statistics, since they are less affected by differences in reporting and/or official recording.[19]

The understanding that our lives are interdependent has increased scholarly interest in comparative studies. Many organizations contribute to the international information flow that is so vital to comparative study:

"For comparative purposes, survey victimization rates may well be a more valid measure of the burden of crime . . . than police statistics. . . ."
Jan J. M. van Dijk, Pat Mayhew, and Martin Kilias, *Experiences of Crime across the World*, 1990.

- The Office of International Criminal Justice, of the University of Illinois, Chicago, with its newsletter *Criminal Justice International*, its conferences, and overseas visits

- The Comparative Criminal Law Project, Wayne State University, Detroit, with its *American Series of Foreign Penal Codes* (29 volumes) and its other publications
- The International Association of Penal Law (and its American National Section)
- The Division on International Criminology of the American Society of Criminology
- The International Society of Social Defense

Professional journals increasingly publish comparative studies, and several journals are devoted exclusively to comparative criminal justice and criminology, including:

- The International Review of Criminal Policy (U.N.)
- The Crime Prevention and Criminal Justice Newsletter (U.N.)
- The International Journal of Comparative and Applied Criminal Justice (Wichita State University)
- The Journal of Offender Therapy and Comparative Criminology (Oregon Health Sciences University)
- The International Criminal Police Review (INTERPOL)[20]

Comparative criminal justice has matured into an academic discipline, which in a relatively short period has produced a number of major multinational studies on trends in crime rates,[21] on the impact of modernization on crime,[22] and on crime prevention policies and planning.[23]

THE PRACTICAL WORK OF THE UNITED NATIONS IN CRIME PREVENTION AND CRIMINAL JUSTICE

Over the last few decades, the U.N. programs in crime prevention and criminal justice have become the focal point of activities in international and comparative criminal justice. These programs consist of the Secretariat's Crime Prevention and Criminal Justice Branch, located in Vienna, Austria; several interregional[24] and regional[25] research and training institutes; and several supporting services.[26] These U.N. programs are monitored by the U.N. Commission on Crime Prevention and Criminal Justice, composed of forty member states on a rotating basis. Policy is set by the U.N. Congress on the Prevention of Crime and the Treatment of Offenders, which has met every five years since 1955.[27] All national governments have the right to participate.

U.N. activities in crime prevention and criminal justice are broad ranging. Many aim at assisting individual countries in their own crime prevention and criminal justice efforts. Some are designed to provide technical assistance to individual countries. Some aim at improving the capacity of governments to deal with their domestic crime problems in a humane manner; others are directed at dealing with international and transnational crime. Of particular significance are the norms, guidelines, standards, and models pertaining to a wide range of criminal justice issues, among them:

- The United Nations Standard Minimum Rules for the Treatment of Prisoners
- The Code of Conduct for Law Enforcement Officials
- The United Nations Standard Minimum Rules for the Administration of Juvenile Justice (the Beijing Rules)
- The United Nations Guidelines for the Prevention of Juvenile Delinquency (the Rijadh Guidelines)[28]

OPPORTUNITIES FOR COMPARATIVE CRIMINAL JUSTICE

No country has a monopoly on experience and achievement in controlling crime humanely, effectively, and efficiently, whether through criminal justice systems or social control measures. Experts agree that even the poorest and least developed countries can point to achievements in crime control—for example, mediation and victim compensation—that other, perhaps far more developed, countries could use as models. Comparative criminal justice aims at the exchange of experiences, not their imposition on others.

With the collapse of the Soviet state came the collapse of its secret police apparatus and the beginnings of the rule of law. Russians toppled the statue of Felix Derzhinsky, founder of the KGB, in a Moscow square and replaced it with a monument to those tortured and killed by the KGB.

Humane Criminal Justice

Considering that only forty years ago there was no agreement among the governments of the world as to what constitutes humane criminal justice procedures, the world has come a long way in a short period of time. The countries of the world have agreed on a basic set of standards for the humane administration of criminal justice. These standards extend to all areas of criminal justice, from crime prevention to policing to prosecution and adjudication to corrections. Some countries have taken the standards very seriously, by enacting them into law or by adjusting their laws accordingly, and by using them in the training of officials. Some have ignored them. And some are undergoing change. By way of example, with the fall of the Communist dictatorship, Russians are working to introduce rule-of-law standards and humane principles into their criminal justice system. With the standards as guides, legislators and criminal justice specialists are in the process of building a new criminal justice system.

Effective and Efficient Criminal Justice

Some of the U.N. norms and guidelines aim primarily at making criminal justice humane. Others seek to improve the effectiveness of crime control, frequently by using methods outside the criminal justice system. One example is the Guidelines for the Prevention of Juvenile Delinquency, adopted by the U.N. General Assembly in 1990. These stress the role of the family, of education, and of social and community-based services; the avoidance of unnecessary labeling; and the encouragement of youth participation.[29]

Similarly, the United Nations Standard Minimum Rules for the Administration of Juvenile Justice (1985) incorporate the best of the world's collective experience in administering a juvenile justice system, including the experience after the U.S. Supreme Court decision *In re Gault* (see Chapter 17).[30] Any nation can use these standard minimum rules and, allowing for cultural diversities, construct a juvenile justice system.

While we have emphasized macro-system comparisons and the work of the United Nations, there is perhaps more benefit to be derived from micro-comparisons focusing on a single question or issue. This work is undertaken largely by individual scholars and private or government research agencies.

Obviously, the more specific a comparative study in the field of criminal justice, the less costly it is, the less it need rely on national statistics, and the more it can rely on data the researchers themselves generate. As the number of such studies increases, so does our understanding of our own system in comparison with others. Recent comparative research includes studies of perception of police power by the citizens of different countries,[31] the role of women as line police officers in different cultures,[32] white-collar crime challenges to law enforcement in contrasting economic systems,[33] social control in contrasting cultural settings,[34] the relation of informal (family, school) to formal (police) social con-

In the non-Western societies of the world, both industrialized and wealthy and nonindustrialized and poor, social control—and crime control—are accomplished in very different ways. These Saudis may have the latest Western toys, but their lives continue to be sanctioned by tradition.

trols in ten very different countries,[35] the impact of crime coverage in newspapers on public attitudes and reactions in a variety of countries,[36] AIDS, law and social control in China,[37] homicide and deterrence in Japan,[38] women's prisons in Japan,[39] offender profiles in Saudi Arabia,[40] Islamic social control (synnomie),[41] unemployment and crime in Japan,[42] prisons in China,[43] victims in the Polish justice system,[44] Danish-American comparison of punishments,[45] a similar Canadian-French comparison,[46] the relationship between the economy and crime in the former Soviet Union during and after Communism,[47] Indian delinquency in comparative perspective,[48] delinquent youth in the culture of the U.S. and India,[49] or Hungarian prisons,[50] to mention but a few of the growing number of comparative studies. Such studies contribute to the growing pool of information on the functioning of the criminal justice system, in support of reform efforts everywhere. It is exciting to realize that just as crime has become globalized, so has criminal justice.

"Just as crime has become globalized, so has criminal justice."

REVIEW

International criminal justice is the system and the process by which offenders under international criminal law, or under the laws of several countries, may be dealt with. Comparative criminal justice is the study of two or more criminal justice systems, their functioning, their interdependencies, and the lessons to be learned from comparisons. International crimes are those that threaten the peace and security of humankind collectively. Violent crimes (e.g., aggressive war and genocide) were the first to be recognized. But increasingly, such criminal activities as terrorism and international narcotics transactions are included among international crimes. Transnational crimes, on the other hand, are offenses that violate the laws of more than one country; some of these are so dangerous and complex as to call for collective action. To explain international and transnational crimes, we need the concept of "jurisdiction," meaning the right and power to define crimes and to punish criminals. Criminal jurisdiction is now in the process of expanding to a yet higher level, the world level.

The machinery for dealing with international/transnational crimes is still developing; success depends largely on international cooperation. But an international criminal justice system is now ready to be activated.

The differences between various legal systems permit us to make comparative studies for the benefit of our own and every other system. Various organizations are devoted to the study of comparative criminal justice, and there are many tools for such study at the disposition of students and researchers. The United Nations Crime Prevention and Criminal Justice Branch and the various U.N. institutes and supporting organizations have become the focal point of practical comparative criminal justice. Their work has an increasing impact on the practical administration of criminal justice in many countries around the world.

Notes

1. Ethan A. Nadelman, "Global Prohibition Regimes: The Evolution of Norms in International Society," *International Organization* 44 (1990):479–526; Gerhard O. W. Mueller, "Four Decades after Nuremberg: The Prospect of an International Criminal Code," *Connecticut Journal of International Law* 2 (1987):499–507.

2. Agreement for the Prosecution and Punishment of Major War Criminals of the European Axis (London Agreement), 8 August 1945, 82 U.N.T.S. 279, 59 Stat. 1544, E.A.S. No. 472.

3. Draft Articles of the Draft Code of Crimes against the Peace and Security of Mankind, adopted by the International Law Commission on First Reading, United Nations, New York, 1991.

4. For a complete listing, see M. Cherif Bassiouni, *International Criminal Law—A Draft International Criminal Code* (Alphen an den Rijn, Netherlands: Sijthoff & Noordhoff, 1980). For recent discussions of all international crimes, see M. Cherif Bassiouni, ed., *International Criminal Law*, Vol. 1, *Crimes* (Dobbs Ferry, N.Y.: Transnational, 1986); M. Cherif Bassiouni, *A Draft International Criminal Code and Draft Statute for an International Criminal Tribunal* (Dordrecht, Netherlands: Martinus Nijhoff, 1987); Farhad Malekian, *International Criminal Law* (Motala, Sweden: Borgstroms Trycker, 1991), 2 vols.

5. André Bossard, *Transnational Crime and Criminal Law* (Chicago: Office of International Criminal Justice, 1990); Harold E. Smith, ed., *Transnational Crime: Investigative Responses* (Chicago: Office of International Criminal Justice, 1989).

6. See Draft Articles, Article 25.

7. Report of the International Law Commission on the Work of its Forty-Second Session, G.A. A/45/10, 1990. See also Draft Statute, International Criminal Tribunal, International Institute of Higher Studies in Criminal Science, Eighth United Nations Congress on the Prevention of Crime and the Treatment of Offenders, A/CONF. 144/ NGO ISISC, 31 July 1990; Robert H. Dickson, "Libya Case Shows Need for Terrorism Court," *The New York Times*, April 24, 1992, p. 34.

8. In general, see M. Cherif Bassiouni, ed., *International Criminal Law*, Vols. 2 and 3, *Enforcement* and *Procedure* (Dobbs Ferry, N.Y.: Transnational, 1986, 1987).

9. *Ker v. Illinois*, 119 U.S. 436 (1886). See Theodore C. Jonas, "International 'Fugitive Snatching' in U.S. Law: Two Views from Opposite Ends of the Eighties," *Cornell International Law Journal* 24 (1991):521–562. The U.S. Supreme Court has in effect maintained that position in its most recent opinion: *United States v. Alvarez-Machain*, 112 S.Ct. 2188 (1992).

10. G. O. W. Mueller, "United Nations Norms and Guidelines in Crime Prevention and Criminal Justice," *UNAFEI Resource Material Series* 33 (1991):34–45 (Fuchu, Tokyo, Japan). See also *Compendium of United Nations Standards and Norms in Crime Prevention and Criminal Justice*, A.CONF. 144/INF.2, 11 May 1990 (New York: United Nations).

11. The first comprehensive course book on international criminal law was published as late as 1965. See Gerhard O. W. Mueller and Edward M. Wise, *International Criminal Law* (South Hackensack, N.J.: Fred B. Rothman; London: Sweet and Maxwell, 1965).

12. Jean Graven, *Le Code Penal de l'Empire d'Ethiopie* (Paris: Centre Francaise de Droit Comparé, 1959).

13. On comparative law and social theory, in general, see Jerome Hall, *Comparative Law and Social Theory* (Baton Rouge: Louisiana State University Press, 1963).

14. G. O. W. Mueller, *Comparative Criminal Law in the United States*, Vol. 4, Monograph Series of the Comparative Criminal Law Project (South Hackensack, N.J.: Fred B. Rothman, 1970). See also Hermann Mannheim, *Comparative Criminology* (London: Routledge and Kegan Paul; Boston: Houghton Mifflin, 1965), 2 vols.; J. A. Coutts, *The Accused: A Comparative Study* (London: Stevens & Sons, 1966); Francis L. Sullivan, Paul Hardin III, John Huston, Frank R. Lacy, Daniel E. Murray, and George W. Pugh, *Cases and Materials in the Administration of Criminal Justice* (New York: Foundation Press, 1966).

15. In lieu of many, see Richard S. Frase, "Comparative Criminal Justice as a Guide to American Law Reform: How Do the French Do It, How Can We Find Out, and Why Should We Care?," *California Law Review* 78(3):539–683, and many references there. Also see Albin Eser and George P. Fletcher, *Justification and Excuse—Comparative Perspectives* (Freiburg, Germany: Max-Planck Institut, 1987).

16. International Criminal Police Organization, *International Crime Statistics*: INTERPOL, (eighty-six countries reporting for 1987–1988). See also Michael Fooner, *INTERPOL: Issues in World Crime and International Criminal Justice* (New York: Plenum, 1989).

17. See Badr-El-Din Ali, "Methodological Problems in International Criminal Justice Research," *International Journal of Comparative and Applied Criminal Justice* 10 (1986):167–176.

18. A/32/199, of 1977 (first survey); A/CONF. 121/18 and Corr. 1, of 1985 (second survey); A/CONF. 144/6, of 1990 (third survey). See also Matti Joutsen, *International Surveys of Crime and Crime Control* (Baltimore: American Society of Criminology, 1990); Carol B. Kalish, *International Crime Rates* (Washington, D.C.: U.S. Bureau of Justice Statistics, Special Report, 1988). However, eighty-nine countries, of which at least seventeen maintain crime statistics, have not participated in the world crime surveys. See G. O. W. Mueller, *World Survey on the Availability of Criminal Justice Statistics* (Washington, D.C.: Bureau of Justice Statistics, 1993).

19. Jan J. M. van Dijk, Pat Mayhew, and Martin Kilias, *Experiences of Crime across the World* (Deventer, Netherlands: Kluwer Law and Taxation Publishers, 1990), p. 100.

20. In addition there are the journals published by the various nongovernmental organizations in criminal justice, including the so-called big four: the International Association of Penal Law, The International Society for Social Defense, the International Society of Criminology, and the International Penal and Penitentiary Foundation; as well as the professional organizations: the International Federation of Senior Police Officers, the International Association of Chiefs of Police, the International Police Association, the International Prisoners Aid Association, the Howard League for Penal Reform, the International Association of Youth Magistrates. In addition, a number of international human rights organizations devote a considerable portion of their efforts in research, publication, and advocacy to matters of human rights in criminal justice. Two of the most well known are Amnesty International and the International Commission of Jurists.

21. Freda Adler, *Nations Not Obsessed with Crime*, Vol. 50, Publications of the Comparative Criminal Law Project (Littleton, Colo.: Fred B. Rothman, 1983); Marshall B. Clinard, *Cities with Little Crime: The Case of Switzerland* (Cambridge, Mass.: Cambridge University Press, 1978).

22. Marshall B. Clinard and Daniel J. Abbot, *Crime in Developing Countries: A Comparative Perspective* (New York: Wiley, 1973); Louise I. Shelley, *Crime and Modernization* (Carbondale and Edwardsville: Southern Illinois University Press, 1981).

23. Hardy Wickwar, *The Place of Criminal Justice in Development Planning*, Monographs of the United Nations Crime Prevention and Criminal Justice Section (New York: New York University

Press, 1977); William Clifford, ed., *Crime Prevention Planning* (Canberra, Australia: Australian Institute of Criminology, 1977); Hernando Gomez Buendia, ed., *Urban Crime: Global Trends and Policies* (Tokyo: United Nations University, 1989). And see Jorg-Martin Jehle, ed., *Criminological Research and Planning in State and Supranational Institutions* (Wiesbaden, Germany: Kriminologische Zentralstelle, 1990). See also, Elmer H. Johnson, ed., *International Handbook of Contemporary Developments in Criminology* (Westport, Conn.: Greenwood Press, 1983), 2 vols.; Richard J. Terrill, *World Criminal Justice Systems* (Cincinnati, Ohio: Anderson, 1984); George F. Cole, Stanislaw J. Frankowski, and Marc K. Gertz, *Major Criminal Justice Systems: A Comparative Survey*, 2d ed. (Newbury Park, Calif.: Sage, 1987). Brunon Holyst, *Comparative Criminology* (Lexington, Mass.: Lexington Books, 1979); V. Lorne Stewart, ed., *Justice and Troubled Children around the World* (New York: New York University Press, 1980–1983), 5 vols.; Anthony P. Travisano, ed., *International Corrections: An Overview* (College Park, Md.: American Correctional Association, 1987).

24. The United Nations Interregional Crime and Justice Research Institute (UNICRI) at Rome, Italy; the International Centre for Criminal Law Reform and Criminal Justice Policy, affiliated with the United Nations, at Vancouver, Canada, and the Institute of Higher Studies in Criminal Sciences, at Siracusa, Italy.

25. The United Nations Asia and Far East Institute for the Prevention of Crime and the Treatment of Offenders (UNAFEI), at Fuchu, Tokyo, Japan; the United Nations Latin-American Institute for the Prevention of Crime and the Treatment of Offenders (ILANUD) at San José, Costa Rica; the European United Nations Institute for Crime Prevention and Control (HEUNI) at Helsinki, Finland; the United Nations African Institute for the Prevention of Crime and the Treatment of Offenders (UNAFRI), at Kampala, Uganda; the Australian Institute of Criminology, at Canberra, Australia, affiliated with the United Nations, and the Arab Security Study and Training Center, at Rijadh, Saudi Arabia.

26. The International Scientific and Professional Advisory Council for United Nations Programs in Crime Prevention and Criminal Justice (ISPAC), at Milan, Italy; the United Nations Criminal Justice Information Network (UNCJIN), at the State University of New York, Albany, New York; and the World Criminal Justice Library Network, at Rutgers University, Newark, New Jersey.

27. 1955: Geneva, Switzerland; 1960: London, U.K.; 1965: Stockholm, Sweden; 1970: Kyoto, Japan; 1975: Geneva Switzerland; 1980: Caracas, Venezuela; 1985: Milan, Italy; 1990: Havana, Cuba.

28. Most of these may be found in pamphlets published by the United Nations, or in the *Compendium of United Nations Standards and Norms*. See also G. O. W. Mueller, "United Nations Norms and Guidelines in Crime Prevention and Criminal Justice," *UNAFEI Resource Material Series* 38 (1990):34–45 (Fuchu, Tokyo, Japan). As to the U.N. standards on juvenile justice, see Antoinette Viccica, "The Promotion and Realization of Children's Rights through Development and Recognition of an International Notion of Juvenile Justice and Its Child-Centered Perspective in the United Nations," *Nordic Journal of International Law* 58 (1989):68–93.

29. U.N. General Assembly Resolution 45/112, 1990. See *The United Nations and Crime Prevention* (New York: United Nations, 1991), pp. 83–90. Adler, *Nations Not Obsessed with Crime*, pp. 80–91.

30. U.N. General Assembly Resolution 40/33, 1985. See also *The United Nations and Crime Prevention*, pp. 72–76; Rules for the Protection of Juveniles Deprived of Their Liberty, U.N. General Assembly Resolution 45/113, 1990; *The United Nations and Crime Prevention*, pp. 90–103.

31. Anastassios D. Mylonas, *Perception of Police Power: A Study in Four Cities*, Vol. 8, Monograph Series of the Comparative Criminal Law Project (South Hackensack, N.J.: Fred B. Rothman, 1973).

32. Mangai Natarajan, *Women's Perception of Their Role as Line Officers in Law Enforcement in India and the United States* (Ph.D. dissertation, Rutgers University, Newark, N.J., 1991).

33. Wojciech Cebulak, *White Collar Crime in Socialist and Capitalist Urban Settings* (Ph.D. dissertation, Rutgers University, Newark, N.J., 1989).

34. Sesha Kethineni, *Delinquency and Substance Abuse in India and the United States: A Test of Strain, Control and Social Learning Theory* (Ph.D. dissertation, Rutgers University, Newark, N.J., 1991).

35. Adler, *Nations Not Obsessed with Crime.*

36. See Harry L. Marsh, "A Comparative Analysis of Crime Coverage in Newspapers in the United States and Other Countries from 1960–1989: A Review of the Literature," *Journal of Criminal Justice* 19(1):67–79.

37. Allen F. Anderson, "China Report: AIDS, Law, and Social Control," *International Journal of Offender Therapy and Comparative Criminology* 35 (1991):303–309.

38. David Merriman, "Homicide and Deterrence: The Japanese Case," *International Journal of Offender Therapy and Comparative Criminology* 32 (1988):1–16.

39. Elmer H. Johnson, "Women's Prisons in Japan: A Comparative Analysis," *International Journal of Comparative and Applied Criminal Justice* 5 (1991):1–14.

40. Komanduri S. Murty, Julian B. Roebuck, and Mohammad A. Almalhem, "Profile of Adult Offenders in Dammam Central Prison, Saudi Arabia, *International Journal of Comparative and Applied Criminal Justice* 15 (1991):89–97.

41. Adel A. Helal and Charisse J.M. Coston, "Low Crime Rates in Bahrain: Islamic Social Control—Testing the Theory of Synnomie," *International Journal of Comparative and Applied Criminal Justice* 15 (1991):125–144.

42. Michael S. Vaughn, "The Relationship between Unemployment and Crime in Japan from 1926 to 1988: Trends during Emperor Hirohito's Reign," *International Journal of Comparative and Applied Criminal Justice* 15 (1991):153–173.

43. John M. Klafas, "Considering Prison in Context: The Case of the People's Republic of China," *International Journal of Comparative and Applied Criminal Justice* 15 (1991):175–186.

44. Ewa Bienkowska and Edna Erez, "Victims in the Polish Criminal Justice System: Law and Reality," *International Journal of Comparative and Applied Criminal Justice* 15 (1991):217–225.

45. William L. Selke, "A Comparison of Punishment Systems in Denmark and the United States," *International Journal of Comparative and Applied Criminal Justice* 15 (1991):227–242.

46. Marc Ouimet and Maurice Cusson, "Severity of Sanctions: A Comparison between Canada and France," *International Journal of Comparative and Applied Criminal Justice* 15 (1991):243–250.

47. Nanci Adler, "Planned Economy and Unplanned Criminality: The Soviet Experience," *International Journal of Comparative and Applied Criminal Justice* 17 (1993): 189–201.

48. Clayton A. Hartjen and Sesharajani Kethineni, "Delinquency in Comparative Perspective: India," *International Journal of Comparative and Applied Criminal Justice* 16 (1992):317–328.

49. Clayton A. Hartjen and Sesharajani Kethineni, "Culture, Gender, and Delinquency: A Study of Youths in the United States and India," *Women and Criminal Justice* (1993).

50. Jess Maghan, "The National Prison Service of Hungary," *American Jails* 5(2) (1991):92–96.

APPENDIX:
THE CONSTITUTION OF THE UNITED STATES OF AMERICA[1]

We the People of the United States, in Order to form a more perfect Union, establish Justice, insure domestic Tranquility, provide for the common defence, promote the general Welfare, and secure the Blessings of Liberty to ourselves and our Posterity, do ordain and establish this CONSTITUTION for the United States of America.

ARTICLE 1

Section 1. All legislative Powers herein granted shall be vested in a Congress of the United States, which shall consist of a Senate and House of Representatives.

Section 2. The House of Representatives shall be composed of Members chosen every second Year by the People of the several States, and the Electors in each State shall have the Qualifications requisite for Electors of the most numerous Branch of the State Legislature.

No Person shall be a Representative who shall not have attained to the Age of twenty-five Years, and been seven Years a Citizen of the United States, and who shall not, when elected, be an Inhabitant of that State in which he shall be chosen.

[Representatives and direct Taxes[2] shall be apportioned among the several States which may be included within this Union, according to their respective Numbers, which shall be determined by adding to the whole Number of free Persons, including those bound to Service for a Term of Years, and excluding Indians not taxed, three fifths of all other Persons.][3] The actual Enumeration shall be made within three Years after the first Meeting of the Congress of the United States, and within every subsequent Term of ten Years, in such Manner as they shall by Law direct. The Number of Representatives shall not exceed one for every thirty Thousand, but each State shall have at Least one Representative; and until such enumeration shall be made, the State of New Hampshire shall be entitled to chuse three, Massachusetts eight, Rhode-Island and Providence Plantations one, Connecticut five, New York six, New Jersey four, Pennsylvania eight, Delaware one, Maryland six, Virginia ten, North Carolina five, South Carolina five, and Georgia three.

When vacancies happen in the Representation from any State, the Executive Authority thereof shall issue Writs of Election to fill such Vacancies.

The House of Representatives shall chuse their Speaker and other Officers; and shall have the sole Power of Impeachment.

Section 3. The Senate of the United States shall be composed of two Senators from each State, chosen by the Legislature thereof, for six Years; and each Senator shall have one Vote.

Immediately after they shall be assembled in Consequence of the first Election, they shall be divided as equally as may be into three Classes. The Seats of the Senators of the first Class shall be vacated at the Expiration of the second Year, of the second Class at the Expiration of the fourth Year, and of the third Class at the Expiration of the sixth Year, so that one-third may be chosen every second Year; and if Vacancies happen by Resignation, or otherwise, during the Recess of the Legislature of any State, the Executive thereof may make temporary Appointments until the next Meeting of the Legislature, which shall then fill such Vacancies.

No Person shall be a Senator who shall not have attained to the Age of thirty Years, and been nine Years a Citizen of the United States, and who shall not, when elected, be an Inhabitant of that State for which he shall be chosen.

The Vice President of the United States shall be President of the Senate, but shall have no vote, unless they be equally divided.

The Senate shall chuse their other Officers, and also a President pro tempore, in the absence of the Vice President, or when he shall exercise the Office of President of the United States.

The Senate shall have the sole Power to try all Impeachments. When sitting for that purpose they shall be on Oath or Affirmation. When the President of the United States is tried, the Chief Justice shall preside: And no person shall be convicted without the Concurrence of two thirds of the Members present.

Judgment in Cases of Impeachment shall not extend further than to removal from Office, and disqualification to hold and enjoy any Office of honor, Trust, or Profit under the United States: but the Party convicted shall nevertheless be liable and subject to Indictment, Trial, Judgment, and Punishment, according to Law.

---

[1] This version follows the original Constitution in capitalization and spelling. It is adapted from the text published by the United States Department of the Interior, Office of Education.
[2] Altered by the Sixteenth Amendment.
[3] Negated by the Fourteenth Amendment.

Section 4. The Times, Places and Manner of holding Elections for Senators and Representatives, shall be prescribed in each State by the Legislature thereof; but the Congress may at any time by Law make or alter such Regulations, except as to the Places of Chusing Senators.

The Congress shall assemble at least once in every Year, and such Meeting shall be on the first Monday in December, unless they shall by Law appoint a different Day.

Section 5. Each House shall be the Judge of the Elections, Returns and Qualifications of its own Members, and a Majority of each shall constitute a Quorum to do Business; but a smaller number may adjourn from day to day, and may be authorized to compel the Attendance of absent Members, in such Manner, and under such Penalties, as each House may provide.

Each House may determine the Rules of its Proceedings, punish its Members for disorderly Behaviour, and, with the Concurrence of two thirds, expel a Member.

Each House shall keep a Journal of its Proceedings, and from time to time publish the same, excepting such Parts as may in their Judgment require Secrecy; and the Yeas and Nays of the Members of either House on any question shall, at the Desire of one fifth of those Present, be entered on the Journal.

Neither House, during the Session of Congress, shall, without the Consent of the other, adjourn for more than three days, nor to any other Place than that in which the two Houses shall be sitting.

Section 6. The Senators and Representatives shall receive a Compensation for their Services, to be ascertained by Law, and paid out of the Treasury of the United States. They shall in all Cases, except Treason, Felony, and Breach of the Peace, be privileged from Arrest during their Attendance at the Session of their respective Houses, and in going to and returning from the same; and for any Speech or Debate in either House, they shall not be questioned in any other Place.

No Senator or Representative shall, during the Time for which he was elected, be appointed to any civil Office under the Authority of the United States, which shall have been created, or the Emoluments whereof shall have been increased, during such time; and no Person holding any Office under the United States shall be a Member of either House during his continuance in Office.

Section 7. All Bills for raising Revenue shall originate in the House of Representatives; but the Senate may propose or concur with Amendments as on other bills.

Every Bill which shall have passed the House of Representatives and the Senate, shall, before it become a Law, be presented to the President of the United States; If he approve he shall sign it, but if not he shall return it, with his Objections, to that House in which it shall have originated, who shall enter the Objections at large on their Journal, and proceed to reconsider it. If after such Reconsideration two thirds of that House shall agree to pass the bill, it shall be sent, together with the objections, to the other House, by which it shall likewise be reconsidered, and if approved by two thirds of that House, it shall become a Law. But in all such Cases the Votes of both Houses shall be determined by Yeas and Nays, and the Names of the Persons voting for and against the Bill shall be entered on the Journal of each House respectively. If any Bill shall not be returned by the President within ten Days (Sundays excepted) after it shall have been presented to him, the Same shall be a Law, in like Manner as if he had signed it, unless the Congress by their Adjournment prevent its Return, in which Case it shall not be a Law.

Every Order, Resolution, or Vote to which the Concurrence of the Senate and House of Representatives may be necessary (except on a question of Adjournment) shall be presented to the President of the United States; and before the Same shall take Effect, shall be approved by him, or being disapproved by him, shall be repassed by two thirds of the Senate and House of Representatives, according to the Rules and Limitations prescribed in the Case of a Bill.

Section 8. The Congress shall have Power To lay and collect Taxes, Duties, Imposts and Excises, to pay the Debts and provide for the common Defence and general Welfare of the United States; but all Duties, Imposts and Excises shall be uniform throughout the United States;

To borrow money on the credit of the United States;

To regulate Commerce with foreign Nations, and among the several States, and with the Indian Tribes;

To establish an uniform rule of Naturalization, and uniform Laws on the subject of Bankruptcies throughout the United States;

To coin Money, regulate the Value thereof, and of foreign Coin, and fix the Standard of Weights and Measures;

To provide for the Punishment of counterfeiting the Securities and current Coin of the United States;

To establish Post Offices and post Roads;

To promote the Progress of Science and useful Arts, by securing for limited Times to Authors and Inventors the exclusive Right to their respective Writings and Discoveries;

To constitute Tribunals inferior to the Supreme Court;

To define and punish Piracies and Felonies committed on the high Seas, and Offenses against the Law of Nations;

To declare War, grant Letters of Marque and Reprisal, and make Rules concerning Captures on Land and Water;

To raise and support Armies, but no Appropriation of Money to that Use shall be for a Longer Term than two Years;

To provide and maintain a Navy;

To make Rules for the Government and Regulation of the land and naval forces;

To provide for calling forth the Militia to executive the Laws of the Union, suppress Insurrections and repel Invasions;

To provide for organizing, arming, and disciplining the Militia, and for governing such Part of them as may be employed in the Service of the United States, reserving to the States respectively, the Appointment of the Officers, and the Authority of training the Militia according to the discipline prescribed by Congress;

To exercise exclusive Legislation in all Cases whatsoever, over such District (not exceeding ten Miles square) as may, by Cession of particular States, and the acceptance of Congress, become the Seat of the Government of the United States, and to exercise like Authority over all Places purchased by the Consent of the Legislature of the State in which the Same shall be, for the Erection of Forts, Magazines, Arsenals, Dock-yards, and other needful Buildings;—And

To make all Laws which shall be necessary and proper for carrying into Execution the foregoing Powers, and all other Powers vested by this Constitution in the Government of the United States, or in any Department or Officer thereof.

Section 9. The Migration or Importation of such Persons as any of the States now existing shall think proper to admit, shall not be prohibited by the Congress prior to the Year one thousand eight hundred and eight, but a tax or duty may be imposed on such Importation, not exceeding ten dollars for each Person.

The privilege of the Writ of Habeas Corpus shall not be suspended, unless when in Cases of Rebellion or Invasion the public Safety may require it.

No bill of Attainder or ex post facto Law shall be passed.

No capitation, or other direct, Tax shall be laid unless in Proportion to the Census or Enumeration herein before directed to be taken.

No Tax or Duty shall be laid on Articles exported from any State.

No Preference shall be given by any Regulation of Commerce or Revenue to the Ports of one State over those of another: nor shall Vessels bound to, or from, one State, be obliged to enter, clear, or pay Duties in another.

No Money shall be drawn from the Treasury, but in Consequence of Appropriations made by Law; and a regular Statement and Account of the Receipts and Expenditures of all public Money shall be published from time to time.

No Title of Nobility shall be granted by the United States: And no Person holding any Office of Profit or Trust under them, shall, without the Consent of the Congress, accept of any present, Emolument, Office, or Title, of any kind whatever, from any King, Prince, or foreign State.

Section 10. No State shall enter into any Treaty, Alliance, or Confederation; grant Letters of Marque and Reprisal; coin Money; emit Bills of Credit; make any Thing but gold and silver Coin a Tender in Payment of Debts; pass any Bill of Attainder, ex post facto Law, or Law impairing the Obligation of Contracts, or grant any Title of Nobility.

No State shall, without the Consent of the Congress, lay any Imposts or Duties on Imports or Exports, except what may be absolutely necessary for executing its inspection Laws; and the net Produce of all Duties and Imposts, laid by any State on Imports or Exports, shall be for the use of the Treasury of the United States; and all such Laws shall be subject to the Revision and Control of the Congress.

No state shall, without the Consent of Congress, lay any duty of Tonnage, keep Troops, or Ships of War in time of Peace, enter into any Agreement or Compact with another State, or with a foreign Power, or engage in War, unless actually invaded, or in such imminent Danger as will not admit of delay.

ARTICLE II

Section 1. The executive Power shall be vested in a President of the United States of America. He shall hold his Office during the Term of four years, and, together with the Vice President, chosen for the same Term, be elected, as follows:

Each State shall appoint, in such Manner as the Legislature thereof may direct, a Number of Electors, equal to the whole Number of Senators and Representatives to which the State may be entitled in the Congress: but no Senator or Representative, or Person holding an Office of Trust or Profit under the United States, shall be appointed an Elector.

[The Electors shall meet in their respective States, and vote by Ballot for two persons, of whom one at least shall not be an Inhabitant of the same State with themselves. And they shall make a List of all the Persons voted for, and of the Number of Votes for each; which List they shall sign and certify, and transmit sealed to the Seat of the Government of the United States, directed to the President of the Senate. The President of the Senate shall, in the Presence of the Senate and House of Representatives, open all the Certificates, and the Votes shall then be counted. The Person having the greatest Number of Votes shall be the President, if such Number be a Majority of the whole Number of Electors appointed; and if there be more than one who have such Majority, and have an equal Number of Votes, then the House of Representatives shall immediately chuse by Ballot one of them for President; and if no Person have a Majority, then from the five highest on the List the said House shall in like Manner chuse the President. But in chusing the President, the Votes shall be taken by States, the Representation from each State having one Vote; a quorum for this Purpose shall consist of a Member or Members from two-thirds of the States, and a Majority of all the States shall be necessary to a Choice. In every Case, after the Choice of the President, the Person having the greatest Number of Votes of the Electors shall be the Vice President. But if there should remain two or more who have equal votes, the Senate shall chuse from them by Ballot the Vice President.][4]

The Congress may determine the Time of chusing the Electors, and the Day on which they shall give their Votes; which Day shall be the same throughout the United States.

No person except a natural-born Citizen, or a Citizen of the United States, at the time of the Adoption of this Constitution, shall be eligible to the Office of President; neither shall any Person be eligible to that Office who shall not have attained to the Age of thirty-five years, and been fourteen Years a Resident within the United States.

In Case of the Removal of the President from Office, or of his Death, Resignation, or Inability to discharge the Powers and Duties of the said Office, the same shall devolve on the Vice President, and the Congress may by Law provide for the Case of Removal, Death, Resignation, or Inability, both of the President and Vice President, declaring what Officer shall then act as President, and such Officer shall act accordingly, until the disability be removed, or a President shall be elected.

The President shall, at stated Times, receive for his Services a Compensation, which shall neither be increased nor diminished during the Period for which he shall have been elected, and he shall not receive within that Period any other Emolument from the United States, or any of them.

---

[4] Revised by the Twelfth Amendment.

Before he enter on the execution of his Office, he shall take the following Oath or Affirmation:—"I do solemnly swear (or affirm) that I will faithfully execute the Office of President of the United States, and will, to the best of my Ability, preserve, protect, and defend the Constitution of the United States."

Section 2. The President shall be Commander in Chief of the Army and Navy of the United States, and of the Militia of the several States, when called into the actual Service of the United States; he may require the Opinion, in writing, of the principal Officer in each of the executive Departments, upon any subject relating to the Duties of their respective Offices, and he shall have Power to Grant Reprieves and Pardons for Offenses against the United States, except in Cases of Impeachment.

He shall have Power, by and with the Advice and Consent of the Senate, to make Treaties, provided two-thirds of the Senators present concur; and he shall nominate, and by and with the Advice and Consent of the Senate, shall appoint Ambassadors, other public Ministers and Consuls, Judges of the supreme Court, and all other Officers of the United States, whose Appointments are not herein otherwise provided for, and which shall be established by Law: but the Congress may by Law vest the Appointment of such inferior Officers, as they think proper, in the President alone, in the Courts of Law, or in the Heads of Departments.

The President shall have Power to fill up all Vacancies that may happen during the Recess of the Senate, by granting Commissions which shall expire at the End of their next Session.

Section 3. He shall from time to time give to the Congress Information of the State of the Union, and recommend to their Consideration such Measures as he shall judge necessary and expedient; he may, on extraordinary occasions, convene both Houses, or either of them, and in Case of Disagreement between them, with respect to the Time of Adjournment, he may adjourn them to such Time as he shall think proper; he shall receive Ambassadors and other public Ministers; he shall take care that the Laws be faithfully executed, and shall Commission all the Officers of the United States.

Section 4. The President, Vice President and all civil Officers of the United States, shall be removed from Office on Impeachment for, and Conviction of, Treason, Bribery, or other high Crimes and Misdemeanors.

ARTICLE III

Section 1. The judicial Power of the United States, shall be vested in one supreme Court, and in such inferior Courts as the Congress may from time to time ordain and establish. The Judges, both of the supreme and inferior Courts, shall hold their Offices during good Behaviour, and shall, at stated Times, receive for their Services, a Compensation, which shall not be diminished during their Continuance in Office.

Section 2. The judicial Power shall extend to all Cases, in Law and Equity, arising under this Constitution, the Laws of the United States, and Treaties made, or which shall be made, under their Authority;—to all Cases affecting ambassadors, other public ministers and consuls;—to all cases of admiralty and maritime Jurisdiction;—to Controversies to which the United States shall be a Party;—to Controversies between two or more States;—between a State and Citizens of another State;[5]—between Citizens of different States—between Citizens of the same State claiming Lands under Grants of different States, and between a State, or the Citizens thereof, and foreign States, Citizens, or Subjects.

In all Cases affecting Ambassadors, other public Ministers and Consuls, and those in which a State shall be Party, the supreme Court shall have original Jurisdiction. In all the other Cases before mentioned, the supreme Court shall have appellate Jurisdiction, both as to Law and Fact, with such Exceptions, and under such Regulations as the Congress shall make.

The trial of all Crimes, except in Cases of Impeachment, shall be by Jury; and such Trial shall be held in the State where the said Crimes shall have been committed; but when not committed within any State, the Trial shall be at such Place or Places as the Congress may by Law have directed.

Section 3. Treason against the United States, shall consist only in levying War against them, or in adhering to their Enemies, giving them Aid and Comfort. No Person shall be convicted of Treason unless on the Testimony of two Witnesses to the same overt Act, or on Confession in open Court.

The Congress shall have power to declare the Punishment of Treason, but no Attainder of Treason shall work Corruption of Blood, or Forfeiture except during the Life of the Person attainted.

ARTICLE IV

Section 1. Full Faith and Credit shall be given in each State to the public Acts, Records, and judicial Proceedings of every other State. And the Congress may by general Laws prescribe the Manner in which such Acts, Records and Proceedings shall be proved, and the Effect thereof.

Section 2. The Citizens of each State shall be entitled to all Privileges and Immunities of Citizens in the several States.

A Person charged in any State with Treason, Felony, or other Crime, who shall flee from Justice, and be found in another State, shall on demand of the executive Authority of the State from which he fled, be delivered up, to be removed to the State having Jurisdiction of the crime.

No Person held to Service or Labour in one State, under the Laws thereof, escaping into another, shall, in Consequence of any Law or Regulation therein, be discharged from such Service or Labour, but shall be delivered up on Claim of the Party to whom such Service or Labour may be due.

Section 3. New States may be admitted by the Congress into this Union; but no new State shall be formed or erected within the Jurisdiction of any other State; nor any State be formed by the Junction of two or more States, or parts of States, without the Consent of the Legislatures of the States concerned as well as of the Congress.

The Congress shall have Power to dispose of and make all needful Rules and Regulations respecting the Territory or other Property belonging to the United States; and nothing

---

[5] Qualified by the Eleventh Amendment.

in this Constitution shall be so construed as to Prejudice any Claims of the United States, or of any particular State.

Section 4. The United States shall guarantee to every State in this Union a Republican Form of Government, and shall protect each of them against Invasion; and on Application of the Legislature, or of the Executive (when the Legislature cannot be convened) against domestic Violence.

ARTICLE V

The Congress, whenever two-thirds of both Houses shall deem it necessary, shall propose Amendments to this Constitution, or, on the Application of the Legislatures of two-thirds of the several States, shall call a Convention for proposing Amendments, which, in either Case, shall be valid to all Intents and Purposes, as part of this Constitution, when ratified by the Legislatures of three-fourths of the several States, or by Conventions in three-fourths thereof, as the one or the other Mode of Ratification may be proposed by the Congress; Provided that no Amendment which may be made prior to the Year One thousand eight hundred and eight shall in any Manner affect the first and fourth Clauses in the Ninth Section of the first Article; and that no State, without its Consent, shall be deprived of its equal Suffrage in the Senate.

ARTICLE VI

All Debts contracted and Engagements entered into, before the Adoption of this Constitution, shall be as valid against the United States under this Constitution, as under the Confederation.

This Constitution, and the Laws of the United States which shall be made in Pursuance thereof; and all Treaties made, or which shall be made, under the Authority of the United States, shall be the supreme Law of the Land; and the Judges in every State shall be bound thereby, any Thing in the Constitution or Laws of any State to the Contrary notwithstanding.

The Senators and Representatives before mentioned, and the Members of the several State Legislatures, and all executive and judicial Officers, both of the United States and of the several States, shall be bound by Oath or Affirmation to support this Constitution; but no religious Tests shall ever be required as a qualification to any Office or public Trust under the United States.

ARTICLE VII

The Ratification of the Conventions of nine States shall be sufficient for the Establishment of this Constitution between the States so ratifying the same.

Done in Convention by the Unanimous Consent of the States present the Seventeenth Day of September in the Year of our Lord one thousand seven hundred and Eighty seven, and of the Independence of the United States of America the Twelfth. In Witness whereof We have hereunto subscribed our Names.[6]

GEORGE WASHINGTON

PRESIDENT AND DEPUTY FROM VIRGINIA

New Hampshire
John Langdon
Nicholas Gilman

Massachusetts
Nathaniel Gorham
Rufus King

Connecticut
William Samuel
    Johnson
Roger Sherman

New York
Alexander Hamilton

New Jersey
William Livingston
David Brearley
William Paterson
Jonathan Dayton

Pennsylvania
Benjamin Franklin
Thomas Mifflin
Robert Morris
George Clymer
Thomas FitzSimons
Jared Ingersoll
James Wilson
Gouverneur Morris

Delaware
George Read
Gunning Bedford, Jr.
John Dickinson
Richard Bassett
Jacob Broom

Maryland
James McHenry
Daniel of
    St. Thomas Jenifer
Daniel Carroll

Virginia
John Blair
James Madison, Jr.

North Carolina
William Blount
Richard Dobbs
    Spaight
Hugh Williamson

South Carolina
John Rutledge
Charles Cotesworth
    Pinckney
Charley Pinckney
Pierce Butler

Georgia
William Few
Abraham Baldwin

Articles in Addition to, and Amendment of, the Constitution of the United States of America, Proposed by Congress, and Ratified by the Legislatures of the Several States, Pursuant to the Fifth Article of the Original Constitution[7]

[AMENDMENT I]

Congress shall make no law respecting an establishment of religion, or prohibiting the free exercise thereof; or abridging the freedom of speech, or of the press; or the right of the people peaceably to assemble, and to petition the Government for a redress of grievances.

[AMENDMENT II]

A well regulated Militia, being necessary to the security of a free State, the right of the people to keep and bear Arms shall not be infringed.

[6] These are the full names of the signers, which in some cases are not the signatures on the document.
[7] This heading appears only in the joint resolution submitting the first ten amendments, known as the Bill of Rights.

[AMENDMENT III]

No Soldier shall, in time of peace, be quartered in any house, without the consent of the Owner, nor in time of war, but in a manner to be prescribed by law.

[AMENDMENT IV]

The right of the people to be secure in their persons, houses, papers, and effects, against unreasonable searches and seizures, shall not be violated, and no Warrants shall issue, but upon probable cause, supported by Oath or affirmation, and particularly describing the place to be searched, and the persons or things to be seized.

[AMENDMENT V]

No person shall be held to answer for a capital or otherwise infamous crime, unless on a presentment or indictment of a Grand Jury, except in cases arising in the land or naval forces, or in the Militia, when in actual service in time of War or public danger; nor shall any person be subject for the same offence to be twice put in jeopardy of life or limb; nor shall be compelled in any criminal case to be a witness against himself, nor be deprived of life, liberty, or property, without due process of law; nor shall private property be taken for public use, without just compensation.

[AMENDMENT VI]

In all criminal prosecutions, the accused shall enjoy the right to a speedy and public trial, by an impartial jury of the State and district wherein the crime shall have been committed, which district shall have been previously ascertained by law, and to be informed of the nature and cause of the accusation; to be confronted with the witnesses against him; to have compulsory process for obtaining witnesses in his favour, and to have the Assistance of Counsel for his defence.

[AMENDMENT VII]

In suits at common law, where the value in controversy shall exceed twenty dollars, the right of trial by jury shall be preserved, and no fact tried by a jury, shall be otherwise reexamined in any Court of the United States, than according to the rules of the common law.

[AMENDMENT VIII]

Excessive bail shall not be required, nor excessive fines imposed, nor cruel and unusual punishments inflicted.

[AMENDMENT IX]

The enumeration of the Constitution, of certain rights, shall not be construed to deny or disparage others retained by the people.

[AMENDMENT X]

The powers not delegated to the United States by the Constitution, nor prohibited by it to the States, are reserved to the States respectively, or to the people.

[Amendments I–X, in force 1791.]

[AMENDMENT XI][8]

The Judicial power of the United States shall not be construed to extend to any suit in law or equity, commenced or prosecuted against one of the United States by Citizens of another State, or by Citizens or Subjects of any Foreign State.

[AMENDMENT XII][9]

The Electors shall meet in their respective States and vote by ballot for President and Vice-President, one of whom, at least, shall not be an inhabitant of the same State with themselves; they shall name in their ballots the person voted for as President, and in distinct ballots the person voted for as Vice-President, and they shall make distinct lists of all persons voted for as President, and of all persons voted for as Vice-President, and of the number of votes for each, which lists they shall sign and certify, and transmit sealed to the seal of the government of the United States, directed to the President of the Senate;—The President of the Senate shall, in the presence of the Senate and House of Representatives, open all the certificates and the votes shall then be counted;—The person having the greatest number of votes for President, shall be the President, if such number be a majority of the whole number of Electors appointed; and if no person have such majority, then from the persons having the highest numbers not exceeding three on the list of those voted for as President, the House of Representatives shall choose immediately, by ballot, the President. But in choosing the President, the votes shall be taken by states, the representation from each state having one vote; a quorum for this purpose shall consist of a member or members from two-thirds of the states, and a majority of all the states shall be necessary to a choice. And if the House of Representatives shall not choose a President whenever the right of choice shall devolve upon them, before the fourth day of March next following, then the Vice-President shall act as President, as in the case of the death or other constitutional disability of the President.—The person having the greatest number of votes as Vice-President, shall be the Vice-President, if such number be a majority of the whole number of Electors appointed, and if no person have a majority, then from the two highest numbers on the list, the Senate shall choose the Vice-President; a quorum for the purpose shall consist of two-thirds of the whole number of Senators, and a majority of the whole number shall be necessary to a choice. But no person constitutionally ineligible to the office of President shall be eligible to that of Vice-President of the United States.

[AMENDMENT XIII][10]

Section 1. Neither slavery nor involuntary servitude, except as a punishment for crime whereof the party shall have been duly convicted, shall exist within the United States, or any place subject to their jurisdiction.

Section 2. Congress shall have power to enforce this article by appropriate legislation.

---

[8] Adopted in 1798.
[9] Adopted in 1804.
[10] Adopted in 1865.

[AMENDMENT XIV][11]

Section 1. All persons born or naturalized in the United States, and subject to the jurisdiction thereof, are citizens of the United States and of the State wherein they reside. No State shall abridge the privileges or immunities of citizens of the United States; nor shall any State deprive any person of life, liberty, or property, without due process of law; nor deny to any person within its jurisdiction the equal protection of the laws.

Section 2. Representatives shall be apportioned among the several States according to their respective numbers, counting the whole number of persons in each State, excluding Indians not taxed. But when the right to vote at any election for the choice of electors for President and Vice-President of the United States, Representatives in Congress, the Executive and Judicial officers of a State, or the members of the Legislature thereof, is denied to any of the male inhabitants of such State, being twenty-one years of age, and citizens of the United States, or in any way abridged, except for participation in rebellion, or other crime, the basis of representation therein shall be reduced in the proportion which the number of such male citizens shall bear to the whole number of male citizens twenty-one years of age in such State.

Section 3. No person shall be a Senator or Representative in Congress, or elector of President and Vice-President, or hold any office, civil or military, under the United States, or under and State, who, having previously taken an oath, as a member of Congress, or as an officer of the United States, or as a member of any State legislature, or as an executive or judicial officer of any State, to support the Constitution of the United States, shall have engaged in insurrection or rebellion against the same, or given aid or comfort to the enemies thereof. But Congress may þy a vote of two-thirds of each House, remove such disability.

Section 4. The validity of the public debt of the United States, authorized by law, including debts incurred for payment of pensions and bounties for services in suppressing insurrection or rebellion, shall not be questioned. But neither the United States nor any State shall assume or pay any debts or obligation incurred in aid of insurrection or rebellion against the United States, or any claim for the loss or emancipation of any slave; but all such debts, obligations, and claims shall be held illegal and void.

Section 5. The Congress shall have the power to enforce, by appropriate legislation, the provisions of this article.

[AMENDMENT XV][12]

Section 1. The right of citizens of the United States to vote shall not be denied or abridged by the United States or by any State on account of race, color, or previous condition of servitude—

Section 2. The Congress shall have power to enforce this article by appropriate legislation.

[AMENDMENT XVI][13]

The Congress shall have power to lay and collect taxes on incomes, from whatever source derived, without apportionment among the several States, and without regard to any census or enumeration.

[AMENDMENT XVII][14]

The Senate of the United States shall be composed of two Senators from each State, elected by the people thereof, for six years; and each Senator shall have one vote. The electors in each State shall have the qualifications requisite for electors of the most numerous branch of the State legislatures.

When vacancies happen in the representation of any State in the Senate, the executive authority of such State shall issue writs of election to fill such vacancies: *Provided,* That the legislature of any State may empower the executive thereof to make temporary appointments until the people fill the vacancies by election as the legislature may direct.

This amendment shall not be so construed as to affect the election or term of any Senator chosen before it becomes valid as part of the Constitution.

[AMENDMENT XVIII][15]

Section 1. After one year from the ratification of this article the manufacture, sale, or transportation of intoxicating liquors within, the importation thereof into, or the exportation thereof from the United States and all territory subject to the jurisdiction thereof for beverage purposes is hereby prohibited.

Section 2. The Congress and the several States shall have concurrent power to enforce this article by appropriate legislation.

Section 3. This article shall be inoperative unless it shall have been ratified as an amendment to the Constitution by the legislatures of the several States, as provided in the Constitution, within seven years from the date of the submission hereof to the States by the Congress.

[AMENDMENT XIX][16]

The right of citizens of the United States to vote shall not be denied or abridged by the United States or by any State on account of sex.

Congress shall have power to enforce this article by appropriate legislation.

[AMENDMENT XX][17]

Section 1. The terms of the President and Vice-President shall end at noon on the 20th day of January, and the terms of Senators and Representatives at noon on the 3d day of January, of the years in which such terms would have ended if this article had not been ratified; and the terms of their successors shall then begin.

[11] Adopted in 1868.
[12] Adopted in 1870.

[13] Adopted in 1913.
[14] Adopted in 1913.
[15] Adopted in 1918.
[16] Adopted in 1920.
[17] Adopted in 1933.

Section 2. The Congress shall assemble at least once in every year, and such meeting shall begin at noon on the 3d day of January, unless they shall by law appoint a different day.

Section 3. If, at the time fixed for the beginning of the term of the President, the President elect shall have died, the Vice-President elect shall become President. If a President shall not have been chosen before the time fixed for the beginning of his term or if the President elect shall have failed to qualify, then the Vice-President elect shall act as President until a President shall have qualified; and the Congress may by law provide for the case wherein neither a President elect nor a Vice-President elect shall have qualified, declaring who shall then act as President, or the manner in which one who is to act shall be selected, and such person shall act accordingly until a President or Vice-President shall have qualified.

Section 4. The Congress may by law provide for the case of the death of any of the persons from whom the House of Representatives may choose a President whenever the right of choice shall have devolved upon them, and for the case of the death of any of the persons from whom the Senate may choose a Vice-President whenever the right of choice shall have devolved upon them.

Section 5. Sections 1 and 2 shall take effect on the 15th day of October following the ratification of this article.

Section 6. This article shall be inoperative unless it shall have been ratified as an amendment to the Constitution by the legislatures of three-fourths of the several States within seven years from the date of its submission.

[AMENDMENT XXI][18]

Section 1. The eighteenth article of amendment to the Constitution of the United States is hereby repealed.

Section 2. The transportation or importation into any State, Territory, or possession of the United States for delivery or use therein of intoxicating liquors, in violation of the laws thereof, is hereby prohibited.

Section 3. This article shall be inoperative unless it shall have been ratified as an amendment to the Constitution by conventions in the several States, as provided in the Constitution, within seven years from the date of the submission hereof to the States by the Congress.

[AMENDMENT XXII][19]

No person shall be elected to the office of the President more than twice, and no person who has held the office of President, or acted as President, for more than two years of a term to which some other person was elected President shall be elected to the office of the President more than once.

But this Article shall not apply to any person holding the office of President when this Article was proposed by the Congress, and shall not prevent any person who may be holding the office of President, or acting as President, during the term within which this Article becomes operative

18 Adopted in 1933.
19 Adopted in 1961.

from holding the office of President or acting as President during the remainder of such term.

This article shall be inoperative unless it shall have been ratified as an amendment to the Constitution by the legislatures of three-fourths of the several states within seven years from the date of its submission to the states by the Congress.

[AMENDMENT XXIII][20]

Section 1. The District constituting the seat of Government of the United States shall appoint in such manner as the Congress may direct:

A number of electors of President and Vice-President equal to the whole number of Senators and Representatives in Congress to which the District would be entitled if it were a State, but in no event more than the least populous State; they shall be in addition to those appointed by the States, but they shall be considered, for the purpose of the election of President and Vice-President, to be electors appointed by a State; and they shall meet in the District and perform such duties as provided by the twelfth article of amendment.

Section 2. The Congress shall have power to enforce this article by appropriate legislation.

[AMENDMENT XXIV][21]

Section 1. The right of citizens of the United States to vote in any primary or other election for President or Vice-President, for electors for President or Vice-President, or for Senator or Representative in Congress, shall not be denied or abridged by the United States or any state by reason of failure to pay any poll tax or other tax.

Section 2. The Congress shall have the power to enforce this article by appropriate legislation.

[AMENDMENT XXV][22]

Section 1. In case of the removal of the President from office or of his death or resignation, the Vice-President shall become President.

Section 2. Whenever there is a vacancy in the office of the Vice President, the President shall nominate a Vice President who shall take office upon confirmation by a majority vote of both Houses of Congress.

Section 3. Whenever the President transmits to the President Pro Tempore of the Senate and the Speaker of the House of Representatives his written declaration that he is unable to discharge the powers and duties of his office, and until he transmits to them a written declaration to the contrary, such powers and duties shall be discharged by the Vice-President as Acting President.

Section 4. Whenever the Vice-President and a majority of either the principal officers of the executive departments or of such other body as Congress may by law provide, transmit to the President Pro Tempore of the Senate and the Speaker of the House of Representatives their written declaration that the President is unable to discharge the powers

20 Adopted in 1961.
21 Adopted in 1964.
22 Adopted in 1967.

and duties of his office, the Vice President shall immediately assume the powers and duties of the office as Acting President.

Thereafter, when the President transmits to the President Pro Tempore of the Senate and the Speaker of the House of Representatives his written declaration that no inability exists, he shall resume the powers and duties of his office unless the Vice President and a majority of either the principal officers of the executive departments or of such other body as Congress may by law provide, transmit within four days to the President Pro Tempore of the Senate and the Speaker of the House of Representatives their written declaration that the President is unable to discharge the powers and duties of his office. Thereupon Congress shall decide the issue, assembling within forty-eight hours for that purpose if not in session. If the Congress, within twenty-one days after receipt of the latter written declaration, or, if Congress is not in session, within twenty-one days after Congress is required to assemble, determines by two-thirds vote of both Houses that the President is unable to discharge the powers and duties of his office, the Vice President shall continue to discharge the same as Acting President; otherwise, the President shall resume the powers and duties of his office.

[AMENDMENT XXVI][23]

Section 1. The right of citizens of the United States, who are eighteen years of age or older, to vote shall not be denied or abridged by the United States or by any State on account of age.

Section 2. The Congress shall have power to enforce this article by appropriate legislation.

---

[23] Adopted in 1971.

GLOSSARY

accessoryship *Criminal liability of all those who aid the perpetrator of an offense.*

accomplice *Person who helps another to commit a crime.*

acquittal *Judicial finding or jury verdict finding the defendant not guilty of the crime charged.*

administration bureau *Unit of a police department responsible for the management of the department as an organization; includes personnel, finance, research, and planning.*

aggravated assault *Attack on a person in which the assailant inflicts serious harm or uses a deadly weapon.*

aggression *Use of armed force by a state against the sovereignty or territory of another state, inconsistent with the Charter of the United Nations. An international crime.*

aggressive patrol *More frequent intervention of patrol officers in what are considered suspicious circumstances.*

aging-out phenomenon *The concept that offenders commit less crime as they get older.*

alternative sanctions *Punishments or other dispositions imposed instead of the principal sanctions currently in use, such as imprisonment or probation.*

anomie *Societal state marked by "normlessness," in which disintegration and chaos have replaced social cohesion.*

appellate court *Court with the power to review the judgment of a trial court, examining errors of law.*

arraignment *First stage of the trial process, at which the indictment or information is read in open court and the defendant is requested to respond thereto.*

arrest *Seizure of the person; the taking of a person into custody.*

arrest warrant *Written order from a court directing the police to effect an arrest.*

arson *The malicious burning of the dwelling house of another, or the burning of other structures or even personal property.*

assault *Unlawful offer or attempt with force or violence to hurt another.*

assigned counsel system *Judge appoints a private lawyer selected from a list of attorneys to represent indigent defendants in criminal proceedings.*

attrition (mortality) rate *Rate at which the numbers decrease in the course of the criminal process because persons are diverted out of the system.*

bail *Security given to ensure the reappearance of a defendant, in order to obtain his or her release from imprisonment.*

bailiff *Officer of the court who administers formal procedures, keeps order, announces a judge's arrival, and administers oaths.*

beat *Territory covered by a police officer on patrol; derived from hunters' "beating" the bushes for game.*

blue curtain *Screen that separates police from civilians in society; isolation of police who spend time only with other police officers and their families.*

bondsmen *Private business operators, paid by the defendant, who post the amount required by the court to secure the release of the defendant.*

Bow Street Runners *Earliest salaried police force in England.*

bribes *Offers of money or goods to police to ensure that they do not enforce the law.*

burden of proof *In criminal cases, the legal obligation of the prosecution to prove the charges against the defendant beyond a reasonable doubt.*

burglary *At common law, the nighttime breaking and entering of the dwelling house of another, with the intention to commit a crime or larceny therein; a felony.*

case study *Analysis of all pertinent aspects of one unit of study.*

challenge for cause *Challenge to remove a potential juror because of his or her inability to render a fair and impartial decision in a case. See also peremptory challenges; voir dire.*

circuit courts of appeal *Federal appellate courts with the power to review judgments of federal district courts (see appellate court).*

civilian police review boards *External control mechanism composed of persons usually from outside the police department.*

classical school of criminology *Criminological perspective suggesting that criminals choose to commit crimes after weighing the consequences of their actions, and that crime can be controlled by criminal sanctions.*

classification *Process that consists of regular procedures through which the custodial, treatment, vocational, and educational needs of each prisoner are determined.*

collective incapacitation *Imprisonment of many offenders for long periods.*

common law *Law as developed in England and later in the United States on the basis of court decisions (precedents) and as supplemented by legislation.*

community policing *Strategy that relies on public confidence and citizen cooperation to help prevent crime and make the residents of a community feel more secure.*

community service *Sanction that requires an offender to spend a period of time performing public service work.*

community service order *Sanction in which sentencing judge orders the convict to perform any of a range of services to the community.*

comparative criminal justice *Science of evaluating the features, successes, and failures of various distinct criminal justice systems.*

complainant *Person who files an official complaint with the police, a prosecutor, or a court, usually alleging personal damages and possibly a criminal offense.*

conditional pardon *Pardon that depends on the fulfillment of specified conditions.*

conduct norms *Norms that regulate the daily lives of people and reflect the attitudes of the groups to which they belong.*

conflict theory *Model of crime in which the criminal justice system is seen as being used by the ruling class to control the lower class.*

consent search *Warrantless search conducted when the party to the search provides "voluntary and intelligent consent" to police.*

conspiracy *Agreement among two or more persons to commit a crime, making each guilty of conspiracy and all other crimes committed in furtherance of the conspiracy.*

constable *Official charged with enforcing the law at the township level.*

contract system *Private attorneys from law firms or local bar associations provide defense services to indigent defendants.*

conventions *International agreements by which many nations commit themselves to common, legally binding obligations.*

corporate crime *Criminal act committed by one or more employees of a corporation that is subsequently attributed to the organization itself.*

correctional facility *Facility where convicted offenders serve their sentence; includes county jails and state and federal prisons.*

court administrator *Chief administrative officer of the court, usually appointed by the state court of last resort, the chief justice of the court of last resort, or a judicial council.*

court fragmentation *The specialization of state courts into separate tribunals for probate, juvenile, small claims, domestic relations cases, and others.*

court officers and marshals *Persons who provide courtroom security and maintain order. See also* bailiff.

court unification *Term used to describe reform efforts to con-* solidate various specialized state courts into one or two courts of broader jurisdiction.

courts of general jurisdiction *Major trial courts that have regular, unlimited jurisdictions over all cases and controversies involving civil and criminal law.*

courts of limited jurisdiction *Courts (with a justice of the peace, magistrate, or judge presiding) that handle minor criminal cases, less serious civil suits, traffic and parking violations, and health law violations.*

courts of special jurisdiction *Courts that specialize in certain areas of law: family courts, juvenile courts, probate courts (transfer of property and money of deceased).*

crackdown *Intensified effort by the police to deal with a problem in a particular area, or to reduce the incidence of a particular crime.*

criminal attempt *Act or omission constituting a substantial step in a course of conduct planned to culminate in the commission of a crime.*

criminal homicide *Unjustified, unexcused killing of another human being.*

criminology *Study of the causes, detection, correction, and prevention of criminal behavior.*

cultural deviance theories *Theories that criminal behavior results from cultural values that permit, or even demand, behavior in violation of the law.*

cultural transmission *Theory that views delinquency as a socially learned behavior transmitted from one generation to the next in disorganized urban areas.*

culture conflict theory *Theory that two groups may clash when their conduct norms differ.*

custody *Suspect under arrest or deprived of freedom in a significant way.*

data *Collected facts, observations, and other pertinent information from which conclusions can be drawn.*

decoy *Police officer disguised as a potential crime victim to attract criminal attacks precipitating an arrest.*

defense attorney (in criminal cases) *Lawyer retained by an individual accused of committing a crime, or assigned by the court if the individual is unable to pay.*

delinquent children *Children who have committed an act that if committed by an adult would be a crime or an act considered deviant in a child (truancy, running away from home) that is not so considered in an adult.*

dependent children *Legal status (granting jurisdiction to a juvenile court) reflecting inadequate and/or abusive parents or guardians.*

deprivation model *Explanation of prison subculture that suggests norms, language, roles, and traditions are developed in the prison to help prisoners adjust to the pains of imprisonment.*

detention facility *Facility that houses persons arrested and undergoing processing, awaiting trial, or awaiting transfer to a correctional facility.*

determinate sentence *Sentence to prison that has a fixed term; also called a flat sentence.*

deterrence *Theory of punishment that holds that potential offenders will refrain from committing crimes for fear of punishment (sometimes called general prevention).*

differential association theory *Theory based on the principle that an individual who learns more definitions favorable to violation of law than unfavorable becomes delinquent.*

differential opportunity theory *Theory that analyzes both legitimate and illegitimate opportunity structures available to individuals and posits that illegitimate opportunities, like legitimate ones, are unequally distributed.*

differential response *Response strategy that involves classifying calls for service and using various responses.*

directed patrol *Patrol officers assigned to specific activities, such as patrolling a high-crime area, chosen after an analysis of crime patterns.*

district courts *Trial courts in the federal and in some state systems.*

diversion *Removal of the defendant from the normal path of the criminal justice process to an alternative path (for example a treatment program).*

due process of law *According to the Fourteenth Amendment, a fundamental mandate that a person should not be deprived of life, liberty, or property without reasonable and lawful procedures.*

electronic monitoring *Computer-assisted checks on offender's movement to ensure that he or she is not going to places in violation of restrictions.*

entrapment *Illegal police practice of persuading an initially unwilling party to commit an offense.*

exclusionary rule *Rule prohibiting use of illegally obtained evidence in a court of law.*

exigent circumstances *Certain emergencies that call for immediate action and therefore do not allow time for a search warrant to be obtained.*

experiment *Research technique in which an investigator introduces a change into a process in order to measure or observe the effects of the change.*

extradition *Process of ancient origin by which an alleged offender is transferred from one sovereign country to another for trial.*

federal courts *Courts of the federal system, applying federal law, with power to test the constitutionality of state law and adjudicate controversies arising between residents of two or more states.*

Federal Witness Protection Program *Program under the Organized Crime Control Act of 1970 to protect witnesses who testify in court by relocating them and assigning them new identities.*

felony *Serious crime, subject to punishment of one year or more in prison, or to capital punishment.*

felony murder *Criminal liability for murder for one who par-*

ticipates in a felony that is dangerous to life and causes the death of another.

fine *Sum of money paid as a penalty and/or as an alternative to or in conjunction with incarceration.*

focal concerns *Set of six values passed down from generation to generation in lower-class urban slums: trouble, toughness, smartness, excitement, fate, autonomy.*

frankpledge *Ancient system whereby every male member of the community over the age of 12 was bound by a mutual pledge to keep the peace.*

fraud *Acquisition of the property of another through deception.*

frisk *Patting down a suspect's clothing to search for concealed weapons, under reasonable suspicion.*

fruit of the poisonous tree *Evidence obtained through other, illegally obtained evidence, inadmissible because it is tainted by the illegality of the initial search, arrest, or confession.*

general deterrence *Threat of punishment intended to induce the general public not to engage in criminal acts.*

genetic fingerprinting *Use of DNA as a technique for identifying suspects.*

genocide *International crime defined by convention (1948) and consisting of specific acts of violence committed with intent to destroy, in whole or in part, a national, ethnic, racial, or religious group.*

good faith exception *Exception to the exclusionary rule in which evidence obtained by police acting in good faith with a search warrant issued by a neutral and detached magistrate is admissible, even though the warrant is ultimately found to be invalid.*

good time system *System under which time is deducted from a prison sentence for good behavior within the institution.*

grand jury *Panel of sixteen to twenty-three citizens who screen the prosecution's evidence, in secret hearings, to decide whether someone should be formally charged with a crime.*

grass eaters *Officers who accept payoffs for rendering police services or for looking the other way when action is called for.*

habeas corpus *Writ requesting that a person or institution detaining a named prisoner bring him or her before a judicial officer and give reasons for the detention.*

halfway house *Residential correctional facility in which an offender may have to serve the last portion of his or her sentence outside prison, but not yet in the community.*

homicide *The killing of one person by another.*

hot pursuit *Exception to the rule requiring police to have a warrant to conduct a search; applies to cases of pursuit of vehicles and of suspects on foot.*

house arrest *Sentence in which convicts are confined to their own residence in lieu of imprisonment in an institution.*

hue and cry *Old English call for assistance in the pursuit of felons.*

hundred *Group of ten tythings.*

hustling *Inmate activity that involves obtaining goods and services that are unavailable through legitimate channels.*

importation model *Explanation of prison subculture that suggests norms, language, roles, and traditions are brought into the prison from outside the walls.*

incapacitation *Preventing persons from committing crime by physical restraint, for example, incarceration.*

incarceration *Sanction that requires a defendant to serve a term in a local jail, state prison, or federal prison.*

independent untainted source exception *Exception to the exclusionary rule in which evidence is admissible if police obtained it from a source that is sufficiently independent of the illegally obtained evidence.*

indeterminate sentence *Sentence for which the legislature allows the judge to impose a minimum and/or a maximum term, the actual length of service depending on the discretion of corrections officials.*

index crimes *The eight major crimes included in Part I of the UCR: criminal homicide, forcible rape, robbery, aggravated assault, burglary, larceny-theft, motor vehicle theft, and arson.*

indictment *Accusation against a criminal defendant rendered by a grand jury on the basis of evidence constituting a prima facie case.*

inevitable discovery exception *Exception to the exclusionary rule in cases where it is inevitable that police would have discovered the evidence regardless of an illegally obtained confession.*

information *Accusation against a criminal defendant prepared by a prosecuting attorney.*

inmate code *Informal set of rules that reflect the values of the prison society.*

insider trading *Use of material, nonpublic financial information about securities to obtain unfair advantage.*

intensive supervision probation (ISP) *Alternative to prison for convicted nonviolent offenders who do not qualify for routine probation; probation subject to stringent supervision.*

internal affairs *Department responsible for receiving and investigating charges against the police.*

International Court of Justice *Court of the United Nations with jurisdiction to adjudicate disputes among states. Also known as World Court.*

international crimes *Crimes, established largely by conventions, violative of international law, including but not limited to crimes against the peace and security of mankind.*

international criminal court *Court created by the Security Council of the United Nations, with power to adjudicate charges of international crimes by states and individuals, so far restricted to crimes on the territory of the former Yugoslavia.*

international criminal justice *Emerging international system for dealing with international and transnational crime.*

interrogation *Explicit questioning or actions that may elicit an incriminating statement.*

involuntary manslaughter *Unintentionally but recklessly causing the death of another by consciously taking a grave risk.*

jail *Place of confinement administered by local officials and designed to hold persons for more than 48 hours but usually less than one year.*

judge *Public officer lawfully instituted (by appointment or election) to decide litigated questions according to law, presiding in a court of law.*

jurisdiction *Power of a sovereign state to make and enforce its own laws. Also, the power given to a court to adjudicate matters in dispute within its competence and territory.*

just deserts *Philosophy of justice that asserts that the punishment should fit the crime and the culpability of the offender.*

justice of the peace *Originally (est. 1326) an untrained man, normally not learned in the law, usually of the lower nobility, assigned to investigate and try minor cases. Today a judge of a lower court, local or municipal, with limited jurisdiction.*

justifications *Defenses in which the law authorizes the violation of another law within limits of proportionality.*

kidnapping *The seizure and abduction of a person by force or threat of force and against the victim's will; under federal law, the taking of a person across state lines and holding of that person for ransom.*

labeling theory *Explanation of deviance in terms of the way a person acquires a negative identity, such as "addict" or "ex-con," and is forced to suffer the consequences of outcast status.*

larceny *Trespassory taking and carrying away of personal property belonging to another with the intent to deprive the owner of the property permanently.*

legalistic style *Style characteristic of police departments where work is marked by a professional orientation with an emphasis on law enforcement.*

legality *Principle that every crime must be clearly defined by common law or legislation prior to its commission.*

legislative exclusion *Elimination of juvenile court jurisdiction for certain serious offenses (e.g., murder and sexual assault) through the passage of legislation.*

levels of authority *Organizational structure within a police department in which all officers of equal authority are headed by superior officers of equal rank.*

line functions *Law enforcement functions of a police department.*

mala in se (Latin) *Offenses deemed inherently evil.*

mala prohibita (Latin) *Wrongs that are merely prohibited.*

mandatory sentence *Sentence prescribed by the legislature, which a judge has no choice but to impose.*

marshal *Federal law enforcement officer of the U.S. Marshal Service. Formerly, federal law enforcement officer in territories.*

mass murder *The murder of several persons, in one act or transaction, by one perpetrator or a group of perpetrators.*

maximum security prison *Penal institution designed and* operated with the principal goal of preventing escape and avoiding violence on the part of prisoners, virtually to the exclusion of rehabilitation or other programs.

meat eaters *Officers who solicit bribes or cooperate with criminals for personal gain.*

medium security prison *Penal institution with emphasis on control and custody, but not to the exclusion of rehabilitative or other programs.*

mens rea (Latin) *Guilty mind; awareness of wrongdoing. Intention to commit a criminal act, or recklessness.*

minimum security prison *Penal institution allowing inmates and visitors internal freedom of movement and program participation consistent with incarceration.*

Miranda warning *Warning that explains the rights of an arrestee, and that police recite at the time of the arrest or prior to interrogation.*

misdemeanor *Crime less serious than a felony and subject to a maximum sentence of one year in jail or a fine.*

modus operandi *Means and method by which a crime is committed.*

moral developmental theory *Theories of moral reasoning in relation to development.*

motion *Oral or written request to a judge, asking the court to make a specified ruling, finding, decision, or order; may be presented at any appropriate moment from arrest until the end of the trial.*

murder in the first degree *Killing done with premeditation and deliberation or, by statute, in the presence of other aggravating circumstances.*

murder in the second degree *Killing done with intent to cause death but without premeditation and deliberation.*

nolo contendere *Defendant pleads no contest (admits criminal liability for purposes of this proceeding only).*

objective classification *Process that uses a standardized form with well-defined legal factors and personal characteristics to assess every inmate's custody and program needs.*

observation *Recording the activities of groups being studied in their natural settings.*

operations bureau *Unit of a police department responsible for the functions associated with the primary law enforcement mission.*

pardon *Release from the legal penalties of an offense.*

parens patriae *(Latin, "parent of the country") Assumption by the state of the role of guardian over children whose parents are deemed incapable or unworthy.*

parole *Release of a prisoner into the community during the last part of a prison term, on promise of good conduct and under supervision.*

parole board *Group of citizens, usually appointed by the governor of a state, who determine the eligibility of prisoners for release from prison and the dates for their release from prison and from parole.*

parole hearing *Meeting held by members of the parole board to decide whether prisoners will be granted parole.*

parole officer *Officer of the executive branch of government responsible for the supervision of convicts released from prison on parole.*

penitentiary *Prison or place of confinement and correction for persons convicted of criminal acts; originally a place where convicts did penance.*

peremptory challenges *Challenges (limited in number) by which a potential juror may be dismissed by either the prosecution or the defense without assignment of reason. See also challenge for cause; voir dire.*

person in need of supervision (PINS) *Juvenile (or adult) requiring supervision but usually not incarceration.*

plain view *No warrant is needed to conduct a search when the fruits or instrumentalities of a crime are in plain view.*

plea *Response to a criminal charge. Traditional pleas are* guilty, not guilty, nolo contendere, *and not guilty by reason of insanity.*

plea-bargaining *Agreement made between defense and prosecution for certain leniencies in return for a guilty plea.*

police brutality *Use of excessive physical force against another person (usually a suspect) by law enforcement officers.*

police subculture *Set of norms and values that govern police behavior, brought about by stressful working conditions plus daily interaction with an often hostile public.*

police–community relations (PCR) programs *All initiatives, whether from the police or the community, to bridge the gap between law enforcement professionals and the people they serve.*

positivist school of criminology *Perspective that uses the scientific methods of the natural sciences and suggests that human behavior is a product of social, biological, psychological, or economic forces.*

posse comitatus *Latin for "power of the county" or the entire force of the* shire.

preliminary hearing *Preview of a trial held in court before a judge, in which the prosecution must produce sufficient evidence for the case to proceed to trial.*

presentence investigation report *Report prepared by the probation department for a judge; contains information about the offense, the offender, and the history of prior offenses and may include a recommendation of a sentence.*

presentment *Grand jury's accusation of crime without the application of a prosecutor.*

preventive detention *Pretrial incarceration of an accused deemed dangerous.*

preventive patrol *Police officers driving or walking through a designated geographic area of responsibility in a varied pattern so that their presence is not predictable.*

prima facie case *Case in which there is evidence that would warrant the conviction of the defendant unless otherwise contradicted; a case that meets evidentiary requirements for grand jury indictment.*

principal *Perpetrator of a criminal act.*

prison *Federal or state penal institution in which offenders serve sentences longer than one year.*

prison argot *Unique vocabulary used by prisoners.*

prison hulks *Decommissioned ships converted into prisons.*

prisonization *Socialization process in which new prisoners learn the ways of prison society, including rules, hierarchy, customs, and culture.*

probable cause *Set of facts that would induce a reasonable person to believe that the accused committed the offense in question; the minimum evidence requirement for an arrest, according to the Fourth Amendment.*

probation *Serving a sentence in the community in lieu of a prison term, on condition of good conduct, compliance with conditions, and under supervision.*

probation officer *Officer attached to the trial court who is responsible for administering the court's probation program.*

problem-oriented policing *Strategy that seeks to identify the underlying problems within a community so that community and police can work together to solve them.*

prosecutor *Attorney and government official who represents the people against persons accused of committing criminal acts.*

psychoanalytic theory *Theory of criminality that attributes delinquent and criminal behavior to a conscience either so overbearing that it arouses excessive feelings of guilt or so weak that it cannot control impulses.*

psychopathy *Condition in which a person has no sense of responsibility; shows disregard for truth; is insincere; and feels no sense of shame, guilt, or humiliation.*

public defender system *Public or nonprofit organizations (with staff) provide defense services to indigent defendants.*

purged taint exception *Exception to the exclusionary rule in which a voluntary act by the defendant removes the taint of prior illegal evidence-gathering by the police.*

radical theory *Theory that crime is the result of a struggle for power and resources between owners of capital and workers.*

reasonable suspicion *Warranted suspicion (short of probable cause) that a person has been or may be engaged in the commission of a crime.*

recidivism *Repeated or habitual relapses into criminal behavior.*

reformation *Voluntary, self-initiated transformation of an individual lacking in social or vocational skills into a productive, normally functioning citizen.*

reformatory *Institution designed to reform criminals through individualized treatment, education, and vocational training.*

rehabilitation *Punishment philosophy that asserts that through proper correctional intervention, such as educational and vocational programs and psychotherapy, a criminal can be reformed into a law-abiding citizen.*

release on recognizance *Release of a defendant on his or her promise to return to court as required.*

restitution *Compensation (normally court ordered) on the part of an offender to the victim, or a victim substitute, for any losses or harm inflicted, usually in money or services.*

retribution *"Eye for an eye" philosophy of justice.*

revocation of parole *Return of an offender to prison for the violation of parole conditions.*

robbery *The taking of the property of another, or out of his or her presence, by means of force and violence or the threat thereof.*

saturation patrol *Increasing the number of units patrolling a particular area, sometimes to target a particular type of offense, such as burglary or subway crime.*

search *Any governmental intrusion upon a person's reasonable expectation of privacy.*

seizure *Exercise of control by a government official over a person or thing.*

selective incapacitation *Targeting of high-risk and recidivistic offenders for rigorous prosecution and incarceration.*

selective incorporation *Supreme Court practice of incorporating the Bill of Rights selectively, by identifying federal rights that are "implicit in the concept of ordered liberty" and applying them to states through the Fourteenth Amendment's due process clause.*

self-report survey *Survey that respondents answer by confidential interview or anonymous questionnaire.*

sentencing guidelines *System for the judicial determination of a relatively firm sentence based on specific aggravating or mitigating circumstances.*

serial murder *Killing of several victims over a period of time.*

service style *Style characteristic of police departments in suburban communities where residents expect and receive a high level of service from local government.*

services bureau *Unit of a police department which provides technical services to assist in the execution of line functions, such as keeping records.*

shire *Territory composing many hundreds.*

shire reeve *Person responsible for maintaining peace within the shire (term from which the word "sheriff" is derived).*

shock incarceration *Short term of incarceration that subjects offenders to hard work, intense drills, and other character-building exercises.*

shock probation *Sentence that allows for brief incarceration followed by probation, in an effort to induce law abidance by shocking the offender.*

shoplifting *Stealing of goods from stores or markets.*

simple assault *Attack that inflicts little or no physical harm on the victim.*

social control theory *Explanation of criminal behavior that focuses on control mechanisms, techniques, and strategies for regulating behavior, and posits that criminality results when* social controls are weakened, so that individuals are not motivated to conform to them.

social disorganization theory *Theory that criminal behavior is associated with the disintegration of conventional values in neighborhoods characterized by rapid industrialization, increased immigration, and urbanization.*

social learning theory *Theory that delinquent behavior is learned through the same psychological processes as nondelinquent behavior, that is, through reinforcement.*

span of control *Number of subordinates reporting to a superior officer.*

special deterrence *Threat of punishment that deters an offender from engaging in any additional criminal behavior, based on the disagreeable experience with a past punishment.*

split sentence *Sentence that requires the convicted criminal to serve time in jail followed by probation.*

standard operating procedure (SOP) manual *Collection of departmental directives governing the performance of duties.*

state attorney general *Chief legal officer of the state; state counterpart to the U.S. attorney general.*

state supreme court *State court of last resort (except in certain jurisdictions, where the supreme court is a trial court of unlimited jurisdiction).*

status offenders *Juveniles who engage in behavior that violates the juvenile law but would not be considered a crime if committed by an adult; includes neglected children.*

sting operation *Deceitful but lawful technique in which police pretend to be involved in illegal activities to trap a suspect.*

stop and frisk *Technique used by police to "pat down" a person suspected of being armed or in possession of the instrumentalities of a crime.*

strain theory *Theory that a gap between culturally approved goals and legitimate means of achieving them causes frustration, which leads to criminal behavior.*

stranger homicide *Murder and nonnegligent manslaughter committed by a person unknown and unrelated to the victim.*

styles of policing *Classifications based on officers' particular approaches to the job (for example, "problem solver," "tough cop").*

subculture *Subdivision within the dominant culture that has its own norms, beliefs, and values.*

subculture of violence *Subculture with values that demand the overt use of violence in certain social situations.*

survey *The systematic collection of information by asking questions in questionnaires or interviews.*

team policing *Strategy where teams of police officers are assigned to a particular neighborhood, and are responsible for all police services in that area.*

terrorism *Use of violence against a target to create fear, alarm, dread, or coercion for the purpose of obtaining concessions or rewards.*

third degree *Torturing a suspect to gain information.*

tort *Wrong committed by one person against another, other than mere violation of a contract, which entitles the victim to compensation.*

transnational crimes *Criminal activities extending into, and violating the laws of, several countries.*

trial by ordeal *In medieval England, subjecting accused to cruel procedures to reveal God's judgment of the person's guilt or innocence.*

trial jury *Body of persons legally selected and sworn to inquire into any matter of fact and to give their verdict according to the evidence.*

tythings *In Anglo-Saxon law, an association of ten families bound together by a frankpledge.*

United States Attorney *Attorney and government official who prosecutes cases at the federal level.*

United States Attorney General *Highest ranking official in the United States Department of Justice.*

United States Supreme Court *Federal court that has ultimate authority in interpreting the Constitution as it applies to federal and state law; final authority in interpreting federal law.*

unity of command *Principle that each person should be accountable to only one superior.*

victim compensation *Scheme, usually based on statute, by which victims of violent crime may receive a limited financial award out of public funds for criminal harm suffered.*

victim precipitation *Opening oneself up, by direct or subliminal means, to a criminal response.*

victimology *Systematic study of the role played by the victim in a criminal incident and in the criminal process.*

vigilante group *Group of private citizens taking the law into their own hands by tracking down criminals and punishing them.*

violation *Infraction of the law for which normally only a fine can be imposed.*

voir dire *Process in which lawyers and a judge question potential jurors to select those who are acceptable.*

voluntary manslaughter *Intentionally but without malice causing the death of another person, as in the heat of passion.*

waiver hearing *Hearing in juvenile court that determines whether jurisdiction shall be waived and granted to an adult criminal court.*

watch and ward *System (established in A.D. 1285) of townspeople standing guard at the gates of walled towns.*

watchman style *Style characteristic of police departments that concentrate on the order maintenance function.*

white-collar crime *A sociological concept, encompassing any corporate or individual criminal activity marked by fraud and deception.*

working personality *Effect of police work on an officer's outlook on the world. Danger and authority are important factors.*

writ of certiorari *Document issued by a higher court directing a lower court to prepare the record of a case and send it to the higher court for review.*

ACKNOWLEDGMENTS

PHOTO CREDITS

2: Comstock; 5: Bill Nation/Sygma; 6: Mary Ellen Mark Library; 7: Les Stone/Sygma; 10: Ohlinger's; 12: Patrick Landmann/Gamma Liaison; 17: Terry Ashe/Gamma Liaison; 31: Bruce De Lis/Picture Group; 32: Left and right, Alon Reininger/Contact/Woodfin Camp & Associates; 33: Donna Ferrato/Black Star; 34: AP/Wide World Photos; 40: Mark Lennihan/Wide World Photos; 48: Najlah Feanny/SABA; 51: Anonymous Danish folk artist/PhotoEdit; 56: Pete Cosgrove/UPI/Bettmann; 62: Boys & Girls Clubs of Boston; 65: Alon Reininger/Woodfin Camp & Associates; 70: John Paul Filo/Valley Daily News, Taretum, PA; 76: Christopher Brown/Stock, Boston; 81: Brad Bower/Stock, Boston; 83: Top, Rick Friedman/Black Star; center, Rick Rickman/Black Star; bottom, Ron Haviv/SABA; 87: Frontispiece of *The Criminal Prosecution and Capital Punishment of Animals* by E. P. Evans (London: Faber, 1987); 91: Courtesy Freda Adler; 92: Left, UPI/Bettmann; right, AP/Wide World Photos; 102: Jeffrey Scott/Impact Visuals; 111: Rick Friedman/Black Star; 112: Kenneth Jarecke/Woodfin Camp & Associates; 115: UPI/Bettmann; 117: Tom Lynn/SABA; 121: ABAJ/Wide World Photos; 123: Alex Webb/Magnum; 128: Bettmann; 131: Scala/Art Resource; 132: Top to bottom: from *Civilization*, Volume I, page 48, CRM Books, 1973; Fathy/Published in *The History of Ships*, by Peter Kemp (Orbis Pub. Ltd., London); Bettmann; 133: Top to bottom: Bettmann; Bettmann/Hulton; Bettmann; source unknown; Culver; source unknown; Culver; Nancy Siesel/NYT Pictures; Giraudon/Art Resource; 135: Mary Evans/Photo Researchers; 140: Top, Roy Platnick/Culver; bottom, Bob Daemmrich/Stock, Boston; 147: Bettman; 149: Rob Knijff; 152: Steve Starr/SABA; 164: P. Chauvel/Sygma; 171: Yvonne Hemsey/Gamma Liaison; 173: Frank C. Dougherty/NYT Pictures; 178: John Giordano/SABA; 182: Top, Cynthia Johnson/Gamma Liaison; bottom, Steve McCurry/Magnum; 190: Jim West/Impact Visuals; 200: Library of Congress; 203: Bettmann; 205: AP/Wide World Photos; 208: J. B. Diederich/Woodfin Camp & Associates; 211: Patti McConville/Image Bank; 213: UPI/Bettmann; 219: Mike Albans/Wide World Photos; 221: Rob Crandall/Stock, Boston; 223: Reuters/Bettmann; 226: Omar Bradley/Picture Group; 228: Omar Bradley/Picture Group; 235: Susan May Tell/SABA; 237: Gilles Peress/Magnum; 242: AP/Wide World Photos; 245: Agence-France Photo; 246: Federal Bureau of Investigation; 247: Frances M. Roberts; 254: Comstock; 256: Comstock; 257: Top, Culver; bottom, James Duncan Phillips Library/Peabody & Essex Museum; 258: Top to bottom: Culver; David M. Grossman/Photo Researchers; reprinted in *Law: A Treasury of Art & Literature*, Hugh Lauter Levin Assoc.; Bettmann; illustration by Sally Sisson Anderson, reprinted in *History of Criminal Justice*, copyright 1988 by Anderson Publishing Co.; 259: Top to bottom: Bettmann; source unknown; UPI/Bettmann; Reuters/Bettmann; 269: Frank Fisher/Gamma Liaison; 273: Courtesy Visitor Services, U.S. Supreme Court; 280: John Neubauer/Photo Edit; 282: Culver; 284: Gehrz/SABA; 288: Palm Beach Post/Sygma; 291: Courtesy Pantheon Books (New York: 1990); 296: John W. Emmons/Impact Visuals; 307: UPI/Bettmann; 308: Top, Shepard Sherbell/SABA; center, Terry Ashe/Gamma Liaison; bottom, Martin Simon/SABA; 314: Tina Gerson/Sygma; 318: Rick Friedman/Black Star; 325: Michael Albans/Wide World Photos; 330: Frank Fournier/Woodfin Camp & Associates; 331: Angela Peterson/Gamma Liaison; 333: Andrea Brizzi/Stock Market; 338: Faye Ellman; 342: Gary Gladstone/Image Bank; 347: Top, Art Resource; center, from *Atlas of Ancient Egypt* by Baines & Malek, Phaidon Press Ltd., Oxford; bottom, Anthony Edgeworth/Stock Market; 351: Roger Sandler/Picture Group; 357: Susan Van Etten/Picture Cube; 366: Phil Huber/Black Star; 367: J. Patrick Forden/Sygma; 374: Bill Swersey/Gamma Liaison; 377: Culver; 378: Top to bottom: Culver; illustration by Michael Hague/*Cinderella and Other Tales from Perrault* (New York: Henry Holt & Co.); Vatican Museum/*The History of Ships* by Peter Kemp-Orbis Publishing Ltd.; from *Halsgericht* by Max Peter Maass-copyright 1968 by S. Toeche-Mittler Verlag, Darmstadt; Bettmann; Pim Donkersloot; 379: Top to bottom: Mary Evans Picture Library/Photo Researcher from *The Cradle of the Penitentiary* by Negley K. Teeters/copyright 1955 by Negley K. Teeters & The Pennsylvania Prison Society; N. Curry, from *Criminology: A Cultural Interpretation* by D. Taft, Macmillan; F. M. Kearney/Impact Visuals; 392: Top, Glenn Morimoto/AP/Wide World Photos; center, Allen Green/Photo Researchers; bottom, W. Campbell/Sygma; 397: From the 1991 Amnesty Int'l Report/copyright 1991 Amnesty Int'l. Publications; 400: Ed Kashi/Gamma Liaison; 404: Larry Downing/Woodfin Camp & Associates; 407: Top, Peter Menzel/Stock, Boston; bottom, Renato Rotolo/Gamma Liaison; 414: Stephen Ferry/Gamma Liaison; 417: Frank Fournier/Woodfin Camp & Associates; 424: Bettmann; 426: John Ficara/Woodfin Camp & Associates; 429: Jeffrey D. Scott/Impact Visuals; 436: Jacques M. Chenet/Woodfin Camp & Associates; 449: UPI/Bettmann; 456: Top, William Snyder/Gamma Liaison; bottom, J. P. Laffont/Sygma; 457: George Cohen/Impact Visuals; 468: Marilyn Church/Wide World Photos; 473: Top, Mary Ellen Mark; bottom, Jean-Marc Giboux/Gamma Liaison; 481: Shepard Sherbell/SABA; 484: Comstock; 487: Ed Kashi/Gamma Liaison; 496: Luc Novovitch/Gamma Liaison; 501: Dale Dunaway/Cincinnati Post; 502: Spencer Grant/Photo Researchers; 506: Karen Schulenburg/Gamma Liaison; 512: Jon Levy/Gamma Liaison; 523: Donna Binder/Impact Visuals; 526: L. Van Der Stockt/Gamma Liaison; 529: Reuters/Bettmann; 534: AP/Wide World Photos; 537: AP/Wide World Photos; 539: Keerle-Parker/Gamma Liaison; 543: Victor Engelbert/Photo Researchers; 547: Top, Pinkhassov/Magnum; bottom, Abbas/Magnum.

ILLUSTRATION AND TEXT CREDITS

3: From Bill Turque with Bob Cohn and Anne Underwood, "A New Line Against Crime," from *Newsweek*, August 27, 1990. © 1990, Newsweek, Inc. All rights reserved. Reprinted by permission; 3: From Stephanie Mencimer, "D.C.'s New Death Row: AIDS Is Devastating the District's Prisons and Busting Its Budget," *The Washington Post*, January 31, 1993. © 1993 The Washington Post. Reprinted with permission; 3: From Peter Truell and Larry Gurwin, "False Profits: The Inside Story of BCCI . . ." as it appeared in *Newsweek*, December 7, 1992. Copyright © 1992 by Peter Truell and Larry Gurwin. Reprinted by permission of Houghton Mifflin Co. All rights reserved; 13: From James Bennet, "New York Crime Statistics vs. Reality," *The New York Times*, August 16, 1992. Copyright © 1992 by The New York Times Company. Reprinted by permission; 19: Figure from "Hate Crimes: 'Litany of Shame,'" *USA Today*, March 13, 1992. Copyright 1992, USA Today. Reprinted with permission; 27: Drawing by Levin; © 1990 The New Yorker Magazine, Inc; 31: Table, "Worst Mass Shootings In U.S. History," *The New York Times*, October 17, 1991. Copyright © 1991 by The New York Times Company. Reprinted by permission; 34: *The Far Side* cartoon by Gary Larson is reprinted by permission of Chronical Features, San Francisco, CA. All rights reserved; 37: Graph, "What's Tempting For Light Fingers?" *The New York Times*, September 19, 1991. Copyright ©1991 by The New York Times Company. Reprinted by permission; 54: Drawing by Mankoff; © 1991 The New Yorker Magazine, Inc.; 58: From James

Willerth, "From Killing Fields to Mean Streets," *Time*, November 18, 1991. Copyright 1991 Time Inc. Reprinted by permission; **59:** Figure, "Time Line of New York City's Chinese Gangs: 1960–1990" in Ko-lin Chin, *Chinese Subculture and Criminality.* Copyright © 1990, Greenwood Press, an imprint of Greenwood Publishing Group, Inc., Westport, CT. Reprinted with permission; **62:** Table, "The Escalating Cost of Disorder." Reprinted from May 18, 1992 issue of *Business Week* by special permission, copyright © 1992 by McGraw-Hill, Inc.; **69:** Figure, "Residential Security Systems in the United States," *The New York Times*, February 9, 1992. Copyright © 1992 by The New York Times Company. Reprinted by permission; **82:** Text from Jean F. Moreau and Gerhard O. W. Mueller, *The French Penal Code*, Vol. I. Reprinted by permission of New York University School of Law; **82:** Illustration by Siné, from *Code Penal—Text Officiel*, Maurice Gonon, Editeur, 1959; **90:** Cartoon, © 1962 *The Saturday Evening Post*; **94:** Drawing by Ross; © 1992 The New Yorker Magazine, Inc.; **103:** From Richard Emery, "Courts Can't Do It All," *The New York Times*, July 16, 1983. Copyright © 1983 by The New York Times Company. Reprinted by permission; **109:** Figure from Samuel Walker, *Sense and Nonsense about Crime*, 1985, Wadsworth, Inc. Reprinted by permission; **109:** Figure reprinted from Huey-Tsyh Chen, "Dropping In and Dropping Out: Judicial Decision-making in the Disposition of Felony Arrests," *Journal of Criminal Justice*, *19*, 1990, pp. 1–18, with permission from Pergamon Press Ltd., Headington Hill Hall, Oxford OX3 OBW, UK.; **110:** Figure from R. F. Sparks, H. G. Genn, and D. J. Dodd, *Surveying Victims: A Study of the Measurement of Criminal Victimization, Perceptions of Crime, and Attitudes to Criminal Justice.* Copyright © 1977. Reprinted by permission of John Wiley & Sons, Ltd.; **114:** From Fred Plog, Clifford Jolly, and Daniel Bates, *Anthropology: Decisions, Adaptation, and Evolution.* Copyright © 1976. Reprinted by permission of McGraw-Hill, Inc.; **121:** Table from Daniel Klaidman, "Bureaucracy that Works: 'Mr. Lost and Found' Woos Court's No-Shows," *Legal Times*, February 25, 1991. Reprinted with permission of Legal Times. Copyright 1991; **145:** Figure from Larry Gaines, Mettie Southerland, and John Angell, *Police Administration.* Copyright © 1991. Reprinted by permission of McGraw-Hill, Inc.; **153:** Figure from Donald A. Torres, *Handbook of State Police, Highway Patrols, and Investigative Agencies.* Copyright © 1987, Greenwood Press, an imprint of Greenwood Publishing Group, Inc., Westport, CT. Reprinted with permission; **159:** Table from William A. Geller and Norval Morris, "Relations between Federal and Local Police," in Michael Tonry and Norval Morris (eds.), *Modern Policing.* Copyright © 1992. Reprinted by permission of The University of Chicago Press; **160:** Figure from Robert J. Fisher and Gion Green, *Introduction to Security*, 5th Edition, 1992, Butterworth-Heinemann; **165:** From Carl B. Klockars and Stephen D. Mastrofski, *Thinking About Police*, 2nd Edition. Copyright © 1991. Reprinted by permission of McGraw-Hill, Inc.; **176:** Graph, "Number of Calls to Police" from "Mental Patients Overload Emergency System" by Marjorie Miller, *Los Angeles Times*, March 12, 1992. Copyright, 1992, Los Angeles Times. Reprinted by permission; **176–177:** From Carl B. Klockars and Stephen D. Mastrofski, *Thinking About Police*, 2nd Edition. Copyright © 1991. Reprinted by permission of McGraw-Hill, Inc.; **180:** Table from Jack R. Greene and Carl B. Klockars, "What Police Do," in Carl B. Klockars and Stephen D. Mastrofski, *Thinking About Police*, 2nd Edition. Copyright © 1991. Reprinted by permission of McGraw-Hill, Inc.; **186:** *Far Side*, copyright 1985 Farworks, Inc. Reprinted with permission of Universal Press Syndicate. All rights reserved; **189:** Figure from "Computerization at the General Secretariat," *International Criminal Police Review*, November/December 1989, pp. 6–19; **206:** Adaptation of table reprinted by permission from pages 906–907 of *Constitutional Interpretation*, 3rd Edition, by Craig R. Ducat and Harold W. Chase; Copyright © 1983 by West Publishing Company. All rights reserved; **212:** Table from Rolando del Carmen, *Criminal Procedure: Law and Practice*, 1991, Brooks/Cole. Reprinted by permission of Wadsworth Publishing Co.; **216:** Table from Rolando del Carmen, *Criminal Procedure: Law and Practice*, 1991, Brooks/Cole. Reprinted by permission of Wadsworth Publishing Co.; **217:** Figure from Rolando del Carmen, *Criminal Procedure: Law and Practice*, 1991, Brooks/Cole. Reprinted by permission of Wadsworth Publishing Co.; **229:** Table from Harold P. Slater and Martin Reiser, "A Comparative Study of Factors Influencing Police Recruitment," *Journal of Police Science and Administration*, *16*, 1988, International Association of Chiefs of Police, Inc.; **230:** Figure from David L. Carter, Allen D. Sapp, and Darrel W. Stephens, *The State of Police Education: Policy Direction for the*

21st Century, 1989. Reproduced by permission of the Police Executive Research Forum, Washington, D.C.; **235:** Figure from Samuel Walker, *The Police in America*, 2nd Edition. Copyright © 1992. Reprinted by permission of McGraw-Hill, Inc.; **239:** Cartoon from William H. Kroes, *Society's Victims—The Police*, 2nd Edition, 1976. Courtesy of Charles C. Thomas, Publisher, Springfield, Illinois; **244:** From Michela Wrong, "French Police Traumatized by Lurid 'Inspector Jobic' Case," *The Reuters Library Report*, July 3, 1988. Reprinted by permission of Reuters Information Services; **260:** Table from Bradley Chapin, *Criminal Justice in Colonial America.* Copyright © 1983. Reprinted by permission of The University of Georgia Press; **263:** Figure from William E. Hewitt, *Courts that Succeed: Six Profiles of Successful Courts*, 1990, National Center for State Courts, Williamsburg, Va. Reprinted by permission; **264:** Figure adapted from Abraham S. Blumberg, *Criminal Justice: Issues and Ironies*, 1979, New Viewpoints; **268:** Figure from Freda Adler, Gerhard Mueller, and William Laufer, *Criminology.* Copyright © 1991. Reprinted by permission of McGraw-Hill, Inc.; **274:** Entry from CBS/*New York Times* Poll, *The New York Times*, August 18–21, 1986. Copyright © 1986 by The New York Times Company. Reprinted by permission; **274:** Two entries from *Los Angeles Times* poll, July 3, 1989. Reprinted by permission; **274–275:** Two entries from Harris Survey, June 3–September 12, 1988 and one entry from Harris Survey, January 11–February 11, 1990; **274–275:** Three entries from Gallup Poll, April 10–13, 1987, April 8–10, 1988, and June 9–16, 1988. Reprinted by permission; **275:** Figure adapted from Thomas R. Marshall, "Public Opinion and the Rehnquist Court," *Judicature*, vol. 74, no. 6, April–May 1991. Reprinted by permission of American Judicature Society; **290:** From *Rough Justice* by David Heilbroner. Copyright © 1990 by David Heilbroner. Reprinted by permission of Pantheon Books, a division of Random House, Inc.; **295:** Drawing by Stevenson; © 1990 The New Yorker Magazine, Inc.; **304:** Table from Henry R. Glick, *Courts, Politics, and Justice*, 3rd Edition. Copyright © 1993. Reprinted by permission of McGraw-Hill, Inc.; **307:** From *Black Robes, White Justice* by Bruce Wright. Copyright © 1987 by Bruce Wright. Published by arrangement with Carol Publishing Group. A Lyle Stuart Book; **309:** Figure from Charles R. Swanson and Surette M. Tularico, *Court Administration: Issues and Responses*, The Institute of Government, 1983; **334:** Drawing by Lorenz; © 1977 The New Yorker Magazine, Inc.; **337:** Figure, "The Story in the Juror's Mind," *The New York Times*, May 12, 1992. Copyright © 1992 by The New York Times Company. Reprinted by permission; **343:** From Dennis Cauchon, "Michigan Drug Law: No Exceptions—No Mercy," *USA Today*, April 17, 1992. Copyright 1992, USA Today. Reprinted with permission; **350:** Drawing by Levin: © 1992 The New Yorker Magazine, Inc.; **359:** Figure based on Hans-Jorg Albrecht, "Fines in the Criminal Justice System," in Klaus Sessar and Hans-Jurgen Kerner, *Developments in Crime and Crime Control Research*, 1991. Reprinted by permission of Springer-Verlag New York, Inc.; **360:** Figure from *The Sentencing Commission and Its Guidelines* by Andrew von Hirsch, Kay A. Knapp, and Michael Tonry. Copyright 1987 by Andrew von Hirsch, Kay A. Knapp, and Michael Tonry. Reprinted with the permission of Northeastern University Press, Boston; **368:** From Robert M. Bohm, Louise J. Clark, and Adrian F. Aveni, "The Influence of Knowledge on Reasons for Death Penalty Opinions: an Experimental Test," *Justice Quarterly*, 7, 1990. Reprinted by permission of the authors; **384:** Table based on Geoffrey P. Alpert (ed.), *Legal Rights of Prisoners.* Copyright © 1980. Reprinted by permission of Sage Publications, Inc.; **387:** Cartoon by Paul Conrad. Copyright, 1992, *Los Angeles Times.* Reprinted with permission; **397:** Table from Todd Clear and George Cole, *American Corrections*, 1986, Brooks/Cole. Reprinted by permission of Wadsworth, Inc.; **398:** Figure from "Americans Behind Bars: A Comparison of International Rates of Incarceration," 1991, The Sentencing Project. Reprinted by permission; **405:** From Jim Quillan, *Alcatraz from Inside*, 1991, Golden Gate National Park Association; **409:** Table from Frieder Dunkel and Dirk van Zyl Smit, "Conclusion," in Dirk van Zyl Smit and Frieder Dunkel (eds.), *Imprisonment Today and Tomorrow.* Reprinted with permission of Kluwer Law and Taxation Publishers; **412:** Two figures from George M. Camp and Camille G. Camp, *The Corrections Yearbook*, 1991, Criminal Justice Institute. Reprinted by permission of George Camp; **420, 422:** From Paul La Rosa, "Babies Behind Bars: in 3 New York Prisons . . .," *Los Angeles Times*, May 12, 1992. Reprinted by permission of Paul La Rosa; **438:** John Augustus Memorial Plaque. Used by permission of N.C.C.D., School of Criminal Justice Library, Rutgers University; **439:** Table reprinted with permission of The Free Press, a Division of Macmillan, Inc., from *Probation and Parole in America* by Harry E. Allen, Chris W. Eskridge, Edward J. Latessa, and Gennaro F. Vito. Copyright © 1985 by The Free Press; **451:** From Kriss A. Drass and J. William Spencer, "Accounting for Pre-Sentencing Recommendations." © 1987 by The Society for the Study of Social Problems. Reprinted from *Social Problems*, Vol. 34, 1987, pp. 227–293, by permission; **458–459:** From James Austin and Barry Krisberg, "Wider, Stronger, and Different Nets: The Dialectics of Criminal Justice Reform," *Journal of Research in Crime and Delinquency, 18,* 1981. Reprinted by permission of Sage Publications, Inc.; **462:** Figure from Joan Petersilia, *Expanding Options for Criminal Sentencing,* 1987. The Rand Corporation; **467:** From Michael Riley, "Corridors of Agony," *Time,* January 27, 1992. Copyright 1992 Time Inc. Reprinted by permission; **479:** Table from Simon I. Singer and David McDowall, "Criminalizing Delinquency: The Deterrent Effects of the New York Juvenile Offender Law," *Law & Society Review,* Vol. 22:3, 1988. Reprinted by permission of the Law and Society Association; **481:** Table adapted from Victor L. Streib, "The Eighth Amendment and Capital Punishment of Juveniles," *Cleveland State Law Review, 37,* 1986. Reprinted by permission; **484:** Figure from Barry C. Feld, "The Juvenile Court Meets the Principle of the Offense: Legislative Changes in Juvenile Waiver Statutes." Reprinted by special permission of Northwestern University School of Law, Volume 78, Issue 3, *Journal of Criminal Law and Criminology,* pp. 512–514, (1987); **485:** Reprinted with the permission of Macmillan Publishing Company from *Process and Impact of the Juvenile Justice System* by Edward Eldefonso and Alan F. Coffey. Copyright © 1976 by Macmillan Publishing Company; **490:** Figure from Philip Cook and John H. Lamb, "Trends in Child Abuse and Juvenile Delinquency," in F. Hartmann (ed.), *From Children to Citizens: The Role of Juvenile Courts,* 1987. Reprinted by permission of Springer-Verlag New York, Inc.; **493:** Figure from *The Cycle of Juvenile Justice* by Thomas J. Bernard. Copyright © 1991 by Oxford University Press, Inc. Reprinted by permission; **497:** From Marcia Chambers, "Life Term in Rooftop Slaying of Aspiring Actress," *The New York Times,* August 6, 1985. Copyright © 1985 by The New York Times Company. Reprinted by permission; **500:** From Alan Riding, "550 Years Later, a Bluebeard Has His Day in Court: Not Guilty," *The New York Times,* November 17, 1992. Copyright © 1992 by The New York Times Company. Reprinted by permission; **501:** Table from Hugo A. Bedau and Michael L. Radelet, "Miscarriages of Justice in Potentially Capital Cases," *Stanford Law Review, 40*(l), 1987. Reprinted by permission of the authors; **507:** Table from David Shichor, "Corporate Deviance and Corporate Victimization: A Review and Some Elaborations," *International Review of Victimology, 1,* 1989, A. B. Academic Publishers; **511:** Table from Barbara Harff and Ted G. Gurr, "Victims of the State: Genocides, Politicides, and Group Repression Since 1945," *International Review of Victimology, 1,* 1989, A. B. Academic Publishers; **513:** "Sample Victim Impact Statement," *Washington Legal Foundation Court Watch Manual,* 1982. Reprinted by permission of Washington Legal Foundation; **520–521:** Table from Andrew Karmen, *Crime Victims,* 2nd Edition, 1990, Brooks/Cole. Reprinted by permission of Wadsworth Publishing Co.; **542–543:** From John Henry Wigmore, *A Kaleidoscope of Justice,* 1941, West Publishing Co.

INDEXES

NAME INDEX

Abadinsky, Howard, *46*
Abbot, Daniel J., *549*
Abraham, Henry J., *313*
Abrahamse, Allan F., *197, 198, 370*
Acker, James R., *371*
Adams, Alison K., *44*
Adams, Edward A., *312*
Adams, K., *126*
Adamson, Patrick B., *161*
Adler, Freda, *44, 46, 47, 65, 69, 73-74,*
    159, 196, 402, 433, 434, 531, 549
Adler, Jeffrey S., *74*
Adler, Jill, *224*
Adler, Nanci, 149, *550*
Ageton, Suzanne S., *73*
Agnew, Robert, *73, 74*
Aguste, Filberto, *46*
Ainsworth, Janet A., *475*
Akers, Ronald L., *73, 524*
Albanese, Jay S., *47, 59*
Albert, Geoffrey P., 384
Albini, Joseph, *47*
Albonetti, Celesta A., *75, 311*
Albrecht, G. L., *225*
Albrecht, Hans-Jorg, 359
Ali, Badr-El-Din, *549*
Allan, Emilie Anderson, *44*
Allen, Donald, 417
Allen, Harry E., *250, 439, 463-465*
Allen, J., *403*
Allen, M. H., *47*
Allingham, Margery, 150
Allinson, Richard, *494*
Almalhem, Mohammad A., *550*
Alozie, Nicholas O., *313*
Alpert, Geoffrey P., *195, 225, 233, 248,*
    250, 312, 402
Alschuler, Albert W., *312, 340*

Alston, Henry, 63
Altman, Jack, *72*
Amdur, Richard L., *74*
Amsterdam, Anthony, 111, *126*
Ancel, Marc, *126*
Andenaes, Johannes, 115
Anderson, Allen F., *550*
Anderson, Andy B., *369*
Anderson, Deborah, *249*
Anderson, Kristine L., *74*
Andes, Steven M., *249*
Andrews, D. A., *370, 434*
Angell, John E., 145, *162, 195*
Angelos, Claudia, *402*
Anglin, M. Douglas, *47, 434*
Annan, Sampson O., *197*
Anson, Richard H., *250, 433*
Anspach, Donald F., *370*
Anthony, Aimee Michelle, *44*
Arbuthnot, Jack, *73*
Archambeault, William G., *194, 433*
Archer, Dane, *371*
Ares, Charles, *340*
Arnold, W. R., *494*
Ascolillo, Victor H., *313*
Ash, Michael, *524*
Ash, Philip, *248*
Ashcroft, John, *198*
Ashworth, Andrew, *369*
Atkinson, Maxine P., *74*
Auerbach, Barbara J., *403, 525*
Augustus, John, 379, *463*
Aultman, Madeline G., *74*
Austern, David, *525*
Austin, James, *340, 403, 432, 459, 464,*
    466, 495, 525
Austin, W. Timothy, *72*
Avary, D'AunnWester, *46*

Aveni, Adrian F., *371*
Avery, John, 177
Aylward, Jack, *248*
Ayres, Marilyn B., *196*
Ayres, Richard M., *195*

Babb, Susan, *432*
Babbili, A., *525*
Bachman, Jerald G., *43, 47*
Bacich, Anthony R., *198*
Badillo, Herman, *402*
Bahn, Charles, *251*
Bailey, Walter C., *433*
Bailey, William C., *45, 159, 371*
Baird, S., *465*
Bakeman, B. A., *403*
Baker, Mary Holland, *195*
Baker, Newman F., *311*
Baldus, David C., *311, 371*
Balkwell, James W., *44*
Ball, John C., *47, 433*
Ball, R., *466*
Ballard, Veronica Smith, *464*
Ballow, Deanna Bellew, *465*
Baltimore, Michael Riley, *493*
Bandura, Albert, *73*
Bannon, James D., *198*
Barker, L., *525*
Barnes, G. E., *251*
Barnes, Harry Elmer, *401, 402, 431,*
    434, 464
Barnett, Arnold, *197*
Baro, Agnes, *44*
Barr, William, 471
Barrett, B. J., *74*
Barringer, Felicity, 353
Barrow, Deborah J., *313*
Barry, Robert P., *369*

Note: Italicized page numbers indicate names found in the chapter-end Notes sections.

Johnston, David, 233
Johnston, Lloyd D., *43, 47*
Johnston, Michael, *251*
Jolin, Annette, *466*
Jolly, Clifford J., 115
Jonas, Theodore C., *548*
Jones, David M., *194*
Jones, Joretta, *433*
Jones, Peter R., *340, 466*
Joutsen, Matti, *549*

Kaci, Judy Hails, *198*
Kadish, Sanford H., *433*
Kagan, Robert A., *279*
Kagehiro, Dorothy K., *224, 466*
Kahan, Bernard, *45*
Kaiser, Günther, *465*
Kalish, Carol B., *549*
Kalven, Jr., Harry, *126*, 337
Kamisar, Yale, *224*
Kant, Immanuel, *369*
Kappeler, Victoria E., *248*
Karacki, Loren, *495*
Karchmer, Clifford, *197*
Karmen, Andrew, 521, *524*
Kartes, Jr., Michael J., *46*
Kassebaum, Gene G., *433*
Katel, Peter, *403, 433*
Kauffman, Kelsey, *432*
Keci, Indy Hails, *225*
Keil, Thomas J., *311, 371*
Keitges, Susan, 159
Kelling, George L., *162*, 171, *196, 197*
Kelly, Martin A., *161*
Kelly, Robert J., *47*
Kelly, Thomas V., *195*
Kempe, C. H., *45*
Kempf, Kimberly L., *43, 44*
Kempinen, Cynthia A., *371*
Kendall, Raymond E., 189
Kennedy, Daniel B., *194, 196, 199, 249*
Kennedy, David M., *196*
Kennedy, John F., *196*
Kennedy, John H., *340*
Kennedy, Leslie W., *45, 126*
Kenney, Dennis, *194, 196, 197*, 230, *248, 249*
Kenney, John P., *195-197*
Kennish, John W., *198*
Kerber, Kenneth W., *249*

Kerby, Judith, *340*
Kercher, Kyle, *44*
Kerner, Hans-Jurgen, 359
Kerper, Hazel B., *493*
Kerstetter, W. A., *524*
Kethineni, Sesharajani, *402, 550*
Keve, Paul W., *494*
Kidd, Robert F., *126*
Kifner, John, *225*
Kilias, Martin, 545, *549*
Kilkenny, Robert, *72*
Kimball, Peter, *402, 433*
Kimmins, Dick, *312*
Kindley, Karen, *45*
King, Jon, 491
Kingsnorth, Rodney F., *369*
Kinkade, Patrick, *402*
Kinlock, Timothy W., *47*
Kirby, Michael B., *340*
Kirchheimer, Otto, *401*
Kirchner, Jr., Robert E., *197*
Kirkham, George, 237, *250*
Kirkpatrick, John T., *45*
Kittrie, Nicholas N., *74*
Klafas, John M., *550*
Klaidman, Daniel, 121
Kleckner, Simone-Marie Vabriescu, 84
Kleiman, Mark A. R., *197, 199*
Klein, Fannie J., *278*
Klein, Malcolm W., *45*, 59, *196, 495*
Klein, Richard, *312*
Klein-Saffran, Jody, *465, 466*
Kleinfeld, N. R., *195*
Klockars, Carl B., *43, 74*, 172, 180, *194-196, 199, 250, 251, 434, 465*
Kluegel, J. R., *494*
Klyman, Fred I., *195*
Knapp, Kay A., 360, 363, *370, 371*
Knapp, Whitman, *251*
Knatz, Hilary F., *248*
Knightly, Phillip, *46*
Knudten, Mary S., *524*
Knudten, Richard D., *524*
Koenig, Dorean M., *341*
Koepf, G. F., *72*
Koester, Pat, *371*
Kohfeld, Carol W., *369*
Kohlberg, Lawrence, *72*
Kollke, Gregory J., 191

Korn, Richard, *432*
Koper, Christopher S., *370*
Kosin, Thomas E., *199*
Koss, M. P., *45*
Kotts, R., *47*
Kowalski, G. S., *494*
Kraft, Lois P., *197*
Krajick, Kevin, *403, 463*
Kramer, Geoffrey P., *341*
Kramer, John H., *363, 371*
Kratcoski, Peter C., *44, 432, 433*
Kravitz, M., *225*
Krisberg, Barry, *74, 340, 459, 466, 493, 495, 525*
Krmpotich, Sharon, *433*
Kroes, William H., 239, *251*
Krohn, Marvin D., *74*
Kronick, R. F., *465*
Krooth, Richard, *341*
Kruckenberg, Joanna, *195*
Kruse, John, 327
Kruttschnitt, Candace, *433*
Kunstler, William M., *313*
Kuntzman, Gersh, 171
Kurland, P. E., *371*
Kuykendall, Jack L., *162, 199, 249, 250*

Lab, Steven P., *43, 196, 370, 434, 495*
Lacayo, Richard, *162*, 353
Lacy, Frank R., *549*
LaFave, Wayne R., *101, 126, 224, 225*
LaFleur, Laurence J., *369*
LaFraniere, Sharon, *162*
LaFree, Gary, *369*
LaGreca, Anthony J., *524*
Lamb, John H., 490
Lamborn, Leroy, *525*
Land, Kenneth, *44*
Landis, Debra T., *101*
Landry, Jr., Pierre H., *494*
Lane, Roger, *161, 162*
Lang, R. A., *45*
Langan, Patrick A., *340*
Langevin, R., *45*
Langworthy, Robert H., *194, 195, 199, 239, 250*
Lansing, Douglas, *495*
Lanza-Kaduce, Lonn, 46, *369*
Lardner, J., *225*

SUBJECT INDEX

Note: Boldfaced entries indicate terms that are also found in the Glossary.
Boldfaced page numbers indicate where terms are defined within chapters.
Persons cited in this index are found in text and boxed material. Persons listed in
chapter-end Notes are found in the Name Index.

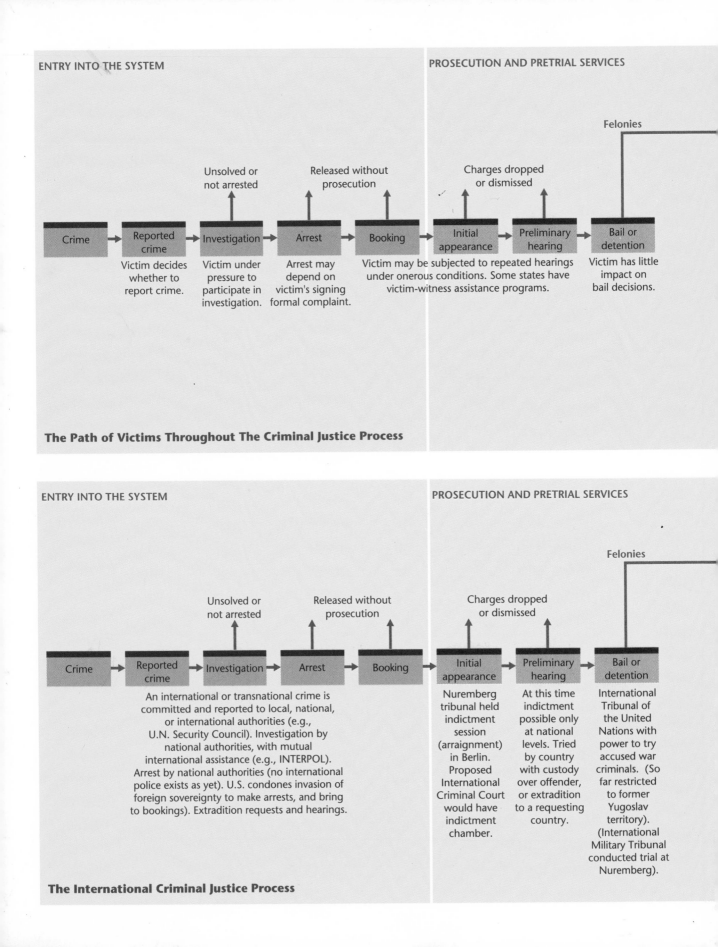

The Path of Victims Throughout The Criminal Justice Process

ENTRY INTO THE SYSTEM

Crime → Reported crime → Investigation → Arrest → Booking

Unsolved or not arrested

Released without prosecution

Reported crime: Victim decides whether to report crime.

Investigation: Victim under pressure to participate in investigation.

Arrest: Arrest may depend on victim's signing formal complaint.

Booking / Initial appearance / Preliminary hearing: Victim may be subjected to repeated hearings under onerous conditions. Some states have victim-witness assistance programs.

PROSECUTION AND PRETRIAL SERVICES

Felonies

Initial appearance → Preliminary hearing → Bail or detention

Charges dropped or dismissed

Bail or detention: Victim has little impact on bail decisions.

The International Criminal Justice Process

ENTRY INTO THE SYSTEM

Crime → Reported crime → Investigation → Arrest → Booking

Unsolved or not arrested

Released without prosecution

An international or transnational crime is committed and reported to local, national, or international authorities (e.g., U.N. Security Council). Investigation by national authorities, with mutual international assistance (e.g., INTERPOL). Arrest by national authorities (no international police exists as yet). U.S. condones invasion of foreign sovereignty to make arrests, and bring to bookings). Extradition requests and hearings.

PROSECUTION AND PRETRIAL SERVICES

Felonies

Initial appearance → Preliminary hearing → Bail or detention

Charges dropped or dismissed

Initial appearance: Nuremberg tribunal held indictment session (arraignment) in Berlin. Proposed International Criminal Court would have indictment chamber.

Preliminary hearing: At this time indictment possible only at national levels. Tried by country with custody over offender, or extradition to a requesting country.

Bail or detention: International Tribunal of the United Nations with power to try accused war criminals. (So far restricted to former Yugoslav territory). (International Military Tribunal conducted trial at Nuremberg).